Human Resource Management
in a Business Context

Human Resource Management in a Business Context

Second Edition

ALAN PRICE

THOMSON™

Australia • Canada • Mexico • Singapore • Spain • United Kingdom • United States

THOMSON

Human Resource Management in a Business Context, second edition

Copyright © Thomson Learning 2004

The Thomson logo is a registered trademark used herein under licence.

For more information, contact Thomson Learning, High Holborn House, 50-51 Bedford Row, London WC1R 4LR or visit us on the World Wide Web at: http://www.thomsonlearning.co.uk

British Library Cataloguing-in-Publication Data

A catalogue record for this book is available from the British Library

ISBN 1-86152-966-X

First edition 1997 published by International Thomson Business Press
Reprinted 2000 by International Thomson Business Press
Reprinted 2000 and 2001 by Thomson Learning
This edition published 2004 by Thomson Learning
Reprinted 2004 by Thomson Learning

Typeset by Saxon Graphics Ltd, Derby

Printed in Italy by G. Canale & C.

Contents

PART 2   HRM and the business environment   85

4   Human resources and the global economy   87

5   HRM and the state   118

6   The employment market   146

PART 5   The employee resourcing process   373

14   Recruitment and preliminary candidate information   375

15   Employee selection   407

PART 6   Managing diversity   433

16   Equality of opportunity   435

List of figures

List of tables

Preface

This book is intended to provide a comprehensive account of the critical issues in human resource management (HRM), taking the reader from an introductory level to a relatively sophisticated understanding of an increasingly important business topic.

We will see that there is no universal agreement on the meaning of HRM. In fact, there are varying and contradictory models. Yet they embody common elements that distinguish them from previous approaches to managing people – specifically, personnel management.

The book takes a distinctive approach, locating the subject of human resource management and its various perspectives within a business context. We recognize that readers will come from a variety of backgrounds, that some will become HR specialists but that many are interested in the relationship between human resource management and other business functions. This is not a 'cookbook' of best practices: it is firmly focused on human resource management in the real world. Accordingly, we set out to understand the role and meaning of HRM from a number of practical and theoretical perspectives.

Framework for the book

The material in this text has a systematic framework with which we explore the complexities involved in managing people at work. There are four levels of discussion: environmental, organizational, strategic and operational. At the environmental level we see that the activities of people managers are constrained by a number of factors. For example:

- The economy, affecting business growth and, subsequently, the balance between demand and availability of employees.
- The actions of government and supranational structures such as the European Union and the North American Free Trade Agreement (NAFTA).
- Legislation on a wide range of employment issues, including hours, diversity, working conditions, minimum pay, redundancy rights, consultation and so on.
- Competing demands from stakeholders such as customers, trade unions, shareholders and senior managers.

At the organizational level, the dimensions of size, structure and culture constrain and sometimes determine the way in which HRM takes place. Organizations range from one-person 'start-ups' to transnationals employing hundreds of thousands of people. As a consequence, HRM can vary from simply managing individuals at a very human level to the strategic and logistical issues involved in controlling vast numbers. Not surprisingly, HRM in small businesses tends to be commonsensical, with an emphasis on solving day-to-day problems. People management is a natural part of the owner-manager's role, along with finance, production, marketing, customer service and everything else.

By contrast, large organizations require a more sophisticated and structured human resource function. Even where the notion of HRM as an integrated approach has been adopted as a strategy, with operational responsibility delegated to line managers, there is likely to be a major role for a specialist HR function. Such a function may be focused on coordination with operational activities such as resourcing, counselling, employee relations, communications and training/development provided on an in-house or external consultancy basis.

The next level – strategic decision making – is particularly relevant for this topic because HRM is often viewed as a strategic alternative to traditional personnel management. Employees are a major cost to organizations of any size. Hence decisions about employee requirements are strategic issues with important consequences for the profitability and growth of organizations.

The final (operational) level encompasses the activities of people managers, including recruitment and selection procedures, performance assessment, training and development, and employee relations. These are areas traditionally associated with 'personnel.' In this volume we see that they are individually important but also form part of a much wider approach to managing people.

Learning features

The book includes a number of features to help students make the most of this text as a key element in their learning experience:

- *Objectives* – the main learning outcomes that a student should aim to achieve from each chapter.
- *Key concepts* – highlighted concepts of considerable significance in understanding HRM and related topics.
- *HRM in reality* – boxed examples and illustrations relating the topic under discussion to human resource management in the real world. Many include discussion questions.
- *Tables and figures* – providing detailed information and graphical representation of major concepts.
- *Chapter summaries* – brief but comprehensive outlines of the content and main points in each chapter.
- *Further reading* – suggested articles and books providing greater depth and alternative perspectives on chapter topics.
- *Review questions* – to check understanding of the principal issues raised in every chapter.
- *Problems for discussion and analysis* – provided at the end of each chapter, designed to stimulate critical analysis, discussion and reflection on the issues raised.
- *Glossary* – an alphabetical list of key terms used in the book with succinct explanations for easy reference.

Plan of the book

The book is divided into nine parts, each composed of a number of related chapters, and a conclusion. We commence the book in Part 1 by addressing the development and scope of HRM as a philosophy of people management, critically examining the claim that it is a coherent and integrated approach to managing people. Part 1 also addresses the link between HRM and 'high-performance' or high-commitment' management, and the effects of new technology on its practice.

The chapters in Parts 2–4 take us through the environmental, organizational and strategic levels, also covering the employment market, human resource planning, organizational change and the nature of resourcing decisions in some detail. The remainder of the book, parts 5–9, addresses the key activity areas, including recruitment and selection, the management of diversity, performance management, reward management, human resource development and employee relations. Finally, the conclusion evaluates the effectiveness of HRM in real organizations and its likely development in the future.

Each chapter includes a number of boxed articles designed to illustrate particular themes within a real-life context. The flavour of reality is emphasized throughout the book with references to contemporary issues in the media and debate in academic journals. HRM really happens out there – even if it is labelled as 'economics', 'labour' or 'industrial relations'.

Related websites

This text benefits from its companion websites in the HRM Guide Network (http://www.hrmguide.net), one of the largest and most comprehensive sources of human resource management information available on the internet. Each chapter has dedicated pages within the HR Topics section, linked to hundreds of articles for further reading, tips and ideas for answering discussion questions in the book, and frequent updates. HRM Guide is international in its scope with separate sections for a number of countries, including Australia, Canada, the United Kingdom and the United States of America. There are also direct links to human resource journals, societies, associations and business organizations throughout the world.

Alan Price
April 2003

Acknowledgements

My thanks are due to past colleagues, students and website visitors from many countries who helped me develop and test the contents of this book. I am also indebted to a number of people at Thomson Learning who have contributed to its production, including Jenny Clapham, who was involved with both editions; Jennifer Pegg, Marie Taylor and Fiona Freel who helped me in its preparation; and Amie Barker and Emily Ferguson who saw it through to fruition. I am also grateful to Simon Perry and Annette Abel for their professional scrutiny prior to publication. Lastly, it must be stated that this book still owes much to the rigorous and supportive editorial advice provided for the first edition by Eugene McKenna and David Needle.

PART I

Introduction to HRM

The first part of this book introduces the essential elements of human resource management (HRM), its origins and applications. HRM is viewed as an all-embracing term describing a number of distinctive approaches to people management. Part 1 helps you to understand and evaluate the different and sometimes ambiguous views of HRM by investigating its origins, explanatory models, technology and practice.

The chapters in Part 1 address a number of specific issues:

- Where do the fundamental concepts of HRM come from?
- What distinguishes HRM from other approaches to managing people – particularly personnel management?
- Is HRM here to stay or is it just another management fad?
- Is HRM a coherent and integrated approach to managing people?
- How prevalent is HRM?
- What is the link between HRM and high performance?
- HRM and 'knowledge management'.
- How has technology changed the practice and delivery of HRM?
- Does its use lead to greater organizational effectiveness?

1

Managing people

Objectives

The purpose of this chapter is to:

- Provide an overview of the history of people management.
- Outline significant developments that led to modern HRM.
- Discuss the main differences between 'traditional' personnel management and HRM.
- Introduce the key roles played by human resource specialists.

People management

In this chapter we set out to understand the purpose of human resource management (HRM), how it developed and the range of tasks covered by human resource specialists. Arguably, HRM has become the dominant approach to people management in English-speaking countries. But it is important to stress that HRM has not 'come out of nowhere'. There is a long history of attempts to achieve an understanding of human behaviour in the workplace. Throughout the 20th century and earlier, practitioners and academics developed theories and practices to explain and influence human behaviour at work. HRM has absorbed ideas and techniques from a wide range of these theories and practical tools. In effect, HRM is a synthesis of themes and concepts drawn from a long history of work, more recent management theories and social science research.

Over and over again, managers must deal with events that are clearly similar but also different enough to require fresh thinking. For example:

● businesses expand or fail
● they innovate or stagnate
● they may be exciting or unhappy organizations in which to work
● finance has to be obtained
● workers have to be recruited
● new equipment is purchased, eliminating old procedures and introducing new methods
● staff must be reorganized, retrained or dismissed.

Some items we have listed are clearly to do with people management (for example, recruiting or reorganizing staff). Others – such as innovation or stagnation – are less obviously so. However, they are likely to be affected by having trained, motivated people with suitable skills in place. Some seem irrelevant to HRM, and you might have identified 'raising finance' in this category. But compare two businesses: one has an excellent industrial relations record with no strikes or disputes, while another has many such problems that have been reported in the media. For which company would you find it easier to raise extra finance? Businesses are made up of people and there is no business activity that might not be touched on by HRM.

Human resource management draws on many sources for its theories and practices. Sociologists, psychologists and management theorists, especially, have contributed a constant stream of new and reworked ideas. They offer theoretical insights and practical assistance in areas of people management such as recruitment and selection, performance measurement, team composition and organizational design. Many of their concepts have been integrated into broader approaches that have contributed to management thinking in various periods and ultimately to the development of HRM (see Figure 1.1).

Background and origins of people management

The roots of people management (and, therefore, of HRM) lie deep in the past. Just as the tasks that have to be carried out in modern organizations are allocated to different jobs and the people who perform those jobs, humans in ancient societies divided work between themselves. The division of labour (see Key concept 1.1) has been practised since prehistoric times: family groups shared the work of hunting and gathering; tasks were allocated according to skills such as ability to find food plants, track animals or cook; age, strength

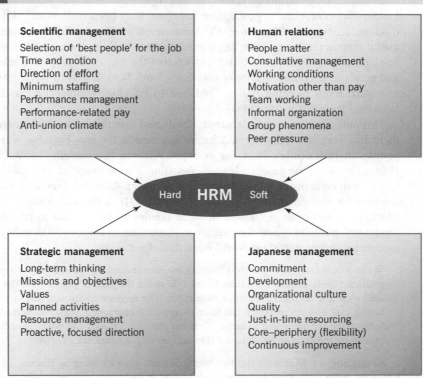

Figure 1.1	Influences on the development of HRM

Scientific management
Selection of 'best people' for the job
Time and motion
Direction of effort
Minimum staffing
Performance management
Performance-related pay
Anti-union climate

Human relations
People matter
Consultative management
Working conditions
Motivation other than pay
Team working
Informal organization
Group phenomena
Peer pressure

Hard **HRM** Soft

Strategic management
Long-term thinking
Missions and objectives
Values
Planned activities
Resource management
Proactive, focused direction

Japanese management
Commitment
Development
Organizational culture
Quality
Just-in-time resourcing
Core–periphery (flexibility)
Continuous improvement

and health were taken into account and the oldest and youngest members were not expected to travel far from home or to be involved in the dangers of hunting.

Social customs determined separate roles and tasks for males and females. Traditional self-sufficient communities, depending on agriculture or fishing, rarely had more than 20–30 categories of labour in contrast to modern industrial states that have thousands of different job types. Some functions, such as religious and political leadership or medicine, were restricted to individuals with inherited or specialist knowledge. As civilization and technology evolved, however, specialization led to a proliferation of different forms of work, and farmers and fishermen were joined by skilled craftworkers using metal, pottery and wood.

Key concept 1:1

Division of labour The subdivision of work so that specific tasks or jobs are allocated to individuals deemed most suitable on the basis of skill, experience or cultural tradition. All societies practise division of labour. Some cultures traditionally allocated tasks to particular social groups, such as castes in India. In others, higher status jobs have been reserved for members of a power elite such as the products of the British 'public school and Oxbridge' system or the French 'grandes écoles'. Modern HRM aims to identify and develop the best people for specific jobs, regardless of background, class or gender.

Every generation believes that its problems and achievements are greater than those of the past. Modern business is seen as being uniquely complex and on a larger scale than the enterprises of earlier times but, in the ancient world, large numbers of people were organized to build great pyramids, fortresses and irrigation systems; military leaders marshalled huge armies; slave owners operated massive plantations and mines. Leadership, power and organization, therefore, have been matters of study and debate for thousands of years. The *Farmer's Almanac*, a 5000-year-old Sumerian text, includes useful tips on the supervision of farm labourers – making it the oldest known HRM text-book (Kramer, 1963, p.105). The text advised the farmer to prepare a selection of whips and goads to keep men and beasts working hard. No idleness or interruptions were to be tolerated. Even planting barley seed had to be closely supervised as the unfortunate labourers were not trusted to do it properly.

This authoritarian approach has predominated throughout most of recorded history, but there has been a continuing and increasing search for less coercive ways of managing people. In 16th century Italy, for example, Niccolo Machiavelli (1469–1527) wrote *The Prince* (by which he meant a leader), detailing a wide range of strategies and tactics that continue to offer insights into the exercise of power. Although famous for advocating ruthlessness in the conduct of public (i.e. political) activities, Swain (2002) considers Machiavelli to be the originator of three themes more relevant to private management: modernity, publicness and the executive. According to Swain (2002, p.281) Machiavelli's modernity distinguished his world from that of antiquity:

> When Machiavelli jettisons the Christian religion and ancient philosophy as sources of guidance in the human condition, he may do so for the sake of politics, but the ramifications spill over into all other aspects of human life. The modern enterprise, simply put, is humankind taking care of itself as best it can in an otherwise pretty lonely universe. Science and technology are harnessed to make life more pleasant. Politics and political orders are mostly guided by the ends of political stability and serving humankind's needs.

According to Machiavelli, the ideal leader should have a degree of virtue and be regarded with both fear and love – although, if only one was possible, it was better to be feared than loved. Among his other prescriptions, the leader should be both a Fox and a Lion, able to exercise cunning and be a champion.

The division of labour required the most suitable people to perform skilled tasks, producing an early interest in the differences between individuals. According to Smith (1948, p.10):

> In the 16th century John Huarte wrote a book in Spanish concerning what we should now refer to as vocational guidance and selection. It was translated into Italian, and from this version an English translation was made under the title of 'The Tryal of Wits', which, translated into modern speech, means the testing of intelligence. He maintained that it is nature which enables a man of ability to learn, and that it is quite superfluous for good teachers to try to teach any particular subject to a child who has not the disposition or the ability required for it. Each person, unless he is a dolt, has some predominant quality which will enable him to excel in some way.

Huarte produced the following classification (Smith, 1948, p.11):

(1) Some have a disposition for the clear and easy parts, but cannot understand the obscure and difficult.
(2) Some are pliant and easy, able to learn all the rules, but no good at argument.
(3) Some need no teachers, they take no pleasure in the plains but seek dangerous and high places and walk alone, follow no beaten track; these must fare forthwith, unquiet, seeking to know and understand new matters.

Activity 1:1

The world was a different place when writers such as Huarte and Machiavelli expressed their opinions. Their views would not be regarded as 'politically correct' today. What value can we attach to their views on dealing with working people?

Individuals perform their jobs within a wide environmental context. In 1776, Adam Smith (1723–90) published *An Inquiry into the Nature and Causes of the Wealth of Nations*. This foundation text for the science of economics began by emphasizing the importance of the division of labour in achieving increased productivity, thereby anticipating the Industrial Revolution. The UK is conventionally regarded as the first country to experience this process which then spread throughout Europe and North America and continues to transform developing countries. However, Cannadine (1992, p.18) observes that:

> The view that Britain was the first industrial nation, whose achievements all others consciously emulated, has also been severely undermined, especially in the case of France where, it is now argued, industrialization was taking place in a different way and where, in any case for much of the eighteenth century, its productivity was higher than Britain's.

'Revolution' implies a rapid transition from craft to industrial methods but British industrialization was a relatively slow process in comparison with the recent development of the 'tiger' economies of east Asia. At the end of the 18th, and the beginning of the 19th centuries, workers were gradually concentrated in factories and work centres, more or less under their own free will. This concentration was linked to increasing mechanization and the consequent need for machine-operating skills. Developing from older craft-based industries, work was divided between employees according to the nature of their skills. One worker would no longer be totally responsible for all stages of production, such as making a piece of furniture. In the industrial system the task was subdivided into simpler, less skilful jobs. Different people would deal with parts of the process: one would turn chair legs, another would prepare seats, yet another would stain and polish, and so on.

By the late 19th century, the size and complexity of the new industries demanded more sophisticated methods of control and organization, eventually evolving into modern management. Until this time, workers were not directly employed by large capitalists: their employers were gang bosses, subcontracted to provide and organize labour. In the developed world, subcontractors of this kind continue to exist in the building sector and in fruit and vegetable-picking. In developing countries their power is even greater. Under autocratic but loose control, skilled or unskilled workers largely organized their own efforts, forming autonomous teams. However, as factories grew larger and people were concentrated in greater numbers in specific locations, this indirect approach became increasingly unworkable. People were needed to control permanent workforces, which were directly employed by factory owners.

Initially they took the form of overseers, foremen or supervisors; exercising 'coercion by means of observation' (Foucault, 1977, p.175). At first they were people promoted from the workforce: the concept of a distinct managerial class with separate recruitment paths evolved slowly. Jacques (1997) points out that 'the foreman was not in any sense a middle manager, but a key player in a form of control in the works radically different from and preceding *management*'.

In the 19th century industry was dominated by individual owners, family businesses and partnerships. The principals of these companies managed their businesses in a direct, personal way, partly because the numbers of people involved were small enough to be within the span of control of a few individuals. Family-controlled businesses became a major economic force and many achieved considerable importance. Some of the most successful were happy to publicize their methods and were featured in the media of the time. Biographies were written glorifying their achievements and presenting their ideas in largely uncritical terms. George Cadbury is one such example and he is featured at the end of this chapter. Along with explorers, scientists and colonial adventurers, business heroes were presented as role models for the masses. Such books met the demands of a reading population who preferred to perceive the world in terms of good and bad, heroes and villains, and required a presentation of success in simplistic terms. Examination of modern 'pop management' books suggest that little has changed.

Key concept 1:2

Alienation A state of estrangement, or a feeling of being an outsider from society. Karl Marx observed that although work in a traditional, agricultural or craft-based society had been exhausting, workers had control over their own jobs. Their work required considerable knowledge and skill that had been removed from many factory jobs. Dull, boring and repetitive work induces a feeling of alienation. Assembly line workers are involved with a small part of the final product, have little control over the rhythm of their work and may have no idea of the significance of their contribution. Their work can appear to be alien with no relationship or meaning to their lives other than to produce income. As a consequence they may feel little enthusiasm and, often, active hostility towards what seems like forced labour.

Activity 1:2

What problems would have resulted from personal control of businesses when they began to develop into large work organizations employing hundreds, and sometimes thousands of workers?

Professional managers

The literature on organization is both extensive and old, but organization is not the same as management. Much of the literature on management history is American in origin and, not surprisingly, attributes most of the credit for the development of management to US originators. Jacques (1997) comments:

> Moderns appear to be superior to other people because we see clearly what has hitherto been seen through the eyes of bias and superstition; English are superior among Moderns because they are the ones who produced the entire body of early work; Americans are superior to British because they have superior character. That this hierarchy of ethnocentrism is commonplace in American writing makes it no less worthy of comment.

One of the principal originators of modern management highlighted in the US literature was, in fact, neither English nor (born) an American. The Scot, Daniel McCallum, was general superintendent of the Eric Railroad in the USA. This railroad, in common with other large rail companies, was finding it difficult to operate profitably, unlike smaller local railroads. He wrote (see Chandler, 1962) that:

> A superintendent of a road fifty miles in length can give its business his professional attention and may be constantly on the line engaged in the direction of its details; each person is personally known to him, and all questions in relation to its business are at once presented and acted upon; and any system however imperfect may under such circumstances prove comparatively successful.

However, McCallum contended, when the railroad is 'five hundred miles in length a very different state exists. Any system which might be applicable to the business and extent of a short road would be found entirely inadequate to the wants of a long one.'

He set about creating a management system in which responsibility for the railroad was split into geographical divisions, each of manageable size. Superintendents were given responsibility for operations within their respective divisions but had to provide detailed reports to the central headquarters. There McCallum and his assistants were able to coordinate the whole operation. McCallum advocated a number of management principles:

- good discipline
- specific and detailed job descriptions
- frequent and accurate reporting of performance
- pay and promotion based on merit
- clearly defined hierarchy of superiors and subordinates
- enforcement of personal responsibility and accountability
- the search for and correction of errors.

The lines of authority from headquarters to superintendents and then to their subordinates were laid out clearly on paper – effectively on an organizational chart. Other railroads copied this system and were able to become effective and profitable. In turn, these ideas spread to other US businesses.

By 1900 the USA had undergone several decades of rapid, large-scale industrialization. Large American companies such as Heinz and Singer Sewing Machines had the characteristics of modern, highly structured organizations. They produced standardized consumer durables for the mass market. These organizations required a supply of trained managers. Notionally selected on the basis of ability and expertise – rather than family connections – they needed to know how to organize, reward and motivate their staff. In the USA, state and private universities were opened to cater for this new professional need.

The first companies of equivalent size and organization did not arise in Britain and the Commonwealth until the 1920s and management education was similarly late in developing. Like most European or Asian companies they still tended to employ relatives or to promote long-standing workers to management roles. Reliability and ability to impose discipline were held to be more important than technical knowledge. Increasingly, however, managers (especially those at a senior level) developed vested interests incompatible with those of the working classes (labour) and shareholders (capital).

Scientific management

In 1903, F.W. Taylor – an American engineer – published *Shop Management*, outlining a system for extracting maximum output from workers. Later, his methods were presented as *The Principles of Scientific Management* (1911). Controversial at the time, and still the subject of debate, Taylor is quoted frequently as the inspiration for many modern industrial practices, including Japanese production methods. He outlined a systematic but controversial programme based on:

- rudimentary time and motion studies
- selection of 'first-class men' for the job
- premium pay for a 'fair day's work'.

Taylor's ideas were not original. They embodied attitudes of the time, including strict discipline to control soldiering ('slacking' or 'skiving'). Taylor saw two forms: (a) 'individual' soldiering where workers were naturally lazy; and (b) 'systematic' soldiering where workers conspired to maintain a comfortable work rate. Activities were timed to prevent employees from taking it easy. As chief engineer at the Midvale Steel Company Taylor sacked slow workers, cut piece-rates and brought in non-union workers. Productivity was raised by standardizing and simplifying procedures into specified and unvarying jobs. Employees were not allowed to think about their jobs, bring in new ideas, or vary tasks to alleviate boredom. Broad craft knowledge was no longer required – knowledge was transferred to the manager.

▶

Taylor's basic concept was the 'task idea': planning out every job in minute detail; giving precise instructions on what to do, in what order, at what speed; and eliminating wasteful or unnecessary actions. This produced 'one best way' for any task. At the Bethlehem Steel Company he applied his principles to shovelling and handling pig iron (Taylor, 1947, p.43):

> Now, gentlemen, shoveling is a great science compared with pig-iron handling. I dare say that most of you gentlemen know that a good many pig-iron handlers can never learn to shovel right; the ordinary pig-iron handler is not the type of man well suited to shoveling. He is too stupid; there is too much mental strain, too much knack required of a shoveler for the pig-iron handler to take kindly to shoveling.

The plant employed 400–600 men to move several million tons of material each year. Taylor found the optimum load for shovelling, designed better shovels and scheduled carefully timed rest-pauses. He was able to achieve the same output from 140 men with an average 60 per cent bonus, virtually halving costs. He argued that the men were not being overworked but simply doing their jobs more sensibly.

Taylor used Henry Knolle – a 'first-class' labourer immortalized in management literature as 'Schmidt' – to demonstrate the motivating effect of premium pay. Knolle's pig-iron handling increased four-fold to 50 tons a day, for a bonus equivalent to half his normal pay. Only one in eight workers could match this performance, the remainder being given lower-paid work. Many employers used Taylor's system to increase productivity, but without extra pay. In fact, wages were often reduced on the grounds that the rationalized jobs could be classified as unskilled. The work was given to people, such as new immigrants, who would accept lower pay.

In his writings, Taylor presented his work at Bethlehem Steel as a success. In fact, there were angry reactions from workers, managers and others. Press publicity on likely redundancies, threats of industrial action and management resentment led to Taylor's dismissal. He spent the rest of his life publicizing his theories. He believed that he had developed a science that would legitimize the professional status of managers. Rose (1975, p.32) describes Taylorism as 'an instructive reminder of how "scientific" theories of workers' behaviour which fail when actually applied in industry can none the less acquire a substitute vitality as managerial ideologies'. In other words, ideas that do not work in practice can still be sold to other managers!

As an early management guru, Taylor used recognizable tactics:

- he developed a relatively simple set of principles
- took personal credit for devising them
- gave them a pretentious name – scientific management
- and publicized them extensively.

A distinctive form of scientific management was taken up in the new high-volume production industries. This came to be known as Fordism after the mass production methods used by Henry Ford for automobile manufacturing. Jelinek (quoted in Mintzberg, 1994, p.21) considers that Taylor 'for the first time made possible the large-scale co-ordination of details – planning and policy-level thinking, above and beyond the details of the task itself'. This produced a new division of labour, splitting tasks and their coordination into different roles. So management had become 'abstracted' from day-to-day activities, allowing it to 'concentrate on exceptions'.

Taylor's ideas were developed further by Frank and Lilian Gilbreth who made valiant efforts to turn human beings into automatons. Their bizarre concepts included the 'therblig' (Gilbreth backwards) as a measure of work (Rose, 1975, p.84). Frank Gilbreth became famous for his study of bricklaying in which he reduced the movements involved from 15 to eight, and increased the number of bricks laid from 120 an hour to 350. Smith (1948, p.144) gave an example of a simple motion study using the Gilbreths' terminology, a bottle of gum and a brush:

Actual movements	*Generalized description*
1 Reach for the gum bottle	Transport empty
2 Grasp the brush	Grasp
3 Carry the brush to the paper	Transport loaded
4 Position for gumming	Position
5 Gum the paper	Use
6 Return the brush to bottle	Transport loaded
7 Insert the brush	Pre-position
8 Release the brush	Release
9 Move the hand back	Transport empty

What was the point of such a motion study? Smith (1948) quoted a paper by H.G. Maule from the *Journal of the Institution of British Launderers*, May 1935, which reported on use of the methodology to investigate the process of folding sheets:

> The sequence of movements was: collect a sheet as it came from the calendar, fold it, place the folded article on a table. In the course of timing he noticed that a disproportionate amount of time was taken in the last movement owing to the position of a table on which the folded articles were placed. By calculating the time taken and multiplying it by the number of sheets folded in a week he found that 20 miles a week were walked unnecessarily. ... By a slight rearrangement of the table this was altered, and yet no one had noticed it before this.

Huczynski and Buchanan (2000) argue that Taylorism and related techniques are more prevalent today than ever. Japanese just-in-time techniques bear a number of similarities to some aspects of scientific management. Scientific management was one of the first of the 'one best way' methodologies of dealing with people management.

Henry Ford

Ford made his first car in 1893 and formed the Ford Motor Company in 1903. He started the company with 11 other men, together putting up US$28,000. Eventually he bought out his associates and Henry Ford became the company. According to Beynon (1973, p.18): 'He was The Man. And he was to remain The Man until his death. Throughout his life he maintained a single-minded, autocratic hold over his company, entirely convinced of his right to run it as he thought fit.'

Ford standardized products ('any colour as long as it's black'), applied modern technology to a flowing production line and allocated workers' jobs according to Taylorist principles. Ford's plant at Highland Park, Michigan was dedicated to a single mass market car – the Model T. His major innovation, the moving assembly line, was inspired by Chicago slaughterhouses where vast numbers of cattle were 'disassembled' on a moving line. At Ford every worker had one task, such as fitting a door to each car as they moved up the line. This development was given great publicity and Ford made every effort to present himself as a great engineer. In fact, there

▶

was nothing new about the equipment. The distinctive feature of the assembly line was the organization of human resources. Assembly workers were allowed a minimum time to complete an operation before the car continued to the next stage: 'The idea is that the man ... must have every second necessary but not a single unnecessary second' (Ford, 1922, quoted in Beynon, 1973, p.19).

A harsh attitude permeated the company. Employees were watched closely and were regarded as objects rather than human beings. They were to do as they were told, and to be hired and fired arbitrarily. While maximizing production efficiency, assembly line manufacturing led to high rates of absenteeism and employee turnover. In 1913 Ford needed 13 000–14 000 workers, but over 50 000 came and went in that year. Something had to be done. In 1914 Ford announced a package deal for his workers, the 'Five Dollar Day', presented as a profit-sharing system that more than doubled workers' wage rates. However, it included a number of changes that benefited the company. Ford did not agree with Taylor's simplistic incentive system. He never paid on a 'piece-work' basis, believing that it led to rushed or 'botched' work. Instead his new scheme increased management control of workers' performance through a combination of:

● Job evaluation, leading to a thorough rationalization of work flow.
● Pay grades, matched to the 'value' or difficulty of jobs.
● Disqualifying clauses, which prevented workers with less than six months' service, men under 21 and all women from receiving US$5 a day. 'Young ladies' were expected to get married and leave the company.

Finally, eligible workers only received the full pay rate if their behaviour and personal habits at work and home were deemed to be satisfactory. Alcohol and tobacco were frowned upon; gambling or taking in boarders was unacceptable. Ford believed that high wages should be paid only to the morally deserving, since the others would spend it unwisely. A Sociological Department was established with 30 investigators checking workers' domestic circumstances and spending habits. Within two years, 90 per cent of Ford workers were thought good enough to receive US$5 a day, but investigators could recommend the loss of six months' bonus at any time if their lifestyles were not acceptable. Ford believed in the virtue of hard work but did not value charity – the poor deserved their fate. He never expressed any concern about the drudgery and boredom of the assembly line, considering most people to be incapable of any better.

Ford's conditions were more attractive than the alternatives open to immigrants in Detroit. Some 10 000 unemployed people mobbed the factory looking for jobs. Absenteeism and employee turnover dropped dramatically: in 1914 only 2000 workers left their jobs. The assembly line speeded up and the average cost of a car actually dropped, despite the wage increases. A reduction of working hours from nine to eight hours a day was easily absorbed. Ford's approach offered an unstoppable competitive advantage over more humane, craft-based companies. By 1923 Ford produced two million cars a year. Mass production dominated the world economy.

The American car industry gradually consolidated into General Motors, Ford and Chrysler. They dominated the US automobile market until the coming of the Japanese in the 1980s. After the initial success of the Model T, Ford lost market share to General Motors. At first, he tried to compete by cutting costs and producing a cheaper product, achieved by relentlessly speeding up the assembly line. Eventually he recognized the need for a new model. He began construction of a new plant to manufacture the Model A. Using more extensive technology it needed far fewer men than the Model T assembly line. In its last year (1927) he drove the Model T line flat out until he had sufficient stocks of the car. Then he shut the plant and laid off 60 000 employees for six months – without pay. He considered this to be a useful lesson to the workers who would appreciate that 'things are not going along too even always'.

Ford became increasingly dictatorial and suspicious. He avoided technical experts – for a long time he did not hire college graduates. As ambitious employees rose in the hierarchy, he found reasons to sack them when their authority threatened his. His cars became technically obsolescent. His marketing and planning were poorly organized – he banned advertising for several years. By the 1930s the company was losing money heavily and was only to be saved by Ford's death and new management.

Sources: Beynon (1973) and Galbraith (1967).

The human factor

The 'science' in scientific management was doubtful. At the same point in time, however, academic researchers had begun to take an interest in the practical aspects of work. Work psychology was pioneered by the German psychologist Hugo Munsterberg (1863–1916) who moved to the USA and became responsible for a research laboratory at Harvard. Between 1900 and 1914 he applied the techniques of the young science of psychology to issues such as the selection of engineers to operate new machines, and the efficiency of various industrial practices (Thomson, 1968, p.133). Work psychology is deemed to have taken off after the publication of his *Psychology and Industrial Efficiency* in 1913. In Germany and the UK the demands of war boosted further research. In Britain, the Health of Munition Workers Committee (1915–17) was required to: '… consider and investigate the relation of hours of labour and other conditions of employment, including methods of work, to the production of fatigue, having regard both to industrial efficiency and to the preservation of health amongst the workers' (quoted in Thomson, 1968, p.345).

In 1919 the researchers involved formed the UK National Institute of Industrial Psychology (NIIP), a body similar to the Australian Institute of Industrial Psychology founded in 1917. These organizations investigated and researched working conditions, and developed vocational guidance and selection techniques. In New Zealand, vocational guidance dates from 1913 and was organized by the Christchurch branch of the YMCA. Initially the work of occupational psychologists bordered on physiology as they investigated fatigue and monotony. It had been believed that fatigue was caused by a build-up of toxins in the blood. It was even thought that an elixir could be found that would neutralize these chemicals; when injected into exhausted workers this could allow them to work indefinitely! The researchers proved conclusively that fatigue was not purely physiological – it was also psychological (Rose, 1975: p.70).

Their work directly countered the myth that working longer hours produced greater output. In their research on monotony they took a deliberate anti-Taylorist perspective. They confirmed Taylor's views on the value of rest-pauses but argued against the notion of 'one best way by a first-class man'. The simple truth was that individual tasks could be done equally effectively in a variety of ways by a diverse range of people. Different people had their own ways of performing effectively: they worked more efficiently when allowed to vary their own working methods. It became clear also that money was not the sole motivator for working people: the social relations between workers influenced their attitude to the job and their productivity. Workers were human beings and should be treated as such: the researchers had identified the importance of human factors.

In effect they had anticipated the conclusions of the more famous 'Hawthorne studies', but their reports – expressed in dry scientific language – made for dull reading and were not accessible to a wide audience. Moreover, their income came from industrial commissions, which were expected to be confidential. The most positive response came from the chocolate makers Cadbury and Rowntree, which were Quaker-owned and humanitarian in attitude. They were receptive to ideas about training, vocational guidance, staff welfare and joint worker–management councils. Many, if not most, employers were not like-minded. The soft approach of the NIIP also had a hard centre, in the shape of efficiency measures such as selection tests to identify suitable workers for specific jobs.

Psychological tests for selection, or 'psychometric tests', were extensively developed in the USA and the UK from World War I through to World War II. Some two million Americans were tested during World War I alone. Their particular priority was the identification of 'subnormals' at one extreme and officer material at the other. After the war, testing became a lucrative commercial activity in the USA but introduced a worrying element of 'scientific' racism that has not been entirely eliminated.

The Union Bank of Australia: HR 100 years ago

Personnel, payroll and other records from the Union Bank of Australia were examined for employees who joined between 1888 and 1900. The researchers found that employment was characterized by limited ports of entry, impersonal rules for pay and promotion, well-defined career ladders, shielding from the external labour market, and a long-term employment relationship. Additionally tenure within the bank was rewarded considerably more than experience elsewhere, and pay increased significantly after 25–30 years' service.

Source: Seltzer and Merrett (2000).

Human relations

The US human relations movement dominated management thinking until the 1950s and was a significant influence on the development of modern HRM. The movement gained most of its inspiration from the famous Hawthorne studies at the Western Electric Company plant of that name in Chicago from the 1920s to the early 1940s. The plant employed 40 000 people and was regarded as progressive. The studies were organized by the company, with some assistance from the Harvard Business School. The intention was to find out how productivity might be affected if working conditions such as lighting, heating and rest-pauses were varied. Elton Mayo, an Australian professor at Harvard, picked up these studies and publicized a new approach in American management philosophy that spread to many other countries.

Mayo is credited often with the Hawthorne research. In fact, as Rose (1975) points out, there is no evidence that Mayo did any 'leg-work' at the plant. Different accounts of the research provide contradictory descriptions. It seems that early research at Hawthorne was conducted using Taylorist 'time and motion' and industrial psychology techniques. The latter were similar to the methods of the 'human factors' researchers in Britain.

In early experiments on changed lighting conditions, the researchers observed two groups. In one group, regardless of whether lighting was worsened or improved, output increased. The other group was used as a control, with no variation in lighting, yet output also increased.

The Relay Assembly Test Room was set up in April 1927 to investigate this phenomenon. Six cooperative women were selected to work in an area partitioned from the main workroom. Relay assembly was their normal work and their output had been measured secretly before the experiment began. They had regular briefing meetings and their comments were taken into account. Also, they were given periodic medical checks. An observer was stationed in the room to ensure that the women paid full attention to the test. The experiment continued for five years, but the significant findings came from the first two years.

During this period, systematic changes were made in the women's working conditions. They were put on a group incentive scheme. Frequency and duration of rest-pauses were increased, while free meals and shorter working days and working weeks were introduced. In general, the improvements were incremental. Output increased with virtually every change. This has been called the 'Hawthorne effect'. Even when – for a period – conditions were returned to their original levels, output did not drop significantly. After two years, output stood at around 30 per cent higher than at the start of the experiments.

The group became cohesive, helped by the replacement of two uncooperative women. Other workers envied their conditions. Gradually the observer developed a friendly relationship with the women, shielding them from their official supervisors. Mayo described the situation in his book on the Hawthorne studies, *The Human Problems of an Industrial Civilization* (1933):

> It was also noticed that there was a marked improvement in their attitude towards their work and working environment. This simultaneous improvement in attitude and effectiveness indicated that … we could more logically attribute the increase in efficiency to a betterment of morale than to any of the alterations made in the course of the experiments.

Mayo argued that the women were responding to the interest shown in them and their work. The experiment was presented as evidence of the importance of human relations. However, from 1929 to 1932 morale and performance steadily deteriorated. In particular, the women became anxious about their security as the economy slumped. Eventually there was so much bitterness and hostility that the experiment was concluded.

Among many other studies at Hawthorne, the 'Bank-wiring Room' is most significant. It led to an appreciation of group norms and conformity. It appeared from this study of 14 men that they had determined the level of 'a fair day's work' between themselves. Anyone doing too much ('rate-busters'), or too little ('chisellers'), or who 'squealed' to management, was picked on and pressurized to conform. Strangely, these group effects were played down by the researchers because most recommendations from the human relations school were geared towards individual worker satisfaction.

The human relations movement shifted management thinking towards 'soft' people management – away from the 'hard' approaches of Taylor and Ford. According to Wendy Holloway (1991, p.71), the Hawthorne studies caused:

1 A shift from a psycho-physiological model of the worker to a socio-emotional one.

2 An appreciation of the fundamental importance of the worker's attitude to the job in determining performance.

Later Hawthorne studies depended on interviews. Sympathetic interviewing produced valuable information for management, and interviews could also change workers' attitudes. In the 1930s, companies such as Kimberly-Clark introduced attitude surveys among their workers. Questioning gave workers extra insight into the nature of their jobs and feelings about work. This was a major discovery in a country dominated by gigantic factories, where individual workers were unknown to managers. What was unthought of before was now a part of common sense: workers have feelings!

Activity 1:3   How would you describe the main differences between the 'scientific management', 'human factors' and 'human relations' approaches?

Management theory

The human relations and human factors approaches were absorbed into a broad behavioural science movement in the 1950s and 1960s. This period produced some influential theories on the motivation of human performance. For example, Maslow's hierarchy of needs provided an individual focus on the reasons why people work. He argued that people satisfied an ascending series of needs from survival, through security to eventual 'self-actualization'.

In the same period, concepts of job design such as job enrichment and job enlargement were investigated. It was felt that people would give more to an organization if they gained satisfaction from their jobs. Jobs should be designed to be interesting and challenging in order to gain the commitment of workers – a central theme of HRM.

Classic theories were produced in the 1950s and 1960s within the human relations framework. By the 1970s most managers participating in formal management training were aware of: Theory X and Theory Y (McGregor, 1960); of Maslow and Herzberg's motivation theories; and knew where they should be in terms of the managerial grid (Blake and Mouton, 1964). These theorists advocated participative, 'soft' approaches to management. However, only a minority of managers in the USA received such training, with even fewer in other countries. Most operational managers – concerned with production, engineering or distribution – had worked their way up from low-level jobs: they were probably closer in spirit to F.W. Taylor than the theorists of the 1950s and 1960s. This contrasted with personnel departments with a higher proportion of people who had received academic training; additionally, 'personnel' was an area where women were prevalent, as opposed to production which was male dominated. Were women naturally more open to human relations concepts than men?

In Britain, the influence of industrial psychology persisted in Alec Rodger's slogan 'fitting the man to the job and the job to the man'. Wendy Holloway (1991) quotes from an undated student handout issued by Rodger in the 1970s, which appears to ignore the concept of the working woman:

. Fitting the man to the job

- through occupational guidance
- personnel selection
- training and development.

Fitting the job to the man

- through methods design
- equipment design
- design and negotiation of working conditions and
- (physical and social) rewards.

Key management theories

Management by objectives

Based on work by Drucker in the 1950s, and further developed by McGregor, management by objectives (MBO) linked achievement to competence and job performance. MBO primarily focused on the individual, tying rewards and promotion opportunities to specific agreed objectives, measured by feedback from performance assessment. Individual managers were given the opportunity to clarify the purposes of their jobs and set their own targets.

MBO developed into modern performance management schemes and performance-related pay.

Contingency

Many researchers found difficulty in applying academic theories to real organizations. The socio-technical school developed models of behaviour and performance that took into account the contingent variables, or 'it depends' circumstances, found in particular work situations (Burns and Stalker, 1961; Woodward, 1980). They argued that employees were part of a system that also included the equipment and other resources utilized by an organization. The system could not function optimally unless all its components – human and non-human – had been considered. The HRM concepts of coherence and integration derive, in part, from this line of thought.

Organizational development (OD)

Also drawn from the long tradition of organizational theory, organizational development (OD) offered a pragmatic approach to change. Theory and practice were mixed in a tentative process called 'action research'. OD familiarized managers with the idea that changes in processes, attitudes and behaviour were possible and that organizations should be thought of as whole entities.

Strategic management

Directing people to achieve strategic objectives so that individual goals are tied to the business needs of the whole organization, strategic management has become a dominant framework for organizational thinking since World War II. It is based on concepts first used for large-scale military and space programmes in the USA. Frequently, it employs project and team-based methods for planning and implementation. Lately, internal (including human) resources and key competencies have been identified as crucial elements of long-term competitive success.

Strategic management has become the major unifying theme of undergraduate and (especially) postgraduate business courses. The concern with strategy distinguishes HRM from personnel management.

Leadership

Many writers have concluded that a visionary leader is essential, particularly in developing and inspiring teams. McGregor's (1960) *The Human Side of Enterprise* linked leadership and management style to motivation. McGregor expressed the contrast between authoritarian people management ('Theory X') and a modern form based on human relations ideas ('Theory Y'). His ideas parallel 'hard' and 'soft' HRM. Effective managers do not need to give orders and discipline staff, they draw the best from their people through encouragement, support and personal charisma. Later

▶

authors (such as Peters and Waterman, 1982) featured the leader's vision and mission as a quasi-religious means of galvanizing worker commitment and enthusiasm.

Corporate culture

Deal and Kennedy (1982) popularized the belief that organizational effectiveness depends on a strong, positive corporate culture. They combined ideas from leadership theory and strategic management thinkers with prevailing beliefs about Japanese business success. Managers were exhorted to examine their existing organizational climates critically and work to change them into dynamic and creative cultures. The excellence movement inspired by Peters and Waterman (*In Search of Excellence*, 1982, and others) has been particularly influential with practising managers, despite criticisms of the research on which it was based.

Question: Some people believe that managing people is just a matter of common sense. What benefits have human resource specialists to gain from the theories and ideas we have outlined here?

Development of the personnel specialism

Personnel management has been a recognized function in the USA since NCR opened a personnel office in the 1890s. American personnel managers worked within a unitarist tradition, identifying closely with the objectives of their organization (Key concept 1.3). It was natural for HRM to emerge comparatively smoothly from this perspective.

In other countries, notably Australia, South Africa and the UK, the personnel management function arrived more slowly and came via a number of routes. Moreover, its orientation was not entirely managerial. In Britain its origins can be traced to the 'welfare officers' employed by Quaker-owned companies such as Cadbury. At an early stage it became evident that there was an inherent conflict between their activities and those of line managers. They were not seen to have a philosophy compatible with the world view of senior managers. The welfare officer orientation placed personnel management as a buffer between the business and its employees. In terms of 'organizational politics' this was not a politically viable position for individuals wishing to further their careers, increase their status and earn high salaries.

Key concept 1:3

Unitarism A managerialist stance which assumes that everyone in an organization is a member of a team with a common purpose. It embodies a central concern of HRM – that an organization's people, whether managers or lower-level employees, should share the same objectives and work together harmoniously. From this perspective, conflicting objectives are seen as negative and dysfunctional. By definition it is the opposite of pluralism: the acceptance of several alternative approaches, interests or goals within the same organization or society. Arguably, in the field of HRM, unitarism represents a US tradition, whereas pluralism is more typical of European attitudes towards people management.

Tyson (1989) distinguished between three 'types' of personnel management jobs:

- *'Clerk of works'*: The majority, involved in the routine of administration, record-keeping, letter-writing, setting up interviews and welfare matters. Reports to personnel or senior line manager.

- '*Contracts manager*': Likely to be found in large organizations with formal industrial relations structures. Involved in detailed short-term policy making and resolving problems. A 'fixer' with some degree of influence with trade unions and senior management.
- 'Architect': Probably highly qualified but not necessarily in 'personnel'. Broad portfolio with a significant strategic role. A business manager first and personnel manager second.

The second tradition – industrial relations – further compounded this distinction between personnel and other managers. In the acrimonious industrial relations climate prevailing in many developed countries throughout much of the 20th century, personnel/industrial relations managers played an intermediary role between unions and line management. Their function was legitimized by their role – or, at least, their own perception of that role – as 'honest brokers'.

But from the 1980s onwards governments with a neo-liberal or free market orientation, such as Margaret Thatcher's administration in the UK, reined in union freedom severely. Overall, there was a marked reduction in the importance of collective worker representation in many English-speaking countries. The perceived importance of collective bargaining reduced as managerial power increased. Trade union membership declined along with centralized pay bargaining and other forms of collective negotiation – and with them, the importance of the personnel manager with negotiating experience. The focus switched from the collective to the relationship between the employer and the individual employee. To support this change, a variety of essentially individualistic personnel techniques were applied to achieve business goals. These included performance measurement, objective setting and skills development related to personal reward.

Table 1.1	Specialist functions of traditional personnel departments
Function	Description
Recruitment	Advertising for new employees and liasing with employment agencies
Selection	Determining the best candidates from those who apply, arranging interviews, tests, references and so on
Promotion	Running similar selection procedures to determine progression within the organization
Pay	A minor or major role in pay negotiation, determination and administration
Performance assessment	Coordinating staff appraisal and counselling systems to evaluate individual employee performance
Grading structures	Comparing the relative difficulty and importance of functions as a basis for pay or development
Training and development	Coordinating or delivering programmes to fit people for the roles required by the organization now and in the future
Welfare	Providing or liasing with specialists in a staff-care or counselling role for people with personal or domestic problems affecting their work
Communication	Providing an internal information service, perhaps in the form of a staff newspaper or magazine, handouts, booklets or videos
Employee relations	Handling disputes, grievances and industrial action, often dealing with unions or staff representatives
Dismissal	On an individual basis as a result of failure to meet requirements or as part of a redundancy or closure exercise, perhaps involving large numbers of people
Personnel administration	Record-keeping and monitoring legislative requirements, for example related to equal opportunities

Activity 1:4   Using Tyson's classification of personnel work into 'clerk of works', 'contracts manager', and 'architect', what role would each of these three types play in the functions listed in Table 1.1?

As we can see from the list of functions in Table 1.1, personnel had become a well-defined but low-status area of management by the 1980s. Associations such as the British Institute of Personnel Management (now the Chartered Institute of Personnel and Development) recruited members in increasing numbers, developed a qualification structure and attempted to define 'best practice'. Although the knowledge and practices they encouraged drew on psychology and sociology, they were largely pragmatic and common-sensical and did not present a particularly coherent approach to people management. Moreover, in some instances training and industrial relations were considered to be specialist fields outside mainstream personnel management. Traditional personnel managers were accused of having a narrow, functional outlook. Storey (1989, p.5) commented that personnel management '... has long been dogged by problems of credibility, marginality, ambiguity and a 'trash-can' labelling which has relegated it to a relatively disconnected set of duties – many of them tainted with a low-status "welfare" connotation'.

In practice, the background and training of many personnel managers left them speaking a different language from other managers and unable to comprehend wider business issues such as business strategy, market competition, labour economics, the roles of other organizational functions – let alone balance sheets (Giles and Williams, 1991). The scene was set for a reintegration of personnel management with wider trends in management thinking.

Management thinking

Like fashions in hairstyles and clothing, management ideas come and go. Today's best-selling management concept will not survive long before being overtaken by the next 'big idea'. Significantly, however, a consistent theme has prevailed for more than two decades: the most successful organizations make the most effective use of their people – their human resources.

The emergence of HRM was part of a major shift in the nature and meaning of management towards the end of the 20th century. This happened for a number of reasons. Perhaps most significantly, as we will see in Part 2 of this book, major developments in the structure and intensity of international competition forced companies to make radical changes in their working practices (Goss, 1994, p.1).

From the 1970s onwards, managers in the industrialized countries felt themselves to be on a roller coaster of change, expected to deliver improved business performance by whatever means they could muster. Their own careers and rewards were increasingly tied to those improvements and many were despatched to the ranks of the unemployed for not acting quickly and imaginatively enough. Caught between the need to manage decisively and fear of failure, managers sought credible new ideas as a potential route for survival.

The development of dynamic new economies in the Asia-Pacific region emphasized the weakness in traditional Western – specifically American – management methods. To meet competition from east Asia, industries and organizations in older developed countries were forced to restructure. The Japanese, in particular, provided both a threat and a role model that Eastern and Western companies tried to copy. Frequently, reorganized businesses in Australasia, Europe, North America and South Africa adopted Japanese techniques in an attempt to regain competitiveness. The term 'Japanization' came into vogue in the mid-

1980s to describe attempts in other countries to make practical use of 'Japanese' ideas and practices, reinforced by the impact of Japanese subsidiaries overseas. Initially, the main interest lay in forms of technical innovation and manufacturing methods such as 'continuous improvement' and 'just-in-time'. And their ways of managing people also attracted attention.

Stakeholders Employees have rights and interests beyond pay. They are stakeholders along with members of other recognizably separate groups or institutions with a special interest in an organization. These include shareholders, managers, customers, suppliers, lenders and government. Each group has its own priorities and demands and fits into the power structure controlling the organization. Employees have limited importance in free market countries such as the USA and the UK in comparison with most European and many Asian-Pacific countries. Notionally, shareholders are paramount in English-speaking countries. In reality, top managers normally have effective control and pursue their own interests, often at the expense of their staff. (This topic is dealt with at some length in Chapter 2.)

The Japanese role model

Until 1868 Japan had been sealed from the outside world for 300 years. The sense of being 'different' remains. Kobayashi (1992, p.18) comments that Japan has never set out to be integrated into the international community. Rather, the country adapted selective aspects of foreign cultures that seemed useful to its development. The Japanese borrowed freely from Western ideas, both at the turn of the century and again during the period of reconstruction after World War II. However, Japanese industrialists did not simply copy American management methods, they revitalized Asian values (Chung, 1991).

A key to Japanese industrial progress was the development of 'Japan Incorporated': the close-knit cooperation between government and business. Specific industrial sectors were targeted for long-term market penetration and dominance. Supposedly competing businesses acted cooperatively at the expense of foreign firms, sacrificing immediate profits for later success.

Economic problems hit the West increasingly from the 1970s onwards and Japan's growing industrial dominance became obvious. This stimulated a flow of influential writing (for example, Ouchi, 1981 and Pascale and Athos, 1981) leading to a continuing debate on the applicability of Japanese management methods to other countries. Ironically, Western managers have examined Japanese techniques just as intently as the Japanese studied the West half a century ago. Developing countries in east Asia took Japan rather than the USA as their model.

The term 'Japanization' came into vogue in the mid-1980s to describe attempts in other countries to make practical use of 'Japanese' ideas and practices as well as the impact of Japanese subsidiaries overseas. Japanese practice emphasized human resources as an organization's key asset. A core feature of Japanese businesses in the 1970s and 1980s was the emphasis on worker commitment, flexibility and development. Books such as Pascale and Athos' (1981) *The Art of Japanese Management* highlighted the competitive advantage that the Japanese gained through effective people management. The message came through that 'essentially, it is the human resource among all the factors of production which really makes the difference' (Storey, 2001, p.5).

Initially, the main interest lay in forms of technical innovation and manufacturing methods such as 'continuous improvement' and 'just-in-time'. More recently their ways of managing people have attracted attention. People management became a central strategic issue rather than a 'necessary inconvenience' (Goss, 1994, p.4). We will see in later chapters that the component ideas of HRM parallel elements of Japanese people management in that period. But, whereas HRM is still a matter of rhetoric for most Western managers, the Japanese viewed it as a way of life: an instrumental approach to ever-increasing efficiency focused on employee commitment and skill. Traditionally, Japanese companies placed the interests of their employees first amongst their stakeholders (see Key concept 1.4), followed by customers and lastly the shareholders. This is virtually the opposite situation to that found in free market Western countries such as Australia, Britain, Canada or the USA. But the recession of the 1990s forced a number of Japanese companies to adopt Western ways.

The Japanese role model is a mixture of racial stereotyping, myth and reality. It is difficult to tell when truth ends and myth begins. Foreign commentators encountering a radically different culture tend to emphasize the points of difference rather the similarities. The Japanese were seen as workaholics, rarely taking holidays and eager to work every available hour. They were conformists with a distinctive form of decision making based on consensus. They worked in teams and hated to be seen as individuals. They searched for continuous improvement and were proud to be identified with their employing organization. Large businesses offered slow but steady promotion paths and lifelong careers in return for total commitment. However, Japan is constantly changing. Most accounts of Japanese business practice refer to the behaviour and beliefs of a generation who had to work hard to restore the economy after World War II. The younger generation do not necessarily share their view of life.

Japanese companies first drew on their profits in lean times in order to keep their workforce. Companies in English-speaking countries would have been unable to withstand the wrath of shareholders demanding dividend payments. Responsibility for the security of their workforce was not simply a matter of goodwill or obligation but the necessary price for commitment from employees. This was difficult for companies operating in a global environment, exposed to fluctuations in the value of the yen or overseas economic demand. These companies made considerable use of peripheral workforces – primarily their suppliers' employees – who took the brunt whenever demand fell. These peripheral workers received little or no income for prolonged periods while favoured employees in multinational organizations maintained their privileges. But as recession deepened closures and retrenchments became a new feature of the Japanese industrial scene.

Question: What were the most significant influences of Japanese people management on the development of HRM?

From personnel to human resource management

HRM-type themes, including 'human capital theory' (discussed in Part 2) and 'human asset accounting' can be found in literature dating as far back as the 1970s. But the modern view of HRM first gained prominence in 1981 with its introduction on the prestigious MBA course at Harvard Business School. The Harvard MBA provided a blueprint for many other courses throughout North America and the rest of the world, making its interpretation of HRM particularly influential (Beer *et al.*, 1984; Guest, 1987; Poole, 1990). Simultaneously, other interpretations were being developed in Michigan and New York.

These ideas spread to other countries in the 1980s and 1990s, particularly Australia, New Zealand, parts of northern Europe – especially the UK, Ireland and Scandinavia – and also South and South-East Asia and South Africa. Today, the HRM approach is influential in many parts of the world. Typically in this period, HRM was presented in four distinctive ways. First, as a radically new approach to managing people, demarcated sharply from traditional personnel management (Storey, 1989, p.4). Personnel management was commonly viewed as having an operational focus, emphasizing technical skills and day-to-day functions such as recruitment and selection, training, salary administration and employee relations. 'Personnel' remains a detached and neutral approach to staff. By contrast, HRM was often portrayed as being proactive – looking at people in economic terms as either assets or costs to be actively managed. HRM was seen to be strategic, tying people management to business objectives. It was an attempt to manage people – not necessarily employees – in the long-term interests of the business.

Secondly, HRM was seen as an integrated approach that provided a coherent programme, linking all aspects of people management. Whereas personnel managers employed a piecemeal range of sophisticated techniques for assessment or selection, HRM integrated these within a meaningful and organized framework. Each element needed to fit into a pattern that ultimately met business needs. Additionally, HRM was seen to be holistic: in other words, it was concerned with the overall people requirements of an organization. It implied a significant shift towards more conceptual, higher-level concerns such as the structure and culture of the organization and the provision of necessary competences.

Thirdly, HRM represented a consistent view of people management in which employees were treated as valuable assets. An organization's reward systems, performance measures, promotion and learning opportunities were to be used to maximize the utilization of its human resources. In particular, they were focused on the attitudes, beliefs and commitment of employees to achieve behavioural consistency and a culture of commitment.

Finally, HRM was presented as a general management function. Personnel management was often viewed as the work of specialists, while HRM was the responsibility of all managers. In some organizations human resource experts provided an internal consultancy service to line managers. There was a particular stress on the role of top management and an overall increase in the status of people management. Traditional personnel managers had little power or prestige.

Why should HRM have attracted such attention, particularly from senior managers? From a strategic viewpoint, Lengnick-Hall and Lengnick-Hall (1988) identify a clear rationale for adopting the HRM approach:

- HRM offers a broader range of solutions for complex organizational problems.
- It ensures that an organization's people are considered as well as its financial and technological resources when objectives are set or capabilities assessed.
- It forces the explicit consideration of the individuals who implement and comprise the strategy.
- Two-way links are encouraged between the formulation of strategy and its human resource implications, avoiding problems that might arise from: (a) subordinating strategic considerations to human resource preferences; and (b) neglecting an organization's people as a potential source of organizational competence and competitive advantage.

Activity 1:5

Summarize the main differences between personnel management and HRM as you see them.

The renewed emphasis on the importance of human resources drew attention to the practice of people management. Conventionally, this has been divided between line and personnel managers – now frequently called human resource managers. For some, HRM was simply a matter of relabelling 'personnel' to redress the criticisms made about traditional personnel management and sceptics have argued that familiar personnel functions were repackaged and given a more upmarket image – 'old wine in new bottles' (Armstrong, 1987). Indeed, until the early 1990s, human resource management textbooks tended to be slightly revised personnel management texts covering familiar topics in a prescriptive manner.

Torrington and Hall (1991, p.15) concur that the term was adopted in order to get away from the ineffectual image of previous eras: '… personnel managers seem constantly to suffer from paranoia about their lack of influence and are ready to snatch at anything – like a change in title – that might enhance their status'. It has also been fuelled by long-standing criticisms by other managers. This includes a general prejudice that is often expressed within organizations and sometimes finds its way into print. Thus the following from an article entitled 'Support for an old-fashioned view' in *The Independent*, 12 May 1994:

> Many of us have long held the view that personnel management, or human resource management as companies sometimes insist on calling it, is a uniquely irrelevant executive function fulfilling no obvious purpose other than to stifle initiative, flair and creativity.

'Averagely derogative' remarks

The following is from 'Inside Track: A prelude to platitudes: Handing out staff guidelines to good and bad "behaviours" is surely a sign that an organisation is in deep trouble', Lucy Kellaway, *Financial Times*, 17 December 2001.

> Last week I printed a piece of incomprehensible HR waffle that purported to lay out the future of HR. I made a few averagely derogative remarks about it and asked for help in translating it.
>
> In response I have received 120 translations, 115 of which referred to the HR profession with scepticism, sarcasm, rudeness or obscenity. One manager e-mailed me a hostile reply and the following day got his secretary to e-mail me again, begging me to disregard it.
>
> It would seem that HR is now in the same category as Railtrack. No one has a good word to say for it. So demoralized are HR people that they churn out junk and when you attack it they do not even have the spirit to get angry. Hay Management Consultants, which penned the original guff, has responded cheerily, offering champagne for the best answer.

Where does this prejudice come from? Some commentators have argued that personnel people should relinquish their ambiguous roles and adopt unashamedly managerialist positions. Others concluded that if human resources were fundamental to business success they were too important to be left to operational personnel managers. One of Lucy Kellaway's e-mailers stated: 'For HR to work it should (a) rename itself personnel and (b) stick to the basics, e.g. payroll, healthcare, training – of other people, not themselves – and pensions.'

Other commentators have argued that major human resource decisions should be made by top managers and the consequences of those decisions should be carried through by line management. These considerations place HRM on a strategic rather an operational footing and therefore make HRM a concept of greater interest than personnel management to senior executives. Whatever the underlying level of hostility, or press disdain, it remains the case that, in larger organizations, there has been a reappraisal of the previously unfashionable and low-status personnel department. 'Personnel' cannot be regarded as peripheral if it controls an organization's people because the rhetoric states that they are its greatest resources. Many businesses have adopted some form of HRM as a recognition of this importance. As Fowler (1987) famously stated: 'HRM represents the discovery of personnel management by chief executives.'

Activity 1:6

Summarize the attitude of personnel specialists and their critics towards the profession. Is 'relabelling' personnel as HRM anything more than a make-over – a cosmetic change?

The new managerialism

Schuler (1990) emphasized that the human resource function had an opportunity to shift from being an 'employee advocate' (associated with personnel management) to a 'member of the management team'. Schuler's view was that this required human resource professionals to be concerned with the bottom line, profits, organizational effectiveness and business survival. In other words, human resource issues should be addressed as business issues.

In fact, line and general managers have been instrumental in the adoption of HRM, often pushing changes through despite the resistance of personnel specialists (Storey, 2001, p.7). Radical changes in business structures and supportive – largely right-wing – governments encouraged a renewed confidence in the power of managers to manage. The balance of power moved away from workers and their representatives with the collapse of traditional heavy industries. High levels of unemployment allowed managers to pick and choose new recruits. Existing employees felt under pressure to be more flexible under the threat of losing their jobs. As a result, managers were able to design more competitive organizations with new forms of employment relationships.

Encouraged by the writing of management gurus such as Peters and Waterman (1982) and Kanter (1989), managers eagerly adopted new forms of organization. Businesses moved away from multi-layered, rigid hierarchies and long-term career paths. Instead we have seen an increase in flatter, project-oriented forms of organizations resourced in a flexible way – including short-term, part-time and contract workers. People managers found themselves needing a framework within which to comprehend and justify these innovative practices. The stage was set for HRM, which was presented as a coherent and integrated philosophy by its originators, covering every aspect of people management (Beer *et al.*, 1984, p.1).

Laughing gurus

The use of humour is one key to the success of management gurus. A UK ESRC-funded research study shows that successful gurus employ skilful communication techniques, especially humour, to promote their sometimes uncomfortable messages. Filling a lecture theatre or conference venue with laughter avoids alienating their audiences and brings people 'on-side'.

▶

Researchers Dr Tim Clark and Dr David Greatbatch of King's College London analysed the techniques used by world-famous gurus such as Tom Peters, Rosabeth Moss Kanter and Gary Hamel: 'Examining live and video recorded performances of leading international gurus enabled us to analyse the presentational techniques they use to disseminate their ideas during live presentations,' said Dr Greatbatch.

Gurus are faced with the problem of advocating unorthodox organizational practices that their audiences are probably not using, and disparaging the practices they are using. This is a delicate task with an inherent risk of alienating their audience members. So how do they do it? Dr Clark argues: 'These gurus remain highly regarded on the world speaking stage and we wanted to discover their grammar of persuasion – in other words the communication techniques which underpin their frequently charismatic and persuasive public speaking performances.'

The study shows that gurus avoid offence by evoking laughter and telling stories. 'Basically, whenever the guru says anything potentially uncomfortable to audiences of managers they use humour and wrap it up as a joke,' said Dr Greatbatch. The researchers found that gurus used a number of specific techniques to 'invite' laughter. 'Collective audience laughter is not simply a spontaneous reaction to humour or jokes,' argued David Greatbatch. 'Rather the gurus invite laughter by indicating when it is appropriate for the audience members to do so.'

Gurus used verbal and non-verbal actions to invite laughter, including:

- laughing themselves
- using exaggerated, ironic or comedic gestures
- showing their teeth in a 'laughing' smile.

Having achieved laughter from the audience, the gurus played on this bonding to encourage the audience to feel part of an 'in group' sharing a common viewpoint with the gurus. The audience then began to turn against the management practice(s) being criticized by the guru.

Storytelling seemed to be particularly important in the two processes of evoking laughter and deflecting criticism. The researchers found that more than two-thirds of audience laughter studied occurred within the context of stories. Stories make the gurus' messages more entertaining and memorable and also reinforce the authority of the gurus' knowledge. So their stories make constant references to famous and respected managers and organizations, personally known to the gurus. Audience research confirms that those speakers who use funny stories to develop their arguments are those who are most remembered.

'Our research clearly shows that gurus deploy humour at those points in their presentation where they face possible dissent,' asserts Dr Greatbatch:

> Because they package their ideas in a non-offensive way, the world's leading gurus are never booed from the stage and typically generate very positive audience reaction and a high feel-good factor. Anyone can learn the techniques which they use and public speakers ranging from politicians to trainers could benefit from having a greater range of presentation techniques to deploy when necessary.

Source: *HRMGuide.co.uk* (http://www.hrmguide.co.uk), 26 April 2001.

Table 1.2	Core roles in HRM

Function	Roles
1. Planning and organizing for work, people and HRM	Strategic perspective Organization design Change management Corporate 'wellness' management
2. People acquisition and development	Staffing the organization Training and development Career management Performance management Industrial relations
3. Administration of policies, programmes and practices	Compensation management Information management Administrative management Financial management

Source: Plenary group of the Steering Committee for HRM Standards and Qualifications, South Africa, 1999.

Question: Does this list of core HR roles differ in any significant way from the list of personnel functions given in Table 1.1?

Summary

In this chapter we introduced the concept of human resource management. HRM has evolved from a number of different strands of thought and is best described as a loose philosophy of people management rather than a focused methodology. It derives largely from the 20th century but incorporates older notions about the management of people at work. These ideas have many different roots and they do not fit comfortably within one coherent and self-consistent body of knowledge. One major point of debate has been the difference – if any – between HRM and 'traditional' personnel management. The development of HRM continues today as new management theories, fashions and fads continue to be developed.

Further reading

There are many introductory texts on HRM, several with an orientation towards a single country. The following texts are of more general use. Wendy Holloway's (1991) *Work Psychology and Organizational Behaviour* (Sage) remains one of the best overviews of scientific management, human factors, human relations and other early approaches. The various earlier editions of *Organizational Behaviour* by Andrzej Huczynski and David Buchanan (2000) also contain useful discussions of these early movements, complete with illustrations. The issues involved in the development of personnel management and HRM are best covered in texts edited by John Storey, including the second edition of *Human Resource Management: A Critical Text*, published by Thomson Learning in 2001.

Review questions

1 How would you explain the difference between 'organizing' and 'managing' people?

2 What is HRM? Is it really different from personnel management?

3 How much does the concept of HRM owe to Japanese management practices?

4 List the major tasks of 'traditional' personnel management. How do these functions compare with the core roles of HRM?

5 Which theoretical developments do you consider to have contributed most to modern people management?

6 What is meant by 'management gurus'? What value can be placed on the ideas they have popularized?

Problem for discussion and analysis

Read the following case study which is largely based on a 'eulogy' of George Cadbury, designed to present both the man and the company in a good light. How many of today's methods of people management can you identify?

George Cadbury (1839–1922)

George Cadbury took on people management without the benefit of a business education or the advice of management gurus. Along with other Quaker manufacturers, Cadbury was eulogized as a hero of Victorian industry. A champion of paternalist management, he exemplified the virtues of thrift and hard work tempered with a concern for the welfare of his workers.

Virtuous hard work

His father, John Cadbury, started a tea and coffee business in Birmingham, England in 1824. Forty years later, aged 22, George Cadbury took on the ailing company with his brother Richard. Brought up with stern discipline, self-denial was their way of life, believing in hard work and a frugal lifestyle.

George removed every distraction, even a morning paper. He abstained from tobacco and alcohol, and later tea and coffee. This was reflected in the business, which concentrated on cocoa and chocolate. He loved sport, especially cricket and boating, but these were largely sacrificed. Each day was planned for maximum effectiveness. In winter he started work by 7.00 am – earlier in summer – rising at 5.15 am. Frequently, he worked until 9.00 pm. Breaks consisted of a walk home for lunch and a later meal at work: bread and butter and water. George Cadbury followed Emerson's maxim that 'the one prudence in life is concentration; the one evil dissipation'.

Total quality

The business became profitable and expanded. As with other manufacturers in an age of low standards, Cadbury's products contained only one-fifth cocoa, the rest being potato starch, sago flour and treacle. In 1861, for example, the company was manufacturing 'Iceland Moss', containing 10 per cent 'Icelandic moss gelatine'. A 'comforting gruel', it probably tasted medicinal and was marketed as having healing properties. Unhappy with such poor products, Cadbury became the first UK firm to make pure cocoa for drinking. They imported Dutch machinery that pressed out some of the cocoa butter, making it unnecessary to add starchy material to counter the natural fat. The medical press was drawing attention to the danger of food additives and Cadbury's new product received favourable mentions in the *British Medical Journal* and *The Lancet*. The Adulteration of Food Act 1872 required manufacturers to state clearly the nature of any additives to their products. Cadbury gradually abandoned inferior products and adopted the motto 'absolutely pure', eventually becoming the leading producers in the UK.

The greenfield site and the all-embracing company

In 1879 development began on a new factory and workers' housing at a greenfield site outside Birmingham. The development was presented as a rare appreciation, for the time, that industrial success depended on people more than machines. There were two motives: business efficiency and staff welfare. As 'our people spend the greater part of their lives at their work … we wish to make it less irksome by environing them with pleasant and wholesome sights, sounds and conditions'. At the same time, having new, efficient premises had considerable marketing value. The British chocolate industry was keen to emulate the French – regarded as the best producers. The French Menier company advertised extensively in the UK, featuring model premises and employee welfare. They had started to build workers' accommodation in 1870. Cadbury chose the French-sounding name of Bournville and set about constructing a village for their key employees. The village and 370 houses were handed over to an independent Bournville Village Trust in 1900 to avoid the accusation of using tied housing.

Employee relations

Unions barely existed at the time. Employers and workers were normally hostile, but the Cadburys had a close, sympathetic relationship with their workers. They believed that business success lay in cooperation rather than friction. Despite initial heavy losses, they gradually pushed workers' pay above the wretched levels normal at that time. They used incentives to encourage punctuality and other improvements but loyalty and commitment were largely won through positive personal relations. Cadbury was the first company in Birmingham to adopt a Saturday half-holiday. The brothers addressed everyone by their first names and played cricket with the workers on spare afternoons.

Between 1879 and 1899 the workforce increased from 230 to 2685, including 1885 women production workers. The Cadburys' business methods were relatively gentle but they were frequently accused of being autocratic. They were deeply concerned with workers' welfare and standards of morality, watching over them keenly. Their own code of business ethics removed many of the evils of the factory system. For them the factory was a centre of learning, fostering good hygiene and intellectual development.

The brothers required female employees to wear company dresses at work. The firm provided the material, free for the first dress and subsidized thereafter. Workers were asked to put on a clean frock every Monday morning. This gave them a clean appearance and encouraged self-respect, making a favourable impression on visitors. Until the 1940s, Cadbury did not employ married women. As explained by Dean Kitchin (1910), quoted in Gardiner (1923):

In this vast multitude, all dressed in pure white and ready for a day's active work, there was not a single married woman. For Mr Cadbury will never take the mothers away from their homes and children; he told me, with a grave smile, that when he had allowed married women to work with him, he found that their husbands were quite content to loaf about doing nothing, living on the wages of their wives; and, he added, that the poor things invariably came back after child-bearing to work long before they were fit to work.

George Cadbury reintroduced his grandfather's practice of a brief daily service with the workpeople. This was also a custom followed by the chocolate firm of Fry at Bristol. According to Joseph Fry:

> In addition to the religious benefit which may be looked for, I think that there is a great advantage in bringing the workpeople once a day under review. It is often a means of observing their conduct and checking any tendency to impropriety.

Valuing the human resource

Traditionally, it was believed that labour should be bought in the cheapest market like any other commodity. Improved pay or conditions were undesirable expenses. George Cadbury believed that economizing on labour was unethical and also bad business. He considered employees' safety, health, and even pleasure to be positive investments. Commonly thought optional, Cadbury regarded them as essential for efficient management.

He considered that people were infinitely valuable and should be used effectively. Work should be well paid but directed to make best use of expensive labour: using low-paid workers to compete with automation was foolish. New technology and efficiency went along with high pay. Inevitably, new machinery displaced workers and, if required, he did not shirk at dismissal. However, the business was always growing so redundant workers from one department could transfer to another.

Sources: Gardiner (1923); Smith, Child and Rowlinson (1990).

2

The concept of HRM

Objectives

The purpose of this chapter is to:

- Outline the variety of ways in which HRM is defined.
- Offer a working definition for the purposes of this book.
- Discuss the most influential early models of HRM.
- Review some of the evidence for the adoption of HRM.

Defining human resource management

Maps and models of HRM

HRM policies and their consequences

A harder approach – people as human *resources*

Adopting HRM

Different interpretations of HRM

Professional certification

HRM in other countries

Summary

Further reading

Review questions

Case study for discussion and analysis

Defining human resource management

In the previous chapter we introduced the concept of human resource management and outlined the territory of people management covered by specialists in personnel or HRM. But what exactly is 'human resource management'? In Chapter 1 we discussed some of the theoretical and other developments that led to HRM being distinguished to some extent from 'traditional' personnel management. In this chapter we will examine the concept in greater detail.

Many people find HRM to be a vague and elusive concept, not least because it seems to have a variety of meanings (see Table 2.1). Pinning down an acceptable definition can seem like trying to hit a moving target in a fog. This confusion reflects the different interpretations found in articles and books about human resource management. HRM is an elastic term (Storey, 1989, p.8). It covers a range of applications that vary from book to book and organization to organization.

Simple reflection on the three words 'human resource management' does not provide much enlightenment. 'Human' implies it has something to do with people; 'management' places it in the domain of business and organization; but 'resource' is a highly ambiguous concept that many people find difficult to relate to.

<table>
<tr><td>HRM
in reality</td><td>

Human resources

'Sir, – While visiting a patient in Edinburgh's Western General Hospital, I was shocked to see a six-foot long board with large letters proclaiming HUMAN RESOURCES. This distinguishes people who work in the hospital – doctors, nurses, porters, office workers, painters, managers – from other resources such as computers, laser beams, toilet rolls, refuse bins, beds, etc.

If these human resources are ill, are they labelled "out of order" or "broken down" and when being treated, are they being repaired? Are babies listed as "in process of being manufactured" with an expected date when they will be "operational"? Are old and dead people "non-usable human resources" or can they be listed as "replacement parts"?

When we define humans as resources, we are in danger of forgetting that we are dealing with people!'

Source: Cited in Price (1997).

</td></tr>
</table>

In fact, much of the academic literature suffers from forgetting the human element in HRM. Most of us would not take kindly to being classified as a 'resource', along with our desks and computers. It seems that there is a fundamental difficulty in considering a person's worth or value to an organization. This arises from that person's humanity. People are different from other resources and cannot be discussed in exactly the same way as equipment or finances. This difference lies at the heart of the antagonism and ambiguity that surrounds HRM in practice.

From an organizational perspective human resources encompass the people in an organization – its employees – and the human potential available to a business. The people in an organization offer different skills, abilities and knowledge that may or may not be appropriate to the needs of the business. Additionally, their commitment and motivation vary. Some people identify with an organization and are motivated to help achieve its objectives. Others regard their employing firm as a vehicle for personal goals. Some may be overworked while others are underutilized. Invariably, there is a gap or mismatch between the actual performance of employees and the ideal requirements of a business.

HRM focuses on closing this gap to achieve greater organizational effectiveness. As we shall see later in this section, this has been referred to as the 'matching model'.

The human potential available to a business includes the recognition and development of unrealized skills and knowledge. Ingenuity and creativity can be tapped to develop innovative services and products. This also extends to people outside an organization – contractors, consultants, freelancers, temporary and part-time workers – who can add expertise, deal with unusual problems and provide the flexibility to give a competitive advantage.

Storey (2001) introduces *Human Resource Management: A Critical Text* by saying:

> It is hard to imagine that it is scarcely much more than a decade since the time when the term 'human resource management' (HRM) was rarely used – at least outside the USA. Yet nowadays the term is utterly familiar around the globe and hardly a week goes by without the publication of another book on the subject.

But he observes that despite the proliferation of books, journals, conferences, academic sub-groups, etc., the subject remains 'and always has been from its earliest inception, highly controversial'. Specifically, he highlights questions about the nature of HRM, the domain it covers, the characteristics of HR practice, the reach of the subject and its antecedents, outcomes and impact.

Table 2.1	Textbook definitions of HRM	
Definition		*Source*
Human resource management involves all management decisions and actions that affect the relationship between the organization and employees – its human resources.		Beer *et al.*, 1984, p.1
A method of maximizing economic return from labour resource by integrating HRM into business strategy.		Keenoy, 1990, p.3
A strategic, coherent and comprehensive approach to the management and development of the organization's human resources in which every aspect of that process is wholly integrated within the overall management of the organization. HRM is essentially an ideology.		Armstrong, 1992, p.9
Perhaps it is best to regard HRM as simply a notion of how people can best be managed *in the interests of the organization*.		Armstrong, 1994
A diverse body of thought and practice, loosely unified by a concern to integrate the management of personnel more closely with the core management activity of organizations.		Goss, 1994, p.1
HRM is a discourse and technology of power that aims to resolve the gap inherent in the contract of employment between the capacity to work and its exercise and, thereby, organize individual workers into a collective, productive power or force.		Townley, 1994, p.138
Human resource management is a distinctive approach to employment management which seeks to achieve competitive advantage through the strategic development of a highly committed and capable workforce, using an integrated array of cultural, structural and personnel techniques.		Storey, 2001, p.6
Human resource management is the attraction, selection, retention, development and use of human resources in order to achieve both individual and organizational objectives.		Cascio, 1998, p.2
Human resources can be described as the organizational function accountable for obtaining and maintaining qualified employees. In today's complex environment, fulfilling that mission is a major contributor to an organization's success.		American Management Association, 2000

Along with management writers (primarily American) on HRM, Storey pinpoints inputs from a wider field that have supported the increased importance of HRM:

- the resource-based theory of the firm
- the 'learning organization'
- 'knowledge management'.

We will discuss these inputs further in later sections of this book.

Table 2.1 gives a selection of definitions taken from various textbooks published over the past 20 years. Generally they offer an academic view of HRM. Would the definitions be any different if decided by practitioners who were actively involved in human resource management? A plenary group – including practitioners – of the Steering Committee for HRM Standards and Qualifications in South Africa produced the following working definition in 1999:

It is proposed that we take human resource management to be that part of management concerned with:

- all the decisions, strategies, factors, principles, operations, practices, functions, activities and methods related to the management of people as employees in any type of organization (including small and micro enterprises and virtual organizations);
- all the dimensions related to people in their employment relationships, and all the dynamics that flow from it (including in the realization of the potential of individual employees in terms of their aspirations);
- all aimed at adding value to the delivery of goods and services, as well as to the quality of work life for employees, and hence helping to ensure continuous organizational success in transformative environments.

We will see that the variety, scope and intention found in definitions of HRM can be explained, in part, by some of the theories and models of human resource management to be explored in the next section.

Activity 2:1	Compare and contrast the textbook and practitioner definitions of HRM. In what ways (if any) are they different?

We conclude this section by reflecting on Storey's (2001) comment that HRM is 'an amalgam of description, prescription and logical deduction' and that it is an 'historically situated phenomenon'. Moreover, for Storey, HRM reflects the beliefs and assumptions of influential 'leading-edge' practitioners. As we shall see in the next section, there are grounds also to believe that it arose when confidence had been lost in more traditional approaches to people management because of new levels and types of competition.

HRM has often been presented as a proactive approach to managing people (Storey, 2001). This entails an emphasis on long-term thinking, anticipating changes and requirements before they become critical. But, in reality, HRM is a mixture of anticipation and reaction (Price, 2000). Tamkin, Barber and Dench (1997) pointed out that human resource managers may have to deal with unexpected problems and radical changes in employer policy – for example, site closures and redundancies because of market changes. To do so, they must react quickly and competently within the bounds of employment law and contractual agreements. This requires that HRM should be both pragmatic and eclectic (Price, 2000): pragmatic because it aims to achieve practical solutions to real work problems; and eclectic because those solutions can be drawn from a variety of theoretical and managerial traditions, as we saw in Chapter 1.

**HRM
in reality**

Reuters: 'Our people'

A major source of competitive advantage for Reuters comes from the energy, ideas and commitment of its employees. 2001 was not an easy year for our people and we recognize with gratitude the continued dedication shown by them. The reorganization of our company, whilst widely recognized to be in the best interests of the business, also brought with it the personal uncertainty that accompanies change. In addition we carried out a job reduction programme, designed to avoid compulsory redundancies wherever possible, which resulted in more than 1000 people leaving in 2001.

To provide employees with the information they need to understand and achieve our business objectives, we make extensive use of the company's intranet as a communications tool. Meetings are regularly held between the management and employees and union representatives so that the views of employees can be taken into account in making decisions which may affect their interests. Reuters European Employee Forum operates as a pan-European works council. The chief executive and other executive directors meet with the Forum regularly. We undertake regular employee surveys to evaluate morale and to identify any employee issues that need to be addressed. The results are communicated throughout the group.

We are committed to the training and development of our people. It is our policy that selection of employees including for recruitment, training, development and promotion should be determined solely on their skills, abilities and other requirements which are relevant to the job and in accordance with the laws in the country concerned. Reuters provides training for employees on health and safety and provides occupational healthcare in its major locations. In view of the deaths in 2001 of six of our colleagues in the World Trade Center and two journalists in Afghanistan we have reviewed the adequacy of our policies, training and procedures for employees generally and for those working in dangerous places in particular. We have reaffirmed the standing instructions to employees to avoid risks wherever possible and for hostile environment training and protective equipment to be provided to all employees who need them.

Reuters is dedicated to a policy of equal opportunities for its employees. We maintain a strict policy prohibiting discriminatory practices on the basis of sex, race, religion, disability, age or any other characteristics protected by applicable law.

Source: Reuters Group plc *Annual Review 2001*.

Question: To what extent do these statements reflect a HRM perspective?

Before we finish this section we need to determine our working definition of HRM for the purposes of this book. This is set out in Key concept 2.1.

**Key
concept
2:1**

Human resource management A philosophy of people management based on the belief that human resources are uniquely important to sustained business success. An organization gains competitive advantage by using its people effectively, drawing on their expertise and ingenuity to meet clearly defined objectives. HRM is aimed at recruiting capable, flexible and committed people, managing and rewarding their performance and developing key competencies.

Maps and models of HRM

Keenoy (1999, p.14–15) compares HRM with a hologram:

> As with a hologram, HRM changes its appearance as we move around its image. Each shift of stance reveals another facet, a darker depth, a different contour. As a fluid entity of apparently multiple identities and forms, it is not surprising that every time we look at it, it is slightly different. This is why, conceptually, HRMism appears to be a moving target, and why, empirically, it has no fixed (fixable) forms.

Keenoy's comparison is helpful in explaining why there are so many divergent definitions of HRM. There are numerous, widely different interpretations, some in the shape of formal models. The two most influential are the Harvard and Michigan models from the 1980s, which we will consider later in this chapter. Consistent with the confusion over the definition of HRM, the major models are to some extent contradictory but also have common elements. Partly this is because some of the key concepts have arisen several times in different contexts. Sisson (1990) contends that there are four major features that appear to some degree in all HRM models and theories:

- Integration of human resource policies with each other and with the organization's business plan. HRM is a key instrument of business strategy, viewing employees as important assets.
- Responsibility for managing people moves from personnel specialists to senior (line) managers. Specialists provide a consultancy service for line managers.
- Employee relations shifts away from collective bargaining – dialogue between management and unions. Instead, direct discussion between management and individual employees is encouraged.
- A stress on commitment to the organization and personal initiative.

Key concept 2:2

Hard and soft HRM   Storey (1989) has distinguished between hard and soft forms of HRM, typified by the Michigan and Harvard models respectively. 'Hard' HRM focuses on the resource side of human resources. It emphasizes costs in the form of 'headcounts' and places control firmly in the hands of management. Their role is to manage numbers effectively, keeping the workforce closely matched with requirements in terms of both bodies and behaviour. 'Soft' HRM, on the other hand, stresses the 'human' aspects of HRM. Its concerns are with communication and motivation. People are led rather than managed. They are involved in determining and realizing strategic objectives.

Softer models of HRM typically suggest that human resource managers should become:

- *Enablers*: structuring organizations to allow employees to achieve objectives.
- *Empowerers*: devolving decision making to the lowest level.
- *Facilitators*: encouraging and assisting employees.

From this perspective, managers are no longer supervisors. Organizations move away from rigid hierarchies and power distinctions towards people taking responsibility for their own work. Guest (1987) provides a fusion of various HRM approaches into a theory of HRM that incorporates a number of policy goals:

- Aim for a high level of commitment from employees, so that workers identify with the organization's goals and contribute actively to its improvement and success.

- This enables the organization to obtain a high-quality output from workers who want to continually improve standards.
- An expectation of flexibility from workers – willingness to depart from fixed job definitions, working practices and conditions.
- Strategic integration – all these strands link the organization's strategy. They are directed towards agreed objectives and interact with each other in a cohesive way.

These goals require support from top managers and integration of human resource strategy with business policy. The activities we outlined in Table 1.1 in the first chapter of this book are linked and overlaid by HR staff so as to improve communication and increase involvement, commitment and productivity. They are integrated and match the requirements of the organization's strategic plans. We cannot take a decision or make a change in one without having repercussions in at least some of the other areas.

The central aim of the HRM approach is to combine all personnel or human resource activities into an organized and integrated programme to meet the strategic objectives of an enterprise. It moves us away from common-sense solutions for day-to-day problems, such as 'get someone to fill that job', towards a conscious attempt to think through the consequences of hiring that 'someone'. Do we want a recruit who is perfect for that particular position right now, or an individual who might require considerable training but shows great adaptability? Do we hire someone for an overworked production department, knowing that the sales department is forecasting a drop in orders later in the year? The essential point of HRM is that the functions should be managed as a whole, and not as stand-alone activities.

Activity 2:2	What do you understand by the statement that 'functions should be managed as a whole, and not as stand-alone activities'?

Karen Legge (1989; 1995; 2001), for example, has been a steadfast critic of simplistic or evangelistic interpretations of HRM. The rhetoric of HRM claims that personnel and human resource management are distinctively different forms of people management. She demonstrates some flaws in this argument (see Legge, 1989, p.20; 1995, p.36). First, we have seen that 'hard' and 'soft' models of HRM themselves describe very different approaches. The 'soft' model can be identified readily with the welfarist tradition in personnel management in countries such as the UK and Ireland, Australia, New Zealand and South Africa. Secondly, most texts do not actually compare like with like:

- Accounts of HRM are normative – they are theoretical models of how human resource management could or should take place. That is to say, they express an 'ideal' or a set of intentions for HRM. They do not tell us how human resource management actually happens in the real world. Moreover, the intentions of soft HRM are often pious and contradictory. We saw earlier that they are derivative of much older concepts and techniques. What makes them 'HRM' is that their components are welded together into expressions of a particular – if divergent – philosophy of people management.
- In contrast, accounts of personnel management are generally descriptive of personnel practice. Models of personnel are grounded in decades of activity whereas HRM is still comparatively new and empirical evidence of its conduct is only beginning to emerge.

In short, we are comparing the theory of a young form of people management (HRM) with the practice of an old form (personnel management). If we seek out normative models of personnel management, Legge concludes that there is not much difference with normative models of HRM. We can do so by examining textbook accounts of personnel management in the 1980s, which used the same terminology of 'integrating with organizational goals' and 'vesting control in the line' as newer HRM literature of the 'soft' variety. However, she finds differences in emphasis:

- Personnel management focuses on the non-managerial workforce. HRM concentrates on managers and the 'core workforce'.
- HRM is vested in line managers in their role as business managers not people managers. The focus is on managing all resources to maximize profit.
- HRM models feature the role of senior managers in managing the culture of organizations.

Cakar and Bititci (2001) argue that whereas a number of authors, including Legge, have attempted to classify the various models of HRM using terms such as 'descriptive', 'normative' and 'prescriptive' (see Table 2.2), they do not offer precise definitions of these terms. They identify two sources of confusion: (a) confusion over the different types of classification – e.g. the difference if any between 'normative' (Legge, 1995) and 'prescriptive' (Storey, 1994); and (b) lack of clear definitions for each classification.

Activity 2:3	Given Cakar and Bititci's criticism, how useful are 'typologies' of HRM such as Legge's?

From a business process perspective, Cakar and Bititci (2001) state that:

> One may summarize that the 80s were all about automation. In the manufacturing industry FMS, FAS, Robots, AGV'S etc. were commonplace. The 90s have been about people, this is evident in the development of TQM concepts throughout the 90s focusing on delegation, involvement, ownership cross functional teamwork, self managed works teams and so on. The European Business Excellence Model (EFQM) together with other developments, such as Investor In People in the UK, makes the role and importance of people and the need for robust processes to manage people explicit.
>
> HRM (People Management) is a critical input enhancing the business results. In EFQM, HRM criteria covers the planning, managing and improving the Human Resources; identifying, developing and sustaining people's knowledge and competencies; involving and empowering people. All these things have an effect on business results, because Human Resources are key assets. HRM has a significant impact on the performance of the manufacturing business.
>
> Furthermore, the 90s were also about business processes. Since the seminal paper by Hammer and Champy (1993) there has been a lot of work investigating and researching business process architectures and models. The CIM-OSA Business Process Architecture … classifies business processes as Manage Processes, Operate Processes and Support Processes… Within this architecture HRM is classified as a support process together with finance and IT. Therefore there is a need to understand HRM as a Business Process in order to improve manufacturing performance.

Table 2.2	Classifications of HRM models		
	Storey (1994)	*Legge (1995)*	*Tyson (1995)*
	Conceptual	Normative	Normative
	Descriptive	Descriptive-functional	Descriptive
	Prescriptive	Descriptive-behavioural	Analytical
		Critical evaluative	

The same argument can apply to service, non-profit and public organizations. Fitz-Enz (1994) argues that businesses can adopt one of three approaches to HRM, offering the practitioner one of three career choices:

- *Zombies*: those that take the traditional 'staff as expense' approach to people management. Estimating that 30–50 per cent of companies took this approach, especially small–medium, family-owned enterprises described as the 'living dead' with no real professionalism in any of their managerial activities.

- *Reactors*: where line managers have grabbed back HR responsibilities as they have (probably) never seen a professional HR function. Fitz-Enz describes this as the 'outsource-decentralize' model. Line managers don't really want some of the HR responsibilities but think they have no alternative. Perhaps 20–30 per cent of organizations followed this approach.

- *Confidants*: a small, trusted group of HR talents are in place as trusted experts, consultants and brokers of external services. Fitz-Enz regards this as the most desirable, again perhaps found in 20–30 per cent of organizations.

More recently, 'best practice' approaches have featured, the best known of which are those presented by Jeffrey Pfeffer and David Ulrich. Pfeffer stresses (in a series of books) that the greatest competitive advantage is to be obtained from people rather than technology. He contends that investment in technology is not enough, because that technology is (or soon will be) available to competitors. And the more complex the technology, the more it requires people skills anyway. Instead we need that variant of HRM described as 'high-performance management' (USA) or 'high-commitment management' (elsewhere). This topic will be discussed in Chapter 3.

Ulrich (1997, pp.16–17) argues that:

> HR professionals must focus more on the deliverables of their work than on doing their work better. They must articulate their role in terms of value created. They must create mechanisms to deliver HR so that business results quickly follow. They must learn to measure results in terms of business competitiveness rather than employee comfort and lead cultural transformation rather than to consolidate, reengineer, or downsize when a company needs a turnaround.

Ulrich contends that modern HR professionals should have four roles: strategic partner, agent of change, administrative expert and employee champion. Each role furthers the goals of both the business and its employees:

- *Strategic partner*: as strategic partner, the HR function must make sure that its practices, processes and policies complement the overall organizational strategy. It must also develop the capacity to execute that strategy in the minimum amount of time.

- *Agent of change*: as we shall see in later sections of this book, organizational change has become a major issue due to speedier communication and global communication. The HR role as change agent, according to Ulrich, is that of a facilitator, involving modelling change to other departments, being a positive advocate of change across the entire organization, resolving employee issues arising from change, and embedding change by implementing efficient and flexible processes.

- *Adminstrative expert*: the HR function spends most of its time as administrative expert, and rightfully so according to Ulrich. This role covers the infrastructure of people management: recruiting, hiring, compensating, rewarding and disciplining, training, record-keeping and terminating – and all the other processes that involve people. HR's focus should be on ensuring that these processes are both efficient and optimized. The HR function must continuously track, monitor and improve on these basic processes to give credibility to its own existence.

- *Employee champion*: this final role draws on the welfare manager roots of the personnel profession. This requires the HR function to know the concerns of employees and spend time talking to them and listening to their concerns. Moreover, according to Ulrich, the HR function should promote all possible methods of communication, including employee surveys, suggestion programmes, team meetings and any other means of sharing information and views. A key element of this role is ensuring that employees receive a fair hearing.

> **Activity 2:4**
>
> Evaluate the contributions of Fitz-Enz, Pfeffer and Ulrich towards understanding the purpose of human resource management. Are they stating anything beyond the obvious?

The Harvard map of HRM

We noted that the Harvard Business School generated one of the most influential models of HRM. The Harvard interpretation sees employees as resources. However, they are viewed as being fundamentally different from other resources – they cannot be managed in the same way. The stress is on people as *human* resources. The Harvard approach recognizes an element of mutuality in all businesses, a concept with parallels in Japanese people management, as we observed earlier. Employees are significant stakeholders in an organization. They have their own needs and concerns along with other groups such as shareholders and customers.

The Harvard view acknowledges that management has the greatest degree of power. Nevertheless, there must be scope for accommodation of the interests of the various stakeholders in the form of trade-offs, particularly between owners, employees and different employee groups. The model also acknowledges the need for mechanisms to reconcile the inevitable tension between employee expectations and management objectives.

Beer *et al.* (1984) argue that when general managers determine the appropriate human resource policies and practices for their organizations, they require some method of assessing the appropriateness or effectiveness of those policies. Beer and colleagues devised the famous Harvard 'map' (sometimes referred to as the Harvard model) of HRM shown in Figure 2.1. This map is based on an analytical approach and provides a broad causal depiction of the 'determinants and consequences of HRM policies'. It shows human resource policies to be influenced by two significant considerations:

- *Situational factors* in the outside business environment or within the firm such as laws and societal values, labour market conditions, unions, workforce characteristics, business strategies, management philosophy and task technology. According to Beer *et al.* these factors may constrain the formation of HRM policies but (to varying degrees) they may also be influenced by human resource policies.

- *Stakeholder interests*, including those of shareholders, management, employees, unions, community and government. Beer *et al.* argue that human resource policies should be influenced by all stakeholders. If not, 'the enterprise will fail to meet the needs of these stakeholders in the long run and it will fail as an institution'.

The emphasis is on psychological objectives: the 'human' side of human resource management, including (a) motivating people by involving them in decision making and (b) developing an organizational culture based on trust and teamwork.

| Figure 2.1 | The Harvard interpretation of HRM |

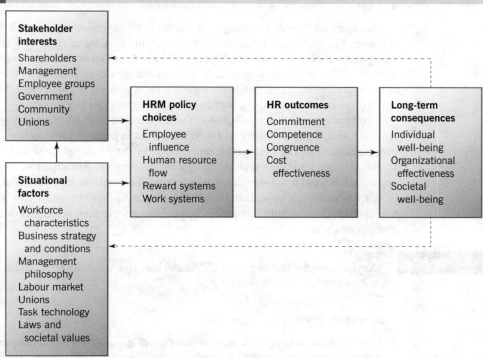

Source: Beer *et al.* (1984:16). Reproduced by permission of The Free Press, a division of Simon & Schuster from *Managing Human Assets* by Beer, M., Spector, B., Lawrence, P.R., Mills, D.Q. and Walton, R.E. Copyright © 1984 by The Free Press.

Within the Harvard 'map' four strategic policy areas are addressed:

1 *Human resource flows*: managing the movement (flow) and performance of people. This involves managing movement and performance:

- Into the organization by means of effective recruitment programmes and selection techniques that result in the most suitable people.

- Through the organization, by placing them in the most appropriate jobs, appraising their performance, and promoting the better employees.

- Out of the organization, by terminating the employment of those no longer required, deemed unsuitable or achieving retirement age.

Human resource policies must ensure the right mix and number of staff in the organization. This is achieved by means of the processes of resourcing and development of employee competences.

2 *Reward systems*: including pay and benefits designed to attract, motivate and keep employees.

3 *Employee influence*: controlling levels of authority, power and decision making.

4 *Work systems*: defining and designing jobs, so that the arrangement of people, information and technology provides the most productive and efficient results.

These policies result in the 'four Cs':

- *Commitment* of employees to the organization's mission and values in a way thought to be typical of Japanese workers.

- *Congruence*, linking human resource objectives with the organization's goals.

- *Competence*, developing an appropriate mixture of skills, abilities and knowledge.
- *Cost-effectiveness*, delivering performance in a competitive manner.

The Harvard model is strongly influenced by behavioural research and theory and stands in the tradition of 'human relations'. This is a humanistic and anti-authoritarian viewpoint which holds that employees will only adopt an organization's objectives if they wish to. They will not demonstrate enthusiasm and commitment if they are forced to comply. Accordingly, although strategic decision making is channelled through top managers there is an emphasis on participation throughout the organization.

A further key point is that HRM is the responsibility of all managers – not just human resource specialists. Delivery of HRM initiatives is pushed down to line managers wherever possible. The Harvard model applies HRM to any manager with staff responsibilities. It should consider issues such as delegation, leadership, participation, team-building and organization from a non-specialist perspective. This will be further explored in Chapter 7 in our discussion of organizational HRM. Taken to its extreme, it can be argued that if managers are sufficiently competent in handling people then personnel or human resource specialists are unnecessary.

| Activity 2:5 | Do you consider that the 'four Cs' model can give us a complete evaluation of HRM in a particular organization? |

Beer *et al.* (1984, p.15) argue that:

In the long run, striving to enhance all four Cs will lead to favourable consequences for individual well-being, societal well-being, and organizational effectiveness [i.e. long-term consequences, the last box in Figure 2.1]. By organizational effectiveness we mean the capacity of the organization to be responsive and adaptive to its environment. We are suggesting, then, that human resource management has much broader consequences than simply last quarter's profits or last year's return on equity. Indeed, such short-term measures are relatively unaffected by HRM policies. Thus HRM policy formulation must incorporate this long-term perspective.

Beer *et al.* (1984) state that these 'four Cs' do not represent all the criteria that human resource policy makers can use to evaluate the effectiveness of human resource management, but consider them to be 'reasonably comprehensive' although they suggest that readers may add additional factors depending on circumstances.

HRM policies and their consequences

Beer *et al.* (1984) propose that long-term consequences (both benefits and costs) of human resource policies should be evaluated at three levels:

- *Individual*. They argue that the well-being of employees must be considered separately and distinctly from that of the organization. Employees can be affected economically, physically or psychologically by HRM policies. But managers have different values and will weight those consequences differently according to those values. Some will focus on the organization at the expense of workers whereas others will regard employees as having legitimate claims to fair treatment.

- *Organizational*. Obviously, human resource policies have to be evaluated in terms of their contribution to business goals and organizational survival. Specifically, HRM policies can increase an organization's efficiency, adaptability, service performance, price performance, short-term results and long-term results.

- *Societal*. HR practices can have wide consequences on society. For example, Beer *et al.* (1984, p.16) ask: 'What are the societal costs of a strike or a layoff?' They point out that 'alienated and laid-off workers may develop both psychological and physical health problems that make them burdens to community agencies funded by the local, state or federal government. Today employers pass on many of the costs of their management practices to society.'

Beer *et al.* suggest that managers use the four Cs to analyze the questions raised above.

1 *Commitment*. Do HRM policies enhance the commitment of employees to their work and their organization – and to what extent? Improved commitment may lead to more loyalty and better performance for the business. It can also benefit the individual through enhanced self-worth, dignity, psychological involvement and identity. And there is a societal spin-off because of these psychological benefits.

2 *Competence*. Do HRM policies serve to attract, keep or develop employees who have valuable skills and knowledge, both now and in the future? Again there are benefits at all three levels. If skills and knowledge are there when required, the organization benefits, and its employees 'experience an increased sense of self-worth and economic well-being'.

3 *Cost-effectiveness*. The cost effectiveness of particular HRM policies can be evaluated in terms of wages, benefits, turnover, absenteeism, strikes, etc. The costs can be judged for organizations, individuals and society as a whole.

4 *Congruence*. The question can be raised about the level of congruence in HRM policies between, for example: management and employees; different employee groups; the organization and the community; employees and their families; and within the individual?

| HRM in reality | ## Stakeholder theory |

'We must commit ourselves to "wrestling" with this stakeholder stuff,' say Steven F. Walker and Jeffrey W. Marr in *Stakeholder Power: A Winning Plan for Building Stakeholder Commitment and Driving Corporate Growth* (2001). They continue:

> Only a brave leader explores what the troops really think. … But to be a true leader in the new economy, we must earn the trust of all our key stakeholders by learning to place faith in people and by weighing their needs and opinions into our business decisions. If we as managers use tools to listen to them, then collaborate with them fairly and intelligently, we will take care of the business and its constituents and, as a result, take care of ourselves as well.

It is a fairly obvious truism that a wide range of people and interest groups have an involvement with any organization, including stock/shareholders, customers, suppliers, employees, the local community, government and others. Clearly, they also have different and varying degrees of influence on the conduct and progress of the organization. There is a cultural context: the American stockholder approach contrasts strongly with the continental European or Japanese.

The US approach (mirrored to some extent in countries like Australia, Canada, New Zealand, South Africa and the UK) places power (and reward) in the hands of the stockholder. According to Windsor (1998):

> Stakeholder theory is a critique of the strong stockholder doctrine in US corporation law and financial-economics theory positing that management's clear fiduciary responsibility is to maximize economic rents on behalf of the firm's legal owners (the residual claimants). Strong stockholder doctrine was articulated in *Dodge Brothers v. Ford*

▶

(1919), in which the Michigan Supreme Court ordered Ford Motor Company to pay a special dividend.

In the stockholder model, other stakeholders – particularly employees – do not count. But Marr and Walker (2001) contend that:

> It is always a mistake to operate as if employees are dispensable or easily interchangeable, because they are not. By definition, we cannot have an organization without the right employees – people who fit our cultures, who bring the right combination of talent, experience and personality to our organizations. These people are never easily replaced. Further, how humanely they are treated when they leave has a lasting impact on those who stay. It certainly sends a clear message about the company's commitment to workers.

You might think that stakeholder theory has its origins in HRM. Certainly Beer *et al.*'s (1984) Harvard map of HRM makes considerable use of the concept. But the main protagonist is regarded as being R. Edward Freeman, Olsson Professor of Applied Ethics at the University of Virginia's Darden School. He argued that managers should serve the interests of everyone with a 'stake' in (that is, affect or are affected by) the firm.

Stakeholders include shareholders, employees, suppliers, customers and the communities in which the firm operates – termed by Freeman the 'big five'. According to Freeman the purpose of the firm is to serve and coordinate the interests of its various stakeholders. The firm's managers are morally obliged to strike an appropriate balance among the big five interests when directing the firm's activities. The influence of business ethics as an increasingly influential discipline is indicated by the following comment (Marcoux, 2000, p.1):

> … among business ethicists there is a consensus favouring the stakeholder theory of the firm – a theory that seeks to redefine and reorient the purpose and the activities of the firm. Far from providing an ethical foundation for capitalism, these business ethicists seek to change it dramatically.

Windsor (1998) points out that stakeholder theory is arguably at an early stage of intellectual development, identifying Donaldson and Preston (1995) as having 'only recently revolutionized our conception of stakeholder theory by delineating nested descriptive, instrumental and normative dimensions with the latter at the core'. Windsor also notes that Donaldson and Preston (1995, p.66) characterize 'the bulk of earlier stakeholder literature as blurred theorizing'. Windsor (1998, p.537) states that:

> The lack of an explicit specification of the relationship between stakeholder and economic reasoning is a major lacuna. While stakeholder theory has achieved a degree of acceptance in the strategic management literature, now being commonly noted in new textbooks as a tool of strategic analysis, there is substantial resistance to stakeholder reasoning in the financial-economics literature. There is a counter-movement favouring stronger stockholders' rights and corporate-governance standards; shareholder value and economic value-added notions are gaining currency.

Shareholder theorists such as Milton Friedman argue that managers should serve the interests of a firm's owners – shareholders. They contend that the social obligations of the firm are limited to making good on contracts, obeying the law and adhering to ordinary moral expectations. Briefly, 'obligations to nonshareholders stand as sideconstraints on the pursuit of shareholder interests' (Marcoux, 2000).

Marcoux (2000, p.1) asks, in the Friedman vein:

> … why firms are obligated to give something back to those to whom they routinely give so much already. Rather than enslave their employees, firms typically pay them wages

and benefits in return for their labor. Rather than steal from their customers, firms typically deliver goods and services in return for the revenues that customers provide. Rather than free ride on public provisions, firms typically pay taxes and obey the law. Moreover, these compensations are ones to which the affected parties or (in the case of communities and unionized employees) their agents freely agree. For what reasons, then, is one to conclude that those compensations are inadequate or unjust, necessitating that firms give something more to those whom they have already compensated?

Activity 2:6   What do you understand by the concept of 'stakeholder'?

Even if one accepts the validity of stakeholder theory as a general approach, there remains a dispute over the meaning of 'stakeholder'. For example, Windsor (1998) considers that: 'who is logically a stakeholder is in fact an unresolved matter in the literature …'. Whereas Freeman's seminal conception was that the stakeholder community should include everyone who affected or was affected by an organization – a widely accepted definition – Donaldson and Preston (1995, p.86) distinguished between non-stakeholder *influencers* and 'true' stakeholders. They argued that stakeholdership as a concept is more than just a union of influence and impact. Windsor (1998) describes this restricted class of stakeholders as 'contributing beneficiaries'.

A harder approach – people as human *resources*

A different view of HRM is associated with the Michigan Business School (Tichy, Fombrun and Devanna, 1982). There are many similarities with the Harvard 'map' but the Michigan model has a harder, less humanistic edge, holding that employees are resources in the same way as any other business resource. People have to be managed in a similar manner to equipment and raw materials. They must be obtained as cheaply as possibly, used sparingly, and developed and exploited as much as possible.

Moreover, the same approach should be applied to all people who resource an organization, not just its employees. Human beings are 'matched' to business needs. They are recruited selectively and trained to perform required tasks. Whereas the Harvard approach was inspired by the behavioural sciences, the Michigan view was strongly influenced by strategic management literature. HRM is seen as a strategic process, making the most effective use of an organization's human resources. Hence there must be coherent human resource policies that 'fit' closely with overall business strategies.

In fact, HRM is seen as a secondary product of strategy and planning rather than a primary influence. Within this model, the purpose of human resource strategy is to assist in the achievement of an organization's goals. This requires an alignment of all HR systems with the formal organization. Since the nature of HRM is determined largely by the situation and the environmental context, there is little freedom of operation for human resource managers. At best, human resource managers can only choose from a menu of possible initiatives that fit business strategy. The Michigan model identified the following key areas for the development of appropriate HR policies and systems:

- Selection of the most suitable people to meet business needs.
- Performance in the pursuit of business objectives.
- Appraisal, monitoring performance and providing feedback to the organization and its employees.

| Figure 2.2 | The Michigan model of HRM |

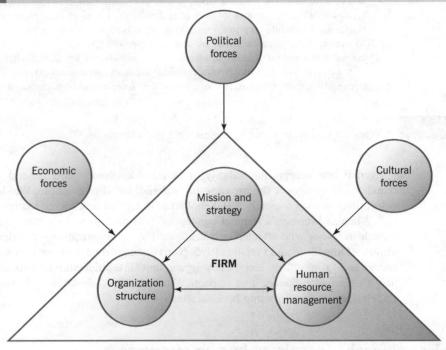

Source: Devanna *et al.* (1984) in Fombrun *et al.*, *Strategic Human Resource Management* © 1984 John Wiley & Sons Inc. Reproduced by permission of John Wiley & Sons Inc.

- Rewards for appropriate performance.
- Development of the skills and knowledge required to meet business objectives.

The Michigan model (see Figure 2.2) takes a top-down approach. In contrast with the Harvard viewpoint, control of human resources lies firmly in the hands of senior management. People are selected and trained to meet the performance needs of the organization. However, this is not sufficient. Their attitudes and behaviour must also fit the strategic requirements of the business. The Michigan model advocates that HRM requires that employees show behavioural consistency with the ways of thinking and operating necessary to achieve business goals. For example, if strategy focuses on sales, employees will be expected to be extrovert, responsive and attentive to customer needs. On the other hand, an innovative strategy based on research and development will emphasize creativity, technical skill and long-term diligence. Behavioural consistency is an objective of change management, discussed in Chapter 12.

| Activity 2:7 | What are the main differences between the Harvard and Michigan models? |

Adopting HRM

So far, we have tried to establish a reasonably clear concept of HRM, despite the different emphases between the two major early models. At this point, however, we must inject a necessary element of caution. Human resource management has been presented as a radical alternative to personnel management. So much so that it has been regarded as a new paradigm (Kuhn, 1962) – a framework of thinking – consisting of exciting, modern ideas which would replace the stale and ineffective prescriptions of personnel management. Enthusiasts saw the transition from 'personnel' to 'human resources' as an inevitable and unstoppable process – a paradigm shift. In fact, the process has proven to be somewhat slow.

The HR function can be organized in a variety of ways. Adams (1991) identifies five main types of HR service:

1 The traditional personnel department with a range of specialist human resource services.

2 In-house HR agencies which act as cost centres, charging client departments for activities such as recruitment.

3 Internal HR consultancies, selling their activities to the organization – possibly competing with outside agencies.

4 Business-within-business HR consultancy, selling services within and outside the company.

5 Outsourcing human resource services to an external provider.

Different interpretations of HRM

As we have seen, HRM is primarily North American in origin but in the USA, far from causing a revolution in people management techniques, acceptance of the new interpretation has not been universal. Kochan and Dyer (2001, pp.272–3) comment that, despite an explosion of interest in human resource management:

> … even today we find that the human resource function within many American corporations remains weak and relatively low in influence, relative to other functions such as finance, marketing and manufacturing … little progress has been made in developing systematic theory or empirical evidence on the conditions under which human resources are elevated to a position where the firm sees and treats these issues as a source of competitive advantage. Nor is there much research that actually tests the effects of different strategies on the competitive position of the firm.

Why is this so? A number of explanations can be considered. Firstly, there is the issue of perception: many US businesses fail to see the difference between HRM and earlier forms of people management. We observed at the beginning of the chapter that the term 'human resource management' had been used interchangeably with 'personnel management' in the USA. This continues to be the case. For example, many American 'HRM' texts are concerned with the functional activities of personnel specialists – their philosophy is little different from 1970s texts. In part, this is due to the managerialist and anti-union tradition of personnel management in the USA. For US practitioners, HRM was not such a radical departure from previous practice as it seemed to be for welfare-orientated personnel managers and industrial relations specialists in other countries.

Kochan and Dyer (2001, p.282) also point to the 'market failures' problem. HRM is generally portrayed as a long-term perspective. Within this context an organization's people are investments for the future. They are not to be hired and fired for short-term purposes. But this concept sits uneasily with the prevailing short-termist ideology of business in the English-speaking world. Long-term investment is expensive and requires the use of money that might otherwise be diverted to dividend payments. This draws unfavourable comment from shareholders. If all businesses in an industry were to take the same human resource initiatives there would be no problem. This is unlikely. Moreover, expensively developed staff can be creamed off by competitors unwilling to invest in training but prepared to pay a premium for competent recruits.

In the case study at the end of this chapter we see how the difficulties associated with long-term, soft HRM are reflected in the history of IBM. As one of the world's major businesses, IBM was used as an example of excellence by Peters and Waterman (1982). It hit its high point in 1984 with profits of over US$6 billion – a sensational 25 per cent return on equity for shareholders. At that time it was the dominant force in world computing with 37 per cent of the total market. IBM was also featured by Beer and his colleagues as an example of a corporation that utilized the Harvard form of HRM. However, recent years have seen a significant shift towards a harder model as the company encountered serious problems in the 1990s. Despite increases in overall revenues, IBM was forced into major restructuring and job losses.

The IBM case study emphasizes a number of difficulties associated with the adoption of 'soft' HRM. When business is good and continued growth seems probable, a company can afford to manage its people in a humane and considerate way. However, when the going gets tough and significant change is demanded, profitability becomes the prime consideration. The pressure for action from other stakeholders becomes overwhelming. It appears that, in such circumstances, managers have no alternative to adopting a 'hard' approach. The choice between hard and soft models is governed as much (if not more) by the prevailing market situation as it is by any question of managerial humanitarianism.

According to Weiss (1999, p.3):

In the past the HR department attempted to meet the company's needs without actively focusing on the company's direction and the return on investment. Today, however, the conditions under which HR needs to operate have changed ... Just as the Finance Department is responsible for overseeing the financial assets of the business, Human Resources' role is to oversee and be accountable for the investment in human capital (the money it takes to cultivate people and their talents). The company will maximise its return on this investment in human capital when HR maximises the contribution people make to the company's strategic direction.

Weiss argues for the transformation of the human resource function in terms of its priorities, accountabilities, roles and organizational design. He emphasizes:

● *Strategic value*: ensuring that HR focuses on transforming organizational processes and people management practices in order to achieve competitive advantage.

● A *competitive mindset*: awareness that people management processes can be supplied by an outside specialist provider if the HR department is not efficient and proactive.

● *Process outcomes*: achieving a balance between the need for measurable outcomes from HR initiatives and practices and 'excellence in process' – i.e. doing it well. In the past, human resource departments could have been accused of an obsession with the quality of practices, and showing little concern for the value of their outcomes.

Weiss (1999) contends that some companies have transformed their HR function, giving it due importance in their corporate strategies – but most have not. Also, the meaning of 'strategy' has changed in recent years. In the past it meant a fairly relaxed 'high-level game plan' played over a long period of, say, five to seven years. But in today's unstable and unpredictable business environment such a strategy would be indulgent if not impossible. Modern strategy is rather more immediate and Weiss offers an operational definition for strategy as 'a plan to achieve relative advantage against the competition'.

Kochan and Dyer (2001) could find no evidence that American businesses (in general) had taken the value of HRM seriously. They argued that there was little in US management history – or in the behaviour of present-day American managers – 'to suggest that management alone, left to its own devices, will produce the transformation in organizational principles needed to sustain and diffuse the delineated human resource principles'. Accepting that some senior executives may share general values such as those outlined by

Weiss, Kochan and Dyer contend that other pressures tend to force them into short-term actions (such as firing people) in order to placate major shareholders.

Activity 2:8	To what extent has HRM – particularly of the softer variety – been adopted in North America?

Professional certification

Human resource specialists have found it difficult to achieve the same esteem and influence as their colleagues in other business functions such as finance and marketing, although their status is probably higher in the USA than most other countries. There have been some attempts at a professionalization of HR practice through certification programmes and encouragement of wider-ranging business knowledge within HR qualifications. Recent surveys give an indication of the prevalence of certification.

Some argue that to be taken seriously, HR professionals need to understand the work of other business specialists, particularly in finance and strategy. The increasing need to quantify the costs of HR activities such as recruitment and the benefits from new initiatives require human resource practitioners to be comfortable with budgets and plans. Weiss (1999) agrees, concluding that human resource practitioners can only be taken seriously at a senior level (in other words, as 'strategic partners') if they have the following:

- A broad understanding of the business.
- A knowledge of how all the activities need to align.
- A professionalism in investing in human capital and HR processes.
- A unique perspective – one not provided by any other business specialist.

How do HR professionals obtain and demonstrate these qualities? A number of organizations provide certification that can increase credibility and career opportunities for newcomers and experienced HR practitioners (see http://www.hrmguide.net). Certification is intended to demonstrate an understanding of human resource practices and their link to wider business issues. Sunnoo (1999) quotes two surveys demonstrating the prevalence of certification:

1 A *Workforce* reader survey conducted in 1998 showed that 56 per cent of respondents had a HR certification of one form or another, while 67 per cent believed that HR certification gave human resource practitioners increased credibility with colleagues and senior managers. But 96 per cent said that their current employers did not make certification a requirement for recruiting HR staff.

2 A survey from 1997–8 conducted by the Bureau of National Affairs (BNA) found that certification had been obtained by 37 per cent of 286 HR executives surveyed at HR director or vice-president level. Some 17 per cent of respondents held the SPHR (senior practitioner in human resources).

HRM in other countries

When HRM was imported into other countries, it arrived with many of the contradictions inherent in American practice. Further confusion was created as its principles were considered in the light of local people management traditions. As many commentators have been quick to point out, there is a 'central uncertainty' as to exactly what HRM is (Blyton and Turnbull, 1992, p.2). The nature of HRM has been the focus of a particularly vigorous debate in the UK. Its meaning and distinctiveness from personnel management have been the topic of numerous articles, texts and conference papers.

| HRM
in reality | **Chartered Institute of Personnel and Development** |

'HRM' has never been a favoured title among HR practitioners in the UK. In fact the HR community seems to have gone out of its way to avoid using the term. Currently the lead body in the UK calls itself the 'Chartered Institute of Personnel and Development', but this is just the latest in a long list of titles.

It originated as the 'Welfare Workers' Association' in 1913, changed to 'Industrial Welfare Workers' in 1924, changed again to the 'Institute of Labour Management' in 1931 and then the 'Institute of Personnel Management' (IPM) in 1946. The IPM label lasted for almost half a century.

Then in 1994 the 'Institute of Personnel Management' merged with the 'Institute of Training and Development' to become (very imaginatively) the 'Institute of Personnel and Development' (IPD). This was a time when management fashion dictated that basic human resource management should be conducted by line managers and it seemed that the old personnel profession might soon dwindle to a small number of recruitment, development and other specialists. Mike Bett, IPD president, argued that: 'There should be a professional personnel and development specialist on all top management teams: in the boardroom and on the executive committees.' The role of the IPD was to be 'the pre-eminent professional body influencing and improving the quality, thinking and practice of people management and development'. But there was little evidence that the influence and authority of personnel specialists increased during the late 1990s.

From 1 July 2000 the Chartered Institute of Personnel and Development replaced the IPD. Geoff Armstrong, director-general of the CIPD said that: 'To all intents and purposes, the two organizations are the same.' In terms of staff, organization and mission that is. But he identified three benefits from proclaiming the chartership:

- A recognition of professionalism, a body of knowledge and the practical competence of the membership.

- It emphasizes the 'must belong' status of the organization for anyone involved in people management and development.

- A recognition in the charter that this is a body that government and other influential bodies should consult.

Technology, globalization and competition are making renewed demands on the way people are managed. According to Geoff Armstrong: '… we are the specialists, the experts in the field. As the knowledge economy gathers pace, our colleagues increasingly look to us to deliver the strategies that make the winning difference.' Time will tell!

Source: http://www.HRMGuide.co.uk.

Paradoxically, attempts to define HRM too precisely seemed to have resulted in confusion and contradiction rather than clarity. However, perhaps only for the moment HRM has the advantage of appearing to be contemporary and innovative. This is particularly the case in comparison with personnel management. Nevertheless, personnel departments have refused to go away. A casual examination of job advertisements in the press will reveal that

Table 2.3	Perceptions of HRM		
Perspective	*Audience*	*Focus*	*Interest*
HRM as people management	General/line managers	Managing people as a direct, interpersonal activity	Commitment Performance Leadership Team-building
HRM as personnel management	Personnel specialists	Technical skills for assessment, selection, training, etc.	Appraisals Recruitment Selection methods Development
HRM as strategic management	Senior managers	People as assets (and liabilities)	Strategic planning Performance management Development Managing change

applications are sometimes still to be sent to 'Personnel Managers', 'Personnel Departments', and even 'Staffing Officers'. At the same time, advertisements for 'human resource' jobs are common – particularly at a senior level – even if applications are to be sent to the Personnel Office!

It is evident, therefore, that defining and accepting HRM comes down to a matter of opinion – or vested interest. Indeed, some interpretations have a strong constituency. It can be seen from Table 2.3 that each of these views has a natural audience able to identify their own interests with a particular interpretation. Hence it is possible to find accounts stressing one of the following:

- *HRM is really personnel management.* Human resource management is a modernized form of 'personnel', repackaged to enhance the status of personnel managers. It has a hard edge, entitling HR managers to the same respect as finance professionals. HRM is based on integrated and coherent recruitment, assessment and development programmes. It is sophisticated, requiring rigorous training under the auspices of a professional body or university.

- *HRM is a strategic model.* It employs the techniques of strategic management for the utilization of human resources. It focuses on senior managers' concern with achieving objectives and containing costs. HRM aims for a seamless link between business policy and recruitment, performance assessment, reward management, development and dismissal. HRM is a mechanism for control and the exercise of power by top management. It encourages employee attitudes and behaviour that are consistent with business goals. HRM is just one aspect of a senior manager's strategic repertoire. It requires a wide appreciation of the industry and the organization and fits resource-based theories that are familiar from business strategy literature. This interpretation owes its inspiration largely to the Michigan model.

- *HRM is people management.* It covers all aspects of managing employees in its widest sense and emphasizes the role of line managers in overseeing their own staff. From this perspective, HRM is a new generic label for all the techniques and tactics available to manage people. It concentrates on translating organizational objectives into operational achievement by winning employee commitment and gaining high-quality performance. HRM is practical and pragmatic. This interpretation derives from the Harvard model. With some reservations, this is the approach taken in this book.

The value and popularity of HRM may derive from its openness to varied interpretations. It is possible to argue that the term is a useful, 'catch-all phrase, reflecting general intentions but devoid of specific meaning' (Guest, 1989). This allows it to be applied in a variety of circumstances. Individual authors and practitioners interpret HRM according to their own background, interests and intended audiences. Applying the principle from *Alice in Wonderland*, it is almost as if HRM is whatever you want it to be (Armstrong, 1989, p.60). Indeed, Keenoy and Anthony (1992, p.238) consider that we should not look too closely:

> … once we seek to explain HRM, to subject it to any analysis or criticism, it ceases to function as intended. Its purpose is to transform, to inspire, to motivate and, above all, to create a new 'reality' which is freely available to those who choose or are persuaded to believe. To explain it is to destroy it.

Summary

The meaning and prevalence of HRM are topics that continue to attract debate and disagreement. As a consequence, practitioners and textbook authors use a diverse and sometimes contradictory range of interpretations. We found that HRM has a variety of definitions but there is general agreement that it has a closer fit with business strategy than previous models, specifically personnel management. The early models of HRM take either a 'soft' or a 'hard' approach, but economic circumstances are more likely to drive the choice than any question of humanitarianism. The extent of adoption of HRM is also problematic, with many commentators disputing its prevalence and the evidence for adoption still slow in coming.

Further reading

Human Resource Management: A Critical Text (2001) (2nd edition), edited by John Storey and published by Thomson Learning, provides a wide ranging and authoritative account of the origins and development of HRM. David Ulrich's *Human Resource Champions* (1997), published by Harvard Business School Press, has been a best-seller among practitioners and outlines much of his thinking on the key roles of the HR function. *How to Measure Human Resource Management* (2001) (3rd edition) by Jac Fitz-Enz and Barbara Davison, published by McGraw-Hill, is one of the few books that addresses the need to measure the effectiveness of HRM as a business discipline.

Review questions

1 Is HRM a fashion or is it here to stay? What is the probability that HRM will be the dominant framework for people management in the 21st century?

2 Evaluate the following statement: 'HRM is in reality a symbolic label behind which lurk multifarious practices, many of which are not mutually dependent on one another' (Storey, 1992).

3 Is managing people just a matter of common sense? If so, what value can we attach to theories and models?

4 The Harvard model of HRM is an idealistic representation of people management. In the real world it is bound to be displaced by harder models of HRM. Do you agree or disagree with these statements?

5 HRM theorists argue that employees are assets and not just costs. What does this
   mean in practice?

6 Compare and contrast the 'hard' and 'soft' forms of HRM. Of the two, which is the
   best approach to people management?

Case study for discussion and analysis

Read the following case study. Trace the main ways in which the management of people
has changed during IBM's history.

Human resource management at IBM

Origins

IBM was originally formed as Computing Tabulating and Recording (CTR), a combination of three companies put together by Charles Flint, a former arms dealer.
Flint recruited Thomas Watson, who became chairman in 1924. Watson renamed
the company International Business Machines in 1929. IBM has a long history of
dominance: at this early stage it already had 95 per cent of the market in punched-
card machines – a mechanical predecessor of the electronic computer.

Watson had previously worked for NCR and had a reputation for aggressive sales
activity, to the extent that he had been indicted in an anti-trust suit. From these
inauspicious beginnings, however, Watson modelled a salesforce on a highly
ethical basis. He required his staff to behave in an 'honest, fair and square way'.
This sober behaviour was expected at home as well as work and included wearing
the familiar dark suits and white shirts. The company benefits included lifetime
employment and IBM country clubs which developed a collective feeling.
Company songs and slogans (such as THINK) were encouraged and inculcated at
company training schools.

This approach was eventually transmitted to Japan. In the 1950s, Japanese management style was deliberately modelled on IBM by the Ministry of International
Trade and Industry (MITI), which found the IBM way eulogized in American business textbooks. Ironically, the company resembled civil service organizations more
than other industrial corporations. Its style was paternalist and hierarchical, offering employment for life and excellent career paths for its brightest workers.

Computing began in Britain and the USA in the 1940s and the first significant
commercial product, Remington Rand's UNIVAC, was launched in the early 1950s.
IBM entered the market soon after and it used its powerful resources to take a
leading position. Under Watson's son, Thomas J. Watson Jr, IBM and computing
became virtually synonymous, controlling 70 per cent of the world market in the
1960s. 'Big Blue' became one of the largest corporations in the world, its international workforce reaching a peak of 405 000 in 1985.

Its overwhelming control of the computing industry was symbolic of the USA's
technological and economic dominance in the post-war world. This strength was
based on an integrated product range of highly expensive mainframe computers,
peripherals and software that locked users into IBM once they had made their initial
purchase. Gradually, however, cracks appeared in this dominance. Despite being an
IBM invention, the personal computer liberated individual users from the mainframe. PC 'clones' were supplied more cheaply by competitors with much lower

▶

overheads. PCs became more powerful, not just because of increasingly faster processing chips but also from the software this speed allowed. Profitability moved from the mainframe sector to the PC, and particularly to software producers such as Microsoft.

People management

IBM was traditionally a non-unionized organization. In fact the corporation was accused of being anti-union, but most of its staff seemed to like it that way. An ACAS survey in 1977 showed that only 4.9 per cent of the company's British employees wanted a union with 91 per cent saying they would refuse to join if there were one. For half a century its culture was strongly based on lifetime employment and excellent working conditions. The company did not possess a formal system of employee relations as such: the nature of the employment relationship was implicit in the corporation's human resource policies. Needle (1994, p.332) describes these as taking the form of:

- A sophisticated system of human resource planning, recruitment and training.
- A system of lifetime employment in which staff changed their jobs as and when required by the organization.
- Equal status for all IBM employees in terms of fringe benefits, staff restaurants and other facilities, although company cars were restricted to senior management and some sales staff.
- Centrally determined salaries, geared to bettering those of competitors and reviewed annually; increases based on a performance objective system.
- Considerable emphasis on training, particularly related to people management and averaging 40 days a year for managers.
- An audit of staff opinion held every two years, focused on attitudes towards work methods, HR practices, pay and conditions.
- A model HRM approach with decision making and people management delegated to line managers at the lowest possible level.
- Formal communication procedures designed to encourage debate about business problems and to allow aggrieved staff to appeal against local management decisions.

By the early 1990s, however, IBM was in serious trouble. The company had been cutting costs for six years under the chairmanship of John Akers, a lifelong IBM man in his late 50s. A former navy pilot, he joined IBM as a sales representative and was soon identified as senior management material. Silver-haired but youthful, he was the image of the IBM corporate employee. The severity of the problem and Akers' bleak assessment of sales performance and poor productivity came to light in 1991. A middle manager who attended a confidential briefing inadvertently distributed his summary of the meeting through IBM's internal electronic mail network. This soon brought the media spotlight on the corporation, publicizing Akers' attempts to correct the situation. One failure was the recruitment of 5000 additional sales representatives – to boost the existing 20 000 – which increased revenues by less than 4 per cent. He then announced 14 000 job cuts, increased to 17 000 shortly afterwards. In IBM-speak these were referred to as 'management-initiated-separation' (MIS). Some 47 000 IBM employees had already had an MIS experience over the previous five years but the latest announcements would still leave the company with a worldwide workforce of over 350 000.

The media and industry analysts increasingly criticized the momentum of change. Forecasts of reduced profits and static turnover led to calls for more radical action. IBM's strong points – its culture and structure – had apparently become its major weaknesses. The company was described as insular and complacent, slow to react to the move away from large expensive mainframe computers to powerful PCs and workstations.

IBM's bureaucratic decision-making structure dragged down its ability to react at a time when the industry was becoming increasingly fast moving. Whereas a local office in Europe, for example, had to refer to its regional head office and possibly to New York, competitors could take the initiative immediately. Procedures that functioned adequately when product development had a four-year cycle were hopelessly ineffective when the lead time had shrunk to a year. IBM had a tradition of producing virtually everything in-house, further increasing its insularity and inability to react quickly to market changes.

A loss of over US$4 billion in 1992 led to Akers' replacement by the first outsider, destined to take the serious decisions that Wall Street analysts had demanded. Despite making IBM's first-ever job cuts the conclusion had been that Akers was too imbued in the IBM culture to be able to take sufficiently drastic measures.

New broom sweeps ...

Louis Vincent Gerstner Jr, 51, was appointed chairman in April 1993 with no experience of running a computer business. Gerstner, a devout Catholic, was the son of a truck dispatcher from Long Island. He started his career with management consultants McKinsey after Harvard Law School and later became head of RJR Nabisco. 'There will be no pussyfooting, no more salami-slicing,' he told shareholders a month later. He quickly hired two experienced cost-cutters as aides: Jerome York, former chief financial officer of Chrysler; and Gerald Czarnecki, who had implemented reductions in staff at Honolulu's HonFed Bank. Gerstner listed four immediate priorities:

- major staff reductions, reducing IBM's workforce worldwide to about 250 000 and including the first compulsory redundancies in the company's history
- defining IBM's core areas
- improving customer relations
- decentralization.

In 1993 Gerstner announced a record quarterly loss of US$8 billion that included an US$8.9 billion charge for laying off 50 000 employees that year – double the previous estimates. Gerstner said: 'Getting IBM's costs and expense structure in line with the revenue realities of our industry – right-sizing the company – is my highest near-term priority.' But he declined to break up IBM's eight product groups and disappointed stock market analysts who were looking for more radical surgery.

One key element of cost was, of course, the company payroll. Gerstner's team made significant changes to IBM's compensation (pay) plan:

- *Look to the market-place.* The single salary structure (for non-sales employees) was changed to different salary structures with merit budgets for different job families. This allowed IBM to pay employees in different job families according to market-oriented rates.

- *Fewer, faster jobs in a flatter organization.* The traditional salary grades were scrapped in the USA, and the number of separate job titles cut from over 5000 to less than 1200.
- *Reward for performance.* The old compensation plan based pay increases on a complex formula linking performance assessments to salary increases measured in tenths of 1 per cent. Under the new system, managers were given a budget and told to differentiate between the pay given to 'stars' and 'acceptable performers' on the grounds that otherwise the stars would not stay too long.

According to Czarnecki: 'IBM *did* deliberately foster paternalism, with a social contract between employer and employee. But economic realities forced us to rethink the relationship. Now we're no longer asking people for total commitment to us. They're eager to stay but prepared to leave' (Sampson, 1995, p.229).

The company still refrained from using terms such as 'lay-off', but employees soon got the message. At the original IBM site, Endicott in New York State, the process was called ETOP – the Endicott Transition Opportunity Program. Cynical staff translated this as 'Eliminate the Older People'. Local mental health services reported a massive increase in requests for stress counselling. 'Surplused' staff felt stigmatized and rejected by the firm. For the company itself, however, the picture was looking better. By 1995 the corporation returned to profitability.

Restructuring HR

When the business units were given autonomy in the early 1990s, the HR department had to react without an expansion of staff (Shugrue *et al.*, 1997). HR was turned into a separate business with a national benefits call centre. Separate human resource functions were consolidated into a number of geographical regions where experts were relocated. Their expertise was offered to other companies on a commercial basis. Small teams of HR advisers were left at individual IBM locations. The business made a saving of more than US$100 million from these changes in just two years.

Following this event, IBM's new CEO recentralized the autonomous business units and indicated to the HR department that its costs should be cut by 50 per cent. Taking the national benefits centre as its model, the company then consolidated the remaining regional HR units within the National Human Resource Service Center in Raleigh, North Carolina, so that all human resource functions were under one roof.

3 | HRM and business effectiveness

Objectives

The purpose of this chapter is to:

- Introduce the concept of high-commitment/performance work systems.
- Provide an overview of human resource systems.
- Evaluate the contribution of HRM and HR technology to business effectiveness.
- Provide a checklist of HRM principles.

High-performance organizations
Knowledge management
Knowledge management practice
Business effectiveness
HR professionals and the HR system
Measuring the impact of HRM
Where does the HR profession go from here?
A ten-Cs checklist for effective HRM
Summary
Further reading
Review questions
Problem for discussion and analysis

High-performance organizations

In all the debates about the meaning, significance and practice of HRM, nothing *seems* more certain than the link between HRM and performance. But is it? Karen Legge (2001), one of the most respected and astute commentators on human resource management, states:

> And what, might it be asked, are the present day concerns of HRM researchers, who ... are of a modernist, positivist persuasion? In a word, their project is the search for the Holy Grail of establishing a causal relationship between HRM and performance. And in this search some success is claimed, in particular that the more the so-called 'high-commitment/performance' HRM practices are adopted, the better the performance.

Legge argues that in order to examine the relationship between performance and HRM we need to address three fundamental questions:

1   How are we to conceptualize HRM?

2   How are we to conceptualize performance?

3   How are we to conceptualize the relationship between the two?

The theoretical meaning of HRM was addressed in the previous chapter. Here we will look at HRM operationalized (according to Legge's approach) in terms of high-commitment or high-performance work practices. In practice, unpicking the meaning of 'high-performance management' from wider notions of management can be difficult. For example, the US Department of Labor (1998) defines high performance as: 'A comprehensive customer-driven system that aligns all of the activities in an organization with the common focus of customer satisfaction through continuous improvement in the quality of goods and services.'

You will probably have recognized that the roots of this definition lie in 'total quality management'. In the past, the practice of TQM has often been procedural and bureaucratic but the high-performance approach has brought in elements of human relations or 'soft' HRM such as commitment and empowerment. The term was publicized by David Nadler *et al.* (1992) within his 'organizational architecture' approach, focusing on 'autonomous work teams' and 'high-performance work systems'. Edward E. Lawler III (1991) used the term 'high-performance involvement' as an alternative to empowerment, advocating the use of small teams of highly committed employees.

The Institute of Work Psychology (2001) at the University of Sheffield states that high-performance work systems usually involve three main sets of management practices designed to enhance employee involvement, commitment and competencies. They describe these as:

1   Changing the design and conduct of jobs through flexible working (especially functional flexibility – broadening the pool of 'who does what' through training), teamwork, quality circles and suggestion schemes.

2   Ensuring that employees are given the knowledge and competencies to handle high-performance work through teamwork training, team briefings, interpersonal skills, appraisal and information-sharing.

3   Resourcing and development practices designed to attract and keep the right people with the right motivation. These include some guarantee of job security, an emphasis on internal selection, sophisticated selection techniques, and employee attitude surveys with feedback to the workers involved. Here there are further indications of an integration of 1970s and 1980s management techniques together with a certain amount of repackaging for the 21st century.

Activity 3:1 Do you consider the concept of high-performance management to be fundamentally different from HRM?

Pfeffer (1998) acknowledges that building a high-commitment organization is not easy and that CEOs are often too busy or distracted to focus on the people. However, he advocates the following as key elements of high-commitment management: (a) building trust so that everyone in the organization can share knowledge; (b) encouraging change; and (c) measuring what matters, arguing that financial data tends to be historical rather than what matters now. He advocates use of the 'balanced scorecard' – a technique that also weighs non-financial criteria in the equation.

Key concept 3:1

Balanced scorecard A conceptual framework used to translate an organization's vision into a set of performance indicators, including measures of financial performance, customer satisfaction, internal business processes, and learning and growth. Both current performance and efforts to learn and improve can be monitored using these measures.

Pfeffer (1998) presents his model of the high-performance work system as including seven key factors:

1 *Employment security*. This is fundamental to gaining employee commitment. If employees are not in fear of working themselves out of their jobs, they will contribute freely to improved productivity. When employees are secure they are prepared to think and act with the long term in mind.

2 *Selective hiring*. Employment resourcing has to be disciplined to ensure that the right people are in the right places. Pfeffer advocates competency-based selection aimed at identifying critical skills and job-related attributes. The quality of employees has a direct impact on organizational effectiveness and market success.

3 *Self-managed teams and decentralization of decision making*. Traditional supervision should be replaced by peer control, allowing a large proportion of the workforce to accept accountability and responsibility for company performance. They are more likely to understand how their work affects the work of other employees. Ideas can be pooled and layers of unnecessary hierarchy disposed of.

4 *High compensation contingent on organizational performance*. Profits can still be made with higher pay rates if the right pay format is used, such as gain-sharing, stock options and pay for skill. When employees feel that they are fairly rewarded they are more likely to show commitment.

5 *Training*. Employees possessed of up-to-date skills and knowledge are more flexible and prepared to initiate change, predict and solve problems, and take responsibility for product and service quality.

6 *Reduction of status differences*. Creating a more egalitarian workplace encourages open lines of communication. Employees have a greater sense of common purpose.

7 *Sharing information*. Making financial information available to employees encourages trust and commitment to the company. Employees can also prioritize multiple and conflicting goals.

In the public sector, the US Department of Labor (1998) sees high performance revolving around three main principles: (a) an organizational focus on achieving customer satisfaction; (b) a constant search for continuous, long-term improvement in all organizational processes and outputs; and (c) taking steps to ensure the full involvement of the entire workforce in achieving quality.

Activity 3:2 'High performance' and 'high commitment' are terms used to describe the same or a similar concept. What are the implications of the different terms on the management of staff?

So what are the key operating practices of such a high-performance system? According to the US Department of Labor they are:

- *Leadership and support from top levels of management* – the most critical element of the process. Top managers must develop a climate of trust where risk taking and innovation are encouraged and rewarded. This means that workers and managers must together develop a shared vision of where they want the organization to go. It also means that there must be tolerance shown towards the inevitable setbacks and mistakes along the way. And managers must be open to suggestions and requests from workers for the removal of barriers to good customer service. This implies a considerable change from the top-down 'I'm in charge and all mistakes will be punished' attitude prevalent among higher management.

- *Strategic planning* – mapping out how the organization will achieve its strategic objectives. But such a plan must be constantly reviewed.

- *Ongoing commitment to training and development for all employees* – not just top–middle ranking staff where organizations concentrate their funds too often. Neglecting the training and development of customer-facing staff has potentially damaging consequences. Somehow, an organization must also withstand the pressure from budget-cutters to reduce training levels as an easy (and stupid) way of reducing costs.

- *A focus on the customer* – not just meeting customer expectations but exceeding them, and devoting considerable energy to finding out the changing expectations of customers through surveys, feedback and other mechanisms. This applies to internal as well as external customers.

- *A focus on quality* – advocating a TQM approach to dealing with problems as they occur and providing a perfect end-product. This differs from the traditional 'inspect, reject or deal with complaint' approach.

- *Empowering front-line employees and an emphasis on teamwork* – the buzzwords empowerment, employee involvement and teamwork come in here. Harness the intelligence and energies of your employees and 'the potential for successful and quality results is virtually limitless'.

- *Developing measures of progress* – data collection mechanisms to ensure that customers are receiving reliable and satisfactory service and that internal processes are functioning properly.

Activity 3:3 What differences would you see in using the high-performance approach for private and public sector employees?

The US Department of Labor (1998) identified the following problems, which also apply in most cases to all non-manufacturing sectors:

1 High performance is conceptually easier to understand in a manufacturing than a service context.

2 Competitiveness is a main motivating factor in the private sector, but scarcely a consideration in the public sector. 'Government is mission-driven rather than profit-driven.'

3 'Government is viewed by many as the archetypal, inflexible, hierarchical structure, and, therefore, incapable of change.'

4 The traditional measurable outcomes of the manufacturing sector – reduced production costs, improved market share, increased profitability – are not so easy to measure in the service sector.

Gardner, Wright and Gerhart (2000, p.4) query the nature of the evidence supporting the supposed value of HR initiatives in improving performance:

> While extremely promising, this research, with few exceptions, has relied on the survey responses from one knowledgeable informant per company to measure the quantity and quality of firms' human resource management systems. Reliance on just one informant makes the measurement of the human resource management construct susceptible to excessive random (i.e. unreliability) and systematic (i.e. bias) measurement error.

As they point out, this threatens the validity of the construct that HR practices are directly related to high performance. Paradoxically, however, the two types of error may be having opposite effects. Citing earlier statistical work by Gerhart, the authors argue that random errors from single-informant surveys may be obscuring and therefore undervaluing the financial benefit of HR practices. Conversely, there is likely to be an overestimate from systematic errors.

Where do these systematic errors come from? Gardner, Wright and Gerhart (2000) argue that:

> This type of error will occur if respondents report HR practices based not on accurate valid estimates, but rather based on an implicit theory that high-performing firms must be engaged in progressive HR practices while low-performing firms must not be engaged in such practices.

They cite the example of a large diversified, perhaps multinational company. If a senior HR person is asked to state the percentage of employees covered by a 'progressive' human resource practice, where does the HR person get the information from? Hopefully from a sophisticated human resource management system, but probably not. Instead, the authors contend, the respondent will provide an answer based on their own implicit theory (see Key concept 3.2) of what is happening in the firm.

Key concept 3:2

Implicit theory An internal or mental model of how and why a set of events or behaviours takes place. A belief system developed by individuals to explain part of their world or organization based on their own interpretations and experiences.

Discussing coverage of this issue in research literature they point out that surveys typically ask for the views of senior managers who, to paraphrase, are likely to believe in their own upbeat propaganda aimed at shareholders and employees. In more academic terms, they say that, surveying the literature, 'there is general consensus that executives' descriptions of past events suffer from low reliability'. They also point to studies which show that outsiders' judgements of a firm are based on financial performance and conclude that it is reasonable to assume that insiders are also likely to be influenced in the same way. They formulated two hypotheses:

1 The estimated extent of the usage of human resource practices for high-performing firms will be greater than low-performing firms.

2   The evaluation of the effectiveness of the HR function for high-performing firms will be higher than for low-performing firms.

These hypotheses were tested on line managers, HR executives, MBAs and HR masters students who were given scenarios of high- and low-performing companies and asked to rate a range of HR practices. The scenarios did not provide any information on HR practices, so judgements were based entirely on implicit theories. The conclusion was that the hypotheses were confirmed to some extent in all four groups. This places a question mark on the supposed evidence from much of the survey research on the relationship between HR practices and high performance.

Activity 3:4	Have Gardner, Wright and Gerhart proved that the link between HR procedures and high performance is imagined rather than real?

Knowledge management

Quoting Stewart (2001, p.5):

> The knowledge economy stands on three pillars. The first: knowledge has become what we buy, sell, and do. It is the most important factor of production. The second pillar is a mate, a corollary to the first: knowledge assets – that is, intellectual capital – have become more important to companies than physical or financial assets. The third pillar is this: to prosper in this new economy and exploit these newly vital assets, we need new vocabularies, new management techniques, new technologies, and new strategies. On these three pillars rest all the new economy's laws and its profits.

Storey (2001) states that knowledge management has become one of the most significant developments in management and organization theory in recent years. It seems to give fresh insights into the theory of the firm and it is also the subject of claims about a completely new kind of economy – the 'knowledge economy'.

Knowledge is scarcely as novel a concept as many protagonists of knowledge management claim, but it has only become a management topic relatively recently. Moreover, a large number of organizations are attempting knowledge management projects – not always successfully.

Key concept 3:3	**Knowledge management** 'Knowledge management caters to the critical issues of organizational adaption, survival and competence in face of increasingly discontinuous environmental change.... Essentially, it embodies organizational processes that seek synergistic combination of data and information processing capacity of information technologies, and the creative and innovative capacity of human beings.' (Malhotra, 1998, p.59)

What knowledge management is not

- Knowledge management is *not* a new religion or spiritual calling.
- It is *not* an attempt to rally disgruntled employees around an appealing physical concept.
- It is *not* an existential search for the truth. (Actually, it's about the entirely worldly task of making money.)
- It is *not* a science or a discipline – yet.
- It is *not* the latest management fad.

Source: O'Dell and Essaides (1998). Note: Authors' emphases.

O'Dell and Essaides (1998) argue that knowledge management is not a fad because:

- The power of learning will never be obsolete.
- Some people may treat knowledge management as a religion but real knowledge management is practical rather than theoretical and should have bottom-line results.
- Technology is not relied upon to make processes efficient, instead, technology is used to facilitate the sharing of knowledge in people's heads.
- It is consistent with modern team and process-based approaches to management.

We will see later that there are criticisms of the way that information technology has come to dominate conferences and publications on knowledge management and, in doing so, often lost the point. In fact, if you think that buying (or rather, *being sold*) a software package to collect information is 'knowledge management' you are probably wasting your money. Knowledge is more than technology.

'Teamworking': better for organizational learning than IT

The Institute of Employment Studies launched a report stressing the importance of learning in teams straddling cross-functional boundaries. Based on in-depth research among teams in a number of leading British employers, one of the authors of the report – IES Research Fellow Polly Kettley – concludes that this is neglected potential deserving proper recognition.

Modern businesses tend to stress sophisticated networks and 'groupware' but they tend to leave their project teams or special task forces unsupported by their colleagues. And their objectives are often not understood or misused. According to Polly Kettley:

Few of the lessons of even successful teams make it into the 'organizational memory', and new teams repeat many of the mistakes of the past. Organizational learning has been hijacked by IT, in the guise of 'knowledge management', and employers are struggling to address the human issues associated with knowledge creation and exchange.

The reality is that the majority of knowledge sharing and innovation within organizations occurs through the interaction of people with people – especially within networks, groups or teams of people who cross conventional organisational boundaries. Moreover, for the ambitious employee, time spent on a cross-functional team is now one of the most popular, and potentially rewarding, forms of career development – though it is not without risks.

Before this study there was little empirical evidence about why cross-functional teams are used, what team members learn in the process or the factors that influence the way they learn. The study found that team members learn:

- About themselves and thus enhance their personal effectiveness.
- About the organization and its processes, complexities and interdependencies together with the part these factors play in managing change.
- About other specialisms in the organization: acquiring or appreciating particular functional or job competencies; what tools and techniques are used by other specialisms or business functions; and their methods of work, professional standards or regulatory requirements.

What helps team members learn? It seems that it helps if:

- Learning is made an explicit and important part of teamworking for team members and their organization(s) before, during and after this team 'experience'.
- Team members' departments have a positive attitude and interact well across their boundaries with other parts of the organization.
- There is a diverse membership within the team.
- Members can organize their own work within the team.
- They can work together in one place.
- Team membership is continuous and consistent because this 'maintains the team dynamic' and builds the mutual trust that is essential for team learning.
- They use recognized team processes for learning and are able to discuss problems honestly.

Source: *HRMGuide.co.uk* (http:www.hrmguide.co.uk), 30 October 2000.

Knowledge management: a big idea

According to Stewart (2001), three big ideas have been fundamental in the past decade or so in changing the ways in which organizations are run:

- *Total quality management.* O'Dell and Essaides (1998) say that this 'may not have yielded big-time change, but it laid the foundation for a corporate-wide systematic initiative for measurement and change and cross-functional teaming, all of which … are critical to the successful management of knowledge'.
- *Business process re-engineering.* O'Dell and Essaides (1998, p.6) comment that BPR 'may not have not delivered sustainable success but it has "delivered" the mind-set of the process-oriented organization. Processes can be made explicit, and knowledge about how to make them work can be transferred.'
- *Intellectual capital.* Stewart divides intellectual capital or knowledge assets into two main forms: 'hard' assets such as patents, copyrights, software and databases; and, most importantly, 'soft' employee-focused assets including skills, capabilities, expertise, culture and loyalty.

Information is already a major component of economic activity. Stewart points to the scale of the knowledge economy:

● Worldwide we produce between 700 and 2400 terabytes of information annually. One terabyte is equivalent to approximately a thousand billion bytes.

● This estimate does not include the services provided by the likes of accountants, lawyers, doctors, psychologists and consultants – information that is not necessarily provided in documentary form.

● Knowledge was the USA's most valuable export in 1999, accounting for US$37 billion in licensing fees and royalties. By comparison, aircraft exports amounted to US$29 billion.

Knowledge management has been approached from a number of perspectives, with information management and organizational being two of the most important. In fact, within organizations and especially in conferences and journals, information technology and human resources have competed for the lead role but IT has tended to be the dominant force – not always beneficially (Storey and Quintas, 2001).

Tacit and explicit knowledge

Knowledge management owes its inspiration to the work of the philosopher Michael Polanyi and the Japanese organization learning 'guru' Ikijuro Nonaka. Both of these theorists argued that knowledge has two forms termed explicit and tacit, which have some similarity to Stewart's hard and soft knowledge assets.

Key concept 3:4

Explicit versus implicit knowledge   Explicit knowledge is the obvious knowledge found in manuals, documentation, files and other accessible sources. Implicit, or tacit knowledge is found in the heads of an organization's employees, and far more difficult to access and use – for obvious reasons. Typically, an organization does not even know what this knowledge is. Worse, the knee-jerk reaction of top managers who fire employees at the first sign of any downturn means that the knowledge is often lost.

Grant (1997) argues that HRM can improve an organization's competitiveness through its impact on the 'knowledge base' of a business: the skills and expertise of its employees. Management of human resources can provide a competitive advantage through a knowledge management perspective. One strategy is to encourage replication of tacit knowledge within an organization without allowing it to replicate outside. From this perspective, organizations should:

1 Accept that knowledge is a vital source of value to be added to business products and services and a key to gaining competitive advantage.

2 Distinguish clearly between explicit and tacit knowledge.

3 Accept that tacit knowledge rests inside individuals and is learned in an unstructured and informal way.

4 Somehow, identify and tap this tacit knowledge and make it part of the 'structural capital' of the business so that it can be made available to others.

Activity 3:5

What do you consider to be the main benefits to an organization of the ability to manage knowledge?

Drucker (1998) contends that knowledge management will have a major impact on the structure of future organizations. He predicts that knowledge-based organizations will have half the number of management layers found in businesses today, and that the number of managers will be cut by two-thirds. Drucker considers that the organizational structures featured in current textbooks are still those of 1950s manufacturing industries. In the future, businesses will come to resemble organizations that today's managers and students would not pay any attention to: hospitals, universities and symphony orchestras. In other words, knowledge-based organizations 'composed largely of specialists who direct and discipline their own performance through organized feedback from colleagues, customers and headquarters'.

In the 20th century information was collected in order to monitor and control workers. 'Knowledge' was held at the top of the organization where strategies were determined and decisions made. But this Tayloristic view of organizations ignored the wealth of knowledge held by ordinary workers. In Drucker's opinion, specialist knowledge workers will resist the primitive 'command and control' model of people management in the same way as professionals such as doctors and university teachers do already.

Davenport and Prusak, in *Working Knowledge* (2000), possibly the best introduction to knowledge management, say that knowledge, data and information are not identical concepts. In their clearly written account, they point out that confusion between the three has resulted in many organizations investing large amounts of money in the technology of knowledge management without achieving any useful results. They consider (at p.1) that understanding the difference between the three concepts is crucial:

> Organizational success and failure can often depend on which one of them you need, which you have, and what you can and can't do with each. Understanding what these three things are and how you get from one to another is essential to doing knowledge work successfully.

So data is hard, factual information often in numerical form; it can tell you when, and how often something happened, how much it cost and so on but it does not say why it happened. Organizations love accumulating vast quantities of data, the sheer bulk of which serves to confuse and obscure any value.

For Davenport and Prusak, information comes in the form of a message (and it is the receiver rather than the sender of the message who determines that it is information) through some communication channel, whether voice, e-mail, letter, etc. It is different from data in that it has meaning or shape. In fact, data can be transformed into information with the addition of meaning and the authors list a number of ways (each beginning with C):

- *contextualized* – the purpose of the data is known
- *categorized* – the unit of analysis or key component is known
- *calculated* – perhaps through a statistical or mathematical analysis
- *corrected* – through the removal of errors
- *condensed* – by being summarized or tabulated.

Knowledge transcends both data and information in a number of ways. Davenport and Prusak (2000, p.5) define it as follows:

> Knowledge is a fluid mix of framed expertise, values, contextual information and expert insight that provides a framework for evaluating and incorporating new experiences and information. It originates from and is applied in the minds of knowers. In organizations it often becomes embedded not only in documents or repositories but also in organizational routines, processes, practices and norms.

Activity 3:6	How can organizations capture knowledge? Write down as many ways as you can think of.

Knowledge management practice

Proponents of knowledge management argue that long-term competitive advantage can come from mapping and tapping tacit knowledge. But simply agreeing with this principle on the grounds of common sense does not tell us how to do it. And many accounts of knowledge management fall down on this issue.

One notable exception is Tiwana (1999, p.29) who points out that:

> In the technology industry, companies that have prospered are not the companies that have invented new technology, but those that have applied it. Microsoft is perhaps a good example of a company that had first relied on good marketing, then on its market share, and now on its innovative knowledge – mostly external.

Tiwana considers that Microsoft has also learned a great deal from its past failures, describing its founder Bill Gates as 'the richest man in the world: a fierce, tireless competitor who hires people with the same qualities'. Microsoft uses knowledge management without a specific knowledge management agenda and gains by applying knowledge rather than creating it. In fact, according to Tiwana, tangible business assets such as technology, patents or market share can only provide a business with a temporary advantage. Eventually, a particular market-leading technology, for example, becomes the staple of every business in the same industry. Tiwana instances Citibank, which introduced the automated teller machine (ATMs or 'hole in the wall' cash machines). This development was a competitive advantage initially but now every bank has them.

Often organizations do not know what they know. And if they do know what they *did* know:

- That knowledge can be out of date.
- The person(s) who possessed it may have gone – perhaps to a competitor.
- The knowledge may have been replaced or updated.
- The location or possessor of the new knowledge may not be known.

Corrall (1999) gives examples of how knowledge can be stored and accessed:

- *Knowledge databases and repositories (explicit knowledge)* – storing information and documents that can be shared and reused: for example, client presentations, competitor intelligence, customer data, marketing materials, meeting minutes, policy documents, price lists, product specifications, project proposals, research reports and training packs.
- *Knowledge route maps and directories (tacit and explicit knowledge)* – pointing to people, document collections and datasets that can be consulted: for example, 'yellow pages'/'expert locators' containing CVs, competency profiles and research interests.
- *Knowledge networks and discussions (tacit knowledge)* – providing opportunities for face-to-face contacts and electronic interaction: for example, establishing chat facilities/'talk rooms', fostering learning groups and holding 'best practice' sessions.

**HRM
in reality**

Knowledge management gives Canadian businesses a competitive edge

A study by Ipsos-Reid for Microsoft Canada Co. shows that 91 per cent of Canadian business leaders believe knowledge management practices have a direct impact on organizational effectiveness. Knowledge management may be defined as a formal, directed process of determining what information an organization has which could benefit other people in the business, and then devising ways of making this information easily available.

This is one of the first studies on the prevalence of knowledge management. It was designed to investigate the specific knowledge management practices used by Canadian organizations and to measure the success and impact of those KM practices. The study indicates that the top three knowledge management processes in place are:

- development of an intranet
- holding events to share knowledge throughout an organization
- using software to encourage sharing and collaboration.

The study indicates that 65 per cent of Canadian businesses practising knowledge management believe that it has given their organization a competitive advantage. It also shows that despite recent criticisms, knowledge management has been a considerable success in most Canadian organizations that have implemented KM practices:

- 91 per cent of respondents agree that knowledge management practices have been successful in creating value in improving organizational effectiveness
- 88 per cent agree that KM practices have succeeded in delivering customer value
- 89 per cent of respondents felt that the positive impact of KM practices also extended to employee satisfaction
- the average return to date is 41 per cent among those organizations able to calculate a return on investment – the average dollar value being C$41 278
- 89 per cent of respondents considered that their organization has a culture that encourages and provides opportunities for communicating ideas, knowledge and experience internally
- one-third of organizations without KM practices in place have plans to implement one in the next 12 months.

'The results indicate that the positive impact of knowledge management processes in Canadian companies extends throughout all different departments, creating value in customer service, product development, human resources, sales and marketing,' said Chris Ferneyhough, vice-president, technology research, Ipsos-Reid Canada. 'We see the implementation of KM practices expanding over the next few years, helping to make even more Canadian companies competitive in the global marketplace.'

The Ipsos-Reid Knowledge Management Study was sponsored by Microsoft Canada. It was based on survey responses from 402 Canadian organizations with no fewer than 50 PCs. The survey targeted senior business and information technology decision makers.

'The primary goal of knowledge management is to deliver the intellectual capacity of a firm to the employees who make the day-to-day decisions that in turn determine the success or failure of a business,' according to Anne McKeon, product manager, Microsoft Canada. 'The Ipsos-Reid Knowledge Management Study results support Microsoft's view that knowledge management should be a priority for Canadian business leaders because it shows there is competitive advantage and return on investment gains to be made when a knowledge management solution is implemented.'

Source: *HRM Guide Canada* (http://www.hrmguide.net/canada/), 14 March 2001.

Business effectiveness

One of the most significant issues faced by modern organizations is the use of technology to streamline activities, cut costs and increase business effectiveness. Perhaps later than many other business functions, technology has recently come into human resource management in a major way. There is still a considerable debate on its cost-effectiveness and ability to provide what is required. Walker (2001) states that if HR technology is to be considered successful, it must achieve the following objectives:

- Strategic alignment must help users in a way that supports the users.
- Business intelligence must provide the user with relevant information and data, answer questions, and inspire new insights and learning.
- Efficiency and effectiveness must change the work performed by the human resources personnel by dramatically improving their level of service, allowing more time for work of higher value and reducing their costs.

But, despite extensive implementation of enterprise resource planning (ERP) projects, human resource information systems (HRIS) and HR service centres costing millions of dollars, Walker concludes that few organizations have been entirely happy with the results. Why is this?

HRM in reality

HR systems

Human resource systems can differ widely. They may be:

- Intranets using web-type methods but operating purely within one organization or location.
- Extranets encompassing two or more organizations.
- Portals offering links to internal information and services but also accessing the World Wide Web.

Advantages
- Familiarity (looking like web pages).
- Attractiveness (colourful, clearly laid out, graphics).
- Integration (linking different HR systems such as basic personnel records, employee handbooks, terms and conditions, contracts, various entitlements and payroll).
- Allowing employees and managers to enter, check and amend controlled ranges of personal and other information.

▶

◀

- Eliminating printing, enveloping and mailing of personnel and other employee information.
- Reducing the need for telephone handling of routine enquiries by HR staff.

Basic system requirements

1 Desktop PCs for accessing and inputting information locally. Standard browsers are used to access information (e.g. Netscape or Internet Explorer).

2 Organization-wide server. In a small company this need be nothing more than a PC as well. The server must have an intranet server software package installed (Microsoft Internet Information Server and Netscape Communications Server are examples).

3 Server-side software such as HTML, Java, Javascript or Perl.

4 Intranet communications protocol running on both PCs and the server.

5 Relational database/information processing software for records, payroll, etc. If data is to be accessed then the procedure is made slightly more complicated with the need for CGI scripts and database server software on the server.

6 Basic documents such as policy manuals typically loaded in HTML, but formats such as Adobe Acrobat PDF are an alternative.

Cost–benefit analysis

This is difficult to quantify because the greatest return is in improved morale. Robert Musacchio, CIO with the American Medical Association in Chicago is quoted as having installed 50–60 intranet applications for 1400 employees at US$10 000 to US$20 000 per application. According to *Information Week Online* (24 May 1999):

> Musacchio says a self-service employee benefits site, which provides information on benefits and lets employees pick healthcare, daycare and retirement investment options, was built for 'almost six figures.' Musacchio figures it provided a 40 per cent return on investment, based on the time saved by human resource managers who don't have to answer employees' questions about these topics because they're answered by the application.

Many systems have been implemented by cutting HR staff, outsourcing and imposing technology on what was left. Arguably this approach should, at least, have cut costs. But Walker (2001) argues that survey results demonstrate that overall HR departments have actually *increased* their staffing levels over the past decade to do the same work. Moreover he considers that: 'Most of the work that the HR staff does on a day-to-day basis, such as staffing, employee relations, compensation, training, employee development and benefits, unfortunately, remains relatively untouched and unimproved from a delivery standpoint.'

Walker advocates business process re-engineering the HR function first, then re-engineering the HR work. He suggests the formation of re-engineering teams of providers, customers and users to examine the whole range of HR activities – including those which are not being done at present. The end-product is a set of processes organized into broad groupings such as resourcing, compensation or training and development. These processes should then be examined by the re-engineering team and redesigned to: (a) be better aligned with organizational goals; (b) streamlined so as to be cost-effective in comparison with the 'best in class'; and (c) have a better integration with other processes.

From this redesign comes the picture of a new HR function. What next? The organization could be restructured and the tasks handed out to existing or new staff. But Walker argues that the most effective approach is to introduce new technology to deal with the redesigned processes.

Walker (2001) also discusses a range of technologies available for re-engineered HR processes, contending that they are all capable of dealing with HR activities in a secure and confidential manner.

1 *Work flow*. Walker describes this as being 'like e-mail with a database and built-in intelligence'. Essentially, a user accesses a range of employee records (perhaps their own) through a computer terminal, keys in data such as a change of address and submits the data electronically to the next person in the chain. The system is configured so that only certain individuals are authorized for a specific range of access or actions. The work flow chain is organized to ensure that the most suitable person approves an action. For example, a bonus payment would be authorized by a line manager's own manager. Also, the system can be structured so that bonuses over a certain level can be monitored by an HR specialist. The paths and actions are all specified in accordance with company rules.

2 *Manager self-service*. Managers can have access to 'front-end' applications on their desktops in the form of HR portals. Typically, they are able to view a range of personal details and aggregate information. They are also allowed to change and input certain details and model the consequences on their budgets of salary increases or bonus payments. More generally, policy manuals, plans and strategies can be made available. Walker highlights the facility to 'push' information requiring attention to managers – including those dreaded employee performance appraisals.

3 *Employee self-service*. Similarly, employees can view company information, change selected personal details, make benefit enquiries (such as pension plans or sick pay entitlement), book leave and apply for training programmes. Walker makes the point that 'portal technology will personalize this data further and "push" relevant data to them as well'.

4 *Interactive voice response (IVR)*. A low-tech method, using the push-button control facility found in most modern telephones. Most of us are familiar with automatic responses such as: 'If your call is about vacancies in the accounts department, press 3 followed by #' when we dial large organizations. The system is restricted but easy to use and inexpensive in comparison to web-based methods. It is suitable for job openings and training course details where straightforward information can be recorded as simple scripts.

5 *HR service centre*. Walker notes that this has become one of the most widely used solutions to re-engineered HR in large organizations. Such centres centralize a number of HR processes and may deal with geographically widespread users. For example, the Raleigh, North Carolina service centre can deal with all of IBM's North American current and former staff. Operators or 'agents' take enquiries by phone, e-mail or online that may already have been filtered through interactive voice response scripts or desktop HR systems. In effect, they deal with the relatively non-routine issues that cannot be handled by basic technology. However, they do use recognizable call centre techniques such as scripted protocols. The agent can enter keywords or a question into a knowledge database and bring up relevant information with which to answer the caller's query. If that query is not covered by information in the knowledge database it can be referred to a supervisor using work flow. HR service centres also have a fax, e-mail and postal facility to send information, confirmations, follow-up queries and printed brochures to users. They are also monitored in the same way as conventional call centres and can generate useful statistics on types and frequency of enquiries. Walker contends that most reports show

that organizations find HR service centres to be highly cost-effective and provide faster and more consistent answers than traditional HR departments.

6 *Human resource information systems (HRIS) and databases*. According to Walker (2001, pp.8–9): 'The HRIS system is the primary transaction processor, editor, record-keeper and functional application system which lies at the heart of all computerized HR work. It maintains employee, organizational and HR plan data sufficient to support most, if not all, of the HR functions depending on the modules installed.' It will also supply information to other systems and generate reports.

7 *Stand-alone HR systems*. There is a massive choice of applications available from commercial vendors which can be linked to an HRIS. They include online application forms, tests, appraisal databases, 360-degree performance assessments and so on.

8 *Data-marts and data-warehouses*. Sources of information, usually held as relational databases, which can be interrogated. Data-marts normally hold data from single sources, such as HR; data-warehouses amass information from multiple sources.

HRM in reality

HRIS survey

A survey for *Conspectus* (Sweet, 2002) in the UK indicates that the downturn in economic conditions has plunged many companies into a battle of survival. However, the implications for human resource information systems (HRIS) are that: 'HR management systems are becoming the front-line weapons in a new fight to ensure that organizations are working as effectively and efficiently as possible.'

The *Conspectus* survey finds that HR issues are being taken seriously at the highest levels of many of their sample businesses. Some 74 per cent of their respondents said that the most senior HR person was a member of the overall management group or main board of the company – in 68 per cent of cases reporting directly to the CEO.

With human resource information systems being the key source of information about an organization's intellectual assets, it may not be so surprising that HRM is achieving a higher profile. But there are still qualms about the ability of HRIS to do what is required.

The *Conspectus* HR survey in the previous year found that users were evenly split about whether or not the software they used met all their needs. But, in the recent survey, just 34 per cent considered that their HR IT systems were meeting their needs and only 16 per cent felt that their systems exceeded their expectations. There was considerable ambivalence about the value of their HRIS and two-thirds of respondents were considering upgrading their systems.

An intriguing aspect of the survey is that when asked if the HR IT function had a reporting relationship to the HR manager, or solely into the IT department, twice as many respondents (46 per cent) indicated a report only to IT, in comparison to 22 per cent reporting to HR and 24 per cent reporting to both. The conclusion is that:

> This tendency for HR information technology to be dealt with by IT experts, rather than HR specialists, may be one reason why the systems themselves fail to satisfy requirements for half of our respondents. Perhaps the emphasis is too much on the latest on the technology front, and not enough on HR-based requirements.

According to Sweet, respondents are making slow progress towards web-enabling their HR applications. Around 66 per cent of the sample had a company portal allowing employees to access information and a third (34 per cent) allowed relatively free desktop access, with most of the others giving access to between a quarter and three-quarters of their staff. But the businesses surveyed are 'not making that much more use of internet and intranet facilities for HR applications at the moment' – in fact, just 28 per cent provided access to HR applications via the web.

Not surprisingly, 54 per cent of respondents said that the internet has had 'little or no' impact on their HR strategy so far.

Source: *HRMGuide.co.uk* (http://www.hrmguide.co.uk), 18 March 2002.

Activity 3:7

- What positive outcomes have been attributed to human resource systems?
- What are the disadvantages of such systems?

HR professionals and the HR system

The pressure is on for proactive HR innovations that contribute directly to the bottom line or improve employee morale and efficiency. Ajuwon (2002) points out that the typical HR professional gets involved with one step in many different flows of work. Very often the involvement of HR has no purpose except to validate the process in some way and acts as an interruption to the flow of work. In other words, the HR function is a 'gatekeeper for information that's been deemed too highly classified for the data owner'.

So HR is not actually making a measurable contribution – in fact, the opposite. HR involvement creates a queue or delay in the process. We should ask if the HR involvement is really necessary. Once upon a time the HR database had an 'all-or-nothing' quality, probably because it was paper-based. But now technology allows controlled access to various portions of the database. So an employee can safely amend his or her own address or bank account details, while the ability to change certain appraisal details might be confined to the line manager. In either case, there is no reason for HR to be involved. HR should move on from the role of intermediary.

Not surprisingly, the use of employee self-service systems for records, information, payroll and other functions is becoming increasingly common. Libraries of forms can be kept online to be downloaded as and when required. Systems can be enhanced to include streaming video and other new software providing wide access to corporate videos, training, etc. Obviously, e-mail announcements and newsletters can also be used to alert employees to new developments or urgent requests.

Ajuwon (2002) argues that HR should be proactive in the process and highlights three different perspectives for action:

- *The process perspective* – getting the fundamental building blocks (people processes) right and ensuring their relevance at all times. This demands close and detailed knowledge of HR processes and a commitment to improvement and efficiency. HR professionals need to understand their own objectives and the relationship with business strategy.

- *The event perspective* – a focus on providing a framework for knowledge management. In other words, capturing the experience and information available in the organization and making it available to individuals.

- *The cultural perspective* – acknowledging that HR has a 'pivotal role in the proactive engagement of the entire organization in a changing climate'.

During the 1990s the business process re-engineering approach resulted in many organizations taking a 'root and branch' look at HR and other processes. Subsequent reorganizations may have produced fresh, streamlined processes but often they became inappropriate or inefficient as circumstances changed. It is not enough to design a corporate human resource strategy or acquire a piece of technology. There has to be some way of ensuring effective operational delivery. A more fluid, constantly changing methodology is required. Ajuwon (2002) contends that we have the means:

> It's more than innovating and/or streamlining your HR processes; or building an HR portal or introducing a culture change programme. It's about weaving together all three in a way that sustains change, engages the entire organization and deploys the organization's knowledge assets to gain competitive advantage and deliver profitability, even in times of economic downturn.

HRM in reality	HR technology focus has significant impact on company shareholder value

Businesses focusing HR technology initiatives on achieving specific, quantifiable improvements can see as much as a 6.5 per cent increase in company shareholder value. But companies with 'softer' goals may find themselves with negative returns. These conclusions come from consulting group Watson Wyatt's *2001 Human Capital Index*® (HCI) study. 'When it comes to implementing HR technologies, the focus of the initiative is the key driver in achieving financial results,' says Ed McMahon, National Practice Leader, eHR Canada, Watson Wyatt. 'The same technology initiative implemented in two similar organizations, but with a different focus, can actually result in a dramatically different impact on company shareholder value.'

The HCI study shows that returns on that investment can be significant when technology is used primarily to help reduce costs, improve employee service and increase transaction accuracy. But where HR service technology is focused on less quantifiable goals – for example enhancing communication and promoting culture change – it is associated with a significant decrease (–14.3 per cent) in shareholder value.

HR technology and shareholder value

Primary focus for HR technology	Expected change in shareholder value (per cent
Reduce costs	+2.3
Improve service to employees/managers	+2.3
Increase transaction accuracy/integrity	+1.9
Promote common corporate culture	–6.6
Enhance employee communication	–7.7

'The important point here is not that HR technology shouldn't be used to enhance employee communication and build organizational culture. Both are important components of organization success, and both are valuable results of successful HR technology implementations,' notes McMahon. 'But making them the primary focus of those technology implementations negatively impacts the results.'

The data can also be used to measure factors such as impact of HR technology choices on total returns to shareholders over five years. Most HR organizations are now dependent on a combination of enterprise resource planning (ERP) systems, outsourcing and individual 'best-of-breed' HR applications. The HCI study shows that those decisions may also have an impact on market value, depending on company size.

Five-year total return to shareholders (in per cent), by company size

Primary HR technology choice	Fewer than 1000 employees	1000–10 000 employees	More than 10 000 employees
ERP	–19	33	92
Total outsourcing	–12	–3	71
Integration of multiple HR applications	5	78	82

'Clearly, larger organizations are achieving significant returns for their shareholders from properly focused HR technology initiatives, regardless of the primary HR technology chosen for service delivery,' observes McMahon. 'For small and mid-size firms, however, the technology choice itself can severely restrict any positive impact on financial results.'

The HCI study was based on a comprehensive survey of HR practices at a total of 750 North American and European companies, each with a track record of at least three years of total returns to shareholders (TRS), 1000 or more employees and/or a minimum of US$100 million in revenues or market value. According to Watson Wyatt: 'The survey data is matched to objective financial measures of a company's worth, including its market value, three- and five-year TRS, and its Tobin's Q, which measures a company's ability to create economic value beyond its physical assets.'

Source: *HRM Guide Canada* (http://www.hrmguide.net/canada/), 19 February 2002.

Measuring the impact of HRM

Human resource departments are often targeted by senior managers wanting to cut budget costs, so it makes sense for HR managers to know how to optimize their practices within tight financial constraints. A study by US benchmarking specialists, Best Practices LLC (2001), explored how businesses focus their limited HR assets into critical areas. They found that most of the 'benchmark partners' (companies identified as using best practices) they examined outsourced a number of HR tasks in order to release staffing resources for more important functions. The most commonly outsourced functions were benefits and compensation.

Benchmark Partners also tracked their HR metrics (measurements) carefully in order to determine return on investment and to evaluate performance. One company used a balanced scorecard, measuring a wide range of financial, quality, operational and strategic metrics to determine the HR department's performance and contribution to business profitability.

Key concept 3:5

Benchmarking Direct comparisons of different measures between an organization and 'best practice' competitors in the same business sector. This indicates the gap in performance, costs, morale, etc., between that organization and industry best practice.

The following data analysis and best practice lessons were identified through quantitative surveys and executive interviews:

- *Coordinate HR roles and responsibilities.* Most benchmark companies – whether centralized or decentralized, assigned corporate human resource functions the following responsibilities: managing benefits; compensation; leadership development/management; and human resource information systems and other HR technologies. They also found that few business units had sole responsibility for any specific HR activity. In decentralized companies, business unit HR groups were also responsible for: staffing and recruiting; employee communications; and generalist functions.

- *Centralize HR performance measurement.* Every benchmark company monitored their competitiveness for compensation/benefits, and over half tracked their overall headcount, employee turnover rates and safety incidents. But monitoring methods varied considerably. Decentralized companies gave responsibility for HR performance measurement decisions to individual business units or locations, letting each decide which metrics to track and how to collect them.

- *Maximize use of staffing and budgeting resources.* The ratio of employees to HR generalists among the companies surveyed ranged from 141:1 to 318:1. But the researchers pointed out that companies at the high end of this spectrum ran the risk of short-changing some of the tasks assigned to generalists.

- *Self-service technologies.* Companies were increasingly creating HR call centres and incorporating self-service HR software programs within company websites in order to: reduce administrative costs and time; increase information access to employees and managers; enable strategic HR; reduce overall HR headcount; and improve information accuracy. In fact these companies regarded their HR call centres as valuable entry points and training grounds for future full-time HR employees. HR assistance offered through self-service software and call centres included: clarifications on benefits plans; performance management worksheets and monitoring; questions about company policies; incentive compensation allocations; and monitoring employee training administration.

| HRM in reality | **HR needs to measure up** |

An Arthur Andersen survey has shown that HR executives say they're missing two things that could improve their effectiveness – support from top management and sufficient financial resources.

The survey of over 90 Australian-based HR practitioners from 70 different firms, with more than 2 million global employees, found that HR executives believe HR and people strategy can significantly improve profitability. But it seems that top company managers are less likely to see a direct link between people and profits, and this divergence of views exists in spite of the presence of a HR director on the executive committee of each of the organizations in the survey.

'Closing the gap in thinking between executives and HR directors is possible,' said Nick Pond, Arthur Andersen's Head of Human Capital in Australia. 'But today's discussion is very different from even six months ago,' he said. 'Executives today are asking two questions of HR: first, can you reduce your costs? And, second, can you do it while still implementing the programs that will improve the bottom line?'

HR directors are now starting to follow common practice in other business functions – measuring input costs, establishing ongoing performance metrics and building business cases for new initiatives. 'We've found that when we help HR directors build stronger financial measures around HR, they end up having a different kind of conversation with their executives,' Pond said. 'They develop a shared understanding of where the real costs are, and they agree on which metrics to put in place. The result is often that costs come down and the bottom line improves. The end result for both HR and top management is that the most important HR initiatives get the broad support and the funding they need.'

'Survey respondents stated their top two organizational challenges as developing new markets and improving profitability,' Pond said. 'HR strategy has been shown to be invaluable in both areas, yet organizations still see HR as an administrative rather than a strategic function.' He went on to explain that '55 per cent of those surveyed said they had moved to online HR administration systems.' 'This means HR practitioners have more resources to contribute at a strategic level. However, they need to be more proactive in communicating this message to stakeholders.'

Arthur Andersen's survey highlighted a need for better HR effectiveness measures, particularly in respect of employee productivity, satisfaction and retention rates. 'If HR is to be taken seriously as a strategic function, measurements should better reflect the scope of practitioners' roles and encompass all stakeholders. This will enable practitioners to better articulate the importance of HR to senior management,' Pond concluded.

Source: *HRM Guide Australia* (http: //www.hrmguide.net/australia/), 9 May 2001.

Where does the HR profession go from here?

Ferris *et al.* (1999) argue that 'strategic HRM, international HRM, and political influences on HRM, appear to be the three dominant perspectives that theory and research in HRM have taken in the past 15 years'.

Addressing the future, they argue that there are 'multitudes of interesting questions to ask and research streams to develop and pursue' for HRM scholars. And Ferris *et al.* go on to say that:

We have perhaps never witnessed more intellectually stimulating times in this field than the present, and it encourages (no, demands!) creative, innovative, uninhibited, and nonlinear thinking if we are to make significant contributions to new knowledge, and truly develop a more informed understanding of HRM.

Similarly for HRM practitioners, there are 'exciting opportunities to make a difference'. But practitioners are continually faced with escalating demands from their organizations to be 'accountable and demonstrate tangible and quantifiable bottom-line impact'. So they see HRM as both a demanding and rewarding profession, but not one for the timid and faint of heart. Whereas businesses in the past would tolerate a 'welfarist' personnel function, modern organizations expect strategic business partners who:

- are HR professionals anticipating and articulating key HRM opportunities and challenges
- are internal experts proactively dealing with the business environment, embracing and leading change
- can justify the statement that 'HRM is, indeed, the source of sustained competitive advantage.'

Ferris *et al.* concur with Ulrich (1997) in seeing effective practitioners as 'human resource champions', concluding that 'HRM will be a "mentality" or way of thinking, so pervasive that it is interwoven into the very fabric of organizations, and integral to all of its decisions and actions.'

A ten-Cs checklist for effective HRM

At this point, and conscious of the risk of 'destroying it' (HRM), we will conclude the first part of this book with a discussion of the principles that appear to be essential to understanding HRM. First, why do we need a concept such as HRM? Surely, people management is a matter of common sense. Certainly, some good people managers have – from many years of experience – developed an internal model which guides them well in the way they deal with their employees. However, there are many indifferent managers who appear to have learned little from their careers. In any case, students need to acquire a comprehensible and communicable framework without the benefit of years of experience. Secondly, if HRM has been in existence for at least two decades, has it not fulfilled its role? Unfortunately not. Comparing the early 1980s – the birth period of the subject – with the situation in the early 21st century, the need for a coherent approach to people management continues to be justified by some obvious deficiencies:

- In the 1980s personnel management had its own agenda: its priorities were not necessarily matched to those of the organization, and its professional training and structure focused on a narrow range of techniques at the practitioner level rather than emphasizing a global view of business needs. It is arguable that the 'personnel profession' has become aware of these criticisms and has gone some way towards addressing them. However, there is still room for improvement.

- Other managers practised people management through a ragbag of often dubious and counter-productive methods, usually developed from intuition and experience. This continues to be largely the case.

- In the 1980s theories of strategic management concentrated on areas such as finance and marketing, tending to ignore human resources. Since then, theoretical accounts have become much more people-conscious, but there is still a gap between theory and practice.

As a consequence, the people in many organizations were, and are, dealt with in a largely inconsistent and parochial manner. The 'you are our most valuable asset and, by the way, you're fired' approach describes people management in so many organizations. As we shall see in later chapters, the evidence shows that a meaningful form of HRM still does not prevail in many organizations. Little has changed.

So how should we practise meaningful HRM? At this point we introduce a systematic framework incorporating ten principles, each conveniently beginning with 'C' – in the best management guru style – for use as a checklist as we go through the various aspects of HRM discussed in this book (see Table 3.1). In fact, terms beginning with 'C' have a considerable track record in HRM and, therefore, the principles are not intended to be novel or surprising. The Harvard model has its central four Cs – commitment, congruence, competence and cost-effectiveness – three of which have been incorporated in our checklist. These and the other principles have been chosen because they are measurable in some way and are sufficiently broad in their totality to reveal the tension and balance that is the essential feature of effective HRM within the 'high-commitment' or 'high-performance' approach.

This may appear to be somewhat 'prescriptive' but HRM is not an academic subject like sociology, which can afford to dissect ideas and argue over interpretations without worry-

Table 3.1	Ten-Cs checklist of HRM		
	Principle	Purpose	Action
1	Comprehensiveness	Includes all aspects of people management	People management must be organized, rather than left to ad hoc decisions at local level
2	Coherence	HR management activities and initiatives form a meaningful whole	Clear link between individual performance/reward and business needs
3	Control	Ensures performance is consistent with business objectives	Participative management, with delegation of *how* an objective is achieved
4	Communication	Objectives understood and accepted by all employees; open culture with no barriers	Clear, simple and justified strategies; cascading process of communication with feedback to the top
5	Credibility	Staff trust top management and believe in their strategies	Top managers are sincere, honest and consistent
6	Commitment	Employees motivated to achieve organizational goals	Top managers are committed to their staff
7	Change	Continuous improvement and development essential for survival	Flexible people and working systems; culture of innovation; skills training
8	Competence	Organization competent to achieve its objectives – dependent on individual competencies	Resourcing strategies, selection techniques and human resource systems in place
9	Creativity	Competitive advantage comes from unique strategies	System for encouraging and tapping employee ideas
10	Cost-effectiveness	Competitive, fair reward and promotion systems	Top managers pay themselves on equivalent basis to staff

ing too much about its usefulness in real life. Real people managers have to deal with real situations, often with major cost implications. There is no time for sterile academic debate – they have to deliver. Learning comes from the consequences. As with medicine and engineering, HRM is a practical subject with a foundation in theory, previous experience and forward thinking based on a carefully assessed degree of risk.

Comprehensiveness

All people management activities should be part of a single, comprehensive system. This implies that the attitudes, behaviour and culture of every individual in an organization – especially those with people management responsibilities – should be integrated within a deliberate framework. This approach ensures that HRM is holistic and systematic, with every aspect – together with their interrelationships – brought into consideration. It reflects the perspective that business problems, especially those involving people management, are highly complex. The relevant variables are densely interconnected (Checkland, 1981). In other words, simple solutions are rarely possible.

Coherence

The second principle addresses the internal balance and integration of the people management system. Strategies and actions must be consistent with each other. For example, if a business has a strategy of increasing sales of high profit margin products, rewards in the sales department should be focused on these products rather than less profitable items. Similarly, if the organization has chosen to take a team-based approach, recruitment and training should emphasize team skills rather than strong individualism.

Control

As with any other form of management, HRM is aimed at directing and coordinating employees to meet an organization's objectives. As such, it cannot be anarchic nor totally democratic in its approach. However, the nature of control must be consistent with the remaining principles. Human resource literature mostly advocates a participative approach with a high degree of empowerment and delegation. An autocratic approach is unlikely to encourage good communication and employee commitment.

Communication

Effective communication facilitates coherence. Serious attention must be given to communicating the organization's strategic objectives, together with the parameters – acceptable behaviour, cost and time – within which they can be achieved. Good communication is essential to the smooth running of the people management system. It must be a two-way process. This can involve a cascaded flow of information from the top and also feedback from lower levels through surveys, performance measures and open meetings. An open culture should be encouraged: employees need to feel confident that they can express their opinions and concerns without fear of retribution.

Credibility

Many organizations spend a great deal of money and effort in their attempts to communicate with their employees. Often, however, employees dismiss glossy brochures and time-consuming team briefings as so much management propaganda. A degree of healthy cynicism is unavoidable, but in today's downsized workplaces this frequently extends into mistrust of and contempt for senior management. This feeling reflects the way many staff feel they are themselves regarded by management. Regaining trust depends on personal credibility which, in turn, can only come from honesty and sincerity.

Commitment

Earlier, we noted that the Harvard model of HRM places a strong emphasis on the notion of commitment. It embodies a 'can-do' approach, going further than is normally asked. Committed employees can give that competitive edge – the extra something that distinguishes a successful company from its lesser rivals. However, commitment is difficult to achieve. As we will find in our discussion in Chapter 10, it is dependent on confidence in the organization, the people who lead it, the reward mechanism and the opportunity for staff to develop themselves. More than anything, it depends on the degree of commitment that managers show to their own people. As we saw in the IBM case in Chapter 2, economic realities can jeopardize this commitment.

Change

Businesses must change to survive. However, change is a difficult management task. Effective change requires sure-footed, considerate people managers who can take employees through the process with minimum anxiety and maximum enthusiasm. It requires the recognition that an organization's people should not be the pawns of strategy but active participants in change. In Chapter 12 we will see that their detailed job knowledge, customer contact and ingenuity can be harnessed to provide ideas for improvement.

Competence

Organizations must have the capability to meet changing needs. In current parlance this is often expressed in terms of competencies – skills, knowledge and abilities. These are qualities possessed by the people who work for those organizations. Competencies can be brought into businesses through the recruitment of skilled individuals. They can also be developed within existing people by investing in training, education and experiential programmes. The establishment and cultivation of a high level of relevant competencies leads to a distinct competitive advantage.

Creativity

Advantages can also come from the ingenuity of staff. Creativity is underemphasized in management training but it can lead to new products and services, novel applications and cost savings. Competencies such as detailed knowledge of products and procedures are required before innovation can occur. A creative environment develops from a trusting, open culture with good communication and a blame-free atmosphere. Conversely, creativity is inhibited by lack of trust or commitment and fear of the consequences of change.

Cost-effectiveness

One of the original Harvard 'four Cs', it provides the hard kernel of an otherwise 'soft' model of HRM. Expressed in terms of profitability, it has been extensively used as the justification for large-scale job cuts. This aspect has attracted considerable criticism, primarily because of the obsessive way in which many senior managers have pursued 'downsizing' at the expense of commitment to their staff. However, as a reflection of the value of its human assets, an organization has a duty to use its people wisely and cost-effectively. In itself, there is nothing wrong with an attention to cost – provided that it does not become the one and only management criterion.

These checklist principles are developed further in later chapters. It can be seen that they are interlocked – failure to observe any one of them can lead to the breakdown of the people management system. Throughout the remainder of the book we will find illustrations of such failure, usually attributable to management belief that HRM initiatives and practices can be adopted on a 'pick and mix' basis.

Summary

In this chapter we discussed recent and ongoing ways in which the human resource management function is changing – perhaps more radically than ever before. The HR function and its activities are being examined in microscopic detail in many large organizations.

Human resource processes, especially those involving the collection and dissemination of information, are being computerized and automated, potentially eliminating routine clerical activities. HR information and knowledge is being linked and integrated with other information systems, breaking down departmental barriers.

As HR processes become more easily measurable, the need for justification and the means to do so become more obvious. Concepts such as the high-performance organization and knowledge management offer HR specialists the chance to push HRM to the fore. HR processes and their outcomes are central to these concepts and the introduction of technology allows more exact methods of determining whether or not human resource initiatives do affect the 'bottom line' and shareholder value.

Yet there is some cynical scepticism coming from HR practitioners and academics, some of it associated with dogged technophobia, together with justifiable questioning of the methodology, rationale and, not least, the capabilities of the systems and concepts we have discussed.

Further reading

Karen Legge provides a carefully reasoned critique of the high commitment/performance concept and its links to HRM in a chapter of Storey (ed.) (2001) *Human Resource Management: A Critical Text*. In the same book, John Storey and Paul Quintas provide a through overview of knowledge management and its implications on HR in their chapter on the topic. *How to Measure Human Resource Management* (2001) (3rd edition) by Jac Fitz-Enz and Barbara Davison, published by McGraw-Hill, contains practical information on measuring elements of HR. *If Only We Knew What We Know: The Transfer of Internal Knowledge and Best Practice* (1998) by Carla S. O'Dell and Nilly Essaides (published by the Free Press) provides a good explanation of how applying the ideas of knowledge management can help employers identify their own internal best practices and share this intellectual capital throughout their organizations.

Keep an eye on further developments in these areas as new articles and updates appear on the HRM Guide Network of websites (http://www.hrmguide.net).

Review questions

1 How would you define the following terms?
   ● high-performance work system
   ● knowledge
   ● knowledge management
   ● human resource information system
   ● workflow
   ● human resource service centre.

2 To what extent are HR processes and outcomes measurable?

3 Do progressive HR policies and activities lead to higher levels of performance?

4 In what circumstances would you *not* introduce HR technology into an organization?

Problem for discussion and analysis

Read the following article. What is the likelihood of achieving a high-performance work system in the circumstances decscribed?

High-quality workplaces in the health services

CPRN has recently published a discussion paper that focuses on a number of human resource issues in Canada's health services (Koehoorn *et al.*, 2002). Other countries are experiencing similar problems. The paper begins by noting that healthcare is still the number one public policy issue in Canada. Employees are at the heart of healthcare and their wages and professional fees make up a high proportion of service costs. But they have been asked to do more with less for a decade as budgets have been squeezed. Yet they work in high demand/low control environments:

> The people who deliver the care do not control these complex systems, which are regulated by governments and professional bodies, technology intensive, and exposed to media scrutiny. The rules of the game change often, as governments change and new ministers are appointed – 73 in the last nine years in Canada and the provinces.

People have coped but at a considerable price to themselves and the system through burnout, declining morale and staff shortages. There is concern about the recruitment and retention of trained staff in these circumstances.

The paper reflects a need to treat employees as 'assets to be nurtured rather than costs to be controlled'. There is a need to create a virtuous circle of high-quality workplaces, a good quality of working life for individuals and high-quality organizational performance. The recommendations in the paper envisage health services built around recruitment, retention, staff development and quality of working life.

Current problems

- The crisis is multi-dimensional in terms of symptoms, underlying causes and consequences.
- Employee relations have been deteriorating for years, including strikes and other actions by health workers.
- Employee (lack of) commitment to employers has reached new depths.
- Nurses have the highest national rates of sickness absence due to ill-health or injury.
- Burnout and other forms of psychological distress are prominent. The paper cites the comment by the Clair Commission about 'moroseness' among Quebec health workers.
- A predicted shortage of 60 000 nurses by 2011 (one-quarter of requirement).

The situation has been made worse by political decisions to cut healthcare budgets and demographic changes (an ageing population) leading to fewer available trained staff but more patients. In turn, these pressures cause more pressures as staff are exposed to greater physical demands, refused leave and given compulsory overtime. High demand, low personal control leads to stress ... leading to more absences ... causing more stress for remaining staff.

▶

Often, attempts to improve matters by creating teams or allowing local decision making have been thwarted by the cost-cutting imperative. Short-term bottom-line priorities inevitably produce damaging long-term consequences. The authors say that the solution demands a recognition that organizational performance depends on 'motivated, knowledgeable and well-resourced employees'. Moreover, the qualities that would produce such employees are exactly those required for effective organizations. Hence the need for a virtuous circle.

Achieving a high-quality workplace?

Studies show that autonomy, improved communication and respect are associated with job satisfaction, recruitment and positive assessments of people's working environments. Job redesign and integrated HR initiatives such as the 'bundling' of elements (for example, teamwork, decision making and work allocation) found in high-performance approaches would be beneficial but, in the case of high-performance HR, have been rarely tried in the health sector. Specifically, the following are highlighted as being significant improvers of nurses' job satisfaction:

1 Autonomous clinical practice where nurses are involved in decisions and believe they have some control.

2 Status, significance and value given to the nursing profession by administrators and physicians.

3 Supportive relationships between nurses, physicians and managers with mutual respect and care for the quality of healthcare.

Work–life conflict has been largely ignored. In fact, the paper cites a study which shows that work–life conflict cost Canadian industry C$2.7 billion in work absences in 1997 and cost the health industry C$425.8 million in physicians' visits, and makes a memorable and scathing point: 'Yet employers may not see a need to address either of these problems because their accounting systems are unable to measure the economic impact of employee health.'

The authors argue that a crucial point learned from studies of high-performance work systems and lean performance is that the former have positive results on workers' perception of their working environment while the latter has entirely negative consequences. Yet the health industry has focused on a 'lean production' mentality. Never mind the consequences on employees' health and general well-being.

Source: *HRM Guide Canada* (http://www.hrmguide.net/canada/), 20 March 2002.

PART 2

HRM and the business environment

At first sight it may seem strange to devote a large and early part of this book to the relationship between HRM and the business environment. But people management within individual organizations cannot take place in isolation from the rest of the world: 'HRM does not exist within a vacuum' (Hollinsead and Leat, 1995, p.7). As we saw in Part 1, this is reflected by the somewhat understressed inclusion of outside stakeholders in the Harvard model of HRM.

Many practitioners and academics have neglected HRM's environmental context, preferring to concentrate on technical detail. This is consistent with criticisms of traditional personnel management for its narrow focus on functional or 'micro' matters such as recruitment. In fairness, however, it must be recognized that personnel managers have always required a detailed knowledge of employment legislation, together with an understanding of industrial tribunals and trade union organization. Nevertheless, this represents a restricted selection from the wide range of environmental factors impacting on people management.

Often exponents of HRM have been no better than traditional personnel managers in this respect. Kochan and Dyer (2001, p.272) argue that despite the obsession with strategy, HRM theories have a fundamental weakness: 'a myopic viewpoint which fails to look beyond the boundary of the firm'. Without the ability or the interest to locate their activities in a wider environmental setting, human resource practitioners can lose contact with the 'bleeding edge' of organizational survival. To counter short-sightedness and parochialism, HR managers must widen their perspectives beyond their own organizations (Beardwell and Holden, 1994, p.613). In contrast to colleagues in marketing, production and finance, people managers seem less prepared to function in a competitive world.

The chapters in Part 2 address this wider perspective and introduce a number of fundamental issues that are developed further within later chapters in the book. For example:

- What is the connection between education and skill levels and national success?

- To what extent is the nature of people management determined by prevailing political ideology and national culture?
- Is HRM simply a managerial reaction to the spread of market economies throughout the world?
- Is there a contradiction between HRM's long-term emphasis and the short-term priorities of the stock market?

We observed in Part 1 of this book that the essence of HRM lies in the competitive advantage to be gained from making the most of an organization's human resources. However, it is obvious that we are constrained by the availability of suitable people – a factor that is heavily dependent on environmental variables such as:

- The implications of world and national economic conditions for business growth.
- The effect of inflation on the perceived value of wages.

- The traditions of local business culture.
- The particular nature of national employment markets.

These variables have a 'macro' effect on the utilization of human resources. Additionally, in Part 2 we consider other effects caused by the activities of external stakeholders, such as:

- Competitors' utilization and demand for human resources.
- Multinational organizations and strategic alliances leading to restructuring or integration on a global basis.
- Economic and legislative actions by governments.
- Resistance or cooperation from trade unions.
- Pressure on senior managers to cut costs and maximize shareholder value.

4

Human resources and the global economy

Objectives

The purpose of this chapter is to:

- Outline positive and negative aspects of the globalization of trade and production that affect human resource management.

- Provide an overview of the HR implications of economic growth and stagnation.

- Critically evaluate the importance of regional trading blocs and multinational companies in the process of globalization.

- Highlight human resource issues specific to developing countries.

- Investigate the roles of supranational organizations such as the International Labour Organization and the European Union regarding the management of people.

Globalization

International human resource management

Trading blocs

Productivity comparisons

Economic growth and employment

Multinationals and global competition

Supranational organizations

Summary

Further reading

Review questions

Problem for discussion and analysis

Globalization

'The modern business has no place to hide. It has no place to go but everywhere' (Lane, Distefano and Maznevski, 1997).

We concluded the previous chapter by considering HRM as a people management system, acknowledging its intricate and interdependent principles. However, HRM is a system within other systems. The most complex of these is the international business environment (see Key concept 4.1). The forces that act on people management are not purely internal to an organization. They encompass innumerable active players in the world economy, including international agencies, governments, competitors, unions, speculators and consumers – each pursuing their own goals.

Key concept 4:1

The business environment 'All factors which exist outside the business enterprise, but which interact with it' (Needle, 1994, p.26). Traditionally, human resource managers have been closely involved with employment legislation, industrial tribunals and trade unions at a functional level. HRM's strategic emphasis requires a focus on other environmental variables. Government economic, social security, education and training policies affect the supply, cost and quality of available employees. International competition, strategic alliances and supranational organizations such as the European Union are exercising increasing influence on people management.

Changes in the business environment have major consequences for people managers. As we saw in the case of IBM (Chapter 2), these forces may be so powerful that an individual organization loses the discretion to pursue its own strategies (Kochan and Dyer, 2001, p.282). In essence this means that factors outside a company's control will affect its requirements for human resources and the way they are managed. For example, unexpected changes in competitor technology or currency exchange rates may compel a business to abandon long-term human resource plans and shed staff in order to survive. Globalization is frequently cited as the most significant factor affecting the deployment of human resources worldwide.

Why is globalization (Key concept 4.2) important to our understanding of human resource management? Examine the business pages of any national newspaper and you are almost certain to find examples of businesses engaged in cross-border mergers, takeovers or expansion overseas. Moreover, domestic mergers of banks, airline companies and even retailers are often explained as defensive moves by national organizations attempting to build sufficient critical mass to withstand competition from giant multinationals. Businesses simply cannot ignore the global dimension, and neither can human resource managers. An example is the extent of foreign control of large businesses in Canada.

Key concept 4:2

Globalization A systematic trend towards integration of production and marketing with brand-named goods and virtually identical 'badge-engineered' products such as cars being made available throughout the world. This process has been fostered by 'transnational' or 'multinational' companies operating in more than one country. Such companies are relatively free to switch resources and production country from one country to another. Typically this is done in order to maximize the benefit (to the corporation) of greater skills availability and lower employee costs. This has been described as the new international division of labour.

HRM in reality

Foreign interests in Canada

Statistics Canada maintains a database of the 86 000 largest corporations among the country's 1 million businesses. Of these, more than 13 000 corporations are controlled by foreign interests. US interests control 7115 corporations, followed by those from the European Union (3796) and Pacific Rim countries (1452). Within the European Union, the most significant participants are the United Kingdom (1272), Germany (942) and France (662). These three countries account for 75 per cent of all EU-controlled corporations operating in Canada.

Summary of foreign control of Canadian companies

Country or region	No. of corporations controlled
1 United States	7 115
2 European Union	3 796
United Kingdom	1 272
Germany	942
France	662
Netherlands	392
Italy	136
Sweden	90
Belgium	78
Finland	57
Denmark	44
Other EU	123
3 Pacific Rim	1 452
4 Other countries	1 131
Total	13 494

Source: *HRM Guide Canada* (http://www.hrmguide.net/Canada/), 15 March 2002.

Scholte (2000) argues that globalization involves 'the growth of "supraterritorial relations" among people'. Physical location is becoming steadily less relevant as new technology and increasingly complex international supply links are developed. This has considerable implications on culture, language and working practices throughout the globe. Globalization is driven by marketing to a considerable extent. Large corporations are attempting to achieve global recognition in their particular market sectors. Brands such as Coca-Cola, McDonald's, BP and Shell are internationally recognized and have become drivers for growth and market dominance. The implications for the nature and availability of work and its management are profound.

Branded products are becoming less diverse across the globe. Consequently employees in one country increasingly use the same manufacturing processes as any other and are expected to achieve equivalent standards of productivity. As a result, the costs and skills of human resources have become a matter of competition between countries. And giant corporations can take advantage of this competition. The car industry is a clear example in which a few major players, especially Ford and General Motors, manufacture specific models (or basic 'platforms') in a number of global locations with parts coming from competing sources. Ford, for example, ceased car production in Dagenham, England after several decades in that location following unfavourable comparison with sites in Belgium, Germany and Spain.

Will standardized products and production techniques lead to virtually identical human resource practices throughout the world? We will see later in this book that significant cultural and linguistic differences between and within countries provide major obstacles to an 'homogenized' global HRM. But some degree of standardization is inevitable. This issue has been the subject of debate for some time. In the 1980s it was discussed under the heading of the 'internationalization of labour'. Some commentators considered that different regions or countries should specialize in specific industries depending on the factors that gave them a competitive advantage (Legge, 1995). Two main types of economy were envisaged:

1 Countries that had cheap, low-skilled labour focusing on assembling low-cost, high-volume products or producing agricultural or mineral commodities. This was typical of 'third-world' countries in an early stage of development.

2 Countries with well-paid, skilled 'knowledge workers' who concentrated on the provision of goods and services with a high value-added component.

In reality, economies are more complex and most countries demonstrate characteristics that are between these two extremes (Dicken, 1998; Fishlow and Parker, 1999). But this kind of analysis led some economists in developed countries into discounting the importance of mass production. Instead they advocated that advanced countries should concentrate on high-value sectors such as financial services and information technology. Similar ideas today are addressed in the concept of the 'knowledge economy'.

Activity 4:1	What do you consider to be the advantages and disadvantages of globalization for working people?

The International Labour Organization (2000) has concluded that globalization intensified in the latter years of the 20th century, especially in terms of trade, investment, financial liberalization and technological change. By 1998 international trade accounted for 22.9 per cent of world gross domestic product (IMF, 1999) (not including national production of global brands). In the 1990s direct international investment increased worldwide from US$192 billion at the beginning of the decade to US$400 billion in 1999 (World Bank, 1999). And the liberalization of private capital and developing e-commerce increased the net flow of private capital into low/middle-income countries from US$43 billion in 1995 to US$298 billion in 1999 (World Bank, 1999).

The ILO states (International Labour Organisation, 2000, p.vii) that:

> The benefits of globalization have been very unevenly distributed both between and within nations. At the same time a host of social problems have emerged or intensified, creating increased hardship, insecurity, and anxiety for many across the world, fuelling a strong backlash. As a result, the present form of globalization is facing a crisis of legitimacy resulting from the erosion of popular support.

Some of the main factors that have been identified as being at the root of the problems and widespread public disquiet are:

● Reduction in job security because work (and therefore jobs) can be moved from one country to another.

● Undercutting of one country's wages by another, leading to erosion of wage rates.

● Exceeding generally accepted working hours and exposure to health and safety risks in order to cut costs.

The 1995 Social Summit of the United Nations highlighted the positive and negative consequences of globalization, concluding that 'globalization ... opens new opportunities for sustained economic growth and development of the world economy, particularly in developing countries'. It also recognized that rapid changes and adjustments 'have been accompanied by intensified poverty, unemployment and social disintegration'. Overall, the Summit identified that the key challenge was 'to manage these processes and threats so as to enhance their benefits and mitigate their negative effects upon people' (United Nations, 1995).

HRM in reality	**Nokia to shift proportion of mobile phone manufacturing from the USA to factories abroad**

Nokia has announced 'action intended to increase market and cost leadership'. In other words, it will switch production of mobile phones to Latin America and South Korea from its manufacturing operations in north Texas.

Nokia is the world's largest mobile phone supplier and the new strategy will shift some of its manufacturing to Korea and Mexico. As a consequence, Nokia will cut jobs at its two north Texas manufacturing facilities by around 800 full-time employees over the next five months. Nokia currently employs around 5500 in the area.

Nokia has increased production of mobile phones considerably in the past year with the massive growth in demand for wireless products. But most of this increase has come from factories in Mexico, Brazil and Korea. 'We continue to grow faster than the market', K-P Wilska, president, Nokia (Americas), said:

> In recent months we have increased the capacity of our factories by installing newer machinery and improving our manufacturing processes. This means we can achieve higher volumes than before, with less labour. In the future, as we begin to make new products that were designed for manufacturability as well as performance, we will have even more capacity. Because of this, we are taking actions designed to increase our market and cost leadership.

Manufacturing will be switched to South Korea and Mexico from the Diplomacy Road/Centreport factory in Fort Worth (opened in 1991) and will be subleased. Nokia's newer Alliance factory will refocus on increased engineering support for the Americas and fulfilment for the United States market, and will continue to manufacture mobile phones. Nokia also plans to consolidate all of the Fort Worth operations at its Alliance facility. Nokia's Americas regional headquarters is located in Irving, Texas where its 'Nokia Campus' houses administrative, sales, marketing and R&D employees: 'We are firmly committed to building on our market-leading position as our products and our business evolve. Likewise, we remain firmly committed to our Alliance facility and to the City of Fort Worth, and we intend to be here for many years to come,' Wilska said.

Source: *HRM Guide USA* (http://www.hrmguide.net/usa/), 2 February 2001.

Weisbrot (2002, pp.10–12) makes the following observation:

> Consider this: In Latin America and the Caribbean, where gross domestic product grew by 75 per cent per person from 1960 to 1980, it grew by only 7 per cent per person from 1980 to 2000. The collapse of the African economies is more well known, although still ignored: GDP in sub-Saharan Africa grew by about 34 per cent per person from 1960 to 1980; in the past two decades, per capita income actually fell by about 15 percent. Even if we include the fast-growing economies of East Asia and South Asia, the past two decades fare miserably. For the entire set of low- and middle-income countries, per capita GDP growth was less than half of its average for the previous 20 years. Also, as might be expected in a time of bad economic performance, the past two decades have brought significantly reduced progress according to

such major social indicators as life expectancy, infant and child mortality, literacy, and education – again, for the vast majority of low- and middle-income countries.

Sen (2002) tries to balance positive and negative views of globalization. He notes that proponents and opponents of globalization tend to perceive it as global Westernization. Those who have a positive view of globalization consider it to be a 'marvellous contribution of Western civilization to the world'. Many see a stylized sequence of history in which everything important happened in Europe: the Renaissance, the Enlightenment and the Industrial Revolution. These led to the improved living standards of the West that are now being spread to the rest of the world. From this perspective, 'globalization is not only good, it is also a gift from the West to the world'.

But those with the opposite point of view see globalization as an extension of Western imperialism. They see contemporary capitalism as being 'driven and led by greedy and grabby Western countries in Europe and North America' using 'rules of trade and business relations that do not serve the interests of the poorer people in the world'.

On the other hand, Jackson (1998) argues that the concept of globalization has been demonized by opponents of the free market, contending that 'they have shamelessly used it to exploit fear and ignorance'. He considers that claims that globalization leads to lowered real wages and 'destroys jobs, causes financial crises, creates social tension and undermines national sovereignty' are false. Jackson refutes such claims despite a prevailing but naive public belief in their status as 'self-evident truths'. He considers that globalization is not a new phenomenon. On the contrary, it is just an alternative name for 'free trade' and an ongoing process of the internationalization of trade and capital, concluding that: 'What many fear today was commonplace a hundred years ago. Globalization is no more damaging or destabilizing now than it was in the 1890s.'

Similarly, Sen (2002) points to the longer-term nature of globalization:

> Is globalization really a new Western curse? It is, in fact, neither new nor necessarily Western; and it is not a curse. Over thousands of years, globalization has contributed to the progress of the world through travel, trade, migration, spread of cultural influences, and dissemination of knowledge and understanding (including that of science and technology). These global interrelations have often been very productive in the advancement of different countries. They have not necessarily taken the form of increased Western influence. Indeed, the active agents of globalization have often been located far from the West.

The degree of perceived job insecurity is highlighted in the OECD survey shown in Table 4.1.

Key concept 4:3

The insecurity thesis   Heery and Salmon (2000) identify a connection between globalization and the 'insecurity thesis', a belief that: 'Employment in the developed economies has become more insecure or unstable in the sense that both continued employment and the level of remuneration have become less predictable and contingent on factors which lie beyond the employee's control.'

Activity 4:2

Why is the debate about globalization of concern to human resource managers?

Perception of the effects of globalization is coloured by such views. One consequence is that the media take a keen interest in human resource practices throughout the world – no matter how remote the location. The coverage inevitably increases public awareness and hostility towards practices that may be viewed as unfair or exploitative. This creates pressures to bring such practices within the remit of international bodies.

Table 4.1	Job insecurity across the OECD in 2000

Country	Unsure of a job even if they perform well (per cent)
Korea	46
United Kingdom	41
Japan	38
United States	37
Australia	37
France	37
Sweden	36
Czech Republic	35
New Zealand	34
Germany	34
Italy	32
Finland	31
Unweighted average	**30**
Greece	29
Spain	27
Canada	27
Hungary	26
Switzerland	26
Belgium	26
Austria	23
Ireland	23
Netherlands	22
Denmark	20
Portugal	21
Norway	17

Source: International Survey Research, OECD 2001.

The World Economic Forum commissioned a survey of 25 000 people in 25 countries during the last few months of 2001. Contrary to some of the opinions we have discussed, the attitude towards globalization was broadly favourable. They found that:

- The majority of people in most countries surveyed expected that more economic globalization would be positive for themselves and their families.

- Globally, more than six in ten citizens see globalization as beneficial, with just one in five seeing it as negative.

- Positive views of globalization had grown over the previous year, especially in North America and Europe.

- People (especially citizens of poorer countries) had high expectations that globalization would deliver benefits in a number of economic and non-economic areas. But, on average, people also believed that globalization would worsen environmental problems and poverty in the world, and reduce the number of jobs in their country.

● Most citizens of the richest countries (G-7) did not believe that poor countries benefited as much as rich countries from free trade and globalization. But the opposite was true in low GDP countries.

Table 4.2 shows a breakdown of opinions solicited by the survey.

The complexity of globalization and its effects reduces the ability of national governments to deal with social and economic problems, for example by means of employment legislation. According to Sen (quoted in ILO, 2000): 'The market economy itself is not merely an international system. Its global connections run beyond the relation between nations: it is very often relations between individuals in different countries, between different parties in a business transaction.' Such interconnections have significant consequences for the ways in which employees are organized and managed in multinational businesses.

| Activity 4:3 | Given the evidence provided, are you for or against globalization? |

International human resource management

Globalization has been driven largely by issues of marketing, cost and competition. International HRM is a subject that has developed in the wake of these driving forces. Consequently, people management on the international scale has often lagged behind other

Table 4.2	Perception of the effects of globalization across 25 countries	
	Better (per cent)	Worse (per cent)
Access to foreign markets	66	22
Availability of foreign products	63	25
National culture	60	28
Family's quality of life	60	23
Human rights, freedom/democracy	57	28
National economy	56	33
Income and buying power	54	27
Economic development in poor countries	51	36
Quality of jobs	48	39
Workers' rights	47	40
Peace and stability	47	38
Economic equality	45	40
Number of jobs available	42	46
Poverty and homelessness	41	45
Environmental quality	41	47

Source: Adapted from World Economic Forum media release 1 February 2002.

management functions (such as production and finance) at both practical and theoretical levels. Adler (1997) argues that:

> Although the other functional areas increasingly use strategies that were largely unheard of or that would have been inappropriate only one and two decades ago, many firms still conduct the worldwide management of people as if neither the external economic and technological environment, nor the internal structure and organization of the firm, had changed.

Growth in international business has led to massive interest in the ways people are best and, perhaps, differently managed in various countries. Yet American business school models of management have been assumed to be normal – the 'best practice' methods to be applied universally, regardless of local tradition, culture or business history. Throughout much of the 20th century and into the 21st century, US corporations have dominated world trade and it is not surprising that North American business methods – focused on tight financial controls and marketing – have been widely copied. But there have been occasions when the universality of these methods has been questioned. For example, when international competition and recession damaged the US economy in the 1970s and 1980s, it became clear that there were HR practices employed in countries such as Japan and Germany that could be usefully studied and adopted elsewhere.

The US Human Resource Planning Society conducted a state of the art/practice survey among HR practitioners in several countries (Tebbel, 2000). Survey questions focused on key issues facing human resource managers in the following three to five years. The key environmental trend identified as having the greatest effect on organizations (and, therefore, the HR function) in the near future was 'the increasingly dynamic and unpredictable nature of globalization'. Intriguingly, however, one of the authors of this study (cited in Tebbel, 2000) commented that: 'Globalization will continue to have a great impact on human resource management. But whenever the Human Resource Planning Society offers seminars [on the subject] they barely fill up.'

The short-term attitudes of senior American executives have been much criticized. Managers with financial or legal backgrounds have gravitated to the top at the expense of those with technical or scientific expertise. This has led to a prevailing management style emphasizing cash management with fast measurable returns. Mergers and takeovers, disposals and closures fit neatly into this mindset whereas long-term research, product development and people management have been neglected. Senior managers elsewhere in the English-speaking world have followed the US lead. American practice was enthusiastically copied in the UK, for example, where it fitted a long-standing class prejudice against 'dirty hands' and 'trade'. 'New Right' policies ensured government support for such attitudes, defended within the mythology of 'market forces'.

In Part 1 of this book we saw that Japan served as a role model for Western businesses in the 1980s. HRM owes much of its inspiration to the long-term and people-orientation, rather than cash-orientation, of Japanese business. For some time it was believed that the Japanese had the 'magic answers' for people management and that these could be identified and translated into Western businesses. Teamworking, quality circles and continuous improvement produced discernible benefits in car manufacturing in the UK, for example. However, in the 1990s the Japanese role model lost some of its mystique. Despite a record trade surplus of US$145.8 billion (£93.5 billion) in 1994, Japanese industrial dominance had peaked – for the time being at least – with the remainder of the decade being a period of stagnation. Ironically, given the previous influence of Japanese manufacturing practices on North American, European and Australasian management thought, major Japanese companies began to introduce Western methods of people management.

In fact, no single approach to people management can ever be guaranteed to be more effective than any other. Different business environments generate different forms of managerial structures that can be equally successful in world markets. Different approaches develop because organizations are dependent on the social, political and financial institutions of the countries in which they operate. Hegewisch and Brewster (1993) found that the country involved was much more significant in the way people management is handled than business size or commercial sector. Contrary to former UK prime minister Margaret Thatcher's confident ideological statement that 'there is no society' it is evident that societies determine what organizational structures and managerial practices are acceptable and 'normal' (Tyson, 1995). The perception of normality varies widely from country to country and is attributable to the business cultures of those countries. As is indicated in other chapters, the concept of culture features prominently in human resource literature, both at a corporate and national level.

Torrington (1994, pp. 5–6) goes as far as denying that many of the most familiar topics in HRM such as recruitment and selection are within the scope of international HRM:

> Employees are selected in one country or another, and wherever the selection is undertaken there are a range of conventions and legal requirements that have to be met. The person appointed will usually have a contract of employment that will fit within the legal framework of one country but probably not another. Recruitment and selection is therefore a national activity, not an international activity. Similarly, negotiation with trade unions and the nature of agreements vary markedly between countries, so industrial relations is a national rather than an international activity.

Activity 4:4	What are the main reasons for distinguishing 'international HRM' from mainstream human resource management?

Trading blocs

Partly due to the activities of multinational firms, international trade has grown to colossal proportions in recent decades. The bulk of this trade is concentrated in three major trading blocs:

1 The North American Free Trade Area (NAFTA) – essentially Canada, Mexico and the USA.

2 The European Union with 15 member states at the time of writing and a substantial queue of countries waiting to join.

3 The Asian-Pacific region with various trading arrangements and including Australia, Japan, New Zealand, Singapore and many developing states.

Globalization and the consolidation of trade within such regional trading blocs is leading to a shift from trade between countries with distinct economic boundaries, to a world economy where national boundaries are not so significant. Instead cross-border manufacturing and trade in goods, services and financial products are now commonplace (ILO, 2000).

The boundaries of the trading blocs are shifting and generally expanding. The most obvious example is the European Union. It has accommodated Austria, Finland and Sweden, and is looking eastwards. Eastern Germany has been absorbed by the Federal Republic. Former members of the Soviet Union – Estonia, Latvia, Lithuania – and satellites such as Poland, the Czech and Slovak republics, Hungary and others are in the queue to join.

Integration of former communist countries into the free world brings different philosophies and practices of management into focus and possible conflict. Currently the eastern

European countries have a much lower standard of living than most of the EU's long-standing members. The Czech Republic is closest to the western European norm with tourism booming and exports to the EU replacing business lost in the former communist countries. It seems reasonable to assume that inequalities between eastern and western Europe will gradually even out as businesses move to the regions with lower costs. However, the evidence of recent economic history indicates that this may not happen quickly, if at all. The reality has been that whereas poorer areas have cut employee costs to maintain their competitiveness, more affluent regions have been unwilling to consider this tactic and have turned to more upmarket quality products instead.

Countries such as South Korea, Taiwan and Singapore have shown much faster rates of economic growth than those of the West and have benefited considerably from the export of Japanese jobs. Comparatively low labour costs and strong adherence to the work ethic have appeared highly attractive to foreign investors. Adjacent countries are making efforts to join in this success. For example, Australia has made political moves away from its Anglo-Celtic ways in an effort to make the country more acceptable to its Asian neighbours. According to Chung (1991, p.419):

> Business people from and in the Asian-Pacific area have become more self-confident, and they are demanding respect for Asian culture if European or American business people want to co-operate with them. The one-way street is a thing of the past, and what is needed now is the ability to engage in culture-specific dialogue. The ability to communicate interculturally has become a crucial factor for success in the global business of the future.

Within the trading blocs, there is increasing scope for integration and rationalization. This is exemplified by the defence and aerospace industries in the EU. Cuts in defence expenditure following the ending of the Cold War, together with ever-escalating costs for the development of new planes and other equipment, have encouraged a consolidation between the former national defence specialists. Closer working arrangements such as those employed by Airbus Industrie will replace joint development and marketing agreements. The consequences on employment will probably include overall staff reductions within the sector, increased specialization and a demand for higher language and technology skills.

HRM in reality

Productivity gap widens

Canada's inability to compete successfully in the 21st century's global economy is posing a serious threat to the country's standard of living, according to Jan Grude, National Chair of the Canadian Association of Management Consultants. Speaking to students and consultants at the Simon Fraser University in Vancouver, British Columbia in 2002 he said that: 'our ability to compete in the economic playing field of liberalized trade has been eroding for decades and is reaching crisis proportions'.

Jan Grude cited a new Association study – *Enhancing Productivity Through Innovation* – which paints a bleak picture of Canada's deteriorating economic position, including:

- A 25 per cent widening of Canada's productivity gap with the USA during the past 20 years.
- A 20 per cent decline in Canada's standard of living relative to the USA since 1961.
- A significant lag in personal income: the average Canadian family of four would have had additional income of C$10 000 in 1999 had Canada maintained its productivity ranking among OECD countries.

◀   The study concludes that unless these gaps are closed, Canada will experience 'continued erosion of our standard of living and a self-fulfilling spiral of losing or being unable to attract the skills and talents needed in a knowledge-based economy'.

Jan Grude said that the primary task of management consultants in the 21st century is to reverse this generation-long trend:

> Management consultants must be the oracle and the spearhead of Canadian business, first bringing to clients a global vision of innovation acquisition, productivity enhancement and market development and then driving home solutions. Canadian companies that fail to adapt to the rigours of worldwide competition have nowhere to hide. They will either be driven into oblivion or taken over by those who are more innovative, more productive and more enterprising.

Source: *HRM Guide Canada* (http://www.hrmguide.net/canada/), 18 March 2002.

Productivity comparisons

Productivity has a direct relationship with the wealth of any country (see Key concept 4.4). A study by the Conference Board (2002) shows that US productivity continues to outpace most other countries and that information and communication technologies were the major drivers of US productivity growth. It was a year of economic turmoil in 2001 but, despite the sharp slowdown in gross domestic product, US labour productivity growth rose 1.8 per cent against an average 0.9 per cent for the member nations of the Organization for Economic Cooperation and Development (OECD). The 'HRM in reality' boxed article indicates Canadian concerns about the productivity gap with their nearest neighbours. Meanwhile, average productivity grew by only 0.6 per cent in the European Union during 2001 – half the growth between 1995 and 2000.

US output per hour in 2001 was US$4.67 higher than the European Union, up from US$4.21 in 2000 and US$2.86 in 1995.

Key concept 4:4

Productivity   Productivity may be defined as the amount of output (what is produced) per unit of input used. Labour is one input among many. Total productivity is dependent upon a variety of diverse and hard to measure inputs. One simple measure of productivity is the gross domestic product (GDP) per person-hour worked. But it is also a simplistic measure of productivity because it neglects a number of factors such as capital investment.

Japan has suffered a decade of stagnation, losing ground to both the USA and the European Union. In fact, during 2001 productivity growth even turned negative, at –0.3 per cent. The country's productivity relative to the USA dropped to 72 per cent in 2001 from about 74 per cent in 2000. Japan's productivity was US$5.66 per hour lower than the EU and US$10.33 behind the USA.

The Czech Republic, Hungary, and Poland improved their productivity in 2001 by between 2.6 per cent and 3.2 per cent – considerably more than the 0.6 per cent recorded by the average EU member state. But they still trail the EU by about 60 per cent.

Overall, the comparative performances of OECD countries were widely divergent since the mid-1990s, reflecting a break in a long-term convergence in productivity levels. 'Following World War II, most OECD economies were "catching-up" with the US', says Robert H. McGuckin, Director of Economic Research at The Conference Board and a co-author of the report. 'This process was particularly rapid in the 1960s and continued until the 1990s. Since about 1995, information and communications technology-driven US productivity growth has brought convergence to a standstill, with some notable exceptions like Ireland and Finland.'

Productivity and per capita income

Labour productivity is clearly connected to living standards as measured by per capita income: the more hours spent on work and the higher the level of productivity, the higher is per capita income.

EU labour productivity in 2001 came within 13 per cent of the US level (in fact, four European countries had even higher productivity levels than the USA) but this did not translate into comparable personal wealth. Average per capita income in the European Union was 33 per cent below US levels in 2001 – only Switzerland, Norway and Denmark had income levels within 20 per cent of the US figure.

According to McGuckin: 'These figures mean that Europe is not translating its productivity into per capita income at the same rate as the US as a result of shorter work weeks and lower percentages of the population working, despite Europe's recent rise in labour input.'

HRM in reality

Productivity surge

Unexpected sectors of the services industry are driving the recent improvement in Australian industry productivity, said Productivity Commission Chairman, Gary Banks at the Outlook 2002 conference in Canberra last week. 'The real surge originated from some new and unexpected contributors in the services sector, especially wholesale trade, finance and construction,' Mr Banks said. 'Microeconomic policy reforms also contributed by sharpening incentives to be more productive and providing greater flexibility for businesses to adjust to a more competitive environment.'

According to Gary Banks, Australia has been advantaged by the country's quick uptake of information and communications technologies during the 1990s. This has contributed to growth, but it will also enable future productivity gains in the services sector in addition to 'traditional' industry contributors, such as agriculture, mining and manufacturing.

Harry Colebourn, Manager, Network Pricing and Marketing for Energy Australia, agreed with Gary Banks, adding, 'historically, there has been a progressive improvement in the productivity of the energy supply industry.' But he also pointed to a number of challenges as well as regulatory design issues for the energy market in Australia following the structural changes, and David Barker, Australia Post's HR group manager said that Australia Post was an example of an organization that has shown substantial productivity increases in recent years: 'Australia Post has achieved cumulative productivity growth of 67 per cent over the last decade. One of the key drivers of this growth has been a change in organizational culture including giving the workforce an ownership of the reform process,' he said.

Source: *HRM Guide Australia* (http://www.hrmguide.net/australia/), 11 March 2002.

Economic growth and employment

The growth of the economy is the most significant overriding variable for people management because it determines overall demand for products and services and hence employment.

Table 4.3	International comparison of GDP per capita	
Country	GDP per capita (US dollars)	Ranking
Luxembourg	36,400	1
United States	36,200	2
Bermuda	33,000	3
San Marino	32,000	4
Switzerland	28,600	5
Aruba	28,000	6
Norway	27,700	7
Monaco	27,000	8
Singapore	26,500	9
Denmark	25,500	10
Hong Kong	25,400	11
Belgium	25,300	12
Austria	25,000	13
Japan	24,900	14
Canada	24,800	15
Iceland	24,800	16
Jersey	24,800	17
Cayman Islands	24,500	18
France	24,400	19
Netherlands	24,400	20
Germany	23,400	21
Australia	23,200	22
Liechtenstein	23,000	23
Finland	22,900	24
United Arab Emirates	22,800	25
United Kingdom	22,800	26
Sweden	22,200	27
Italy	22,100	28
Ireland	21,600	29
Guam	21,000	30
Qatar	20,300	31

Table 4.3	International comparison of GDP per capita (continued)	
Country	GDP per capita (US dollars)	Ranking
Faroe Islands	20,000	32
Greenland	20,000	33
Guernsey	20,000	34
Falkland Islands	19,000	35
Israel	18,900	36
Man Isle of	18,800	37
Andorra	18,000	38
Spain	18,000	39
New Zealand	17,700	40
Brunei	17,600	41
Gibraltar	17,500	42
Macau	17,500	43
Taiwan	17,400	44
Greece	17,200	45
Korea South	16,100	46
Cyprus – Greek Cypriot Area	16,000	47
British Virgin Islands	16,000	48
Bahrain	15,900	49
Portugal	15,800	50
Bahamas The	15,000	51
Kuwait	15,000	52
New Caledonia	15,000	53
Virgin Islands	15,000	54
Barbados	14,500	55
Malta	14,300	56
Argentina	12,900	57
Czech Republic	12,900	58
Northern Mariana Islands	12,500	59
Slovenia	12,000	60
Netherlands Antilles	11,400	61
Hungary	11,200	62
Martinique	11,000	63
Saint Pierre and Miquelon	11,000	64
French Polynesia	10,800	65
Saudi Arabia	10,500	66

Table 4.3	International comparison of GDP per capita (continued)	
Country	GDP per capita (US dollars)	Ranking
Mauritius	10,400	67
Malaysia	10,300	68
Slovakia	10,200	69
Chile	10,100	70
Estonia	10,000	71
Puerto Rico	10,000	72
Trinidad and Tobago	9,500	73
Uruguay	9,300	74
Mexico	9,100	75
Guadeloupe	9,000	76
Libya	8,900	77
Poland	8,500	78
South Africa	8,500	79
Anguilla	8,200	80
Antigua and Barbuda	8,200	81
American Samoa	8,000	82
Oman	7,700	83
Russia	7,700	84
Seychelles	7,700	85
Belarus	7,500	86
Fiji	7,300	87
Lithuania	7,300	88
Turks and Caicos Islands	7,300	89
Latvia	7,200	90
World	7,200	91
Palau	7,100	92
Saint Kitts and Nevis	7,000	93
Turkey	6,800	94
Costa Rica	6,700	95
Thailand	6,700	96
Botswana	6,600	97
Brazil	6,500	98
Tunisia	6,500	99
Gabon	6,300	100
Iran	6,300	101

Table 4.3	International comparison of GDP per capita (continued)	
Country	GDP per capita (US dollars)	Ranking
Bulgaria	6,200	102
Colombia	6,200	103
Venezuela	6,200	104
French Guiana	6,000	105
Panama	6,000	106
Romania	5,900	107
Croatia	5,800	108
Dominican Republic	5,700	109
Algeria	5,500	110
Cyprus – Turkish Cypriot Area	5,300	111
Cook Islands	5,000	112
Kazakhstan	5,000	113
Lebanon	5,000	114
Montserrat	5,000	115
Nauru	5,000	116
Guyana	4,800	117
Paraguay	4,750	118
Georgia	4,600	119
Peru	4,550	120
Saint Lucia	4,500	121
Grenada	4,400	122
Macedonia Former Yugoslavia	4,400	123
Namibia	4,300	124
Turkmenistan	4,300	125
Dominica	4,000	126
El Salvador	4,000	127
Swaziland	4,000	128
Ukraine	3,850	129
Philippines	3,800	130
Guatemala	3,700	131
Jamaica	3,700	132
China	3,600	133
Egypt	3,600	134
Jordan	3,500	135
Morocco	3,500	136

Table 4.3	International comparison of GDP per capita (continued)	
Country	GDP per capita (US dollars)	Ranking
Suriname	3,400	137
Sri Lanka	3,250	138
Belize	3,200	139
Samoa	3,200	140
Syria	3,100	141
Albania	3,000	142
Armenia	3,000	143
Azerbaijan	3,000	144
Ecuador	2,900	145
Indonesia	2,900	146
Niue	2,800	147
Saint Vincent and the Grenadines	2,800	148
Honduras	2,700	149
Kyrgyzstan	2,700	150
Nicaragua	2,700	151
Bolivia	2,600	152
Iraq	2,500	153
Moldova	2,500	154
Papua New Guinea	2,500	155
Saint Helena	2,500	156
Zimbabwe	2,500	157
Lesotho	2,400	158
Uzbekistan	2,400	159
Yugoslavia	2,300	160
India	2,200	161
Tonga	2,200	162
Equatorial Guinea	2,000	163
Maldives	2,000	164
Mauritania	2,000	165
Micronesia Federated States of	2,000	166
Pakistan	2,000	167
Solomon Islands	2,000	168
Wallis and Futuna	2,000	169
Vietnam	1,950	170
Ghana	1,900	171

Table 4.3	International comparison of GDP per capita (continued)	
Country	GDP per capita (US dollars)	Ranking
Haiti	1,800	172
Mongolia	1,780	173
Bosnia and Herzegovina	1,700	174
Cameroon	1,700	175
Cape Verde	1,700	176
Central African Republic	1,700	177
Cuba	1,700	178
Laos	1,700	179
Marshall Islands	1,670	180
Côte d'Ivoire	1,600	181
Senegal	1,600	182
Bangladesh	1,570	183
Burma	1,500	184
Kenya	1,500	185
Togo	1,500	186
West Bank	1,500	187
Nepal	1,360	188
Cambodia	1,300	189
Djibouti	1,300	190
Guinea	1,300	191
Vanuatu	1,300	192
Tajikistan	1,140	193
Bhutan	1,100	194
Congo Republic of the	1,100	195
Gambia The	1,100	196
Liberia	1,100	197
Sao Tome and Principe	1,100	198
Tuvalu	1,100	199
Uganda	1,100	200
Benin	1,030	201
Angola	1,000	202
Burkina Faso	1,000	203
Chad	1,000	204
Gaza Strip	1,000	205
Korea North	1,000	206

Table 4.3	International comparison of GDP per capita (continued)	
Country	GDP per capita (US dollars)	Ranking
Mozambique	1,000	207
Niger	1,000	208
Sudan	1,000	209
Tokelau	1,000	210
Nigeria	950	211
Malawi	900	212
Rwanda	900	213
Zambia	880	214
Guinea-Bissau	850	215
Kiribati	850	216
Mali	850	217
Yemen	820	218
Afghanistan	800	219
Madagascar	800	220
Burundi	720	221
Comoros	720	222
Eritrea	710	223
Tanzania	710	224
Congo Democratic Republic	600	225
Ethiopia	600	226
Mayotte	600	227
Somalia	600	228
Sierra Leone	510	229

Source: *World Factbook 2001*, CIA.

Table 4.3 shows a ranking of OECD countries in terms of gross domestic product (GDP) per capita. The British economy has the longest industrial history but UK growth has been consistently slow, rarely exceeding 3 per cent per annum. There is a tendency for countries that are lower in the GDP league to have higher rates of growth in a 'catching-up' process. Consequently, high rates of growth in east Asia have accompanied medium growth in the developed countries. However, this is not universal – there has been consistently low growth in Africa, for example.

The reasons for differing rates of growth have been endlessly debated but the effective exploitation of human resources appears to be a crucial factor. The nature of the link between human resources and economic success is not simple. This is illustrated by attempts to provide an index of international competitiveness.

For some years the World Economic Forum (WEF), an international business organization, and the Institute for International Management Development (IMD), a Swiss business school, cooperated in the production of such an index. Since 1996, however, they have produced independent league tables. We can see in Table 4.4 that their conclusions differ markedly.

Both organizations calculate their competitiveness indices by combining hundreds of different measures. These range from GDP per head to estimates of the competence of a country's managers. The main difference lies in the relative weightings given to the measures. The WEF regards government regulation and welfare provision as negative factors for national growth, whereas openness to international trade and investment are viewed favourably. Hence, for example, the UK's comparatively low pension burdens and flexible employment market are seen as strengths. The IMD, on the other hand, emphasizes investment in higher education and vocational skills – areas of weakness in the UK. Significantly, both organizations rate the quality of British management as low. These ratings reflect two important perspectives of the role of human resources in the competitiveness debate. We can regard them as the 'hard' and 'soft' versions of macro HRM.

Table 4.4	Relative competitiveness		
Combined	*IMD*	*WEF*	
1995	*2001 (index)*	*2001*	
1 USA	1 USA (100)	1 Finland	
2 Singapore	2 Singapore (87.66)	2 USA	
3 Hong Kong	3 Finland (83.38)	3 Netherlands	
4 Japan	4 Luxembourg (82.81)	4 Germany	
5 Switzerland	5 Netherlands (81.46)	5 Switzerland	
6 Germany	6 Hong Kong (79.55)	6 Sweden	
7 Denmark	7 Ireland (79.20)	7 UK	
8 Netherlands	8 Sweden (77.86)	8 Denmark	
9 New Zealand	9 Canada (76.94)	9 Australia	
10 Norway	10 Switzerland (76.81)	10 Singapore	
11 Austria	11 Australia (75.81)	11 Canada	
12 Sweden	12 Germany (74.04)	12 France	
13 Canada	13 Iceland (73.75)	13 Austria	
14 Taiwan	14 Austria (72.54)	14 Belgium	
15 UK	15 Denmark (71.79)	15 Japan	
16 Australia	16 Israel (67.92)	16 Iceland	
17 Luxembourg	17 Belgium (66.03)	17 Israel	
18 Finland	18 Taiwan (64.84)	18 Hong Kong	
19 France	19 UK (64.78)	19 Norway	
20 Chile	20 Norway (63.10)	20 New Zealand	
	21 New Zealand (61.73)	21 Taiwan	
	22 Estonia (60.20)	22 Ireland	
	23 Spain (60.14)	23 Spain	
	24 Chile (59.84)	24 Italy	

Table 4.4	Relative competitiveness (continued)	
Combined 1995	IMD 2001 (index)	WEF 2001
	25 France (59.56)	25 South Africa
	26 Japan (57.52)	26 Hungary
	27 Hungary (55.64)	27 Estonia
	28 Korea (51.08)	28 Korea
	29 Malaysia (50.03)	29 Chile
	30 Greece (49.96)	30 Brazil
	31 Brazil (49.66)	31 Portugal
	32 Italy (49.58)	32 Slovenia
	33 China (49.53)	33 Turkey
	34 Portugal (48.36)	34 Trinidad and Tobago
	35 Czech Rep. (46.68)	35 Czech Republic
	36 Mexico (43.67)	36 India
	37 Slovak Rep. (43.59)	37 Malaysia
	38 Thailand (42.67)	38 Thailand
	39 Slovenia (42.48)	39 Slovakia
	40 Philippines (40.60)	40 Jamaica
	41 India (40.41)	41 Poland
	42 South Africa (38.61)	42 Latvia
	43 Argentina (37.51)	43 Greece
	44 Turkey (35.44)	44 Jordan
	45 Russia (34.57)	45 Egypt
	46 Colombia (32.84)	46 Uruguay
	47 Poland (32.01)	47 China
	48 Venezuela (30.66)	48 Panama
	49 Indonesia (28.26)	49 Lithuania

Sources: Adapted from International Institute for Management Development, World Economic Forum.

The developing world

In 1993 the United Nations Industrial Development Organization report (UNIDO, 1993) indicated that international trade had replaced aid as the principal vehicle for industrialization. Currently, foreign aid from industrialized to poorer countries runs at about US$50 billion a year. By contrast, foreign direct investment (FDI) in developing countries averages about US$200 billion a year, but fell from US$300 billion in 1997 to US$150 billion in 2001. UNIDO's report showed that the developing world's share of manufacturing trade increased from 11.7 per cent to 14.5 per cent between 1975 and 1990. As we noted in our earlier discussion of multinationals, private capital is being moved around the world in search of profit from flexible and open economies. Complex factors attract this capital: it is not simply a case of the cheapest employees.

The 1993 UNIDO report indicated that the cheapest global human resources were available in Tanzania, averaging US\$6.32 per US\$100 worth of output against US\$24.98 in Germany. Yet German jobs were not being transferred to Tanzania. This was because employee productivity in Germany was 48 times as great and material costs in Tanzania were significantly higher. Tanzania's disadvantages outweighed the benefits to investors despite the poor levels of pay. In fact, direct employee costs rarely contribute more than 10 per cent of the total costs of manufacturing. They can be dwarfed by transport charges.

Japanese manufacturers have opened factories in the UK and other parts of Europe where employee costs are high in comparison with developing countries. They have done so in order to avoid EU import restrictions and cut transport costs. But they have also created jobs in developed rather than developing countries in order to make use of better skills and education.

Uncontrolled globalization has not gone unquestioned. The possibility of social dumping puts societies and national economies under intense pressure and is generally destabilizing (see Key concept 4.5).

Key concept 4:5

Social dumping The concept of social dumping describes the practice of switching production from countries with relatively high employee costs to those with cheap labour. It is an accusation made against large multinational corporations. Social dumping has led to long-term structural changes including the closure of older, heavy manufacturing industries such as steel and shipbuilding in established industrial countries.

Activity 4:5

Summarize the relationship between labour productivity and the economic well-being of a country. What other factors are involved?

Multinationals and global competition

Businesses are not entirely passive or helpless. They are also active players in their environment. They can influence and, sometimes, control their markets. Effectively, major industrial sectors such as petroleum, information technology, aerospace and automobile manufacture are dominated by a small number of multinational corporations. At a local level, strategic alliances between small companies can have the same effect: establishing a degree of control and predictability on the market.

It has been estimated that some large corporations operating internationally, described as multinationals, are responsible for a greater proportion of international trade than most independent states. At one time, companies such as IBM in the USA, ICI in the UK, Volkswagen in western Germany and Toyota in Japan were viewed as national champions. They were key players in those countries' economic activities. Their senior managers influenced governments. As long as profits flowed, shareholders, banks and employees were relatively content. In recent decades, however, industrial competition has become global. National champions have become multinational corporations moving functions around the world without loyalty to any nation. Research and development takes place in one country, manufacturing in a second, with sales in different continents.

This importance has given them the power to play one country against another and to take actions that would be unacceptable for companies operating within single states. Their ability to switch investment from one country to another has been a significant cause for concern. Multinationals are major determiners of action on the world scene, able to move their operations from country to country in defiance of government attempts to maintain minimum wages or workers' consultation.

Initially, corporations such as Ford adopted a policy of dual-sourcing, in which two or more plants in a regional trading bloc such as Europe or North America had the same function, for example building engines. If there were engineering or industrial relations problems in one plant, the other could supply the required components. This insurance policy became less necessary as quality control improved but afforded the opportunity of shifting production, and hence employment, from the country with the greater labour costs to the cheaper. Potentially, this had the effect of driving down employee costs. Deliberate government policy has made dismissal cheaper and easier in the UK than in other European countries, thereby encouraging manufacturers in volatile industries to consider the UK for inward investment. However, this policy has rebounded. Short-term expediency induced corporations to close UK plants because this was effectively easier than tackling less competitive European plants protected by social legislation.

Another feature of multinational activity has been the sourcing of components of manufactured products in different countries. Low-skill items were the first affected, but more sophisticated items have followed. Wage levels and required skills are not constant factors and it can be argued that this form of sourcing is a natural and progressive feature of industrial growth. Alternatively, it could be described in terms of unscrupulous corporations chasing low wages around the world with the connivance of desperate and sometimes corrupt politicians. A number of countries have tried to attract foreign direct investment by creating special economic zones, free of the usual taxation arrangements. The most famous of these – maquiladoras – are concentrated on the Mexican–US border.

HRM in reality

UAW attacks NAFTA model

The president of the UAW (United Auto Workers) Stephen P. Yokich argued that President Bush and 33 other heads of state and prime ministers participating in the Summit of the Americas in Quebec City should reject the NAFTA model as the basis for the proposed Free Trade Area of the Americas (FTAA): 'The results from seven years of NAFTA are in, and it is clear that NAFTA has failed to deliver on its backers' promises that it would create good jobs, raise workers' living standards, and improve public health and the environment,' Yokich said.

He continued:

> Hundreds of thousands of American, Canadian, and Mexican workers have lost their jobs as a direct result of NAFTA, and US employers routinely use the threat of moving jobs to Mexico to kill union organizing drives or force workers to take concessions on wages and benefits. Employment in the maquiladora plants of northern Mexico has soared to over 1.3 million workers since NAFTA was adopted. But Mexican workers have seen their real wages drop, poverty and inequality in their country worsen, and many of their cities and villages turn into environmental nightmares.

Referring to President Bush's recent address to the Organization of American States, Yokich said:

> NAFTA's glaring failures have forced George W. Bush to try out a new sales pitch for the FTAA – that free trade strengthens democratic values and democratic institutions, but, while Bush won't admit it, the hard truth is that NAFTA has seriously weakened the ability of democratically elected municipal, state, provincial, and national governments to protect the interests of their citizens.

Here, Yokich was pointing to the investment section of NAFTA (Chapter 11), which gives corporations (but not citizens) the right to directly sue governments. 'Chapter 11 of NAFTA is an outrageous shift of power away from citizens and their governments to multinational corporations,' he added.

Yokich concluded:

We can expect to hear a lot of lofty rhetoric from President Bush this weekend about how a Free Trade Area of the Americas is essential to strengthening democracy in the western hemisphere. But those words will ring hollow to the millions of workers, small farmers and businesspeople, students, environmentalists, human rights and religious activists, and other concerned citizens who have been denied a voice in the FTAA negotiations, as reflected in the complete absence of worker rights and environmental standards in the draft FTAA text. The highest priority of President Bush and the other heads of state at the Summit of the Americas must be to develop a path of sustainable economic development that improves living standards and our environment while reducing economic inequality and poverty. And that can only be done by putting the interests and rights of ordinary citizens first.

Source: *HRM Guide USA* (http://www.hrmguide.net/usa/), 20 April 2001.

The maquiladoras programme

The Mexican in-bond industry, or maquiladora programme, has mushroomed, producing manufacturing exports geared to the US market (Ransom, 1994). The Mexican government copied similar plants in the 'tiger' economies of South-East Asia, almost all owned by US multinationals. The term maquiladora has its derivation in '*maquila*' – the fee collected by a miller for processing grain in Mexico's colonial period (Teagarden, Butler and Von Glinow, 1992).

The programme is restricted to Mexican-registered companies formed with the purpose of manufacturing, assembling, repairing, or other processing of goods destined mainly for the export market – but they can be wholly owned by partner operations in other countries. They were introduced as part of a Mexican government human resource strategy described as the 'Border Industrialization Programme'. According to Teagarden, Butler and Von Glinow (1992), the aims of this programme were to:

- increase the level of industrial activity in Mexico, particularly in the border area
- create new jobs
- increase the domestic income level
- facilitate technology transfer into Mexico and encourage absorption of relevant skills
- attract foreign exchange.

Foreign multinationals benefited from significantly lower costs than similar operations in the USA – especially wages, energy and rent. Creating jobs is a key part of maquiladora operations. According to Mexican law, maquiladora companies must create a minimum of 25 jobs. But the Ministry of Commerce and Industrial Development can authorize an operation to begin with fewer than 25 jobs as long as the number of jobs increases from year to year.

According to Mexican employment law, nine out of ten workers taken on by an employer must be Mexican nationals. But this rule has been enforced flexibly for management and technical personnel in the case of maquiladora companies. Moreover, the rule does not apply to foreign workers who are not employed by the Mexican maquiladora company but rather by a foreign partner company.

Maquiladora employment reached 1.3 million in October 2000, and then fell to 1.1 million, with about 400 of the 3700 maquiladoras closing during 2001. At the time of writing (2002), however, maquiladora employment has begun to rise again. The emphasis has switched to a more balanced workforce making technologically advanced parts for major US companies in the automobile, electronics and textile industries. The companies that have made use of maquiladoras include General Motors, Ford, General Electric, Honeywell, Fisher Price, Mattell, Sony, Sanyo, Matsushita, Hitachi and Lucky Goldstar.

Working and living conditions in the maquiladora regions have been heavily criticized. Employers have resisted unionization, frequently ignored Mexican employment legislation and paid low wages to employees living in squalid shanty towns. US labour activists have been particularly critical as up to 800 000 relatively well-paid manufacturing jobs have disappeared across the border. But average rates of pay have moved upwards in recent years and the Mexican government has indicated its intention to follow the path of countries such as Malaysia into higher-skilled jobs. Higher wage rates have already led to the departure of many sweatshop textile manufacturers for more vulnerable countries in central America.

Activity 4:6	What alternative job creation strategies are open to developing countries that need to provide employment for growing populations?

International outsourcing and subcontracting

The marriage of global telecommunications and advanced information technology has resulted in a phenomenon known as 'teletrading'. Airlines such as British Airways, Lufthansa and Austrian Airlines have transferred data processing work to Bombay and New Delhi. Similarly Data Management Services, an associate of American Airlines, took on large numbers of staff in Barbados and the Dominican Republic handling much of the airline's data processing work, along with claim forms for a number of US insurance companies. In fact, the company became the largest private employer on Barbados. Initially, teletrading focused on low-skill work being handled by low-wage workers, but the trend is towards transferring more skilled programming and query handling.

Heeks (1996) identified five main factors to explain the massive growth in software subcontracting to Indian suppliers:

1 Indian software programmers were paid substantially less than their counterparts in the West. According to Heeks this meant that Indian subcontractors were typically charging about 70 per cent of Western contract rates and 40 per cent for work carried out offshore.

2 The Indian education system was producing a huge pool of software workers who were highly educated and fluent in English. Conversely, most Western countries had skill shortages in this sector.

3 The Indian software market was itself growing so that use of Indian subcontractors laid the ground for future strategic penetration of Indian markets.

4 Indian companies were enthusiastic about cooperating with foreign high-tech organizations in order to gain access to new markets and technology.

5 The Indian government had become more open towards inward foreign investment and collaboration.

Despite the criticisms of multinationals, many governments – including those of developed countries such as the UK and those of underdeveloped economies – have devoted much energy and money into attracting overseas investment. The British have focused on

American and Japanese manufacturers of computers and electronic equipment. The Pacific Rim countries have wooed the same companies. Developing countries in Africa, the Caribbean and south America have been more restricted, often dependent on mining and plantation conglomerates supplying the supermarkets of North America.

Lasserre and Schutte (1999) argue that outside investment depends upon the level of economic development. Looking at east Asia, for example, they identify five levels:

1 *Platform countries*, such as Singapore and Hong Kong, which can be used for regional coordination, initiating new contacts and gathering intelligence.

2 *Emerging countries*, for example Vietnam.

3 *Growth countries*, particularly China.

4 *Maturing economies*, as in South Korea and Taiwan.

5 *Established economies*, such as Japan.

Multinationals have ruthlessly played one country or region against another, accepting the highest subsidies and lowest controls over pollution and workers' welfare. Environmental and employee legislation in their 'home' countries has been cynically avoided by transferring production overseas. Trade unions have been slow and largely ineffective in providing employee protection to match global managers.

Admittedly, however, despite the bad press multinationals also produce clearly positive benefits. Multinationals have introduced innovative human resource practices including: mobility packages; cross-cultural and language training; greater sensitivity to national management practices; recruitment and development of local employees; and some exciting international careers.

Even in such quasi-monopolistic sectors, however, management is constrained by a range of environmental factors. Western economies have experienced alternating periods of global recession and recovery. Spurts of growth have been followed by cuts in both production and employment. In a dynamic economy businesses expect growth in sales, production and ultimately in employee numbers. Conversely, companies experiencing recession or intense competition may have to retrench – 'downsize' in modern management-speak. For instance, in the mid-1990s air travel recovered slowly from recession. Airlines struggled to meet competition and cut costs to remain in existence. Orders for new aeroplanes were deferred or cancelled. The consequences on aeroplane manufacturers were severe. The world's largest aircraft manufacturer, Boeing, was forced to cut production, leading to thousands of job losses. Similarly, losses at the Dutch company Fokker, leading producer of medium-sized aircraft, impacted heavily on its major German shareholder Daimler-Benz. By 2000 production of aircraft was brisk once more.

Then, on 11 September 2001 the sudden impact of terrorism at the World Trade Center in New York brought airlines to their knees and the aircraft production industry back into the doldrums. Employment in tourism, airlines and aircraft production was dramatically affected throughout the world by the events of one day. No human resource strategist could have forecast such sudden changes in employment needs.

Supranational organizations

The International Labour Organization

The International Labour Organization (ILO) is the highest international authority responsible for the conduct and development of human resources. It has a global programme on decent work (ILO, 2000) with the overall goal for the global economy of providing 'opportunities for all men and women to obtain decent and productive work in conditions of freedom, equity, security and human dignity'. It outlines four objectives:

- *Creation of employment*. Developing a positive environment in which investment and enterprise creation can take place both nationally and internationally with due regard to good practice. Specifically, the ILO considers that there should be worldwide recognition of 'the interdependence between respect for freedom of enterprise for investors and freedom of association for workers'. It calls for a particular focus on stimulating creativity, innovation and entrepreneurship and promoting small enterprises.

- *Promotion of human rights at work*. With a special focus on the rights of women. Among these rights, the ILO highlights freedom of association, collective bargaining, non-discrimination, forced labour and child labour. The ILO measures annual progress in these areas.

- *Improvements in social protection*. These include legislation governing dismissal and redundancies.

- *Promotion of strong institutions* to improve social dialogue between business and labour. Such institutions may include works councils, arbitration systems, joint consultative committees and a variety of other institutions.

World Trade Organization

According to the World Trade Organization website: 'The World Trade Organization (WTO) is the only international organization dealing with the global rules of trade between nations. Its main function is to ensure that trade flows as smoothly, predictably and freely as possible.'

The WTO came into existence in 1995 as successor to the General Agreement on Tariffs and Trade (GATT) established after World War II. It began as a result of the tariff reduction negotiations known as the Uruguay Round. It is not designed to deal with employment regulation but, by its actions, it has a major influence on human resources around the world. Its member states account for 97 per cent of world trade.

It has been severely criticized by environmentalists, union activists and others. For example, the International Forum on Globalization (IFG) describes the WTO as follows (see http://www.ifg.org/wto.html):

> … among the most powerful, and one of the most secretive international bodies on earth. It is rapidly assuming the role of global government, as 134 nation-states, including the US, have ceded to its vast authority and powers. The WTO represents the rules-based regime of the policy of economic globalization. The central operating principle of the WTO is that commercial interests should supersede all others. Any obstacles in the path of operations and expansion of global business enterprise must be subordinated. In practice these 'obstacles' are usually policies or democratic processes that act on behalf of working people, labour rights, environmental protection, human rights, consumer rights, social justice, local culture, and national sovereignty.

The WTO has also been accused of not addressing the impact of unfettered free trade on employment rights, although countries that enforce employment rights are at a disadvantage compared with countries that consistently violate employment conventions promulgated by the International Labour Organization.

Summary

Human resource management takes place within a business environment that is increasingly global in its reach. Globalization is a hotly debated subject with many implications on the practice of HRM, both within and between countries. The allocation of human resources depends on comparative issues such as international competitiveness and productivity, factors that are themselves dependent upon a wide range of variables. Foreign inward investment and subcontracting can bring benefits in terms of increased employment opportunities, earnings and economic development but this may be at the expense of comparatively low pay, poor working conditions and denial of employment rights. However, along with a trend towards reduction of trading barriers and encouragement of international trade, there is an increasing call for worldwide regulation of labour issues.

Further reading

There are numerous books on globalization, many with a markedly political agenda. *The Silent Takeover: Global Capitalism and the Death of Democracy* by Noreena Hertz (published under the Heinemann, Arrow and Free Press imprints, 2001, 2002) takes a highly critical view of the uncontrolled behaviour of multinationals in the globalization process. *Globalization and Its Discontents* by Joseph E. Stiglitz (published by W.W. Norton in 2002) adopts an all-round view of the process of globalization. *Globalization – The People Dimension: Human Resource Strategies for Global Expansion* by Stephen J. Perkins and John Banham (2000, published by Kogan Page) takes matters further than our discussion by considering the practitioner implications of global HR. *The Global Competitiveness Report 2001–02: World Economic Forum* (2002) by Klaus Schwab, Michael E. Porter and Jeffrey D. Sachs is the latest in a regular series on international competitiveness published by Oxford University Press. *The Maquiladora Reader: Cross-Border Organizing Since NAFTA* (1999) edited by Rachael Kamel and Anya Hoffman is a union-minded text published by the American Friends Service Committee. *Smart Sourcing: International Best Practice* (2002) by Andrew Kakabadse and Nada Kakabadse takes a managerial perspective on wider subcontracting issues (published by St Martin's Press).

Review questions

1 What is globalization? Why should globalization concern human resource managers?

2 Outline the positive and negative attributes of globalization for:

   (a) employees in the developed world;

   (b) employees in the developing world.

3 What is the relationship between a country's international competitiveness rating and employment prospects in that country?

4 What do you understand by 'labour productivity'? How is it measured?

5 As an international HR consultant you have been asked to consider the merits of introducing a 'maquiladora' programme for a Caribbean country. What would you advise?

6 Outline the factors to be evaluated before a major computer supplier outsources software development to a developing country.

7 What is the role of the International Labour Organization in the growth of global employment?

Problem for discussion and analysis

Read the following case study and answer the questions that follow.

Change in Japan

The recession of the 1990s and early 2000s seemed to be of a different order from those of the past. In just one year – from October 2000 to October 2001 – the number of people with jobs fell to 64.05 million, a drop of 1.03 million. The Labour Ministry estimated that for every 100 people seeking work, only 55 jobs were available. At the end of October 2001, 49.3 per cent of high school students who had graduated in June and were looking for jobs were still unemployed – the worst level ever recorded. Overall, unemployment reached 5.4 per cent in May 2002, the highest for 50 years.

Smaller Japanese companies without financial muscle suffered badly. In October 2001, 1804 businesses employing 19 550 workers went bankrupt. This was the 32nd consecutive month in which more than 10 000 people lost their jobs due to bankruptcy.

At the start of the recession in the 1990s, the larger companies tried to avoid compulsory redundancies through redistributing human resources, freezing recruitment and early retirement. Major companies also laid off 'temporary' workers, typically comprising 10 per cent of the staff. This was followed by reduction in overtime – possibly 20 per cent of an average worker's pay packet. Then came the first announcements of redundancies in core workforces.

Nissan, the country's second-largest car maker, announced heavy losses and began a restructuring involving 5000 fewer staff (9 per cent of its employees). The most dramatic part of the announcement was the closure of the Zama plant employing 2500 workers. This was a showcase factory capable of making 260 000 cars a year, using the most advanced technology, including extensive employment of robots. However, Nissan did not anticipate any job losses at all from this move, offering transfers to other Nissan plants. Then Nissan received an injection of cash and an equity investment from Renault on condition that Western management techniques were introduced. By 2002 profitability was soaring – at the expense of traditional Japanese employment practices and job levels.

During much of the recession the rising value of the yen made overseas production cheaper than domestic manufacturing for Japanese multinationals. This had the effect of exporting jobs. After a period of huge investment in Japan and overseas, much of the domestic production capacity was standing idle. Initially the overcapacity was not tackled by sacking workers. Redundant executives were left within organizations as *Madogiwazoku,* the 'window-gazing tribe' with nothing to do but stare out of their windows. Western managers would not have hesitated to close surplus factories and make large numbers of workers redundant. Japanese businesses had to overturn their basic philosophy in order to come to terms with firing their people.

At first, many Japanese companies exerted pressure on higher paid salarymen to leave of their own accord. Managers over 45 earning ¥10 million or more were the main target. Ironically, this generation had been accustomed to doing what their employers asked them to do. Now they were asked to leave and found it difficult to say no. Companies exerted psychological pressures on them, for example appealing to their sense of duty by leaving and helping the company's financial situation.

In general, Japanese manufacturing companies employed large numbers of people they did not need. More critically, overstaffing in the Japanese retail and distribution system was remarkably high in comparison with manufacturing and with retailers in the West. One estimate put the surplus at 1.5 million people in manufacturing alone, with around 4 million overall. If these workers were dismissed, the true level of unemployment would be 11–12 per cent.

Japanese attitudes towards workers in overseas operations were less sympathetic. American employees of Japanese subsidiaries falsely assumed that, if not having a job for life, their employment was virtually secure. Instead, American employees were shed quickly when orders fell. Americans were not the only people to lose their jobs: hundreds of Japanese executives were sent home to lower-status positions.

Underlying the reaction to the recession is a change in Japanese beliefs. The attitudes of the workaholic senior executives of the post-war era are not shared by their middle-aged successors and even less by young graduates. They have different values and are prepared to take on some of the risks of the Western way of business. Whether or not the recession is quickly overcome, a falling birth rate and increasing independence for young people require long-term changes. Excellence in manufacturing has disguised organizational inefficiency. The commitment expected from employees can no longer be guaranteed. Younger men and women with career aspirations are not prepared to work 'long hours for little money while waiting to fill dead men's shoes'. For the first time, there is a debate about fast-track career paths, appointment on merit and performance pay.

By 2002 a survey of companies listed on Section 1 of the Tokyo Stock Exchange showed that the lifetime employment and seniority systems considered typical of Japanese companies were being severely questioned. Just 19.5 per cent of the companies that responded said that they would continue the lifetime employment systems into the future, while 53.9 per cent said that they were considering re-examining them.

Discussion questions

1 Why were Japanese people management practices unable to withstand global economic changes?

2 Why should Japanese multinationals treat Japanese and foreign employees in different ways?

5

HRM and the state

Objectives

The purpose of this chapter is to:

- Provide an overview of the role played by governments in creating the context for human resource management.

- Outline the concept of human capital and its implications on development throughout the world.

- Introduce the legal frameworks that regulate employment in the major economies.

- Describe initiatives taken by the European Union as examples of governmental initiatives with a human resource focus.

Key concept 5:1

Labour market   The setting in which people who can provide labour meet those who need labour. Labour markets can be internal, within an organization, or external, outside the organization. 'Labour market' is a somewhat old-fashioned term that implies physical labour as opposed to the time, knowledge and intellectual effort required in many modern jobs. 'Job market' or 'employment market' is more meaningful in today's context.

The state and intervention

'Losses of work or assets providing subsistence are often the first shocks that lead to poverty and destitution. Hence, labour markets are central mechanisms for rehabilitation programs when adversities occur, to reverse the spiral of poverty' (Abrahart and Verme, 2001).

National and regional (state or province) governments have a powerful influence on the practice of HRM because they set the legislative, regulatory and economic contexts in which people work. Economists typically describe the political and regulatory initiatives taken by governments as 'labour market policies'. Abrahart and Verme (2001) distinguish three broad types of labour market policies adopted by governments around the world: the Japanese, European and American models.

The Japanese model relied (at least, until the early 1990s) on full employment as one basic principle of a stable society. The emphasis was on the 'internal labour market' rather than the external job market. In other words, firms were hierarchical and protected their own workers from the consequences of economic fluctuations. In turn, employees were expected to be fully committed to their employing organizations. The role of government was to support firms through skills upgrading and training or finding production alternatives for changing markets. Labour market policies were seen to be part of a wider group of economic and industrial policies managed by the ministries of economy and industry. Abrahart and Verme describe this as an 'enterprise-centred and industry-driven form of labour market management'. The Japanese model was the main frame of reference for many Asian governments until relatively recently.

Abrahart and Verme perceive the European model as one that accepts market laws and the existence of unemployment – but only as a 'necessary temporary condition to facilitate and maximize the allocation of labour'. There is limited government intervention in support of firms. Instead, governments support the unemployed by maintaining their income and providing training schemes to help them find jobs. The European model accepts that the market will fail to protect the public interest from time to time and that governments need to step in to mitigate the short-term economic and social consequences. Unemployment support tends to be generous and is meant to provide a basic standard of living. Responsibility for labour market policies lies with ministries of employment. Abrahart and Verme describe this as a 'mediating, public interest-driven labour market management style'.

The American model limits government intervention to a considerable extent. Firms can dispense with employees to match economic fluctuations. The role of government is to 'maximize mobility of workers and minimize labour market rigidities such as hiring costs and mismatching of the supply and demand of labour'. Unemployment benefits are provided in the short term but the unemployed are expected to be very active in seeking jobs. Abrahart and Verme perceive this as an individualistic model. For example, in the area of employee relations:

● Employment conflicts have been rare in Japan as workers expected to be protected by their enterprises and the government.

- In the European model the government is seen as a mediator that can protect the interests of both employees and enterprises.

- In the American model, however, labour disputes are viewed as civil disputes between individuals for the courts to settle with an army of lawyers available to service them.

Abrahart and Verme describe the American model as a 'liberal market-driven labour management system'.

Activity 5:1	Abrahart and Verme describe their typology as a broad generalization. How useful is the typology in describing government policies in your country?

The USA is an exception among developed countries, having generated more new jobs than any other through flexible job markets, minimal welfare benefits and comparatively low wages for unskilled work. However, the cost has been considerable social inequality and a high crime rate. In most other developed countries the employment market is subject to a greater level of governmental control as a result of traditionally greater concerns for the welfare of the whole population, not just the economically successful. Governments attempt to exercise a major influence on the quantity and quality of workers in their employment markets by means of economic, social and employment legislation, and investment in human capital through education and training programmes.

Underlying beliefs regarding the degree of employment protection, benefits for the unemployed, and acceptable wages have become tougher throughout the developed countries indicating a general swing towards the 'American model'. Against an agenda primarily set by 1980s right-of-centre leaders, especially Ronald Reagan in the USA and Margaret Thatcher in the UK, even left-wing parties have adjusted their views to fit what is now termed a 'neo-liberal' perspective. Hence, parties supposedly at opposite ends of the political spectrum such as 'New Labour' in the UK and the Liberals in Australia have adopted policies advocating:

- restrained and affordable public sector spending (fiscal prudence)
- control of inflation
- encouragement of inward investment
- tax rates that compare favourably with those of international competitors
- employment protection that does not cause rigidity or inflexibility in the job market
- maintenance (in the case of the UK Labour Party) of some of the 1980s Conservative government legislation restricting the scope of trade union activities
- partnership between public and private sectors to revitalize investment-starved infrastructure – for example, railways and roads
- the reform of education to boost the nation's skill base.

In the European Union, the pursuit of a single market has led increasingly to measures allowing free circulation of employees and freedom of residence in any EU country. Other barriers to job mobility are being removed with recognition of different educational qualifications and further social and economic cohesion. There are increasing moves towards standardization of employment regulation and protection measures to further promote a single European job market with the goal of full employment. The result is an apparent hybrid between a US-style, 'free for all' employment market and the more rigid, social protectionism of mainland western Europe between the 1950s and 1980s.

HRM in reality	**The new agenda**

According to UK Prime Minister Tony Blair, speaking in 1998 (cited in Economic Research Forum, 2000): The industrial order was built on raw materials, heavy industry, unskilled manual employment, great concentrations of economic power and antagonism between capital and labour. The old politics of the left was an expression of old industry – raw materials, large factories and armies of unionized labour. The new economics – like the new politics – is radically different. Services, knowledge, skills and small enterprises are its cornerstones.... Its most valuable assets are knowledge and creativity.

Outside these comparatively rich areas of the world, governments have an uphill battle to achieve high growth and reduced unemployment in the face of rapidly increasing populations and low levels of industrialization. In the Middle East and North Africa, for example, the ILO projects an annual increase of more than 3 per cent between 2000 and 2015. In total, these countries will need to provide more than 5 million new jobs each year, rising to 6.18 million in 2015. But, according to World Bank estimates, the region already has 20 million unemployed. Unemployment rates are estimated to be between 10 per cent and 19 per cent in Oman, Egypt, Syria, Jordan, Tunisia, Bahrain, Morocco and Lebanon. The unemployment level reaches between 25 and 30 per cent in Libya, Algeria, Iran and Yemen. Worryingly, these levels remained the same (or worse) throughout the 1990s.

One of the major contributing causes is the population explosion in the region during the 1970s and 1980s when the birth rate was among the highest in the world. Population growth has slowed considerably since that time but it will take at least 20 years for this to be translated into slower growth in the labour force. On a more optimistic note it may be that the rapid growth in available workers may fuel high economic growth as happened in east Asia during the 1980s.

Analysis of statistics from the 1990s suggests that there are additional problems to be overcome, with a reduction of productivity and a decline in real wages being seen in Kuwait, Algeria and Jordan, for example. Whereas the rate of GDP growth was double the growth rate of the labour force in east Asia during 1970–80, GDP growth and labour force growth were more or less the same in the Middle East and North Africa during the 1990s.

The Economic Research Forum (2000) suggests that almost all countries in the region should focus on:

1 macroeconomic stability

2 human resource development

3 promotion of exports

4 reforming the state and empowering the private sector.

Dickens (1998) concludes that successfully developing economies have one thing in common:

Despite many popular misconceptions, none of today's NIEs (newly industrialising economies) is a free-wheeling market economy in which market forces have been allowed to run their unfettered course. They are, virtually without exception, *developmental* states: market economies in which the state performs a highly interventionist role.

Activity 5:2	In reality, how much power do governments have to influence employment and the development of their human resources? What factors can you identify that would act as obstacles to government initiatives?

The Economic Research Forum (2000) also takes a neo-liberal stance on the purpose of the state, arguing that most governments in the region still perceive their role as employers and producers of public goods. They contrast this to the growth model of the newly industrialized countries (NICs) which they see as 'a deliberately selective approach to intervention by the state to provide an optimal institutional environment'.

This selective approach is made up of a number of elements:

● Maximizing the flow of knowledge to all market players (market information, technology, quality education and training) through the establishment of a modern information infrastructure connecting them with knowledge networks.

● Transforming government bureaucracy from being a passive or even obstructive element in the economy into an active agent of development. This requires creation of an elite technocracy recruited on the basis of merit and operating in a transparent environment with clear objectives, rewards and penalties; grounded in an effective system of monitoring and performance evaluation.

● Aiming for rapid insertion into the global market and opting for openness and flexibility of their political and economic institutions so as to realize the potential productivity gains of the second economic revolution.

HRM in reality	**The ILO view on the role of the state**

The International Labour Organization (ILO, 2000) considers that one of its roles is in:

> ... promoting greater awareness of the continuing importance of the role of the state in dealing with market failures and providing public goods, especially in economies where markets remain underdeveloped and inefficient. This includes the state's role in alleviating poverty and reducing inequality, in maintaining adequate financing for basic social services, and in developing and maintaining the regulatory frameworks and institutions that are necessary for the efficient and equitable functioning of markets. This promotion of greater awareness needs to be supported by action to strengthen the capacity of the state to discharge these functions effectively. We need a 'better' state that is respected and respects itself in the institutional function it performs for the benefit of its citizens.

Question: Can you reconcile this statement from the International Labour Organization with the views of the Economic Research Forum on the purpose of government? What are the differences and similarities in the two perspectives?

It should be noted that changes in economic or political circumstances can lead to decline as well as growth in employment opportunities and living standards. Table 5.1 shows a large number of countries where the average income in 2002 was lower than in previous decades.

Human capital

Personal and national success is increasingly correlated with the possession of skills. Skilled individuals can command a premium salary in periods of high economic activity. Worldwide, unemployment levels remain high, while organizations have difficulty in filling vacancies that require specific expertise. A shortage of skilled people can act as a limiting factor on individual organizations and on the economy as a whole. For example, in Canada and the UK small businesses report an inability to expand because of the difficulty in finding people with the right skills. Small firms are also vulnerable because their owners do not possess basic marketing and finance skills. It is in the interest of any country to maximize its human resources by investing in the skills of its workforce: its human capital (see Key concept 5.2). Human capital is a crucial component of a country's overall competitiveness.

Key concept 5:2

Human capital   It can be argued that economic growth, employment levels and the availability of a skilled workforce are interrelated. Economic growth creates employment, but economic growth partly depends on skilled human resources – a country's human capital. The concept encompasses investment in the skills of the labour force, including education and vocational training to develop specific skills.

Table 5.1   Per capita income higher then than in 2002

1975	1976–80*	1981–85*	1986–1990*
Jamaica	Angola	Albania	Armenia
Madagascar	Bolivia	Algeria	Azerbaijan
	Central African Republic	Comoros	Bahamas
	Chad	Congo	Belarus
	Côte d'Ivoire	Ethiopia	Bulgaria
	El Salvador	Gambia	Cameroon
	Gabon	Georgia	Croatia
	Ghana	Paraguay	Estonia
	Guatemala	Peru	Jordan
	Haiti	Philippines	Kazakhstan
	Honduras	Rwanda	Kenya
	Iran	Sierra Leone	Kyrgyzstan
	Kuwait	South Africa	Latvia
	Mali	Trinidad and Tobago	Lithuania
	Mauritania		Macedonia (TYFR)
	Namibia		Moldova
	Nicaragua		Mongolia
	Niger		Russian Federation
	Nigeria		Tajikistan
	Saudi Arabia		Turkmenistan
	Senegal		Ukraine
	Togo		Uzbekistan
	Venezuela		
	Zambia		

*Refers to a year within the specified period.

Source: United Nations Development Report 2002, UNDP. Copyright © 2002 United Nations Development Programme. Reproduced by permission of Oxford University Press Inc.

The United Nations Development Programme produces an annual Human Development Index (HDI) (see Table 5.2), which is a composite of life expectancy, education and income.

Table 5.2   Human Development Index 2002

High human development	Medium human development	Medium human development	Low human development
1 Norway	46 United Arab	93 Ecuador	138 Pakistan
2 Sweden	Emirates	94 Dominican	139 Sudan
3 Canada	47 Seychelles	Republic	140 Bhutan
4 Belgium	48 Croatia	95 Uzbekistan	141 Togo
5 Australia	49 Lithuania	96 China	142 Nepal
6 USA	50 Trinidad and Tobago	97 Tunisia	143 Laos
7 Iceland	51 Qatar	98 Iran	144 Yemen
8 Netherlands	52 Antigua and	99 Jordan	145 Bangladesh
9 Japan	Barbuda	100 Cape Verde	146 Haiti
10 Finland	53 Latvia	101 Western Samoa	147 Madagascar
11 Switzerland	54 Mexico	102 Kyrgyzstan	148 Nigeria
12 France	55 Cuba	103 Guyana	149 Djibouti
13 United Kingdom	56 Belarus	104 El Salvador	150 Uganda
14 Denmark	57 Panama	105 Moldova	151 Tanzania
15 Austria	58 Belize	106 Algeria	152 Mauritania
16 Luxembourg	59 Malaysia	107 South Africa	153 Zambia
17 Germany	60 Russian Federation	108 Syria	154 Senegal
18 Ireland	61 Dominica	109 Vietnam	155 Congo (Dem Rep)
19 New Zealand	62 Bulgaria	110 Indonesia	156 Côte d'Ivoire
20 Italy	63 Romania	111 Equatorial Guinea	157 Eritrea
21 Spain	64 Libya	112 Tajikistan	158 Benin
22 Israel	65 Macedonia (TFYR)	113 Mongolia	159 Guinea
23 Hong Kong (China	66 St Lucia	114 Bolivia	160 Gambia
SAR)	67 Mauritius	115 Egypt	161 Angola
24 Greece	68 Colombia	116 Honduras	162 Rwanda
25 Singapore	69 Venezuela	117 Gabon	163 Malawi
26 Cyprus	70 Thailand	118 Nicaragua	164 Mali
27 Korea (Rep. Of)	71 Saudi Arabia	119 Sao Tome and	165 Central African
28 Portugal	72 Fiji	Principe	Republic
29 Slovenia	73 Brazil	120 Guatemala	166 Chad
30 Malta	74 Suriname	121 Solomon Islands	167 Guinea-Bissau
31 Barbados	75 Lebanon	122 Namibia	168 Ethiopia
32 Brunei Darussalan	76 Armenia	123 Morocco	169 Burkina Faso
33 Czech Republic	77 Philippines	124 India	170 Mozambique
34 Argentina	78 Oman	125 Swaziland	171 Burundi
35 Hungary	79 Kazakhstan	126 Botswana	172 Niger
36 Slovakia	80 Ukraine	127 Myanmar	173 Sierra Leone
37 Poland	81 Georgia	128 Zimbabwe	
38 Chile	82 Peru	129 Ghana	
39 Bahrain	83 Grenada	130 Cambodia	
40 Uruguay	84 Maldives	131 Vanuatu	
41 Bahamas	85 Turkey	132 Lesotho	
42 Estonia	86 Jamaica	133 Papua New Guinea	
43 Costa Rica	87 Turkmenistan	134 Kenya	
44 Saint Kitts and Nevis	88 Azerbaijan	135 Cameroon	
45 Kuwait	89 Sri Lanka	136 Congo	
	90 Paraguay	137 Comoros	
	91 St Vincent and the		
	Grenadines		
	92 Albania		

Source: United Nations Development Report 2002, UNDP. Copyright © 2002 United Nations Development Programme. Reproduced by permission of Oxford University Press Inc.

Countries that have shown some of the highest rates of growth, for example Singapore and Malaysia, are investing heavily in the education and technical skills of their populations. Similarly, South Korea aimed for 90 per cent of its young people to have an 18-plus qualification with 60 per cent undertaking higher education. Britain, conversely, was only able to provide 28 per cent of its youth with higher education at the beginning of the 1990s. Yet industry recognized the value of human capital – unskilled people were paid at just 40 per cent of the graduate rate. Belatedly, the UK government set targets for higher levels of achievement. The 'HRM in reality' article looks at action in Wales regarding skills achievement.

**HRM
in reality**

Wales action on skills progress report

The Welsh Minister for Education and Lifelong Learning released a progress report that outlines measures taken to help provide Wales with the skills it needs for future growth. The report describes the actions taken on the key recommendations proposed by the Wales Skills Task Force in their report to the Welsh Assembly last year. The Minister said:

> The report of the Wales Skills Task Force made 50 challenging recommendations, which put skills firmly at the centre of our economic and learning agendas. This has given us a head start in highlighting what needs to be done to upgrade skills in Wales and has helped to inform our comprehensive Education and Lifelong Learning Programme – 'The Learning Country'.
>
> Since we received the Task Force report the Assembly has not been standing still or playing for time; where there is a clear need then we have acted. We have done that in respect of the all-age skills programme called for by the Task Force.
>
> Until recently Assembly-funded training support has only been available for the under 25s and for the unemployed, yet it is clear that many over-25s in work need to acquire new or higher-level skills and that employers cannot always meet this alone. In April we introduced a new pilot programme called the Modern Skills Diploma for Adults. This is a unique 'made in Wales' solution and will help older workers to have modern apprentice-type training that will help them and their employers compete effectively and deliver the good quality jobs that we so badly need.
>
> We have also removed the upper age limit for the Modern Apprenticeship Programme so that apprentices in Wales can complete their training beyond age 25. And we have launched our basic skills strategy backed up by an investment of £27.3 million over the next three years.
>
> Today's report summarizes progress on the action that has been set in hand by the National Assembly and its partners to ensure that we meet the Task Force's vision for Wales to be a place of learning and skills acquisition for all. It shows that a good start has been made to tackle the skill needs identified in the Task Force report but we recognize that continuous action is needed to ensure that we keep apace with emerging technology, changing working patterns and ever higher demands for skills. We therefore propose to publish an Employment and Skills Action Plan for Wales alongside the National Economic Development Strategy at the end of the year. This strategy will build upon the recommendations of the Wales Skills Task Force and develop further the action outlined in the progress report I am publishing today.

Source: *HRMGuide.co.uk* (http://www.hrmguide.co.uk), 3 October 2001.

Skill requirements are particularly critical at the managerial level. For example, the arrival of multinational corporations in China has led to an increased demand for professional managers. In the past, Chinese colleges have produced large numbers of technicians but few accountants, lawyers or marketing specialists. Without a modern commercial tradition, Western companies such as Motorola and Price Waterhouse are using in-house training programmes (Reuters, 12 February 1995). Motorola's own 'university' in Beijing announced its intention to send 60 students each year for on-the-job training in its plants elsewhere in Asia and the USA. Price Waterhouse opened its own US$600 000 training centre in Shanghai.

Competition is not restricted to marketing and product development. It also entails competition for staff. Availability of skilled employees in the external job market may constrain growth. Additional expensive advertising may be required, together with the offer of enhanced salaries to attract suitable applicants. We saw in Part 1 that businesses are inhibited from investing in training by the non-activity of other businesses in the same sector. Companies like Motorola and IBM, which invest heavily in training and development, are at risk of losing their investments (Kochan and Dyer, 2001, p.282). Their staff can be poached for higher wages by businesses that spend little on training. In turn, this may lead good trainers to conclude that training is not worthwhile.

Human capital theory also deals with personal investment in self-development, such as enrolling on a degree course. It presupposes that individuals balance the cost of education and training (time, loss of income, fees) against the benefits of a higher income in the future. As such it predicts that the young are more likely to invest in training because their losses are relatively less – and the potential gains greater – than for older people. In general, the income of employees with degrees and other higher education qualifications is significantly more than that of people who ceased education at an earlier point.

It has been suggested that the value of education may lie not in any real investment in skills but in its 'screening' power (Sapsford and Tzannatos, 1993, p.89). Recruiters assume that individuals with 'pieces of paper' are better candidates than those without. Qualifications are used as a cheap and easy selection filter. However, a survey designed by the US National Centre on the Educational Quality of the Workforce at the University of Pennsylvania produced evidence to show that improved workers' education directly increased productivity (*The Times Higher*, 26 May 1995). The survey of owners and managers in 3000 businesses showed that whereas a 10 per cent increase in capital investment (machinery, tools, buildings, etc.) produced a 3.4 per cent increase in productivity, a 10 per cent improvement in education attainment increased productivity by 8.4 per cent.

The survey found that organizations that used education grades as selection criteria and were linked to schools through work placement arrangements or training schemes also showed higher levels of productivity and innovation. However, most employers disregarded school grades and reports in favour of 'attitude', communication skills and previous work experience.

| HRM in reality | **European science and technology skills observatory needed** |

There is a risk to Europe's prosperity if the supply of graduate science and technology skills does not match market needs. This is the conclusion of *Assessing the Supply and Demand for Scientists and Technologists in Europe* (Pearson *et al.*, 2001), a report from the Institute for Employment Studies.

The report is based on in-depth research across the European Union conducted for the European Commission by IES. It reveals shortages in specific skills such as IT, together with underutilization of other skills in life sciences and some areas of engineering that are expensive to develop. But the report also shows that there are considerable problems in providing accurate data about supply and demand of skills that are fundamental to Europe's economic performance.

Richard Pearson, Director of the Institute for Employment Studies (also an author of the report) said that action was necessary:

> A good supply of science and technology skills is an essential element of our prosperity. Yet knowledge about the flows of scientists and technologists into and out of higher education, in employment and around the EU, is inadequate. The effective operation of these critical labour markets, with skill shortages co-existing with over-supply, requires better information. Existing data sets have major deficiencies and inconsistencies. The establishment of a European science and technology Observatory would be a significant first step, building on our research, to monitor and report regularly on the key trends.

The report argues that the proposed Observatory should report on supply and demand trends, together with their imbalances across the European Union. It should advise on future information needs by coordinating inputs from experts drawn from every member state of the EU, these in turn drawing from their own local information sources.

So what information do the report authors think that we need to know about Europe's scientists and technologists? Employer demand can be influenced by numerous factors – for example, national and international economic climate, historic patterns of national development and structural change, and corporate competitiveness, including competition for skills. On the supply side it is clear that higher education is in a state of flux with many universities trying to be more responsive to the demands of students and the job market.

Europe is a diverse continent and the job market for scientists and technologists shows huge and rapidly changing differences between occupations, sectors, countries and locations. Basic trends may be well reported but some of the studies that have been most widely publicized 'have been rather ad hoc and based on poor research, or undertaken to lobby for more publicly funded resources', indicating a need for better quality information on which impartial decisions can be taken.

Main findings of the study

The number of research scientists and engineers within the EU increased from 500 000 in 1985 to 800 000 in 1995. Almost two-thirds were in Germany, France and the UK.

There is no evidence to support theories of a 'brain drain' from the EU. Most R&D employers conduct recruitment within their own countries. Technical skills are no longer enough: R&D employers increasingly look for recruits with personal skills as well. They cite ability to communicate, adaptability, problem solving and business awareness as being important.

Other key findings included:

- Just 20 per cent of research scientists and engineers in the research and development establishments surveyed were women. But women make up more than half of people graduating in most EU member states.

- Natural sciences account for 18 per cent of people graduating in the EU, with Ireland and France having the largest share.

- Engineers and technologists feature prominently in Germany, Finland and Denmark, with 24 per cent of graduates.

◄

● Unemployment among newly qualified scientists and technologists has been comparatively high in some countries. Underemployment and underutilization of
skills can be seen in Germany, the Netherlands, Sweden, the UK and (at Doctoral
level) in France. This is particularly the case for some engineers and life science
graduates.

Source: *HRMGuide.co.uk* (http://www.hrmguide.co.uk), 12 March 2001.

Figure 5.1	Human capital and major HR activities

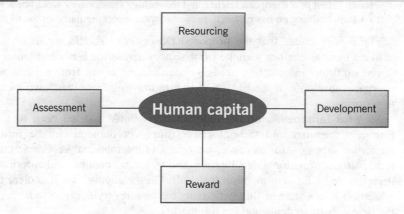

We can see from Figure 5.1 that human capital is a significant unifying concept in HRM.
It links four major people management activities – resourcing, assessment, development
and reward – with an environmental variable that is a key to both organizational and
national success. Each of these areas is further explored in later chapters in this book.
Table 5.3 locates macro HRM in the context of a changing world and a background of economic uncertainty.

Table 5.3	Macro HRM in context

	Levels of analysis			
	Environment	Organization	Strategy	Activities
HRM type	Macro HRM	Organizational HRM	Strategic HRM	Operational HRM
Features	Economy	Structure	Mission	Recruitment
	Labour market	Culture	Objectives	Development
	Culture	Power	Policy	Reward
	Political climate	Functions	Planning	Dismissal
Traditional responsibility	State	Senior management	Senior management	Personnel
Modern responsibility	Supranational	Managers	Senior and	Line managers
	National	Employees	middle	HR specialists
	Multinationals		management	

| Activity 5:3 | What are the most effective measures open to a government for improving a country's human capital? |

Legislative frameworks

One of the most important environmental constraints on the job market and the activities of people managers comes from the law. Employment law changes continuously and varies extensively in different parts of the world. Much of the legislation relating to business derives from custom or precedent. Precedents are also decided by judges working to the system that 'like cases be decided alike'. Within the Anglo-Celtic countries these have been systematized into a common law framework. Many of these countries, such as the USA, also have a written constitution which provides a further code. Most European countries employ an entirely code-based system called civil law descended from the law code of the Roman Empire. A further element is that of 'equity', which is discretionary and has relevance to cases involving non-monetary actions or injunctions, for example against an illegal strike.

By the 21st century, national governments have become law-making machines, creating a complex legal environment for businesses. Governments implement statutes for strategic reasons, ensuring, for example, that employees who are disciplined or dismissed are dealt with in a particular manner. Organizations that fail to meet their legal obligations must compensate aggrieved individuals appropriately. Not only does this apply to current employees but also ex-employees and potential recruits such as job applicants. But one of the major complications for human resource managers is that such laws differ from country to country, and also between different states within countries with a devolved or federal structure.

The European Union is a useful example to examine in greater detail because there are still marked differences in employment legislation covering operating units in different locations. Unlike the USA, for example, it is made up of countries with widely different employment laws, traditions and practices. The variations in European employment law can be attributed largely to different legal systems, national traditions and accidents of history. The different legal systems in the EU can be divided into three broad groupings (Due, Madsen and Jense, 1991; Gold 1993):

- The Roman-German system prevailing in Austria, Belgium, France, Germany, Italy and the Netherlands. Government has a pivotal role in employee relations, guaranteeing a fundamental core of constitutional rights. These provide the foundation for national industrial relations. Legislation covers significant aspects of employment market conditions such as working hours and trade union representation.

- The Anglo-Celtic system in the United Kingdom and the Irish Republic. A minimalist approach to the role of the state with limited legislative protection.

- The Nordic system, covering Denmark, Finland, Norway and Sweden. The 'basic agreement' between employers and unions forms the foundation of employee relations. The state plays a limited role, intervening only at the request of these two parties.

The central and dominant group of the EU follows the Roman-German model. Not surprisingly, their way of thinking has shaped many proposals to the European Commission. The European Court of Justice has also contributed to harmonization with an increasing body of case law (Gold, 1993, p.16). However, debate on employee relations reflects changing business practices and a shifting balance of attitudes within an enlarging EU.

In our earlier discussion of globalization we observed that the EU is not sealed off from other trading areas such as east Asia and North America – its industries are often in direct competition. We also noted that the process of 'social dumping' (see Key concept 4.5) has led to a questioning of the fitness of traditional methods of industrial relations within the EU. Institutionalized worker participation can function smoothly in a growing company but what happens when employees are asked to participate in determining their own redundancies?

Many governments and employee groups have been concerned that social dumping can also take place from one country to another within the EU. They have proposed improvements in employment rights for all workers across the Union. Gold (1993, p.17) has described this approach as 'social protectionist' (Key concept 5.3) in contrast to the largely deregulatory views of the UK Conservative government and, to a considerable extent, its Labour successor. Indeed, the Conservative UK government refused to sign the 'Social Chapter' of the Maastricht Treaty in 1991 arguing that it would lead to higher employee costs and a reduction in the country's competitive position. It was agreed that the other 11 members at the time would implement a common social and employee policy whether or not the UK acquiesced. Later in the decade an incoming Labour government accepted this policy.

> **Key concept 5:3**
>
> **Social protection**   According to the World Bank, social protection measures improve or protect human capital, ranging from labour market interventions, unemployment or old-age insurance, to income support, for individuals, households and communities.

Whereas HRM in the USA has been predominantly within non-unionized firms, this has not been the case in Europe. In Britain and Ireland, where HRM has had its earliest and greatest impact, there is a long-standing pluralist tradition of collective bargaining. In the pre-Thatcher era, the industrial relations scene in the UK, especially, could be described as confrontational and competitive, with unions and management in a state of frequent disagreement and strikes or other forms of industrial action being commonplace.

During the Thatcher period, the UK witnessed a massive reduction in union power: a phenomenon associated with large-scale redundancies and restructuring within the British economy. The old labour-intensive industries, where the major union power lay, were particularly affected by these processes. By the mid-1990s fewer than half of Britain's commercial sector employees were covered by collective bargaining arrangements. UK-wide agreements were being eroded in the public sector, with government pursuing a policy of breaking up structures such as the National Health Service into local trusts with separate bargaining powers. There was a marked move towards authoritarian styles of management in this period with union rights to take industrial action being considerably reduced – partly through government legislation but also due to awareness of economic reality among the workforce and a reluctance to run the risk of further job losses. This has been described as a 'new industrial relations' within which: 'management has seized the initiative to change working practices and unions have become less confrontational, more flexible, more accommodating to "local" conditions, and generally more "realistic"' (Goss, 1994, p.140).

This new realism was reinforced by a succession of changes in legislation with four main consequences:

- *Making it easier for people not to join a union*. For example, by strengthening rights for non-union workers within a 'closed shop'. Protection for workers who lost their jobs, or who were victimized for not being members of a trade union when a closed-shop agreement prevailed between a union and employing organization. Protection for employees who chose not to join a union because of personal conviction. In effect, closed shops became unworkable.

- *Making unions financially liable for their members' actions*. A union could be held responsible for any damage caused by an individual member to property during a strike.
- *Curtailing the power of solidarity*. For instance, through the restriction of picketing, limiting numbers to six at any one entrance and only allowing picketing at their own place of work. Limiting secondary industrial action to situations where the employers involved had a contractual relationship and the action was directly related to the dispute. This prevented any sympathetic action by other union members. This was further reinforced by redefining a trade dispute to refer only to a dispute between workers and *their* employer (the previous definition had been 'employers *and* workers'); the dispute had to be *wholly* or *mainly* related to (formerly *connected* with) one or more specific issues – such as terms and conditions, recruitment or dismissal, duty allocation, discipline and negotiation.
- *Increasing the accountability of union leaders*. A secret postal ballot was required before any industrial action, including strikes, overtime bans and working-to-rule. Similarly, senior union officials were required to offer themselves for re-election every five years by secret ballot.

This approach contrasts markedly with the so-called 'Rhineland' model – the form of social market (see Key concept 5.4) developed in Germany and adjacent countries. According to Bolkestein (2000):

> The Rhineland model may be seen as a regulated market economy with a comprehensive system of social security. Government, employers' organizations and labour unions consult each other on economic goals and on the policy instruments to be used. In the Rhineland, therefore, the welfare state is combined with a so-called 'consultation economy'.
> Rhineland participants in the economic process (widely known as stakeholders) try to achieve a harmony of interests. In such a stakeholder economy the primary goal, it is said, is not the maximization of short-term profits for the benefit of the shareholders. The main concern is a sustainable, stable and continuous economic growth and a high level of employment.

Activity 5:4

To what extent is the UK's employment context more similar to other English-speaking countries such as Australia, Canada and the USA than to other member states of the European Union?

Much of the UK Conservative legislation remains in place. The 'HRM in reality' article looks at the implications for multinationals when deciding which plants to close during a period of retrenchment.

HRM in reality

Damaging myths?

Digby Jones, Director-General of the Confederation of British Industry, criticized a number of 'damaging myths' about the consultation rules that govern company plant closures. He said that it was untrue that multinational companies either choose to shut British plants before other European sites simply because of UK redundancy law, or deliberately tell the media about redundancies before informing their staff.

He also rejected claims that British redundancy legislation does not require meaningful consultation at present or that it needs to be overlaid by a proposed EU Directive on information and consultation.

He said:

> Nobody likes to see factories close down and people losing jobs – no employee, no trade unionist, no politician and certainly no employer. But it will not help anyone if we allow damaging myths to become accepted facts. So let's be clear. It's naive to believe one-off redundancy costs are the main reason for closing one factory over another. Firms have many other long-term issues to consider like skilled labour, productivity, taxes, proximity to market, transport, communication, exchange rates and capacity.

Digby Jones argues that UK redundancy rules are actually challenging and do offer meaningful consultation – contrary to perception:

> In reality, firms must discuss timing and implementation of redundancies plus the decisions behind them. Failure to consult leads to stiff penalties. Of course, companies take making people redundant extremely seriously so consultation rarely reveals startling new facts. But the possibility of changing the original decision does exist and that means meaningful consultation can and does take place.

He added that it was nonsense to argue that companies deliberately tell the media before telling staff:

> It must be appalling to hear about redundancy on the radio, but let's not pretend this happens at the instigation of management – they are equally appalled. With the best security in the world, organisations can still fall victim to a leak. But the first priority for an employer will always be to comply with the law of the land and inform both the workforce and shareholders as soon as possible.

The CBI and the TUC are participating in a government review of UK redundancy law and Digby Jones will urge ministers to continue resisting pressure for a European Directive on information and consultation:

> When it comes to UK redundancy rules, the EU Directive is a red herring because it would simply overlay the existing rigorous requirements and add yet another raft of red tape. The vast majority of companies consult happily with employees in any event. Naturally, trade unions support the proposed Directive because it offers consultation rights on a range of day-to-day management decisions, not just plant closures. But a one-size-fits-all rule is not the way to get the unemployed into work or more productive businesses creating better jobs.

He concluded: 'Of course people get angry and frustrated about redundancies – we're talking about their livelihoods and futures. But we risk even more jobs and much-needed inward investment if we prevent companies from reacting quickly to changing market conditions.'

Responding to the CBI's claim that UK redundancy rules have not played a part in a succession of recent closures in the UK, TUC General Secretary, John Monks, said:

> There is no doubt it is easier, cheaper and quicker to sack staff in the UK. Just ask anyone who works for Marks and Spencer hit by their recent round of redundancies in Britain or France.
>
> It is a shame to see UK business leaders describing minimum decent standards for employers to keep their staff informed about their business and to take their views into account as red tape. No doubt there were nineteenth century employers who said ending child chimney sweeps imposed intolerable burdens on business.

There are two main differences between the limited consultations that occur in the UK and elsewhere in much of Europe. First information and consultation is continuous elsewhere, not just after the event when it's generally too late to consider real alternatives. Secondly, as Mark and Spencer discovered, the courts elsewhere get tough with companies that do not consult their staff.

Of course there are other factors behind recent redundancies such as exchange rate problems and our continuing exclusion from the euro as the TUC has often said. But there can be no doubt hire and fire is easy in the UK.

Source: *HRMGuide.co.uk* (http://www.hrmguide.co.uk), 4 May 2001.

Europe-wide initiatives

The European Union has created a new dimension for people management in its member states. The European Commission has undertaken a number of initiatives aimed at improving economic conditions in less privileged regions. The differences in income between the EU's richest and poorest regions are dramatic, ranging between 30 per cent and 209 per cent of the average. It was once believed that the division between rich and poor could be described simply in terms of location. The rich were concentrated in a belt from south-east England, through northern France, Belgium, the Netherlands into northern Germany. The peripheral areas along the Mediterranean and Atlantic seaboard were thought to be poorer. Today, the situation has become far more complex. For a variety of reasons, rich and poor regions are found next to each other in a patchwork throughout the EU.

In particular, there was pressure from the then president of the European Commission, Jacques Delors, for the EU to take a unified and strongly interventionist approach to the problem of 17 million people without work. This was an area of conflict between the majority social market (Key concept 5.4) position in Europe and the UK's free market stance. Both Conservative and Labour governments in the UK advocated a 'hands-off' approach to the issue, arguing that the 'market' would take care of the problem if employment laws were loosened and 'flexibility' encouraged. However, it is clear that having a pool of unskilled people in rundown industrial or mining areas is not sufficient to attract industry. Companies need to be able to draw on an infrastructure of transport facilities, service companies and highly trained potential employees.

Key concept 5:4

Social market   A term coined by Alfred Müller-Armack, Secretary of State at the Economics Ministry in Bonn, Federal Republic of Germany between 1958 and 1963. He defined the social market as an economic system that combined market freedom with social equilibrium. In this kind of economic system the government plays a regulating role and creates the framework for market processes, going beyond securing competition to ensure social equity.

Worries about job losses in the EU led to a decision at the Essen summit of 1994 to adopt a monitoring procedure based on five recommendations:

- improving employment opportunities
- increasing the intensity of employment growth
- reducing non-wage employment costs
- developing active labour market polices
- targeting measures on the long-term unemployed.

Member states were required to produce annual reports and money was made available from the European Social Fund.

A few years later, the European Council meeting in Lisbon, March 2000, formulated new strategic goals for the first decade of the 21st century. The strategic goals demand an ambitious programme through which the EU aims to 'become the most competitive and dynamic knowledge-based economy in the world, capable of sustainable economic growth, with more and better jobs and greater social cohesion' (Bolkestein, 2000). The goals are based on the assumption that that the EU can reach an average annual economic growth of around 3 per cent and a labour participation rate rising from 61 per cent in 2000 to 70 per cent in 2010.

HRM in reality

The 1999 European Union employment guidelines

Pillar 1: Employability

The first of the four pillars focuses on employability and on tackling the skills gap. While skill development and lifelong learning remain a key objective for the whole workforce, there is a particular emphasis in this part of the guidelines on ensuring that young people and the unemployed (particularly the long-term unemployed) are equipped to take advantage of new employment opportunities in the fast-changing labour market. A key element of the employability pillar is the recognition of the need for early intervention, before individuals become long-term unemployed, and the provision of help which is customised and targeted to individual needs. Also noteworthy is the inclusion, for the first time, of clear quantified targets for member states in giving a new start to young and long-term unemployed people, and in increasing access to training for the unemployed.

Tackling youth unemployment and preventing long-term unemployment

In order to influence the trend in youth and long-term unemployment, the member states will develop preventive and employability-oriented strategies, building on the early identification of individual needs; within a period to be determined by each member state, which may not exceed five years and which may be longer in member states with particularly high unemployment, member states will ensure that:

- Every unemployed young person is offered a new start before reaching six months of unemployment, in the form of training, retraining, work practice, a job or other employability measures.

- Unemployed adults are also offered a fresh start before reaching 12 months of unemployment by one of the aforementioned means or, more generally, by accompanying individual guidance.

These preventive and employability measures should be combined with measures to promote the re-employment of the long-term unemployed.

Transition from passive measures to active measures

Benefit and training systems – where they prove necessary – must be reviewed and adapted to ensure that they actively support employability and provide real incentives for the unemployed to seek and take up work or training opportunities. Each member state will endeavour to increase significantly the number of persons benefiting from active measures to improve their employability. In order to increase the numbers of unemployed who are offered training or any similar measure, it will in particular fix a target, in the light of its starting situation, of gradually achieving the average of the three most successful member states, and at least 20 per cent.

Encouraging a partnership approach

The actions of member states alone will not suffice to achieve the desired results in promoting employability. Consequently the social partners are urged, at their various levels of responsibility and action, to conclude as soon as possible agreements with a view to increasing the possibilities for training, work experience, traineeships or other measures likely to promote employability. Also, the member states and the social partners will endeavour to develop possibilities for lifelong training.

Easing the transition from school to work

Employment prospects are poor for young people who leave the school system without having acquired the aptitudes required for entering the job market. Member states will therefore:

- Improve the quality of their school systems in order to reduce substantially the number of young people who drop out of the school system early.
- Make sure they equip young people with greater ability to adapt to technological and economic changes and with skills relevant to the labour market, where appropriate by implementing or developing apprenticeship training.

Pillar 2: Entrepreneurship

The second of the guidelines' four pillars derives from the recognition that the creation of more and better jobs requires a dynamic and enterprising climate for businesses to expand and hire workers. This pillar is, therefore, about entrepreneurship, defined in a broad way, to cover the start-up and running of new enterprises, the development of existing enterprises and the encouragement of initiative within large firms. It also supports measures to generate new sources of employment (including self-employment), and to create networks among enterprises and between enterprises and local authorities.

Making it easier to start up and run businesses

Aiming to provide a clear, stable and predictable set of rules and improve the conditions for the development of risk capital markets. The new facilities offered by the European Investment Bank (EIB) combined with the member states' efforts will enable new businesses to be set up more easily. The member states should also reduce and simplify the administrative and tax burdens on small and medium-sized enterprises. To that end the member states will:

- Give particular attention to reducing significantly the overhead costs and administrative burdens for businesses, and especially small and medium-sized enterprises, in particular when hiring additional workers.
- Encourage the development of self-employment by examining, with the aim of reducing, any obstacles which may exist, especially those within tax and social security regimes, to moving to self-employment and the setting up of small businesses.

Exploiting the opportunities for job creation

If the European Union wants to deal successfully with the employment challenge, all possible sources of jobs and new technologies and innovations must be exploited effectively. To that end the member states will investigate measures to exploit fully the possibilities offered by job creation at local level, in the social economy and in new activities linked to needs not yet satisfied by the market, and examine, with the aim of reducing, any obstacles in the way of such measures.

Making the taxation system more employment-friendly

Reversing the long-term trend towards higher taxes and charges on labour (which have increased from 35 per cent in 1980 to more than 42 per cent in 1995). Each member state will set a target, if necessary and taking account of its present level, for gradually reducing the overall tax burden and, where appropriate, a target for gradually reducing the fiscal pressure on labour and non-wage labour costs, in particular on relatively unskilled and low-paid labour, without jeopardizing the recovery of public finances or the financial equilibrium of social security schemes. It will examine, if appropriate, the desirability of introducing a tax on energy or on pollutant emissions or any other tax measure. Member states will also examine, without obligation, the advisability of reducing the rate of VAT on labour-intensive services not exposed to cross-border competition.

Pillar 3: Adaptability

As we have already noted, part of the diagnosis of the employment challenge is that there is a need for greater adaptability on the part of businesses, but also on the part of the workforce. The third pillar focuses, therefore, on the adaptability of enterprises and workers to changing technology and markets, industrial restructuring, and the development of new products and services. It covers adaptability in terms of the organization of work, working patterns and contracts, as well as adaptability in terms of regulatory and training systems. It recognizes explicitly that a balance must be struck between the need of businesses for flexibility, and the needs of employees for security and employability, and that striking this balance will not always be an easy task.

Modernising work organisation

In order to promote the modernisation of work organisation and forms of work:

- The social partners are invited to negotiate, at the appropriate levels, in particular at sectoral and enterprise levels, agreements to modernize the organization of work, including flexible working arrangements, with the aim of making undertakings productive and competitive and achieving the required balance between flexibility and security. Such agreements may, for example, cover the expression of working time as an annual figure, the reduction of working hours, the reduction of overtime, the development of part-time working, lifelong training and career breaks.

- For its part, each member state will examine the possibility of incorporating into its law more adaptable types of contract, taking into account the fact that forms of employment are increasingly diverse. Those working under contracts of this kind should at the same time enjoy adequate security and higher occupational status, compatible with the needs of business.

Support adaptability in enterprises

In order to renew skill levels within enterprises, member states will re-examine the obstacles, in particular tax obstacles, to investment in human resources and possibly provide for tax or other incentives for the development of in-house training; they will also examine any new regulations to make sure they will contribute to reducing barriers to employment and help the labour market adapt to structural change in the economy.

Pillar 4: Equal opportunities

The final pillar of the guidelines prioritizes equal opportunities, with the twin social and economic objective of modernizing societies so that women and men can work on equal terms with equal responsibilities, to develop the full growth capacities of European economies. It recognizes both the social need to counter discrimination and inequalities between women and men, and the economic loss resulting from not making full and effective use of the productive capacities of all sections of the population.

In addition to this focus on closing the gender gap in Europe's economic and social life, this pillar emphasizes the integration of people with disabilities into working life. This is an important first step towards recognition that the full integration of disabled people is a fundamental issue of equal opportunities. This, in turn, is a move also towards a wider implementation in the employment field of the important new anti-discrimination clause of the Amsterdam Treaty, under which the Council may take: '... appropriate action to combat discrimination based on sex, racial or ethnic origin, religion and belief, disability, age or sexual orientation' (Article 13).

Tackling gender gaps

Member states should translate their desire to promote equality of opportunity into increased employment rates for women. They should also pay attention to the imbalance in the representation of women or men in certain economic sectors and occupations. Member states will attempt to reduce the gap in unemployment rates between women and men by actively supporting the increased employment of women and will act to reverse the under-representation of women in certain economic sectors and occupations, and their over-representation in others.

Reconciling work and family life

Policies on career breaks, parental leave and part-time work are of particular importance to women and men. Implementation of the various Directives and social partner agreements in this area should be accelerated and monitored regularly. There must be an adequate provision of good quality care for children and other dependants in order to support women's and men's entry and continued participation in the labour market. The member states will strive to raise levels of access to care services where some needs are not currently met.

Facilitating reintegration into the labour market

The member states will give specific attention to women, and men, considering a return to the paid workforce after an absence and, to that end, they will examine the means of gradually eliminating the obstacles in the way of such return.

◀

Promoting the integration of people with disabilities into working life

The member states will give special attention to the problems people with disabilities may encounter in participating in working life.

Source: The European Commission.

Question: Are these guidelines more consistent with a free market or a social market approach to employment?

The Europeanization of employment policies has already aroused academic debate within the European Union. Bertozzi and Bonoli (2002) point to a new policy instrument adopted by the EU to bring governments to heel. This is described as the 'open method of coordination'. Used first for the European Employment Strategy, it involves a complex framework beginning with adoption by the Council of the European Union of common objectives and agreed targets. Member states are then required to submit reports to the European Commission detailing their efforts and progress towards meeting those objectives and targets. Recommendations for the Employment Strategy were first issued in 1999. The process is repeated each year and culminates in an assessment by the Commission of the progress made by each country.

Bertozzi and Bonoli assume that this process will have the most impact on the countries that show the greatest 'misfit' between their current employment practices and those put forward in the Employment Strategy, stating that: 'we assume that the EU develops a European model of employment policy and that the OMC will be applied most forcefully on those countries that are furthest from this model, whereas it will just mildly try to reorient policies in countries that are closest to the model.'

Further pressures on member states come via three routes (Leibfried and Pearson, 2000):

- *Direct positive pressures of integration*. Actions taken directly by the European Commission to create a social dimension.

- *Direct negative pressures of integration*. Through the market-building process that encourages labour mobility and freedom of provision of services.

- *Indirect pressures of integration*. Due to tax harmonization, common European currency (with implications for the setting of a unified interest policy) and other economic initiatives.

As regards the Employment Strategy, Bertozzi and Bonoli (2002) distinguish between four different European traditions: the English-speaking countries, continental and southern European countries, and the Nordic countries. This classification is broadly similar to the different legal traditions we identified earlier.

- *English-speaking countries* – specifically the UK. Here, employment markets have been left to themselves to survive the changes of the 1980s and 1990s. Redundancies in the old heavy industries such as coal, steel and shipbuilding have not been accompanied by major changes in employment policy. Benefits have been kept to subsistence level 'so that people are prepared to accept low-paid jobs in the service sector'. Women have been modestly encouraged to join the employment market through tax changes but nothing more radical. Bertozzi and Bonoli conclude that: 'The road followed by the UK, that can be characterized as liberal, has been relatively successful in terms of job creation in the service sector (although not as successful as in the US), but has resulted in growing wage inequality and social problems of poverty and exclusion.'

- *Continental and southern Europe*. High levels of social protection but relatively low levels of childcare and tax arrangements that are based on household income in a number of northern countries such as the Netherlands and Germany. France has attempted to absorb job losses by severely curtailing working time, other countries have offered generous benefits for early retirement. In southern Europe the 'black economy' accounts for a great deal of untaxed economic activity.

- *Nordic countries*. These are characterized by relatively weak employment protection but generous unemployment benefits. They also have a tradition of active labour market policies, including retraining, childcare and generous parental care. These policies, together with a relatively large public sector have encouraged a high level of female participation in the job market. They have produced high levels of employment and low wage equality at the cost of expensive state intervention in the job market.

Bolkestein (2000) draws attention to the particular success of the Netherlands economy in achieving an average of 1.6 per cent growth in the number of jobs over the past 15 years. This equals the US job gain and is four times the European average. This job growth is attributed to wage moderation, itself encouraged by tax cuts. But he also points to the fact that this success is 'merely relative to a worse past'. Bolkestein quotes a 1997 McKinsey report on the Dutch economy. Four key barriers were identified as having a significant role in holding the Netherlands back:

1 *Lack of competition*. In the past, Dutch legislation on competition has been relatively lax. Stricter rules are now in place that will have to be enforced vigorously.

2 *Inflexible labour market rules*, including those on working hours, on hiring and firing, and stringent collective bargaining agreements.

3 An *unattractive climate for starting new companies* in fast-growing sectors. Strict regulation drives up employee costs, especially for small businesses.

4 *Lack of incentives* for the low skilled to find jobs. Social security benefits in the Netherlands are among the most generous in the world, so that many unemployed are stuck in a poverty trap. If everyone able to work but receiving social benefits were included in the official jobless statistics, the unemployment rate would rise to over 20 per cent of the labour force.

Bolkestein does not agree that the Netherlands should follow the so-called 'Anglo-Saxon' model, but concludes that:

> If the Netherlands still have a long way to go, that goes even more for those European countries which are still firmly stuck in the Rhineland rut. European unemployment is a man-made disaster. Policy harmonization may cause this blight to spread. According to conventional wisdom the coordination of economic policies is considered the key to creating employment. This belief is often professed by governments, which espouse unsuccessful policies. They say they fear that tax rates will suffer a race to the bottom. Harmonization, though, is more likely to result in a race to the top. High tax rates will undermine economic incentives and thus be inimical to investments, growth and employment. Altogether, harmonization would lessen the pressure to carry out necessary but unpopular structural adjustments to the welfare state.

Instead he advocates:

- wage moderation and differentiation
- liberalization of legislation on job security
- less generous and more strictly administered unemployment and other welfare state benefits
- a policy that would reduce the market power of established parties.

Activity 5:5

Can you differentiate between Bolkestein's views and those of people favouring the social and free markets?

HRM in reality

IMF says UK economic performance impressive – but watch employee productivity

While concluding that 'the overall performance of the UK economy remains impressive' and labour market policies 'continue to be exemplary' the IMF believes that in comparison with other European countries there is still a problem with employee productivity.

The IMF praises government efforts to get people off welfare and into work and the drive on improving productivity but says that 'the UK's comparatively weak labour productivity performance ... may be the Achilles heel of an otherwise strong economy.' But the Fund also says that 'as regards productivity growth, the authorities' approach to this complex issue – combining a stable policy environment with key structural reforms – is certainly appropriate in terms of direction and emphasis.'

Extracts from UK 2000 Article IV Consultation: Concluding Statement of the Mission

1. The overall performance of the UK economy remains impressive. Output is growing at a brisk pace, the unemployment rate is at its lowest level in a quarter century ... These achievements reflect ... sound macroeconomic policies ... as well as a decade and a half of fundamental structural reform that should, in many respects, be an example for many other European countries. ... some aspects of the economic performance remain disappointing. In particular, the UK's comparatively weak labour productivity performance in relation to other countries – due mainly to past underinvestment in physical and human capital – may be the Achilles heel of an otherwise strong economy.

2. Looking to 2001, the ongoing economic expansion appears set to continue with output growth in the range of 2.5 to 3 per cent. Private demand growth may slow down, but total domestic demand would still be buoyed by a sizeable increase in government spending. ...

3. Given these broadly favourable economic developments, ... uncertainty stems from two sources: first, how much further the unemployment rate can fall before setting off wage pressure; and second, how fast productivity can grow on a sustained basis. On the first, the moderate behaviour of wages in 2000 is suggestive of a substantial fall in the economy's structural rate of unemployment since the mid-1990s. However, this moderate behaviour could also reflect, at least in part, pressures from the appreciation of sterling in recent years as well as a lag in the response to the increase in headline inflation this year. On the second, productivity gains in recent quarters are tantalizing, but cannot necessarily be extrapolated forward. Thus, we agree with the authorities that further efforts must be made to increase labour supply and the trend growth in productivity. ...

6. Turning to medium- and long-term issues, the authorities have set their policies with the broad purpose of enhancing the economy's productive potential. The strategy is rightly multifaceted. Macroeconomic and financial sector stability underpinned by strong policy frameworks should continue to make an important contribution to raising both productivity and private investment. This is complemented by many targeted initiatives to enhance productivity as well as investment and private saving, encompassing medium-term fiscal plans to increase public investment in human and physical capital, policies to enhance prospects for the 'New Economy', labour market reform, pension

reform, deregulation, and measures to promote competition – including in the provision of financial services. While we support the broad thrust of these initiatives, some adjustments in specific areas would be desirable.

7. ... areas such as education – where there is a clear need to improve the UK's relative performance – may benefit more from well-targeted, cost-effective reforms (e.g.) to address low skill levels) than from greatly increased spending. ...

10. Turning to structural issues, we broadly agree with the priority areas identified by the authorities for fostering productivity growth: promoting innovation and research and development (R&D); strengthening competition; and encouraging enterprise. ...

11. An important aspect of the productivity issue is the potential for accelerated gains from the production and use of ICT as illustrated by the 'New Economy' experience of the United States. The productivity growth of some ICT-intensive sectors in the United Kingdom provides some early, circumstantial evidence that the New Economy may be taking hold following years of relatively high rates of ICT investment on a par with those of the United States. However, we would caution against relying too heavily in the next few years on the effects of ICT investment to raise economy-wide productivity given the difficulty of determining the timing of potential productivity gains associated with the use of ICT equipment. Preliminary evidence suggests that the productivity gains realized to date in the United Kingdom come mainly from increases in the ratio of ICT capital per worker, underscoring the need to maintain high rates of growth in private investment accompanied by improving skill levels. The multifaceted approach envisaged by the authorities to enhance productivity growth in general will, of course, also enhance the development of ICT. However, there may be a need for more targeted measures, such as the recent decision to set up ICT learning centres. A good example would also be the removal of existing hindrances to low cost connections to the internet. Looking ahead, given the recent sharp decline in equity prices in the high-tech sector, care should also be taken to ensure that avenues remain open for financing viable enterprises.

12. The labour market is an area where – particularly by comparison with most other European countries – UK policies continue to be exemplary. The targeted measures adopted over the past three years, including various New Deal initiatives and in-work benefits for low-income workers, appear to have created further incentives for and facilitated transitions from both unemployment and non-employment to work. In many respects, these measures have complemented and built upon the reforms initiated in the 1980s and early 1990s. Yet, some concerns remain. While employment and activity rates have continued rising for women, these measures have been declining for men, indicating the increasing marginalization of men with low skills.

Moreover, notwithstanding recent progress, the non-employment rates for some groups such as lone parents remain very high. Hence, more emphasis is needed on integrating various components of the welfare and unemployment benefits systems; programs directed towards raising participation rates of specific groups such as lone parents and those on disability benefits; and measures to increase the supply of workers with vocational and intermediate skills – an area where the United Kingdom remains deficient. Furthermore, unemployment benefits could be tapered in a manner that increases disincentives for rotating through the different options of the New Deal while remaining unemployed over long periods. An important concern going forward is that, although the National Minimum Wage (NMW) appears not to have affected employment or inflation thus far, significant increases in the NMW or changes that would bring the youth rate up to the standard NMW could have adverse implications for the prospects of integrating low-skill and younger workers into the workforce.

> The IMF comments follow another positive report from the OECD pointing to recent sustained growth in the UK economy and noting government labour market policy.
>
> Source: *HRMGuide.co.uk* (http://www.hrmguide.co.uk), 22 November 2000.
>
> **Question: Does the IMF take a social market or free market stance on the UK's employment policies?**

Summary

In this chapter we examined the role played by governments in creating the context for human resource management through labour market policies, regulation and legal frameworks. We emphasized the particular influence of state intervention in developing human capital and growth of the employment market. Employment legislation sets a framework for the practice of human resource management but these frameworks vary widely and embody different traditions and views on the nature of the employment market. We took the European Union as an example and highlighted a number of initiatives with a human resource focus that were interpreted differently in member states.

Further reading

Texts on labour market policies include: *Why Deregulate Labour Markets?* edited by Gosta Esping-Andersen and Marino Regini, Oxford University Press (2000); *Changing Labour Markets in Europe: The Role of Institutions and Policies* edited by Peter Auer, International Labour Office (2001); *Innovations in Labour Market Policies: The Australian Way* by D. Grubb, Douglas Lippoldt and Peter Tergeist, OECD (2001); *Labour Market Inequalities: Problems and Policies of Low-Wage Employment in International Perspective*, edited by Mary Gregory, Wiemer Salverda and Stephen Bazen, Oxford University Press (2000).

Most books about human capital are focused on the firm, but more generally *Rethinking Development Theory and Policy: A Human Factor Critique*, by Senyo B.S.K. Adjibolosoo, Praeger Publications (1999) looks at failure within the context of development. There is a huge selection of books available on employment policies in the European Union. *European Labour Law*, 8th and revised edition by Roger Blanpain, Kluwer Academic Publishers (2002) is an exhaustive review of employment legislation in the EU. More generally, *Unemployment in the New Europe*, edited by Nancy Bermeo, Cambridge University Press (2001) advocates a European way forward.

Review questions

1 If businesses have little control over economic growth or recession, is there any point in attempting to follow long-term human resource strategies for employee development?

2 Define the concept of human capital in your own words. Is it possible to quantify a nation/company's human capital?

3 It has been said that a successful multinational must have a strong presence in each of the three main trading blocs. What are the human resource implications for an organization undertaking this strategy?

4 In what ways do approaches to people management differ between 'social market' and 'free market' countries. Relate these differences to hard and soft models of HRM.

5 What can be gained from comparing people management practices in different countries?

6 To what extent are the policies of the European Union encouraging identical employment legislation in member countries of the EU?

Problems for discussion and analysis

1 You have been appointed general manager at a new European subsidiary of a Japanese television manufacturer. The subsidiary is controlled by three senior Japanese managers who have been seconded from the parent company for a five-year period. Your first task is to identify and shortlist suitable locations for production and then participate in choosing suppliers and staff. Describe the likely decision processes and contrast them with the way a typical local company would have dealt with the same problem. What elements of employment legislation, government support and industrial relations would encourage you to locate in a particular country?

2 Leyanne has recently graduated with a degree in business studies, specializing in finance. She has been recruited as a trainee by a large conglomerate involved in airport management and cargo distribution. The company operates in Australia, Singapore, Europe and the Caribbean. Corporate headquarters are in Sydney, Australia but the largest operational units are in Singapore and Germany. The organization prefers to develop its own management and expects a broad range of experience and grasp of different cultural traditions. Leyanne is ambitious and wants to become a senior manager in the company. Outline a possible career plan for Leyanne, including aspects that the company should take responsibility for and issues for her own self-development.

3 Read the following case study and answer the question at the end.

Case study: South Africa

With the demise of apartheid, President Nelson Mandela's government of national unity faced a formidable challenge. Some 4.7 million South Africans were unemployed, or 32 per cent of the available workforce. Half of them were under 30, with a further 400 000 school-leavers joining the queue for jobs each year. In 2002, according to *The Economist* country briefing, under President Mbeki the official unemployment rate is 26.7 per cent but estimates range up to 40 per cent depending on the definition used. The annual growth rate has averaged around 3.0 per cent in GDP – nowhere near the level required to reduce unemployment significantly. Inequality in income is considerable and the informal economy has grown at the expense of formal employment.

Reforming the economy

The strategy for reforming the moribund economy included:

- the partial privatization of South African Airways
- partial sale of the telecommunications utility Telekom
- encouragement of tourism and
- an unbundling of private conglomerates.

Government policy did not include large-scale privatization along New Zealand or British lines. Politicians were unlikely to accept the image of closures, heavy redundancies and large capital gains for a few shareholders. The intention of privatization – where it happened – was to empower the disadvantaged and spread wealth more widely.

Foreign businesses began to renew investment. Ford and IBM bought back into former subsidiaries that had been sold off in the 1980s. Microsoft, Apple, Pepsi and Procter and Gamble were new investors. Pepsi made a point of putting black managers in charge of their operation. Rover said it would make South Africa its major production hub for Land Rovers in Africa. Other investors were holding back because of a perception of relatively high wage levels and low productivity, inflexible working practices and poor management (Horwitz and Smith, 1998).

Productivity levels

A *Monitor* company report commissioned by the then National Economic Forum found that – in almost every industrial sector examined – identical products were being made at much lower cost or to a higher quality in other countries. Many industries could only survive through protectionism and subsidy. The *Monitor* report demonstrated how South Africa lost its international competitiveness because of low levels of productivity. They compared South African vehicle assembly with Mexico and the USA:

	Employee cost per hour (US$)	Employee hours per car	Employee cost per car (US$)
South Africa	5.6	63.5	355
Mexico	6.0	24.3	145
USA	38.0	18.6	705

The same pattern was found in the textile industry. Paradoxically, a long-term cure for unemployment requires short-term job losses in order to increase productivity. Both the public and private sectors were regarded as inefficient and overstaffed. Rising expectations among workers, however, meant a likely clash with trade unions.

Affirmative action

Around 75 per cent of South Africa's population is black, but only a minority of its managers are black. Under apartheid, blacks had been prevented from having business accommodation in many city sites. They had been denied skills training and access to capital. Black empowerment required a nurturing of small businesses, backed by extra training and finance. Franchising and joint ventures with overseas companies offered considerable possibilities. Kentucky Fried Chicken and McDonald's actively sought black franchisees.

Many firms used affirmative action programmes to recruit black professionals, partly in an attempt to appease the government and public opinion. Job-hopping – the 'pinball syndrome' – became normal, with educated black employees moving from one job to another every six to eight months. People have attempted to climb up the status and responsibility ladder much faster than their experience and training will allow. Skilled, experienced black professionals remain such a valued resource that they have been offered salaries 20–50 per cent higher than their white counterparts. Jobs have imposing titles and may be accompanied by cars and cellular telephones. In practice, these positions often turned out to be disappointing: the responsibilities bearing no comparison to the titles. Black professionals became frustrated as high salaries were not matched with the opportunity to develop self-esteem.

Officially, according to South African Department of Labour figures (1999) the proportion of non-white managers had increased to junior 39 per cent, middle 25 per cent, senior 22 per cent and executive director 7 per cent. Many employers were seen as cynical, hiring black faces for 'soft' jobs such as human resources but not for financial and line management positions. Support in the form of training, development or mentoring was frequently absent. The process was usually initiated by the board of directors without consulting existing managers who subsequently did little to help the new appointees.

Discussion question: From your reading of this chapter, outline a programme of possible government initiatives that could lead to improved and real employment in South Africa.

6

The employment market

Objectives

- Outline some of the major theories about why people work.
- Develop an understanding of the conditions and salaries for which people work and the expectations they have of employers.
- Explore the relationship between human capital and national employment levels.
- Determine some of the effects of competitor activities on employee availability.
- Investigate the patterns of work that are replacing 'nine-to-five' jobs.

The employment or job market (see Key concept 6.1) is the ultimate source of all new recruits. Human resource managers must be aware of the dynamics of this market in order to deal properly with resourcing, to set competitive salaries and obtain people with essential skills. They need to understand the expectations of prospective employees and have an insight into issues such as those raised in the objectives for this chapter.

We begin by exploring the reasons why people seek employment and examine their expectations of working life. This is evaluated first from an economic perspective, introducing competitive market and institutional theories, and from social and individual viewpoints. The chapter moves on to consider the issue of unemployment. Finally, the characteristics of the flexible job market are debated, including new forms of part-time working and the effects of greater female participation in the working economy.

Key concept 6:1

The employment market   The employment market comprises all those people who are available for work. Neo-classical economics views this potential workforce as forming a labour market. The market is affected by national or regional supply and demand for appropriately skilled employees. It is constrained by demographic factors such as the number of young people leaving schools and universities and by cultural variables such as expectations for mothers to stay at home looking after children.

Why do people work?

The simple answer in most cases is that they have to. Few of us have the private resources needed to maintain a satisfactory lifestyle without an income from employment. This seems obvious but the issue becomes much more complex on examination. For example, many wealthy people (or lottery winners) continue to work even though they do not 'need' to. Moreover, unless they are in a desperate financial state, people pick and choose the type of work they are prepared to do. Professions such as nursing and social work attract large numbers of people despite relatively low rates of pay in many countries. Clearly, there are many other factors, other than money, that have to be taken into account in understanding people's motives in the employment market. Economists, occupational psychologists and industrial sociologists have contributed to our knowledge.

The issue has been made all the more complicated because economists have provided several different and contradictory theories in this area. They can be divided broadly into two main approaches: competitive and institutional. Pure competitive theories of the employment market have little to do with HRM because they are not 'concerned with what goes on inside organizations' (Claydon, 2001, p.70).

Competitive market theories

These are derived from the neo-classical economic concepts of rational choice and maximization of utility. The assumption here is that individuals choose jobs that offer them maximum benefits. The utility or value of these benefits – money, vacation time, pension entitlement and so on – varies for different individuals according to their personal preferences. People move from one organization to another if improved benefits are available. At the same time, employing organizations attempt to get the most from their employees for the lowest possible cost.

The outcome of this process is a dynamic and shifting equilibrium in which both employees and organizations compete to maximize benefits for themselves. Within a specific region or industry there is a balance between supply and demand for human resources. Pay and conditions for employees are determined by the relative scarcity or abundance of their skills and abilities in the employment market. Competitive forces push wages up when demand for products – and hence employees – increases, and downwards when the economy is in recession. In the latter case a 'market clearing wage' is arrived at eventually which is sufficiently low to encourage employers to increase recruitment and eliminate unemployment. This discourse reinforces the view that employees are objects to be traded like any other commodities in the market – human resources in the hardest possible sense. Supposedly, they offer themselves – their skills and human qualities – for sale to the highest bidders. Within this mindset they could just as well be vegetables on a market stall.

| Activity 6:1 | How useful is the competitive market model in describing the ways in which the employment market functions in the real world? |

According to Claydon (2001, p.74) 'this model is a heroic simplification of the real world. It has nothing to say about the internal processes of managing people at work.' In reality, it is obvious that the job market does not work in such a simple fashion: people do not move readily between organizations in search of higher wages; most firms do not cut pay when unemployment levels are high and cheaper workers are available. Indeed, in the 1980s wages soared for those in work at the same time as unemployment levels increased. Such contradictions are partly explained by the omission of HR development issues such as training and career structures in competition theories. More generally, they assume that employment markets are purely external when, in fact, large organizations have internal job markets operating through promotion and transfer of existing employees.

Competition theories assume that job-seekers have perfect knowledge of available jobs and benefits. Job-searching is an expensive and time-consuming business. The unemployed do not have money and those in work do not have time. The result is that few people conduct the extensive searches required to find jobs that meet their preferences perfectly. In practice, most individuals settle for employment which is quickly obtained and which exceeds the 'reserve minimum wage' they have in mind. There is a considerable element of luck involved. Moreover, the job-seeker does not make the choice: in most cases the decision is in the hands of the employer.

Entry barriers to skilled jobs provide a further constraint on the competitive job market. Many jobs are restricted to people possessing key skills – often specific to a particular firm or industrial sector. In fact, the external job market is made up of many sub-markets with widely different circumstances and constraints. For example, between 1989 and 1995 the job market for construction workers – particularly house-building – in the UK experienced a contraction of half a million posts. Conversely, other sectors were unable to find enough suitable workers. Although the reduction in housing construction was a feature of the recession of that time, failure of many workers to find jobs elsewhere reflects the consistent trend away from unskilled, manual work. As we shall see in later chapters, full employment is no longer likely to come from low-paid and low-skilled jobs.

Institutional theories

An alternative approach places its main focus within the firm rather than the external job market. Institutionalists do not accept the principle of individual maximization of utility, arguing that both individuals and organizations cooperate to some extent and take account of the preferences of others in similar situations. Individual workers are less concerned with maximum benefits than achieving a fair rate compared to their peers. But this comparison may be restricted to employees within the same organization: most people appear indifferent (much of the time, at least) to benefits offered by other employers and large variations occur between firms in the same sector. Employers set wages for a variety of reasons ranging from profitability to tradition – competition with other firms is a relatively minor consideration. As a result, pay levels within many firms are relatively rigid. Wage rates are more likely to go up than down and are largely immune to influence from the external job market.

Competition theories assume that hiring and firing in reaction to changing market conditions is good practice. There are close parallels between this way of thinking and 'hard' HRM. In fact, most firms take active steps to avoid employee turnover. This is because turnover is disruptive and costs money. Recruitment advertising and redundancy payments are expensive and training new employees represents a considerable investment in time and effort. Organizations may encourage workers to remain with them by means of HR policies that increase benefits such as annual leave and pensions in line with length of service.

Key concept 6:2

Insiders and outsiders   Union negotiators are more aware of the interests of their employed members (insiders) and their pursuit of increased benefits than of the interests of the unemployed and non-members (outsiders). Equally, as we discussed earlier, employers know that replacing existing workers with others from the ranks of the unemployed has inherent costs. These costs and the associated disruption outweigh the advantages of cheaper workers from outside. Consequently, insiders can demand an 'economic rent' or premium above competitive wages. Established workers can use their insider-power in other ways, including a refusal to cooperate with new recruits, if there is a perceived threat to this premium.

Reflecting on our discussion in Part 1, we can conclude that institutional approaches to the job market have a greater affinity with 'soft' HRM. They recognize that group effects underlie notions of fairness and loyalty, fundamental to the notion of employee commitment. They are consistent with the stakeholder concept, recognizing the important roles played by government and trade unions. For example, the 'insider-outsider' model offers an explanation for simultaneously high wages and high levels of unemployment (Lindbeck and Snower, 1988). Insiders have stakeholder status whereas outsiders do not (see Key concept 6.2).

At the organizational level, human resource managers also affect the nature of the market as a result of their recruitment and redundancy strategies. When business is optimistic recruitment numbers increase; if conditions are bad, employees may be shed. Technological change is a further complicating factor, leading to fewer but more highly skilled employees.

Figure 6.1 demonstrates some of the forces that shape the employment market, including elements discussed in Chapter 5, such as the major role played by government, particularly in the shape of legislation. The interactions between organizations and the job market are debated again later in the book when we consider human resource strategy. At this stage it is appropriate to note some omissions from most discussions of this subject. These include the influence of social class, age, status, gender and ethnic origin in the job expectations of employees and the attitudes of employers towards these characteristics. As we shall see in later discussions on equal opportunities, suitable people can appear invisible to managers who associate competence for high-level jobs with a particular age, accent, sex or colour.

Figure 6.1	Competing influences on job creation within an organization

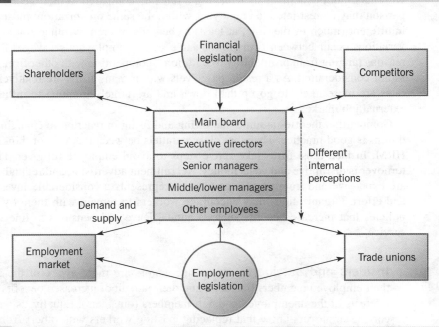

Activity 6:2	Summarize the main differences between competitive market and institutional models of the employment market.

HRM in reality	**Still tied to Mum's apron strings**

The future of the job market may lie in mobility, but most of us will just pop around the corner this Sunday to deliver Mothers' Day cards and flowers. Research by the Future Foundation – entitled *The Renaissance of Regional Nations* – shows that almost two-thirds of adult Britons live within an hour's journey of their mother with almost a third living less than 15 minutes away! On average Brits live within 12.6 miles of their mothers – and fathers, sisters and brothers are not much further away.

The likelihood of British workers upping sticks and moving to areas of skill shortage seems remote. The report concludes that we are 'a relatively static nation, strongly attached to our local communities and interests'.

The Future Foundation's research shows that:

- UK inhabitants live most of their lives – working, school, shopping, leisure and entertainment – within a 14-mile radius.

- More than half live within a 30-minute drive of their places of birth.

- Over half have lived in their current home for more than ten years.

- Nine in ten homeowners will move within a ten-mile radius.

'In the future, increases in homeworking, continued pressure on time and demographic shifts will mean that the local sphere becomes still more vital to people's day to day lives,' says the Future Foundation report. 'Whatever is happening on the global stage, people's everyday lives remain rooted in the physical local space within which they live and work.'

Source: *HRMGuide.co.uk* (http://www.hrmguide.co.uk), 23 March 2001.

Social preferences

It is important to understand that participating in employment is not an 'all-or-nothing' decision. Individuals also determine the amount of time they are prepared to devote to paid work. The allocation of time is affected by 'expected market earnings', taking travel, clothing and taxation into account. Traditionally, time given to 'market work' is distinguished from that devoted to any other activity – described as 'leisure'. However, it is recognized that time outside paid work is not necessarily devoted to pleasure. Far from lying on a beach, sipping a cool drink, people spend much of their 'leisure' time on some form of work without pay. This could be housework, maintenance, looking after children, cooking or providing a voluntary service.

Deciding to take a job, or not, involves a trade-off between family members. If an additional member works, there must be a reduction or reallocation of that person's unpaid activities. Employment may change lifestyle significantly. In developed countries this can result in the purchase of labour-saving devices such as a microwave oven, changing from fresh to ready-prepared food and hiring a cleaner or child-minder.

Becker (1965) recognized that the decision to seek employment can be complex and is likely to be taken in conjunction with other members of the household. The household is viewed as the 'decision-making unit'. The household chooses how to allocate its members' time, evaluating the comparative advantages of working as against not working. For example, the emphasis can be on working for money in order to buy the largest possible house, a brand new car, expensive holidays and consumer goods such as convenience foods. Alternatively, the household can minimize working time and maximize leisure, making do with a more modest home and car, spending effort on home-grown and prepared food.

Doing without paid work in order to maximize free time is an opportunity cost. In other words, if paid work is available, not working has a cost for the household. There may be preferences for particular family members to stay at home – typically mothers – whereas others (fathers) are expected to earn a wage. As we will see later in this chapter, this pattern has changed radically in most industrialized countries in recent years.

Recognition of household preferences is important to people managers because there are strong cultural differences between one region and another. There are considerable pressures on potential and actual workers to behave in the way perceived as normal for their particular society. However, most organizations pay little attention to the domestic influences on an employee's motivation and performance. Employees are recruited and their performance assessed as if they were entirely free agents with no domestic responsibilities or interests outside work.

When is it worthwhile going to work? The total available resources of the household unit may be weighed up in the equation, including the time available for all its members, other income and total wealth. The financial benefit of work can only be gauged when tax, social security deductions, travelling, child-minding costs and so on have been calculated. This benefit may prove insignificant.

Mathematical models have been developed to predict the hours that people are prepared to work. They take into account factors such as the availability of overtime work, the effects of taxation, opportunities for self-employment and payment by results (Sapsford and Tzannatos, 1993, p.27). Empirical studies do not necessarily support this approach – unemployment is an experience that can arrive like a tidal wave. There may be no opportunity to make a free decision on whether or not to work. During the 1980s recession, for example, it was common for both husband and wife to lose their jobs in quick succession (Morris, 1987). The latter were often in highly vulnerable part-time jobs. Morris argues that his research contradicts the notion of the household decision-making model. He concludes that such models take no account of the local social network that influences beliefs and expectations of employment. Neither do they accommodate local differences in employment opportunities and cultural ideas of gender behaviour. Job choices also reflect individual career plans and preferences.

HRM in reality	**Out of work couples targeted in jobs drive**

The government announced today that young unemployed couples without children (in Great Britain) will be expected to both actively seek work in order to claim Job-seeker's Allowance. The Employment Minister, Tessa Jowell said that these changes would provide more people with access to training programmes and New Deal assistance and would boost the labour supply by bringing around 27 000 additional people into the job market, including about 10 000 current claimants.

Unemployed couples without dependent children – with at least one partner aged between 18 and 24 – will be required to make a joint claim for Job-seeker's Allowance. This will be a change from previous circumstances in which one could make a claim while the other was treated as a dependent partner. Provisions for joint claims for JSA were brought in by the Welfare Reform and Pensions Act 1999. Ms Jowell said this would ensure that when both partners were capable of working, they both looked for work.

Tessa Jowell added:

This is a radical change to help get both members of a couple back into work, giving equal assistance and ensuring they have the same rights and the same responsibilities. We have made a clear distinction between those who have children and those who don't – this is aimed at those who don't and will offer direct help to another 27 000 people a year. It will also prevent couples from adjusting to benefit dependency at an early age.

Over 85 per cent of partners of claimants are women, who have previously been regarded as 'dependants' on a Job-seeker's Allowance claim. Today's change scraps this outdated view of the world, where 72 per cent of all women are now economically active, and makes sure we are no longer missing the opportunity to help these people.

Source: *HRMGuide.co.uk* (http://www.hrmguide.co.uk), 19 March 2001.

Activity 6:3	To what extent do people behave as individuals – as opposed to households – when they seek work? Consider your family, relatives or friends as examples.

Individual preferences

We have seen that people do not behave as mere commodities. Human behaviour involves deep complexities that bring unpredictability and apparent contrariness into the employment market. Most people's motives and ambitions involve much more than seeking the highest salary. Money is important but to a degree that varies between individuals. People will remain in comparatively lowly-paid jobs such as nursing because the satisfaction that comes from helping other people can be valued above a high salary. An economic model based purely on income will go some way to explain employment behaviour on the large scale but it will not explain *individual* human behaviour. Other motivations come into play in determining people's approach to work. Psychologists have attempted to provide explanations at the individual level (see for example: McKenna, 1994, p.63; Mullins, 1996, p.479).

Table 6.1	Psychological benefits of work

Factor	Characteristics
Opportunities for control	Limited control over work, or no job at all, leads to higher levels of anxiety, depression, tiredness and psychosomatic symptoms. Also lower general life-satisfaction and self-esteem.
Opportunities for skill use	People benefit from stretching jobs. Morale, self-esteem, sociability and life satisfaction are reduced when a worker's job is de-skilled or lost. Some people can compensate through hobbies or voluntary work, but many are unable to fill the gap.
Goal and task demands	Jobs set demands on our lives in general. Many unemployed people find it hard to fill their time, often spending a high proportion sleeping, sitting around or watching TV, further contributing to lowered morale.
Variety	Work can increase variety, providing a contrast with home life. It also provides the income to pay for experiences such as cinema, music, sporting activities and holidays.
Environmental clarity	Work helps us understand and predict the world around us. Mental health is better if we are clear about our roles and purpose in life. Conversely, uncertainty is detrimental, especially over a lengthy period.
Availability of money	The unemployed have a lower income level (40–60 per cent on average) than those in work. This can make it difficult to repay credit and keep up mortgage payments, adding further stress. Expensive activities are curtailed, contributing to feelings of isolation and boredom.
Physical security	In Western cultures people are brought up to value personal and private space. To provide feelings of personal security, self-worth and well-being they need a home to call their own. This requires an income to achieve.
Opportunity for interpersonal contact	Interaction with other people reduces feelings of loneliness and provides emotional support.
Valued social position	Work provides a self-identity and a feeling of worth.

Source: Adapted from Warr (1987).

It is common to ask the question, 'What do you do?' For many of us, self-identity is provided by a job. Table 6.1 lists a number of other psychological benefits obtained from work. These include social needs such as companionship, group cohesion, and a sense of belonging. In contrast, unemployment carries connotations of worthlessness. For example, in a period of increasing unemployment, a Coopers and Lybrand study of jobless executives found that 43 per cent did not reveal their lack of a job in applications (*Personnel Management*, March 1992, p.3). In the next section we go on to explore some of the consequences of participating, or not, in the job market and the relevance of unemployment to the formation of modern work patterns.

Participating in the employment market

Who is involved in the job market? We have seen that the resourcing of organizations is affected by national or regional availability (supply) and demand for appropriately skilled

Table 6.2	Comparative levels of unemployment (April 2002)

Country	Unemployment (per cent)
Australia	6.3
Belgium	6.8
Canada	7.6
Denmark	4.1 (March)
Finland	9.1
France	9.1
Germany	8.1
Ireland	4.3
Israel	8.8 (2000)
Italy	8.8 (March)
Japan	5.3
Netherlands	2.7 (March)
New Zealand	5.3 (March)
Mexico	1.6
Norway	3.7 (2001)
Poland	18.2 (2000)
Portugal	4.4
South Africa	25.4 (2000)
Sweden	5.3
Turkey	7.3 (1999)
UK	5.1
USA	6.0

Source: OECD.

employees. On the supply side of this balance, people can be divided into three groups, the first two of which are described as 'economically active' (Key concept 6.3).

Key concept 6:3

Economically active   The economically active comprise two groups: (a) *the employed* – those in paid work; and (b) *the unemployed* – those who are looking for paid work but are unable to find it.

Economically inactive people are neither in paid work nor seeking jobs, including people in education, with medical conditions, looking after dependants, and the retired. Proportions of these categories vary from country to country, depending on economic conditions and custom. Accurate figures for each group are not easily calculated as our 'HRM in reality' example on hidden unemployment in Australia shows. In particular, it is difficult to estimate true unemployment because the unemployed are identified on the basis of registration with state agencies. As an illustration, Table 6.2 shows official figures for a number of OECD countries in 2002. Usually the registration of individuals as unemployed is linked to the payment of unemployment relief or other social security benefit. If the benefit system is generous, people are more likely to register. Conversely, if benefits are restricted the registered unemployment figure decreases. As a result, Mexico has the lowest official rate of unemployment in the OECD! In the 1990s the British Conservative government was also accused by the opposition of massaging figures in this way.

HRM in reality

Hidden unemployment

Real unemployment in Australia is currently at 10.7 per cent according to a poll of 13 000 people conducted by Roy Morgan Research. The poll regards someone as unemployed if they are not employed and are looking for work.

Labor used the poll to justify an attack on government policies. Cheryl Kernot, Shadow Minister for Employment and Training said:

> This poll shows why job creation and job security must be central issues in the election campaign. This poll comes on the same day as up to 850 jobs may be lost at Optus.
>
> What this poll highlights, is the very high extent of hidden unemployment in Australia. Melbourne academic Dr Peter Brain has previously stated that the 'true' level of unemployment in Australia is much higher than official estimates indicate. In fact according to other Australian Bureau of Statistics figures there are 437 400 underemployed part-time workers who don't have enough work to make ends meet and an additional 1 159 000 Australians who don't have a job but would like one. This is all in addition to the 669 000 people who are officially unemployed.

The Shadow Minister continued:

> Labor has pledged to tackle the unemployment and underemployment problem head on. To help do this Labor made a policy announcement in February of this year that it would require the ABS to collect additional information about the extent of underemployment in Australia. In addition Labor will use this extra information to help workers and employers to tailor a better work life balance. This policy can be found on the ALP website. The 100 policies found here stand in stark contrast to the 0 policies on the Liberal website.

Source: *HRM Guide Australia* (http://www.hrmguide.net/australia/), 10 October 2001.

Developed countries have experienced considerable variations in unemployment levels. This is reflected in changes in public expectations and concern over the level of unemployment.

It can be argued that more people would work if jobs were easy to find – but they do not search when work is scarce. This has been called the 'discouraged worker hypothesis' (see Key concept 6.4). Workers calculate the probability of finding a job in relation to the wage they are likely to get and conclude that the effort is not worthwhile. This hypothesis suggests that the number of active job-seekers decreases in times of high unemployment, leaving an unmeasurable hidden unemployment rate behind the official statistics.

Key concept 6:4

Discouraged worker hypothesis   Workers calculate the probability of finding a job in relation to the wage they are likely to get and conclude that the effort is not worthwhile.

HRM in reality	**London worst region in the UK for unemployment**

The TUC has highlighted the fact that there has been a significant increase in the level of unemployment in London, making it Britain's most severely affected region. Some 3.5 per cent of manufacturing jobs in London were lost in the year to June, 23 000 service sector jobs were lost during the same period, and more jobs are likely to go in finance and banking.

The rate of unemployment in London is now 7.5 per cent – almost one percentage point higher than any other region – compared to the national average of 5.3 per cent. London's total of 287 000 unemployed is more than the totals for Wales and Scotland combined, more than the entire Midlands and more than the north-west and north-east combined. Six London boroughs have unemployment levels of more than 6 per cent: Tower Hamlets 12.3 per cent, Hackney 12.2 per cent, Newham 11.7 per cent, Southwark 10.7 per cent, Haringey 10.4 per cent and Lewisham 10.3 per cent.

Mick Connolly, Regional Secretary for the TUC London Region said:

> Unemployment is a personal tragedy and an economic waste. There are problems of unemployment throughout Britain and the TUC campaigns for full employment and decisive action to promote employment and quality jobs in all parts of Britain. But the media, many policy makers and some politicians seem blind to the level of unemployment in London. The government's own figures show the true extent of the problem and prove that the situation is worsening. Is it any wonder that a huge proportion of children in London are raised in poverty when nearly 300 000 workers who live in London are unemployed.

SERTUC, the TUC for the London region has called for the following measures from the government:

- A cut in interest rates.
- A national strategy for renewal of manufacturing that seeks to strengthen manufacturing in every region in Britain.
- Additional resources for the five Learning and Skills Councils in London, to address skills deficiencies, and for the London Development Agency to support employment creation and equalities programmes.
- Additional resources to support the implementation of a 'child-care strategy' for London, to address the immense barrier to employment that the shortage of low-cost high-quality child-care represents, especially to women.

Unemployment in Britain, September 2002, by country/region

Country/Region	ILO Unemployed (thousands)	Rate of unemployment (per cent)
London	287	7.5
Scotland	171	6.6
West Midlands	164	6.2
North-east	74	6.2
North-west	198	6.0
Yorkshire/Humberside	145	5.8
Wales	74	5.4
East Midlands	106	4.8
South-east	178	4.1
South-west	106	4.1
East	117	4.0

Source: *ONS Labour Market Statistics*, November 2002 (not seasonally adjusted).

Source: *HRMGuide.co.uk* (http://www.hrmguide.co.uk), 18 November 2002.

Activity 6:4	What is the relationship between levels of welfare payment or unemployment benefits and the level of employment?

Organizations in free market countries focus on the external employment market, seeking new staff from outside the business. This is compatible with a competitive market approach in which employees are recruited when needed and dispensed with when no longer required. This view also provides a clear rationale for the hard HRM form of employee planning which we will discuss in a later chapter. In the first chapter of this book we observed that the softer Harvard model of HRM emphasizes commitment between organizations and their employees. The latter approach is more consistent with social market and east Asian capitalist models. In Germany and Japan – together with the ideal organizations of soft HRM rhetoric – the traditional focus has been on the internal employment market with:

- Recruitment taking place almost entirely at the lower levels from the pool of available school-leavers and graduates.
- Organizations offering a structured career on a lifetime basis.
- Little movement, or labour turnover, between organizations.

You will remember from the earlier discussions on Japan that, until recently, major Japanese companies offered life-long employment and career development. German organizations emphasize the recruitment of apprentices who will eventually fill middle and senior posts, whereas in free-market countries companies advertise vacancies externally at all levels. An OECD study quoted by Thomson and Mabey (1994, p.1) showed that people stayed with one employer for an average of around 22 years in Japan, Germany and France. This compared with around 13 years in the USA, and similar average periods of time in Australia, Canada, the Netherlands and the UK.

Despite the current slump and recent boom, job tenure has increased for women and decreased for men in the USA. But overall there is little change according to the Employee Benefit Research Institute (EBRI) (*HRM Guide USA*, 19 March 2001). They contend that underlying economic factors – which seem to have changed in the late 20th century – may have played an important role in the interpretation of job tenure data in the recent past.

Analysing job tenure data from the US Bureau of Labor they found that between 1983 and 2000 the proportion of all wage and salary employees with up to two years of tenure with current employers was in the 36–39 per cent range. Male job tenure fell for all age groups between 1983 and 2000, but seems to have levelled out during the last couple of years. Conversely female job tenure has been rising for almost all age groups since 1951 – increasing the most for women between 45 and 54 years of age.

EBRI President Dallas Salisbury commented that job tenure data do not necessarily provide a good yardstick to gauge employment security, unless the underlying economic factors are also considered. For instance, many analysts may regard increases in employee tenure as a sign of improving job security and decreasing tenure as a sign of a decline in job security, when in fact the opposite could be true. According to Salisbury:

> An increase in employee tenure may reflect lower overall job security if it occurs during a recession, when relatively junior workers lose their jobs more rapidly than do workers with longer tenure. Conversely, a decrease in employee tenure can result during economic expansion, particularly in a tight labor market, as more job opportunities become available and experienced workers find better jobs.

Whereas the median tenure for working men between 25 and 64 years increased between 1951 and 1983 for all age categories, it actually declined between 1983 and 2000:

- from 15.3 years to 10.2 years for males aged 55–64
- from 12.8 years to 9.5 years for males aged 45–54
- from 7.3 years to 5.4 years for males aged 35–44.

But male tenure figures have been relatively stable since 1998.

Female tenure levels rose for every age category between 1951 and 2000. After 1983, tenure increases became most evident for the 45–54 age group, growing by a year over the 17-year period. In comparison, tenure grew by under six months for women between 35 and 44, and actually declined for women aged 25–34. It grew slightly for those aged 55–64.

The proportion of employees with 20 or more years of tenure with current employers increased slowly but steadily throughout the 1990s, reaching just over 10 per cent in 2000.

Trends and levels vary significantly between public and private sectors. Data for 1983–2000 indicate much higher tenure levels in the public sector and trends have moved in opposite directions between the two sectors. At the end of the 20th century, public sector tenure levels were over twice those of the private sector. This may be partly explained by the tendency of government workers to be older than their counterparts in private industry. Also, there is a lesser likelihood of public sector employees being laid off or being affected by cyclical factors to the degrees experienced by private sector workers – for example those in construction or wholesale and retail trade.

Intriguingly, the archetypal east Asian economy, Singapore, has seen high rates of employee turnover to match its remarkable growth rate due to competition for scarce skills. Similarly, Japanese companies have changed their traditional practices to attract electronics experts with premium technological skills.

Projections of the future size of the employment market are critical to planned economic development. On a local basis, individual companies need to anticipate the availability of suitable recruits to meet business planning needs. These are normally calculated from:

- Demographic trends (Key concept 6.5), including the birth rate at least 16 years previously.
- Retirement rates (in the last few decades there has been a pronounced trend towards earlier retirement in developed countries – see Table 6.3).
- Numbers of people in higher education.

Table 6.3	Percentage of older males in the workforce (aged 60–64)		
Country	1960–61	1994	per cent decrease
Australia	79.6	48.7	39
Austria	66.0	12.7	81
Finland	79.1	23.9	69
France	71.1	18.2	74
Germany	72.5	34.9	51
Italy	70.1	37.2	46
Japan	81.9	75.6	8
Netherlands	80.8	18.0	88
Sweden	82.5	57.8	29
UK	87.4 est.	52.2	40
USA	77.1	54.9	29

Source: *World Labour Report 1995*, International Labour Organization.

Reductions in demand for manual work have seen many unskilled workers leaving the employment market. In the UK, the Institute of Public Policy Research found that the proportion of men of working age in employment fell from 91 per cent in 1977 to 80 per cent in 1992. But 10 years later there had been little change with 79.3 per cent in employment during April–June 2002.

| **HRM in reality** | **Where will tomorrow's public service employees come from?** |

Two reports released at the US state legislators' conference – *Taking Action Against the Quiet Crisis in Recruitment and Retention* and *AFT Public Employees Compensation Survey* – show that ageing workforces, inadequate compensation, and lack of planning will leave almost every state government with critically low pools of employees to provide essential public services. 'States can't ignore this crisis any longer. In fewer than ten years, states will lose their best employees while the supply of people interested in these jobs runs dry,' said Jim McGarvey, chair of AFT Public Employees, the 100 000-member public employee division of the American Federation of Teachers. 'States are barely getting by now, and they should be actively recruiting the best talent and making sure public service jobs are attractive to these people.'

Taking Action Against the Quiet Crisis in Recruitment and Retention says that states will be left short of essential employees as a consequence of:

- a massive wave of baby-boom retirements, exacerbated by raids on public reserves
- cutbacks due to budget shortfalls
- a major drop in the economy.

According to the report, the most skilled and expert employees will be gone from public service, and vital resources will be drained from government programmes. To support this view, the report quotes US Bureau of Labor Statistics projections which show that 45 per cent of all government employees are eligible to retire in the next five to ten years.

It also argues that public employee unions, state legislators, government administrators and those setting the course for government policy need to act now to address the clear threat facing quality public services. According to Jo Romero, president of the Colorado Federation of Public Employees and a 20-year employee of the state of Colorado: 'There are two problems here. One is that while there's a gratifying sense of altruism with public employment, it doesn't pay the bills like similar jobs in the private sector. Also, when the availability and quality of public services are reduced, everyone loses.'

Taking Action Against the Quiet Crisis in Recruitment and Retention is based on results from a recent survey of 500 public employees across the USA conducted by Peter Hart Associates. The main findings include:

- Some 57 per cent of respondents said that retention of qualified employees was a major or moderate problem in their agency, while 61 per cent indicated that recruiting qualified employees was a major or moderate problem. Low pay and the need for more professional or career development opportunities were cited most often as the reasons for these problems.

▶

- Around 65 per cent of respondents said they would be very likely or fairly likely to retire if offered a financially attractive early retirement option.

- Staff turnover is increasing at every level of government with almost one-fifth of the public workforce turning over each year in some areas of the country.

- Turnover costs are rising. Texas alone spent US$254 million on employee turnover in 2000. In fact, the report says that it costs a state as much as 150 per cent of an employee's annual salary when lost productivity is factored in.

- The median age of the nation's workforce rose from 34.8 years in 1978 to 38.7 years in 1998 and is projected to reach 40.7 years by 2008.

- The report says that state government services are far more diverse than the range of products and services offered by any private company. This means that the public sector requires an even more diverse and well-educated workforce.

'Inadequate compensation packages are making it more difficult to encourage young people to enter public service and keep the high-quality, experienced employees. There indeed is a quiet crisis rippling across the country that must be addressed,' McGarvey said.

The *AFT Public Employees Compensation Survey* reveals the major salary and benefits inequities between jobs in public and private employment and among states. It shows a direct correlation between states that are 'haemorrhaging public employees' and these states' comparatively low pay and other compensation packages. 'We hope union officials, state legislators and government administrators use the survey to compare wages job by job and examine changes taking place across the country for specific job titles,' McGarvey said.

Source: *HRM Guide USA* (http://www.hrmguide.net/usa/), 25 July 2002.

Key concept 6:5

Demographic trends   Long-term changes in the overall population level and age distribution in countries, regions and localities due to variations in birth, death and migration. These changes affect the availability of employable people.

Employee supply and demand

Individuals determine how much time they will devote to paid work for a variety of reasons. The proportion of people of working age in work, or seeking jobs, is described as the labour force participation rate. In the year 2000, for example, 64.7 per cent of the working age population of Australia were in work or seeking jobs. This compared with 65.9 per cent in Canada, 62.0 per cent in Japan, 63.5 per cent in the Netherlands, 63.3 per cent in the United Kingdom and 67.2 per cent in the United States.

The flow of young people into the workforce is fundamental to the employment market. The underlying demographic pattern is changing throughout the world. Whereas most developing countries have seen an explosion of growth in the youngest age groups, the developed world is experiencing a reduction in birth rate. This follows a baby boom after World War II which produced a wave of people who will mostly retire in the first quarter of the 21st century. In western Europe and North America, numbers of people entering the employment market have been falling. This will reduce the overall size of their workforces, shifting the age balance towards older employees. This has been compensated by a massive increase in working women, especially in part-time jobs.

In Australia, more than a third (39 per cent) of the country's unemployed are aged between 15 and 24, according to the Australian Bureau of Statistics (ABS) (*HRM Guide Australia*, 3 April 2002). Exactly one-half (50 per cent) of unemployed 15–19-year-olds were looking for full-time work, compared with 76 per cent of unemployed people of all ages.

The most frequent difficulty in gaining employment cited by unemployed people aged 15–24 was insufficient work experience (18 per cent). Other difficulties referred to were 'no vacancies at all' (cited by 15 per cent of those aged 15–19 and 10 per cent of those aged 20–24) and 'lacked the necessary skills/education' (11 per cent and 13 per cent respectively).

Among 613 000 unemployed people aged 15 and over in July 2001, the main difficulties referred to trying to find work were:

● being considered too young or too old by employers (12 per cent)

● too many applicants for the jobs available (12 per cent)

● insufficient work experience (12 per cent)

● no vacancies at all (11 per cent).

Around 75 per cent of unemployed people searching for full-time jobs were registered with Centrelink (the government job search service). This compares with just 22 per cent of unemployed people looking for part-time jobs.

Some 24 per cent of all unemployed people were 'long-term unemployed'– defined as being unemployed for a year or longer. Most of these (89 per cent) were looking for full-time jobs, but 90 per cent had not received any job offers during the previous 12 months. A fifth of the long-term unemployed reported that being considered too young or too old was the main barrier to finding employment.

Of the 613 000 unemployed people 75 per cent had their highest educational qualifications at Year 12 level or below. People with their highest qualification at Year 10 or below had been unemployed for an average of 64 weeks. This compared with 31 weeks for those with Bachelor degrees or above.

HRM in reality

Record number of women in work

The UK has the third highest rate of female employment in Europe with a record 70 per cent of women at work: 12.5 million (843 000 more than there were ten years ago). This is revealed in a government study – *Trends in Female Employment* – which shows that 65 per cent of women with dependent children are working. This ranges from 54.4 per cent of women with children under five, to 75 per cent with children between 11 and 15, and 78.2 per cent for those with children aged 16–18.

The employment rates for lone mothers in work are considerably lower, averaging just 48.6 per cent. And whereas 60.5 per cent of married women with pre-school children are working, only 31.6 per cent of lone mothers with children under five are in employment. But growth in employment was higher among lone mothers (5.2 per cent) than married mothers (2.4 per cent) over the last three years.

According to Employment and Women's Minister Tessa Jowell the study shows excellent progress in women's employment over the years, with many women able to get the work–family balance right. Ms Jowell said:

> This is good news for women. The report shows that women continue to be an integral part of the workforce. It is vital that we recognize this achievement and continue building on this success – making sure there is support for women returning to work

▶

after having a family and helping people balance their work and family life. That is why we are encouraging employers to introduce flexible working policies such as job sharing and term-time working as well as traditional part-time working in a way that has not always happened in the past.

I am especially pleased to see that lone mothers are taking advantage of the employment opportunities that exist. In just two years over 72 000 single mothers have got jobs through New Deal for Lone Parents. And the introduction of the Minimum Wage, Working Families Tax Credit and the National Childcare Strategy are all supporting lone mothers who want to work.

We are determined to eliminate age discrimination in employment, so I am particularly encouraged to see that in the past three years employment growth has been strongest among women aged between 50 and 59, an increase of 3.3 percentage points.

No matter which region of the UK you live in, the employment rate for women is higher than the European Union average. But there is still much to do – 88 per cent of women are concentrated in service industries and in non-manual occupations whereas nine out of ten workers in the manufacturing sector are men.

The report is by National Statistics in *Labour Market Trends*. It also reveals that the number of women in permanent employment rose by more than 500 000 (5.2 per cent) over the past three years. Most of the growth has taken place among full-time employees. But the report also indicates that 90 per cent of women who have dependent children do not want full-time work.

Female employment rates in the UK (per cent)

	Spring 1997	Spring 2000
All women aged 16–59	67.5	68.9
All married/cohabiting	71.0	73.0
Married/cohabiting without children	74.7	76.2
Married/cohabiting with children	67.7	70.1
All single	60.3	61.7
Single without children	65.2	66.8
Single with children	43.4	48.6

Source: *HRMGuide.co.uk* (http://www.hrmguide.co.uk), 7 February 2001.

Key demographic trends include the following:

- Populations in developed countries are stabilizing or declining. Birth rates are tending to fall below replenishment rates.
- Ageing populations in 'first-world' countries may be counter-balanced by immigration. For example, North Africans to France.
- Developing countries experience a period of rapid population growth as infant mortality rates are reduced – well in advance of birth control measures being adopted.
- Most developing countries experience population pressure for decades until stability is achieved.
- The population balance will change markedly between the developed and developing world. Eventually the developed world will decline in importance, in line with their reduced working population.

HRM in reality

Canada on verge of labour crisis

The 7 May edition of *Time Magazine* carried a special report on a looming national shortage of skilled workers. It concluded that 'Canada's future belongs to its new immigrants.'

The article states that Canada is 'about to reach the climax of its most important demographic event since World War II', with an increasing number of immigrants required to fill jobs as diverse as high tech, nursing and teaching. The problem is exacerbated by a continuing 'brain drain' into the USA and retirement of the baby-boomer generation. National Bureau Chief Steven Frank agues that 'the natural rate of population growth in Canada, without immigration, is less than half a percentage point a year.' And the country may need twice the 220 000 currently arriving each year.

Observing that 'the Canadian Federation of Independent Business put the national shortage of [skilled] people at between 250 000 and 300 000,' and that 'the Conference Board of Canada foresees a national shortage of 1 million skilled workers by 2020,' Frank says that provinces like Manitoba are already feeling the pinch. 'The problem is likely to get worse,' he writes. 'These days, a boomtown like Calgary is not only competing against Edmonton and Vancouver for skills and talent, but it increasingly has to fight against the lure of such places as Dallas, Geneva or Tokyo in the struggle to retain a competitive edge.'

In the same issue, Sandy M. Fernandez says that Canada's skilled employee shortage is not helped by the fact that 'immigrants can choose to stay at home because their own economies are growing.' Fernandez argues in her article 'The Call of the Homeland' that Canada is faced with a difficult – if not impossible – mix of: an impending mass retirement of baby-boomers; a lack of natural population growth; and reliance on an educated immigrant workforce.

Using Hong Kong as a case study, Fernandez explains that 'in the 1990s, Hong Kong was Canada's third largest source of skilled immigrants.' Now Hong Kong's economy has changed 'from finance and real estate to a knowledge base,' she contends that the 'numbers (of Hong Kong immigrants coming to Canada) won't be the same in the future.' Places like Hong Kong and other major sources of skilled immigrants such as Ireland and India are making great efforts to keep their brightest people at home.

Source: *HRM Guide Canada* (http://www.hrmguide.net/canada/), 7 May 2001.

HRM in reality

Shortage of qualified labour a serious problem for nearly half of all smaller firms in Canada, as total number of unfilled jobs ranges from 250 000 to 300 000

Two national surveys by the Canadian Federation of Independent Business (CFIB) show that the shortage of qualified labour has become a major problem for almost half the small- and medium-sized firms in Canada. There are 250 000 to 300 000 vacant jobs due to this problem. In some provinces demand for skilled workers is at its highest level since CFIB began monitoring this issue 25 years ago.

CFIB's tracking survey showed that, across Canada as a whole, an average 46 per cent of small business respondents identified the shortage of qualified labour as a problem. But the problem is viewed more seriously in Manitoba (59 per cent),

Alberta (55 per cent) and Ontario (51 per cent). By contrast, Newfoundland respondents registered the lowest concern at 33 per cent.

CFIB's president in Toronto, Catherine Swift, describes the shortage of qualified labour as a 'difficulty in finding the right people to fill available jobs'. She says that the problem has grown rapidly since 1996 and widened to cover a cross-section of jobs across all skill levels. Swift added that the CFIB was spurred by members' concerns into conducting a specialized national survey during October and November of 2000.

Results from this detailed survey gave additional details and highlighted the negative impact of this problem on small- and medium-sized firms. Swift points out that 67 per cent of respondents who hired during the past year felt that long-term growth had been compromised by this problem. She said this had severe consequences since small businesses created the vast majority of jobs in Canada. When their growth is stunted, so is job creation. 'It is important to understand also that the shortage of qualified labour is not just an inconvenience to business owners, but has a real impact on firms' productivity and their bottom lines,' said Swift. 'Given that small- and medium-sized business accounts for more than half of GDP in this country, this is a serious economic issue.'

Swift states that one out of every 20 jobs remains unfilled because of the inability to find suitable people. 'For a smaller business, unfilled jobs can mean a poorer standard of service, losing customers or not developing new products,' she said. 'The fact that 4.7 per cent of jobs in the small business sector are left vacant is unacceptable when there is a 6.9 per cent national unemployment rate. On the other hand, lack of necessary skills also deprives the unemployed of badly needed job opportunities.'

The problem is experienced in different degrees by specific industries. Construction firms reported the highest rate (7.7 per cent), followed by the business services sector (6.8 per cent) and agriculture (5.3 per cent). Compare this with financial, insurance and real estate firms which had the lowest job vacancy rate at 3.7 per cent.

Half of respondents (51 per cent) indicated that appropriate candidates for entry level and low-experience positions were most difficult to find. But the other half (49 per cent) found the greatest difficulty in their searches for positions with mid-level and high-level experience requirements.

What qualities were they looking for in prospective employees? Some 73 per cent of respondents identified 'willingness to learn' as the most important requirement, while 61 per cent identified willingness to stay with the firm, and 60 per cent cited the ability to be customer-focused as being of major importance. More teachable skills were also identified, including: technical trade know-how (49 per cent), understanding of the industry or business (46 per cent), computer knowledge (42 per cent), and writing/communications skills (38 per cent).

'There is no one cause of the shortage of qualified labour and no single solution to this problem,' said Whyte. But some policies that exacerbate the problem – including the decision to loosen employment insurance regulations when businesses are crying out for people – must be re-examined and new strategies developed, he added.

CFIB's tracking survey collected 22 203 responses during the last half of 2000, while the other survey drew 8767 responses.

Source: *HRM Guide Canada* (http://www.hrmguide.net/canada/), 21 February 2001.

Activity 6:5

What are the most important demographic consequences on the employment market in your country?

Employee demand

Demand for workers is linked to the economic cycle, increasing in boom times and decreasing in recession. Other factors include the adoption of new technology, productivity improvements and changing skill requirements. Superficially, calculating employment supply and demand seems easy. In practice, the combination of variable consumer demand, development of new products and technology, and economic turbulence make it extremely problematic. In the last decade, for example, commentators have confidently predicted both permanently high levels of unemployment *and* shortages of labour.

As we observed in the last chapter, the role of the state is important in this respect: through fiscal or monetary policy, governments can directly increase or diminish consumption and economic activity. Such actions lead quickly to changes in demand for human resources as firms relate their requirements to production or provision of services. Activity in service and manufacturing services may follow different patterns. The decline in manufacturing in the UK, for example, has been dismissed as unimportant by some commentators who believed that production jobs would be replaced by new work in financial and other services. The reality is that these sectors have proven incapable of generating enough employment to compensate for the loss of full-time jobs in manufacturing. As we shall see shortly, there has been a widespread trend for well-paid jobs to be replaced with low-paid, part-time work.

HRM in reality

Saskatchewan jobs programs create employment

The 'Jobs First' initiative celebrates its first anniversary in Regina today. 'The Jobs First initiative helps people access local job opportunities as a first choice before becoming involved in the welfare system,' Social Services Minister Glenn Hagel said. 'By using the resources of Canada-Saskatchewan Career and Employment Centres across the province, participants not only find out about local job opportunities, but can also access a full range of services including career counselling, job search and interview skills.'

'Regina was one of two pilot projects in Saskatchewan where this unique program was tested,' Hagel said. 'These two pilot projects helped create a service that will be of tremendous benefit to people who want to connect to the labour market.'

Jobs First involves group meetings where participants are made aware of local job opportunities. They can select employment opportunities from these to match their skill level and experience. Facilitators also provide instruction in job search skills and help participants prepare for and attend interviews.

'During the pilot projects in Regina and Yorkton, 30 to 45 per cent of participants in Jobs First went to work instead of welfare,' Hagel said. 'Based on this success, we are now making Jobs First available to the rest of the province.' Jobs First is the newest component of Saskatchewan's 'Building Independence' strategy. Since its introduction in 1997, Building Independence has helped 6000 families, including 13 000 children, leave welfare.

'Phase 1 of Building Independence is successful because it removes the barriers to the workforce that prevent people from leaving welfare,' Hagel said. 'The second phase of Building Independence is focusing on renewing the way welfare is

◀

delivered and strengthening supports for low-income people outside of the welfare system.' Other measures introduced in Phase 2 include:

- A call centre as the first point of access for new applicants. Call centre staff can direct new applicants to other programs that may allow the applicant to remain independent.

- First Step orientation sessions providing general information to new clients about other community resources and programs, as well as information on an individual's rights and responsibilities while receiving social assistance.

- Transition planning – a new approach to social work for people on social assistance which builds on client strengths and addresses barriers that prevent participation in the labour force.

Source: *HRM Guide Canada* (http://www.hrmguide.net/canada/), 11 May 2002.

Active labour market programmes

Active labour market programmes (ALMPs) are government initiatives to reduce unemployment and increase participation in the employment market. They include public works, training and retraining, job search assistance, support for self-employment or new enterprises and wage subsidies (Dar and Tzannatos, 1999). Such programmes are justified in a variety of ways. For example, the provision of public works is a demand side intervention, whereas training is intended to have an effect on supply side skills availability. However, all such interventions are based on the assumption that the employment market is failing in some way or that the social outcomes (particularly unemployment) are unacceptable.

Dar and Tzannatos (1999) review 100 evaluations of such programmes undertaken in OECD and developing countries (including Turkey, Hungary, Poland, the Czech Republic and Mexico) and draw some general conclusions:

- Public works may help the most disadvantaged groups such as older workers, the long-term unemployed, and people in distressed regions by acting as a poverty/safety net. However, they are ineffective in providing a channel into permanent employment.

- Job search assistance programmes have a greater positive impact and are more cost-effective than other ALMPs. They are most effective when the general economic climate is favourable. However, they do not appear to significantly improve either the employment prospects or wages of young job-seekers.

- Training for the long-term unemployed is useful when the economy is improving. The best returns are offered by small-scale, tightly targeted, on-the-job training programmes, especially those aimed at women and older groups. In general, however, they are rarely cost-effective and no more successful than job search assistance programmes in terms of post-programme placement and wages.

- Mass retraining for redundant workers is usually ineffective and, as in the case of the long-term unemployed, is also more expensive and no more effective than job-search assistance.

- Training for young people has no positive impact on either their employment prospects or post-training earnings. Such programmes generally offer a negative return on the investment.

- Start-up assistance for small business is usually taken up by a small proportion of the unemployed and the failure rate of these businesses is high. Targeting at women and older individuals increases the likelihood of success.
- Wage subsidy programmes are unlikely to be effective and may be exploited by unscrupulous employers.

HRM in reality	**Toronto surveys people who left Ontario Works**

A Toronto City survey of people leaving social assistance shows that they still face a poverty trap from which it is difficult to escape.

Toronto's Social Services Division commissioned the random telephone survey of more than 800 people who left Ontario Works (OW) in the first quarter of 2001 to find out how they fared, and whether they are better off after leaving. The survey indicates that people are not significantly better off than they were while on OW, or than they were five years ago. The survey data revealed three key findings: 77 per cent of survey respondents worked at some point after leaving OW; just 43 per cent said their finances had improved; and 17 per cent returned to OW in 2001 (a third of these were ill or disabled).

'Having a skilled workforce is vital to Toronto's economic health and development,' said Councillor Brad Duguid, Ward 38 Scarborough Centre, Chair of the Community Services Committee. 'We encourage senior levels of government to re-invest in strategies that recognize education, supports and skills upgrading for people on social assistance. Not only do people need to connect to the labor market, they need to secure stable jobs and increase their earning potential over time.'

Education is a key factor in determining who is likely to return to OW – returners in 2001 were more likely to have less than a high school education. And 38 per cent of survey respondents said they required access to education and skills upgrading to help them keep their current job or find a better one. Unfortunately, funding cuts at both federal and provincial levels over the last five years have substantially reduced access to education and training.

'Many people can't break the cycle of moving back and forth between social assistance and marginal employment,' said Heather MacVicar, General Manager of Social Services. 'While our clients obtain jobs, they are typically unstable and low paying with few benefits. Our survey finds that our clients want to work, and most of them use at least one job-related service that the City provides.'

Source: *HRM Guide Canada* (http://www.hrmguide.net/canada/), 29 May 2002.

Activity 6:6	Summarize the advantages and disadvantages of 'active labour market programmes'.

Part-time and temporary working

Part-time employees contract to work for anything less than normal full-time basic hours. Part-time working has grown consistently in developed countries for 30 years. For example, in the UK part-timers made up just 4 per cent of the employment market in 1951. This had risen to 16.4 per cent in 1979 and 23.5 per cent in 1992. European figures varied considerably, with around a third of all employees in the Netherlands working part-time,

26.9 per cent in Norway, 10.2 per cent in France and just 9.5 per cent in Germany (*Financial Times*, 12 December 1995). Advantages to employers include: more intensive work with less time used for breaks; lower absenteeism among part-time workers; enthusiasm and commitment can be higher (less opportunity for boredom); and little unionization among part-time staff.

The main forms of part-time work include:

- *Classical.* Work that does not require full-time cover, typically taking a few hours a day. For example, office cleaning and staffing a canteen.
- *Supplementary.* Where a part-timer replaces overtime, perhaps performing an evening shift, or working short days to cover peak periods.
- *Substitution.* In which part-timers replace full-timers through job-splitting. It is common for older workers to be retained as part-timers before full retirement.

More recent types of part-time work include key working and job sharing. Key working is typically found in service industries such as retailing. Service work differs from 'traditional' work. Peak activity occurs on days and at times when other workers are at leisure. Peak times may be so short that it is impossible for an employer to use full-time workers effectively. In these circumstances few 'core' full-timers are required. Correspondingly, a large number of 'peripheral' part-timers work at busy periods. Peripheral numbers can be shrunk or expanded as required. This allows greater flexibility than would be possible for a completely full-time workforce.

Job sharing is where two people are responsible for one full-time job, dividing pay and benefits in proportion to the hours worked. Days or weeks may be split or alternate weeks worked. An advantage for some employees, job sharing can also benefit employers. For example:

- Sharers can overlap hours so that busy periods receive double cover.
- Jobs are at least partly covered when one person is away through illness or annual leave.
- Two individuals can bring greater experience and a broader range of views to a job than a single employee.

Job sharing allows skilled people to be retained if they give up full-time employment. However, there are some disadvantages such as:

- Training, induction and administration overheads for two people.
- Finding a suitable partner with matching skills and availability if one sharer leaves.
- Communication on tasks that cannot be dealt with quickly ('hand-over' problems).
- Responsibility for staff can be problematic; people may find difficulty in working for two supervisors.
- Fair allocation of work.

HRM in reality

Leaving Job-seeker's Allowance for part-time work

An in-house report for the Department of Social Security identifies characteristics of clients leaving Job-seeker's Allowance (JSA) for part-time work (defined as work of under 16 hours per week) between 1996 and 1998, comparing them with characteristics of people leaving JSA for full-time work (over 16 hours per week).

The authors are Karl Ashworth and Rachel Youngs from the Centre for Research in Social Policy at Loughborough University. Based on secondary analysis of the second cohort of the JSA claimant survey their study has the following main findings:

- A majority of part-time workers were qualified – many with professional, managerial or technical backgrounds. There was no predominant type or sector of work undertaken but professional jobs were over-represented.

- People taking up work of under 16 hours were 'well attached to the labour market', reporting high levels of satisfaction with the return-to-work jobs and stating that these jobs made use of their skills.

- Clients moving into part-time work tended to be older and were more likely to have a partner than people entering full-time work. Partners were likely to be in full-time work of 30 or more hours a week.

- Having considered a range of variables the authors conclude that part-time workers did not seem any more disadvantaged than full-time workers. However – as in the case of people working 16 hours or over – a fifth of part-time workers were unqualified, one-fifth reported health problems and one-quarter were unskilled.

Source: *HRMGuide.co.uk* (http://www.hrmguide.co.uk), 2 March 2001.

Part-time workers come especially from specific groups, including:

1 *Female parents with children*. The largest group, typically working when children are at school.

2 *Retired or semi-retired*. Supplementing pensions, filling time and using their skills. Again, they tend to work during the day period.

3 *Moonlighters*. With full-time jobs elsewhere, supplementing income in the evening or at weekends. For instance, driving mini-cabs, delivering free newspapers or bar work.

4 *Students*. Supplementing pocket money or grants by delivering papers, pizzas, serving in fast-food outlets. They may also work in vacation periods or undertake seasonal work, in the summer tourist industry, etc.

Paradoxically, many managers question part-timers' commitment, seeing them as being primarily home-oriented. They are excluded from interesting and senior positions. Part-time workers get few training and promotion opportunities. Managers have contradictory beliefs about women part-timers. On the one hand they believe them to be reliable, loyal and flexible. At the same time, they also consider that they take time off to be with children and give precedence to partners' careers.

Temporary workers

Overall, temporary job contracts are increasing but this statement 'needs to be heavily qualified' (Martin and Stancanelli, 2002). An analysis of 1985–2000 data from 13 OECD countries shows that the share of temporary employment in total salaried employment has risen (on average) by less than 3 per cent. France, Italy, the Netherlands and Spain are responsible for much of this less than massive increase. In five other countries, the share actually reduced. This includes the United States. Martin and Stancanelli (2002) suggest that 'one reason for the low recourse to temporary work in the United States may be that US permanent positions are less rigidly protected than in Europe, for instance, so there is less incentive for employers to offer temporary contracts.'

The largest temporary staff agency, Manpower Inc. places 2 million people in a year, over 40 per cent of whom go on to permanent employment. More than 10 per cent of workers in the EU have temporary jobs, with the highest level (30 per cent) in Spain. A UK *Labour Force Survey* found that 1.6 million British workers were employed on a temporary basis.

Apart from the familiar 'temps' obtained from specialist agencies, two main groups of temporary workers can be highlighted:

● *Contingent employees.* In the UK there are 500 000 professional and highly skilled people working on temporary contracts. For example, 'interim managers'. These are generally freelance executives aged over 40. Most assignments last for 40–80 days, allowing for short-term problems to be handled without long-term commitment to expensive staff. Specialist expertise can be bought in for specific tasks or projects. Contingent managers have been rated highly in functions such as human resources, finance, information technology, marketing, operations and property.

● *Seasonal employment.* Seasonal workers are hired to cope with fluctuations in demand – to keep down stock volumes, and hence cost. For example, the chocolate industry has especially high periods of demand at times when gifts are commonly given, such as Christmas.

Implicitly, two classes of workers are created. One class has employment rights. The other is disposable. In the public sector, government action (particularly in New Zealand and the UK) has seen the distancing of many activities (and workers) who were formerly civil servants or local government employees.

From the employee's point of view, it is undeniable that part-time or temporary work is both convenient and attractive to many people. However, they are no substitute for the loss of full-time jobs. The 20th century concept of the nine-to-five job and a lifetime career is disintegrating in favour of much more flexible arrangements. Levels of insecurity and stress are rising as people have increasingly uncertain working lives. It has become a truism that most people will experience at least two or three careers in their lifetime. Handy (1989, p.146) sees work becoming part of a portfolio of activities. At any one time, individuals may have a number of part-time jobs, together with leisure or study periods. Flexibility and career development will be further explored in Chapter 7.

Summary

In this chapter we discussed some important features of the employment market. We considered factors that lead to people seeking work and joining that market. We examined key economic and psychological concepts and identified a number of links with fundamental elements of HRM. Participation in the job market was investigated, comparing rates in different countries. Different working patterns were described as a prelude for later discussion of flexibility.

Further reading

The range of books on the employment market is vast but tends towards political or economic analysis. The following are of interest: *The Jobs Gap in Britain's Cities: Employment Loss and Labour Market Consequences* by Ivan Turok, Policy Press (1999); *Work to Welfare: How Men Become Detached from the Labour Market* by Peter Alcock,

Christina Beatty, Stephen Fothergill, Rob MacMillan and Sue Yeandle, Cambridge University Press (2002); *Europe: One Labour Market (Work and Society)* edited by Lars Magnusson and Jan Ottosson, Peter Lang Publishing (2002); *Europe's Population and Labour Market Beyond 2000* (Population Studies No. 2), Council of Europe Publishing (2001).

Two books of particular Canadian interest: *Federalism, Democracy and Labour Market Policy in Canada* (Social Union Series) edited by Tom McIntosh, McGill-Queen's University Press (2001); and *Aging and Demographic Change in a Canadian Context* (Trends Project) edited by David Cheal, University of Toronto Press (2002).

Books on unemployment include: *Losing Work, Moving On: International Perspectives on Worker Displacement* by Peter Joseph Kuhn, W. E. Upjohn Institute (2002); *Stress and Distress Among the Unemployed: Hard Times and Vulnerable People* (Plenum Studies in Work and Industry) by Clifford L. Broman, V. Lee Hamilton and William Sydney Hoffman, Plenum Publications (2001).

For flexibility and the future of work see: *The Future of Work* by Charles Handy, Blackwell, 2002; and *Flexibility at Work: Balancing the Interests of Employer and Employee* by Peter A. Reilly, Ashgate Publishing Company (2001).

Review questions

1 How is it possible to regard jobs as being in a market?

2 Describe in your own words what is meant by the 'labour force participation rate'.

3 Is full employment a practical goal for every country?

4 How will demographic trends affect employment in your country in the 21st century?

5 How do competitive and institutional models of the job market relate to hard and soft versions of HRM?

6 Outline the advantages and disadvantages of part-time jobs for employers and employees.

7 Why has the introduction of new technology not led to a 'leisure revolution'?

Problems for discussion and analysis

1 Rob is a student on placement with a thriving media marketing company. He enjoys the challenges of dealing with customers and other staff. He prefers placement work to university where, academically, he is an average performer. Rob enjoys some parts of his course but dreads other aspects – particularly the end of semester assessments. He was pushed into higher education by an ambitious father whose own career was limited by his lack of qualifications. Personally, Rob cannot wait to complete the course and get on with his career.

Rob's placement company has lost a number of key staff to a competitor. Senior managers have looked at the younger staff and highlighted Rob as a potential high-flyer. He has the energy and the enthusiasm to cope with the long hours and the considerable travelling required. They have offered Rob a higher level position which is now vacant. The rewards are high and the prospects for the next few years are excellent. However, Rob has been told that he cannot

▶

accept this position and return to full-time education to complete his final year.

Rob has to make a choice quickly. What factors should he take into account in making his decision?

2   Jefford Trading is a medium-sized business selling high-quality designer furnishings. Originally started 20 years ago from one small shop, Jan and Keith Jefford have built the company into a multi-shop retailer with ventures around the country. In the last three years business has become a struggle: other firms have entered the same market and rental and other costs have risen sharply. The company continues to make a profit but further expansion will be hard work.

There are 57 employees. Apart from the founders there is one other director, Paul Stevens the company secretary (49), who looks after major contracts and personnel. He is competent but not ambitious. There are five middle managers, all graduates under 35 picked by Paul, with responsibilities for buying, logistics, finance, marketing and retailing respectively. The logistics and retail managers are responsible for most of the staff. Junior managers run the shops, all without higher education qualifications but are keen. The other head office staff are of mixed ages with little potential for advancement.

The Jeffords have worked long hours developing the company, taking few holidays and little money out of the company. Keith is 48, looks much older and has some health problems. Jan is 43, more determined but worried about her husband. The managers have suggested that they take over the running of the company, allowing the owners to sit back and enjoy life.

The Jeffords' accountants have little faith in the managers: they believe them to be too young and inexperienced. The accountants have advised the sale of the company and investment of the proceeds. The Jeffords accept this is sensible advice but would prefer to keep the company going.

You have been brought in as a consultant to advise them. What would you do? How would you conduct your investigation? What are the options? What do you anticipate your recommendations to be? How are the Jeffords likely to react?

PART 3

Organizational HRM

This part of the book examines HRM within the organization. Human resource practices are enabled and constrained by a variety of organizational factors, including organizational size, structure, culture and employee commitment.

The chapters in Part 3 address a number of specific issues:

- What are the different structures found within organizations and what effect do they have on human resource management practices?

- Are there any significant differences between people management practices in small and large organizations?

- What are entrepreneurs like as people managers?

- How do organizations grow and what are the implications on HRM?

- How do national business cultures impact on international HRM?

- What is the relationship between corporate culture and human resource management?

- What is employee commitment and how is it achieved?

- Is employee branding a road to commitment or a method of brainwashing employees?

- How do we manage professionals without losing their trust and commitment?

7

HRM in large organizations

Objectives

The purpose of this chapter is to:

- Investigate why organizations structure their people management systems in different ways.
- Determine the influence of organizational goals on the management of human resources.
- Outline the advantages and disadvantages of alternative organizational structures.
- Compare and contrast the work of human resource specialists in different forms of organization.

Introduction

This is a world of organizations: more and more elements of life that were once matters of personal action are now integrated into organizational frameworks. Modern society depends on people working together effectively to solve problems and achieve objectives that are beyond the scope of individuals. It is a truism to say, therefore, that all people management takes place within organizations. But what are they? We talk about familiar corporations such as CNN, the BBC and IBM as if they were objects. Yet we cannot see them in their totality. We recognize them as entities but they are also intangible: 'Although organizations are real in their consequences, both for their participants and for their environments, they are essentially abstractions. They cannot be picked up and dropped, felt or fulfil any of the other tests that we apply to physical things' (Butler, 1991, p.1).

The very idea of something, which everyone is aware of but no one can fully grasp, is fascinating in itself. It has spawned an entire field of academic enquiry – organization theory. Key concept 7.1 outlines some of the main characteristics identified by organization theorists. In this chapter we focus on how they can be understood in terms that have meaning for people managers.

Key concept 7:1

Organizations   Organizations are the means by which human and other resources are deployed so that work gets done. They can be defined by a number of characteristics:

- They are social entities created by humans.
- They have purpose expressed in the form of common goals.
- They are unrestricted in range – from corner shops to multinational corporations.
- Each organization has a boundary which leads to the inclusion of some people and excludes others.
- Within this boundary, people are patterned into a structure composed of formal and informal relationships.

First, we must recognize that the term 'organization' is wide-ranging: it can be used to describe bodies as disparate as Microsoft and scout troops. For our purposes, the concept has to be defined more narrowly. The key lies with the nature of control within organizations functioning on business lines, exercised through the employment relationship between staff and management. Business organizations such as Volvo or News International are set apart from 'social arrangements' – for example lunch clubs or photographic societies – by a preoccupation with controlled performance (Huczynski and Buchanan, 2000, p.10). They are set financial, service or production targets that determine the activities of their employees. People managers have a critical role in monitoring and controlling performance in order to achieve these targets. In the first part of this book we stressed that HRM is a 'holistic' approach to people management. To make the best use of an organization's human resources, it is necessary to manage not only its people but also its corporate structure and culture.

Organizations are highly complex, and not amenable to simple analysis, but managers must attempt to predict and control their activities in order to conduct business. Rosemary Stewart (1993, p.3) explains the value of theoretical understanding to practising managers:

> … even the most practical managers can think about a problem more easily if they have some frame of reference that will help them to decide what kind of problem it is. … Organizations

are highly complex. We do not understand enough about how they work to have developed comprehensive theories. Instead we have a number of partial explanations which have been put forward by writers from different backgrounds. Each represents a different way of looking at organizations. An understanding of these different viewpoints can help managers to identify what kind of problem they are worrying about.

The formal allocation of people management responsibilities is fundamental to the process. Businesses vary considerably in this respect: small firms tend to incorporate people management within line or general management; larger organizations are likely to have specialist functional roles. We noted that these roles might have titles such as 'human resource manager', 'personnel officer' or 'staff administrator'. These titles do not give much indication of the activities undertaken or the power vested in the jobs. In fact, they differ significantly from one firm to another. This chapter explains some of the major reasons for these variations. We begin by placing organizations in their environmental context: the competitive business world. We go on to discuss how and why organizations are formed and their implications for the nature of the people function.

| Activity 7:1 | Think of situations where human beings are collected together. List five that can be described as organizations and five that are not. What are the main reasons for classifying some as organizations and some not? |

Organizations and the business environment

Competitive pressures on businesses and national economies have increased markedly in recent decades. As a consequence, the organizations that impact on our lives are constantly changing. Powerful entities have arisen at the international level – the European Union being a prime example – and multinational corporations increasingly dominate particular sectors such as cars and aerospace. New competitors are emerging and forcing older organizations to adapt and reform themselves in order to survive.

Like Russian dolls, most organizations are parts of larger entities with one business unit fitting within another, larger structure. They are the complex products of a world subject to the international division of labour, geographic rationalization and product differentiation. There is nothing unusual in a business section in Cork reporting to a Dublin-based department within the Irish operating division of the European subsidiary of a US multinational. For marketing purposes some firms deliberately obscure these relationships. Walking down a typical high street or shopping mall in a developed country, we find an apparent diversity of retail traders. In fact, many are brand names controlled by just a few conglomerates.

In Part 2 we saw that organizations also interact with their environment through the regulatory, economic and cultural framework in which they operate. Different levels and types of organization supervise, support and impede each other's operations with contradictory demands. External stakeholders such as governments, financiers, customers and shareholders exercise their influence through legislation, tax benefits, interest rates, consumer demand and the purchase and sale of shares.

Organizations reflect the values and norms of society, supplying products and services that meet the needs of the culture in which they function. They structure and manage themselves in ways that are acceptable to those societies. Inevitably, therefore, there are differences in the nature of organizations between one country and another. For example, French companies have a tradition of bureaucratic, hierarchical organization whereas German firms have tended towards flatter, less rigidly differentiated structures (Sparrow and Hiltrop, 1994, p.270).

Different structures affect the way in which people are managed. HRM is intimately bound up with the way firms are organized. Businesses throughout the world require the same basic human resource activities: they recruit new employees; they develop and train their staff; they have reward systems; they have control and feedback mechanisms; and people must interrelate and make decisions (Brewster and Tyson, 1991, p.9). But these issues are handled in different ways, reflecting the expectations and acceptable behaviour patterns within national business cultures. Similarly, employee values and attitudes are shaped to a considerable extent by people's native culture. Since national cultures are so pervasive, we will see in Chapter 9 that they strongly influence the cultures within organizations (Hofstede, 1980).

This chapter focuses on organizational structure but we must be aware that structures are influenced by culture. People have strong feelings towards the organization in which they work. Siemens, Saab and Qantas are psychological entities to which employees react positively or negatively (Schein, 1988, p.8). Internal stakeholders – employees, managers and owners – expect organizations to operate in an acceptable manner but the notion of acceptability is culturally determined and varies from one country to another. For example, Korean employees expect and accept more authoritarian management than their Japanese neighbours. Expectation and acceptability are important factors in determining the range of possible organizational structures that can operate successfully in a particular country.

To a considerable extent, therefore, environmental factors constrain the operations of commercial enterprises; but, conversely, businesses must control elements of the environment to ensure their own survival. Organizations are not passive – they can take a number of actions that increase their freedom in meeting environmental demands. Managers do so by devising strategies for survival and growth that can prove to be beneficial or counterproductive. They can influence public perception through advertising, or achieve competitive advantage by developing new products.

Equally, an organization's prospects can be improved by deploying its human resources in a novel and effective way, drawing on their competencies and creativity. Throughout the world, the use of human resources is moving away from the employment of inflexible, full-time workers with expectations of lifelong careers in a single organization. Businesses can make strategic choices between a range of alternatives: part-timers, contingent workers, contractors, franchises and so on, as we shall see in our discussion of flexibility later in this chapter.

Some organizational strategies have been misguided. In the 1980s and 1990s most large corporations indulged in tumultuous restructurings, variously described as 'downsizing', 'rightsizing', 'de-layering', and 'focusing on core areas'. These dramatic disruptions were justified largely on financial grounds. Often the consequences for employees – including those remaining – were negative. Older redundant workers had to accept early retirement. Others faced long periods of unemployment. Morale then slumped and stress increased among surviving employees who were expected to work harder in a climate of uncertainty.

In many organizations blind pursuit of cost-effectiveness destroyed the credibility of senior managers in the eyes of their staff, leading to a marked reduction in employee commitment. In this chapter we seek to pinpoint more positive approaches in the organization of people management.

Dimensions of organization

How can we differentiate one organization from another? Large companies spend considerable amounts of money on developing strong images for themselves. Corporate logos, decoration schemes, uniforms, marketing literature and advertisements are all designed to create a favourable impression on customers and share analysts. But public image tells us little about an organization as an employer. In fact, it obscures the nature of people management.

From our perspective the first question to ask in any organization is: who manages the people? In Part 1 we noted that early HRM models placed the responsibility for people management with line managers. This is a debate in itself: should the management of people be part of the function of every manager in an organization; or does it demand an expertise that can be expected only from trained specialists? Opinions have changed markedly, sometimes due to fickle fashion and sometimes to the idiosyncratic opinions of senior managers. One view is that managing people is what business is all about and, therefore, that every manager and supervisor should deal with the individuals within their area of responsibility. Conversely, it can be argued that the detailed aspects of people management such as resourcing and reward management are too complex for the average sales manager, accountant or engineer – untrained in the behavioural sciences – to handle satisfactorily.

In reality, examples are found along the entire length of the dimension from specialist to non-specialist. The decision to manage people in a particular way depends on a number of factors, including the basic organizational dimensions we shall consider next: goals, size and structure.

Organizational goals

According to Simon (1955, p.30):

> Organizations are formed with the intention and design of accomplishing goals; and the people who work in organizations believe, at least part of the time, that they are striving towards these same goals. We must not lose sight of the fact that, however far organizations may depart from the traditional description ... most behaviour in organizations is *intendedly rational behaviour*.

As we have seen, the rhetoric of HRM attaches great importance to strategy and the linking of employee performance to organizational goals (Key concept 7.2). What are these goals? They are expressions of a company's purpose and long-term objectives. Often written in the form of a mission or values statement, they give purpose or direction to an organization. They are intended to influence the behaviour of employees but few small companies have a written statement and many larger companies provide woolly verbiage without clear meaning. We will discuss mission statements in more detail later in this book when we consider HR strategy.

Key concept 7:2	**Organizational goals** The logical starting point for human resource management lies in an organization's goals – the reasons for its existence. Most modern businesses express these goals in the form of a mission statement. The allocation and control of human resources serves to assist or constrain the achievement of these objectives.

Taken at face value, mission statements appear to show that businesses have clear objectives. Traditionally, competitive market models portray the firm as a single decision-unit engaged in maximizing profits. This approach ignores the possibility of conflict between owners, managers and employees. Organizations are political structures – usually surface unity is purely cosmetic. Needle (1994, p.99) observes that, as abstract entities, organizations do not have goals – their public objectives are those of some dominant person or group. Hidden behind the published goals of a business we find a series of conflicting agendas held by various individuals or work units. So, for example, the human resources or personnel department may have its own priorities, inconsistent with those of senior management. The HR department may be concerned with being 'professional', using the best selection techniques and careful job evaluation whereas senior executives may be more concerned with short-term employee costs.

Size

Organizations can range from single-person businesses to multinational corporations employing hundreds of thousands of people. Generally, the sophistication and importance of people management is greater in larger organizations. However, sophistication does not lead necessarily to effective people management. In small companies all management functions – including human resources – are dealt with by the owners. By 'professional' standards these activities – especially selection and training – often are inadequately handled, yet the quality of the employment relationship can be high. Owners and employees work on a down-to-earth, personal level. Some are genuine friends and there may be mutual trust and confidence.

Conversely, larger organizations employ highly trained human resource practitioners using advanced selection, assessment and reward techniques. But size also brings problems in meeting the need for comprehensiveness, coherence, control and communication, resulting in the possibility of remote and conflict-ridden relationships between people at the top and bottom of the firm. Analysis of the UK 1998 Workplace Employee Relations Survey (WERS) data shows that large workplaces (over 500 employees) are five times more likely to have a HR specialist than workplaces with 25–49 employees (Cully *et al.*, 1999, p.50). Similarly, titles including the words 'human resource' were more likely to be used in larger workplaces, although a greater proportion of personnel specialists in workplaces with fewer than 50 employees (40 per cent) were using such titles than in any other size group (Sisson, 2001). Also, the HR practices we identified as 'high commitment or high performance' in Chapter 3 were more common in larger workplaces.

To make sense of size differentials, it is useful to divide business enterprises into three categories (Curran and Stanworth, 1988):

- Small-to-medium enterprises (SMEs), further subdivided by the European Commission into: micro-enterprises, with less than ten employees; small enterprises, with 10–99 employees; and medium enterprises, employing 100–499 people.
- Large commercial enterprises with over 500 people.
- Organizations within the public or state sector. These continue to have distinctive characteristics despite government attempts to place them on a business-like footing.

Activity 7:2   How would the management of people differ between small and large organizations?

Cooperatives

The origins of this form of organization are lost in history. The first successful cooperative in North America was initiated by Benjamin Franklin in 1752. The Philadelphia Contributionship for the Insurance of Houses from Loss by Fire provided fire insurance for its members in Pennsylvania – and still does so at the time of writing (2002). In fact, the 'Contributionship' was the first mutual in the USA and is now the third oldest corporation in the country. But Benjamin Franklin probably copied a model of fire insurance pioneered in Britain in the 17th century.

Other ventures in Britain included a corn cooperative formed by workers in the Chatham and Woolwich areas of south London in the 18th century. Most significantly, the 19th century development of retail and wholesale cooperative societies pioneered in Rochdale in the north of England brought fair priced groceries to the working classes. By the 1970s, however, the number of cooperatives in the UK had dwindled to around 20. Elsewhere, however, the concept took root throughout the world.

According to Iain Williamson (1994, republished by International Cooperative Alliance, ICA):

> Today, the cooperative idea has been taken up by more than 700 million people in over 100 countries, with co-ops providing jobs for skilled craft workers in India, marketing expertise for farmers in the United States, healthcare for Japanese and precious credit for rural peasants in Africa.

The work team became a fashionable obsession among human resource theorists and consultants in the 1990s. In the small cooperative the work team *is* the organization. This offers us an opportunity to examine the supposed benefits of teamworking in a relatively pure form. According to Foley and Green (1989, p.8), cooperative relationships are based on six principles:

1 an open and voluntary membership

2 a democratic method of control, usually based on 'one member, one vote'

3 limited interest on the capital invested

4 fair and equal distribution of any profit

5 education in the principles of cooperation

6 cooperation among cooperatives.

Cooperatives arise in three ways:

- as new business start-ups, deliberately created in this fashion
- as buy-outs of existing factories or companies by the workforce
- conversion of existing enterprises into cooperatives.

Of these, the first has been the most common. They tend to be providers of services, usually benefiting from the different skills of the participants, rather than manufacturers. Most start-ups of this nature have been established with groups of fewer than five people who feel that the cooperative relationship fits their social values and need to structure their own work. But some are larger. However, there are many instances of cooperatives failing. An examination of such organizations can tell us a great deal about the advantages and disadvantages of the 'softer' aspects of HRM such as participative management, commitment and the functioning of self-organized teams. Table 7.1 summarizes the nature of people management in smaller cooperatives, using our familiar ten-Cs checklist for HRM.

Larger cooperatives such as mutuals and agricultural cooperatives may employ managers but ultimate power lies in the democratic voting system. Similar structures are found in legal and medical practices, where specialists are independent but obtain administrative support and accommodation from the practice in which they operate. Success in such a system requires much tolerance and goodwill. Many cooperatives have failed because of a lack of clear strategy and leadership; often the maintenance of a harmonious relationship has obscured the need for financial viability. However, some have expanded to a considerable size; for instance the John Lewis Partnership is a major retailing force in the UK and over 100 million Americans invest with mutuals and other cooperatives. But even large cooperatives face structural problems that impact on people management because of their size.

Table 7.1	HRM in cooperative businesses

Principle	Range	Comment
1 Comprehensiveness	Cooperatives are uniquely focused on their working members	People systems such as resourcing and training are not necessarily sophisticated
2 Coherence	Medium–good, depending on mutual understanding between members	Where specific aspects have not been discussed and agreed, members may 'do their own thing'
3 Control	Generally decentralized	Assertive members can have undue influence
4 Communication	Tends to be fairly good with shared and well-understood objectives	Generally open with intermittent conflict and possible political factions
5 Credibility	Strategies have to be discussed and agreed (or accepted) by all	Management and staff are the same in smaller cooperatives
6 Commitment	Belonging implies commitment	People vary and there are committed activists and less committed 'passengers'
7 Change	May be slow because of the need for consensus agreement	A sensitive and highly political subject and may be the major cause of conflict
8 Competence	Competent initially but needing to bring new partners in as requirements change	What happens to the partners whose skills are no longer appropriate?
9 Creativity	Can be high	Where members are free to deal with own areas of work
10 Cost-effectiveness	Depends on realism of the partners	Transparent and equitable as pay is agreed among members

Activity 7:3	What HRM issues might be problematic for larger cooperatives?

Managerial structures

As organizations grow larger and technology becomes more complex, it becomes increasingly difficult to coordinate the people involved in an enterprise (see Key concept 7.3). Beyond a certain size it is impossible for one person to know what people are doing or even what their names are. It is necessary to introduce some form of managerial structure as a framework for control and coordination. Large businesses – including sizeable cooperatives – have to be organized in a deliberate, formal way, probably with groups of workers reporting to individual managers or supervisors.

Along with a formal structure there is likely to be a clearer division between specialist functions, including that designated to look after aspects of people management – usually labelled 'Personnel' or 'Human Resources'. Someone, at least, has to keep basic records.

Typically HR managers are closely involved in the effective distribution of people and the development of management structures. The focus is on matching human resources to strategic objectives. Larger organizations display some degree of specialization, centralization and hierarchy (see Key concepts 7.4, 7.5 and 7.6). This applies to people management as much as any other activity.

Key concept 7:3

Coordination   Tasks divided amongst a group of individuals must be synchronized and integrated in some way so as to achieve the overall objectives of the group. Jobs must fit into a coherent flow of work. Coordination involves the distribution of decision making. This can be formal, with rigid rules and regulations, or informal, giving freedom for local decisions. Coordination may be routine, because of structure and control mechanisms, including a performance management system, or direct, by management action.

Key concept 7:4

Specialization   The division of work between individuals or departments, allocating responsibilities for specific activities or functions to people who can achieve a high standard of work in a relatively narrow range of activities. They may require specific training or expertise. For example, HR managers are concerned with organization of the HR function and resourcing of all other functions.

Key concept 7:5

Centralization–decentralization   This depends on where decisions are taken. The human resource function may be held within a separate headquarters department or devolved to local sections. Alternatively, it may be allocated to line managers, with an in-house 'consultancy' provided by specialists for procedures such as selection, development and performance measurement.

Key concept 7:6

Hierarchy   Pattern of responsibility and authority, usually represented by a tree and branch organization chart. It reflects senior managers' perception of the organization. 'Vertical complexity' of an organization is indicated by a tall or flat hierarchy. Taller organizations tend to be bureaucratic but have clear lines of command. Each individual has one boss. Flatter organizations are fashionable. They demand more responsibility and self-control from staff, but decision making and authority are less clear.

For a long time, large organizations were bureaucratic – typified by precise job titles, grading structures and segregated departmental activities. Status and responsibility were matched accordingly. We noted earlier that French organizations have continued to follow this pattern. The 'people function' was identified with the personnel department, which primarily had a supportive, maintenance role in a comparatively rigid framework. This department held an intermediate position – part of the 'glue' which held the balance between differentiation (allowing specialist tasks to be fulfilled by relatively expert people) and integration (combining all those tasks into a coordinated whole).

Nowadays organizations are structured more diversely and the people function has taken on a variety of forms. The diffusion of HRM ideas on the one hand and simple cost-cutting on the other have led to a move away from 'all-embracing' personnel departments in many companies, particularly in Scandinavia and the UK. Line managers have become more involved in activities such as selection, recruitment and performance appraisal. Typically, there is a division of work between various aspects of people management. Senior management may take responsibility for human resource strategy; line managers assume operational responsibility for their people; human resource specialists provide specific services ranging from administration to selection programmes and counselling.

In line with the fundamental HRM principles of comprehensiveness and coherence, the basic elements of people management must be interdependent. Supervision, recruitment and selection, training and development, reward systems and performance management cannot be considered in isolation. Each activity has implications for a number of other functions and subtly influences many more. Interactions throughout an organization's systems have to be assessed before making changes in any one function. The move away from permanent, nine-to-five jobs towards short-term contracts, part-timers and subcontracting offers a particular opportunity for human resource specialists with expertise in training, contracting and controlling workers in these categories.

Large organizations cannot be discussed as a homogeneous group. Their human resource and other management functions are dependent on the nature of their structures.

Organizational structures

Organizations can be regarded as people management systems. They range from simple hierarchies along traditional lines to complex networks dependent on computer systems and telecommunications. Structures may be relatively formal, following strict reporting lines. Alternatively, they may be based on informal working relationships. Structures are power and control systems that constrain or facilitate the freedom of employees to act and make decisions.

Chandler (1962) argued that structure follows on from strategy. Human resource managers can encourage strategies that foster both cost-effectiveness and employee commitment. Whether as line managers or specialist practitioners, they are able to use employee information and assessments to gauge the effectiveness of a particular structure. As managers they can influence or determine changes leading to improved employee performance and productivity. Organizational structures can be classified into a number of types, including functional, divisional, federations, matrix and networks.

Functional structures

Early organizational design divided enterprises into relatively simple parts, splitting them into defined activities such as production, marketing or personnel. This is still a common structure in medium-sized companies but it has become unusual in large (particularly multinational) organizations except, paradoxically, Japanese corporations (Sparrow and Hiltrop, 1994, p.284). Such a design normally divides human resource management between specialized activities dealt with by a designated department (Figure 7.1) and day-to-day aspects handled by the operational functions.

As we can see from Table 7.2, there are both advantages and disadvantages to such an arrangement. On the one hand, functional organizations are simple to understand with clear lines of command, specified tasks and responsibilities. Staff can specialize in a particular business area such as production or marketing and follow well-defined career paths. This is equally true of human resource specialists who can develop expertise in specific areas such as employee relations or reward management. Table 7.3 details a number of

Figure 7.1   Functional structures in HR

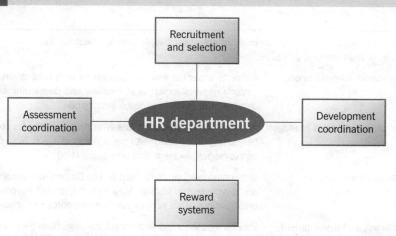

Table 7.2   HRM in functionally structured organizations

Principle	Range	Comment
1 Comprehensiveness	Different functions are likely to be treated differently	Specific people systems such as resourcing and training may be sophisticated
2 Coherence	Low–medium, as functional managers block or value different aspects, e.g. performance-related pay	Organization is divided into separate camps
3 Control	Split between functions	Some functions are more powerful than others
4 Communication	Good vertically within a function but dreadful horizontally between functions	Prone to 'us and them' misunderstanding and warfare between departments
5 Credibility	Promotion and reward policies not understood if they do not fit functional needs	Parochial view restricts comprehension of overall business objectives
6 Commitment	Focused on functional department, not whole organization	People march in different directions
7 Change	Structural change regarded as threatening	Managers fight to preserve departmental power
8 Competence	High at functional and individual levels	Limitations on developing generalists with all-round abilities
9 Creativity	Limited	Little cross-fertilization between functions
10 Cost-effectiveness	Can be good if management kept to minimal levels	Specialist managers expect professional rates: jealously between functions

Table 7.3	Specialist HR roles in large organizations

Role	Activity
Human resource director/manager	Head of specialist people management function.
Personnel administrator	Formerly a clerical function concerned with maintaining paper records. Latterly requires expertise in creating and developing computer databases of human resource information.
Employee relations manager	A long-standing specialist role with responsibility for collective bargaining and liaison with trade union officials. Now extends to employee involvement and communication.
Recruitment specialist	Less common than they used to be. Trained in interviewing techniques and psychometric testing. May be occupational psychologists in larger organizations. This activity is often outsourced to specialist firms.
Training and development specialist	Previously concerned with direct training. Now becoming an internal consultancy role. Often possessing a psychology qualification.
Human resource planner	Statistical and planning expert providing projections of human resource requirements for strategists.
Employee counsellor	Comparatively new but increasingly common role. May be part-time or outsourced. Requires counselling qualification and knowledge of stress reduction techniques. Typically replaces the welfare role of personnel management.
Health and safety officer	Ensures that legislation on workplace health and safety is complied with. Liaises with local authority and other enforcement officials.

Source: Adapted from Torrington and Hall (1995, p.18)

specialist roles performed by human resource specialists in functional and other large organizations.

However, there are also major disadvantages to functional structures. People managers have to tread carefully because this form of organization is prone to inter-departmental conflict, often degenerating into 'them and us' tribal warfare. Coherence and good communication are particularly hard to achieve between virtually independent functions. Moreover, HR development is complicated as it is difficult for individuals to gain a broad range of experience and an overview of the organization as a whole. Additionally, functional organizations have a tendency towards rigidity and ever-increasing layers of management. Since the 1980s, however, larger organizations of this type with tall and bureaucratic hierarchies have suffered the brunt of reorganization and de-layering. Our case study on the Home Products company provides a simple illustration of de-layering. Restructuring is further considered in a later chapter on human resource strategy.

HRM in reality

Home Products

Home Products came into existence in 1975 and grew to be a medium-sized importer and distributor of plastic and wood domestic goods. Spreading over the entire country, a network of distribution points and sales offices was gradually built up employing 80 staff. By the early 1990s the company began making heavy losses. Eventually, the managing director was replaced and management consultants brought in to recommend changes in the structure of the organization.

▶

The consultants examined the operation of the company in detail. They found a traditional, functionally split company with a low level of computerization and a high level of middle management for its size. They recommended the streamlining of the company, development of a team-based structure and investment in networked personal computers. Over a period of two years the company was transformed by eliminating expensive layers of management. Apart from financial savings, the improved communication and devolved decision making produced a higher quality of service to customers. Before and after organization charts are set out in Figure 7.2.

Figure 7.2	Tall versus flat hierarchy

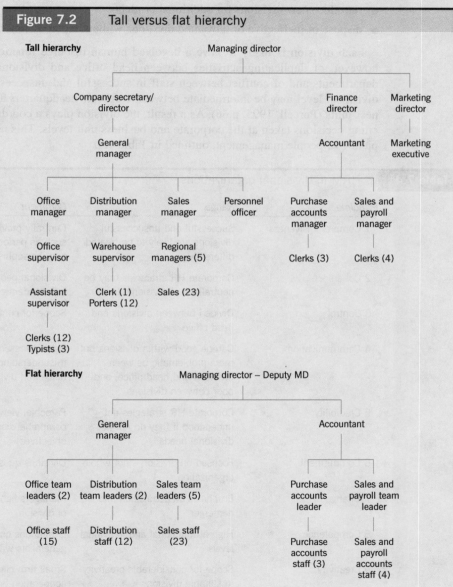

Source: Based on a real situation.

Discussion question: Summarize the advantages and disadvantages of both structures in your own words.

Divisional structures

Divisions may be based on specific products or product ranges, as in the pharmaceutical industry, or alternatively on a territorial basis.

Divisions encourage team spirit and identification with a product or region. Managers can develop broad skills as they have control of all basic functions. Performance of business units and their employees can be readily monitored because costs and productivity are tied to product or territory. This allows organizations to:

- increase investment with certainty
- introduce new divisions for additional products
- dispose of ineffective or unwanted divisions without repercussions on the remainder.

Each division is likely to have a devolved human resource function. There is a risk, however, of duplicating activities between head office and divisional human resource departments and of conflict between staff in successful and unsuccessful divisions. The divisional level may be intermediate between corporate headquarters and individual business units (Purcell, 1995, p.66). As a result, the division plays a coordinating role, reconciling decisions taken at the corporate and business unit levels. This results in a complex picture of people management, outlined in Table 7.4.

Table 7.4	HRM in divisional organizations	
Principle	*Range*	*Comment*
1 Comprehensiveness	Successful and unsuccessful divisions are likely to be treated differently	Centrally provided people systems such as performance management may be sophisticated
2 Coherence	Corporate HR strategies may be neutralized at divisional level	Divisional people managers behave independently
3 Control	Divided between divisions and head office	Scope for conflict and confusion
4 Communication	Can be good within divisions but more problematic between divisions and head office, and poor between divisions	Prone to resentments and misunderstandings between head office and divisions
5 Credibility	Corporate HR strategies not understood if they do not fit divisional needs	Parochial view restricts comprehension of overall business objectives
6 Commitment	Focused on division – not whole organization	Divisions quasi-independent
7 Change	Emphasis on acquisition and demerger	Managers fight to preserve integrity of division
8 Competence	High at functional and individual levels	Limitations on developing generalists with all-round abilities
9 Creativity	Scope for considerable creativity in suitable divisions	Small firm climate encourages cooperation between functions
10 Cost-effectiveness	Tendency for managerial/ administrative jobs to be duplicated	Little consistency between divisions

The key issue for people managers is the relationship between division and corporate head office. According to Purcell (1995, p.73) 'there are no obvious roles for a corporate personnel department'. A few large organizations do without HR specialists at this level but most assign a role, usually of a policy nature, to the centre. Hence central HR departments in companies such as Ford, Barclays and Sainsbury were comparatively large. This makes sense where the activities in different locations or divisions are closely related. In practice, the more diversified and unrelated the divisions, the more likely it becomes that HRM is fully devolved to divisional level. In very diverse conglomerates, even senior managers are recruited and developed locally.

Activity 7:4	What are the main differences between functional and divisional organization structures?

Federations

One variant of the divisional form which has a particular relevance because of its human resource implications is the 'federation', a loosely connected arrangement of businesses with a single holding company or separate firms in alliance. For example, the Cable & Wireless group functioned as a worldwide federation of equals with a small corporate centre. HRM operated on a partly formal, partly informal basis. The central human resource function offered an extensive support facility for international managers. This form of organization attracted criticism from stock market analysts who found difficulty in comprehending its subtle informality.

Matrix structures

As we have seen, both functional and divisional forms suffer from the 'them and us' problem between different parts of the organization. A number of large businesses have experimented with matrix structures to try and overcome these difficulties. Matrix structures focus on project teams, bringing skilled individuals together from different parts of the organization. Individuals are responsible to their line manager and to the project manager for different aspects of their jobs.

Their effectiveness is dependent not only on the provision of skilled people but also clear information on location and activities. This is difficult to achieve and many matrix experiments have resulted in failure, largely due to the 'matrix muddle': a general confusion of roles and responsibilities. Some activities may be duplicated because no one understands the structure and others may be neglected because it is assumed that someone else is responsible. Some of these difficulties have been overcome in more recent 'network' structures.

New structures

Older accounts of people management within organizations propose a highly structured, directive role for managers. This kind of management style and the rigid organizational context that it requires is inconsistent with the 'tight-loose' frameworks advocated by gurus such as Peters and Kanter. They propose new relationships that offer the flexibility to respond quickly to changing market demands but also allow retention of effective managerial control. Such organizations require a fine balance between centralization and decentralization. The key lies in organization design (see Key concept 7.7).

Organization design   The design of an organization patterns its formal structure and culture. It allocates purpose and power to departments and individuals. It lays down guidelines for authoritarian or participative management by its rigidity or flexibility, its hierarchical or non-hierarchical structure. Appropriate design is crucial to effective use of resources and long-term success and survival.

In recent years the emphasis has been towards differentiated but integrated organizations. This paradoxical view stresses that individuals work for the business rather than for specific departments that might compete rather than cooperate with each other. Communication and information distribution systems in earlier days were based on paper memos and reports. Paper-based systems could only work if functional activities were broken down into defined, quasi-independent sections.

Today, developments in telecommunications and computing allow raw or analyzed data to be collected electronically and distributed to any point in the organization. This makes it easier for an organization to be managed as a whole. As we have seen, such an organization is likely to be slimmed down, 'de-layered' and focused on core activities. Non-core functions, including HR activities such as recruitment and training, can be subcontracted. Integrated information technology allows previously unimagined control mechanisms and organizational forms. The boundaries between organizations become increasingly blurred and the nature of people management takes on a new and complex level of intricacy. For example, we can ask how one manages 'employees' who have no employment contract with one's own organization?

Managers, including human resource specialists and others, must play a new role. They cease to be checkers and order-givers. Instead they are more likely to become:

● enablers, structuring organizations to allow employees to achieve objectives

● empowerers, devolving decision making to the lowest level

● facilitators encouraging and assisting employees.

In such a context, people managers are no longer supervisors. Their organizations move from rigid hierarchies and power distinctions towards an environment where people take responsibility for their own work. Various forms of integrated structure are technically and ideologically feasible within relatively loose arrangements that encompass different organizations, agencies and specialist contractors.

Networks

In the context of organizational design, networks extend firms beyond their own boundaries. Focused organizations concentrate on core activities – those areas in which they believe they have particular strengths. Other functions are provided by subcontractors, which may be different business units within the firm or entirely independent providers. For example, one organization manufactures and sells its products but purchases its research, design and computing functions from other firms within the network. Snow, Miles and Coleman (1992) distinguish a number of network types:

● *Internal networks*. Comprised of business units, mostly owned by the parent organization, each specializing in one function. These units network with other internal units and also interact with external suppliers and customers. This is a development of the divisional system.

● *Stable networks*. Basically working to the core–periphery model of flexibility which we will consider later in this chapter. A small core of professional and managerial staff subcontracts most of its activities to external providers. Television stations frequently work on this basis.

- *Dynamic networks.* A further extension where the core acts as a broker for independent suppliers, producers and distributors.

In general, networking takes some familiar producer-wholesaler-distributor concepts, extends them into new industrial sectors and binds them into a seamless structure with no visible boundaries between individual parts of the network.

Human resource management takes on issues in networked structures that are outside the familiar bounds of the employee–employer relationship. Traditional personnel management is replaced by operational managers with strengths in people management – true 'human resource managers' (Thomson and Mabey, 1994, p.5). People managers in networked structures are diplomats, encouragers and resource-allocators. Table 7.5 outlines the main characteristics of HRM in network structures.

Virtual organizations

Advancing technology allows firms to extend the network concept to form enterprises with no permanent structures. They bring people together for specific projects. Teams dissolve on completion, to reappear in new combinations for other tasks. The network is composed

Table 7.5	HRM in networked organizations		
Principle	Range		Comment
1 Comprehensiveness	Dependent on design of organizational structure – is it formalized or ad hoc?		Flexibility of the organization allows expertise to be bought in for any need
2 Coherence	Amorphous nature of organization can lead to incoherence		Reward, performance and development systems apply to some, but not to others
3 Control	Project or customer-driven		Dependent on software systems
4 Communication	Tends to consist of informal connections forged to solve problems and achieve task goals		Self-managed and problem-solving approach leads to direct communication
5 Credibility	Evident that organization is there to meet project or customer needs		Emphasis on performance gives high credibility to the network
6 Commitment	Focused on project, not whole organization		No long-term commitment to the organization required
7 Change	Organization changes continuously		Structure and processes driven by customer needs
8 Competence	Focus on skilled knowledge workers		Dependent on identification and availability of most suitable people
9 Creativity	Emphasis on people devising their own approach to work		Freedom for creativity comes from self-management
10 Cost-effectiveness	Theoretically, human resources are perfectly matched to work		Minimal supervision requirement

of expert nodes. These are people who add value through their knowledge. Traditional hierarchical structures have no role in this model. Departments, divisions and offices disappear leaving an amorphous mass of people connected electronically and meeting only when required. Through web-based technology and teleworking, there is scope for considerable change in the nature of work.

HRM in reality

Almost 10 per cent of NSW workforce 'teleworks'

A recent survey by Australian Bureau of Statistics (ABS) showed that almost a quarter of a million (or 8 per cent) of New South Wales workers 'teleworked' in the three months to October 2001. Another 355 200 (12 per cent) worked at home after normal business hours.

According to the definition used by the ABS, teleworkers are people 15 years and over employed by a business not based at their own home but who worked at home during normal business hours for a full or part day. A person who worked at home after hours only is defined as someone who worked at home on weekends or took work home after normal business hours.

The majority of teleworkers were aged 35–44 years, with people aged 45–54 years accounting for the largest proportion of employed people who spent all day in the office then only worked at home after normal business hours.

In terms of numbers, nearly three-quarters (74 per cent) of teleworkers were in the private sector. But a greater proportion of public sector employees teleworked. Of those who worked for the government or public service 10 per cent teleworked, while 7 per cent of private sector employees teleworked.

Main reasons for teleworking were given as:

- 'work commitments/job requires it' (33 per cent)
- 'less distractions' (15 per cent)
- 'childcare/family considerations' (13 per cent)
- 'greater productivity' (12 per cent).

'Childcare and family considerations' were the main reason for 21 per cent of women, compared to just 7 per cent for men.

Teleworking employees used a variety of technological facilities that were supplied by either their employer or themselves while working at home. These included:

- the telephone (72 per cent of all teleworkers)
- mobile phone (68 per cent)
- internet (67 per cent)
- e-mail (65 per cent).

But more than a third of teleworking employees were not supplied with any equipment by their employer while they were working at home.

More than half a million people (566 700) employed in NSW do not do any work at home for their job or business, but reported that they would like to telework. Some 75 per cent said they did not telework at present because their type of work was not suitable and 13 per cent that employers were not allowing it.

Details are in *Teleworking, New South Wales, 2001* (Cat. No. 1371.1), Australian Bureau of Statistics.

Source: *HRM Guide Australia* (http://www.hrmguide.net/australia/), 2 May 2002.

Table 7.6	Summary of organizational structures		
Type	*Focus*	*Benefits*	*Disadvantages*
Functional	Department – e.g. sales, accounts, personnel	Simple to understand Clear lines of command Specialist expertise Career structures	Slow to react 'Us and them' Hierarchies tend to grow into vast pyramids Managers have difficulty in gaining organization-wide perspective
Divisional	Product or market, e.g. pharmaceuticals Geographical territory, e.g. brewing region	Self-contained units Can be evaluated separately Can be added to, closed or sold as wholes Team-based, loyalty to division and product Managers obtain overall experience	Conflict between divisional and organizational objectives Morale difficulties in unsuccessful divisions Duplication of functional activities, e.g. marketing, human resources
Matrix	Project or team	Strong focus on project, client objectives	Complex Conflict between reporting lines Conflict over allocation of resources
Federations	Loose relationship	Informal, flexible	Disliked by City commentators
Network	Nodes Individuals as resources	Talents focused on tasks Seamless organization – no departmental boundaries Open to external contributors	No job security Potentially anarchic

Activity 7:5 In what ways would the activities of human resource specialists differ between networked or virtual organizations and more traditional organizational structures?

Organizational strategies

If the purpose of organizations is to coordinate people's activities to achieve certain objectives, why do they go about it in such different ways and why are some organizations spectacularly poor at achieving their goals? A partial explanation comes from organizational design. This may be strategic or unplanned. Some organizations have come into being almost through accidents of history. Perhaps they started as small enterprises with individuals taking on regular or specialist roles, looking after stock, keeping financial records, going out to meet customers and so on. As the business expanded individual jobs grew into departments – following the same division of work; eventually, the original job-holders moved on but their functions remained to be carried out by other people. A mature organization is still shaped according to the skills and personalities of people who are no longer there.

Other organizations are designed in a particular way from their inception. Government departments may be set up to achieve a particular social purpose. Their objectives, form and operation will be determined by conscious thought. To some degree, organizing (patterning) of all enterprises is deliberate. Even the 'accidental organization' will be remodelled and reshaped at some time. As Torrington and Hall (1995, p.102) explain:

> For most people the organization is in a steady state of being not right: a pattern of working relationships bedevilled by inefficiency, frustration and obsolescence. For them organization design is a process of tinkering, pushing and shoving, achieving piecemeal improvements where possible and occasionally coping with a cataclysm – such as a need to shed half the workforce – that seems to leave the worst possible combination of human resources in its wake.

Some enterprises contain the remnants of a succession of reorganizations. Most large organizations are diversified. They operate in different product areas. In the free market model prevalent in English-speaking countries, this has happened mainly by acquisition of other firms. This has a number of implications on the overall organization of such firms. In many cases they will display 'hybrid' characteristics, preserving much of the character and structure of the original businesses. Such organizations are prone to inconsistencies and misunderstandings on people management issues.

Some strategists have insisted on the 'one best way' approach to organizational design, advocating a specific method. Conversely, others have preferred the contingency view which adopts the line of: 'it depends ...' Contingent strategies can range between two extremes: determination and strategic choice.

Determinism holds that critical variables are decisive. Woodward (1980) pointed to the importance of technology in determining the span of managerial control – how many staff one person can manage realistically – and therefore the organizational structure. The span of control is highest in mass production where activities are relatively predictable and a low number of managers is required. Another example is where environmental factors such as market or economic conditions determine which form of organization is most appropriate. Burns and Stalker (1961) advocated 'organic' – flexible and adaptive – forms of organization for periods of technological change; and 'mechanistic' (rigid) structures for stable, long-term processes.

At the other extreme is strategic choice. Essentially it is 'up to you!' based on your perception of the situation with no necessary constraints from external conditions. Peters and Waterman (1982) shifted the emphasis to people. Their concept of 'simultaneous loose and tight controls' advocated fuzzy (loose) controls over employee decision making, requiring tight adherence to the central mission of the enterprise. Mintzberg (1983) used the term 'adhocracy' to describe a flexible, fuzzy structure able to adapt its form continuously to meet changing circumstances. Three factors are particularly relevant:

- *Uniformity of organization*. A firm with one product range or branded outlet is likely to have a centralized human resource function to preserve a common approach.

- *Attenuation*. De-layered and otherwise slimmed-down companies have a limited number of specialist roles. Probably, there is a senior HR figure and administrators at clerical level but no specialist support in between. Line management has been given the bulk of people management activity.

- *Decision making*. Each organization has a decision-making style. This varies from democratic – as in cooperative organizations – to the autocratic where decisions are taken by the powerful or self-elected. Autocratic (centralized) decision making is common in small firms but it is seen also in large businesses where delegation (decentralized) is the more usual style.

Butler (1990) considers that decision making is the driving force of an organization. Its structure is the decision framework: the enduring set of decision rules that allow or constrain uncertainty. The elasticity of the rules produces a fuzzy (organic) or a crisp (mechanistic) structure so that fuzziness indicates the flexibility of the rules. Butler argues that every organization or part-organization should be designed to optimize the quality of managerial decision making. This can be done by selecting the appropriate degree of fuzziness or crispness, based on the uncertainty of the decisions involved.

A fuzzy structure eases decision making in conditions of high uncertainty. Correspondingly, decisions with relatively certain outcomes should be given comparatively crisp, if not rigid organizational structures. Further, an individual organization can have zones of relative fuzziness or crispness to reflect the differing functional decisions.

Crisp structures restrict the level of individual decision making. Fuzzy structures give a high degree of decision freedom, loosely determining:

- who can do what
- who is involved in decisions
- how operating procedures can vary
- who reports to whom
- how they are rewarded
- how much analysis is required for a decision.

As a consequence of such thinking, large firms may take on a variety of forms. An organization does not have to be homogeneous, with identical structures and processes throughout. It can take on varied characteristics to suit its activities in different parts of the firm. These activities can be classified into (Handy, 1993, p.201):

1 *Steady-state*. Routine, programmed activities typically making up 80 per cent of work in the average organization.
2 *Innovation*. Researching and developing new products and methods or opening new markets.
3 *Crisis*. The branch of management known as 'fire-fighting' or dealing with the unexpected, emergencies and industrial disputes.
4 *Policy*. Identifying goals, setting standards, allocating scarce resources and generally getting people to do things.

This implies also that: different people need to be employed to fit the requirements of these activities; these workers should be motivated in diverse ways; and management style needs to be tailored to the job and the personal characteristics of individual employees.

What does this mean for ordinary workers? Effectively, job satisfaction and personal challenge depend on specific situations within the organization. One finance clerk may have a domineering boss who does not allow her to make any decisions, whereas another will be given a considerable amount of discretion by a more trusting supervisor. However, the first clerk may have access to a powerful computer information system, allowing her to handle much greater sums of money. Overall, the first employee may feel the greatest sense of personal responsibility and self-importance.

Activity 7:6   Summarize the significance of decision making as a factor in organizational design.

As with any theoretical model, individual organizational theories simplify reality to an excessive degree. They miss out many of the intricacies that we experience in real organizations. From our discussion it has already become clear that organizations are not simply formal structures – they also consist of informal relationships, cultures, power allocations

Table 7.7	Organizational metaphors

Metaphor	Perspective
Organizations as machines	Working machines with visible structures, levels and routines. Typical of bureaucracies, providing continuity and security but limiting people's capacities by prescriptive regulations.
Organizations as organisms	Responsive, dynamic living things. As the environment changes the organization adapts to fit the new circumstances. Best for a fast-moving industry in uncertain market conditions.
Organizations as brains	An organization does more than respond, it appears to be inventive and rational, self-changing, an innovative learning system that is open to self-criticism. Akin to the 'learning organization' concept.
Organizations as cultures	The Deal and Kennedy definition of shared meanings, values and customs outlined in the next chapter. Cultures make each organization unique.
Organizations as political systems	Each organization has its own equivalent to a governmental ethos, which might be comparatively authoritarian or democratic. A recognition that it functions through processes of power and patronage, bargaining and negotiation, alliances and control of information.
Organizations as psychic prisons	Based on Plato's allegory of the people tied in a cave and ascribing meaning to shadows on the wall thrown by the fire. Similarly, people live with the organization's myths and believe in the representation they provide to the world. They are therefore constrained by the image which they have created.
Organizations as flux and transformation	Organizations are constantly in a process of change, the logic and conduct of which has to be understood.
Organizations as vehicles for domination	The recognition that organizations are coercive places.

Source: Based on Morgan (1986).

and political intrigues. People managers have to be aware of all these varied aspects at one and the same time.

Morgan (1986) offers us an alternative way of conceptualizing these complexities by providing us with the eight different metaphors described in Table 7.7. The metaphors reflect the essentially human and changing nature of organizations and can be used to provide an insight into organizational dynamics. Any business can be examined from a number of perspectives because any one organization can be a mix of two or three dominant metaphors.

The HR role in large organizations

Apart from the degree of differentiation, people management functions are affected by organizational strategies. Recent moves to de-layer large organizations and reduce the number of managers have affected HR specialists as much as anyone else. Their activities have been 'balkanized' or parcelled-up into discrete areas (Sisson, 1995, p.96), although this has 'mirrored developments in management more generally' (Sisson, 2001, p.78).

Based on information from a survey of nearly 100 large firms, Adams (1991) found that HRM was organized in a number of ways:

- Traditional 'personnel'-type departments providing a full range of HR services.
- In-house agencies, or cost centres, performing one or more activities such as recruitment. Their costs are automatically charged to client divisions or departments.
- Internal consultancies that 'sell' their activities to other parts of the organization, perhaps in competition with external services.
- Business within a business arrangements that provide an internal and an external service to clients inside and outside the organization.
- External consultancy arrangements, subcontracting HR activities to outside agencies.

By the late 1990s, based on the UK 1998 WERS data, Millward, Forth and Bryson (2000, p.80) could state that: 'One of the most significant changes is that the people responsible for managing employee relations in 1998 were quite different from those who were managing it at the beginning of the 1980s.'

Specifically, responsibility for HRM had shifted away from general managers to HR specialists and line managers. And HR specialists were better qualified: whereas 57 per cent held personnel management qualifications in 1980, this had increased to 72 per cent in 1998. Conversely, Cully *et al.* (1999) found that 30 per cent of workplaces had never given supervisors training in people management skills and a further 25 per cent only gave it to a few. They also noted that use of external sources of expertise, such as ACAS and employment lawyers, had increased from a third to over half of workplaces between 1980 and 1998.

Marginson *et al.* (1993a) differentiated between UK-owned and foreign-owned organizations in the UK. Foreign-owned companies tended to move their managers between divisions in different companies and to grade them on the same rating scales. They were more likely than British companies to have a central department responsible for training and development. Twice as many foreign-owned companies had HR directors on their main board in comparison with British-owned firms. In fact, Cully *et al.* (1999) noted a reduction from 73 per cent to 64 per cent of overall board HR representation between 1980 and 1998. Similarly, HR specialists were twice as common (57 per cent) in non-UK owned workplaces than British-owned (27 per cent) according to the UK 1998 WERS data. Foreign-owned companies were also much more likely to spend money on training and communication and to have a corporate committee of senior managers to establish HR policies (Marginson *et al.*, 1993b).

Activity 7:7	Using the UK as an example, how has the organization of the human resource function changed over the last few decades?

Flexibility

Quoting Wood (1989, p.1):

> In Japan ... it began after the 1973 oil shock ... [and] has recently concentrated on how to handle reductions in labour demand, whereas in the USA attention has especially centred on changing work rules which are thought to inhibit intra-organizational job mobility. In Britain ... much of the concern has been with the balance between non-standard and regular contracts.

Sociologists have long perceived industrialization as a process leading through a sequence from agriculture, to heavy industry to service economies. In Chapter 2 we noted that the process is particularly visible in the older industrial countries such as the UK and the USA. These countries are described sometimes as 'post-industrial' in that the service element of their economies is a bigger proportion than manufacturing. This is reflected in the nature of employment which has changed from predominantly manual and blue-collar jobs to white-collar. Work has have been revolutionized by the introduction of information technology which puts a premium on skilled, competent 'knowledge workers'.

We have already observed that one of the most pronounced trends in recent years has been the replacement of full-time, long-term jobs with other types of positions. These include part-timers, 'temps', consultants, franchisees and so on. Business strategies have focused increasingly on flexible working in order to reduce employee costs of products and services (see Key concept 7.8). As we saw, this is exemplified in the concept of the virtual organization.

Key concept 7:8

Flexibility   The concept covers a combination of practices that enable organizations to react quickly and cheaply to environmental changes. In essence, flexibility is demanded from the workforce in terms of pay, contractual rights, hours and conditions, and working practices. This extends to the employment market, requiring job-seekers to show a willingness to move location, change occupation and accept radically different terms of employment.

Flexibility has become a much-quoted term. Neo-liberal politicians argue that, at the environmental level, competitiveness comes from the reduction of perceived 'rigidities' in the employment market. Rigidities in the job market have been pinpointed as causes of industrial decline and flexibility has become an unquestioned 'good'. Rigidity includes lack of mobility, refusal to accept new conditions, unorthodox working hours and so on. By scrapping minimum pay rates, removing legislation that limits employers' rights to hire and fire, and generally deregulating the job market, they believe that businesses will achieve the maximum degree of competitiveness.

HRM in reality

Flexible working reduces absenteeism

New research reported by the Industrial Society indicates that flexible working patterns can help to reduce absenteeism. *Managing Attendance*, the Industrial Society's recent survey report on absence, shows that absence rates fell from an average of eight days per employee to 6.5 days during the last 18 months among almost 300 firms surveyed: 49 per cent of survey respondents linked this improvement to having flexible annual leave; 40 per cent to the ability to work from home on occasions; and 55 per cent to flexible working hours.

HR specialists from 292 organizations were surveyed, including Boots the Chemist, Inland Revenue, London Underground, Norfolk Probation Service, Sheffield City Council and Vauxhall. Absence reporting is becoming more common: 40 per cent of surveyed organizations report all absences with an additional 33 per cent reporting nine out of ten instances. Overall, this is an increase of 8 per cent since 1999 but, strangely, there has been a reduction in the number of firms who measure the cost of absenteeism, from 54 per cent of organizations in 1996 to 41 per cent now.

Reported reasons for absences have not changed, with 91 per cent of employees reporting time off for flu or colds, 74 per cent giving stomach upsets or food poisoning as the reason for being off sick and 54 per cent citing headaches or migraines. But employers felt that only 65 per cent cited colds and flu as the main reason for employee absence with 43 per cent blaming stress and emotional problems. Some

37 per cent of HR specialists also thought that a proportion of sickness absence was due to the need for employees to take time off to look after a child or other family member.

Motivation (64 per cent) and return-to-work interviews (63 per cent) were cited by employers as the most effective ways of managing attendance.

According to Theo Blackwell, Policy Specialist at the Industrial Society, 'Left unchecked, absenteeism hits productivity and erodes morale in organisations. Firms should regularly examine the causes of absence and take appropriate action – by promoting workplace well-being or flexible working practices.' He added that:

> This report provides even more evidence of the business case for flexible working. According to HR professionals more flexibility seems to equal less time off sick and a healthier, happier and more loyal workforce. Now the government's new Taskforce on Flexible Working has yet more evidence backing up the business case behind a meaningful legal right for employees to have their request to change the terms of their contracts considered fully and fairly by the employer.

Source: *HRMGuide.co.uk* (http://www.hrmguide.co.uk), 12 July 2001.

Simplistically, it can be argued that the terms have an implicit political agenda: rigidity equates with worker protection and therefore left-wing, socialist attitudes; flexibility matches with hard HRM, exploitation of workers and hence a right-wing, capitalist approach.

Flexibility takes a number of forms:

- *Numerical flexibility*. Matching employee numbers to fluctuating production levels. This is difficult to achieve with 'regular' workers on full-time, long-term contracts.
- *Functional flexibility*. Abolishing demarcation rules and skill barriers so that workers can take on a variety of jobs.
- *Pay flexibility*. Offering different rates of pay for the same work – depending on geographical location and skills availability.

A further requirement is 'flexible specialization'. Consumer demand increasingly reflects individual tastes. Purchasers want an ever-wider choice of goods, making it difficult, if not impossible for mass production techniques to satisfy the market. The Fordist assembly line is outmoded – even if it does offer cars in colours other than black. Producers must switch equipment and employees from one product to another in a flexible but economic way. Staff must have versatile skills. Proponents of flexible specialization hold that mass production – the dominant industrial force of the 20th century – along with Taylorism and Fordism is obsolete. Organizations will become like major Japanese businesses. They will employ a multi-skilled, highly flexible core workforce able to turn their hands to a wide variety of tasks.

HRM in reality

Flexible working is increasing

At a special briefing on the future of flexible working, the Industrial Society refuted employer claims that the legal right to flexible working is likely to harm business competitiveness.

A recent Industrial Society survey of 516 human resource specialists found that 91 per cent of respondents' organizations use some form of flexible working. This

◄

compares with 84 per cent in 1998. Around 75 per cent of respondents said that flexible working made good business sense for the organization, with almost two-thirds (63 per cent) saying that it builds trust, loyalty and commitment. But many businesses (31 per cent) apply flexible working practices only at an informal level. The Industrial Society argues that there is a risk that informal policies can short-circuit employee consultation and lead to inconsistencies.

Other, less significant problems may prejudice some employers against the concept, including:

- communication difficulties (cited by 43 per cent of respondents)
- difficulty in managing varying working arrangements (31 per cent)
- and resentment from staff on standard contracts (27 per cent).

Theo Blackwell, Industrial Society policy specialist says:

Our survey shows that far from seeing flexible working as burdensome, the vast majority of employers already recognize the compelling business case in favour of flexible working. Yet in too many organizations flexible working arrangements are informal and patchwork. Firms practising flexible working should do so in the open, through formal policies which clearly explain their stance on flexibility. This will make the change to flexible working easier for employers and help to manage some of the transitional problems sometimes associated with working flexibly.

The challenge of the Work and Parent Taskforce is to develop a legal right that can be easily understood by employers and employees alike, and help shift workplaces from informality to clarity on flexible working.

Christine Gowdridge, Director of Maternity Alliance added:

The Taskforce has the opportunity to establish a straightforward right which will make flexible working an everyday reality benefiting mothers, fathers, employers and children. We hope they respond to employers' genuine concerns in a constructive way, but not to unfounded fears that flexible hours will harm business. This is a rare chance to transform working lives and must not be lost.

Source: *HRMGuide.co.uk* (http://www.hrmguide.co.uk), 28 August 2001.

Activity 7:8	What do you understand by 'flexibility'? Is it becoming more prevalent?

Atkinson's (1984) 'flexible firm' model combines flexibility with Japanese concepts of 'core' and 'peripheral' workforces (see Figure 7.3). Core workers are employed on standard contracts. Peripheral workers are employed by subcontractors, or on short-term contracts. However, Atkinson's model does without mutual obligations essential to the Japanese system: core workers provide functional flexibility – but without lifelong employment; peripheral workers and subcontractors are not rewarded with close, long-term relationships.

Against a background of high unemployment, workers have been forced to accept a reduction in employment rights, unsociable working hours, short-term contracts and lower pay rates. This is a development that has occurred throughout the industrialized world. It has been driven by competition – particularly from the Japanese – whose production techniques embody a process of continuous improvement. It is also a development that has attracted a considerable degree of theoretical and ideological debate. Flexibility enables

Figure 7.3	Core and peripheral workers

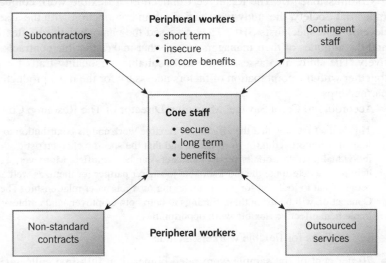

organizations to react quickly and cheaply to environmental changes. In free market countries there is a trend towards replacing full-time, long-term jobs with other employment relationships. Nevertheless, this is still a minority situation. For example, in the UK 70 per cent of workers have been employed by the same organization for over 20 years.

The idea of flexibility has definitely taken root but its theoretical basis has weaknesses. On the one hand, it is consistent with the concept of the 'virtual organization' discussed earlier, forming and re-forming to meet particular demands. Conversely, it is doubtful that we are really moving to a 'world of quasi-bespoke production concerned with gratifying fleeting market whims' (Hyman, 1988). Rather, niche marketing is concerned with defined 'varieties' of mass produced products. Consumers are not purchasing unique cars made to their specific requirements, but red 2.0 litre GL models, or white 1.3 litre basic models from a controlled choice – built in factories that Henry Ford would find recognizable. The availability of such varieties has more to do with computer-controlled robots, switchable from one program to another, than with a flexible, multi-skilled workforce.

Further problems arise in practice. Where are the necessary skilled people supposed to come from? A true transition to total flexibility requires a system for training non-permanent workers. Most employers are not equipped to provide this. Companies in countries such as Australia and the UK have been heavily criticized for under-investing in training their permanent employees. Ironically, the same countries have a weak record of providing such training on a national basis as well. We will return to this issue in our discussion of training and development.

HRM in reality	**Work–life balance boosts the bottom line**

Research released at today's British Psychological Society conference demonstrates that senior executives who can work flexibly perform better than full-time managers.

Flexible working and job sharing have not been widespread among the UK's managers but a new study shows that those who can make use of flexitime, reduced hours or home working can improve their performance significantly. In fact the study reveals that managers of both flexible and job sharing executives give them higher output ratings than their full-time equivalents.

▶

Commissioned by The Resource Connection, a flexible work company, and the Industrial Society, the study was carried out in conjunction with the assessment and development specialists SHL. They assessed the characteristics of flexible workers and the attitudes of their managers to see what makes flexible contracts work effectively. The study also assessed the most suitable personality traits for job sharers, together with the combination of factors necessary for the most productive job share partnerships.

According to Carol Savage, Managing Director of The Resource Connection:

> This is the first time that the efficacy of flexible work and its contribution to the bottom line has been proved through research, and that the specific characteristics that determine individual flexible workers versus jobsharers can be identified. Moreover, we are able to help people determine the most suitable jobsharer partner for them, as well as showing people what to look out for when embarking on a jobsharer relationship. The Resource Connection will be using these findings to help both employers and employees implement effective flexible work opportunities.

Key findings for flexible workers included:

- 70 per cent of the sample were rated higher than full-time colleagues, and their own output in previous full-time work
- 60 per cent were given very good/excellent rankings at problem solving and analysis
- 60 per cent were rated very good/excellent at resilience in the face of setbacks
- higher ratings on resilience, leadership and commitment than their full-time equivalents.

For job sharers:

- 70 per cent of job sharing executives were perceived to have 30 per cent increased output over one person doing the same job
- job sharers were rated highly on problem solving, teamwork and flexibility.

Karen Janman, Head of Assessment at SHL UK said:

> This research is especially exciting as it provides invaluable insight to employers and employees alike about characteristics that best suit an individual to job share or more individual flexible working. This vital information can then be used to form the basis of the management, coaching and developmental process.

And Dr John Knell, Deputy Director of Futures, the Industrial Society, commented:

> There have been two significant barriers to flexible working among senior managers. Firstly, employers find it very hard to believe that flexible working amongst their senior executives can work. Secondly, senior managers often regard making such a request as 'career death'. This research knocks both these misconceptions on the head. To show that work life balance and high performance can go hand in hand will be a significant contribution to the work life debate, but the research also has significant implications for working in a globalized 24-hour society.

Source: *HRMGuide.co.uk* (http://www.hrmguide.co.uk), 4 January 2001.

Summary

Organizations are taking increasingly divergent forms but the key dimensions of size and structure still constrain the people function. HRM is conducted in a variety of ways, partly due to these constraints but also because of strategic decisions taken to meet organizational goals. Businesses can choose to vary their structures and their people management systems for a number of reasons. Increasingly, flexibility is required from employees and managers to meet new circumstances. Centralized personnel departments have been largely replaced with more specialized units, some of which may be subcontracted outside the organization. Nevertheless there are opportunities for human resource specialists dealing with complex issues arising from new organizational structures and flexible working patterns. These include contract arrangements, selection, control, assessment and training.

Further reading

The literature on large organizations is vast. *Organization Theory and Design* by Richard L. Daft, South-Western College Publishing, 7th edition (2000) is a classic in its field. *Competing by Design: The Power of Organizational Architecture* by David Nadler and Michael L. Tushman, Oxford University Press, 2nd edition (1997) links organizational design to competitive advantage. *Re-Creating the Corporation: A Design of Organizations for the 21st Century* by Russell Lincoln Ackoff, Oxford University Press (1999) treats organizations as organic wholes. *Understanding Organizations* by Charles Handy, Oxford University Press, 4th edition (1993) remains the most user-friendly introduction to organization theory.

Review questions

1 What are the principal dimensions by which organizations vary? What are the implications for the management of their human resources?

2 What are the major differences between the following types of organization: (a) functional structures; (b) divisional structures; and (c) networked organizations? How is people management likely to be organized in each of these? What priorities and constraints will human resource specialists experience within each type of structure?

3 Discuss the consequences of advances in information technology on business organization and the work of employees.

4 How would you implement a major reorganization in a large company involving a change from a tall, hierarchical structure to a flatter organization based on self-managing teams?

5 What are the advantages and disadvantages of flexibility to employees and employing organizations? Is total flexibility possible?

6 Distinguish between numerical and functional flexibility. How would demands for flexibility differ between organizations in the following sectors: (a) public service, e.g. local government; (b) production; (c) retailing; (d) the hotel industry.

7 What opportunities are there for human resource specialists in diversified, flexible organizations?

Problem for discussion and analysis

Rapid Supply Company

The Rapid Supply Company is a large electronic and mechanical parts wholesaler, supplying independent outlets throughout the country. The company purchases and distributes items from manufacturers throughout the world, supplying many to special order. The progress department chases orders from placement to delivery. Dealing with customers, warehouse and manufacturers, the department has to maintain a careful and diplomatic relationship with both suppliers and customers.

As a wholesaling organization, Rapid Supply credits its success to the ability to obtain and deliver a wide range of parts. Five years ago the company was purchased by its managers from a large multinational conglomerate. The business has thrived due to the determination and hard work of managers and key staff. Its market share has increased by 30 per cent in the last two years. The catalogue range of parts has grown extensively with an additional 53 listed manufacturers.

The owners and the venture capital company supporting the organization have decided to float the business on the stock market next year. This will allow them to realize a proportion of their investment and will make millionaires of the senior executives. To maximize the potential share value of the company, their advisers have recommended a number of cost-cutting efficiency exercises. These include a reduction in warehouse stocks, increasing the proportion of items supplied to special order.

The progress department is divided into two sections: the five record clerks enter changes and information from manufacturers onto individual order records; the six order-chasing clerks deal with telephone and postal enquiries from customers. The former lead a comparatively peaceful life, steadily working through the daily pile of paper acknowledgements and amendments. In contrast, the order-chasing clerks have a hectic existence, barraged with phone calls and emails, frequently experiencing abuse from irate customers. The department's work has increased considerably over the last two years but staff levels have been held down. Progress is managed by Julie Dee, a tough, self-resilient and detached person. She is polite but adamant with customers and staff, and can rebuff the most irate client. She seems to have an impenetrable shell. Around her, young employees wilt and fall under the onslaught of enquiries. The average length of employment is three to four months but there are a few experienced people who have worked in the department for several years.

Most enquiries are from customers requesting updates on delivery of their goods. The order-chasers first check goods-inwards records to see if the items have arrived. If they have been received, customers are forwarded to the despatch section to arrange a delivery date. More often, the parts have not arrived, requiring onward phone calls to the manufacturers and return calls to customers. At its simplest, a progress enquiry can be dealt with during the customer's first telephone conversation; at its worst, a succession of calls might be required over several days. Matters are complicated by delays elsewhere in the system. There is no guarantee that the goods are not in the warehouse even if they are shown as 'not arrived' on the computer screen. They might not have left the manufacturer, may be in transit, or have actually arrived at the warehouse but not been recorded as yet.

Order-chasing irritates other staff and the suppliers. There have been complaints from manufacturers about progress calls from Rapid Supply regarding parts that were delivered to the warehouse days ago. An instruction has been sent around stating that progress clerks must check with the warehouse first, before going on to the manufacturers. This has caused a great deal of friction between progress and the warehouse. Progress staff complain about the apparent slowness of recording receipt of goods; the warehouse complains of being pestered about parts which sometimes are not due for several days. There is a further conflict with the despatch clerk whose telephone is frequently engaged for lengthy periods. Similar problems are experienced with suppliers, often needing several calls, emails or fax messages in order to obtain an answer. Manufacturers require their own acknowledgement numbers to be quoted: sometimes these have been entered incorrectly, or not entered at all, by the records clerks.

Progress clerks have a difficult role to play and run the risk of upsetting everyone they deal with. Customers become irate if:

- The progress telephone system is engaged.

- They are put on hold and lines take a long time to answer because they are dealing with other enquiries.

- They cannot be provided with an immediate answer.

Progress staff become frustrated when:

- As soon as one customer is cleared, another comes onto the line, making it impossible to deal promptly with the first enquiry (this could be true for a whole succession of calls).

- On particularly busy days, especially when staff are missing for any reason, it proves impossible to follow up all the calls; as a consequence many customers phone back, increasing the overall volume of calls and making it even more difficult to deal with enquiries.

As the work level has grown, individual enquiries have increasingly trailed from one day to another. Enquiries by email, fax and post do not seem quite as urgent and tend to be left to last. This has made some valued customers extremely cross, demanding to speak to the manager. Julie now spends much of her time dealing with complaints about the service received from her staff.

The marketing department have completed a customer survey which shows high levels of dissatisfaction with the progress department. The senior managers are furious and have seconded you to work alongside Julie and 'sort things out'. What will you do?

8 | HRM in small and medium-sized organizations

Objectives

The purpose of this chapter is to:

- Outline the nature of entrepreneurship.
- Evaluate the consequences of business growth on human resource practice.
- Discuss research findings on human resource management in small and medium-sized businesses.
- Consider the consultancy as a special instance of the small business.

HRM in smaller organizations

Serious appreciation of HRM in small to medium-sized enterprises (SMEs) is a comparatively recent phenomenon. HRM researchers have largely ignored the SME sector, preferring to concentrate on large organizations with recognizable 'personnel' structures (Hendry, 1994, p.106). Yet the SME sector is an important aspect of any country's economy, already employing large numbers of people and embodying future growth potential. But the information available on people management in these organizations is sparse. Researchers attempting to investigate the topic have found access difficult, largely because small business owners are busy and perhaps regard academics with some suspicion. However, smaller companies should be fruitful subjects for study because many conduct people management in the direct fashion advocated by HRM models.

HRM in reality

Around 40 per cent of new jobs created by small businesses

Small businesses hired twice as many people as large companies during the first six months of 2002, according to CIBC. And, over the last 12 months, 40 per cent of all new jobs in Canada were generated by small businesses.

The study released by Benjamin Tal, senior economist of CIBC World Markets, indicated that firms with fewer than 20 employees increased their labour forces by 2.8 per cent compared with the first six months of 2001. This compares with an increase of just 1.2 per cent in employment at companies with more than 500 employees.

Tal's study seems to explain reports of strong growth in the Canadian employment market despite massive lay-offs after the bursting of the 'tech bubble'. 'Downsizing in large firms has given small business owners a golden opportunity to tap into a new pool of workers,' says Tal. 'And small business owners are capitalizing on it, especially in the case of highly skilled workers.'

In fact, growth in the number of professional employees in small businesses is dramatic, showing an increase of 9 per cent during the first six months of 2002. This is three times the rate of growth in total small business hiring.

Arguing that small business is often the bell-wether of changes in the overall economy, Rob Paterson, a senior vice-president who has worked for six years in CIBC's small business group, notes: 'Small business tends to be the first to experience the effect of an economic downturn, and the first to respond positively to a pick-up in economic recovery. Therefore, the fact that small business activity is accelerating is good news for all of us.'

Source: *HRM Guide Canada* (http://www.hrmguide.net/canada/), 10 July 2002.

International research

Aldrich (2000) summarizes international research on entrepreneurship:

- Entrepreneurship research, while improving, is still of limited topical concern and value to entrepreneurs.
- Research on entrepreneurship has developed in partial isolation between Europe and North America. Surprisingly, government and foundation support has been greater in Europe.
- Research on both sides of the Atlantic has a strong normative and prescriptive orientation. European researchers focus on fieldwork while North American

researchers prefer survey methods. But North American researchers tend to assume that their findings have universal applicability whereas European researchers show an awareness of national differences.

● Entrepreneurship as a research field includes scholars of many different disciplines and each views entrepreneurship from their own academic perspective.

Aldrich observes that entrepreneurship research in both continents has four common features:

1 Research on entrepreneurship and research on organizations has developed separately to a considerable extent, so that similar disputes have been repeated between the two sets of researchers in both cases.

2 The strong normative and prescriptive approach has meant that they have kept in close touch with practitioners and policy makers.

3 They have concentrated on description rather than hypothesis-testing although there is now a trend towards model-building.

4 There has been a focus on established businesses to the neglect of the start-up and growth phases.

Aldrich observes that organization studies in North America had moved from sociology and psychology departments into the business schools by the 1990s. The same trend appears to be taking place in Europe in the following decade.

Business start-ups

'It's important to understand that the rewards of small business ownership are not instantaneous. You must be ready to defer gratification and make sacrifices to ensure the rewards eventually do come' (Lesonsky, 2001, p.14).

One in ten adults in the US today has started a business. Australia is not far behind with one in 12, and Brazil is ahead with one in eight according to the *Global Entrepreneurship Monitor, 2000*. By contrast, the older established countries are less entrepreneurial: for example, Germany (one in 25), the UK (one in 33), Finland and Sweden (one in 50) and Ireland and Japan (fewer than one in 100).

What is an entrepreneur (see Key concept 8.1) and why do people start businesses?

Key concept 8:1

Entrepreneurship   A classic definition of entrepreneurship is provided by Timmons (1994, p.7): 'Entrepreneurship is the process of creating or seizing an opportunity and pursuing it regardless of the resources currently controlled.'

HRM in reality

Would-be entrepreneurs

Some 40 per cent of Australians would like to be self-employed and/or their own boss, according to a new survey by global recruitment agency, Kelly Services.

A total of 3000 people were surveyed in four countries – Australia, New Zealand, Malaysia and Singapore. New Zealanders were most enthusiastic about becoming entrepreneurs with 50 per cent stating they would like to be self-employed and/or their own boss; followed by Malaysia (48 per cent), Singapore (42 per cent) and Australia (40 per cent).

Among the Australian respondents, men wanted to be their own bosses more than women – 44 per cent against 38 per cent. People in the 25–34 age group were most attracted to self-employment with 42 per cent wanting to become their own boss/self-employed.

According to managing director of Kelly Services, Garie Dooley, the findings point to a trend of increasing entrepreneurialism from people who would once have been happy to remain employees:

> New technology and the internet have opened up a host of opportunities which would previously have been unattainable without the significant resources of a large firm. It is possible for many people to set up a business with little more than a mobile phone and an internet connection. They are able to operate with a minimum of overheads and resources; they can stay in touch with their customers; and even promote themselves globally at relatively low cost.

Another question on the survey asked employees if they were to receive the offer of a very attractive job with the security of a contract, how long they would sign it for? Around 67 per cent of Australian respondents said they would sign it for five years or less. Just 12 per cent would sign it for 10 years or longer. Women were less likely than men to commit to a long-term contract.

The youngest respondents were the least willing to commit themselves, even for an attractive job. A mere 5 per cent of 15–19 year olds, 7 per cent of 20–24 year olds, and 6 per cent of 25–34 year olds were willing to sign a contract for ten years or more for an attractive job. This compared with 19 per cent for 35–44 year olds and 40 per cent for those aged 55 and older.

'We are seeing employees much more prepared to change their careers and their jobs and this appears to be the result of personal choice, not because it will be forced upon them,' Garie Dooley said 'Employees seem to have embraced the end of the job for life and they are certainly not prepared to give their undying loyalty to one employer, even where the job package is considered very attractive.'

Participants in the survey were also asked to rate their chances of becoming unemployed at some time in the future. Queensland respondents were most concerned about their futures with 13 per cent imagining they will be unemployed at some point in the future. This was followed by New South Wales (12 per cent), Victoria (11 per cent), South Australia (10 per cent) and Western Australia (8 per cent). Those aged over 55 were the most uncertain about their jobs with almost 20 per convinced of facing near-term unemployment.

Source: *HRM Guide Australia* (http://www.hrmguide.net/australia/), 17 May 2002.

According to Stolze (1999, p.13):

> Long ago I read one author's comment that, 'Entrepreneurship is a profession for which there is no apprenticeship.' No matter how many books you have read, no matter how many courses or seminars you attend, no matter how much advice you get from 'experts', no matter how many small companies you work for, there is no substitute for the actual experience of doing it yourself.

Catlin and Matthews (2001, p.6) list the following classic entrepreneurial strengths:

- vision and a pioneering spirit
- being able to see possibilities where others do not
- always searching for new opportunities and challenges

- possessing energy and passion
- having a drive to succeed and achieve results with high standards of excellence
- being creative – idea generators, able to 'think out of the box'
- constantly striving to do things better
- proactive and focused on the future
- intelligent, capable and decisive
- having a strong sense of urgency
- confident about taking risks
- problem solvers seeking new challenges and believing that nothing is impossible
- a determination to succeed, be wealthy or 'make a difference'

Stolze (1999, p.16) divides the reasons why entrepreneurs start businesses into two categories: reactive reasons and active reasons. Reactive reasons are negatives that push people out of working for other people; active reasons are the positives that pull people towards the idea of working for themselves.

Reactive reasons include:

1 *Inequity between contribution and reward.* People who are high achievers tend not to enjoy working in large organizations. According to Stolze: 'They want rewards based on accomplishment – not on seniority, conforming to the corporate culture, or political clout.'

2 *Promotion and salary policy.* Large organizations tend to categorize people and mavericks do not fit the conventional promotional paths and salary bands.

3 *Adversity.* One of the commonest reasons – basically, job insecurity. When the job is not safe, people tend to think about alternatives. According to Stolze: 'I get very upset when a young college graduate seems unduly concerned about a retirement plan, fringe benefits and so forth. Long ago, I concluded that there is only one kind of job security that means anything – your ability to get another job fast.' Redundancies may also mean severance packages, allowing people to fund their own businesses.

4 *Red tape and politics.* Stolze says they are 'shortcomings of all large organizations that drive the entrepreneurial type bananas. Politicians and bureaucrats are rarely entrepreneurs.'

5 *Champion of orphan products.* Those of us who have cared about products or services outside the mainstream can understand how negative a large organization can be about 'orphan products'. This can be a first step towards the entrepreneurial leap.

Active reasons include:

1 *Wanting to be one's own boss.* According to Stolze: 'Many entrepreneurs have personality traits that make it difficult (if not impossible) for them to work for others.' Running their own business is the only solution. But also, there is the opportunity of professional satisfaction, seeing a job through, using time more flexibly, and so on.

2 *Fame and recognition.* Stolze does not consider this to be a common reason for starting a business, considering that there are 'more extrovert egotists' in established large organizations. In fact, he believes that starting one's own business is often a lesson in humility.

3 *Participation in all aspects of a business.* The all-round experience is elating and challenging. Being able to see the whole picture is more interesting than being one 'cog in the wheel'.

4 *Personal financial gain*. This can be important for some people, but not all. Potentially, the gains are much greater than normal wages.

Lesonsky (2001) considers that, according to surveys and research, entrepreneurs share some common personality traits – confidence being the most important. They have confidence in themselves, in their ability to sell their ideas, set up their own businesses, and trust in their intuition. Confidence is essential in the fiercely competitive world of small business. The value of confidence is shown in a commonly held belief that the critical determinant of entrepreneurship is the ability to raise significant amounts of money from investors: 'If you can make people believe in your dreams and share your goals so that they are willing to invest hard-earned cash in your venture, chances are you have what it takes' (Lesonsky 2002, p.14).

Activity 8:1	Are entrepreneurs special people?

HRM in reality	**New Deal creates jobs in Britain**

Kerry Marks, a 24-year-old from Brighton, unemployed on and off since leaving school, now runs her own business, Squeaky Clean, with three employees because of New Deal. She says:

> I can't believe what has happened in the last couple of years. I've changed so much. Before I had nothing to my name and had a problem sticking any job out. I couldn't handle it when they started to order me around. In the new year I'll need to take on another member of staff. I don't think that I have ever been as happy as I am now.

Similarly, Sam Robinson from Huddersfield joined the New Deal self-employment programme after six months of unemployment. He was given help writing his business plan and also conducting basic research before launching a specialist website (http://www.allballs.co.uk) selling sports balls, rackets and accessories. The site sells all over the world: 'I have shipped products to Portugal, Bermuda, Malaysia, Indonesia and Japan,' says Sam. Sam feels that starting your own company can be a lonely experience. Support from the New Deal helped him stay motivated and he continues to meet the programme advisers regularly. 'The ongoing support has proved invaluable,' he says.

According to Employment Minister Tessa Jowell, the New Deal scheme is helping to create new jobs in addition to helping unemployed people find work:

> New Deal is an individually tailored programme that aims to meet the hopes and aspirations of young people. The programme has helped over 2600 people kick-start business, with almost 600 now independent self-employed entrepreneurs. A key element of this programme is the level of support New Deal clients receive before they go it alone. They are put in touch with a business mentor, they receive a £400 grant and training towards a relevant qualification and using their training provider to co-manage their accounts.

The scheme works through three stages:

- Stage 1 – a one-day awareness raising session
- Stage 2 – a four-day course/counselling which leads to production of a business plan
- Stage 3 – (test trading) taking place as part of the Employment Option.

On Stage 3, participants get a training allowance and 'passported' benefits; a £400 grant; help from a business mentor; training towards an approved qualification; and co-management of their own trading account with the training provider acting as joint signer of cheques.

New Deal also meets the needs of more-established employers. More than 81 500 businesses have signed up to New Deal and all but 500 of these are small or medium-sized enterprises. Steve Hickling is one such employer. He set up World of Koi 15 years ago. His company imports ornamental fish from Japan, selling them on to British customers, as well as constructing and maintaining specialist ponds for his customers' fish. According to Steve: 'My experience of schemes such as YTS and Work Experience left me disillusioned. I felt that there was a lack of support and back-up. It's time consuming and costly to train a young person into a fully function-ing member of staff, especially when you're a small company like ours.' After a poor response for his advert for a trainee landscaper Steve tried his local Job Centre and selected Anthony Bearman from a number of applicants. World of Koi received £60 a week towards training Anthony. Steve went on to employ three more people through the programme.

Source: *HRMGuide.co.uk* (http://www.hrmguide.co.uk), 2 January 2001.

Key concept 8:2

Collaborative entrepreneurship   Cooperation between two or more individu-als in order to found or acquire a business. The degree and nature of collaboration may vary from one company to another in terms of financial input, time devoted, skills and knowledge.

Collaborative entrepreneurship

There has been extensive research on collaboration between enterprises (to be considered later) but little on the relationship between entrepreneurs within an organization. This is despite the fact that it has been well known for decades that 40–60 per cent of small busi-nesses have been collaboratively funded or acquired.

The evidence is limited but it appears to be the case (Quince, 2001, p.3) that 'collabo-ratively funded firms are more likely to survive and achieve faster growth' and that 'there is evidence from the US in particular that collaborative entrepreneurship is a feature of high-technology firms'. Whittaker (1999) also cites a study of over 500 high-technology entrepreneurs in the UK which found that over two-thirds (68 per cent) had been collabo-ratively funded.

Quince (2001, p.5) identifies three types of relationship within collaborative entrepreneurship:

1 The enterprise is an economic entity, having economic relations with other organizations and individuals. Moreover, there is an economic relationship between the co-founders or acquirers. Co-owners both provide and *are* resources: their own human capital in terms of skill, knowledge and experience, labour and often finance. In return, they are entitled to a share in the profits of the firm.

2 The co-owners or co-founders have an organizational relationship in which roles, responsibilities and accountability have been allocated.

3 An interpersonal relationship exists, typically embedded in a pre-existing social or personal friendship with friends, work colleagues, family or life partners.

Most of the research into small businesses has focused on the economic dimension. But there are also issues of self-identity and notions of possession. As Quince points out, the 'I am the business' and 'My baby' elements of possession are 'common if potentially psychologically damaging, entrepreneurial perspectives'. Like many other perspectives, the business is perceived as an extension of the self.

Quince (2001, p.7) reports on a study of almost 500 East Anglian businesses in the manufacturing and business services sectors, each employing between 15 and 250 workers. A high incidence of collaborative entrepreneurship was found with 238 (60 per cent) of the 395 first generation independent firms having been founded or acquired collaboratively. Of these, 50 were family firms. Intriguingly, of the other 188 (non-family) firms that had been founded or acquired collaboratively, almost a half (43 per cent) were now owned by just one of the collaborators. According to Quince:

> Follow up telephone conversations with 47 remaining owners suggested that in 60 per cent of these cases the break-up of the team had been acrimonious. These conversations indicated the level of personal trauma associated with such conflict, including one case of attempted murder, several cases of serious assault and fraud, attempted suicides, depressions, and mental or family break-ups.

Activity 8:2   What do you consider to be the main advantages and disadvantages of collaborative entrepreneurship?

Small firm growth

Most small businesses never become large, and many are unsuccessful. Some of the reasons why can be traced back to the start-up. Goltz (1998) describes a number of the common-sense elements of starting a business, for example:

1 Going into business for yourself is more responsibility than you can possibly imagine. You may start off thinking that when you go into business for yourself, you do not have to answer to anyone. In fact, the list is endless: your bank, your customers, your spouse, the Revenue people and so on.

2 Behind every failed business are a dozen friends who said it was a great idea. And they did – enthusiastically – along with your life partner. It is always best to get an expert opinion and not to rely on people who want to be supportive and not hurt your feelings.

3 If you've got it, use it. Even if it's a great smile. Hard work is not enough – you need to leverage the assets you have. And assets could be just about anything.

4 It's easier to steal a share of the market than create a market. Remember that Bill Gates was not the first in the computer software market. You might believe that a totally original idea is the key to success but if you have no competition you cannot be sure that there is a market out there.

<table>
<tr><td>

HRM in reality

</td><td>

UK firms do well in European small business league

</td></tr>
</table>

Reacte, the first European benchmarking report, compared 1390 small businesses in nine different countries – the UK, Austria, Germany, Spain, Greece, Ireland, Italy, the Netherlands and Portugal – and measured their performances against each other in key aspects of their businesses. The firms sampled were split between the manufacturing and the service sector. The report is intended to help small businesses compete more effectively in Europe by allowing them to compare themselves to the best and worst in each category.

The UK scored the highest marks in 20 of the 70 categories. Report findings include:

- The UK had the highest pre-tax profit margin (relating to turnover) of all nine European countries. Portugal and Spain had the lowest.

- British manufacturers were least likely to go bust because they had sufficient liquid assets to cover their liabilities if creditors called in their debts. Conversely, the UK service sector came last in this category. Overall, German firms came out consistently best in both sectors.

- German companies received the highest number of customer complaints – UK firms had least.

- German workers took the highest number of sick days of all European countries surveyed.

- Italian firms were least likely to send out defective goods.

- UK manufacturers and German service sector companies were most likely to have more new customers than old ones, with Spain and Italy retaining old clients but not attracting new ones.

Nigel Griffiths, the UK minister responsible for small business commented:

I want to give our millions of small businesses the competitive advantage in Europe, and this report gives them a unique opportunity to do that by comparing themselves to their international competitors. The SBS's benchmark scheme provides invaluable help to small companies by giving a no-holds-barred analysis of their strengths and weaknesses and comparing them to similar businesses in the same sector. This allows them to boost their productivity and helps to develop their economic growth – as so many companies across Britain who have already taken part in our benchmarking scheme have so successfully done.

Comparing the top 25 per cent of manufacturing and service sector firms across Europe with the bottom 25 per cent, the report came up with some intriguing results, including:

- The bottom 25 per cent of manufacturing firms report double the complaints per customer than the top 25 per cent.

- The top 25 per cent of firms have an average of 12 per cent of their turnover as cash in the bank, whereas the bottom 25 per cent have on average just 1 per cent.

- If their creditors called in their debts tomorrow, 25 per cent of the companies surveyed across Europe would go bust.

- The bottom 25 per cent of companies surveyed only receive 50 per cent of their supplies on time.

Other results from the report include:

- Spanish manufacturers were weakest when it came to delivering goods on time.
- Employees in UK manufacturing firms had the highest number of reported accidents.
- British manufacturers invested most in staff training in relation to turnover, but were only average in terms of spending per employee. Ireland and Austria came out top.
- Greece and Spain had the highest proportion of graduates working for small firms, with the UK at the lowest level.
- Greek and German firms were most likely to plough their sales turnover back into the company, with British firms the least likely to do so.
- UK manufacturers spent most money on marketing in their sector but, overall, German service sector firms spent the most.
- Germany makes the most money from developing new or innovative projects, while UK firms make the least.

Source: *HRMGuide.co.uk* (http://www.hrmguide.co.uk), 2 May 2002.

**HRM
in reality**

Self-employment will continue to grow strongly in Canada

bizSmart, a division of CIBC, reports that the recent dip in self-employment is temporary. And self-employment will continue growing strongly over the next decade, according to Benjamin Tal, CIBC's senior economist and author of the report.

Between 1989 and 1999 the number of self-employed in Canada reached 2.4 million, largely due to a significant increase in one-person businesses. But last year the number fell by nearly 150 000. The report concludes that these were mainly low-skilled people forced into self-employment by the poor state of the job market. These people were able to find paid jobs again when the situation improved.

Benjamin Tal says that: 'The dramatic growth in self-employment over the past decade is not a temporary phenomenon. In the next 10 years, self-employment will become even more dominant in the Canadian labour market.' Pointing out that the recent drop in the number of self-employed people represents the late stages of the economic cycle, Tal continues: 'Most of these formerly self-employed people who have taken on paid employment are young and less educated. At the same time, self-employment among older and more skilled workers has continued to rise as many of these workers are less tempted by the increased availability of paid employment.'

Some 16 per cent of the Canadian workforce is now self-employed – up from 13 per cent in 1989. Most of the difference is accounted for by one-person operations, a big change from the 1980s when just 30 per cent of growth in self-employment came from these solo firms. The greatest increase was seen in IT fields such as computer system analysis and computer programming. This was followed by human resources and business services. There was also a big jump in traditional personal service occupations such as drivers and hairstylists. But clerical, farming and contracting segments showed a drop in numbers.

Regionally, the fastest growth has been in western provinces and Ontario: increasing by 60 per cent in British Columbia, with Ontario and Alberta close behind.

▶

'Manitoba and Saskatchewan have seen a more moderate rate of growth, largely reflecting the reliance of these provinces on the agricultural sector,' Tal said.

Two-thirds of all self-employed are males, compared with their 52 per cent share of the paid labour force. But the growth in one-person operations has been led by women. And they have also done better than men in taking on paid employees of their own. 'Of the 630 000 self-employment jobs created since 1989, more than 320 000 were created by women – and 250 000 of those were one-person operations,' said Tal.

Tal points to the main factors responsible for growth in self-employment over the next ten years:

- *An ageing labour force:* The older you are, the more likely it is that you will choose self-employment and a growing number of baby-boomers are now reaching their 50s. In fact, the self-employed tend to be older than paid employees. Just 20 per cent of self-employed people are under 35, compared with 43 per cent in paid employment.

- *Increasing demand for personalized products:* Small-scale businesses can meet the increasingly specialized demand for niche products and services.

- *Immigration:* Over 20 per cent of self-employed are immigrants, nearly twice the rate of the 1980s. And since 1991 a third of immigrants have possessed university degrees, again increasing the likelihood of self-employment.

- *Increased interest in self-employment among young Canadians:* Self-employment is increasingly fashionable among younger people. And US research shows a trend for self-employment to reinforce itself through the generations. If your parents are self-employed, you are also likely to choose this career path.

- *Increased availability and lower cost of technology:* Making it easier and cheaper to start a business and develop the connections that allow an operation to succeed in non-traditional locations.

- *Government and corporate outsourcing:* Encouraging the self-employed to provide the services previously done in-house.

But there are some obstacles ahead, including shortages of skilled staff and the increasing problem of balancing work and family responsibilities. Self-employed people with employees work 48 hours a week on average. This compares with 39 hours for one-person operations and just 36 hours for paid employees.

Source: *HRM Guide Canada* (http://www.hrmguide.net/canada/), 10 January 2001.

Activity 8:3

Summarize the reasons why people start their own businesses. Why does the level of entrepreneurship vary between countries?

Until the late 1970s and early 1980s it was assumed that small businesses were a thing of the past: 'big is beautiful' was the prevailing view. Since then it has become clear in countries such as Hong Kong, Singapore and latterly the UK and the USA, that small firms are the basic seeds of a successful economy. They are a dynamic force for growth in comparison with the relatively slow movement of large and bureaucratic organizations. For example, in a number of east Asian countries the Chinese family-owned business is a key economic unit. Few of these businesses are large as younger members tend to spin off their own enterprises.

Table 8.1	Types of business owner

Type	Characteristics
Craftsmen	Self-employed in order to spend as much time as possible expressing their creativity. This freedom would not be possible in a large organization. They would prefer to make the product or provide the service personally and are reluctant employers. They probably experience difficulties in marketing or sales, and resent spending time on paperwork and administration. Many are 'hobbyists' and fail to create a viable business.
Promoters (opportunists)	With the ambition of creating personal wealth through 'deals'. Many have a succession of different businesses with varying degrees of success. They are not committed to a specific product or service. Proactive individuals, they are focused on marketing and finance and capable of rapid rates of growth in the right circumstances.
Professional managers	Aim to develop businesses with the hierarchical characteristics of larger organizations. They aim for controlled and sustained growth and take a long-term view of their businesses.

Source: Based on Hornaday (1990, p.29).

The growth process

Flamholtz and Randle (2000, p.9) state that:

> The first challenge entrepreneurs face is that of establishing a successful new venture. If they have the ability to recognize a market need and to develop (or to hire other people to develop) a product or service appropriate to satisfy that need, their fledgling enterprise is likely to experience rapid growth. It is at this point, whether the entrepreneur recognizes it or not, that the game begins to change. The firm's success creates its next set of problems and challenges to survival.

Entrepreneurs such as Richard Branson of Virgin, Bill Gates of Microsoft, Anita Roddick of the Body Shop and Michael Dell are unusual. Rarely do the founders of start-up businesses remain in charge as their businesses become large organizations. Catlin and Matthews (2001, p.4) point out that: 'The irony of entrepreneurial leaders is that the very behaviours and habit patterns that lead to success at one stage of growth can contribute to failure at the next stage. It seems that just when you get good at something, you discover it's the wrong thing to be doing!'

Flamholtz and Randle (2000) identify the following stages of successful business growth:

1 new venture

2 expansion

3 professionalization

4 consolidation

5 diversification

6 integration

7 decline and revitalization.

Catlin and Matthews consider that entrepreneurs begin with an intuitive leadership style. In the start-up phase they can make decisions 'on the fly', improvise when required and manage everything on a day-to-day basis. As the business expands, this approach results in more and more frenzied activity, less time to think and a gradual feeling of being overwhelmed. Flamholtz and Randle point to characteristic organizational growing pains such as:

- people feeling that there are not enough hours in the day
- people spending too much time 'fire-fighting'
- people not knowing what other staff are doing
- a failure to understand the organization's goals
- not enough good managers
- an attitude of 'I have to do it myself if I want it done properly'
- meetings are generally felt to be a waste of time
- plans are rarely made and where they exist they are seldom followed, so that things are often not done
- some people do not feel secure about their positions
- sales may be increasing, but profits are not.

These problems are symptomatic of a lack of organizational and managerial infrastructure that can support a larger and more complex operation. The original leadership style has become inappropriate and inadequate. Now there is a need for leadership to be more deliberate and for growth to be designed rather than accidental. Nevertheless, a successful owner needs to combine this approach with the best of their entrepreneurial characteristics to achieve consistent growth.

Flamholtz and Randle consider that the firm (and therefore the entrepreneur) has to go through 'a fundamental transformation or metamorphosis from the spontaneous ad hoc, free-spirited enterprise that it has been to a more formally planned, organized and disciplined entity'. Catlin and Matthews contend that if the founder is to remain in charge of the expanding business, he or she has to:

- Develop strategies, products/services, customers and markets.
- Develop organizational processes for planning, management and work flow – and also the infrastructure to accommodate growth and expansion.
- Recruit new people and develop teams to handle growth.
- Create a business culture to align people and teams so that they work together effectively.
- Monitor the evolution of the business and adapt their own leadership style as the business expands and changes.

But what if the owner-entrepreneur is unable to meet these requirements? Flamholtz and Randle contend that there are four alternatives:

1 Resign and let someone else be brought in to run the organization.
2 Move up to chairperson, allowing a new manager to run day-to-day operations.
3 Carry on as before and hope the problems will go away.
4 Sell out and start a new entrepreneurial venture.

In general, they conclude that: 'Founder-entrepreneurs typically experience great difficulty in relinquishing control of their businesses. Some try to change their skills and behaviour but fail. Others merely give the illusion of turning the organization over to professional managers.'

Activity 8:4 What difficulties are human resource specialists likely to experience in dealing with a founding entrepreneur as a business grows?

HRM practices in the small business

Defining the role of HRM in small organizations is problematic because of the limited research findings available:

> Given the importance of SME employees to the US economy, it is disheartening to note that scant attention in the SME research literature is given to the study of human resource management practices. No matter where you look ... scholars are lamenting the dearth of information about human resource management practices in SMEs. (Heneman, Tansky and Camp, 2000)

Heneman, Tansky and Camp (2000) reasonably ask how useful or valid HR theory can be if it is based almost entirely on research conducted in large organizations. Is it relevant to the needs of practitioners or general managers in small or medium-sized enterprises? And the bulk of businesses fall into the SME category. The authors point also to the mismatch between the concerns of SME owners and the focus of HR researchers, quoting recent survey results on the importance of labour shortages and the 'handful' of research

Table 8.2	HRM in SMEs		
	Principle	*Range*	*Comment*
	1 Comprehensiveness	All people management handled by owner/small executive team	Tends to the extreme: comprehensively good, or totally ineffective
	2 Coherence	Dependent on owner's personality	May be haphazard and idiosyncratic
	3 Control	Often completely centralized	Can be either autocratic or 'clubby'
	4 Communication	Highly variable: objectives may be a mystery to staff	Dependent on owner: often an open culture with direct communication
	5 Credibility	Highly variable, employees tend to develop a fixed opinion of the owner	Owner's personality is visible to all
	6 Commitment	Can be exciting and challenging for people of the right type	People who relate to the owner will stay – others will quickly leave
	7 Change	Varies between static and growth businesses	Change usually reactive rather than strategic
	8 Competence	Dangerously dependent on the abilities and knowledge of the owner and core staff	Often erratic and personalized resourcing: 'development' unsystematic and restricted to the chosen few
	9 Creativity	Most SMEs do the same as their competitors: the few exceptions are destined for success	Creative owners generally make use of their own ideas
	10 Cost-effectiveness	Often run on a shoe-string: minimal staffing and low pay	Most owners do not reward themselves and their staff on the same criteria

studies on SME recruitment practices compared with hundreds of studies on recruitment in large organizations.

Table 8.2 summarizes the position of SMEs in relation to the ten principles of HRM outlined in Chapter 3. It is obvious that the nature of people management varies widely in small businesses but they tend to be characterized by a number of factors illustrated in Figure 8.1:

- *Centralized control.* A spider's web, with the owner at the centre. Limited financial and organizational resources ensure that people management is a non-specialist activity. The small business tends to be direct and informal. The character of the principal determines the climate, the morale of the workforce, and whether it is a friendly or unfriendly place to work. Employees have poorly defined responsibilities and little authority. The principal normally controls all major functions. Job tasks, pay rates and benefits are negotiated with the owner. The boss hires and fires, determines pay and conditions and requires considerable flexibility from the workers.

- *Strategy.* There is little forward planning. Decisions are taken when problems are met. Staff development and training are often neglected. Succession and career planning is rare. Performance assessment is rudimentary and arbitrary.

- *Fire-fighting or crisis management.* Employees are expected to be totally flexible, prepared to work long or irregular hours. They must perform a variety of tasks without necessarily having appropriate skills or training.

- *People function.* Companies with fewer than 50 employees are unlikely to have an identified human resource function.

Wilkinson (2000) provides an analysis of responses to questions about the practice of HRM in the 1997 CBR survey of 2520 small and medium-sized, independent, manufacturing and business service firms. This revealed that: 35 per cent of respondents used job rotation/multi-skilling; 31.9 per cent used performance-related pay; 29.6 per cent used

Figure 8.1	HRM in the small firm

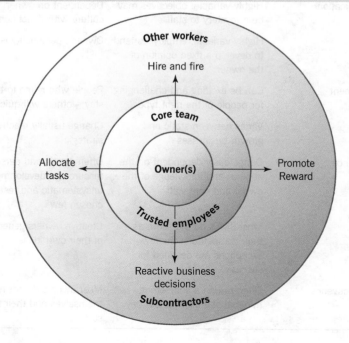

total quality management; and 13.1 per cent used quality circles. Grouping the last two procedures together as 'quality management', 39 per cent of firms used none of these categories, 30 per cent used one only, 23 per cent used two and just 9 per cent used all three.

Firms that used HRM-type procedures were more growth-oriented than those that did not. But these companies also saw the greatest obstacles to growth, identifying shortages of skilled labour and marketing, sales and management skills as significant constraints. HRM users rated these limitations 10 per cent higher in significance than non-users. The most marked difference was seen between firms that used performance-related pay and those that did not.

According to Wilkinson (2000, p.9):

> The positive associations between the growth and related business objectives, and HRM, and between HRM and non-price competitive strategies, are not difficult to explain. Firms looking to grow, expand their market share and increase the return on assets in highly competitive conditions, can be expected to adopt non-price competitive policies, and to support these by HRM strategies geared to: involving employees more in reducing costs; improving quality and productive performance; increasing their skill and flexibility to make this possible; and linking their pay to performance to reward their effort. In this sense, product market and HRM strategies are complementary and proactive means of securing the firms' objectives in a hard competitive environment.

HRM-using firms were found to be dedicating a greater proportion of total employee costs to formal training than non-HRM-using firms. In fact, roughly twice as many firms using quality management procedures had formal training than did companies not using quality management. HRM-using companies were also more innovative than non-users, citing an extension of their product range, improving product quality and gaining market share as the main reasons for innovation.

A further means of improving performance is to network with other companies. A third of the firms surveyed had some form of formal, informal or partnership arrangements with other businesses. Most commonly these were suppliers, customers or other companies in the same business sector. A few SMEs had developed links with colleges or universities. The reasons given by firms involved in some form of external collaboration were to: expand the range of expertise (75 per cent); assist in development of specialist services or services required by customers (70 per cent); provide access to UK markets (54 per cent); provide access to overseas markets (45 per cent).

HRM-using businesses were significantly more likely to collaborate with other firms than non-users. HRM-using firms were also more likely to use services or advice from outside agencies, contractors and consultants. Another striking finding was that companies that used 'bundles' of HRM practices fared better than those using a more restricted range. Firms that used all three HRM practices did better than those that used none by the following percentages: innovation (+80 per cent), exporting (+124 per cent) and increased employment (77 per cent).

Activity 8:5

Is it the case that: (a) Firms using HRM procedures benefit because of those procedures? (b) Firms that are forward-looking and growing are more likely to use HRM procedures because they are forward-looking and growing?

HRM in reality

Employee issues come first

Employee issues take more time than e-commerce, globalization or growth planning. And Canadian entrepreneurs say it's more stressful to run a company now than five years ago. These are the main conclusions of a poll conducted by Research Dimensions for Grant Thornton LLP, which asked owner-managers to rank their top 10 business headaches, ranging from customer relations to succession planning.

Globalization, e-commerce and growing threats of litigation seemed to be back-burner issues for most Canadian entrepreneurs. Time-crunched owner-managers said that business growth should be their number one priority, but employee issues took up most of their time.

'This survey is a bit of a wake-up call for Canadian entrepreneurs,' says Alex MacBeath, executive partner at Grant Thornton LLP, a leading firm of chartered accountants and business advisers with offices across Canada. It suggests 'Canadian entrepreneurs feel there are not enough hours in the day to address fundamental issues to growth such as business planning or improving customer service,' says MacBeath who is based in Toronto.

The survey highlights a number of regional differences. For instance, the challenge of running a business is felt most acutely in British Columbia, with 80 per cent of respondents feeling that there is more stress these days, followed by Alberta (69 per cent), Ontario (68 per cent) and Atlantic Canada (67 per cent).

There are ten key issues affecting today's business owners according to the survey (percentage of owner-managers saying that the following issues are extremely or very important to them):

1 strengthening customer relationships (97 per cent)

2 finding and keeping good people (89 per cent) – 63 per cent agree there is an extreme shortage of skilled labour in their region

3 minimizing corporate and personal taxes (81 per cent)

4 growing the business (73 per cent)

5 keeping pace with technology (68 per cent) – basic skill levels of employees lead the list

6 managing cash flow (66 per cent)

7 current business climate (65 per cent)

8 creating and executing strategy (62 per cent)

9 retirement and succession planning (55 per cent) – personal retirement and succession planning are essential in respondents' business plans

10 finding expansion capital (50 per cent).

Source: *HRM Guide Canada* (http://www.hrmguide.net/canada/), 18 October 2001.

Entrepreneurship and business growth research

Howard E. Aldrich has been a considerable influence on the topic of entrepreneurship. In his *Organizations Evolving* (1999) he makes the point that:

Organizational scholars have done an excellent job in explaining how things work in organizations that have been around for a while, but not how they came to be that way. In contrast, I am interested in the genesis of organizations, organizational populations, and communities. Even really large organizations started small, usually, but the absolute miracle of their creation does not seem to interest most organization theorists. It should.

He advocates an evolutionary approach to the emergence and change of organizations. Using Darwinian language he describes the creation of new organizational structures as 'variation', the way in which entrepreneurs modify those structures and use resources to meet changing circumstances as 'adaptation', the circumstances leading to survival or extinction as 'selection' and imitation of successful concepts by other entrepreneurs as 'retention'.

Aldrich points to the weakness of traditional (romantic) views of the entrepreneur, when most are only modestly successful and that success is often dependent on others. He draws attention to the issue of the 'nascent entrepreneur' – someone who initiates a series of activities that are intended to result in a business start-up but often do not end up doing so (Reynolds, 1994). Every year, between 4 and 6 per cent of working Americans embark on actions aimed at a business venture, and 40 per cent of Americans do so at some point in their adult lives, according to Reynolds and White (1997).

Activity 8:6	How would you explain the difference between 'nascent entrepreneurs' and entrepreneurs who succeed in starting business ventures?

HRM in reality	**Small firms lose staff to large companies**

The belief that small companies poach trained staff from large businesses is a myth, it seems. A NatWest Small Business Research Trust (SBRT) Quarterly Survey of Small Business suggests the opposite: small firms lose more staff to large organizations than they gain from bigger companies.

Most small firms get new employees from other small firms and the pool of unemployed. Just 20 per cent of their new recruits come from large organizations, whereas more than 40 per cent of full-time workers recruited by small firms in the survey over the last 12 months came from businesses with fewer than 100 employees. Around 20 per cent of recruits were unemployed and another 13 per cent were students. This finding is all the more remarkable given that more people work in large than small firms across the economy as a whole. The survey also shows that more people leave small firms to set up their own businesses than to become small firm employees.

According to Peter Ibbetson, Head of NatWest Business Banking:

> These findings yet again underline the considerable contribution small firms make to the UK economy in terms of employment. Overall, small firms appear to recruit from the unemployed and students and then lose them, probably after providing much valuable training and experience, to large firms.

Source: *HRMGuide.co.uk* (http://www.hrmguide.co.uk), 17 April 2001.

Working in small businesses

Entrepreneurs start small businesses in order to obtain freedom, challenge and personal income. Starting one's own business offers a way around the lack of equal opportunities. Women are strongly represented in the SME sector. Immigrants often overcome prejudice, language difficulties and barriers in the employment market by starting their own businesses.

The picture is different for employees, however. Staff in small businesses can feel insecure because of the lack of structure and planning. Career aspirations are frustrated as most owners either do not wish their businesses to expand beyond their personal span of control or do not have the management skills necessary for effective delegation. Few corner shop owners have the skills or inclination to develop large businesses and many of their children are disinclined to carry on with the family firm. In contrast, the best entrepreneurs have a range of general business skills – including people management – or have the good sense to obtain specialist assistance from:

- *Consultants.* Providing advice on recruitment, pay and benefits, management structures and organizational change associated with growth.

- *Training agencies.* Providing local or regional skills training.

- *Networks.* Small businesses can link together to pay for resourcing and development assistance, possibly through chambers of commerce and business clubs.

Entrepreneurial structures can only function up to a certain size. When they become too large for personal relationships they must evolve into a more clearly defined organization. The nature of people management must change fundamentally when this occurs. However, it is possible to preserve some of the informal and non-hierarchical characteristics of the small business by setting up a formal cooperative or, informally, a team-based organization.

The problems and concerns of small and medium-sized businesses are also seen in other organizations such as schools, colleges, religious institutions, charities, trusts – and ships. Abrashoff (2002, p.13) describes taking on command of a US Navy ship:

> ... as the new captain of *Benfold*, I read some exit surveys, interviews conducted by the military to find out why they are leaving. I assumed that low pay would be the first reason, but in fact it was fifth. The top reason was not being treated with respect or dignity; second was being prevented from making an impact on the organization; third, not being listened to; and fourth, not being rewarded with more responsibility. Talk about an eye opener.

Abrashoff observes that the same findings appear in exit surveys from the civilian sector and concludes that leaders all make the same mistakes. As a naval captain there was little he could do about the pay scales, so he concentrated on the other four 'gripes'. He advocates a simple organizational approach: 'The key to being a successful skipper is to see the ship through the eyes of the crew. Only then can you find out what's really wrong and, in so doing, help the sailors empower themselves to fix it.'

But he also observes that the Navy applauds this approach in principle, and negates it in practice because officers are taught never to say the words 'I don't know'. Many entrepreneurs have worked themselves into the same psychological position – an unwillingness to admit that they do not know everything about their business. Abrashoff describes their behaviour as being 'on constant alert, riding herd on every detail'. They micromanage everything and thereby disempower their employees. He concludes that: 'A ship commanded by a micromanager and his or her hierarchy of sub-micromanagers is no breeding ground for initiative.'

| Activity 8:7 | How can knowledge about effective people management aboard a ship be regarded as relevant to small business management? |

HRM in reality	**Why female enterprise is an uphill struggle**

Britain's businesswomen are an underfunded minority according to a new report published by the Industrial Society. The report – *Unequal Entrepreneurs: Why Female Enterprise is an Uphill Struggle* – shows that the UK government has failed to support an increase in the number of women-owned businesses. The report recommends greater government support for UK businesswomen including: a national centre for women's enterprise, an Office for Women's Business Ownership in the DTI and a women's business charter to encourage better treatment for women from law firms, banks and financial advisers.

The report indicates that women business-owners are younger on average than male entrepreneurs – 43 per cent are under 44 compared to 30 per cent of men. Compared to their male equivalents, women entrepreneurs also have less access to start-up capital, less management experience and are less welcome in the informal business networks that often provide vital support to small firms. The report concludes that these gender differences stifle both start-up and growth of businesses owned by women.

Increases in numbers of working women, 'feminised' markets and the expansion in service sectors have all failed to generate the expected growth in women-owned businesses. Currently women make up just 26 per cent of the UK's self-employed – a figure that has barely changed since 1990. The report's authors attribute this, in part, to the inferior position of women in the labour market. Dr Eleanor Shaw of Strathclyde University said: 'Most women hold low-paid, unskilled or semi-skilled positions, women earn on average 72 per cent of male earnings and only 10 per cent of the UK's 200 largest companies have female board members. Women's experiences of the labour market are a major constraint on their ability to set up their own businesses.'

Also, women in business find it more difficult (than men) to finance their companies. The reasons include:

- Guarantees required for external financing are often beyond the scope of their personal assets and credit track record.
- Women face sexual stereotyping from banks.
- There are informal financial networks, which women find it difficult to penetrate.
- Women rely heavily on personal savings – between 80–99 per cent of initial capitalization compared to 30–59 per cent for men.

Dr Eleanor Shaw said: 'The economic argument that self-employed people create jobs and wealth is well-documented. Women constitute an overwhelmingly untapped pool of entrepreneurial talent, and if we can encourage more women to start their own businesses we can add to our economic prosperity.'

Women in the USA have benefited from a number of initiatives producing an increase in women entrepreneurs from 5 per cent in 1970 to 38 per cent of all small businesses in 1999. The report urges similar initiatives in the UK, including:

- *National Centre for Women's Enterprise.* The centre should take a lead in advocacy, research and development, networking and dissemination of best practice and awareness-raising. Its key role would be to ensure there is a cohesive and strategic approach to women's enterprise development in the UK.
- *National Policy on Women's Enterprise.* Recognizing the needs of women as a

▶

diverse group and requiring high level government support to overcome the piecemeal approach to support for women's enterprise.

- *Business support.* Projects to improve women's experiences of small business should become a political priority, both centrally and locally. To achieve this, female economic development professionals would have to be paid well and rewarded well – providing an important signal.

- *Women's Business Charter.* Championed by the Small Business Service and, in Scotland, the Scottish Executive. The Charter would encompass the complete range of professional services supporting businesspeople – including banks, accountants, lawyers and careers advisers – encouraging best practice for supporting women's enterprise. It would also require its signatories to monitor progress and outcomes with respect to their female clients.

- *Office for Women's Business Ownership.* A similar body to the Office for Women's Business Ownership in the USA (established in 1979) should be established under the auspices of the DTI. The mission statement of the USA Office is equally relevant to the UK: 'to advocate for women-owned business, one of the fastest-growing segments of the nation's economy' and 'to create programmes and policies that help women entrepreneurs become full partners in the national and global economies'. Acting as a policy development unit, in conjunction with the National Centre, the Office would have overall responsibility for ensuring the delivery of a cohesive approach to women's enterprise development in the UK.

- *Access to finance.* Traditional credit scoring mechanisms discriminate against women because they tend to have a less detailed and more fragmented financial track record. The report also recommends specific initiatives to improve women's access to finance. These include a microcredit programme, improved information on and access to informal investment, as well as an online business credit union that would attract savings and funds from existing businesswomen and provide financial and networking support. The report further suggests that there is a need for more female 'angels' for funding the creation and growth of women-owned ventures. It says that 'business angels' are an important source of capital, but only a small proportion of these are female.

According to Will Hutton, chief executive of the Industrial Society:

In the British labour market, women are still second class citizens. They lag behind men in terms of pay, promotion, benefits and more. They are drastically under-represented in management, and routinely invisible in the average boardroom. Less well-documented is the discrimination women entrepreneurs encounter when it comes to establishing themselves in business. For an economy whose lifeblood is new enterprise, and particularly diverse enterprise, this situation is literally intolerable.

Source: *HRMGuide.co.uk* (http://www.hrmguide.co.uk), 18 October 2001.

Consultancies

Business organizations rarely have the expertise or spare resources to conduct large-scale change initiatives without outside assistance. What options do they have? They may turn to the academic world which contains a large number of 'experts' who research and theorize in this area. Alternatively – and far more likely – they use business consultants (Key concept 8.3). Whereas academics appear to have played a major role in the appearance of HRM, consultants have taken the lead in the wider area of change management.

Key concept 8:3

Consultants   Biech (2001, p.1) describes a consultant as someone who 'provides unique assistance or advice to someone else, usually known as the client. The work is defined by the consultant's expertise, the structure in which the consultant works, and the process the consultant uses.'

Astute consultants understand how important packaging is in marketing their services. More than anything, they sell themselves. As we have noted in earlier chapters, image plays a disproportionate role in business credibility. Academics appear to believe that the quality of the ideas is what matters. In fact, sound methodology and process value are virtually irrelevant when it comes to client acceptability. The average academic is not as adept at the self-marketing and impression management necessary to win over top managers. Consultants play the business game, dress and behave appropriately knowing that 'their clients will be acutely aware of the messages that are sent by such small things as the type of watch, size of briefcase and elegance of technology used' (Furnham, 1992, p.xix).

According to Furnham, academics look for puzzles, consultants are given problems; the researchers are 'satisfied to know and understand, while the latter want to use the knowledge and sell it'. The former veer towards 'pure' understanding for its own sake; consultants focus on the 'applied'. University researchers tend to be overcautious, taking a considerable time to develop ideas and theories. Their detached, independent view does not fit business managers' expectations of enthusiastic commitment to 'owning the problem'. Unlike academics brought up in the dense waffle school of explanation, the most successful consultants are polished presenters. They have a considerable store of supportive anecdotes and make a point of expressing ideas clearly and simply. Consultants are aware of managers' urgent timescales; of the requirement to provide 'solutions'; of a need for face-to-face reassurance.

Furnham finds different personality traits in academics and consultants, outlined in Table 8.3, describing successful consultants as 'time-conscious, high-urgency people, driven by deadlines'. Their use of time is quite different from that of academics who

Table 8.3	Characteristics of academics and consultants	
	Academics	*Consultants*
Major aims	Insight and knowledge	Action and operation
Speed of solution	Low urgency	High urgency
Type of solution valued	Elegant and critical	Applicable and comprehensible
Source of data	Direct empirical base	Second-hand empirical base
Level of complexity	Frequently complex	Frequently simple
Dealing with uncertainty	Dealt with statistically	Dealt with personally
Preferred medium or presentation	Written documents/tables	Face to face
Self-presentation	Irrelevant, often shabby	Crucial, fashionably smart
Means of persuasion	Empirical data	Rhetorical
Cost–benefit analysis	Irrelevant	Crucial
Type of personality valued	Introvert	Extrovert

Source: Based on Furnham (1992).

appear sluggish and hesitant in comparison. Given that most businesses turn to established consultancies, what services do they provide?

According to Wood (1983), reasons for using consultants include:

1 Specialist knowledge and expertise. For instance, a venture in a new country is made easier by using consultants familiar with the local language and business practices.

2 An independent perspective on the organization's problems. This requires mutual trust and respect between client and consultant.

3 Acting as a catalyst for change. Consultants can provide cautious managers with reassurance, having been through similar circumstances before. By reducing the level of anxiety, decisions can be taken more swiftly and risks accepted with greater confidence.

4 Provision of additional resources for temporary needs. Within the context of flexibility, this is a form of outsourcing or subcontracting of management tasks.

5 To help develop a consensus when views are divided.

6 Demonstrating impartiality and objectivity about changes to the organization's employees.

7 To provide the justification for unpleasant decisions.

We can distinguish between (Torrington, 1994): (a) resource consultancy, transferring knowledge or understanding from consultant to client, and (b) process consultancy, in which the consultant helps the client organization to develop new skills of analysis and diagnosis for themselves.

Of course, consultants are not without their critics. According to Townsend (1970, p.97):

> The effective ones are the one-man shows. The institutional ones are disastrous. They waste time, cost money, demoralize and distract your best people, and don't solve problems. They are people who borrow your watch to tell you what time it is and then walk off with it. Don't use them under any circumstances. Not even to keep your stockholders and directors quiet. It isn't worth it.

Ironically, the many consultant-inspired de-layering and downsizing programmes have unleashed a mass of redundant managers who have elected to become consultants themselves! Faced with an employment market saturated with middle-aged, middle managers, consultancy may be seen as the only way of generating income. However, consultancy and the practice of management require different skills. Many would-be consultants do not have the appropriate qualities; others can put on an impressive performance of impression management but have little specialist knowledge or ability in diagnosis and facilitation.

Torrington (1994, p.77) provides a sequence of steps to determine whether a consultant should be used at all, and if so which:

1 Check the experience of previous clients. Consultants will provide the names themselves and professional bodies such as the Chartered Institute of Personnel and Development may be able to help. Useful questions to ask include:

- What was the assignment and how was it performed? How long did it take? Were there any unexpected findings or developments?

- What were the benefits to the client? How did they compare with initial expectations?

- Was the exercise completed within initial budget estimates? Were expenses detailed clearly?

- Would the organization use the same consultant again? If yes, would the client make changes in briefing or monitoring the exercise?

2 Describe what you want done. Clarifying a problem in precise detail can lead to a solution that does not require outside assistance. Alternatively, it may establish a requirement for specific expertise.

3 Formulate an approach. Decide roughly which approaches to a problem seem viable. A consultant cannot be briefed without some idea of the possible solutions. A vague grasp of the problem may result in unending expense.

4 Work out how you could do it without external assistance. Calculate the degree of disruption involved, extra resources required and the costs incurred. If these are reasonable, a consultant is not required.

5 Obtain proposals from consultants. They should be asked to quote for exactly the same task, the brief for which can be derived from stages one and two. They can be compared in terms of expected results, time to be taken, cost and the resources the consultant will require from you. Great care should be taken in examining the draft contract.

6 Decide between the alternatives. Torrington emphasizes the following points:

- Does the proposal meet the specific requirements? How important are any variations?

- What are the anticipated results claimed in the proposal? Are there any unexpected benefits in addition?

- How is the consultant's progress and performance to be assessed during the exercise? Are there specific stages which can act as milestones?

- Consultants invariably send senior staff to negotiate a contract but who will actually do the work? What qualifications and experience do they have? What other assignments will they be involved in at the same time?

Torrington concludes that the responsibility for the exercise is inescapably the client's. Clearly, there are considerable risks of entering into an open-ended and expensive relationship that will not result in the desired consequences.

| Activity 8:8 | Why should small businesses consider using consultants? What are the key issues to take into account when commissioning consultants and evaluating results? |

Summary

This chapter introduced entrepreneurship and people management issues in small and medium-sized enterprises. This remains an inadequately researched area in HRM terms despite its importance to job creation and national economies. There is a fair amount of knowledge about individual entrepreneurs and their aspirations but comparatively little 'hard evidence' regarding collaborative entrepreneurship and the human resource aspects of the business growth process.

Further reading

International differences and similarities in small business research are outlined by Howard Aldrich in 'Learning together: national differences in entrepreneurship research' in D.L. Sexton and H. Landstrom (eds.) *The Blackwell Handbook of Entrepreneurship*

(Blackwell Handbooks in Management), published by Blackwell (2000). His evolutionary approach to business growth is described in *Organizations Evolving*, Sage (1999). Good texts on the growth process in SMEs include: Catlin and Matthews' *Leading at the Speed of Growth: Journey from Entrepreneur to CEO*, published by John Wiley & Sons (2001); and Flamholtz and Randle's *Growing Pains: Transitioning from an Entrepreneurship to a Professionally Managed Firm*, published by Jossey-Bass (2000).

Huge numbers of 'how-to' and 'real life problem-solving' books exist, including: Goltz's *The Street Smart Entrepreneur: 133 Tough Lessons I Learned the Hard Way*, LPC (1998); Lesonsky's somewhat immodestly titled *Start Your Own Business: The Only Start-Up Book You'll Ever Need*, 2nd edition, Entrepreneur Media Inc. (2001); and D. Michael Abrashoff's engaging *It's Your Ship: Management Techniques from the Best Damn Ship in the Navy*, Warner Books (2002).

Review questions

1 How does the size of a small business limit the practice of human resource management?

2 Outline some of the ways in which people management skills could be made available to entrepreneurs.

3 Why do entrepreneurs start business ventures?

4 Why do collaborative ventures often end as single-owner companies?

5 Few small companies become major corporations. In terms of people management, why do you think this is so?

6 What is 'micro-management' and what is its significance to a growing business?

7 Summarize the advantages and disadvantages of the use of consultants by small and medium-sized enterprises.

Problems for discussion and analysis

1 New Age Finance is a venture recently started by two experienced graduates. They have launched a range of financial services geared towards middle-aged suburban house owners. The products have proven to be very successful and have attracted the interest of a large insurance company who has agreed to fund a major expansion. A sales forecast suggests that around 40 sales and administration staff need to be in place by the end of the year. The business plan envisages regionally grouped sales staff with administrative functions located at head office.

What are the possible organizational structures for this company? On what basis should the decision be made for the chosen structure?

2 The Craft Partnership is a cooperative of 20 independent producers. They are based at an old factory site on the outskirts of town which is divided into small workshops. Personnel, marketing and finance services are provided by an office manager and two staff. The cooperative has grown successfully over the last five years. Now they have the opportunity of taking on a much larger site adjacent to the tourist centre.

Opinion is divided among the partners on the way forward. Some are content to stay as they are. A few have said that they will leave and set up on their own if the cooperative gets much larger. Others are excited by the prospect of better facilities, room for growth and space for new members in the cooperative. They also see big advantages in being accessible to tourists.

The office manager sees this as the opportunity to make more radical changes. She is concerned that the partnership is unwieldy and makes external finance difficult. She spends much of her time sorting out squabbles between partners and trying to get them to share resources sensibly. Some partners are overworked and others do not have enough to do. She can see many ways of increasing efficiency if the partnership becomes a conventional business. This could be done by creating a holding company, making the existing partners both shareholders and employees. A local venture company is prepared to make a substantial investment for a 50 per cent share in the new organization. However, they would require a formal structure with defined management roles. They feel that the office manager would make a suitable managing director.

She has arranged a meeting with the partners and the venture company. (a) How should she proceed? (b) What is the reaction likely to be? (c) What is the way forward?

3   The Royal Ocean is a well-established resort hotel. Its clients are in the middle to upper income bracket and many return year after year. It has developed a reputation for attentive service and is regarded as expensive but good value. In recent years, however, a new marina development further down the coast has provided extra competition. The new hotels are larger and more modern, boasting a choice of restaurants, bars and leisure facilities. They have affected the Royal Ocean's profitability seriously.

The hotel is on a restricted site and the owners, a small regional chain, cannot afford substantial capital investment. Like most hotels it has a highly seasonal pattern of business. Despite the competition, the Royal Ocean has no difficulty in filling rooms during peak periods. Occupancy rates have been mainly affected during quieter periods. The company has decided to encourage more business out of season through selective promotions to group travel organizers. During the low season, the country has a national holiday when, traditionally, the hotel has allowed most of its staff to take two days off. The small number of remaining employees have been sufficient to cater for the few guests. In the past, visitors at this time of year have tended to be middle-aged people seeking quiet relaxation. They have been happy to tolerate restricted service in the restaurant, bar and pool area.

This year, the hotel has achieved 80 per cent occupancy over the holiday period. The regular clients have been vastly outnumbered by families with young children. Rooms have been sold cheaply to low-income groups who are not expected to spend heavily on the more profitable services. Accordingly, the hotel general manager decided not to increase staffing to normal weekly levels. He felt that the low return would not justify upsetting employee morale.

However, the consequences have proved to be unfortunate. The regular clients have been angered by the inability of the hotel to provide even the basic service experienced in previous years. Most shops, restaurants and visitor facilities in the area are closed because of the holiday. The clients are forced to remain within the hotel. The restaurant has been besieged by noisy family groups. The pool area

◄

has become a playground. Clients are waiting for up to 20 minutes for an elevator because children are continuously going up and down in them. The quiet middle-aged regulars are complaining vociferously to any member of staff they can find. It seems that they are largely affluent professionals who are accustomed to having their way. They are becoming increasingly demanding and are threatening never to come back.

What can be done (a) now and (b) in the future?

9 | Organizational culture

Objectives

The purpose of this chapter is to:

- Introduce the concept of culture at international, national and organizational levels.
- Describe and evaluate theoretical approaches to culture, especially that of Hofstede.
- Evaluate the contribution of Deal and Kennedy to the debate on corporate culture.
- Discuss how cultures may be managed.

Culture and international HRM

To quote Bunge and Ardila (1987, p.225):

> Culture is the great social matrix within which we are born, we grow, and we die. It gives meaning to human action, and we transmit it to our biological and spiritual descendants (our children and our students). It has many philosophical, political, and practical implications: it tells what is good and bad; how to live and die; how to talk, dress, and love; things to eat and when to eat them; how to express happiness and sadness; what to consider desirable and what to detest.

Management practices vary throughout the world. Culture, history and language obviously underlie much of this variation. More than any other business function, the practice of people management is closely linked to national culture (Gaugler, 1988). This is readily seen in many texts produced over the last decade or so (such as Evans, Pucik and Barsoux, 2002; Dowling, Welch and Schuler, 1998; Sparrow and Hiltrop, 1994; Torrington, 1994; Hegewisch and Brewster, 1993; and Brewster and Tyson, 1991). They catalogue significant differences between major countries and indicate a wide diversity in philosophies of people management. Comparing one country with another we find that basic activities are regarded with different degrees of importance; they are carried out differently; and the activities undertaken by HR managers vary from one country to another. As a consequence it is possible to distinguish practices that are universally applicable from those based on a particular national culture.

Key concept 9:1

Culture   The anthropologist Edward Tylor (1871) defined culture as 'knowledge, belief, art, morals, law, custom and any other capabilities and habits' acquired through membership of society. In a narrower sense the term is used to describe the differences between one society and another. In this context, a culture is an all-pervasive system of beliefs and behaviours transmitted socially. Specifically it consists of the set of values – abstract ideals – and norms or rules held by a society, together with its material expressions (Giddens, 1989, p.30).

Cultural differences are seen also at the organizational level. Human resource literature places considerable emphasis on corporate culture. We saw in Chapter 2 that the classic Harvard model of HRM emphasizes the link between a culture that fosters appropriate employee attitudes, behaviour and commitment in order to achieve competitive performance. This requires sophisticated people management systems allowing careful selection and development of people with suitable characteristics, plus accurate performance assessment and reward packages to encourage desirable behaviour.

International comparisons

International comparisons of HRM focus on similarities and differences between people management practices in different countries (Sparrow and Hiltrop, 1994, p.3).

For example, Pieper (1990) finds that most comparative texts ask questions such as:

● How is HRM structured in individual countries?

● What strategies are discussed?

● What is put into practice?

● What are the main differences and similarities?

● To what extent are corporate policies and strategies influenced by national factors such as culture, government policy and educational systems?

The answers to these questions are not simply of theoretical interest. They provide lessons that we can learn from other cultures (Brewster and Tyson, 1991, p.2). For the international manager operating in more than one country they define the cultural elements and behaviours that must be learned in order to be effective. We noted in Part 2 that the market-place is global and the key players are multinational organizations. Modern people managers cannot confine themselves to an understanding of people management in their own countries. Everyone must develop an awareness of international HRM.

Torrington (1994, p.5) argues that international HRM has the same basic dimensions as HRM in a national context, but with added features:

● it operates on a greater scale
● strategic considerations are more complex
● operational units vary more widely and require coordination across more barriers.

Torrington considers that we all operate within the 'learned frameworks' of our own cultures. People managers need to transcend these frameworks. Human resource managers often have responsibility for developing and training staff for subsidiaries in several countries. They must provide training programmes to meet the needs of international managers including:

● language training
● cultural awareness
● economic and political understanding
● appreciation of different legal systems
● awareness of management style and conventions.

Activity 9:1 Summarize the main benefits from gaining an understanding of international HRM.

Respecting cultural differences

'One of the major dangers of any discussion of HRM is that it is easy to fall into the trap of ignoring the difference between national cultures' (Sparrow and Hiltrop, 1994, p.60). There is a misleading assumption that the social, class and cultural values underlying management ideas are – or should be – 'normal' for every country. Scientifically based management methods are regarded as culturally neutral and universal (Chung, 1991). In fact, they are mostly North American and based on that particular culture, but Western managers have regarded methods such as performance-related pay and particular methods of selection as best practice everywhere.

Rooted in 19th century imperialism, this misconception is founded on the belief that important ideas are conveyed in one direction – from Western 'civilization' to less developed countries. Political and industrial world power moved from Europe to the USA as long ago as 1945 but the transmission of ideas continues to have a colonial pattern.

English is the major business language, allowing the spread of largely American business concepts via colonial/post-colonial routes and multinational corporations (Brewster and Tyson, 1991). These methodologies were accepted as 'received wisdom' in large areas of the world, including Africa, the Middle East and India. They were also adopted by countries in Europe and Asia which had been brought within the American orbit after World

War II. North American business ideas continue to flourish in both continents as a managerial 'lingua franca' in highly diverse markets where no single local culture dominates.

Walton (1999) distinguishes between a global mindset and an international mindset. Managers in an internationally minded company are 'more one-directional, ethnocentric, outward looking from the country in which they are based'. Whereas a true global organization will feature (Rhinesmith, 1996): (a) highly adaptable managers, and (b) an organizational value structure that allows managers to detach themselves from their original national roots and thereby shed their ethnocentric outlook.

This global-oriented mindset suggests that multinationals should become 'free-floating' – not tied to any specific country. Instead, the location of their operations should take into account a balance of factors including:

- Differing national employment legislation, ways of doing business, customs, national investment policies, fiscal incentives, attitudes to foreign investment and other competitors.

- Issues related to physical location, including local market potential, geographical and cultural distance from the company's base, transport logistics and communications.

- Employee costs including wages, training needs, skills availability, social and industrial infrastructure.

- Fit of new locations with existing customers, management and production.

- The organizational structure of the firm.

It is doubtful that many transnational companies are truly global multinationals, most having strong ties to one or more countries.

Activity 9:2	What are the arguments against employing the same human resource practices throughout the world?

The following list (based on the work of Campbell and associates, cited in Triandis, 1990, p.35) highlights key conclusions from studies of ethnocentrism. Characteristics of the 'in-group' are that everyone tends to:

- Define their own culture as 'natural' and 'correct' and other cultures as 'unnatural' and 'incorrect'.

- Perceive in-group customs as universally valid – what is good for us is good for everybody.

- Think that in-group norms, rules and values are obviously correct.

- Consider it natural to help and cooperate with members of one's in-group.

- Act in ways that favour the in-group.

- Feel proud of the in-group.

- Feel hostility towards out-groups.

Cultures and standards

Cultures are human creations but, unlike bridges, buildings, roads and other material objects of our making, cultures are subjective (Triandis, 1990, p.36). They are made up of elements such as attitudes, beliefs, norms, roles and values (see Key concept 9.1). We take our own culture for granted. In fact, we are scarcely aware of it until we interact with another. Each culture has a 'world view' – a set of values and beliefs. This is meaningful to its members but alien to others. As a consequence, we look at people from other cultures, see that their ways are different and often dislike these ways. It is normal to 'use our own culture as the standard and judge other cultures by the extent they meet the standard' (Triandis, 1990, p.34). As we have seen, this ethnocentrism can be related to the concept of the 'in-group' – those people we identify with. It can be argued that the export of Western (American) management methods by multinationals and business schools – including HRM and its associated paraphernalia of assessment, performance-related pay and related ideas – is an example of ethnocentrism on a massive scale. Trompenaars and Hampden-Turner (1997, p.2) consider that:

> Even with experienced international companies, many well-intended 'universal' applications of management theory have turned out badly. For example, pay for performance has in many instances been a failure on the African continent because there are particular, though unspoken, rules about the sequence and timing of reward and promotions. Similarly, management-by-objectives schemes have generally failed within subsidiaries of multinationals in southern Europe, because managers have not wanted to conform to the abstract nature of preconceived policy guidelines.

Trompenaars and Hampden-Turner (1997) point out that international HR (and other) managers have a particularly difficult task. They have to operate in three different cultures at the same time: their culture of origin; the culture within which they are currently working; and the corporate culture of the organization.

Cultural variety

Cultures should not be confused with countries or so-called 'nation states'. There is a danger in examining cultures as 'wholes': there are not only differences between cultures but also within cultures (Brewster and Tyson, 1991). For example, Australian culture can be identified with that of the majority Anglo-Celtic population but the nation's culture also encompasses a number of distinctive sub-cultures. These include that of the indigenous Aboriginal population and a number of significant immigrant groups, such as Italian, Greek and Vietnamese communities. More accurately, Aboriginal culture is itself plural, composed of hundreds of different cultural and linguistic groups. Hofstede (1991, p.10) argues that an individual's culture has several levels:

● National, according to country (countries for migrants).

● Regional and/or ethnic and/or religious and/or linguistic.

● Gender – different assumptions and expectations of females and males.

● Generation – differences between age groups.

● Social class – linked to educational opportunities and occupations.

● Organizational – different organizations have their individual cultures.

We can see readily that this mixture provides an intriguing cocktail for a selector to attempt to disentangle; for a performance assessor to misunderstand; a management developer to 'correct'. All in all, there is massive scope for a clash of cultures – and prejudices. As we shall see in Part 6 on the management of diversity, there is a major issue on the real meaning of 'equal opportunities' in this context.

Activity 9:3

How many different cultures can you identify in your own country? What are the implications of the differences between these cultures for human resource managers?

The perception of time

Managing people depends a great deal on our perceptions and expectations of others. We assess, we select, we reward on our own criteria. We have our inbuilt standards, the origins of which we rarely question and which, as we have seen, we interpret as 'normal'. Given that this is the case, can we identify firm dimensions of difference that people managers can be taught to recognize and respect?

Triandis (1990) identifies a number of such dimensions, or cultural syndromes. One example is 'cultural complexity', which particularly affects the perception of time. Think about time for a moment and consider how many basic business activities depend on people 'doing something within three hours', 'arriving for an interview at 10 am', 'achieving an objective in six months' and so on. In fact, our judgement of other people depends heavily on our conception of time. How do we feel about people who do not turn up to an interview on time, or fail to complete a task within the agreed period? If we live in an industrial culture we will regard them unfavourably.

But what if their concept of time is not the same as ours? Of course, an hour, a day or a month is the same for everyone, but we vary in our beliefs about the significance of these periods. Albert Einstein showed that time is relative and this notion is as significant for human resource management as it is for space travel.

Triandis argues that different cultures have different attitudes towards time. Time-keeping is treated tolerantly in undeveloped societies – with few things to do, they can be done in any order. However, as societies become industrial and technological, people must pay increased attention to time. In industrialized countries there are many things to do and they must be coordinated with other people. Hence, time becomes more important. Time is regarded as something precise and highly significant. So, if a manager moves to a less developed country, what standard is it fair for that person to expect?

Another significant time characteristic is that of short or long-term orientation (Hofstede and Bond, 1988). East Asians tend to have a much longer time perspective than, for example, nationals in Australasia, Nigeria, North America, Pakistan and the UK. In Part 1 we identified HRM as a philosophy of people management that is long term in its intent. The root of this orientation lies in comparisons of US and Japanese management and criticism of the former's short-term attitudes towards human resources. In effect, the adoption of HRM requires short-termist cultures to take on Japanese attitudes towards time. As we saw in earlier chapters, this does not come naturally and provides a partial explanation for the failure of many organizations to take on true HRM.

Hofstede and Bond (1988) attribute the long-term orientation in east Asians to 'Confucian Dynamism'. It embodies values from the teaching of Confucius such as perseverance, a need to order relationships by status, a sense of shame and a habit of thrifty saving. Kahn (1979, p.121) also saw the rise of the east Asian 'tiger' economies as being due to the Confucian ethic, including factors such as sobriety; placing a high value on education; a need for accomplishment in various skills; seriousness about job, family and obligations; and a sense of hierarchy. However, as we will see later in this chapter, it has been pointed out that since Kahn contributed to the argument, the tiger economies have come to include countries with Buddhist or Islamic rather than Confucian traditions.

Roles

Triandis also relates cultural complexity to the way we define our working and other roles. In complex societies roles become increasingly specific – compartmentalized into separate mental boxes. We can be finance managers, parents, social club officials and behave differently in each role. In less complex societies, on the other hand, roles are diffuse, affecting every aspect of people's lives. Religion, politics and matters of taste are important in diffuse cultures. They are less important in role-specific cultures. Developed countries tend to be role-specific, avoiding role confusion. Theory and best practice in key HRM areas such as selection, performance measurement and development assume an equal opportunities approach in which people are dealt with without favour or prejudice. However, this notion is alien to diffuse-role cultures in which it is natural to favour members of one's own family or community.

Diffuse-role cultures value politeness and courtesy – even towards people who are disliked – something that would be regarded as hypocrisy in specific cultures. Again human resource texts assume that outright, if tactful, honesty is required in rejecting job applicants, counselling for performance weaknesses and dismissal. In short, if we feel that someone is not up to the job we more or less say so. This approach can appear arrogant and aggressive to people from diffuse societies.

Related cultures

Haire, Ghiselli and Porter (1966) surveyed 3500 managers in 14 different countries and estimated that 28 per cent of discernible differences in management attitudes were culturally based and identified four main cultural groups: Nordic-European, Latin-European, Anglo-American and developing nations. This started a trend to try and divide the world's complex pattern of cultures into neat, analytical groupings – with all the attendant risks of historical inaccuracy and gross insensitivity. Take for example, an attempt by Leeds, Kirkbride and Duncan (1994): '… we can distinguish a number of reasonably clear country clusters … which parallel the work of other commentators … These would include:

1 Scandinavia: Denmark, Finland, Norway and Sweden.

2 Anglo: Ireland and the UK in Europe but also other English-speaking countries including Australia, New Zealand and Canada (excluding Quebec), and the United States.

3 Germanic: Austria, Germany and Switzerland.

4 Latin and Mediterranean: Italy, Portugal and Spain.

5 Near Eastern: Greece and Turkey. The Turks and Greeks are close culturally, and both are proud of their European and Oriental associations. However, the Greeks have also been considered very close to the Italians culturally.

6 Northern (quasi) Latin: France and Belgium have frequently been placed in a separate cluster of two. However, France is often also put in the Latin and Mediterranean group.

7 Miscellaneous: regions such as Alsace (France), the Flemish and German-speaking Belgium and countries such as Luxembourg are difficult to categorize. They possess their own special identity as well as cultural traits based on national identity, and are also influenced by values from neighbouring countries such as Holland and Germany. Holland … has been placed in the Nordic group … but shares many of the traits associated with the Anglo group.'

The authors speculate on the historical origins of these patterns and qualify this classification with the caveat that reality is much more complex. However, they do not accept the Thurley and Wirdenius (1990, p.33) criticism of 'the tendency to over simplify national culture and make comparisons based on exaggerated cultural stereotypes'.

Strangely, many authors seem to have picked up the curious French habit of using the terms 'Anglo' or 'Anglo-Saxon' when describing countries in Australasia, the British Isles and North America. Notwithstanding the considerable irritation this creates for those of us with Celtic origins, it demonstrates also an ignorance of ethnic relationships that leads one to question the overall value of the exercise. If the Irish can be wrongly classified as 'Anglo-Saxons' (Ronen and Shenkar, 1985; Sparrow and Hiltrop, 1994), how much faith can be placed in the supposed validity of any other grouping?

Activity 9:4	Do attempts to classify cultures into groups or types enhance our understanding of international HRM?

Psychology and culture

Classification difficulties aside, there is no denying that cultural differences can be deeply embedded. Chung (1991), for example, draws on the psychology of thinking styles to explain differences between business cultures, arguing that Europeans are taught to think in a linear way, whereas Asians see things as a whole (see Table 9.1).

We can see from the table that, according to Chung, Europeans value rational logic while Asians think intuitively in circles and leaps. Whereas Europeans are individualistic and dependent on legalistic controls, Asians are community-minded and prepared to build and work on the basis of trust. European thinking is comparatively short term whereas Asians look further ahead. This model provides a cultural explanation of the different forms of people management: contract-based in the West; commitment-based in the East. Despite the additional insight this model provides, again, however, we have a case of two groups of very diverse cultures being lumped together to suit an argument.

Table 9.1	Ways of thinking	
	European	*Asian*
Thinking styles	Causal, clear-cut, single-track thinking – one thing follows another	Network, whole vision, complex, taking in different perspectives
Decision styles	To suit controls Individual, free To suit the majority	Based on trust Group solidarity Reaching consensus
Behaviour	True to principles Based on legal principles Dynamic, facing conflict Open, direct, self-confident, extrovert	To suit a situation To suit a community Harmonious, conservative Restrained, indirect, with self-assurance, introvert

Source: Adapted from Chung (1991).

Culture and business behaviour

Western observers recently have come to appreciate the diversity of cultures in Asia. Religions go beyond Confucianism to include Buddhism, Islam, Christianity and others, with wide-ranging effects on people management. In Malaysia and Indonesia, for example, a predominantly Moslem culture has produced distinctive role differences between men and women at work. There can be restrictions on employment of female workers in 'male' areas of a factory and in promoting women to be in charge of men. For Western people managers this can cause a conflict between moral commitment to equal opportunities and respect for local traditions, an issue we will develop further in Part 6 on the management of diversity.

The constitutional context and role of the state also varies considerably throughout the region with political arrangements ranging from democracy to one-party rule. At the level of individual behaviour, we can also see that variations in rules on politeness and directness produce contrasting ways of conducting business:

- National cultures vary widely within the region.
- Courtesy and politeness are valued highly in all these cultures.
- Business structure is family-based in some, but not all, of these countries.
- There is widespread contact and cooperation between Chinese communities throughout the region.
- Business practices are changing because younger people are being trained in Western-style business schools.

HRM in reality

Diversity in Asia

Western observers have tended to regard Asian countries as one business culture, primarily based on the Japanese model. In fact the region contains a wide diversity of cultures, including several large countries such as Bangladesh, China, India and Pakistan – some of which are not homogeneous in themselves – and a number of smaller countries with very different traditions and economic problems. Failure to appreciate the contrasts between cultures is not confined to Westerners: the variations in business practices in these countries are just as surprising to the Japanese.

Perhaps the only issue they have in common is a keen attention to etiquette and politeness. Rudeness and over-eagerness can be the downfall of visiting executives who must expect some obligatory courtesies. Thereafter, however, diversity begins. In Singapore and Malaysia, long accustomed to Western business, negotiations can be relatively direct, whereas in Indonesia and Thailand the participants must engage in further elaborate ritual. Sensitivity to these variations is essential for negotiations to succeed.

As a relatively recent creation, Singapore pays less attention to tradition than countries such as Thailand, and business is less dependent on family or clan connections. In a region where corruption is still not uncommon, Singapore's stringent legislative system encourages transparent honesty in business activities. Familiarity with Western ways and good command of English also lead to a greater readiness among Singaporeans and Filipinos to ask questions or challenge instructions than, for example, Thais and Malays.

Chinese minorities are widespread throughout South-East Asia and have their own ways of conducting business, sharing a similar management philosophy. In many

▶

◀

countries they dominate business but in Malaysia and Indonesia they are constrained by nationalist sensitivities. Throughout the region, and especially among the Chinese communities, there is a gradual trend away from family-owned business towards free market joint-stock arrangements. In conjunction with this development, and partly due to contrasting business traditions, it is becoming common for younger managers to be trained according to American principles.

Source: *Financial Times*, 4 December 1995, Edward Luce, 'SE Asia: singularly different'.

Discussion questions

1 **Outline the main similarities and differences in people management between the countries described in this review.**

2 **To what extent do you consider that the Western concept of HRM is likely to replace prevailing forms of people management in these countries?**

Cultural training

Human resource managers have a considerable role to play in preparing staff for work overseas. Given the range and sensitivity of cultural differences, it is clear that people working in an international context can benefit from tuition in the business customs and social manners of the countries they will work in. Human resource managers can play a major part in developing programmes for sales and other staff whose behaviour must be fully acceptable in target countries. For example, it is evident that export managers travelling to other countries in east Asia need to have considerable awareness of cultural differences. Consultants from the West have even greater hurdles of understanding to overcome.

What kind of training can HR managers arrange for travelling staff? We provide an answer to this question in Chapter 20 when we examine development programmes for international managers. At this stage, it is sufficient to say that training can encompass language, social behaviour, local business structure and practice, and table etiquette. However, the most critical area is that of non-verbal behaviour. Stories abound of contracts being lost because of inappropriate expressions, overeagerness, unacceptable familiarity and general insensitivity. Argyle (1991) details a number of key behavioural features that differ from one culture to another.

Non-verbal behaviour

● *Proximity, touch and gaze.* Cultures can be classified as contact or non-contact. For example, Arabs and Latin Americans stand much closer to each other than east Asians and northern Europeans. In Greece, staring is regarded as an expression of interest and politeness, even at a complete stranger in the street. Conversely, a Caribbean employee may avoid eye-to-eye contact with a manager during a conversation, having been taught to regard this as discourteous. Opportunities for misunderstanding here are boundless.

● *Expressiveness.* The Japanese are reluctant to be too expressive for fear of causing offence. Many northern Europeans are also reticent in showing emotion. By contrast, African-Caribbeans are more likely to be open about expressing opinions, including negative emotions and attitudes.

- *Gestures*. It is dangerous to make use of one's own familiar gestures in another country. In all innocence you may indicate a threat or pornographic meaning.
- *Accompaniments of speech*. People often expect listeners to show obvious attention while they are talking. Failure can be interpreted as lack of interest or boredom. This feedback is not expected in all cultures. According to Argyle, 'black Americans often annoy white interviewers by their apparent lack of response while listening'.
- *Symbolic self-presentation*. Dress, badges and uniforms have significance for individuals in a particular culture but may mean nothing to outsiders.
- *Rituals*. Seating positions at a dining or conference table may be highly significant to one culture – for example Japan – and virtually irrelevant to another.

Customs or rules

- *Bribery*. A bribe in one culture is a gift in another. In many cultures it is normal to pay a commission to people involved in a transaction. People such as civil servants, managers and sales representatives expect a percentage of the contract value. Western European and North American tradition regards this as unethical if not illegal.
- *Nepotism*. Cultures that feature personal obligations to large extended families expect powerful individuals to look after relatives. For instance, by giving jobs or contracts. This 'social welfare' system is normally governed by codes of conduct that regulate its abuse.
- *Gifts*. Every culture expects its members to give presents in certain circumstances such as weddings or birthdays. Some cultures extend gift-giving to everyday business meetings. For example, the Japanese spend a great deal of money on standard presents from special gift shops.
- *Buying and selling*. The importance of bargaining varies from 'fixed price' cultures where haggling is regarded with distaste, to others where negotiation is expected in any transaction.
- *Eating and drinking*. Each culture has taboos on various foods. For example, the eating of pork is unacceptable in religious Jewish and Moslem communities. Alcohol is particularly problematic. It is a feature of business transactions in parts of Europe, but drinking is increasingly frowned upon in North America and abhorred in many Arab countries. The ritual of eating, commonly described as 'table manners' also varies considerably. The international manager risks causing offence and prejudicing business if local eating customs are not observed.
- *Rules about time*. Being on time is regarded as polite and a demonstration of business efficiency in Western countries. Conversely, lateness is taken as normal in other cultures – the more powerful the individual, the later that person will appear.

Language

The use of language has critical implications. For example, in appraisal feedback meetings or interviews people managers must be aware of cultural differences covering directness and politeness.

As regards directness, Westerners often begin an informal meeting with a joke, but at this stage in a Japanese relationship such familiarity would be regarded as extremely offensive. The Japanese expect formality until each other's status and authority are clearly understood. People of different status would not expect to conduct discussions at an informal level. Americans discuss business in a direct way.

Northern Europeans, being sometimes reserved and formal, are closer to east Asians – but only slightly. According to Chung: 'Asians prefer indirect communication, they want the correct form, they esteem absolute politeness and reserve with self-control.' The Japanese, for example, may leave sentences unfinished to allow listeners to draw their own conclusions. Westerners live with confrontation and conflict, but this would cause considerable loss of face in Japan. The extent and importance of 'face' is difficult for a Westerner to understand.

As regards politeness, all cultures employ polite forms of address that are expected in particular circumstances. For instance, senior staff expect to be addressed more formally than colleagues at the same level. In several languages the word for 'you' has to be used carefully. In French, respect is traditionally shown to individuals by using the plural '*vous*', rather than the singular '*tu*'.

Politeness is socially supportive behaviour that maintains harmony and respect between individuals. It varies considerably both in importance and practice. Politeness is so important in Japan that it is even regarded as rude to say 'no'. Foreign business visitors are famously advised that 'yes' does not mean agreement but 'yes, I have heard you'.

Torrington (1994, p.19) describes the end-product as 'inter-cultural self-confidence'.

Key concept 9:2

Attitudes   Attitudes are dispositions held by people, towards or against people, things and ideas. They have individual components based on factors such as personality and understanding, and social elements derived from shared experiences and cultural history. Attitudes are complex systems of belief, evaluation, emotion and behaviour (Eiser, 1994; McKenna, 1994, p.251).

Activity 9:5   Does the analysis provided by Argyle go beyond cultural stereotyping?

National and organizational cultures

We have identified some of the broader implications of culture on people management. In this section we examine some specific contributions to cross-cultural understanding, including the classic research conducted by Hofstede (1980). In our earlier discussion we touched on the danger of stereotyping. For example, France has a culture that is perceived in a highly stereotyped way in other countries. Images of beret-wearing peasants and long, leisurely lunches with impeccably cooked food obscure the complexity and variety of French culture. Our cultural stereotypes are composed of a few accurate notions mixed with generalizations and misconceptions, some dating from previous centuries. They take no account of change in a modern, technologically advanced country that also has distinctive regional cultures. Is it possible to define real differences between countries such as France and others, avoiding the trap of stereotyping?

Organizations are microcosms of national cultures, reflecting crucial differences. Hofstede (1980; 1994) compared several thousand IBM employees in over 50 countries using attitude questionnaires (see Key concept 9.2). He found significant differences between employees in one country and another, despite their similar jobs and membership of an organization which, as we saw in Chapter 2, is renowned for its strong corporate culture.

Using factor analysis, a sophisticated statistical method, Hofstede analysed the employees' responses and attributed the variation to four main dimensions: power distance; collectivism versus individualism; masculinity versus femininity; and uncertainty avoidance.

Power distance

How marked are the status differences between people with high and low degrees of power? Questions tested whether:

- people were afraid of expressing disagreement with their managers
- management style was perceived as paternalistic, autocratic, participative and so on
- employees preferred a particular management style.

Table 9.2 shows ratings on power distance and other dimensions. Individuals in countries with autocratic management styles preferred their own bosses to have that style. Individuals in countries with low power distance scores preferred consultation. Consistent with our discussion on diversity in Asia, it is not surprising to find that the highest score was found in Malaysia where workers have been known to ask Western managers to be more 'bossy'. In a culture where respect for authority is a valued quality, participative management can make people feel uncomfortable (Beardwell and Holden, 1994, p.603).

Collectivism versus individualism

Is a culture focused on individuals or groups? Hofstede describes most societies as 'collectivist' in a non-political sense. In these cultures people obtain their identity from an

Table 9.2	Cultural dimensions (after Hofstede, 1980, and others)		
Dimension	High	Medium	Low
Individualism (versus collectivism)	Argentina, Australia, Belgium, Brazil, Canada, France, Ireland, New Zealand, Spain, UK, USA	Austria, Germany, Israel, Italy, Japan, Netherlands, Scandinavia, Switzerland, South Africa	Chile, Greece, Hong Kong, India, Iran, Mexico, Pakistan, Peru, Portugal, Taiwan, Singapore, Turkey, Yugoslavia
Power distance (inequality between levels in organizations)	Belgium, France, Iran, Hong Kong, Nigeria, Philippines, Singapore, South America, Spain, Taiwan, Thailand	Japan	Australia, Germany, Italy, UK, USA
Uncertainty avoidance (intolerance of ambiguity)	Austria, Argentina, Belgium, France, Germany, Greece, Iran, Israel, Italy, Japan, Spain, Turkey, South Africa, Switzerland		Australia, Canada, Ireland, Netherlands, New Zealand, Scandinavia, UK, USA
Masculinity (competitiveness)	Japan, Austria, Venezuela, Italy, Switzerland	Canada, Jamaica, Greece, India, Hong Kong, Pakistan, South Africa, UK, USA	Chile, Netherlands, Scandinavia, Costa Rica, Yugoslavia
Work centrality	Japan	Belgium, Israel, USA, Yugoslavia	Germany, Netherlands, UK
Job satisfaction	Canada, UK, Germany, Netherlands, Scandinavia		Greece, Spain, Italy, Portugal, Japan

extended family or a work organization. This is especially relevant to people management, and HRM in particular, because most of its concepts come from the USA – a strongly individualistic country. Indeed, Hofstede found the highest scores for individualism in the USA, followed by Australia and the UK (both countries that have followed US management developments keenly). Individualistic cultures are characterized by:

- An emphasis on care for self and immediate family – if necessary, at the expense of others.
- 'I' consciousness – heightened awareness of the distinction between oneself and other people.
- Self-orientation – looking for advantage and career progression for the individual.
- Keen defence of the right to a private life and personal opinions.
- Emphasis on decisions being made individually.
- Emotional independence from the work organization.
- Autonomy and individual financial security.

The least individualistic scores came from Latin America and east Asia. High power distance and collectivism usually go together. France and Belgium are exceptional, combining medium power distance with high individualism. In collective cultures such as Taiwan, socially respected jobs are valued highly. In contrast, individualistic cultures value personal success, responsibility and self-respect. Triandis (1995, p.33) points to key differences leading to reward and promotion: 'People in individualistic countries have the tendency to emphasize *ability* more than is necessary, and to underemphasize *effort*. In collectivist cultures, the reverse is true.'

Hui (1990, p.193) argues that Hofstede's notion of the collective is too vague: people in collective cultures relate to particular in-groups, not to everybody. For example, the Japanese identify with the organization in which they work. The important distinction is a sharper distinction between 'in' and 'out' groups in collectivist cultures, compared to individualistic cultures where boundaries tend to blur. Hence, recruitment may be restricted to members of a particular in-group, especially the extended family. Collectivist cultures emphasize harmony, and avoidance of shame or loss of face. These are social elements of culture emphasizing obligations to others within the in-group. This point is further developed later in this chapter in our discussion of commitment in Japanese organizations.

Masculinity versus femininity

Hofstede rates the aggressiveness of a culture as masculinity – its level of individual assertiveness and competition. Positive responses to questions relating to high earnings, recognition, advancement and challenging work rated highly on masculinity. Good working relationships, cooperation, living in a desirable area and employment security were scored at the 'feminine' end of the dimension. Japan scored highest on this dimension with the lowest levels in Scandinavia and the Netherlands.

The dimension has practical consequences on people management:

- *Recruitment.* Applications in 'masculine' cultures are expected to be couched in positive, achievement-orientated language. Interviews are searching and sometimes aggressive. In contrast, applicants from 'feminine' cultures are expected to be modest about their achievements, giving the opportunity for interviewers to 'discover' undeclared talents. Thus Americans applying for jobs in the Netherlands can appear brash and boastful, whereas Dutch people may appear soft and unassertive to American interviewers.

● *Meetings.* In Scandinavia and the Netherlands, meetings are held to achieve cooperation, exchange ideas and solve problems. The intention is positive and participative. In masculine cultures, such as Australia and the UK, meetings are more competitive and are used for displays of power, posturing and political point-making.

The masculine–feminine dimension helps to explain the different forms of market found in Part 2, and the styles of management and employee relations prevalent in those markets. The welfare-focused social markets in Scandinavia and the Netherlands emphasize mutual respect and care for all members of the community at the expense of individual wealth. Employee relations take place within a context of extensive worker participation and protection. The 'masculine' countries, on the other hand, feature highly competitive free markets, an imbalance of power and income between management and workers, and comparatively low levels of social security. There are exceptions, of course, since Japan and Germany are high on masculinity but do not show the same range of characteristics.

Uncertainty avoidance

How do people deal with conflict, particularly aggression and the expression of feelings? Hofstede's fourth dimension measures people's reactions to unusual situations. High uncertainty avoidance favours precise rules, teachers who are always right and superiors who should be obeyed without question. Low uncertainty avoidance leads to flexibility, arguing with superiors is acceptable and students are happy with teachers who do not claim to know everything. According to Hofstede (1994, p.145):

> In weak uncertainty avoidance cultures, like the USA and even more in the UK and, for example, Sweden, managers and non-managers alike feel definitely uncomfortable with systems of rigid rules, especially if it is evident that many of these were never followed. In strong uncertainty avoidance cultures, like most of the Latin world, people feel equally uncomfortable without the structure of a system of rules, even if many of these are impractical and impracticable.

Dimension mix

The characteristics of national business cultures are further defined by the particular mix of these four dimensions. In the last chapter we outlined a range of organization structures. Hofstede argues that the choice of structure is strongly influenced by the prevalent culture. For example, matrix structures have never been popular in France because the idea of having more than one boss to report to does not meet the French need for clearly defined authority. A culture with high power distance and strong uncertainty avoidance prefers a functional 'pyramid of people' hierarchy. Lower power distance but high uncertainty avoidance, as in Austria, Germany and Israel, encourages a 'well-oiled machine': an organization with a clear structure, rules and procedures. Anglo-Celtic and Scandinavian cultures, with low power distance and uncertainty avoidance favour a flexible structure focused on human relations: a 'village market'. Finally, the large power distance and low uncertainty avoidance typical in east Asia features a strong boss, equivalent to the father, and hence an organizational model based on the family.

Hofstede's statistics have been questioned but the thesis remains popular. It fits conventional wisdom and common stereotypes. Such research has relevance to HRM in cross-border mergers and acquisitions. Olie (1990) found that British–Dutch mergers were more successful than German–Dutch mergers. Netherlands and UK cultures had greater synergy than those of the Netherlands and Germany. Similarly, Olie observed the difficulties of American managers in the US subsidiary of a Japanese bank. Americans expected firm performance targets from head office. Japanese managers could not understand why the Americans could not identify their own objectives, based on the parent's banking philosophy. Olie found differences also between British and Americans. Directors from the two countries disagreed about information required for decisions. The Americans wanted far more data than the British.

A study by Pheng and Yuquan (2002) compared construction workers in Singapore and two cities in China on Hofstede's dimensions. Although apparently from related cultures, their different histories seemed to result in some interesting variations:

- *Power distance.* Singapore workers showed a higher power distance than their Chinese counterparts. In Singapore, superiors and subordinates were more likely to consider each other as unequal. Pheng and Yuquan state that 'the hierarchical system is felt to be based on some existential inequality; power is the basic fact of society that antedates good or evil and where its legitimacy is irrelevant. Indigenous organizations centralize power more and subordinates are expected to be told what to do. Superiors are believed to be entitled to privileges.'

   Construction employees in China felt themselves to be more equal, whether they were subordinates or superiors. They were likely to regard the hierarchical system as an inequality of roles, established for convenience, which could change in different circumstances. This attitude leads to more decentralized organizations with flatter hierarchies and fewer supervisors.

- *Uncertainty avoidance.* Singapore respondents had a low index value for uncertainty, in contrast with Chinese respondents who had a high index value. According to Pheng and Yuquan: 'In Singapore, people feel less threatened by ambiguous situations. Emotions are shown less in public. Younger people are trustworthy. People are willing to take risks in life. The authorities are there to serve the citizens. Conflicts and competition can be contained on the level of fair play and are used constructively.'

   In China, on the other hand, 'people tend to establish more formal rules, reject deviant ideas and behaviour, accept the possibility of absolute truths and the attainment of unchallengeable expertise. Younger people are looked upon suspiciously. People are concerned with security in life. Ordinary citizens are incompetent, unlike the authorities. Conflict and competition can unleash aggression and should therefore be avoided.'

- *Individualism/collectivism.* Singapore workers are more individualistic than their counterparts in China, tending to think of themselves as 'I' and also tending to classify people by individual characteristics, rather than by group membership. Employees in China are less inclined to differentiate an individual from the group and put a lower emphasis on self-actualization.

- *Masculinity/femininity.* The masculinity score in the Singapore construction industry is lower than that for respondents in China, meaning that Chinese employees tend to place a greater emphasis on work goals such as earnings and advancement and also on assertiveness. In Singapore, by contrast, respondents showed a greater concern with personal goals, a friendly atmosphere, getting along well with the boss and others, etc.

| Activity 9:6 | Summarize Hofstede's analysis of culture in your own words. |

Converging cultures?

The accelerating trend towards the internationalization of business is eroding these cultural differences. For example, the development of business within the European Union has led to talk of 'Euromanagers' (Tyson *et al.*, 1993). But attempts to create pan-European businesses can still founder due to national differences. Throughout the world, younger and more travelled managers are more alike in attitudes and practices than colleagues less open to foreign influences. They prefer to associate with people who have similar ideologies and personalities – even if they come from different cultures. Additionally, technological development is leading to an increasing convergence of business methods.

Corporate culture

As Deal and Kennedy (1982, p.15) propose: '… people are a company's greatest resource, and the way to manage them is not directly by computer reports, but by the subtle cues of a culture.' In this section we turn to the cultures that distinguish one organization from another, whether or not they are in different countries. It has been long recognized that the organization cannot simply be described in terms of its formal structure (Bakke, 1950). Often this is no more than window dressing: the illusion of order that senior management believe they have created.

Key concept 9:3

The informal organization   An organization is both a formal and informal entity. The formal aspect of an organization is its official structure and public image visible in organization charts and annual reports. The informal organization is a more elusive concept, describing the complex network of psychological and social relationships between its people. The informal organization is an unrecognized world of cliques and politics, friendships and enmities, gossip and affairs.

Behind and in parallel with the 'official' system there is the reality of action and power commonly described as the 'informal' organization: 'those patterns of coordination that arise among members of a formal organization which are not called for by the blueprint' (Schein, 1988, p.16).

Formal organization design is concerned with only certain activities which are felt important to the organization. All other aspects of working life, from gossip on the line to complaining about management, are the territory of the informal organization (see Key concept 9.3). Real action depends on this informal structure of opinion leaders and power-brokers (Brunsson, 1989, p.7). The formal organization is there for 'demonstration and display to the outside world … defined as rituals'. Management literature earlier in the 20th century frequently regarded informal behaviour as undesirable: 'Basing their actions on the logic of formal organization, they try to neutralize or do away with the informal behaviour through directive leadership, management controls, and pseudo human relations programs' (Argyris, 1957, p.231).

This was typical of the North American business schools that tended to view organization structure as a prescriptive matter of 'one best way' with scant regard for functional purpose or cultural location. This form of management served to increase feelings of dependence, submissiveness and subordination among employees. Ironically, workers coped by increasing the scope of the informal organization, using it as a mechanism to counter management initiatives.

By the 1980s, however, the informal organization was regarded in a new and more favourable light. From being perceived as something to be ignored or bludgeoned out of existence, it was realized that features of the informal organization could be harnessed for competitive advantage. This notion developed along with the concept of corporate culture – a central theme of the 'excellence' literature (Peters and Waterman, 1982) as well as HRM and total quality management (see Key concept 9.4). Its major exponents presented a 'strong' corporate culture as a key factor in enhancing competitive performance through greater employee commitment and flexibility (Deal and Kennedy, 1982). Employees in strong cultures know what is expected of them. Conversely, staff in weak cultures waste time trying to discover what is required. Employees identify with a strong culture and take pride in their organization.

Key concept 9:4

Corporate culture   The simplest – and probably most often quoted – definition is Bower's (1966) 'the way we do things around here'. Trice and Beyer (1984) elaborated this as: 'the system of ... publicly and collectively accepted meanings operating for a given group at a given time'. Hofstede (1994) describes corporate culture as 'the psychological assets of an organization, which can be used to predict what will happen to its financial assets in five years' time'.

The creation – or even the definition – of such a culture is not easy. In managing people to achieve organizational goals, organizations prefer clarity, certainty and perfection (Pascale and Athos, 1981, p.105). However, those same organizations have people as their basic building bricks. Their human relationships involve ambiguity, uncertainty and imperfection. The trick of good management is to honour, balance and integrate these. One way to do so is somehow to use the information channels of the informal organization to transmit and reinforce messages of commitment to management goals.

Unlike many other 'new' management ideas, corporate culture has endured and appears to have had a 'material effect upon the politics of work' (Willmott, 1993, p.515). We will see in Chapter 12 that a whole industry has arisen to supply management of change programmes, much of it devoted to changing and strengthening corporate cultures. However, it is worth noting that although a wealth of literature exists publicizing the importance of culture change, most of this is relatively uncritical.

Activity 9:7

In what ways are the informal organization and the corporate culture of that organization (a) the same; (b) different?

HRM in reality

Men dress smarter than women in the office

A survey commissioned by Austin Reed reveals that men dress more smartly than women in the office. The Consumer Analysis Group surveyed 500 men and women in England, Scotland and Wales and 53 per cent of both sexes agreed that men were the smartest dressers in their office. Also, one in six men (described as 'hopeful') admitted to choosing work clothes in order to attract female colleagues.

The survey also found solicitors and barristers to be the most unfashionable and 'un-cool' office workers in Britain – or so said 28 per cent of survey respondents. They were followed in the 'un-cool' stakes by bankers and accountants (22 per cent), IT professionals (17 per cent) and journalists (15 per cent).

More details:

- 69 per cent of men claimed to favour more relaxed businesswear over dark suits.
- 63 per cent of men favoured a relaxation of the dress code for men in offices and 45 per cent of women agreed.
- 37 per cent of male respondents considered that relaxed, coordinated jackets and trousers were appropriate workwear these days, but only 15 per cent of men would want to dress down in jeans or cords; just 4 per cent of men said they would feel comfortable wearing a t-shirt, and 9 per cent a sweatshirt.

Of the people who would like a change to office dress code, colour was identified as the most important factor with 84 per cent of women and 70 per cent of men wanting more 'colour coordination' and more 'colourful styles'.

Some 66 per cent of women felt that the clothes worn by men in the office had an effect on colleagues' opinions of their ability, but only 41 per cent of men agreed. One in three men admitted to sometimes wearing odd socks to work, with young men being the most haphazard. Almost half of male office workers claimed to look after laundering of their shirts and ties (43 per cent), but only 10 per cent of women agreed. Around 80 per cent of women with partners working in offices said they laundered their partner's shirts.

Source: *HRMGuide.co.uk* (http://www.hrmguide.co.uk), March 2001.

Question: To what extent does the dress code in an organization indicate the influence of cultural factors?

The Deal and Kennedy model of corporate culture

We have noted that, together with Peters and Waterman's *In Search of Excellence* (1982), Deal and Kennedy's *Corporate Cultures* (1982) was inspirational in this area. As a prelude to discussion of the role of corporate culture in people management, it is appropriate to outline Deal and Kennedy's model. It incorporates five critical elements: the business environment; values; heroes; rites and rituals; and the cultural network.

The business environment

In line with our discussion in Part 2, Deal and Kennedy argued that the activities of governments and competitors, changes in technology, customer demand and general economic conditions are instrumental in shaping the cultures of organizations with survival potential. The orientation of organizations within this environment – for example a focus on sales or concentration on research and development – develops specific cultural styles.

Values

Values are at the heart of corporate culture. They are made up of the key beliefs and concepts shared by an organization's employees. Successful companies are clear about these values and their managers publicly reinforce them. Often values are unwritten and operate at a subconscious level.

Heroes

Personifications of the organization's values: achievers who provide role models for success within the company. Heroism is an element of leadership that has been virtually forgotten by modern managers: 'since the 1920s, the corporate world has been powered by managers who are rationalists, who do strategic planning, write memos, and devise flow charts' (Deal and Kennedy, 1982, p.37). Heroes, on the other hand, create rather than run organizations; are intuitive rather than decisive; have all the time in the world because they make time; are experimenters rather than routinizers; are playful; get things 'just right'. Heroes have vision and break the existing order if necessary in order to achieve that vision. Deal and Kennedy describe this process in terms of 'making success attainable and human'.

A figurehead such as Richard Branson is presented as 'being' the Virgin group, serving the purpose of 'symbolizing the company to the outside world' (Deal and Kennedy, 1982, p.40).

Rites and rituals

Ceremonies and routine behavioural rituals reinforce the culture. Examples include product launches, sales conferences or the Friday afternoon 'beer-bust'.

The cultural network

The carrier of stories and gossip that spreads information about valued behaviour and 'heroic myths' around the organization. The degree of factual content involved is questionable. Michelson and Mouly (2000, p.339) attempt to draw a distinction between rumour and gossip:

> While the basis of rumour is information that is unsubstantiated, gossip may or may not be a known fact …. This distinction is more a matter of degree than substance and the issue becomes problematic in the context of celebrity or political gossip. In such cases the 'facts' or 'truth' are likely to be highly elusive. It is also conceivable that the initiation of rumour may be underpinned by some element of 'truth', no matter how obscure or circumstantial the evidence. The extent of factuality or truth is hard to determine any way, and one can never know if something is a 'white lie' or 'half truth'.

Key concept 9:5 **Rumour and gossip**   Rumour is typically regarded as unsubstantiated talk that is not supported by evidence or authority. Gossip is commonly held to have a factual basis of some kind.

HRM in reality ### New code of conduct for NHS managers

A new code of conduct has been published for consultation until mid-July 2002 by National Health Service chief executive Nigel Crisp. It sets out the ethics and standards of behaviour expected of managers. A breach of the code will be regarded as gross misconduct, leading in many cases to dismissal. If the breaches are serious – financial fraud, providing false information or negligence in providing for the safety of patients are given as examples – then the managers responsible are unlikely to be employed again in the NHS.

▶

The code will cover all NHS managers and was developed following the investigations into medical scandals, including practices at Bristol Royal Infirmary and Alder Hey in Liverpool, and also the inappropriate manipulation of waiting lists. The code says NHS managers must:

- make the care and safety of patients their first concern
- respect the public, patients, relatives, carers, NHS staff and partners in other agencies
- be honest and act with integrity
- accept accountability for their work, the performance of those they manage and their own organisation
- cooperate with colleagues in the NHS and the community.

Addressing the NHS Confederation conference in Harrogate, Nigel Crisp said:

This code of practice is about the values we as NHS managers stand for. We decided to introduce this Code in order to have a means for holding managers to account for their own professional behaviour. It will be used in that way and breaches of this code will be taken very seriously indeed.

The vast majority of managers in the NHS are highly principled and value-driven people who will welcome the code. But we must deal with failure. We simply must not repeat the mistakes of the past. We cannot have people re-employed in positions of trust if they have betrayed that trust in other parts of the NHS. We must have national standards applied nationally. This is about trust and about trust in us all as the NHS. It is corrosive if not handled well. We must be firm and fair.

However, the code is also a set of values and should inform development programmes and training for managers. It should make us all think exactly how we are going to work, how we make the care and safety of patients our first concern and how we respect the public, patients, relatives and carers.

But breaches of the code must be investigated fairly. Just as the code sets out how managers should behave and their responsibilities, they also have rights. They have the right to be treated with respect, judged consistently and fairly, encouraged to maintain and improve their knowledge and skills and to be helped to balance their work and home lives properly.

I am delighted with the work put in to this Code by Ken Jarrold, Chief Executive of County Durham and Tees Valley Health Authority, in partnership with the NHS Confederation, the Institute of Health Management, the British Association on Medical Managers, the Health Financial Management Association and the NHS Modernisation Centre.

Source: *HRMGuide.co.uk* (http://www.hrmguide.co.uk), 23 May 2002.

Question: Is a code of practice a method of managing the culture of an organization?

Table 9.3 outlines an anthropological classification of the elements of corporate cultures.

Deal and Kennedy's types of culture

Deal and Kennedy produced a framework with two key dimensions: the 'risk' attached to the company's activities and the speed of 'feedback' to employees. Taking the extreme combinations of these two dimensions they described four types of culture:

Table 9.3	Elements of corporate culture

Element	Ingredients
Company practices	*Rites*: planned, dramatic events in the life of the organization. *Ceremonial*: a series of rites such as the launch of a product, a graduation ceremony, the annual shareholders' meeting. *Ritual*: standardized, unimportant activities such as the Friday afternoon pub session which used to be a commonplace.
Company communication	*Stories*: based on true events. *Myths*: untrue stories, old-timers' stories. *Sagas*: heroic company histories. *Legends*: involving heroes and heroines in the organization's history. *Folk tales*: fiction with a message indicating successful behaviours that led to promotion or reward. *Symbols and slogans*: these are powerful components of a corporate identity, serving to create a recognizable image for people inside and outside the organization. They include colour schemes, letterheads, logos and uniforms.
Physical cultural forms	*Artefacts*: tools, furniture styles, appliances and other equipment used in a factory or office. Some companies collect these in a haphazard way over the years, others have central purchasing policies that ensure harmonization. *Physical layout*: as with equipment, offices, production areas and canteens may be laid out in an ad hoc manner or they may be planned to follow an organizational theme.
Common language	Organizations develop their own terminology and ways of expression. For example, in Disneyland theme parks the staff are not employees but 'cast members' who wear 'costumes' (uniforms) 'onstage' (at work). 'Guests' (customers) use the 'attractions' (rides). The use of such terminology helps employees to slip into their roles and reinforces their belief in the characters they play. At Land Rover, employees were called 'associates', and all wore company overalls (including the managing director).

Source: Adapted from Trice and Beyer (1984).

1 *Tough guy culture* – characterized by entrepreneurial, high-risk-taking individuals, receiving quick feedback, but with a low level of teamwork. Such companies tend to follow a cycle of boom and bust, with the possibility of high earnings during the successful period.

2 *Work hard, play hard* – where work is fun and there is plenty of action with low risk and quick feedback on success. A high volume sales company is a typical example. The individual works alone but has a supportive team.

3 *Bet-your-company* – high-risk, long-term industries usually requiring significant technical expertise, such as the oil and aerospace businesses.

4 *Process culture* – low-risk, low-feedback organizations, typical of traditional models of public institutions, banks, civil service, etc., where the focus was on the actual conduct of the work. In this kind of culture, status issues such as the right to sign off memos and use of graded titles were of paramount importance.

Different kinds of people have varying degrees of success in these cultures. Someone who reacts well to a high-pressure, fast-moving 'work-hard, play-hard' culture will be unhappy and unsuccessful in a process culture. With the wrong cultural style an individual can lose self-esteem and confidence. Deal and Kennedy (1982, p.17) reasoned that 'culture shock may be one of the major reasons why people supposedly "fail" when they leave one organization for another.' Cultural fit is often ignored in selection procedures, leading to unhappy and non-productive experiences for some.

Activity 9:8	Briefly describe Deal and Kennedy's model of corporate culture in your own words.

HRM in reality	**Only a quarter of NHS employees feel secure about challenging how things are done at work**

A mere 24 per cent of NHS employees feel secure about challenging the way things are done within their organization, according to data from employee research specialist ORC International's latest benchmarking study. These findings are drawn from ORC International's benchmarking database, *Perspectives*, which contains results of employee surveys conducted in a range of companies and sectors. The database represents the opinions of over a million UK employees, including nearly 50 000 staff employed by 20 NHS trusts.

The recent data set shows that employee opinion in the NHS contrasts significantly with the opinions of those working in other commercial sectors. Further examples of the findings of the study include:

- NHS staff are the least satisfied with their physical working conditions, with only 51 per cent being satisfied: this compares with 71 per cent of retail employees being satisfied and an overall average of 61 per cent.

- When asked about job satisfaction, NHS employees were actually the most likely to say that they enjoyed their work, with a figure of 87 per cent, compared with 76 per cent in the financial sector and an average of 62 per cent overall.

- The NHS scores well below average when employees are asked if they think their organization offers favourable opportunities for career progression, with a figure of 28 per cent. The public sector scored the lowest at 25 per cent, with the retail sector the highest at 41 per cent.

- Some 41 per cent of NHS employees believe they are treated with fairness and respect by employers. This compares to an overall average of 55 per cent.

ORC International director, Rory MacNeill commented: 'The *Perspectives* database is an exceptional tool, not only because it gives our clients the opportunity to compare their survey results with other organizations, but also because it provides invaluable insight into employee opinion in a variety of sectors.'

Source: *HRMGuide.co.uk* (http://www.hrmguide.co.uk), 1 May 2002.

Corporate culture and people management

The concept of corporate culture continues the tradition of human relations and 'Theory Y'. It fuses the two and moves further away from the logic of scientific management and Fordism towards a view of self-motivated employees who have internalized the values of the business (Wilmott, 1993, p.524). If the culture is strong, people do not need orders or directives. Social norms constrain individual discretion so that employee values are those of the organization. In HRM terms the focus on values and norms is important to achieve behavioural consistency and commitment to the objectives of the business. The key point is that corporate culturalism requires the management of culture so that the 'correct' values are acquired. In effect 'normal', rational techniques of management are applied to the affective (emotional) domain (Wilmott, 1993, p.532). In other words, culture management is a 'hard' approach in thoroughly 'soft' territory.

Based on Handy (1993), corporate culture and organization types can be classified as follows:

1 *The club culture*. Typical of a small company. A personal, informal culture focused on the owner. The leader is all. This form of culture is suitable for new ventures needing strong personalities and fast responses.

2 *Role culture*. Hierarchical with an organizational chart portraying an orderly set of job boxes (roles). Individuals are less important than the roles they fill. A role culture is managed not led, with a formal communication system. Such a culture is best for stable, unchanging organizations with routine tasks. There is a strong tendency to adopt the role culture with increasing size, leading to a mechanistic, bureaucratic organization.

3 *Task culture*. The main focus is on groups such as project teams. Organization is based on trust and respect and geared to plans not procedures. This is a problem-solving environment – exciting and challenging but expensive to run. Work is based on projects. There is little job security: staff leave when tasks are finished.

4 *The person culture* – which is radically different. This is suited to professionals who are self-managing and require minimal structure or supervision. The focus is on talent and professional expertise – management has low status. This is reflected in non-managerial titles such as 'Dean'. Such a culture is best suited for professional practices and educational establishments.

However, there is an underlying tension between the 'humanizing' and the 'control' aspects of people management which is evident in this process. Whereas Theory Y (McGregor, 1960) was unashamedly humanistic, delegating discretion and freedom of choice to individual workers, corporate culturalism advocates: 'a *systematic* approach to creating and strengthening core organizational values in a way that *excludes* (through attention to recruitment) *and eliminates* (through training) *all other values*' (Wilmott, 1993, p.524, original emphases).

People are promoted, appraised and rewarded according to management perception of their acceptance of core values. Hence the view in the Deal and Kennedy approach and much other corporate culture literature is that culture can be created and managed from the top. In this respect it is a departure from older ideas about informal organizations which are more closely aligned to the view that an organizational culture emerges from social interaction (Meek, 1988, p.293). In fact, the literature appears to transfer culture from the informal to the formal organization. As such it becomes the property of management and open to manipulation on their part. This has become the underlying logic for major change initiatives in many large organizations.

Furthermore, there is a common assumption that a unified culture – a 'monoculture' – exists to which all members of the organization belong. Earlier, we saw that narrow, simplified stereotypes of national cultures are misleading: most countries are pluralities with different regional, ethnic and class cultures. In the same way every organization has different cliques and minority groups with varying perspectives of culture. Far from being a management tool, culture can be regarded as a form of collective consciousness, reflecting the diversity of opinion, politics and ambition to be found in any organization. Indeed, as a product of the great mass of employees interacting with each other, it is often anti-managerial.

Legge (1995, p.185) asks 'If senior managers seek to manage "organizational culture", what exactly is it they are seeking to manage?' We can distinguish, therefore, between corporate culture as it is presented in most of the literature, and organizational culture. The former reflects the view that culture is something that an organization 'has', the latter that an organization 'is' (Smircich, 1983). Corporate culture is portrayed as something created by management which employees must accept. If we choose the organization culture view, however, we must acknowledge its long-term interactionist basis. From this perspective, it is difficult to see how senior management can control the culture of a firm – it is too diffuse, embedded and ever-changing. Indeed (Legge, 1995, p.186):

> Corporate culture – that shared by senior management and presented as the 'official' culture of the organization – may be only one of several sub-cultures within any organization, and may be actively resisted by groups who do not share or empathize with its values. If the corporate culture makes no sense of the organizational realities experienced by the employees other than senior management, it will not become internalized outside that small sub-group.

This idea of a small 'official' corporate culture floating on top of a multi-cultural informal organization is mirrored earlier in Handy's classification of cultures above. Senior managers typically form a dynamic club culture which they believe to be universal in the organization whereas, in reality, it sits uncomfortably on top of a depressed and antipathetic role culture. From the managerial point of view, therefore, culture is a major variable to be influenced rather than a creation to be managed.

Summary

We commenced this chapter by recognizing that international HRM can be considered analytically and that differences between national cultures are important to that analysis. However, descriptions of cultural differences tend to be stereotypical and do not pay sufficient attention to the diversity found in regions such as Asia. We discussed the work of Hofstede (1994) on dimensions such as cultural complexity, power distance, individualism, assertiveness and uncertainty avoidance. We extended our discussion to cover corporate culture with an account of Deal and Kennedy's (1982) model and more recent debates on the subject.

Further reading

Riding The Waves of Culture: Understanding Diversity in Global Business by Fons Trompenaars and Charles Hampden-Turner, 2nd edition (1997), published by McGraw-Hill, remains a good introduction to the subject of management in an international context. *When Cultures Collide* by Richard D. Lewis (2000), published by Nicholas Brealey, is an enlightening account of national cultural differences. Hofstede's (1994) updated version of *Cultures and Organizations: Software of the Mind*, published by HarperCollins, provides a stimulating account of his research and ideas. Deal and Kennedy's (1992) *Corporate Cultures* is one of the classic texts on culture within organizations.

Review questions

1 What is 'culture'?

2 To what extent do national cultures determine corporate cultures?

3 How can the concept of 'in-groups' help to explain the inadequacies of equal opportunities policies?

4 Is it possible to describe national business cultures without resorting to stereotypes?

5 Explain the following terms in your own words:
- power distance
- uncertainty avoidance
- role specificity.

6 How does the notion of time vary around the world?

7 Explain the difference between organizational 'culture' and 'structure'. Is there a difference between the two concepts?

8 What insights have Deal and Kennedy provided to further our understanding of corporate culture?

Problem for discussion and analysis

Volvo

In the 1970s Volvo was a model for the future of work: a partnership between management and employees. The company's policies recognized workers as human beings and moved manufacturing away from the production line towards team-based methods. Volvo's long-term commitment to its workforce placed it – together with many other Swedish companies – in the 'social market' or 'soft-HRM' model of capitalism (see Chapter 2). Workers were offered job security, high wages and comparatively short working hours. By the late 1980s, competition was severe and the company struggled to maintain its generous policies in a worsening financial situation.

In the 1990s a relationship developed between Volvo and the French car manufacturer Renault. It began with a cooperation agreement. This involved Volvo taking a 20 per cent shareholding in Renault and Renault taking 10 per cent of Volvo shares. Then, in September 1993, Pehr Gyllenhammer, Volvo's chairman, and Louis Schweitzer, his Renault equivalent, signed a deal in Paris which announced their intention to merge on 1 January 1994. Both groups had shed thousands of workers in previous years and there were immediate fears that the merger would lead to further job losses. According to Louis Schweitzer, designated chief executive of the new Renault-Volvo Automobile (RVA), they would expect savings of Ffr30 billion (£3.3 billion) within the car and truck operations. RVA would maintain two distinct ranges of vehicles and separate dealerships. These savings would come from rationalizing research and development, lower investment costs and joint purchasing. They would also be able to launch new cars more quickly using common components. Pehr Gyllenhammer presented the deal as a large French investment in Sweden. The remainder of Volvo would be concentrating on other core activities

▶

such as Branded Consumer Products which had a leading share of the Scandinavian food, drinks and tobacco market.

The merger would have produced the world's sixth largest vehicle manufacturer with over 200 000 employees and sales of 2.4 million cars and small commercial vehicles a year. Despite the high-quality market served by Volvo it was the junior partner, with a total production of 300 000 vehicles in 1992 leading to a loss of Skr1.8 billion. The Volvo directors felt that this was too small a company to support the ever-increasing development costs of launching new models. There was never any doubt that Renault would be in charge, with a holding of 65 per cent of the joint company. Renault was still in French government ownership with an intention to privatize by the end of 1994. The deal was supported initially by the major institutional shareholders such as insurance companies. However, it enraged private Swedish shareholders who could not accept the effective takeover of Sweden's largest company and industrial flagship. The media took a keen interest and the Volvo share price dropped immediately.

The Volvo shareholders' meeting to vote on the merger was postponed from 9 November to 2 December. This was because top managers felt they were unlikely to be able to muster sufficient support. On 2 December – virtually at the last minute – the Volvo board decided not to proceed with the merger. Pehr Gyllenhammer, the Volvo chairman for 22 years, resigned immediately along with three other directors, including Raymond Levy, the former Renault chairman who had been instrumental in setting up the link. The reason for not proceeding was a revolt among the top managers. The managing director, Soren Gyll, said that the necessary support had not been available to proceed with the plan, either from within the company or among the shareholders. Mr Gyll had consistently backed Pehr Gyllenhammer in public but had become disenchanted with the latter's handling of the issue and had held secret meetings to discuss his misgivings with other managers.

Discussion questions

1 Why do you think that the negotiations fell through?
2 If shareholders had not objected too, would the views of the workforce have been sufficient to prevent it going through?

10

Commitment and employer branding

Commitment and brand values

Organizational commitment is a central concept in HRM (see Key concept 10.1). It is one of the four 'Cs' featured in the seminal Harvard model discussed in Chapter 1 and one of the measurable criteria in our ten-Cs checklist of HRM effectiveness (see Part 1). Rhetorical accounts of human resource management have claimed that organizations that adopt the philosophy of HRM gain integration and coherence in their people management processes and systems. Integration is dependent on a strong and binding link between employee behaviour and the goals of the organization. According to this viewpoint, commitment to the mission and values of the organization is a fundamental principle. As a concept it is clearly related to that of 'strong' corporate culture. Commitment goes further than simple compliance: it is an emotional attachment to the organization. For example, Osborne and Cowen (2002) make the claim that:

> A 'true believer' mentality pervades high-performing organizations. Everyone believes in the vision of the business and that it will bring certain success. People believe that they are involved in something bigger than simply their own self-interest. They have a strong sense of identity with the organization and act as if they were owners.

In particular, the Harvard approach views employee commitment as the key determiner of competitive performance. In Chapter 3 we observed that people working within a culture of commitment are prepared to work longer, apply greater ingenuity to resolve a problem, try that much harder to win an order. In effect they are in a high-commitment culture.

From this perspective, commitment comes within a climate of trust. There must be a shared understanding between employees at all levels as mutual stakeholders in the future of an enterprise. Workers cannot be expected to make suggestions leading to a reduction in the time and effort required to perform a task if there is a risk of job loss as a result.

It is easy to see how commitment can arise in a high-trust culture such as that which prevailed in Japan until the 1990s. It can be understood also within the context of the consensus social market where jobs have a considerable degree of protection, employees are consulted through works councils and there is generous social security provision for people without jobs. But how can commitment arise in free market businesses where there is an imbalance of power between different stakeholders? Why should people be committed to organizations whose senior managers reward themselves disproportionately for the efforts of others?

Key concept 10:1

Commitment Commitment is defined as the degree of identification and involvement that individuals have with their organization's mission, values and goals (Mowday, Steers and Porter, 1979). This translates into: their desire to stay with the organization; belief in its objectives and values; and the strength of employee effort in the pursuit of business objectives (Griffin and Bateman, 1986).

Commitment has been the subject of research for some time because of its strong psychological connotations. Initially, attention was paid to commitment as behaviour. For example, Salancik (1977) identified four behavioural elements:

- *Explicitness*. Is it clear that an act of commitment took place? Can it be denied? Was it consciously determined?
- *Revocability*. Can we change our minds? Can the act be undone?
- *Volition*. Is an act performed under our own volition or under the control of someone else?
- *Publicity*. Has an expression or act of commitment been made in public?

Commitment arises as individuals perform acts such as joining a firm, working long hours and speaking well of the organization to customers or friends. Employees reflect on their own behaviour and conclude that because they have done something which is favourable towards their own organization, and done so in front of others, apparently of their own free will, they must have a commitment to that organization. In other words, free choice and public behaviour reinforce a feeling of commitment. This has been described as a 'neat theory' and there is some evidence in support (Arnold, Robertson and Cooper, 1991, p.147).

The emphasis has shifted towards a significant framework in social psychology that revolves around the concept of 'attitudes'. Attitudes are seen to have three components (McKenna, 1994, pp.251, 287). These are: belief (cognitive), feeling (affective) and action (behavioural or conative). Each can be positive or negative. The emotional (affective) component seems to be of greatest significance, able to influence or override the other two. From this viewpoint, commitment is seen as having three key elements (Allen and Meyer, 1990):

- *Affective* – the individual's emotional attachment to an organization.
- *Continuance* – an individual's perception of the costs and risks associated with leaving the organization (equivalent to the behavioural component).
- *Normative* – the obligation and responsibility a person feels towards the organization (equating to the cognitive component).

Research on attitudes indicates that these components usually show a considerable degree of consistency with each other. But this is not always the case. For instance, employees can feel proud of a company and believe that they owe an obligation for past good treatment, training or promotion. However, they may be aware that pay is relatively low and other organizations offer more attractive prospects. It is clear, therefore, that commitment is not as simple a concept as some HR theorists hold. In practice, many of us hold ambivalent attitudes towards our employing organizations, perhaps enjoying our own jobs and the company of our fellow employees but wary of the intentions of senior executives.

Nevertheless, committed employees are crucial to high performance, not least because (Gotsi and Wilson, 2001, p.102):

> ... staff and their behaviour represent the reality of the organisation to the customers and therefore, if their behaviour does not live up to the expectations created through the organisation's external communication campaigns, the organisation's overall reputation will be damaged. Consultants argued that visionary organisations realise that front line personnel are the company. 'Because they know that when you walk into a store it doesn't matter about the big corporation, what matters is that moment of transaction, it's just you and that 19-year-old person, and so that person has to deliver the reputation. And if they don't, millions of pounds on advertising and products are lost' (Consultant A).

Activity 10:1

What do you understand by 'commitment'? To what extent are you committed to the organization in which you work or study?

Employer branding

Many commercial organizations are well experienced at promoting and cultivating a relationship between themselves and their clients through their brand image. Coca-Cola, BMW, McDonald's, Sony and BP are just some of the organizations whose brands are recognized throughout the world. Brands are not simply logos or names: by their existence they encourage people to develop a faith in the products or services provided by an organization and a belief in the integrity and reliability of its staff. Well-regarded brands are valuable in themselves and companies work hard at maintaining their brand images. Recently, the concept of branding has been extended from the organization as supplier of goods and services to the organization as an employer (see Key concept 10.2).

Key concept 10:2

Employer branding   The practice of developing, differentiating and leveraging an organization's brand message to its current and future workforce in a manner meaningful to them. Using the methodology of corporate brand-building strategy to attract and keep quality employees. Employer branding is aimed at motivating and securing employees' alignment with the vision and the values of the company. From a HR perspective, the concept has subsumed the older term 'internal branding' which was essentially the process of communicating an organization's brand values to its employees.

The basis of employer branding is the application of the same marketing and branding practices to a company's human resource activities (specifically, recruitment and retention) as it uses for consumer-targeted marketing and branding efforts. In other words, the business markets its brand image to its staff. And just as customers will cease buying a company's products or services when a promise is unfulfilled, its employees will also leave if the company fails to live up to its employer brand promises.

HRM in reality

Employer branding

A study from The Conference Board (*Engaging Your Employees Through Your Brand, Report no. 1288*) found that many large organizations were using the methodology of corporate brand-building strategy to attract and keep quality employees. Their survey found that 'employer branding' was being used by 40 per cent of respondents in a survey of 138 leading companies to increase their attractiveness to potential and current employees. Yet most of these initiatives were relatively new, and many started in the year 2000. However, funding and awareness of 'employer branding' seems to be increasing, particularly in companies whose corporate brand image is not strong among the general public because, for example, they are suppliers to businesses rather than consumers. In other words, prospective employees are not so likely to have heard of them.

The report was sponsored by Charles Schwab and examined these businesses in relation to their branding experiences and practices. Two broad categories of managers were interviewed: communications/marketing and human resources.

'The challenge to employers is not only to make potential employees aware of the company as a good place to work and bring the best applicants successfully through the recruitment and hiring process, but to retain them and ensure their understanding of the company's goals and commitment to them,' said David Dell, Research Director of The Conference Board's Capabilities Management and Human Resources Strategies area. 'Companies have found employer branding programs provide a real edge in competing for talent.'

'The findings suggest the amplification of a trend we noted in our 1998 research on corporate branding,' commented Kathryn Troy, Director, The Conference Board's Performance Excellence and Operations Management Research. 'Executives told us that their brand was being used as a rallying point for employees in a time of extensive change. Moreover, they expected employees to exemplify the promises the brand makes to the firm's customers.'

▶

Some businesses were using separate, dedicated employer branding efforts aimed at aligning employees with their organizations' vision and values whereas others were pursuing this goal as one element of broader corporate branding strategies.

Comparing corporate branding and employer branding

For the corporate brand, the communications/marketing executives identified four goals as being most important:

- delivering the brand promise to customers (through employees)
- helping employees to internalize company values
- recruiting and retaining customers
- instilling brand values into key processes (e.g. customer service).

The HR executives gave a very similar response, with their highest priorities for the corporate brand being:

- delivering the brand promise to customers
- helping employees to internalize the company values
- recruiting customers
- achieving a reputation as an employer of choice.

For the employer brand, the two sets of responses were more different. The communications/marketing executives identified the following as their top goals:

- helping employees internalize the company's values
- achieving a reputation as an employer of choice
- recruiting and retaining employees
- instilling brand values into key processes.

Priorities for HR executives were:

- helping employees to internalize the company's values
- recruiting employees
- retaining employees
- achieving a reputation as an employer of choice.

These findings show considerable overlap and muddling of the two concepts. Differences seem to be a matter of emphasis. And only 20 per cent of organizations seemed to have metrics to measure the consequences of employer branding initiatives. Elsewhere in the study they also report that senior managers are most concerned with corporate branding at the strategic level. But it is realized at a senior level that 'mergers, acquisitions, spinoffs, and other forces of change increasingly blur company identity, with adverse impact on the effectiveness of the workforce.'

The report notes that the 'employer of choice' concept emphasizes improvement of recruitment and retention, but indicates that true employer branding goes further. Employer branding is aimed at motivating and securing employees' alignment with the vision and the values of the company. The authors argue that employer branding can be a stimulus to the improvement of all of those people-related processes that create organizational excellence.

Source: *HRM Guide USA* (http://www.hrmguide.net/usa/), 1 March 2002.

The concept of employer branding draws on the notion that employees who fully understand and embrace an organization's culture, values and business objectives are more
likely to share common goals with the organization, work for those goals and share information with other people. Employer branding reinforces perception of the organization's
culture (as top managers perceive it) through a variety of messages, behaviours and other
forms of communication.

Employer branding begins with the recruitment process because this offers a number of
tools that can be used to create perceptions of an employing organization, including:

- job advertisements and descriptions
- the interview process
- offer letters
- information packs for new recruits
- employee handbooks
- induction and training.

Effectively managed, and this should be comparatively simple to professional marketers,
the recruitment process can be used to create a positive relationship between candidates and
the organization. It depends on comparatively simple, thought-through procedures that consistently project a company's image and values in order to create strong, positive views of
the organization. This can even extend to unsuccessful candidates.

Activity 10:2	Is employer branding an ethical form of 'internal marketing' or an attempt at brain-washing staff?

Gotsi and Wilson (2001) found in their research that PR consultants considered it essential to have an alignment between employee behaviour and the values that an organization's brand stands for. They quote one consultant who stated that: 'aligning brand actions
with brand promises is a critical test for managers.' The consultants they investigated highlighted the need to ensure that there was no gap between what an organization was saying
in the outside world and what people believed inside that business. Employees were perceived as 'brand ambassadors' and brand marketing would only be successful if they 'lived
the brand'. From this perspective, organizations have to (a) encourage employees to 'buy
in' to the business vision and values; and (b) ensure that everyone within the organization
clearly understands the purpose of the common set of values.

It is necessary for these conditions to be realized for employees to be able to reflect them
through their own behaviour. There has to be an understanding of the brand, if staff are to
'live the brand' and its values (see Key concept 10.3). One of their interviewees observed
that for this to happen 'reputation has to be based on reality in order to be credible'.

It is worth observing that, while it may be comparatively easy to convince a new recruit
of the positive nature of a company's culture, employer branding can be quickly undone if
the organization turns out to be rather different from the recruit's initial perceptions. In
fact, an employer brand that departs considerably from reality can be counter-productive,
leading to rapid disillusionment rather than sustained commitment.

Key concept 10:3	**Living the brand** Identifying with an organization's brand values to such an extent that employees' behaviours fit exactly with the image that the business is trying to portray to its customers.

| HRM in reality | **Branding aligns employees with organizational goals** |

Treatment of employees and the quality of products and services rate highest in job-searchers' perceptions of organizations they want to work for even though recent big-name collapses and lay-offs might be attributable to financial health and market conditions. In fact, a recent survey found that 77 per cent of adult respondents did not rate a company's financial health as their top priority in determining its reputation as a place to work.

The survey, conducted by The Cherenson Group (http://www.cherenson.com), a New Jersey-based public relations and recruitment ad agency firm in the week of 11 February 2002, included 800 completed interviews with New Jersey residents age 18 and older. With a margin of error of plus or minus 3.5 per cent at the 95 per cent confidence level, the survey indicated that the most important factors in determining a company's reputation as a place to work are the way employees are treated (36 per cent) and the quality of the company's products or services (27 per cent).

In keeping with results from the previous year's survey, people earning more than US$75 000 annually were more likely to consider financial factors as their most important factor. In the 2001 Reputation Survey, 78 per cent of respondents said they would rather work for a company with an excellent reputation than for a company with a poor reputation – even if they were offered a higher salary. 'Our first study indicated that people would actually accept a lower paying job, in order to work for a company with an excellent reputation,' said Michael Cherenson, vice-president, The Cherenson Group. 'This study indicates once again that nearly 8 in 10 people think with their hearts and not just their wallets.'

According to the survey, a mere 4 per cent cited the CEO as being the most important factor, 3 per cent pointed to a company's charitable contributions and community support with 6 per cent citing a combination of factors. 'While these factors may not have ranked as a top concern, other research offers strong evidence that a company's leadership and commitment to community concerns are critical to the overall reputation and relationship building process,' Cherenson said.

'Our 2001 study clearly indicated that a company's reputation is an asset that needs to be developed and secured,' said Cherenson. 'This year's study provides a deeper understanding of that asset and shows an obvious correlation between reputation and relationships, specifically the relationship between employee and employer.'

Cherenson argues that findings from both studies also confirm that by investing in reputation and relationships, businesses can realize bottom-line savings in the form of recruitment, retention and overhead costs: 'While this study looked at reputation from the recruitment/retention viewpoint, other reputation research clearly indicates the power of reputation as it relates to consumer spending and investing.'

Source: *HRM Guide USA* (http://www.hrmguide.net/usa/), 1 March 2002.

Gotsi and Wilson (2001) indicate that the twin tasks of aligning staff behaviour with brand values and getting employees to 'live the brand' are very difficult – far more difficult than other aspects of conventional brand marketing such as creating a visual identity for an organization. They quote a consultant as saying: 'It's much harder to get people's behaviour and culture aligned with a brand, because people are much more unpredictable than graphics. People talk, walk, think, do things; graphics just stay there.'

To achieve these goals, it is necessary to treat employees as an audience for corporate communications to ensure that all stakeholders receive the same message. The aim of internal communications, according to Gotsi and Wilson's respondents, is to encourage employees to believe that they can live up to projected brand values. This is done by talking and listening to staff and being aware of their need to believe in the organization's vision and values. But, whereas most consultants proposed a top-down communication exercise from senior managers to lower levels of employees, Gotsi and Wilson are more impressed by a minority view that communication should be two-way. They argue that communication should be a learning exercise in which ideas are shared and feedback obtained from the 'front line'.

Specifically, they contend that for employees' behaviour to reflect brand values organizations must align human resource management practices with their brand values. Recruitment policies, performance appraisal, training and reward systems must fit with brand values, otherwise conflicting messages will be sent about the behaviours that are really important for the business. Recruitment policies must be aimed at attracting the type of people who can fit the desired culture; performance management must identify and encourage behaviours that relate to brand values; reward systems should benefit people who live the brand.

Blumenthal (2001, p.37), using the term 'internal branding' (IB), concludes that:

> While searching for meaning is uncomfortable and putting power in the hands of frontline employees is risky, it may also be the only way to actually find the kind of meaning that transforms employees' lives. If employees 'can live with it or without it,' then the brand is not living up to its potential. As Bergstrom points out, people are looking to be a part of something special, something connected, something that they can be a proud of building. Brand, and its particular application internally, has the potential to be wielded in that way. Although at its worst, IB can prove a cynical exercise, at its best there is potential for more than just profit. IB can provide a basis for mutual respect, community, and honest win-win relationships that profit the organization precisely because it improves the quality of people's lives.

Activity 10:3   Take a well-known brand name as an example. What are its values and how should HR practices be aligned to fit?

Commitment and culture

Western companies have long striven to obtain the degree of commitment shown by Japanese workers. However, Japanese organizations have a significant and possibly insurmountable advantage: Japanese culture. The traditional Japanese managerial scale of values was different from those of Western cultures (Whitehill, 1991). Most crucially, commitment was a two-way process – managers are committed to their people (Pascale and Athos, 1981, p.191). Physical status symbols that are so important to Western managers – such as named car parking spaces, large personal offices and executive dining areas – have little value for the Japanese. In contrast, traditionally minded Japanese managers and workers share fundamental values that lie at the heart of their commitment – a work ethic, conformity and avoidance of shame.

The 'work ethic' centres on being seen to work hard and typically being in the office for long hours. Key to this culture is the belief that 'duty – in the form of work – must come first' (Briggs, 1991, p.41). Dissatisfaction, boredom and exhaustion are brushed aside in the commitment to duty. Indeed, surveys show poor job satisfaction in many Japanese companies. Commitment, therefore, is not to specific corporations so much as to 'duty' in general. Because of this cultural underpinning, it may be that Western managers are pursuing a futile goal in copying Japanese 'commitment'. If the national culture does not feature a similar pressure – for example the Protestant work ethic – then organizations may never achieve the same levels of employee commitment.

| HRM in reality | **Overworked Americans can't use up their vacation** |

Americans have the least annual vacation entitlement (13 days) in the industrialized world. This compares with Italy 42; France 37; Germany 35; Brazil 34; Britain 28; Canada 26; South Korea 25; and Japan 25.* But one in six US employees are unable to use up their entitlement because of overwork. This is the conclusion of a landmark national survey released in February 2001. 'If you take off a week, you've got three times as much work to do when you get back,' said Bob Boudreau, 42, a computer analyst in Poughkeepsie, NY, who has gone without a vacation in two of the last four years.

Sheri Hinshaw, 31, of Seattle, Washington, quit her job, partly because she hasn't been able to take a vacation in five years. She remembers thinking, 'I can't go – I've got too many things to do.' She recently left her job as a program manager at Microsoft and took a less demanding position overseeing computers for the Seattle Opera in order to 'have a life' and possibly take a vacation next summer.

'This survey is a wake-up call for Americans to realize that taking a vacation is not frivolous behaviour. It's essential to staying healthy,' said Alan Muney, MD, chief medical officer and executive vice-president at Oxford Health Plans, Inc., which sponsored the national survey. 'Regular vacations are preventive medicine – they cut down on stress-related illness and save health care dollars.'

The survey of 632 men and women shows that workers often endure a high level of stress on the job:

- 34 per cent of respondents said their jobs were so pressing that they had no down time at work
- 32 per cent work and eat lunch at the same time
- 32 per cent do not leave the building during the working day
- 19 per cent said that their job makes them feel older than they are
- 17 per cent said work caused them to lose sleep at home.

The survey also showed that:

- Most employers make it easy to keep medical appointments (70 per cent) and return to work after illness (68 per cent) – but some have a corporate culture that discourages healthy behaviour
- 19 per cent said workplace pressures make them feel they must attend work even when injured or sick
- 17 per cent said it is difficult to take time off or leave work in an emergency
- 8 per cent believe that if they were to become seriously ill they would be fired or demoted
- 14 per cent believe their employer makes it difficult to maintain a healthy diet
- 14 per cent felt that company management only promotes people who habitually work late.

Stress may be relieved by taking a vacation but there is another motivating factor – medical research linking vacation to a lowered risk of death, commented Dr Muney. 'Taking a vacation is a serious health issue that should not be ignored. It could save your life,' he said. In fact researchers at the State University of New York at Oswego published a study in September 2000 based on 12 866 men, aged 35 to 57, that found regular vacations lowered risk of death by almost 20 per cent. The random telephone survey was conducted from 17 August to 1 September 2000 by Central Marketing Inc. of New York City, with a margin of error of plus or minus 4 per cent.

More recently a survey conducted for Expedia.com® found an average of 1.8 unused vacation days per employee each year in the USA. They calculate this to be worth US$19.3 billion a year to their employers. Yet 71 per cent of the workers surveyed wished that their employers gave an extra week's paid vacation each year. And 53 per cent of respondents did not know that US employees receive considerably less annual vacation time than their counterparts in other industrialized countries.

* These figures come from a World Tourism Organisation study and appear to refer to average vacation days taken by nationals from those countries, including public holidays.

Source: *HRM Guide USA* (http://www.hrmguide.net/usa/), 31 May 2001.

Discussion question: Is the fact that Americans do not use their (low) vacation entitlement an illustration of national culture or commitment to their organizations?

Secondly, on conformity, as we observed in earlier chapters, individuals have little importance in comparison with the in-group. There is a psychological need to belong and not to be isolated from one's community. The high degree of interdependence leads to the 'high trust' characteristics of Japanese business culture. Western companies are far more individualistic. Conformity comes from external control, as we shall see later in Chapter 18 on performance management, not from a deep compulsion. The result is that workers often conform only when the boss is watching. The unpredictability of individualists also leads to an inevitable reduction in mutual trust.

Thirdly, as regards avoidance of shame, the Japanese manager has obligations and responsibilities derived from traditional culture rather than an employment contract or job description. Failure to discharge these according to the normal social rules can bring shame – loss of face – and isolation on managers and their families. This may be brought about, for example, by a breach of obligation (psychological contract) such as the guarantee of continued employment for one's staff. In the past this has reinforced a high-trust relationship and mutual commitment. However, as we observed in Chapter 2, the 1990s have brought economic reality to bear on traditional values and large organizations in Japan have been forced to shed people, albeit by oblique methods such as early retirement and coerced resignations. Many Western managers have no concept of shame. Any obligation to staff is tempered by the need to maintain their own careers.

Commitment also depends on organizational culture. Indeed a 'culture of commitment' is frequently cited as a goal for organizational change. Paradoxically, however, change programmes designed to instil modern business methods and 'lean-mean' management structures can rebound, leading to a reduction in employee commitment.

Osborne and Cowen (2002) see a culture of commitment as a crucial basis for high performance. They identify a number of characteristics of such a culture:

1 *Emotion-packed vision.* A simple, compelling vision for the future that resonates with employees. It must be easy to understand and visualize and go 'beyond simply making money'.

2 *'True believer' mentality.* Every employee having a belief in the vision of the business and convinced that it will bring certain success. The key is a strong sense of identity with the organization so that ordinary employees act as if they are owners.

3 *Plain vanilla values.* Three or four essential and basic values that may be formally expressed or implicit in the way the business is conducted. They need to be simple and have some emotional appeal. For instance, Jack Welch, formerly of General Electric, who highlighted self-confidence as the core of employee success, and also added speed and simplicity as basic values. Fair treatment is another typical 'high-commitment' value.

4 *Pride and dissatisfaction.* An apparently contradictory mix of intense employee pride in the company combined with a dissatisfaction with their current performance. According to Osborne and Cowen: 'Edgy ideas and attitudes are pervasive. High performers have a commitment to learning from every mistake and every success.'

5 *Peer respect.* From Osborne and Cowen's observations, high-performing organizations rarely rely on fear to motivate employees. Instead, an urge to earn and maintain mutual respect appears to govern the behaviour of senior managers. Respect for oneself comes as a result of respect from others. According to Osborne and Cowen: 'Cynicism is regarded as weakness, an excuse for not getting the job done.'

6 *Long-term relationships.* Instead of switching jobs frequently, from one company to another, long-term relationships are seen as the path to personal success. Employees expect to work for their company and with each other for a long time. This is related to peer respect because short-term 'one-upmanship' is not seen as a positive way forward in a high-performance organization.

7 *Fun.* Success is celebrated publicly and loudly.

Activity 10:4	Is Osborne and Cowen's description of a high-commitment organization idealistic or realistic?

HRM in reality	TUC's campaign on call centre working

There were almost 400 calls to a TUC hotline in the first week of its campaign on call centre working. A total of 397 call handlers contacted the TUC in six days, complaining about issues such as:

● bullying

● being set impossible sales targets

● not getting their wages on time

● hostility towards union representation.

Although calls came from all over the UK, almost a third were from people working in South Wales (15 per cent of all calls) and Scottish (14 per cent) call centres. Just 30 per cent of the calls were from men, indicating that this is a female-dominated industry. And 68 per cent of callers were non-union members.

Specific complaints included:

● being made to go into work to report in sick rather than make a simple phone call

● being required to put their hands up when they wanted to go to the toilet

● then having the length of time they were there monitored

● being allowed just three seconds' break between calls

- being restricted to no more than three days' leave in one go, making it impossible to book a proper holiday.

According to TUC General Secretary, John Monks:

Many call centres already treat their staff with respect and others are making a real effort to clean up their act. But these figures show there are still too many centres using bullying tactics to pressurize and intimidate employees. According to reports on our hotline, some call centres seem to be openly flouting the law.

The TUC cite a number of particularly bizarre instances:

- One call handler was disciplined for being idle – after leaving a six-second gap between calls.
- Refusal to allow Christmas decorations in one office because (bosses claimed) it was a health and safety hazard. But the mice in the office were not, the staff were told.
- A claim that one call centre manager took disposable nappies into work and said that staff using the toilet the most would be told to wear one.
- The same call centre was said to have a 'shame' board to monitor staff progress. Anyone on the board for three weeks would be dismissed.

Source of calls

Region	Per cent of calls to hotline	Per cent call centre employment
North-west	9.0	17.1
South-east	12.0	15.8
Scotland	14.0	12.0
Yorkshire and Humberside	7.0	8.5
East Anglia	3.0	8.1
West Midlands	7.0	8.0
South-west	8.0	6.9
North-east	8.0	6.8
Greater London	9.0	6.6
East Midlands	5.0	4.7
South Wales	15.0	4.7
North Wales	2.0	n/a
Northern Ireland	0.5	0.8

The facts about call centres

Call centres currently employ more than 400 000 people – more than the coal, steel and vehicle manufacturing industries put together. It is predicted that there will be more than 665 000 full-time equivalent jobs in the call centre industry by 2008. But staff turnover is a significant problem, with turnover rates of 20–30 per cent a year

▶

◀

– although the TUC claims that these are 'public' figures. In reality, they say that turnover may be double the admitted figures.

Low pay is typical, according to the TUC report on call centres (*It's your call*), with average earnings of less than £8000 per annum. In general salaries amount to only 60 per cent of average earnings in a specific region. But standards and pay are being driven up by concentration in some areas such as Glasgow and South Wales where it is possible to earn in excess of £20 000 as employers compete with each other to keep staff. About 44 per cent of call centres are unionized – mainly in the public sectors, privatized utilities and finance, which also tend to pay better.

As well as the incidents detailed by recent callers to the TUC hotline, the report also highlights:

- being listened to on the phone when discussing union business
- having pay withheld while serving probationary periods
- being expected to pay for their own headsets
- suffering 'acoustic shock' which can result in short-term memory loss and an inability to bear loud noises.

Case studies

The report includes a number of illustrative cases. For example, that of Jayne (not her real name), a student employed by a call centre in South Wales for three months. Anonymity is required because she (and her colleagues) signed a contract which stipulated that she could not speak to the media about her working conditions.

When she started work, Jayne signed up to a 'training loyalty bond' and was told to go through one-month's training, but she would be paid for only two weeks. The other two weeks' pay was held until she completed a three-month probationary period that started when her training finished. She considers that her pay isn't bad – £4.50 an hour – but Jayne has been required to buy her own headset.

Another case highlights Anthony Samaroo. He had been working for BT for four years when he suffered two acoustic shocks in his left ear. He felt these like a high-pitched sound from a fax machine, but ten times worse:

> The shocks made me feel dizzy and disoriented and now, eighteen months later, I'm still suffering from tinnitus. I find it difficult to concentrate on conversations with several people at a time. I can't go to the theatre or to concerts any more and even squeaky brakes on a bus can leave me with terrible migraine-like pains.

He now wears cotton wool in his ears most of the time, which can cause ear infections. Nevertheless, the London BT centre where he works will not recognize his problem:

> I've taken myself off any duties involving a headset. BT aren't happy about it, but I can't work any other way. I'm frustrated they won't take responsibility for what's happened. Just because you can't see the effects of acoustic shock, doesn't mean it's not real.

Good practice

The report is not all bad. Some call centres are trying to be models of best practice. And some employers operate ethical policies and use good employee relations to achieve deals with new clients. They can offer flexible working patterns, including term-time working. They may also get rid of targets such as call-handling times and offer training and personal development to staff. BT has accepted a 'blueprint' for best practice including such features, agreed with the Communication Workers Union.

TUC General Secretary John Monks concludes:

> As the positive stories in our report show, many call centres don't deserve the sweatshop image they're tainted with. The good call centres we highlight prove the industry can offer good working conditions and still be profitable. But there are still too many call centres exploiting their staff. That's why we're running this campaign – to make sure call handlers know their rights and to raise the status of call centres by encouraging shoddy employers to improve their standards.

Source: *HRMGuide.co.uk* (http://www.hrmguide.co.uk), 20 February 2001.

Discussion question: What are the shortcomings of the call centres highlighted in this report in achieving employee commitment?

O'Malley (2000, p.7) considers that commitment is not easy to obtain:

> Companies that are able to create commitment realize that commitment ultimately is personal. This is the hard part of commitment that has profound implications for corporate conduct. It requires being consistent in what one does even though there may be short-term costs attached; it requires being flexible and making exceptions; and it requires making choices about what employees are prepared and unprepared to do – and providing reasons. Commitment is not created through a grab bag of trendy corporate goodies. It requires the patient and concerted attention of the whole organization.

O'Malley lists a number of reasons why companies feel they cannot create a culture of commitment:

1 *Too hard.* The process is perceived as being too difficult. In essence, the company has decided that its management is not good enough to obtain commitment.

2 *Too costly.* When changes are considered to improve conditions for employees, the immediate focus is on the costs involved rather than the ultimate benefits: 'If it costs money and is not related to physical or financial capital, the answer is *no*' (O'Malley, 2000, p.7).

3 *Too different.* Business is supposed to be hard-nosed whereas treating employees in a way that will foster their commitment is seen as 'soft'. HR professionals worry about their soft image in the company, especially if a commitment programme fails.

4 *Too hopeless.* Companies may assume that they are in a competitive industry where staff are constantly being poached from other organizations. They conclude that there is nothing that can be done – unaware that other businesses *are* doing something.

Commitment strategies

According to Smither (1994) there are five barriers that are commonly encountered in changing organizations: disruption of personal relationships; the perceived threat to status; a preference for the status quo; economic factors; and problems arising from the use of consultants. If there is a risk that commitment may be a casualty of change initiatives, how is it best protected and developed? The answer seems to be that it must be regarded as a specific strategic objective in itself. This is best achieved by giving it a clear focus (Armstrong, 1992, p.102). In addition, it must be remembered that 'hearts and minds' commitment cannot be gained by top-down imposition of changes that run counter to the beliefs of employees.

Total quality management (TQM) programmes have been shown to be particularly effective in obtaining commitment. This may be due to their systematic and apparent objectivity, employing project management and other documentation to verify quality standards. These standards are externally justified: they are required to satisfy customers and are not seen as a local management invention. Commitment is reinforced by inbuilt feedback mechanisms that inform staff and management of quality levels.

A more sinister implication is the extension of this mechanism within Japanese production techniques into insidious forms of control – 'management by shame' and 'management by blame' (Garrahan and Stewart, 1992). Social pressure and individual feelings of guilt help to pressurize workers into meeting ever-increasing performance standards.

More positively, a commitment programme should involve a thought-through package of measures that addresses:

- *Communication.* Outlining the direction that the organization's strategy is taking and the purpose of any changes. Staff need to understand why decisions have been taken before they will cooperate in their implementation. Additionally, they must be encouraged to contribute to the process from their experience and ideas.

- *Education.* Where change involves new technology, systems or procedures there must be a suitable training package available to provide confidence in their use. Training also builds commitment and respect through direct contact with managers involved in planning developments.

- *Ownership.* Commitment is encouraged by involving people in decisions and making them responsible for implementing specific actions.

- *Emotional identification* is more likely in an atmosphere of enthusiasm. This can be created by acknowledging and encouraging responsibility and recognizing hard work and results.

- *Performance* assessment and reward structures should be focused on commitment.

- *Rewards* in the form of pay, bonuses and prizes can be linked to visible commitment behaviour. The introduction of performance-related pay has been extensive in recent years. Normally this has been justified as a method of increasing commitment. However, as we shall see in Chapter 19, evidence shows that performance-related pay can encourage a small proportion of good performers at the expense of demotivating the majority. In practice it reduces morale and leads to accusations of unfairness.

- *Employment contracts* can include clauses to prevent employees from publicizing information or opinions that might disadvantage the organization. Regrettably, such 'gagging' clauses have been used by management in public sector organizations, where staff feel themselves committed to public service rather than a particular hospital trust, for example.

Activity 10:5

Design a commitment programme for an organization you know well.

HRM in reality

Actively disengaged workers cost US hundreds of billions a year

A Gallup study indicates that 'actively disengaged' employees – workers who are fundamentally disconnected from their jobs – are costing the US economy between US$292 billion and US$355 billion a year. This finding appears in the inaugural issue of Gallup's new quarterly, the *Gallup Management Journal* (*GMJ*).

These estimates are based on a recent Gallup 'Q12' employee engagement survey of the US workforce, which calculates that 24.7 million workers (19 per cent) are actively disengaged. The survey found that actively disengaged workers are absent from work 3.5 more days a year than other workers – or 86.5 million days in all.

Gallup research consistently shows a tendency for actively disengaged workers to be (in comparison with colleagues):

- significantly less productive
- report being less loyal to their companies
- less satisfied with their personal lives
- more stressed and insecure about their work.

Gallup has developed a proprietary formula to measure levels of employee engagement based on worldwide survey results and performance data in its database. In fact, over the past three years, Gallup's employee engagement consulting practice has surveyed more than 1.5 million employees at more than 87 000 divisions or work units.

Gallup intends to administer the national Q12 survey every quarter to a representative sample of American working adults. The results will be published in *GMJ*. The Q12 survey takes its name from 12 core questions (see below) that Gallup asks the employees at its clients' work units. The results allow Gallup clients to see and understand links between levels of employee engagement and productivity, growth and profitability.

Q12 survey

1 Do I know what is expected of me at work?
2 Do I have the materials and equipment I need to do my work right?
3 At work, do I have the opportunity to do what I do best every day?
4 In the last seven days, have I received recognition or praise for doing good work?
5 Does my supervisor, or someone at work, seem to care about me as a person?
6 Is there someone at work who encourages my development?
7 At work, do my opinions seem to count?
8 Does the mission or purpose of my company make me feel my job is important?
9 Are my co-workers committed to doing quality work?
10 Do I have a best friend at work?
11 In the last six months, has someone at work talked to me about my progress?
12 This last year, have I had opportunities at work to learn and grow?

▶

Cost calculations

The US$292 billion estimate of the annual cost of actively disengaged employees was derived through a three-step process:

1   The proprietary formula was applied to the Q12 survey results in order to calculate the number of actively disengaged employees in the USA.

2   Standard utility analysis methods (statistical guides) were applied to the US$30 000 per year US average salary, yielding US$2246.

3   This was multiplied by 130 million US workers who are 18 years old or older, resulting in the US$292 billion estimate.

Gallup's US$355 billion estimate had its basis in a different economic measure – the USA's US$10 trillion gross domestic product in the year 2000.

● The GDP figure was divided by the total number of US workers, yielding US$73 870 worth of goods or services per worker last year.

● Also using standard utility analysis methods, Gallup statisticians found that a 3.7 per cent increase in output for each employee would be attributable to eliminating active disengagement from the workforce.

● The 3.7 per cent increase, applied against the US$73 870 average output figure amounts to US$2733 per person in the workforce, or US$355 billion overall.

Note: 'Gallup', 'Q12 Advantage', 'The Gallup Poll', and 'The Gallup Poll Monthly' are trademarks of The Gallup Organization.

Source: *HRM Guide USA* (http://www.hrmguide.net/usa/), 23 March 2001.

Justifying commitment

In practice, Western managers have often imported the concept of commitment without a supporting framework which parallels that provided by Japanese culture. Some have appealed to the good sense of employees – a management rhetoric which presents commitment as voluntary. Supposedly, people are won over by the sound sense of strategic objectives and the 'obvious' view that commitment produces positive benefits for both staff and management. What are these benefits? First, management is made easier. A committed workforce consists of self-motivated staff who can function without the need for orders or managerial control. Left to themselves, they will work in a manner consistent with business objectives. Secondly, employees gain from management trust. They are empowered to make decisions and are rewarded through achievement. But what if the rhetoric is not matched by reality?

There are a number of contradictions inherent in the notion of commitment. Earlier, we discussed commitment in terms of three elements: emotion, belief and behaviour. As a combination of these, commitment can range between 'affective identification' and mere 'behavioural compliance' (see Key concepts 10.4 and 10.5) (Legge, 1995, p.44). For instance, it can be confused with the phenomenon of 'presentism' – the idea that putting in long, and perhaps ineffectual, hours is a demonstration of commitment to the organization.

Key concept 10:4

Affective identification   A real intellectual and emotional identification with the organization.

Key concept 10:5

Behavioural compliance Presenting an appearance of the attitudes and behaviours expected by senior managers without any real commitment.

Kunda (1991, cited in Willmott, 1993, p.538) found evidence of 'distancing' in a study of middle managers in a company where the rhetoric of commitment and corporate culturalism was strong. Managers deftly played the game of appearing to be committed to the organization's culture while, in reality, maintaining a sense of detachment from the process. In fact, many Western organizations have a prevailing climate of cynicism with employees and managers alike acting out their roles with little faith in the outcome of their actions. Watson (1994, p.74) questioned managers in one organization and obtained the following response from one participant: 'We are a pretty committed bunch but I don't think ZTC knows what to with that commitment.'

Activity 10:6

How easy is it to identify real commitment?

HRM in reality

Top talent and passionate employees

'The war for talent has shifted, now it's the war for the right talent,' said David Ulrich, a business administration professor at the University of Michigan and leading human resources author and speaker. 'It is not enough to say that people are our most important asset; but to believe that people are the customer's most important asset.'

Egon Zehnder International, a human capital consulting and executive search firm, has just released results from a survey of more than 60 senior-level HR executives based at companies throughout the United States. The results indicate that businesses could lose top performers in a recovering economy if they do not have comprehensive talent management strategies.

'From our survey, we discovered both large companies, such as Texas Instruments and General Electric, and smaller, high-growth companies, like Intercontinental Exchange and CES, are successful in retaining top talent because they have made "talent management" an integral part of their culture,' said Andrew Dietz, a consultant for Egon Zehnder International who, with Greg Hiebert, co-authored the report on *Talent Management*. Dietz observed:

> Unfortunately, we also discovered many companies that had no talent management strategies or those that were under-supported and ineffective. Top performers in these companies are at risk as the economy recovers. Our study offers prescriptive measures to ensure that business leaders are employing the best practices that have helped companies like GE succeed. The survey itself includes specific answers and actions not just for human resources executives, but for CEOs and boards as well.

The researchers argue that the 80: 20 rule means that 20 per cent of a company's top employees yield 80 per cent of the positive results. In their view employers need to give exceptional treatment to the strongest executives – people with the ability to drive and deliver superior results on a consistent basis.

Key findings of the Talent Management study

Survey participants that excelled at talent management had:

▶

◄

- CEOs who were directly involved in the talent management process
- empowered, strategic human resources leaders
- attentive boards of directors
- unified, comprehensive and integrated approaches to focusing exceptional care upon top-performing executives.

Some senior employees are reassessing their values as economic and social conditions have changed. Monetary rewards are not so strongly emphasized as motivators. Consequently, proactive employers are looking to a broader and more personalized range of non-financial motivators, including:

- executive education
- personal coaches
- individualized development programmes
- allowing employees to select how they are rewarded.

Most respondents were unhappy with current talent development programmes and succession potential of their senior teams. The survey noted heightened succession planning considerations (perhaps sparked by the events of 11 September) driving increased high-potential employee development activities.

Finally:

- HR departments tended not to have formal budgets for talent management – costs being mostly incurred and driven at line management level.
- Absence of performance metrics and accountability around talent management programmes contributes to a lack of action in moving such programmes forward.
- Respondents said that finding and attracting the best talent is still a problem despite the increase in resumé volume brought on by recession.

Top performers foster passionate employees

Last year, the Jesse H. Jones Graduate School of Management, Rice University hosted lectures by Gordon Bethune, Chief Executive Officer of Continental Airlines, and Ralph Eads, President, Merchant Energy Group for El Paso Corp. These executives discussed formulae for growth and success in their businesses. Both pointed out that top performers differentiate themselves by harnessing the power of the most important asset within any organization – their people. Top-notch processes and strategies need to be paired with happy, productive employees to sustain success and ensure continued improvement within any organization.

Still in the midst of reorganization efforts, El Paso Corp. is in a transitional phase. Rapid growth due to mergers and acquisitions has required the largest natural gas company in the world to closely examine its corporate culture. 'It's hard for a company to sustain superior performance when growth is substantial and rapid,' Eads told students.

El Paso Corp., headquartered in Houston, owns and operates a significant portion of the North American natural gas delivery grid and is the nation's third largest natural gas producer. Growth has only bolstered the company's passion to do more. The company is moving toward a less structured business environment, where ideas emerge from conceptualization to execution quickly. 'We want to do things faster than anybody else in America,' Eads said.

El Paso's emphasis on speed and efficiency embodies the rules for success in the 'new economy', said Eads. 'We're eager to translate these and other new economy concepts of experimentation, imagination, creation, diversity and network into the El Paso culture to drive our business forward,' he explained. The result was a reorganization effort to create a culture of passion, integrity, empowerment and high performance at El Paso. 'We wanted to create an environment where people feel passionate about their work, where people feel inspired,' Eads said.

When Gordon Bethune joined Continental Airlines in 1994, the challenge extended beyond reorganization: the airline needed a complete overhaul. Continental had twice been bankrupt and customer complaints had been consistently high:

'When I took over as CEO, some of my friends expressed their deepest sympathy,' Bethune told students at his 5 March lecture. 'My first challenge at Continental was to keep the airline away from the brink of bankruptcy.'

Bethune moved quickly to implement a reorganization plan to reinvent the image of the ailing company. He found that 'doing a few things right' while keeping focused on a clear, simple vision was important in this goal. Bethune's leadership and communication skills translated well into the new corporate culture. Company goals, plans, and initiatives were routinely communicated to all employees, from senior management to the pilots to baggage handlers. 'We wanted to let our people feel involved, that they belonged, that they were important – no matter what their role or position is in the company,' Bethune said.

Beyond promoting a culture of openness within the company, Bethune also believed in rewarding good, hard work with more than just a pat on the back. Monetary incentives were awarded to employees who reached or surpassed their goals. 'The incentives serve as a way for us to acknowledge good or superior performance, to let our people know that we appreciate [their efforts],' Bethune said. His formula for success in the customer-driven airlines business, is simple: 'We treat our people well, and in turn, they treat our customers well. Happy employees equal customer satisfaction.'

In March 2002, Continental Airlines was ranked 30, the highest-ranking commercial airline, on the 'Top 50 All Stars' list of the 'World's Most Admired Companies' by *Fortune* magazine, up from its previous rank of 48. 'After the struggles of 2001, it is a tremendous honour for my co-workers and me to be named among the most admired companies in the world,' said Gordon Bethune, chairman and chief executive officer of Continental Airlines. 'Our commitment to clean, safe and reliable service has earned recognition from our customers and peers.'

Continental Airlines is the fifth largest airline in the USA and recovering from the effects of 9/11. Continental was named the 2001 Airline of the Year by *Air Transport World*, as well as the 1996 Airline of the Year, making it the only carrier to receive this honour twice in five years. For the fourth consecutive year, Continental was named one of the 100 'Best Places to Work' by *Fortune* magazine, and is ranked the nation's number one airline in customer satisfaction for long and short-haul flights by *Frequent Flyer Magazine* and J.D. Power and Associates.

Source: *HRM Guide USA* (http://www.hrmguide.net/usa/), 10 April 2002.

Committed to what?

Individuals may identify with their work at a variety of levels: their job, profession, department, boss or organization. Realistically, commitment may be diverse and divided between any or all of these. For example, there may be a significant conflict between commitment to the organization and commitment to a trade union. Multi-union situations diffuse commitment even further: they encourage identification with themselves and their own sectional interests; they become combatants in a power game and compete with each other for management attention. Single-union agreements and healthy consultation arrangements help to unify and refocus commitment to the strategic objectives of the company. Japanese 'enterprise unions', linked to and funded by individual organizations, further enhance a unified focus. Abolition of union representation removes the alternative focus completely, at the expense of a useful mechanism for developing a cohesive workforce.

Commitment conflicts with the notion of flexibility. Numerical flexibility has been a predominant feature of recent years, with 'downsizing' and 'de-layering' being an obsession for many large companies. A climate of fear has been created for those people remaining. Staff keep a wary eye on senior managers who have demonstrated a ruthless ability to cut employee costs. The workload has not been diminished in equal measure to the reduction in staff, imposing extra burdens on remaining staff.

Extra work, longer hours and fear of redundancy have increased stress and reduced commitment to employing organizations. Peak performance in the short term requires a significant level of commitment but this can only occur if managers 'ensure that a perception of healthy longevity is achieved' (Watson, 1994, p.111). In other words, insecurity does not lead to motivated employees.

This is so obvious that one is hesitant to make the point. Nevertheless, many people in charge of organizations behave in a way that suggests it is beyond their awareness. Employees are far more likely to be committed to their employing organization if they can feel confidence in their employers' commitment to them. Recent evidence shows that such confidence is misplaced in many free market companies which, seemingly, are controlled by people concerned largely with furthering their own careers. There is no possibility of achieving real commitment without mutual trust.

| **HRM in reality** | ## Managing workplace negativity |

Earlier this year, ComPsych Corporation, a major provider of 'Guidance Resources' (including employee assistance programmes, managed behavioural health, work–life, legal and financial services, personal convenience services and outsourced human resource functions), produced strategies for overcoming negativity in the workplace in its 'Managing Workplace Negativity' workshops.

'The softening economy and accompanying layoffs has workers feeling insecure and defensive, which manifests in negative behaviour such as pessimistic talk and bad attitudes,' said Dr Richard Chaifetz, CEO of ComPsych. 'Negativity is especially apparent in situations where employers aren't honest about the financial conditions of their organizations and when employees aren't sure who's the next to go.' Chaifetz argues that signs of negativity include: an increase in customer complaints; a jump in absenteeism; and loss of loyalty by individual employees or entire departments.

He points to the extremely contagious nature of negativity and feels that employers should set out to identify negative workers and make efforts to address their behaviour before it starts an epidemic. 'Cite examples that illustrate to the employees how their negative conduct affects their work,' said Chaifetz. 'Then offer them opportunities to change their negative attitudes by involving them in culture building activities, like managing a special project or event. Bringing negative employees into the fold gives them reason to commit to your organization.'

Chaifetz believes that employers should build trust within their businesses to overcome negativity. 'Keep employees informed about significant decisions, like reorganizations and layoffs, and openly discuss the situation,' he said. 'Employees should feel they're able to approach managers to get the straightforward facts about the security of their position and the future of the company.'

Source: *HRM Guide USA* (http://www.hrmguide.net/usa/), 6 November 2001.

Discussion question: What factors contribute to lack of trust and employee negativity?

HRM in reality

Just 30 per cent of Canadian workers take a one-hour lunch

A new survey of job hunters visiting workopolis.com shows that only around a half of respondents (53 per cent) take a lunch break every day. A third eat lunch at their desks (or on the run) every day and another 36 per cent do so two or three times a week. And when they do eat lunch the largest proportion (42 per cent) take just 15–30 minutes.

'This survey shows that a surprising number of workers are foregoing the traditional lunch hour and instead staying at their desks or continuing to work,' says Kim Peters, President of Workopolis, Canada's biggest job site. 'As the day to day pressures of work continue to grow, many workers may find it's easier to continue working on a task that's already been started rather than put it aside to take a break.'

Workopolis.com survey: 'Taking Lunch'

- Do you take a break for lunch every day at work? Yes 53 per cent; No 47 per cent.
- How often do you eat at your desk or on the run? Every day 33 per cent; 2–3 times a week 36 per cent; Almost never 31 per cent.
- On average, how much time do you take for lunch? Less than 15 minutes 26 per cent; 15–30 minutes 42 per cent; 30–60 minutes 30 per cent; Over 60 minutes 2 per cent.

And when asked 'If you are having a bad day at work, what are you most likely to choose to have for lunch?', respondents came out with a wide variety of answers, the most common being: fast food, chocolate bars, pizza, soup and potato chips. Some responses were a little unusual, including: pork and beans, gummy bears, pork rinds, alcohol and 'whatever is left in the fridge'.

Source: *HRM Guide Canada* (http://www.hrmguide.net/canada/), 11 April 2001.

Managing professionals

Employee commitment faces one of its most difficult challenges in the management of people who regard themselves as professionals – for example, accountants, artists, designers, doctors, engineers, lawyers, scientists and teachers. Strictly speaking, they are salaried professionals in that they conduct their craft within the organization rather than in private practice (Raelin, 1991). The tendency has been to superimpose conventional management practices on these individuals despite several important differences affecting status, power, motivation, etc. According to Raelin: 'There is a natural conflict between management and professionals because of their differences in educational background, socialization, values, vocational interests, work habits and outlook.' He encapsulates the essential problem in the following way:

> As a manager of professionals, how often in your career have you had to confront attempts by your professional associates or subordinates to challenge your authority? As a salaried professional, how much longer can you put up with managers who interfere with your right to work autonomously on the problems to which you have been assigned?

Conventionally, professionals will have been trained and socialized in their professions outside the organization in which they are now working. Managers, on the other hand, will have had a comparatively short and non-specialized training and will probably gain much of their expertise on the job. The organization expects professionals, as employees, to obey its rules and procedures. Professionals may feel that these procedures conflict with the ethics or practices of their profession.

Their commitment and loyalty may take a number of forms: to their profession, to the organization or both. Sociologically, individuals primarily committed to the former are regarded as 'cosmopolitan', those to the organization as 'local'. This commitment may vary at different stages in a career and with different circumstances. There are also clear cultural tendencies: in Japan, commitment is overwhelmingly to the organization whereas the Anglo-Celtic economies such as the UK and the USA have encouraged a cosmopolitan attitude. This tendency matches prevailing attitudes towards job-change between organizations.

Professional status

To be classified as a professional, an individual needs to satisfy such criteria as the following:

1 Possession of expertise or detailed grasp of a recognized body of knowledge, usually after a prolonged period of formal training.

2 Autonomy: the freedom to choose the methods by which they conduct their profession.

3 Commitment to a specific profession.

4 Identification with a group of like-minded professionals – e.g. an association.

5 Ethics: a recognized code of conduct.

6 Standards, the maintenance of which requires the policing of colleagues' activities and being policed in return.

Conflict factors

The interaction of professionals and their managers involves conflict between the aspirations and attitudes of the two. Systematic factors are likely to be responsible.

Overspecialization

There are forces from both management and the profession towards the overspecialization of the individual. From the organization's viewpoint, greater efficiency is obtained by only using the professional for tasks where the specialization is specifically required. The professional is treated like a tool. Very often, the professional is happy to fit in with this process since it involves recognition of their expertise. However, the end-result of this practice is to produce an individual lacking in the general experience and integrative skills required for senior levels within the organization.

Employment a loose attachment

The professional will tend to regard management as being unnecessary: self-management is the ideal. Obviously, this view is not shared by the professional manager who will regard the professional attitude as disrespectful and obstructive. Furthermore, the professional will readily share opinions and information with their network of professionals outside the organization thereby revealing information that the manager could regard as being commercially sensitive. This process is further encouraged by the pressure on professionals to enhance their status through publication of papers in journals and attendance at conferences. Local commitment will operate against the perceived professional status of an individual who is more likely to gain respect among colleagues by frequently moving between jobs. Their reputation is reduced by staying with one organization.

Demand for autonomy

The organization holds the view that professional employees are 'hired to do the job' for which they have been taken on: the task requiring trained expertise. Management sets this agenda and normally finds little resistance from the professional who tends to be happy to fit in with it. Whereas the ends of the organization are not so important to the professional, the means by which the job is done is a considerably more sensitive issue. Bad managers will exacerbate the situation by getting involved in the details of job methodology and demand constant reports.

Conflict situations

The conflict between manager and professional can be brought to a head in a number of specific circumstances: project termination; close supervision; and management by non-professionals.

Project termination

Professionals are often employed as members of project teams. Inevitably, a high proportion of projects fail to achieve their objectives and many organizations deliberately start a large number of projects knowing that only a small proportion will produce marketable products or services. In these circumstances, the management decision to close a project will be clinical and unemotive. However, the staff involved will probably have invested a great deal of emotional commitment to the project and are unlikely to want to abandon it.

Close supervision

As we discussed earlier, professionals tend to be ready to accept the specification of ends and allow managers to determine what tasks the organizations will undertake. However, they will not be ready to accept the supervision of the means by which these tasks are completed and will resent any attempt by managers to closely supervise them. Professional work inevitably requires the flexibility to interpret rules and determine which techniques should apply. In these circumstances, self-supervision and peer control should replace traditional supervision.

Management by non-professionals

In many organizations, the overriding respect for technical competence has led traditionally to professionals managing their own institutions. Since the advent of neo-liberal agendas, the trend (e.g. in hospitals) has been to promote administrators as a separate cadre of professional managers. Achieving the correct balance of management between close or laissez-faire supervision has tended to be problematic.

Activity 10:7   What are the main points of friction between professionals and managers?

HRM in reality

Are employers taking advantage of their loyal tech employees?

An online survey by TechRepublic, the specialist IT site, suggests that the answer is 'Yes' – because IT professionals find it difficult to achieve a work–life balance.

The website (www.techrepublic.com) surveyed 3900 IT professionals online as a part of an ongoing study of the phenomenon known as the 'pervasive workplace'. This refers to the opportunity for confirmed workaholics – and exploited workers – to work anywhere, anytime through new technology such as cell phones and personal digital assistants (PDAs).

There is nothing new in IT pros working long hours – they have a reputation for this. Grabbing midnight pizzas and spending just a few hours sleeping under the desk in order to meet deadlines are common stereotypes of the IT professional. The survey confirms that many IT pros work long hours:

- 81 per cent of IT professionals work 40–60 hours per week
- 8 per cent work 60–70 hours a week
- 3 per cent claim to work over 70 hours a week
- just 7 per cent admit to working 30–40 hours a week
- a mere 1 per cent say they work fewer than 30 hours per week.

Significantly, 77 per cent of respondents felt they had to work more than 40 hours per week in order to be successful at their jobs.

Two-thirds believed they worked too much, with many reporting that this feeling of being overworked indicated an imbalance between personal and working lives. Some 81 per cent said the lack of balance caused them stress, either at work or at home – or both. The blame was often directed at employers with 40 per cent saying their overwork was due to understaffing and 18 per cent feeling that management had no idea of the time required to complete specific tasks.

IT pros were not being paid for the extra time at work – probably because a high proportion were salaried employees. More than half (56 per cent) were not compensated at all, with a mere 12 per cent getting overtime pay. Some got time off in lieu.

'As businesses today look to further streamlining operations, demands on the IT pro will continue to rise,' said Bob Artner, vice-president of content development at TechRepublic. 'The jobs that IT pros do are central to the success of today's enterprise and should not be under-appreciated. Our members are telling us that the demands of the job are incredibly trying on their professional and personal lives.'

'The 40-hour workweek no longer exists for the IT professional – and that's not necessarily in the best interests of the IT pro or their organization,' added Artner.

Source: *HRM Guide USA* (http://www.hrmguide.net/usa/), 19 March 2001.

Summary

In this chapter we examined the concept of commitment, particularly in relation to the concept of employer branding. Commitment has been a particular feature of human resource literature since the 1980s as a result of its inclusion in the influential Harvard map of HRM and the apparent advantage it gave Japanese firms over their Western counterparts. In recent years, internal brand management has been subsumed by the process of 'employer branding' – an attempt to build organizations that embody brand values by attracting, keeping and developing employees who 'live the brand' through the alignment of marketing communications and HR practices. We reconsidered the link between commitment and culture and questioned its true justification and meaning and addressed the issue of commitment in the management of professionals.

Further reading

Karen Legge provides a powerful analysis of commitment in *Human Resource Management: Rhetorics and Realities* (1995), published by Macmillan Business. Michael O'Malley's *Creating Commitment: How to Attract and Retain Talented Employees by Building Relationships That Last* (2000), published by John Wiley, is a highly readable practitioner account on developing commitment and identifying employees who 'fit'. There are hundreds of brand management books in print, but few go into employer branding in detail. *Integrated Branding: Becoming Brand-Driven Through Companywide Action*, by F. Joseph LePla and Lynn M. Parker (1999), published by Quorum Books, takes a holistic approach to branding, including its impact on employees. *Brand Manners: How to Create the Self Confident Organization to Live the Brand,* by Hamish Pringle and William Gordon (2001), published by John Wiley, and *The Brand Mindset: Five Essential Strategies for Building Brand Advantage Throughout Your Company* by Duane E. Knapp and Christopher W. Hart (1999), published by McGraw-Hill, also contain some material on employees and branding.

Review questions

1 Define commitment in your own words. Why is the term significant in human resource literature?

2 What is the relationship between brand management, employer branding and commitment?

3 How can individuals retain their individuality and freedom of expression in an organization that emphasizes employer branding?

4 If Japanese commitment is dependent on Japanese culture, how useful is the concept likely to be in other parts of the world?

5 To what extent is true commitment attainable? Is it just an example of management rhetoric?

6 What is the relationship between the concepts of 'strong culture' and 'commitment'?

7 Is it possible to obtain commitment in a situation where redundancies are inevitable?

8 What are the principal drivers and barriers to effective employee commitment?

Problem for discussion and analysis

Ark Nurseries

Ark Nurseries is a specialist wholesaler of fresh and freeze-dried herbs and vegetables. These are grown within the country or brought in from other parts of the world and packaged in a small, chaotic factory. Most of the sales are to small retailers and restaurants in middle-class areas. The company was founded ten years ago and has prospered as its products have become familiar and customers have been increasingly interested in a more varied range of foods. The managing director founded the company with her late husband and has taken complete control of the company since his death three years ago. She was always accustomed to working hard and now spends virtually all her waking hours at the company. Her main interest is selecting and marketing new products and she is happy to spend a lot of her time travelling to meet growers and attending trade fairs and exhibitions. She is frequently away from the office for weeks at a time.

The staff have gradually increased in number over the years, most of the more senior managers having been with her for several years. She deals directly with her managers, usually on a one-to-one basis as problems come up, and dislikes committee-type meetings. An outgoing and energetic person, she takes decisions quickly, based on intuition and her experience of the market. She takes advice from her staff but does not feel obliged to follow it. Generally, she is a talker rather than a listener and is accustomed to having her way. She insists on vetting all staff recruitment, promotion and pay increases and takes all equipment-purchasing decisions herself. There is no one specifically in charge of human resources, each functional manager being responsible for their own staff. Pay is good for the area and employees are generally pleased to work for the company. The factory has a five-day week and is open for ten hours a day. There is no appraisal or performance management system, with senior staff being paid salaries and factory workers receiving wages based on a piece-rate system.

The sales manager has just clinched a deal with a major supermarket group which has agreed to take Ark produce for its 60 stores. The MD was surprised by his success but is delighted that it has finally been achieved. The contract was announced last week but reactions within the company have been mixed. The managing director has spent years trying to break into this market and is astonished by the attitude of most of her senior staff. They have been accustomed to steady but undramatic growth and are now faced with tripling sales over the next three years. They argue that their regular growers could not meet the demand at the right level of quality, especially as the supermarket group will expect stringent standards and exact financial penalties for late delivery.

Over the last few days, fierce arguments have broken out between the MD and her staff and there have been threats of resignation. However, the MD is convinced that the contract is feasible and that resignations will not happen because of the unemployment situation. As a human resources consultant, how would you analyse the situation and how could you help?

PART 4

Strategic HRM

This part of the book discusses the basis, preparation and implementation of strategic HRM. Human resource management is closely identified with business strategy by many authors. In fact, HRM is typically distinguished from traditional personnel management by its concern with meeting business objectives in a strategic fashion.

The chapters in Part 4 address a number of specific issues:

- What is strategy?
- What is the role of HRM in the strategic process?
- How are human resource strategies prepared and implemented?
- What is the relationship between strategic HRM and human resource planning?
- How does HRM impact on the process of organizational change?
- What is the role of HR practitioners in mergers and acquisitions?
- How can behavioural change be achieved?
- What strategies are available for recruitment and retention?
- How are resourcing strategies prepared?

11 | People strategies

Objectives

The purpose of this chapter is to:

- Determine the nature and prevalence of strategic HRM.
- Evaluate the influence and involvement of people managers in high-level decision making.
- Identify different approaches to strategic HRM, and outline their strengths and weaknesses.
- Consider how people strategies and practices can be adapted to meet perceived threats and opportunities in a changing business environment.

Strategy and HRM

Armstrong (1994) has posed the question:

> What *is* this thing called strategic HRM? It seems to be part of the brave new worlds of strategic management and human resource management. But have these terms any real meaning? How many people actually put either strategic management or human resource management into practice? And if they do, what do they look like and what impact, if any, do they make on organizational performance?

In Part 1 we saw that many theorists consider a strong link with strategy to be the key difference between HRM and earlier philosophies of people management. Exponents of HRM emphasize the importance of an organization's people in achieving its overall business objectives. Typically, it is claimed that human resource strategies combine all people management activities into an organized and integrated programme to meet the strategic objectives of an enterprise. It is claimed also that HRM is different from personnel management primarily because of its supposed emphasis on the link between people policies and overall business strategy. For example, Guest (1993, p.213) distinguishes traditional personnel management from HRM 'by virtue of the way in which the former ignored, but the latter embraces strategy'. This contrasts with the 'technical-piecemeal' approach of personnel management.

Purcell (2001, p.59) concludes that 'the integration with strategy is central to all models of HRM and virtually all authors are agreed that this is *the* distinctive feature of HRM, compared with personnel.' Personnel management, we are told, is essentially reactive whereas HRM, exemplified by HR strategy, is proactive. The personnel model focused on short-term, largely operational matters of little interest to strategists. HRM, by contrast, takes a longer perspective and is closer to the heart of the organization. HRM is portrayed as 'having come out of the shadows to claim a rightful place alongside other core management roles' (Beardwell, 2001, p.13). It takes a proactive stance towards the competitiveness and efficiency of the organization, unlike the mundane and reactive, day-to-day orientation of personnel management. However, this distinction is by no means accepted unanimously: 'HRM's claim to take a strategic approach to employment touches a particularly raw nerve among personnel managers. "*Of course*" personnel management has "*always*" advocated a strategic approach' (Hendry, 1995, p.12).

Moreover, human resource strategies are not easy to identify. For example, Marginson *et al.* (1988) found that 80 per cent of senior people managers claimed to have overall HR strategies – but few could describe what those strategies were! In fact, both academics and practitioners have found it difficult to understand what HR strategy means in practice. Hendry (1994), for example, acknowledges that strategy is the dominant theme in HRM but it is also a misunderstood concept. He concludes that 'the perspective writers on HRM offer on strategy is often glib and lacking in sophistication'. Hendry attributes this to HR theorists being 'strategically illiterate'. They use strategic concepts that are outmoded and defective. The problem is compounded by the lack of case studies to give us insight into the way strategies arise in practice.

We can compare these comments from the UK, where (as in Australia, India, Ireland, Malaysia, New Zealand, Singapore and South Africa) there is a perceived dichotomy between 'personnel management' and HRM, with the situation in North America where Rothwell, Prescott and Taylor (1998, p.5) compare 'traditional HR' and its more modern (and dynamic) form, 'strategic HR':

1 Traditional HR practitioners do not have enough 'working knowledge of what business is all about or of the strategic goals of the organizations they serve'. Instead they present what appears to be a social (i.e. dangerously liberal) agenda without

explaining the organizational benefits. As a result the impression is created that they have little concern for business results.

2 They lack leadership ability, especially if they have no line management experience and are viewed as having less interest in helping line managers solve their problems than they have in meeting HR objectives, such as complying with employment legislation.

3 HR practitioners are viewed as reactive. For example, insisting on individual pay scales when the organization has otherwise decided on a team-based approach. 'They appear unresponsive – and even resistant – to line management needs, interests and business pressures.'

4 They sometimes seem unable to take on 'the lead in establishing a vision for change and garnering the support necessary to lead the change'. The result is that they lose credibility and respect.

5 They are seen as 'fad-chasers' who try to use solutions for problems in other workplaces and 'drop them in place without taking into account the unique business objectives, corporate culture, organization-specific politics, and individual personalities of key decision makers found in their own organizational settings'.

Such criticisms of 'personnel management' or old-school HR are common and strategic HRM is seen as a possible solution. For example, Beardwell (2001, p.13) states:

> In this respect one of the traditional stances of the personnel practitioner – that of the 'liberal' conception of personnel management as standing between employer and employee, moderating and smoothing the interchange between them – is viewed as untenable: HRM is about shaping and delivering corporate strategies with commitment and results.

Strategic management

Strategy is about choice. The underlying assumption is that firms can make deliberate decisions about their markets, the products or services they provide, prices, quality standards and the deployment of human and other resources. According to most discussions of the subject, strategic thinking is based on rational decision making, taking into account the competitive and financial pressures on an organization and the resources available to it, including its people. It imposes orderly, logical thinking on a messy real world, modelling the present situation and predicting the consequences of specific actions (see Key concept 11.1). In order to evaluate these outcomes there is an emphasis on quantitative statements – such as the number of people needed – based on an explicit set of objectives. But we will see that this approach has been questioned and alternative approaches have been proposed for strategic human resource management.

Under the influence of the Harvard MBA, business strategy has become an influential and integrative discipline at the organizational level. The emphasis on a planned approach to development and growth brings together the functional elements of operations management, marketing, finance and human resource management into a cohesive whole. Strategic management is a process by which organizations determine their objectives, decide on actions and suitable timescales, implement those actions and then assess progress and results (Thompson, 1993, p.xiv). Fundamentally, it is the task of senior managers, although more junior employees contribute to the process and the implementation of strategy.

Key concept 11:1

Strategy   A strategy is the means by which an organization seeks to meet its objectives. It is a deliberate choice, a decision to take a course of action rather than reacting to circumstances. It focuses on significant, long-term goals rather than day-to-day operating matters.

As we observed in Part 1, rhetorical accounts paint a picture of HRM as being focused and managerial, unified and holistic, and driven by strategy. According to Armstrong (1992, p.47):

> A strategic orientation is a vital ingredient in human resource management. It provides the framework within which a coherent approach can be developed to the creation and installation of HRM policies, systems and practices. ... The aim of strategic human resource management is to ensure that the culture, style and structure of the organization, and the quality, commitment and motivation of its employees, contribute fully to the achievement of business objectives.

But there is a considerable debate about what 'strategic human resource management' (SHRM) actually means (Key concept 11.2). There are many definitions, including:

- 'A human resource system that is tailored to the demands of the business strategy' (Miles and Snow, 1984).
- 'The pattern of planned human resource activities intended to enable an organization to achieve its goals' (Wright and McMahan, 1992).
- 'By *strategic* we mean that HR activities should be systematically designed and intentionally linked to an analysis of the business and its context' (Schuler, Jackson and Storey, 2001, p.127).

Such definitions range from a portrayal of SHRM as a 'reactive' management field where human resource management is a tool with which to implement strategy, to a more proactive function in which HR activities can actually create and shape the business strategy (Sanz-Valle, Sabatar-Sanchez and Aragon-Sanchez, 1998).

Key concept 11:2

Strategic HRM   Strategic HRM takes a long-term perspective and is concerned with issues such as corporate culture and individual career development as well as the availability of people with the right skills. It incorporates redundancy and recruitment planning and is increasingly focused on the concept of the flexible workforce.

The range of activities and themes encompassed by SHRM is complex and goes beyond the responsibilities of personnel or HR managers into all aspects of managing people and focuses on 'management decisions and behaviours used, consciously or unconsciously, to control, influence and motivate those who work for the organizations – the human resources' (Purcell, 2001, p.64). For example, Mabey, Salaman and Storey (1998) look at the subject from four perspectives:

1 The social and economic context of SHRM – including the internal (corporate) and external environments that influence the development and implementation of HR strategies.

2 The relationship between SHRM and business performance, emphasizing the measurement of performance.

3 Management style and the development of new forms of organization.

4 The relationship between SHRM and the development of organizational capability, including knowledge management.

Other authors have attempted to provide more analytical frameworks for SHRM. Delery and Doty (1996), for example, make distinctions between three different theoretical frameworks:

- *Universalistic*: where some HR practices are believed to be universally effective.
- *Contingent*: the effectiveness of HR practices are supposed to be dependent on an organization's strategy.
- *Configurational*: where there are believed to be synergistic effects between HR practices and strategy that are crucial for enhanced performance.

Wright and Snell's (1998) model of SHRM aims to achieve both fit and flexibility. They emphasize a distinction between HRM practices, skills and behaviour in their relation to strategy on the one hand, and the issue of tight and loose coupling of HR practices and strategy on the other.

Activity 11:1	What is 'strategic human resource management' and what does it encompass?

HRM in reality	**Strategy and planning**

Planning and strategy have a long history (Mintzberg, 1994, p.6). Writing in 1916, Henri Fayol (1916/1949) described having ten-yearly forecasts, revised every five years. Fayol supported the maxim that 'managing means looking ahead', regarding foresight as an essential part of management. Strategic thinking can occur at a number of levels. We have seen already that governments and multinational organizations can shape the future of whole economies and engage in strategic human resource planning at a macro level.

Mintzberg observes that, ironically, planning achieved its greatest importance in two of the most divergent societies on earth: the command economies of the communist world and in corporate America. However, many observers have argued that the Japanese economy is the best illustration of integrated government and corporate strategic planning (Whitehill, 1991, p.256). Japan has targeted and supported successful industries but that success has not just been a matter of good fortune. 'Winners' have been created by means of strategic thinking and careful planning at a joint national and organizational level.

Strategic HRM: theory and practice

Why do management theorists stress the importance of strategy? A number of reasons are apparent:

- Strategic literature largely emphasizes the internal resources of a business as the source of competitive advantage. This 'resource-based' perspective (Boxall, 1996) views a firm as a bundle of resources. Such resources must possess four qualities for advantage to be maintained:
  - *Value*. They must add value to the organization's activities.
  - *Rarity*. They must be rare and (preferably) unique.

- *Inimitability*. Competitors should have difficulty in copying them.
- *Non-substitutability*. They cannot be replaced by technology.

Although the resource-based view originally came from economics, commentators such as Boxall have argued that it is particularly applicable in the case of human resources. The resources embodied in an organization's people are found in the form of skills, expertise and experience (Storey, 1995, p.4). Knowledge management (discussed in Chapter 3) can be viewed as a development of the resource-based view of the firm but focused on one particular aspect – tacit knowledge.

- HRM models focus strongly on strategy. Certainly, this is the case. However, models of human resource management largely derive from American business schools. The prevailing philosophy in these schools has been analytic, and strategic. This line of reasoning offers an explanation but not a justification. In fact, it is circular because if one asks why they devised strategic models for HRM, the answer might simply be that 'they would, wouldn't they.'

- Strategy is intellectual and, therefore, interesting – to management theorists. It is analytical and can be conceptualized in terms of models, abstractions and even numbers. In other words, it deals with a business subject within an orthodox academic framework. This contrasts with forms of operational management that deal with 'boring admin'. Day-to-day management tends to be commonsensical, uses ragbags of techniques that – from experience – have been found to work, and deals with messy problems. It is unteachable and difficult to intellectualize. Students without business experience find discussion of real-life people management hard to relate to. It does not have the tidiness and coherence of a proper subject with 'right' answers. Far easier to regard it with contempt!

- Degree courses major on strategy. Since the advent of the Harvard MBA, there has been a steady trend towards a final year focus on 'business policy' for undergraduate business studies degrees. The underlying rationale is the provision of an integrative subject that prepares students for high-level business jobs. It is taught by looking backwards – retrospective examination of case studies that are prepared within recognized frameworks. Essentially, it is a case of 'where did they go wrong' and, occasionally, right. Intriguingly, however, employers consistently ask for practical business skills such as presentation and teamwork – not strategic thinking. Essentially, strategy is for senior managers. In a time of mass higher education few students will ever become senior managers, and those who do will not achieve such jobs for at least a decade.

- Strategy is important. It deals with high-level decisions, concerning itself with the 'big agenda'.

If strategy is deemed so important by theorists, how much impact has strategic thinking had on practitioners? First, the emphasis given to strategy by HRM theorists has led to significant interest from senior managers. For example, there is a stress on the importance of maximizing the performance and potential of an organization's people. This does not come necessarily from an altruistic and soft-hearted interest in their welfare. More likely, it derives from a hard-headed appreciation of the long-term contribution they can provide to the business. 'Soft' HRM focuses on an organization's people as assets so that time spent on training and development is an investment in human capital (see Part 2). This investment provides long-term benefit for an organization.

Hence strategic HRM can fit the interests of senior executives. But what of lower-level managers? There are two major difficulties for HR practitioners brought up in the personnel tradition. First, as we have noted, knowledge of wider business functions has not been a strength of the personnel profession. There is a gulf in personality between those attracted to strategy and the people actually dealing with human resources at company level. Differing interests and outlooks on life can lead to a serious failure of communication.

On the one hand, business school strategists have tended to minimize human resource considerations because of the ambiguity and uncertainty attached to human behaviour. Humans are the most unpredictable of strategic resources. Michael Porter, the doyen of strategic management, virtually discounted the HR aspects of strategy. On the other hand, personnel departments generally employ practitioners who view themselves as pragmatists dealing with practical issues such as recruitment, pay and discipline 'on the ground', remote from the grand theories of strategists (Beardwell and Holden, 1994, p.7).

The second difficulty comes from their historic role of independent arbitrators between staff and management. As conciliators and apologists personnel managers depended on the ability to find compromises and reconcile the two sides rather than developing a clear agenda of their own. As a result, they make uncomfortable stakeholders, unable to fight their corner. Instead they are forced to react to the decisions of more powerful stakeholders. In practice then (Giles and Williams, 1991, p.31):

> ... personnel specialists find strategy difficult. Personnel specialists have not developed the strategic skills needed to contribute to their organization's effectiveness. Current education and training programmes give them little insight into how to link business, technical and human resource management skills in times of great uncertainty. Personnel specialists do not speak the language of top management in marketing and manufacturing and often seem to clam up when confronted with all the noughts on a company balance sheet.

Herein lies the source of difficulty between the planning mentality and human resource management. Good people managers, through intuition or experience, are profoundly aware of their lack of control over people. In a high proportion of situations, the most carefully constructed and devious tactics will fail to get people to behave in a desired way. Experienced managers will regard this as normal and inescapable. People are not puppets and it is not surprising that they do not behave as such. Coming to terms with this is very much a matter of personality. Managers with a high tolerance of ambiguity, able to operate in fluid, uncertain situations, gravitate towards jobs with a considerable people element.

In contrast, human quirkiness and unpredictability do not fit the planning mindset which demands ordered, rational and entirely predictable behaviour. Communication between dedicated planners and people managers can be a painful business. To the HR manager a plan can seem to be a statement of intentions, an attempt to forecast an ideal world – but not to be stuck to rigidly. If circumstances change, surely the plan can be bent to accommodate this? To the planner, human resource thinking seems woolly and vague. HR managers do not convey a feeling of confidence: they are far too tolerant of deviant behaviour and seem incapable of *making* employees toe the line. They are incorrigible 'firefighters' and hence unsuitable for senior, strategic roles.

Activity 11:2

Is it fair or reasonable to criticize traditional personnel practitioners for their attitudes towards strategic management?

Michael Porter and business strategy

Michael E. Porter is the world's most influential business thinker, according to an Accenture study conducted in 2002. His book, *Competitive Strategy: Techniques for Analyzing Industries and Competitors* (Free Press, 1980) has been required reading on numerous Business Strategy courses ever since it was published over two decades ago. His notion of strategy has been debated and criticized in academic circles but Porter's ideas have often been adopted uncritically (and, perhaps, misunderstood) by business leaders throughout the world (Hammond, 2001).

According to Harfield (1998):

> The question, 'what is strategic management?' often leads to the work of Porter. Strategic management texts inevitably contain his models, theories and frameworks which imply that they are 'fundamental' to the field. An historical journey through six prominent management/organization journals, *Strategic Management Journal, Academy of Management Journal, Academy of Management Review, Journal of Management Studies, Organization Studies, Advances in Strategic Management*, shows that Michael E. Porter was not a constant contributor, in fact he is almost absent from the journals, but his work is often the study of empirical testing or theoretical debate.

In fact, Harfield argues that 'strategic management' is a myth with Michael E. Porter as its principal myth-maker.

Porter spent most of the 1990s concentrating on the competitive advantage of nations. Recently he has returned to look at corporate strategy and comments, according to Hammond (2001, p.150):

> It's been a bad decade for strategy. Companies have bought into an extraordinary number of flawed or simplistic ideas about competition – what I call 'intellectual potholes'. As a result, many have abandoned strategy almost completely. Executives won't say that, of course. They say, 'We have a strategy'. But typically, their 'strategy' is to produce the highest-quality products at the lowest cost or to consolidate their industry. They're just trying to improve on best practices. That's not a strategy.

He argues that this course has been adopted for three main reasons:

1 That people simply found strategy too difficult in the 1970s and 1980s – they had problems with it and it seemed artificial.

2 They were distracted by the pre-eminence of Japanese production techniques. This seemed to be about implementation rather than strategy: produce higher quality products at lower prices than your rivals and keep refining the process of production continuously.

3 More recently it was believed by many that change was happening too quickly for strategies to be of any value. Strategy was seen as rigid and inflexible in a world of speed and dynamic reinvention.

Porter argues that strategy and operational effectiveness need to be distinguished from each other:

> There's a fundamental distinction between strategy and operational effectiveness. Strategy is about making choices, trade-offs; it's about deliberately choosing to be different. Operational effectiveness is about things that you really shouldn't have to make choices on; it's about what's good for everybody and about what every business should be doing (Hammond, 2001).

He contends that business leaders have concentrated too much on operational effectiveness rather than strategy. He points to the popular managerial enthusiasms of the late-20th century – total quality, just-in-time, business process re-engineering – as examples of this. In his view, they were driven by the incredible competitiveness of the Japanese up to the 1990s when some companies 'turned the nitty-gritty into an art form'.

Forming HR strategies

Identifying the relationship between HRM and strategy, it seems, is simpler in theory than it is in practice. Frequently, strategic HRM is a matter of rhetoric. Organizations can usefully be grouped into five alternative categories on the basis of their approach towards human resource strategy (Torrington and Hall, 1995, p.47):

1 Businesses in which there is no consideration whatsoever of human resource issues in the preparation of organizational strategy. Typical of firms 20 years ago and still found in many small companies.

2 Organizations in which there is a growing understanding of the role of human resources in implementing corporate strategy. Human resource strategy cascades on from organizational strategy, very much along the lines of the Michigan model described in Chapter 1. The purpose of HR strategy is to match the requirements of organizational strategy, ensuring the closest possible fit in terms of employee numbers, skills and so on.

3 Businesses in which the relationship becomes two-way with some ideas initiated by HR managers. There is an element of debate about the people management consequences of particular strategies before they are implemented.

4 Organizations in which the HRM concept has been accepted and people are seen as the key to competitive advantage. Corporate and human resource strategies are developed simultaneously. They are coherent and comprehensive.

5 Companies where human resources become the driving force in the development of strategy. There is an overriding emphasis on developing their skills and capitalizing on their competencies.

In practice, organizations may adopt any of these approaches although, at present, the first and last are rarely encountered in large businesses.

Strategies can encompass many issues. Whether or not a business gives prominence to its human resource strategies, when the organization takes decisions on its intended market and product or service range it also determines the types of job and skills required (Purcell, 1995, p.63). Where organizations are genuinely concerned with their people, HRM normally focuses on certain strategic sub-goals, or second-order strategies in Purcell's terminology, as shown in Table 11.1. For example:

● Resourcing an organization with the most suitable people at the right time, in the right place. We will consider this issue in depth later in the book but for the moment we will note that, from a strategic viewpoint, there are two important elements:
(a) knowledge of and participation in the formulation of 'official' strategy; and
(b) awareness of underlying developments that will produce 'surprises' that lead to about-turns in the official policy, typically with little or no notice.

Table 11.1	Levels of strategy affecting HRM		
Level	*Organizational focus*	*Environmental constraints*	
First-order strategies	Long-term objectives Range of activities, markets, locations	Supranational authorities Government Culture and tradition	
Second-order strategies	Internal operating procedures, organizational structure	Capital market Product market Consumers	
Third-order strategies	Strategic choice in HRM	Job market Workforce Law	
Outcomes	Style, structure, conduct of HRM		

Source: Adapted from Purcell, 1989.

- Planning the redeployment or dismissal of staff who are no longer required for specific tasks. The emphasis varies between free market and social market companies with the former taking a hard-HRM line and the latter being committed to a softer approach.

- Determining the cultural characteristics appropriate to an organization's business objectives. Implementation requires us to plan the socialization, performance assessment, development and change programmes needed to realize that culture.

- Developing key skills for new products or equipment. This includes consideration of external and internal resourcing, training programmes, formal education and job rotation.

Examining HR strategy within our ten-Cs checklist of HRM we can see in Table 11.2 how each element, or combination of elements, can be made the focus of strategy. Guest (1987), for instance, identifies a circular relationship between a number of strategic goals:

- As we have seen, HRM aims for a high level of commitment from employees, so that they identify with the organization's goals and contribute actively to its improvement and success.

- In turn, this enables the organization to obtain a high-quality output from workers who want to continually improve standards.

- Within this environment, there is an expectation of flexibility from workers: a willingness to depart from fixed job definitions, working practices and conditions.

- Strategic integration – all these strands link the organization's strategy. They are directed towards agreed objectives and interact with each other in a cohesive way.

Activity 11:3   Summarize the main goals of strategic human resource management as outlined above.

Key concept 11:3

Mission statements   A mission statement should convey the essence of what an organization is about: why it exists, what kind of business it intends to be, and who its intended customers are. The mission is translated into objectives or goals within the strategic management process.

Table 11.2	Checklist for strategic HRM	
Principle	*Definition*	*Action*
1 Control	Effective organizations require a control system for cohesion and direction	Clear, unambiguous mission statement supported by strategies and organization able to meet objectives
2 Contiguity	Human resource management should be closely matched to business objectives	HR strategies developed at board level and integrated with all other strategies
3 Coherence	Allocation and activities of human resources integrated into a meaningful whole	People management must be organized, rather than left to ad hoc decisions at local level
4 Communication	Strategies understood and accepted by all employees. Open culture with no barriers	Clear, simple and justified strategies: cascading process of communication with feedback to the top
5 Credibility	Staff trust top management and believe in their strategies	Top managers are sincere, honest and consistent
6 Commitment	Employees motivated to achieve organizational goals	Top managers show the same commitment to staff
7 Competence	Organization competent to achieve its objectives – dependent on individual competencies	Resourcing strategies, selection techniques and human resource development systems in place
8 Compensation	Competitive, fair reward and promotion systems	Top managers pay themselves on equivalent basis to staff
9 Creativity	Competitive advantage comes from unique strategies	System for encouraging and tapping employee ideas
10 Change	Continuous improvement and development essential for survival	Flexible people and working systems; culture of innovation; skills training

Business goals

Organizations are formed to achieve certain goals. Strategic thinking focuses on these long-term objectives. Thompson and Strickland (1998) provide a framework for strategic management based on five major activities that incorporate objective-setting:

- Deciding the type of business in which the organization will operate, developing a strategic vision and producing a set of values together with a general strategy.
- Identifying the strategic issues for the business and setting strategic objectives.
- Developing strategic action plans.
- Creating and implementing strategic action plans for units within the business.
- Evaluating, revising and refocusing strategy for the future.

Human resource strategies are derived from overall business objectives in the same way as investment or marketing strategies. We noted also in the previous chapter that commitment is seen to be particularly crucial for competitive advantage. For true commitment to occur, conventional management wisdom sees the need for employees to accept and believe in an organization's goals.

A mission statement communicates these goals to everyone in a company (Key concept 11.3). Mission statements have a particular significance in large companies where communication can be difficult and, as we have seen, departments and 'political' groups frequently focus on their own sectional interests. A small business may not need such a statement since its employees and owners have a clear understanding of its reasons for existence. Mission statements can be wide-ranging. For example, the Ford Motor Company states:

- *Our vision.* Our vision is to become the world's leading consumer company for automotive products and services.

- *Our mission.* We are a global family with a proud heritage, passionately committed to providing personal mobility for people around the world. We anticipate consumer needs and deliver outstanding products and services that improve people's lives.

- *Our values.* The customer is Job 1. We do the right thing for our customers, our people, our environment and our society. By improving everything we do, we provide superior returns to our shareholders.

What prevents such a statement from being no more than a set of banal platitudes? It can be tied to some form of performance measure, perhaps in the form of detailed objectives. The mission statement is locked into the company's 'first-order' strategies (see Table 11.1). These are major decisions on its long-term aims and the scope of its activities (Purcell, 1995, p.67). As we can see in the 'HRM in reality' article, Ford is an example of a diversified firm that has made both acquisitions and diversifications in recent years. The company has attempted to rebalance its activities to give long-term growth and profitability. The human resource implications are evident in terms of industrial relations, job security, career expectations and human resource development.

| HRM in reality | **Ford Motor Company announces restructuring actions** |

Ford Motor Company today announced several restructuring actions as part of its Ford Revitalization Plan. Five plants are to be closed – Edison Assembly, Ontario Truck Plant, St Louis Assembly, Cleveland Aluminum Casting and Vulcan Forge. Also, new products have not been identified for two plants: Ohio Assembly and Cuautitlan Assembly. Woodhaven Forging Plant will be sold. Major downsizing and shift reductions will take place at 11 plants with line speed reductions and changes to operating patterns at nine plants.

'Our revitalization plan is based on executing the fundamentals of our business to build great products,' said chairman and chief executive officer Bill Ford. 'What we are outlining today is a comprehensive plan that builds for the future. It's going to take everyone in the extended Ford family – employees, suppliers and dealers – working together, over time, to make it work.'

Actions include:

- *New products.* Twenty new or freshened products in the US annually between now and mid-decade.

- *Plant capacity.* Reducing North American manufacturing capacity by about 1 million units by mid-decade to realign capacity with market conditions.

- *Hourly workforce.* About 12 000 hourly employees in North America will be affected by actions completed in December and those to be taken in 2002 and beyond: 3000 hourly employees were affected in 2001. The company intends to reassign as many plant employees as possible.

- *Salaried workforce*. Voluntary separation for salaried employees and other actions led to a reduction of 3500 in the North American workforce last year. The program will be extended to produce a further 1500-person salaried workforce reduction. 'If necessary to meet this goal, an involuntary separation program will be used.'
- *Global workforce*. Since January 2001 about 35 000 employees will be, or already have been, affected around the world. These include 21 500 in North America – 15 000 hourly, 5000 salaried and 1500 agency employees – and 13 500 in the rest of the world.
- *Material costs*. A squeeze on North American suppliers, with Ford receiving 65 per cent of implemented cost reductions and suppliers receiving 35 per cent in the first year.
- *Discontinued low-margins models*. The Mercury Cougar, Mercury Villager, Lincoln Continental and Ford Escort to be discontinued this year.
- *Beyond North America*. Revitalization plans beyond North American automotive operations including continued implementation of the European Transformation Strategy (involving the end of production of Ford-badged cars in the UK).
- *Divestitures*. Proposed sale of non-core assets and businesses, realizing US$1 billion in 2002.

Other actions include: a 7 per cent pay reduction to contract labour firms; a voluntary separation program for North American salaried employees; elimination of bonuses and raises for senior managers; 'sharing' of healthcare costs with US salaried employees and retirees; and elimination of the company match for US salaried employee 401(k) plans.

'Although the actions we're outlining today are difficult, they are necessary steps to lead Ford back to a strong financial and competitive position,' said Nick Scheele, president and chief operating officer. 'They will help us to address our problems, while at the same time permitting us to keep a sharp focus on delivering great products. Quality and value will be the hallmarks of our cars and trucks.'

'In order to remain competitive and profitable, we must make some hard decisions to align capacity with our anticipated sales,' said Scheele. 'At the same time, the company is continuing its commitment to North American manufacturing operations with investments of about US$20 billion over the next five years in new product programs and spending to add flexibility and increase our ability to respond quickly to changes in market demand.'

'We are confident we can achieve these goals through the efforts of our dedicated employee team,' Bill Ford said. 'We know we have immediate challenges to face. It will be difficult, and in some cases, painful to turn things around. But we will turn things around.'

Source: *HRM Guide USA* (http://www.hrmguide.net/usa/), 12 January 2002.

Discussion question: To what extent were these restructuring actions consistent with Ford's vision, mission and goals as outlined above?

It has to be conceded that many businesses have a mission statement simply because it is the done thing to have one. Often they serve no clear purpose. As Whitehill (1991, p.123) points out, this has not been the case in large Japanese firms:

> A statement of mission, or overall philosophy, is particularly significant within the Japanese management system. It is this broad policy declaration which establishes the corporate culture within which regular employees will spend their working lives. Becoming 'socialized' within the corporate culture, and internalizing the company spirit (*shafu*), are important foundations for building the Japanese employee's remarkable loyalty and dedication to the company.

Hence the mission statement plays a crucial role in developing the uniquely Japanese forms of organizational culture and commitment discussed in Part 3.

HRM in reality

Nissan UK

As a Company we aim to build the highest quality car sold in Europe. We want to achieve the maximum possible customer satisfaction and ensure the prosperity of the Company and its staff.

To assist in this, we aim to achieve mutual trust and cooperation between all people within the Company and make Nissan a place where long-term job satisfaction can be achieved. We recognize that people are our most valued resource and in line with this spirit believe the following principles will be of value to all.

People

We will develop and expand the contributions of all staff by strongly emphasizing training and by the expansion of everyone's capabilities.

We seek to delegate and involve staff in discussion and decision making, particularly in those areas in which each of us can effectively contribute, so that all may participate in the efficient running of Nissan.

We firmly believe in common terms and conditions of employment.

Teamworking

We recognize that all staff have a valued contribution to make as individuals but, in addition, we believe that this contribution can be most effective within a teamworking environment.

Our aim is to build a Company with which people can identify and to which we all feel commitment.

Communication

Within the bounds of commercial confidentiality we will encourage open channels of communication. We would like everyone to know what is happening in our Company, how we are performing and what we plan.

We want information and views to flow freely upward, downward and across our Company.

We will agree clear and achievable objectives and provide meaningful feedback on performance.

Flexibility

We will not be restricted by the existing way of doing things. We will continuously seek improvements in all our actions.

> These are tough targets and we aim high. With hard work and goodwill we can get there.
>
> Source: http://www.nissanrecruitment.co.uk/culture.htm.

Strategy formation

Strategic management takes into account all the complexities of the business environment, the pressures that prevail upon an organization, and the resources available to it. Despite a concentration on objective planning, it remains essentially an art rather than a science and draws on a range of theories, models and practical techniques. There is no single approach that guarantees formulation of a successful strategy. Business strategy draws heavily on management theory and is sometimes criticized for employing 'psycho-babble' or 'management speak'. Good strategies should be simple to understand. Sensible plans and changes can be obscured and discredited by excessive use of terminology that conveys little meaning to employees who do not have management literature as their favourite bedtime reading.

Several distinctive approaches to strategic management have arisen. Ansoff (1968) provided some classic principles:

1 Strategy formation should be a controlled, conscious process of thought. In other words it should not be the result of intuition or accident – it should be as 'deliberate as possible'.

2 Responsibility for the process must rest with the chief executive officer. This fits the 'leader is all' mentality that sees the top person as being the major influence on the organization.

3 The model of strategy formation must be kept simple and informal.

4 Strategies should be unique. The best result from a process of creative design. They should build on the particular 'core competencies' of the organization.

5 Strategies must come out of the design process fully developed.

6 Strategies should be made explicit and, therefore, have to be kept simple.

7 Finally, once these unique, full-blown, explicit and simple strategies are fully formulated, they must then be implemented.

More or less at the same time as this approach was developed a significant variant emerged from Harvard. It emphasized strategic planning as a process and played down the role of the chief executive. Its basic premises were that (Mintzberg, 1994, p.42):

1 Strategy formation should be controlled and conscious as well as a formalized and elaborated process, decomposed into distinct steps, each delineated by checklists and supported by techniques.

2 Responsibility for the overall process rests with the chief executive in principle; responsibility for its execution rests with the staff planners in practice.

3 Strategies come out of this process fully developed, typically as generic positions, to be explicated so that they can then be implemented through detailed attention to objectives, budgets, programmes and operating plans of various kinds.

Both models view strategy as encompassing all aspects of a business, including its people. Thus strategic thinkers envisaged a major role for human resource planning before

HRM was conceived as a separate philosophy of people management. For example, Steiner (1969, p.34) wrote:

> The model that may be covered in strategic planning includes every type of activity of concern to an enterprise. Among the areas are profits, capital expenditures, organization, pricing, labour relations, production, marketing, finance, personnel, public relations, advertising, technological capabilities, product improvement, research and development, legal matters, management selection and training, political activities and so on.

Steiner presented strategic planning as an orderly sequence of steps:

1 Objectives-setting develops and quantifies the organization's purposes and goals. This takes a variety of forms, the most sophisticated of which is the Delphi technique. Integral to this step is a determination of the enterprise's fundamental values.

2 External audit for gaining information about the firm's position in the environment. Intricate techniques have been developed to provide exhaustive measures of virtually every external factor that has ever been thought of. Similarly, elaborate forecasting techniques can be employed including scenario building, exploring alternative views of the enterprise's future.

3 A similar internal audit examines the internal, organizational and functional factors that produce the 'competence profile' of the firm.

4 Strategy evaluation taking the above into account within a framework such as SWOT, outlining strengths, weaknesses, opportunities and threats, and comparing the consequences of a variety of strategic options.

5 The strategy operationalization phase which produces a hierarchy of objectives and actions, cascaded down throughout the organization.

The orthodox view of strategy is that it is a deliberate, conscious process coming from the top of the organization (Ansoff, 1968). Figure 11.1 outlines a sequence of activities from this perspective.

However, this model cannot explain organizational strategies and the means of evaluating their relative usefulness. A business can choose between recruiting and training its own direct sales people or subcontracting the function to outside agents. It has to be recognized that all options may not be apparent and that trial and error may be the only practical method of evaluation. Other factors such as competition, organizational politics or the absence of resources may limit the choice. As we saw earlier, in order to reduce costs and increase quality Ford outlined plans in 2002 to reduce its workforce worldwide, partly by outsourcing component manufacture to subcontractors located alongside its car assembly plants.

Moreover, this model cannot explain the strategic process entirely. As the future is not perfectly predictable, a feedback mechanism must be built into the process to correct for unexpected developments. An alternative approach is that of Johnson and Scholes (1984), which divides the process into three components:

● *Strategic analysis.* A successful organization is one that understands its market and is sensitive to changes in the business environment. It must be able to analyse its current position, the strengths and weaknesses of its current resources – for example, the skill and flexibility of its human resources – and assess the opportunities and threats present (and likely) to its continuing success.

● *Strategic choice.* Determination of all the courses of action that are open to the organization and the means of evaluating their relative usefulness. So, a business can choose between recruiting and training its own direct sales people or subcontracting the function to outside agents. It has to be recognized that all options may not be

| Figure 11.1 | The strategy process |

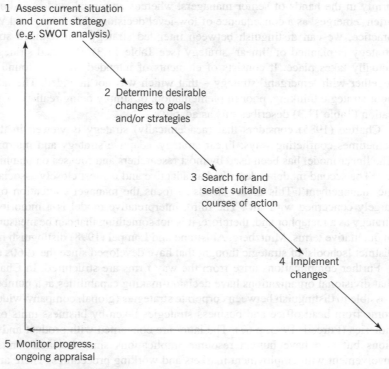

1 Assess current situation
and current strategy
(e.g. SWOT analysis)

2 Determine desirable
changes to goals
and/or strategies

3 Search for and
select suitable
courses of action

4 Implement
changes

5 Monitor progress;
ongoing appraisal

Source: Adapted from Thompson (1993, p.32).

apparent and that trial and error may be the only practical method of evaluation. Other factors such as competition, organizational politics or the absence of resources may limit the choice.

- *Strategic implementation*. Senior managers may believe that by determining strategy they have decided the future of the organization. In fact, as we have seen in previous chapters, the structure and culture of the organization and the commitment of lower-level managers can influence or hinder the implementation of strategy. This is particularly evident in decentralized and loosely controlled organizations that require higher levels of consultation and communication to ensure cooperation. Later in this chapter we will consider these issues in relation to organizational change.

Coherent strategies and integrated practices sound fine in theory but how are they to be translated into action? This 'surface neatness' hides an organizational reality that is far from simple (Blyton and Turnbull, 1992, p.2). Mintzberg (1994, p.26) argues that the strategies which are actually carried through into practice include an unintended element that he terms 'emergent strategies'. This might result from poor strategic thinking, poor implementation or a sound state of realism. It reflects the view that strategic management should not be confined to the top layers in an organization. Emergent strategy rarely comes from the centre but rather from bright ideas and initiatives at a local level, which were not predicted but were found to work and then adopted more widely: '... big strategies can grow from little ideas (initiatives), and in strange places, not to mention at unexpected times, almost anyone in the organization can prove to be a strategist. All he or she needs is a good idea and the freedom and resources required to pursue it' (Mintzberg, 1994, p.26).

Orthodox strategic thinking tends to underestimate the limitations of people – their 'bounded rationality' (Simon, 1960). It supposes also that responsibility for strategy lies firmly in the hands of senior managers, whereas empirical evidence shows that strategy often 'emerges' as a consequence of low-level decisions (Mintzberg and Waters, 1985). In practice, we can distinguish between intended strategy and realized strategy. Intended strategy is planned or 'linear' strategy (see Table 11.3). Realized strategy is that which actually takes place. It consists of elements of intended strategy, found to be practical, together with 'emergent' strategy – that which was not intended. The latter results from poor strategic thinking, poor implementation, or simply being realistic. Chaffee's classification (Table 11.3) describes this as adaptive.

Chaffee (1985) considers that (academically) strategy is viewed in three distinct but sometimes conflicting ways: linear strategy, adaptive strategy and interpretative strategy. The linear model has been used by most researchers and focuses on planning and forecasting. The second model is described as adaptive and is most closely associated with 'strategic management'. This model 'tends to focus the manager's attention on means' and is largely concerned with 'fit'. The third, interpretative model is a minority view that sees strategy as a metaphor and, therefore, it is not something that can be measured but is viewed in qualitative terms. Mintzberg, Ahlstrand and Lampel (1998) distinguish no fewer than ten distinct 'schools' of strategic thought that have developed since the 1960s (see Table 11.4).

Further complications arise from the way firms are structured. In Chapter 7 we noted that divisional organizations have decision-making capabilities at a number of levels. It is possible to distinguish between corporate strategies (global, company-wide initiatives) that come from head office and business strategies taken by business units or operating subsidiaries (Purcell, 1995, p.67). The latter are concerned with product and marketing decisions but also have human resource implications since business units have a closer involvement with employment markets and working procedures. There are no recognized rules on the relation between corporate and business strategies, but it has been argued that strategic HRM should be focused at the business unit level. Nevertheless, business units cannot operate in isolation from the rest of the firm. Overriding issues such as succession planning and media comment on industrial relations demand corporate people strategies.

Table 11.3	Interpretations of strategy
Strategy	Interpretation
Linear strategy	A planning process that determines basic long-term goals for an organization and then uses strategic decision making to determine appropriate courses of action and allocate resources to achieve those goals.
Adaptive strategy	Matching process, continuously aligning an organization to a changing environment. Incremental or iterative, attaching more importance to the means by which this alignment can take place. This model views the involvement of operational managers as being important in the strategic process.
Interpretive strategy	A more thoughtful development of the adaptive model, it bears some resemblance to the approach advocated by Peters. Managers are expected to have a 'cognitive map' of the environment and its interactions with the organization and its resources. An understanding of these relationships allows the strategist to anticipate developments and plan accordingly. This model emphasizes the culture of the organization and the motivation and values of its members.

Source: Based on Chaffee (1985).

Table 11.4	Ten 'schools' of strategy research developed since the 1960s

Title	Concept
1 The Design School	Strategy as a process of conception
2 The Planning School	Strategy as a formal process
3 The Positioning School	Strategy as an analytical process
4. The Entrepreneurial School	Strategy as a visionary process
5 The Cognitive School	Strategy as a mental process
6 The Learning School	Strategy as an emergent process
7 The Power School	Strategy as a process of negotiation
8 The Cultural School	Strategy as a collective process
9 The Environmental School	Strategy as a reactive process
10 The Configuration School	Strategy as a process of transformation

Source: Adapted from Mintzberg, Ahlstrand and Lampel (1998).

Management theory normally stresses order and control. Recently, however, chaos theory has been applied to business. In contrast to strategic thinking, which attempts to plan and predict, chaos theory states that much of the future is unknowable. Planning assumes straightforward relationships with a few measurable variables. In fact, most business problems – particularly those involving people – are highly complex. Often it is impossible to connect what happens to any individual actions that have been taken deliberately.

Peters (1987, p.510) argues that organizations become too safe and predictable. Managers should destabilize their business structures so that new, competitive relationships and activities can emerge. He considers that strategic planning is 'irrelevant, or worse, damaging'. In his view, formal plans should be replaced by adding value to human capital. There are no good strategic plans but there is a good process which:

- gains commitment by getting everyone involved – it is not left to professional planners
- is open to radical ideas
- encourages creativity by asking new questions
- is considered and debated.

For Peters (1987, p.511), the plan should be short, have an emphasis on strategic skills, and should not be regarded as an icon. Its value lies in the thinking process, not in slavish implementation:

> The plan, whose development involves everyone, should be shared with everyone after completion. At that point, there is a serious case to be made for destroying it – if not in practice, at least in spirit. Its value is as an assemblage of thoughts, not constraints. The process of developing it is close to 100 per cent of its value – or perhaps more than 100 per cent of its value. Slavishly following the plan despite changing conditions (now the norm), because of the time and political capital spent in assembling it, is counterproductive.

This form of strategic planning is a 'bottom-up' rather than the traditional centralized, 'top-down' process. It is focused on front-line employees, their skills, creativity and commitment – although senior managers are involved in the debate. Its function is in attuning employees to be able to react quickly to opportunities – 'environmental scanning'. Peters' conception is similar to Chaffee's interpretive strategy (described in Table 11.3).

Mintzberg (1994, p.268) agrees with Peters that strategic planning should not be left to full-time planners on the grounds that they are likely to be out of touch with the front line. Strategic planning posts are often resourced with young graduates, MBAs and finance experts in the belief that planning is an abstract and theoretical exercise. It is scarcely surprising if plans emerging from such a department turn out to be unrealistic and impractical. More intriguingly, Mintzberg also draws attention to the 'tacit' knowledge that line managers use to make judgements. This unverbalized and often subconscious knowledge is the stuff of the informal organization, being political and based on unofficial opinions and personal relationships. It is not passed on to planners but is crucial to the operation of the company.

Other aspects of strategy involve people making decisions about capital equipment, finance or marketing; HR strategy requires people to make decisions about themselves. It is, according to Stacey (1993, p.2):

> important ... to think of strategy as a game that people play, because when it is discussed more seriously there is a strong tendency to slip into talking about it as a response that 'the organization' makes to an 'environment'. ... The inevitable result is a lack of insight into the real complexities of strategic management because in reality organizations and their environments are not things, one adapting to the other, but groupings of people interacting one with another.

However, it is a deadly serious game with people's careers and livelihoods at stake (Stacey, 1993, p.9). The reality is that faced with a choice between profit and the well-being of employees, most commercial organizations will select the former. 'Softer' human resource issues continue to be secondary and subordinate to financial matters. Regardless of well-meaning statements to the contrary, within the free market capitalist model there is an emphasis on short-term improvement in financial performance. In Western organizations, financially knowledgeable managers have taken the lead as the 'bottom line' of profit or loss drives business. Strategic actions derived from technological or financial considerations can have direct and relatively immediate effect on an organization's people. Human resource initiatives are accommodated within a broad financial picture in which benefits or changes to people management compete with other resources. In reality, long-term HRM goals such as training and developing skills for the future are rarely considered. If employee commitment, flexibility and product quality are valued, they are sought for profit and not pursued as beneficial for workers.

Activity 11:4	What deficiencies are commonly found in strategic human resource plans?

Strategy, thinking and decision making

According to Haslam and Baron (1994, p.33):

> Decision making is the thinking, or lack of thinking, that determines what to do when we are faced with more than one option about what to do and when we have time to think. In general, thinking consists of some sort of search process plus some inference that we draw from what the search has found. In decision-making, the search is for alternative options, evidence bearing on the advantages and disadvantages of each option, and goals, which are criteria by which we evaluate the options in the light of the evidence. Decisions are typically made according to rules or habits, without much thinking. But the creation of these rules and habits results from earlier decisions, and thinking can come into play at several points in the formation of these rules and habits.

In recent years, a new approach to strategic management has developed based on cognitive science – the study of thinking and decision making (Hodgkinson and Sparrow, 2002). This approach takes issue with the rationalist view of strategy presented by Michael Porter and others. Cognitive science can trace its origins to Craik's 1940s concept of the 'mental model'. This is an elegantly simple concept. Craik argued that through life the brain builds and maintains an internal, simplified model of the world on which it conducts mental operations before we take any action. In his words, 'thought models, or parallels, reality in some form of symbolism'. In modern technical terminology this is described as mental representation.

Craik postulated that this involved three processes of reasoning:

1 A 'translation' of external process into an internal representation in the form of words, numbers or other symbols.

2 The derivation of other symbols from them by means of an inference process. Ideas are tested against the mental model so that dangerous or unsuitable options are discarded before being tried in the real world.

3 'Retranslation' back into actions.

Mental representations take a variety of forms, including imagery (visual, sounds, etc.), analogies and symbols such as words and numbers. There are contradictory theories on the structure of representations. Some writers identify a single mental model. Others consider that we have mental maps, schemata (mini-models) or 'scripts' for familiar activities. Whatever rationale is employed, this approach indicates that strategic thinking is not the simple, rational activity portrayed in 'classical' accounts. Instead, it involves assumptions, intuition, simplification, 'rules-of-thumb' and emotion. It is just like every other kind of thinking or decision-making activity engaged in by human beings.

HRM in reality	**Thought and logic**

How rational is normal thinking? Naturally, our thinking is influenced by both cold logic and emotion. Rationality does not mean the denial of emotion. Basic rational thinking can be described in terms of a search–inference framework. Within this framework, thinking is a form of exploration or search for choice alternatives. We search for three types of information:

● Possibilities, which can be solutions to a problem or resolutions of doubt.

● Goals are your personal objectives and provide the criteria by which you judge the possibilities. Goals may be present at the beginning of your thinking or they may emerge during your search.

● Evidence is used to help make the judgement, taking the form of information or opinion.

Search makes use of observation, memory, knowledge and external aids – books, computer files, balance sheets and so on. Together with these search processes we employ inference: using the evidence to evaluate the possibilities against our goals. Search and inference go on together – they do not have to be placed in any particular order. When we are solving a problem, the search-inference framework can be represented diagrammatically – for instance, in the form of a decision tree. Positive or negative evidence could be represented in terms of probabilities. The calculation could also be described in terms of subjective expected utility. The search inference framework provides us with the basis for decision modelling.

▶

This approach gives us some insight into the process of trial and error, which is the simplest form of decision making. Trial and error can be active – for example, when we try to get out of a maze. Alternatively, it can be mental: working through the possibilities in our heads, using our mental models of the problem situation. This can be partly unconscious, leading to an apparently spontaneous answer popping into your head. This is called insight. It is a process similar to remembering a name some time after you tried to recall it. It also plays a role in creativity. An early group of psychologists called the Gestalt movement described it as a process of closure. Gestalt means 'form' or 'shape' in German. The Gestaltists argued that the brain constantly tries to form tidy 'wholes' out of the untidy or incomplete information it receives. The brain attempts to create rational forms or shapes and fills in any gaps in the information it has. Often this takes the form of a relationship between one thing and another.

As we develop through childhood we move away from inventing fresh solutions for every problem. More and more, we rely on stock solutions from memory and rules for thinking. There is a danger of becoming mechanical in our thinking and of ignoring novel solutions. One set of rules we acquire is that of formal logic. Logic and rationality are frequently assumed to be the same. Many prescriptive (do it like this) approaches to decision making emphasize logical analysis of a problem. There is plenty of evidence that formal logic is not a natural method of thinking for humans. For example, the following is an example of a totally logical statement taken from instructions on UK National Insurance contributions:

> A Class 1 contribution is not payable for employment by any one employer for not more than 8 hours in any week – but if you normally work for more than 8 hours in any week for any employer, a Class 1 contribution is payable except for any week when you do not do more than 4 hours work for any employer.

Most people lose the thread of logic half way through the paragraph. Logic suffers the same defects as utility. Logic can only work when the problem is relatively simple, self-contained and with complete information (evidence) on goals and possibilities. Most real-life problems do not come in such a neat package.

Translating strategy into action

At this point we turn to the issue of implementing human resource strategies. The classic approach follows the 'matching' process outlined in the Michigan model of HRM outlined in Chapter 1. The goal is a realization of the organization's strategic human resource requirements in terms of numbers and, more importantly: attitudes, behaviour and commitment. According to Miller (1989), the key lies with 'the concept of "fit": the fit of human resource management with the thrust of the organization'. Truss (1999, p.44), reviewing a number of authors, finds that 'there is no evidence that a tight fit leads to positive outcomes and the concept of fit implies inflexibility and rigidity which could, in themselves, be detrimental to organizational outcomes.'

She also notes the underlying assumption of some 'matching models' of hard HRM which contend that every business strategy has one appropriate human resource strategy. This implies a 'simple, linear relationship between strategy and human resource strategy' that does not exist. Such models fail to acknowledge the complex relationship between strategy and HRM and they ignore issues of power politics and culture. She concludes that: 'The matching model is based on a narrow classical view of strategy formulation which assumes that formulation and implementation are separate activities and, consequently, that strategies in the HR area can simply be "matched" to business strategies at the formulation stage.'

Armstrong (1992, p.53) argues that the significant issue in HR strategy is that of integration with overall business strategy. In practice, this integration is difficult to achieve. Armstrong outlines some crucial difficulties:

- *Diversity of strategic processes, levels and styles.* As we have seen, many organizations do not use neat, traditional approaches to business strategy based on rational planning. In line with the criticisms of Mintzberg and others, it may be more sensible to be open-minded and intuitive. However, from the perspective of people management it becomes difficult to discern appropriate HR strategies and the corporate strategies they are supposed to match. Further, in a diversified organization composed of strategic business units (SBUs), each unit may have its own idiosyncratic strategies. Consequently it becomes difficult to provide corporate HR strategies – such as management development – which can be reconciled with the different needs of individual SBUs.

- *The evolutionary nature of business strategy.* It is not possible to provide a rational HR strategy if corporate strategy is evolving quickly and in a piecemeal way. In fact, the concept of 'rational' strategic planning is culture-bound: it is a product of free market economies. Other cultures naturally employ a more diffuse, emergent or evolving method of business planning (Legge, 1995, p.104).

- *The absence of written business strategies.* This is particularly the case in smaller companies and overwhelmingly in cultural contexts where evolutionary planning is the rule. This does not help to clarify those corporate strategic issues with which HR strategy is expected to fit.

- *The qualitative nature of HR issues.* Business plans have tended to be expressed in numerical terms, such as financial data, sales forecasts and competitive position. As we shall see later, traditional 'manpower planning' fitted this mould. Equally, human resource strategy has been identified with the 'hard' rationalist model of HRM. However, 'soft' or qualitative issues such as culture, motivation and employee relations have become increasingly important – even in free market countries.

Armstrong's solution to these problems is to emphasize the need for human resource practitioners to achieve an understanding of how business strategies are formed. They should adopt a wider point of view and an understanding of key business issues such as:

- Corporate intentions for growth or retrenchment, including strategic alliances (mergers, acquisitions, joint ventures – discussed earlier), product and market development, disposals.

- Methods of increasing competitiveness such as improvements in productivity, quality and service, reducing costs.

- A perceived need for a more positive, performance culture.

- Other cultural consequences of the organization's mission such as 'commitment, mutuality, communications, involvement, devolution and teamworking'.

Organizations vary considerably in the formality of their strategic planning, ranging from detailed 200-page documents to unwritten 'orientations'. Neat theoretical approaches with successive stages of analysis, choice and implementation are rarely seen in practice. The organizational characteristics of a firm, and the environmental constraints upon it, affect and sometimes transform the process. As Whipp (1992, p.33) explains:

> Seldom is there an easily isolated logic to strategic change. Instead that process may derive its motive force from an amalgam of economic, personal and political imperatives. ... The

application of over-rational, linear programmes of HRM as a means of securing competitive success is shown to be at odds with experience both in the UK and elsewhere.

Whipp concludes that control of the environmental, organizational and strategic aspects of both competition and human resources is so problematic that the relationship between the two can only be indirect and fragile. Another critical factor is that the human resource is but one of the resources of the firm. Strengths and weaknesses in other areas, such as marketing and finance, may obscure the best people management.

Whipp also points to the environmental context within which HR strategy is implemented. We have discussed cultural influences already. Individual companies also have their own control and industrial relations traditions. Attempts to import HRM into companies outside North America and link it to business strategy have foundered because many organizations have no tradition of strategy.

Activity 11:5	What do you see as the main barriers to successful implementation of strategic HRM?

The greatest difficulties are experienced in large, diversified organizations with a wide range of interests. They are highlighted in recession when the business needs do not fit with 'soft' HR values. HR strategies may focus on redundancies, and sacking employees inevitably damages or destroys a caring corporate image. Legge (1995) outlines a strategy described as 'tough love' – being cruel to be kind – in which employees are expected to be both dedicated and disposable. In fact, human resource strategy may only be unproblematic in the ideal circumstances described by Guest (1987):

1 It should take place within a purpose-built modern location, a greenfield site employing carefully selected 'green' labour. Such staff would have no previous experience of the industry in which the company operates and therefore would be untarnished by an 'undesirable' industrial sub-culture. They would not be hidebound by traditional but outmoded ways of doing things.

2 The organization requires highly professional management, preferably Japanese or American.

3 Employees should be given intrinsically rewarding work rather than uninteresting functions for which pay is the sole motivation.

4 Workers should have security of employment and not be constantly in fear of losing their jobs.

Guest acknowledges that these conditions are difficult to achieve in practice since most organizations – Japanese transplant factories excepted – have pre-existing staff, buildings and equipment that cannot be discarded. They bring with them patterns of power and behaviour that may be contrary to the HR philosophy.

More positively, human resource strategies can be aimed at improving an organization's competitiveness by increasing its 'knowledge base' or competence. This includes shedding old values and techniques in favour of new ones. It requires a collective change of the organization's shared world view – including perceptions of the company and the market. Proactive SHRM is particularly important in highly competitive conditions. Writing at the end of the 1990s, Kane, Crawford and Grant (1999, p.512) observe that Australia and New Zealand are entering a new millennium as developed countries in an Asia-Pacific region experiencing an economic downturn:

This downturn has exacerbated the need for Australian and New Zealand organizations to maximize competitive advantage. Since there appears to be little opportunity for them to do so by focusing solely upon price-based competition, there is general agreement that strategies which focus upon innovating quality and service are likely to be more effective. Such strategies tend to rely upon highly skilled, committed and innovative workforces. Thus the strategic application of a developmental approach to HRM can be argued as essential for many of the organizations in these two countries.

Yet Kane, Crawford and Grant conclude that the barriers to effective HRM remain in place and that Australian and New Zealand organizations 'appear to be adding to their present difficulties through what is tantamount to a self-inflicted handicap'.

Summary

Strategic thinking has its basis in rational thinking. In practice, strategists have accepted that there must be a place for the unexpected. Strategy and planning provide a framework for human resource requirements over a defined period but traditional personnel managers have experienced difficulty in understanding and implementing strategy. Human resource strategies tend to focus on numbers and also attitudes, behaviour and commitment in line with harder 'matching' models of HRM but their implementation is problematic. Recent thinking has accommodated the notion that HR strategy is not as simple as some rationalist accounts imply and that strategy itself has the same emotional, irrational and intuitive components as any other form of thinking or decision making.

Organizational competencies are the sum product of the competencies of the workforce. This suggests that people management should drive rather than follow business strategy, by building employee competencies through selection, assessment, reward and development. In the next chapter, we elaborate further on the building of organizational competence with an examination of a fundamental aspect of people management – resourcing.

Further reading

Mintzberg, Ahlsrand and Lampel (1998), *Strategy Safari: A Guided Tour Through the Wilds of Strategic Management*, published by Free Press provides an interesting excursion through the different types or 'schools of strategic management. Good reviews of strategic human resource management are found in the articles by Purcell and by Schuler *et al.* in J. Storey (ed.) *Human Resource Management: A Critical Text*, 2nd edition, published by Thomson Learning (2001). Rothwell, Prescott and Taylor (1998), *The Strategic Human Resource Leader: How to Prepare Your Organization for the Six Key Trends Shaping the Future*, published by Davies-Black Publications, is a practitioner-oriented primer on strategic human resource management.

Review questions

1 What is a strategy? What is meant by first, second and third-order strategies?

2 Is HRM really 'strategic'? How does human resource strategy fit into the business planning process?

3 In your own words, describe the difference between strategic and operational HRM.

4 Is it possible to demonstrate that human resource strategies are vital for business success?

5 Within any organization, how are management styles and corporate culture likely to influence human resource strategy?

6 What are the ideal conditions for the implementation of a human resource strategy?

7 Is strategic human resource management more important in some countries/industries than others?

Problem for discussion and analysis

Supreme Sportscars

Supreme Sportscars makes high-powered luxury cars. Due to limited manufacturing capacity, for many years sales have been steady at 190 vehicles a month, with a two-year waiting list. The factory is poorly equipped with a large proportion of the work being done by traditional hand methods. However, the company has always been profitable at this level. The staff are loyal but modestly paid. They take pride in their craftsmanship and the reputation of the cars. They have close relationships with the lower-level managers, most of whom were promoted from the ranks.

Five years ago, the company was acquired by a major US manufacturer. Initially, the American company had significant expansion plans based on a small and cheaper sports car. Under a new chief executive, the corporate strategy has changed and now the parent company is looking to dispose of Supreme, possibly in the form of a management buy-out. Design of the small car is virtually complete but nothing has been done to increase production capacity. There are two key executives at Supreme.

The current managing director is Arnold Davies, a 45-year-old marketing man. He was recruited by the parent company last year after a career spent mainly in promoting and advertising washing machines and refrigerators. He has few academic or technical qualifications but is an intelligent, decisive man with a reputation for getting things done. A flamboyant character, he drives a bright red Supreme from the top-end of the range. The staff have accepted him but have no great respect for his managerial qualities. He believes in leading from the front and has asked your management consultancy to advise him on the merits of a management buy-out.

You are aware that a large multinational car manufacturer is interested in acquiring Supreme and badging its own cars under this name. They would establish a new production facility to make these cars. They would not consider a joint venture but they might be prepared to take some of the management team and the design unit. The parent company of Supreme is wary of selling the company to the multinational in case of encouraging further competition for their other products.

The divisional accountant, Jeff Mathias, is an important figure in any decision. He is a long-term staff member of the US company, well qualified and experienced. He is a quiet but firm person, known to be open to new ideas but also very loyal to his employers. He is respected by the other managers, although the nature of his work isolates him from the day-to-day running of the factory. He is well paid but is conscious that he will never become rich working for the US company. Mathias is also aware that the parent company is about to announce major job cuts worldwide because of heavy losses in the US and declining sales in Europe.

This is your first impression of the problem. How would you proceed with collecting relevant information, determining the crucial issues and devising the decision strategy?

12

Change strategies

Objectives

The purpose of this chapter is to:

- Introduce the concept of transformational human resource strategies.
- Compare incremental and packaged change programmes.
- Discuss the HR role in mergers and acquisitions.
- Consider the issue of behavioural transformation and negative change.

Transformational HR strategies

Enthusiasts have seen a transformational power in HRM, quoting major corporations such as IBM and Marks & Spencer that emphasize HRM-type values in their mission statements (Tyson, 1995, p.28). In fact transformation, or change, is an inevitable consequence of many human resource strategies. In this chapter we will consider various kinds of change initiatives from both a strategic and implementational perspective. Change initiatives fall into one of two catagories: turnaround change and behavioural transformation (Bertsch and Williams, 1994):

1 *Turnaround change.* This is financially driven, often to ensure corporate survival by cutting unprofitable products and services. It involves the redesign of organizational structures, disposal of non-core activities and large-scale redundancies. This kind of change is painful but straightforward because existing hierarchical control systems can administer the process.

2 *Behavioural transformation.* This involves changing behaviour patterns throughout the company. Hierarchical control is inadequate because different power centres are likely to conflict and differences between business units make behavioural consistency a difficult objective to achieve.

Whatever the strategic purpose and product of change, its organization is likely to take the form of one of three models (Buchanan and Boddy, 1992):

● *Project management.* A rational, linear problem-solving approach, very much in the tradition of classical business strategy. Decisions are generated at the top and orchestrated by a project manager who assigns objectives, allocates budgets and responsibilities and sets deadlines. The project management model embodies a control mechanism that monitors progress in the determined direction.

● *Participative management.* This model takes more account of the skills and concerns of people affected by the change at lower levels of the organization. It involves a degree of emergent strategy. This approach is more time-consuming for managers and runs the risk of deviating into side issues. Participative management may lead to changes being blocked by inflexible interest groups. In general, however, it is more compatible with concepts of empowerment, commitment and team management.

● *A political perspective.* This framework goes further in accepting and dealing with interpersonal and cultural aspects of change. It reflects an awareness of power distribution within an organization and of the reasons for resistance. It is most useful when there is a lack of clarity or agreement over the objectives of the firm, or the need for strategic change. This approach has particular relevance in comprehending the effects of mergers and takeovers. It requires front stage political 'performances' from senior managers, together with Machiavellian intrigue in building behind the scenes power blocks and undermining resistance.

Each model has its merits and disadvantages. Individual organizations may also employ combinations of more than one approach.

Activity 12:1   What do you see as the main advantages and disadvantages of these three models?

Restructuring

Restructuring is the most common form of major organizational change (Key concept 12.1). According to its protagonists, restructuring should not be a defensive cost-cutting process but rather a proactive attempt to achieve innovative products and services: 'focus without fat' (Kanter, 1989, p.58). The goal should be synergy (Key concept 12.2).

Restructuring usually involves reorganization – a move from one form of organization to another. For example, a business may change from a divisional to a network structure. This requires the breaking up of the previous hierarchy or departmental structure. Some organizations are notoriously prone to reorganizations at intervals of two to three years or less, with the consequences of the last restructuring not being fully absorbed and analysed before being swept up in the next.

Key concept 12:1

Restructuring Breaking up and recombining organizational structures. Advantages include: reduced costs; eliminating duplication; and greater efficiency. Disadvantages include: disorder; interfering with normal activities; destruction of long-term commitment; loss of direction, especially in careers; and overwork from excessive cost-cutting. Recent strategic thinking has also emphasized the importance of relating business objectives to core organizational competencies. In other words, organizations should do what they are good at, leading to a new trend for companies to demerge, splitting into focused activity areas on which separate management teams can concentrate.

Activity 12:2

List as many possible organizational changes as you can think of that would involve human resource specialists in their planning or implementation.

Change and organizational structures

According to Fritz (1996, p.4):

> Structure is an entity (such as an organization) made up of elements or parts (such as people, resources, aspirations, market trends, levels of competence, reward systems, departmental mandates, and so on) that impact each other by the relationship they form. A structural relationship is one in which the various parts act upon each other, and consequently generate particular types of behaviour.

Fritz points out that organizational structures are rarely designed in a deliberate manner. Small structures grow into larger ones and individual units become the focus of managerial power. Fritz (1996, p.5) says that: 'Departments and divisions become entrenched as power systems.' Any structural change is likely to meet resistance from these power systems.

Fritz also argues that organizations are structured either to 'advance' or to 'oscillate'. Advancement is a positive move from one state to another that acts as a foundation for further advances. Fundamental to structural advancement is the concept of 'resolution' when an outcome is achieved and a particular problem is resolved. According to Fritz (1996, p.6), management in an organization that is structured to coordinate in advance 'individual acts into an organizational tapestry of effective strategy'. When all the individuals in this utopian organization are acting together, the result is synergy, allowing the achievement of 'enormous feats'.

The alternative is structural oscillation. Fritz (1996, p.6) explains this: 'Oscillating behaviour is that which moves from one place to another, but then moves back towards its original position.' So many organizations set out on some change programme, full of enthusiasm and energy. But, six months later, the enthusiasm has evaporated and the programme peters out leaving very little changed.

Labovitz and Rosansky (1997, p.7) consider that senior managers can achieve alignment to ensure advancement through:

- Carefully crafting and articulating the essence of their business and determining the 'main thing'.
- Defining a few critical strategic goals and imperatives and deploying them throughout their organizations.
- Tying performance measures and metrics to those goals.
- Linking those measures to a system of rewards and recognition.
- Personally reviewing the performance of their people to ensure the goals are met.

Labovitz and Rosansky criticize traditional structures of organization that are based on the notion of breaking up a managerial problem into pieces: departments and divisions. As they point out (1997, p.8):

> Psychologists have long recognized that human beings like people who are like themselves and tend to reject people who are different from them. Yet organizations continue to create differences between people in the interest of efficiency. Line versus staff, management versus labour, field versus corporate, international versus domestic, East versus West, accounting versus sales – the list goes on. No wonder it's so hard to focus people around common goals when they are so different from each other simply by virtue of what they do and where they do it. Specialization and expertise can be a wedge that drives people further apart and makes it difficult for them to work together.

Key concept 12:2	**Synergy** Making the new whole worth more than its old parts, sometimes described as '2+2=5'. Synergies involve economies from integrating activities, horizontally or vertically; but also unrealized potential for new ideas, products or processes by melding expertise from the different sources into centres of excellence.

The difficulty for corporate management comes in the attempt to achieve both synergy and workable new diversified or decentralized structures at one and the same time (Marginson *et al.*, 1993, p.7). Public statements through the media and shareholder information normally present such changes as deliberate and thought-through, the implication being that restructuring would be dealt with by means of a project management approach. However, the notion that restructuring is usually decided at the most senior level on the grounds of balance sheet rationality is often illusory (Purcell, 1995, p.70). As we observed in earlier discussions on strategy and management, when faced with uncertainty, complexity situations and conflict within the organization, managers typically resort to 'political' decision making.

Unfortunately, as we concluded earlier, employees are a secondary consideration of change in free market organizations (Willmott, 1995, p.313). Participative management is squeezed out in favour of the project management or political approach. Developing on Willmott's remark that 'the turkeys are unlikely to vote for Christmas', it is evident that they are generally kept in the dark until it is too late. Hence, little account is taken of the people who will be disrupted by the process and those who have to maintain quality and value during a period of major upheaval. Often the principal role of people managers is to sort out the resulting mess and smooth ruffled feathers.

Shrinkage

As we observed earlier, focusing on core activities and disposing of others has become particularly fashionable. In some cases, businesses have decided that management control and shareholder value are best served by a demerger, for example the hiving off of Zeneca from ICI, or the split of British Gas into distribution and retailing companies. More commonly, shrinkage involves downsizing – reducing the number of employees. In either case, HR managers are involved with communicating the change, conducting union negotiations and arranging redundancies or redeployment.

A particular concern is the cost-effectiveness of individual employees and departments. The more expensive, the greater the degree of justification required to retain them. For example, the 'de-layering' initiatives of the 1980s and 1990s focused on expensive middle managers. Kanter (1989, p.94) suggests that 'overhead' functions such as divisional headquarters have a duty to justify themselves to the business units they are meant to support. Approval and checking delay decision making, hindering the ability to compete. Wherever possible, these should be eliminated completely or transferred to the business units whose activities are involved. Decentralization is a dominant force, leaving small, slimmed down central functions. Restructuring can be dangerous when companies treat people purely as costs rather than as assets. Kanter points to the inevitable 'discontinuity, disorder and distraction' that interfere with people's normal activities. She concludes that 'top management typically *overestimates* the degree of cooperation it will get and *underestimates* the integration costs'.

Cowboy management in these circumstances can destroy long-term commitment since restructuring removes many of life's certainties. Most of us try to create a state of order and predictability around our jobs. Restructuring can destroy this. No longer can we count on a job for life with any one company, but some sense of direction is essential to preserve motivation and obtain the best performance. Neither can people be expected to cope with overwork caused by excessive cost-cutting. According to American experience, much downsizing is really 'dumb-sizing', since two-thirds of the companies who have slashed workforces in recent years report no increase in efficiency. Often the principal role of human resource specialists is in rescuing the situation after the change has happened. Motivation and commitment must be rebuilt and skills training made available for staff involved in new tasks.

HRM in reality	**How CEOs can make the most of their top teams**

The most powerful CEOs often fail to create and manage the right environment in which top executive teams can be effective. This is the conclusion of research by Hay Group, the global professional services firm, published in the Hay Group Working Paper, *Top Teams: Why Some Work and Some Don't: Five Things the Best CEOs Do to Create Outstanding Executive Teams*.

The research was based on a four-year study of executive-level teams at leading global corporations in the telecommunications, airlines, beverages, computer software and manufacturing sectors. In each case, the team was led by a CEO or other executive decision maker and was made up of top business unit or geographic area leaders.

CEOs under pressure to make teams deliver – quickly

The study was begun in 1998 and coordinated by Hay Group senior vice-president, Debra Nunes in conjunction with researchers from Harvard University and Dartmouth College. She said:

> Average tenures of CEOs today are only about 18 months. As a result, they're under tremendous pressure to deliver results quickly. Assembling, managing and leading a top executive team is increasingly seen as critical to both the CEO's success, and the

organization's. Given the increasingly important role of top teams, it's striking how many fall short of being truly effective. In our study, two-thirds of the teams failed to excel according to our criteria, and we discovered this was substantially tied to the team leader, usually the CEO, who often lacked an understanding of the dynamics of top teams. Because executive teams are generally charged with issues central to the company's future, the cost of an underperforming team is great – both in terms of unrealized opportunity and in the loss of executives' commitment to the strategic agenda of the organization. On the other hand, truly effective teams can have a tremendously positive influence on the performance of the organization, and can be a critical driver of shareholder value.

Corporate success is dependent on top teams

The Hay Group study suggests that:

- effective top teams can help advance the CEO's strategy and agenda more quickly
- make the organization more nimble and responsive to market changes
- lead to higher perceived valuations from institutional investors.

According to Debra Nunes:

Institutional investors are increasingly aware of the importance of top teams in executing a company's 'big picture' strategy. In fact, a recent study of institutional portfolio managers suggests that 35 per cent of an investment decision is driven by non-financial data, primarily 'execution of corporate strategy' and 'management credibility.' Since top teams exist primarily for these reasons, they are fast becoming a key component of a company's shareholder value proposition. And over time, we believe the role of top teams will only increase in importance. In fact, Gillette's bond rating was recently upgraded by agencies which cited the top executive team created by the new CEO.

What constitutes a 'real team'?

It seems that many CEOs hold the (mistaken) belief that their 12–15 key 'reports' are the top team. Probably this is not the case. These people exist in order to share information from each 'silo' of the business – they are not there to address the organization's biggest challenges and opportunities. And, significantly, they do not have a team dynamic.

Conversely, a real top team has 'collective tasks and challenges that demand a high level of interdependency among its members.' Also they have clear and stable boundaries so that membership is not constantly changing. The most effective top teams were found to have only six to eight members, handpicked by the CEO. Larger teams are likely to lack interdependence, have an unfocused agenda and unclear boundaries. And there is no need for a representative from every business unit so long as someone represents their interests.

The most effective teams tend to focus on the most consequential issues facing the business. They tend to stay away from operational matters and concentrate on big-picture mandates, including:

- mergers
- expansion into new markets
- sweeping reorganizations
- e-business strategy.

Debra Nunes argues that: 'Top executive teams have the potential to become entities that are smarter, more effective and more productive than the sum of their parts. In fact, resilient companies depend on top teams. But for those that are falling short, and risk becoming also-rans, there are steps that can maximize top team performance.'

CEOs need to be democratic but retain control

CEOs and other top executives have a variety of leadership styles – for example, coercion (expecting employees to comply with orders without question) or pacesetting (demonstrating performance standards by personally modelling the way). But the Hay Group research suggests that these styles are often ineffective, serving to alienate team members and retard the collaborative process. Debra Nunes explains:

> One of the most interesting anecdotal findings of our research is that the most charismatic CEOs make some of the worst team leaders. In a sense, their mythologies precede them, and their strong, forceful presences simply suck the air out of the room, creating an environment of worship rather than teamwork. The challenge for these types of leaders, and others, is to turn off some of the skills and behaviours that have served them so well in their rise to the top, and turn on the listening and social skills that are not always reinforced in a hierarchical corporate culture.

Strong leaders were authoritative, gave strong direction, communicated the big picture and clearly articulated goals and behaviours expected of the team. But they were also democratic, allowing the team to be a team and encouraging members to believe their voice would be heard, and that what they say matters.

Debra Nunes added: 'The most successful team leaders have a spectrum of managerial styles that they deploy based on the situation. In general, they create the right conditions for teamwork and then step into the background to act as moderator and guide.'

CEOs should provide more direction – even to the most insightful members of their team

There is an assumption that team members are powerful and committed and have the same core agenda. Not necessarily so. Team leaders need to be forceful and provide direction. According to Debra Nunes:

> One leader of an oil refining business gave his team a quick quiz asking each member to write down the team's number-one priority. When the ten team members listed several different priorities related to safety, cost-cutting, environmental compliance and new markets, the leader was shocked. 'Don't you guys realize that if we can't cut our refining costs by three cents a gallon, they're going to shut us down?' The team members were equally stunned by the simplicity of the mission. In fact, over the following year, the team took steps that reduced costs by five cents per gallon. The lesson here: You can never be too clear, or overstate the team's primary goal.

Top teams need members with empathy and integrity

The members of the most successful top teams are neither brighter, more driven nor more committed than people in less successful teams. But the members of the most successful teams excelled at working with others, bringing a high degree of emotional intelligence to the 'team dynamic'. Emotionally intelligent team members:

- have self-control
- are adaptable
- exude self-confidence and self-awareness
- display high levels of empathy and integrity.

In fact, empathy and integrity are particularly significant. Hay Group research shows members of outstanding teams to be far more empathetic, having an understanding of the emotional make-up of others, than team members of less successful teams. Additionally, on high-performing teams, the research showed that 71 per cent of participants said their team peers were sensitive to the unspoken emotions of their fellow members. On average-performing teams, only 44 per cent showed this characteristic.

According to Debra Nunes: 'Empathy is incredibly important to the successful team's dynamic. This is because members of a team will only "buy in" to the team process if they feel they are being heard and understood. Resentment and withdrawal are the inevitable result if people feel their ideas and input are not being fairly evaluated.'

The research also identified perception of integrity among and between team members as being essential for team success. A team member with 'integrity' was defined as one who 'behaves consistently with the organization's or the team's values – even when it is personally risky to do so.' The researchers justified the importance of integrity through the trust it fosters among team members.

Just 3 per cent of team members in average-performing teams had taken the personal risk of challenging the team to live up to its values, compared to 44 per cent of the members of high-performing teams. As Debra Nunes explains:

> No one wants to commit professional suicide by challenging his or her peers, especially the CEO. But if the team dynamic is healthy enough, members should feel comfortable about raising an opposing point of view. In fact, productive conflict is desired as long as it's about ideas, not personalities. Top teams must be comprised of people who not only have the courage to identify, even create, conflict over ideas, but also the social skills to resolve friction constructively.

Necessary support and development

The research identifies strong operational support as a necessity if a top team is to be successful. This support must include sound data and forecasts; teamwork training; and appropriate compensation tied to its ability to meet its goals.

Debra Nunes concluded that:

> Outstanding team leaders also periodically review the team's performance, providing helpful feedback, encouragement and continuous reinforcement and refinement of the team's goals. Some effective team leaders even provide individual coaching, taking aside a team member who's not contributing enough, or speaking privately with someone who's personality may be getting in the way. Again, the team leader must learn to wear several hats to make the team function as smoothly and effectively as possible.

Source: *HRM Guide USA* (http://www.hrmguide.net/usa/), 2 October 2001.

Activity 12:3

How important is leadership in achieving permanent change within an organization?

Incremental change

In the 1960s and 1970s, change often came under the label of organizational development (OD). This is an undramatic – but effective – long-term change process based on incremental improvements, essentially a continuous flow of emergent strategies. With the advent of modern change programmes such as 'business process re-engineering', this low-risk and long-term approach has gone out of fashion to a considerable extent. As we can see from Table 12.1, its underlying principles are similar to Japanese methods of continuous improvement and the methodology has considerable parallels with radical change initiatives described later in this chapter.

Action learning

What is action learning? Rothwell (1999, p.5) states that it is a 'real-time learning experience that is carried out with two equally important purposes in mind: meeting an organizational need and developing individuals or groups'. Rothwell notes that Reg Revans, the originator of action learning, avoided defining the term, preferring to say what it was not. But there are many formal definitions, including the following by Dean (1998, p.3): '… a voluntary, participant-centred, evolutionary process to solve real, systemic, and so-far-up-till-now-unresolved organizational work-cum-learning problems in the workplace as it applies the principle of democratic values and team learning.'

Marquardt and Revans (1999, p.4) feel that: 'Perhaps action learning's greatest value is its capacity for equipping individuals, teams, and organizations to more effectively respond to change.' They go on to contend that action learning has a 'unique and inherent capacity' to deal simultaneously with five pressing organizational needs:

1 *Problem solving*. The more difficult the problem. the better suited is action learning to meet the challenge.

Table 12.1	Themes of organizational development
Theme	Features
1 Top management support	Initiatives will not succeed unless higher management levels are fully committed to the change process and its maintenance.
2 Problem-solving and renewal process	Allows adaptability and viability to be generated in an organization that may be living in the past. This should allow the organization continually to redefine its purpose.
3 Collaborative diagnosis and management of culture	The process of change must involve all levels within the organization in a search for ideas that will lead to improvement. This is a non-hierarchical, shared evaluation of the culture and long-term goals of the organization.
4 Formal work team	Focusing on work groups, group dynamics and team development.
5 Consultant facilitator	Bringing in an external change agent or catalyst, experienced in the mechanics of change, able to spot resistance and unbiased by any prevailing agenda.
6 Action research	A primary feature of classic OD that is absent in many modern packaged initiatives.

Source: Adapted from French and Bell (1990).

2 *Organizational learning*. Action learning provides a valuable focus for company-wide learning.

3 *Team-building*. Helps build teams and team skills for future team-building.

4 *Leadership development*. Prepares leaders to deal with future problems.

5 *Professional growth and career development*. Action learning facilitates high levels of self-awareness, self-development and continuous learning.

The whole process revolves around a real-life problem that needs to be important to the organization. Marquardt and Revans (1999, p.5) say that:

> The problem should be significant, be within the responsibility of the team, and provide opportunity for learning. Selection of the problem is fundamental to action learning because we learn best when undertaking some action, which can then be reflected upon. The problem gives the group something to focus on that is real and important, that is relevant, and that means something to them.

This democratic – or, at least, participatory – process may follow a sequence such as (Rothwell, 1999, p.5):

- pinpoint the cause(s) of problems
- solve the problems
- formulate goals
- work toward achieving goals
- establish a shared vision of the future.

People are chosen for an action learning team (composed of four to eight members) for their experience and ability to contribute to the learning process – and also for the developmental benefit to them. So they must already possess relevant knowledge or skills for the particular issue they are working on. It is beneficial to have participants from a wide range of departments or functions, representing a number of views. They need to be positive and open-minded about the issue and possible solutions. It is also customary to appoint a team facilitator who is not a leader but helps the team work together effectively.

But there are times when action learning is not appropriate according to Rothwell (1999, p.18):

- When the issue or need to be addressed is simple or straightforward.
- It is pressing or urgent, such as an emergency or catastrophe.
- The organization does not have the expertise to deal with the problem.
- Managers do not value their employees or see merit in the developmental benefits.

HRM in reality	**Business-driven action learning**

Business, in the past, was not particularly interested in fostering learning and the self-development of its people, says Dr Yury Boshyk, author and international expert on business-driven action learning. But, he argues, the situation is changing with more companies worldwide – such as General Electric, Siemens, Boeing, Baxter Healthcare, DuPont, Fujitsu, Johnson & Johnson and Volvo Car Corporation – adopting business-driven action learning as a way to explore new business opportunities and develop their best people.

Dr Boshyk, chairman of the Global Executive Learning Network, addressed the 7th Annual Global Forum on Business-Driven Action Learning and Executive Development held last week at the Gordon Institute of Business Science (GIBS) in South Africa. The Forum was sponsored by Standard Bank. According to Dr Boshyk:

> As a philosophy, business-driven action learning is based on the belief and practice that learning should be tied to business realities, and that some of the best business solutions can and should come from fellow executives and employees. Many of the companies that utilise business driven action learning are those who also have a high respect for their people and who appreciate that learning often comes from the sharing of experiences in an open exchange, which in turn encourages reflection and practical application.

Boshyk's Global Executive Learning Network and Victoria Marsick, co-director of the J.M. Huber Institute for Learning in Organizations at Columbia University, New York, USA, claim from survey results that between 60 per cent and 65 per cent of 45 top multinational companies were using action learning. According to Boshyk:

> Product life cycles, globalization, and indeed, the entire pace of business life and decision-making took on a new meaning in the 1990s. The new business mantra included the key words: speed, flexibility, shareholder value and customer focus, and therefore, the need for change. Many senior executives realized the need to align their organizations to these new objectives.

Changing corporate culture was perceived as a top priority with companies' cultural 'baggage' and old ways of thinking as the greatest obstacles to success. Education and hence the learning organization were 'discovered' by chief executives and it became important in their eyes to learn quickly, and faster than competitors. Reg Revans, one of the founders of action learning, used to say that for competitive reasons, 'learning must be equal to or greater than the rate of change'. But, at the turn of the 21st century it seems clear that individuals and organizations who learn faster than the rate of change gain competitive advantage.

Boshyk argues that as traditional executive education provided to companies was seen not to be translated into business results, chief executives began looking to action learning as a more relevant approach to their new emerging educational needs. As Boshyk explains:

> Companies began to realize that knowledge, with an emphasis on 'actionable knowledge', was a corporate asset and therefore had to be developed for competitive advantage. The past emphasis on individual development and learning was replaced with a view that individual learning should be tied more directly and clearly to organizational objectives as well.

Business-driven action learning (as practised in some of the world's best companies) involves five key elements:

- The active involvement and support of senior executives.
- Participants working in teams on real business issues and exploring new strategic business opportunities.
- Action research and learning focused on internal and external company experiences and thinking that can help resolve business issues.
- Leadership development through teamwork and coaching.
- Follow-up on the business issues and leadership development, thus enhancing positive business results and ensuring that learning is greater than the rate of change.

◀

According to Professor Peter Pribilla, head of Corporate Human Resources at Siemens AG:

> The speed at which a corporation can learn and employ new knowledge is a decisive factor in competition. It is not enough to learn and work. Learning and working must be integrated. Only then can a corporation be a learning organization. Action learning addresses this challenge very efficiently.

Gerard van Schaik, president of the European Foundation for Management Development and former chairman of the executive board of Heineken, says:

> Real progress in business is only achieved by corporations and individuals trying out creative ideas and making them work, running into problems and solving them, by pooling talent and scoring with it, and most of all … by having fun and learning while doing. Business-driven action learning is a superb vehicle for achieving this.

Source: *HRMGuide.com* (http://www.hrmguide.com), 27 May 2002.

Activity 12:4	Is action learning most effective for change management or developing employees?

Competitive pressures often demand a faster, more dramatic process than that provided by organizational development or action learning. Many modern managers would question whether their organization had the time required. More pertinently, we can ask if ambitious executives on short-term contracts have enough time to make their mark with such a slow methodology. It is likely that a glossier and more public method will be better appreciated. This is provided by 'packaged', or 'off-the-shelf' approaches, which begin with top management and are cascaded down the organization. They are normally dramatized with considerable emphasis on communication and a spotlight placed on the lead personality.

In the 1980s most large organizations engaged in 'total quality management' (TQM) programmes, focusing on continuous improvement, quality assurance and zero faults. TQM programmes are geared to organizational processes such as production. HR involvement includes the selection of flexible people who are amenable to increasingly demanding levels of quality.

Business process re-engineering

Re-engineering is a methodology of the 1990s (see Key concept 12.3) that has inspired many change strategies. The technique was first publicized by Hammer (1990) in a *Harvard Business Review* article with the somewhat dramatic title of 'Re-engineering Work: Don't Automate, Obliterate'. In typical guru fashion he outlined amazing benefits in a range of companies, proclaiming the existence of seven fundamental principles of re-engineering:

● Organize around outcomes, not tasks.

● Those who use the output should perform the process.

● Information processing work should be subsumed into the real work that produces the information.

● Geographically dispersed resources should be used as though they were centralized.

● Link parallel activities instead of integrating tasks.

- Decisions should be taken where work is performed and control built into the process.
- Information should only be captured once – at source.

Business process re-engineering (BPR) appears under the guise of a number of similar terms and a variety of definitions. Depending on the definition used, re-engineering can involve: change in individual work tasks; in interpersonal work processes within a department; between sections of a business; or beyond the boundaries of a firm in a networked or virtual organization. Critics argue that perhaps it is no more than organization and methods (O&M), TQM and just-in-time 'dusted down and repackaged' (Burke and Peppard, 1995, p.28).

Nevertheless, BPR swept the Western business world. Companies such as AT&T, BT, Ford, Mercury and Rank Xerox have used the methodology. A recent search on the Google search engine for the phrase 'business process re-engineering' found 47 200 items in response. Why was it apparently so popular? Instead of 5–10 per cent improvements from other methods, the proponents of re-engineering promised 30 per cent, 50 per cent or even more. But BPR requires total rethinking of the organization from the bottom up, rather than tinkering with an existing situation.

Key concept 12:3

Business process re-engineering A 'fundamental rethinking and radical redesign of business processes to achieve dramatic improvements in critical contemporary measures of performance, such as cost, quality, service and speed' (Hammer and Champy, 1993).

Hammer and Champy presented a process perspective in contrast to the functional basis of most businesses. Hence, organizations and departments are not re-engineered but processes are. For instance the process of order fulfilment is everything from an order request to its delivery to the customer, regardless of department or level. Hammer and Champy argue that traditional hierarchical structures 'stifle innovation and creativity'. Instead, new technology should be introduced to cut out stages and people in a process. Moreover, a multi-skilled team should be employed, able to deal with a process as a whole. In all, they describe ten interrelated changes that Grint (1995, p.83) traces to much earlier origins (see Table 12.2). In fact, an examination of these change principles reveals some strong links between BPR and concepts, such as empowerment and facilitatory management, associated with HRM elsewhere in this book.

Business process re-engineering also has close parallels with the notion of a 'learning organization' discussed in Chapter 21. BPR works on the principle that an organization cannot learn before it has first unlearned. BPR does this by starting with a 'blank piece of paper' approach using techniques such as cognitive mapping and soft systems methodology. These are diagrammatic methods aimed at tapping creativity and ensuring that a holistic approach is taken.

1 Have a vision
2 Identify and understand the current processes
3 Redesign the processes
4 Implement the redesigned processes.

Matters become even more confusing when one asks 'who does it?' It is simultaneously presented as an empowering programme, with fine rhetoric about teamworking, multi-skilling and flattened hierarchies, and as a top-down exercise demanding (as ever) commitment from senior executives! Of course, consultants have to remember who pays the bill. Perhaps the true emphasis is reflected in the key roles required for re-engineering as presented by Hammer and Champy:

- Leader – a visionary and motivator.
- Process owner – sufficiently senior to oversee the entire process to be re-engineered.
- Re-engineering team – composed of insiders who understand present activities; and outsiders to question assumptions.
- An optional steering committee to oversee the organization's re-engineering as a whole.
- 'Re-engineering czar' – the operational head of the organization's re-engineering activities.

Clearly, this is a directed process. Employees may be 'permitted and required to think, interact, use judgement, and make decisions' but this only applies to the workers who are allocated jobs after the process has been re-engineered – eliminating one or two departments along the way. The attractiveness to senior executives is evident in the promise of redundancy; the benefits to employees are somewhat less obvious. Conceivably, Willmott's 'turkeys' may be less than keen to cooperate, but this appears not to be a problem to the proponents of BPR (Willmott, 1995, pp.311–12):

> ...any employee hostility to BPR is interpreted not as warrantable resistance but as irrationality or inertia which can be overcome by effective leadership and commitment from top management. Hammer notes that the disruption and confusion generated by re-engineering can make it unpopular. But he is equally confident that any opposition can be effectively surmounted by top-level managers.

Table 12.2	Origins of change principles in BPR
Principle	**Origins**
1 Switch from functional departments to processes	Principle of 1950s socio-technical systems and Volvo Kalmar experiment
2 Move from simple tasks to multi-dimensional work	1970s quality of working life and job enrichment
3 Reversal of power relationship from superordinate to subordinate empowerment	Seen in both above
4 Shift from training to education	A criticism of British 'education' since the 19th century
5 From payment for attendance to payment for value added	Common in Ancient Greece
6 Bifurcation of link between reward for current performance and advancement through assessment of ability	The 'Peter Principle' – every employee tends to rise to his (or her) level of incompetence
7 From concern for boss to concern for customer	See modern Japan
8 Managers become coaches rather than supervisors	Hawthorne experiments – USA 1930s
9 Flattening of hierarchies	Kalmar experiments
10 Executives move from scorekeepers to leaders	Human relations

Source: Adapted from Grint (1995, p.85).

Burke and Peppard (1995, p.34) identify a number of further barriers to implementing BPR:

- There is a paradox in that people with knowledge of a particular process are unlikely to have the authority to redesign it, and vice versa.

- Redesign disturbs existing patterns of power in an organization. The power base may not coincide with senior management but with a 'dominant coalition' that has a vested interest in frustrating BPR.

- The firm's culture may work against a process-based organization and consequent changes in work practices, job content and relationships.

- Within multinational companies, processes may cross national boundaries, bringing in further difficulties.

Given the importance of employees in implementing BPR, and the embodiment of strong ideas about people management in its basic texts, it is surprising to find that human resource issues have scarcely been addressed (Willmott, 1995, p.306). Tinaikar, Hartman and Nath (1995, p.109) in a survey of 248 articles on BPR found that:

> Almost all of the articles (95.9 per cent) portray BPR as being concerned with only technical issues. The few articles discussing social issues such as empowerment of the lower levels, resistance to change, etc, focused primarily on the managerially relevant benefits of BPR. Cost-cutting through technology and downsizing, or the politically correct 'rightsizing', were some of the most common themes. However, the implications of this potential job loss through BPR were singularly neglected.

They conclude that the human aspect has been trivialized in the BPR literature. However, it is not unreasonable to wonder if this lack of concern for people may be partly responsible for the high failure rate of re-engineering initiatives. Pink (2001, p.108) considers that: 'In the beginning [of the new economy] there was reengineering. And it was good. Then it was big. Then it got scary.' Pink goes on:

> Reengineering corporations quickly became a $50 billion industry. The craze turned Hammer, a former MIT computer-science professor, into a rock star of the then-fledgling new economy. His bearded face began appearing at corporate conferences, inside boardrooms, and on lists of America's most influential people. He scolded CEOs for not zeroing in on first principles. He exhorted them to repent. Some of his warnings verged on the apocalyptic: 'Reengineering,' he wrote, 'is the only thing that stands between many US corporations – indeed, the US economy – and disaster.'

It seemed at one stage that BPR could be regarded as the answer to everything. But business process re-engineering is just one more set of practices in a long list of methodologies that have been in and out of fashion over recent decades. Perhaps it is not too surprising to read in Hammer (2001, p.5), a decade further on from his seminal paper:

> It is told that Albert Einstein once handed his secretary an exam to be distributed to his graduate students. The secretary scanned the paper and objected, 'But Professor Einstein, these are the same questions you used last year. Won't the students already know the answers?' 'It's all right, you see,' replied Einstein, 'the questions are the same, but the answers are different.' What is true of physics is true of business. Today's business world is not that of Drucker or of Peters and Waterman, and it calls for a new edition of the management agenda.

Of course, Hammer argues that a new agenda is required because circumstances have changed. 'Executives of the most powerful companies now tremble before their independent and demanding customers.' This implies that customers were somehow not independent or demanding in the past. An alternative explanation is that the last agenda (for which you can read 'fashion') did not work all that well. Among the recent innovations, he lists:

- just-in-time inventory management

- total quality management and its avatar 'six sigma quality'
- cross-functional teams
- portfolio management and stage gates (in product development)
- supply chain integration, including vendor-managed inventories and collaborative planning and forecasting
- performance-linked compensation
- competency profiling in human resources
- measurement systems based on EVA (economic value added) or balanced scorecards
- customer–supplier relationships
- business process reengineering.

But Hammer (2001, p.8) regards these as being no more than the first phase in dealing with customer expectations. In fact, innovative as they were, 'yesterday's innovation is baseline today and obsolete tomorrow.'

Activity 12:5	Is business process re-engineering just a passing fad or a significant breakthrough in change management?

Strategic alliances

Redesign or restructuring may take place within one organization, or go beyond its boundaries, perhaps resulting from the combination of one firm with another. There are several relevant variables to consider at the strategic stage:

- *Strategic intent.* Regardless of negotiated positions and public positions of the partner companies, what are their long-term intentions? Are they committed to a joint venture? Does one partner intend to achieve control? Managers will be wary of losing their power.
- *Consolidation.* How much autonomy and organizational independence is to be allowed? Mergers and acquisitions tend towards much greater consolidation than joint ventures and consortia. Employees feel threatened by obvious opportunities for staff reduction.
- *Cultural integration.* Is cultural plurality to be respected? Does the alliance intend a common culture? If so, will it be based on the culture of the dominant partner or a negotiated hybrid? Being forced to change familiar ways is threatening.

Key concept 12:4

Mergers and acquisitions   'A merger occurs when one corporation is combined with and disappears into another corporation. For instance, the Missouri Corporation, just like the river, merges and disappears corporately into the Mississippi Corporation. Missouri Corporation stock certificates are turned in and exchanged for Mississippi Corporation stock certificates. Holes are punched in the Missouri certificates, and they are all stuck in the vault. The Missouri Corporation has ceased to exist. Missouri is referred to as the *decedent*, while the Mississippi Corporation is referred to as the *survivor*.' (Reed and Lajoux, 1998, p.7). Acquisition, on the other hand is a generic term used to describe a transfer of ownership. Here, the two parties in the transaction may continue as entities in some form or other after the acquisition.

Alliances and mergers draw on the capacity and potential of participants but they have a poor history of success. Surveys shown that over 50 per cent of mergers and acquisitions fail to achieve strategic objectives – often disastrously. An often-quoted McKinsey and Company study of mergers between 1972 and 1982 (involving 200 of the largest US corporations) found increased value to shareholders in just 23 per cent. The greatest proportion, 33 per cent, was seen in relatively small takeovers of closely related businesses. The explanation seems to have attracted yet another analogy with poultry, although the meaning is quite different: 'You don't put two turkeys together and make an eagle!' (unnamed economist quoted in Peters, 1987). Often the advantages are outweighed by (Porter, 1990; Buono, 1991):

● Restructuring costs – including redundancy payments, consultancy and legal fees, accommodation transfer.

● Strategic difficulties – harmonization of goals and objectives.

● Organizational problems. Difficulties in coordinating two different structures; overloading the parent organization's management systems; reorganization taking attention away from day-to-day activities.

● Behavioural problems and barriers. Managers fight to preserve their territories or take over others; motivation falls when staff feel they have been taken over by remote managers.

According to Mackay (1992, p.10):

Most of the evidence suggests that a failure to acknowledge the human dimension undermines many potentially successful ventures. ... There is a feeling that if 'the figures are right' all else will follow smoothly. Wrong! It is precisely 'all else' that can frustrate the best laid plans of marketing men and accountants as cultures fail to gel and key executives engage in destructive battles for dominance.

The nature of the power relationship is particularly significant. Many studies show that acquisitions are notoriously unsuccessful because of the manner of the takeover. Specifically, the benefits of an acquisition or merger can be destroyed by the way in which the merger process is handled. Staff working for new owners tend to feel defensive and threatened. It is almost as if they have been colonized. Similar feelings are experienced when internal restructuring results in merged departments or the absorption of one section by another. Frequently, takeovers are handled insensitively. Acquisitions and mergers bring power differences into sharp and highly visible focus. There is a temptation to charge into the acquired firm or department or to take a condescending attitude. Many takeovers have parallels with the sack of Rome. The new managers are inclined to feel superior and to regard methods that are different from their own as inefficient or second-rate.

Arrogance and organizational chauvinism on the 'conqueror's' part lead to defensiveness and concern on the other side. People sense a loss of power to determine their own fate (Kanter, 1989, p.65):

Arrogance can destroy the essence of the company. Strangers in suits wander about the organization, misunderstanding what they see. Observation is accompanied by sniggers and sneering comments, serving to boost the acquiring management team's egos and sense of superiority. Mackay describes this as 'tribal warfare' – one culture trying to assert pre-eminence over the other.

The consequences are serious. This is not simply a matter of upsetting workers, important though that may be in terms of its consequences on morale and cooperation. There is a considerable risk of throwing the baby out with the bath water by obliterating the victim's processes before their consequences and rationale are fully understood. The 'HRM in reality' case describes the merger of Sperry and Burroughs to form Unisys, which has been presented as a model of successful communication.

Unisys

Unisys originated in a 'hostile' takeover of Sperry by Burroughs. Initially, the merger was heavily criticized by Wall Street analysts. However, the chief executive, Michael Blumenthal, had a clear vision of the combined firm and set out to confront anxieties and uncertainties directly. Good communication was required to prevent the 'merger syndrome': conflict, apathy, depression, departure and low productivity. This syndrome comes from unanswered questions going through the minds of the staff who have been acquired:

● Will I lose my job?

● Will I be promoted or demoted?

● Will my salary and benefits change?

● Will I have to move?

● What will the organization be like: will its values, kind of people employed and commercial objectives change?

● How long will the transition period take?

Blumenthal formed a merger-coordination council, including senior executives from both businesses, supported by task forces that investigated ways of structuring and consolidating the merged organization. Efforts were also made to create a unified culture with:

● 'the Power of 2', a clear vision of the new business

● supporting speeches by senior managers

● developing a sense of partnership between the two companies

● sensitization groups and counselling sessions

● newsletters reporting merger activities

● a 'name the company' competition

● continuing feedback to the employees throughout the process.

The merger was not devoid of problems. There were instances of 'in-fighting' between rival executives, of politics, distrust, and fear of losing jobs to the 'other side'. Nevertheless, in terms of staff turnover and satisfaction, the merger seemed to be successful.

Sources: Buono (1991, p.95); Mackay (1992, p.14).

Employee fears and anxieties can be minimized but research shows that people who have been 'taken over' continue to be suspicious and uncomfortable in the new organization for some time. Maurer (1996, p.11) notes that:

> Change is unsettling. It disrupts our world. Some fear they will lose status, control, even their jobs. The larger the change, the stronger the resistance. Successful change requires vision, persistence, courage, an ability to thrive on ambiguity, and a willingness to engage those who have a stake in the outcome.

Why do so many mergers and acquisitions fail?

Mergers and the HR function

Clemente and Greenspan (1999, p.1) point out that:

> There are literally hundreds of reasons why the M&A failure rate is so high. But many can be traced to the exclusion of human resource professionals in the pre-deal planning phase and the function's last-minute inclusion after the transaction has closed. It's a classic case of 'too little, too late'.

Clemente and Greenspan (1999) present a description of the typical merger or acquisition. The focus is on 'making the numbers work' and the sequence begins with an investment banker or equivalent presenting an apparently suitable candidate company to management. If this makes 'financial sense' the process is launched.

The 'due diligence' phase then begins, involving a detailed examination of financial, legal and regulatory, accounting and tax issues. If these check out, the merger partners 'plunge forward', assuming that all the strategic aspects will somehow fall in line. As the authors point out, the statistics on failure suggest that this is often highly erroneous thinking. Clearly, the 'ledgers and liability' aspects of the process are extremely important but the all-consuming focus on these matters ignores people issues. Clemente and Greenspan ask: 'If people issues are so important to the success of the deal, how can such little focus be paid to those issues in the strategy development, target company screening and due diligence phases?'

They answer their own question by stating that in most cases the merger partners have not looked closely enough at the 'people component' – strategic variables at the very heart of the deal. Most M&As are driven by apparent cost-cutting synergies and stock prices. But if they were driven by true strategic vision instead, HR professionals would need to be involved from the beginning to assess the people implications that do not feature in balance sheets or income statements. The authors conclude that:

> … identifying key human assets in a target company and quickly taking steps to prevent them from walking out the door on announcement of the deal is an HR-related imperative every company must take. Yet, historically, HR comes into the M&A process too late to make this vital contribution.

In most cases, the deal-making is more or less complete by the time that HR gets involved. HR specialists are left with the difficult role of developing communication strategies; aligning payroll, benefits and compensation systems; and melding different and possibly incompatible processes and cultures. But by this time a number of key personnel may have gone and those remaining may be confused or hostile.

Instead, Clemente and Greenspan argue, HR professionals should be involved in the earliest stage of any acquisition involving people. This means that human resource specialists must be familiar with the organization's strategic objectives, and its business and marketing plans. HR professionals must contribute to 'target screening' to identify and evaluate the worth and 'integrate-ability' of the proposed merger partner's human assets. This includes an evaluation of the two cultures and their potential compatibility.

Hanson (2001) observes that early coordination between HR specialists in both companies is ideal but due to the 'sensitive nature of many organization transactions, it is possible that the HR team on the receiving side of the transaction will be notified before the team on the sending side, or vice versa.' Tellingly, as someone writing from experience, she concurs with Clemente and Greenspan, noting that: 'The deal negotiators and attorneys will usually dictate when the intercompany communications can begin in the HR planning process.'

Mergers and acquisitions: project planning

Hanson (2001) advocates the use of a project plan as an organizational tool to schedule necessary actions and set deadlines. A simple plan document would have columns for the following:

1 major steps in the process
2 a breakdown of specific tasks within each step
3 ownership of each step/task – i.e. who is responsible
4 completion date for each task
5 comments/state of progress.

A wide variety of project and spreadsheet software can be used with the updated project plan being made available to the integration team through web technology. In Hanson's opinion the project plan is a mechanism for communication and control of the integration process. But the project manager, she argues, must be tenacious in the following respects:

● documenting necessary actions as they surface
● assigning them to a reliable owner
● determining appropriate deadlines that are compatible with other deliverables
● communicating with applicable parties
● following up to ensure that progress is on track
● escalating problems
● closing actions as they are completed.

HR due diligence

Hanson highlights the importance of HR due diligence as an early stage in the project plan. A due diligence investigation is designed to establish liabilities and vulnerabilities *before* signing the final agreement. According to Hanson the HR review offers the following possibilities:

1 Discovery of liabilities that could impact on the financial viability of the transaction.
2 Discovery of discrepancies that might be addressable in the agreement to both parties' satisfaction.
3 Discovery of variations in policy and practice that will be essential when integrating and communicating with employees.

The investigation may have to take place in two stages: a preliminary overview before the letter of intent is signed; and a more thorough investigation thereafter when confidentiality can be guaranteed, but before the final agreement. According to Hanson, the investigation involves a number of data-gathering components that divide into hard and soft. Hard facts are those that can be found in written records, reports, surveys, documented policies and statistics. They include information on pay, benefits, bonuses, employment regulations, third-party claims, employee relations, safety and so on. Soft data are less easily established but can be critical, including key employee losses, management style, CEO reputation and senior management integrity.

Hanson points to the particular importance of compensation and benefits plan information, not only in the due diligence stage but also later when close comparison is required. Issues of long-term liability are critical as regards pension plans and medical benefits.

In later stages of the integration plan, pay and other benefits have implications on the cost of 'golden parachutes' for people no longer required. Serious differences between salary structures, overtime and 'perks' may also have significant consequences on morale and retention. Inevitably the question arises as to whether the more generous schemes are to be pushed down or the less generous increased in the future.

Activity 12:7

Summarize the concept of HR due diligence in your own words. Why is it important in increasing the probability of successful mergers and acquisitions?

HRM in reality

5000 managers surveyed on change

Contrary to some beliefs, a survey of 5000 mid-to-upper level managers shows that most are very open to change.

Discovery Learning, a developer of training products, also used its *Change Styles Survey* to identify strategies for successful change management, placing respondents on a continuum between 'conserver' and 'originator,' with 'pragmatist' in between. Not surprisingly, most individuals are a blend of conserver-pragmatist or pragmatist-originator. Of the entire population surveyed between 1996 and 2001, 52 per cent of managers (57 per cent men/43 per cent women) scored in the pragmatist range, 26 per cent in the originator range and 22 per cent in the conserver range.

Survey developer Dr Chris Musselwhite characterizes the types as:

- *originators* – people who welcome dramatic change
- *conservers* – more comfortable with gradual change
- *pragmatists* – most enthusiastic about change that will address current circumstances.

'Americans are attracted to innovation, so we think being an originator is best,' says Musselwhite (president and CEO of Discovery Learning). 'But it takes all of these personality types to build a successful business.' Taking Enron as an example, he says: 'Conservers at Enron tried to warn of problems, but the leadership culture was apparently skewed so much toward originators charged with "reinventing business" that conservers were viewed as resisters and were either silenced or ignored.'

What can we learn from the survey? First, it is clear that a specific change will not meet with universal approval. Managers would benefit from knowing the change styles of staff and colleagues. 'You have to be gradual and clear with conservers, who are most concerned with the details of implementing the change,' says Musselwhite. 'You win the pragmatists over when they can see how the change will positively address current circumstances. And you may have to reel in the originators, who welcome dramatic change and sometimes move too fast for other team members' comfort.'

Musselwhite has an interesting perspective on the people who appear to resist change. He says that there are two kinds of resisters in the world. The most devoted staff sometimes voice the biggest objections to change and listening to them gives managers the opportunity to head off unanticipated problems. But some people are 'hard core' resisters. 'You want to be able to tell the difference,' explains Musselwhite. 'If someone's simply a conserver who's seeing red flags, you can benefit from their insights. They'll feel heard and will be more ready to move forward. But hard core resisters will fight the change no matter what.' Managers need to be careful not to treat every sceptic as a hardcore resister – there is a risk of breeding dangerous alliances between the two groups. 'People may resist change on an emotional level,' says Musselwhite. 'It might have nothing to do with the change itself, but with territorial issues, problems at home, etc.' He also says that originators can cause problems on the other extreme – wanting to move too fast or in too many

▶

directions. In some cases, he argues, there's no way to get these people to work at a pace that's best for the organization, and you have to let them go.

Other findings of the survey include:

- Men (28 per cent) are more likely than women (23 per cent) to be originators, with women (27 per cent) being much more likely to be conservers than men (17 per cent). 'This may be due to women being more mindful of the implications of change, rather than being less open to change in general,' says Dr Musselwhite.

- Among industries surveyed, communications had the highest percentage of pragmatists (71 per cent) and the lowest percentage of conservers (11 per cent). Petroleum had the lowest number of originators (4 per cent).

- Among professions, soldiers (46 per cent), school principals (42 per cent) and business consultants (40 per cent) had the highest percentage of originators. The lowest percentage of originators were security/police (3 per cent), support staff (8 per cent) and bankers (12 per cent).

- Among age groups, there are a substantially higher percentage of originators among 'baby boomers' (born 1946–65) than among earlier 'post war and depression' generations (born 1928–40) or the later 'generation X' (born 1966–81). Over 33 per cent of boomers were originators, compared to 26 per cent of gen X-ers and 26 per cent of post-war/depression generations.

'The bottom line: the more aware people are of their co-workers' change styles, the better they work together, which improves business performance,' says Musselwhite.

Source: *HRM Guide USA* (http://www.hrmguide.net/usa/), 20 June 2002.

Behavioural transformation

If you ask people to brainstorm words to describe change, they come up with a mixture of negative and positive terms. On the one side, *fear, anxiety, loss, danger, panic*; on the other, *exhilaration, risk-taking, excitement, improvements, energizing*. For better or worse, change arouses emotions, and when emotions intensify, leadership is key. (Fullan, 2001, p.1, original emphases)

We noted earlier that the most difficult form of change involves modifying employees' attitudes, behaviour and commitment. Initiatives may come about as a result of deliberate strategic planning. Frequently, however, the process begins with a vague feeling among board members that there is 'something wrong' within the organization even though they are uncertain as to what it might be. The feeling may be fuelled by customer dissatisfaction, failure of innovation, conflict between departments or financial difficulties. The popularity of guru ideas and the spread of HRM have encouraged many senior executives to look to their people in order to improve overall organizational performance, quality of service and productivity. Black and Gregersen (2002, p.20) describe the realization of a need for change in the following way:

Clearly, if you do not see a truck racing toward you, you are unlikely to jump out of the way. Likewise, if you do not realize that you are standing on a treasure of gold, you are unlikely to bend down and pick it up. It is no brilliant observation to say that if people fail to see the need for change (whether threat or opportunity driving it), they will not change.

It is impossible to plan an effective change programme without first defining what cultural change aims to achieve and how this differs from the existing situation. The objective of many organizations in managing cultural change is to move from a static or rigid culture to one that is flexible and adaptable (Fowler, 1993).

Fowler suggests that the process could begin with a theoretical comparison of static and adaptable cultures. Such a scale might include 30 items and would focus on the nature of the initiative – for example quality or customer care. The current organization is then scored on this scale. Frequently, detailed and accurate information does not exist in a form that allows this to be done. This can be gathered from a 'where are we now' exercise, normally taking the form of survey research and feedback. Typically this involves the use of questionnaires and structured interviews at all levels of the organization. Research can focus on employee attitudes towards:

- the organization
- its methods
- communication channels
- company culture
- customers
- mechanisms for initiating and sustaining innovation and change.

Data is collated and a preliminary analysis fed back to the 'top team' and other interested parties, such as trade unions. After discussion – possibly involving a reappraisal of the company's mission and core values – action is agreed with the consultancy. To gain full cooperation it is best to discuss and agree the programme with employees and their representatives. Conventionally, the purpose and manner of any change is introduced to staff through presentations, discussions, videos, staff magazines and newspapers.

Action to improve such a situation could involve a cascading process in which groups of interested employees are asked to considering the data in relation to the company's core values. Staff could then be encouraged to suggest improvements and innovations and to take responsibility for seeing them through. There are instances of successful behavioural transformations of existing businesses, using a culture-change approach. The 'HRM in reality' example describes changes at Land Rover.

HRM in reality

Land Rover

Terry Morgan, managing director of the company, attributed success to 'working with people'. According to Morgan, manufacturing technology is no longer changing quickly. Competitive advantage comes from making the best of staff, or rather 'associates', on the production line.

Associates work to the maxim: 'each associate has two jobs, their work and the improvement of their work'. Many employees are middle-aged and have been with Land Rover for most of their working lives. Yet they have adopted the Japanese 'transplant' ways that supposedly require 'green labour'.

Associates work together in teams. Team members have been trained for a variety of jobs so that anyone missing due to illness or other cause can be covered by the team. Of course, absenteeism has been reduced considerably. Personal responsibility for their own performance, together with an emphasis on teamwork, produced a productivity gain of 28 per cent in two years.

All associates wear identical green overalls, including the managing director. They are expected to regard the next worker in the production process as a customer. Similarly, work teams regard other sections within the company as their customers.

▶

This has led to a considerable increase in quality. Ideas for improvement are generated in two-hour discussion groups every week. Six to eight associates come together to brainstorm and work on honing new improvements.

The management hierarchy has been flattened dramatically. Now there are just three levels between the managing director and the shopfloor associate. The reduction in middle management was a painful process with most managers choosing to leave the company rather than work at a lower level of responsibility.

Source: Solomon (1994).

Discussion question: Despite the positive impression created by this case, and increasing demand for Land Rover products, some quality problems remained. What more could the company do to improve its quality performance?

Negative change

If the cost of failed change is high for organizations, the cost is equally dear for people. The first casualty is trust: people start to blame one another. Too many botched plans, and people become afraid to try again. Even so-called 'successful' efforts often leave a bitter taste in the mouths of those who were forced to change. The toll on individuals is enormous. (Maurer, 1996, p.11)

Implicitly, anyone opposing change is viewed as negative. Often, however, change is a destructive process and the end-product inferior to the original. This may be disguised by redefining quality requirements so that the lowering of standards becomes invisible or obscured. Newcomers to the situation know no better. Many may be involved in the change process and have a commitment to perceiving it as being necessary.

A redefinition of quality coincides inevitably with a change in the nature and flow of information, making a true 'before and after' comparison impossible. The proponents of change are unlikely to present their initiatives as failures; antagonists will never be happy with modifications in methods they have cherished. In the absence of objective evidence, debate is reduced to political confrontation with opponents of organizational change labelling new approaches as 'change for change's sake'. In fact, this is rarely the case. Change is difficult and disruptive and is not lightly entered into, but the true reasons for change may differ from its public justifications.

For example, we noted earlier that change is commonly associated with new management. This is not a coincidence. New managers have to work hard if the status quo is left alone. They are forever at the mercy of old networks and power balances. Far easier to highlight deficiencies in the current situation, pronounce it to be lacking in quality, and sweep it away to be replaced with another of their own making. Power-holders in the old networks can be eliminated or sidelined; there are always ambitious replacements available who are willing to become loyalists of the new regime. Young, or formerly disaffected, staff will show a naive enthusiasm for their new-found opportunities. Even better – from this somewhat cynical perspective – people can be imported from outside the organization who will be anxious to perform as required.

| Activity 12:8 | Is it possible for negative attitudes towards change to have positive benefits for an organization? |

Who would make the best corporate chief executive?

A survey of 150 top executives at Fortune 1000 companies asked them to choose who would make the best CEO from the following: George W. Bush, Colin Powell, Bill Clinton, Dick Cheney, Donald Rumsfeld, Al Gore, Tony Blair or Rudy Giuliani.

The survey was conducted for the Council of Public Relations Firms, the trade association for the public relations industry. The main conclusions were that:

- Vice President Cheney and Secretary of State Powell were regarded as being the most suitable CEO-types, followed by President Bush and ex-New York Mayor Rudy Giuliani. Then came Secretary of Defense Rumsfeld and British Prime Minister Tony Blair. Bill Clinton came out badly from the survey (3 per cent of the vote) but not as badly as former Vice President Al Gore who received zero votes!

- Almost one half (47 per cent) of the executives surveyed singled out the ability to effectively communicate and motivate as the most important quality for a CEO to have in tough times like these. The next most important were decisiveness (31 per cent) and being a visionary (15 per cent). The other qualities surveyed, including being tireless and hard-working, barely scored.

According to Kathy Cripps, president of the Council of Public Relations Firms:

> The survey shows that America's executives put a premium on the ability of corporate leaders to communicate company policy and give direction with clarity and conviction, and to energize and motivate managers and workers alike. In this difficult economic environment, effective communication, both internal and external, can inform, motivate, build trust and reassure.

Survey results

1 Thinking about leadership, if you could select one of the following to be CEO of your company at this time, who would you choose?

Choice	Per cent
Dick Cheney	23
Colin Powell	23
George Bush	15
Rudy Giuliani	15
Donald Rumsfeld	9
Tony Blair	9
Bill Clinton	3
Al Gore	0
Don't know/refused	2

2 Which one of the following do you believe is the most important quality for a CEO in tough times?

Choice	Per cent
Effective communicator and motivator	47
Decisiveness	31
Being a visionary	15
Openness	4
Tireless and hard-working	2
Compassion/empathy	1
Don't know/refused	0

▶

◄

CEO reputation

If these men were appointed as CEOs they would not have much time in which to prove themselves, according to another study conducted by consulting firm Burson-Marsteller in 2001. The study, *Building CEO Capital*, showed that today's CEOs have just five earnings quarters on average to prove themselves.

'The job of chief executive officer is exceedingly complex and increasingly short-lived,' said Dr Leslie Gaines-Ross, chief knowledge and research officer of Burson-Marsteller. The study, conducted with RoperASW, also found that new CEOs are given, on average, eight months to develop a strategic vision, 19 months to increase share price and 21 months to turn a company around. And if they failed, why did they fail? 'The inability to execute well' and 'a lack of strategic vision' were cited as the main reasons.

The Burson-Marsteller study included 1155 US chief executives, senior managers, financial analysts, institutional investors, business media and government officials. It shows that almost half (48 per cent) of an organization's reputation can be attributed to the reputation of its CEO – a significant increase on the 40 per cent recorded in 1997. The companion survey in the United Kingdom matched the US results with 49 per cent attributed to the CEO.

'CEO reputation matters the world over,' said Christopher Komisarjevsky, president and CEO of Burson-Marsteller worldwide. 'Four years of research confirms that the CEO is arguably a company's most critical intangible asset driving the brand and the reputation of the company both internally and externally.' Credibility, ethical standards and good internal communications are viewed as the leading three drivers of CEO reputation – with credibility having increased in importance since the previous survey in 1997.

'Delivering on promises made is an integral part of how CEOs build and sustain reputation today,' remarked Dr Gaines-Ross. 'Furthermore, in light of the events of September 11, good CEO communications was put to the highest test as most Americans first heard the tragic news in the workplace. Many employees had a chance to re-evaluate the effectiveness of their CEO's ability to communicate clearly and sincerely.'

Five factors were cited as critical in building CEO capital:

1 being believable

2 demanding high ethical standards

3 communicating a clear vision inside the company

4 maintaining a high quality top management team

5 motivating and inspiring employees.

Intriguingly, increasing shareholder wealth did not feature in the top five drivers for building CEO reputation. 'Financial performance is often considered a given and a price of entry for CEO favorability,' says Gaines-Ross. 'It is necessary but clearly not all there is to building an admirable CEO reputation.'

CEO reputation influences the decisions of 'business influentials' to invest in a company (95 per cent), believe in a company when it is under pressure from the media (94 per cent), recommend it as a good alliance/merger partner (93 per cent) and maintain confidence when the share price is lagging (92 per cent). Also, business influentials are more likely to recommend an organization as a good place to work (88 per cent) if the CEO is favourably regarded.

Source: *HRM Guide USA* (http://www.hrmguide.net/usa/), 26 February 2002.

Summary

In this chapter we investigated transformational or change management. Nowadays, change initiatives are common elements of human resource strategies as companies and public sector organizations struggle to achieve their objectives in a competitive environment. Frequently these involve some form of organizational restructuring using a change programme such as business process re-engineering. Change programmes are fashion-driven and quickly become obsolete, to be replaced by the next heavily touted set of magic solutions. Some of the most difficult aspects of change management for human resource practitioners come from mergers and acquisitions where their involvement is often late – if not too late to rescue a disastrous situation. Finally we looked at behavioural transformation involving attempts to change corporate culture, and recognized that negative attitudes to change are to be expected and are not necessarily unhealthy.

Further reading

Hanson's *The M&A Transition Guide: A 10-Step Roadmap for Workforce Integration*, published by John Wiley & Sons (2001), takes a step-by-step approach to HR involvement in the merger and acquisition process. Michael Hammer presents a review of recent thinking on change interventions in *The Agenda: What Every Business Must Do to Dominate the Decade*, published by Crown Publications (2001). His collaboration with Champy in *Re-engineering the Corporation: A Manifesto for Business Revolution*, Harper Business (1993), was probably the best-selling business book of the 1990s. Black and Gregersen's *Leading Strategic Change*, Financial Times Prentice Hall (2002), is focused on the leadership of change but pays particular attention to resistance and harnessing negative attitudes.

Review questions

1 What is a transformational HR strategy?

2 Define: (a) synergy; (b) restructuring; (c) business process re-engineering.

3 How would you distinguish between incremental and programmed methods of change management?

4 Why do people resist change?

5 What role should human resource practitioners play ideally in a merger or acquisition? How does this differ from reality?

6 What is action learning?

Problem for discussion and analysis

West Five Care Trust

The West Five Care Trust controls four hospitals in a suburban area. Two of the hospitals are modern and have extra accommodation space. The other two are old but prestigious specialist units located in expensive areas. The trust considers that it would make considerable financial sense to close the older hospitals and transfer their functions to the modern sites. Several specialist consultants are extremely unhappy about the consequences and have launched a public campaign to save the specialist units. This has angered the general manager who has only just presented the plan as a proposal to the management committee. He considers the consultants to be disloyal as they have taken a confidential business matter to the press. He is also baffled since the new hospitals would offer them far better facilities.

The general manager was recently recruited from industry and has been keen to exercise his right to manage. In his first six months, he successfully contracted out cleaning and catering, brushing aside union opposition. He has also instituted stringent cost-control measures and now vets all budget requests personally, including expenses for attending conferences.

As human resources manager, how would you analyse the situation and how could you help?

13

Resourcing strategies

Objectives

The purpose of this chapter is to:

- Provide an overview of employee resourcing strategies.
- Discuss the purposes and methods of human resource planning.
- Outline the process of job analysis.
- Debate resourcing strategy in the context of staff retention and redundancy.

Resourcing

The basis of people management lies in how work gets done and who does it. Therefore, the rationale behind *why* we should decide on one solution rather than another is fundamental to HRM. There are important issues involved at all levels of analysis. At the environmental level, employee resourcing takes place against a background of:

● fluctuating economic conditions and global competition
● choice and availability within the local job market
● competition for scarce skills.

At the organizational level, the structure and functions of an enterprise are composed of the tasks that people perform. Allocating work to unsuitable or inadequately skilled people reduces the effectiveness of the whole organization. The consequences can be significant and – particularly with high-level or specialized work – may be critical to its future performance. Employee resourcing is no longer a matter of recruiting and selecting new people to fit existing posts. As we saw in earlier chapters, organizations have a range of 'flexible' alternatives.

At the strategic level, employee resourcing involves decisions on:

● subcontracting or creating vacancies
● allocating tasks
● choice of selection methods.

As an activity, it is a major element of the work of human resource specialists, involving considerable technical expertise. Employee resourcing can involve sophisticated methods intended to realize long-term objectives and balancing considerations such as (Price, 2000): (a) satisfying the immediate need to minimize employee costs while maximizing worker contribution to the organization; and (b) fulfilling a longer-term aim of obtaining the optimal mix of skills and commitment in the workforce.

Employee resourcing is also a subject of vital importance at a personal level because most of us have to apply for a job: probably the first practical aspect of human resource management we encounter. In many cases it is a frustrating and sometimes baffling process of rejection. Readers in employment may well participate on both sides of the issue – as selectors or as applicants. Inevitably, therefore, resourcing deserves serious discussion. In this chapter we focus initially on *why* resourcing decisions are taken.

The first section of the chapter begins with a consideration of the environmental constraints on resourcing and discusses the implications of the move towards flexible organizations. Next we determine the nature of resourcing strategy and consider various types.

In the next major section we discuss human resource planning, examining the hard or 'people as numbers' approach – involving forecasting methods – and soft planning which takes commitment and culture into account.

Next we consider the use made of information gained from job analyses. We discuss the role of the job description and person specification in resourcing decisions. The chapter moves on to a debate on the merits of the 'best practice' approach in flexible organizations. Finally we discuss strategy and planning in relation to redundancies.

Key concept 13:1

Employee resourcing Resourcing is the process by which people are identified and allocated to perform necessary work. Resourcing has two strategic imperatives: first, minimizing employee costs and maximizing employee value to the organization; secondly, obtaining the correct behavioural mix of attitude and commitment in the workforce. Employees are expensive assets. They must be allocated carefully and sparingly. In terms of costs and efficiency, effective resourcing depends on the care taken in deciding which tasks are worthwhile and the levels of skill and ability required to perform them.

Employee resourcing is a fundamental aspect of people management (see Key concept 13.1). We can define four key stages:

- *Strategy and planning*. Determining future human resources needs in terms of availability, expertise and location. We observed in Part 1 that HRM literature stresses the integration of resourcing activities with other people processes, such as performance management and human resource development, as well as the overall objectives of the enterprise

- *Research and data collection*. Determining the nature of work to be done and the criteria or competencies necessary to perform them. Additionally, obtaining adequate information about the people who possess these competencies, whether as employees, consultants or subcontractors.

- *Marketing*. Making the work known – and attractive – to potential applicants in the internal and external job markets. Conventionally this function is contained within the term 'recruitment'.

- *Decision making*. Selection or allocation: choosing individuals to perform the work.

Activity 13:1 Why is employee resourcing a core activity for human resource staff?

Marketing and decision making are discussed in Chapters 14 and 15 on recruitment and selection. In this chapter we will concentrate on strategy and planning and the research necessary to establish the need for particular jobs.

Environmental constraints on resourcing

Unlike many other aspects of people management, employee resourcing involves direct interaction between organizations and their environment. In Part 2 we observed that, ultimately, businesses are dependent on the external job market for the supply of suitable staff. It is the source of school-leavers and university graduates for junior posts and experienced people for senior or specialized positions. Even in conditions of high unemployment there are shortages of people with skills that are in demand. Countries such as Australia and Britain, for example, have a long record of failure to provide their young people with appropriate vocational training. If companies are unable to find staff or subcontractors with appropriate skills, their growth prospects and competitiveness are constrained. This may be so severe that companies are forced to relocate. Some multinationals have been forced to transfer operations from low-cost economies to high-wage countries, such as Germany, where skilled workers are available. Alternatively, businesses may compete for scarce skills through increased remuneration packages and benefits. Purcell (1989), for instance, sees star companies identified by the Boston Consulting matrix (discussed later in this chapter) as being prepared to pay above market rates to recruit and retain the best employees.

Economic changes over the last two decades have led to systematic responses in the attitudes and practices of employers. In his discussion of the flexible firm, Atkinson (1984) identifies a number of themes that underpin the employment plans of businesses in free market countries:

- *Market stagnation*. Prolonged periods of recession and the increased competitiveness of world markets have produced a managerial obsession with the permanent reduction of unit employee costs.

- *Job loss*. Most large firms have undergone dramatic reductions in levels of employment. These reductions have been expensive in redundancy costs and have had significant negative effects on relations with remaining employees.

- *Uncertainty*. Despite continuous announcements of recovery, firms have been cautious about preparing for growth. In particular, they have been wary of a commitment to more full-time employees.

- *Technological change*. This is happening at increasing pace and reducing cost, requiring organizations – and their employees – to respond quickly by changing products, manufacturing methods and ways of working.

- *Working time*. Employers have maximized the value of employee time through restructuring work patterns to match periods of demand. This has led to a preference for part-time workers.

These factors have encouraged a move towards flexible jobs in flexible organizations.

| Activity 13:2 | Summarize the main environmental factors that affect employee resourcing strategies. |

| HRM in reality | **Higher proportion of people working on casual basis** |

A fifth of all employed people consider themselves to be employed on a casual basis, according to recent results from the Australian Bureau of Statistics (ABS). The current rate of 20 per cent represents an increase of three percentage points since the last Forms of Employment Survey conducted in 1998.

Employees with paid leave entitlements still make up the predominant group (58 per cent) of workers recorded in November 2001 – little different from the 59 per cent recorded in 1998. A further 19 per cent of employed people had their own business in November 2001. The remaining 3 per cent consisted of employees who were not receiving paid leave entitlements but did not identify themselves as casual.

The report shows that gender differences are significant with women making up the majority (59 per cent) of self-identified casuals in November 2001, while over two-thirds (69 per cent) of people working in their own business were men. There were also age differences: 42 per cent of self-identified casuals were aged between 15 and 24 while 60 per cent of people working in their own business were aged between 35 and 54 years.

People work longer for their own businesses. Most employees with paid leave entitlements (70 per cent) worked at least 35 hours in their main job during the reference week – with 17 per cent working 49 hours or more. This compared with 68 per cent of people employed in their own business working at least 35 hours and 40 per cent working 49 hours or more. In contrast, the majority (76 per cent) of self-identified casuals worked less than 35 hours in their main job.

At November 2001, 288 100 employees (4 per cent) worked on a fixed-term contract, and 451 900 persons employed in their own business (26 per cent) undertook contract work. Overall, 8 per cent of employed persons were working under some form of contract arrangement.

Source: *HRM Guide Australia* (http://www.hrmguide.net/australia/), 17 September 2002.

Resourcing and the flexible organization

According to Blau and Schoenherr (1971, p.347): 'The recruitment of employees with the required skills becomes a crucial responsibility and a major mechanism of control.' During periods of relatively high unemployment in the 1980s and 1990s, organizations in many countries felt able to dictate the terms of employment they were prepared to offer new recruits, often moving away from traditional nine-to-five work patterns. As we have previously observed, there is a pronounced trend away from full-time work towards other job patterns. For example, in the late 1990s, nine out of ten posts created in the UK were part-time. We also noted earlier that many businesses have distanced non-core activities – such as catering and cleaning – allocating them to external contractors. Similarly, technically specialized functions, such as the management of computer and telecommunications networks, have been subcontracted to specialist firms.

A modern, flexible organization may adopt a structure along the lines of Handy's three-leaf 'shamrock' model (Handy, 1989, p.70):

● A professional core made up of managers, technicians and qualified specialists.

● Contractors, providing non-core activities, who are not direct employees of the organization.

● The flexible labour force composed of part-timers, temporary staff, consultants and contract staff performing tasks as and when required.

The allocation of work between the 'leaves' of the shamrock organization is generally decided upon at a senior level. The implications are considerable, often requiring main board approval, particularly for the employment of subcontractors. The decision to 'outsource' activities is usually taken on purely financial grounds, leaving people managers to clear up the resulting employee relations mess.

Key concept 13:2

Grow or buy?   Organizations can focus on internal or external job markets, or draw from both. Firms with an internal focus recruit at junior levels and 'grow' their employees into valuable assets through training, development and experience in the organization. Alternatively, companies can buy talent at a variety of levels from the external employment market. A mixed strategy offers a balance of continuity and commitment from long-term staff together with fresh ideas from imported 'new blood'.

Resourcing strategies

Most large organizations employ human resource or personnel specialists to conduct or, at least, coordinate employee resourcing. This is a role that has long been regarded as part of the domain of personnel management (Iles and Mabey, 1992, p.255) and personnel textbooks conventionally describe resourcing as a passive, technical procedure – a matching of available candidates to the requirements of the organization. In fact, successful recruitment must be proactive. Organizations can take one of three actions to fulfil their employee resourcing needs:

1   *Reallocate tasks* between employees, so that existing staff take on more or different work. This may be part of an organizational change programme, such as restructuring or reorganization. The emphasis is on flexible working practices, requiring multi-skilled workers and sophisticated assessment and development programmes.

2   *Reallocate people* from the internal employment market, through promotion or transfer between different departments. Traditionally, German and Japanese organizations have filled their supervisory and management posts from existing staff. Large Japanese organizations expect their potential managers to move between different functions during their careers. Japanese human resource managers, for instance, are likely to have worked in finance, production and marketing rather than specializing in 'personnel'.

3   *Recruit* new staff from the external job market. Countries in the free market tradition have focused most of their resourcing activities on bringing in people from outside the organization. Employers have a choice between:

   ● *Recruiting anybody and everybody.* Until comparatively recently, many workers in heavy industry were employed casually at the factory gate. In many parts of the world construction labourers and seasonal agricultural workers continue to be taken on in a casual fashion. With no commitment on either side, a rigid chain of command then rules. This approach predominates for employment at low skill and wage levels. It is especially common in small low-technology companies.

   ● *Recruiting selectively.* Skilled and motivated workers are selected. These employees can be allowed to get on with the job with only broad guidelines or a policy framework to observe. This approach predominates in large organizations. The result has been the creation of an internal and external recruitment industry, including selection experts, recruitment consultants and headhunters.

External recruitment has the virtue of bringing in a wider range of experience but limits career opportunities for existing employees. It is predominantly a free market approach to resourcing but even Japanese businesses have begun to recruit externally, particularly for scarce technological skills such as computer programming. *Heddo-hantas* have become common in Japan, recruiting for small to medium-sized enterprises and foreign companies (Whitehill, 1990, p.129).

Activity 13:3	Summarize the main resourcing strategy options open to modern organizations.

Types of resourcing strategy

Resourcing is a dynamic process: the movement of human resources through an organization. In terms of systems theory this can be represented as:

- input
- throughput
- output.

Businesses can assign people largely from existing staff or from the external job market. Companies that focus on internal supply are likely to view people as assets, carrying long-term value, rather than as costs. This is in line with practice in social market and Japanese organizations. It also reflects the spirit of the Harvard model of HRM discussed in Chapter 2. In essence the choice is between 'growing' or 'buying' (see Key concept 13.2). 'Growing' is the central theme of human resource development discussed in Chapter 20. Needless to say, firms in free markets such as the UK and the USA have a tendency to 'buy' – and dispose of – employees as required.

Choices between 'growing' or 'buying' can be related to environmental conditions and organizational culture. In an early discussion of human resource strategy, Miles and Snow (1978) devised a typology based on the degree of risk taken by businesses in stable or unstable environments. They classified organizations as defenders, prospectors, analysers and reactors. A similar typology by Sonnenfeld, Peiperl and Kotter (1988) shown in Table 13.1 uses slightly more dramatic terminology: clubs, baseball teams, fortresses and academies.

- *Defenders*. These are firms with small niche markets or narrow product ranges. As organizations they have an equally narrow focus, requiring stability and reliability. They need loyal employees with a long-term commitment. Staff enter at junior levels and are 'made' into worthwhile employees through extensive training and career development along largely functional routes. Incremental growth allows for new career opportunities within an internal job market grounded in a strong culture. Loyalty and commitment are encouraged through performance assessment based on behavioural compliance characteristics. Staff turnover is low, partly because employees are chained by organization-specific skills and a degree of institutionalization. This strategy is employed by 'clubs' in Sonnenfeld, Peiperl and Kotter's (1988) classification.

Table 13.1	Resourcing strategies		
Type	*Characteristics*	*Key HR function*	*Sectors*
1 Academies	Active growers Low staff turnover Long-term service	Development	Office products Pharmaceuticals Electronics
2 Clubs	Passive growers Seniority Commitment Status Equal treatment	Retention or 'maintenance'	Public utilities Government Insurance Military

3 Baseball teams	Active buyers
	Staff identify with
	  profession more than
	  firm
		Recruitment of star
		performers
			Accounting
			Law
			Consulting
			Software
			Advertising

4 Fortresses	Cautious buyers Survival Cost-cutting	Recruitment of generalists Redundancies	Publishing Textiles Retailing Hotels

Source: Based on Sonnenfeld, Peiperl and Kotter (1988).

- *Prospectors*. Innovative firms, moving in and out of markets to capitalize on opportunities and avoid competition. Top management consider themselves to be dynamic. Equating to Sonnenfeld, Peiperl and Kotter's 'baseball teams', they are typical of sports and entertainment businesses. The instability of their market-place requires constant flexibility and environmental scanning. In the eyes of 1970s and 1980s theorists, locked into the 'right person' recruitment models, which we will discuss shortly, this could only be met by buying rather than making talent. Uncertainty does not allow for career systems, the focus being on recruitment from the external job market. New recruits have to be able to 'hit the ground running' (Rousseau, 1995, p.188). Rewards are high and geared to immediate results. However, commitment is low on both sides of the employment relationship: recruits are seen as 'passing through'. Learning is personal rather than organizational and knowledge leaves with the employee.

- *Analysers*. These firms are cautious innovators, waiting for prospectors to open up new markets before entering themselves. Analyser organizations are structured into stable and efficient production units with highly flexible and responsive marketing or service units. They emphasize quality and skill and equate to Sonnenfeld, Peiperl and Kotter's 'academies'. As hybrids they take a mixed approach to making and buying employees: stable business units rely on internal promotion and development; flexible units buy in expertise as and when required.

- *Reactors*. These are 'fortresses' in Sonnenfeld, Peiperl and Kotter's classification: failed defenders, analysers or prospectors, desperately attempting to survive. Their strategies are often incoherent, unable to 'make' employees but often 'buying' and selling. In their attempts to recover or instigate the 'turnaround' changes discussed in Chapter 12, the emphasis is likely to be on redundancies.

Activity 13:4

Compare and contrast the classification systems proposed by Miles and Snow and Sonnenfeld, Peiperl and Kotter.

Human resource planning

For resourcing strategies to be implemented they must be translated into practical action. The strategic process can be organized logically – for example, following the decision sequence shown in Figure 13.1. For these decisions to be taken, information must be obtained, consequences gauged, political soundings taken and preferences assessed.

It is clear that many of these decisions are fundamental to an organization. If the implications are major, strategic decisions are taken at the centre of the business. The role of the human resource function is two-fold:

1 To participate in the decision process by providing information and opinion on each option, including:

- redundancy or recruitment costs
- consequences on morale
- redeployment/outplacement opportunities
- availability of skilled staff within the organization
- availability of suitable people in the job market
- time constraints

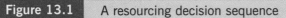

Figure 13.1   A resourcing decision sequence

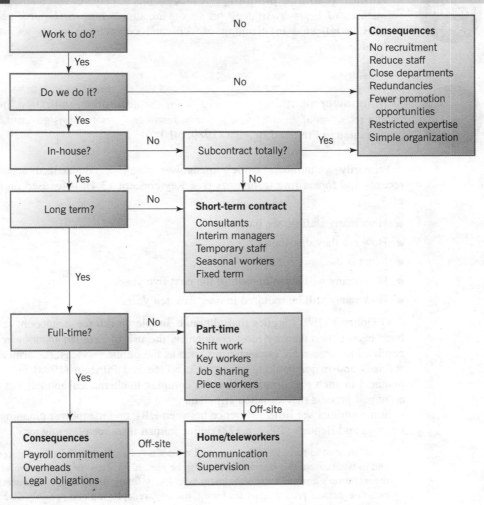

- development/training needs/schedules
- management requirements.

This forms part of the information collated from the organization as a whole.

2 To support line managers dealing with the people consequences of implementing the decision. Information already gathered provides the basis for a human resource plan.

In other instances, decision making has consequences of lesser significance to the business. Resourcing decisions taken at an operational level may lead from departmental expansion or cost-saving, transfer of activities, new product ranges and comparatively small changes in function. In practice, therefore, human resource planning has short, medium and long-term aspects (see Key concept 13.3).

Older texts refer to this topic as 'manpower planning'. (Presumably 'womanpower planning' was not much different!) Use of this quaint term has declined – but not disappeared – in favour of human resource planning (HRP). Some authors distinguish between manpower planning and HRP as distinct approaches (Hendry, 1995, p.190).

Key concept 13:3 **Human resource planning**   A process that anticipates and maps out the consequences of business strategy on an organization's human resource requirements. This is reflected in planning of skill and competence needs as well as total headcounts.

Key concept 13:4 **Manpower planning**   'A strategy for the acquisition, utilization, improvement and retention of an enterprise's human resources' (anonymous government publication cited in Pratt and Bennett (1989, p.101)).

Primarily a 'numbers game', manpower planning emphasized accurate personnel records and forecasting techniques (see Key concept 13.4). It focused on questions such as:

● How many staff do we have/need?

● How are they distributed?

● What is the age profile?

● How many will leave in each of the next five years?

● How many will be required in one, five, ten years?

O'Doherty (1997) argues that although simple workforce headcount predictions may have been undertaken by most companies, the use of detailed manpower forecasts was confined to large-scale organizations such as the public services, the armed forces, postal services and major banking groups. Corbridge and Pilbeam (1998) note that specialist planners in such organizations devised complex mathematical models but this was often an unreal process that attracted criticism.

Some authors see little difference between HRP and manpower planning. For example Graham and Bennett (1992, p.172) define human resource planning as:

… an attempt to forecast how many and what kind of employees will be required in the future, and to what extent this demand is likely to be met. It involves the comparison of an organization's current human resources with likely future needs and, consequently, the establishment of programmes for hiring, training, redeploying and possibly discarding employees. Effective HRP should result in the right people doing the right things in the right place at precisely the right time.

The manpower planning approach regards the human resource manager as a personnel technician. Within this framework, the function of the human resource planner is to provide 'management' with the necessary advice with which to make decisions on issues such as:

● recruitment

● avoiding redundancies

● training – numbers and categories

● management development

● estimates of 'labour' costs

● productivity bargaining

● accommodation requirements.

In this tradition, Graham and Bennett (1992, p.175) envisage a long-term human resource plan as a detailed specification, by location, function and job category of the number of employees 'it is practicable to employ at various stages in the future' (see Table 13.2). A plan should include:

- jobs which will come into being, be ceased, or changed
- possibilities for redeployment and retraining
- changes in management and supervision
- training requirements
- programmes for recruitment, redundancy and early retirement
- implications for employee relations
- a feedback mechanism to company objectives
- methods for dealing with HR problems such as inability to obtain sufficient technically skilled workers.

Table 13.2	Steps for long-term human resource planning

Step	Aspects
1 Create a company HRP group	This should include the main functional managers of the company, together with human resource specialists.
2 State the organization's human resource objectives	Within the context of the overall business objectives and considering: - capital equipment plans - reorganization such as centralization or decentralization - changes in products or in output - marketing plans - financial limitations.
3 Audit present utilization of human resources	Sometimes described as the 'internal manpower audit', detailing: - number of employees in various categories - an estimate of employee turnover for each grade, analysing the effects of high or low turnover on performance - amount of overtime worked - assessment of performance and potential of current employees - comparison of payment levels with local firms.
4 Assess the external environment	Placing the organization in its business context in terms of: - the recruitment position - population trends - local housing and transport plans - national agreements dealing with conditions of work - government policies in education, retirement, regional subsidies, and so on.
5 Assess potential supply of labour ('external manpower audit')	Including: - local population movements (emigration and immigration) - recruitment and redundancy by other firms - employing new work categories – e.g. part-time workers - productivity improvements, working hours and practices.

Source: Based on Graham and Bennett (1992, p.174).

Such a plan requires organization, belief in the process and detailed information. Not surprisingly, many organizations cannot meet these criteria. Tyson (1995, p.77), reporting on a study of 30 large UK-based organizations, found that most had plans of three to five years' duration. Shorter-term plans were used by some retail firms which kept detail down to a year or so, whereas capital-intensive firms were more likely to favour long-term planning. Generally, managers were unhappy about five-year plans, regarding them as 'a constraint on business'. Tyson (1995, p.80) identifies three distinct approaches to planning:

- *Formal, long-range planning.* Creating a planning framework, usually expressed in financial terms with verbal commentaries. Notably, all the companies studied that used this approach consulted widely with interest groups.

- *Flexible strategies.* Covering most of the organizations studied. Plans changed frequently in response to market changes. Plans were intentionally short term, often with minimal written detail.

- *Attributional strategies.* 'One step at a time'. Previous actions can be rationalized but, in truth, organizations using this approach are cautious and are not really committed to any specific strategy. This can be compared with Mintzberg's concept of 'emergent strategies' discussed in the previous chapter.

In general it is worth observing (Price, 2000) that:

Modern human resource planners have tended to move away from predicting headcounts towards building 'what if' models or scenarios which allow the implications of different strategies to be debated. However, traditional HR planning techniques have become considerably easier to implement with the spread of Human Resource Information Systems which trap key employee information and generate reports and analyses as a matter of course.

HRM in reality	**Planning for health human resources**

Evidence is replacing guesswork for planning health human resources in Nova Scotia. 'We are learning how to plan health human resources based on what we know about the age, sex, and health status of a population,' says Gail Tomblin Murphy, Associate Professor of Nursing at Dalhousie University. 'Health human resource planning is moving into a new stage. We are now collecting the evidence that will enable policy makers to make decisions based on need.'

And the days of predictions based solely on doctor/patient and nurse/patient ratios are over, she adds:

For years we have tried to determine health human resource planning needs in ways that make no sense. We had no evidence. We only looked at supply – how many physicians do we have, how many nurses, how many physiotherapists, etc. – not how many do we require based on the health needs of people.

Her research, which is funded by the Canadian Health Services Research Foundation (CHSRF), the Nova Scotia Health Research Foundation (NSHRF) and the Ontario Ministry of Health and Long-Term Care, will help decision makers determine their health human resource needs. Together with Dr Linda O'Brien-Pallas, National Chair in Nursing Resource Planning (CHSRF/CIHR) and Professor at the Faculty of Nursing at the University of Toronto, Professor Tomblin Murphy is working on developing a model for future planning. Her team of researchers are collating records of nursing use with a national population health survey. They will use this information to estimate the relationship between health services use and population health needs to look for patterns to help predict future resource needs.

Professor Tomblin Murphy was a speaker at a workshop hosted by NSHRF that brought about 50 experts from Atlantic Canada together to explore the issue of health human resources. Intended to help establish working partnerships among researchers, policy makers and clinicians to create collaborative research projects and address major issues in health human resources, the workshop also encouraged frank discussion aimed at identifying research gaps and needs.

'We are committed to building capacity among Atlantic Canadian researchers,' says Krista Connell, NSHRF executive director and host of the workshop. 'We hope that workshops like this one will give researchers the insight into what granting agencies are looking for.'

'Collaboration is the key to winning major research awards,' she adds. 'Granting agencies want to see partnerships among researchers, clinical managers, and policy makers that ensure projects will be used, not just sit around in journals.'

Source: *HRM Guide Canada* (http://www.hrmguide.net/canada/), 4 January 2002.

Activity 13:5	Is human resource planning a worthwhile activity?

People as numbers

Generally, it is accepted that modern human resource planning should have a wider perspective, in tune with the philosophy of HRM, including 'softer' issues such as competence, commitment and career development. Modern human resource planning continues to use the 'hard' techniques of manpower planning but also includes a new focus on shaping values, beliefs and culture, anticipating strategy, market conditions and demographic change.

Nevertheless, in line with the tradition of formal, observable and 'objective' planning, numerical measurement and forecasting have been favoured over qualitative studies of opinion, attitude and motivation. 'Hard' data allows managers and planners to sit in their offices and wait for information. 'No need to go out and meet the troops, or the customers, to find out how the products get bought ... all that just wastes valuable time' (Mintzberg, 1994, p.258). The growth of information technology and management information systems has made numerical data readily available and possibly further discouraged collection of qualitative information. Numbers give a comforting feeling of unarguable objectivity and allow managers to detach themselves from shopfloor emotions. It is much easier to sack a number than a real human being.

Forecasting methods

Human resource planners have a choice of techniques available to them, for example:

1 *Extrapolation*. This method assumes that the past is a reliable guide to the future. Various techniques are suitable for short and medium-term forecasting, such as time series, trend analysis and measures of cyclical requirements. Since they rely on present knowledge and cannot take the unpredictable into account, forecasts are best in a stable environment. They tend to do little harm if kept pessimistic, but enthusiasm and political considerations often lead to overestimation. This can have expensive consequences.

2 *Projected production/sales information.* As a normal part of the planning process, production, sales and marketing departments will prepare their own forecasts. Intelligent use of this data, taking the introduction of new technology and quality improvements into account, will provide an estimate of the quantity and nature of the human resources needed. Work study, managerial judgement and a certain amount of scepticism – particularly regarding sales forecasts – can be used to transform this information into employee requirements.

3 *Employee analysis.* Modern computer packages offer extensive possibilities for modelling the total profile of an organization's human resources. Employees can be classified in a variety of ways, such as function, department or grade. Age and length of service are important predictors of future availability. Skills levels and training or development needs can be compared with annual performance assessments.

4 *Scenario building.* Scenarios are not strictly forecasts but speculations on the future. It is impossible to predict what will happen in 20 – or even five – years' time, but it is possible to describe some alternatives. Working through a variety of possible states can identify the uncertainties, help us gain an understanding of the main driving factors and produce a range of options. Given the dramatic changes and discontinuities experienced today, scenario building seems to be one of the most realistic and useful forms of planning. Instead of prescribing detailed plans, the process allows strategists to work through the consequences on resources and costs of different courses of action.

| **HRM in reality** | **Forecasting and reality** |

Instruments may be made by which the largest ships, with only one man guiding them, will be carried with greater velocity than if they were full of sailors. Chariots ... will move with incredible rapidity without the help of animals. Instruments of flying may be formed in which a man, sitting at his ease ... may beat the air with his artificial wings after the manner of birds ... also machines ... will enable men to walk at the bottom of the seas. (Roger Bacon c.1214–92)

Planners attempt to anticipate future events but few strategists are likely to equal Bacon's powerful imagination. For most of us, crystal-ball gazing or prediction is fraught with difficulty. Arthur C. Clarke (1973), a noted science fiction writer who invented the concept of satellite communications, concluded that 'it is impossible to predict the future ... all attempts to do so in any detail appear ludicrous within a few years'. In the table we can see that many of today's major industrial products were not expected. Nevertheless many management texts insist that the future should be anticipated and planned for: it is assumed that we have a good appreciation of what the next few years will bring us. This means that the training and development of tomorrow's managers is geared to the requirements of the future as we see them now.

Normative models tend to suggest that strategic decision making is an entirely rational and orderly process: what *ought* to happen. Usually, of course, events get in the way and there will be some variation from intended strategy. As we saw in Part 2, the business environment is complex and uncertain. It is impossible to predict the future with any degree of precision. Prediction is a dangerous business because it relies mainly on what has already happened. It depends on information that might be incomplete or inaccurate. Circumstances can change quickly. For example, it is probably just as well that the renowned Dr R. Woolley, space 'expert' and Astronomer Royal, was not employed as a strategist at NASA. In 1956 he confidently announced that 'Space travel is utter bilge' – the first satellite, Sputnik 1 was launched in the following year!

The expected and the unexpected

Unexpected	Expected	Still expected?
X-rays	Cars	Teleportation
Nuclear energy	Flying machines	Invisibility
Relativity	Robots	Time travel
Radio, TV	Telephones	Telepathy
Photography	Steam engines	
Sound-recording	Submarines	
Electronics	Spaceships	

Source: Adapted from Clarke (1973, p.38).

HRM in reality

Attracting and keeping top employees is still difficult

The economy may be slowing but most HR executives find attracting and retaining talent to be a big problem, according to a new study (*Sustaining The Talent Quest: Getting and Keeping the Best People in Volatile Times*) from The Conference Board. Some 90 per cent of the 109 surveyed executives say that they are finding it difficult to attract and keep the best people for their organization.

Respondents cited corporate turmoil and limited career opportunities as the key reasons for unwanted turnover. Non-competitive pay and benefits are also barriers. 'While labor shortages in the 1990s were driven by technology skills and initiatives, employers are currently putting a high premium on general leadership competency,' says David Dell of The Conference Board, co-author of the report with Jack Hickey, Research Consultant, The Conference Board:

> For this reason, the quest for top-flight talent has to be the job of everyone within an organization from CEO to junior employee. Even with unlimited funding and resources and the best intentions and programs, HR cannot conquer a turnover problem alone. Success requires a corporate-wide integrated recruitment and retention strategy that can respond quickly to change. Most companies still take a shotgun approach to keeping employees happy, and most still consider their efforts too reactive, especially in regard to retention.

Behaviours that can drive away talent

These include:

- *Failure to make talent supply a long-term strategic priority*. New technology and tools are now available to address getting and keeping talent, but if HR is not actively engaged in the planning process and does not receive corporate commitment from the top, the supply of talented employees will almost certainly be limited to ad hoc clusters of programmes and boom and bust cycles of hiring and reductions that waste talent and inevitably cost more.

▶

◀

- *Not making the business case on turnover*. Senior managers are not likely to recognize and treat employee turnover as a problem if they do not understand how it affects their business. HR executives need to quantify relevant costs and benefits in clear, concrete terms.

- *Just throw money at the problem*. Pay and benefits are not the only reasons why employees leave their jobs. But companies frequently raise or sweeten the compensation package when valued employees look like leaving, even when compensation is not ranked among the most important staff turnover factors. This response is likely to be inadequate.

- *Organizational denial*. Employers should acknowledge that employees' first loyalty is to themselves, followed by their craft or professional skills. Companies have to be aware that people make decisions to leave or stay not only on their career prospects with their current employers but also on how it might prepare them to move on elsewhere.

Translating turnover into numbers that executives understand is not only essential because they need to appreciate the true costs, but also because they have the solutions within their spheres of control. Individual managers control skills, behaviour and job design and are 'fairly inaccessible to HR's intervention'. But, although HR may take the lead on attacking turnover, responsibility for their own turnover numbers and any behaviours that may cause employees to leave the firm have to be delegated to line managers.

The HR executives surveyed cite five major objectives for their staffing management activities:

- organizational stability
- opportunities for career and personal development
- multi-level involvement and accountability for talent
- integrated talent strategies
- emphasis on employer brand and reputation.

Keeping the best talent

Companies are increasingly using the internet and intranets/enterprise portals to manage part, at least, of the recruitment and retention process. Web-based HR systems have often become the key to broader outreach strategies – they are especially cost-effective in accessing passive job-seekers, college students and minorities.

E-recruiting is particularly efficient in cost and time, eliminating expensive headhunters and agencies and may significantly reduce the duration of the recruiting cycle. Speed matters, with each day of delay in hiring meaning a loss of potential revenue from a new employee. Online recruiting also vastly expands employers' access to some of the most desirable segments of the talent market – even high-level executives.

E-recruiting assembles more candidate information and makes it easier and cheaper to gather, track, organize and store applicant data. It is especially valuable for highly competitive campus recruiting, appealing to college students as leading-edge and dynamic.

Source: *HRM Guide USA* (http://www.hrmguide.net/usa/), 15 September 2002.

Employee turnover

In recent years managers have been preoccupied with reducing the size of the workforce, closing plants and encouraging people to leave. In times of economic growth the emphasis changes to retaining the people with required skills. Human resource planning has a role in anticipating wastage. In its 'manpower planning' days, it received considerable attention from planners for whom 'the statistical possibilities ' were enormous (Pratt and Bennett, 1989, p.106). Turnover covers the whole input-output process from recruitment to dismissal or retirement and takes the consequences of promotion and transfer into account. Wastage deals only with leavers. Its importance lies in the freedom of employees to leave when they choose and hence its relative uncontrollable nature for employers.

Control of staff turnover or wastage is critical when there is a general skills shortage. Ahlrichs (2000, p.2) comments that:

> Employers have not ignored the hiring and retention crisis, but their choice of responses has been inadequate at best and off-target at worst. Misled by memories of applicants lined up outside the door, they have focused on the recruiting portion of the problem and largely ignored retention. They have regarded employees as mere lists of hard skills, as plug-in parts who are inter-changeable as long as the resumé matches the job description. They continue to hound their HR departments for more and better candidates while ignoring the cost of turnover and HR's strategies to bond with, develop and retain existing employees.

Early work by Rice, Hull and Trist (1950) identified three main phases of turnover:

1 *Induction crisis.* Individuals who leave shortly after joining an organization: uncommitted employees tend to leave in the first few months. Recent research appears to show that there are several kinds of induction crisis experienced in different ways in different organizations.

2 *Differential transit.* During the first year or so, when some employees conclude that the organization is an unsuitable career vehicle or source of income.

3 *Settled connection.* Becoming a long-term 'stayer'.

Despite the increase in flexible approaches to employment and the demise of the 'job for life' this pattern remains common.

Dibble (1999, p.19) suggests a working assumption that a company's employee population follows a normal distribution:

- Crucial to the organization's success, so we want to do everything we can to keep them (3 per cent).
- Very important and we are willing to do a lot to keep them (13 per cent).
- Employees we are happy to have and whose requests we will try hard to accommodate (68 per cent).
- Need to improve or leave (13 per cent).
- In a process leading to termination of employment (3 per cent).

The degree of wastage can be determined by a variety of turnover indices of varying sophistication. Three examples are:

1 The British Institute of Management (BIM) Index (annual labour turnover)

$$\frac{\text{Leavers in year}}{\text{Average number of staff in post that year}} \times 100 = \% \text{ wastage}$$

2 Cohort analysis – a survival curve is drawn of employees taken on at the same time to determine what happens to a group.

3 Census method – for example, providing a histogram of the length of employee service.

Costs of staff turnover

An annual survey conducted by the Chartered Institute of Personnel and Development (CIPD) finds that the cost and rate of staff turnover is at record levels. More than two-thirds of organizations surveyed report negative effects from such levels of turnover with the average turnover cost of management and professional staff being over £6000, or 28 per cent more than last year. Overall, the average cost of turnover per employee is now £3933.

According to Nick Page, author of the report:

> The escalation in the rate of labour turnover is a big concern for business and is clearly impacting on organizational performance. However, it is encouraging to see employers responding to such activity with one in four planning to introduce work–life balance measures and many more planning to use exit interviews and change pay and benefit structures.
>
> Interestingly, public sector workers such as teachers are less likely to leave their jobs than their counterparts in the private sector. Even so, the public sector continues to have difficulties in recruiting new staff. It appears that the poor performance of this sector in managing both turnover and recruitment is a key reason for their severe labour shortages, rather than people leaving the sector in droves.
>
> However, if employers are to solve what is becoming a major problem for them, they need to find ways of reducing labour turnover. For example in the retail and leisure sectors turnover is now over 50 per cent of staff per year. The solution lies in offering better career and reward structures to retain staff – something which many are clearly struggling to achieve.

Source: *HRMGuide.co.uk* (http://www.hrmguide.co.uk), 3 October 2001.

Activity 13:6

Why is it important to measure and forecast staff turnover?

'Soft' planning

HRM implies that planning has to go beyond the 'numbers game' into the softer areas of employee attitudes, behaviour and commitment. These aspects are critical to HR development, performance assessment and the management of change, which are considered in some depth in Chapters 20, 18 and 12, respectively. At this point, we can consider an outline of the process:

1 *Where are we now?* Information needs to be gathered through some form of human resource audit. This can be linked to a conventional SWOT analysis of the organization's human capital:

- *strengths* such as existing skills, individual expertise and unused talents
- *weaknesses*, including inadequate skills, talents that are missing in the workforce because they are too expensive, inflexible people and 'dead wood'
- *opportunities*, such as experience that can be developed in existing staff and talent that can be bought from the external job market
- *threats*, including the risk of talent being lost to competitors.

Table 13.3	In-house and external human resources

In-house resources	Out-sourcing
● Management control	● Legal contract
● Long-term people (can be developed; build experience; understand organization)	● Focus on paying only for work you need
● People are hassle	● No extra pay/commitment
● Contractual arrangements (talent expensive; overheads; large structure; hierarchy; support systems)	● Range of options, e.g. consultants (variable expertise; expensive) or contingent workers (usually ex-managers; best for operational work) or homeworkers (lower level/specialist; low overheads; supervision issues) or sub-contracting
● People are ambitious (require advancement; can go elsewhere – taking knowledge)	

2 *Where do we want to be?* Essentially, a clear strategic vision and a set of objectives.

3 *What do we need to do?* For example, following the logical sequence in Figure 13.1 decisions must be made on the use of in-house or external staff (see Table 13.3).

4 *Devise an action plan.* Some kind of resource planning is used by as many as 60 per cent of large organizations but it has to be conceded that it is often done poorly. Ideally, it should be linked to corporate strategy but corporate planners tend to ignore the human dimension.

Iles (2001, p.139) argues that the extension of human resource planning to include 'soft' issues such as motivation, commitment and culture has its dangers since it:

> ... tends to conflate HRP with HRM as a whole, and takes the specificity away from HRP as a discrete dimension of employee resourcing concerned with forecasting and assessing the extent to which the organization will meet its labour requirements (or perhaps increasingly its knowledge requirements, which may take the focus of HRP away from labour supply concerns to an interest in knowledge supply, and away from focusing on employees alone to emphasizing knowledge resources, chains and intermediaries).

Resourcing information

Effective in-house resourcing requires accurate and comprehensive information. Strategies and human resource plans must be translated into actual jobs and people found or developed to perform them. Some basic questions can be asked:

● What tasks are involved?
● What skills or competencies are required to do the work?
● Are they to be found within the organization?
● If not, should extra people be recruited?

Researching the job

Conventionally, the first question is answered by a job analysis (Key concept 13.5). Reminiscent of Taylor's techniques of 'scientific management', discussed in Part 1, it is a more-or-less detailed examination of the sub-tasks within an identified job. Jobs vary between the 'crystallized', such as manufacturing assembly where the job is precisely defined, to managerial and professional jobs in which individuals have considerable freedom to vary their work (McCormick and Ilgen, 1987, p.38). The degree of freedom is determined partly by technology or personal expertise and partly by the organization. Job analysis is geared towards tasks that are already being done in some form or can be easily extrapolated from current activities.

Job analysis techniques vary from the rudimentary to the sophisticated. The latter require specialist skills and are more commonly used in the USA where equal opportunities legislation is more stringent than in most countries. Long-regarded as a somewhat tedious aspect of the personnel or work study function, job analysis has been highlighted as a valuable technique in ensuring compliance with anti-discrimination legislation in the USA. Conversely, the move towards flexible working has turned many organizations elsewhere away from closely defining jobs.

Key concept 13:5

Job analysis   The process of job analysis is that of gathering and analysing job-related information. This includes details about tasks to be performed as part of a job and the personal qualities required to do them. Job analysis can provide information for a variety of purposes including determining training needs, development criteria, and appropriate pay and productivity improvements. For resourcing purposes, job analysis can generate job and personnel specifications.

The simplest forms of job analysis are conducted by observing or interviewing existing job-holders and supervisors. Alternatively, the same people can produce a self-report according to an agreed format. Information is also available from records, 'experts', training materials, equipment descriptions and manuals. A basic six-step approach could be conducted as follows (Smith and Robertson, 1993, p.15):

1 Make use of relevant existing documents such as training manuals.

2 Ask the line manager responsible about the main purposes of the job, the tasks involved and the links with other people.

3 Ask the same questions of job-holders, preferably backed by a detailed activity record over a week or two.

4 Where possible, sit in and observe job-holders at work – preferably on more than one day and at different times.

5 Try to do the job yourself. (This is not possible if specialist machinery or training is required.)

6 Write the job description.

The job-related information produced by job analysis can be arranged according to a number of headings (see Table 13.4) to ensure that all relevant details are covered.

This method is cheap and relatively easy. However, more complex methods may be justified, such as:

1 Questionnaires, generally purchased 'off-the-shelf' from specialist companies. Questionnaire techniques can provide a wealth of information but are often expensive and time-consuming. Examples include:

  ● McCormick's position analysis questionnaire (PAQ). Worldwide, probably the best known. It includes 150 scales with benchmarks covering a variety of jobs (McCormick and Ilgen, 1987, p.44).

  ● The work profiling system (WPS) is a modern, computerized and professionally packaged questionnaire system produced by Saville and Holdsworth. This is made

Table 13.4	A basic job analysis checklist
Heading	*Subject matter*
Job identification	Job title, department, grade or level.
Relationships	Name or title of immediate boss; number and type(s) of staff job holder is responsible for; links with other departments.
Outputs	What are the end-products or results of the job.
Activities	The behaviours or actions of the worker in achieving these outputs.
Performance	Required standards, agreed objectives.
Individual requirements	Abilities, skills, experience, temperament, training, languages, etc.
Working conditions	The physical and social surroundings of the job such as workspace, working hours, leave entitlement.
Equipment	Computers, machine tools, vehicles etc. used as an essential part of the job.
Other information	Promotion outlets, training available, transfer opportunities.

up of three overlapping tests, each of 300–400 items. The package is analysed by computer to give a detailed job description and a profile of the ideal recruit.

2 The critical incidents technique can provide a rich, qualitative perspective on a job. Incumbents are asked to describe a number of specific real-life incidents in which they participated. The most effective incidents are those that detail qualities required to do the job well.

Job analysis is not a value-free source of information. Employees are prone to:

● *Exaggeration*. Making jobs seem more demanding or complex than they really are.
● *Omission*. Humdrum tasks are forgotten in favour of less frequent but more interesting activities.

In contrast, information given by supervisors may lead to:

● *Understatement*. Jobs are portrayed as being easier and less complex than they are in reality.
● *Misunderstanding*. Frequently bosses do not know workers' jobs in any detail.

The various systems of job analysis also differ in the kind of information collected:

● *Job-oriented methods*. Detailed specifications of the tasks involved in specific jobs, for example 'spray chassis with anti-corrosive'. This approach produces accurate descriptions of individual tasks but it is difficult to extrapolate these to other jobs.
● *Worker-oriented methods*. More generalized accounts of required behaviour that can be compared with those employed in other jobs. Both the PAQ and WPS systems use this approach.
● *Competence-oriented methods*. Sometimes termed 'attribute' or 'trait'-oriented approaches. Highly descriptive in terms of the skills, experience and personal qualities needed. Require considerable skill on the part of the analyst in translating job content into competences. The 'HRM in reality' article describes the use of competence criteria in retailing.

Activity 13:7	When and why would you conduct a job analysis?

<table>
<tr><td>

HRM in reality

</td><td>

Resourcing retail management

The UK's largest retailers are among the most efficient in the world. They employ sophisticated management techniques in a number of areas including resourcing. Eight major groups – Marks & Spencer, Boots, CWS, the John Lewis Partnership, Kingfisher, Safeway, Sainsbury and Tesco – formed the Consortium of Retail Training Companies (Cortco). This organization promotes retailing as a career with opportunities in fields as diverse as computing, design, engineering, marketing, logistics, food technology, finance and surveying as well as store management.

Four core competencies have been identified that are expected from applicants:

- self-confidence and personal strength
- capacity for leadership and teamwork
- planning and organizational abilities
- analytical and problem-solving skills.

Evidence of leadership is held to be particularly important – for example being president of the student union, course representative or organizing a major social event.

Source: Neil Buckley, 'Retailing' in *Career Choice*, FT Surveys, Financial Times (1995).

Discussion questions: (a) Why do you think these four core competences are particularly important for retail organizations? (b) How would you rate yourself on these competences?

</td></tr>
</table>

The job description

Whatever the degree of sophistication, the common outcome of job analysis is the job definition or description. In the past, job descriptions have been used as quasi-legal documents, with employees declaring its contents to be a definitive list of the tasks they were expected to perform. Uncooperative employees would refuse to do anything that was not on the list and unions and employers would enter into trench warfare over any changes. Today, in a climate of change and flexibility, employers are reluctant to agree to a rigid list of tasks, preferring the employee to be ready to take on any required function. Job descriptions are out of date almost as soon as they are written and cannot be seen as documents to be adhered to rigidly.

Conventionally, job descriptions detail information such as:

- job titles
- summaries of main functions
- more detailed lists of activities within each job.

We will see later in the chapter that the 'flexible job description' has a significant role in modern selection strategies.

Researching people

Depending on the method used, job analysis provide a detailed description of the work to be performed but may not indicate the knowledge, skills or abilities needed to do so. The 'right person' model of resourcing advocates a personnel specification for this purpose.

Personnel specifications represent 'the demands of the job translated into human terms' (Arnold, Robertson and Cooper, 1991, p.95). Personnel specifications list 'essential' criteria which must be satisfied, and other criteria which rule out certain people from being able to do the job. Competence analyses and sophisticated forms of worker-oriented job analysis, such as WPS, generate personnel specifications as part of the package. The step from job to person specification never is entirely objective, requiring inference or intuition. In fact, it is a wonderful opportunity to introduce discriminatory criteria that rule out particular groups (Ross and Schneider, 1992, p.150). Personnel specifications may be no more than blueprints for clones, a matter that will be explored further later in this chapter.

Checklists such as Rodger's Seven-Point Plan (Rodger, 1952) have been commonly used for preparing personnel specifications. The desired qualities are categorized under the following headings:

1 physical qualities, including speech and appearance
2 attainments – qualifications, membership of professional associations
3 general intelligence
4 specific aptitudes, such as numerical ability
5 interests and hobbies
6 personality
7 domestic circumstances.

Slavish use of such a plan leads to evident danger. Items one and seven could easily cause discriminatory choices and require rigorous and critical examination. As we shall see in the next chapter, further information is obtained by using selection techniques including formal interviews, psychometric tests, assessment centres and biodata.

Activity 13:8	What is the difference between a job description and personnel specification?

Strategies for redundancy

Most of the discussion so far in this chapter has addressed human resource strategies relating to successful, growing companies. As we noted with reactor strategies, managers are also expected to implement redundancies and closures as a result of strategic decisions. Sir John Harvey Jones once observed that most companies refer to their workers as 'our greatest resource' but, in practice, do little to make them feel that way. We have observed in earlier chapters that the workforce is one group of stakeholders among many and within the free market model of capitalism they are probably the weakest. Presenting a caring image to staff and the consuming public may have advantages but greater attention is paid to more powerful voices when action is required. Directors and financiers ensure that their interests are satisfied first – well before those of the employees. This reflects a 'people as objects' rather than 'people as people' approach.

Handy (1993, p.222) argues that the concept of employees as assets is rarely treated with the same seriousness as football teams regard their players:

> ... in a football club, the players truthfully are human assets. They have a productive capacity, an earning power, that is potentially far greater than their cost. That cost has both a capital and a maintenance element. Rewards are proportionate to group performance, the asset has a finite life. There is no question of the organization assuming responsibility for the asset beyond the limits of its useful life, nor is there any stigma in the declaration that the asset has grown too old to be worth maintaining. The care and attention and protection given to key assets by

leading clubs is of a different order of people maintenance than any known in industry. Training and development become vital, for if you can increase the productive potential of the asset, in a short time you not only have greater productivity, but also an appreciated asset in terms of capital value.

He speculates whimsically that one day all businesses will require transfer fees for their best performers but concedes that this is unlikely.

Most job losses are due to age-old causes: business failures and cutting back on capacity in response to lower sales levels. Generally, the term 'redundancy' is losing its old stigma. In fact, a survey by Right Associates, in association with the *IPM* journal, found that out of 550 companies responding, some 46 per cent used the term as a cover for dismissal on the grounds of incompetence (*The Guardian*, 10 July 1992).

Planning for redundancies

There are some new features to job-cutting that are indicative of systematic changes in the way that human resource strategists view the process. Despite the emphasis on job security as a prerequisite for an effective human resource strategy, reality in free market economies demands planning for redundancies. These may result from company failure, rationalization or reduction in demand for products and people. There are several terms for the process of losing a job, all with different connotations and nuances: being made redundant, 'letting you go', 'getting the sack' and so on. One currently fashionable euphemism is 'deselection'. This implies that some form of systematic or thought-out procedure has been used to decide who will lose their jobs.

Hendry (1995, p.202) details a number of key issues:

● To what extent can over-staffing be corrected through natural wastage or redeployment?

● What agreements constrain the redundancy process. For example, 'last in, first out'?

● When should a redundancy programme be announced? How much consultation is required?

● How are redundancy entitlements to be calculated?

● Is it possible to have an entirely voluntary process? What restrictions should be placed on key staff leaving?

● Should the organization play an active role in outplacement?

● When will savings in salary and related items pay for the redundancy costs?

Large companies often employ portfolio management systems that view business units as growth, closure or disposal prospects. A classic, if simple, portfolio planning model is based on the Boston Consulting matrix shown in Figure 13.2. This offers a further typology for resourcing strategy:

1 *Stars*. Profitable business units with a dominant market position. Good prospects for employees with promotion opportunities and competitive salaries.

2 *Cash cows*. Mature companies with a high market share but low growth rate. They produce a cash surplus as investment costs are low but profits are good. Secure but unchallenging for employees – promotions are only possible when staff leave or retire. The focus may be on managing a steady decline, squeezing as much profit out of the enterprise as possible. Comfortable salaries until later stages when hard cost-cutting is required.

3 *Wild cats*. New ventures with low market share but high growth rates. A risky environment for employees. If lucky, the group will invest and there will be

| Figure 13.2 | Boston Consulting Group portfolio planning matrix |

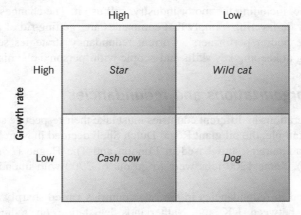

considerable career opportunities and rapid promotion – provided they work for potential stars. Employees are expected to be flexible and the work can be exciting and fast-moving. If unlucky, they face closure or disposal to another organization. This type closely parallels the 'prospector' strategy discussed earlier.

4 *Dogs*. Certain failures. Low growth, low share of market and no strategic potential. The only hope for employees is sale to a more positive owner. Essentially, these are 'reactor' companies.

Companies using portfolio planning are likely to take decisions on purely financial criteria without regard to the welfare of employees. HRM in such organizations tends to be tough-minded, favouring employees in profitable business units. Those in less successful areas are likely to be disposed of unceremoniously.

Redundancy and retention

Managers in charge of redundancy programmes typically focus on target numbers, with little or no thought about the quality of the staff leaving the business. Retention strategies for key staff are even more important during periods of redundancy:

> It is the quality of the staff … not the quantity, which is the essential factor in downsizing. As we all know from experience, where there are programmes of voluntary redundancy, it is often the most skilled employees who go first because they are more marketable outside. (Thomson and Mabey, 1994, p.11)

An obsession with numbers leads to a haemorrhaging of valuable skills: years of work on building a strong competence base can be undone in a matter of weeks.

The inspiration for many of the redundancy strategies of the last two decades can be attributed to Tom Peters, the US management guru. In *Thriving on Chaos* (1987, p.355), Peters argues that most large companies are hopelessly over-managed. Specifically, he considers that there are too many managers in too many layers – not that there are not enough Indians but there are certainly too many chiefs. This over-management leads to inefficiency. He quotes a study by McKinsey and Company into 38 advanced manufacturing technology systems. The study concludes that:

> The first step in accomplishing successful plant floor implementation of new manufacturing approaches is the clearing out of all the middle managers and support service layers that clog

the wheels of change. These salaried people are often the real barriers to productivity improvement, not the hourly workers on the floor.

'Last in, first out', was a common rule. Nowadays, however, redundancies are much less likely to happen on this basis. Sectors such as banking have virtually abandoned the principle, although some, including the motor industry, still use it. The changes advocated by Peters – specifically de-layering – imply that companies are 'getting rid of dead wood' or 'winnowing out the poorer performers'. Current redundancy strategies seem to follow Peters' lines, aiming at keeping key skills and people with 'personal chemistry'.

International organizations and redundancies

Businesses with operations in different countries must take their respective severance rules into account. For example, the oil giant Royal Dutch Shell decided in March 1995 to slim down corporate headquarters staff based in London and The Hague (*Financial Times*, 14 November 1995). Some 1200 jobs were to go out of 3900 with intended savings of £190 million a year.

The costs involved in redundancies in the two countries varied sharply, reflecting the marked difference between UK and Netherlands legislation on redundancies. The Netherlands was committed to the EU's Social Chapter and enforced significantly higher entitlements for both voluntary and compulsory redundancy. Accordingly redundancies in the two capitals had widely different consequences. Whereas staff taking voluntary redundancy in the UK were given a lump sum based on years worked and final salary, Netherlands staff received a further year's salary with a minimum of £60 000 ($90 000). People made redundant compulsorily in The Hague were entitled to 12 months' full salary, 85 per cent of eight months' salary, and 70 per cent of a further four months. This was equivalent to 21 months' salary in contrast to the six to nine months to which London staff were entitled.

Although Shell cannot be accused of doing so, other – less scrupulous – organizations may well concentrate their redundancies in the country where severance costs are lowest.

HRM in reality	**Tips for handling lay-offs**

Consulting firm Drake Beam Morin (DBM) warned employers against short-sighted workforce decisions and badly handled employee terminations. Lay-offs may be necessary at times, but they can have a negative impact on an organization's productivity levels and affect their ability to retain and attract talented employees in the future.

'From a company's standpoint, the decision to terminate a group of employees is fraught with potential legal, financial and public relations consequences,' said Thomas Silveri, president and chief executive officer of DBM. 'It is critical that managers communicate the news of lay-offs in a professional, legal and humane way in order to treat the departing employees with sensitivity and to maintain a respectful corporate image.'

DBM recently conducted a global study which revealed that one out of every ten individuals who lost their jobs involuntarily in 2000 told a colleague first of their job loss. So the manner in which employees are laid off can have a direct impact on the morale, commitment and retention of remaining staff.

DBM has experience in working with organizations undergoing restructuring over three decades and has come to know that there are right and wrong ways to handle

▶

a lay-off. We quote DBM's recommended five-step process for managers to ensure a successful termination:

1 *Prepare the materials*. Explain the rationale and prepare all severance information in writing (notification letter; salary continuation/severance period; benefits; outplacement, etc.).

2 *Prepare the message*. Write the script you will use during the meeting and the key information you will convey to remaining employees. Keep it short and to the point.

3 *Arrange the next steps*. Schedule meetings with your organization's human resources and outplacement professionals. Review what should be done with the departing employees' personal belongings and specify when the employees should leave the organization.

4 *Prepare yourself emotionally*. Don't assume personal responsibility for the termination. Remember it is a business decision based on business needs. Acknowledge your anxiety, prepare your approach and talk about your feelings with the human resource and outplacement professionals.

5 *Anticipate employee reactions*. There are typically five reactions to termination: anticipation, disbelief, escape, euphoria or violence. By acknowledging these various reactions and learning to recognize them, you will ensure that no matter what the reaction, you will be prepared to handle it in the best way.

DBM recommends that the following 'Dos and Don'ts' should be followed when conducting a termination meeting:

'Dos'

- do invite the employee in to sit down
- do get right to the point
- do explain the actions taken and the reasons
- do listen to the employee and wait for a response
- do restate the message if necessary
- do use your prepared notes/guidelines
- do clarify the separation date
- do give an overview of the separation package
- do explain the logistics for leaving the company
- do provide appropriate written materials
- do close the meeting within 15 minutes
- do escort the employee to the next appointment.

'Don'ts'

- don't say 'Good morning', 'Good to see you', or 'How are you?'
- don't engage in small talk
- don't use humour
- don't be apologetic
- don't defend, justify or argue

- don't threaten
- don't discuss other employees
- don't sympathize
- don't try to minimize the situation
- don't make promises
- don't personalize the anger
- don't use platitudes like 'I know how you feel,' or 'You will be just fine,' etc.

'Managers need to learn how to manage this process in a way that preserves the current productivity levels and the company's ability to attract top talent in the future,' said Silveri.

Source: *HRM Guide USA* (http://www.hrmguide.net/usa/), 2 February 2001.

Recently, critics have argued that the cutting process has gone too far: as we have noted before, de-layering or downsizing have led to 'dumbsizing' – a condition described by Hamer as 'corporate anorexia' (*Financial Times*, 22 November 1995). Organizations have slimmed down to the point where they are denuded of the skills needed to grasp new opportunities and remaining staff are demoralized and overworked.

Summary

Employee resourcing is a wider issue than recruitment and selection. In this chapter we discussed strategies for determining resourcing from either the internal or external employment markets. We considered a variety of models for resourcing strategies. We also discussed some approaches to human resource planning and the use made of information collected during the resourcing process. We reviewed the issue of retention, staff turnover and wastage in terms of measurement, forecasting and action. Some of the limitations of job descriptions and personnel specifications were identified. Finally, we considered redundancies as an aspect of resourcing strategy.

Further reading

Ahlrichs' (2000) *Competing for Talent: Key Recruitment and Retention Strategies for Becoming an Employer of Choice*, Davies-Black Publishing, examines the topic of employee resourcing in a practitioner context. Miles and Snow's typology is debated in Sonnenfeld, Peiperl and Kotter (1988). The planning process is discussed in Hendry (1995), *Human Resource Management: A Strategic Approach to Employment* (published by Butterworth-Heinemann) and Tyson (1995), *Human Resource Strategy*, published by Pitman. Rothwell ('Human resource planning' in J. Storey (ed.) 1995, *Human Resource Management: A Critical Text*) takes a fairly technical overview of the subject and also provides a useful attempt at explaining why HRP is a 'textbook' topic rather than widespread practice. Iles' article on 'Employee resourcing' in the second (2001) edition of the same book places human resource planning in its context. Dibble's *Keeping Your Valuable Employees: Retention Strategies for Your Organization's Most Important Resource*, published by John Wiley & Sons (1999), addresses retention and staff turnover in a comprehensive manner.

Review questions

1 How does employee resourcing relate to organizational strategy?

2 Consider an organization of your choice. (a) Does it obtain its human resource requirements from existing staff where possible? (b) At what levels are people brought in from the external employment market? (c) Would it be beneficial to change these practices?

3 Distinguish between 'hard' and 'soft' human resource planning. Which is of greatest value to modern businesses?

4 Are resourcing decisions normally taken on a short-term operational basis or at a strategic level?

5 Are long-term resourcing strategies realistic?

6 To what degree are resourcing strategies constrained by the nature of the external employment market?

7 How has the concept of flexibility affected resource decisions?

8 What is the relationship between resourcing strategy, HR planning and job analysis?

9 Is there merit in the claim that resourcing strategies should focus on employee retention rather than recruitment?

10 Are redundancies inevitably a matter of cynical expediency?

Problem for discussion and analysis

Pribake

Pribake manufactures biscuits ('cookies'). The company requires a steady stream of new product ideas, a small proportion of which will form a permanent element of its range. The board are considering a new appointment but cannot agree on the nature of the post. The production director feels that there is a need for an operational manager to look after chocolate-coated products. Conversely the marketing director wants an 'ideas' person to devise new products and enliven the company's range. The two cannot agree and the managing director has imposed a compromise. She has asked the human resource manager to find an individual who can meet both requirements. After some dispute they have produced a basic job definition along the following lines:

1 *Job title*. New Products Production Manager.

2 *Job summary*. Reporting at a high level with responsibility for development team and – possibly – maintenance staff. Overseeing manufacture of chocolate-coated range. Developing new product ideas and progressing through from trial to production stages.

3 *Desirable qualities*. General management skills. Able to manipulate technology effectively and realistically. If the successful candidate does not have direct knowledge of the actual machinery and techniques used in the company's factories, then he/she must have the ability to appraise systems and technology quickly.

▶

◀

After much discussion the HR manager has produced a list of additional competencies that seem to meet the requirements of the post:

- Creativity – to develop marketable products that can be produced at a reasonable cost.
- Experience of, or familiarity with market research techniques and able to formulate research programmes and evaluate results.
- Ability to design and test product manufacturing processes.
- Familiarity with the properties and possibilities of available materials: for example, what can and cannot be done with different kinds of chocolate.
- Familiarity with production line equipment including ability to appraise production line speeds, error factors and quality improvements. New products must not pose insurmountable problems for production machinery or workforce.
- Versatility – the fewest development problems arise when products can be manufactured on existing equipment and are made from simple and easily obtainable raw ingredients.
- Managerial skills to motivate and control the development team and ensure its effectiveness. A solitary genius will not work well in this environment.
- Ability to communicate persuasively with management and the workforce, especially when products are trialled and inevitable teething problems occur. Also to communicate with senior management and the marketing staff in promoting products within the company and in the market-place.

The directors have also agreed on the following criteria:

1 Academic qualifications: likely to be a graduate with a production or engineering speciality.
2 Ability: above average. Strong in mechanical aptitude. High on creativity scores. High on verbal fluency. A flair for design.
3 Personality: neither highly introverted nor extraverted. Good leadership and persuasion skills.
4 Experience: there are significant elements of the job that seem to demand familiarity with this particular industry.

Discussion: What deficiencies are apparent in the job description, competence list and additional selection criteria? How would you conduct the recruitment and selection exercise for this vacancy? What is the likelihood of finding a suitable candidate?

PART 5

The employee resourcing process

This part of the book addresses one of the core aspects of human resource practice: recruitment and selection. These areas of employee resourcing are extensively covered in critical academic literature and prescriptive ('how to') books for people involved in hiring or being hired. Our discussion attempts to strike a balance between these two approaches, allowing you to gain an understanding of the wide range of practical techniques in use as well as an appreciation of some of the weaknesses and inconsistencies in the methodology and underlying theory.

The chapters in Part 5 address some key issues, including:

- Why are some recruitment channels more popular than others?
- What are the most cost-effective recruitment and selection methods?
- How is candidate information collected?
- What use is made of that information?
- Are interviews an effective method of determining the 'best' candidates?
- How prevalent are more sophisticated or non-traditional selection techniques such as psychometric tests, biodata and assessment centres?
- How valid are these selection techniques?

14

Recruitment and preliminary candidate information

Objectives

The purpose of this chapter is to:

- Discuss the meaning and significance of recruitment in its organizational context.
- Provide a typology of recruitment strategies.
- Critically review preliminary information-gathering techniques.
- Discuss the merits of references and biodata.

Recruitment as a textbook subject

Matching people and jobs

Selectors and strategies

Marketing jobs

Informal recruiting

Web-based recruitment

Formal recruiting

Targeting and diversity

Researching candidates

Applications

Qualifications

Biodata

References

Summary

Further reading

Review questions

Problems for discussion and analysis

Recruitment as a textbook subject

In Chapter 13 we discussed the 'why' of resourcing, evaluating strategies and plans that guide the process. We considered also the initial information gathering from job analysis and the – sometimes unwise – strategies employed by selectors. This chapter and the next follow on with an examination of the operational elements of resourcing, commonly termed recruitment and selection.

Recruitment and selection are major issues for human resource specialists. Additionally, HRM and other management literature puts great emphasis on the process of selecting and socializing new recruits (Guest, 1992; Storey, 1989). There is no shortage of material on these topics and, together with performance assessment, they are critical elements of effective people management. Not surprisingly, therefore, these aspects of employee resourcing have attracted a great deal of attention from human resource practitioners and occupational psychologists. But, as Murphy (1994, p.58) observes: 'The very substantial volume of research in the areas of selection and appraisal is both a blessing and a curse.'

Textbooks in the personnel management tradition devote considerable space to *how* recruitment and selection are best conducted. As we will see in Chapter 15, the topic range has a well-rehearsed familiarity because selection methods are regarded as basic tools for personnel managers. Indeed, the underlying 'best practice' model has achieved the status of holy writ in certain quarters, with any deviation regarded as heresy.

Many recent HRM texts have followed this line. Others, particularly those written by commentators with a firmly academic background, have gone to the opposite extreme, sniffily avoiding discussion of mere 'tools'. Instead the subject is skirted or else discussed at a high – and somewhat unreal – socio-political level. We can take our choice, it seems, between superficial accounts of selection techniques and incomprehensible debates about post-modernist resourcing. Neither approach seems satisfactory.

There is a pronounced tendency for textbook accounts to be prescriptive, dealing with the subject in a 'do it like this' fashion, almost invariably using an underlying 'right person for the job' resourcing model. However, since the early 1990s this approach has been challenged (Sparrow, 1994, p.15; Iles and Salaman, 1995, p.203). For example, Iles and Salaman (1995, p.203) argue that: 'The limitation of the psychological and personnel-driven approaches to selection is that they are entirely, if understandably, concerned with improving the efficiency of the processes, and not with understanding their wider provenance and significance.' And again (Iles, 2001, p.134): '... despite the need for a fuller understanding of these processes, the bulk of existing social science and HR literature is concerned primarily and solely with assessing the efficiency of these processes, often in rather descriptive, prescriptive and atheoretical ways.'

As we noted in the last chapter, we cannot discuss how recruitment and selection take place without asking why certain techniques are used in preference to others. Iles (2001) sees much deeper consequences, meaning and significance in the exercise and justification of recruitment and selection processes. Within the HRM paradigm, they are not simply mechanisms for filling vacancies. Recruitment and redundancy can be viewed as key 'push' and 'pull' levers for organizational change. Recruitment and selection allow management to determine and gradually modify the behavioural characteristics and competencies of the workforce. The fashion for teamworking, for example, has focused on people with a preference for working with others as opposed to the individualist 'stars' preferred by recruiters in the 1980s. Attention has switched from rigid lists of skills and abilities to broader-based competencies. In general, as we noted in Chapter 13, there is a greater regard for personal flexibility and adaptability: a reorientation from present to future suitability.

Iles (2001) contends that the issue of resourcing is not 'simply, or even perhaps primarily, one of efficiency or rationality but of power: the capacity of, and the forms of knowledge and associated technologies through which organizations identify, define and assess individuals against structures of necessary competences or similar behavioural frameworks.'

Activity 14:1	Why is employee resourcing more than a matter of filling jobs?

Matching people and jobs

Focusing on in-house resourcing, how can we make the best use of people? In practice, it is rarely possible to match perfectly the requirements of an individual job with the skills and abilities of the people available. Square pegs in round holes are not only bad for the organization. Wrongly placed workers are often unhappy and bored, or anxious about being out of their depth. In line with the three basic recruitment strategies outlined in Table 14.1, any mismatch between person and job can be resolved in one of the following ways (Drenth and Algera, 1987):

- Select the best qualified person for the job ('right person' approach).
- Change job characteristics to fit the abilities of the people employed ('culture-fit' model).
- Train people to perform more effectively (flexible person approach).

An organization may choose any one or a combination of these methods. However, all depend on the ability to identify and measure the characteristics necessary for successful job performance. At first sight this seems simple and obvious but a close examination reveals how complex it can be. People can perform a particular job successfully for varied and sometimes contrasting reasons. For example, a good manager may be personally well-organized and able to clear mountains of paperwork quickly. Another manager may deal with similar tasks equally efficiently through skilful delegation. As such, it is the *totality of effectiveness* of the individual that matters rather than specific skills and abilities. Effectiveness also depends on context. Most jobs require an individual to work within a team where required skills or qualities can be spread between its members. In such a case it may not be necessary for every team member to possess all qualities needed for effective performance.

Table 14.1	Recruitment strategies			
	Approach	Objective	Organization	HR emphasis
	1 *Suitability* – right person for the job	Get the job done	Traditional Hierarchical Fixed job categories	Job analysis HR planning Selection
	2 *Malleability* – fit the culture	Fit in with today's organization	Small core Strong culture Variable periphery	Appraisal Job training
	3 *Flexibility* – employee for tomorrow	Build a competitive organization	Flexible Lean	Performance Skills training Development

Companies may be forced to review their strategies to take account of new market conditions or technological changes. After several years of sustained growth the British supermarket group Sainsbury's faced competition from discounters. With 120 000 employees and a salary bill of over £1 billion a year, the company decided to examine its human resource requirements. With the maxim of 'retail is detail' Sainsbury's had achieved a reputation for high quality by ensuring that goods and procedures were extensively checked by staff. Management consultants were brought in to investigate the use of information technology in eliminating clerical and management tasks. Head office functions were subjected to a 'business process re-engineering review'. Automatic reordering linked to electronic point of sale (EPOS) terminals eliminated the need for several management layers in stores and offices. This programme produced a need to reduce staff numbers overall, changed the roles of remaining staff and required a major revision in human resource planning.

The right person?

Resourcing strategies should maintain the required number and quality of staff within an organization. They should also ensure suitability for its future development. There are two underlying and apparently contradictory approaches in common use (Haire, 1959). The first methodology emphasizes the right (or best) person for the job. The individual is the variable element in the search; the job is fixed. This approach is associated with traditional Western personnel management. People are sought with appropriate abilities and experience to perform the job with minimal training. It implies that individual jobs are relatively long term and unchanging and that people can be 'bought in 'at any stage in their careers. Vacancies are filled from the internal or external employment market. When the job is no longer required, the incumbent is disposed of.

This model is conventionally described as 'best practice' in the UK and other free market countries. Accordingly, most personnel or human resource management textbooks traditionally outline a 'prescriptive approach to recruitment based on a systematic analysis of the requirements of an individual job' (Wright and Storey, 1994, p.192). Almost invariably the account focuses on a series of selection techniques with limited discussion of the logic behind the resourcing process. There is rarely a suggestion that any other approach may be worth considering, although there may be references to the exotic practices of the Japanese in the obligatory 'international' section. Wright and Storey also rightly point out that 'best practice' only takes place in the largest organizations. Small and medium-sized enterprises generally recruit in an informal manner and rarely use sophisticated selection methods.

The 'right person' approach attempts to be 'objective'. It requires clear answers to questions such as:

● Is there a job to fill?

● If so, what tasks and responsibilities are involved?

● What qualities, skills or experience are required to perform the tasks?

● What process will identify these criteria best?

In essence, it is an attempt to find a seven-sided object to fit a seven-sided hole. It is a *discrimination* rather than a selection process: a matching technique that attempts to pin down the 'right' or 'best' applicant. By definition it excludes those people who are believed not to fit – a view of people as objects (Townley, 1994, p.94). Townley perceives an underlying belief that 'employees who are carefully and appropriately matched to their jobs are satisfied and productive'. Matching involves generating a taxonomy of qualities and skills (criteria) which are believed to be essential or desirable – including qualifications and experience. In turn a matrix is constructed that ranks candidates in relation to the job criteria and imposes a decision point at which some people are accepted and others rejected. In the simplest case, this process can take place inside a selector's head. In the most complex, it involves elaborate selection techniques, multiple dimensions and rating scales and requires a computer to calculate the resulting matrix. The 'right person' approach functions well when:

- it is possible to define a job tightly
- the job is discrete and separable from other functions
- the job is best done by an individual with a specific range of skills.

Frequently, however, these criteria do not apply and jobs are identified for less rational reasons such as:

- we have *always* had a 'major accounts manager'
- department 'x' *must* handle the task
- people *like* it done in a particular way.

The 'right person' model is geared to static, self-satisfied organizations. It meets the needs of the 'job box' model of organizational structure discussed in Chapter 7, where people come and go but the job continues indefinitely. It leads to positions being offered to people who match traditional criteria – the kind of people we have always had. It closes the appointments process to people who traditionally have been unsuccessful. In terms of equal opportunities this approach continues to disadvantage people from 'different' backgrounds and alternative outlooks. In essence it is a cloning process: resourcing a firm with more of the same people (see Key concept 14.1). It eliminates any opportunity for the organization to be creative or experimental.

Key concept 14:1

Cloning Cloning, or 'elective homogeneity' is the tendency for selectors to pick people like themselves, thereby reducing the breadth of skills and personalities in an organization. Simply matching the set of characteristics possessed by previous successful post holders, it is a safe, conservative way to fill jobs. As a low-risk, but backward-looking approach, it is unlikely to meet the future needs of the organization.

Fit with the organization

The second approach described by Haire focuses on fitting the person to the organization. Jobs are changed and reshaped to make the best use of individuals' skills within the organization. People are permanent but jobs can be varied. If more employees are required, a search is made for individuals who appear to have the personal qualities necessary to 'fit in' with the organization's culture. Personality is more important than technical skills in this context.

HRM in reality

Cultural fit and web-based recruiting

Around 90 per cent of large US businesses use the web in some form for recruiting, making access to the application process easier for job-seekers and cutting the time employers take to fill jobs. Web-based recruiting can also reduce recruitment costs

▶

by as much as 95 per cent compared to more traditional methods. But are these businesses attracting applicants who fit their company cultures?

'Companies are not only interested in skills and abilities; they want to know if an applicant will fit in their culture,' said Raymond A. Noe, Robert and Anne Hoyt Designated Professor of Management at The Ohio State University's Fisher College of Business. Raymond Noe argues that a clearly defined culture can 'help with employee commitment, allow the employees to understand what the company stands for, and provide growth opportunities for those who match well.' It follows that enabling potential recruits to understand a company's culture should be a key part of its efforts to attract and retain high performers.

A recent study by Dineen, Ash and Noe, published in the August 2002 issue of the *Journal of Applied Psychology* found that feedback concerning cultural fit can affect a web-based applicant's attraction to an organization. Noe, Dineen and Ash conducted an experiment using a fictitious company website to examine person–organization fit and how feedback influenced job-seekers. Applicants completed a preliminary screening regarding their values preferences and were then given feedback about their likely fit with the organization's culture. Perhaps not surprisingly, those who did not seem to have a good match were less attracted to the company. But the results were more complex when looked at in detail.

As part of the study, student participants were asked to review background information about the business, what it did and how it had grown. They completed a 'tool' designed to collect their values preferences and then received random, predetermined feedback about their fit with the business. Participants then viewed values information about the organization. Finally they were asked if they were interested in and attracted to the company.

Findings

- Feedback from a preliminary cultural screening can have an influence on the participant's level of attraction to the organization. But study participants did not just rely on this feedback. Instead, they acted as 'somewhat discerning consumers of the feedback, evaluating their fit based on their inferences about material on the website, as well as integrating the feedback into their assessment of fit.'

- The self-esteem of individual participants played a role in how the feedback was received. Students with high self-esteem were more likely to trust their own judgment above a low cultural fit score. Random test scores more easily swayed participants with low self-esteem even if they were a good match.

- Organizations can influence potential applicants by providing feedback about their cultural fit. The interactive capability of web-based recruitment makes this a significant feature compared to other forms of recruitment such as newspaper and recruitment brochures.

According to the authors, the research findings point to significant benefits of web-based recruiting that incorporates an organizational fit component, providing a win-win situation for both the job-seeker and the organization. 'Specifically, it helps job-seekers more accurately decide up front whether or not they would be a good fit with a company. If they decide they would not be a good fit, they can elect to forgo the application process, saving themselves and the organization time and administrative resources.' They conclude:

- When jobs are plentiful, the culture fit tool allows job-seekers to 'deselect' themselves, by reducing their options to those companies they believe would match well with their values.

- When the job market is less favorable to job-seekers and businesses are swamped with applications, the inclusion of a culture fit tool can help to narrow applicant pools by giving job-seekers with a poor match the encouragement to opt out of the application process.

- This type of organizational feedback could help companies of various sizes, including the smaller ones.

While large organizations may have very public cultures, 'job-seekers don't have a preconceived notion of fit with smaller organizations,' the authors say. Including the feedback tool in their web-based application process may help smaller organizations publicize their culture. That, in turn, would help job-seekers make better choices about pursuing employment with small companies.

The researchers suggest future areas of study, including the financial outcomes of using tailored feedback and evaluating the applicant pool before and after implementation of a cultural fit assessment tool.

The use of web technology has just begun to reshape the recruiting process for companies, they say. The person–organizational culture fit tool has the potential to make job-seekers more savvy while also providing a smaller, 'better fitting' applicant pool for organizations. 'There is so much traffic on the internet, people need ways to filter through all the information. The culture fit tool can serve as an accurate shortcut that benefits both organizations and job-seekers.'

Points to consider when developing a web-based cultural fit tool

1 Consult with professionals in organizational culture measurement and use established methods to help assure that you are accurately measuring the nature of your company's culture and providing accurate feedback to job-seekers.

2 Design your culture fit feedback tool so that it is anonymous, and let job-seekers know this up front. Otherwise, job-seekers may attempt to put their 'best foot forward' and not gain an accurate assessment of their culture fit.

3 Provide the culture fit tool before describing the culture of the organization to avoid influencing the job-seekers' responses.

Source: *HRM Guide USA* (http://www.hrmguide.net/usa/), 24 September 2002.

This method predominates in the traditional large Japanese company. The emphasis is on matching individuals to organizational culture rather than to organizational structure. Recruitment focuses on young people who can be socialized into the company's way of working. Recently Western managers have taken an interest in this approach. It has been justified in terms of attracting creative and innovative employees. However, there is a distinction between creative and plastic minds. In reality, it is a means of hiring more potential clones who have the further 'advantages' of being young, cheap and easy to manage.

Flexibility

A third, more demanding, approach can provide a significant competitive advantage for organizations: recruiting 'flexible employees', prepared for future change and able to contribute rather than conform. Rather than aiming for rigid skills and ability profiles or malleable and gullible personalities, recruit people who are versatile and adaptable. This reflects a long-term strategy, geared towards realizing talent for tomorrow's requirements and not simply meeting current needs or filling the organization with compliant clones. The emphasis is on diversity. Organizations should identify a range of individuals required for the future – including 'mavericks to buck the system' and not just 'conformist clones' (Armstrong, 1992, p.135). They will require training and development; they will not be docile and managing them may be difficult; but their potential is massively greater than any clone.

Taking this approach, some of the rhetoric of HRM must become reality. Instead of viewing resourcing as a matter of recruiting individuals, it is seen as a means of adding to the total pool of competencies in an organization's human capital (Sparrow, 1994, p.13). There is a genuine need for integration and coordination between resourcing strategies and people management processes such as assessment, development and reward. Creative people must be freed from overbearing control. They cannot be managed through compliance: commitment is the only 'glue' which can bind individual talents and innovation to organizational objectives. Fine words have to be translated into sincere action.

All options, including subcontracting, must be considered carefully before hiring new people. This form of flexibility offers long-term benefits but needs people ready for new demands and hence a need for a detailed knowledge of individual jobs, people's capabilities and the range of work to be performed now and in the future.

| Activity 14:2 | What do you see as the main advantages and disadvantages of the 'right person', 'culture fit' and 'flexibility' models of recruitment? |

| HRM in reality | **Job-hoppers worry potential employers** |

There are signs that potential employers are becoming cautious about hiring job-hoppers – those with a pattern of changing jobs every year or so.

Jerry Weinger, chairman of Bernard Haldane Associates, says that job-seekers need to be able to demonstrate a strong record of success in the down economy. Weinger points to a number of signals that are especially worrying to potential employers, including resumés listing positions that indicate backwards career steps, repeated lateral moves or changes that look like a digression.

'Our booming economy enticed many people into job-hopping,' says Weinger. 'But as the job market tightens, they will be forced to justify the high turnover on their resumés.' Weinger advises job-seekers to look for signs of concern from the interviewer. For example, watch out for questions such as: 'Why didn't you pursue that project for longer?' or 'I see you earned your degree in a different field; why didn't you go into that?'

Weinger lists the following tips:

● Put together an accomplishment-oriented resumé with your qualifications highlighted on the first page. Save your work history for the second page.

● Don't list positions older than 10–15 years – they are out of date.

● Short assignments with various companies should be listed under one job title such as 'consultant' or 'programmer'. Then give dates for the entire time you worked in that capacity.

- Plan to discuss the actual dates you spent at each company during the interview. Explaining turnover is easier in person than on paper, if you are mentally prepared to address the issue.

- Avoid stating that you left jobs for 'a better opportunity.' Instead demonstrate that the changes were strategic moves to acquire new skills and experiences.

- Prepare 30-second examples of how experience in one area led to success in another.

- Communicate why you expect to stay in your next position for an extended period of time.

- Always be honest about your career history, but don't volunteer damaging information.

Source: *HRM Guide USA* (http://www.hrmguide.net/usa/), 29 March 2001.

Discussion question: How are job-hoppers regarded by prospective employers?

Selectors and strategies

The 'right person' approach is entirely concerned with the individual, whereas the 'cultural fit' model is consistent with a focus on teamworking. In practice, the models are easily confused with each other and many selectors apply a mixture of both. Frequently, selectors believe they are using 'best practice' to find the person who meets the specified criteria. In fact, the person chosen is the one whose face fits. All too often resourcing emphasizes the selection of people who fit existing culture and practice at the expense of future needs.

Why does this occur? Employee resourcing involves risk and uncertainty. Above all, assessors want to avoid the consequences of picking the 'wrong' person. This may be for the valid reason that an unsuitable person will not perform to required standards. However, selectors are also aware of the consequences of an unfortunate choice rebounding directly on themselves (and their reputations). This encourages selectors to take 'safe' decisions minimizing risk of error. The individual clearly identified as a 'good bloke' by the organization and its senior managers becomes an attractive choice (Townley, 1989).

The in-breeding found at higher levels of management has been described as 'organizational dry rot' (Smith, 1991, p.29). Poverty of ideas, stultified thinking and blinkered behaviour can be due to a narrow range of experience. It is imperative, therefore, that resourcing activities should increase the breadth of experience within an organization. To do this the interests of the organization should be divorced from those of any specific stakeholders, including those of its senior managers. However, resourcing costs money directly (e.g. advertising) and indirectly (the time occupied by comparatively well-paid people). As a consequence many organizations avoid the hassle and expense by taking a casual approach to one of the most critical aspects of people management.

HRM in reality

Virtual career fair

The Petroleum Services Association of Canada (PSAC) has launched what is described as 'a unique Virtual Career Fair on the internet' in conjunction with Human Resources Development Canada (HRDC). To help deal with a growing

▶

labour shortage, the new website (www.careersinoilandgas.com) will provide information on career opportunities in service, supply and manufacturing sectors of the upstream oil and gas industry.

Roger Soucy, president of PSAC, said: 'We're proud of this breakthrough site. We've taken everything great about a career fair for students and put it onto our Virtual Career Fair site. Anyone can log on and explore upstream oil and gas industry jobs in amazing detail.' PSAC represents some 240 companies working on oil and gas exploration and production. They employ more than 28 000 Canadians and account for 80 per cent of revenue in the sector. The new site took a year to plan and was launched in the Career Centre at Crescent Heights High School, Calgary, Alberta.

Students and others can access online videos, day-in-the life occupational profiles, job descriptions, scheduled interactive chats, training and mentoring information, links and more. 'We believe it's the first of its kind and we're excited about what it will do for students planning their careers,' said Elizabeth Aquin, Manager of Operations at PSAC. 'All our focus group testing showed that students are serious about their futures and [the site] will make it so much easier for them to make informed decisions.'

Source: *HRM Guide Canada* (http://www.hrmguide.net/canada/), 9 May 2001.

Marketing jobs

Following on from our discussion in Chapter 13, if resourcing strategy and planning have identified the need for new or additional work to be performed in-house, it is obviously necessary to make potential applicants aware of any vacancy. Essentially, this is a marketing process conventionally termed 'recruitment' which Lewis (1985, p.29) defines as: 'the activity that generates a pool of applicants, who have the desire to be employed by an organization, from which those suitable can be selected.'

Potential candidates may come from an internal trawl of the organization, or from the external job market. The latter are reached through channels such as recruitment advertising, employment agencies, professional associations or word of mouth. We saw in Chapter 9 that organizations with a strong culture are likely to seek malleable new employees at school-leaving or graduate levels. More senior jobs are filled from the internal job market. When companies look for the 'right person', however, detailed personnel specifications may rule out internal candidates. In each case, the recruitment phase is critical because it determines the range of choice available to the selectors: 'The more effectively this stage is carried out the less important the actual selection of candidates becomes: if a firm can attract 20 high flyers for a job it hardly matters whether they choose amongst these high flyers with a pin, an interview or tests' (Smith, Gregg and Andrews, 1989, p.24).

Internal recruitment marketing can take place by word of mouth, staff notices, newsletters and vacancy journals. Recruiting may be on a 'one-off' basis or linked to a development programme as discussed in Chapter 20. External recruitment marketing can include media advertisements, various public and private employment agencies and headhunting. The role of the state varies, with some countries such as Italy requiring official notification to state employment agencies. As with other marketing campaigns the selection of appropriate channels, creativity of vacancy presentation and size of budget will determine success.

| HRM in reality | **Billboard recruitment** |

A Toronto pharmaceutical company is targeting their competitors' employees on their way to work in an attempt to fill 400 job openings. The Apotex Group campaign uses billboards across the Greater Toronto Area which are strategically placed near their competitors' facilities.

The billboard campaign strategy is simple, says Ron Davidson, vice-president human resources:

> We will use every means at our disposal, including billboards to communicate our job openings directly in locations where we know potential candidates can see them. We believe that this is a very unique way to find employees. We have a multi-million dollar expansion, and without the people, we can't grow our business.

The majority of the jobs are for technical professionals required to work in manufacturing and R&D areas at some of Apotex Group's 14 facilities across Toronto. The Apotex Group is the largest Canadian-owned pharmaceutical company. It employs nearly 5000 people and has an R&D budget of C$1 billion over the next ten years.

Having taken on 1000 employees over the last 12 months and 2000 over three years, Apotex is finding it more and more difficult to find qualified candidates.

Source: *HRM Guide Canada* (http://www.hrmguide.net/canada/), 12 September 2002.

Informal recruiting

Cultural factors are important in determining the orientation between internal and external job markets. They also influence the nature of recruitment. Papalexandris (1991) compared multinational corporations operating in Greece and Greek-owned companies. She found that Greek employers preferred to recruit from among relatives and friends of the owners or existing employees. Advertisements and agencies were used only when this failed to produce suitable candidates. Greek employers paid more attention to recommendations and previous experience than to qualifications such as degrees. In contrast, foreign-owned companies followed 'best practice' and focused on younger, inexperienced graduates attracted through agencies and advertisements. Acknowledging the usefulness of personal acquaintance and experience in providing information for the selection process, Papalexandris considers that Greek firms risk nepotism and depriving themselves of competent younger staff.

Formalized introduction schemes along similar lines occur in other countries, serving to perpetuate recruitment from pools of like-minded people. However, they have the benefit of supplying candidates who have a more realistic view of the organization, compared with people attracted by recruitment advertising. The former have gained their knowledge from the informal network, the latter from PR information. As a result, word-of-mouth applicants are likely to stay longer and be more suitable than recruits obtained by advertising. Word of mouth is discriminatory since it restricts applications to established communities and excludes recently arrived minority groups who have not had time to become part of informal networks (Smith, 1991, p.31). Inevitably, people will recommend others from their own in-group even if they have no intention of discriminating.

Informal recruitment is common. More widely, Table 14.2 shows findings of a study conducted by the Chartered Institute of Personnel and Development in the UK in 1999 and 2000.

Table 14.2	Recruitment methods		
		Per cent	
Recruitment method		2000	1999
Ads in specialist/trade press		86	87
Local newspaper ads		81	87
National newspaper ads		68	75
Job centre/employment services		68	62
Employment agencies		66	61
Speculative applications		56	65
Word of mouth		53	53
Internet		47	36
Links with education		44	50
Headhunters		29	33
Local radio ads		12	11

At a senior level, headhunting has become a common, if not predominant, method of recruitment. Otherwise known as executive search, consultancies are used to locate supposedly 'outstanding' people. The marked absence of women and ethnic minorities in senior positions reveals this to be a further mechanism for cloning.

Activity 14:3

Review the advantages and disadvantages of the recruitment marketing channels we have considered so far.

HRM in reality

Any jobs going for astronauts?

Superhero, trapeze artist, goddess, astronaut and slave are just some of jobs people have looked for online, according to an analysis of 6 million career searches made on Fish4jobs during the past month. 'The vast majority of searches done on our site every month are serious ones,' says Fish4jobs publisher Ian Sprackling. However, he continues:

A lot of workers seem to fantasize about a completely new career as a 'superhero' for example, or hope to see a position open as an 'astronaut'. Though we unfortunately can't claim to hold current vacancies for 'billionaires', we do have an enormous range of dream jobs available. For example, the people who thought it would be a laugh to type in 'tree surgeon', 'tarot card reader', 'wine taster' and 'lap dancer' will have been in for a surprise as positions for all four have been advertised on the Fish4jobs website over the past month!

The research found that more than 1000 people could not spell common job titles correctly, including 15 different misspellings for 'secretary':

sercretary

secrretary

secetary

sectary

sacretery

sacratary

scretary

secretie

secraterie

secritarie

secreatarie

secutery

secitery

secreatire

secrectree.

Apart from 110 people spelling 'secretary' wrongly, 51 people replaced reception-ist with anything from 'recepshionist' to 'receiptionist'. Manager became 'meneger', 'managar' and 'manger' for 34 applicants.

According to Ian Sprackling:

Though it's easy to miss out the odd letter here or there when doing a search on a PC, attention to detail is one of the most important things employers look for. Therefore let's hope that the person wanting to become a 'manger' hasn't made the same mistake on his/her CV. However, the people who got it completely wrong and decided they want to become a 'recepshionists' or 'secreties' should maybe consider a career change!

Top ten searches for jobs that don't exist comprised:

1 mover and shaker

2 billionaire

3 superhero

4 nun

5 busy bee

6 slave

7 astronaut

8 layabout

9 male porn star

10 trapeze artist.

Top ten unusual searches – where there have been vacancies on Fish4jobs – comprised:

1 lap dancer (posted for a club in Blackpool)

2 'car jockey' (an excusive hotel in Scotland wanted 'car jockeys' to park guests' cars)

3 tarot card reader (two vacancies available, one working from a call centre)

4 trainee forensic psychiatrist (postgraduate post in Newcastle)

5 tree surgeon (several vacancies)

◄

6 footwear designer (design company in West Yorkshire)

7 drag racer (company in Basingstoke has sought professional drag car drivers)

8 rectal surgeon (a vacancy was posted for a health professional specializing in 'colo-rectal surgery'!)

9 reporter for the local paper (several positions nationwide)

10 lollipop lady (over the summer, several councils were seeking lollipop ladies or men).

Source: *HRMGuide.co.uk* (http://www.hrmguide.co.uk), 5 September 2001.

Web-based recruitment

A survey commissioned by Workthing.com, an employment network owned by the Guardian Media Group, investigated recruitment and the internet in the UK in a number of stages. The *Online Recruitment and Employment Survey (Spring 2000)*, conducted by independent research consultancy, BMRB, was based on interviews with over 3000 internet users. The survey objective was to ascertain the size and growth potential of the online job market and provide a snapshot of current and potential users. The research showed that:

- Job-seeking online was a rapidly growing mainstream market.
- Some 31 per cent of internet users had looked at job opportunities online in the previous six months, amounting to 4 million people in the UK. This compared with 21 per cent who bank online.
- Of those who applied online, 400 000 had been interviewed and 170 000 had been offered jobs.
- Around 50 per cent of internet users who had never visited a recruitment site were likely to do so the next time they looked for a job – implying that the market could grow by an estimated 4 million new users.
- Some 3 million internet users currently in work were likely to change jobs in the next six months.

The more individuals use the internet, the more likely they are to look for a job online.

Online job-hunters want more than just a job

The survey found online job-seekers to be very demanding – requiring a wealth of advice aimed at improving their career prospects including employment news, industry reports, career advice, discussion forums, CV tips and salary surveys. Most importantly job-seekers are concerned with confidentiality – only one-in-eight currently upload CVs. The survey authors identified eight main types of use, based on attitudes towards recruitment, the internet and work, which they entitled: Clock Watching Clickers, Nervous Netty, Work Steady Eddies, Stiff Upper Clicks, Super Surfers, Mouse Potatoes, Digital Man and Net Workers. For example:

- *Work Steady Eddie*. The oldest of all the groups and most likely to be married and have a mortgage. A third of this group have not changed employer for over 10 years. Work Steady Eddie believes that the internet can lack personality, and is looking for a 'human face' from sites. In terms of recruitment he is worried about confidentiality and security on the internet, and is looking for lots of ongoing work support in the form of careers advice.

- *Digital Man.* The most likely of all groups to access the internet from work. His use of the internet is driven by business and personal productivity. He is unlikely to use the internet for entertainment or shopping. Digital man is a confident job-changer and eagerly seeks out the ammunition he needs, such as salary surveys and industry news.

Six months after the initial report, a follow-up by BMRB found that:

- Around 5.4 million people – 38 per cent of UK internet users – had searched for jobs online in the previous six months (1.4 million more than six months before).
- Some 400 000 people had already found jobs through the internet.
- There were 2 million people now expecting to find their next job through this medium.
- One-in-five online job-seekers had uploaded their CV onto a recruitment site, compared with one-in-eight six months previously.
- Some 76 per cent of online job-seekers wanted employment news or industry-specific news as well as jobs from recruitment websites.

Generally, research into online recruitment has judged the success rate of online job postings by the number of online applications completed. But the latest ORES data shows that only 20 per cent of job-seekers apply by filling in the form online – four times as many apply by other methods such as postal applications, telephone calls or other online methods such as e-mailing the contact at the employer.

By June of 2001 results showed strong growth with 6.3 million internet users who have used an online recruitment site – a growth rate of over 50 per cent in the last 12 months. When asked about the advantages of the internet, respondents rated it above trade magazines, recruitment consultants and newspapers in terms of use, convenience, selection of jobs and the ability to remain anonymous. The survey found online recruitment to be the second most popular method through which people think that they will find their next job, behind only word of mouth, and ahead of national newspapers, local newspapers, trade magazines and recruitment consultants.

| **HRM in reality** | **Switch to online graduate recruitment** |

More and more of Australia's largest employers are moving to online graduate recruitment and away from slow and costly 'traditional' methods. This reflects market demand as recent surveys show that as many as 94 per cent of undergraduate and MBA job-seekers visit corporate websites to gather information and evaluate prospects before they make their applications.

Shell, Orica, Arthur Andersen, Ford Australia, MIM Holdings, Cap Gemini Ernst & Young, and Westpac are just a few top businesses that are adding recruitment functionality to their websites with products such as GradManager from nga.net in Melbourne. GradManager was designed specifically for large organizations needing to collect and process applications at a fraction of normal recruiting costs.

Richard Ogier-Herbert, general manager of nga.net in Melbourne, claims administrative cost savings in the region of 70 per cent from the use of GradManager as a recruitment tool. 'The ease of access, centralized location, automated processing and communication and its position at the leading edge make GradManager ideal for large organizations to manage their volume recruitment,' he said. He expects up to

▶

◀

95 per cent of Australia's top 500 companies to adopt this type of technology to meet volume recruitment needs.

Shell Australia takes on about 30 graduates a year in engineering, business and IT. From this year all graduate applications will be handled online. Candice Topp, who deals with graduate applications for Shell Australia comments that the group had switched to online graduate recruiting because 'it is the way the market is heading.' She added that 'With more and more students using the internet, we saw significant benefits in encouraging online applications for our annual placement of graduates.'

With a turnaround time of just 24 to 48 hours, compared with a week or more for paper-based applications, there is a major benefit for applicants. According to Ms Topp:

> If you regard graduate applicants as customers, as we do, then it is in their best interests to have their interest and our determination acknowledged as quickly as possible. We can avoid so much time consuming manual processing by capturing data electronically, uploading it into information systems and doing all sorts of tracking.

Natalie Rice, graduate program coordinator for Orica, considers that online graduate recruiting indicates a more professional approach and improves organizational efficiency. Orica has 1500 graduate applications each year for around 20 places on the Graduate Leadership Program in engineering, science, IT and marketing. As she explained:

> The paper-based system was becoming more and more demanding on us. The online application system will streamline the process, increasing our internal efficiencies and allowing us to screen and respond to applicants in a timely manner. It's a two-way thing: we need to be quick off the mark to ensure we get the right people and the applicants themselves deserve a timely response.

Source: *HRM Guide Australia* (http://www.hrmguide.net/australia/), 19 February 2001.

HRM in reality

Online recruiting best practice

An iLogos 'Best Practices' report defines recruiting industry standards for career website features. One of the main recommendations is incorporating a link from the corporate home page directly to the careers section on the company's website, and 73 per cent of Fortune 500 companies do this. Another best practice feature, utilized by 55 per cent of Fortune 500 companies, is to make information available to candidates about a company's culture and work environment.

According to Yves Lermusiaux, president, iLogos Research:

> This personalized assessment for companies helps them to measure their current performance against the standard for online recruiting and presents them with an opportunity to make a marked improvement in interacting with job-seekers on the careers sections of their websites. It is critical that all companies make the most effective use of their corporate career websites, to brand their companies with potential candidates, who may also be customers and shareholders. Benchmarking practices against those of the Fortune 500 provides a useful measurement and perhaps motivation to implement best online recruiting practices.

Canadian companies have a lower rate of adoption and usage of online recruiting best practices compared to their Fortune 500 counterparts. This can be explained by lower overall penetration of corporate career websites among Canadian companies (64 per cent versus 89 per cent). Take away the Canadian companies without career sites and we find that the remaining Canadian companies lead the Fortune 500 in over half of the best practices and by greater margins – and are well ahead in some of the most innovative best practices.

The top 100 Canadian companies lead the Fortune 500 in their use of some leading best practices on career websites, including:

- urgent jobs highlighted (4 per cent versus 3 per cent)
- submission of formatted resumés (13 per cent versus 9 per cent)
- e-mail to a friend (10 per cent versus 9 per cent)
- anonymous applications (3 per cent versus 1 per cent)
- online job agents (8 per cent versus 6 per cent)
- customized pre-assessment tools (5 per cent versus 1 per cent).

But the top Canadian companies fared less well in a number of other respects:

- Just 64 per cent of the top Canadian companies had career sections on their corporate websites, compared with 89 per cent of Fortune 500 companies.
- Some 45 per cent of the top Canadian companies posted job positions on their websites, compared to 76 per cent of the Fortune 500.
- Only 42 per cent of Canadian companies surveyed studied posted job positions and accepted online applications, compared to 71 per cent of the Fortune 500.

Key areas where Canadian companies are behind their Fortune 500 counterparts include:

- ability for job-seekers to search a database of available jobs (17 per cent versus 42 per cent)
- link from the corporate home page to the career website (47 per cent versus 73 per cent)
- one click to apply for a job (36 per cent versus 56 per cent)
- information about company benefits (21 per cent versus 55 per cent)
- information about company culture (37 per cent versus 44 per cent)
- separate college recruiting section (21 per cent versus 42 per cent)
- automatic connection of an application to a job posting (24 per cent versus 39 per cent)
- candidate profiling (16 per cent versus 19 per cent)
- reuse of candidate information for multiple applications (9 per cent versus 18 per cent)
- ability for candidates to cut and paste their resumé or use a resumé builder (9 per cent versus 14 per cent).

According to Yves Lermusiaux, president and founder of iLogos Research:

The identification of the best practices is the result of more than three years of iLogos Research monitoring the online recruiting activities of Fortune 500 companies. These results have become the benchmark against which corporate online recruiting practices are measured. By failing to adopt key practices, Canadian companies will continue to fall behind Fortune 500 companies in the race for qualified talent.

▶

◄

Canadian companies were selected and ranked for this report on the basis of revenue. The online recruiting practices of these top Canadian companies were compared with corporate career websites of the Fortune 500. In the view of Louis Têtu, CEO of Recruitsoft:

> The corporate career website is an important, yet underutilized tool for Canadian companies. More than 14 million Canadians have access to the internet at home and we have seen a significant rise in the number of people conducting job searches online, yet only 64 per cent of the top 100 Canadian companies have a career section built into their corporate website, compared to 89 per cent of Fortune 500 companies. In fact, six per cent of the top 100 Canadian companies still do not have a corporate website. In order for Canadian corporations to effectively compete for top talent globally, they will need to be more innovative in their online recruiting practices.

Source: *HRM Guide Canada* (http://www.hrmguide.net/canada/), 2 May 2001.

Formal recruiting

Equal opportunity demands equal access. This can only be achieved through public and open recruitment. However, recruitment marketing is expensive and time-consuming. For example, PA Consulting conducted a survey of 91 UK companies recruiting graduates (*Times Higher*, 21 January 1994). They recorded 318 988 applications for 3372 vacancies in 1993. This averaged 95 applicants for every post, rising to 272 applications per vacancy for the major high-street and 'blue chip' companies. Organizations recruiting more than 100 graduates spent between £50 000 and £800 000 on recruitment programmes, with advertising taking a small proportion of the cost in comparison with stationery and travel. They averaged a remarkable 1172 hours processing applications and arriving at a shortlist.

The effectiveness of recruitment is usually measured in terms of expediency: 'whether vacancies are filled with minimally qualified people at acceptable cost' or a sufficient number of applicants are attracted (Iles and Salaman, 1995, p.213). Rarely are the long-term consequences to the organization of cloned and barely adequate employees or the costs of recruitment taken into account. Doubts have also been expressed about the quality of people who are engaged in recruiting. Remarkably, the advertisements placed by recruitment agencies for their own staffing vacancies rarely ask for any knowledge of people management or selection techniques. Almost invariably they emphasize selling skills such as communication, dynamism and youth.

The likelihood of attracting 'suitable' applicants depends on the detail and specificity of the recruitment advertisement or literature. Key factors such as salary, job title, career and travel opportunities obviously influence response rates. As examples of marketing, considerable effort and money can be invested in the effectiveness of recruitment advertisements. However, employers do not wish to be swamped with applications from clearly unsuitable people. In some instances, honest job descriptions are designed to put off unwelcome applicants.

HRM in reality

'In' and 'Out' in the job hunt

Today's competitive market requires considerably more effort than in recent years, notes Tracey Turner, executive director of The Creative Group, a specialized staffing firm placing creative, advertising, marketing and web professionals. According to Turner, methods that may have worked in a robust economy should be replaced with more focused, aggressive strategies.

'As competition for employment intensifies, job-seekers are branching out beyond obvious tools such as job-board postings and classified ads,' says Turner. 'They're networking harder and smarter, and using their resumés to paint vivid pictures of the value they can add to companies.'

Adds Turner, 'The most successful applicants thoroughly research prospective employers before initiating contact. They approach job interviews with a "sales pitch" on how their skills and expertise can directly benefit the company.'

These are the 'in' and 'out' tactics to landing a new position in 2002 according to Turner:

Out	In
Working the want ads	Working a room
Free time while job hunting	Freelancing, volunteering or continuing your education while job hunting
Mass mailing generic resumés	E-mailing resumés tailored to specific companies and positions
Listing creative job titles (e.g. 'innovation guru') on resumés	Using creative job-search strategies to identify leads
Providing a laundry list of previous job duties on resumés	Highlighting and quantifying specific achievements on resumés
Waiting by the phone	Calling potential employers
Using business buzz words and jargon in application materials	Using clear, simple and persuasive language in application materials
Including references with resumés	Preparing references for phone calls
Cover letters addressed 'To Whom It May Concern'	Personalized cover letters that complement information on the resumé and 'sell' your skills
Telling people you're 'between jobs'	Asking everyone you know if they have job leads
Ending the interview by asking when they'll be contacting you	Ending the interview by asking for the job

Source: *HRM Guide Canada* (http://www.hrmguide.net/canada/), 16 April 2002.

For example, at Nissan UK job adverts emphasized the demanding nature of the work, clearly stating that (Wickens, 1987):

- the pace of work will be dictated by a moving production line and will be very demanding;
- work assignments will be carefully defined and will be repetitive.

Table 14.3	Satisfaction with recruitment	
	Method	*Satisfaction (1–5)*
	Internal	4.1
	Local press	3.7
	National press	3.5
	Trade journals	3.2
	Consultants	2.8
	Agencies	2.7
	Headhunters	2.5
	Job centres	2.2
	Professional registers	1.9

A British Institute of Management/IPM study completed in 1980 compared ratings of satisfaction between various methods of recruitment available to employers and found the levels of satisfaction with their effectiveness set out in Table 14.3. The survey showed that trade or professional journals attracted the most suitable candidates, whereas the local press showed the greatest cost-effectiveness. This is a poorly researched aspect of resourcing but it seems that employers are happier making a choice between an unexpectedly large pool of candidates than a small pool generated by an unsuccessful recruitment campaign (Van Ours and Ridder, 1992).

Specific journals or magazines are favoured for particular occupations with employers and job-seekers gravitating towards the same titles on the same days. These change with time, dependent on the effectiveness of their advertising sales departments, and good response rates require awareness of the state of play before placing any advertisements.

The approach to recruitment reflects cultural priorities. Recruitment marketing in English-speaking countries normally features salaries and benefits but French equivalents are vague in this respect, reflecting different approaches to rewards (Barsoux and Lawrence, 1990, p.47). Base pay in English-speaking countries depends on job requirements; in France it depends on the candidate's qualifications. French advertisements define educational requirements in detail, sometimes indicating the number of years of study after the baccalaureat as the main heading. Specific *grandes écoles* may be requested. Management in France is regarded as an intellectual rather than an interpersonal matter. Hence recruitment is geared towards cleverness (Barsoux and Lawrence, 1990, p.47). Instead of the managerial buzzwords, such as 'dynamic', 'energetic', 'high calibre' and 'outstanding' found in British advertisements, French equivalents seek out '*les elements les plus brilliants*'. The nuance is telling.

HRM in reality

The job-seekers

Around the world, job-seekers find similar problems in gaining employment. They feel unfairly treated by insensitive employers. Unemployed people who are too young or too old, or come from unfavoured areas or disadvantaged groups are particularly susceptible to callous treatment. Two letters from different continents describe the treatment experienced by some job hunters.

First letter: 'Sad conclusions of job-seekers' (Trinidad Guardian)

The editor

Kindly publish the following letter in your newspaper on our behalf.

Dear employers, we are a group of young and middle-aged persons from different social backgrounds and educational levels, ranging from CXC passes to university degrees, plus experience.

We recently compared notes as to our lack of success in obtaining employment over the past year, and have come up with the following conclusions and observations:

(1) On a number of occasions, the jobs advertised were 'filled', and the advertising and interviewing process was merely to fill a 'requirement'.

(2) Too many recruiters and interviewers use the opportunity of the interview to let us know how powerful they are, that they have the right to employ or not, to dehumanize, insult, embarrass, mentally abuse and to generally show us that we the unemployed are the lowest form of life on this earth.

(3) If you live in a depressed area, it is recommended that you use as your mailing address and point of contact the address of a friend or relative in a more respectable area. Few invitations for interviews are sent out to Laventville or Maloney.

(4) Instead of the popular phrase, 'only suitable applicants will be acknowledge' (sic), we recommend that the statement 'only successful applicants will be acknowledged by dd/mm/yy' be used. Please understand that it is extremely frustrating not knowing whether you are to be shortlisted for an interview weeks after mailing out a letter.

(5) Those of us who have been used during the interview process, tend, on the average, to relate our stories to at least eight other persons. This means that the company whose employees were the abuser receive negative public relations. In one case, a major account was moved from a bank. Take note, employers.

(6) Executive placement services are a waste of time. They play the 'skin' and 'club/lodge/contact' game. Over the past year, not a single search company has even acknowledged any of the 11 letters which we all sent to them.

(7) The only success which we have had by way of employment were not through advertisement in the newspapers but by way of contact – someone knowing of the vacancy before it could be advertised. This to us is the saddest fact of all.

We, however, still are hopeful that we can obtain gainful employment.

The Group of Anxious Job-seekers, Maraval.

Second letter: 'Be more caring with job-seekers' (Cape Times)

I am an outplacement consultant specializing in assisting retrenched personnel. To those in positions of power over the unemployed may I remind you that the unemployed person, in many instances, could be your father, mother, brother, sister, friend or even yourself. Put systems in place to ensure that advertising response is dealt with in a pleasing and caring manner. It is dehumanizing to have someone bark questions at you when your confidence is at a low ebb.

I understand the pressure of the job, having owned and run my own recruitment agency, and I know there are many chancers out there. However, if it were not for the chancers and the irritation attached, big business would not need your services.

◄

I ask that companies looking for staff check up on the agencies they use by phoning in anonymously to check up on the treatment meted out to job-seekers. In my view, it leaves a lot to be desired.

What amazes me is the dignified way the unemployed people I work with handle themselves and the undignified response they very often receive from so-called human resource professionals.

Colleen Ingram
Somerset West

Sources: *Trinidad Guardian*, 23 July 1992; *Cape Times* (Cape Town, South Africa), 25 January 1996.

Discussion question: What are the implications of dissatisfied job applicants to employing organizations?

Targeting and diversity

In the UK, the recent massive increase in higher education has produced a consequent increase in the number of new graduates. British employers have begun to copy US organizations in targeting specific universities, courses and even lecturers. As we observed in Chapter 2, the pecking order favours 'old' universities, reflecting the prejudices of employers. A Glasgow consultancy, Yellowbrick Training and Development, indicated five 'insights' into targeting (*Financial Times*, 25 October 1995; *Guardian*, 26 October 1995):

● Competition for the 'best' graduates requires employers to have a clear idea of what they mean by 'best'. Recruitment needs to send a strong, distinctive message to these people.

● There must be a move away from junior staff indiscriminately attracting as many applicants as possible to a more selective process involving senior management.

● Target key institutions and specific courses.

● Recruit whenever the needs of the business dictate, rather than to a fixed 'milkround' calendar.

● There will be a diminished role for glossy brochures. Instead, vacation and placement jobs will be used to provide 'two-way interviews'.

It is clear that many employers are likely to use this form of targeting to ring-fence jobs so that only specific groups are considered. Essentially, they discriminate against institutions where ethnic minorities and working class people are more heavily represented.

The choice and variety of new graduates has extended considerably in the UK during recent years as the result of government initiatives to widen access to higher education. A number of institutions have achieved university status, largely catering for students with a lower economic status, ethnic minorities and adult learners. But the people who were intended to gain the most benefit of this expansion in higher education actually 'gain somewhat less than their middle-class peers from achievement of a degree' (Purcell 2002). And they earn less, on average, than people with similar qualifications who enter the job market with a 'traditional' graduate background.

The UK has moved from an elite to a mass market system of university education but recruiters have not changed their practices in line with this development. On the contrary, a significant number have introduced or emphasized recruitment practices that act against graduates from non-traditional backgrounds. This is a matter of critical concern to people considering an investment in time and money in order to gain a degree.

Purcell (2002) point to a situation where:

- graduates with non-traditional backgrounds complain that they are finding it difficult to access jobs that offer them the fullest range of opportunities and make the most of their skills; while

- companies appear to find difficulty in understanding the diversity of higher education courses and say that they cannot fill jobs with the right *calibre* of graduates.

Purcell (2002) contends that many of these problems result from the conservative recruitment strategies adopted by many organizations. Additionally, there is evidence to show that such strategies impact more on some groups of 'non-traditional' graduates than others – specifically those in older age groups. They appear to show the highest degree of dissatisfaction with the quality of their subsequent jobs and the value of having a degree. Also, the social background of graduates, regardless of age, has a correlation with their levels of pay and job satisfaction after graduation. The lower their economic status before they embarked on higher education, the lower the consequent pay and job satisfaction.

Recruitment can be used to present a more positive, welcoming image to groups that are under-represented but, to be successful, this must be reinforced by similar initiatives further on in selection, induction and development mechanisms. Purcell (2002) identifies a number of key characteristics of 'leading practice employers', a similar concept to that of 'employers of choice' in North America:

- In line with the concept of employer branding, they understand that recruitment is intimately connected with marketing. This means that they have to actively sell their organizations as equal opportunity employers.

- They are clear about the skills and competencies they need for specific jobs and do not confuse these with (irrelevant) attributes. They target sources of these skills and competencies and design their recruitment and selection processes to identify them.

- Where skills shortages exist they work with regional bodies and higher education institutes to draw attention to vacancies and opportunities, so that under-represented groups are positively encouraged to apply.

- Expectations of recruits (internal and external) are managed to ensure that they understand the nature of the work, the culture of the organization and the career opportunities available.

- Work experience and placement opportunities are offered through higher education institutes, to encourage students to gain employment skills and experience and to allow them to make sensible career choices.

- They provide training and development programmes, plus assessment of progress, making internal progression possible wherever possible.

- They recognize the diversity and changing needs of their staff through work–life balance, flexibility and people-friendly working policies.

Activity 14:4

What are the critical characteristics of leading practice employers or employers of choice?

Researching candidates

Recruitment attracts a pool of applicants from whom successful candidates may be chosen. We now move on to the selection stages of the employee resourcing process. If a job analysis has been conducted, the criteria or competencies that are deemed necessary have been identified. These may be well-defined and focused on experience and skills, as in the 'right person' approach; or general and related to education, intellect and personality for the 'cultural fit' and 'flexible person' models. Since decision making is based on these criteria, relevant information must be obtained from applicants. The initial response to a vacancy announcement can take a number of forms but each offers the opportunity for: (a) recruiters to obtain information on applicants; and (b) applicants to gain an understanding of the job and the organization.

The commonest responses requested are by telephone or letter. Telephone responses may be used for an exchange of information or as a means of eliciting an application form and literature describing the job and organization.

Applications

Application letters, CVs and resumés

Cover letters and resumés or CVs (curriculum vitae) are typically used as initial applications. There is some variation between cultures. North American resumés are intended to present career objectives and history (usually in reverse chronological order, starting with the present) on one tightly written typed page. CVs in the British tradition are typically more detailed, running into two and sometimes more typed pages. The latter approach is also used by professionals in North America. In France, by contrast, advertisements often request a handwritten application letter, CV and photograph. (Many French companies use graphologists in the selection process.) French CVs are shorter and more factual than the British model and include little or no personal information such as hobbies or sporting interests. Japanese recruiters expect an official family registry record, a physical examination report and letters of recommendation in addition to CV and photographs. The use of photographs arouses disquiet in countries where equal opportunities are a major issue since they imply that selection will be influenced by appearance and colour.

Watkins and Johnston (2000) investigated the effect of physical attractiveness and resumé quality on how job applicants were evaluated during the screening phase of the selection process. A total of 180 participants read a job advertisement and one of two differing quality versions of a curriculum vitae. Each CV had a passport-sized head-and-shoulders photograph of either an average or an attractive female attached. A control study was also conducted where a photograph was not attached. Participants were asked to state how likely they were to offer an interview to the applicant, rate the quality of the application and state the likely starting salary to be offered to the applicant. Overall, attractiveness had no impact with high-quality applications but was an advantage when the application was mediocre. For example, average quality resumés were evaluated more positively when a photograph was attached and attractive photographs increased the rating of a mediocre application.

Job clubs and career advisers spend a great deal of time coaching job-seekers on the preparation of polished application letters, resumés and curriculum vitae. Paradoxically, however, coaching often results in a bland, standardized application that does not stand out amongst hundreds of others. Applicants might be best advised to try some cautious experimenting in layout, paper quality and typeface to achieve a more distinctive product.

A survey by online recruiter reed.co.uk found that employers now prefer electronic resumés/CVs over paper versions (AGR online, 26 April 2002). Of the 400 firms surveyed, almost 80 per cent said that given two equal candidates, they would favour a candidate who had supplied them with an electronic resumé or CV.

Nearly two-thirds said they would favour candidates with electronic versions when selecting for interviews. Not only are they quicker and easier to process, they also give a favourable impression of candidates' computer literacy levels. Around 40 per cent of recruiters surveyed said that they currently receive more than 90 per cent of resumés or CVs electronically, but 15 per cent did not receive any electronic versions at all.

Such applications are often scanned into computers and screened by proprietary software, which may use a simple keyword rating system or more intelligent 'knowledge-based' rating systems. Many people are worried by the implications of this process but hiring staff in large organizations typically give no more than 30–40 seconds to reviewing CVs and resumés and machines are more likely to be consistent in dealing with large numbers of such applications. The privacy and data protection issues arising from this practice are complex and the European Union has attempted to control the use of automated selection processes through a Directive that forms the basis, for example, of the UK's Data Protection Act 1998 (PPRU, 1999). The code of practice for this Act states in respect of shortlisting:

1 Be consistent in the way personal data are used in the process of shortlisting candidates for a particular position.
2 Inform applicants if an automated shortlisting system will be used as the sole basis for making a decision. Make provisions to consider representations from applicants about this and to take these into account before making the final decision.
3 Ensure that tests based on the interpretation of scientific evidence, such as psychological tests and handwriting analysis, are only used and interpreted by those who have received appropriate training.

Activity 14:5

Write a covering letter and a resumé or CV that would be suitable for an application to a HR department in a large multinational company. You wish to apply for a post in that department.

HRM in reality

Resumé 'padding'

A survey by *The New York Times Job Market* research team indicates that 89 per cent of job-seekers and 49 per cent of hiring managers in the New York metropolitan area believe that a significant number of candidates pad their resumés.

The researchers define resumé padding as falsifying information on a resumé to make a candidate look stronger. The hiring managers who believe that a significant number of resumés are padded consider that (on average) 52 per cent of the resumés they receive are padded. But just 13 per cent of job-seekers surveyed admitted to ever having padded their resumés.

Some 82 per cent of responding job-seekers say they think companies are aware of resumé padding and believe that companies perform background checks on the following: some items on the resumé (70 per cent); all items on the resumé (17 per cent); none of the items on the resumé (13 per cent).

The survey identified the following techniques used by hiring managers to verify job candidates' claims made on their resumés:

▶

◀

- checking of references (47 per cent)
- evaluating candidates during the interview process (30 per cent)
- checking of past employers/schools listed on resumés (17 per cent)
- asking questions of candidates to see how specific their answers are (6 per cent)
- evaluating new employees once they are on the job (4 per cent)
- requiring samples of candidates' work (2 per cent)
- requiring candidates to complete tests during the hiring process (2 per cent).

What happens if someone is hired and then found to have padded his/her resumé? It seems that 68 per cent of larger firms (100 or more employees) and 50 per cent of smaller firms (less than 100 employees) have policies to address the situation. Most often the policy is to terminate the employment (79 per cent). Disciplining the employee (7 per cent) and an undetermined action depending upon what was padded (5 per cent) are distant second and third choice actions.

Some 29 per cent of hiring managers and 21 per cent of job-seekers consider that any resumé padding is a serious matter. Both groups believe the following to be the items most frequently padded on job-seekers' resumés:

	Hiring managers (per cent)	Job-seekers (per cent)
Job responsibilities	53	51
Length of employment	18	14
Education level	13	10
College attended/previous employment	11	14

Source: *HRM Guide USA* (http://www.hrmguide.net/usa/), 31 May 2002.

Discussion question: What are the arguments for and against being scrupulously honest in presenting a career history?

Application forms/blanks

Both letters and CVs/resumés present a problem in a large recruitment programme: applicants may not provide all the relevant information and what there is will be presented in different ways. Comparison of applicants is easier if data is supplied in a standard form. Therefore, applicants replying to a job advertisement typically receive an application form (usually termed an application blank in North America), asking often for information already supplied.

Candidates face a paradox with application forms. Because information is regimented into a particular order and restricted space, job-seekers may present very similar applications. As with application letters, if candidates do not include details that distinguish them from (sometimes hundreds) of others they stand little chance of being shortlisted. Conversely, if their responses are too unorthodox, the form immediately becomes a test of conventionality:

Application forms are of doubtful benefit; they torment applicants rather than motivate them. They blunt any initiative in presentation. ... inane questions such as: 'Describe yourself in one hundred words' or: 'What are your greatest achievements and failures?' ... create sarcastic answers in the mind and false answers on paper. The curriculum vitae is a better tool; it is a chance for the applicant to sell him or her self. Its presentation and its content are also more useful and less boring to the member of staff who has to scrutinize them (*Sunday Times*, 8 August 1993).

An applicant's heart sinks when a carefully crafted resumé or CV appears to be ignored and a standard form arrives in the post. Hours are wasted completing forms which are not read because applicants are rejected on decision criteria, such as qualifications, that are not mentioned in the marketing process. However, an organization which does not use application forms has a major problem dealing with hundreds of applications. How are they to be analysed and compared? How is the choice of a shortlist to be made? Applicants will leave out crucial items of information, particularly when they are likely to have a negative impact. When and how is this information to be acquired? Interviews are expensive methods for filling in the gaps in a CV or resumé. Moreover, it is unfair to raise hopes, cause inconvenience and possibly expense for interviewees who are disqualified on the basis of information that could be picked up from an application form.

Provided that they are not devised as mediaeval instruments of torture, short and pertinent application forms will continue to have a major role in recruitment. Purcell (2002) found that employers were increasingly tailoring application forms to identify specific competencies required for individual jobs.

| **Activity 14:6** | What types of information are best obtained through the use of application forms? |

Qualifications

We noted that educational qualifications are of major importance in some cultures, for example France and Japan. In other countries their value varies, depending on the level and nature of the vacancy. Purcell (2002) found that employers tended to use degrees as thresholds for considering applicants in order to guarantee minimum potential and ability. Also, with the massive increase in degree-qualified candidates in the UK, many employers were questioning the need for a degree as a basic qualification for a wide range of jobs. Many had moved, or were in the process of moving away from qualifications as a key element in the selection process. Instead they were looking for evidence of competencies, particularly generic competencies such as communication and teamworking or personal attributes such as resilience and commitment. In particular, they were increasingly valuing experience.

Purcell (2002) noted a clear difference between employers seeking to fill professional and technical jobs and those looking for general management or administration candidates. The former emphasized degrees as a qualification, particularly in subjects that featured numeracy. Whereas degrees were often thought unnecessary for entry jobs in more generalized fields. They quote the instance of one high-street bank which sought to obtain A-level (high-school graduate) candidates for a five-year management programme rather than university graduates. They targeted working-class applicants who might consider the programme more attractive than a debt-incurring degree course.

Biodata

Application forms and model CVs invariably include sections on experience, hobbies and other spare-time activities. Applicants frequently have serious difficulties in providing answers if they have fairly mundane interests. Does a passing interest in stamps and a small collection of CDs allow us to describe our hobbies as philately and music? Do holiday snapshots justify 'photography'?

Traditionally, little use was made of this type of information. But it can be useful in discriminating (and that word is used advisedly) between applicants who are similar in most other respects. In fact, as we have already mentioned, an increase in coaching, books and professional writers aimed at preparing CVs or resumés and answering conventional forms has resulted in applications becoming more and more similar. Suppose an employer advertises for trainee customer service assistants. The response is likely to include numerous applications from school-leavers with insufficient qualifications to proceed into higher education. These applicants may seem much the same on paper, but some have greater initiative or people skills than others. Biodata (biographical data) forms have been developed to identify non-academic qualities such as these. Biodata consists of systematic information about hobbies, interests and life history. The underlying rationale is described by Smith, Gregg and Andrews (1989, p.54):

> Biodata methods are based on the assumption that *either* our characteristics are formed by the experiences we are subjected to in the course of our lives *or* our abilities cause us to select or become involved in certain types of life event. In either case, it follows that if we can accurately assess the events of a person's life, we can deduce something about their skills and abilities.

Key concept 14:2

Biodata   Roberts (1997, p.10) describes biodata as a 'set of questions framed around "coincidences" in the lives of good performers'. People who are good at a particular job are likely to be more similar to each other than to individuals selected at random from the general population. Such similarities extend beyond work-related factors into hobbies, sports and social activities.

Biodata forms request detailed information of this kind, normally in the form of a multiple-choice questionnaire, covering:

- age, sex, place of birth, residence
- family background, number of brothers and sisters, parental history
- education, work experience
- marital status, number of children
- physical characteristics (weight, height) and medical history
- hobbies and leisure interests
- reading habits: newspapers, magazines, type and frequency of books read.

Questions items are largely factual or 'hard' and could be checked with other sources if necessary. Other items are 'soft' and include opinions, attitudes and feelings. It is also possible to collect the same data in a structured interview. Biodata is an expensive procedure to set up but cheap to administer, especially if the data can be entered on computer by optical scanning.

A typical biodata exercise follows the following sequence (Smith, Gregg and Andrews, 1989):

1   Job analysis identifies criteria for good performance.

2   A 'brainstorming' exercise generates relevant biodata items, such as 'interest in people', 'stability', 'imagination'.

3   Draft questionnaires are given to a large number – ideally over 300 – existing employees.

4 Replies are correlated with job performance. Items that correlate poorly or discriminate against particular groups should be discarded.

5 The revised questionnaire is then given to applicants.

6 Biodata items become out of date quickly. They should be rechecked every two years.

Biodata cannot be used in small organizations or for a 'one-off' job. A simplified version could be provided as a decision aid in such circumstances. This would entail interviewers collecting narrative personal histories and scoring the information against a previously determined scale. The main use of biodata is in pre-selection of basic or entry-level jobs such as apprenticeships or posts for trainees. The logic is that if candidates are matched with existing staff, people with similar interests can be found who are likely to be suitable for the job. The greatest value of the technique is its ability to reduce staff turnover.

Biodata is specifically used to select people who are similar to those employed already. Although designed to eliminate unfairness, in a less obvious way it consolidates and makes 'scientific' an embedded practice that is prejudicial to the disadvantaged. Furnham (1992, p.231) reviews a number of studies comparing biodata with job performance and finds strong supporting evidence for its usefulness. He instances Russell *et al.* (1990) who examined the life details of 900 naval recruits and measured five biographical features:

- life problems and difficulties
- aspects of task performance
- work ethic/self-discipline
- assistance from others
- extraordinary goals or effort.

These were found to relate to other measures such as military performance rating. Furnham notes that factor analyses of biodata information relate to well-attested personality dimensions. Roberts (1997) observes that we do not need to know why biodata items are significant in order to use them. In many respects it is similar to the actuarial techniques used by insurance companies to quote for car insurance cover. Clearly, however, there are distinct implications for equal opportunities in a technique which, it could be argued, is designed not to promote diversity and which raises a possibility of breaching anti-discrimination laws unless the biodata items are carefully assessed. There is also the issue of faking to consider (Lautenschlager, 1994). The 'correct' (expected) answers to questions on non-cognitive tests such as biodata questionnaires are often easy to guess. In fact present-day biodata questions may be indistinguishable from items on personality tests and may attract the same problems of impression management and dishonesty. The consequent uncertainty about the effect of distorted responses on selection decisions and validity is a matter of concern (Snell, Sydell and Lueke, 1999).

| Activity 14:7 | Review the positive and negative aspects of using biodata questionnaires. |

References

Virtually all employers request references as a matter of course, usually without any thought as to their purpose and value. Where a purpose is expressed, they tend to serve one or both of the following functions: (a) a factual check to maximize the probability of a truthful application; (b) to provide evidence of character or ability.

The latter assumes that the referee is disinterested and capable of making a valid judgement and is frequently misused. Candidates are most unlikely to offer referees who will write unfavourably. A classic study is frequently quoted to demonstrate the dubious value of the reference (Mosel and Goheen, 1958). In the study 1000 applications for the US civil service were examined and it was found that:

- less than 1 per cent had poor references for ability or character
- approximately 50 per cent were described as outstanding by the referees
- the remaining references were at least satisfactory.

Moreover, when the work performance of successful candidates described by referees as being particularly suitable for the job were compared with those that were not, no difference was found between the two groups.

There is a growing and welcome trend for references to be simple factual checks rather than a source of 'evidence' for the selection process. There is also an issue regarding a referee's liability for the consequences of their comments. This is dependent upon employment law within specific countries.

| HRM in reality | **Ontario moves forward with mandatory criminal background checks** |

Education Minister Janet Ecker announced today that criminal background checks for teachers and other school employees will start in September 2001 to improve safety and security in Ontario's classrooms.

'We recognize that the vast majority of teachers and school staff have earned and deserve the respect of their students,' said Ecker. 'However, mandatory criminal background checks will provide school boards with an additional tool to assist them in creating more secure learning environments.'

As part of the Harris government's election commitment to a province-wide Code of Conduct to improve safety within schools, local police services would conduct a one-time criminal background check designed to show all criminal convictions. About 200 000 employees in schools across Ontario would be affected by these mandatory criminal background checks. Checks would be phased in over two school years, beginning in September 2001 and running to August 2003.

The initiative forms the basis of a new regulation under the Safe Schools Act, 2000. Over the next month the government will solicit input from the Ontario College of Teachers, the Ministry of the Solicitor General and other partners on implementing criminal background checks for September.

According to Ecker, criminal background checks are consistent with practices used in a variety of other professions such as social workers and early childhood education workers. This initiative is intended to establish a province-wide standard, setting out necessary procedures for handling this type of information. 'Parents, teachers and students have told us that safe, secure learning environments are a priority,' said Ecker. 'This is another key step in fulfilling the government's commitment to make all publicly funded schools safe, respectful places for learning and teaching.'

Source: *HRM Guide Canada* (http://www.hrmguide.net/canada/), 12 March 2001.

Summary

Recruitment and selection are core areas of human resource management but are frequently discussed in a prescriptive manner. They are not simply techniques for filling jobs – they are also levers for organizational change, sustaining employee commitment and achieving high performance. In free market countries, the personnel profession has adopted a 'best practice' model that fits the prevailing business ideology. This model prescribes a quest for the 'right (best) person for the job'. The 'best-person' or psychometric model has achieved the status of orthodoxy in free market countries. But different models of resourcing have been developed with a greater concern for personality and attitude than presumed ability. Recruits may be sought who will 'fit in' with the culture of the corporation; who will be content to build a career within the organization; who will absorb the goals of the organization.

Further reading

There are many titles available covering the topic of recruitment, usually in conjunction with selection. Some of the best include: *Competing for Talent: Key Recruitment and Retention Strategies for Becoming an Employer of Choice* by Nancy S. Ahlrichs (2000), Davies-Black Publishing; *Assessment and Selection in Organizations: Methods and Practice for Recruitment and Appraisal, Volume 2, International Handbook of Selection and Assessment* edited by Neil Anderson and Peter Herriot (1997), published by John Wiley & Son; *Competency-Based Recruitment and Selection* by Robert Wood and Tim Payne (1998), John Wiley & Son; *Recruitment and Selection* by Gareth Roberts (1997), published by the CIPD; *The Graduate Recruitment Manual* by Rajvinder Kandola, Robert Wood, Bindi Dholakia and Carol Keane (reissue 2001), Gower Publishing Limited; *Staff Recruitment and Retention* by Alastair Evans (2001), Chandos Publishing.

Review questions

1 Distinguish between recruitment and selection. What is the purpose of recruitment?

2 Describe in your own words what is meant by: (a) the 'right' person model; (b) culture fit; and (c) the flexible employee. Which approach is most commonly used for employee resourcing in your locality?

3 What role do the internet and company websites have in recruitment?

4 Evaluate the role of the line manager in the resourcing process.

5 What are the best ways of obtaining basic candidate information? Clarify your interpretation of the word 'best'.

6 What are the legal pitfalls in the recruitment process?

Problems for discussion and analysis

1 The general manager of Saveplenty Stores has been interviewing applicants for sales and management jobs for 23 years. She believes that she can identify good and bad candidates by chatting to them for ten minutes. You have been placed in her department as a graduate trainee and have been given the task of organizing recruitment for a new superstore. How would you do this and what role should the general manager play?

▶

2 You are a human resource specialist with a large software company. The company has agreed to set up a joint venture in Paris with a major French computer manufacturer. The venture will adapt and distribute software in French-speaking countries. Being fluent in French, you have been chosen as HR manager. Most of the other senior staff are long-standing managers from the French company. Your first task is to recruit approximately 60 junior managers and technical staff. The procedures and choices have to involve your French colleagues. How would you conduct the exercise and what difficulties would you expect?

15

Employee selection

Objectives

The purpose of this chapter is to:

- Evaluate the screening or pre-selection stage of employee resourcing.

- Introduce the concepts of validity and reliability in relation to different selection methods.

- Provide a critical overview of selection methods.

- Investigate the frequency of use of different selection methods.

Resourcing decisions

According to *The Dictionary of Daily Wants* (1859):

> In seeking employment, much depends upon the applicant's manner and dress; if he is rude and ungainly, and expresses himself in an awkward manner, an employer will at once conceive a prejudice against him, and curtly decline the proffer of his services. But if, on the other hand, he is pleasing in his manners and dress, he will not only be engaged to fill a vacancy, but will sometimes be taken into the establishment, although no vacancy exists. Applicants for employment should also be scrupulously neat in their attire, and clean in their persons; for an employer naturally argues that a person who is careless of himself will be equally so about his business.

Selection is a decision-making activity: 'the psychological calculation of suitability' (Townley, 1994, p.94). If the recruitment process is open, selection decision making normally takes place in a series of stages. Recruitment marketing may attract hundreds – sometimes thousands – of responses. The first decision stage is termed pre-selection. Its purpose is to reduce applications to a manageable number with the emphasis on rejection rather than selection. Evidence is gathered from letters, resumés/CVs, application forms, and possibly biodata or screening tests. Regardless of the methods used, the intention is to arrive at a comparatively small number – the shortlist of apparently well-suited applicants.

Pre-selection is open to considerable abuse and plays a major role in the cloning process. Frequently decisions are made on arbitrary grounds, ranging from the absurd – use of the 'wrong' colour of ink, for example – to the discriminatory, excluding particular groups such as women, ethnic minorities, graduates from other than specific schools or universities and people over a certain age. Pre-selection offers those so inclined an ideal opportunity to reject unwanted candidates without having to give detailed reasons. Unless the organization has an equal opportunities monitoring system, with each application logged, categorized and tracked throughout the selection procedure, this a glaring loophole, allowing hidden and illegal discrimination to take place. It is common for two identical applications to be treated differently if one is sent with an obvious ethnic minority name and the other is evidently from the majority population. Herriot and Fletcher (1990) note the irony that pre-selection and initial interview result in rejection of the largest proportion of candidates and yet these stages are the least valid and reliable.

After pre-selection screening, surviving applicants meet the formal decision-making procedure termed 'selection'. Biased selection processes can result in hiring unsuitable people (false positives); or may lead to a failure to hire applicants who would have been suitable for the job (false negatives). In the 'best person' model, selection is a matching process where:

- an applicant's qualities are compared with criteria deemed necessary for the job
- when the measurement of the former is extremely difficult, and
- evidence for the latter is a matter of opinion.

In contrast, 'culture fit' focuses on personality and compatibility with existing staff. In Japan, attention is given to such matters as political views, family background and personal finances. These would not be relevant to the average Western company (Whitehill, 1990). We have noted that these two models are frequently confused and decision making is a matter of identifying the 'ideal' or clone candidate, a process rationalized by talk of 'fitting in'.

An alternative explanation comes from the cognitive process interpretation of selection (Vandenberghe, 1999). For whatever reason, selectors develop a cognitive schema (mental picture) of the 'ideal' candidate for a specific job, or more generally as a recruit for their particular organization. The cognitive schema may be a complicated mental network of beliefs and attitudes shared by a group of selectors against which prospective candidates are assessed.

Sophisticated selection methods are not common in small companies, most of which continue to depend on informal methods for selection decisions – typically references and one or two interviews. In contrast, large organizations have adopted a range of methods to aid decision making. This is especially true for employment categories such as blue-collar workers where it had not previously applied (Townley, 1989). The trend is most obvious in Japanese and US-owned firms but it is also apparent in UK and other European companies. Regardless of the resourcing model employed, procedures have become more elaborate. At Mazda in Michigan USA, for example, the process involved several weeks' assessment and included application forms, aptitude tests, personal interviews, group problem solving and simulated work exercises. These were designed to weed out 'druggies, rowdies, unionists'. Selection emphasized teamworking behavioural traits rather than technical skills and successful candidates had an average age of 31, little or no factory experience and were overwhelmingly (70 per cent) male.

Townley argues that this has not resulted from the increasing professionalization of human resource specialists. Neither is it a reaction to the difficult task of selecting from the large number of applicants attracted by any job advertisement during an economic recession. She attributes the trend to the increasing prevalence of HRM with its emphasis on the 'attitudinal and behavioural characteristics of employees'. Guest (1992) observes that the 'excellence literature', authored by Tom Peters and others, together with accounts of Japanese management methods have focused the minds of many Western managers on the importance of recruitment, selection and socialization of employees. This leads to an interest in factors that can be assessed by a range of technical methods such as psychometric tests. In recent years their use has increased in Europe, particularly in the UK, whereas equal opportunities legislation has forced a different approach in the USA.

HRM in reality	**Looking good, sounding right: style counselling in the new economy**

A new Industrial Society report claims that there is a danger of social exclusion as UK employers increasingly choose staff who 'look and sound the part'. Society is becoming more and more style-obsessed and this is reflected by a growing trend among UK companies to opt for staff who reflect their company image. But the report highlights the need for employers to remember the importance of equal opportunities and customer demand for high-quality service and not to be blinded by the desire to pick recruits who look or sound the part.

Chris Warhurst and Dennis Nickson of Strathclyde University, authors of *Looking Good, Sounding Right: Style Counselling in the New Economy*, have examined the trend for recruiters to select staff with self-presentation skills in preference to experience or technical skills. This trend is particularly prominent in the rapidly expanding service sector. They argue that government training policy should be focused on this demand. If not, there is a risk of a new employment underclass appearing made up of people who don't meet 'aesthetic' standards required by prospective employers.

The rise in 'aesthetic labour' could lead to an increase in potential discrimination, but the authors believe that it would be more effective to create impression management training programmes than to ignore or condemn the trend. They argue that 'aesthetic labour' is here to stay. Middle-class liberals might find social engineering –

▶

◀

they term it the Eliza Doolittle syndrome – offensive but providing unemployed people with aesthetic skills can enhance self-confidence and increase employability. Among the findings in the report are:

- A survey of skills needs in hotels, restaurants, pubs and bars indicated that 85 per cent of employers ranked personal presentation and appearance in third place – above initiative, communication skills or even ability to follow instructions.
- Glasgow employers rated technical skills 23 out of 24 as criteria for recruitment and selection.
- In January 2000, the government announced that all New Dealers would be offered personal presentation skills.
- Job advertisements for the hospitality and retail sectors frequently ask for people who are 'stylish', 'outgoing', 'attractive' or 'trendy' and 'well spoken and of smart appearance'.
- A 1996 survey of recruitment consultants indicated that strong regional accents – particularly those of Liverpool and Birmingham – were viewed negatively.
- Research in Glasgow shows that employers are, to a considerable extent, recruiting on the basis of physical appearance or accent.

Chris Warhurst says:

Aesthetics have always been important to companies and to certain groups of employees. Politicians, managers, professionals and city types recognize the career benefits of dressing for success. And the name and visual style of an organization are sometimes the most important factors in making it appear unique. What is startling is the application of highly prescriptive aesthetic values in the wider job market. The danger is that many people in deprived areas are being denied work because of a lack of cultural capital. Take Glasgow as an example: 50 per cent of jobs are now filled by commuters from the middle-class suburbs. This situation is likely to be repeated in similar urban restructuring economies, such as Liverpool, Manchester and Newcastle.

Examples of this kind of discrimination highlighted by the authors include:

- A supermarket check-out girl sent home by her boss to shave her legs so she wouldn't 'put customers off'.
- A pregnant sales assistant who was sacked for becoming 'too fat and ugly'.
- A male offshore oil worker who was dismissed for being too fat.

Richard Reeves, director of futures at the Industrial Society says:

In the service-crazy US, the reality of aesthetics has been accepted for decades. Charities exist to take cast-off clothes from professional women to help their jobless counterparts get work. We Brits are traditionally more squeamish about admitting that how you look, dress, talk – or even smell – might be as important as your GCSE results. Not everyone can enter the style labour market and, of course, not everyone would want to. But as the economy shifts towards 'high touch' jobs, the premium on presentation is rising. A key task for government is to reconcile these commercial imperatives with those of fairness and social justice. Employers need to tread carefully too. Aesthetic labour should be about great service, not great teeth.

Source: *HRMGuide.co.uk* (http://www.hrmguide.co.uk), 12 February 2001.

So, confining our discussion to 'best-person' and 'culture-fit' models for the moment, is selection best conducted subjectively or objectively? Smith and Robertson (1993, p.255) compare the two approaches:

- *Clinical*, or subjective. Just as a doctor diagnoses a medical condition on the basis of perceived symptoms, an 'expert' or experienced person reviews information on candidates. Choice is based on the expert's experience and expertise.

- *Actuarial*. Comparable to calculating an insurance premium. Various factors are quantified and put into a weighted equation. For example, experience may be given twice the value of educational qualifications. The candidate scoring the highest number of points is selected.

They conclude that the actuarial approach is better than the clinical method, but not to a very major extent. But what happens in practice? Nowicki and Rosse (2002) note that the state of practice in employee selection differs markedly from the state of research. They conducted interviews with 166 line managers and asked them to describe their own successes and failures in hiring. The managers attributed successful hiring largely to luck and intuition, but they also acknowledged the value of more systematic and rigorous approaches to selection. From their comments it seemed that they simply lacked awareness of research on selection such as comparative validities, rather than choosing to ignore this information.

Activity 15:1   Suggest some reasons why hiring managers do not necessarily use the best decision-making practices in employee selection.

Psychometric tests

Psychological tests have become commonplace. Psychometric means 'measurement of the mind'. Psychometric tests purport to measure psychological characteristics including personality, motivation, career interests, competencies and intellectual abilities. Traditionally they take the form of pen and paper multiple-choice questionnaires but modern forms can also be presented on computer screens. Most tests require applicants to work through a large number of items in a given amount of time. Some ask candidates to choose between various alternatives, as in the following example:

'Which of the following best describes you?'

1 I never take time off from work because of illness.
2 Sometimes I take time off work if I am very ill.
3 I believe in taking care of myself. If I am ill, I stay at home.

This kind of item is typical of personality and motivation tests. Other tests use pictures and geometrical shapes. Tests of number ability might offer a series of numbers and ask for the next two:

  2   4   8   16   ?   ?

This is a simple illustration – tests normally include items of increasing difficulty. The limited amount of time allowed ensures that few people can complete all items correctly.

Users argue that such tests provide valuable evidence that is not revealed by other methods. Additionally, there is a widespread belief that they are somehow objective, contrasting strongly with the subjectivity of interviewing. Candidates often feel that they may justifiably 'sell' themselves in an interview, creating an excessively favourable impression, whereas tests will magically reveal the truth. They give resourcing the semblance of scientific professionalism (Townley, 1989).

Tests are based on the psychometric model (Key concept 15.1) which: '... assumes that there is an optimal set ... of psychological characteristics for success at any human activity (in this instance, success at a particular job)' (Kline, 1993, p.374). Kline states that this is so obvious as to be banal. However, in our discussion of human resource planning we have seen that identifying such optimal sets is extremely difficult in practice. Specifically, job or personal specifications derived from traditional job analysis are backward-looking – they do not describe requirements for the future (Iles and Salaman, 1995, p.219). As we have seen, the traditional tightly prescribed 'job' is disappearing in favour of a more fluid, flexible role. Consequently, older notions of psychological 'dimensions' by which jobs and people are matched are being replaced by the more complex multi-dimensional concept of competencies.

Key concept 15:1

The psychometric model   The dominant approach to selection in British and US textbooks. In its traditional form, it grounds the 'best-person' model in psychological theory and testing. It embodies the use of refined techniques to achieve the best 'match' between job characteristics identified by formal job analysis and individual characteristics measured by psychological tests, structured interviews and other assessment methods.

Psychological testing has been used for different purposes in mainland Europe and North America, with the UK taking an intermediate view (Drenth, 1978). The reasons for this are complex and reflect different traditions. The 'softer' European approach has relied on more descriptive, observational methods such as projective techniques and qualitative performance tests that draw on psychoanalytic theory. Conversely, the American approach was dominated by behaviourist attitudes, emphasizing 'objectivity' and the quantitative use of data. This led to development of a massive range of 'paper and pencil' tests, suitable for individual or group use. Many European selection theorists have never been convinced of their merits. However, in recent years, growth of a more systematic methodology has meant that the two approaches have converged to a considerable extent.

Jenkins (2001) reviewed 17 surveys of psychometric test usage published between the early 1970s and 2000. The wide variation in methodology, sampling sizes and sample frames made it difficult to provide precise estimates of test usage for specific periods. However, a clear growth in use was seen from the 1980s onwards, with evidence of widespread adoption by large organizations in particular.

Jenkins (2001) considers that large organizations are more likely to use tests because: they have a greater number of vacancies across which to spread the fixed costs associated with testing; and they are more likely to have human resource specialists who are familiar with and trained for psychometric testing.

Key concept 15:2

Personality   Many lay people and psychologists believe that personality is a definite 'something' with a continuing existence at all stages of an individual's life, manifesting itself in every situation that person encounters. Generally expressed in terms of types or traits, the latter form the basis of most personality tests used for resourcing and the documentation employed for many performance appraisal systems. An alternative approach is to regard personality as an artefact of a particular set of circumstances. In other words, apparent personality depends on the meaning individuals give to a particular situation.

Table 15.1	Advantages and disadvantages of tests

Advantages	Disadvantages
● Test results are numerical – allowing direct comparison of applicants on the same criteria.	● Responses can be faked on many tests to give a 'desirable' score. Some include 'lie detectors' to overcome this.
● Tests provide 'hard' data that can be evaluated for their predictive usefulness in later years – i.e. compare predicted with actual performance.	● Some people lack sufficient self-insight to give accurate responses.
● Tests provide explicit and specific results unlike interviews and references which can be vague or 'coded'.	● Tests are unreliable – temporary factors such as anxiety, headaches, illness can lead to variable results.
● Tests measure substance rather than image.	● Tests are invalid – many tests do not measure what they say they measure.
● A battery of tests can cover a comprehensive range of abilities and personal qualities.	● Tests are irrelevant – many tests do not measure qualities that are relevant to a specific organization, such as honesty and punctuality.
● Tests are 'scientific' – empirically based with a grounding in theory. They are reliable, valid and discriminate between good, average and mediocre.	● Tests require minimum literacy and a grasp of American jargon.
● Tests provide a conceptual language to users, enhancing understanding of behaviour.	● Good norms do not exist for most populations – comparison with white, middle-class, male US students has little practical value.
● Empirical data from tests provide objective evidence to justify decisions.	● Tests are unfair to anyone who is not a white, middle-class, male American because most have been constructed using them as a reference population.
● Tests provide insights and explanations for behaviour. They can be used to justify individual rejections.	● Freedom of information legislation opens 'objective' data to greater scope for challenge than vague, unrecorded interview data.
	● Firms tend to use the same tests so that practice effects and knowledge of desirable answers can destroy their value.

Source: Adapted from Furnham (1992, p.39).

Table 15.2	Reasons for using selection tests

Reason	Per cent citing as a reason	Per cent citing as main reason
To predict job performance	76.1	39.4
To provide additional information before interview	73.5	27.9
To assess ability of applicants to 'fit into' organizational culture	67.3	25.0
To screen people for emotional stability	20.4	1.0
Other	12.4	6.7

Source: Adapted from IRS (1997).

Activity 15:2   Review the advantages and disadvantages of using psychometric tests for small and large organizations.

Criticism of psychological testing

Increasing use has caused some disquiet among psychologists, particularly the proliferation of personality assessments (Bartram, 1991). There are many available on the market promoted by people without adequate training and making extravagant claims about their value and effectiveness. Many employers, including those with human resource specialists, do not have the ability to identify good and bad products. In an attempt to distinguish the trained from the untrained, the British Psychological Society has introduced a Certificate in Occupation Testing Competence.

Furnham (1992, p.5) criticizes the underlying research which 'justifies' specific personality measures on a number of grounds:

● The personality characteristics chosen are often arbitrary and uninformed. Often they are historical relics, long-abandoned and condemned by psychologists but still exploited as commercial products.

● Statistical analyses tend to be simple and naive, leading to more findings of significant differences than there are in reality (Type II errors). Usually, simple correlations are used – rather than 'robust and sensitive' multivariate statistics – when all the variables involved are multi-factorial.

● Most studies are exploratory, with no theoretical basis and are not part of systematic programmes. As a result, they tend to be 'one-off', sometimes with interesting implications but no particular consequence.

● Organizational and social factors are often ignored – personality may not be the only relevant factor.

Blinkhorn and Johnson (1991) criticize personality tests as predictors of job performance compared to ability and aptitude tests. They argue that their validity coefficients are often no better than chance. However, other specialists consider that personality tests are still valuable if they are used carefully and are not taken to be the main predictors. For example, 'conscientiousness' is linked to job performance and 'extraversion' scores are useful predictors for sales ability.

The greatest fault of personality tests is that candidates can lie. Individuals may score highly on extraversion because they are extraverts. Alternatively they can present themselves as outgoing because it is clear from the job description that selectors are seeking extraverts. It has also been argued that, since tests are based on personality theory, they cannot be interpreted without knowledge of the theory in which most selectors are untrained. Another contentious issue is the effect of practice. If applicants are exposed to the same test on more than one occasion, they gain from the previous experience, often remembering answers.

Wood and Baron (1992) consider the effect of psychological tests in terms of 'adverse impact' on ethnic minority groups: '"Adverse impact" occurs when there is a significant disparity in test scores between ethnic groups, resulting in one group being disproportionately preferred over the other. The test is then said to have an adverse impact on the lower-scoring group.' They argue that the greater degree of adverse impact, the more this has to be justified. Employers must be careful to test strictly for qualities that can be proven to be required for the job. Even when this can be demonstrated it remains important to find the method of measurement with the least adverse impact. A common problem is the effect of language proficiency on test performance. Typically, ethnic minority candidates are undergoing a selection procedure in the dominant community language, such as English, when they are stronger linguistically in another, such as Hindi or Italian. Their performance is masked by their comprehension of the questions and their ability to express their answers in a manner that is meaningful to the testers. Often, tests are time-limited. This is a reasonable gauge of mental speed for native speakers because their use of language is automatic. However, it is detrimental to people answering out of their native languages, because they need to translate at a conscious mental level. In effect the test becomes an assessment of 'proficiency in English' rather than a measure of its true objectives such as 'problem-solving ability' or 'motivation'. The test has become unfair for anyone whose first language is not English.

In a case involving British Rail (BR), it was shown that, in an analysis of 4000 tests taken by potential drivers, white people were twice as successful as ethnic minority candidates. Eight guards of Asian origin took BR to an industrial tribunal on the grounds that the tests were discriminatory. The verbal reasoning tests employed were not directly related to the job and were particularly difficult for people who spoke English as a second language. BR admitted that the tests had adverse impact on Asian workers and undertook to seek the advice of the Commission for Racial Equality in developing revised selection techniques.

Similarly, the Council for Legal Education (CLE) introduced a critical reasoning test for around 2300 applicants to the English Bar's training school. The CLE had attempted to provide a test that was as fair as possible and involved two firms of occupational psychologists and Birkbeck College of the University of London. However, the test was trialled on a group of existing students which included very few from ethnic minority groups. According to Makbool Javaid, chair of the Society of Black Lawyers, it was felt that 'some of the questions would be difficult to answer for anyone who was not from a middle-class public school kind of background' (*Times Higher*, 18 March 1994). The results produced a storm of protest and the tests were soon reconsidered. These reservations are widely known among human resource specialists and may explain Storey's (1994a) report of a reduction in use of personality tests around that time.

Activity 15:3	Are psychometric tests fair?

Interviewing

The interview is a social ritual expected by all participants, including applicants. It is such a 'normal' feature of filling vacancies that candidates for a job would be extremely surprised not to be interviewed at least once.

Informal interviews

Many employers invite applicants for informal interviews prior to the main selection procedure. These interviews are useful for information exchange, particularly in the case of professionals (Breakwell, 1990, p.10). They provide the opportunity to discuss the full nature of the job, the working environment, prospects for further development and promotion. Candidates who decide that the job is not for them can elect to go no further. To avoid interviews degenerating into pointless chats, Breakwell emphasizes that both interviewer and applicant need to have checklists of essential points to cover. Interviewers should:

● Give a balanced picture of the job, including an honest account of its disadvantages together with a (larger) number of positive aspects. Honesty might seem dangerous but is best in the long run.

- A description of the organization in the same terms.
- Introduce the interviewee to other people in the department. This also allows interested parties to vet the applicant.

Blackman (2002a) investigated the practice of telephone interviews – a common way of conducting informal interviewees. The study was aimed at determining if impoverished personality judgements of job applicants would come from telephone interviews in comparison to face-to-face interviews, given the lack of crucial non-verbal communication. Mock job interviews were used in both face-to-face format and telephone format. A significantly higher correlation was found between personality ratings of face-to-face interviewers and other sources of an applicant's personality ratings. Not surprisingly, face-to-face interviewers also rated applicants significantly higher or more favourably on personality traits that are normally best-revealed by non-verbal communication.

There seems to be some ambiguity as to whether informal interviews should be used as part of the pre-selection process by the employer rather than self-selection by the candidate. The crux of the issue depends on what interviewees have been told. If they have been led to believe that it is a truly informal information session they will not consider the process to be fair if they are subsequently told that they have not been shortlisted as a result.

Key concept 15:3

Person perception   The perception of other people. Cues such as facial expression, posture, gesture, body movement, tone of voice, etc., are used to evaluate their current mood and overall personalities (McKenna, 1994, p.144). Each one of us has an 'implicit personality theory' based on our experience, assumptions about people, beliefs and prejudices. The evidence of our senses is used to collect data about the perceived person and attribute characteristics to them according to our implicit theory. This is a simplification process and leads to a number of well-known errors of judgement, including:

- *Logical error:* assuming that certain traits are always found together – e.g. if a person is described as 'objective' we tend to perceive them as 'cold'.
- *Halo effect:* the tendency to perceive people as all 'good' or all 'bad'.
- *Stereotyping:* seeing all members of a particular group – e.g. Africans, Scots – to have the same characteristics. Stereotyping leads to prejudice.

Activity 15:4   When would you use an informal interview?

Formal interviews

A selection interview can be defined neatly as 'a conversation with a purpose' but not infrequently the purpose is obscure to the point of invisibility. More often than not 'purposeless chat' would be nearer the mark. It is a form of social interaction in which the interviewer is engaged in active person perception of the interviewee (see Key concept 15.3). From the interviewee's perspective 'one is managing a demonstration of knowledge or ability through a social vehicle, and one inevitably needs to attend to the social as well as the cognitive aspect of the interview' (Sternberg, 1994, p.181). In other words, the impression created depends as much on social factors as any demonstration of experience or expertise.

For many unskilled or semi-skilled jobs, the formal interview tends to be perfunctory and can be over in a few sentences. This is not necessarily a bad thing. For decades, the evidence has been that the more sophisticated and lengthy proceedings entered into by major organizations often have been no better in terms of outcome. According to Sternberg (1994, p.182): 'Interviewers tend to prefer interviewees who are relaxed, who put the interviewers at ease, who are socially as well as verbally facile, and who have some degree of interpersonal sparkle.'

In fact, the interview has attracted severe criticism for a very long time. W.D. Scott is quoted as having said in 1915 that the selection interview is not a dependable selection method (Lewis, 1985, p.150). Since then the interview has been attacked on the grounds of its subjective nature, questionable validity and unreliability. Webster (1964) noted some significant findings:

- First impressions count. Interviewers make their minds up in the first few minutes, then seek evidence to support their opinion.
- The candidate's appearance is the most significant factor, followed by information on the application form.
- Unfavourable evidence is valued more strongly than favourable evidence.
- The interviewer's opinion 'comes over' to the candidate during the interview and influences the candidate's further performance in an unfavourable or favourable direction.

Nevertheless, in a survey of 60 interviewers and 90 candidates in a 'milkround' exercise, 95 per cent of interviewers and 85 per cent of candidates considered interviews to be fair (*Personnel Management*, March 1992). Comparing panel with one-to-one interviews, 52 per cent of the interviewers said panel interviews were fairer, 35 per cent were unsure and 13 per cent preferred one-to-one interviews. In contrast, nearly two-thirds of the candidates preferred one-to-one interviews, with only 13 per cent indicating a positive preference for the panel approach.

Evaluating methods

How do we judge the value or effectiveness of interviewing – or any other method of selection? Before going further it is useful to consider the four basic requirements (Smith, 1991, p.32):

1 *Practicality.* Selection methods must be practical in a given situation – for example cost, convenience and time available. Attitudes of employers and candidates to the methods are also relevant.

2 *Sensitivity.* The ability of a method to distinguish one candidate from another. Interviews may rank a number of candidates fairly closely, whereas tests may give a wide range of scores.

3 *Reliability.* How consistent are the results? Conventionally, there are three forms of reliability measure:
   - Comparison over time. If a method is used on the same group of candidates on different days, are the scores likely to be similar? This is sometimes called test-retest or intra-rater reliability.
   - Inter-rater reliability. If two or more assessors are involved, how much agreement is there between them?
   - Internal consistency. If several items in a test or procedure are meant to measure the same characteristic, such as sociability, how close are the ratings?

Table 15.3	Comparative validities	
Validity range	Methods	Rating
0.4 to 0.5+	Work sample tests Ability tests	Good–excellent
0.3 to 0.39	Biodata Assessment centres Structured interviews	Acceptable
Less than 0.3	Personality tests Typical interviews References Graphology	Poor
Chance (0)	Astrology	

Source: Adapted from Smith (1991).

4 Validity. Does the method achieve its purpose in distinguishing the most suitable applicants from the others? Three measures of validity are available:
- Face validity. Does the method appear to be measuring what it is supposed to measure? This is important because it is essential that candidates believe that they have been fairly treated. Disappointed applicants frequently complain about apparently irrelevant interview questions or test items. For example, one selection test includes the question: 'Do you like tall women?' Whether or not this has deep psychological significance, its appearance is enough to bring derision on the test.
- Construct validity. To what extent does the method measure a particular construct or human quality such as commitment?
- Predictive validity. How well does the method predict the suitability of a successful candidate?

Reliability and validity are expressed as correlational coefficients where perfection is represented by 1.0 and pure chance is shown by zero. Establishing the validity of a particular procedure logically requires the employer to take on a large number of applicants, good and bad, and then compare their job performance with that predicted by the selection method. This kind of predictive validity study is impractical in most circumstances. Sometimes termed 'the one that got away' problem, we never know how the people we did not select might have performed.

Research shows that similar results can be obtained by a method termed 'concurrent study' where selection methods are employed on existing employees at the same time as the selection procedure is taking place. Performance of existing employees is then correlated with prediction scores of the selection method. Again, however, this is rarely done, partly because accurate performance measures are difficult to obtain for many jobs.

Fairness is a further requirement: specifically, candidates' perceptions of the equity of the process. As we see in the Toyota 'HRM in reality' illustration, good candidates are more likely to accept an offer if they consider that the procedure has been fair, effective and considerate. Moreover, candidates must receive full and accurate description of the job and their prospects in the company. Misleading impressions can lead to wastage sooner rather than later as the new recruit realizes that expectations and reality do not match. This is particularly the case with young employees – for example graduates who tend not to have clear 'vocational maturity' or awareness of their own skills and career needs (Herriot and Fletcher, 1990).

Activity 15:5	Explain the difference between validity and reliability in your own words.

HRM in reality

Toyota in Europe

In common with several other major Japanese car manufacturers, Toyota has established a production facility in Europe. By 1994 it had spent nearly £1 billion on its factories in Britain and development facilities in Brussels. Production in 1995 was forecast to be 90 000 cars with a workforce of 1950. The cars included 80 per cent local content, derived from 200 European suppliers. In the long term Toyota aims to employ 3000 staff producing 200 000 cars at its factory in Burnaston, Derbyshire, UK. Its resourcing practices were typical of Japanese transplant ventures. The first 1100 staff included just 78 Japanese, over 90 per cent of the employees being locals living within 35 miles of the factory. The average employee was male, aged around thirty and had no experience of car production. Workers were called 'team members' and had typically gone through a six to seven-month recruitment process. According to Bryan Jackson, director of human resources: 'We want people who can work as a team and who have ideas for improvements and can demonstrate an ability to learn.'

The resourcing procedure included:

- A five-page application form with biodata items 'designed to test commitment'. These included questions about personal values and achievements.

- A three-hour 'testing and orientation phase'. This was a series of tests to measure numerical skills, attitudes and learning ability. They included a 'Video-Interactive Test of Learning' which asked candidates to give responses to a number of situations.

- Then came the interview phase. Bryan Jackson explained that:

  We didn't want the traditional 20-minute interview, and the 'you-go-to-the-same-football-match-as-me-so-you-must-be-okay line'. Instead candidates received a 'targeted behavioural interview' which consisted of 75 minutes of questions on situations they had experienced. Their decisions were assessed on the basis that 'It's well known that past behaviour is a good predictor of future behaviour.'

- Having survived so far, candidates were then given a work sample: six hours on a simulated production line making wheel trims or fuel filters under realistic conditions.

- The final hurdles were a further (one hour) interview, two references and a medical.

Prior to the first car being manufactured, 400 production staff were employed from over 20 000 applicants for the 39-hour a week jobs.

The British workers had achieved comparable quality standards to the company's Japanese plants. However, Japanese factories made further productivity gains in reaction to the recession. European manufacturing is not expected to be profitable until production has reached 130 000–140 000 vehicles a year.

Interviews revisited

Since the late 1980s there has been a revision of opinion concerning the value of interviews (Smith, 1991; Eder and Harris, 1999). Earlier research findings were based on small samples. The use of meta-analytic techniques allows the combination of statistics from a number of small studies to give much larger samples. For example, Weisner and Cronshaw (1988) combined validity coefficients from 150 studies and concluded that interviews can be more valid than suspected. In fact, their validity depends on the type of interview. Traditional, or unstructured interviews comprise the vast majority and are generally no more than cosy chats. Their validity was found to be 0.2 (very poor) whereas structured interviews, especially those based on job analysis, were found to be significantly better with a validity of 0.63.

Structured interviews are conducted to a format – rather than a script – and focus questioning on the job rather than irrelevant incidentals such as holidays and golf. Some standard methods are:

- Criterion referenced interviews, based on job analysis with a set of questions geared to experience and skill for interviewers to choose from.

- Situational interviews, based on the 'critical incidents' technique. A reasonable number (typically 20) of real-life work incidents are obtained from job-holders or their supervisors. Possible ways of dealing with these situations are outlined and rated as suitable or unsuitable, frequently on a points system. These situations are presented to candidates as hypothetical problems and responses evaluated against predetermined ratings.

Moscoso (2000) reviewed evidence on the criterion and construct validity of the interview. Based on the content of questions included in selection interviews, Moscoso identified two types of structured interview: the conventional structured interview and the behavioural structured interview. Criterion validity studies generally support the view that behavioural structured interviews show the highest validity coefficients. Moscoso found a lower level of investigation into construct validity but concluded from studies available that conventional structured interviews and behavioural structured interviews were clearly measuring different constructs. Also, behavioural structured interviews seemed to produce more frequent negative applicant reactions than conventional structured interviews.

A further study by Salgado and Moscoso (2002) included a series of meta-analyses on the construct validity of conventional interviews and behavioural interviews. Conventional interviews typically include questions aimed at checking credentials, description of experience and self-evaluative information. Behavioural interviews consist mainly of questions regarding job knowledge, job experience and behavior descriptions. They found that conventional interviews assessed general mental ability, job experience, the 'Big Five' personality dimensions and social skills. Behavioural interviews, on the other hand, mainly assessed job knowledge, job experience, situational judgement and social skills. Although there was some overlap, the two main forms of interview seemed to be different.

To be effective, an interview must be more than a friendly chat. The greater the degree of planning beforehand, the greater the likelihood of a higher degree of validity as a selection tool. The function of the interview is to obtain predictive evidence regarding a candidate's likely performance on specific criteria. The questioning style can be linked to the kind of evidence required and may take one of three principal routes:

- *(Hypothetical) problem-solving questioning* in which the candidate is presented with situations to evaluate or solve and which can be expected to test the candidate's abilities in a number of respects – e.g. intellect, grasp of information, problem-solving ability, lateral thinking, practicality, creativity, etc.

- *Behavioural (past) event questioning,* which assumes that previous handling of situations and problems predicts an individual's future performance in similar circumstances.

- *Patterned behavioural event (life) questioning*, which attempts to identify an individual's career or life strategy, establishing how rational and sensible changes in that person's life have been and drawing conclusions about stability, seriousness of application and likely motivation. The 'culture fit' approach emphasizes this perspective. For example, Japanese companies such as Toyota are more interested in personality than technical skill. They look for a personal philosophy that fits the corporate culture. Modern call centres similarly seek a range of competencies from customer care through to commitment-related qualities (Callaghan and Thompson, 2002).

Blackman (2002b) investigated structured and unstructured employment interviews in relation to the assessment of applicants' job-related personality traits. The hypothesis was that unstructured interviews would lead to more accurate personality assessments since interviewees would feel less constrained by a script and more readily manifest their true selves. Behaviour in mock job interviews (structured and unstructured) was coded by an independent rater. Self-ratings of job-related personality traits on the California Q-set were obtained for each interviewee, together with ratings of their personality from the interviewer and a peer of the interviewee. A correlation analysis supported the original hypothesis, showing that average self-interviewer and peer-interviewer agreement was significantly greater when interviews had used the unstructured method.

Barclay (2001), however, comes out in favour of the behavioural structured interview. A survey of the use of behavioural interviewing in selection for UK organizations showed that both interviewers and applicants were positive about the method. Barclay identifies the following as key benefits:

- better quality information-gathering leading to improved selection decisions
- more consistency and improved skills of interviewers
- better opportunities for applicants to explain their skills.

But Barclay also recognizes limitations in respect of training, practice and time required, scoring.

Other approaches that have ethical considerations to take into account include stress interviewing and 'sweet and sour'. Stress interviewing, where the candidate is pressurized, sometimes aggressively, are justified on the basis that the job is pressurized and, therefore, it is important to establish how the candidate is likely to perform under stressful circumstances. One study asked interviewers if they ever deliberately put candidates under stress in interviews to see how they would cope (*Personnel Management*, March 1992). The findings were disturbing with 13 per cent saying they often did, 27 per cent saying sometimes and 27 per cent rarely.

'Sweet and sour' are where interviewers take completely different approaches, one pleasant, one unpleasant in an attempt to gain a wider range of responses from the candidate.

Activity 15:6	Review the merits and disadvantages of unstructured, structured and behaviourally structured interview methods.

Preparation for interviews

Training for interviewers stresses a number of factors conducive to making a good impression on the candidate. The interviewer should ensure that relevant information (application forms, etc.) is read beforehand – it is surprising how many interviewers are found to be reading such material for the first time *during* the interview. The interview should take place in an appropriate environment – a quiet room without interruptions, with comfortable but business-like furniture and so on. The candidate should be put at ease as much as possible.

A major change in recent years has been the improvement in applicants' interview techniques. Redundant staff are commonly given the opportunity of outplacement counselling, which normally includes advice on CV preparation and coaching in interview technique. Managers who are rarely involved in selection, perhaps only conducting interviews once or twice a year, are at a disadvantage against trained applicants. Interview coaching is similar in principle to training politicians for television appearances. Astute trainees can learn how to mask insincerity and to promise the earth with apparent conviction.

Against trained interviewers, the most useful tactic for applicants is to become familiar with the company they are applying for. This requires research on the company's history, products or services and its reported strategy. Knowledge of the industry or sector in which it operates is also valuable. This information should not be acquired by pestering the recruitment section on the telephone. Given the number of applications to advertised vacancies at present, this is likely to be unwise. Whether or not any direct questions are asked on these subjects, applicants who have researched the territory will be able to form their responses in a way that makes it clear that they have done so.

Interviewing techniques

There are significant variations in the way employers conduct interviews. The most common method is the 'singleton' interview when the candidate's fate is determined by one session with a single interviewer. For obvious reasons, this method is likely to be regarded as unfair by interviewees who are not selected. There is no check or record of bias on the part of the interviewer who may have made a judgement on a complete whim.

A long-standing method which attempts to overcome this problem is the panel or board interview, involving a number of interviewers. Typically, two or three people ask questions in turn. A classic format involves an 'operational' interviewer, usually a line manager from the department offering the job and a personnel interviewer, normally from the personnel department. There may be an additional chair person. Each asks questions appropriate to their areas of expertise, the operational assessor asking task-related questions and the personnel assessor investigating career aspiration and motivation. The board is sometimes much larger: there are instances of seven or nine interviewers.

Superficially, the panel interview is judged to be fairer since all questioning takes place in a public arena and candidates' responses are heard by all parties. It also offers the candidate a more varied range of questions, expanding the evidence available to the assessors. As a consequence, personal bias should have less effect. However, the situation is likely to be more stressful for candidates. There are also opportunities for organizational politics to enter the situation, especially when the procedure is an internal selection.

Dipboye *et al.* (2001) looked at unstructured panel interviews for corrections officers and found a weak aggregate level of validity in the prediction of job performance and training success. Aggregate analyses also showed only a small incremental contribution to the prediction of job performance from panel judgements relative to paper credentials and found the two sources of information to be only weakly related. But there was a considerable variation in simple and incremental validity at the level of individual panel members and among sub-groups of panels. They conclude that aggregate analyses underestimate the validity of the typical unstructured panel interview.

A further variant is the 'sequential' method, with two or more interviews but with the candidate only being expected to face one interviewer at a time. This method carries most of the advantages of singleton and panel interviews with fewer of the disadvantages.

It is possible to use group interviews in certain circumstances. We will see later in this chapter that they are useful within assessment centre programmes as information sessions.

As with many other aspects of selection, interviewing has been formalized and packaged into training programmes available for both selectors and candidates. Untrained assessors are likely to conduct interviews in an unstructured way. Interview training is a useful component of management training. The best training programmes encourage people to become aware of their body language and questioning styles, helping them to develop interview techniques that open up fresh areas of evidence. Many junior managers and job club participants have had the opportunity to see themselves 'in action' on video taking part in mock interviews. Initially demoralizing (for most), it is an invaluable method of feedback.

Packaged training methods have led to a certain sameness, however, and seasoned job applicants and interviewers now enter into formalized duals where each participant is aware of the underlying dynamics. Typically, interviewers are taught to:

● Ask open not closed questions to elicit the maximum information. Questions beginning with how, what, why, when reduce the frequency of yes/no answers and force candidates to think about their replies.

● Provide supportive body language which suggests interest in what the candidate is saying without indicating approval or disapproval.

● Employ questioning styles such as the use of funnelling. Here the interviewer asks a succession of how, what, why questions on the same subject in an attempt to achieve a depth of evidence.

● Consider factual or hypothetical questions, such as 'How would you go about setting up a telephone system for a remote island in the Pacific?' Provided that the interviewee is not a qualified telecommunications engineer, an applicant for a totally unconnected job will have to think hard to provide a full, imaginative but practical answer.

Tom Peters dismissed this 'quick analysis' technique as honouring glibness (*Independent on Sunday*, syndicated article 8 May 1994). Many interviewers have strong opinions on what they are looking for and how they should set about it. Peters held that 'interviews should be the centrepiece of a respectful courting process' foregoing 'pop quizzes and sadistic questioning rituals'. Arguing that the past was the only guide to future performance he set out an interviewing programme in typical guru style.

1 *Put the candidate's resumé under a microscope.* Pull an applicant's CV apart, following up experiences and achievements, including:
   ● 'the kid who went through college without participating in extracurricular activities – without *leading* those activities – is not likely to be a tiger on the job'
   ● scrutinize college grades
   ● an extensive check of references, previous work samples and work commendations ('employee of the month certificates or their equivalents').

2 *Look for a legacy.* Good performance in the past is not enough – how did they make their previous jobs better and different?

3 *Examine their turn-ons.* Talk about the applicant's 'peak experiences at work or school'. Apparently 'what a person brags about is a key to future job performance.' Essentially, is the candidate a solo performer or a teamworker?

4 *Seek deviance, defiance and adventure.* Has the applicant broken with convention and done something in an unusual way? For example, by taking time out from education and travelling the world. 'Curiosity and productive kinkiness in the past will raise the odds of getting more of the same in the future.'

5 *Pursue animal energy.* If the 'spirit and zest' of the candidate exhaust you by the end of the interview, 'hire that one on the spot'.

6 *Trust your gut.* Ignoring interview nervousness, is the applicant 'the kind of person you would like to hang around with?'

| Activity 15:7 | Evaluate Peters' approach against our discussion on the various types of interview. |

Work samples

Interviews suffer from a basic problem: they obtain answers from candidates which, in effect, are unverifiable claims. When asked what they would do in a particular situation it is only natural for candidates to give the answer they feel the interviewer wants to hear. There is no guarantee that a candidate would actually behave in that way in a real situation. In addition, it is common for candidates to exaggerate their abilities or experience and play down their inadequacies.

The work sample technique attempts to overcome this problem by asking candidates to take on 'mini jobs' in a selection situation. Properly designed work samples capture key elements of a real job. As such, they are realistic rather than hypothetical or abstract and should include features of the context in which the job functions. Work samples have shown some of the highest validity scores compared to other selection methods (Smith, Gregg and Andrews, 1989, p.70). They are comparatively easy to organize and even the smallest of companies could employ the simpler forms such as:

- a typing test for jobs requiring keyboard skills
- bricklaying
- role playing
- group decisions
- presentations
- reports.

The most sophisticated of work sample procedures include in-basket tests, sometimes called in-tray exercises. Normally used for managerial jobs, candidates are given a typical in-tray containing a selection of material such as letters to be answered, reports to be analysed, items to be prioritized, etc. They are given instructions on what to do and a time limit. Standard scoring methods are available. Work samples are often used as part of an assessment centre programme.

Assessment centres

Recent surveys indicate increasing use of assessment centres, especially by large companies. They have been heavily researched in recent years, with the emphasis on their reliability and predictive validity. They show up well in comparison with most other forms of selection or assessment such as interviews and personality tests. Meta analyses indicate much more respectable validity coefficients for assessment centres in predicting managerial success than with any other method. However, as we will discuss shortly, their use is not entirely without difficulties.

Assessment centres are procedures and not necessarily places. They function on the principle that no individual method of selection is particularly good and no individual assessor is infallible. Accordingly, they use multiple methods and several assessors in structured programmes which attempt to minimize the inadequacies of each method and cancel out the prejudices of individual selectors. Inevitably, assessment centres are very expensive methods of selection. However, cheaper methods are focused towards past or present performance. This may be adequate where applicants are being assessed for jobs that are broadly similar to their current or previous work. When this is not the case, and applicants are being considered for more stretching tasks, they fail to provide the evidence as to how candidates are likely to perform. Most management promotions come into this category. Good managers need to demonstrate knowledge, skills and abilities that may not have been required at lower levels. How can we identify these characteristics? Assessment centres are particularly useful in this respect because they are focused on potential. They bring taxing problems and challenges to candidates in a situation that allows systematic observation and measurement of their performance.

The origins of the assessment centre lie in the violent history of the 20th century and the need for officer selection. Originally devised by the German army in the 1930s, assessment centre techniques were soon taken up in other countries. The British War Office Selection Board subjected candidates to a three to four day assessment geared to evaluating leadership and organizational abilities. This included exercises in which intending officers had to negotiate obstacles such as rivers with a motley collection of squaddies and an assortment of ropes, planks and oil drums. They also included lengthy interviews and long written reports.

Some modern assessment centres with an 'outward bound' inclination continue to include such exercises, but most consist of group discussions, psychometric tests, interviews and exercises such as 'in-basket' work samples and presentations. The underlying intention is to measure applicants on the competencies deemed to be appropriate to the job. Simulations in the assessment centre are designed to bring out the behaviour that demonstrates possession of these competencies. The intention is not to estimate current ability but to predict future performance, possibly at higher management levels.

After World War II the method spread to the public sector and then to industry. The first industrial application was at the American Telephone and Telegraph Company (AT&T). Their experience had a major influence on subsequent use elsewhere following a number of studies in which employees were compared with initial assessment centre evaluations. These studies showed a significant correlation between the evaluations and subsequent work performance (Smith, Gregg and Andrews, 1989). The model form of assessment centre is an expensive process (Byham, 1984).

A typical assessment centre involves six participants and lasts from one to three days. As participants go through the simulations they are observed by assessors (usually three) who are specially trained in observing and evaluating behaviour. Assessors observe different participants in each simulation and take notes on special observation forms. Then, after the simulations are completed, assessors spend one or more days sharing their observations and reaching agreement on evaluations of participants. Their final assessment, contained in a summary report for each participant, gives a detailed account of participants' strengths and development needs as well as an evaluation of overall potential for success in the 'target' position. Based on Blanksby and Iles (1990), the following list sets out the seven conditions that classically characterize assessment centres.

1 A number of assessment techniques must be used, of which at least one must be a simulation. Simulations could take the form of work samples, group exercises and in-baskets. Simulations are designed to bring out behaviours that are related to dimensions of performance on the actual job in question.

2 There must be multiple trained assessors.

3 Ratings must be pooled between assessors and assessment techniques in order to provide a judgement on a selection, training or development programme.

4　Overall assessment of behaviour has to take place at a different time from the observation of behaviour.

5　Simulation exercises must be pre-developed to elicit a number of desired behaviours. They must be tested in advance to ensure that the results are relevant to the organization and that they are reliable and objective.

6　All dimensions, qualities, attributes or characteristics to be measured by the assessment centre must be determined by some form of job analysis.

7　The assessment techniques used must be designed to provide evidence for the evaluation of these dimensions.

Problems with assessment centres

Whether or not it is costed in financial terms, the impact of assessment centres on management time is considerable. Managers may appreciate the value of high-quality selection procedures, but will be reluctant to devote so much time. Additionally, the traditional process is group-based and is unusable in situations where only one or two candidates are being considered.

The effectiveness of an assessment centre depends upon its design and the anticipation of problems. Common design faults have been well documented (Dulewicz, 1991):

- The criteria for measurement are too woolly. Often, the competencies on which candidates are being assessed are very poorly defined and not expressed in behavioural terms that can be measured.

- The competencies are not mutually exclusive and overlap each other. Candidates are rewarded or penalized twice, depending on their strength in a particular area.

- Criteria are tied to the past, rather than being forward-looking.

- Exercises are badly designed and do not relate to experiences that are likely to occur within the organization. Alternatively, and perhaps because of this, they do not relate to the assessment criteria.

- Assessment centres contain a wide range of procedures, from group exercises to psychometric tests. Results from these procedures take a variety of forms. Integrating the results is complex, particularly when combining evidence on single competencies from a number of procedures. Poor technical design at this stage will lead to misleading findings.

- Poor assessor training. Line managers are unlikely to be good assessors unless they have been trained to avoid pitfalls such as 'halos and horns'. Also they require guidance on the range and skew of their assessments. Assessors need to be consistent in how they pitch their ratings, avoiding over-leniency or severity.

- Poor pre-selection and briefing of candidates. The consequence is that some candidates flounder from the beginning of the programme. Others become hostile towards a procedure that appears to them to be unfair or disorganized.

- Poor programming, leaving both assessors and candidates unsure of what they are supposed to be doing. They may be allotted too little or too much time at different points in the assessment.

- Inadequate handling of the programme events due to lack of coordination or commitment.

- Inadequate (or non-existent) follow-up. This may occur in the form of badly handled feedback counselling or inaction on assessors' recommendations.

● Poor evaluation of candidates' experience and assessors' performance on the programme.

Dulewicz (1991) considered that there were three broad phases that accounted for most of these difficulties:

1 programme design
2 selection and training of assessors
3 effective follow-up action.

He attributed many of the shortcomings to inexperience. Assessment centres are involved and complex. Good design is dependent on the knowledge and skills to design and develop what is a 'highly precise and sophisticated tool'.

Activity 15:8	Assessment centres are infrequently used. Why is this so?

Graphology

Graphology, or handwriting analysis, has a long history on the mainland of Europe. It originated in Italy in the early 17th century and was further refined in France and Germany where it is used widely. The essence of graphology is that analysts claim to be able to describe an individual's personality from a sample of their handwriting. Their theoretical base is that of trait psychology, which holds that personality has a number of fixed dimensions that are relatively unchangeable and do not depend on the situation. This is not to say that people do not change, indeed many graphologists believe their strongest asset to be the identification of neurotic or stress-related conditions that may be transient. Some graphologists also claim to be able to detect such characteristics as alcohol problems, homosexuality and dishonesty.

The British company S.G. Warburg have used graphology in selection for a long time:

> The recent candidate interviewed for a junior job in Warburg's computer department provided an excellent CV, and seemed able and confident in the course of two interviews. His handwriting sample, however, was abnormally cramped. The lines were crooked and the letters spidery and badly squashed. At best, it seemed the writing of an ill-educated child. But Mrs Nezos [graphologist] thought otherwise. For an employer like Warburg, the prospect of hiring a drug addict is too frightening to contemplate. The man was turned down for the job.
> (*Independent on Sunday*, 20 October 1991)

Evidently, the graphologist believed that spidery, squashed writing indicated drug addiction!

Handwriting analysis is routine and highly regarded in many continental European countries but is generally regarded with disdain in most English-speaking countries. Moss (1992) reported high levels of use in France including large companies such as St. Gobin, Elf Aquitaine, Crédit Lyonnaise and Peugeot. In Switzerland, Crédit Suisse, Sandoz and most banks and insurance companies use graphology. Curtis Casewit, an American graphologist, claimed that West Germany had as many graphologists as dental surgeons in 1980 (*The Economist*, 16 June 1990).

Cox and Tapsell (1991) compared analyses by graphologists and non-graphologists of 50 handwriting samples provided by managers on a training course. When assessment centre results were compared with the handwriting analyses, they found that the graphologists did slightly worse than the non-graphologists in rating the candidates. Moreover, the two graphologists failed to agree with each other!

The different attitudes towards graphology were highlighted in Shackleton and Newell's (1991) comparison of selection methods in the UK and France. They extended the methodology of an earlier UK study by Robertson and Makin (1986), comparing responses from companies in the 'Times Top 1000' list and similar French firms in 'Les 200 Premières Groups des Echos' (Table 15.4). Apart from use of graphology, other differences were apparent on the two sides of the English Channel. Unlike British firms, French companies rarely used multiple-interviewer panel or board interviews but do use the sequential system. Whereas references continued to be considered in many UK decisions (but less so

Table 15.4	Comparison of British and French selection methods	
Method	UK (per cent)	France (per cent)
Application forms	93	98
Interviews	93	94
More than one interview	60	92
References	74	11
Cognitive tests	70	50
Handwriting	3	77
Biodata	19	4
Assessment centre	59	19

Source: Shackleton and Newell (1991).

Table 15.5	Selection methods used in US states public service	
Method		Percentage
Written tests for job knowledge		85
Oral exams		68
Training and experience evaluations		67
Resumé screens		63
Criminal record checks for certain positions only		44
Pre-employment drug testing for certain jobs only		44
Criminal record checks for *all* jobs		42
Assessment centres		40
Written aptitude tests		37
Skills inventories		28
Personality tests		23
Computerized written exams		18
Computerized skills inventories		17
Written intelligence tests		16
Video tests		14
Honesty tests		13

Source: 1998 HR Practices Benchmarking Project, IPMA 1998.

Table 15.6	Selection methods in the UK, 1999 and 2000		
Method	1999 (per cent)	2000 (per cent)	
Interviewing	100.0	99.6	
Application forms	82.1	80.9	
CVs	77.6	74.0	
Covering letter	58.2	63.4	
Ability/aptitude tests	60.8	54.2	
Personality questionnaires	42.5	36.3	
Assessment centres	30.2	26.0	
Telephone screening	18.3	17.6	
Biodata	4.1	6.9	
Graphology	1.1	1.9	

Source: CIPD (2000).

than in 1986), they were only used as factual checks in most large French companies. Tests tended to be used by the larger companies and exclusively so in France. Compare these findings both with the later survey of selection methods used in the public services of US states conducted by the IPMA in 1998 (Table 15.5) and a survey of UK companies by the CIPD (Table 15.6).

Summary

In free market countries, the personnel profession has adopted a 'best practice' model which fits the prevailing business ideology. This model prescribes a quest for the 'right (best) person for the job'. To achieve this goal, criteria are used to rate prospective applicants by means of selection techniques, including biographical data, interviews, psychometric tests, group exercises, simulated work samples and even handwriting analysis. The most definitive form of selection is likely to take place within the context of assessment centres, which involve several assessors and a variety of selection techniques. The 'best person' or psychometric model has achieved the status of orthodoxy in free market countries. Elsewhere different models of resourcing apply. For example, in Japan there is a greater concern with personality and background than presumed ability. Recruits are sought who will 'fit in' with the culture of the corporation; who will be content to build a career within the organization; who will absorb the goals of the organization.

Further reading

Competency-based Recruitment and Selection by Robert Wood and Tim Payne (1998), published by John Wiley & Sons, takes a 'best practice' approach to the selection process. *Human Resource Selection* by Robert Gatewood and Hubert Field, 5th edition, 2000, published by Thomson Learning, has a more technical approach. Books on interviewing include: *The Selection Interview* by Penny Hackett, CIPD (1998); and *Effective Interviewing* by Robert Edenborough, Kogan Page (2002).

Review questions

1 Are selection methods objective?

2 Discuss the advantages and disadvantages of the following: (a) structured and unstructured interviews; (b) assessment centres; (c) psychometric tests.

3 What criteria can be used to judge the effectiveness of selection methods? Define 'validity' and 'reliability' in your own words.

4 Evaluate the role of the line manager in the resourcing process.

5 Why are some selection methods used more often than others?

6 Is it possible to guarantee equality of opportunity in a resourcing process?

Problem for discussion and analysis

Everylang

Everylang is a small, fast-growing translation bureau. It needs to keep tight control of its costs in a very competitive market. The owner considers that its success depends on quality, presentation, speed of work and the ability to provide translations to and from any language. Most of the work is from the main European languages and into English. The company employs 12 staff, while the remaining work (over half) is farmed out to freelance translators who are only paid for the work they do. They deal with the office by a variety of means, including courier, post, fax and computer modems. It is sometimes difficult to get and maintain relationships with top quality freelancers, especially those with good word-processing equipment and able to transfer work electronically.

Situation

Everylang has now grown to the point where the owner-manager is too busy with marketing, finance and developing new customers to be able to cope with the day-to-day operations. You have been invited as an external consultant to advise on selecting an office manager for Everylang. It is apparent that the owner knows a great deal about the translation market but is inexpert in managing people. The owner is keen to promote a member of the existing staff, partly in order to improve motivation but mainly in order to keep costs down. Five have applied and you have been provided with the following job summary on which to base your initial thoughts.

- *Title*. Office Manager.

- *Pay*. Translator salary + 30 per cent + profit-related bonus and benefits.

- *Main purpose of job*. Day-to-day running of Everylang office, ensuring that incoming work is dealt with and returned to the agreed standard of quality and delivery time.

- *Functions*. Providing quotations for customers; dealing with enquiries by phone, post and fax; allocating work to full-time staff or freelancers; recording and progressing all incoming work, delivery on time and to the agreed quality; dealing with complaints; finding and monitoring new freelancers; completing personal computer records for billing and administration; and dealing with any personal problems among staff.

- *Personnel specification*. None existing.

Applicants

Helen. Age 42. Five years with Everylang. No formal qualifications. Translates French and Spanish. Ex-secretary. Has been translating for almost 20 years and knows a large number of other translators. Very efficient, quick and accurate. She is keen on long legal translations and has developed a considerable knowledge of business law in French-speaking countries. Pleasant personality but a little short-tempered. She has a good working relationship with other staff members but tends to keep her distance and does not socialize with them. Likes to take a six-week holiday at her parents' home in France every summer. She has an arrangement with the owner to take this partly as unpaid leave.

John. Age 36. Has been 12 years with Everylang. High school qualifications in French and Italian. Also has a diploma in translating and interpreting in the same languages. A great language enthusiast, he is proud of his standard of work. He translates mostly from French, specializing in letters and product information. Takes a keen interest in the welfare of the other staff. They have a considerable regard for him, respecting his professionalism and his interest in them. Over the last year he has had arguments with the owner over policy and thinks the company is growing too fast. He believes that the ever-increasing pressure of work is leading to inadequate checking of translations. Personally, he is quite efficient but pays too much attention to small details. Has been thinking of going self-employed.

Jill. Age 32. Three years with Everylang. Left school at 16. Took evening classes in French for several years. Cheerful, chatty person who gets on well with customers. Not a particularly good translator but useful for short French translations needed quickly. Can understand Scandinavian languages quite well, particularly Norwegian – she worked in Norway as a managing director's personal secretary for two years. The other staff do not respect her as a translator and often patronize her. She copes well, brushing off their remarks and getting on with her job. She has applied for a number of other jobs recently – without success.

Francesca. Age 26. Graduate in Spanish and Italian. Diploma in Translating. Also speaks Portuguese. Has 18 months' service. Undoubtedly the best translator in the office. She had considered becoming a language teacher but dropped out of the training programme after a year and joined Everylang. She is much younger than the other staff and relations are not particularly good. Gets on extremely well with major clients who find her vivacious personality attractive to deal with. She gives customers a feeling of confidence in her abilities. Francesca sees Everylang as a long-term career job, is ambitious and enthusiastic about major expansion. At the moment, she is having major problems with her pre-school age child who suffers from asthma. Sometimes she takes time off with little notice. She has promised the boss that her difficulties will be sorted out soon.

▶

David. Age 55. Three years with company. BA and MA in German Literature. Former export manager, made redundant from a major company. He translated on a freelance basis before joining Everylang. He is the only full-time German translator. A workaholic – he never seems to leave the office and is always ready to work overtime to complete a piece of work. He is regarded as bookish by the other staff. Sometimes David is extremely critical of other people's standard of work. He considers the qualifications of some of the other translators to be inadequate for the jobs they are doing. In general, he thinks that the owner is unimaginative and has failed to capitalize on non-European languages. He is very unhappy about his salary which is much lower than his pay as export manager. However, he knows that he cannot cope with the uncertainties of being a freelancer.

The company does not have a performance assessment system.

Activity brief

1 What criteria would you employ in seeking the most suitable applicant?

2 What methods would you use to obtain further information about these candidates?

3 What are the likely advantages and disadvantages of promoting any one of these individuals?

PART 6

Managing diversity

This part of the book discusses the subject of equal opportunity in the workplace. We consider the prevalence of discrimination on the grounds of gender, race, religion, disability and age, and discuss the use of anti-discriminatory legislation. Also we evaluate the effectiveness of proactive policies and initiatives aimed at the management of diversity within organizations.

The chapters in Part 6 address questions such as:

- Why should we encourage diversity in human resources?

- What is the purpose of anti-discriminatory legislation and why have some countries adopted different approaches?

- Why do people from certain backgrounds figure so prominently at the upper levels of virtually all professions?

- What is the empirical evidence for various types of discrimination?

- Is there any evidence for the effectiveness of legislation or management of diversity initiatives?

PART 6

Managing diversity

16 | Equality of opportunity

Objectives

The purpose of this chapter is to:

- Define and distinguish between the concepts of equal opportunity and the management of diversity.

- Assess the scope and effectiveness of legislation and other anti-discriminatory initiatives.

- Identify the significant barriers to equality and diversity in employing organizations.

- Outline the nature and extent of discrimination on the basis of sex and gender.

The meaning of diversity

People are different. They vary in gender, culture, race, social and psychological characteristics. But our attitudes towards these differences can be negative or positive, depending upon individual perspectives and prejudices. In earlier chapters we identified the tendency to form like-minded 'in-groups', to favour members of one's own group and for those in authority to recruit people like themselves. This may seem natural or normal and often goes unquestioned – but it is unfair. The consequences can be seen in a lack of opportunity for women, ethnic minorities, the disabled, the middle-aged and other disadvantaged sections of the community as the best jobs are ring-fenced and barriers are placed to prevent their progress.

As members of organizations, it is difficult to challenge the often subconscious actions and elaborately entrenched justifications for unfairness. Not least, because discrimination and prejudice are expressions of power entailing the ability to prevent, inhibit or punish critical comment. Yet, if people are the key assets of a business it is important to realize the maximum benefit from their human capital. True competitive advantage requires the best from everyone, without restrictions; it demands a prejudice-free and inclusive attitude towards actual and potential employees. It requires diversity (see Key concept 16.1).

> **Key concept 16:1**
>
> **Diversity**   'Diversity is the variation of social and cultural identities among people existing together in a defined employment or marketing system' (Cox, O'Neill and Quinn, 2001, p.3).

In reality, this has to be viewed as an ideal since discriminatory and non-inclusive behaviours have a deep psychological basis. Research shows that prejudice is difficult to remove. For example, if someone is prejudiced against a particular group, meeting someone with positive qualities from that group does not dispel the prejudice. As McKenna (1994, p.260) states:

> ... the prejudiced person is capable of rationalizing the situation in such a way as to conclude that the person he or she met is unique in some respects, and is unlike the stereotype. ... For example, an anti-Semite will not be swayed in his or her view of Jews by evidence of their charitable behaviour, nor will those who have a deep prejudice against black people be persuaded by coming in contact with intelligent and industrious people in this group.

Nevertheless, equality of opportunity is an objective worth striving for. It can be addressed at all levels: governments have a role to play through legislation to prevent discrimination; organizations need to focus on the management of diversity, making the most of a wide pool of talent; strategists should consider equal opportunity policies, targeting and positive development of under-represented groups; people managers can monitor their activities and increase awareness to minimize discrimination.

> **Activity 16:1**
>
> Are there any circumstances in which jobs should be reserved for specific individuals or groups without being unfair?

Society and opportunity

Anthony Jay is reputed to have said that 'success is when preparation meets opportunity.' Preparation depends on personal effort but opportunity is linked to social factors such as economic conditions, education and other people. Effectively, society determines who is given opportunity and who is not through the process of discrimination. Overt prejudice is comparatively easy to observe but the true nature of unfairness lies in the way opportunity has been institutionalized within society. The status quo is constructed to benefit certain types of individual from particular backgrounds or those who are able to adapt most easily to its requirements. Typically this has denied opportunity to women and minority groups.

Most countries have a concentration of particular social groups at the top of their institutions. Others are found further down. As a consequence, skills and abilities are not used to the full – a situation that is detrimental to society as a whole. However, the advantaged are unlikely to admit that their positions come from privilege rather than competence. For them, change is not a priority. An example can be seen in India where government attempts to assist disadvantaged castes have met with violent protests by the privileged. Other instances are readily found in developing African states where paid employment is scarce. Managers are under pressure to offer jobs to people from their family or tribe (Akinnusi, 1991) and this has extended to politicians and civil servants to the extent of threatening the economic development of sub-Saharan Africa. This is a form of 'particularism' (see Key concept 16.2) that is important still in South Africa, although the influence of convergent forces such as globalization, information technology and increased competition is becoming much more prominent (Horwitz *et al.*, 2002).

Key concept 16:2

Particularism   Discrimination favouring particular groups and individuals over others. It derives from a reliance on personal relationships such as ethnic origin, religion or tribal community. It contrasts with 'universalism' in which personal relationships are ignored and emphasis is on other criteria such as qualifications, expertise and ability to do the job.

Particularism leads to discrimination. Worldwide, this mechanism can be extended to include a number of forms, including discrimination on the grounds of:

- *Age.* Arbitrary age boundaries excluding younger and older workers.
- *Appearance.* Preferring people of a certain height or weight, for example.
- *Disability.* Discriminating against people with special needs.
- *Gender.* Limiting certain types of jobs to either males or females.
- *Ethnic origin.* Preference for particular racial or linguistic communities.
- *Nationality.*
- *Religion.*
- *Background.* Often seen as cliques – networks of people from similar backgrounds reserving the best jobs for themselves. In addition, people with socially undesirable backgrounds, such as ex-offenders, are actively discriminated against.
- *Nepotism.* Common in small companies which rely heavily on family members.

Marti, Bobier and Baron (2000) found that some forms of discrimination, specifically gender and race, are more easily observed and recognized than others, such as age and weight. Participants in their studies were more likely to label actions of gender or racial discrimination as prejudice and also tended to rate such prejudice as more severe than in cases of prejudice on the grounds of age or weight. Harper (2000) reports on a study of longitudinal cohort data covering 11 407 individuals born in Britain in 1958. The results showed that physical appearance had a significant effect on earnings and employment patterns for both men and women. Regardless of gender, people assessed as unattractive or short were penalized. At the extremes, taller men tended to receive higher pay than the average, while obese women were paid less than average women. The researchers attributed the bulk of the pay differential for appearance to employer discrimination.

Discrimination can be direct (Key concept 16.3) or indirect (Key concept 16.4). It can also extend into victimization when employers or their agents treat employees less favourably as a result of actions taken by those employees to assert their non-discriminatory rights. Many countries use legislation to reduce such discrimination, for example, in areas such as equal pay, selection and promotion. The effectiveness of such legislation is seen in the proportion of disadvantaged groups achieving responsible positions. Often this has been disappointing. We will see that, in most parts of the world, the presence of women and people from ethnic minority groups becomes increasingly rare towards the top of most organizations, while some groups, such as the disabled and the over-50s, are conspicuously absent from many firms.

Key concept 16:3 **Direct discrimination**   Treating an individual or group less favourably on grounds such as disability, race, religion, age, gender or sexual orientation. Direct discrimination is fairly obvious because of its explicit nature (Corbridge and Pilbeam, 1998). The use of different criteria for promoting or paying male or female employees is an example of direct discrimination.

Key concept 16:4 **Indirect discrimination**   A less obvious form of discrimination than direct discrimination. This may take the form of applying certain conditions or requirements that are more easily satisfied by one group than another (Corbridge and Pilbeam, 1998). One example would be to specify a fixed minimum height requirement for entry into a police force. This is a requirement that would be more easily met by male than female applicants. Another example would be a requirement for an unnecessarily high standard of spoken or written English, which would favour people with a particular educational background.

Examples of national anti-discrimination legislation

Lappalainen (2001) observes that different countries have essentially chosen one of two paths for laws dealing with discrimination. Some have focused on a single law covering all the grounds of discrimination, while others have issued separate laws for each type of discrimination. Legislation has been in place in the USA since the 1960s with separate laws and programmes designed to protect women, individuals aged over 40, people with disabilities, war veterans and racial minorities (see the 'HRM in reality' box).

HRM in reality **Federal anti-discrimination laws in the USA**

A number of federal laws prohibit discrimination in the workplace.

Title VII of the Civil Rights Act 1964

Title VII prohibits employers from discriminating against applicants and employees on the basis of race or colour, religion, sex, pregnancy, childbirth and national origin (including membership of a Native American tribe). It encompasses all terms, conditions and privileges of employment, including hiring, firing, compensation, benefits, job assignments, shift assignments, promotions and discipline. There are limited exceptions, termed bona fide occupational qualification (BFOQ) exceptions, covering sex, religion and national origin, but not race. Title VII also prohibits employers from retaliating against any applicants or employees who assert their rights under the law (e.g. firing someone who has complained about race discrimination). Title VII is restricted to the following types of organization:

- private employers with 15 or more employees
- state governments and their political subdivisions and agencies
- the federal government
- employment agencies
- labour organizations, and
- joint labour–management committees and other training programmes.

It is enforced by the US Equal Employment Opportunity Commission (EEOC). Title VII makes it illegal for employers to use apparently neutral practices that have a disproportionate impact on a protected group of people. There has to be a valid reason for using any such practice. Height and weight requirements are typical examples. Title VII also prohibits the harassment of someone because of their race or colour, religion, sex, pregnancy, childbirth or national origin (including membership of a Native American tribe). Sexual harassment is the most common form of harassment covered by Title VII.

The Age Discrimination in Employment Act (ADEA) 1967

The ADEA prohibits discrimination against employees who are age 40 or older. It also covers all aspects of employment and makes it illegal to retaliate against anyone exercising their legal rights. The range of employers covered by the ADEA is slightly different to Title VII. It does not apply to state governments or their agencies and private employers with fewer than 20 employees. However, it does apply to the federal government and its agencies, private employers with 20 or more employees, interstate agencies, employment agencies and labour unions. The ADEA is also enforced by the EEOC.

The Equal Pay Act 1963

The Equal Pay Act requires that employers give men and women equal pay for equal work. Equal work is defined as work done under similar working conditions or requiring equal skill, effort and responsibility. The job titles used have no bearing on whether two jobs are equal. However, employers can pay men and women different salaries for equal work if the difference is based on a seniority, merit or incentive system, or if the difference is based on factors other than gender.

The Equal Pay Act applies to virtually all employers. Again, the Equal Pay Act is enforced by the EEOC.

The Americans with Disabilities Act (ADA) 1990

The Americans with Disabilities Act prohibits discrimination against people with disabilities in employment, transportation, public accommodation, communications, and activities of state and local government. The Act was signed into law in 1990 but its various elements come into force on different dates including: state and local

▶

government activities (January 1992); employers with 25 or more workers (26 July 1992); employers with 15 or more workers (July 1994).

The Act requires that employers, employment agencies, labour organizations and joint labour–management committees must:

- Have non-discriminatory application procedures, qualification standards, and selection criteria, and in all other terms and conditions of employment.

- Make reasonable accommodation to the known limitations of a qualified applicant or employee unless to do so would cause an undue hardship.

The Act makes exceptions regarding the employment of a person with a contagious disease, a person who illegally uses drugs or alcohol, employment of someone by a religious entity, and private membership clubs.

The ADA does not apply to the federal government and its agencies. The EEOC and the US Department of Justice oversee the Americans with Disabilities Act. Other federal laws that encompass discrimination include: Sections 501 and 505 of the Rehabilitation Act of 1973, which prohibit discrimination against qualified individuals with disabilities who work in the federal government; and the Civil Rights Act of 1991, which, among other things, provides monetary damages in cases of intentional employment discrimination.

New Zealand

New Zealand passed a Race Relations Act in 1971 and an Equal Pay Act in 1972. The Race Relations Act was passed primarily in order to allow the government to ratify the International Convention for the Elimination of All Forms of Racial Discrimination in the following year. Intriguingly, many people felt at the time that race relations in New Zealand were so good that such an Act was unnecessary!

Unlike the US court-based system of enforcement, the New Zealand Act created the Office of the Race Relations Conciliator with the aim of resolving incidents of discrimination, although the Conciliator could recommend to the Attorney-General that proceedings be taken against an offender in extreme cases.

The Human Rights Commission Act (1977) introduced a new element, the Equal Opportunities Tribunal, to which the Conciliator could take civil proceedings. That Act also outlawed discrimination on the grounds of sex, marital status and religious or ethical belief. The Human Rights Act (1993) consolidated earlier legislation and the Human Rights Amendment Act (2001) amalgamated the Race Relations Office with the Human Rights Commission.

Australia

The Australian Commonwealth Government passed its Racial Discrimination Act in 1975. The Sex Discrimination Act (1984), Human Rights and Equal Opportunity Commission Act (1988) and Disability Discrimination Act (1992) followed to cover most of the country's equal opportunities arena. However, individual Australian states inclined towards comprehensive anti-discriminatory laws, as in the New South Wales Anti-Discrimination Act (1977). The trend to comprehensiveness continued such that Tasmania's Anti-Discrimination Act (1998) encompassed the following:

Age, breastfeeding, carer status, disability, family responsibilities, gender/sex identity, industrial activity, irrelevant criminal activity, irrelevant medical record, lawful sexual activity, marital status, parental status, physical status, political activity, political belief or affiliation, pregnancy, race, religious activity, religious beliefs or affiliation, sexual orientation, personal association with a person who has, or is believed to have any of these attitudes or identities, sexual/sexist harassment, victimization, inciting hatred, publishing displaying or advertising matter that promotes, expresses or depicts discrimination or prohibited conduct.

The Australian Human Rights and Equal Opportunities Commission is led by a single Commissioner with some overall responsibility but there are separate Commissioners for each of the nationally recognized discrimination grounds (gender, race and disability). This approach retains a broad human rights focus but also pays attention to the separate issues involved in each form of discrimination.

United Kingdom

For many years the UK was the only country in Europe with comparatively comprehensive civil legislation on workplace discrimination, having had anti-discriminatory laws covering race and ethnicity since the 1970s. The main pieces of legislation covering equal opportunities were: the Equal Pay Act (1970), providing for equal pay for comparable work; the Sex Discrimination Act (1975), which makes discrimination against women or men (including discrimination on the grounds of marital status) illegal in the working situation; the Race Relations Act (1976) with subsequent amendments; and the Disability Discrimination Act (1995). Subsequent UK and EU legislation has generally improved women's rights in the area of pregnancy and maternity. These Acts were supported by a Commission assigned to each piece of legislation. The Commission for Racial Equality (CRE) oversees the Race Relations Act. The Equal Opportunities Commission (EOC) was established under the Sex Discrimination Act of 1975 with powers to monitor implementation of both the Sex Discrimination and Equal Pay Acts. The Disability Rights Commission was set up in 2000 in line with the Disability Rights Commission Act (1999).

The equality guarantee contained in Article 14 of the European Convention of Human Rights also came into effect in October 2000 with the implementation of the Human Rights Act 1998 (Fredman, 2001). At the time of writing, further changes are taking place in accordance with the EU anti-discrimination Directives, which will be discussed later in this chapter.

HRM in reality

Biggest review of equality in 25 years

Barbara Roche, the minister responsible for equality coordination across the UK government, says that there are good arguments in favour of a single equality body and that the government is now looking at the longer-term feasibility of this.

In a speech at the British Bankers Association in London, she said:

> We are looking at the longer-term options for the UK's equality framework. This doesn't mean ignoring the voices of any particular group represented by the current Commissions. It does mean finding ways of involving those who think they aren't being catered for.
>
> Equality isn't a minority issue and discrimination legislation is not just about protecting a few, important though that is – it's relevant to all of us. But we also need to achieve a lasting culture change by looking beyond legislation, at the broader economic inequalities that still persist in our society.
>
> Women still lose out to a tune of £250 000 during their working lives; a groundbreaking PIU report for which I'm Sponsor Minister shows that a black man is still 2.5

times more likely to be unemployed than a white man; and people with disabilities are seven times more likely to be out of work than a non-disabled person.

We are committed to an open and inclusive process and will be drawing on the expertise of those working in the field of equality, including the Equal Opportunities Commission, the Commission for Racial Equality and the Disability Rights Commission.

The EOC and the CRE were established in the mid-1970s and the DRC was set up by the government in 2000. Following a Directive from the European Commission, the UK government is committed to outlawing unfair discrimination at work for the first time on the grounds of religion and sexual orientation by 2003, and age by 2006.

The DTI recently conducted extensive consultation under the title of *Towards Equality And Diversity*, which took views from business, trade unions and interest groups. Respondents showed support for the concept of a 'joined-up approach'. But Barbara Roche emphasized there would be no changes to structures within the life-time of this parliament. A project team in the Cabinet Office will report on the initial conclusions of the Single Equality Commission (SEC) Project in September.

SEC Project terms of reference

One of the government's main aims is to create opportunity for all. The promotion of equality for individuals, business and service providers is a key part of this. It also means that if people are unlawfully discriminated against they should have access to advice and support to resolve, if needs be through legal means, their cases. The Equal Opportunities Commission, the Commission for Racial Equality and, more recently, the Disability Rights Commission, have statutory powers to carry out these functions in their respective regimes.

Legislation currently being introduced to implement the EU Article 13 Employment Directive will extend the grounds for protection against discrimination in employment and training to include sexual orientation and religion by 2003 and age by 2006. In anticipation of this, the prospect of a single equality body in the 'longer term' was signalled in the consultation document on Article 13, launched on 13 December 2001. A new, more unified approach to equality has some clear attractions. It could provide a single point of contact for employers and employees, service providers, customers and members of the wider public, by offering advice and support on the broad range of common grounds for discrimination.

However, there are various models for achieving greater unity and these may impact in different ways on the work of the existing commissions. The advantages, disadvantages and the timescales need to be carefully examined. It is also necessary to consider the relationship between possible new arrangements for promoting equality and those for promoting and protecting human rights more widely.

A focused project is therefore needed to look at these issues, and to consider key relevant policy developments including:

- the creation of interim arrangements relating to sexual orientation, religion and age under the new legislation mentioned above
- alternative disputes resolution policy
- modernized delivery of public services.

As regards objectives the project will examine the pros and cons of possible arrangements, in the long term for:

- promotion of equality in relation to sex, race, disability, sexual orientation, religion and age, to individuals, business and service providers
- resolution of discrimination cases
- production of statutory codes of practice and other guidance
- 'last resort' enforcement mechanisms
- review of anti-discrimination legislation
- assistance to individuals.

Source: *HRMGuide.co.uk* (http://www.hrmguide.co.uk), 15 May 2002.

Ireland (Republic)

Ireland introduced an Anti-Discrimination (Pay) Act in 1974 which established the right to equal pay for 'like work', defined in terms of skill, physical or mental requirements, responsibility and working conditions. This was followed in 1977 by the Employment Equality Act prohibiting discrimination in recruitment, training, conditions of employment and promotion opportunities on the grounds of sex or marital status. The Employment Equality Act (1998) combined the earlier Acts and prohibited discrimination in respect of all aspects of employment. It extended the grounds for discrimination to cover gender, marital status, family status, sexual orientation, religion, age, disability, race and membership of the Traveller community.

Irish legislation is also affected by the EU anti-discrimination Directives discussed later in this chapter.

Canada

Canada's approach to anti-discrimination has long been distinctive, especially in comparison with its southern neighbour. Canadian legislation is grounded in human rights. The Canadian government signed the Universal Declaration of Human Rights in 1948 and has made universal human rights a key part of Canadian law. Four principal mechanisms are designed to protect human rights: the Canadian Charter of Rights and Freedoms (1982), the Canadian Human Rights Act (1977), Human Rights Commissions, and provincial human rights laws and legislation.

The Canadian Human Rights Act (1977) prohibits discrimination in federal or federally regulated organizations on grounds of race, colour, national or ethnic origin, religion, age, sex (including pregnancy and child-bearing), marital status, family status, physical or mental disability (including dependency on alcohol or drugs), pardoned criminal conviction and sexual orientation. Similar laws have been enacted in the provinces and territories banning discrimination in their areas of jurisdiction. The Act is enforced by the Canadian Human Rights Commission.

By the 1980s there was an awareness that despite this legislation there was a need for a more proactive approach and, following the report of a Royal Commission, the first Employment Equity Act was passed in 1986. The Royal Commission had been asked to 'explore the most efficient, effective and equitable means of promoting equality in employment for four groups: women, native people, disabled persons and visible minorities.' The term 'employment equity' was chosen to distinguish the Canadian approach from American affirmative action programmes associated with quotas.

The 1986 Employment Equity Act covered federally regulated companies with 100 or more employees, operating primarily in the banking, transportation and communications industries. These employers were required to identify workplace barriers and to develop and implement equity plans for the four designated groups. Employers were also required to report annually to the responsible minister but the Act had no enforcement mechanisms, other than for failure to report.

Over the next few years it was recognized that the Act had to be toughened and extended. A new Employment Equity Act came into effect in 1996 which also covered the federal public service and mandated the Canadian Human Rights Commission to conduct on-site compliance reviews. It also provided for final enforcement by an Employment Equity Review Tribunal which had the power to hear disputes and issue orders.

South Africa

The Canadian approach had a major influence on South Africa's Employment Equity Act which came into force in 1999 and bans direct or indirect unfair discrimination in employment policy or practice, on the grounds of: 'race, gender, sex, pregnancy, marital status, family responsibility, ethnic or social origin, colour, sexual orientation, age, disability, religion, HIV status, conscience, belief, political opinion, culture, language and birth.' Fair discrimination includes affirmative action that is designed to redress previous exclusion from education and employment of black people, women and those with disabilities. The Employment Equity Act is regulated by the Commission for Employment Equity.

Activity 16:2	Compare and contrast the approaches taken by the countries we have discussed.

The emphasis of anti-discrimination legislation

Countries with legal systems based on common law, including Australia, Canada, Ireland, New Zealand, the UK and the USA, have used civil rather than criminal law as the main method of counteracting discrimination. Government bodies may assist, but, in essence, it is up to individuals to pursue their case. Possible costs are a negative aspect of this approach but there is a benefit in the lower burden of proof required in civil law (Lappalainen, 2001). There is also room for compromise and conciliation, possibilities not usually available in criminal law. The Netherlands had a tradition of using the European criminal law model. However, it was determined that this approach was not working and, in 1994, the Equal Treatment Act was introduced based on civil law, substantially influenced by Canada's Human Rights Act (Lappalainen, 2001).

Legislation can take a number of forms:

● *Positive action.* Measures to prevent discrimination and remove inequalities by insisting, for example, on non-discriminatory recruitment procedures, training programmes and pay rates. This does not include any preferential treatment for disadvantaged groups. UK and Irish legislation takes this approach.

● *Affirmative action* or positive discrimination. A long-standing approach in the USA, designed to advantage the disadvantaged, including women, African-Americans and Hispanics. Laws only applied to the public sector and its suppliers. Affirmative action came under severe criticism in the 1990s from white, middle-class males who argued that laws intended to encourage equality were unfair to them.

● *Targeting.* Quotas for the employment of particular groups have been enforced in the USA. In Europe quota systems existed for some time in respect of disability and, in a few countries, other groups such as ex-servicemen, but enforcement was not usually strict.

The European Union adopted two new Directives in 2000: the first concerned discrimination on grounds of racial or ethnic origin; and the second extended the principle of equal treatment to prevent discrimination on the grounds of age, disability, religion and sexual orientation. The Directives form the basis for national legislation on these matters, which member states such as the UK and Ireland are obliged to implement. By 2003 laws must be in place that prevent employers from discriminating against workers because of their sexual orientation or religion. By 2006 unequal treatment on the grounds of age or disability (the latter already covered by legislation in the UK for organizations employing 15 or more staff) must also be made unlawful. Belatedly, the EU has taken responsibility for anti-discrimination on a par with developments in North America and Australasia and introduced a positive duty to promote equality, albeit in a somewhat vague fashion (Fredman, 2001).

More widely, it should be emphasized that legislation is only effective if institutions and individuals charged with its implementation are themselves committed to the concept of equal opportunity. Barnard, Deakin and Kilpatrick (2002) point to the fact that English law (which also provides the foundation for law in many other countries) lacks a general principle of equality of the kind found in constitutional texts in some European countries. They argue that anti-discriminatory legislation not founded on such a principle stresses formal rather than substantive equality, so that discrimination is described in terms of unequal treatment of individuals and ignores the structural sources of group disadvantage. They believe that this provides a partial explanation for the relatively limited impact of legislation, in the UK at least.

Activity 16:3	What are the advantages and disadvantages of using separate laws for each form of discrimination?

In practice, the number and range of disadvantaged groups is so huge that true fairness is a difficult objective to achieve. Well-meaning advocates can find themselves embroiled in endless verbal battles over the subtle nuances and implications of the concept. We turn next to its practical consequences on people management at the organizational level.

HRM in reality	**Female and minority job-searchers look for diversity in the workplace**

One-third of survey respondents have eliminated companies that lacked gender and ethnic diversity from employment consideration.

Actions speak louder than words when it comes to diversity, according to results of a WetFeet study – *Diversity Recruitment Report 2001*. The study for the recruitment specialists found that 16 per cent of respondents were looking for a diverse workforce as a significant pointer to an organization's commitment to diversity. And a third of respondents indicated that they would not consider employment in a company that did not demonstrate gender or ethnic diversity. African-American candidates showed an even higher degree of reluctance, with 44 per cent of those surveyed reported to have dismissed a company on that basis.

'Improvement in diversity recruiting is one of the highest priorities of companies today – and it's driven by their recognition that a diverse workforce will strengthen their organization and increase their business success,' said Steve Pollock, president of WetFeet. 'However, our research shows that companies that are the most

▶

successful in this area utilize creative recruitment practices, supported by a strong track record of deployment and promotion of diversity within their organizations.'

WetFeet's *Diversity Recruitment Report 2001* is based on a survey of 748 female and minority candidates and interviews with 12 leading corporations on their diversity recruitment practices. The report explores career expectations, job search methods and effective recruitment messaging and is designed to help companies develop more effective recruitment strategies.

Other findings from WetFeet's *Diversity Recruitment Report 2001* include:

- Diverse candidates are most motivated by the opportunity for advancement and competitive compensation. Some 95 per cent of respondents rated 'opportunity for advancement' as 'very' or 'extremely' motivating to an employment decision, while 92 per cent rated competitive compensation and 91 per cent rated comprehensive benefits as 'very' or 'extremely' motivating. Accordingly, one-third of respondents looked at the make-up of a company's executive team and employees as key indicators of that company's commitment to diversity.

- Women and men are influenced by different value propositions. Women place higher value than men on flexible work arrangements, comprehensive benefits and vacation time. Around 57 per cent of female respondents rated comprehensive benefits as 'extremely motivating' to an employment decision, whereas just 39 per cent of men did. Some 52 per cent of women were seeking work–life balance initiatives, in comparison to 38 per cent of men. Finally, 42 per cent of women were motivated by generous vacation time against 28 per cent of men surveyed.

- Diverse candidates are in demand. The war for experienced candidates is still a top concern for companies. Candidates in the survey were interviewed by an average of 4.7 companies and received 2.3 job offers.

- The internet is a key job searching tool. The internet remains the most popular job search tool for candidates. Around 70 per cent of respondents use corporate websites to search for jobs with 67 per cent using general job posting websites. Female and minority candidates preferred general job posting and employment sites, with just 13 per cent of respondents using diversity specific websites.

Source: *HRM Guide USA* (http://www.hrmguide.net/usa/), February 2001.

Diversity and the organization

'Fairness, justice, or whatever you call it – it's essential and most companies don't have it. Everybody must be judged on his performance, not on his looks or his manners or his personality or who he knows or is related to' (Townsend, 1970, p.59). Why should business organizations and their managers offer equal opportunities to a diverse range of employees? Two fundamental perspectives are identifiable which can be related to different models of HRM (Goss, 1994, p.156):

- *Human capital.* 'Artificially' blocking the progress of any group results in less than optimal use of an organization's human capital. Discrimination is irrational since it limits the resource value of employees. This view is compatible with 'hard', or free market HRM discussed in Part 1 of this book.

- *Social justice.* A moral or ethical interest in social equality, compatible with 'soft' or social market HRM. Economic benefits are secondary to this social duty.

Goss sees the human capital perspective as fluctuating and opportunistic: a shallow commitment '... capable of being adopted or abandoned, in line with legal or economic expediency'. It is also narrow, restricted to legal requirements and short-term employment market conditions. This contrasts with the more principled social justice viewpoint, which embodies a deeper and wider commitment, extending beyond minimum legal requirements.

Organizations benefit from a deep, principled commitment to equality of opportunity because it leads to (according to Ross and Schneider, 1992):

● A diverse workforce that enriches ideas and perspectives within an organization.

● Imaginative ideas to assist total quality management.

● Recruitment or promotion of the most talented people.

● An environment that encourages them to stay.

● Improved motivation and commitment that raises productivity.

● Reduced wastage and recruitment costs that increase profitability.

In recent years, the UK Equal Opportunities Commission has argued strongly for the human capital approach pointing, in particular, to the waste of women's abilities. However, some commentators contend that, whereas this is valid for the economy as a whole, equal opportunity practices may be a significant expense rather than a benefit for individual firms.

All businesses operate within the national or supranational legislation governing equal opportunities in a specific country. As we noted earlier, the USA and South Africa have required a number of employers to take measures of positive discrimination, typically requiring them to fill quotas from under-represented sections of the community. To do so, recruitment criteria such as qualification or skill requirements may be relaxed for members of those groups. This is an attempt to achieve the equal share level of opportunity outlined in Straw's model (detailed in Table 16.1).

Alternatively, positive action may be required or undertaken voluntarily by governments or employers. Under-represented groups are assisted and encouraged to participate in training and development initiatives, support groups and mentoring schemes. This requires that organizations are aware of their disadvantaged employees and the jobs they

Table 16.1	Levels of opportunity	
Level	Opportunities	Barriers
1 Equal chance	Everyone has same chance, e.g. right to apply for vacancies; be considered for a position.	Formal or informal barriers, e.g. employers may ignore applications from people living in ethnic minority areas.
2 Equal access	Disadvantaged groups not barred from entry into organizations but may be confined to lower levels of work.	Institutional barriers, e.g. appraisal methods that favour certain groups, or promotion requirements – such as mobility – which, effectively, bar many married women.
3 Equal share	Access is free. Representation achieved at all levels. Legislation may require quotas for disadvantaged groups, e.g. disabled.	Only those lawful, justifiable and necessary, e.g. specific language speakers to work with ethnic groups.

Source: Based on Straw (1989).

are doing, so that the problem of occupational segregation can be tackled (see Key concept 16.5).

Occupational segregation   Disproportionate representation of particular groups in specific sectors, job types or levels of responsibility. Horizontal segregation places men and women, for example, in different jobs, such as chambermaids (women) and porters (men). Vertical segregation places one group in better-paid positions than another group, so that men are better represented at managerial levels while women are concentrated in lower, administrative jobs.

Turnasella (1999) suggests that the employment process is itself responsible for the persistent pay gap between men and women and between ethnic minorities and non-minorities. Specifically, employers usually require a salary history from job applicants and frequently ask questions about salary expectations during their selection procedures. If the applicant has a history of relatively low pay, employers tend to give lower offers of remuneration. Intriguingly, in an experimental study involving 100 participants (50 men and 50 women), Blanton, George and Crocker (2001) found that women compared themselves with other women to gauge satisfaction with a pay rate when it was framed as compensation for past work but compared themselves with the men when framed as part of an offer for future employment.

Corbridge and Pilbeam (1998) also point out that networking and headhunting are inevitably discriminatory because they involve recruitment from a restricted pool of friends, social acquaintances and school or university peers. People from disadvantaged groups, if they are employed at all, tend to be confined to 'boring jobs with no prospects' in the secondary sector (Molander and Winterton, 1994, p.96).

The impact of discrimination on equality of pay is less in a unionized environment than in a non-union environment (Metcalf, Hansen and Charlwood, 2001). The authors attribute this to two factors:

- Union members and jobs are more homogeneous than their non-union counterparts.
- Union wage policies narrow the range of pay rates within and across firms and bring up the lowest wage rates.

HRM in reality

Woman truck driver wins compensation for sex discrimination

£5600 has been awarded to a woman truck driver from Grangemouth, Scotland in compensation for injury to feelings and loss of earnings in a sex discrimination case brought against a former employer. She had been made redundant after she complained about a male colleague who refused to work with her because she was a woman.

Yvonne McLeod had worked for Drummond Distribution as a driver of 38-tonne trucks. She claimed that other workers had begun making derogatory remarks to her shortly after she had been made a permanent employee by the company. One particular driver had frequently been rude to her, saying that she was 'doing a man out of a job' and refusing to work with her. Ms McLeod complained to two of the company's directors, but no action was taken. She was made redundant in December 1999 when she returned to work after a period of sick leave. According to Ms McLeod:

I am an experienced driver, but because I'm a woman one of the other drivers tried to make my life difficult. I just ignored the comments or laughed them off for quite a while, but when he refused to drive with me his attitude began to affect other drivers' work too and I felt I had to do something about it. I just wanted to be able to get on with my job, but not long after making a complaint I was made redundant.

Julie Mellor, chair of the Equal Opportunities Commission, said:

There is no place for outdated ideas about what is 'women's work' and what is 'men's work' in today's labour market. Employers need to ensure that women and men are judged purely on their ability to carry out a job, rather than on their sex. Giving everyone the opportunity to fulfil their potential in the field of work they choose does not only benefit individuals, it also gives employers more choice and so boosts the British economy. This case also demonstrates how important it is that employers take complaints of discrimination very seriously and ensure that anyone who has made a complaint is not victimized as a result.

Source: *HRMGuide.co.uk* (http://www.hrmguide.co.uk), 30 March 2001.

Activity 16:4   Why are women and members of minority groups placed in unfavourable occupational categories?

Strategies for diversity

Many organizations have adopted equal opportunities policies – statements of commitment to fair human resource management. However, equal opportunities policies are notoriously ineffective, often no more than fine words decorating office walls, designed to appease politically vociferous activists and soothe consciences. They disturb vested interests too rarely. The obstacles to creating a diversified workforce are embedded in organizational culture – particularly the sub-culture at the top. A serious equal opportunity policy requires (Molander and Winterton, 1994, p.102):

- Allocation of overall responsibility to a specific senior executive.
- Agreement of the policy with employee representatives.
- Effective communication of the policy to all employees.
- An accurate survey of existing employees in terms of gender, ethnic origin, disability, etc. and the nature and status of their jobs.
- An audit of human resource practices and their implications for equal opportunities.
- Setting equal opportunity objectives within the human resource strategy.
- Resources, such as training and development capabilities, to back up these objectives.

Key concept 16:6

Management of diversity   The management of diversity goes beyond equal opportunity. Instead of merely allowing a greater range of people the opportunity to 'fit in', or be an honorary 'large, white male', the concept of diversity embodies the belief that people should be valued for their differences and variety. Diversity is perceived to enrich an organization's human capital. Whereas equal opportunity focuses on various disadvantaged groups, the management of diversity is about individuals. It entails a minimization of cloning in selection and promotion procedures and a model of resourcing aimed at finding flexible employees.

This approach can be incorporated within an integrated framework termed the 'management of diversity' (outlined in Key concept 16.6). The pitfalls in the process are evident. A 1995 report (*Targeting Potential Discrimination*) produced by the UK Equal Opportunities Commission detailed findings from 2000 companies that showed that over two-thirds did not collect information about the gender and ethnicity of their employees. Auditing HR systems is also problematic.

However, the main difficulties arise from cost and lack of commitment, exemplified by 'tokenism' – the employment or promotion of isolated individuals to represent their gender or colour. This is no more than an inadequate sop to equal opportunities: 'We have done as much as we need to – we have a disabled person in the office.' 'Paternalism' is a related attitude, where discriminatory decisions are taken for the 'benefit' of particular groups, as illustrated in the 'HRM in reality' case of American Cyanamid.

HRM in reality

American Cyanamid

In an attempt to eliminate any liability for toxic damage to unborn children, American Cyanamid decided in January 1978 to remove all women of child-bearing age from contact with any chemical which, in the company's opinion, carried a risk. In effect, the company banned all women aged between 16 and 50 from production areas at its Willow Island, West Virginia plant. The only exception was for women who could prove they had been surgically sterilized or accepted such a sterilization at the company's expense. Five women accepted this offer.

The other women in the plant were only offered lower-paid jobs. Thirteen women and a union representative took legal action that was eventually settled out of court. In addition, the Occupational Safety and Health Administration (OSHA) cited American Cyanamid for violating a clause in the OSHA Act of 1970 which required employers to provide employees with a place of work that was free from recognized hazards. However, this was defeated by a summary legal judgement. This decision was confirmed by the OSHA's Health Safety Review Commission, which considered that the hazards that required sterilization for foetal protection were not cognizable under the OSHA Act. A further appeal by the Oil, Chemical and Atomic Workers Union to the District of Columbia Circuit Court of Appeals failed to overturn the judgement.

Source: Nelkin and Tancredi (1989).

Discussion questions: (a) Was the company right to take the action it did? (b) If not, how should the company have dealt with the problem?

The case of American Cyanamid is a rather horrific example of heavy-handed action to 'protect' staff but it illustrates how people strategies can sometimes lose any sense of humanity.

Women's social attitudes

The *Women's Social Attitudes* survey shows that women are increasingly confident and determined to make the most of their opportunities – inside or outside work.

This research covers changes in women's views between 1983 and 1998. Topics range across social, economic, political and moral issues, including government and politics, money, paid work and the family. The report compares different groups of women as well as those of women and men in general.

The main findings include:

- Women are now financially better off and live more comfortably on their earnings than they did in 1984. Some 83 per cent of women in 1998 felt they were coping or living comfortably in comparison with 72 per cent in 1984. Around 59 per cent of 1998 respondents felt that having a job was the best way for a woman to be an independent person.

- Women have a more positive attitude than men about accepting opportunities for advancement. Specifically, they are more positive about the provision of skills by schools – and value post-16 education and university.

- Women are not satisfied that their current jobs give them the opportunities they want. In 1997, 74 per cent of women said they wanted advancement at work but just 19 per cent felt that they had this opportunity in their present job. This difference was found across all social and educational levels and across ages.

- Women are finding work more stressful. In 1997 one-third of women found work stressful 'often' or 'always' compared with a quarter in 1989.

- Women are more favourably disposed to working mothers than they were. In 1998, 73 per cent of women agreed that if children are well looked after, it is good for a woman to work, in comparison with 61 per cent in 1987.

- Women no longer tend to view men as breadwinners. A mere 16 per cent of women in 1998 endorsed the view that 'a man's job is to earn the money, a woman's job is to look after home and family', compared with a quarter of women in 1989.

Minister for Women, Margaret Jay, commented:

This report provides valuable information on the views and preferences of women in different circumstances at different stages in their lives. Specific information on women's views is essential to better policy making and *Women's Social Attitudes* provides just the sort of sound data that policy makers need.

Women's Social Attitudes was produced for the Women's Unit by the National Centre for Social Research. It is a gender analysis of the *British Social Attitudes* survey between 1983 and 1998, an annual survey of 3500 men and women.

Source: *HRMGuide.co.uk* (http://www.hrmguide.co.uk), 23 November 2000.

A study by the Industrial Society (2001) – now the Work Foundation – found that 67 per cent of UK managers regard diversity and equality of opportunity as matters of high priority over the next two years. Some 77 per cent expect these issues to become even more important to their organizations in the next couple of years. But fewer than half (45 per cent) of organizations responding to the survey have the strategies in place to achieve this. Their diversity strategies may reflect a lower priority in the past two or three years as the percentage of respondents who said that diversity had been high or very high priority during that period was also 45 per cent.

Knowledge of company equal opportunities policies within organizations seems inadequate. While 46 per cent of respondents said that senior managers had a working knowledge of their company's equal opportunities policy only 18 per cent felt that their senior managers had extensive knowledge. Middle managers were (slightly) better rated with 53 per cent of respondents saying that middle managers had a working knowledge of the company's equal opportunities policy. One in five (20 per cent) said that employees had a working knowledge, while only 2 per cent believe employees had extensive knowledge.

The monitoring of potential discrimination seems to be a variable commodity. It is most common in the recruitment stage, followed by promotion and then at exit stage. In contrast, training does not seem to be monitored closely for potential discrimination.

The apparent emphasis on diversity has not stopped employees from being dissatisfied: 41 per cent of the organizations that responded had been involved in industrial tribunal cases about diversity/equality issues. Respondents pointed the blame at three main barriers:

- organizational culture (46 per cent)
- attitudes of line managers (42 per cent)
- business pressures on line managers (41 per cent).

A third of respondents also pinpointed senior managers as a significant obstacle to achieving true diversity.

The management of diversity is a natural consequence of human resource strategies that focus on flexible working arrangements. Part-time work and, especially, homeworking are particularly attractive to some women and disabled employees. But (see the 'HRM in reality' section) fathers also may have reasons for more flexible working arrangements.

HRM in reality

Dads nervous about taking paternity leave

Working fathers believe that bosses discriminate against men with childcare responsibilities and they are missing out on time with their children as a result. This is the conclusion of *Dad's Army* – a report out today from the Work Foundation – which also argues that real equality of opportunity for women will not be achieved until this situation changes.

Drawing on new research from the Equal Opportunities Commission, the report says that attitudes towards gender equality are still being defined by a generation of 'Dinosaur Dads' – the older generation of corporate men who were supported by stay-at-home wives. They know they now employ mothers, but do not seem to have realized that this means they now employ a different kind of father:

> A new and important divide in the workplace is the one between fathers in their fifties and those in, say, their thirties. Most of the former group have wives who stayed at home to raise their kids, at least in the pre-school years. Most of the latter group have wives or partners who work.

Currently, 59 per cent of married or co-habiting mothers with pre-school children are also working outside the home. As a consequence, more men are accepting responsibility for at least some of the childcare and domestic tasks. But, the report contends, how these new responsibilities affect working fathers has not yet registered on the corporate radar.

According to the report, working fathers are nervous about taking paternity leave, or asking for time off or flexible working to help them manage their childcare responsibilities. Instead, they may parent by stealth, using off-site 'client meetings' as a means of covering up for time spent looking after their children. Fathers appear to be afraid of appearing uncommitted or less masculine in front of their colleagues. The result is that women continue to take most of the responsibility for childcare, at the expense of their careers – and an average cost of around £140 000 in terms of lifetime earnings.

Richard Reeves, author of the report and research associate at the Work Foundation says: 'To achieve gender equality we have to recognize that equality at work and equality at home are inescapably intertwined. We can't get one without the other. Until there is a redistribution of unpaid work towards men, women will never be able to achieve full parity in the labour market.'

The report highlights the advantages of father-friendly working. Research shows that dads who are hands-on at home are happier at work. Involved fathers are also more likely to have the 'emotional intelligence' considered essential for modern management.

Tom Beardshaw of Fathers Direct comments: 'A lot of the skill set that employers want has been called "feminine" when a more accurate description would be "parental" – they come from the experience of nurturing and raising kids. Dads who are actively involved in their children's lives will bring the same benefits to work as mothers do.'

According to the Work Foundation's director of research, John Knell: 'Rather than women conforming to a male model of work, men and women need to join forces to overthrow it. The focus should no longer be on the dual-career couple but the dual-carer couple with both taking on the rearing of their children without either suffering a setback to their careers.'

Companies may point to their paternity leave as evidence of their father-friendly policies but only 65 per cent of firms offer paternity leave. And fathers often fail to take it because of a fear of discrimination for wanting time off for childcare reasons. 'Paternity leave is a great start but does not in itself constitute a "father-friendly" approach to work,' adds Reeves. 'Workplace culture is hugely important and this is not just created by Dinosaur Dads at the top. Men's lack of participation to date in companies' work–family programmes perpetuates an environment where both men and women unwittingly allow childcare to be come sidelined as a mothers only issue, rather than a parenting issue.'

There are five recommendations in the report for companies that want to think more creatively about the parents on their payroll.

- *Daddy diagnostic* – find out what men want; it may not be paternity leave but leaving early on a Friday to pick up their kids for the weekend.
- *Paternity leave* – the necessary starting point but companies must think beyond it; children will need two parents throughout their lives.
- *Time sovereignty* – grant employers more control of their working hours and provide a range of options: flexitime, compressed hours, term-time working, etc.
- *Culture shift* – this has to come from the top but also requires staff changing their behaviour and assumptions.

▶

◄

● *Good work* – improving the quality of the job and the working environment, as opposed to reducing hours, will have positive effects at home which will be reflected back at work.

Source: *HRMGuide.co.uk* (http://www.hrmguide.co.uk), 22 October 2002.

Key concept 16:7

The glass ceiling   The term glass ceiling describes the process by which women are barred from promotion by means of an invisible barrier. This involves a number of factors, including attitudes of people in power and the inflexible processes and requirements geared to the cloning process that ensures that 'men of a certain sort' will generally succeed. In the USA, the term is also used to describe the barrier that prevents progress for other disadvantaged groups – for example, ethnic minorities.

Gender and sexual discrimination

Many countries have sex discrimination and equal pay legislation. However, informal psychological and organizational barriers continue to bar the progress of women. In 1999, for instance, the Canadian Workplace and Employee Survey (WES) showed that women were paid an average of 80 cents for every dollar earned by men. Expressed in average rates per hour this meant that women received C$17.14 per hour compared with the C$21.54 per hour earned by men (*Statistics Canada*, 2002). The reasons for this wage gap are complex.

Whereas women's participation in the employment market has increased rapidly, in most countries their share of senior jobs is still low. The first annual FTSE Female Index published in 2000 demonstrated that few women are present on the boards of Britain's biggest businesses. As part of the campaign, FTSE 100 companies were ranked according to the number of women board directors. Although women made up over half of the UK workforce in that year, fewer than 2 per cent of FTSE 100 executive directors and fewer than 8 per cent of non-executive directors were female. Very nearly half (49 per cent) of these companies had no women on their boards; 54 per cent had no women non-execs; and a staggering 91 per cent had no female executive directors.

The processes of occupational segregation and 'sex-typing' of jobs continues to be prevalent, so that women are concentrated at the base of most organizational hierarchies in jobs that are less prestigious and lower paid than those favoured by men.

HRM in reality

Number of UK women directors in the FTSE 100 falls again

Gender equality takes a backward step in the boardroom as a new report shows that the number of UK women directors in the FTSE 100 has fallen for the third year running.

Research carried out by the Centre for Developing Women Business Leaders, Cranfield School of Management (specializing in studying women in corporate leadership) builds on what was described last year as the 'FTSE Female Index' and shows that 57 per cent of Britain's leading businesses have women directors. This compares with 58 per cent last year and 64 per cent in 1999. In addition, 43 firms in the FTSE 100 have no women on their board, and a mere 2 per cent of executive directors are women.

But intriguingly, the most successful companies are more likely to have women on their boards. Of the top 20 FTSE businesses, 17 (85 per cent) have women directors. Conversely just 10 of the bottom 20 firms had at least one female director.

Other main findings include:

- Only one company has a female CEO.
- Ten women hold executive directorships.
- Industry sectors with the least women directors are media, tobacco and energy.
- Retail, pharmaceuticals and financial services have the most women directors.
- 15 FTSE 100 companies have two or more female directors.
- 58 women hold 66 non-executive directorships and 10 women hold executive directorships this year out of 1166 available seats. This is a marginal increase from last year, when 52 women held 58 non-executive directorships and 11 women held executive directorships out of 1188 available seats.

Some companies are bucking the trend. For the first time in the history of the FTSE 100, three companies – Marks and Spencer, Legal and General and AstraZeneca – have three female directors. And until November Legal and General had a record four female directors – the first time for any FTSE 100 company.

The 2001 league table places Marks and Spencer at the top with a 25 per cent female board. Logica is second with two female non-executive directors from of a total of eight. Legal and General and AstraZeneca are joint third with three women out of 13. In last place are BHP Billiton and Standard Chartered – both with 18 board members, none of whom were women.

Harriet Harman said:

British boardrooms are one of the last remaining 'no-go' areas for women. We lag far behind the US, where business recognizes the value of diversity and reflects on their boards the importance of women employees and women consumers. The task is to continue to expose the extent of the problem, to work for change, to achieve our target that within the next two years, there should be no all-male boards in the FTSE top 100, to monitor progress and to provide a support network to the women who make their way onto boards. The boards of British business should be a meritocracy – not just 'chairman's chums'.

Sue Vinnicombe, professor of organizational behaviour and diversity management, and director of the Centre for Developing Women Business Leaders at Cranfield School of Management, co-authored the report. She said:

It is disappointing to see another drop in the number of companies in the FTSE 100 with women directors. It is also interesting that this is seen as a women's issue. Until male chairmen and CEOs are willing to engage in this debate I feel the situation will not improve. They are the key catalysts for boardroom change.

Angela Ishmael, head of Dignity at Work at the Industrial Society said:

Women are proving their ability in education, as entrepreneurs and in the workplace – against their success in these areas, the inability of boardrooms to include women amongst their numbers begins to look like sheer resistance. UK employers must harness the ability, talent, creativity and determination that many women in the workplace so clearly possess.

Mary-Ann Stephenson, director of the Fawcett Society, commented:

▶

Successful businesses know that they cannot afford to miss out on the talents of half the population, but while women are moving up into senior management, change at board room level is still too slow. Too many boards of directors remain all male clubs. It's not that there are not able women out there – it's time some businesses took advantage of what they have to offer.

Val Singh, co-author of the research and senior research fellow at Cranfield, said:

The fact that more women are being appointed to boards where there are already women directors indicates that the pioneer women have done very well. This means there should be fewer concerns about whether women can do the top jobs. The appointments within Marks and Spencer and Legal and General provide some hope for the future. Our report highlights that women directors have a wealth of experience and a range of skills to complement existing boards. Why are so many chairmen and CEOs still not managing this valuable resource?

Source: *HRMGuide.co.uk* (http://www.hrmguide.co.uk), 25 November 2001.

**HRM
in reality**

Women still working more than men

The trend for a narrowing of the gap between men and women in terms of income, work and learning is continuing according to Canada's Economic Gender Equality Indicators 2000, measuring human well-being or quality of life.

Main highlights of the indicators are:

- The income imbalance between women and men is declining, but women's after-tax income is just 63 per cent of men's.

- Women continue to work longer than men – an extra 15 minutes a day, equivalent to more than two additional weeks a year.

- There is an increasing gender balance in many fields of education and women are making slow but steady progress into previously male-dominated professions. But women's share of female-dominated areas is increasing as men continue to stay away.

- The female share of job-related training is increasing, particularly in training sponsored by employers.

- Male and female university graduates are both less likely to be in high-level jobs than used to be the case.

Hedy Fry, Secretary of State (Multiculturalism) (Status of Women) commented:

Overall, the Economic Gender Equality Indicators show that Canada is moving towards a better gender balance. However, despite the gains, there is still work to be done. There remain areas of concern and we must be mindful these gains are not necessarily benefiting all women. A surprising disparity highlighted in this update of the Economic Gender Equality Indicators is the difference in total workload of young women and men. Women aged 15–24, when compared to their male counterparts, work 18 per cent more. While the share of paid work done by young women is high, their share of unpaid work is even higher.

Source: *HRM Guide Canada* (http://www.hrmguide.net/canada/), 12 March 2001.

Internationally, the United Nations concludes that women are facing a global glass ceiling (Key concept 16.7) and that 'in no society do women enjoy the same opportunities as men' (*Financial Times*, 11 December 1995). In developing countries women represent under a seventh of administrators and managers. In the most developed country, the USA, the Glass Ceiling Commission stated that between 95 and 97 per cent of senior managers in the country's biggest corporations were men. According to Robert Young, Director General of the Institute of Management: 'men are the prime barrier to women in management. Despite some progress, old fashioned sexist attitudes are still common and represent a real, not an imagined, barrier.'

Helena Kennedy, a prominent lawyer and one of Britain's few women QCs at the time, commented (*Independent*, 19 December 1992) a decade ago:

> What we have to fight is the idea that access to these jobs is based on merit and it will only be a matter of time before women break through. What it is actually based on is men choosing people who are like themselves. It's all about cloning. That's why it's so hard to make the breakthrough and that's why it has to be consciously tackled.

Employer prejudices explain some of the difficulties that women experience. Central to many employers' attitudes is a belief in the Victorian model of the family, where the woman stayed at home looking after the children and the man went out to work. This pattern has become uncommon in much of the developed world. Dual-career and one-parent families, equal parenting and the dismantling of life-long career structures have eroded the distinction between male and female roles. Misra and Panigrahi (1996) looked at attitudes among people of different ages regarding female labour force participation. Using National Opinion Research Centre Social Survey data they found that younger people are more favourably disposed towards women working outside the home than older people. Women had more positive attitudes towards this than men. But both women and men disapprove of women working if pre-school children might suffer as a result. A positive attitude towards women working outside the home was also associated with higher education, higher family income, residence in urban areas and generally liberal viewpoints.

HRM in reality

Pregnancy still means the sack for thousands, says CAB

A report from the National Association of Citizens Advice Bureaux (NACAB) claims that thousands of working parents will not benefit from improved maternity and parental rights because employers are ignoring legislation. In fact tens of thousands of women are being sacked illegally or threatened with dismissal simply because they are pregnant.

NACAB is strongly in favour of government proposals to improve maternity leave and introduce two weeks' paid paternity leave. But it says that the government is ignoring the extent to which existing benefits are flouted by employers. The report is based on case evidence provided by Citizens Advice Bureaux throughout England, Wales and Northern Ireland.

Pregnant women who are dismissed are often asked to resign or work reduced hours. They may also be denied their right to time off to attend ante-natal appointments or the right to return to the same job after maternity leave. Women returners frequently find that their job has changed, or hours and pay have been cut. Men are often advised (by employers) that there is no right to parental leave, or that it does not apply in their organization.

Most of the employees denied their rights are in low-skilled and low-paid jobs, usually employed by small businesses. Denial of these rights is often part of a pattern

◀

where other rights such as paid holidays, sick pay and proper rest periods or breaks are also not given. Examples of case studies include:

● A pregnant shop worker dismissed on the grounds that pregnant women are not an attractive sight to customers.

● A nursery employee sacked just before she was due to start her maternity leave. She had been employed for two years on less than the minimum wage – and the employer illegally docked her wages for time off taken to attend ante-natal appointments.

● A woman was contacted on maternity leave and told that her job had been filled and that there was no job for her, regardless of her legal rights.

● Another sales assistant returned to the full-time job she had held for seven years after maternity leave and discovered that her working hours were reduced to three days a week and that her pay had been cut by 35 pence an hour.

Often women do not know their rights or how to enforce them. If they are aware of their legal rights, many are afraid of confronting their employers, anticipating victimization or loss of their jobs. The 'dauntingly adversarial nature of the employment tribunal system' puts dismissed women off taking action – plus, of course pregnant women and new parents have a great deal else to be anxious about at a time when life is particularly demanding and stressful. And if they are successful at a tribunal, compensation levels are low and they will still be out of work.

NACAB proposes a dedicated employment rights agency – or Fair Employment Commission – to be founded with the following tasks and powers:

● Proactive enforcement of a range of basic rights at work.

● Provision of advice, guidance and specialist business support to those employers facing the greatest challenge in meeting their statutory duties to their workforce.

● Powers to investigate individual and anonymous complaints, carry out random checks and impose fines.

The report also recommends establishing a statutory right for both mothers and fathers to work 'child-friendly' hours after the birth or adoption of a child.

Source: *HRMGuide.co.uk* (http://www.hrmguide.co.uk), 21 March 2001.

Gender differences

Key concept 16:8

Gender   All human societies divide themselves into two social categories called 'female' and 'male'. Each category is defined on the basis of varying cultural assumptions about the attributes, beliefs and behaviours expected from males and females. The gender of any individual depends on a complex combination of genetic, body, psychological and social elements, none of which are free from possible ambiguity or anomaly (Helman, 1990). Traditionally, sexual differences have been used to justify male-dominated societies in which women have been given inferior and secondary roles in their working lives.

A further contributor to the problem is our perception of gender differences, real or imagined (see Key concept 16.8). There are differences between men and women, other than the physical, but there is little agreement as to what they are. For example, Bevan and Thompson (1992) found evidence that men and women rated working behaviour differently:

- Males tended to favour and aspire towards qualities that were essentially individualistic and competitive, such as intelligence, dynamism, energy and assertiveness.

- Women stressed qualities of a more cooperative and consensual nature: thoughtfulness, flexibility, perceptiveness and honesty.

They concluded that since male managers are prevalent, females are disadvantaged by being evaluated against male standards of behaviour. This has been described as the 'male-as-norm syndrome' (Wilson, 1995, p.3). Given similar jobs and appraisal ratings, men are more likely to be offered training or promotion. For example, Kramer and Lambert (2001) examined a large, random sample of female and male employees using a survival analysis technique to investigate the time taken from being hired to being promoted to supervisor. They found evidence for significant pro-male bias in promotion decisions that could not be attributed to differences in time on the job, education, or parenting responsibilities.

Also, women are more likely to underestimate their own skill levels and, therefore, inhibit their own progress. However, not all women meekly accept the male order. Some deal with the situation by playing the game according to male rules. In a study of Greek organizations employing both female and male managers, Bourantas and Papalexandris (1990) found no difference between leadership styles. Their explanation was that women were imitating male patterns of behaviour in order to achieve success. This approach attracts mixed and complex reactions, particularly from other women. For instance, Margaret Thatcher, former UK prime minister, sometimes regarded as being a better man than most men, was an object of some fascination. According to Webster (1990, p.2):

> Mrs Thatcher has acted out a role which is forbidden to women within conventional notions of femininity, revelling in power, dominating, 'handbagging' and humiliating men, a role which can be incorporated and allowed within the 'nanny' image, under the cover of rectitude. A common reaction from women is often mixed, a combination of a recognition that Mrs Thatcher has done little or nothing for her own sex, and of an admiration, sometimes unreserved, for the way in which she has shown rather conspicuously and publicly that women are not weak and indecisive, nor deficient in stamina and guts.

Margaret Thatcher saw toughness, practicality and the ability to cope as being particularly female qualities (Webster, 1990, p.51). Nevertheless, she surrounded herself with a cabinet of men and did little to benefit other women politicians. Thatcher appears to have been an exception in trying to assert her views over others. In general, women are more likely to regard themselves as 'enablers' of other people, seeing themselves as opening up information to employees, building up the confidence of their staff and encouraging them to develop and use their skills.

There is no denying, of course, that not only are men and women sometimes different in their approach but that this may sometimes lead to conflict. Indeed, as we see in the 'HRM in reality' example, a woman who speaks her mind may suffer the consequences.

HRM in reality

Tribunal awards £1.4 million for sex discrimination

Share analyst Julie Bower was awarded £1.4 million compensation for sex discrimination after a tribunal found that she had been forced out of her job at Schroder Securities. The case was supported by the Equal Opportunities Commission (EOC). The remedy hearing took place on 7–10 January 2002 with Julie Bower being represented by Nicola Dandridge.

Julie Mellor, chair of the EOC, commented:

▶

For too long, City firms have accepted a culture of secret pay deals for their staff. This perpetuates discrimination against anyone who is deemed not to 'fit in', regardless of their capability. This record payout sends a strong message to employers that they must have a fair and transparent pay and bonus system. It also reflects the seriousness of the discrimination that Julie faced during her employment with Schroders and the impact on her career.

This case highlights the need for all firms to take a good, hard look at their pay system to check they are rewarding all staff fairly. If employers don't act soon, a legal requirement to carry out pay reviews will be the only way forward.

Background

An Employment Tribunal found that Julie Bower, City share analyst, was forced to resign by former employer, Schroder Securities, as a result of sex discrimination. The Employment Tribunal found that the amount of Ms Bower's bonus for 1998 was a figure that had been 'picked from the air' as part of her manager's deliberate plan to drive her out.

The Tribunal agreed with the contention that Ms Bower's bonus for 1998 (£25 000, later increased to £50 000) did not reflect the market rate for an analyst, did not reflect a genuine valuation of her performance and that her work was undervalued because she was a woman.

Jenny Watson, deputy chair of the Equal Opportunities Commission (EOC) said:

> This case raises important issues for all employers. The Tribunal found that Schroders had no transparency in their pay system and that employees were forbidden to discuss pay and bonuses. Such a culture makes it all too easy for discrimination to occur, which is why the EOC's Equal Pay Task Force has called for legislation requiring employers to review pay systems to ensure they are not biased. Until reviews are carried out on a routine basis no employer can be confident that they pay fairly.
>
> I hope employers will take notice of the lessons to be learned from this case. Equal opportunities are not an optional extra and there is no case, as is sometimes claimed, for the City to 'do things differently'. Employers in the City are bound by the same laws as everyone else.
>
> Many other companies will identify with the broader issues highlighted by the Tribunal, such as the low proportion of women in senior roles at Schroders, and their complete absence among the higher levels of director. Recruitment methods that are likely to replicate existing male hierarchies simply aren't sustainable for companies looking to recruit from the broadest pool of potential employees.

The Tribunal concurred that Ms Bower had received an unfair appraisal in early 1999, and that her boss told her that a senior corporate financier 'wanted her head on a plate' in order to deliberately unsettle her, instead of trying to resolve the problem. Julie Bower said:

> I'm pleased that the Tribunal has concluded that the level of my bonus for 1998 and the fact that I was forced to leave my job were a result of sex discrimination. The way in which Schroders dealt with my complaints about the way I was being treated was completely unacceptable and I hope that no one else ever has to go through the same sort of thing again.

The tribunal also found:

- Of the bonus setting process: 'it was hard to conceive a process more lacking in transparency'.

- In her appraisal Ms Bower was told she had the lowest score of any team leader. That was untrue; overall she ranked 37th out of 68.

- Employees engaged in recruitment and appraisal had no training in equal opportunities (other than those in the Personnel Department).

- Recruitment above graduate level was done with no regard for equality of opportunity in the sense that it is advocated by the EOC.

- Schroders did not monitor or observe either its recruitment or its pay levels to establish whether they were discriminatory.

- There was a laddish or sexist air about some of the corporate entertaining in which the Respondent engaged in that it involved taking clients to places where there were scantily dressed women.

- The proportion of women employed in client-facing roles while Ms Bower was at Schroders was around 15 per cent (not out of line with what competitors achieved).

- When Ms Bower left Schroders 100 per cent of men (27 out of 27) at team leader or senior analyst level were directors, compared to 71 per cent of women (five out of seven).

Source: *HRMGuide.co.uk* (http: //www.hrmguide.co.uk), 11 January 2002.

It is clear that much of the debate about male and female behaviour revolves around sexual stereotyping, which has a significant cultural basis. Hofstede (1994, p.16) argues that, within any society, there is a men's culture which is different from the women's culture. This difference may explain why traditional gender roles are so difficult to change. Stereotyping can also influence career aspirations. Harper and Haq (2001) examined British cohort data and found that 16-year-old boys and girls showed significant differences in their occupational aspirations, appearing to follow a traditional pattern. They argue that these occupational preferences influence the decisions of young people to apply for certain types of job. Harper and Haq used a conditional hiring model in order to separate the effects of such preferences from the hiring decision of employers. They found no evidence of hiring bias against women except in manual and craft occupations and that the effect of sex discrimination could be exaggerated if occupational aspirations were not taken into account.

Kraus and Yonay (2000) compared the way in which women and men attained workplace authority in female-dominated, mixed and male-dominated occupations. They found that women have the greatest chances of being given authority when they work in 'male' occupations, arguing that the competition between men and women is weaker in such occupations so that men have less reason to discriminate against women. They observed that men have similar chances regardless of the type of occupation in which they are employed. By contrast, in a meta analytic study, Davison and Burke (2000) found that female and male applicants received lower ratings when being considered for an opposite-sex-type job.

Sexual harassment

Some aspects of male culture are distinctly unattractive – even to many men. From school to shopfloor, locker room to office, the culture of masculinity expresses itself in 'jokes' revolving around three stereotypes of sexuality (Mills and Murgatroyd, 1991, p.78):

- the ideal, or 'real man' syndrome – toughness, football and so on
- definitions of males as 'not-females'
- the normality of heterosexuality.

Ford (2000) found experimental evidence to suggest that when people who are high in hostile sexism are exposed to sexist jokes they become increasingly tolerant of sex discrimination. The process appears to involve the activation of a non-critical mindset. In traditionally all-male factories, workshops and warehouses, joking is reinforced by sexually explicit, homophobic or racist language, swearing, pictures of nude women (where they have not been banned), sexual bragging and suggestive horseplay. This serves to create an immensely threatening atmosphere for women and others, discouraging any attempt to enter this 'man's world'.

In office and managerial environments these elements are less evident but sexual harassment – ranging from unwelcome comments on appearance to physical advances – remains common although surveys give conflicting evidence. Canadian surveys show that as many as 70 per cent of women have been sexually harassed at some time during their working lives (Moynahan, 1993). A survey by the Employment Law Alliance (www.employmentlaw-alliance.com, 6 February 2002) shows that 21 per cent of US women polled said that they had suffered sexual harassment at work, compared to 7 per cent of men.

Sexual harassment is a difficult topic for managers to deal with, since it involves personal relationships and the individual interpretations of those involved (see Key concept 16.9). The issue has often been trivialized or ignored in a 'conspiracy of silence'. In a survey of top British companies, Davidson and Earnshaw (1991) found that only 64.8 per cent of respondents regarded it as a serious management issue. Given that this was based on a response rate of only 22 per cent from their sample, this finding probably overestimates management concern.

Few cases develop into formal complaints or tribunal cases but the consequences on morale are severe, with victims frequently leaving to escape harassment. The effects on victims can include nervousness and depression. In the work context, this affects concentration and productivity and increases the likelihood of absenteeism (Wright and Bean, 1993). The effects can spill over into the home, possibly leading to the breaking up of relationships.

Key concept 16:9   **Sexual harassment**   Definitions vary considerably but most are agreed that it is sexual attention which is unwanted, repeated, and affects a woman's work performance or expectations from her job. However, it is possible for one incident to be sufficiently severe to be regarded as harassment. It differs from sexual banter or flirting since it is one-way; it does not have the involvement and acceptance of both parties. In the USA, the Equal Employment Opportunity Commission has extended the definition of sexual harassment to include a range of actions that lead to a 'hostile work environment'. This definition includes unwelcome touching, joking, teasing, innuendos, slurs and the display of sexually explicit materials.

Employers have a moral duty to protect staff from sexual harassment. In general, if employers tolerate sexual harassment they convey the impression that one gender does not deserve respect; they are prepared to sacrifice motivation and commitment; and they must accept the consequences on efficiency. Organizations can deal with sexual harassment by (Moynahan, 1993):

- Surveying the organization to determine the extent of sexual harassment.
- Writing and circulating a strongly worded policy indicating possible disciplinary action.

- Providing an effective reporting mechanism, protecting the rights of accusers and the accused.

- Packaged workshops, which help to define harassment and prevent 'misunderstandings'.

- Assertiveness training, appropriate for women working in jobs that have traditionally been regarded as male, which encourages the ability to provide verbal or even written feedback to unwanted behaviour. The ability to say 'no' firmly and at an early stage is particularly effective.

- Gender-awareness training to emphasize different perceptions of teasing and 'harmless fun' between men and women.

Increasingly, employing organizations are liable to legal action for sexual harassment by one employee against another.

HRM in reality

Sexual harassment is no joke

A new leaflet, provocatively entitled *What Would You Do If Your Boss Asked You For a Blow Job?* has been published by the EOC. But Jenny Watson, deputy chair of the Equal Opportunities Commission (EOC), says that sexual harassment is no laughing matter for hundreds of thousands of British workers who experience it. In fact, the EOC's analysis of Employment Tribunal cases over the last three years shows that 90 per cent of successful claimants had lost their job or resigned because of the harassment.

Earlier research shows that more than half of female employees and almost 10 per cent of male workers have experienced some form of sexual harassment at work. But only 5 per cent of employees experiencing sexual harassment at work make a formal complaint – and a mere 10 per cent of these get as far as an Employment Tribunal hearing.

Consistent with earlier findings, the EOC's analysis also showed that:

- Many of the people who suffer harassment are young women in a job for less than a year.

- They are often in low-paid jobs such as shop workers, carers or factory workers.

- A third of the harassers were directors or owners of the employing organization.

- In a third of cases they were the immediate manager of the person being harassed.

Sexual harassment, far from being 'just a bit of fun' as some people try to claim, makes people's lives a misery, affecting their confidence and their health, as well as their performance at work, said Jenny Watson:

> Our analysis of Employment Tribunal cases paints a grim picture, but this is only the tip of the iceberg. Nearly half of the people bringing a case had not made a formal complaint to anyone at work because there was no one they felt they could complain to, they were too embarrassed, they feared that they would not be believed or they thought they could handle it for the sake of their careers. Many of the people we talk to have put up with harassment for months or even years before contacting the EOC.
>
> It is time to get this issue out in the open. We have launched online advice on our website, a leaflet for individuals, *What Would You Do If Your Boss Asked You For a Blow Job?* and a good practice guide for employers. No one should have to suffer in silence.

▶

◄

> The EOC calls on employers to take responsibility for preventing sexual harassment in the workplace. They recommend that employers:
>
> ● Adopt a clear policy that sexual harassment will not be tolerated in the workplace.
>
> ● Spell out what kinds of behaviour are unacceptable.
>
> ● Make sure victims know how to raise concerns and feel confident in doing so.
>
> ● Investigate problems and take firm action to stamp out harassment when it occurs.
>
> Source: *HRMGuide.co.uk* (http://www.hrmguide.co.uk), 1 September 2001.

Legal definitions of sexual harassment fall into one of two types:

● *Quid pro quo*. A narrow, traditional definition of sexual harassment as a demand by a person in power, for example a supervisor, for sexual favours from a subordinate in return for a job, pay increase, promotion, transfer or other benefit.

● *Hostile environment*. A wider definition, including unwelcome sexual advances that have the effect of creating a hostile, intimidating, abusive or offensive working environment.

Summary

Equality of opportunity is both a matter of social justice and sound economic sense. Voluntary approaches to minimize discrimination have been largely ineffective and most developed countries have introduced some form of anti-discrimination legislation. There has been a tendency towards all-embracing laws in recent years, increasingly linked to human rights legislation. Granting opportunity is beneficial to organizational effectiveness as well as personal success. The strategic management of diversity leads to a wider range of ideas and abilities, offering greater scope for innovation and competitive performance in the future.

Further reading

Anti-discriminatory Practice, 3rd edition by Neil Thompson (published by Palgrave Macmillan, 2001) provides a comprehensive review of the topic. *The Diversity Training Handbook* by Phil Clements and John Jones (published by Kogan Page, 2002) is another practical book, as is *Dynamics of Managing Diversity* by Gill Kirton and Anne-Marie Greene (published by Butterworth-Heinemann, 2000). *Discrimination Law Handbook* by Camilla Palmer, Gay Moon, Tess Gill, Karon Monaghan and Mary Stacey (published by the Legal Action Group, 2002) is a comprehensive, practical and accessible guide to anti-discrimination law. Written by experts, it tells readers all they need to know about UK, European and human rights laws. *Global Diversity at Work: Winning the War for Talent*, 2nd edition by Trevor Wilson (John Wiley & Son, 2002) provides a practical Canadian perspective. *The Affirmative Action Debate*, 2nd edition, edited by Steven M. Cahn (published by Routledge 2002) is a collection of articles about the range of arguments surrounding contemporary discussion of affirmative action. *Discrimination, Jobs and Politics: The Struggle for Equal Employment Opportunity in the United States Since the New Deal* by Paul Burstein (University of Chicago Press, 1998) provides an interesting historical perspective. *Justice in the Workplace: From Theory to Practice* (Applied Psychology Series) edited by Russell Cropanzano (Lawrence Erlbaum Associates Inc., 2000) and *Durable Inequality* by Charles Tilly (University of California Press, 1999) take a deeper approach to the study of persistent social inequality. *Breaking Through the Glass Ceiling* by Linda Wirth (published by the International Labour Office, 2001) is a revised account of her study on the status of women's employment in a number of countries.

Review questions

1 Distinguish between equal opportunities and the management of diversity. How is it possible to justify either in a commercial organization?

2 Is positive discrimination an effective method of ensuring equal opportunities?

3 Is it true to say that anti-discrimination legislation has had a major effect on equal opportunities in the workplace?

4 Why have different countries chosen to take their own distinctive approaches to anti-discrimination legislation?

5 What is occupational segregation and what part does it play in the process of discrimination?

6 How important is 'cloning' in discriminatory behaviour?

7 Romantic relationships commonly start in the workplace. What distinguishes such a relationship from sexual harassment?

Problems for discussion and analysis

Frank and Margaret

Most people think Frank is a nice guy. He is a good networker, knows everyone in the company and is always the first to buy a round of drinks at any social event. He is married, has three children and an attractive house in a very expensive area. He is the Senior Accounts Controller in the Purchasing Contracts Department and is thought to run a very efficient department. For several years he had a relationship with Margaret from Government Sales. This broke up in a somewhat emotional fashion last December when he finally told her that he had no intention of leaving his wife.

Audrey, the Government Sales Coordinator, has come to see you regarding some stories that are being told in her department. It seems that Margaret has been telling people that Frank is not entirely honest. She has claimed that he has been taking bribes from contractors, accepting cash, holidays and improvements for his house in return for signing contracts. Margaret has not said this in Audrey's presence because Audrey is a rather straightlaced person who has always made it clear that she disapproved of the relationship. Audrey and Margaret do not get on very well as a result.

Question: You are the General Manager responsible for these departments. How would you proceed?

Read the following article. Are men or women the most disadvantaged gender in the employment market?

White male culture and dis/advantage

In the September edition of *HRMagazine*, Michael Welp, a principal at EqualVoice is quoted as saying that white men need to view themselves as part of a culture and a group. He says that:

> Many organizations define diversity as simply respecting everyone's different culture. This attitude ignores the fact that there are systemic advantages for the white male culture. For one thing, we never have to leave our own culture and enter someone else's. This allows us to continue to think of ourselves as individuals, not as part of a white male culture. Everyone else, however, must become bi-cultural in order to fit into our culture.

In the same article, Jeff Hitchcock, author of *Unraveling the White Cocoon* (Kendall/Hunt Publishing, 2001) says that:

> I had never thought of myself as needing to be involved in a diversity process. I had evolved to the point where I realized that we, as white males, had all of the privileges, but I still thought that only people of colour had a need for a sense of community. I realized then that white men also have a part to play in diversity.
>
> I'm not sure it's a good idea to make white men too much of an entity and tell them that they have their own culture.

He offered two reasons for concern:

1   There is a lot of collusion between white men and white women regarding who we are as white people. When you place the focus on white men, it is sometimes difficult to get to the elements of privilege and culture for white men and white women. That is, when you remove white women from the discussion, you lose something. You give white women a 'break' on issues of racism that they don't always deserve.

2   Just as there is a lot of collusion between white men and white women on the issue of race, there is also a lot of collusion between white men and men of color on sexism.

Again he argues that a focus on white males 'gives black men a "break" on the question of how they think about and treat women.'

A study for British think-tank CIVITAS concluded that men are now at a disadvantage in the workplace. In the study, *Women or Men: Who Are The Victims?* (Pizzey, Shackleton and Urwin, 2000), the authors argue that, in many ways, the modern work environment favours women rather than men:

● Male jobs are less secure. Male unemployment is higher than female unemployment. Redundancy rates are higher for men.

● Male jobs are more dangerous. Men are more likely to suffer injuries, including fatal injuries, at work.

● Jobs have been falling in manufacturing, where men predominate, and rising in female-dominated service industries.

● Women are more likely to receive in-work training than men.

● Workplace legislation usually favours women workers, including the right to take time off work for family emergencies. Meanwhile, the trade unions, most of whose members are men, have had their powers reduced.

- Women have more time off work for sickness than men.
- The state pension and most occupational pensions are actuarially unfair to men.
- Women live longer, which means that 'a man and a woman with similar characteristics, retiring at the same age and on the same salary, can expect different benefits from the same contributions'.

Pizzey, Shackleton and Urwin (2000) point out that the often-quoted comparison between the average earnings of men and women – the rate for women is 75 per cent of that for men – does not take into account the difference made by the personal choice to marry. Married men earn more than single men, presumably because they are motivated by their family responsibilities, argue the researchers. But marriage has the opposite effect for women. They may drop out of the employment market completely or change from full-time to part-time working to allow for the demands of childrearing. In fact, the gap in pay between single men and single women is small, and often insignificant.

Decisions about marriage and childbearing are freely taken, they argue, so it is difficult to see how government action could narrow the gap in average earnings without unacceptable interference in people's private lives. The authors warn that 'the labour market is a very complicated place' (p.22), and that attempts to even out differences between broad groups like men and women can lead to laws and regulations that endanger jobs by imposing a burden on employers, rather than achieving their stated aims.

Source: *HRM Guide USA* (http://www.hrmguide.net/usa/), 6 October 2001.

17

Race, disability and age

Objectives

The purpose of this chapter is to:

- Evaluate the causes and extent of racial discrimination in the employment market.

- Analyse the basis and effects of institutional racism.

- Assess the effectiveness of legislation in the reduction of disability discrimination.

- Consider the increasing significance of anti-age discrimination initiatives.

Ethnic diversity

For historical reasons, most countries have populations of different ethnic origins. Typically these are highlighted by colour or religious differences. Few countries have true equality between these groups. Stelcner (2000) reviews considerable disparities between incomes earned by 'visible minorities' and aboriginals in Canada in comparison with the white population. Carmichael and Woods (2000) confirm that black, Indian, Pakistani and Bangladeshi workers in the UK are disadvantaged relative to whites, experiencing higher rates of unemployment and tending to be under-represented in higher-paid, non-manual occupations. Elvira and Zatzick (2002) found that whites are less likely to be laid off in the USA than non-whites and that Asians are less likely to be laid off than African-Americans or Hispanics. We could mention numerous other examples.

Racism is usually equated with hostility and prejudice. The media encourages this simplistic picture by linking it to the racial abuse and violent behaviour of neo-fascist parties. Their members' antics are a product of frustration with their own inadequacies – projected onto a visible minority. In general, however, fascists have little power and influence and the perception of racism as obvious prejudicial opinions and attitudes obscures subtler, more insidious forms of discrimination (Sivanandan, 1991). Racism cannot be reduced to 'human nature and individual fallibility' which leave the state, politics and 'major structural aspects of contemporary life out of focus' (Husband, 1991, p.50). The complexity of the phenomenon is illustrated by Augoustinos, Tuffin and Rapley (1999) who analysed the way in which two groups of students discussed Aboriginal people in Australia. They found four modes of discourse:

- An imperialist narrative of Australian history that denied any blame for colonialism.
- Economic-rationalist or neo-liberal talk of 'productivity' and entitlement to distance themselves from the contemporary Aboriginal 'plight'.
- A superficially balanced and even-handed account that discounted the seriousness of discrimination and racism in Australia.
- A nationalist belief in the necessity for everyone in the country to identify themselves as 'Australian'.

In the same vein, Howitt and Owusu-Bempah (1990, p.397) point to a 'new racism' characterized as 'being a far more complex and subtle form of racism which, superficially, lacks the traditional emotive denigration of black people'. They conclude that 'seeing racism solely as a form of interpersonal antagonism not only sanitizes it, but prevents us from defining ourselves as racist if we do not *feel* racial hatred'. Hence stereotypes appear that are not seen as 'prejudiced': '… Asian women are seen as "passive" or "hysterical" or subject to oppressive practices within the family; there is the stereotype of the strong dominant Afro-Caribbean woman as the head of the household; and the description of the over-aggressive African woman' (Sayal, 1990, p.24).

Stewart and Perlow (2001) looked at applicant race, job status and interviewers' racial attitudes in relation to unfair selection decisions. They found that interviewers with more negative attitudes toward black people showed greater confidence in their decision to hire a black applicant rather than a white applicant for a low-status job and to give a high-status job to a white candidate rather than a black candidate. Frazer and Wiersma (2001) conducted an experiment with 88 white US undergraduates who were asked to look at paper credentials and then interview a high or low-quality black or white applicant. Black and white applicants were 'hired' in equal proportion. But when the interviewers were asked to recall the experience one week later, they rated the answers from black applicants as being significantly less intelligent than the answers given by whites. Frazer and Wiersma explain this by postulating that the undergraduates had negative schemas towards black people which they suppressed in the public situation of making a hiring decision, but these negative stereotypes were revealed when unobtrusive measures were used.

Another significant aspect of the problem is not so much racial discrimination as racial disadvantage. This arises from the inability of the liberal-minded middle classes to perceive the structural advantages that contribute to their own success. Dominelli (1992, p.165) argues that:

> it is the subtle presence of racism in our normal activities, coupled with our failure to make the connections between the personal, institutional and cultural levels of racism which make it so hard for white people to recognize its existence in their particular behaviour and combat it effectively.

Mason (2000) evaluates the concept of 'pre-labour market inequality' – essentially, the class and cultural background of individuals – and concludes that it has an undoubted impact on individual well-being and intergenerational mobility. But the manner in which class background has its effects is not clear. A higher class position may create an advantage in skill acquisition. Alternatively, higher social status may increases access to people in positions of power and authority. Stelcner (2000) also speculates that the shortfall in earnings experienced by aboriginal people in Canada may be due to the apparent lack of certain work-related characteristics more commonly found as part of the culture of white Canadians.

In a British study, Shiner and Modood (2002) observe that young people from ethnic minority backgrounds are admitted into university in large numbers but class or culturally based institutional biases cause ethnic minority candidates to be filtered into the new university sector. The new universities are grossly under-funded in comparison with institutions with more long-standing university status and are also less favoured by 'blue chip' recruiters.

Ben-Tovim *et al.* (1992) criticize the ideology of 'colour blindness' which: fails to appreciate the pervasiveness of racism; confuses racism with urban deprivation and class inequality; is conveniently compatible with a range of political opinions; accommodates the 'universalistic ideologies and practices of public administration' ; denies racism purely as overt and deliberate discrimination. They note some rationalizations for ignoring other forms of racism: that raising the question of racism is divisive; that the problems of the ethnic minorities are the same as those of the white population, or the working class, the inner cities, and so on.

Activity 17:1	Review the evidence for racial discrimination being a more subtle process than overt prejudice.

The financial impact of race discrimination

According to the TUC (2002) unemployment is up to three times higher among black and Asian workers than it is among white workers in some parts of the UK (Table 17.1). Nationally, unemployment among black and Asian workers is at 11 per cent in comparison with 5 per cent for white counterparts.

Blackaby *et al.* (1999) examined the employment prospects of different ethnic groups using a sample of over 100 000 males from the UK Labour Force Survey. They found significant differences across groups, particularly Indian and Pakistani/Bangladeshi groups. They argue that the differences do not result from different levels of discrimination by the white majority. Instead they propose that this is due to the predominately Muslim

Table 17.1	Unemployment in selected English regions	
Region	White workers (per cent)	Black and Asian workers (per cent)
London	5	12
North-west	5	12
South-east	3	6
Yorkshire and Humberside	5	11
West Midlands	5	15

Source: TUC, based on Labour Force Survey September–November 2001. (Other UK regions did not include sufficiently large samples for reliable figures.)

Pakistani/Bangladeshi community being less assimilated in comparison with other ethnic minority groups.

Being a woman from an ethnic minority is doubly disadvantageous. In a US study, Lapidus and Figart (1998) show that if measures of equal worth were applied to jobs, 50 per cent of women of colour and 40 per cent of white women who were earning less than the federal poverty threshold for a family of three would be lifted out of poverty. Overall, they conclude that being a woman, an African-American or a worker of Hispanic origin negatively and significantly affected pay levels. In another US study, using a large sample of recent college graduates, Weinberger (1998) found that white male and Hispanic male graduates earn 10 to 15 per cent more per hour than comparable female, black male or Asian male graduates.

In common with women and the disabled, members of ethnic minorities are rarely found among the senior executives of large companies. This can be linked to the frequent ineffectiveness of equal opportunities policies. A Commission for Racial Equality survey (*Guardian*, 25 February 1995) of the largest 168 companies in Britain found that 88 per cent had issued statements committing themselves to racial equality. However, just 45 per cent had a serious plan to implement racial equality.

HRM in reality

Black and Asian workers suffer wage discrimination

A new report – *Black and Excluded* – released by the TUC reveals that black and Asian male workers earn on average £97 per week less than white counterparts.

Launched to coincide with the TUC's Black Workers' Conference in Southport, the report highlights alarming differences in pay within black and Asian communities. On average:

- Pakistani and Bangladeshi men earn £150 per week less than white men.

- Caribbean men earn £115 and Africans £116 per week less than white men.

- Black and Asian women earn £7 per week more than white women – mainly because they are more likely to be in full-time jobs

- But Pakistani and Bangladeshi women earn £34 per week less than white women.

Average weekly earnings in Britain (£)

Origin	Men	Women
White	332	180
All black	235	187
Caribbean	217	210
African	216	199
Indian	327	194
Pakistani/Bangladeshi	182	146

The TUC is asking for all employers to be legally required to promote good race relations in their organizations. This is a legal duty in the public sector at present, but not in the private and voluntary sectors. The TUC also wants a further change in the law so that trade unions and the Commission for Racial Equality can take collective cases on behalf of individuals or groups of members. The government should also encourage employers to regularly monitor pay data to ensure equality, says the TUC. Apart from direct racial discrimination, factors affecting pay include black and Asian workers being trapped in low-paid jobs and economic sectors such as textiles; language problems, despite high educational achievement; and being concentrated in deprived areas of the country with a dependence on public transport.

John Monks, TUC general secretary, said:

> New laws in the public sector will make a difference – these must now be extended to end the unfairness in pay for black and Asian workers. These workers already suffer twice the levels of unemployment, lack of promotion opportunities and racial harassment. Unions are seeking to work in partnership with employers and the government to end this disadvantage.

Source: *HRMGuide.co.uk* (http://www.hrmguide.co.uk), 12 April 2002.

Activity 17:2   Why does racial discrimination affect some minority groups more than others?

Race and performance

As we have already observed, the problems of discrimination and job market disadvantage have complex causes. One aspect is the judgement of performance. A report from the Institute for Employment Studies – *The Problem of Minority Performance in Organizations* (Tackey, Tamkin and Sheppard, 2001) – concludes that apparent 'underperformance' of minority ethnic employees is due more to the perceptions of white managers than to true measures of their performance or abilities. According to IES Director Richard Pearson:

> Blanket claims of institutional racism are notoriously imprecise, inevitably emotive, and not particularly helpful for finding answers to the challenges of managing diversity in the workplace. Over time, organizational cultures and systems evolve their own subjectivities, and these only emerge as people become more aware of potential side effects. By actively looking for unconscious or indirect bias in systems, processes and attitudes at work, the real problems of workplace discrimination can begin to be eliminated.

The report reviewed published literature to help answer a key question: are the observed differences in performance between individuals from minority ethnic groups and their white counterparts due to real differences in performance or biased perceptions by appraisers in the organizations in which they work? IES research fellow and co-author, NiiDjan Tackey observes:

> While some studies have found real differences in performance, the weight of evidence suggests that many of the observed differences are due to bias on the part of those making performance judgements. In other words, some white managers assess their minority ethnic subordinates on criteria other than their ability alone.

There are two theories that attempt to explain why this difference in perception occurs:

1 The first theory is that managers who assess employees' performance subconsciously look for evidence to confirm broader stereotypes – for example those based on gender or race. When a particular group has negative attributes associated with it, all members of that group are seen in the same light. People who stand out as clear exceptions to the 'rule' are explained by luck or extraordinary effort, rather than genuine ability.

2 Theory two says that, within an organization, people are allocated to one of two kinds of groups: (a) those identified primarily by the physical characteristics of their members (such as race, ethnicity, gender or disability); and (b) those identified by the roles and functions of their members.

Managers – according to this theory – have a tendency to assign people to groups based on a combination of these characteristics, treating them differently according to whether they are in an 'in-group' (i.e. share the same group membership), or an 'out-group'. In-group people get more favourable treatment; out-group people are managed in a more authoritarian, contractual style.

The ways in which individuals are treated form part of organizational culture. Self-limiting patterns are then set up as minority ethnic individuals hold themselves back because of previous lost opportunities, or become demotivated because they feel less valued or overlooked.

The report provides advice to organizations that are seeking to understand if they unwittingly discriminate against minority ethnic groups, and what they might do to address any identified problems. It recommends the kinds of information and analysis that are needed to establish and locate any problems. Penny Tamkin, IES principal research fellow, offers the following advice:

- Review your workforce thoroughly to identify any areas of concern.
- Is the issue in recruitment or in the treatment of people once employed?
- Where are differences focused: e.g. shortlisting, promotion, assessment?
- Where might the causes lie: systems, processes, attitudes or behaviours?
- How might you challenge written and unwritten rules of how things are done?
- What needs to be changed if behaviour is the problem? How much is possible?
- Review the impact of all your actions and revisit the solutions.

| Activity 17:3 | How does workplace culture affect the perception of an individual's performance? |

Institutional racism

Braham, Rattansi and Skellington (1992, p.106) suggest that widening our definition of discrimination to include indirect or 'institutional' racism gives a much better understanding of the barriers faced by ethnic minorities (see Key concept 17.1). Institutional racism is virtually unrecognized in commercial organizations but it is an extremely contentious issue in the public sector – for instance social work and housing. At one extreme, there are those obsessed with race issues, ignoring other forms of disadvantage. At the other, those who consider that 'there is no such thing as institutional racism and that those who say there is are totalitarian monsters, running amok, reducing nice white people to tears' (Alibhai-Brown, *The Independent,* 11 August 1993).

Key concept 17:1

Institutionalized racism Institutionalized racism is an indirect and largely invisible process that can be compared with cloning and the glass ceiling. It is a term encompassing the, often unintentional, barriers and selection/promotion procedures that serve to disadvantage members of ethnic minority groups.

Braham, Rattansi and Skellington (1992) caution that it is important to acknowledge the wide range of practices involved – some much more obvious than others. Rejecting the proposition that all institutions are uniformly racist, they argue that 'the kind of procedures ... that disadvantage black people *also* disadvantage other groups'. We noted in Chapter 14 that the process of cloning is focused on replicating the people in power rather than discriminating against any particular group.

The British civil service is a good illustration of the existence and strength of institutionalized disadvantage. A Cabinet Office report in 1995 concluded that it was a bastion of the white, male middle classes, making it difficult for ethnic minorities to progress into its upper reaches. The report concluded that the main barriers to career development were: prejudice and/or ignorance among line managers; and a lack of confidence in themselves among ethnic minority staff. These barriers were derived from attitudinal or cultural stereotypes that limited expectations and opportunities on both sides.

HRM in reality

More aboriginal participation required in Manitoba's workforce

Manitoba's Aboriginal and Northern Affairs Minister Eric Robinson has advocated more aboriginal participation in the province's workforce to match overall growth of the aboriginal population.

The aboriginal population of Manitoba will grow significantly in the next decade. At present just 10 per cent of the province's workforce is of aboriginal descent. But, by the year 2011, as many as one in four workers will be of aboriginal descent.

'We have a responsibility to ensure that aboriginal people are represented in the workforce,' said Robinson. 'Statistics indicate that the unemployment rate for aboriginal people in Manitoba is significantly higher than that of non-aboriginal people. By working to increase the participation of aboriginal people in the workforce we will also provide a hope and a viable future for our young people.'

Robinson also highlighted the potential benefits to the business community from an increase in the percentage of aboriginal people in the workforce. 'The fact that the aboriginal population will increase in the upcoming years also means that the number of aboriginal consumers will increase,' said Robinson. 'This is a large market opportunity and I challenge the private sector to work in partnership with aboriginal organizations to meet this challenge. After all, hiring aboriginal people is just plain good business.'

According to Eric Robinson, the Manitoba government has made a number of practical moves to boost aboriginal representation in the province's workforce. 'I am pleased that our government has made steps in meeting this challenge,' said Robinson. 'Recently, our government, in partnership with Manitoba Hydro and the Winnipeg Regional Health Authority, have announced two initiatives designed to increase the representation of aboriginal people in both organizations.'

Source: *HRM Guide Canada* (http://www.hrmguide.net/canada/), 4 April 2001.

The Parekh report

The Parekh report (report of the Commission on the Future of Multi-Ethnic Britain) published in 2000 had a significant impact on the future of race relations in Britain. Set up by the Runnymede Trust in 1998 the Commission consisted of 23 distinguished individuals chaired by Bikhu Parekh. The Runnymede Trust is an independent think-tank which aims to promote racial justice in Britain. The Commission was asked to:

● Analyse the present state of Britain as a multi-ethnic country.
● Suggest ways in which racial discrimination and disadvantage can be countered.
● Suggest how Britain can become 'a confident and vibrant multi-cultural society at ease with its rich diversity'.

Commission members came from a wide range of community backgrounds and professions and had extensive experience of academic or practical involvement with race issues. Two years of deliberation and discussion resulted in the consensus represented by this report.

According to Bikhu Parekh:

Given the fluidity of social life and the constant emergence of new ideas and insights, no report can claim to be the last word on its subject, and this one most certainly advances no such claim. However, as a carefully researched and thought-out document, hammered out in searching discussions conducted in a spirit of intellectual and moral responsibility, it represents, we hope, a major contribution to the national debate.

Recognizing the moral equality of worth of individuals from each of Britain's many communities, Parekh advocates the recognition of differences while stressing the need to combat racism. Bikhu sees racism as 'a subtle and complex phenomenon' which:

may be based on colour and physical features or on culture, nationality and way of life; it may affirm equality of human worth but implicitly deny this by insisting on the superiority of a particular culture; it may admit equality up to a point but impose a glass ceiling higher up.

Method of working

The Commission visited many of Britain's regions, asked a wide range of relevant organizations for their views, conducted interviews and focus group discussions and read hundreds of written submissions. Activists and experts in race-related issues were invited to day-long seminars in which specific issues were debated in detail. Papers were commissioned from experts in particular areas for Parts Two and Three of the report and these were commented on by other experts and debated in meetings of the full Commission.

Overview

The nations of Britain (England, Scotland and Wales in this instance) are viewed as being 'at a turning point in their history'. Two scenarios are presented:

1 Narrow, inward-looking countries unable to forge agreement between themselves or between the regions and communities from which they are composed.

2 Alternatively, they could become a 'community of citizens and communities' at the level of Britain as a whole and also within every region, city, town or neighbourhood.

If the latter is the preferred choice, it will be necessary to:

- rethink both 'the national story and national identity'
- understand the transitional nature of all identities
- achieve a balance between cohesion, difference and equality
- address and eliminate all kinds of racism
- reduce the inequalities in material benefits
- build a 'human rights culture'.

The report looks at a number of areas including: police and policing; the education systems of England, Scotland and Wales; cultural policy; health and welfare; employment; immigration and asylum policy; responsibilities of politicians; religious motivations and affiliations; and strategies for change at governmental, organizational and other levels.

Employment issues

The report makes the following specific recommendations on employment:

1 The government should 'place a statutory duty on all employers to create and implement equity employment plans' and do so as a matter of priority.

2 The award of 'Investors in People' status should be made conditional on an organization having formulated and implemented an employment equity plan. Also issues of equity should be 'explicitly and comprehensively covered in the Business Excellence Model's guidance materials'.

3 The importance of employment equity should be stressed in such matters as guidance on public procurement and investment subsidies (e.g. Regional Selective Assistance).

4 Organizations involved in delivering New Deal programmes should be asked to demonstrate a positive contribution to employment equity. Failure to do so should lead to responsibilities being transferred to others.

5 Organizations responsible for the provision of personal adviser services should be asked to make sure that people from black or Asian backgrounds are 'equitably involved in their programmes, both as managers and as advisers'.

6 The government should commission research on the contributions made by black and Asian-owned businesses to the UK gross national product or UK trade balances.

7 The Department of Trade and Industry and the Small Business Service (SBS) should sponsor research on black and Asian business start-ups and their survival patterns.

Local targets and SBS national strategies should be based on the findings of this research.

8 Targets should be set at SBS national council and local council levels for increasing the take-up of support by Asian and black small businesses.

9 Undertakings of non-discrimination should be included in the Banking Code and the Mortgage Code.

10 Providers of financial services should be required to monitor and improve procedures, ensuring that their key employees are given race and diversity training.

11 Lending decisions by financial institutions should be monitored by ethnicity.

12 Targets should be set for British Trade International and Business Links partnerships to work more closely with black and Asian business sectors, and to highlight the 'possibility of international trade as a mechanism for encouraging growth'.

13 Business support agencies should be required to develop expertise in helping and advising independent retailers, and each agency involved in urban regeneration or business development should be made aware the value of the independent retail sector.

HRM in reality	'Hidden discrimination' prevents visible minorities and aboriginal people from gaining equal access to jobs, study finds

A study released by the Canadian Race Relations Foundation shows that visible minorities and aboriginal people miss out on promotions and the best jobs. Written by Jean Lock Kunz, Anne Milan and Sylvain Schetagne from the Canadian Council on Social Development (CCSD) the study – *Unequal Access: A Canadian Profile of Racial Differences in Education, Employment and Income* – was based on recent quantitative statistics and focus group discussions with visible minorities and aboriginal peoples in cities throughout Canada.

The authors found that:

- Even though visible minorities typically have higher levels of education than their white compatriots, they have lower levels of both employment and income.

- The greatest difficulty in finding suitable jobs is experienced by foreign-born visible minorities. Just half of those with university education have found high-skill jobs.

- University-educated visible minorities and aboriginal people are less likely to be in managerial and professional jobs than white Canadians. In fact, a half of visible minorities who do have managerial jobs are self-employed. This compares with a third of white Canadians.

- There is a greater representation of foreign-born visible minorities and aboriginals within the bottom 20 per cent of income earners than would be expected from their numbers in the population. They are also under-represented in the top 20 per cent of income earners.

- Comparing people with the same level of education, white Canadians (both foreign-born and Canadian-born) are three times as likely as aboriginal peoples and about twice as likely as foreign-born visible minorities to be in the top 20 per cent of income earners. Even when born in Canada, visible minorities continue to be less likely than white Canadians to be in the top 20 per cent of income earners.

▶

- Some 38 per cent of university-educated Canadian-born whites were within the top 20 per cent of the income scale. This compares with just 29 per cent of Canadian-born visible minorities and 21 per cent of foreign-born visible minorities.

- On average, foreign-born visible minorities earn 78 cents for every dollar earned by foreign-born white Canadians.

'Our findings confirm that the higher you go in the workplace, the whiter it becomes,' says Dr Kunz, senior research associate at the CCSD. 'Racial discrimination is still present in the work place, mostly in covert forms. Diversity is generally seen at the bottom and middle level of the labour force pyramid.'

While most focus group participants agreed that labour market outcomes are dependent on the right skill sets, education and the economic conditions, they observed that racial discrimination existed in employment. Participants found that racism is a 'hidden thing' in the workplace. Examples of 'subtle discrimination' include being passed over for promotion, being assigned unpleasant tasks at work, being stereotyped and being excluded from the 'inner circle' of their workplace.

'This report should be required reading for employers in both the public and private sectors,' says the Honourable Lincoln Alexander, chair of the Canadian Race Relations Foundation. 'The results demonstrate that we need to make greater efforts to eliminate systemic discrimination in Canada.'

Moy Tam, chief operating officer of the Foundation, says that although employment equity laws can play an important role in reducing employment and income disparities, a more sophisticated range of solutions is needed. 'Employment equity alone is not a panacea for eliminating racial discrimination in the workplace,' says Tam. 'We also need to eliminate the barriers faced by immigrants in accessing professions and trades and put more effort into raising public awareness about the existence of systemic discrimination in the workplace.'

Source: *HRM Guide Canada* (http://www.hrmguide.net/canada/), 12 December 2000.

Activity 17:4   Compare and contrast the British and Canadian experiences of race discrimination. Should the solution be the same?

Race and ethnicity legislation

Legislation against discrimination has an important bearing on human resource management in countries such as the USA, UK, Canada, New Zealand and South Africa but virtually none in others. The British Race Relations Act 1976 defined two forms of racial discrimination:

- *Direct discrimination.* This occurs when someone is treated less favourably than another because of his or her colour, race, nationality (including citizenship), or ethnic or national origins.

- *Indirect discrimination.* When a requirement or condition that applies equally to everyone has unequal and detrimental impact on a particular racial group, and cannot be justified irrespective of colour, race, nationality or ethnic or national origins.

Among the predominantly Anglo-Celtic countries, the UK was virtually alone in not having an affirmative action policy until recently. In Canada and New Zealand, for example, it is theoretically possible to enforce targets for the recruitment of particular groups. Within the UK, the Commission for Racial Equality (CRE) is able to:

● Give advice to people who feel they have been discriminated against, attempt to reach a settlement between parties such as employers and employees, and also provide legal representation in a court or industrial tribunal.

● Take action against discriminatory advertisements and in situations where people have been instructed or pressurized to discriminate on racial grounds.

● Investigate organizations that have been accused of racial discrimination. If it is shown that discrimination has occurred, the CRE is empowered to issue a non-discrimination notice which the organization is required to observe.

The CRE provides employers with guidance on their responsibilities under the Act and offers advice on equal opportunities and fair employment. This includes an employment code which has been approved by parliament. The code does not have the force of law but failure to follow its recommendations can be used in an industrial tribunal.

HRM in reality

Race relations legislation takes effect

The Race Relations (Amendment) Act 2000 comes into force today. It strengthens but does not replace the Act of 1976. Among other effects, it fulfils the recommendation of the Stephen Lawrence inquiry report which advocated that the 'full force' of race relations legislation should apply to the police. Chief Officers of Police are now liable for acts of discrimination by officers under their direction or control. As of today, people who feel that they have been racially discriminated against by the police can take their cases to the courts.

Members of the public can also take a variety of other race discrimination issues to court, including decisions to detain under the Mental Health Act and use of regulatory powers by local authorities in environmental health.

Public bodies now have to assess where and how racial equality can be relevant to the manner in which they carry out their work and deal with any problems they become aware of. More widely, the new Act requires public bodies to take positive steps towards racial equality in both their employment practices and the services they give to the public. The Commission for Racial Equality can enforce this requirement if public bodies fail in their responsibilities.

According to Gurbux Singh, chairman of the CRE:

> Britain today moves into a new gear on racial equality. All public bodies have new responsibilities and members of the public have new rights. Areas of discrimination that were immune from the Race Relations Act but which could have a devastating impact on people's lives have now been brought within its scope and individuals will be able to take cases to the courts.
>
> The public sector has not lived up to the justified expectation that it should deliver racial equality. It now has no option but to do so.
>
> Parliament, united with the agreement of all parties on this historic step, has put racial equality at the heart of the responsibilities of public bodies. They will now need to look at what they do, who they serve and who they employ, and make sure that they provide equality of opportunity across all their activities. This will end the waste of talent that discrimination imposes, improve the quality of individual lives and lay the basis for a new and positive relationship between public authorities such as the police and all members of Britain's diverse communities.

▶

◀

The CRE has published a guidance document on the general duty that public bodies have to promote racial equality and a handbook detailing assistance the CRE can provide for members of the public in pursuit of complaints of racial discrimination.

Source: *HRMGuide.co.uk* (http://www.hrmguide.co.uk), 2 April 2001.

Disability

Disabled people are among the most disadvantaged. In 1986, the European Commission estimated that 10 per cent of the Community's population had some form of disability. This amounted to 27 million people. A recommendation was adopted in the same year which encouraged member states to 'take all appropriate measures to promote fair opportunities for disabled people in the field of employment and vocational training'. However, there is no general legislation against discrimination on the grounds of disability. Quota systems for the employment of disabled people have largely been ineffective because of inadequate supervision by governments. Also, where social legislation for the disabled is weak, companies have found it comparatively easy to argue that they cannot provide suitable access or facilities to meet their needs.

HRM in reality

Jobs growth policies must include people with disabilities

With an unemployment rate for people with disabilities well above that for the general population, ACROD (National Industry Association for Disability Services) argues that policies designed to promote employment growth in Australia must include jobs for people with disabilities.

The most recent Australian Bureau of Statistics survey of *Disability, Ageing and Carers* (1998) showed that the unemployment rate for people with severe or profound disabilities who participated in the workforce stood at 12 points above that for the general population.

ACROD argues that governments of both political persuasions have underinvested in disability employment and training services. For every dollar spent on Disability Support Pension payments, the Government invests a mere 5 cents in the 440 organizations that provide specialist services that help people with disabilities find and maintain jobs. There are many social and economic barriers to employment for people with disabilities.

Disabled people are also grossly under-represented in vocational education and training (VET). ACROD says that 'if persons with a disability had the same age-specific participation rate in VET as the wider population, then the participation rate would almost treble, rising from 3.6 per cent to 9.6 per cent. The links between education, training and employment are well established.'

A recent report estimates that increasing VET participation to this level would generate an extra A$2.5 billion for Australia's economy. This benefit is being lost to Australia while the participation rate remains so low.

ACROD concludes that the next government should increase funding for disability employment and training services to ensure fewer disadvantages experienced by people with disabilities and more benefit for the economy from their contribution.

Source: *HRM Guide Australia* (http://www.hrmguide.net/australia/), 12 October 2001.

HRM in reality

Disabilities: It's time to do MORE

The Canadian Labour Congress launched an internal initiative to work better for people with disabilities. The 'It's time to do MORE' initiative is a challenge from the CLC to its affiliates. Canadian unions are asked to find ways to mobilize, organize, represent and educate working people with disabilities about their rights in the workplace.

'The best way to deal with the bare-bones fundamentals, issues like accessibility and accommodation which make work possible for people with disabilities, is to make sure that the workers whose rights we're defending are actively involved in building a better workplace,' says Nancy Riche, secretary-treasurer of the Canadian Labour Congress.

'Work works better when we belong to a union,' says Derek Fudge, CLC vice-president for disability rights, 'but unions need to make this fact more obvious to more people. They need to ensure that organizing strategies and other union activities include workers with disabilities. We need to see ourselves as part of the labour movement and we need to know how important it is to have a say in how our work is organized.'

The Canadian Labour Congress launched a long-term campaign on this year's Labour Day to shift the focus of Canada's decision makers towards the quality of life and standard of living of working people and their families. The campaign focuses on a simple question for workers – 'Is work working for you?'

'For most people, work doesn't work as well as it did one or two decades ago,' says Riche:

> There's been a real erosion in the quality of life and standard of living of working people. Longer hours, lower real wages, the loss of benefits and the increasing costs of healthcare and education are widening the gap between the haves and the have-nots in our society and moving us further away from the kind of Canada we worked so hard to build not that long ago.

Riche argues that the MORE initiative fits into the broader campaign which aims to ensure that all workers – including disabled – benefit from an improved standard of living and quality of life in the decades to come.

Earlier this year, the Conference Board of Canada in partnership with the Government of Ontario's Ministry of Citizenship published a new resource guide, *Tapping the Talents of People with Disabilities*, which finds that people with disabilities represent a largely untapped source of workers.

'Most employers have policies and practices in place that encourage the hiring and retention of a diverse workforce. But employers told us that they needed help finding candidates with disabilities for job openings,' says Ruth Wright, author of the guide. 'So we produced this employers' resource based on extensive research. We developed it as a concise, user-friendly resource with examples of good practice companies.' Minister of Citizenship Cam Jackson noted:

> Diversity in the workplace offers us a significant economic advantage in Ontario. This partnership represents an essential aspect of this government's commitment to finding shared solutions to address the needs of people with disabilities. Legislation alone will not achieve our goals. We need other organizations and individuals, like the Conference Board, to work in partnership with us.

▶

◀

About 16 per cent of Ontario's population – some 1.6 million people – have some form of disability. The Conference Board research showed that employers need help to accommodate employees with disabilities – particularly in restructuring jobs due to the nature of work, and with perceived cost-related factors. Employers also reported the need to dispel myths and stereotypes about employees with disabilities, both among co-workers and within society at large.

The guide provides practical steps for employers to improve the workplace representation of people with disabilities as well as recruitment strategies. It includes practical checklists, resources and contacts. Leading organizations such as IBM Canada, Motorola, Canadian Tire and Casino Niagara are cited as 'good practice' examples.

Resulting from a two-year partnership between the Conference Board of Canada and the Ontario Ministry of Citizenship, the report is available in English and French, and alternative formats including braille, diskette, audiocassette and large print. The guide for employers was developed from information gained through a survey of Ontario-based employers, a multi-stakeholder roundtable, interviews with organizations that have retained persons with disabilities, and seminars held across the province.

Source: *HRM Guide Canada* (http://www.hrmguide.net/canada/), 3 December 2001.

Some individual countries outside the EU, including Canada and the USA, have instigated their own legislation. After decades of ineffectual quotas, the UK was the first country in the European Union to introduce a Disability Discrimination Act (DDA) in 1995. This makes it illegal for businesses to discriminate against disabled people as employees or customers. In 1995, there were 3.8 million people of working age in the UK alone with some form of disability. Under 30 per cent of disabled adults in the UK are in full-time jobs. The disabled have also been targeted disproportionately for voluntary redundancies.

The Act requires all businesses employing more than 20 people to make 'reasonable adjustments' to shops, offices and factories where administrative or physical barriers have led to discrimination against disabled people. The government estimated that, on average, this would cost less than £200 per employee. This compares with US research which shows that their tougher legislation can be accommodated for under US$1000 dollars per person in the majority of cases (*Financial Times*, 6 November 1995).

Introduction of the Act did not take place without criticism. Many disability groups and businesses have argued that it is too vague and does not give clear guidelines. For example, whereas it makes direct discrimination against the disabled illegal, this does not apply to people with 'substantial impairments'. The legislation was initially policed by a weak but complex system of monitoring bodies including the National Disability Council and the National Advisory Council on the Employment of People with Disabilities. In 1999 the Disability Rights Commission Act paved the way for a new Disability Rights Commission to start functioning in 2000. The Commission has the following specific tasks:

- *Assistance.* Assisting disabled people to secure their rights, and arranging for legal advice and help where appropriate.
- *Information and advice.* Providing information and advice to disabled people and to employers and service providers about their rights and duties under the DDA.
- *Codes of practice.* Preparing and reviewing statutory codes of practice, which provide practical guidance to employers and service providers on meeting their obligations under the DDA and on good practice.

- *Conciliation*. Providing an independent conciliation service in the event of disputes between disabled people and service providers over access to goods and services, and monitoring the performance of the conciliation service.
- *Investigation*. Undertaking formal investigations into how disabled people are treated in a particular organization or sector, and into unlawful acts by particular organizations.
- *Research*. Carrying out research to inform discussion and policy making and to ascertain how well the law affecting the rights of disabled people is working.

HRM in reality	## Is it fair to put people with disabilities onto the dole queue?

The Brotherhood of St Laurence argues that the federal government should renegotiate its proposed budget policy of moving people with disabilities onto unemployment benefits.

'The federal government should think seriously about negotiating changes in the senate to its proposed policy of transferring people on the disability support pension to unemployment benefits,' says Brotherhood general manager, Stephen Gianni:

> The Brotherhood of St Laurence helps people with physical and psychological disabilities find work and we have found many possess good skills and are extremely willing to work. But there are already seven job-seekers for every vacancy. The need to create more secure full-time jobs is already obvious. It would be even more apparent if 200 000 people with disabilities join the dole queue.
>
> Asking vulnerable people to find jobs that demonstrably do not exist is simply cruel and unfair. 'Unless there is also meaningful job creation, then transferring people from the disability support pension onto unemployment benefits looks like a cynical cost-cutting exercise at the expense of people we should be working to protect.
>
> At the very least, more thought needs to go into how people with disabilities can be supported in their job search without forcing them into a system of mutual obligation that could lead to their benefits being cut. It is important that people with disabilities are not stigmatized and devalued and that we focus on people's abilities and capacities.

The budget plan for the disability support pension (DSP) is to move those assessed to be capable of 15 hours per week (previously 30 hours per week) onto unemployment benefits. Newstart allowance is less than DSP and does not cater for additional costs associated with their disability.

The mental health charity SANE Australia is also warning against budget proposals to limit access to the DSP. 'The government clearly fails to understand mental illness, and what these changes will mean for those affected with a psychiatric disability,' said SANE's executive director, Barbara Hocking. 'The budget ignores the "invisible" symptoms of mental illness and its episodic nature. It ignores the fact that people want to participate fully in society, but are impaired due to illness,' said Ms Hocking.

And Catholic Welfare Australia says that the government's mean-streak towards the disadvantaged continues and budget changes are redefining what it means to be disabled in Australia today. 'The "bad back" scenario offered by [Finance Minister] Costello exposes all people living with disabilities to demonstration,' said Mr O'Connor, National Director of Catholic Welfare Australia:

> Once again we see a pattern emerging from the government that puts everyone within a marginalized group under the microscope in the hope of catching a few people out. First

▶

◄

it was the dole bludgers and jobs snobs, then the queue jumpers and now disability pensioners.

The fact of the matter is that there is no accurate data regarding disabilities. Questions on disabilities were withdrawn from the recent census due to cost.

The government does appear to be making a concerted effort to prepare the nation for our ageing population by increasing funding in the Aged Care sector. A similar approach needs to be taken in the Disability sector. With an ageing population you would expect there to be an increase in age related disabilities. It is an issue of 'wear and tear' for many and it is in the nation's best interest to improve health outcomes for all people.

The government must open up discussion regarding the needs of people with disabilities in much the same way as they are currently doing with the aged. 'If Mr Costello is true to his inter-generational focus then we need to discuss and explore the range of approaches that should be taken to tackle the problem in the long term. The government has not asked what can be done to prevent disability or to better treat disabilities to reduce their impact.'

Mr O'Connor concluded, 'this is not a clear cut issue and the factors involved are complex and diverse – it is unfortunate that the government chose to voice such a narrow-minded view in last night's Budget.'

Source: *HRM Guide Australia* (http://www.hrmguide.net/australia/), 17 May 2002.

Activity 17:5

Are there any aspects of disability discrimination that are fundamentally different from any other form of discrimination in the employment market?

Ageism

Discrimination on the grounds of age is prevalent but often unrecognized. Some countries such as Canada, France, New Zealand and the USA have legislated against ageism and a European Union Directive compels all member states to introduce legislation against ageism by the year 2006. In other countries, employers are allowed to specify age ranges for job applications. For example, in the UK Heasman (1993, p.28) found that 30 per cent of advertisements carried discriminatory references against older workers. Half of these advertisements specified a maximum age limit of 35. Other advertisements used terminology such as 'youthful' and 'dynamic' which carry an implicit message that older workers are not welcome to apply. Most Australian states have gone further than most US states in their age discrimination legislation (Bennington, 2001) but, at the time of writing, there is no national law covering age discrimination. Gomez, Gunderson and Luchak (2002) observe that while the USA has banned the setting of mandatory retirement ages, this issue is still a topic of debate in neighbouring Canada.

HRM in reality

Large employee search firm illegally screened job candidates based on age

The Equal Employment Opportunity Commission substantiated a charge filed by AARP that Spencer Stuart, a large employee search firm, illegally screened job candidates on the basis of age. Spencer Stuart was accused by AARP in October 1998 with routinely violating the Age Discrimination in Employment Act (ADEA) through the practice of limiting searches for suitable job candidates on the basis of the age-based preferences of its clients and disclosing age information to clients during candidates' presentations.

EEOC New York district director Spencer H. Lewis, Jr issued a 'Determination' (final decision) memorandum to AARP and Spencer Stuart on 15 March, stating that the search firm has 'regularly continued to provide the ages of candidates either verbally or in writing to select clients' – a practice illegal under the ADEA.

'Age discrimination in hiring is one of the most critical problems facing older workers,' said Laurie McCann, a senior attorney with AARP Foundation Litigation. 'It is essential that gatekeepers to employment, including employment agencies and search firms such as Spencer Stuart, accept, refer and place candidates in a fair and non-discriminatory manner,' McCann said.

The EEOC's final decision triggers – under the ADEA – a period of informal conciliation during which the commission, Spencer Stuart and AARP will seek to reach a settlement on the charges. Failure to reach such a settlement could lead to court action by EEOC and/or AARP.

The ADEA, enacted in 1967, is the primary federal law prohibiting employment discrimination on the basis of age for persons 40 and older. Over 45 per cent of the AARP membership is employed – and most of these people are protected by the ADEA.

AARP's charge emanated from allegations filed with the EEOC by two former employees of Spencer Stuart that the company engaged in systemic violations of civil rights laws, including prohibitions against age discrimination. AARP's charge stated that the company's discriminatory practices in its US offices took a number of forms: entering age information into a computer database; including the age in candidate presentation packages to the client; or orally relaying such information to clients.

In its Determination memo last week, EEOC said that AARP's claim was supported by a January 1995 widely circulated memorandum in which Spencer Stuart's then chief financial officer wrote:

> Over the past six months, we have had numerous questions raised as to the exposure created by referencing age (birth date) and marital status in candidate reports. We have concluded, after having sought advice from outside counsel, that we are principally creating a legal exposure for our clients by including this information in reports that end up in their personnel files. Therefore, in order to protect our clients (and, to a lesser degree, ourselves) we should not include age (birth date) in candidate reports. The best approach (for our clients) is to provide this information verbally so that their permanent records do not contain this information … If the client wants this information provided in the cover, we should comply with their wishes … Please keep in mind that asking for age or marital/parental status does create a legal exposure. Be very careful about how you obtain this information.

The Determination stated: 'Based on our investigation, EEOC has determined that there is reasonable cause to believe that the Respondent has violated the ADEA in that it provides ages of candidates to prospective employers for a discriminatory purpose … This Determination is final.'

The EEOC statement said that, even after that memo was circulated, Spencer Stuart regularly forwarded the ages of candidates – either verbally or in writing – to select clients.

Source: *HRM Guide USA* (http://www.hrmguide.net/usa/), 26 March 2001.

The delay in adopting anti-age discrimination legislation in the UK can be attributed to a comparative lack of interest among organizations such as the Institute of Personnel and Development and the Confederation of British Industry. These organizations have preferred self-regulation and promoting raised awareness to counter ageism. Such voluntary methods did not work in relation to race and gender and there is no reason to assume that they will in respect of age discrimination (Loretto, Duncan and White, 2000). However, critics point out that the proportion of men over 50 employed in the UK is broadly similar to that in the USA where legislation has been in force since 1967.

Sargeant (2001) points to the strange contradiction in the UK government's highly positive attitude towards lifelong learning and its apparent disinterest regarding combating age discrimination. Sargeant also comments that people who enter or return to higher education as mature students are no more successful at avoiding age discrimination than counterparts who do not take up the opportunity.

A report on older workers by the Industrial Society (2000) (now the Work Foundation) argues that while internet start-ups have become synonymous with youth, the new economy actually depends on the over-50s. Falling birth rates are leading to reduced numbers of young people coming into the job market. This means that employers elsewhere are beginning to look more enthusiastically for older employees – especially as over-50s are much fitter and more flexible than ever before. Once ignored, employers are starting to appreciate the unique skills possessed by older workers.

The report states that there is emerging evidence from the dot-com sector to suggest that firms are increasingly using over-50s in the transition from start-up to long-term success. There is a new demand for 'new elders' possessing health, wealth, wisdom and strategic know-how. These indispensable older workers come in several types:

- *Warhorses.* Seasoned campaigners who have gone through economic downturns in the past and are not afraid of economic cycles.

- *Trusted guides.* Consumers (for example, those looking for mortgage advice) prefer older employees with age and experience over the youthful and enthusiastic but inexperienced.

- *Networkers.* Able to develop good business relationships, particularly with partner companies in Asia where, to quote one employer, 'veneration and respect for age is important, and counterparts find it more comfortable to build relationships with older business people rather than with young dot-com entrepreneurs'.

- *Strategists.* According to Ronald Cohen, from a venture capitalist firm cited in the report that has invested around US$3billion in the new economy, 'young entrepreneurs are coming in and asking for experienced people; increasingly they're realizing that they need this to get the business to the stock markets.'

- *Connectors.* Older workers with team-building skills can provide a balance in the 'lean economy' of new organizations.

Statistics presented in the report show that:

- People over 50 are returning to work at a faster rate than the rest of the population as demand increases for their skill. For example, over the last year the employment rate for women aged 50 and over has gone up nearly three times that for the workforce as a whole. By the year 2020, one-in-four of the employed population will be aged 50 and over.

- In the USA older people make up a tenth of the workforce but have been responsible for 22 per cent of the country's job growth.

- The Australian economy created 360 000 full-time jobs between 1996 and 2000, with three-quarters going to employees aged 45 and over.

- Start-ups by entrepreneurs in their early 50s have double the likelihood of survival than those started by people in their early 20s.

On the downside, many employers have been slow to see the value of older workers – the proportion of people between 50 and 65 who are not working has doubled in the last 20 years. A third of those in this age group do not work.

The report argues for flexibility over the retirement age and for the adaptation of the rules governing occupational pensions so that people can be partly retired and partly working. The government should also 'temper its enthusiasm for youth with a recognition of the values in age'. In conclusion, the report states that:

'we must look to business to set about sweeping away misconceptions about age. The business case for wisdom is compelling, the demographic pressure for change inescapable. Once employers have recognized the value in age, the work of reassessing the meaning of ageing will begin.'

**HRM
in reality**

Mature age workers vital for Australia's future

A new report commissioned by the federal government makes it clear that mature age workers have a vital role in Australia's economic future. Released at the Ageing Workforce Conference held by the Committee for Economic Development of Australia (CEDA), the report emphasizes the importance of Australia's ageing population to the country's future growth.

Minister for Aged Care, Bronwyn Bishop said that the landmark Access Economics report, *Population Ageing and the Economy*, sends a strong signal to all Australian businesses that if they neglect the older worker they do so at their own peril. She pointed out that, in common with other developed countries, the ageing of Australia's population was demographically inevitable:

This Access Economics report examines the micro and macro economic issues flowing from these demographic changes. It provides a comprehensive examination of the projected increase in the supply of mature age workers and the implications of the baby boomer cohort for the labour market and the market place for goods and services in the next couple of decades.

The three chapters in this report will provide a guide to informed future debate on the implications of ageing for our nation: 'Too Valuable to Waste', 'All in it Together' and 'The Silver Market goes Platinum.'

The Access Economics research highlights the range of market forces at work in the economy and the potential for creative outcomes for an ageing population. If mature age workers and their families have the flexibility to make choices which allow them to maximize their participation and contribution to the community, then ageing can be about increasing our economic well-being, not an impending burden.

Source: *HRM Guide Australia* (http://www.hrmguide.net/australia/), 20 March 2001.

Activity 17:6

Given the reducing proportion of younger people in most developed countries, what could be done to encourage the employment of older workers?

There is a common view among employers that people over 45 are not worth recruiting, promoting or training. This is against a demographic trend where, in developed countries, this covers a third of the workforce. The proportion will continue to increase over the next several decades. Common stereotypes about older workers include: being slow to learn; unwilling to accept and adapt to new technology; and lacking enthusiasm for training.

However, research shows that older workers:

- are more reliable and conscientious
- more loyal and committed to stay with their organization
- have greater interpersonal skills
- work harder and more effectively
- show equal levels of productivity to younger staff.

In a survey of Hong Kong and UK workers, Chiu *et al.* (2001) found that stereotyping was linked to respondents' own age although supervisors also took account of perceived work effectiveness. Stereotypical beliefs significantly affected respondents' attitudes towards training, promotion and retention of older workers and their willingness to work with older workers.

Older workers are less effective at work that requires heavy physical activity or the continuous, rapid processing of information. Conversely, they are better than younger people at jobs requiring accuracy and reliability, and the use of knowledge.

Older workers often do not portray the kind of image that many younger managers subscribe to. To appear smart and modern, a youthful customer-facing workforce is preferred. Extensive downsizing in organizations throughout the Western world has concentrated on early retirements. The result is that many companies are entirely staffed by people under 50 (with the exception of senior managers).

HRM in reality	**National age discrimination law a priority, says Human Rights Commissioner**

Human Rights Commissioner Dr Sev Ozdowski has called on the federal government to introduce national age discrimination legislation and also to begin an education campaign against the stereotypes about ageing.

At a speech to the Council on the Ageing National Congress in Canberra, Dr Ozdowski welcomed promises from both major parties prior to the election regarding the introduction of national age discrimination laws: 'Over the past year, I have strongly lobbied the government to develop a national age discrimination law – the missing piece of a national patchwork of sex, race and disability discrimination laws,' Dr Ozdowski said. 'With this legal protection, people may have an effective remedy for violations of these rights – including the right to be free from stereotypes with no factual foundation.'

Some of the key areas in which discrimination occurs (based on complaints received by the Human Rights and Equal Opportunity Commission) include retirement ages, recruitment in employment, superannuation schemes (which differ between states and territories), access to goods and services, training and education. State and territory laws do not cover federal government employees.

Some 46 per cent of 50–64 year olds do not have paid employment and 33 per cent are relying on some form of social security payment. Dr Ozdowski said there was a clear economic imperative for recruiting, retaining and promoting older people: 'It is the best use of available economic resources and expertise while society goes through the process of ageing.'

He called on the government to commence immediately an education campaign to combat stereotypes about ageing and prejudices against older Australians, and for media organizations to support the campaign. Dr Ozdowski said such a campaign would lay the groundwork and hopefully make the wider community more receptive to the early introduction of the law. Dr Ozdowski said he would be happy to assist the new government in developing the legislation and the education campaign.

At the end of March 2001, *Age Limits*, a report into age discrimination in employment affecting workers aged over 45 (jointly funded by the Equal Opportunity Commissions of South Australia, Victoria and Western Australia) found that very significant levels of age discrimination occurred at every stage of the employment process.

Quotes from people interviewed for the report included:

- 'The agency told me that without the age I could still be shaped into a saleable package.'

- 'You feel you should be "up front" about your age, but there are institutionalized consequences of putting your age.'

- 'Recruitment agents are "going through the motions" of recruitment according to an "identikit picture" of what employers want.'

- 'The General Manager came in and winced and wouldn't look at me. They never rang me back. I rang and they gave an excuse that they were going to get someone more experienced.'

- 'I attended a group interview with around 20 other women, all of whom were younger. When the time came to demonstrate how to apply cosmetics I was asked to act as the model for the whole interview.'

- 'There is a perception that you are not likely to change, and that you are not open to new skills and you are not offered new skills. There is no offer of new training, but rather that another person comes back in a new role.'

- 'There seems to be a culture of preferring young people who have had a lot of jobs. I thought that a long history with one firm would be worth more, but they prefer young people who have had six or seven jobs in the last ten years. They like the turnover rather than stable employment.'

Commenting on the report, South Australian Commissioner for Equal Opportunity Linda Matthews said the report was commissioned to find out why more people did not make use of age discrimination legislation despite anecdotal evidence of significant levels of age discrimination in the community, particularly towards people over the age of 45:

> This report confirms that there are high levels of age discrimination in the community. It also found that older workers were unclear about their rights under equal opportunity laws and that older workers are reluctant to make complaints of age discrimination because they fear they will be victimized by employers, or because they will become stigmatized as complainers and because age discrimination can be very difficult to prove.

Chief executive of the Victorian Equal Opportunity Commission, Dianne Sisely noted the report found that strong negative community attitudes persist about the abilities of older workers:

> These attitudes about what a person's working life should be, come from a past era where workers were often worn out from physical labour by the time they were 45 and were unlikely to live much beyond 60. Not only has the nature of work changed so that people are no longer physically burnt out at 45 but we are now also living well into the

◄

80s. This means that the productive capacity of many workers now extends well beyond 45.

West Australian Commissioner for Equal Opportunity June Williams said the report supported anecdotal evidence and evidence from complaints of age discrimination to the Equal Opportunity Commission, as well as other research, that these attitudes impacted negatively on the job prospects of people aged over 45:

> There is no reason why many people cannot continue to be productive contributors to the economy well into their 60s and beyond. Yet despite compulsory retirement being abolished in most states there is no sign of a change to working longer. In fact the opposite is true with a significant trend towards early retirement and the retrenchment of older workers when downsizing occurred.

The report made a number of recommendations including that action be taken:

- To ensure older workers received practical information to upgrade their skills and support to understand the changing nature of work, to maximize their chances of recruitment.

- To assist employers with information on how to value and support their older workers' employment opportunities through training and how to comply with legislation in recruitment.

Source: *HRM Guide Australia* (http://www.hrmguide.net/australia/), 13 November 2001.

Summary

This chapter focused on three areas of workplace discrimination: race, disability and age. We observed that all societies appear to favour certain groups more than others and that most developed societies have attempted to combat prejudice, favouritism and discrimination by introducing relevant laws. Each of the forms of discrimination that we have covered has complex causes that are not easily countered by legislation.

Further reading

Much of the available material on race discrimination at work is to be found in more general books on racism and ethnicity. *Stereotypes and Prejudice* edited by Charles Stangor (published by Psychology Press, 2000) is a collection of readings on stereotypes, prejudice and discrimination. *Theories of Race and Racism* edited by John Solomos and Les Back (published by Routledge, 1999) is another collection of readings. *Responding to Racism in Ireland* edited by Fintan Farrell and Philip Watt (published by Veritas Publications, 2001) and *Race, Colour and Identity in Australia and New Zealand* edited by John Docker and Gerhard Fischer (UNSW Press, 2000) concentrate on those specific countries. *Discrimination and Human Rights* by Sandra Fredman (Oxford University Press, 2001) focuses on the role of human rights law in combating race discrimination. For ageism issues see: *Age Discrimination in the American Workplace: Old at a Young Age* by Raymond F. Gregory (published by Rutgers University Press, 2001); *Older People and Work* by Ali Taqi (International Labour Organisation, 2003); and *Age Discrimination by Employers* written by Kerry Segrave (McFarland & Company, 2001). Texts on disability issues include *Disability Discrimination* by Andrew Hogan (published by EMIS Professional Publishing, 2001 in the UK) and *Employment, Disability, and the Americans*

With Disabilities Act: Issues in Law, Public Policy, and Research (Psychosocial Issues)
edited by Peter David Blanck (published by Northwestern University Press, 2000).

Review questions

1 Outline the differences between racial prejudice and institutional racism. Do other groups experience institutional barriers?

2 Why have some governments shown an apparent reluctance to introduce age discrimination legislation?

3 Discuss the attitudes of young people towards older workers. At what age should people cease paid employment?

4 What are the limitations on the employment of the disabled? What can be done to improve the situation?

5 What are the arguments for and against the introduction of quotas for the employment of certain groups?

Problem for discussion and analysis

The Black Workers' Support Group

The borough of Kenwood is situated on the outskirts of a large city. It is predominantly populated by white, middle-class people and is considered reasonably affluent by comparison with its inner city neighbours. Just under 20 per cent of residents are over pensionable age, of whom 7 per cent are over 75 years. The vast majority continue to live in their own homes, an increasing proportion living alone. The ageing population has significant resource implications for the local authority.

The social services department is responsible for the home help service which comprises three full-time managers and a team of 40 part-time women workers. In addition to providing practical help and social support to their elderly clients, they are often the first people to be alerted to a deterioration in a person's situation. They are a crucial element in enabling people to stay in their own homes, saving the local authority enormous sums of money. However, their status does not reflect their true importance to the community and the section is regularly scrutinized for potential budget cuts.

The local authority has an equal opportunities policy which 'strives towards elimination of discrimination within the workplace'. The social services department had noted that the few black staff recruited were in low-paid or insecure posts and tended not to stay long. To try to prevent the policy remaining no more than a piece of paper, it was decided to set up an equal opportunities monitoring committee. This has met quarterly for the last three years and comprises staff representing all grades within social services, plus representatives from the main personnel department and two co-opted councillors. It is seen as undesirable to have such a group entirely made up of white representatives so the few black staff available are under constant pressure to volunteer for membership.

▶

One exception to the tendency of black staff to stay no more than a few months is Mary, a middle-aged black woman who has worked for the local authority for 17 years, always as a home help. She is a tolerant person who likes the flexibility of the work. She has regularly encountered clients whose questions and comments are inadvertently offensive and insensitive but has said little to her managers. However, having been allocated to a couple whose racism is overt and sustained, Mary made a complaint to her harassed line manager, who sympathized and reallocated a white home help to the couple concerned. Mary got on with her job without further comment. Over the next few weeks the manager thought about her own response, felt it had been inadequate, and referred the incident to the equal opportunities monitoring committee.

The reaction of group members was diverse:

- What do you expect? Old people are always unreasonable about everything.
- They may well be suffering from dementia; if so, they can't be held responsible.
- Living in this area, they're probably not used to black people and don't know how to react.
- Would Mary like any further action?
- We did all we could in practical terms – we can't withdraw the service from them.
- The line manager should have visited and confronted them.
- Oh dear, how awful.
- Has this sort of thing happened before, do we know?
- Black staff are particularly discriminated against and should receive appropriate support.

The final response came from one of two black members. He proposed a Black Workers' Support Group, open to anybody working for the local authority who defined themselves as black. The group would meet every two months within paid working time. The existence and purpose of the group would be made known to other colleagues who would be asked to demonstrate support by enabling participants to attend. Benefits to the local authority might accrue from being seen to be implementing its own equal opportunities policy and potentially retaining staff who would feel less isolated and marginalized.

The majority of group members had considerable reservations about this proposal although most did not say so openly. While most doubts centred on the impact on over-stretched departments and the possible adverse reaction of colleagues asked to cover extra duties, one of the councillors was more direct: 'Where exactly will this end? In no time at all we'll be expected to pay for part-time workers' support groups, Irish workers' support groups, etc., etc.'.

The proposal was referred to the senior managers' meeting for further consideration. There was more support within this forum, but it was felt that the Black Workers' Support Group should be chaired by a senior manager. Black staff pointed out that the group would not operate on such hierarchical terms and, in any event, all managers of the grade proposed were white. Managers' expectation that they would receive copies of the minutes of each meeting met with a similar response. While uneasy with their lack of control, senior managers felt it would be more controversial to refuse permission. The Black Workers' Support Group went ahead and the local authority began to receive enquiries about the scheme from outside the organization and praise for its initiative. With significant cuts proposed to the home help service in the next financial year, and with school-age children to care for, Mary has felt too busy to attend.

Discussion questions: (a) How effective is the equal opportunities policy in Kenwood? (b) Did Mary's supervisor take the right decision? (c) What is the value of the Black Workers' Support Group?

PART 7

Performance and compensation

Performance management is important because it plays a pivotal role in any organization's human resource framework. There are clear benefits from managing individual and team performance to achieve organizational objectives. Similarly, compensation in the form of pay, bonuses, stock options and other benefits can be linked to the achievement of particular goals. But such links do not necessarily produce expected results. This is a problematic and complex area in which common-sense solutions do not work.

The chapters in Part 7 address a number of specific issues, including:

- How have legislative, technological and organizational changes affected the process of performance assessment?
- Why do organizations favour certain stereotypes of good performance?
- What decisions underpin the adoption of performance assessment strategies?
- What are the theoretical and practical problems associated with performance appraisal and counselling?
- How are the HR and payroll functions related?
- How can pay levels be evaluated fairly?
- Does performance-related pay produce the desired results?
- What roles do bonuses, stock options and other forms of non-monetary compensation play in reward management?

Performance and compensation

18 Performance management

Objectives

The purpose of this chapter is to:

- Determine the criteria that distinguish 'good' from less acceptable performance.

- Evaluate the most common techniques for measuring performance.

- Investigate how performance management can be used to reinforce an organization's human resource strategies.

- Consider whether or not performance management really encourages desirable work behaviour.

Performance assessment

In Part 5 we looked at how the performance of potential recruits can be predicted from evidence collected during selection procedures. This was followed by an examination of the difficulties encountered in any attempt to ensure equal opportunities and to overcome the powerful socio-cultural mechanisms that promote the interests of privileged in-groups. In this chapter we extend our debate to the evaluation of current employee performance.

Performance assessment has a long history based on comparative judgements of human worth. In the early part of the 19th century, for example, Robert Owen used coloured wooden cubes, hung above work stations, to indicate the performance of individual employees at his New Lanark cotton mills in Scotland. Various merit ratings were represented by different coloured cubes, which were changed to indicate improvement or decline in employee performance (Heilbroner, 1953, cited in Murphy and Cleveland, 1995, p.3).

As with the employee selection techniques described in Chapter 15, modern performance assessment developed from sophisticated rating systems designed by work psychologists for military use during the two world wars. By the 1950s, such methods had been adopted by most large US business organizations, spreading worldwide thereafter. Initially, performance assessment was used to provide information for promotions, salary increases and discipline. More recently, performance measurement has had wider purposes:

- To identify and enhance desirable or effective work behaviour.
- Reinforcing this behaviour by linking rewards to measured performance.
- Developing desired competencies and building human capital within organizations.

Enthusiasts for performance assessment argue that it serves a key integrating role within an organization's human resource processes. First, it provides a checking mechanism for resourcing policies and procedures, evaluating the quality of recruits and hence the underlying decision-making process. Secondly, it monitors employee commitment and the relevance of their working behaviour to business objectives. Thirdly, it provides a rationale for an organization's pay policies. Taken at face value, these intentions seem entirely compatible with an integrated and strategic approach to human resource management. In reality, however, the definition and measurement of good performance is a controversial matter, involving fundamental issues of motivation, assessment and reward.

Key concept 18:1

Performance management   'A strategic and integrated approach to increasing the effectiveness of organizations by improving the performance of the people who work in them and by developing the capabilities of teams and individual contributors.' (Armstrong and Baron, 1998)

All aspects of performance management (see Key concept 18.1) arouse controversy, especially appraisals and performance-related pay. Critics point to weaknesses in their methodology and basic philosophy. Employees are often dissatisfied with the methods of performance management systems and managers are frequently reluctant to engage in the process because of its confrontational nature. At a deeper level, it can be argued that if true commitment exists performance management is superfluous. In too many organizations it enforces the compliance of an unhappy workforce. However, Pettijohn *et al.* (2001) demonstrated that a positive attitude towards appraisal – from employees and managers – is possible if managers are provided with information designed to increase the benefits of engaging in the evaluation process and more thought is given to the appropriateness of measurement criteria.

Despite its problematic reputation, the use of performance assessment has been reinforced through the increasing prevalence of performance-related pay (PRP). As we will see in Chapter 19 this is based frequently on an oversimplified view of work motivation. Employers, consultants and neo-liberal politicians remain wedded to PRP schemes despite considerable evidence against their effectiveness as motivators. Fletcher (2001) argues that performance assessment has widened both as a concept and as a set of practices, becoming more obviously a part of HRM's strategic integration of human resource activities and business policies. Consequently, research and discussion of the topic has moved beyond measurement issues and criticisms of the accuracy of performance ratings to encompass the social and motivational aspects of assessment. Fletcher divides current concerns into two thematic groups:

- The content of appraisal – contextual performance, goal orientation and self-awareness.
- The process of appraisal – appraiser–appraisee interaction and multi-source feedback that have cross-cultural implications and are open to technological change.

We begin with a discussion of the environmental factors that have led to the widespread use of performance assessment techniques. These include legislation, the demands of technological change, increasing flexibility and diversification, and changes in workforce composition. We proceed to look at the way in which organizations favour certain stereotypes of good performance. The next section evaluates decision making underlying the adoption of performance assessment strategies. Finally we discuss the activities involved in assessment such as appraisal and counselling.

Activity 18:1	Why is performance assessment important?

The environmental context

'The effects of context variables on appraisal processes and outcomes have been the object of speculation but have not been empirically examined in the detail that these effects warrant. We believe that context is the key to understanding appraisal in organizations' (Murphy and Cleveland, 1995, p.407).

The business environment exercises both a direct and an indirect influence on the conduct of performance assessment. Whereas legislation has specific consequences, particularly in the USA, most environmental factors have a diffuse and often unrealized effect on assessment and pay structures. It is likely that different individuals – and organizations – will respond in varying ways to these factors. Some will be highly sensitive to possible legal implications, practice elsewhere and the state of the job market; others will be virtually immune to these influences. The main environmental factors identified as having a contextual influence on performance management are examined in the following subsections.

Business culture

At a national level, culture affects performance management through socio-political traditions and attitudes that determine whether assessment is acceptable, and to what degree. Cultural norms dictate 'acceptable' standards of performance and the management methods by which they are assured. For example, in a number of Asian societies the employment relationship is a matter of honour, and obligations are regarded as morally, rather than contractually, binding between the two parties. In a situation where people are automatically expected to do the job as agreed, the role of performance assessment is questionable. Entrekin and Chung (2001) and Hempel (2001) conducted studies of Hong Kong Chinese and Western managers in Hong Kong. Both studies found considerable differences in attitudes towards appraisal and the attribution of good performance between Hong Kong Chinese managers and their counterparts from the UK or the USA. Entrekin and Chung (2001) concluded that western managers and Chinese managers in Western-owned firms regarded performance assessment more highly than Hong Kong Chinese managers in Hong Kong-owned firms. And, given a choice, supervisory (top-down) appraisal was preferred by Chinese managers over other approaches such as subordinate or peer evaluation. However, Paik, Vance and Stage (2000) examined the characteristics of performance assessment systems in four South-East Asian countries – Indonesia, Malaysia, the Philippines and Thailand – and found significant differences in managerial practices and behaviours relevant to the design and conduct of performance appraisal. They suggest that the cultural context of performance assessment is complex and that the familiar clustering of cultures is too simplistic to explain the differences that exist.

HRM in reality

Personnel evaluation in Latin America and Spain

A study by Bumeran, a HR technology company owned by Terra Lycos, focused on personnel evaluation in Latin American and Spanish companies. The study looked at the issue from both company and employee perspectives. The online survey received a total of 3500 responses from all countries combined. This represented 450 companies.

Results from the employee perspective included: 35 per cent of respondents stated that they never received evaluations from their employers; 53 per cent of Brazilian respondents said they were never evaluated; and 49 per cent of Spanish respondents said that they received annual evaluations.

From the company side: 50 per cent of Brazilian companies stated that they never evaluate their employees; 50 per cent of the companies from Spain said that they conduct annual evaluations of their personnel; and in Brazil, Mexico and Spain a similar percentage of both employers and employees indicated that they know the internal procedures and evaluation methods, and when evaluations are done, they are clear and understandable.

Results varied considerably in Argentina, Chile and Venezuela but this may be due to the high level of unemployed respondents. Obviously the unemployed group does not receive any kind of evaluations.

Source: *HRMGuide.com* (http: //www.hrmguide.com), 20 June 2002.

> **Key concept 18:2**
>
> **The work ethic**   The belief that work is virtuous in itself. Work can be defined as 'an activity directed to valued goals beyond enjoyment of the activity itself' (Warr, 1987). Hard work is to be admired and leisure is equated with laziness. Spare time is perceived as evil: 'the devil makes work for idle hands'. In some societies the work ethic became a fundamental religious principle, the Puritans and Calvinists holding it to be such a virtue that Max Weber termed it 'the Protestant work ethic'. Nineteenth century factory owners used the principle to justify 11 and 12-hour days. The concept is sometimes extended to include the virtue of frugality as against waste. It justifies regarding the poor as sinful, since success and ambition are virtuous and wealth is a sign of God's favour.

Legislation

In free market economies, the employment relationship between workers and employing organizations is seen as a contractual matter. This relationship is expressed in formal or legalistic statements of obligation between the two, such as written employment contracts, job descriptions and performance objectives. Performance measurement has the purpose of ensuring that the employee fulfils the contract. Commitment in Western organizations is rarely a 'hearts and minds' phenomenon and this is exemplified in the policing nature of performance management. It is a modern version of scientific management in which the detail of work is supervised in a sometimes overbearing way. Within English-speaking countries, performance-related pay encapsulates a fusion of the work ethic (Key concept 18.2) and free market ideology: work is virtuous and virtue should be rewarded generously.

Performance measurement has become a sensitive legal issue in the USA because of possible consequences on equal opportunities (Murphy and Cleveland, 1995, p.11). Since the 1970s, assessments have been regarded as tests and are subject to guidelines enforced by the Equal Employment Opportunities Commission. Employers taking personnel decisions on the basis of performance assessment have to be mindful of possible legal action on one of two grounds: (a) the validity or accuracy of assessment ratings as predictors of future performance and promotion potential; the validity or accuracy of ratings as measures of past behaviour. This legislation is specific to the USA, but all human resource managers have to be mindful of possible breaches of equal opportunities legislation in their own countries.

General economic conditions

Prevailing attitudes towards employees and, in turn, their response to performance assessment are considerably affected by issues such as unemployment. In line with our discussion in Chapter 6, growth and shrinkage in the job market is conventionally believed to be followed by changes in the behaviour of workers and employers. At times of high unemployment, workers are thought to be concerned about losing their jobs and hence are more conscientious and tolerant of strict management. When suitable employees are scarce, managers must be cautious – unflattering assessments can trigger an employee's move to another organization.

The relationship between the economy and assessment is circular and complex. Performance management is justified by organizational efficiency, and the overall efficiency of organizations in a country is crucial for its economic well-being. Income generated by effective, as opposed to inefficient, performance encourages economic wealth. Performance management has become the chosen Western instrument to drive out ineffective activity. It incorporates both stick and carrot: the first in terms of sanction, criticism or discipline; the second in the form of praise or cash.

Industry sector

Methods of performance management vary considerably between different industrial sectors, partly as a matter of the nature of the work involved, tradition and fashion. Sales-dominated industries, such as financial services, tend to have clear individual or team objectives that can be translated readily into performance targets. Performance-related pay is common in this sector and commission-only contracts are not unusual. In other sectors, objectives are more diffuse and difficult to measure so that PRP is not easily justified.

Technological change

Computer networking is likely to have a dramatic effect on the nature of supervision, and hence performance assessment (Murphy and Cleveland, 1995, p.408). In Chapter 7 we observed that modern organizations can extend beyond their formal physical boundaries by means of networked systems. Work can be done at a distance by travelling executives, overseas affiliates or telecommuters working from home. This raises intriguing issues for performance management. For instance, how does a manager assess the performance of a homeworker when there is little or no personal contact between the two?

Technology has the power to provide extensive statistics such as the time an individual spends logged on to a system, number of key strokes and volume of output; but does this information provide a meaningful measure of job performance? If the employee's task involves elements of creativity, accuracy and thoroughness, how can these be assessed? If managers become dependent on 'objective' measures of work, they may be forced to bring their personal assessments into line, 'even if they know that the workers who spend the most time at their desks may not be the best performers' (Murphy and Cleveland, 1995, p.408). Being there, and even being busy, is not the same as being effective. Performance management hinges inevitably on results.

Advanced technology requires expert users. It is common for managers not to possess the same level of expertise as their subordinates. Such managers are not qualified to assess their performance and, moreover, subordinates are well aware of the fact. In these cases, supervisors have neither the competence nor the credibility necessary for effective performance management.

Flexibility and diversification

As we have already seen, in the 1980s and early 1990s, the traditional nature of the employment relationship in free market countries changed, moving the balance of power firmly in favour of employers. We noted that job descriptions have disappeared or, at least, have been diluted, so that employees can be asked to do virtually anything required by the organization. Conversely, performance criteria have been more tightly defined, typically expressed in the form of demanding objectives: forever-moving goalposts. Performance assessment has become the crucial means of monitoring this relationship.

Employee relations

Performance management is a means of enhancing managerial control, particularly through individual performance-related pay schemes. In Chapter 22 we will see that the individualization of pay diminishes or neutralizes the role of collective bargaining. The purpose and influence of trade unions is undermined, reducing both their effectiveness and attractiveness as an alternative focus for employee commitment.

Workforce composition

Largely forgotten in the controversy over PRP, the other main function of performance assessment is the identification of individual strengths and weaknesses. As we will see in Chapter 20, the latter can be targeted for improvement through training and development. Strengths may indicate a potential star performer, worthy of a management career route and promotion. Assessment employed to determine development needs ultimately serves to increase a nation's human capital.

Less positively, demographics and a history of unequal opportunities affect the conduct of assessment, since they largely determine who assesses whom. For example, in countries such as the UK, it is likely that performance assessments are largely carried out by white male managers, whereas the people they assess are probably of mixed gender and ethnic origin. This is one of a series of organizational issues we consider further in the next section.

| Activity 18:2 | Summarize the external factors that can affect the process of performance assessment within an organization. Do they help or hinder that process? |

The organization and effective performance

How do organizations decide which performance criteria should be measured? How do they differentiate between a good, average or indifferent employee? On the basis of empirical evidence, Armstrong and Baron (1998) highlight two central propositions used to justify performance assessment:

1 People, either as individuals or teams, put the greatest effort into performing well if they know and understand what is expected of them and have had an involvement in specifying those expectations.

2 Employees' ability to meet performance expectations is based on:
 ● individual levels of capability
 ● the degree of support provided by management
 ● the processes, systems and resources made available to them by the organization.

In practice, according to Armstrong and Barron, performance management has the following aims:

● Assisting in achieving sustainable improvements in an organization's overall performance.

● Serving as a lever for change in developing a more performance-oriented culture.

● Increasing employee motivation and commitment.

● Giving individual employees the means to develop competencies, improve job satisfaction and reach their full potential to their own benefit and that of the organization.

● Improving team spirit and performance.

- Offering a mechanism for regular dialogue and improved communication between individual employees and their managers.
- Providing an outlet for employees to express their aspirations and concerns.

In our discussion of organizational HRM in Part 3 we observed that organizations take many forms. No matter how an organization is structured, its output is the product of an interaction between different employees, departments, divisions and so on. Frequently, it is difficult to determine whose performance has been critical, or most significant, to the completion of a particular task. Current trends towards networking and team-based projects make individual performance even harder to gauge. Claus Offe once stated that identifying an individual's contribution to meeting an organization's goals is like listening to the sound of one hand clapping. Yet some people are singled out as key performers. On what basis? It is arguable that they may not be outstandingly good performers in an absolute sense but, simply, the people who conform most closely to the organization's norms.

Each organization defines effective performance in its own terms: being a 'good' manager in one organization is not the same as being good in another (Gunz, 1989). Company cultures and management styles vary and effective performance often translates as conformity to the house-style. According to Gunz (see Figure 18.1), organizations differ greatly so that:

1 The contexts in which managers operate vary considerably.

2 This leads to different ideas about effective management so that some companies, for example, emphasize engineering quality, others financial performance or market dominance.

3 In each case people find it comparatively easy to recognize good management but may find it hard to say why. This leads to certain types of people being promoted. As these people are seen to succeed everyone else draws their own conclusions about what it takes to get ahead.

4 This closes the loop, reinforcing the dominant image of effectiveness.

Figure 18.1   The renewal of managerial structures

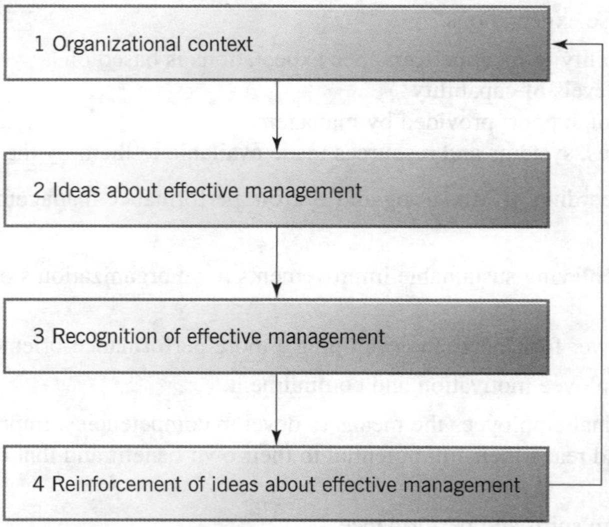

Source: Adapted from Gunz (1989).

As Gunz (1989) concludes:

> ... the figure suggests that promotion patterns in a firm will be resistant to change because of the model's closed loop. The system is remaking itself in its own image, something organizational managers are usually aware of even if they do not always admit it openly.

This is consistent with evidence from a large number of studies reviewed by Campbell *et al.* (1970) who found that judgements of managerial effectiveness or *good*ness are actually measures of personal success. When people are asked to identify a good manager, they do so on the basis of an individual's promotion record, salary, global ranking of success and so on. Often the identification of promotable staff is devolved to individual managers. They tend to favour subordinates who are reliable – that is, they do things in the way the managers would – or who have skills the manager does not possess.

Most of all, as we have noted already in previous discussions of the cloning process, they favour employees who are similar to themselves. Bates (2002) investigated 'liking' and two types of rater–ratee similarity to predict ratings of managerial competencies. The study showed that technical proficiency, rater–ratee liking, and demographic and attitudinal similarity about work were all significant predictors of proficiency ratings. Technical proficiency was the strongest predictor of ratings, followed by attitudinal similarity. A combination of liking, attitudinal and demographic similarity seemed to have a significant influence on ratings, over and above technical performance.

Activity 18:3	What are the implications of the personal relationship between manager and employee on performance assessment?

Morgan (1986, p.144) draws parallels between organizations and political systems in that both vary from autocracy to the democratic decision making seen in some voluntary organizations. He attributes a major role in determining successful performance to political processes such as conflict, power-play and intrigue.

Following this line of logic, it is clear that any performance assessment system is vulnerable to the cloning process. Without thought, performance management can drive out diversity. It is also open to manipulation by employees who can identify the qualities necessary to 'get on' in a particular organization.

Behaviour can be fine-tuned to meet the organization's expectations. The latter can be termed 'impression management' (see Key concept 18.3).

Key concept 18:3	**Impression management** Image is created as part of one's self-identity. It is a product of individual and social elements, constantly shaped and reshaped to fit the expected behaviours of the current role. In other words, people act. An image can be learned or acquired through training – a deliberate process called impression management.

Impression management

Every organization has its cultural symbols and rites: standards of dress and personal appearance, time-keeping, participating in semi-social activities, etc. We choose to conform or not. We may pretend to be enthusiastic, agree with management opinions, or even take up golf for networking rather than sporting reasons. Such behaviour can be described as 'manipulating the impression others gain about us' (Hinton, 1993, p.23). The archetypal example is the selection or promotion interview where most of us make a special effort with appearance and manner to achieve a favourable impression. This is easy to sustain for 20–40 minutes, but not necessarily convincing. Long-term success requires a consistent and believable image sustained over a considerable period.

The most significant quality required for selection to top jobs is the ability to create a good impression (Miller and Hanson, 1991). The key feature of a well-honed image is that it gives the impression that applicants have qualities they do not possess: a false portrayal of abilities, disguising the lack of true competencies behind socially valued characteristics.

Control of one's public image depends on self-awareness. Degrees of self-awareness vary. Some people are invariably 'themselves' whereas others are acutely sensitive to the impression they convey and modify their behaviour constantly. For example, salespeople are much more likely to succeed if they can 'fine-tune' the impression made on customers. Snyder (1974) attributed this to 'self-monitoring'. Good salespeople are high self-monitors, responding quickly to customers' reactions. Low self-monitors make little effort to modify their behaviour, even in an employment interview. Hinton (1993) points to skilled politicians who change their message depending on the audience, and are thereby perceived as being 'in-touch with the people'. Bill Clinton was seen to do this extensively during his campaign for the American presidency, sometimes making contradictory statements to different audiences and portraying himself as a liberal or a conservative as required.

Some images derive from the role models around us: successful people in the company or media stars. In the UK – particularly in England – the class structure, education system and institutions such as the civil service and the City serve to create and promote specific images. In Part 5 of this book we noted the condition described by Smith as 'organizational dry rot'. Picking people like ourselves to join our in-group is symptomatic of this condition at a national or institutional level. Too many organizations are dominated by identikit clones with similar images and ideas, whose concept of talent-spotting is finding more of the same.

Influencers

Miller and Hanson (1991) note that our ability to recognize real ability 'is contaminated by what we have come to call *the smile factor*' – closely related to the halo effect described in Chapter 15. The one-to-one interview is the most susceptible but at assessment centres 'the fish-bowl setting gives influencers/impressers space to perform'. A classic example is the excellent salesman who fails to perform well after promotion to sales manager. Time and time again the different requirements of the two jobs are ignored. Miller and Hanson studied four groups of widely different US executives and people deemed to have 'high potential' by their organizations. They describe their results as: '…to put it mildly, alarming. These organizations seeking leaders for major responsibilities were apparently confusing demonstrated leadership with some of the behavioural characteristics which some leaders exhibit.'

They found that all the people studied were particularly good at influencing others. They communicated well and were able to get other people to accept their ideas. They were generally sensitive and articulate, able to listen as well as talk. However, few had the motivation and the ability to manage or exercise leadership. They termed the majority 'influencers', people who wanted 'to have an impact on others but who did not want continuing or complete responsibility for the performance of others'. They were natural coaches and facilitators but reluctant to confront staff over missed deadlines or other forms of poor performance.

Admitting that influencers are likely to be bright and analytical, Miller and Hanson consider them to be too aware of the complexities inherent in any situation. They lack the confidence to take one direction as opposed to any other and, therefore, cannot be proactive or take risks. Further, because they are not aware in detail of the activities of their staff, they are unable to monitor changes effectively. Leaders are able to take tough decisions, can handle ambiguity and give direction. Miller and Hanson concluded that 'as many as eight out of ten people promoted into executive positions are influencers rather than leaders: most of the people running these organizations are not leaders; they only look as though they are.'

Key concept 18:4

Charisma   Weber (1947) regarded charisma as one of three types of authority (the other two being 'rational–legal' and 'traditional'), portraying it as a magical and hypnotic force based on direct personal contact. In modern life charisma is often fake – a product of carefully orchestrated mass communications.

There is nothing new in saying that 'real self' and 'outward image' are different constructions and that success is probably more dependent on the latter than the former. However, it is worth stressing that organizations do not benefit from this process. Images are distracting and misleading. Promotion on the basis of image does not produce employees capable of doing the job to an internationally competitive standard. Performance assessments tend to value image qualities: apparent self-confidence, the ability to talk charismatically, etc. Indeed, 'charisma' – the essential characteristic of the successful double-glazing salesman – is much admired and respected in a leader (see Key concept 18.4). According to Bryman (1999, p.22):

> In business and management periodicals the term is employed a great deal in the context of discussions of certain prominent figures. In such discussions, the term is often employed to describe someone who is flamboyant, who is a powerful speaker, and who can persuade others of the importance of his or her message. The non-charismatic leader, by contrast, is often depicted as a lacklustre, ineffectual individual.

Charismatics are perceived as having the power to transform organizations; as having a mission; able to inspire awe and obedience. They can also be lethal: a poison-pill for the ultimate well-being of any organization. Yet, like particularly dim lemmings, people managers – from personnel officers to boards of directors – will opt for the charismatic in preference to the non-charismatic.

It can be argued that at senior levels managers need to be figureheads and spokespersons for their organizations. For these roles, the required fluency, credibility and general communicating skills are those of a charismatic person. Indeed there may be a case for such a role to be entirely that of figurehead, not requiring any substantive abilities beyond those required for that role. A monarch or president, for example, can serve as a figurehead without executive power, allowing a prime minister to administer and direct. However, the tendency to overvalue charismatic skills has repeatedly led to foolish choices for 'number one' in large and small organizations. A further danger for performance assessment lies in the tendency to use cloning criteria at junior levels that are only relevant for people at the top of the organization.

Image can be construed as a decorative edifice built on the foundation of substance. An image that satisfies an audience does not necessarily preclude ability. Curiously, failure does not seem to dent common belief in the value of charisma. Similarly, the success of people with image and substance is commonly attributed to charisma – reinforcing belief in its necessity. Countering this process is difficult. It requires a recognition by senior managers that they may have succeeded by cultivating successful images rather than being the best available. Their organizations need assessment methods that are immune to this process: techniques to identify substance or necessary competencies, rather than the obscuring irrelevances of a polished image (Key concept 18.5).

Substance versus image   'Substance' can be defined as that body of competencies, knowledge and experience required to fulfil a particular function. 'Image' is the *apparent* totality of such knowledge and abilities as outwardly presented by an individual or group.

Langtry and Langtry (1991) compare two extreme management types, which are over-simplified but identifiable within most organizations. '*I*' stands for image or 'me', '*O*' equals objective or 'others':

- *I* managers maintain a high profile, speak well at meetings and are particularly effective at interviews. They are good networkers and make a point of getting to know the right people. They develop a good 'veneer', deliberately projecting a positive and confident image. Effective self-publicists, they make sure that everyone knows how hard they work and how successful they are. They are skilled careerists, and with sufficient emphasis and repetition they ensure that myth becomes reality.

- *O* managers do not indulge in such elaborate charades. Innovative and supportive, they are quietly hard-working, getting on with the job as efficiently as possible. They only come to the attention of senior management when they challenge simplistic ideas which the *I* manager enthusiastically adopts. The tendency is for their work to be ignored in favour of the *I* manager's claims and their criticism to be interpreted as negative. Their fatal mistake is to assume that recognition will follow a job well done. Usually, however, the *I* manager goes streaking past them up the career ladder.

Obviously, this delightful typology divides managers too sharply into two simple categories but it captures the essence of the problem.

Activity 18:4   Evaluate a significant business (or political) leader. How much of that person's success is due to charisma or impression management?

Assessment and organizational change

The conduct of performance management is affected also by the success of the organization. Assessors and assessed may vary their standards depending on their perception of the organization's overall performance, career prospects and, consequently, their feelings of security and optimism. The emotional background to assessment can be directly affected by the prevailing culture of the organization. Attempts to develop a strong, cohesive culture encourage closer agreement between raters on the standards they expect.

As we observed in the early chapters of this book, de-layering and downsizing have had the effect of increasing the ratio of staff to managers throughout the Western business world. As a consequence, managers have a greater number of assessments to conduct on people they know less about. Widespread structural changes in large organizations also bring new combinations of people together with little knowledge of each other – but, perhaps, fewer long-standing prejudices.

Intriguingly, managers' routes to power appear to have a direct effect on the way they assess subordinates (Murphy and Cleveland, 1995, p.415):

Attribution theory suggests that raters who have risen through the ranks will have a distorted perception of how well they performed in the job (they will readily recall good performance and will discount poor performance), which may lead to unrealistically high standards.

On the other hand, managers look after their own and assess their own staff generously. It is well known that performance ratings tend to the positive, with more people being judged as good performers than one would expect from a normal population. This is termed 'rater inflation'. It happens generally, but is particularly evident when assessors rate employees they have themselves previously promoted or selected.

Why does this happen? Most explanations are couched in terms of organizational politics:

- *Preserving morale.* A positive performance assessment – whether or not it is deserved – is an act of praise. It offers an opportunity for a manager to say 'thank you' and 'well done', boosting morale and commitment. It engenders good working relationships between managers and subordinates. It maintains a cosy atmosphere.

- *Avoiding confrontation.* Conversely, a critical assessment is likely to have the opposite effects.

- *Management image.* If managers rate staff poorly there is an implication that they make bad selection decisions and run poor-quality departments. This can have unfortunate consequences on their own performance ratings.

From a psychological perspective, it can be argued that managers develop a bonding, or personal working relationship with their favoured staff which inevitably leads to biased assessments of their performance. The organization's human resource strategies should be focused, in part at least, on overcoming this problem. In the next section we consider the strategic choices that are open to us.

Performance strategies

'Organizations face a critical paradox. No other management tool is more critical to productivity than effective performance appraisals, yet they can actually impair employees' performance' (English, 1991, p.56).

As we observed at the beginning of this chapter, performance assessment or appraisal has been in use for a considerable period, particularly for management and sub-management grades in large corporations. The range of jobs covered by performance assessment is steadily increasing but there remain areas of employment where performance measurement does not yet feature and there is a great deal of conflict over its introduction.

From a strategic perspective, the process of assessment is an exercise in management power and control. It is a method by which an enterprise can evaluate its employees and feed back the organization's views to them. Furthermore, evaluation can be linked to 'stick and carrot' measures in the form of: critical comment indicating the firm's disapproval; incentives to reward and encourage 'good' performance in the form of enhanced pay and promotion prospects.

We saw in Part 1 of this book that 'behavioural consistency' is a major focus for models of HRM which hold that business competitiveness is improved by enhancing employee attitudes, behaviour and commitment. To do so, it is imperative that the organization has effective methods of communicating its standards or norms of behaviour. Assessors and assessed may have entirely different perceptions of both the reasons for performance appraisal and the criteria for judgement. Proponents argue that performance management should be: 'a process or set of processes for establishing shared understanding about what *is* to be achieved, and of managing and developing people in a way which increases the probability that it *will* be achieved in the short and longer term' (Armstrong, 1992, p.163).

Performance management strategies are particularly concerned with workforce motivation or, more accurately, management belief in the factors that lead to employee effort and commitment.

Motivation and performance

A considerable body of literature exists on the relationship between motivation and work performance. Theories range from the simplistic rational 'economic man' concepts underlying scientific management – implying that workers are only interested in money – to complex 'expectancy' theories that explain motivation in terms of a calculus of conflicting needs. Morgan (1986, p.149) points to the diverse range of interests that people bring to the workplace:

- *Task interests.* Focused on the job being performed so that, for example, someone in sales is committed to selling, enjoys dealing with customers and takes pride in being able to clinch a sale.
- *Career interests.* Aspirations and visions of one's future – which may or may not include the current job.

These are complemented by extramural interests which incorporate leisure pursuits and domestic relationships. They cannot be divorced from work because they compete for an individual's time and psychological or physical effort. Performance management strategies must take account of people as whole beings, with work forming just a part of their lives.

Achievers and non-achievers

A number of researchers have attempted to identify the important factors leading to successful performance by comparing recognized high achievers with average performers. This method focuses on distinguishing key psychological differences between people in the two groups. However, as Furnham (1990, p.30) notes: 'it cannot be assumed that these factors *caused* the success, indeed they may have been a *consequence* of success.' Factors such as confidence and knowledge of a particular area may have been present at an early stage in a person's career or, alternatively, developed as that career became successful. For example, Charles Handy uses the term 'helicopter view' to describe the broad strategic grasp of business expected from senior managers. They are unlikely to have achieved this perspective without wide experience at lower levels.

Reviewing some of the vast selection of books on the rich and famous, Furnham finds consistent themes such as:

- *Perseverance.* Tenacity, single-minded determination and concentration.
- *Ability.* Especially in creating and exploiting opportunities.
- *Contacts.* Knowing the right people.
- *Self-reliance.* Striving for independence.
- *Thinking big.* But taking modest risks.
- *Time management.* Making the best use of time and planning progress.

The weakness in these studies lies in their essentially retrospective and descriptive nature. They do not set out to test the hypothesis that individuals setting out on a career with a particular set of personality characteristics will be more successful than average. Nevertheless, Furnham (1990, p.31) finds that certain values that he describes as PWE (the Protestant work ethic) recur, providing: 'some evidence for the fact that specific PWE values – namely tenacity, perseverance, autonomy, independence, and hard work – are to be found in financially successful individuals and companies alike.'

Locus of control

Performance management is based on the underlying belief that managers can influence behaviour and, therefore, that rationality is the basis of human action. Unfortunately, the available psychological evidence suggests that this is not the case. Research shows that people vary significantly in their reactions to the persuasion or coercion of others, depending on their perception of the ability they have to control their own lives. At one extreme, some individuals will believe that what happens in their lives is the consequence of their own decisions, abilities and behaviour. These people are judged to have an 'expectancy of internal control'. There is evidence that individuals who have an expectancy of internal control ('internals') are better performers and tend to occupy most of the higher level jobs (Andrisani and Nestel, 1976). Internals take more notice of the feedback provided by performance management but do so according to their own agenda. If good performance produces appropriate rewards, they will deliver more of the same. If it does not, they are likely to devote their internal strengths to finding another job. On the other hand, externals see little connection between their own performance and eventual success. When criticized for below average work they will attribute their failure to causes outside themselves and the disapproval of the appraiser to personal dislike.

At the other extreme are individuals who attribute events to fate, to God, luck or to more powerful people. They consider life to be outside their personal remit and are permanent victims of chance or the wishes of others. They are said to have an 'expectancy of external control' (Furnham, 1990, p.42). People with an expectancy of external control will be more compliant at the surface level, following instructions from supervisors and fitting social expectations. 'Following orders' they will fit neatly into bureaucratic structures but will demonstrate little initiative.

Are you in charge of life, or is life in charge of you? Most people have times when the former is true, and other times when the progress of life is firmly out of their hands. Some are permanently in one camp or the other. It is clear that being in charge of one's own life, career and circumstances leads to feelings of well-being and confidence and equates with successful and happy times. This is true 'empowerment'. However, it is doubtful whether performance management is entirely compatible with this state. In the next section we elaborate on how organizations can place performance assessment within a wider framework of human resource management.

Activity 18:5   What factors determine individual success in an organization?

Performance management systems

Among the ten-Cs checklist criteria for HRM discussed in Chapter 3 and elsewhere we placed consistency, coordination and control. These strategic aspects of performance assessment are exemplified in the integration of appraisal and performance-related pay processes within performance management systems. Armstrong (1992, p.162) sees the functions of such systems as:

- Reinforcement of the organization's values and norms.
- Integration of individual objectives with those of the organization.
- Allowing individuals to express their views on the job.
- Providing the means for managers and staff to share their expectations of performance.

A major British survey of public and private sector organizations showed that: 20 per cent claimed to have such a system; 65 per cent had some kind of performance management process; whereas 15 per cent stated that they had no policy (Bevan and Thompson, 1992). The survey showed no consistency in approach or understanding of the concept of performance management. Bevan and Thompson found two contradictory strategic themes for performance management:

- *Reward-driven integration.* Emphasizing performance-related pay (PRP) based on short-term targets with a consequent undervaluing of any other human resource activities.
- *Development-driven integration.* Using appraisals to provide information for developing an organization's people, in line with our discussion in the next section, geared for long-term objectives. When in existence, PRP is complementary to this.

They concluded that the first theme was dominant in the UK, serving to reinforce the prevalent cash-flow driven, short-termism of British managers.

Management by objectives

The origins of strategic performance management can be traced to the concept of management by objectives (Raia, 1974). This is a technique to establish individual performance objectives which are tangible, measurable and verifiable. Individual objectives are derived or cascaded from organizational goals. Top managers agree their own specific objectives compatible with the organization's goals but restricted to their own areas of responsibility. Subordinates do the same at each lower level, forming an interlocked and coherent hierarchy of performance targets. Hence management by objectives lies within the strategic way

Table 18.1	The management by objectives process
Essential elements	*Key stages*
Goal-setting	1 Establish long-range strategic objectives
	2 Formulate specific overall organizational goals
	3 Agree departmental objectives
	4 Set individual performance targets
Action planning	5 Draw up action plans
Self-control	6 Implement and take corrective action
Periodic reviews	7 Review performance against objectives
	8 Appraise overall performance, reinforce appropriate behaviour, and strengthen motivation through:
	• management development
	• reward
	• career and HR planning

Source: Adapted from Raia (1974).

of thinking which forms a key element in HRM (see Table 18.1). Management by objectives (MBO) encompasses four main stages as detailed in the following sub-sections.

Goal-setting
This is the heart of the MBO process. Goals are specific and desired results to be achieved within an agreed period of time. They must represent real progress. They should be:

- *Challenging* – stretching the individual beyond comfortable performance.

- *Attainable* – realistic within cost and resource constraints.

- *Measurable* – specific, quantifiable and verifiable. Objectives are best set in numerical terms such as 'increased sales by x thousand', 'reduced staff by y per cent'.

- *Relevant* – directly related to the person's job and consistent with overall organizational objectives.

Alternatively, goals are sometimes set against the acronym SMART, linked to: Specific or stretching; Measurable; Agreed or Achievable; Realistic; Time-bounded.

Action planning
Goals or performance targets are the 'ends' of the MBO process, action plans are the 'means'. They require individual employees to ask themselves what, who, when, where, and how an objective can be achieved.

Self-control
MBO is a self-driven process with each person participating in setting their own goals and action plans. This results in greater commitment to their own objectives and an improved understanding of the process. They are expected to control their own behaviour in order to achieve performance targets. In return it is essential that they are given sufficient information and feedback to gauge their progress.

Periodic reviews
It is not sufficient to review progress at the end of the MBO process. Individuals must be provided with an opportunity to check their performance at regular intervals so that obstacles can be identified. Reviews should take a positive, coaching approach rather than critical approach.

MBO pre-dates human resource management and derives from a period when strategic thinking and the integration of organizational objectives were being emphasized by management writers. Since then, the development of HRM has preserved the focus on strategy and integration. This has been reinforced by the fashion for performance-related pay, fostered by the prevalent belief that reward should be firmly tied to results. Whereas MBO concentrated on individual management of one's own performance, the spread of PRP is underpinned by the use of assessment systems to manage the individual. MBO has gone out of fashion to a considerable extent although its basic techniques have been absorbed into newer approaches. It has been criticized for the paperwork involved, the administrative burden and the realization that goals set for individuals are actually dependent on a team, a department or even a substantial part of the organization (Armstrong and Baron, 1998).

| Activity 18:6 | Would an objective-setting method such as MBO produce the same effects on performance for a person with an internal locus of control as it would for someone with an external locus of control? |

Prescriptions for performance management systems

Bevan and Thompson (1992) describe a model performance management system:

- The organization has a shared vision of its objectives or a mission statement that is communicated to its employees.
- There are individual performance management targets, related to unit and wider organizational objectives.
- There is a regular formal review of progress towards achieving the targets.
- There is a review process that identifies training, development and reward outcomes.
- The whole process is itself evaluated – feeding back through changes and improvements.

Rather similar to the MBO approach, the central features of such a system are an objective-setting process and a formal appraisal system. Typically, the performance management system is owned and implemented by line managers. The role of human resource specialists is to aid and advise line managers on the development of the system. In a slightly different approach, English (1991) argues for a 'rational' system of performance management that should have the following characteristics:

- A clear statement of what is to be achieved by the organization.
- Individual and group responsibilities support the organization's goals.
- All performance is measured and assessed in terms of those responsibilities and goals.
- All rewards are based on employee performance.
- Organizational structure, processes, resources and authority systems are designed to optimize the performance of all employees.
- There is an ongoing effort to create and guide appropriate organizational goals and to seek newer, more appropriate goals.

Many organizations consider that they have a performance management system along these lines. Often they do not because one or more of the following conditions are missing:

- Agreement among all critical parties on what is to be performed.
- An effective way to measure desired performance.
- A reward system tied directly to performance.
- An environment conducive to successful performance.
- A communication programme to gain understanding, acceptance and commitment to the system.
- A performance-based organizational culture.

Key concept 18:6

Appraisals Performance assessment is one of the many people management techniques that 'classify and order individuals hierarchically' (Townley, 1994, p.33). Appraisals rate individuals on quasi-objective criteria or standards deemed to be relevant to performance. Traditional appraisals rated individuals on a list of qualities – primarily work-related attitudes and personality traits. Modern assessment is often focused on competencies.

Ontario teacher appraisals

Measures are now in effect giving parents and senior students input into Ontario teachers' performance appraisals. According to Education Minister Janet Ecker: 'Parents and students can provide valuable input into a teacher's appraisal. Their feedback will help to improve student achievement and support teachers in their efforts to inspire and motivate students.'

The new measures are included in regulations that came into force on 15 March and will be phased into Ontario schools, starting this fall. They ensure that students in Grades 11 and 12 or on OAC courses can provide input on areas such as student–teacher communication and a teacher's ability to promote student learning. Parents of students from all grades will be able to provide input in areas such as a teacher's communications to parents and students will also give input.

These measures form part of the comprehensive Ontario Teacher Testing Program and are intended to support teaching excellence. The provincial government's program includes:

- a qualifying test for new teachers, from 27 April.
- ongoing professional learning requirements for practising teachers
- clear and consistent criteria for performance appraisals.

Inputs from parents and students are just one component of the performance appraisals of teachers that will be conducted by principals and vice-principals. Performance appraisals will also include the teacher's level of commitment to the pupils, the teacher's knowledge of the curriculum and other factors. The appraisals will be conducted every three years for experienced teachers and twice in each of the first two years for new teachers or those moving to another school board.

The Ontario Teacher Testing Program is based on programs in other jurisdictions. The government argues that it is similar to the requirements for other professions, such as doctors, lawyers, nurses, architects and occupational therapists. It follows on from recommendations from Ontario's education partners and recommendations from the 1995 Royal Commission on Learning.

'Teachers play a key role in helping students to achieve their potential,' Ecker said. 'It is important that all teachers participate in ongoing professional development so that their skills and knowledge are up to date.' But teachers are not happy: 'Elementary teachers continue to be concerned about the government's Quality in the Classroom Act,' says Emily Noble, first vice-president of the Elementary Teachers' Federation of Ontario (ETFO), representing 65 000 teachers and education workers across Ontario. She explains:

This Act focuses on the mechanics of performance appraisal for teachers and is designed to ensure the process is punitive rather than constructive. For example, we are concerned the appraisals will be governed in part by anonymous complaints from parents and students, against which teachers will not be able to defend themselves.

ETFO has developed a performance appraisal model for teachers that ensures accountability in the classroom.

Source: *HRM Guide Canada* (http://www.hrmguide.net/canada/), 18 March 2002.

The assessment process

'Appraisal is seen as essentially an exercise in personal power. It elevates the role of the supervisor by emphasizing individualism and obscuring the social nature of work' (Storey, 1989, p.14).

In this final section we consider performance assessment as an activity. Traditionally, performance assessment uses a rating system known as appraisal (Key concept 18.6). In most companies it is a matter of something being done to the employee rather than a process in which the employee plays a valued and important part. Assessments are generally an annual exercise, although some organizations may undertake them more frequently, perhaps every six months, especially with new entrants or recent promotees. For lower-grade employees, some companies are content with an assessment every two years.

Appraisal and conformity

Appraisals tend to be formalized. In many organizations they take the shape of pre-printed forms and typed instructions prepared for the appraising manager or supervisor. Dates of completion and return are fixed and the whole process monitored and administered by the personnel or HR department. Theoretically, appraisals can be completed in a number of ways:

- *Self-assessment.* Individuals assess themselves against rating criteria or targeted objectives.
- *Peer assessment.* Fellow team members, departmental colleagues or selected individuals with whom an employee has working interaction provide assessments.
- *Line management.* The employee's immediate supervisor(s) provide the assessment. Alternatively, other line managers may be involved.
- *Upward appraisal.* Managers are appraised by their staff.
- *360-degree or multi-rater feedback.* Raters may include anyone with a direct knowledge of an individual's performance, including colleagues, direct reports, managers and internal customers.

The traditional performance appraisal was completed by the immediate supervisor or line manager with, usually, further comments or countersignature provided by the supervisor's own manager. This has been described as the 'father and grandfather' system – appropriate terms, given the essentially paternalistic nature of the process.

HRM in reality	Annual performance appraisals still the norm

A recent survey shows that two-thirds (66 per cent) of executives polled scheduled formal employee appraisals annually, with just 29 per cent conducting them more frequently.

The survey was conducted by an independent research firm for OfficeTeam, a leading staffing service specializing in highly skilled administrative professionals.

A total of 150 executives were sampled from the nation's 1000 largest companies. Executives were asked, 'How often, if ever, do you conduct formal performance appraisals of your staff?' Responses were: quarterly 10 per cent; twice a year 19 per cent; once a year 66 per cent; as necessary 2 per cent; never/don't conduct formal appraisals 3 per cent.

'Annual performance appraisals are common among companies that tie formal reviews to yearly raises and bonuses,' said Liz Hughes, executive director of OfficeTeam. 'But it's important for managers to provide ongoing feedback to their staff to foster greater productivity and reduce the potential for miscommunication.'

'Don't wait until the formal review to recognize excellent work or raise concerns about weak performance,' advised Hughes. 'Instead, address these situations when they arise and use the review to discuss an employee's overall progress toward established goals.' She offers five tips for conducting an effective meeting:

- *Stick to a schedule.* Decide on a standard review schedule and adhere to it. Consider holding more frequent meetings for new or less experienced employees.

- *Consult the experts.* Your legal and human resources departments may have guidelines and materials to help you plan the review. Ask if there are policies for discussing compensation, documenting the meetings and for following up.

- *Be fair and consistent.* Meet with each staff member privately for the review, ideally in a place where you can focus without interruption. Evaluate all employees according to the same criteria.

- *Request participation.* Ask the employee to prepare a list of accomplishments, obstacles and goals. Review this document prior to the meeting and use it as the basis for discussion.

- *Develop an action plan.* Even the best employees can improve in some ways. Set objectives with each staff member and plan a course for progress checks prior to the next formal review.

Source: *HRM Guide USA* (http://www.hrmguide.net/usa/), 26 February 2002.

Appraisal normally requires rating on a series of categories. Management and lower-level appraisals are commonly conducted in different ways. Management assessments tend to feature results-oriented criteria, typically against objectives agreed at the beginning of the year. Non-managerial appraisals are more likely to be 'trait-ratings' – no matter what the questions may ask overtly, they are actually rating the employee on behavioural or personality criteria. In essence, they are no more than crude personality questionnaires. This remains the case if the criteria are couched in terms of job-related qualities. According to Townley (1994, p.43):

> Received wisdom is now that the appraiser judges the work not the person, with trait-rating being replaced by appraisals which identify and measure some aspect of performance. This, however, introduces the problem of defining and measuring performance, whether this should include for example, skill, knowledge, potential and overall 'worth', etc., and the relative weight which should be attached to behaviour or results.

According to Philp (1990):

> The disadvantages of this approach are numerous. For instance, the terms themselves are extremely ambiguous and it is unlikely that any group of managers would share exactly the same interpretation of any of them. Any appraisal using such words would be extremely subjective and, as a result, totally unfair. Also, because assessment in these terms deals with the individual rather than with the results they produce for the organization, it is very difficult to communicate with the individual involved. The person being appraised is likely to see any critical assessment of this type as a personal attack. The factors deal with the emotive areas closely concerned with personality, and the majority of people will tend to react defensively.

Appraisals are generally disliked by employees and employers alike (Armstrong and Baron, 1998). Human resource practitioners are often made responsible for the paper-distribution and then for policing the process, coercing unwilling participants into completing the paperwork and holding one-to-one confrontations with appraisees.

Despite the fact that most assessors are completely unqualified to make judgements on anyone's personality, even in the most general of terms, the traditional appraisal form asks for a numerical rating on a scale of 1–4 or 1–7 (from excellent to appalling) (see Figure 18.2). Additionally, more detail is asked for as supplementary verbal comments, which could range from one word such as 'good' to a paragraph or more of detailed criticism and/or praise. Moreover, there is usually an overall rating that may be tied to promotability and a section to indicate areas for development or training. Finally, there are normally sections for comments by the person being appraised, possibly in the form of notes of a counselling interview and comments by the appraising manager's own supervisor.

The document is usually signed by all the contributors and forms part of the company's personnel records. It can be used for promotion boards, training and management development programmes. What happens if an employee disagrees with the assessment? Despite its critical consequences for promotion prospects and, perhaps, remuneration, only a half of all organizations allow any form of appeal.

| Activity 18:7 | To appreciate some of the points made in this section more fully, it would be useful for you to photocopy Figure 18.2 and complete an assessment on someone well known to you – or even yourself! |

Upward feedback

The emphasis of performance management has been on top-down assessments open to a degree of power play by managers and senior executives. Over the last decade or so there has been a trend towards constructive, developmental approaches and moving away from a fixation with ratings. It has also become increasingly acceptable to take views of individual performance from a wide range of perspectives. Upward feedback is a process whereby managers receive comments and criticisms from their subordinates. This may be facilitated by an intermediary to organize the process and maintain a positive and non-acrimonious climate.

Upward feedback is not an appraisal as such and is not linked to standardized competencies. Instead (Forbes, 1996):

- It is intended to deliver candid, accurate feedback from a team to its manager.
- The basis lies in the team's perception of the actions of its manager.
- Upward feedback is not a system of judgement 'but only asks him or her for more, less, or the same of a broad series of behaviours'.
- Leadership, management, task and people factors are given equal weight.
- The facilitator gives confidential feedback, initially to the manager, then between the team and its manager.
- Team members and the manager – and that person's manager – can compare their views on what is required, bringing areas of misunderstanding or disagreement out into the open.

Because upward feedback is not formal appraisal, managers do not need to fear being judged. Conventionally, upward feedback begins with the most senior executive and cascades downwards with each level in turn receiving feedback.

Figure 18.2   Traditional appraisal form – 1980s style

J. SMITH & CO. ANNUAL PERFORMANCE ASSESSMENT

This document should be completed by the responsible line manager and returned to the Human Resource Department by ....

Name of appraisee:

Job title:

Department:

Name of manager completing assessment:

		A	B	C	D	E	F
1	**KNOWLEDGE AND EXPERTISE**						

Comments:

		A	B	C	D	E	F
2	**ATTITUDE TO WORK**						

Comments:

Figure 18.2	Traditional appraisal form – 1980s style (continued)

3 **RESULTS**

A B C D E F
|_____|_____|_____|_____|_____|_____|

Comments:

4 **INTERPERSONAL SKILLS**

A B C D E F
|_____|_____|_____|_____|_____|_____|

Comments:

5 **WRITTEN AND VERBAL COMMUNICATION**

WRITTEN

A B C D E F
|_____|_____|_____|_____|_____|_____|

Comments:

VERBAL

A B C D E F
|_____|_____|_____|_____|_____|_____|

Comments:

6 **NUMERICAL AND DATA SKILLS**

A B C D E F
|_____|_____|_____|_____|_____|_____|

Comments:

Figure 18.2	Traditional appraisal form – 1980s style (continued)

                                                              A   B   C   D   E   F
7 OVERALL RATING |__|__|__|__|__|__|

Comments:

_____

NOTES ON COUNSELLING INTERVIEW

Manager's signature ....

Date ....

_____

APPRAISEE'S COMMENTS

Appraisee's signature ....

Date ....

_____

SENIOR MANAGER'S COMMENTS

Senior manager's signature ....

Date ....

_____

Based on Forbes (1996), the benefits of upward feedback can be summarized as follows:

1 Individual/team action plans can improve cooperation between team and manager.

2 Supervisors are encouraged to vary their management style and emphasis.

3 Ideas, problems and suggestions can be collected across a range of individuals or teams. In turn these can be used to set up new cross-functional teams or aid in the management of change.

4 Training requirements can be pinpointed and linked to specific outcomes for the team.

5 It facilitates empowerment and self-management.

6 A benchmark is gradually developed taking the form of an organizational map and data on how employees, managers and senior executives view requirements in 20 defined behavioural areas in up to 100 practices. An annual comparison can be made from this.

7 It opens up a more communicative culture where different forms of performance assessment can be introduced.

Upward feedback also has its disadvantages. Managers may receive negative comments from assertive and ambitious employees intent on undermining their confidence and authority. No one likes to be rated as a poor performer and some managers may be less firm or directive, even when appropriate, in order to avoid criticism. Similarly, managers may be less critical or demanding of their subordinates in order to reduce the probability of unfavourable feedback.

Waldman and Atwater (2001), in a study of upward feedback in a large telecommunications firm, found that managers who receive poor formal appraisal scores from their bosses are more likely to value the usefulness of upward feedback. Managers who receive lower subordinate ratings are more likely to ask for additional feedback. In general, subordinates are more likely than managers to believe that upward feedback scores should be incorporated into formal performance assessments. Waldman and Atwater also found that subordinate ratings were correlated with formal appraisal scores.

360-degree or multi-rater assessments

Multi-rater assessments have been used by large US corporations for over a decade and have gradually become more common in other countries. The evolution of business organizations into flatter, team-based structures has led to multiple reporting lines and wider spans of command for managers, so that assessments by single line managers are not as appropriate as they were in the past (Kettley, 1996). A multi-source rating system such as 360-degree performance profiling typically involves information collected from the people working with the person being appraised, managers, staff reporting to that individual and internal (or, exceptionally) external customers. The process follows a sequence such as the following:

1 A skill model or competence framework is devised that lists essential job skills and behaviours.

2 A performance management survey is defined on the basis of the skill model.

3 Individual employees are each asked to recommend 8–12 raters for their personal reviews. Immediate supervisors choose 6–10 of these to complete performance surveys, rating the employee on each skill area, typically on a scale of 1–10. Raters need to have direct knowledge of the employee's performance but supervisors need to ensure that they are not all friends of the appraisee.

4 The reports are collected together and a summary is given to the appraisee, highlighting both strengths and development needs.

This method of performance assessment has its advantages and disadvantages over more traditional methods. It is clear that the number of people involved, and the amount of form-filling required, can lead to considerable expenditure of time and effort, even when online forms, data-scanning and report producing software are used. The anonymity of the process may also allow malicious and undefended negative ratings to be given.

Activity 18:8

Compare and contrast the processes of upward feedback and 360-degree profiling.

Limitations of performance management

Performance appraisal has become one of the most widely used management tools despite widespread criticism of its effectiveness. To add to the controversy, Strebler, Robinson and Bevan (2001) from the UK's Institute of Employment Studies (IES) argue from research on over 1000 British managers that many performance appraisal systems have a limited impact on overall business performance and fail both employees and organizations.

Many organizations try to use performance appraisal and review as a 'strategic lever', not just for the performance of individuals, but also the performance of the whole business. However, according to Strebler and colleagues:

> This assumes that managers have the ability and motivation to make performance review work, by translating strategic goals into operational practice. Ideally, they should use the appraisal to help the employee see how their contribution adds value to the business as a whole. Too often, however, they are rushed discussions where performance ratings are handed out, where petty lapses in performances are picked upon, or where performance-related pay is awarded.

Additionally, Strebler, Robinson and Bevan (2001) contend that performance review is rapidly becoming an 'over-burdened management tool'. Along with its appraisal and objective-setting aspects, line managers are expected to pinpoint staff training requirements, provide career counselling, identify future star performers and do something about poor performers. These are all important elements of people management but the attempt to do so much at the same time often leads to poor results from appraisal schemes.

Performance review systems are frequently rooted in the hierarchical organizations of the past, and often still drive pay or promotion decisions. Organizations are flatter today and there may be limited opportunities for upward progression. Rewards can also take forms other than pay increases. So, according to Strebler, Robinson and Bevan (2001), new systems are needed that meet the requirements of individual organizations: textbook models might not be suitable for particular strategies or structures.

They advise a transformation of the performance review 'from a beast of burden into a thoroughbred', starting with business strategy, then being clear about the roles, skills and behaviours required for delivering that strategy. There are some simple rules:

● Clear aims and measurable criteria for success.

● Involving employees in design and implementation of the system.

● Keeping it simple to understand and operate.

● Making its effective use one of managers' core performance goals.

● Ensuring that employees are always able to see the link between their performance goals and those of the organization.

● Using it to keep roles clear and the focus on performance improvement.

- Backing up the system with adequate training and development.
- Making any direct link with reward crystal clear, and providing proper safeguards to guarantee equity.
- Reviewing the system regularly and openly to make sure it's working.

Strebler, Robinson and Bevan (2001) conclude that human resources functions that can deliver this will be making a real and visible strategic contribution to their organizations.

Counselling interviews

Having tested the manager's talents as untrained psychologist, the next part of the process expects the manager to be a qualified counsellor! This takes the form of a face-to-face dialogue between (normally) the appraising manager and the appraisee, although it is sometimes done by the countersigning manager. The whole process is designed to focus the power of the organization on a direct and individual basis. However, it is also clear that the scope for conflict and its avoidance are considerable.

Many, perhaps most, managers are reluctant to engage in the appraisal process. First, because it is difficult to criticize someone's performance honestly, knowing that the appraisee will read the comments. Potentially, the whole exercise is confrontational and many counselling interviews have turned sour because of carelessly worded appraisals. Most people find criticism difficult to accept and registering a point with an employee without causing offence requires diplomatic skills.

The process is dependent on the personality and management style of the appraising manager. Some managers will be blunt and, perhaps, brutal in their approach. As a consequence, they may not produce any improvement in behaviour but, rather, sullen resentment and a reduction in quality of performance. Others will regard the whole exercise as something to be avoided. As we noted earlier, the result will be rater-inflation: an assessment that is over-generous or, at best, neutral in order to avoid conflict. The process also depends to a great extent on the quality of the appraising manager. If that individual is not particularly capable, the evaluation of the subordinate may well be inaccurate or misleading and may blight the person's career.

It can be argued there is an increasing tendency to focus on marginal performers in the light of harsh economic conditions. Companies consider that they are unable to carry inefficient employees and the assessment procedure offers a source of data that will support dismissals. In theory, performance appraisal provides documentary evidence of inefficiency that would be hard to refute. In practice, rater-inflation often undermines the process, providing generous appraisals for questionable performances.

Activity 18:9	Summarize the main benefits and limitations of the performance assessment techniques we have discussed in this chapter.

Objectivity and subjectivity in assessment

As we have seen, some of the key issues of performance management revolve around questions of fairness, judgement and interpretation of both results and behaviour. Serious attempts have been made to address these areas. Performance assessment focuses on one or more of the following criteria:

- *Results.* In line with MBO and similar objectives-based systems, employees are rated on their achievements, expressed as well-defined, personal or organizational targets. For example, a sales person may be given the objective of US$x worth of sales in the year. How this is achieved is not the subject of assessment. As we have already observed, objectives are easier to define for some jobs than others. This approach can be complicated by the use of a 'moving target'.

- *Processes.* In this case the emphasis is not on measurable results but on *how* the outcomes are achieved. It can be argued that compliance with quality procedures, or, alternatively, provision of a particular level of service are examples of process assessments. However, if these are measurable in some way, they can be translated into results – for example, proportion of defective items or number of complaints.

- *Behaviour.* Weaker and less objective assessments – but probably the most common – focus on employee behaviour that is only tangentially connected with either achieved results or work processes. A favourite approach for managers incapable of seeing the 'wood from the trees', they allow ample opportunity to dwell on personal prejudices over appearance, dress and manner. Such assessments provide a direct feeder mechanism into culture-bound and organizationally unhealthy practices designed to increase conformity and eliminate diversity. A number of large organizations have countered this tendency by using behaviourally anchored scales.

- *Behaviourally anchored scales (BARS).* These are relatively expensive techniques to maintain, requiring 'experts' to develop rating scales anchored to real-life behaviour through critical incidents. However, they force appraisers to make comparatively objective judgements, placing individual behaviour in the context of the organization as a whole, rather than on inadequate personality categorizations. They are less usable in situations where new technology or procedural changes require frequent updating of scales.

- *Behavioural observation scales (BOS).* There are constructed in a similar way to BARS but assessors are required to list the frequency of occurrence of particular behaviours within a particular period, rather than make comparative judgements of better or worse performance.

Different behaviorally oriented rating formats may enhance or inhibit the value of performance appraisal as a developmental tool. Tziner, Joanis and Murphy (2000) compared the effects of rating scale formats on a number of indices of the usefulness of performance appraisal for employee development. Using simple graphic scales, behaviorally anchored rating scales or behavior observation scales, ratings were made of the job performance of 96 police officers. The BOS ratings produced both the highest ratee satisfaction with the performance appraisal process and the most favourable perceptions of performance goals. Additionally, experts judged the performance improvement goals for officers appraised with BOS to be the most observable and specific.

Competence ratings

In recent years the trend in performance management has been towards assessing people on 'dimensions' of suitable attributes or 'competencies'. These may be derived from job analyses and describe a limited number of core skills or behaviours necessary to do a certain job. In fact, such competencies aggregate to form a key strategic element of business competitiveness – the overall competencies of the firm. There is some ambiguity about the meaning of the term at the level of the individual – it is sometimes used as an equivalent for a psychological trait (perseverance) and, at other times, as a complex hybrid of learning and skill (ability to use computers).

Armstrong and Baron (1998) suggest that competencies should address the following points:

1　What are the 'elements' of the job – its main tasks or key areas?

2　What is an acceptable standard of performance for each element?

3　Which skills and what knowledge does a job-holder need to have in order to be fully capable in each of these job elements – and at what level?

4　How will employees or their managers know that they have achieved the required levels of competence?

Summary

HRM is associated with sophisticated and intensive performance assessment, typically involving performance-related pay. The assessment of performance can be beneficial to personal development. We considered performance management as an integrated system. Theoretical descriptions of such systems emphasize their value to the link between individual employee performance and the achievement of strategic goals. However, there are philosophical issues of what precisely represents 'good' performance, and further technical problems of measurement. We completed the chapter with a critique of appraisal methods and a discussion of recent attempts to objectify their use.

Further reading

Performance Management: The New Realities by Michael Armstrong and Angela Baron (CIPD, 1998) is a wide-ranging text that conveys the full flavour of the subject. *Performance Appraisal: State of the Art in Practice* (Siop Professional Practice Series) edited by James W. Smither (published by Jossey-Bass, 1998) takes a practical approach. *Performance Management* by Robert Bacal (published by McGraw-Hill Education, 1998) is particularly reader-friendly. Kevin R. Murphy and Jeanette N. Cleveland's *Understanding Performance Appraisal: Social, Organizational and Goal-Based Perspectives* (1995) provides a detailed analysis of research on the performance assessment process over three decades. *Abolishing Performance Appraisals: Why They Backfire and What to Do Instead* by Tom Coens and Mary Jenkins (published by Berrett-Koehler Publishers, 2000) takes an original but positive approach to the process of assessment.

Review questions

1　Do organizations prefer conformists?

2　Should males and females be assessed differently?

3　Discuss the view that performance appraisals are unnecessary.

4　Explain the following terms: (a) behavioural consistency; and (b) competencies.

5　Compare and contrast Bevan and Thompson's textbook model of performance management with English's rational model.

6　Discuss the ways in which externals and internals react to performance assessment.

7　Is management by objectives discredited as a performance management technique?

8 How would you conduct a 360-degree performance assessment?

9 Define 'rater-inflation'. What are its causes and implications?

10 Is it possible for appraisals to be objective?

Problems for discussion and analysis

1 As General Manager, the Consumer Relations department has been the source of considerable difficulties for you this year. The manager, Jean Davis, her assistant Lyndon Greaves, and the six staff are involved in a constant battle with Sales. First, they say that the number of complaints has gone up substantially. Jean says that customers seem far more ready to find fault with deliveries than ever before. She blames the salesforce for errors in order-taking. She has become aggressive in the way she deals with Sales and has accused you of ignoring the problem. Lyndon is more reasonable but says that his people are grossly overworked. They have developed a backlog in clearing customers' letters and phone calls and sick leave has increased.

   Conversely, the Sales department is working better than ever before. They have a new PRP system in place, based on targets for orders taken by each person. The field salesforce has embraced PRP enthusiastically with orders 20 per cent up on last year. Most have received generous bonuses. The board are very pleased with this and have asked you to extend PRP to other departments, including Consumer Relations. However, Jean and Lyndon are very negative about the idea, demanding to know how they are likely to be assessed when they are behind on their targets.

   What is your analysis of the situation and how would you deal with it?

2 *International Holidays* is a travel agency group. The company has 43 shop units, each employing between four and eight front-office staff. Each unit has a manager. The company has been suffering from low trading levels in recent years. The situation has not been helped by the devaluation of the currency, which has made foreign travel more expensive. The managing director has asked you to set up a performance management system to improve the motivation of the staff. How would you do this? What difficulties would you expect in ensuring that the system achieved its objectives?

19 | Reward management

Objectives

The purpose of this chapter is to:

- Investigate the relationship between the human resource function and payroll administration.
- Outline the rationale behind different compensation packages.
- Evaluate the link between pay and performance.

Pay and compensation

Pay is an important feature of human resource management – after all, it is the main reason why people work. It is a sensitive and controversial area that has been extensively debated at both practical and theoretical levels. In the USA the term 'compensation' is used to encompass everything received by an employed individual in return for work. For example, Milcovich, Newman and Milcovich (2001, p.6) state that: 'Employees may see compensation as a *return in exchange* between their employer and themselves, as an *entitlement* for being an employee of the company, or as a *reward* for a job well done' (original emphases).

The reward or compensation people receive for their contribution to an organization includes monetary and non-monetary components. Remuneration does not simply compensate employees for their efforts – it also has an impact on the recruitment and retention of talented people.

The term 'reward management' covers both the strategy and the practice of pay systems. Traditionally, human resource or personnel sections have been concerned with levels and schemes of payment whereas the process of paying employees – the payroll function – has been the responsibility of finance departments. There is a trend towards integrating the two, driven by new computerized packages offering a range of facilities. These are described later in this chapter.

There are two basic types of pay schemes, although many organizations have systems that include elements of both:

- *Fixed levels of pay.* Wages or salaries that do not vary from one period to the next except by defined pay increases, generally on an annual basis. There may be scales of payments determined by age, responsibility or seniority. Most 'white-collar' jobs were paid in this way until recently.

- *Reward linked to performance.* The link may be daily, weekly, monthly or annualized. Payment for any one period varies from that for any other period, depending on quantity or quality of work. Sales functions are commonly paid on the basis of turnover; manual and production workers may be paid according to work completed or items produced. Catering staff typically rely on direct payment from satisfied customers in the form of service charges or tips (gratuities).

Both methods work smoothly, provided that scales are easy to understand and the methods of measuring completed work are overt, accurate and fair. However, there has been considerable dissatisfaction with the management of pay on both sides of the employment relationship. In recent years, attempts have been made to remedy the situation through new systems and a greater reliance on performance-related pay.

Key concept 19:1

Reward management   Reward or compensation management is an aspect of HRM that focuses pay and other benefits on the achievement of objectives. Typically, it incorporates other changes in pay administration and policy, including: decentralization of responsibility for setting pay levels; uniform appraisal schemes; flexible working practices; and performance-related pay.

Within HRM literature there is some ambiguity as to whether reward should play a supporting role, a view implicit in the Harvard model of HRM, or, conversely, that it should *drive* organizational performance – an opinion that finds greater favour among exponents of hard HRM (Kessler, 1995, p.10). Milcovich, Newman and Milcovich (2001, p.5) take a broad perspective, arguing that:

In addition to treating pay as an expense, a manager also uses it to influence employee behaviours and improve organization performance. The way people are paid affects the quality of their work; their attitude towards customers; their willingness to be flexible or learn new skills or suggest innovations; and even their interest in unions or legal action against their employer. This potential to influence employees' behaviours, and subsequently the productivity and effectiveness of the organization, is another reason it is important to be clear about the meaning of compensation.

Wolf (1999, p.41) argues that compensation programmes have been structured to meet three primary design criteria. They must be:

1 *Internally equitable* and pay people in proportion to the relative value of the job.
2 *Externally competitive* and pay people in proportion to the market price of the job.
3. *Personally motivating* to employees.

Wolf adds a fourth objective, which is often kept from line managers: ease of administration for staff. Wolf comments on these objectives:

> Unfortunately, the first two are almost always at cross purposes with each other, forcing an organization to sacrifice one to achieve the other, and achievement of the third means a high degree of individualization, which complicates the fourth, administration.

Many countries have minimum pay rates in place which set the base rate for wages across the job market.

HRM in reality

Scrooge bosses

DTI enforcers have discovered £10 million of wages unpaid by scrooge bosses since the minimum wage was introduced. The third national minimum wage annual report also confirms that compliance officers are effectively identifying cases and investigating complaints and that enforcement of the minimum wage is working well.

Employment Relations Minister, Alan Johnson commented:

> The minimum wage is a great success story. The government is committed to making work pay and the national minimum wage, alongside working tax credits and the New Deal, is key to tackling poverty.
>
> I am delighted that the vast majority of employers are complying with the minimum wage. Awareness of the minimum wage is high and the enforcement system is working well when workers are not receiving the pay they deserve. But success has not made us complacent. Substantial extra funds are going into enforcement, we have 20 more compliance officers and the number of enforcement teams around the UK has been increased from 14 to 16.

TUC general secretary, John Monks said:

> The recovery of £10 million in illegally withheld wages is great news for fairness at work. More could be achieved with an even more proactive enforcement regime and less reliance on vulnerable workers reporting their bad bosses.
>
> Working in partnership with the government, we want to stop scrooge bosses and put an end to exploitation. There is no room in the modern British economy for employers who flout the law in the name of cost-cutting and profiteering.

Key findings of the report (covering the period April 2001 to April 2002) are:

- More than £5 million in wage arrears were identified in the year. The total amount identified since the minimum wage was introduced in April 1999 is now well over £10 million.

- Some 36 per cent of employers investigated were found not to be paying the minimum wage. This represents a 6 per cent increase on 2001/02 and a 16 per cent increase on 1999/00 and demonstrates improved efficiency in targeting non-payment.
- The average arrears identified per worker was £495, compared with £418 in 2000/01 and £205 in 1999/2000.
- The regions with the highest number of complaints were the north-west (207) and Yorkshire and Humberside (180).
- The sector with the highest number of complaints (296) was market services (which includes car and other repairs, taxi firms and communications) followed by hospitality (227).
- Usage of the minimum wage interactive website (www.tiger.gov.uk) increased by over 70 per cent. Each month more than 4000 people visited the site.
- More than 79 000 enquiries were received by the minimum wage helpline on 0845 6000 678. Over 94 per cent of calls were answered within 15 seconds. Since 1 April 1999 the helpline has responded to more than 275 000 enquiries and handled over 7500 complaints about non-payment of the minimum wage.

Recent cases where workers have received wage arrears include:

- A worker employed by one of the top 100 blue chip construction companies complained to the helpline that he had not been paid the minimum wage. The compliance officer established that the company had misunderstood the rules for apprentices and accepted that arrears of wages were due: 186 workers benefited from total arrears identified of more than £130 000.
- A worker complained that he and his colleagues were not being paid the minimum wage. All were residential officers at a city university who lived on campus, but although provided with free accommodation they were not paid any wage. Arrears totalling £137 000 were identified for 27 workers.
- In a case involving homeworkers the employer contended that the workers were self-employed and therefore not subject to the minimum wage legislation. An Employment Tribunal decided in favour of the homeworkers. Over £15 000 in arrears was secured for 23 workers.
- Information received from a third party suggested that a bus company had not been paying its drivers the minimum wage. The claim was investigated and enquiries revealed that 14 drivers had been underpaid. Over £5000 in wages arrears was identified.
- Six workers who had been employed as sales representatives for a building hardware retailer complained that they had not been paid for all the hours they worked. The employer was not able to produce any records of pay for hours worked and was keen to pay the arrears identified without recourse to an employment tribunal. Arrears totalling £7477 were identified for the six workers.

Source: *HRMGuide.co.uk* (http://www.hrmguide.co.uk), 13 September 2002.

Activity 19:1   What is pay for? What effect does the minimum wage have on employer and employee attitudes to rates of pay?

HR and payroll administration

Traditionally, payroll sections and the human resource sections that interface with them have suffered from too much administration. Every transaction triggered 'a paper-intensive, repetitive and inconsistent process' (Hitzeman, 1997). Today, businesses want their pay functions to do more than just administration. They demand efficient payroll processes together with expertise and service. According to Hitzeman such changes in delivery and expectations are forcing pay-related departments to sharpen their focus on key issues.

Hitzeman argues that the pay function is becoming increasingly complex because:

- legal aspects have become more involved
- staff expect higher standards of service
- pay staffing levels have been kept steady or even reduced.

To provide the desired level of service to staff and other 'customers', pay departments need to reorganize both tasks and resources around two central themes: transactions and consulting.

Payroll sections typically deal with issues that go beyond simple pay calculations. They can include:

- health benefits such as BUPA
- pension contributions
- savings
- company share option purchases
- sickness and other forms of paid time off
- expenses.

As a result, payroll staff are involved with the following transactions:

- dealing with routine queries
- filling in forms
- issuing forms for staff to complete
- explaining company policies and procedures.

Consequently, payroll departments handle a great deal of repetitive work and generate mountains of paper. At the same time they are inconsistent in the responses they provide – similar queries often receiving different answers, depending on the staff member involved. Partly, this is a function of experience, but also depends on how busy they may be. Basically, traditional pay sections are too clerical in focus. The information they use and collect may be of doubtful quality.

The solution may be to split information away from administrative functions into specialist areas. This allows consolidation and standardization of transaction-handling, leading to a degree of efficiency not possible in a traditional, unspecialized department. In large organizations, such a function can become a centre of excellence, taking advantage of professional techniques and up-to-date information technology. This offers the possibility of: more efficient processes and better customer service; consistent handling of queries and situations; better information; and a recognized 'one-stop shop' for pay-related queries.

| Activity 19:2 | What functions should a payroll department fulfil? |

Technology and the pay unit

Concentration of clerical and transactional tasks in a single unit gives greater opportunity for cross-training. It also exposes staff to wider organizational issues, providing enhanced awareness of the purpose and effects of reward management. A centralized unit can benefit from new technology, such as: interactive voice response (IVR) systems, routing basic enquiries and messages to voice mail boxes and recorded standard answers; corporate intranets which give internet-type access to staff within the organization, including message boards, data gathering and online access to company information.

According to Hitzeman (1997), the other important element of the pay function that deserves attention is the provision of an internal consultancy for staff. This is more than using expertise to provide advice and information. The transaction-handling function is operational, emphasizing cost-effectiveness, efficiency and accuracy. By contrast, consulting services are regarded as strategic and value-added, perhaps offering: benefit package design; the ability to handle unusual (exceptional) pay or taxation problems; and strategic remuneration programmes, aimed at recruiting and retaining talented staff.

To distinguish between transaction-handling and consulting, as many administrative tasks as possible can be removed from 'consultant' staff and transferred to the operations unit. Consultants are then able to concentrate on strategic issues. As a further spin-off from setting up data collecting and information presentation systems for the transaction-handling unit, consultants are provided with more accessible and accurate information. This allows situations to be analysed more quickly and easily because useful data is readily available.

As another step in this process, organizations may choose to outsource some of the more routine 'number-crunching' functions to specialist companies. Pension administration is a long-standing example. The most obvious justification for outsourcing is to cut costs by:

- benefiting from the economies of scale open to a specialist provider
- reducing the number of internal pay administrators
- minimizing capital investment in equipment
- reducing overhead costs such as accommodation, heating and lighting.

Separate operations, consulting and outsourced providers can be difficult to manage for a large organization. One solution is to create a Pay and Benefit Service Centre. Typically, this is contacted through the internal telephone system or an external freefone (toll-free) number. Some 80 per cent of calls are dealt with at the first point of contact. These are the most routine questions that can be answered through an interactive keypad system: pressing a combination of keys provides a recorded response to the most common queries. The other 20 per cent require human contact with a customer service representative (CSR). The CSR has access to information sources such as scripted answers, a corporate intranet a pay manual, etc. Just 5 per cent will be referred to the payroll experts who will deal with policy and exceptional circumstances.

HRM in reality	1998 survey on UK employers' pension provision

The Department of Social Security (DSS) published results of the third survey of pension provision by private sector companies in Great Britain. The survey involved nearly 2000 private sector organizations who were interviewed by telephone

▶

between January and June 1998. This survey provides an update of research previously conducted in 1994 and 1996. The survey investigated:

- types of pensions provided by employers
- extent of employees covered by pension provisions
- contributions and benefits involved
- trustee arrangements for pension schemes
- financial status of and minimum funding requirements for pension schemes
- valuation of employees' pension rights
- awareness of Stakeholder Pensions.

Results were divided into two categories: small organizations (defined as having fewer than 20 employees); and larger organizations (with 20 or more employees). The authors of the report – Jon Hales and Nina Stratford of the National Centre for Social Research – among their findings revealed that:

- Size and employment profiles of private sector companies had changed little since the last survey in 1996. Most employers (93 per cent) had fewer than 20 employees but most workers (67 per cent) were employed in larger organizations with 20 or more employees.
- Around 34 per cent of companies made some form of pension provision in 1998 (compared with 38 per cent in 1996). But the researchers warned that this comparison should be treated with caution due to possible sample bias.
- In both 1996 and 1998 the most common form of provision was through employer contributions to personal pensions. Some 38 per cent of larger organizations had two or more types of pension provision in 1998 but multiple provision did not feature prominently among smaller organizations.
- There was a striking difference between the percentage of employees making some kind of pension provision between large and small organizations. Whereas 90 per cent (89 per cent in 1996) of employees in larger firms did so, just 38 per cent of small organization workers made provision – a drop from 42 per cent in 1996.

Source: Adapted from *Employers' Pension Provision 1998*, published 28 September 2000 in the Department of Social Security's Research Series.

HRM in reality

Retirement planning and employee benefits

Planning retirement and servicing 401(k) plans remain key HR issues in the USA. Fidelity® Investments found 2001 to be the strongest year ever in its institutional retirement and human resources/benefits outsourcing businesses, adding more than 1500 plans and over 1.0 million new participants in the corporate and tax-exempt market-place. In total, by the end of 2001, Fidelity served more than 11 100 employee benefit programs and 11.2 million American workers through its defined contribution, defined benefit, health and welfare and HR/payroll practices. Around 30 per cent of its largest clients now use Fidelity to provide multiple outsourcing services.

'One of the fastest growing areas at Fidelity is our human resources and benefits outsourcing business,' said Peter J. Smail, president, Fidelity Employer Services Company:

> Fidelity's broad understanding of the workplace positions us well to assist employers in achieving their goals of integrated HR/benefits solutions that create excellent long-term value. Our clients are looking for broader multi-service solutions. In 2001, about 61 per cent of requests for proposals from large companies asked for administration services in two or more areas, including HR administration and payroll services, health and welfare programs and defined benefit pension plans.

Fidelity found the outsourcing trend to be driven by companies focused on integrating their employee benefits with just one service provider to benefit from cost efficiencies and to deliver new self-service tools to employees via the internet. 'The web has transformed the employee desktop and has moved us into the world of employee self-service,' Smail said. 'Today, in the 401(k) and benefits outsourcing business, we get more than 350 000 contacts per day and more than 65 per cent are via the web.'

Fidelity provides its service through its NetBenefitsSM site, providing access to a wide range of employee benefit programs – including 401(k) and pension plans, health, dental and other benefit programs, and payroll information. 'In one place, employees can gain direct access to relevant information, online planning and decision-support tools, and conduct a wide range of workplace service transactions with the convenience of the internet,' Smail said.

401(k) and a volatile economy

What happens to employee confidence when stock values are affected by economic downturns? Immediately following the events of 11 September CIGNA Retirement and Investment Services commissioned two separate surveys. They found that half of 1000 Americans surveyed said they would pursue new investment strategies if their retirement account balances were lower at the end of 2001 than they were in the previous January. And, in the other survey, 504 human resource executives involved in the administration of their companies' retirement plans said they were unprepared to provide the retirement planning information employees need to make informed decisions.

The good news was that most Americans were keeping faith in their 401(k)s despite the recent volatility of stock portfolios in most retirement plans. They might be looking to make changes but their interest lay in reallocating portfolios or increasing contribution levels – made possible by recent pension reform.

But the more worrying news was that nearly half of HR executives (47 per cent) said they were unprepared to provide retirement planning advice to employees. And the survey pinpointed the fact that fact HR executives found educating their workforce about retirement benefits was their biggest challenge, with employees giving them low marks – the equivalent of a 'C' – for their efforts.

Just one in five people (22 per cent) relied on their employer as the primary source of retirement-planning information. Plan providers and financial advisers also each garnered 22 per cent, followed by family and friends (12 per cent) and the media (5 per cent).

'These are difficult times, and employees clearly are looking for help in managing their 401(k) portfolios. Employers are struggling to meet this need,' said Tom Jones, president of CIGNA Retirement and Investment Services. 'Retirement

▶

◀

planning is a critical workplace education and retention issue, and the gap between what employees need and what employers are providing is startling. They're not just on different pages, they're on different planets.' Some 31 per cent of consumers said that retirement plans were the most important employee benefit. But a mere 9 per cent of HR executives cited employer-sponsored retirement plans as the most important tool for attracting and retaining employees.

'The 401(k) plan is America's best tool for building employee wealth and financial security. But like any tool, it's only as good as the instructions,' said Jones:

> Particularly in today's environment, employees are looking for retirement education. And it's up to employers, working with their retirement plan providers, to design educational programs that build awareness, encourage increased participation and recognize the individuality and specific needs of each employee.

Source: *HRM Guide USA* (http://www.hrmguide.net/usa/), 8 April 2002.

Pay evaluation

Large organizations have traditionally resorted to job evaluation to provide the justification for different levels of pay. According to the International Labour Organization, 'job evaluation is directed towards rating the job, not the person'. Job evaluation is particularly concerned with:

- tasks involved in fulfilling a job
- duties that have to be completed
- responsibilities attached.

It is not concerned with elements of job analysis required for the recruitment process such as qualifications, experience, proficiency, or the key considerations of performance management – job behaviour, proficiency and attendance.

The outcome of a traditional job evaluation process is a set of job classifications, perhaps expressed as a formal hierarchy of jobs. The next stage – job pricing – results in a pay scale. Therefore, job pricing determines the remuneration or compensation for each job.

Traditional job evaluation involves the comparison of jobs in a formal, systematic way to identify their relative value to an organization. It has an underlying premise: that some jobs are worth more than others. Job evaluation has its roots in the scientific management movement (Taylorism) of the early 20th century. The methodology has had a particularly strong influence in the USA, where it has focused on position-based job evaluation systems. These systems define the scope and value of jobs by using comparatively narrow job classification grades.

The end of the century saw some radical changes in the nature of work. Increasingly, the concept of flexibility has displaced the notion that work should be composed of a rigid set of pre-defined tasks. The job description seems increasingly inappropriate for the way work is organized today since the content of many jobs varies from one day to the next. This makes job rating and pay evaluation more difficult. Traditional job evaluation is focused on unchanging job descriptions and requirements, encouraging staff to take a rigid attitude to their work. If performance assessment and pay are linked to the completion of specific tasks, the need for change and a flexible approach to customers is ignored. Modern organizations have turned to competency profiles instead.

Over the last few decades, pay evaluation systems have swung from having an individual focus to being job-based and, more recently, back again to a stress on the individual. Risher (1998, p.7, cited in Wolf, 1999, p.45) states that:

> ... the new work paradigm, in which jobs are more flexible and duties change as required, undermines the traditional focus on jobs ... The newer concepts for managing base pay, pay banding, competency-based pay and skill-based pay shift the focus to the value of the individual. Value is now determined by what the individual can do, not on what he or she actually does from day to day. A new definition of equity, one that will need to be understood by employees, supports paying the most competent people higher salaries. As organizations move to team-pay environments, it will lead to differences in pay for people in similar jobs.

HRM in reality

The grass is greener ...

A majority of workers believe they can get better pay elsewhere, according to a Watson Wyatt survey of nearly 13 000 employees in the USA.

The Watson Wyatt WorkUSA® 2002 study shows that just 41 per cent of employees think they are paid as much as people in equivalent positions at other companies. And fewer than half (48 per cent) believe they are paid fairly in comparison to workers with similar jobs in their own organizations.

'Companies must take a close look at employees' perceptions of pay fairness both within and outside their own organizations or risk losing people once the economy improves and labour market mobility is restored,' said Ilene Gochman, Watson Wyatt's national practice leader for organizational measurement and author of the 2002 study. 'In fact, other Watson Wyatt research has shown that pay dissatisfaction is a key reason why top performing employees leave their companies.'

Inadequate communication is pinpointed as a significant contributor to employees' dissatisfaction with their pay, according to the survey. Just 43 per cent of workers said their organizations were good at explaining how their pay is determined. This is 13 points down since 2000 and the worst figure for pay communication since 1994. And 20 per cent of employees claimed not to know what their total compensation packages are worth.

The survey's findings on employee benefits demonstrate the value of effective communication: over two-thirds (68 per cent) of employees felt that their organizations are good at providing information on their benefits. This strategy seems to be paying off as shown by a ten-point improvement over the 2000 results in the percentage of employees who believe their benefits packages compare well to packages offered by other companies (42 per cent in 2002).

'The high marks given to companies for benefits communication suggest that improvements in pay communications are possible. Companies clearly know how to communicate – they just need to better apply their communication strategies to their pay-related practices,' said Gochman.

Employees' reactions are mixed on specific benefits strategies. Most workers are satisfied with leave benefits (71 per cent), savings plans (67 per cent), healthcare plans (64 per cent) and pension/retirement plans (60 per cent). But it seems that the economic downturn has affected employee attitudes toward profit-sharing and stock programs. Satisfaction with profit-sharing plans fell by 10 points to 45 per cent between 2000 and 2002. Satisfaction with stock programs declined by 7 points to 50 per cent over the same period.

Gochman said that the study results show that companies must do a better job linking employees' pay to their performance. 'Despite evidence that pay differentials

▶

◀

between strong performers and weak performers boost firms' financial performance, only one-third (35 per cent) of employees told us there is a clear link between how well they do their jobs and the money that they earn.'

Corporate strategy shifts appear to have left many employees confused about the link between their jobs and company objectives. The study shows that fewer than half of employees (49 per cent) understand the steps their organizations are taking to reach new business goals – a drop of 20 per cent since 2000. The study also found that only 35 per cent see clear links between the quality of their job performance and the money they earn.

'Confusion about corporate goals and uncertainty about the link between pay and performance will complicate economic recovery for many companies,' said Ilene Gochman. 'This is extremely unfortunate because we know that there is tremendous positive impact to the bottom line when employees see strong connections between company goals and their jobs. Many employees aren't seeing that connection.'

The study also reveals that three-year total returns to shareholders (TRS) are three times higher in companies where workers understand corporate objectives and the ways in which their jobs contribute to achieving them. 'Companies cannot develop effective teams and working relationships unless everyone involved clearly under-stands the connections between their jobs and objectives,' Gochman added. 'Workers and their companies excel when they know why their jobs matter and they understand what's in it for them.'

'In every case, we found that employee attitudes make a difference when it comes to business performance,' Gochman said. 'For example, companies that instil trust, manage business changes effectively and communicate openly with employees have much higher shareholder return rates than companies that don't.'

WorkUSA® is one of the largest and most current statistically representative surveys on the attitudes of US workers. The 2002 survey includes responses from 12 750 workers at all job levels and in all major industries.

Source: *HRM Guide USA* (http://www.hrmguide.net/usa/), 18 October 2002.

Market-driven criteria

New skills and occupations are characterized by a greater demand for the right people than the job market can supply. The natural response is to increase pay and benefits on offer to these people. However, this has consequences on other staff in the organization and also for any job evaluation system. Scarcity of skills distorts evaluation systems and raises con-cerns about fairness. Short-term solutions produce further problems in the future when appropriately skilled staff become plentiful. This situation is common in information tech-nology where, at first, only a few individuals are able to use new computer programs and packages. Within a matter of months large numbers of trained people become available. A year or two later the packages may be replaced by a new product and the once-valued skills are redundant.

Broadbanding and skill-based pay

Broadbanding has been implemented in a number of different ways, but the basic principle is the same: large numbers of individually rated jobs or job types are clustered into a few, much wider job classifications or 'bands'. Although broadbanding was trumpeted as a panacea in the 1990s, Wolf (1999, p.45) criticizes the exaggerated claims for its effectiveness, stating that these are made on questionable data. It is clear from a number of surveys that managers are not implementing broadbanding thoroughly – for example, bands often are not broad at all. Many organizations are not measuring the cost or effectiveness of broadbanding in comparison with more traditional methods, and improvements in career management (cited as one of the main benefits by proponents) are not being achieved.

Wolf (1999, p.48) is equally dismissive of skill or competence-based pay systems:

> Whether one relies on old-fashioned job evaluation and traditional job-pay structures or moves to competencies and broad bands, employers still pay for what you know and what you do. No matter how you get there, these are the key compensable elements! Attempts to dress this up in modern garb abound, but the underlying premise remains as an eternal verity.

Kessler (2001, p.221) also concludes that competence (and team) based pay are superficially attractive, but they are difficult to put into practice as competencies are difficult to identify and measure as are the standards for judging team performance. Kessler considers that:

> It is difficult to avoid the conclusion that while use of pay to encourage the development of employee competencies and a team-based work environment are readily identifiable as business priorities, driving the formulation of new pay strategies, there is precious little evidence to suggest that such priorities are being translated into practice.

Wolf (1999, p.47) concludes that:

> 'This brave new world of compensation raises many questions. If there are 'no levels, scales or ranges,' what role does 'market competitive pricing' play? Why is it even a factor? Is it subordinate to 'career development' or 'employees' contribution' or are they subordinate to it? Is 'career development' more or less important than 'employees' contribution'?

Activity 19:3	What are the implications of paying different salaries for the same job?

HRM in reality	**PC perks**

Society may be increasingly computer-based but new research indicates that 41 per cent of British employees do not have access to a personal computer at work or at home. *Mouse In The House* is a report based on a survey carried out by MORI in the UK (and also France and Germany) where 44 per cent are without PC access. The report was commissioned by PeoplePC, a global provider of home-based PC and internet benefit programmes.

It highlights the so-called 'Digital Divide' between the people who have PC and internet access and those who do not. Some 18 per cent of those without are afraid of being left behind in the age of technology. People under the age of 35 have the greatest wish to be able to use the internet but often feel they can't afford it. Intriguingly, 32 per cent of survey respondents would be willing to make a contribution to the cost of an employer subsidized home PC. In fact, a home computer is seen as better perk than more familiar benefits such as membership of a health club.

Virtually a half (49 per cent) of respondents wanting employers to provide PCs with internet access anticipate using them for personal development – learning new skills for jobs or careers. They see benefits to themselves, their families and employers. And 17 per cent said they would be happy to use those PCs in order to work flexibly, during evenings or weekends.

Source: *HRM Guide.co.uk* (http://www.hrmguide.co.uk), 2 June 2001.

Motivation and performance

According to Rosenbloom (2001, p.2):

> Employee benefits constitute a major part of almost any individual's financial and economic security. Such benefits have gone from being considered 'fringe' to the point where they may constitute about 40 per cent of an employee's compensation, and the plans under which they are provided are a major concern of employers.

Key concept 19:2

Employee benefits   Broadly defined, 'employee benefits are virtually any form of compensation other than direct wages paid to employees' (Rosenbloom, 2001, p.3).

The US Chambers of Commerce survey of employee benefits (cited in Rosenbloom 2001, p.3) includes the following:

1 Employer's share of legally required payments.
2 Employer's share of retirement and savings plan payments.
3 Employer's share of life insurance and death benefit payments.
4 Employer's share of medical and medically related benefit payments.
5 Payment for time not worked (e.g. paid rest periods, paid sick leave, paid vacations, holidays, parental leave, etc.).
6 Miscellaneous benefit payments (including employee discounts, severance pay, educational expenditure and childcare).

Paid time off is still the most common benefit for employees in US private organizations. According to the Bureau of Labor Statistics, US Department of Labor, paid vacations were available to 80 per cent of employees and paid holidays to 77 per cent of employees in private industry during the year 2000. The data comes from the National Compensation Survey (NCS), which provides comprehensive measures of occupational earnings, compensation cost trends and details of benefit provisions (*HRM Guide USA* [http://www.hrmguide.net/usa/], 19 July 2002). In 2000:

- Some 52 per cent of employees in private industry participated in medical care plans. Premiums were fully paid by the employer for 32 per cent of those with single coverage plans and 19 per cent of those with family coverage. The majority of medical plan participants were required to contribute a flat monthly amount, averaging US$54.40 for single coverage and US$179.75 for family coverage.

- Around 48 per cent were covered by retirement benefits of at least one type: a defined benefit plan (19 per cent); a defined contribution plan (36 per cent). Approximately 7 per cent were covered by both types.

- Life insurance was available to over half of all employees in private industry.

- Short-term disability benefits were available to 34 per cent of employees, while long-term disability benefits were only available to 26 per cent.

- Non-production bonuses were offered to 48 per cent of employees.

- Work-related educational assistance (38 per cent).

- Severance pay (20 per cent).

- Job-related travel accident insurance (15 per cent).

- Long-term care insurance (7 per cent).

Access to most benefits (including availability of fully paid medical care and amount of required contributions to cost of medical care) varied by worker and establishment characteristics.

Worker characteristics

This analysis looked at three categories of employees in detail. Retirement benefits covered 66 per cent of professional, technical and related employees; 50 per cent of clerical and sales employees; and 39 per cent of blue-collar and service employees. Work-related educational assistance was available to 62 per cent of professional, technical and related workers; 37 per cent of clerical and sales workers; and 28 per cent of blue-collar and service workers.

Payment of premiums for medical care coverage also varied by employee characteristics. Some 38 per cent of blue-collar and service workers covered by medical care benefits had their coverage fully paid for by their employers compared with 25 per cent of professional, technical and related employees and 28 per cent of clerical and sales employees.

Full-time employees were far more likely to have benefits coverage than were part-time employees: 55 per cent of full-time employees were covered by retirement benefits compared with 18 per cent of part-time employees. The disparity in healthcare benefits was even greater: 61 per cent of full-time employees were covered by medical care plans compared with 13 per cent of part-time workers.

Establishment characteristics

Benefit incidence varied by the number of employees within an establishment. As an example: 65 per cent of workers in establishments with 100 employees or more (medium and large establishments) were covered by retirement benefits compared with 33 per cent of employees in small establishments (those with fewer than 100 workers); 86 per cent of employees in medium and large establishments had paid holiday benefits compared with 70 per cent in small establishments.

Benefit cover also varied by industry. Retirement benefits covered 57 per cent of workers in goods-producing industries compared with 45 per cent in service-producing industries. Long-term disability coverage was also more common in goods-producing industries (31 per cent) compared with 24 per cent of employees in service-producing industries. Short-term disability benefits covered 45 per cent of employees in goods-producing industries and 30 per cent of those in service-producing industries.

HRM in reality	**Industrial Society survey shows twice as many flexible benefits schemes for staff**

A new report shows that flexible benefits schemes (where employers provide a menu of benefits to staff) are twice as common as they were four years ago. The report into flexible benefits comes in the Industrial Society's 'Managing Best Practice' series.

Benefits most frequently on offer as 'flexible' are healthcare, additional holiday and company cars. Other common benefits in flexible benefit schemes include life insurance, medical insurance, share plans/options, dental care, optical care, gym membership, childcare vouchers and nursery vouchers.

▶

◄

According to Christine Garner, the Industrial Society's head of organizational development, flexible benefits are still relatively uncommon but take-up is increasing rapidly:

> Organizations introduce flexible benefits for a variety of reasons. They show that a company is forward thinking and they allow employees to choose benefits suitable for their needs. Parents may want to take extra holidays to be with their children. Older people may want extra medical benefits or life assurance and younger staff may want extra money rather than extra holidays. For employers they are a way of increasing employees' satisfaction and also of attracting the best recruits.

Together with case studies and best practice tips from Alcatel Telecom Ltd, Cable & Wireless, Cadbury Ltd, EMAP, PricewaterhouseCoopers and Spring Group Plc, the authors used a mixture of qualitative and quantitative research. They found that

- Around 53 per cent of the organizations responding to the survey now operate a flexible benefits scheme.
- The most common reason given for these schemes was to help retain staff (27 per cent). Other reasons included: recognition of employee's individual requirements (16 per cent); competitive pressures (16 per cent); and cost-effectiveness (10 per cent).
- Most organizations (77 per cent) offer their scheme to all employees, but in 19 per cent of responding companies only middle and higher ranking managers were eligible. In 5 per cent of organizations just the top 10 per cent of employees are covered.
- It seems that 92 per cent of employees like to have a degree of choice over benefits. On the drawbacks list, however, 55 per cent of businesses thought administration was costly and 36 per cent found the schemes difficult to manage, while 38 per cent said that employees would rather have their basic pay increased.

Cadbury Ltd's flexible benefits scheme has been running for two years. Jan Johnston, the benefits development manager, says that the response from staff was initially caution and on occasions there was cynicism. However, more people are now using their options and Johnston believes that word of mouth is spreading the good news.

Alcatel Telecom Ltd found their system to be extremely popular. According to a spokesperson: 'Those who do not want to use it do not have to. The majority like being able to change benefits according to their needs.' But there have been problems due to the time-consuming administration, although fewer than originally expected. However, it took considerable effort to break down the initial apathy barrier.

PricewaterhouseCoopers' scheme was also met with some scepticism. But when staff became familiar with the scheme they showed far more enthusiasm. An attitude survey conducted in late 1999 confirmed positive attitudes. However, it obviously needs time for employees to understand how flexible benefits work.

Communication at the start of any flexible benefits scheme has to be very clear to show staff exactly what is and what is not on offer, according to Christine Garner.

'We recommend a sustained, targeted campaign that makes use of a mixture of methods such as staff meetings, posters, e-mail and intranet sites. We also recommend that organizations regularly monitor the take-up for each benefit.'

Source: *HRMGuide.co.uk* (http://www.hrmguide.co.uk), 20 November 2000.

What advantages do flexible benefits offer for individual employees and their employers?

Pay and performance

Many commentators severely criticized the apparently chaotic and disorganized nature of pay management between the 1950s and 1980s. In recent years there has been an attempt to remedy this situation. The fashion has been towards the development of performance-related pay schemes which are related to assessments of performance through individual employee appraisal. Wolf (1999, p.48) sums up a common view:

> Pay for performance is the holy grail of modern compensation administration – widely sought but hard to actually achieve. Pay for performance is the flag, motherhood and apple pie, but it is easier said than done. One primary problem is defining performance properly, so that the organization pays for results and not for effort. Once over that hurdle, there remains the large impediment of finding enough money to make the reward for top performance meaningful.

Pay is a sensitive issue. Most employers have been cautious with the introduction of PRP. Often it is applied to senior managers first, then extended to other employees. Usually, it has been an 'add-on' to normal pay. Rarely does it replace the existing pay scheme completely. More commonly, PRP has:

- formed part or (rarely) all of the general pay increase
- been used to extend pay above scale maxima for employees with high levels of performance
- replaced increases previously paid on the basis of age, or length of service.

Such caution is due to the complexity and sensitivity of performance-related pay in the context of employee relations. People take pay scales seriously. Negotiating and justifying radical changes to a pay structure can be difficult and time-consuming. It is sensible to do so in a gradual way, commencing with senior managers who are more likely to be committed to demanding performance objectives. Even if they are not, it gives experience of the advantages and disadvantages of performance-related pay. It also gives pay administrators experience of pay schemes which are more complicated to operate than traditional methods.

The basis of performance-related pay systems

Simplistically, it seems only fair that people should be paid according to their contribution and a number of studies indicate that most people in business agree with this. In a classic experiment, Fossum and Fitch (1985) asked three groups of subjects – students, line managers and compensation managers – to make decisions on pay increases for hypothetical people, taking into account factors such as seniority, budget constraints and cost of living. All three groups gave far more importance to performance and contribution than other factors. Research into the attitudes of corporate boards and chief executive officers, among others, have all produced similar findings.

Theoretically, performance-related pay schemes can benefit both employers and employees. By emphasizing the importance of efficiency and effective job performance, employers can benefit from higher productivity. Higher pay can be targeted at the 'better' performers, encouraging them to stay with the company and continue to perform to a high standard. Good employees benefit from extra pay in return for extra quality of performance. According to this view, properly directed pay can reinforce appropriate behaviour, focusing effort on organizational targets and encouraging a results-based culture. However, these links must be justified and real if they are not to demoralize other members of the workforce. This is particularly important in relation to senior management, as can be seen in the 'HRM in reality' case of British Gas. Accusations of 'fat cat' behaviour can also seriously affect stock market views of a company's organization.

HRM in reality	**British Gas**

In 1994 the remuneration committee of British Gas recommended pay increases from 11 to 75 per cent for directors earning £200 000 or more. A new structure replaced a complex system that overemphasized share options and bonuses. This included a pay package worth £475 000 for the chief executive, Cedric Brown. This placed Mr Brown on about 20 times the earnings of the average British Gas employee – a ratio typical of British companies. This compared with differentials of five to eight in Japanese companies.

Facing a House of Commons committee Cedric Brown argued that he was paid much less than many other chief executives of large British companies. In the USA a smaller utility company paid its CEO ten times as much. Indeed it could be regarded as modest when compared with a total payout of US$203 million to Michael Eisner, chairman of Walt Disney in 1993. Mr. Brown's remuneration was justified on the grounds that it was 'the rate for the job' and that it would take this kind of salary to attract top international managers. However, Cedric Brown had never worked for any company other than British Gas, had apparently been happy on lower pay in the past, and there was no indication that he was about to be head-hunted by anyone else.

Public criticism was fuelled by the fact that 25 000 British Gas workers were in the process of losing their jobs. Redundancies and relocations were making their mark on employee morale and commitment. The changes also included the closure of half its showrooms. The remaining retail outlets would concentrate on appliance sales. They would no longer accept payment for gas bills, offer advice or accept service complaints. The Gas Consumer Council complained about this reduction in customer service, especially given an increase of 19 per cent in complaints over the previous year.

As part of this process, another executive was reported as being offered a bonus of £36 000 on top of his salary of £120 000 for pushing through changes in the work and payscales of retail workers. The 2600 workers were being asked to take pay cuts from their average £13 000 a year salaries along with reductions in holiday entitlements.

The attendant publicity about 'fat cats' dogged Mr Brown for the next two years. Symbolically, angry shareholders brought a pig named Cedric into the annual general meeting and fed it from a trough. Mr Brown suffered further criticism when it was revealed that British Gas had tied itself to a number of supply deals at inflated prices. In 1996 the continued existence of British Gas as an independent entity seemed uncertain. Mr Brown announced his retirement – with a pension of £250 000 a year.

Discussion questions: (a) Was criticism of Mr Brown reasonable? (b) Were the various payments made to Mr Brown fair (i) to him?; (ii) to British Gas employees?

PRP can be related to the performance assessment of the individual, group (team), department or company. There are several systems in common use.

Appraisal-related pay schemes

Merit pay

This is paid as part of a person's annual increase on the basis of an overall performance appraisal. The method has a long track record and is commonly regarded as an effective motivator. However, it is frequently undermined by budget restrictions, when the merit element often is set too low to motivate.

There are also instances when the payment is used as a 'market supplement' to retain individuals who have skills for which there is demand but whose performance is not particularly meritorious. However, it is known that breaking the clear link between appraised performance and payment of PRP reduces the overall effectiveness of PRP as a motivator for other employees.

Individual incentives

Given as unconsolidated (one-off) payments or gifts such as holidays, golf sets or vouchers.

Collective performance schemes

Bonuses

These are paid to all staff in an organization, department or team. In common with all collective performance rewards, they are designed to reinforce corporate identity and performance. The John Lewis retail group paid out a total of £57 million in 2002 to its 58 000 partner employees in the form of bonuses equivalent to 9 per cent of each person's salary. In 1996 the jeans manufacturers Levi Strauss proposed a payout of a year's salary to each permanent employee at the end of 2001, provided they had worked at least three years and the company reached its objective of a US$7.6 billion a year cash-flow. But the plan failed as the company's sales dropped: US$343.9 million from the proposed incentive plan went back into the company in 2000, instead of being paid to staff.

HRM in reality

American Express extends bonuses and stock plans to all staff

Some 3500 American Express employees are to share in a US$5 million celebration after the business surpassed five-year financial targets and had a record year in 2000. Canadian staff will benefit from:

- A bonus plan for all members of staff (beyond the managers and sales employees who are already on variable pay plans) linking personal and company performance to cash payments.

- A stock purchase plan through which the business will top up employee contributions to a savings program to buy the company's shares.

Bonus notices are being sent to customer service and clerical staff, following celebration parties across Canada recognizing employee contribution to American Express's achievements. 'Five years ago, we set out on an ambitious journey to more than double the size of our business in Canada,' said Alan Stark, president and CEO of Amex:

▶

We asked all our employees at every level to act like they were part owners of the company, and deliver the kind of productivity gains and increases in service and performance levels needed to reach our goal. Our commitment back has been to make this one of the best places to work in Canada, and part of that has been putting in place new and creative reward mechanisms to motivate our employees.

Initiatives like these have helped to put American Express into the number 20 spot on the annual list of the top 35 companies to work for. Other employee benefits include a health and wellness program with an onsite fitness centre and medical facilities, educational assistance and paid sabbaticals. But the main motivation is improved business performance, says Stephen Gould, vice-president of human resources:

We consider any additional investments very carefully, and an investment in our people is really an integral part of our future growth strategies. Particularly for a company like ours that operates in the service sector, attracting, retaining and continuing to motivate a talented workforce is a critical competitive advantage.

American Express in Canada operates as Amex Canada Inc. and Amex Bank of Canada. Amex has doubled its customer base in Canada over the past five years and now has more than 2.3 million cardmembers in the country. It has also increased the number of employees by over a thousand at its Markham, Ontario operating centre and other offices across Canada.

Source: *HRM Guide Canada* (http://www.hrmguide.net/canada/), 28 March 2001.

The reward system in Japan is unusual. According to Hart and Kawasaki (1999, p.4):

Most Japanese workers receive the major part of their direct remuneration via two channels. First, and familiar to workers in other countries, they are paid in the form of regular (usually monthly) wages. Secondly, they receive bonus payments which, typically, are paid twice a year. The bonus constitutes around one-fifth to one-quarter of total cash earnings.

Bonuses paid in other countries are much smaller, so why are Japanese bonuses paid at such a level? Hart and Kawasaki offer a range of alternative explanations, including the possibility that bonuses:

... represent a form of efficiency wage by providing a reward for greater effort. By contrast, and at a general level, wages may reflect more systematic and structural elements of remuneration, such as seniority-based pay scales (the *Nenko* system), while bonuses are used to adjust total compensation to fluctuations in firms' economic experience. In this event, we might expect that the bonus should display more flexibility than the wage. One school of thought in this respect regards bonuses as a form of profit-sharing between the firm and its workforce. Another holds that bonuses reflect shared returns to investments in firm-specific skills and know-how.

Profit-related pay

These are schemes in which employees are allocated a payment equivalent to an agreed proportion of the organization's profits. Profit-related pay has been encouraged in the UK through tax incentives for schemes registered with the Inland Revenue.

Option schemes

Executive share option schemes are particularly prevalent in the USA but have also become common elsewhere. They allow senior managers to benefit from the continued success of the organization through the purchase of shares at designated dates in the future at a fixed price. The more successful the company, and therefore the greater the likely increase in share value, the higher the reward to the executive. This is seen as an important incentive to motivate people who can dramatically affect the prosperity and even survival of the business.

HRM in reality	**Shareholders to vote on directors' pay**

Trade and Industry Secretary Patricia Hewitt today announced that shareholders will be given the right to an annual vote on directors' pay – a move that may strengthen links between pay and performance in the boardroom. The new legislation is intended to:

- ensure greater transparency
- improve accountability
- strengthen links between performance and pay.

Patricia Hewitt said:

> Our companies have to be able to attract and retain the best executives in the world and we support top-class pay for top performances. But all too often directors are lavishly rewarded for lacklustre or even poor performances. We share the view of many shareholders that this is simply unacceptable and goes against the interests of the company, its shareholders and the UK as a whole. That is why I am taking action to strengthen the corporate governance framework for boardroom pay. Today's measures will require quoted companies to hold annual shareholder votes on directors' pay and further build on the proposals outlined earlier this year aimed at improving accountability and transparency of directors' remuneration.

Quoted companies will be required to:

- Publish a report on directors' remuneration as part of the company's annual reporting cycle.
- Disclose within the report details of individual directors' remuneration packages, the role of the board's remuneration committee, and the board's remuneration policy, as well as specific requirements relating to the disclosure of information on performance.
- Put an annual resolution to shareholders on the remuneration report.

The government will introduce secondary legislation to implement these new requirements in the coming parliamentary session. The DTI will publish a consultation document before Christmas inviting comments on the draft regulations.

Source: *HRMGuide.co.uk* (http://www.hrmguide.co.uk), 19 October 2001.

Employee share option schemes apply to less senior staff and tend to be considerably less generous than executive schemes. Generally, a sum is allocated from company profits and used for share purchase for employees. There may also be save as you earn (SAYE) option schemes registered with the taxation authorities. These allow staff to save a proportion of their salary via the pay administration process and have it accumulated for a fixed period. This may be paid to them at the end of that time, with a bonus equivalent to the interest that could have been earned in a savings account. Alternatively, and more beneficially, the sum plus bonus can be used to purchase shares at the price prevailing at the start of the scheme. Preferential tax arrangements have been made for shares held in trust for a fixed period.

<table>
<tr><td>

HRM in reality

</td><td>

Stock options have arrived in Canada

Stock options are becoming an important recruitment and retention tool for top talent in Canada. They benefit employees but also help companies grow – businesses with stock option plans are expected to expand as much as 11 per cent faster than those without, according to *Assessing The Options: Stock Option Plans in Canada*, a new report by The Conference Board of Canada. The report also shows that smaller organizations concentrated in technology or other high-skill industries have the most aggressive stock option plans.

But stock option plans do not come without problems:

- When employees exercise their options to sell the result can be a lowering of a company's earnings per share index.
- As some dot-com employees have discovered, stock options can become almost worthless when a company's share price declines.
- There may be a weak link to employee performance if the company's share value is growing but the company is doing poorly when compared to its competitors.

'In an increasingly tight labour market, compensation is a critical lever for organizations as they strive to attract, retain and motivate talented employees,' said Prem Benimadhu, vice-president with the Conference Board. 'In an attempt to recruit and retain top talent, employers are now offering stock options to employees at all levels within the organization. And this is just the beginning.'

Source: *HRM Guide Canada* (http://www.hrmguide.net/canada/), 28 February 2001.

</td></tr>
</table>

Activity 19:5

What are the practical consequences of using employee stock options as a motivator?

<table>
<tr><td>

HRM in reality

</td><td>

Executive PayWatch upgraded

The AFL-CIO's Executive PayWatch website (http://www.paywatch.org) is being upgraded to include almost 50 new 'e-tools' for shareholders to campaign against excessive boardroom pay.

PayWatch makes the point that (despite recent major falls in stock prices) the average CEO collected a record US$20 million in 2000 – including almost 50 per cent more in stock options plus 22 per cent more in salary and bonuses than the previous year. Contrast that with the 3 per cent raise for a typical hourly worker last year. In 1999, CEOs were paid 476 times the earnings of the average blue-collar American worker compared with 85 times more in 1990 and 42 times in 1980.

PayWatch also lets visitors compare their pay to that received by their own CEO. It tells you how many years it would take you to earn what your CEO receives. For example, according to PayWatch, a telephone line repair person would need to work 1891 years to equal Sprint chairman and CEO William Esrey's year 2000 rewards – equivalent to repairing 6.9 million working phones. He received US$69.3 million in total compensation and stock options in 2000, together with US$64.1 million in stock option exercises from prior grants. And Bank of America's Hugh McColl

</td></tr>
</table>

▶

grabbed a total of US$95.6 million over the last five years, during which Bank of America's stock return underperformed the S&P Index by 34 per cent!

Opinion research by Peter Hart Research Associates in 2001 indicates that 78 per cent of the US public feel that it is important for everyone – and not just CEOs – to have a fair share in a growing economy. Respondents rated this as one of the top three economy-related goals that were seen as important for the future.

You can also find out if your mutual fund has invested in companies that are among those that waste most money on excessive CEO pay. The site provides summaries of CEO rewards in some 1600 companies. You can e-mail individual company board members to demand CEO pay reform, use the internet to blast executives with ill-gotten stock options, or e-mail 'dead beat directors' who received subsidized loans.

'People are sickened by watching this bear market eat up their life savings while CEOs still make out with the big bucks,' said AFL-CIO secretary-treasurer Richard Trumka. 'That's why we're giving working people the e-tools they need to take action and organize against outrageous CEO pay packages which lower the value of everyone's stock.'

Source: *HRM Guide USA* (http://www.hrmguide.net/usa/), 5 April 2001.

Flavour of the (last) month?

Kanter (1989, p.233) observes that whenever any US organization comes up with a 'new' pay scheme a merit element is involved. PRP has also been a prominent feature of the attempt to commercialize practices in the public services, intended as a key factor in encouraging business-like behaviour among managers.

The earliest use of PRP in the British civil service dates back to an experiment in 1985 affecting a range of senior grades (principal to under-secretary). The scheme involved payment of a minimum £500 unconsolidated bonus paid as a one-off lump sum to no more than a fifth of eligible staff. The exercise drew a range of comments but it was decided to extend the scheme to most other grades including non-management staff. Ironically, the Review Body on Top Salaries which covered judges, permanent secretaries, senior military officers and diplomats, felt that PRP was unsuitable for politically sensitive posts.

Performance-related pay was introduced for the 800 National Health Service general managers in 1986 based on annual objectives, individual performance reviews and financial rewards where the achievement of objectives could be clearly demonstrated (Murliss, 1987). For general managers, the process relied on an appraisal procedure called the 'individual performance review' (IPR). The system had the following characteristics:

● The method was objectives-based, stated wherever possible in quantifiable terms.

● Appraisals were conducted on the 'parent–grandparent' system. Unit general managers would be assessed by the district general manager, with the chair of the regional health authority acting as 'grandparent'.

● Managers were rated on one of five bands. 'Grandparents' had final responsibility and were required to ensure that no more than 20 per cent received the highest rating level and 40 per cent the next.

● An individual at the highest level 'consistently exceeds short-term levels of performance and makes excellent progress towards long-term goals' justifying a salary increase of 3–4 per cent a year, up to a maximum of 20 per cent over five years.

● At the lowest level, an individual 'meets few short-term objectives and makes little or no progress towards long-term goals' receiving no increase at all.

PRP has also been a major feature of the managerial transformation of former state-owned industries that have been privatized. Thames Water was privatized in 1989 but began preparing for the process three or four years earlier. Introduction of pay schemes based on performance rather than national wage bargaining started in 1988. By 1992 PRP had been extended to 50 per cent of Thames Water staff. Performance-related pay was seen as one element in the process of culture change, the other features being introduction of a management development scheme, recruiting people from outside the organization and improving internal communication.

If you kept your nose clean, and did not get noticed, you did well. Now we are encouraging people to use their initiative, to push out boundaries, to do more than they are asked to increase productivity. The trick is to reward those who perform above average and to be seen to be doing so. (Richard Marshall, group personnel director, quoted in the *Independent on Sunday*, 15 November 1992)

London Electricity, a privatized utility company, started PRP with senior management then applied it to industrial grades including meter readers and joiners. Meter readers were paid for the number of readings they achieved. Those who achieved the best performance did so by working outside normal hours in order to find customers at home.

Criticisms of PRP

There is a widespread opinion among senior managers that PRP must be a good thing – but the evidence for its effectiveness is not overwhelming. Indeed, the search for a positive relationship between PRP and good performance has been described as being like 'looking for the Holy Grail' (Fletcher and Williams, 1992). As one variable in a complex situation, it is not surprising that a connection cannot be proven.

There may be evidence that people who are rewarded well by PRP are duly motivated, but they are a minority and the effect is outweighed by the demotivation of the majority (Marsden, French and Kobi, 2000). The main criticisms in the literature are highlighted in the following sub-sections.

Fairness

The concept of 'fairness' is problematic and open to interpretation, with some people seeing pay as a measure of justice (Milcovich, Newman and Milcovich, 2001, p.2). Some employers have gone to elaborate lengths in an attempt to make their system appear fair. This may involve sampling the work of lower-level workers, listening in on phone calls, examining files or checking through a proportion of completed work. The Bank of America has been cited as spending over a million dollars a year and employing 20 people to monitor 3500 credit card workers for their merit scheme. Not surprisingly, such attempts at 'fairness' have not been entirely popular among employees. The system seems to be distinctly Orwellian: 'big brother is watching you.'

Managerial judgement

The process is dependent on skilled line managers. As we have observed, for various reasons managers feel under pressure to rate their staff as above average. As Kanter (1989) says, 'far from freeing the energies of employees to seek ways to improve their performance, subjectively based merit pay systems throw them back on the merit of their bosses.' Typically such systems are cynically regarded by employees and attacked by unions as being open to abuse and favouritism. They can also result in a rash of high marks by supervisors who feel exposed to the wrath of their employees. Relationships between managers and employees are often uncomfortable, and this process tends to charge that relationship with even more emotion. But line or middle managers are often obliged to implement performance-related systems that they personally do not believe in (Harris, 2000).

Value of reward

Many senior managers seem more concerned with managing the pay bill than motivating staff, so that PRP is often budget-led, not performance-led. A frequent complaint is that the merit element is too small as a percentage of the whole – commonly from 3 to 10 per cent. This is not enough to be a motivator for improved performance. The solution is obvious at one level: increase the merit element to a significantly motivating level such as 15–25 per cent. But this only serves to highlight the difficulty in making a judgement on who gets an increase and being seen to be fair about it (Isaac, 2001). Most employers have not felt confident enough about the process to go beyond a token percentage level.

Relationship with company performance

Fletcher and Williams could find no correlation between company performance and PRP. PRP schemes were used by both high and low performance businesses.

A demotivator

PRP benefits 20 per cent of employees at the expense of 80 per cent. Consequently it demotivates far more people than it encourages.

PRP and flexibility

PRP increases the likelihood of flexibility and management power. Not surprisingly, PRP has attracted hostility from many unions as collective bargaining is side-stepped. Intriguingly, however, PRP schemes have largely been focused on core (in other words, relatively permanent, well-paid, non-manual) staff, rather than peripheral (often lower-paid and lesser-skilled) workers (Kessler, 1995, p.469).

Conflict with the team philosophy

The obsession with individually based performance pay conflicts with HRM's emphasis on teams.

Employee dissatisfaction was highlighted in an internal review of a performance assessment and payment system covering 68 000 Inland Revenue employees (*Independent*, 5 April 1994). The inquiry surveyed 800 staff and found considerable dissatisfaction, concluding that the performance system was acting as a demotivator for most staff. As well as the familiar complaint that merit payments were too low to provide any incentive, a number of further criticisms of the operation of the system were listed:

- Upward movement of targets: employees found themselves on a treadmill that was continually being speeded up – the goalposts were being moved.
- Employees were being assessed by managers who did not know them.
- Performance pay for junior employees was restricted by 'budgetary constraints' but this limitation did not seem to apply to senior officials.
- Objectives were often imposed rather than negotiated.
- Subjective criteria led to disagreements on the quality of performance, leading to a perception of unfairness.
- Individual targets were not compatible with team performance.

Similarly Kellough and Nigro (2002) investigated GeorgiaGain, a compensation system developed for the state of Georgia (USA). Performance-related pay was the centrepiece of the initiative which was intended to include a state-of-the-art performance management system, providing performance measurement and evaluation procedures trusted by supervisors and subordinates. But Kellough and Nigro's survey of state employees found them highly critical of the reform and complaining that it had not produced the intended outcomes in most areas.

The reduction of the inflation rate to low single figures has further reduced the perceived effectiveness of incentives. Merit payments of 2–3 per cent are not seen as much reward for exceptional performance. Indeed such payments may be viewed as insulting. Performance systems established in a high inflation period have proven to be a financial embarrassment to some companies. British Telecom scrapped a system for junior and middle managers on the grounds that managers were being overpaid in comparison with equivalents in other firms. Consolidated performance pay was restricted to the top 10 per cent in 1994, with one-off bonuses being paid to most.

| Activity 19:6 | How large does a merit payment or bonus have to be in order to provide an incentive for effective performance? |

| HRM in reality | **Are the fat cats getting obese?** |

The rules just aren't the same in that fat cat paradise in the boardroom.

Inflation-linked pay increases (plus a little bit – maybe) might be the norm for 'ordinary' employees, and the government claims that they cannot afford to link state pensions to average workers' pay. Contrast this with rewards for the hardworking directors of the largest companies in the UK.

The latest survey from the New Bridge Street remuneration consultancy shows that the chief executives of the UK's top 100 quoted companies rocketed by 20.4 per cent in the last year. Pensioners and students please note that these guys (not many women around at that level) have to struggle to survive on an average of just £717 000 – just over a million US dollars. In fact the rise in base salary (13.9 per cent) was a little more modest, giving them an average of £486 000. The rest was made up of bonuses but does *not* include pensions and share option schemes.

Looking at the FT-250 companies – bringing in some smaller quoted businesses – the total cash earnings of chief executives grew by a whopping 23.3 per cent (third quarter comparisons between 1999 and 2000). Their average cash earnings reached £488 000. The stock phrase in company reports is that 'our people are our greatest asset'. Clearly there are people and people. If commitment and trust are major goals of people management, why should those at the top be rewarded by pay systems or performance criteria that are any different from those applied to other employees?

One argument is that top executives need to be motivated by pay packages that will get the best from them. But doesn't this argument apply to everyone else? Another view is that they are so special that they need 'golden handcuffs' to stay with their existing companies – otherwise they would be snapped up by 'world-class' businesses. Can we really argue that boardroom inhabitants are so special? Bizarrely, the businesses that rewarded their chief executives most generously were in the general retailing sector where many famous name companies have done badly. Their total cash earnings averaged £616 000 – a rise of 37.3 per cent.

In fact, the mechanism for rewarding top managers has little to do with performance. Pay is typically benchmarked against the highest remuneration or thereabouts in an industry sector (certainly never less than the average). When one person's pay goes up it feeds into the average – ultimately boosting everyone else's rewards. And round the circle goes, spiralling ever upwards. The only stakeholders with the power to do anything about it are the shareholders. Ironically these are often pension funds. And they are notorious for their 'hands-off' approach.

In HR terms, this is bad-value resourcing.

Source: *HRMGuide.co.uk* (http://www.hrmguide.co.uk), 11 November 2000.

Summary

Pay is a key element in the management of people. The importance of pay begins with pay administration that deals accurately and swiftly with payroll-related matters. Much of the information used by pay administrators is shared with the human resource function. Pay evaluation systems also impinge on human resource territory. Free market organizations are particularly concerned with performance-related pay as a motivating factor but this trend appears to be ideological rather than rational since practical PRP schemes that deliver the results intended are extremely difficult to construct. Current evidence shows that performance pay is likely to demotivate more people than it motivates.

Further reading

Ian Kessler's contribution on 'Reward system choices', in J. Storey (ed.) *Human Resource Management: A Critical Text*, 2nd edition (published by Thomson Learning, 2001) provides an in-depth theoretical analysis of recent research and practice. *The Compensation Handbook* edited by Lance A. Berger and Dorothy R. Berger (published by McGraw-Hill, 1999) is a compendium of articles on compensation strategy and design. *Compensation* by George T. Milkovich, Jerry M. Newman and Carolyn Milkovich, 7th edition (published by McGraw-Hill, 2001) includes exercises and in-depth discussion. *Work and Pay in Japan* by Robert A. Hart and Seiichi Kawasaki (published by Cambridge University Press, 1999) provides detailed information on an atypical reward system.

Review questions

1 Is it appropriate to merge the HR function with a payroll department?
2 Does job evaluation have a function in a modern pay system?
3 'A fair day's work for a fair day's pay'. How can a company's pay system be designed to meet this criterion?
4 Outline the arguments for and against the use of performance-related pay.
5 Should executive directors be paid on a different basis from other employees?

Problem for discussion and analysis

Fairness

Scenario 1

A photocopying shop has one employee who has worked in the shop for six months and earns US$9 per hour. Business continues to be satisfactory, but a factory in the area has closed and unemployment has increased. Other small firms have now hired reliable workers working at US$7 an hour to perform jobs similar to those done by the photocopy shop employee. The owner of the photocopying shop reduces the employee's wage to US$7.

Is it fair to cut the worker's wage from US$9 to US$7 an hour? Compare your decision with the second scenario.

Scenario 2

A house painter employs two assistants and pays them US$9 per hour. The painter decides to change his business and go into lawn-mowing, where the going wage is lower. He tells the current workers that he will keep them on if they want to work, but will only pay them US$7 per hour.

Is this employer being fair?

PART 8

Learning and development

This part examines human resource development (HRD) at a number of levels. If people are truly 'our greatest asset' and are the key to 'competitive advantage' we must have mechanisms in place to enhance their capabilities and provide opportunities for learning and development.

The chapters in Part 8 encompass a number of key issues such as:

- What is human resource development?
- How and why does vocational learning vary between different countries?
- What is the role of self-development?
- What are the major differences between training and learning?
- Is the 'learning organization' a meaningful concept?
- Do trainers have a role in the context of strategic HRD?
- Is online learning useful and cost-effective?
- How can we evaluate learning experiences?

20 | Human resource development

Objectives

The purpose of this chapter is to:

- Outline the concept of human resource development.
- Investigate and evaluate HRD initiatives at national level.
- Debate the need for distinctive management and gender-focused HRD programmes.
- Introduce the concept of mentoring.

HRD strategies

HRD at the national level

The meritocratic ideal

Education and training

Vocational education and training

Development programmes

Management development

Developing women

Mentoring

Summary

Further reading

Review questions

Problem for discussion and analysis

HRD strategies

Business page pundits argue that industrialized states must move away from low technology products with poor margins which can be produced more cheaply in low-wage countries. Similarly, developing countries aiming to join the ranks of the advanced nations must acquire a capacity for producing sophisticated products and services. High technology products require long-term research, expensive and sophisticated production equipment and precise quality procedures. Above all, they require skilled human resources capable of performing effectively in this environment.

At the organizational level, enterprises need people with appropriate skills, abilities and experience. These qualities can be bought from outside the organization through recruitment, consultancy and subcontracting, or grown by training and developing existing employees. This chapter focuses on the second approach. The strategic choice between buying and growing is made on the basis of cost-effectiveness, urgency of requirement and the need to motivate staff.

Political, cultural and historical elements also influence the decision. Organizations with an internal job market orientation, for example most large German and Japanese companies, have made a practice of growing their own talent.

Key concept 20:1

Human resource development   Human resource development (HRD) is a strategic approach to investing in human capital. It draws on other human resource processes, including resourcing and performance assessment, to identify actual and potential talent. HRD provides a framework for self-development, training programmes and career progression to meet an organization's future skill requirements.

Throughout this book we have distinguished HRM from previous models of people management by its emphasis on the integration of an organization's people policies and activities. Investment in employee skills to support the needs of advanced technology is a prime example of this approach. Financially obsessed managers in free market countries have preferred cost-cutting to investment in people or new technology. Moreover, there has been a chronic failure to understand the link between the two: investment in new equipment has been viewed as worthwhile only if it leads to a cut in employee costs. Managers in Australia and the UK, for example, have been wedded to a penny-pinching mentality, avoiding the kind of high technology that requires expensive, skilled workers. Their counterparts in Singapore and Korea have invested more readily in new machine tools in order to increase output and profitability, frequently taking on extra staff to meet demand.

The following list (adapted from Thomson and Mabey, 1994, p.7) highlights the principal elements of human resource development:

- Effective resourcing, induction and deployment of high-quality people.
- Identification and improvement of skills and motivation among existing and longer serving employees.
- Regular job analysis in relation to organizational objectives and individual skills.
- Reviewing the use of technology, in particular in replacing routine tasks.
- Performance management and assessment through identification of key tasks.
- A focus on skills and general abilities rather than paper qualifications.
- Training needs identification.

- Provision of training programmes to improve current performance and support career development.
- Provision of opportunities for personal growth and self-development.
- Helping people to manage their own careers.
- Encouraging the acceptance of change as normal and an opportunity.

Systematic human resource development (see Key concept 20.1) maximizes the human capital of an organization, devoting time, money and thought to improving the pool of essential competencies among its staff. It has a general impact on business performance by enhancing product knowledge and service expertise. HRD emphasizes people as people rather than numbers, and it motivates staff, drawing on their talents and demonstrating that they are valued by the organization. It is also claimed to empower staff, allowing individuals to take a measure of control over their own careers and develop life patterns that offer increased opportunity and satisfaction.

How 'real' is HRD? Gibb (2002, p.138) takes the view that:

> The idea of HRD promises a great deal, and is seductive; but whether there is evidence of organizational examples of this being delivered is questionable. Indeed the 'rhetoric' involved is arguably being used to cover changes which are far removed from the espoused aims; instead of better valuing the human resource, such re-inventions can mask the greater exploitation of people.

According to Sambrook (2001) HRD has its roots in the early organization development interventions of the 1940s, but the term was first used by Nadler in 1972. Nadler (cited in Nadler and Nadler, 1989, p.4) described HRD as 'organized learning experiences provided by employers, within a specified period of time, to bring about the possibility of performance improvement and/or personal growth.'

What is the relationship between HRD and training? The two terms are sometimes used to mean the same. However, Goss (1994, p.62) observes that they are regarded often as mutually exclusive activities. He attributes this to the hierarchical nature of most organizations in which training is something done to lower-level workers, whereas development is a process experienced by managers – hence 'management development'. As Goss rightly points out, this approach is incompatible with the central principles of HRM, which hold that all employees are assets whose competencies need to be developed. According to Hendry (1995, p.366): 'Increasingly, we are getting away from the divisive notion that managers are "developed" while the shopfloor are merely "trained". The principles of adult learning apply to each.'

It is appropriate, therefore, to regard training as an integral aspect of HRD. Gibb (2002, p.7) argues that:

> ... past definitions of education, training and development, with their essentially sequential divisions of learning, are no longer useful or acceptable. They would be deemed to draw the boundaries around the subject, in theory and practice, too narrowly, and also inaccurately; they would not capture and deal with the practice and theory of contemporary work and organizations.

Sambrook (2001) argues that HRD can be thought of as a construct, like 'love' or 'quality'. It is intangible in itself since it cannot be found, touched or seen but it may be investigated through features associated with the concept that might distinguish it from training and development. She argues that training and development was focused on operational issues and took a short-term or reactive approach in which specialists 'did training', delivered it to passive trainees and usually conducted it in classrooms.

Sambrook describes this as the 'tell' approach as opposed to 'sell' or 'competent' HRD. Competent HRD focuses on competencies and takes a wider approach, encompassing self-development, employee development, management development and organization development. Probably delivered by facilitators, there is two-way communication and some consultation together with far more diverse training methods. There is an attempt to link HRD to other HR processes and take a wider organizational perspective. Finally, Sambrook identifies strategic HRD or 'gel'. Here the HRD function and the organization are strategically and totally interlinked and there is an emphasis on learning. Individuals are encouraged to take responsibility, to share learning and to be participative and collaborative.

Gibb (2002) prefers the term 'learning and development', considering that it addresses a combination of cognitive capacities, capabilities and behaviours that have to be established or changed in the process. He employs 'cognitive capacities' as a more comprehensive concept than 'knowledge', stating that (Gibb, 2002, p.8):

> ... accumulating 'knowledge' is just one specific kind of cognitive capacity, and it is indeed only the most basic kind. It cannot be treated as being synonymous with what [learning and development] work involves, where a whole set of cognitive capacities are significant and relevant if people are to be 'thoughtful performers'. The brain is capable of far more than memorizing knowledge, and performance at work involves aspects of cognition other than the use of memorized knowledge.

Similarly, Gibb wraps the older concepts of skill and competence within the term 'capabilities', arguing that 'skill' has too many connotations of physical performance and also that 'competence' is increasingly questioned as a valid and useful concept. His third dimension, behaviours, is favoured over abilities since it draws in the influence of emotions, attitudes and values that mediate actual performance.

Activity 20:1	What are the limitations of the following concepts in describing learning in the workplace: training, education, human resource development, 'knowledge, skills and abilities'?

HRD at the national level

Education plays a key role in causing and, potentially, curing institutionalized discrimination in advanced countries. As early as the 19th century, the sociologist Weber held that people should be promoted solely on the basis of relevant qualifications. He proposed this condition in order to overcome the nepotism and patronage that prevailed in the public and private sectors at that time. Since then qualifications have become significant, if not essential, requirements for a successful career.

The importance of education for personal advancement is best illustrated in France, where a clear and simple equation traditionally existed between management success and intellect. Intellect was taken to be the possession of the right qualifications from the right educational institutions. In France, not only was admission to one's first job dependent on educational attainment but attendance at a *grande école* eased (and still eases) the path right to the top. According to *The Times* (16 January 1992):

> *L'Expansion* surveyed how the French business community viewed graduates of every one of the top *grandes écoles*. Among the shortcomings cited, graduates of Polytechnique were considered to be too elitist, those of Centrale unimaginative, those of HEC over-ambitious and those of l'ENA too theoretical. This educational type-casting tendency is reinforced by a fairly rigid pecking order in salaries. The market value of new graduates is closely tied to the intellectual reputation of their alma mater.

The right qualification admitted a recruit to a much higher entry level than would otherwise be the case. Thereafter, *grandes écoles* diplomas did not compensate for lack of effort but they made promotion considerably easier (Barsoux and Lawrence, 1990, p.58). As an employee rose in the organization, technical ability became less important than 'social' skills required to delegate, resolve conflicts and motivate staff. At the higher levels (Barsoux and Lawrence, 1990, p.58):

> ... the effects of attending the 'right' school comes to fruition, as some individuals move from line jobs into positions of power that put a premium on such qualities as distinguished appearance, good manners, tact and good taste. Emphasis on social competence tends to favour the products of the *grandes écoles* who possess the necessary self-confidence and social wherewithal. So while companies ostensibly drop educational credentials as a means of selection, they replace them with credentials which elevate members of the same population.

Whereas in some countries – Germany, for example – training was seen as the key to effective performance, the French were inclined to view intellectual quality as the most important factor. Accordingly, French education was highly selective, emphasizing the production of 'high-fliers' who would be given early responsibility in their business careers. They produced managers with an analytical perspective in which every business issue was seen as an intellectual problem as shown in Table 20.1. People rejected by this process had poor prospects compared with the USA, for instance, where – in theory – anyone could get to the top.

Barsoux and Lawrence observe that the French have identified a class of top business people: *cadres*. The word '*cadre*' may be translated as 'executive' but has a meaning beyond 'manager', entailing considerable prestige and an apparent homogeneity of lifestyle and attitudes. *Cadres* are distinguished from other employees They are targeted by advertisers who regard them as high-spending consumers with taste and style. *Cadres* lie at the centre of an intellectual pecking order with the principal success route being via school physics and engineering, through the *grandes écoles* and then into the major industries. As a consequence, industry is dominated by technologists. Second-ranking students could take Business Studies, Finance or Behavioural Sciences at universities and other less-prestigious educational establishments, proceeding to lower-status sectors such as retailing.

But there are *cadres* ... and *cadres*. As business schools developed and higher education extended in France, junior executive and middle management jobs were increasingly filled by non-*grandes écoles* graduates – and women. This was balanced by the growth in such jobs, now comprising around 15 per cent of the French workforce. Reflecting these status differentiations, traditional French organizations have been divided into rigidly defined social levels (Poirson, 1993):

1 Senior executives (*cadres supérieurs*).
2 Junior and middle management (*cadres*).

Table 20.1	*Grandes écoles* education and management skills	
Strengths	*Weaknesses*
Strong capacity for formulating problems	Interpersonal communication
Marked aptitude for reasoning through data given in figures	Capacity for managing people
Good capacity for planning	Capacity for implementing strategy

Sources: After Barsoux and Lawrence (1990) and Poirson (1993).

3 ETAM – administrative, technical and supervisory staff (baccalaureate plus two years technical studies).

4 Workers (non-baccalaureate).

Potentially, French education offers a route to the top on grounds of merit. In practice, there is a strong bias towards the children of existing *cadres* and government employees who understand the system and its requirements.

In this respect, it is not unlike the British educational system. A survey reported in *The Economist* (19 December 1992) found that two-thirds of top jobs surveyed were occupied by 'public school' men, with over 50 per cent having graduated at Oxford or Cambridge Universities. Without going into a detailed historical explanation it should be pointed out that British public schools are actually fee-paying institutions outside the state system. Of the others, 27 per cent came from the most prestigious institutions such as top Scottish universities, leaving only 11 per cent without higher education.

Similarly, Conlon and Chevalier (2002) found that:

> For individuals graduating in 1985 and 1990 (interviewed in 1996), there was a 46 percentage point difference in average returns between graduates from the best and worst institutions. The range of estimates decreased by approximately 10 percentage points for individuals graduating in 1995 (interviewed in 1998). For the 1985 and 1990 cohorts, Oxbridge graduates achieved a 7.9 percent earnings premium over graduates from 'old' universities, while those attending polytechnics suffered a 3.8 percent wage penalty compared to those attending 'old' universities. For the 1995 cohort, degree holders from former polytechnics suffered a 7.7 percent earnings penalty compared to degree holders from 'old' universities.

This represents virtually no change over the last two decades. We can attribute this partly to clone-seeking selection and promotion procedures. For example, major companies tend to visit the same narrow range of universities for annual recruitment and headhunters tend to assume their clients have conservative requirements.

Education fails to deliver true meritocracy for a number of reasons, for example:

- Life chances are not taken into account. People from privileged backgrounds have a greater opportunity to achieve acceptable qualifications. They have parents who understand the system and, if necessary, can purchase private education. It is infinitely easier for a student with affluent, supportive parents to obtain good grades than it is for those having to work to support themselves and, perhaps, children or relatives.

- Second chances are discouraged or have reduced effectiveness. Educators, particularly university academics, have achieved their status by passing exams and acquiring degrees. Their personal status and function is legitimized by the belief that clearing these hurdles is indicative of underlying intellect and personal worth. They offer limited sympathy and understanding for people who fail examinations at any stage – unless there are overt causes such as illness. In fact, failure can occur because of a whole range of non-intellectual reasons: domestic, financial or motivational. The critical timespan for education leading to paper qualifications (14–21) coincides with the transition from childhood to adult life – a traumatic maturational period for many. However, people who attempt to recover the situation at a later (more stable) age find the way littered with innumerable obstacles.

- Snobbery and class: regardless of the consequences of social circumstances and maturational crises, as we have seen possession of a 'good' degree from a 'good' university is viewed generally as evidence of intrinsic virtue, allowing entry to a range of powerful in-groups. However, in-groups have an unpleasant side to them: prejudice against outsiders. For example, the development of mass higher education in the UK has produced a great deal of snobbish disquiet in certain circles. Worse, a number of major employers now confine their recruitment to a restricted number of older universities where they can continue to find really worthy candidates – people just like themselves. In line with our discussion in previous chapters, this is a low-risk selection strategy from the employer's perspective.

The meritocratic ideal

People in developed – and many developing – countries no longer 'know their place' in society. Those who have a vested interest in preserving plum jobs for a select elite are facing overwhelming opposition from a generation whose career aspirations and expectation of equitable treatment by employers would have been unthinkable a few decades ago. However, there is some way to go before a universal meritocracy prevails (see Key concept 20.2).

> **Key concept 20:2**
>
> **Meritocracy**   Meritocratic procedures aim to make judgements on the basis of evidence of competence such as examination results or the achievement of targets. We have noted already that educational achievement is not simply a matter of merit. Evidence of merit is invariably contaminated by social factors and life chances.
>
> A meritocratic but socially fair system should:
>
> - Take aggregate outcomes into account. In other words, if the process does not produce a balanced proportion of gender, ethnic origin and so on, then it is unfair.
> - Take life chances into account.
> - Require organizations to institutionalize the representation of specific groups within their key decision processes – including selection and promotion.

> **HRM in reality**
>
> **What's in a name?**
>
> 'The City was long a preserve in which what mattered was not *what* you knew but *who* you'd been to school with. Big Bang was supposed to have changed all that and much was made at the time of the new, thrusting, yuppie meritocracy that would leave the old buffers swinging from lampposts by their old school ties.
>
> 'All bullshit, of course, this being Britain. Here is Grand Old Buffer Lord Rothschild (RIP) talking to Bernard Levin about his City career: "Rothschild's bank invited me to go in there. That was very lucky for me indeed." This was enough to wake even Mr Levin. "You say Rothschild's bank invited you as though you were called Smith," said he, incredulously, "but you are called Rothschild after all. It's not all that surprising is it?"
>
> '"Aahm", harrumphed the GOB in his best pompous ass voice, "I think in the modern world less attention is paid to the name Rothschild, whether it's in a bank or anywhere else, and I think that's as it should be. So I went in and I was a stranger there – I didn't understand the language at all – and there came a moment when they said to me, 'We'd like you to be chairman.' And so I said 'OK'." No wonder the Japanese are astonished by the City.'
>
> Source: John Naughton, 'No gnus is bad gnus', *The Observer*, 30 August 1992.

Activity 20:2 Is a truly meritocratic society an impossible ideal? Does it matter in the workplace?

Education and training

In Chapter 5 we introduced the idea of human capital – investing in people as national or organizational assets. Human capital development in the form of education and skills training can be an effective response to constraints imposed on the employment market. Specific skills may be in short supply – even during periods of considerable unemployment – and technological developments outdate some skills and require entirely different competencies.

There is a considerable variation between education and training levels in different countries. For example, technology and production have long been regarded as high-status activities in Germany. Success in these areas demands a high level of technical training among the workforce. As a consequence, German businesses place a higher value on technical merit than, say, those in the UK. Ironically, training systems in the two countries are similar, depending on a mixture of academic education and vocational courses, unlike France, Japan and the USA where there is a greater concentration on full-time education. Significantly, however, there was a markedly greater commitment to training in Germany with levels of participation and achievement that had no comparison in the UK.

Whereas the British apprentice system had been more or less dismantled by the 1980s, it remained intact in Germany. Some 50 per cent of German school-leavers (compared with a mere 17 per cent in the UK) participated in apprenticeship schemes covering over 300 occupations. The consequences are evident. Throughout the 1980s British industry was subjected to a withering series of criticisms. A good illustration is a comparison of UK and German kitchen and metal plants, which showed that in the UK (Steedman and Wagner, 1987) less modern technology was in use; there were frequent breakdowns; long repair times; and there was a low level of technical competence.

German companies had a staggering 60 per cent higher rate of productivity. Underlying this was a dramatic contrast in levels of participation in training and managerial expectation. In Germany, 90 per cent of employees had completed a minimum of three years' craft training; in the UK the equivalent figure was only 10 per cent. Even more worrying was the fact that British managers surveyed seemed unconcerned. Supported by their higher technical skills, it was scarcely surprising that German companies dominated the high-value, quality end of the market while British companies concentrated on cheaper, low-profit products.

HRM in reality

Apprenticeships and training need federal funding support

The ACTU is calling on federal and state governments to resolve differences on growth funding for vocational training and the future of the ANTA (Australian National Training Authority) agreement.

'The federal and state governments should jointly fund the growth in vocational training across Australia. The continued successful introduction of a range of new training opportunities over the last decade will be put at risk if sufficient funds are not made available to cater for the growth in demand for apprenticeships and traineeships,' said ACTU assistant secretary Bill Mansfield.

According to Mr Mansfield, in New South Wales alone in 1999 the number of apprenticeships and traineeships grew by 50 per cent. These increases are likely to continue but States will not be able to meet demand without federal funding. The federal government is a key player in the VET system, it is promoting higher levels of growth and it must accept a greater part of the financial burden which results. The ACTU agrees with the Director-General of Education and Training in NSW Dr Ken Boston when he said in a recent (5 March 2001) speech:

> The Commonwealth offer of A$20 million growth funding in year one, rising by A$5 million per annum in years two and three won't make a dent in the rising training demand. In NSW alone, the present state of growth requires A$50 million per year. Nationally, based on ANTA projections, Australia could require up to A$150 million each year. The Commonwealth is prepared to contribute A$20 million rising up to A$30 million, to be divided between six states and two territories. Meanwhile, when it comes to recurrent VET funding, states and territories contribute four dollars for every Commonwealth dollar. Of the A$3.6 billion in recurrent VET funding that Australia spends, the Commonwealth contributes A$746 million. The states have not received any growth funding for the last three years, and have funded additional demand from greater efficiencies. For NSW, this is the equivalent of an extra A$91 million of investment without a commensurate Commonwealth contribution.

> Mr Mansfield continued: 'The ACTU is calling on the federal government to increase its support for growth in traineeships and apprenticeships by at least A$150 million over the next three years. This issue deserves attention from the highest level of government. The Prime Minister should immediately give Minister David Kemp authority to make a realistic proposal to the states for the federal funds necessary to help meet future demand for apprenticeships and traineeships.'

Source: *HRM Guide Australia* (http://www.hrmguide.net/australia/), 19 March 2001.

Similar criticisms could still be levelled against British industry in the 1990s. According to Stevens and Walsh (1991, p.25):

> It has been argued that a significant fraction of the British labour force is in danger of becoming trapped in a low-skills, low-quality equilibrium with low initial education and poor skills leading to low productivity and a predominantly low-quality market orientation of the companies they work for. Dependency upon low-cost competitive strategies in much of British industry undermines the demand for higher skills.

Differences varied between industrial sectors, some being considerably better than others. In 1994 a National Institute of Economic and Social Research survey evaluated high-level skills in the engineering and chemical industries in Britain and Germany and the resulting effect on industrial competitiveness. Researchers identified a relationship between the much greater employment of technically proficient postgraduates in German engineering firms and the superior levels of innovation in products and processes. British engineering firms were dismissed as technical 'followers', content with their products and blind to the value of research and development. In contrast, UK chemical companies employed a similar level of PhD graduates to their German counterparts, providing a 'virtuous circle' of high-quality postgraduates and employer demand.

In 1996 a skills audit completed as part of a competitiveness White Paper commissioned by the then Deputy Prime Minister, Michael Heseltine, showed that British standards of education and vocational training had still not improved (*The Guardian*, 14 June 1996). The White Paper, optimistically titled *Creating the Enterprise Centre of Europe*, focused on the country's comparatively poor levels of numeracy and literacy among school leavers: 30 per cent of 16–17-year-olds were judged to be inadequate in numeracy; 21 per cent in oral communication. More generally, 32 per cent were regarded as having a poor business ethos.

Table 20.2	Training targets in Wales
Item	Target
Number of 19-year-olds without an NVQ Level 2	Reduced by 1 in 3 to 1 in 5 by 2004
Number of working age adults with an NVQ Level 2	Raised from 5 in 10 to over 7 in 10 by 2004
Number of working age adults with an NVQ Level 3	Raised from 3 in 10 to over 5 in 10 by 2004
Number of working age adults with NVQ Level 4	Raised from 1 in 5 to almost 3 in 10 by 2004
Adults with functional skills in literacy	Raised from 8 in 10 to over 9 in 10 by 2004
Adults with functional skills in numeracy	Raised from below 6 in 10 to over 6 in 10 by 2004
Young people in Modern Apprenticeships	Raised from 8700 to 14 000 by 2003
Total number of Individual Learning Accounts (ILAs)	Raised to 50 000 by March 2002

Source: ELWA (Education and Learning Wales) (http://www.elwa.ac.uk/).

Again and again, British firms report 'skill shortages', even in periods of high unemployment, leading to a reliance on overtime, subcontracting (often overseas) or a containment of growth – instead of creating jobs as in the USA. Significant blame is attached to the inadequacies of the British education system with its focus on cultivating an academic elite, as opposed to developing numeracy and communication skills throughout the population. We noted earlier that the recent explosion in higher education and the establishment of vocational qualification targets may eventually lead to improvements. It has been estimated that those organizations in British industry who do train their staff are paying up to £10 billion a year to make up for the past deficiencies of the education system (*Financial Times Guide to Business in the Community*, 1995).

British companies are not alone in devoting considerable resources towards 'remedial' programmes. The Australian Association of Graduate Employers surveyed 150 of the largest public and private sector employers in the country, asking them about 5000 graduates recruited in the previous three years (*Times Higher*, 25 February 1994). Their criticisms of new graduates echoed those of British school-leavers, including:

- lack of basic knowledge of grammar, sentence structure and spelling
- inability to explain ideas clearly in writing or speech
- inability of many to write or speak clearly 'in a business sense'.

Employers stated that their deficiencies had been noted during the selection process but these faults were so common that they had to be accepted in order to fill vacancies. Academics were criticized for setting a standard for students based on their own use of jargon and inability to express themselves lucidly in simple English. Employers had to compensate by providing communication courses.

Activity 20:3	Why should businesses compensate for deficiencies in the education of young people?

Vocational education and training

The early 1990s actually showed a reduction in job-related training in the UK: from 15.4 per cent of workers to 14.9 per cent (3.16 million workers) reporting that they had received such training. In the same period, the *Employment Gazette* found a disappointing response from young people on various government sponsored schemes such as youth training and employment training and trade apprenticeships. Almost 200 000 young people on these schemes were not aware of having been given job-related training.

Against the backdrop of gloom, CBI figures indicated a more positive attitude among medium to large companies (those employing 200–5000 people). These businesses were planning to increase spending on training. However, bad though the British training performance may be, it has been argued that the real situation is not quite so dire. Whereas the level of technical qualification in the UK appears to be very low, the reported training activities of organizations are much higher. This discrepancy can be explained by the historical absence of recognized basic and intermediate level vocational certification. It may be that the employment market contains many individuals with usable skills but they have no means of proving their worth to employers.

Continuing the changes instituted by the Conservatives, the UK Labour government has focused on target-setting. Individual learning targets have been set for each country in the United Kingdom (see Table 20.2 for Welsh examples). At the time of writing the English targets are:

- Targets for young people: 85 per cent of 19-year-olds with a 'level 2' qualification; 60 per cent of 21-year-olds with a 'level 3' qualification.

- Targets for adults: 50 per cent of adults with a 'level 3' qualification; 28 per cent with a 'level 4' qualification; a 7 per cent reduction in non-learners, 1998–2002.

- Targets for organizations: 45 per cent of medium-sized or large organizations recognized as 'Investors in People'; 10 000 small organizations recognized as 'Investors in People'.

HRM in reality

Rise in number of apprentices

The 'Modern Apprenticeships' scheme appears to have contributed to the largest number of apprenticeships in the UK since 1993. There will be 215 000 people on apprenticeships this year.

Addressing the TUC's Learning Centre Conference in London, Lifelong Learning Minister Malcolm Wicks said:

> The big increase in the numbers of young people doing apprenticeships is very good news. Modern Apprenticeships have made considerable headway into sectors like accountancy and childcare where there was no previous apprenticeship tradition, and I welcome the role that trade unions have played in developing Modern Apprenticeships.
>
> The response of the TUC to the Union Learning Fund has also been tremendous with nearly 7000 people benefiting from it over the past two years, including 2000 Union Learning representatives being trained, 26 new learning centres opened and 91 accredited courses and qualifications established.
>
> Unions have shown considerable energy and imagination in promoting learning in the workplace. They have demonstrated time and time again that they can really add value to the lifelong learning agenda. I congratulate the army of Union Learning representatives promoting learning in the workplace on the impressive results they have achieved, particularly amongst those who are not typical learners and those with basic skills needs.

▶

We must continue to focus on people rather than equipment. Unions represent every type of worker in the UK and encouraging and supporting people is their trademark. It is essential that they continue to lead the way on this.

The following table shows the number of apprentices in employment since 1986:

Numbers of apprentices in employment (thousands)

Year	Males	Females
1986	316	261
1987	322	264
1988	341	268
1989	373	308
1990	357	298
1991	339	270
1992	318	254
1993	236	191
1994	209	167
1995	180	141
1996	174	138
1997	176	141
1998	191	154
1999	197	166
2000	215	179

Source: *Labour Force Survey, 1986–2000*, United Kingdom.

It is worth noting that this improvement almost entirely refers to male apprentice-ships – female uptakes remain comparatively low. Also, the overall totals still compare unfavourably with the late 1980s and early 1990s.

Source: *HRMGuide.co.uk* (http://www.hrmguide.co.uk), 13 November 2000.

Activity 20:4	Should 'new' or 'modern' apprenticeship schemes be restricted to practical skills learning?

HRM in reality	## Hostile reception for new apprenticeships

Teachers and Labor gave a thumbs down to new government initiatives on appren-ticeships and traineeships.

Linda Simon, Secretary of the TAFE Teachers Association said:

The coalition's education policy released yesterday does not give young people the boost into jobs that it suggests. The only new money that is there for apprenticeships and traineeships is incentive funding to employers to take on school based New Apprentices. There is no money to provide the educational support in schools or TAFE colleges that these young people undertaking such apprenticeships would need.

The reality is that in 2000, A$220 million that had been allocated by the government for employer incentives to take on post-school apprenticeships and traineeships, was not taken up. These apprenticeships are generally more attractive to employers than school-based apprenticeships. As usual, the coalition policy looks as though additional money is being used to support young people into jobs, when if they really wanted to provide assistance, the funding would go to schools and colleges to ensure that young people were able to gain the skills and qualifications that employers require.

Employers are telling us that they want extra funding put into pre-apprenticeship and pre-vocational programs in TAFE colleges. These courses provide young people with those initial skills so important in the workplace. But the cuts in funding to TAFE colleges over the last five years, over A$240 million plus cuts to Labour Market Programs, has meant that many of these courses are no longer offered.

Both major parties must make real commitments to the education and training of young people in Australia, and support for apprenticeships and traineeships. The coalition policy does not do this.

Meanwhile Senator Kim Carr, Labor's Parliamentary Secretary for Education said that Dr Kemp had taken his 'misrepresentation of education policy' to new heights with his release today of a policy pretending to improve new apprenticeship opportunities for school students. 'I challenge Dr Kemp on four points,' said Senator Carr:

His claims that a further 30 000 additional places will be created are a cruel fraud. In fact, there are 6000 school based apprenticeships already in place (with 60 per cent in Queensland). He is really trying to claim credit for barely 1500 additional places each year, at a cost of more than A$40 million!

Dr Kemp remains silent on the source of this funding. Dr Kemp must say whether this is new money or is it, as is so often the case with him, simply recycled funding dressed up as new?

According to departmental statistics more than 306 000 students (or 75 per cent of year 11 and 12 enrolments) will take VET related subjects by 2004. Dr Kemp's gesture will aid a few thousand. What of the future of the 300 000 that he continues to ignore?

Finally, Dr Kemp is characteristically silent on quality issues. What is he doing to ensure that these apprenticeships give our young people the quality training they need to get a job?

Dr Kemp must answer these important issues. If he fails to do so, he stands condemned yet again as patently disinterested in the quality and welfare of our education system and Australia's future.

Source: *HRM Guide Australia* (http://www.hrmguide.net/australia/), 11 October 2001.

In fact, the reluctance of many employers to engage in training probably can be pinned down to two issues: (a) the short-term, cost-based approach to all management activities (in this case, demand for a quick and obvious benefit from training expenditure); and (b) the difficulty of proving the connection between training and improved efficiency. Hendry (1995, p.364) argues that the connection has never been proven:

One of the things which gets in the way is the fallacy, promoted by the Employment Department among others, that the benefits of training can somehow be demonstrated on the bottom-line. As a rhetorical device, it may encourage employers to train by saying 'training pays', but no one has ever satisfactorily demonstrated this.

We will expand further on the issue later in this chapter. The development of vocationally inclined qualifications such as the National Vocational Qualifications (NVQs) developed for England, Wales and Northern Ireland and their Scottish equivalents (SVQs), which certificate defined levels of technical competence, may eventually redress the problem. The British scheme uses five levels of achievement from 'shopfloor' to managerial standard.

Vocational training in Scotland: SVQs

Scottish Vocational Qualifications (SVQs) cover all aspects of work from traditional craft jobs to management-level activities. Based on the same standards as the NVQs offered in other parts of the UK, they are work-based and aim to demonstrate that people can carry out particular tasks competently. Individuals can learn at their own speed and are then assessed on the job.

SVQs in management have been developed by the National Forum for Management Education and Development (NFMED). The qualifications are awarded by SCOTVEC in conjunction with other bodies such as the Institute for Personnel and Development, the Marine and Engineering Training Association and the Open University, as well as the NFMED.

For example, the level 3 SVQ demonstrates supervisory competencies, whereas the level 4 qualification is aimed at managerial standards. Candidates awarded level 3 must demonstrate ability to:

- maintain services and operations that meet quality standards
- contribute to proper use of resources
- contribute to training and development of employees, including themselves
- help to plan, organize and evaluate work.

The more demanding level 4 SVQ requires evidence of skills in:

- improving service or product operations
- contributing to organizational change
- recruitment and selection.

It also requires candidates to demonstrate that they are capable of playing an influential part in:

- allocating and evaluating work
- creating and enhancing effective working relationships
- exchanging information for problem solving and decision making.

The advanced, level 5 SVQ is aimed at experienced senior managers.

Source: Adapted from *The Scotsman*, 17 May 1996.

Goss (1994, p.70) observes a contradictory feature in the initiative. On the one hand the emphasis is on outcomes, specifically overt behavioural features of doing a job, giving a narrow focus to the training involved. On the other hand, the opportunity to progress through a sequence of levels is a strong developmental feature. NVQs and SVQs are the end-product of a government initiative to provide a national framework for training activities. In 1993 the UK government introduced the 'Modern Apprenticeship' scheme to provide 16 and 17-year-olds with the opportunity to train for NVQs and SVQs up to level 3 (equivalent to two 'A' levels). However, progress in gaining the interest of employers appears slow. In particular there has been considerable reluctance among smaller companies to participate in the scheme or recognize the value of the qualifications.

A further initiative sponsored by the British government is the 'Investor in People' award, given when an assessor appointed by the Training and Executive Council (TEC) (Local Enterprise Council in Scotland) is satisfied on four national standards:

● Public commitment from the top of the organization to develop all employees to achieve business objectives.

● The organization regularly reviews the training and development needs of all employees.

● The organization takes action to train and develop individuals on recruitment throughout their employment.

● The organization evaluates the investment in training and development to assess achievement and improve effectiveness.

This particular scheme is aimed at tying training and development to business strategy (Goss, 1994, p.70). Achieving the award requires substantial commitment from an organization. It involves a considerable degree of planning, assessment and documentation in support of an application. Again, however, progress has been slow. For example, a major survey in Leicestershire indicated that few employers in the county were familiar with either this programme or a third government programme, the 'Management Charter Initiative' (Storey *et al.*, 1993). The latter takes the NVQ/SVQ framework further to provide management qualifications at four levels: supervisory, certificate (first-line management), diploma (middle management) and masters (senior management). The MCI scheme has focused on generic competencies, considered later in this chapter.

The Adult Learning Inspectorate published its first report in 2002 on standards of education and training received by adults and young people in England (*Training Journal*, October 2002, p.5). David Sherlock, the chief inspector, was quoted as saying that while his inspectors:

> found some examples of world-class provision, too few young people are receiving the quality of training that will prepare them for employment or address the country's skills shortages. Sixty per cent of work-based learning provision was found inadequate. On average, only a third of young people embarking on a modern apprenticeship achieved their qualification.

In particular, inadequacies in the key skills of communication, numeracy and IT use were identified as the biggest cause of young people's failure to succeed with a modern apprenticeship. Key skills were unpopular with both learners and employers, often being left to the end of the programme or omitted entirely.

HRM in reality	**New Learning and Skills Council receives cash boost**

Addressing the first conference of the Learning and Skills Council Chairmen (sic) Education and Employment Secretary David Blunkett announced that the new LSC will receive more than £5.5 billion for 2001–2002. This is a 9 per cent increase (£600 million) on present funding of post-16 education and training. David Blunkett said:

> The creation of the Learning and Skills Council is one of the most significant and far-reaching reforms in post-16 learning in this country. Through the Council, for the first time, all the planning and funding of all school sixth forms, colleges and training outside higher education will be integrated into a single system. The Council will be the leading

▶

agent of change in ensuring that we rise to the skills challenge we face and that we are equipped to close the productivity gap with our major competitors. It will be at the heart of our drive to secure sustainable economic success and prosperity.

The extra money will mean that the Council and its 47 local arms can hit the ground running when they start work next April. For 2002–03 there will be a further funding increase of £400 million, a 5 per cent increase in real terms. This does not include the additional funding we shall be giving to the Councils when they take over responsibility for school sixth forms. The money will allow more young people and adults to take part in education, by making courses more widely available, providing more and better qualified teachers and better facilities across the country. It will help individuals and employers to recognize the importance of regularly updating their skills and it will give them the skills and confidence they need to reach their potential.

I have written to the Learning and Skills Council chairman, Bryan Sanderson, today to set out my strategic priorities for the Council, as well as the framework needed to drive forward the learning and skills agenda. Firstly, I want the Council to maximize the participation and achievement of all young people in education and training as a route to participation in society and work. Too many young people still take little or no part in education or training after 16, failing to achieve their potential. High standard vocational training, with new apprenticeships which replace the failed youth training programmes of the past, will be as important as more vocational education in colleges and schools to attract young people – and to make education and training worthwhile. By working with the new Connexions Service, the new advice and guidance service for all 13 to 19-year-olds, the Council will help to provide a smooth transition for all young people into post-16 education and training.

Secondly, I want the Council to drive up standards of education and training and to raise the level of achievement for all age groups, whether it's helping the one in five adults with inadequate basic skills, updating technical skills, or ensuring that more young people opt to study for 'A' levels or vocational learning.

A third key objective for the Council will be to ensure the provision of attractive and relevant courses. This will help to stimulate demand and to maximize the opportunities for all those in the workforce and those out of work.

Working within the terms of the remit letter which I've issued today, the Council will seek a flexible and responsible approach at a local level to skills and business needs and to the demands of students. Helping communities to help themselves is vital to our drive to increase participation. Increasing demand means offering attractive routes to learning and building on existing initiatives, such as community and family learning projects, where people learn together in familiar, locally based environments. I expect the Council to support a wide range of learning opportunities which will help people to become more actively involved in their communities. We need to develop forms of citizenship which are sensitive to and respect differences between people. That's why I want the Council to take forward our aim of supporting more volunteering in the local community amongst 16–19 year olds.

The challenges I have set for the Council are demanding and significant. I want individuals to have confidence on the vocational and work-related route – the route from school to foundation apprenticeship and on to the new foundation degrees. I also want the Council to help us overcome the institutional divide within different sectors and between the public and private sector.

Over the first two to three years I expect the Council to secure a step change in the performance of the nation's learning and skills. I am pleased that we have secured such high quality people to lead the new Council and the 47 local Learning and Skills Councils. Together with the support and commitment of business and the extra money that I have announced today, we will ensure that, through the Learning and Skills Council, learning can be the key to prosperity, for each of us as individuals and the nation as a whole.

Source: *HRMGuide.co.uk* (http://www.hrmguide.co.uk), 9 November 2000.

Discussion of training and development in the media and management literature tends to become idealistic and evangelical. In reality, many employers take an extremely hard-nosed attitude towards the topic, particularly, as we have seen, in countries such as the UK with a notoriously short-termist view of business. Employer reluctance to embark on training young recruits can be attributed to various factors (Stevens and Walsh, 1991, p.37):

- *Poaching*. Some employers train while others do not. The non-trainers are likely to poach trained workers from those who train. Development requires trainees to acquire general skills as well as skills specific to the training company. Employers are reluctant to offer general skills training for fear of poaching. According to Stevens and Walsh:

  > ... firms may be unwilling to invest in the development of their employees because they are unable to be sure that they, rather than some other employer, may enjoy the benefits of such investment ... investment in training, once completed, is embodied in the individual, and as such is not under the direct control of the firm undertaking the investment.

  Whereas Australian and UK firms are afraid of 'free-riders', their German counterparts see themselves as having a responsibility to contribute to the common good. Along with the activities and support of government this attitude maintains a high level of training in Germany. Elsewhere – in France, Japan and the USA, for instance – the poaching problem is less evident since the training of young people takes place largely within the formal education system. Most of the burden and costs are placed upon the trainees.

- *Cost*. Young trainees anticipate higher wages in comparison to recruits for semi-skilled jobs. The reduction in numbers of young people coming onto the employment market has increased competition and wages for higher calibre trainees. Also, people are paid when training but do not produce anything and occupy trainers who are not managing or supervising during this period.

- *Individual disinterest*. Human capital theory predicts that the young are more likely to choose training than the old because their indirect costs are lower than those of older workers. It also predicts that there should be a direct relationship between additional training and increased income. But the perception of young workers may be that there is no direct link: the skill differential may be small or non-existent. They also see that promotions are not based on qualifications. It is known that qualifications are mainly used as filters in the recruitment process. Their value comes a long way behind previous job performance and the selectors' perceptions of their potential. Hence young workers may not see vocational training as being worthwhile. In Australia, an attempt has been made to tie vocational qualifications directly to pay, resulting in a stimulation of training levels.

- *Weak links between training and performance*. Training does not have strategic importance for many companies partly, as we have noted, because of the difficulty proving the connection between training and improved performance. The problem may be compounded by the delegation of training to personnel specialists or line managers without strategic direction at board level. Lower-level employees are even less likely to be aware of competitor practices than their senior managers.

Activity 20:5

What additional pressures or incentives could be placed on businesses to take vocational education and training seriously?

Development programmes

The fundamental principle of human resource development is that it goes further than piece-meal training. Beginning in this section we examine the organizational and personal decision-making processes that lead to systematic, planned HRD programmes. We focus on key aspects such as induction, fostering star performers and management development. We discuss the part played by individuals in their own development, examine the role of mentors and question whether women and men should be offered separate development programmes.

Where does HRD fit into the human resource strategy of an organization? It should be part of a planned and systematic process in which:

- Competencies or capabilities are identified by a performance management system.
- These are matched with needs specified by the human resource strategy.
- Gaps are addressed by the development programme.

Within a HRD programme, training is geared towards planned development rather than being an isolated activity unconnected to the organization's objectives. In fact, HRD programmes can use a combination of organized patterns of experience as well as formal training. It can be an empowering process that provides (Armstrong, 1992, p.152):

1 A signal that the organization believes its employees are important.

2 The motivation to achieve the skills required by the organization and the consequent reward.

3 Commitment to the organization from an understanding of its values and learning how to uphold them.

4 Identification with the company through a clearer understanding of its aims and policies.

5 Two-way communication between managers and staff as a by-product of workshops and other training activities.

6 Need satisfaction: being selected for training fulfils a need for achievement and recognition in itself.

7 Job enrichment coming from the additional skills obtained from training programmes that can be applied to other aspects of work.

8 Change management: education and training provide people with the understanding and confidence to cope with change.

Based on London and Stumpf (1982), a development programme for new managers might comprise the following steps:

1 Obtain an accurate assessment of individuals' skills and abilities.

2 Reflect their strengths, weaknesses and preferences by giving individual responsibility.

3 Set target job(s) and timeframe(s).

4 Give challenging tasks early on.

5 Assign role models.

6 Provide objective feedback.

7 Ensure accurate and realistic expectations.

8 Give individuals experience of a variety of functions.

9 Ensure everyone is committed – including top management.

10 Allow periodic evaluation and redirection of career plans.

Self-creation can be a conservative process when we are satisfied with our achievements. It is transformed into self-preservation when we can no longer imagine further development, but only see risks and threats. The emphasis for middle ranking executives may be the retention of their current status or standard of living. This produces a need to secure their jobs and defend them from change, blocking the advance of others and stifling development of the organization.

Management development

The main focus of HRD for many organizations lies in management development. In principle, anyone can become a manager and many do so without any formal training or development. However, graduates typically aim for formally designated management trainee positions that promise a structured development programme and steady progression through the management ranks.

The trend has been away from long induction periods and work shadowing towards immediate 'real' jobs in which trainees perform useful activities, often with management responsibilities. Traditionally, trainees remain in particular functions for fixed periods of time – perhaps six months, a year or longer. Of late, competence-driven development programmes have required trainees to achieve a certain standard before moving on.

Storey (2001) justifiably observes that 'the panoply of HRM technology is seen in its fullest form in the management of managers'. General management capabilities are developed in various ways. Companies such as Mars, Proctor & Gamble and Unilever have highly structured programmes. Others are more individually based or informal. Training may also involve academic study. At this point it is useful to consider the role of management education.

Activity 20:6	Why has there been such a strong focus on management development?

Management and professional education

Many development programmes involve formal business education, including diplomas, business degrees and, above all, the Masters in Business Administration (MBA). MBA programmes have emphasized rational decision making and a top-down strategic approach to business. It is worth noting, as we observed in Chapter 1, that introduction onto the Harvard MBA was seminal in the growth of HRM. By 1990, American business schools alone awarded 75 000 MBAs of widely varying quality each year.

In the 1980s, MBA graduates could guarantee substantial salary increases and the likelihood of 'fast-track' careers. More recently, their prospects have become less assured. Employers have questioned the quality of the product they receive for premium salaries. Harold Leavitt expresses the opinion that 'business schools transform well-proportioned young men and women ... into critters with lopsided brains, icy hearts and shrunken souls' (quoted in *The Economist*, 2 March 1991). Such criticisms have encouraged a number of business schools to revise the content and the way in which MBAs are taught, focusing on programmes that are custom-designed to meet the requirements of individual companies.

Nevertheless, academic courses can stretch the boundaries of a manager's experience, exposing them to a wide range of concepts, theories and ideas they would never come across otherwise. They also provide students with the means to understand and communicate with people in different business specialisms. McKenna (1994, p.210) argues that academic and experiential learning should 'coexist and complement each other for the betterment of the provision of management education and learning'. Between them, formal education and experiential learning can be used to build the combination of skills, knowledge and abilities – the management competencies necessary for effective managerial performance.

Developing management competences

What are management competencies? There are two main perspectives on skills necessary for management:

1 *'One best way'*. The generic approach assumes that there is a range of competencies or portable techniques that can be learned and used in a variety of organizational settings.

2 *'It depends'*. The *contingency* view holds that running an organization efficiently requires competencies or methods unique to that enterprise. This approach emphasizes common sense, experience, rule-of-thumb techniques and wisdom. It acknowledges the complexity of the business environment. It also recognizes that what has worked once in a particular situation is likely to work again.

Taking the former approach, in the 1970s the American Management Associations initiated a major study of management competencies, whereby 2000 successful managers were studied over a five-year period with the intention of identifying generic – common – competencies from actual job performance. The research identified 30 statistically significant competencies of which 18 were generic and could be regarded as essential for all successful managers (Boyatzis, 1982). The remainder were related to organizational requirements or individual management styles. The generic competencies could be placed in four groups: intellectual, entrepreneurial, socio-emotional and interpersonal (the largest group). These are elaborated in Table 20.3.

HRM in reality

Competence-based development

The South East Thames Regional Health Authority (SETRHA) was responsible for providing services to 3.2 million people in the south-east of England. It employed 73 000 staff of whom around 15 per cent were in management grades. The Human Resources Department had to arrive at a set of competencies with the agreement of senior managers already in place. Existing managers were employed on a wide variety of jobs and there were no clear models of general management within the public sector. The HR Department gained the public support of the regional general manager to implement a process based on a sample of 30 managers within the region. Using trained interviewers employing the critical incidence technique, repertory grid analysis and expert panels they identified the following competencies:

1 *People orientation*. Promotes team working and cooperation. Takes others' interest and views fully into account. Supports and enables staff to achieve their objectives. Manages in an open manner, establishing good relationships with a wide range of staff.

2 *Personal skills*. Comprising (a) communication and (b) interpersonal skills. (a) Communication skills – (i) Oral: expresses complex issues succinctly. Spoken communication is clear, confident, enthusiastic and appropriate for audience. (ii) Written: expresses complex issues succinctly. Clear, concise, well

researched, grammatically correct and appropriate for audience. (b) Interpersonal skills – Shows listening and empathy skills. Recognizes threads, identifies lines of agreement and keeps order. Negotiates sensitively, keeps in mind key objectives and outcomes. Consults and takes account of a wide range of opinion.

3 *Persuasion/influence*. Able to influence people and 'win the day'. Persuades people to accept and implement controversial decisions. Assists others to see issues in a wider context.

4 *Leadership*. Takes control and manages a situation. Draws on strengths and weaknesses of others. Acts as catalyst giving direction and energy to learn. Gives clear instructions.

5 *Persistence in goal achievement*. Hard-working, accepts responsibility, and follows through issues to completion. Routinely meets tight deadlines. Willing to confront difficult issues with energy to resolve them. Accepts organizational goals and shows high level of personal commitment. Continues to pursue goals despite setbacks.

6 *Consistency under pressure*. Accepts pressure and always meets deadlines. Keeps sense of humour and resilience. Remains accessible to staff.

7 *Creative resource management*. Thinks independently and has original ideas. Finds entrepreneurial solutions but recognizes organizational culture. Manages creatively in crisis. Creative use of budgets enables achievement of goals. Able to respond to shifting priorities by changing use of resources.

8 *Priority and objective-setting*. Sets clear priorities. Recognizes implications of priorities for organization and staff. Delegates and monitors progress towards objectives. Takes short-term action in light of major objectives.

9 *Problem analysis*. Is able to grasp a complex problem quickly. Uses information and analysis effectively to identify options. Considers solutions to problems that are entrepreneurial and new and appreciates possible outcomes. Tackles difficult as well as easy problems.

10 *Planning and organization*. Thinks ahead and plans practical actions to achieve objectives. Recognizes needs and takes action to meet them. Ensures staff are aware of and pursuing plans.

11 *Decision making*. Makes quick decisions without unnecessary consultation or delay, recognizing where further information/support is necessary. Recognizes implications of decisions for long-term goals. Willing to make unpopular decisions if necessary.

Source: Taken from Perkins and Snapes (1992), 'Developing the best managers?' in Vickerstaff (1992), *Human Resource Management in Europe*, Chapman and Hall.

This competence analysis was used as the basis for 48-hour, residential career development workshops, including an assessment centre process and a subsequent career development programme. Participants were given feedback on their performance within the workshop. The aim was to identify individuals with the potential for general management. This process was used to identify competence requirements in a specific business culture. How do we address similar issues in a global context?

▶

► Discussion questions: (a) To what extent do the competencies identified above overlap with the AMA's list of generic management competencies? (b) The Health Authority management expended considerable time and effort in arriving at their list of competencies. To what degree did this process produce better conclusions than a short common-sense exercise would have done? (c) Do Health Service managers need to demonstrate all these competencies in order to do their jobs well?

Table 20.3	Generic management competencies

Competencies	Characteristics
Intellectual	*Logical thought* – being able to think in a logical and organized manner. *Conceptualization* – an ability to relate apparently unconnected events into a meaningful pattern. *Diagnostic use of concepts* – being able to use theories or models, or develop new ones if required.
Entrepreneurial	*Effective use of resources* – planning and organizing, with an image of efficiency and achievement. *Proactive initiation* – a successful manager takes effective action rather than merely responding to events.
Socio-emotional	*Self-control* – an ability to suppress impulses and control personal reactions. This requires self-discipline and a capacity to place organizational requirements above individual needs. *Spontaneity* – free, unconstrained self-expression. *Conceptual objectivity* – impartiality and the preservation of emotional distance. Being able to balance opposing points of view. *Accurate self-assessment* – a realistic appraisal of one's own strengths and weaknesses. *Stamina and adaptability* – the 'stickability' or resilience required to cope with long hours and flexibility to deal with the unexpected.
Interpersonal	*Self-confidence* – showing that as 'natural leaders' they know what they are doing. *Developing others* – coaching, counselling, mentoring and being part of a team. *Impact* – able to influence others. *Use of unilateral power* – the ability to take the leadership role. *Use of socialized power* – negotiating and alliance-building, team roles. *Use of oral communications* – clear and persuasive communication. *Positive regard* – valuing other people, able to delegate and allowing employees to perform. *Managing group processes* – fostering and developing commitment and team-spirit.

Source: Vickerstaff (1992), pp. 122–124.

**HRM
in reality**

Female recruitment is a growing concern

A survey by Andersen (formerly Arthur Andersen) concludes that teenage women who are about to join the US workforce 'have a lukewarm impression of corporate America'. Andersen consider that this poses a major challenge for businesses seeking to attract young talent in what has become the tightest labour market in 40 years.

Bureau of Labor Statistics projections indicate that numbers of people with jobs or available for hire will increase at just 1.1 per cent a year until at least 2006. But the Andersen survey, *Bringing Girls into Corporate America*, reveals a preference among teenage girls for careers in small business or public service. They associate these with happiness and independence – factors of greater importance to them than the purely economic benefits they see in corporate jobs.

Bringing Girls into Corporate America is an in-depth study of teenage girls' perceptions of corporate America, as well as their career aspirations, computer usage, role models and their definitions of success and leadership. The survey polled 500 girls and 150 boys between 15 and 18 years of age.

'It's clear from the survey findings that large corporations need to brush up their image when it comes to enticing young females to work for them,' said Kathy Bellwoar, business consulting partner in the Philadelphia office and local champion of the Growth and Retention of Women (GROW) initiative:

> Recruitment and retention remains an unrelenting challenge. As such, these results serve as a wake-up call for corporate America to overcome the stereotypes teens have that are likely to affect their career decisions. Companies looking to attract young talent can take a step in the right direction by assessing their overall career advancement, mentoring, networking and work–life initiatives.

Other key findings include the following:

Career aspirations

Teen girls most frequently cite medicine or health services (17 per cent), education (10 per cent) and fine arts (10 per cent) as likely college majors. Boys show preferences for computer science (20 per cent) and law (9 per cent).

The likelihood of boys choosing computer science or computer engineering majors in school is five times greater than for girls, even though both genders unanimously agree on the importance of understanding computers for future employment.

Boys show twice as much interest as girls in considering being CEO of a high-tech business or a computer scientist. Girls indicate most interest in considering a job in health services, being CEO of a clothing company, a teacher or small business owner.

Success and leadership

Teens rate being happy, having the respect of family and friends, and a happy family life as the most important signs of success. A good job, making money, and having power and authority are rated the least important.

Leadership is seen as important by both girls and boys, but 87 per cent of girls want to be leaders compared with 80 per cent of boys. According to Dr Judy B. Rosener, Professor in the Graduate School of Management at the University of California, Irvine:

◄

Women bring different leadership styles to the corporate world, yet teenage girls apparently feel this will in no way disadvantage them as future leaders. The perspectives and insights women bring to the workplace, by virtue of their shared experience as women, are a key asset to organizations in the New Economy. Since 51 per cent of the population is female, it seems important to encourage young girls to aspire to leadership roles in the corporate world.

Role models

All teens see role models as important, but girls – especially those aged 17 and 18 – don't believe that there are enough of them. Celinda Lake, president of Lake, Snell, Perry & Associates, a nationally recognized research firm specializing in political issues relating to women and children says that:

> The indifference girls feel toward corporate America may result from their not seeing enough female leaders. Since most girls polled indicate that they view themselves as being leaders both now and in the future, it's a natural fit for them to gravitate to careers that bring out their leadership abilities. From their perspective, it looks like these jobs currently exist within the small business and public service sectors.

Computer usage

As many girls as boys will enrol in computer classes and agree that computers are important – but they are much less likely to consider a job in technology.

Most teenage girls spend less than five hours a week on the internet, but a majority of teenage boys spend more than five hours.

Source: *HRM Guide USA* (http://www.hrmguide.net/usa/), 26 March 2001.

Developing women

The low level of women in management has produced a case for special consideration to be given to the development needs of female managers. For example, the provision of career breaks, refresher training, job-sharing and extended childcare facilities can make a considerable difference in career progress. Hammond (1993) identifies three critical stages in women managers' careers:

- joining organizations
- establishing competence in management jobs
- strategies to progress up the management ladder into more senior jobs.

According to Hammond, in comparison to men, women learn more from others and from facing up to hardships. Conversely, men say they gain more from assignments, but it seems that men tend to be given more challenging assignments.

Specific HRD programmes can be set for women focusing on greater self-awareness, appreciation of career opportunities and encouragement to manage their own careers. This kind of programme boosts confidence. It is equally valuable to young trainees and mature returners. Hammond considers that women make outstanding developers. They appear to have more 'attending' skills than men – the ability to work on and care about several tasks simultaneously. However, there are few senior women managers to act as role models.

Development programmes involving seminars or attendance on women-only courses allows many female managers to compare notes, discuss issues in common and make sense of advancement in what is primarily a male world. Sharing experiences openly and honestly appears to be easier for women than men. Men tend to find it difficult to avoid competing and this leads to exaggeration, denial and an unwillingness to open themselves to criticism. Accordingly, women can gain more from the sharing experience than men. Hammond stresses that they may also bring in life issues outside the immediate work scenario that men tend to ignore.

Activity 20:7

What are the arguments for and against separate development programmes for women and men?

Mentoring

Demand is intense for people with the right combination of skills for a particular industry. The market for talented staff, or 'gold-collar workers', is becoming international and the ability to recruit, develop and keep them 'provides a significant and sustainable competitive advantage ... chief executives ignore this at their peril' (Sadler and Milner, 1993). Four categories of potential star performers can be highlighted:

1 Highly trained specialists – found in large numbers in high-technology industries such as computing, or those with intensive research and development such as pharmaceuticals. Retailing, finance, distribution and administration are highlighted specialist areas.

2 Good managers and leaders, such as retail group managers.

3 Sales and marketing people – able to acquire business.

4 Hybrids – individuals with the potential to cross over from a specialism – such as human resources – into general management.

Development programmes must provide these individuals with:

- A sense of mission, providing a more satisfying cause than just pay and security.
- An organization structure that encourages rather than stifles creativity.
- A performance management system which identifies and rewards talented individuals, giving them opportunities to develop their skills through challenging work.
- A clear statement of the link between strategic objectives and the desire of talented people to excel.

Mentor relationships have been found to be highly effective (Key concept 20.3). Kram (1983) found that mentors offered specific benefits in two main areas:

1 *Career support.* Sponsoring individuals for high-profile, challenging or stretching tasks; coaching in appropriate techniques; protecting the trainee from unfair treatment.

2 Psycho-social support. Offering acceptance of anxieties and concerns, counselling from the basis of dealing with similar experiences, providing a role model and friendship within the organization.

Thomson and Mabey (1994, p.60) consider that successful mentors should be seven to ten years (or, perhaps, more) older than the individuals they are mentoring. The age gap should allow the mentor to reflect on their own careers and work experience and be able to give considered responses. Key points (Thomson and Mabey, 1994, p.61) are:

- Meeting with a mentor, typically on a monthly basis, encourages an individual to collect his or her thoughts and structure the learning experience by talking those thoughts through with the mentor.

- Mentors can help to clarify an individual's thinking by questioning and challenging.
- In order to do so, mentors must have the ability to listen well and to probe into shallow thinking.
- The primary role of a mentor is not to advise – although this can occur – but to provide feedback and provide information on recent developments in the organization.

Mentoring Mentors are established managers who can provide support, help and advice to more junior members of staff. A mentor should not be a direct line manager, but should have an understanding of the employee's job. Ideally, mentor and junior should have the same gender and ethnic background, so that advice is based on similar life experiences.

Mentors can help build the individual's self-confidence in what may initially seem an unfriendly and perplexing environment. Self-confidence is a key requirement for empowerment: the ability to take one's own decisions.

Summary

Competitiveness demands a diverse workforce and up-to-date skills. The free market belief in 'buying-in' skill has proven inadequate, even in times of high unemployment. HRD allows people managers to be proactive, focusing on employees as investments for the organization. One of the great strategic contributions of HRM lies in the planning of skill availability in advance of need. Development programmes involve more than training and may be focused on competencies, gender and role. They require constant accurate assessment, counselling and personal challenge. Development also involves socialization of employees to fit the cultural requirements of the company.

Further reading

Stephen Gibb's *Learning and Development* (published by Palgrave/Macmillan, 2002) provides a good overview accompanied by a number of case study examples. *Employee Training and Development*, 2nd edition, by Raymond A. Noe (published by McGraw-Hill/Irwin, 2001) covers the fundamentals of training and development. *HRD and Learning Organizations in Europe* (Routledge Studies in Human Resource Development) edited by Saskia Tjepkema, Jim Stewart and Sally Sambrook (published by Routledge, 2002) provides case studies from a number of European countries. *Creating a Training and Development Strategy* by Andrew Mayo (published by CIPD, 1998) has been described as an ABC of HRD strategy. *Management Development* by Jean Woodall and Diana Winstanley (also published by CIPD, 1998) takes a multi-perspective view of the topic.

Review questions

1 Consider an organization of your choice: (a) Does this organization offer systematic development? (b) Does it aim to develop employee skills as a long-term strategy?

2 How is human resource development distinguished from training?

3 What are the benefits of apprenticeship systems to a country's human capital base?

4 Should women and men be offered different HRD programmes?

5 Define mentoring and explain its benefits.

6 Why are organizations reluctant to train lower level employees?

Problem for discussion and analysis

Read the following article. How can we rebalance HRD practices so that all employees receive the learning opportunities they need? Answer this question at the national, organizational and individual levels.

Managers more likely to get training than workers

The CIPD's third annual training survey shows that managers and professionals are far more likely to receive training in the workplace than manual workers. The survey was commissioned from the Centre for Labour Market Studies, Leicester University who telephone interviewed over 500 people in December 2000 and January 2001.

Mike Cannell, author of the report and CIPD adviser on training and development says:

> The findings show an alarming gap between the 'haves' and the 'have-nots'. Only 8.4 per cent of our respondents said that managers and professionals in their organizations had received no on-the-job training in the past year, whereas 47 per cent said that their manual workers had received no on-the-job training during the same period. Similarly, although less surprisingly, manual workers are less likely to have a formal coach or mentor than managers and professionals. It is surprising that the main beneficiaries appear to be managerial and white-collar employees given that on-the job training has historically been a case of manual workers 'sitting with Nelly'. This shift may be due to the widespread use of computers, which has forced every manager to learn about information technology which lends itself to on-the-job training.

Nearly half the training managers interviewed said that they found it difficult to obtain adequate assistance from senior line managers or directors to develop an adequate training strategy. And 16.5 per cent believed that their senior managers and directors had a poor understanding of training and development.

Cannell concludes:

> One of the weaknesses of the UK economy is that we have too many people with low skills and low incomes. It is therefore very disappointing to see that the training needs of some of the very people we should be targeting to get out of this circle, manual workers, are being ignored. The UK economy should be moving towards a high performance/high skilled economy but it can only be achieved if more investment in training, particularly through workplace learning, is undertaken. Maybe one of the reasons for this, as our survey suggests, is that a minority of senior managers and directors are insufficiently committed to developing their employees.

Source: *HRMGuide.co.uk* (http://www.hrmguide.co.uk), 3 April 2001.

21

Learning in organizations

Objectives

The purpose of this chapter is to:

- Distinguish between learning in organizations and the 'learning organization'.
- Discuss the relationship between empowerment, self-development and learning.
- Debate the role of the trainer in the context of proactive learning methods.
- Evaluate the state of evaluation.

HRD and the organization

From training to development

The learning organization

Empowerment and HRD

Self-development

HRD as an activity

Induction

Learning methods

Leadership development

Evaluating and costing training

Summary

Further reading

Review questions

Problem for discussion and analysis

HRD and the organization

In this section we see that organizational priorities have changed in recent years. The focus has moved from piecemeal training activities to more systematic human resource development. In fact, many businesses have re-oriented themselves away from training individual employees towards becoming 'learning organizations' with the emphasis on continuous learning. For example, Whipp (1992, pp.45 and 52) argues that one of the critical ways in which HRM can improve an organization's competitiveness is through its impact on the 'knowledge base' of the business:

> The role of knowledge is paramount in the way an HRM approach can help create competitive advantage. That knowledge has both technical and social components. What becomes critical is the extent to which a company's knowledge base matches changing competitive conditions through learning.

Key concept 21:1

Learning   A relatively permanent change of behaviour as a result of past experience. Learning is taken to mean more than acquiring knowledge. It encompasses the way in which outmoded values and techniques are shed in favour of new ones. At an organizational level this requires a collective process of change in its shared worldview, including perceptions of the company and its market.

Competitive advantage comes from the development of an organization's human capital: a learning experience for employees and the organization as a whole (see Key concept 21.1). For some time, this learning experience was encapsulated within a particular model of training: a comparatively straightforward, organized function which depended heavily on planning. The systematic training model pervaded organizations so thoroughly as to be accepted as received wisdom. In the UK this was encouraged by the Industrial Training Boards established in the 1960s. Depending on a series of logical steps it normally involved (Sloman, 1994):

- a training policy
- a method for identifying training needs
- formulation of training objectives
- development of a training plan
- implementation of a planned training programme
- validation, evaluation and review of training.

The systematic training model assumed an organizational environment based on slow change, hierarchical lines of authority and clear requirements. It was a logical series of steps centred on the use of an objective training needs analysis. Normally, this would take the shape of an empirical exercise to identify current needs but bringing in the organization's objectives for consideration. It provided a framework within which the trainer could ensure a thorough and 'professional' job. However, it required a methodical and time-consuming series of activities that do not fit in so well with modern organizations.

Today's organizations are constantly changing and have much looser systems of control than the companies of the 1960s. The systematic training model does not incorporate a link with development and other human resource initiatives and, consequently, offers an inadequate framework for modern trainers. For example, structural changes require the movement of people from activities whose human resource requirements are shrinking to those which are growing. The skills required are those appropriate to the new work area. It is wasteful in both human and budgetary terms to have to dismiss people in one function while simultaneously hiring new people in another.

Learning in organizations can be approached from either a business or educational perspective. Tight (2000) argues that this is an area in which a variety of 'academic tribes' are operating with only limited contacts with each other, including:

- adult/continuing/lifelong education
- organizational behaviour/occupational psychology, and
- management development/learning/studies.

Each of these 'tribes' has a valuable contribution to make to our understanding. There is a conceptual gap between academic literature on the learning organization and that of organizational learning. Huysman (2000) argues that the two streams of theory and research have operated highly independently of each other. The learning organization stream tends to be mainly prescriptive, linking learning to improvement, while the organizational learning stream analyses learning processes without real interest in the outcome.

Whether or not an organization is growing, there is a need to develop skilled people for the future to replace those who are promoted or leave the company. Consistent with human resource strategy, succession planning links development to career structures and promotion policies. It must also take individual career plans and intentions into account. Typically, such a programme is linked to the human resource plans of the company, reflecting its anticipated needs in the relatively long term. Good employers take this seriously.

From training to development

Following the argument in the previous section it becomes clear that, with its incorporation into HRD, training has become a complex topic with a significant shift in emphasis and importance from the systematic training model. Trainers experience a conflict between two contrary trends (Sloman, 1993). On the one hand, organizations are demanding higher levels of training to meet their skill needs, linking training to strategic initiatives such as total quality management, culture change and customer care. But this centralizing trend contrasts with a decentralizing approach to the delivery of the training. There have been changes in responsibility in line with the growth of HRM, de-layering and divisionalization. Increasingly training is seen as the province of line managers with specialist trainers being used as an internal consultancy resource.

The new approach requires an effective communication system between the strategic decision makers, line managers and specialist trainers. Together, these changes have made the traditional model of training management obsolete. Sloman (1994) poses some questions which are vexing training managers:

- It is accepted that training should be closely linked with business strategy. But what does this mean in practice? How should this be done?
- How should training relate to corporate culture?
- How important a breakthrough are competencies?
- Should the training manager be operating as an internal consultant? If so, what does this mean in practice?
- Should the company be attempting to become a learning organization, and if so, how?

The strategic link with competitiveness means that HRD has become more important, but there have been pressures on training budgets. Critical eyes have looked at training departments in search of firm evidence of their ability to deliver. According to Rainbird and Maguire (1993): 'it also includes activities which are more closely linked to developing employees relationships with colleagues, legitimizing new working practices and changing company culture.'

The emphasis on decentralizing training has caused difficulties for trainers. As with many others in the former personnel-related area they are seen more as facilitators and agents of change than as instructors. Trainers have experienced considerable uncertainty. They are more involved with strategic decision makers but often have an unclear career path ahead of them. In many cases they have become managers of externally sourced training, providing advice, and acting as internal consultants.

The idea of regarding training as an internal consultancy has attracted considerable support. It has an obvious appeal for organizations that divide functions into 'buyers' and 'sellers' and provide an internal accounting system which allocates training costs to budget holders. Separate training centres can be accurately costed and their value established.

There are some unsatisfactory aspects, however. If an organization employs external consultants to provide a service such as training it can do so on the basis of single transactions. If these prove to be unsatisfactory, the purchaser has the option of changing to a different supplier. In other than the largest organizations, the buyer of an internal consultancy's services does not have this freedom. Additionally, the emphasis on 'independence' sits uncomfortably alongside current management thought which places responsibility for all human resource activities with line managers. Some businesses have rationalized these conflicts by taking a new perspective: regarding themselves as 'learning organizations'.

Activity 21:1	What are the main forces driving change in the work of professional trainers?

The learning organization

In recent years the learning organization has 'captured the imagination of trainers and others' (McKenna, 1994, p.210). As we can see from Key concept 21.2, it is a view that organizations have to go beyond sporadic training into a permanent state of learning in order to survive in today's business environment. Adapted from Pedler, Boydell and Burgoyne (1989), key characteristics for a learning organization are as follows:

1 The formation of organizational policy and strategy, along with its implementation, evaluation and improvement, is consciously structured as a learning process.

2 There is wide participation and identification in the debate over policy and strategy. Differences are recognized, disagreements aired and conflicts tolerated and worked with in order to reach decisions.

3 Management systems for accounting, budgeting and reporting are organized to assist learning from the consequences of decisions.

4 Information systems should 'informate' as well as automate. They should allow staff to question operating assumptions and seek information for individual and collective learning about the organization's goals, norms and processes.

5 Information on expectations, and feedback on satisfaction, should be exchanged by individuals and work units at all levels to assist learning.

6 Employees with external links – such as sales representatives and delivery agents – act as environmental scanners, feeding information back to other staff.

7 There is a deliberate attempt to share information and learn jointly with significant others outside the organization, such as key customers and suppliers.

8 The organization's culture and management style encourage experimentation, and learning and development from successes and failures.

9 Everyone has access to resources and facilities for self-development.

Garvin (1993) highlights three important areas:

- *Meaning.* A learning organization has the ability to create, acquire and transfer knowledge. It can modify behaviour to accommodate new knowledge and insights.

- *Management.* The organization shows evidence of learning from others, systematic problem solving, experimentation and internal transfer of information, for example by job rotation.

- *Measurement.* The organization possesses mechanisms that assess the rate and level of learning. By taking practical aspects of its key functions, such as quality and innovation, managers can ensure that gains are made from the learning process within an acceptable timescale.

Key concept 21:2

Learning organization   Not simply an organization which carries out extensive training but rather an organization 'which facilitates the learning of all its members and continuously transforms itself' (Pedler, Boydell and Burgoyne, 1989). A learning organization is one that lives and breathes knowledge acquisition and skill development – the ultimate extension of 'learning on the job'.

The concept of the learning organization is evolving and remains fairly abstract or, as a senior consultant engagingly described it, 'quite fluffy' (Prothero, 1997, quoted in Walton, 1999). The seminal ideas of the concept come from two main sources: Pedler, Boydell and Burgoyne's (1989) ideas on the 'learning company' and Senge's 'five disciplines'. According to Senge (1990, cited in Price 2000), learning organizations are organizations in which:

- the capacity of people to create results they truly desire is continually expanding

- new and open-minded ways of thinking are fostered

- people are given freedom to develop their collective aspirations

- individuals continually learn how to learn together.

This set of goals may seem somewhat ambitious but Senge contends that they can be achieved through the gradual convergence of five 'component technologies', the essential disciplines of which are (Price, 2000):

- *Systems thinking.* People in an organization are part of a system. Systems thinking is a discipline which integrates the other disciplines in a business. It allows the 'whole' (organization) to be greater than the 'parts' (people, departments, teams, equipment and so on).

- *Personal mastery..* This discipline allows people to clarify and focus their personal visions, focus energy, develop patience and see the world as it really is. Employees who possess a high level of personal mastery can consistently generate results that are important to them through their commitment to lifelong learning.

- *Mental models.* These are internalized frameworks that support our views of the world, beliefs in why and how events happen, and our understanding of how things, people and events are related. Senge advocates bringing these to the surface, discussing them with others in a 'learningful' way and unlearning ways of thinking that are not productive.

● *Building shared vision*. Developing 'shared pictures of the future' together so that people are genuinely committed and engaged rather than compliant.

● *Team learning*. Senge sees teams as a vital element of a learning organization. Hence there is a great significance in the ability of teams to learn.

It is evident that many of the virtuous aspects of 'learning organizations', such as extensive job rotation, mirror practices commonly found in large Japanese corporations. The concept has been much trumpeted but one can justifiably ask if such idealistic objectives can be met in a harsh, competitive business environment. Critics argue that the concept may be unrealistic and, sometimes, counter-productive. Elkjaer (2001) describes a Danish learning organization that did not last very long and suggests that its short life had been due to the emphasis placed on changing individual employees while the organization itself – its management structures and work practices – had remained fairly constant. This emphasis on individual learning may have arisen because of the general and abstract terms in which learning is discussed in prescriptive accounts of learning organizations.

Sloman (1994, p.27) contends that the goals of the learning organization model are so remote from most trainers' reality that:

> Bluntly, it asks from most managers too great a leap of faith and does not describe situations they can recognize. Indeed, the very phrase 'learning organization' could be regarded as unhelpful; it is firmly 'trainer-speak' and does not carry a high likelihood of achieving resonance with a hard-bitten manager who is struggling to achieve short-term financial targets.

Perhaps the most striking proof that most companies are *not* learning organizations comes from the very existence of training courses. Firms may decide that they require particular sets of behaviours to retain their competitiveness. They may choose to achieve those behaviours by means of training courses. Doing so indicates that the processes which should create and support those behaviours is missing within those organizations.

On the other hand, managers and others learn a great deal on the job – whether or not they are in a 'learning organization'. They learn how their organization works, how to survive within it and how to get things done. This informal education within the organization may conflict with learning from formal courses:

> The problem thus is not that managers won't learn, or that they resist learning but that they have learnt too much and too well. They have 'learnt the ropes' and these lessons about how their organization works may obstruct their openness to further learning. (Salaman and Butler, 1994, p.38)

Organizational learning and its offshoot the 'learning organization' have been criticized as a rhetorical device designed to offer senior managers new mechanisms of control over employees. Huzzard (2001) agrees that the learning organization can be criticized on this basis but considers that it should not be dismissed without an adequate alternative. Ellinger *et al.* (2002) investigated the relationship between firms' financial performance and the learning organization concept. This is one of the few empirical investigations conducted on the practice and effectiveness of learning organizations. They found a positive correlation between seven action imperatives for a learning organization and four objective measures of financial performance.

Activity 21:2 Evaluate the view that 'learning organizations are just hype'.

Empowerment and HRD

The notion of empowerment has become increasingly popular in both North America and Europe. It is particularly relevant in the context of human resource development. There is nothing new in the notion that decision making should be delegated as low down the organization as possible, and that individuals should take responsibility over their own work, but it has significant implications on the career structures and work behaviour of employees. Empowerment is often presented as something provided for the benefit of employees. In fact, its use is driven by financial considerations deriving from:

● *Downsizing*. Slimmer companies typically have fewer management layers. The consequence is that the remaining managers are not available for day-to-day decisions – they *must* be taken by lower-level employees.

● *Speed of response*. In an increasingly competitive market, customers expect fast, authoritative decisions on price availability. There is no time for staff to refer to 'the manager'.

In this environment there is a need for confident, speedy decision making based on a high degree of product expertise. Moreover, in return for empowerment, employees must accept that career opportunities have diminished. Much of the ladder has disappeared and vertical promotion is only available to the few star performers. HRD in this case is focused on building resilient people, able to gain rewards from existing jobs. Their future lies in 'horizontal promotion', regular moves between different jobs on a similar level.

Specifically, development programmes require an emphasis on decision-making and customer-handling skills together with in-depth product and service knowledge. In the absence of managerial backup it is necessary that empowered staff have a wide understanding of the organization's functions and goals. They must be able to function well in unclear circumstances, without detailed prescriptive rules and be flexible and proactive enough to make events happen.

It is evident, therefore, that empowered businesses cannot work with the same personalities – including management – as those found in hierarchical organizations. Neither is there scope for rigid specialists in narrow fields of work. Not surprisingly, workers in these organizations must resemble those in Japanese companies where supervisors have typically managed as many as a hundred individuals. They must be generalists with a broad perspective of their role in the organization. Empowerment is especially significant in fostering an individual employee's self-development.

Self-development

Development is the responsibility of the individual as well as the organization. Career success requires self-control, self-knowledge, systematic career evaluation and frequent role change. Selecting a career path depends on factors such as:

● *Self-awareness*. Being able to accurately assess one's own skills, abilities and interests.

● *Ambition*. Self-esteem, confidence and motivation.

● *Opportunity*. Education, experience and social contacts.

People develop their lives and become distinctive persons through an interaction of three processes: genetic inheritance, life events and self-creation (Glover, 1988). They are so intertwined that we may be unable to attribute a particular event to any one of them.

Genetic inheritance determines much of our physical and mental capabilities. Hence the opportunity to succeed in education or business is constrained, to some extent, by inherited factors outside our control. Even health and the duration of our lives are subject in part to genetic determination.

Our lives also depend heavily on accident or chance because the process of living is predominantly an unsystematic series of incidents. We choose to apply for specific jobs, or particular universities, because they meet our needs at a specific point in time. These decisions produce unanticipated side-effects. For example, later we might find ourselves living in a specific location and engaged in projects we would never have contemplated if we had not taken the job or gone to that university.

However, there are major components of life that are controlled by our own actions, leaving scope for intention and direction. The more we plan and take action, the greater the control we have over our lives. To a degree, we shape our own selves by imagining the kind of person we want to be: perhaps being more successful, being respected, or being seen as kind or helpful. When we take actions that contribute to the achievement of these goals we are involved in a process of self-creation. Few of us have a systematic life plan, but rather a loosely organized collection of sometimes minor aims. Most people have restricted opportunities, so that self-creation is a matter of taking account of reality and adjusting to what is possible. The following independent development checklist (based on Margerison, 1991, p.63) can be useful for this purpose:

- What is the best way to spend my time?
- Who else could do my work?
- What am I improving and why?
- What do I feel strongly about?
- What are my special strengths and weaknesses?
- What am I doing to increase my effectiveness?
- What are the likely benefits and risks of achieving my objectives?
- What have I learned in the last month?
- What motivates me most?
- How many of my objectives do I achieve on time?
- What is my action plan for: one month, one year, five years?

Activity 21:3   Copy the questions in the independent development checklist onto a blank piece of paper. Try answering the questions yourself.

Work is a major area in which self-creation can take place. According to Glover, the search for an imagined self explains much of our working behaviour. Self-creation is not necessarily a fully conscious activity, and people are inevitably constrained in achieving their goals. Some jobs crush any opportunity for advance, forcing people into behaviour that gives a false impression of the personalities they are, or want to be. The apparently unsympathetic social security clerk, for instance, may be a creation of the framework of rules within which that individual must operate. The rules of the job mask any warmth or caring.

Organizations may use customer care programmes to train people in a form of impression management, producing staff who are groomed and dressed in a certain way and use approved body language and facial expressions. This veneer of humanity may be beneficial to some and certainly improves the organization's image, but the end-result is a constraint on true self-expression. We have to be careful that the organization does not take over our true selves. In fact, developing one's self is a learning and a recognition process. Work may teach us about a lifestyle that we do not want (Glover, 1998, p.136):

> We are lucky if work brings out in us things we did not know we had. But we can also discover things about ourselves in a less satisfying way. We take a job because it is well paid, or because others find it interesting, and then find we are stifled by it. Parts of us are denied expression. ('It was not really me', we say afterwards.) Relationships lead to the same kind of self-discovery: in some we flourish and in some we are stifled.

HRD as an activity

In the final sections of this chapter we examine HRD at the activity level, focusing on the training and experiential processes that make up development programmes. We examine the continuing role of training needs analysis, the value of formal training as opposed to experiential 'action learning' and consider similar issues in the context of leadership development. The chapter concludes with a discussion on how training activities can be evaluated in terms of cost-effectiveness and quality.

What should be the aim of HRD activities? Vickerstaff (1992, p.132) argues that:

> ...well-trained employees make better products, serve the customer more effectively, and are likely to have more ideas about how to change the process and the product to improve quality and efficiency. However, the benefits of a well-trained workforce can only be realized if the training effort is properly managed.

Organizations can be described as 'upskillers' or 'de-skillers' (Ashton and Felstead, 1995, p.242). The latter use a scientific management approach to simplify job requirements, remove the opportunity for initiative and reduce employees to a near-robotic state. Training (if it exists) in such cases becomes no more than rote learning of procedures. In many instances, increased skill demands are linked to flexibility, increasing the importance of training attached to multi-skilling and job enlargement. Training and development activities are reaching sophisticated levels in many countries. As an illustration, see the 'HRM in reality' article indicating expectations of training professionals in South Africa.

HRM in reality	**'The top training position in South Africa'**

Woodburn Management Selection advertised a position for a person able to 'develop and implement world class, leading edge performance improvement training and development strategy and practices' for a client company in the Gauteng area. The successful individual was expected to have degree level education and a minimum of five years' training experience including at least two years in a 'progressive, leading edge training and development environment'. This individual would have 'excellent knowledge on the Theory of Learning, the training industry and team behaviour understanding, as well as general business acumen'.

The successful candidate would report to the general manager: human resources. The key areas of activity would include:

● Developing and implementing training and development strategy.

● Managing a world class learning centre.

● Designing, developing and implementing training materials (internal and external).

- Evaluating, validating and monitoring training processes.
- Conducting training needs analyses.
- Managing budgets, reports and staff.

Applicants were expected to be 'assertive, have well-developed communication and inter-personal skills, and the ability to interface effectively across cultural lines'. Applicant were also required to be 'able to see the big picture, think globally and be good idea generators'.

Source: South African *Sunday Times*, 'Business Times' section, 28 January 1996.

The role of the trainer – how to begin

Maresh (1999) argues that trainers should capitalize on the innate nature of the brain to:

- seek and perceive patterns
- create meanings
- integrate sensory experience
- make connections.

The trainer should aim to:

- become proficient at designing and delivering a dynamic curriculum
- assess learning
- effectively administer *true* education.

Maresh argues that 'in the process trainers will release learners' intrinsic drive to acquire knowledge, an admirable outcome from any training.'

People come to learn with a variety of previous experiences, needs and skills, so Maresh advises us to create common ground as a first step in the training process – and every subsequent learning segment. By this she means entering into a dialogue with the members of the training group, acknowledging their experience and speaking directly to 'the familiar frustrations, joys, and challenges that link up to the learning task at hand.'

This is done through a series of questions that highlight the backgrounds of individual members, identify their concerns and gain commitment to the learning process. Maresh suggests 'enrolment' questions beginning with 'How many people have ever …' but not relying on just a show of hands. It is essential to elicit information and comments. Moreover, the trainer should repeat what members have said so that everyone hears and to validate the members who made those statements.

For example, a training session on selection interviewing could begin with enrolment questions such as:

- How many people here have been trained as interviewers?
- How many of you have a lot of experience as interviewers, whether or not you have been trained?
- And how many have very little experience of interviewing?
- Any with none at all?
- But surely you have all been interviewed by someone else?

Questions such as these should involve everyone in the room and also bring out comments, questions and friendly banter – as well as telling the trainer what level of training will be needed for the group. The common ground acts as a basis for group awareness. When the audience begin to see themselves as a group, they begin to relax and feel comfortable entering into the learning process together. The stage is now set for the trainer to address what Maresh calls the 'big why' in the trainees' minds. Remember that we are building connections and relating to previous experiences. So the purpose, method and intended results of the training need to be explained in relation to the answers given to the enrolment questions. The importance of the subject – especially in relation to trainees' own experience – and what can be done with the learned skills when trainees get back to work should be explored.

Then, Maresh advises, the trainer should say something about his or her own background, ideally using a personal story involving the subject of the training session. According to Maresh:

> This connects the leader to the participants in an essential way. People's experiences are dramatic. They include emotions, mystery, tension, climaxes and humor. When personal stories are recounted, learners emotionally identify with the parts that have meaning to them, and this confirms their commitment to participate. Personal stories bond the audience to the instructor, the course content, and other participants.

She also addresses the logical component of the adult learner's mind by stressing the need to provide an agenda or list of learning objectives at this point. The team members need to know what the outcomes of the course will be.

Gibb (2002, p.86) summarizes the characteristics of good instructors:

- Being consistent in their ability to manage repeated delivery of the same learning and development (L&D) event.
- Being meticulous and obsessively organized in order to ensure that all aspects of instruction are effective.
- Being sympathetic to learners of different abilities.
- Being patient with the process of showing and telling, trial and error.
- Being objective in assessing others' knowledge, capabilities and behaviour.

Activity 21:4   Can anyone be a good trainer?

Training needs

Customer demands are driving training for service and product quality but this is generally focused on 'core' staff with career structures rather than part-time and temporary employees. However, the latter tend to be highly visible to customers, particularly in retailing. Studies in this sector and in the hotel and catering industry indicate that, in contrast with the management trainees, most staff receive induction training, some customer care instruction and little else (Rainbird and Maguire, 1993).

In addition we need to distinguish the training needs of the individual and those of the organization. Personal and corporate objectives must be reconciled. Individual employees frequently look for wide-ranging courses that will help them in promotion. They will look to develop transferable skills which are seen as valuable by other employers. In contrast, local management are more interested in training which improves performance on their present jobs leading to improved output quality and productivity. In other words, employees seek training which will make them more marketable whereas organizations prefer training that makes employees more productive.

Taking the organizational viewpoint, Nowack (1991) distinguished these as:

- *Training needs*: for tasks or behaviours that the business considers important and the employee's proficiency is inadequate.

- *Training wants*: when employees desire training for tasks and behaviours in which they are not proficient but which the organization considers unimportant.

Nowack proposes the first purpose of a training needs analysis is to 'weed out' the latter. Rainbird and Maguire found evidence for the balance lying predominantly with the management agenda, with training focused more on organizational rather than individual development. Whereas increasing thought is being given to management and professional development this does not seem to be the case with sub-management grades. Their training appears to be heavily biased towards job and company-specific skills.

A decision must also be taken on whether or not to conduct training in-house or employ outside means. If the choice is made for in-house training, should it be by means of a course or on-the-job? We need to ask (Fowler, 1991):

1 What knowledge do employees need to perform their jobs well? This includes detailed job-specific knowledge, such as product information, and broader knowledge, for example about who is responsible for marketing literature in the organization.

2 What skills or competencies are needed, and to what level? Employees must be able to turn basic knowledge into good performance. Skills can be developed through direct tuition, coaching, planned experience or work simulations.

3 What attitude characteristics do we need? Interest, commitment and enthusiasm are always important but there may be a need for employees to develop a particular type or set of attitudes focused on customer service, for example.

The starting point for any development programme is a clear measure of individual aptitudes and experience. Ideally, individual employees should be developed from where they are now with their own particular requirements being addressed. Different people will benefit from different kinds of training even when performing the same job. If the organization is clear on the level of knowledge, skill or attitude required, development can be geared towards correcting individual shortfalls in meeting these standards. The measure will normally be provided:

- Through the performance appraisal process, which should identify each employee's personal training needs as agreed by the individual's supervisor. Sloman (1993) found this to be the primary source of information among his surveyed companies.

- If there is no formal appraisal system, from an examination of each individual's productivity and quality of output. This method is commonly used in production and manual work.

- Assessment centres can be employed for development purposes. Normally used for employees seen to have potential for advancement, workers are assessed in similar ways to the centres used for selection. Information is obtained from group exercises, job simulations and psychometric tests.

- Checklists or questionnaires given to individual employees and their supervisors with training requirements in mind.

- Succession plans indicating the likely next generation of managers and their training shortfall.

- Various methods can be integrated into a skills audit of the company.

The assessment should be considered in terms of immediate training and long-range development and a balanced plan produced. Ironically, employees who have the most extensive education and higher qualification levels appear to have the greatest access to and participation in continuing training (Rainbird and Maguire, 1993). There is also evidence to show that part-time and manual workers are particularly disadvantaged along with employees in small private firms.

A training needs model

Nowack (1991) proposes a nine-step model for a training needs exercise.

1 Prepare a job profile

Jobs for which training is required need to be identified clearly. The job profile is based on 12–15 dimensions, or job requirements, within which groups of behaviours can be classified. The number of dimensions depends on factors such as what the job involves, its complexity and required skills for effective performance.

Information is obtained from subject matter experts: people who have detailed knowledge of the job(s) being considered. This includes workers currently performing that work, their supervisors and others involved with the input or output to and from those jobs. Information comes from individual interviews, focus groups and survey techniques. Focus groups, for example, discuss the skills deemed important to each job and list them in dimensional categories within broad areas of:

- necessary technical knowledge and experience
- communication skills
- decision making or problem solving
- administrative skills
- management skills.

Each group indicates how important they feel each dimension is to a particular job – from 'very' to 'not' important. They are also asked to estimate the likely frequency of occurrence of each dimension in terms of 'several times a day/week/month/year'. The lists are compared and integrated to form a definitive job profile.

2 Preparing a learning or training needs questionnaire

This is a critical part of the process. Targeted towards particular jobs or job levels in the organization, it is addressed to the people performing the jobs and their immediate supervisors. It includes questions aimed at obtaining three categories of information:

- *Attitudinal* – describing employees' feelings about their work, their perception of organizational procedures and policies, pay, career, management and environment.
- *Dimensional* – summarizing views on the job dimensions in terms of their importance and employees' proficiency (expressed on a 1–5 scale).
- *Demographic* – relevant questions on employees' time within the organization.

3 Administering the questionnaire

A decision must be taken on the size of sample required to complete the questionnaire. This will depend on the resources available and the number of people involved in target jobs. In a relatively small organization the questionnaire can be directed to all relevant employees; in larger organizations where hundreds of people may be performing similar tasks, a sample will be more appropriate. The target audience should offer alternative perspectives of specific jobs, for example by asking workers and their immediate supervisors to evaluate the workers' jobs.

The questionnaire should be accompanied by a covering letter describing: the purpose of the exercise; details on how and when to return the questionnaire; and its voluntary, anonymous and confidential nature.

Standard methods can be adopted to increase the percentage of questionnaires returned, such as offering incentives (prize draw, restaurant vouchers, etc.).

4 Analysing responses

Returned questionnaires are statistically analysed, preferably by means of a computerized package. A simple mathematical method can indicate the most crucial training needs: each respondent's measure of importance (I) is multiplied by the equivalent rating for proficiency (P) for every dimension. The resulting (I×P) scores can be utilized in a variety of ways. For example, mean scores can be compared across dimensions for a specific group or between groups. Alternatively, supervisors' ratings can be compared with employees' judgements of themselves. It is useful also to compare different departments and to check for differences between new and experienced employees.

5 Interpreting the results

Nowack suggests that three follow-up questions should be addressed:

- Is there some commonality between the highest-ranked training needs?
- What is the explanation for any differences between supervisor and employee assessments?
- Is there a reason for differences between groups of employees – e.g. senior and junior workers?

Different levels of employee will inevitably have different perceptions of the importance of particular development needs. Workers on the shopfloor may be particularly concerned with day-to-day matters such as dealing with complaining customers effectively, or working a particular machine. Managers may be more interested in longer-term, strategic requirements, such as filling in stock returns accurately and understanding the fine differences between product categories in order to identify trends. These differences have to be evaluated logically.

6 Follow-up focus groups

Interpretation of questionnaire results will identify a need for further clarification. This is best provided by small focus groups which can consist of workers, managers or a mix. They can review I×P scores and offer further explanation. Groups should provide a final executive summary that will be useful for managers and trainees.

7 Feedback

A feedback of results to managers and respondents is an essential part of the exercise. Planning and presentation of results is crucial for further progress and as a record of the process for future use.

8 Development objectives

The goal is to produce an objective for each dimension identified from the questionnaire and follow-up exercises. They should be tied to an explicit statement of the competencies required for effective performance of the jobs in question. Each training need must be categorized as:

- imparting knowledge
- changing attitudes
- modifying behaviour.

Having done this, the criteria for successful training can be established. For example, if delegation skills are a training need, what behaviour needs to be established by the trainee?

9 A pilot training programme

This is a prototype used to test the conclusions of the training needs exercise and provide further information for the final employee development programme.

Activity 21:5	There has been a trend towards proactive learning and away from passive training. Should the 'training needs analysis' be modified to become more of a 'learning needs analysis'? If so, how?

Induction

Starting a new job has been compared with one's first day at school. The newcomer is bound to be: a little nervous, but hopefully enthusiastic; keen to impress, but not wanting to attract too much attention; anxious to learn quickly, but not wanting to be deluged with names, facts and figures; hoping to fit in, but not look too 'new' and inexperienced.

The reception from the employer should ideally anticipate these feelings. After all, the organization has spent good money hiring the newcomer and should treat that person as an investment to be nurtured and encouraged. In reality, however, new recruits are likely to receive an induction or orientation, which can be anywhere between two extremes:

- *In at the deep end* – expecting the recruit to get on with the job without any real welcome or information.
- *Overwhelming* – providing the newcomer with an avalanche of introductions, site tours, information packs, etc.

Most large organizations inflict at least some of the following on new hires:

- Handing out the employee handbook – the HR department may be proud of it but it is not going to be an easy read.
- Introducing the new recruit to everybody in the business – embarrassing at best, and likely to be off-putting to a new hire who wants to slide into the job quietly. Besides, no one will remember what they have been told nor the names of the people to whom they have been introduced.
- Dishing out even more facts and figures on day one.
- Doing so in the form of a lecture or presentation – with slides.
- Doing it again on day two.
- Not giving the employee their own 'home' – workspace, desk, phone, computer.
- Having the immediate supervisor away on vacation, in a continuous series of meetings, or just too busy to be involved.

These activities run the risk of boring and confusing, rather than helping, the new employee. Obviously, there is information that new recruits need and paperwork (payroll details, social security, etc.) that has to be done. Also, there is a degree of ritual – a 'rite of passage' – expected by the new hire, colleagues and the organization. But the process needs to be thought through, especially in relation to timing, quantity and intensity.

The simple truth is that most people responsible for orienting new employees do not put themselves in the new hire's shoes – i.e. do not take account of just what it is like to start a new job – or think of induction as an adult learning process that has to be designed to take account of the ways in which people learn. Unfortunately, joiners are commonly 'thrown in at the deep end'. Finding themselves in a strange environment and told to get on with it, they are easily forgotten. Raw recruits are left feeling anxious and vulnerable, forced to make sense of new surroundings and to learn correct procedures the hard way. Many managers regard this approach with favour: after all, this was how they learned to cope and get to grips with the business. It is regarded as a test of competence, of machismo, of ability to survive in a demanding environment. This can be a valuable 'growth' experience but there is a considerable risk of individuals becoming disillusioned, leaving or developing bad habits.

As we noted in earlier chapters, there is a well-known 'induction crisis' in which a proportion of new recruits leave within the first few weeks. Effective recruitment and selection takes time and costs money. Careless handling of new recruits can render this easily into waste. It is a questionable way of dealing with a significant investment. In the same way as young seedlings and transplanted cuttings are the most vulnerable plants a gardener has to look after, newcomers and promotees are the employees at greatest risk of disillusionment and failure. They will worry about their ability to fit in, their competence to do the job, and the impression they are creating in the eyes of their bosses and colleagues.

HRM in reality

Induction: getting it right

1 Treat each individual new employee as an individual – i.e. induction must be tailored to orient individual recruits according to their needs. A school-leaver or fresh graduate will require a different approach to a seasoned professional or experienced worker who can 'hit the ground running'. Don't insult the latter – and waste valuable working time – by putting them through the official HR department induction programme! It is not advisable to have an orientation procedure that is applied to everyone regardless.

2 The immediate line manager should be closely involved, even if arrangements are made by the HR department.

3 It is often useful to allocate a 'buddy' or sponsor on the same working level as the new hire. This allows informal learning to take place about unwritten rules of behaviour, location of important services, and all kinds of 'how to's that are obvious to an experienced employee, but not to a newcomer. Pick a positive person for this role.

4 Pace the induction process. It is not necessary to do everything on the first morning. The newcomer will still be learning in six months' time.

5 Give the new recruit a real job to do as soon as possible. There is nothing more demoralizing than feeling oneself to be a 'spare part' or a nuisance in a busy department.

The casual Western approach to induction contrasts sharply with Japanese practice. New employees in large Japanese companies receive intensive and prolonged induction training. For example, at Toyota a typical apprentice (secondary school-leaver aged 18) devotes the first two to four months of employment to learning the Toyota Production System. This includes the intricacies of *kaizen* (continuous job improvement) and *kanban* – a card system which conveys information between factory and suppliers.

Table 21.1	CIPD survey of learning methods	

Method	Percentage
On-the-job training	87.3
Face-to-face	84.3
Coaching/mentoring	59.4
Formal education	49.6
Conference	43.4
Open learning (non-electronic)	34.7
CD-ROM	28.9
Video	26.1
Intranet	23.7
Other computer	22.7
Internet	16.5
Action learning	14.7
Audio based	8.4
Extranets	7.4

Source: *Training and Development in Britain 1999*, CIPD (2001).

After this training, the trainee is ready to start on production. There is additional on-the-job training on a slightly slower than usual production line. It is also the opportunity for the trainee to absorb the 'fighting minds' mentality. This is the ability to withstand the pressure of the full-speed production line in a motivated, positive manner. The pressure is formidable, requiring total and unflagging concentration. The induction programme emphasizes teamwork: fundamentally, it is a process of socialization.

Some overseas subsidiaries have sent new recruits to parent factories in Japan, returning as converts to Japanese practices with 'modelled behaviour patterns'. Intensive induction programmes are designed to produce loyal employees through a process dominated by personality 'development', imbuing workers with the company's history and purpose and thereby fusing the individual and the organization. Similar advanced practices are used in the West, especially for management trainees.

HRM in reality	**Organizations yet to embrace online learning**

The CIPD's third annual training survey shows that online learning is still lagging well behind more traditional training methods (see Table 21.1). The survey was commissioned from the Centre for Labour Market Studies, Leicester University, who telephone interviewed over 500 people in December 2000 and January 2001.

Mike Cannell, author of the report and CIPD adviser on training and development says:

> The tried and tested training methods remain by far and away the most popular. For example, 84.3 per cent of training managers say that they regularly use face-to-face training courses – in contrast, 45.4 per cent of those surveyed claim they have never used the internet for training while only 16.5 per cent use it regularly.

But Cannell believes that online learning is likely to mature in the short to medium term:

Key indicators point to a growing future for online learning. For example, a comparison between this year's survey and that of 1999 shows a 33 per cent increase in the use of intranets and a 28 per cent increase in the use of the internet. However, there seems to be a lot of uncertainty about the new techniques; 40 per cent of those questioned felt unable to respond to questions relating to the use of intranets or the internet. I suspect that this suggests that there is a great deal of nervousness about how to tackle e-learning, not least because one can make expensive mistakes by choosing the wrong solutions. For this reason, the CIPD will be campaigning over the coming months to improve understanding of the benefits – and pitfalls – of e-learning.

Clearly, technology is playing an increasingly important role in training, but the more traditional methods of learning far outweigh online learning. The average spend on training per employee remains a concern; it must be significantly increased if we are to move towards a higher skilled economy.

Martyn Sloman (2001), author of *The E-learning Revolution*, says: 'Existing models of learning and training are being overturned. Those trainers who stay inside their comfort zones and think in terms of traditional models will be the losers in the profession.' Also, John Chambers, CEO of Cisco Systems stated that: 'I truly believe e-learning will change the way schools and universities teach, the way students learn, and the way businesses keep employees up to date with the skills and information for this fast changing internet economy.'

Sloman adds

The pace of change in the global economy and advances in communications technology mean that there is no debate about whether e-learning is the future or not. It clearly is. Latest assessments indicate that competitive organizations will soon be delivering up to a fifth of their training through the internet, intranets or the web.

Martyn Sloman's book advocates that trainers should rapidly gain an understanding of how e-learning allows the delivery of training in an entirely new way. Learners become interactive clients needing differentiation in services and products, rather than passive customers accepting standard products. They will be able to shop around for training providers, just like any other consumers on the web.

Sloman sets out 21 propositions in *The E-learning Revolution*, including:

● How technology offering learner-centred opportunities will demand re-examination of the way adults learn.

● What lessons can be learnt from organizations such as the BBC, Motorola, IBM and the Post Office.

● How corporate universities and virtual business schools can provide radically different learning opportunities.

● Why barriers between knowledge management, performance management and training must fall to achieve competitive advantage.

Sloman concludes that: 'Trainers have to get to grips with these issues and redefine their roles and skills. New skills will need to be developed and customer/client management will become a top priority.'

Source: *HRMGuide.co.uk* (http://www.hrmguide.co.uk), 3 April 2001.

Learning methods

HRD managers are presented with an ever-increasing range of learning methods. Traditionally, they have been divided into:

- *On-the-job training*, including demonstrations of equipment and procedures, instruction manuals and PC-based training packages.
- *Off-the-job training*, such as group briefings, projects and formal courses.

Off-the-job training can be in-house, taking place within the organization, or external, for example at a local college or university.

More recently, e-learning has arrived on the scene. A survey for SkillSoft Corporation conducted in the USA and Canada during January and February 2001 by Taylor Nelson Sofres found that (*HRM Guide USA* [http://www.hrmguide.net/usa/], 17 April 2001):

- Some 43 per cent of businesses involved in the survey were in the process of implementing e-learning initiatives or had already done so.
- Around 85 per cent of these businesses planned to increase investment in e-learning during 2001.
- About 19 per cent of businesses were already using e-learning for business skills training and 39 per cent of large businesses (10 000 or more employees) were delivering business training via e-learning.
- An increase of 79 per cent was projected in the number of organizations expected to use e-learning for business skills in the coming year.
- The main benefits cited by businesses that used e-learning were: improved workforce effectiveness (67 per cent); reduction in training (60 per cent); and improved workforce retention (45 per cent).

However, enthusiasm for online learning is not so pronounced outside the USA. A study from Vanson Bourne published by THINQ Limited found that in a survey of UK IT managers, 65 per cent said that their companies were not using online learning for internal training (*Training Journal*, October 2002, p.4). Smaller companies were most likely (78 per cent) not to be using online learning, compared to 53 per cent of large companies. The most often cited barrier (28 per cent) was that learners preferred 'talk and chalk' or classroom learning to other methods.

Action learning

Many years before the concept of e-learning was thought of, Revans (1972) argued that classroom-based management education is not adequate (see Table 21.2). He devised a systematic, experiential or 'action learning' programme based on job exchanges that placed managers in unfamiliar situations and asked them to take on challenging tasks. These tasks:

1 Must be based on real work projects.
2 Projects must be owned and defined by senior managers and be important to the future of the organization.
3 The process is an investment requiring a real return on cost.
4 Managers must work in groups, learning from each other and crossing boundaries between functions and departments.
5 Projects must go beyond analysis – they should require real action and change.

Table 21.2	Comparison of training and 'action learning'

Traditional	Action learning
Individual-based	Group-based
Knowledge emphasis	Skills emphasis
Input-orientated	Output-orientated
Classroom-based	Work-based
Passive	Active
Memory tested	Competence tested
Focus on past	Focus on present and future
Standard cases	Real cases
One way	Interactive
Teacher-led	Student-led

Source: Based on Margerison (1991).

6 Content (programmed knowledge) and process (questions/methods) of change should be studied.

7 There must be public commitment from participants to action/report.

Revans' ideas are consistent with the principles of the learning organization discussed earlier in this chapter. The emphasis lies with learning rather than training and with meeting the changing needs of an organization in a competitive world. His approach is also mirrored in many current programmes aimed at developing leaders. Margerison (2002), a keen exponent of action learning comments:

> Management courses should not be separated from the reality of work. Indeed, a management programme should be based on the issues identified by those attending, and the tutor needs to have the consulting skills to respond to the demands. Courses should be integral to both work and careers and based on what the participants are doing. By focusing on real issues, they can learn with and from others how to tackle them.

But, he also notes that although this is a nice idea, it is hard to do:

> After all, who is running the management development show – the trainers (and that term says it), or the people who do the line management job? Too often, it is the trainers for they insist on running their role-plays, exercises, case studies and giving their standard talks. They are input led. My view is that we should be output led, and follow the needs of the participants in a more mentoring, coaching and facilitating role.

HRM in reality	**Business-driven action learning**

Business, in the past, was not particularly interested in fostering learning and the self-development of its people, says Dr Yury Boshyk, author and international expert on business-driven action learning.

But, he argues, the situation is changing with more companies worldwide – such as General Electric, Siemens, Boeing, Baxter Healthcare, DuPont, Fujitsu, Johnson & Johnson and Volvo Car Corporation – adopting business-driven action learning as a way to explore new business opportunities and develop their best people.

▶

Dr Boshyk, chairman of the Global Executive Learning Network, addressed the 7th Annual Global Forum on Business-Driven Action Learning and Executive Development held last week at the Gordon Institute of Business Science (GIBS) in South Africa. The forum was sponsored by Standard Bank. Dr Boshyk said:

> As a philosophy, business-driven action learning is based on the belief and practice that learning should be tied to business realities, and that some of the best business solutions can and should come from fellow executives and employees. Many of the companies that utilize business-driven action learning are those who also have a high respect for their people and who appreciate that learning often comes from the sharing of experiences in an open exchange, which in turn encourages reflection and practical application.

Boshyk's Global Executive Learning Network and Victoria Marsick, co-director of the J.M. Huber Institute for Learning in Organizations at the Columbia University, New York, USA, claim from survey results that between 60 per cent and 65 per cent of 45 top multinational companies were using action learning.

According to Boshyk:

> Product life cycles, globalization, and indeed, the entire pace of business life and decision-making took on a new meaning in the 1990s. The new business mantra included the key words: speed, flexibility, shareholder value and customer focus, and therefore, the need for change. Many senior executives realized the need to align their organizations to these new objectives.

Changing corporate culture was perceived as a top priority with companies' cultural 'baggage' and old ways of thinking as the greatest obstacles to success. Education and hence the learning organization were 'discovered' by chief executives and it became important in their eyes to learn quickly, and faster than competitors. Reg Revans, one of the founders of action learning, used to say that for competitive reasons, 'learning must be equal to or greater than the rate of change.' But, at the turn of the 21st century it seems clear that individuals and organizations who learn faster than the rate of change gain competitive advantage.

Boshyk argues that as traditional executive education provided to companies was seen not to be translated into business results, chief executives began looking to action learning as a more relevant approach to their new, emerging educational needs:

> Companies began to realize that knowledge, with an emphasis on 'actionable knowledge', was a corporate asset and therefore had to be developed for competitive advantage. The past emphasis on individual development and learning was replaced with a view that individual learning should be tied more directly and clearly to organizational objectives as well.

Business-driven action learning (as practised in some of the world's best companies) involves five key elements:

- The active involvement and support of senior executives.
- Participants working in teams on real business issues and exploring new strategic business opportunities.
- Action research and learning focused on internal and external company experiences and thinking that can help resolve business issues.
- Leadership development through teamwork and coaching.

- Follow-up on the business issues and leadership development, thus enhancing positive business results and ensuring that learning is greater than the rate of change.

According to Professor Peter Pribilla, head of corporate human resources at Siemens AG:

> The speed at which a corporation can learn and employ new knowledge is a decisive factor in competition. It is not enough to learn and work. Learning and working must be integrated. Only then can a corporation be a learning organization. Action learning addresses this challenge very efficiently.

Gerard van Schaik, president of the European Foundation for Management Development and former chairman of the executive board of Heineken, says:

> Real progress in business is only achieved by corporations and individuals trying out creative ideas and making them work, running into problems and solving them, by pooling talent and scoring with it, and most of all … by having fun and learning while doing. Business-driven action learning is a superb vehicle for achieving this.

Source: *HRMGuide.com* (http://www.hrmguide.com), 27 May 2002.

Activity 21:6   Do we still need training specialists if people can learn for themselves?

Leadership development

'I would argue that more leaders have been made by accident, circumstance, sheer grit, or will than have been made by all the leadership courses put together' (Bennis, 1990).

The skills of leadership have attracted management theorists and trainers alike. Whereas good leaders are comparatively easy to recognize when they are in positions of authority, developing people to achieve the necessary qualities is not so easy. Just as the nature of leadership is not fully understood, the appropriate methods of training and leadership are a matter of controversy. At the same time leadership training is a lucrative area for training consultants, and management gurus have been ready to produce packaged methods. According to Crofts (1991), elective as opposed to despotic leadership 'is all about influence, persuasion and motivation – about making people *want* to do things your way.'

It is arguable that many supposed 'leadership' courses are actually teaching management skills rather than those of leadership. A typical leadership course concentrates on:

- Identifying the nature of leadership and the form which the individual trainee wishes to adopt. This incorporates a range of options from being able to give orders (to 'boss') to a more inspirational form.

- Self-awareness – the identification of those leadership skills which individuals feel themselves to be lacking.

- A general boost in self-confidence.

The focus in each case depends on factors such as:

- Participants' level of seniority. It would be counter-productive to encourage a junior manager to adopt the manner and style appropriate to a managing director.

- The organizational culture in which trainees have to operate. Authoritarian forms of leadership would be disastrous in a participative business.

- Trainees' personalities. People vary in their degrees of assertiveness and sensitivity and need to develop a leadership style that fits naturally with their personality characteristics. It is easier to develop abilities that already exist in an embryonic form than to attempt to change an individual's whole character. The latter is likely to be impossible.

Part of the programme would involve a team exercise requiring the solution of a hypothetical problem.

Many courses have taken on 'outward bound' elements. These use sport or other outdoor physical activities that require skill as a vehicle for experiential learning. Such programmes claim to develop management skills such as leadership, teamwork, communication, problem solving, managing change and coping with stress. However, much of this learning does not translate naturally to the office. There have also been lasting physical and psychological effects of a negative kind – particularly with older, unfit participants.

Perhaps a more positive approach comes from involvement in corporate community initiatives (*Financial Times Guide to Business in the Community, 1995*). De-layered and slimmed-down organizations offer reduced opportunities for promotion, and hence development at lower levels of management but, at the same time, demand from employees greater 'soft skills' – teamwork, listening, negotiating, influencing and general communication. Community projects offer scope for these skills to be honed and tested in 'power without authority' organizations. The UK's Business in the Community (BITC) has originated a number of schemes such as:

- 100-hour development assignments
- career-change 'transitional' secondments
- 'business on board' – trusteeships with voluntary sector groups.

Seconded or voluntary participants have found that they learn from each other, break down barriers and increase their team skills.

Evaluating and costing training

According to Rosania (2000):

> The fact is that trainers do not inherently lack power; what they lack is the ability to use their power in a way that consistently demonstrates the value of their service to their stakeholders. Trainers do not need fancy titles or affiliation with certain departments to demonstrate their value. What trainers need to change is their thinking about how they can contribute to the success of their organizations.

Of course, one basic issue affecting the credibility of trainers is the need to demonstrate the value of training to the organization. In a review of evaluation methods, Rowden (2001) states: 'The "beancounters" in the organization are likely to know exactly how much training "costs" but they may have little idea of its value. HR must be able to supply that information if it is to truly become a strategic part of the organization.'

Kirkpatrick (1994) split evaluation into four levels:

- *Reaction* – is the 'customer' satisfied? If the trainee does not like the programme he or she is unlikely to be motivated to learn.

- *Learning* – Brown and Seidner (1998) state that this 'can be described as the extent to which participants change attitudes, improve knowledge, and/or increase skill as a result of attending the program'.
- *Behaviour change* – how is actual behaviour changed by training?
- *Results* – the return on investment (ROI) or effect of the training on the organization's bottom-line.

Rowden (2001) examines the last two levels in detail. He proposes the following as the most significant for measuring behaviour change: a 360-degree appraisal feedback process and, secondly, a performance-learning-satisfaction evaluation system. In practice, evaluation is seen as a weak link in the learning process. 'It is the step most likely to be neglected or underdone' (Gibb, 2002, p.107).

Sloman (1993) found that organizations were placing increasing importance on training effectiveness and value for money. More than half of his surveyed companies evaluated every training event and many others were examining ways of doing so. Virtually all respondents had training budgets but practice on decentralizing these varied widely. Many training budgets were held by line managers with a charging mechanism for training activities organized by training departments. One respondent (Sony Manufacturing) abandoned this practice because 'training was not high on people's agenda' and departmental budget spends were not being analysed properly. Other sources indicate a wider problem. For example, of 200 organizations which were 'committed to training', attending conferences held by the UK Industrial Society, only 10 per cent had an evaluation system in place (van de Vliet, 1993). However, by 1999 an IPD survey found that at least 75 per cent of organizations were using some form of evaluation.

What methods are used in practice? The most obvious are 'happy-sheets' or questionnaires handed out to participants on completion of a training course. These are forms that ask trainees to rate the presentation and usefulness of the course and invite comments. The inherent flaws of this approach are well-known (Lewis, 1991):

- They are usually completed in the euphoric period at the end of the course when trainees are relieved to have survived, when they are looking forward to going home, and pressure and stress have lifted. At this point in time the world has taken on a comfortable, rosy glow.
- A personal relationship has been developed with the trainers, so criticism is toned down to avoid upsetting them.
- Most of all, the evaluation concentrates on the wrong issues. Often there is cursory attention to the value of the training experience to the trainees, their future job performance and hence the organization. Instead, forms are likely to concentrate on the overall enjoyability of the course and the quality of the environment in which it took place. According to McKenna (1994, p.212): 'It is known for trainees to be thoroughly satisfied with a programme merely because the instructor or trainer did a good job entertaining them'. Happy-sheets are excellent for comments on the comfort of hotel accommodation, speed and service in the restaurant and the stuffiness of seminar rooms. Usually they tell us little about the cost-effectiveness of the programme.

The evaluation of training has attracted considerable attention (Crittan, 1993). A number of models exist of which Hamblin's (1974) is, perhaps, the best known. Hamblin stratified training into five levels, which could be evaluated independently:

- *Level 1*. The reactions of trainees during training to the trainer, other trainees and external factors.

- *Level 2*. Learning achieved during training, assuming basic aptitude and receptiveness on the part of the trainee.
- *Level 3*. Job behaviour in the work environment at the end of the training period.
- *Level 4*. The overall effects on the organization.
- *Level 5*. Ultimate values: factors such as business survival, profit, welfare of interested parties and social/political welfare.

However, the fact that such models exist has not led many organizations to use them! Hendry (1995, p.366) echoes some astute criticisms of evaluation:

> The whole notion of evaluation is based on training as a discrete event – namely the training course – and justifying the substantial visible costs associated with off-the-job courses and full-time training staff. Take these away, as Hamblin (1974) and Crittan (1993) have observed, and the rationale and pressure for evaluation largely collapses. Evaluation of training events was always a fallacy as long as it ignored the equally important process of practice back on the job which ensures that training transfers.

In practice, Hendry (1995, p.364) argues that the most progressive firms use a mixture of:

- *'Hard' evaluation criteria*. Short-term improvements in measurable performance, such as individual productivity and quality adherence.
- *'Soft' criteria*. Indirect benefits from intermediate human resource goals, including reduction in staff turnover, promotability and flexibility.

Tamkin, Yarnall and Kerrin (2002) and Gibb (2002) concur that although evaluation has grown in priority in recent years, most evaluation activity is unsophisticated. According to Gibb (2002, p.120):

> So while L&D evaluation is at least now done more widely than ever before it is stuck at the most basic level possible, with the prevalence and preference in L&D for using the basic recipes of levels of evaluation. … In the end the formulas and techniques for evaluation of L&D have to balance the demands of scientific rigour with those of professional practice, and the theoretical goals of 'truth seeking' with the practical goals of 'pragmatic management'.

Summary

A much-publicized modern approach places development within the learning organization, which contrasts with older notions of learning within organizations. HRD focuses strongly on management development. Career plans, performance objective-setting and training programmes are more often directed at managers than lower-level employees. With the integration of training activities into human resource development programmes trainers are particularly concerned with cost-effectiveness, quality and the merits of formal as opposed to experiential training. A widening range of learning methods allows employees to acquire information and skills in an active, self-directed manner.

Further reading

Telling Ain't Training by Harold D. Stolovitch and Erica J. Keeps (published by ASTD, 2002) is an engaging book written by two training professionals, but useful for a wider audience. *New Directions in Career Planning and the Workplace: Practical Strategies for*

Career Management Professionals edited by Jean M. Kummerow (Davies-Black Publishing, 2000) includes exercises and examples. *The Action Learning Guidebook* by William J. Rothwell (published by Jossey-Bass, 1999) covers the action learning process. See also *The ASTD e-Learning Handbook: Best Practices, Strategies, and Case Studies for an Emerging Field* edited by Allison Rossett (published by McGraw-Hill, 2001) and *Evaluating Training Programs: The Four Levels,* 2nd edition by Donald L. Kirkpatrick (published by Berrett-Koehler, 1998). *How to Measure Training Success* by Jack Phillips and Ron D. Stone (published by McGraw-Hill, 2002) extends Kirkpatrick's methodology to include return on investment (ROI).

Review questions

1 How would you distinguish between learning organizations and learning in organizations?

2 What are the most significant links between performance management and learning and development?

3 What is a learning or training needs analysis? How would you conduct an analysis for a small retail company?

4 How has the concept of career development changed in recent years? What are the implications of the reduction in management layers in many large organizations on individual career aspirations?

5 Outline the essential differences between action learning and formal training.

6 What are the most important features of induction?

7 Is it possible to prove that training is a worthwhile business investment?

8 Draw up your personal career plan for the next five years.

Problem for discussion and analysis

Lisa

Lisa was a recent recruit. The personnel manager was very pleased to have taken her on as her assessment centre results were outstanding. She was a graduate in Chemical Engineering, apparently keen to apply her university training within the organization, a medium-sized manufacturer of aluminium products.

Previous female graduate recruits had received a brief induction period involving visits to all departments, and had then been placed in marketing or personnel jobs. None had risen beyond the junior management grades: higher posts seemed to be reserved for men promoted from production and finance. The board had decided that the company's attitude towards women was old-fashioned and was preventing them from making the best use of their human resources. Lisa was the opportunity to do something positive about the problem. With the support of the MD, the personnel manager set out to offer Lisa a development programme that would give her the opportunity to achieve a senior management post within a reasonable period.

▶

Situation

Tina Johnson was a determined and thorough personnel manager. In her late 40s and without much in the way of academic qualifications herself, she was aware that many bright young recruits were going to university before taking their first job. She was also in touch with the greater expectations of young people qualified to this level. She found that they were unhappy with the idea of several years at a junior level before being offered a seriously demanding job.

Lisa did not seem to be any different to the other graduates taken on by the company. Outside the male-dominated production and service areas, there were many female graduates at the lower management levels. Lisa had been with the company for three months and had completed the 'grand tour' which was the company's induction programme.

Tina decided to conduct a development interview with Lisa. Tina began by asking her how she felt about the company so far.

'It isn't quite what I expected,' said Lisa. She seemed ill at ease and nervous.

'Oh, in what way?' asked Tina in a friendly but quizzical tone.

'Well, I suppose I was expecting to use my university training from the beginning … rather than being shown around places like Marketing and Distribution,' Lisa answered in a very apologetic way.

Tina decided to persist: 'Yes, but we think it's important for you to have a proper induction programme so that you get a basic understanding of the way the company operates. We invest a lot of time and money in our new recruits … three months is a long time to spend just on induction, you know.'

Lisa continued to look doubtful, and clearly wasn't convinced: 'I just don't think I learned very much, that's all.'

'Why was that?' said Tina, sensing that she had a problem she had not anticipated.

Lisa took some time composing her answer. It was clear that she was fumbling for words that would allow her to express her opinion without upsetting the personnel manager: 'I really wanted to show people that I know a lot about chemical engineering but nobody seems interested. Besides, several people told me that I would probably end up in marketing anyway. Most women do, don't they? Or personnel, and I'm definitely not interested in that.' She emphasized 'personnel' with a grimace.

After the development interview Lisa wrote a letter couched in hostile terms, accusing the company of misleading her and having no idea of how to use graduates. She had been offered a scholarship to study for a PhD at an American university and had accepted it. She would be leaving the company in a month's time.

Activity brief: (a) How would you have designed Lisa's development programme? (b) What resistance would you have reasonably expected and how would you have overcome it?

PART 9

Employee relations

In this part of the book we examine the mechanisms by which organizations and workers communicate and resolve conflict within the employment relationship. Why 'employee' rather than 'industrial' relations? The latter has acquired a negative connotation, associated with conflict between trade unions and employers and conveys a picture of acrimonious strikes and lock-outs (Blyton and Turnbull, 1994, p.7). 'Employee relations' avoids such preconceptions and also serves to widen the topic to encompass flexible and cooperative relationships between individuals and organizations. As with much of the terminology associated with HRM, the newer term is broader in perspective and indicates a more proactive approach.

The chapters in Part 9 address a number of specific issues:

- What is the historical and current status of trade unionism?
- How do different cultural and legislative contexts affect the practice of employee relations?
- What formal and informal mechanisms are used for individual and collective workplace bargaining?
- How does negotiation take place?
- What is the role of arbitration?
- How is 'employee involvement' defined and implemented?
- Is work–life balance a feasible objective?
- Why are health and safety matters often neglected in comparison to other organizational priorities?

22 | Unions and collective bargaining

Objectives

The purpose of this chapter is to:

- Debate the concept of collective employee relations.
- Provide an overview of formal employee relations, including the role of trade unions.
- Evaluate comparative employee relations in a range of developed countries.
- Draw lessons from comparative employee relations.

Introduction

In earlier chapters we observed that HRM is generally associated with a move from collectivist employee relations – stressing union–employer bargaining arrangements – towards individual-based negotiation, reinforced by personal contracts and performance-based pay systems. The change has not been total in those countries where HRM has been influential and is certainly not universal. In reality, collective negotiation and representation remain common.

The common perception also relates to an outmoded picture – a Thatcherite or Reaganite world – which in many countries is being replaced by more formalized models such as that of the European Union. In the UK and Ireland, for example, EU legislation is steadily bringing companies into line with the attitudes of the social market, differentiating them from their US cousins. This is exemplified by the requirement that all large multinational companies operating in more than one EU country must have Europe-wide works councils, ensuring an enhanced role for collective representation in the 21st century. Ironically, of course, this also means that US multinationals must also observe what may be a comparatively alien process of compulsory union consultation within their European operations.

Employee relations   Employee relations is not confined to unionized collective bargaining but encompasses all employment relationships. It goes beyond the negotiation of pay and benefits to include the conduct of the power relationship between individual employees and their employers.

The employment relationship also encapsulates different cultural assumptions about the roles, entitlements and obligations of these stakeholders. Accordingly, national employment systems are heavily influenced by their ideological and cultural traditions. We noted in Part 2 that businesses operate within varied legal frameworks, reflecting underlying ideological beliefs in the rights of employers and employees. As an example, we shall see later in this chapter that German companies operate within a social market that places great importance on a balanced relationship between employee and employer. German business culture also emphasizes regulation. Hence the German job market is based on detailed legislation, formalized consultation procedures and protected employee rights. Conversely, legislation in free market countries tends to leave employee consultation to local arrangements and provides little employee protection. Paradoxically, countries such as Canada, the UK and the USA have a history of more advanced equal opportunity legislation than Germany, specifically for ethnicity and reflecting their multi-cultural nature.

We begin this chapter at the environmental level with an evaluation of the role of collective bargaining in different business cultures, ranging from the free market in the USA and UK, through the social market represented by Germany, to Japan as an example of Asia-Pacific approaches. We move on to consider the organizational context and discuss both management and employee strategies.

Collectivization and confrontation

This section considers the problematic concept of the employment relationship. Regarded by neo-classical economists (see Part 3) as an exchange of labour for pay, it is also a power relationship in which the employer has the formal authority to direct effort towards specific goals, whereas the employee can – informally – frustrate the achievements of those objectives. The employment relationship goes beyond money to include a number of secondary issues, such as working conditions, the length of the working day, vacation time, freedom to arrange one's work and measures of participation.

Through collectivization, workers could band together to protect their mutual interests. From the late 19th century, trade unions have fought for improved conditions for their members. The first unions were formed for defensive purposes, often in response to cuts in wages, denying change without payment and setting the scene for future accusations of intransigence.

Adapted from McIlwee and Roberts (1991, p.386) trade unions can be categorized as follows:

1 *Craft unions* – recruiting members from distinct trades or occupations, historically linked to an apprenticeship system. Originally such unions aimed to preserve jobs within the craft exclusively for their members. Technological change has blurred and, sometimes, eliminated the craft skills and unions have survived by changing their membership boundaries to incorporate other areas.

2 *Industrial unions* – for example the National Union of Mineworkers in Britain, IG Metall in Germany. The dominant form in Germany but slow to develop in the UK. They aim to represent all employees in a particular industry regardless of their type of work.

3 *General unions* – broad-ranging unions representing a variety of industries and job types with little restriction on potential membership. Some are so extensive that they have been termed 'super-unions'.

4 *Occupational unions* – recruit members within a particular occupation or group such as teachers, police or fire-fighters.

5 *White-collar unions* – concentrating on non-manual occupations such as banking.

Unions have been described as a mixture of movement and organization (Flanders, 1970). On the one hand, they met workers' individual needs: protecting them from exploitation; negotiating improved wages and conditions; developing career prospects. On the other, unions had a wider, collective purpose which often extended into a political role. Workers were expected to subordinate personal advantage to the greater interests of the membership as a whole. In this respect, trade unions offered an alternative focus for employee commitment and a power base which clashed with the prerogatives of management: '... modern societies have developed a whole range of *labour market institutions*, ranging from social custom and moral codes to labour law and collective agreements, that is, the outcome of collective bargaining at an aggregate level which lies above the private level between employer and employee' (Van Ruysseveldt, Huiskamp and van Hoof, 1995, p.2).

The history of trade unionism varies from one country to another in terms of:

● *Business sector*. Focusing on job conditions within an industry or specific company. Initially, unions in most countries organized around specific crafts such as boiler-makers; this pattern remained dominant in the UK until the late 20th century. In contrast, since 1945 German trade unions have represented all the workers in a specific industry.

● *Ideology*. Extending their role beyond the workplace and influencing social and political change to the advantage of their members. Many unions were instrumental in the creation of political parties, such as Labo(u)r in Australia and Britain. Employee relations have been a battleground for ideology, local disputes being played out as skirmishes in a much larger war.

Employee relations in North America

In the USA the prevailing business culture of scientific management and Fordism created a particular trade union response and an irreconcilable conflict between the interests of 'capital' and 'labour' (see Table 22.2).

Remarkably, the view from the 1920s (expressed in the text panel) remains typical of many US organizations today. In fact, most American management writers ignore trade unionism, taking a unitarist (see Key concept 22.2) rather than a pluralist or collective viewpoint (Guest, 1992). Beaumont (1992) argues that this perspective is reflected in a considerable reduction in US union membership and collective bargaining in recent decades. American HRM literature also emphasizes individual relationships and marginalizes trade unions (Blyton and Turnbull, 1994). Unions have been viewed as restricting the nation's competitive position and protecting insiders (those with jobs) at the expense of those without. However, Van Ruysseveldt, Huiskamp and van Hoof (1995, p.2) contend that '... no modern society has ever accepted a purely individualistic determination of the employment relationship.'

Assumptions of confrontational industrial relations

1 Workers' and employers' interests are generally opposed. Employers: want highest output at least cost; try to lower wages, increase hours, speed up workers; try to remove least efficient workers; maintain worst possible working conditions; discharge workers when possible; replace expensive, skilled workers with cheaper, low-skilled employees; and reduce numbers through automation. Conversely, unions: attempt to obtain continuous employment; seek highest wage rates; and look for the best working conditions.

2 Effort and increased output produce lower wages. Employers prefer reducing prices to increase market share, rather than pass on productivity benefits to workers as higher wages.

3 Wages depend on the relative bargaining strengths of employers and workers.

4 Employers' bargaining strength is always greater than the workers'.

5 Employers' full bargaining strength will be exerted against individuals.

6 Individual bargaining produces competition between workers. This tends to lower wages to the level accepted by the weakest bargaining worker.

7 This applies during employment as well as recruitment. If workers speed up in response to bonuses, there is competition between workers.

Source: Hoxie (1923).

Kanter (1989, p.117) describes the tradition of American management as being firmly rooted in paranoia:

> One of the lessons America's mythologized cowboys supposedly learned in the rough-and-tumble days of the American frontier was that paranoia was smart psychology. You couldn't trust anybody. They were all out to get you, and they would steal from you as soon as your back was turned.

Key concept 22:2

Unitarism versus pluralism   The unitarist view is implicit in American models of HRM. It holds that the interests of employees and the firm should be the same. Pluralism, on the other hand, recognizes that every organization is composed of different interests that are not balanced. Pluralists accept that conflict is natural and are concerned with the means by which it can be managed.

'Self-reliance' became the motto of the country. Everything outside one's own control was treated as an adversary and a potential enemy and had to be dominated. This applied as much to trade unions as it did to competitors. Elsewhere in the democratic world, such an extreme position was unusual. Nevertheless, it cannot be assumed (by benign unitarists, for example) that there is a common agenda between employers and the employed that can be 'managed'. There is an inevitable, if latent, tension between the two (Blyton and Turnbull, 1994, p.4).

Historically, unions attempted to replace all individual bargaining with collective bargaining (see Key concept 22.3) in order to increase employee bargaining power and counter employers' attempts to create competition between workers. This required solidarity between union members. Union goals were to obtain standardized wages and conditions at the best possible level. In contrast, employers have preferred to deal with employees on an individual basis.

Key concept 22:3

Collective bargaining   Collective bargaining takes place between employers and trade unions when: employees are members of trade unions that undertake to negotiate on their behalf in matters such as pay, working conditions, other benefits and work allocation; and employers recognize trade unions and their officials as legitimate bargaining agents.

Braverman (1974) regarded the weakness of workers in the employment relationship as an inevitable consequence of the role of management. He concluded that managers owed a responsibility to the market, over and above their duties to shareholders and employees. If managers did not deliver continually increasing levels of productivity and efficiency then their businesses would not survive. The workforce held the key to survival through their creativity, imagination and problem-solving abilities. However, these same qualities could be used to resist managers' aspirations for change.

Employees were human beings with their own objectives that frequently differed from management goals. Under the 19th century craft-based system of production individual employees held a considerable degree of power through their possession of knowledge. Very often managers had no idea what workers were doing. The value of scientific management and Fordism lay in their ability to de-skill jobs and remove knowledge, and hence bargaining power, from the workforce. Braverman's original analysis has been criticized for oversimplifying the nature of skill because most workers were unskilled or semi-skilled at best. Fordism led to a relative standardization of the employment relationship throughout the developed world until around 1980, with the following characteristics (Van Ruysseveldt, Huiskamp and van Hoof, 1995, p.2):

● Permanent, full-time jobs.

● Wage increases on the basis of experience and training.

● Extra payments for inconvenient or anti-social arrangements, such as weekend working.

- Regular working hours and a clearly defined working week.
- Paid holidays.
- The right to collective representation and a degree of consultation on changes of working practices.

Trade unions conducted negotiations with employers within this framework. This form of employee relations was associated with vertical and horizontal division of labour, hierarchical management and close supervision of work. However, in the last two decades – as has been made evident in this book – this pattern of working life has disintegrated under the pressures of competition from newly developing countries and the arrival of flexibility. In consequence, the 'traditional' role of trade unions has been undermined.

Union activity was focused on people within the internal employment market. New working practices, on the other hand, may reduce the core workforce within the internal market to small and sometimes insignificant numbers. Moreover, in line with our discussion in earlier parts of this book, jobs may be on relatively short-term or part-time contracts. Variable working hours have become a valuable source of flexibility. Extended opening hours have offered employers the opportunity to generate more money from the same equipment and accommodation.

There have been significant differences in union density (proportion of the workforce who are trade union members) between Canada and the USA, and also between and within industry sectors in the United States. In the period 1950–2001 union density in Canada fluctuated in the range around 32–37 per cent, with a marked drop between the top and bottom of this range between 1995 and 2001. By contrast, there was a consistent drop in US union density between 1960 and 2002, down from comparable levels to those in Canada to a mere 13.2 per cent (16.1 million workers) in 2002.

Why is there such a difference? The prevailing view (see Johnson, 2002) is that mandatory voting has discouraged unionization in the USA whereas card-checking (counting the number of existing union members) until recently has encouraged unionization in Canada. In fact, there was a marked change in the proportion of the Canadian workforce covered by mandatory voting between 1993 (18 per cent) and 2000 (62 per cent). Individual provinces have introduced these changes with Ontario being the most significant (because of its population) in 1995.

According to the US Department of Labor:

- Men are more likely to be union members than women.
- African-Americans are more likely to be union members than either whites or Hispanics.
- Nearly four in ten government workers were union members in 2002, compared with fewer than one in ten employees in private sector industries.
- Almost two-fifths of workers in protective service occupations (including fire-fighters and police officers) were union members in 2002. Protective service occupations have had the highest union membership rate of any broad occupation group in every year since 1983.

Van Ruysseveldt, Huiskamp and van Hoof (1995, p.7) argue that the 'classic' analytical and theoretical frameworks for studying employee relations reflect the times in which they were conceived and do not provide a satisfactory perspective for today. The shift in the nature of the employment relationship, introduction of flexible working practices and elimination of large, homogeneous workforces have been so significant that any pre-1980s perspective becomes simply an historical curiosity.

A new role for organized labour?

Ken Georgetti, President of the Canadian Labour Congress, told thousands of union delegates at the opening of the CLC's 23rd Convention that organized labour can become a powerful political force to defend people from corporate greed and capitalist excess.

He pointed out that the structure of the CLC was designed before colour television and called for the organization of the labour movement to be modernized so that it can exercise the muscle that should come from a membership of 2.5 million people. 'To be successful, to give workers the unions and the Canadian Labour Congress they deserve, it is up to us as a labour movement to change our thinking, our culture, our approach ... because if we build on and respect our past and meet the challenges of today, there's no stopping us in the future.'

Georgetti has been leading the country's largest labour organization for three years. He says he has learned that Canada's political leadership – at federal, provincial and local levels – will only listen to working people if they speak with a united voice, from a position of strength, and apply constant pressure.

On the other hand, today's politicians are far too willing to listen to greedy CEOs who, according to Georgetti, do not deserve the attention given the standard they set: 'Even though the TSE 100 Index lost 16 per cent last year, the top 100 chief executive officers in Canada took home a 54 per cent raise. Name me one ordinary worker in this entire country who earned a 54 per cent increase in less than the last 20 years combined.' Georgetti attacked the political agenda of 'these greedy corporate leaders' which he considered was destroying the lives of workers around the world as well as corroding basic standards of decency in Canada. He cited the openly pro-business government of British Columbia who shut down the provincial human rights commission, repealed laws restricting child labour, and passed legislation eliminating overtime and bringing back the 12-hour working day.

'Canada's success is too important to leave it all up to government and business, workers have to be involved too ... and people desperately want us to fight back against the right wing and defend their standard of living and the quality of life they have built together in communities right across this country.'

Source: *HRM Guide Canada* (http://www.hrmguide.net/canada/), 10 June 2002.

Do trade unions have a role to play in the modern workplace?

Employee relations in the UK

The British were once notorious for industrial disputes and walkouts. In fact, they were daily occurrences in the 1960s and 1970s, such that industrial relations was perceived as a 'problem' that brought down governments. Weak management and intransigent unions produced industrial chaos, manifested by low productivity, hostility towards change and highly publicized disputes, fundamentally weakening the UK as an economic power.

The reputation of British personnel managers was not enhanced during this period. When HRM came onto the scene in the 1980s, personnel management had become bogged down in a form of industrial relations characterized by 'fire-fighting' – undermining any claim to being strategic or proactive (Hendry, 1995, p.12). By this time, personnel management had moved away from its neutral balancing role between employees and management. It had become a front-line activity in defence of the organization. Strikes, pay deals and overtime needs were largely dealt with in an ad hoc, piecemeal fashion with little sign of any strategy. In a context of industrial warfare, long-term thinking was displaced by short-term coping.

Hendry (1995, p.13) also attributes the lack of strategy to personnel managers' preference for dealing with industrial relations in an informal and personal manner. Their knowledge of the personalities involved on the management and union sides and their willingness to engage in 'off-the-record' discussions and make compromise deals fostered a quick-witted ability to clinch agreement on the spur of the moment. There was no place for long-term strategy – 'manpower tactics' were the prevailing practice (Atkinson, 1984).

The situation changed dramatically during the 1980s and 1990s. Recessions, 'New Right' politics, restrictive legislation on industrial action (see Part 3) and massive restructuring in many organizations considerably reduced the power and role of unions. They also led to the downfall of the industrial relations 'industry'. Instead:

● Detailed obligations between employer and employee were replaced by informal commitments.
● Job descriptions became flexible.
● Job demarcations diminished in the face of flexible working practices.

Consequently, the new employee relations extends beyond collective bargaining – or rather, two-sided warfare – to include non-unionized organizations where dialogue may be between employers and individual employees and alternative negotiating structures exist. Hendry (1995, p.49) reflects on the perspectives of people in the 'industrial relations orthodoxy' who see a 'persistent weakening of employee power within organizations through the substitution of individualized systems for collective ones'. The development of corporate cultures also offends their confrontational instincts and is perceived virtually as a top management plot. HRM is implicated as an anti-union philosophy (Guest, 1989, p.44) which:

1 Can be aggressively anti-union, advocating the withdrawal of recognition from existing unions.

2 Can produce more generous rewards through individual pay deals, making unions seem unnecessary.

3 Neutralizing or controlling unions through close attention to their activities by means of single-union agreements, no-strike clauses and pendulum arbitration. These can be reinforced with careful recruitment, socialization, communications, teamworking and so on.

Such tactics are theoretically plausible. However, it is difficult to find instances of HRM being responsible for these developments. Rather, HRM tends to coincide with such actions. If anything, it comes into play when dealing with subsequent mending of fences (Hendry, 1995, p.51).

Employees and managers frequently have different goals. Governments have also taken sides. For example, Prime Minister Margaret Thatcher crippled British trade unions in the 1980s. Recent management literature assumes that the worldwide balance of power has swung to employers. This is described by some as a 'new realism' among both managers and employees. Strikes virtually disappeared from the scene in countries such as Britain. In the early 1970s in the UK nearly 13 million days a year were lost through industrial action, while in the 1980s this dropped to an average of just over 7 million days a year. In 1995 the comparable figure was just 440 000, but at the time of writing (2003) a new wave of union militancy seems to be leading the country towards more turbulent employee relations.

Similarly, there has been a substantial reduction in days lost because of strikes in South Africa. In both countries these have been largely restricted to the public sector and have been responses to government attempts to contain public spending. The private sector, meanwhile, has contained industrial action by means of tactics such as:

- elaborate communications techniques
- career development
- quality circles
- performance-related pay
- non-union status.

Further restriction of the union role has come in the form of single-union agreements – limiting negotiating rights to one union rather than several – and no-strike deals. We will see later in this section that single-union arrangements are normal in Germany and that German unions regard them as beneficial. In the UK, however, such developments have led to deep philosophical disagreements and some acrimony among trade unions. Unions such as the mainly electrical EEPTU were accused of 'selling out' to employers and 'poaching' members by actively negotiating for single-union agreements; and, despite the rhetoric, it is clear that realism has driven most major unions into similar deals (Goss, 1994, p.142).

Intriguingly, Brown (1994) finds that during the 1980s average pay rises were higher in non-unionized than unionized businesses. Moreover, this was not due to single-union agreements. He finds no evidence that non-unionism in this period was associated with 'progressive' management developments such as HRM. Non-unionism is linked to the absence of a bargaining structure, but Brown argues that removing trade unions leads to worse people management. This is reflected in inferior training, health and safety, and dismissal practices. By their very existence, unions force managers to manage.

For whatever reason, strikes and other cases of reported industrial action are considerably more common in larger organizations. This is not necessarily due to the atmosphere being better in small companies; an obvious corollary is that far fewer people in small firms are members of unions. This is because employers in small companies actively discourage union organization, while unions are not particularly interested in small groups of staff who would need far more attention and provide relatively little extra benefit in either monetary or political terms.

Matlay (2002) observes that although SMEs are becoming increasingly significant, most of the research on employee relations has been conducted in large organizations. In Matlay's opinion, the few studies that have focused on small firms tend to be prescriptive, categorizing workplaces into simplistic 'small is beautiful' or 'bleak house' alternatives. Matlay's own survey of 6000 organizations finds that small business owners or managers tend to use a personalized and informal management style, and that employee relations are widely varied.

The Employment Relations Act 1999

The Employment Relations Act 1999 introduced:

- A statutory procedure for trade unions to be recognised (or derecognised) for collective bargaining purposes in organizations employing more than 20 workers. The Act provides for recognition to be awarded by an independent public body (the Central Arbitration Committee) where: (a) either a majority of the relevant workforce are union members (so-called 'automatic recognition'); or (b) following a ballot where a majority of those voting and at least 40 per cent of those entitled to vote support recognition.

- The right for a worker to be accompanied by a trade union official at disciplinary and grievance hearings.
- New protections against dismissal for employees taking official, lawfully organized industrial action, making it unfair to dismiss in the eight weeks following the commencement of action and thereafter if the employer has not taken all reasonable procedural steps to resolve the dispute.
- Strengthened rights to belong to a union.
- Measures to promote family-friendly working.
- Reform of tribunal awards for unfair dismissal (for example, by raising the maximum limit of compensatory awards from £12 000 to £50 000).

A DTI review of the Act early in 2003 indicates that it is succeeding in delivering better working standards and promoting a new climate of cooperation between workers and employers. Key findings of the review suggest that the recognition procedure has operated smoothly with cases now decided in less than half the time, and that inter-union disputes and legal challenges are rare. Also, the Act has encouraged voluntary settlement of recognition claims since 1998. Employers and unions have reached over 1000 voluntary recognition agreements.

However, a number of changes are proposed to improve the efficiency and clarity of the law, including: provision of earlier access rights to unions in recognition cases; clarification of the law on the 'right to be accompanied' so companions can contribute during disciplinary or grievance hearings; and, establishment of a new legal right for workers to access their union's services.

The DTI will also consider modifying aspects of trade union law, including the law on political fund ballots and union elections to lighten the administrative burdens on unions. But the review finds no evidence to support changing the central pillars of the Act, such as:

- The rules governing automatic recognition, where the majority are union members.
- The 40 per cent threshold for statutory recognition ballots.
- The exclusion of workplaces with less than 21 employees from statutory recognition.
- The eight-week period of protection for striking workers against dismissal – though the review suggests that days on which workers are locked out might be disregarded.

HRM in reality	**Union recognition still rising**

24 February 2003: Trade union recognition is still rising across the UK, according to the TUC's annual survey, *Focus on Recognition*, but the going is getting tougher as unions are left with smaller, more resistant and obstructive employers to deal with.

There were more than 300 recognition deals in the 12 months up to October 2002, according to the report. This compares with 159 in the 2000 report, which included deals reached before recognition laws came into force. But last year's figure is slightly less than the previous year's when unions achieved some 'easy-wins' in workplaces with union members, as a result of a more favourable atmosphere following the passing of union recognition laws. More than 90 per cent of new recognitions were achieved through voluntary agreement with employers.

Organizations with new recognition deals covered by the latest report include American Airlines, Boots, Meridian TV, Church of Scotland, Kwik-Fit, Greenpeace and Air New Zealand.

The report confirms the link between the legal right for unions to win recognition and the big increase in recognition deals. In the two years following the introduction of statutory recognition there were 50 per cent more recognition deals (770) than the total number of deals made in the previous five years (513). However, there are signs that anti-union employers are increasingly exploiting loopholes in the recognition law to deny staff recognition of their union.

Brendan Barber, TUC general secretary elect, said:

> Once again this report shows the dire warnings that recognition rights would lead to difficulties were wrong. The vast majority of new deals are coming about through voluntary agreement, and the deals are increasingly covering more than the basics of pay and conditions, covering issues such as pensions and training.
>
> The survey also nails the lie that unions only have a role in big businesses. We are much encouraged that so many small to medium businesses are signing voluntary agreements. This provides strong backing for our call to end the exclusion of employees of firms employing fewer than 20 – disproportionately women and from ethnic minorities – from the right to have their voice heard.
>
> But it can be tough going out there. There is still a small minority of employers who are desperate to avoid working with trade unions and now are using intimidation and unfair labour practices to deny staff a voice at work. That is why the government should change the Employment Relations Act to outlaw unfair practices and bullying.
>
> Yet these difficulties should not overshadow the very real advances that unions are making, and the growth of partnership relations at work.

Key findings from the report include the fact that the vast majority of voluntary agreements were for recognition covering at least pay, hours and holidays. Some 91 per cent also covered representation at grievance and disciplinary hearings. There were significant increases in the number of agreements covering training (62 per cent versus 44 per cent in 2001), information and consultation (59 per cent versus 41 per cent in 2001), equal rights (53 per cent) and pensions (36 per cent versus 23 per cent in 2001).

Statutory recognition

The agreement covering the largest number of workers was between Kwik-Fit and the T&G. As a result, 574 workers won recognition following a CAC ballot in which 92.2 per cent voted in favour. Following the CAC ruling, a voluntary agreement was concluded covering 3200 workers in over 600 auto centres across the UK (the statutory agreement only covered workers in London). NUJ recognition at the Bristol Evening Post was a crucial breakthrough in the Northcliffe Newspapers chain, a regional subsidiary of the Daily Mail Group. The deal covers 90 journalists.

Voluntary recognition

At board manufacturing company Norcor, the GPMU won recognition in February 2002 for 160 production workers after a 12-year campaign. Amicus secured recognition for 6000 staff employed by financial company AMP UK across the country. UNISON achieved recognition for 200 domestics employed by ISS Mediclean in South Durham in July.

▶

◄

Trends in recognition 1995–2002

Period	Number of new deals
July 95–Dec 95	54
Jan 96–June 96	54
July 96–Dec 96	54
Jan 97–June 97	26
July 97–Feb 98	55
Mar 98–Nov 98	34
Dec 98–Oct 99	75
Nov 99–Oct 00	159
Nov 00–Oct 01	450 (plus 20 through the CAC)
Nov 01–Oct 02	282 (plus 24 through the CAC)

Source: *HRMGuide.co.uk*, 24 February 2003.

Activity 22:2   What are the principal factors responsible for the changes in union power in the UK over the last few decades?

The European Union

Since the signing of the Treaty of Rome in 1958, there have been several attempts to develop community-wide initiatives on employee participation and corporate industrial relations. Progress in harmonizing this area has been slow but there has been a considerable convergence of employment conditions. The resistance of British Conservative governments towards any control of social policy at a European level is well known. However, the delay can be attributed to deeper philosophical differences within the EU as a whole. There are two perspectives (Cressey, 1993):

● Free market enthusiasts – particularly in the UK – seek deregulation and decentralization of employee relations. They emphasize voluntary, non-statutory arrangements.

● Regulatory minded people in the Commission, European Parliament and the Council of Ministers see a need for a harmonized system of employee relations.

The EU already recognizes employees and their representatives as a 'social partner' in its own institutions. It allows representation, consultation and participation within a number of the EU's tripartite bodies. The argument revolves around an extension of this representation to situations beyond the EU's own institutions.

Brewster (1994) describes Europe as a 'heavily unionized continent'. Membership of trade unions varies from 87.5 per cent in Denmark to a mere 9.1 per cent in France (see Table 22.1). Membership is concentrated in organizations employing over 200 staff. In part, this variation reflects the differing traditions of member states, from the free market capitalist model in the UK to the social market concepts prevalent in Germany. Brewster concludes that, unlike the UK, German unions 'tend to be more involved and to have more positive and less antagonistic relations with employers'.

Table 22.1	Trade union membership in the EU compared to the USA and Japan (trade union density, per cent, 2000)

Country	Union density
Denmark	87.5
Finland	79.0
Sweden	79.0
Belgium	69.2
Luxembourg **	50.0
Ireland	44.5
Unweighted EU average	43.8
Austria	39.8
Italy**	35.4
Greece	32.5
Weighted EU average	30.4
Portugal*	30.0
Germany**	29.7
UK	29.0
Netherlands	27.0
Japan	21.5
Spain	15.0
USA	13.5
France	9.1

* 1999 figure ** 1998 figure.
Source: EIRO and national figures.

During the mid-1990s, government attempts to meet the requirements of the single currency agreement led to extensive industrial action in several European countries, France being a notable instance. Reductions in public spending and cuts in government borrowing hit state sector – or state-subsidized – industries hard, producing wage cuts and job losses. In these cases, efforts to forge pacts with trade unions were generally unsuccessful because governments had nothing to offer in return. Throughout Europe, unions have lost political influence. Ironically, in Belgium and Spain, their allies in government have been instrumental in the imposition of some of the toughest economic measures.

Works councils are required in all companies employing a minimum of 1000 workers in two or more countries in the EU, provided there are at least 150 workers at two sites or more. The councils are to be informed of the state of business and consulted on changes to production or working methods, restructuring and planned closures. Whereas French and German companies have modelled their 'Europe-wide councils' on pre-existing national formats, other organizations are obtaining agreements on widely different bases.

Interpretation and application of EU law by the Commission and the European Court is shaped by their understanding of the 'European social model' which views trade unions as social partners (Bercusson, 2002). The EU Framework Directive on information and consultation further extends the role of employee representatives for companies employing at least 150 employees or workplace establishments with at least 100 employees. This must be implemented by national governments by 23 March 2005. The Directive requires a nine-stage process of information and consultation (Bercusson, 2002):

1 Transmission of information/data.

2 Acquaintance with and examination of data.

3 Conduct of an adequate study.

4 Preparation for consultation.

5 Formulation of an opinion.

6 Meeting.

7 Employer's reasoned response to opinion.

8 'Exchange of views and establishment of dialogue', 'discussion', 'with a view to reaching an agreement on decisions'.

9 'The employer and the employees' representatives shall work in a spirit of cooperation and with due regard for their reciprocal rights and obligations, taking into account the interests both of the undertaking or establishment and of the employees.'

German employee relations

By comparison with many other countries, the management of people in Germany is tightly controlled by legal processes. Indeed many aspects of people management dealt with in an ad hoc way elsewhere are strictly regulated in the Federal Republic. As a result of the various co-determination laws in the period since the end of World War II, Germany has evolved a system that focuses on industrial democracy and harmony. Abandoning the pre-war tradition of small craft-based unions, 15 single-industry unions were organized largely for blue-collar workers. Together with the Police Trade Union, these unions formed the Deutscher Gewerkschaftsbund (DGB) – the Confederation of German Trade Unions – in 1949.

At the time of German unification in 1990 the unions affiliated to the DGB had almost 8 million members, including IG Metall (Metal-Workers' Union) which, with 3.6 million members in west and east Germany, was the largest trade union in the world (Randlesome, 1994, p.109). There are also separate associations representing white-collar workers, civil servants and Christian trade unionists.

Unlike craft and general unions, or professional associations, German unions are industrial: anyone employed in the industry represented by a particular union may be a member. This includes blue-collar and white-collar, skilled and unskilled, manual or supervisory workers. Consequently, demarcation disputes between different grades in a company cannot occur since all are represented by the same union. Some 90 per cent of German employers belong to federations which require them to recognize trade unions (Brewster 1994, p.64). In practical terms, the main instruments of co-determination are the supervisory boards and works councils that characterize large companies.

Supervisory boards

Companies employing more than 2000 workers are obliged to have a supervisory board. This is in addition to the management board, which continues to have final authority. The supervisory board consists of 50 per cent shareholder representatives, with the other 50 per cent being worker representatives elected by the workforce – including both basic and executive staff. Elections take place every four years.

The supervisory board oversees management action and monitors and evaluates performance and change. German employers were reluctant to go along with this procedure but most now believe that it functions well, despite the occasional problem. In fact, the number of occasions when the supervisory and management boards fail to agree is limited – largely as a result of informal discussions to make sure that they achieve consensus in the official forum. If they fail to agree, the chairperson of the supervisory board (a shareholder representative) has the casting vote. The major drawback of the system is that it slows down the process of decision making.

Works councils

We noted earlier that works councils have been extended to all large companies operating in more than one European country. In Germany, three sets of rights have been given to works councils (Lawrence, 1993, p.34). First there is the co-determination right (*Mitbestimmingsrecht*) – the ability to give consent on a number of issues: the appointment of an employee to a new position; transfers within the organization; transfers from one wage group to another; determining starting and finishing times for the working day; and the introduction of shift working, overtime, etc. According to Lawrence (1993, p.36):

> A German company that has a bursting order book cannot just institute overtime by its own authority. It needs the agreement of the works council to do this and even then it cannot engage in unlimited overtime working. ... quite small issues between management and workforce can only be said to be 'settled' when they have been formally agreed with the works council and written down.

Secondly there is the consultation right (*Mitwirkungsrecht*) over planning issues, including plant closure, new factories, investment decisions and business policy matters.

Finally there is the information right (*Informationsrecht*) to receive information about company performance and prospects.

Legislation on the works council system was significantly amended in 2001 (Weiss, 2002). The amendment was intended to improve the conditions for applying the law in SMEs, increase the powers and resources available to works councils in some areas and adapt the traditional organizational structure to better fit modern situations.

Pay negotiations take place between an appropriate employers' federation and the matching union for that industry. Negotiations take place at the state level, with some variation in settlement levels between rich and less affluent states. Bargaining takes place to a predetermined schedule and in a specific order of states (Lawrence, 1993, p.30). Some smaller companies are not members of employers' federations but tend to follow agreements, although they are not obliged to do so. A few large organizations, such as Siemens, conduct negotiations directly with their unions.

Until recently, co-determination brought stability into the German employee relations scene. According to Jacobi and Muller-Jentsch (1990, p.134):

> From the point of view of organization policy, the trade unions have proved to be extremely stable. Their status as a party to collective bargaining has up to now remained unchallenged because of the high degree of juridification and centralization and their monopoly-like legal privileges in collective bargaining and in calling strikes. Whereas the 'institutionalization of class struggle' could be seen as a fetter on the unions' development of power in the years of sustained high employment, institutional protection now constitutes a bulwark against labour-exclusion strategies.

However, in 1996 some cracks began to appear in these apparently sacrosanct arrangements (*Financial Times*, 21 October 1996). Viessmann, a mid-sized producer of heating systems, was sued by the IG Metall engineering union on the grounds that it had negotiated new working hours with its employees without involving the union. Faced with the loss of work to a new (and cheaper) factory in the Czech Republic, Viessmann's workers agreed to work 38 rather than 35 hours a week without increased pay. This improved efficiency by 8.6 per cent, matching the savings that would have been gained by the company had it transferred its work to the Czech Republic. IG Metall objected because the German system accords negotiating rights for pay and working hours to the trade unions. In this case, the union action failed because only some 10 per cent of Viessmann's employees were members of IG Metall.

Other companies have negotiated informal agreements and 'opt-out' clauses which have allowed them to reduce employee costs. There have also been murmurings about the structure of supervisory boards. In fact, the cosy consensus between management and employees is under strain. As we have noted already the economic pressures, firstly of additional taxation to support the unification of East and West Germany and, latterly, of government spending cuts to meet single-currency convergence requirements have caused considerable tensions. Unemployment has climbed rapidly since unification and the combination of high rates of pay and generous social security has led to the export of jobs on a significant scale.

Addison, Schnabel and Wagner (2001) analysed a large-scale database to investigate the effects of the works council system on a number of variables. They found that works councils were associated with reduced labour fluctuation, higher productivity (but only in larger establishments) and no reduction in innovative activity. At the same time they were also associated with lower profitability and higher wages. Flecker and Schulten (1999) contend that the German employee relations system has never been as uniform as it has been presented in comparative literature and that the strains of unification and other social changes are having a considerable impact. Similar points are made by Hassel (1999). Klikauer (2002), on the other hand, argues that the basic system of German employee relations remains intact despite major changes in the public sector and the consequences of unification.

Activity 22:3	How central is the German system of employee relations to the European Union's 'social partnership' model?

HRM in reality	**'Ordinary' working week includes Saturday and Sunday**

A report from ACIRRT shows that an 'ordinary' working week includes Saturday and Sunday in almost a quarter (24 per cent) of current registered enterprise agreements. The implication is that the organizations involved may be routinely asking staff to work Saturdays and/or Sundays as part of their normal working arrangements.

Working days that used to be regarded as being outside normal working hours used to attract a premium payment – even when allowed for in awards. This made weekend working less attractive for employers. But the report concludes that the 'weekend' provisions in agreements mean that the normal working week has effectively been redefined.

This does not necessarily mean that employees are working longer hours. Workers affected by these agreements may be working the same number of hours in total per week. But they may be less certain about the days of the week they may be asked to work.

Organizations are advantaged by these new agreements as they can deploy people more flexibly without the extra costs of premium weekend pay. It may be the case that base rates of pay have been adjusted to compensate for the absorption of penalty payments. This would leave overall earning largely unaffected but there is no conclusive evidence of the effect on overall earnings, according to the report. Most current 'weekend' agreements are concentrated in four industry sectors: mining and construction; wholesale and retail trade; community services; and recreation and personal services.

In fact, working Monday to Friday is a comparatively recent practice. People in postal services, banking and manufacturing regularly were expected to do weekend work involving at least Saturday mornings as recently as 30 years ago.

Commenting on the findings ACIRRT director Ron Callus said:

> This re-emergence of Saturday and now Sunday work raises further challenges for Australian families trying to balance work and family responsibilities. With more two income earning households than ever before, families affected by weekend work provisions are going to find it difficult to find a day when all members of the household are off work together. It's a problem for workers affected, but it is also an increasingly difficult issue for governments and employers that seek labour market flexibility. The efficiencies of greater labour market flexibility may well have a longer run, community wide downside.

Source: *HRM Guide Australia* (http://www.hrmguide.net/australia/), 3 October 2002.

Employee relations in Australia and New Zealand

Throughout much of the 20th century, employee relations in Australia and New Zealand were characterized by industrial conciliation and arbitration (Harbridge and Walsh, 2002). In New Zealand, especially, they were criticized for being highly legalistic and interventionist (Vranken, 1999). But the global pressure for greater flexibility has led to radically different approaches. The old industrial relations system, essentially multi-employer bargaining, was effectively dismantled in New Zealand and replaced with a system that favoured individual contracts. The Australian constitution protected conciliation and arbitration but new legislation considerably weakened the system in the 1990s.

Despite the different approaches, the outcome has been similar in both countries: a drop in collective bargaining and union density, reductions in benefits, and major changes in working time arrangements (Harbridge and Walsh, 2002). However, the number of union members actually increased in Australia in 2001 (Nelson and Holland, 2002). A study by Allan, Brosnan and Walsh (1999) found that New Zealand's decentralized system had encouraged greater employer experimentation (albeit with both positive and negative outcomes), particularly in the private sector. Vranken (1999) found a growing tension between the specialist labour court and the ordinary courts of law, especially the court of appeal.

Briggs (2001) observes that globalization and employers are normally regarded as key agents of change, with unions reduced to a reactive or impotent role. Paradoxically, however, Briggs argues that unions were responsible for the shift to enterprise bargaining in Australia in the early 1990s as a consequence of two industrial campaigns. The Australian Industrial Relations Commission (AIRC) had been reluctant to introduce enterprise bargaining but a loss of union solidarity behind centralized wage negotiations and a power struggle between the AIRC and the Australian Council of Trade Unions (ACTU) created a policy vacuum that had to be filled. As a result the Business Council of Australia (BCA), the employers' organization, was allowed to take the lead in the process of decentralizing pay bargaining in Australia. Similarly, Phillimore (2000) attributes some of the changes to union misjudgements and weak workplace bargaining structures. Wooden and Bora (1999) found that following the changes of the 1990s, workplace-specific factors were responsible for 39 per cent of hourly wage differences.

Deery, Walsh and Knox (2001) looked at employee relations practices and outcomes in non-union and unionized workplaces using the 1995 Australian Workplace Industrial Relations Survey. They found non-union workplaces to be distinctly less innovative in their employee relations practices and had higher dismissal and turnover rates. They also observed that non-union workplaces were notable for the individualistic nature of their contractual, remunerative and bargaining arrangements. Nelson and Holland (2002) note the view of some commentators that a new era of union–management cooperation appears to have begun.

HRM in reality	**Agreements reduce consultation and training but increase casual working**

A report (*Agreement Making in Australia Under the Workplace Relations Act 2000–01*) released by Tony Abbott shows that:

- A mere 20 per cent of non-union agreements provide for employee representation, compared with 81 per cent of union agreements.
- Just 46 per cent of non-union agreements provide for employee consultation, compared with 77 per cent of union agreements.
- Some 67 per cent of non-union agreements provide for employee training, compared with 87 per cent of union agreements.

These details were recently highlighted by Robert McClelland MP, Shadow Attorney-General and Shadow Minister for Workplace Relations, who said that:

> The report confirms that under the non-union agreements advocated by the Howard Government, employees are much less likely to be consulted about important decisions affecting a business, and are less likely to have access to training. How does Tony Abbott expect employees to embrace workplace change if they're not consulted or offered training? Tony Abbott obviously thinks employers should copy his approach, which consists of making threats, bashing unions and talking up conflict. More workplace consultation and training are essential if Australia is to have sustainable productivity growth. They are fundamental, structural long-term issues for the economy.

Robert McClelland also points to the proportion of enterprise agreements that provide for the use of casual labour. These have increased from 43 per cent to 71 per cent in the past two years. To add insult to injury, he says, the figures strongly suggest that the newly casualized workers enjoy fewer protections:

> The proportion of agreements that protect workers by regulating the hours, wages and numbers of casual employees has dropped from 16 per cent to 6 per cent. The proportion of agreements that provide for a casual loading (the extra hourly pay to compensate casual employees for having no leave entitlements and no guarantee of work) has barely risen – from 25 per cent to 29 per cent.

Source: *HRM Guide Australia* (http://www.hrmguide.net/australia/), 3 October 2002.

Activity 22:4

Review the consequences of deregulation in Australia and New Zealand. What were the major effects?

Japanese and east Asian employee relations

Kuruvilla and Erickson (2002) argue that employee relations systems change because of the constraints facing those systems. Until the 1980s east Asian employee relations focused on maintaining labour peace and stability during the early stages of industrialization. Since then the major issues have been numerical and functional flexibility in the face of economic turbulence. Todd and Peetz (2001) observe that employee relations in Malaysia have been characterized by extensive state control, which has guaranteed high levels of managerial prerogative within the workplace, minimal overt conflict and very little bargaining power for workers. They found no evidence of major change and employees remain excluded from the decision-making process. But it is possible for particularly strong unions to make an impact (Peetz and Todd, 2001). In Hong Kong, on the other hand, unions are weak (Chan and Snape, 2000) and in Singapore they have a 'special relationship' with the government with a modest amount of influence (Barr, 2000).

Japanese employee relations methods are particularly relevant in two contexts: Japan itself and transplant factories in the Pacific area, North America and Europe. Nissan, for example, has been particularly active in overseas expansion and – in common with many other Japanese corporations – has a specific attitude towards trade unions (Garrahan and Stewart, 1992, p.9). It established a factory in Tennessee, USA where state laws on the 'right to work' effectively neutralized the power of established unions by allowing the freedom not to belong to unions. Nissan campaigned against the Auto Union with the result that they failed to establish themselves.

In the UK, Nissan took a site in Washington in the north-east of England. The company contracted a single-union deal with the Amalgamated Union of Engineering Workers. This gave the union negligible negotiating powers. In fact, the company staff council had more power.

In Japan itself, Nissan destroyed union power in 1953 after a four-month lock-out of employees, coupled with the use of strong-arm tactics. After the capitulation of the independent national auto union, employees were taken back by the company on condition that they joined a company union: the All Nissan Motor Workers Union. After this episode, employee relations were described by the company in the following way: 'Nissan prides itself on 30 years of smooth labour–management relations' (Garrahan and Stewart, 1992, p.9).

Critics said that Nissan controlled the union, pointing to the history of employee relations since the 1950s. Employee pay was reduced for six years after 1953. It took until 1964 for that level to be achieved again. Thereafter wage claims were always 100 per cent agreed, but this was not too surprising, given that the claims were always modest and restrained. The company gained a massive increase in productivity as a result.

During 1980 union elections, 99 per cent of employees voted with the elected officials receiving 98 per cent of the total votes cast. The voting process was closely surveyed by company officials. Strangest of all to Western eyes is the part played by union membership in career progression. A period as a union officer – on secondment from the personnel department – is an expected part of the career route. Pressure is put on staff to belong to the company union and they can be dismissed for belonging to other unions, or unacceptable political groups.

Organizations and employee relations

Earlier in this chapter we observed that traditional industrial relations assumed a formal structure in which management and staff negotiated pay levels and working conditions such as hours of work, grade demarcation, holiday entitlement and sick pay arrangements. In some organizations the same structure was used for grievance and disciplinary matters, agreeing levels of performance, attendance requirements – such as shift hours – and work procedures. Within this mechanism, staff were represented by one or more trade unions or staff associations.

In recent years large organizations in free market countries have attempted to move away from traditional mechanisms. The focus has switched to individual rather than collective bargaining. This may take place through:

- Introduction of personal contracts, allowing employers to offer pay increases to staff willing to accept such contracts but not to workers wishing to remain as union members.

- Organizational change methods such as team briefings, where managers cascade information throughout the organization by means of a series of meetings (usually on a monthly basis) and also collect ideas and criticisms at the same meetings to be funnelled upwards.

- Quality circles have also served to circumvent the traditional union role by emphasizing direct dialogue between staff and line management on the subject of improving procedures.

It is not surprising that unions have often resisted the introduction of change methods of this nature because they depend on staff and management talking directly to each other, thereby removing a main source of union power – the filter or gatekeeper of information and innovation. In such situations, collective bargaining has often been reduced to the primary subjects of pay, holidays and discipline, removing the unions from the discussion of procedures.

Individualized systems stress commitment from employees, yet the fashion for downsizing and restructuring imposes a 'fear of commitment' among managers and employees alike (Rousseau, 1995, p.xii). HR policies that emphasize the individual contribute to this fear since they do away with any collective employee defence against the employer. 'Divide and rule.' Hendry (1995, p.57) acknowledges a 'more sophisticated pluralist technique which sees the unitary organization as "bad" because the denial of individual and group interests actually makes for a less effective organization.' In other words, there is a valid criticism that the integrating activities of HRM can rub out the healthy diversity that is essential for future development: 'Such paradoxes, discrepancies, and ambiguities highlight the fact that organizational life is beset by paradoxes, and that (mercifully) managers and organizations cannot get a handle completely on human behaviour.'

Peters (1987) distinguishes two contradictory philosophies operating in modern business organizations:

- *Minimize human resources.* Workers are pure costs. New methods and equipment are now available globally. Businesses in the developed world can: cut employee costs to match those of poorer countries; or switch to industries that are not labour intensive. This involves actual and threatened redundancies, transferring operations to lower-wage countries and automation.

- *Increase the value of the people element.* Employees are assets. This approach emphasizes flexibility and creativity and aims to eliminate unnecessary routine by: the intelligent use of technology; and retraining workers for more complex or varied tasks. According to Peters it should be tied to profit-linked bonuses to ensure commitment.

The first approach leads to industrial conflict. Managers must make cuts and be aggressive towards staff. Workers defend their position and oppose change. It is the view which predominated in New Right thinking and predominated in the UK under Conservative rule. The second approach is collaborative. It seeks partnership between workers and employers for mutual benefit. It fits the 'social market' philosophy held by many governments in the European Union. Peters argues that both approaches deliver short-term profits but only the second can maintain competitiveness in the long term.

Other management writers advocate a new form of employee relationship based on cooperation. For example, Kanter (1989, p.127) argues that 'the adversarial mode with its paranoid world view' is unsuitable for the modern world. 'Teaming up' is the route to growth and survival. Corporations need to seek strategic alliances – cooperative arrangements to achieve business goals. Such alliances should be made with unions as well as other businesses. Kanter defines these as 'stakeholder alliances' or 'complementary' coalitions. In 1996, the British Labour Party adopted a similar concept as their 'big idea' for the UK's future. Stuart and Lucio (2002) found that while some unions (such as the MSF) were extremely enthusiastic, most companies did not reciprocate. Oxenbridge and Brown (2002) found a dichotomy between production sector firms that nurtured collective bargaining through informal partnership relationships and service sector businesses that contained collective bargaining tightly through formalized partnership agreements. Haynes and Allen (2001), meanwhile, found equally distinct polarization among unions – some saw partnership as a potentially effective strategy for restoring union influence, others viewed the concept as fatally flawed.

Participation is also a matter of delegation – involving everyone downwards within the organization as well as the stakeholder partners. It requires a change in behaviour from managers who have previously exercised power in a clear-cut, overtly decisive fashion. A consensus style requires patience; willingness to discuss ideas at an early stage; and ability to listen. Not all managers can make the transition. Partnerships require managers with team leadership skills.

Management strategies towards employee relations have been classified in a number of ways (see Table 22.2). These classifications demonstrate the variety of ways in which managers regard employee relations, ranging from authoritarian and anti-unionist to more sophisticated and inclusive strategies. In the same way, employees may take various approaches as we shall see in the next section.

Employee relations strategies

Trade unions in different countries have varying interpretations of their roles and aim for different goals. McIlwee and Roberts (1991, p.390), for example, have outlined the major objectives of British trade unions in the 20th century:

- *Preventing legal interference in the collective bargaining process.* Trade unions in the UK have favoured voluntary collective bargaining and have resisted government attempts to restrict this process – albeit unsuccessfully in the Thatcher era. Unions have been favourably inclined towards (essentially pre-1979) legislation which aimed to protect employees; but have opposed income policies and limitations on industrial action.

- *Improving monetary rewards for members.* Pressing for higher wages, especially in periods of high inflation. This is the principal concern of most union members: unions that are successful in this respect are likely to benefit from additional recruitment and retention of existing members.

Table 22.2	Strategic management styles towards employee relations

Basic	Purcell and Sissons (1983)	Gunnigle et al. (1994)
1 Authoritarian. Typical small company style. Boss rules absolutely – staff have simple 'take it or leave it' choice. Works if employees accept situation – e.g. where there is little or no opportunity to change jobs. Seen in some large organizations.	**1 Traditional**. Fire-fighting – managers pay little attention to employee relations until trouble arises. Low pay levels. Hostile to unions. Prevails in authoritarian small businesses but seen in larger companies when workers have little choice in their employment.	**1 Anti-union**. Little or no consideration of employee relations. No collective arrangements such as union representation. Low concern for employee needs. Aggressive opposition to collective bargaining and union recognition.
2 Individual. Negotiation between management and individuals. Possible for staff teams to discuss common interests jointly. Non-authoritarian. Emphasis on commitment to company goals. Managers reasonable and approachable. No collective body representing staff.	**2 Paternalist**. More benevolent, humanistic style; close parallels with HRM approach. Employers consider unions unnecessary because conditions are so generous. Employee relations concentrate on getting employees to identify with the objectives of the business.	**2 Paternalist**. Concern for employee needs but rejects union recognition and collective bargaining. Little sophistication in human resource policies.

3 Sophisticated paternalist. Emphasizes welfare and well-being of individual staff. Sophisticated HR policies for resourcing, development, reward and communication. Rejects unions and collective bargaining. Equates to 'traditional HRM' – values employees because this is seen to benefit organization. |
| **3 Collective**. Dominant method in Western world from 1945 until approximately 1980. Since then, social and free market economies have taken different paths. Social market economies, e.g. Germany, have industry or company-wide trade unions (or staff associations) negotiating with management on behalf of the staff. Free market economies continue to make extensive use of this approach but management literature and HRM emphasize individual bargaining. Many companies utilize both strategies. | **3 Consultative**. Ideal form of employee relations in some eyes. Emphasis is on informal rather than formal systems of bargaining with continuous dialogue. Unions are fully recognized.

4 Constitutional. Similar to consultative approach but emphasis on formal regulatory agreements to control the relationship between powerful parties on either side. Found in social market economies and strongly encouraged by European Union social policy.

5 Opportunistic. Responsibility for employee relations left to individual divisions/subsidiaries, leaving no common approach and an emphasis on unit profitability. | **4 Sophisticated unionized**. Recognizes trade unions but carefully prescribed union role (e.g. single-union agreement). Mixed collective and individual arrangements, incorporating HR policies. Neo-pluralist model with HRM-type policies designed to foster consensualism and employee commitment.

5 Traditional unionized. Pluralist approach typified by adversarial industrial relations. Collective bargaining but multiple unions complicate matters. |

- *Improving other terms and conditions.* As the nature of work and its rewards change, non-monetary benefits become increasingly important. These include reduction of working hours, earlier retirement, longer holidays, improved pension and sick pay schemes.

- *Involvement in determining national economic and industrial objectives.* Accustomed to 'beer and sandwiches' at 10 Downing Street in pre-Thatcher days, these stakeholders have found themselves virtually ignored by neo-liberal governments –

both Conservative and Labour. However, their (reduced) influence continues through ACAS and Industrial Tribunals.

- *Health and safety at work.*
- *Protection of job opportunities.* Traditionally, unions have fought job cuts in any circumstances, leading to accusations of massive overstaffing in many organizations until the 1980s. Of late, union opposition has been more selective and the 'new realism' has produced a longer-term perspective. Unions have focused increasingly on jobs with a future and have been prepared to negotiate flexible terms with employers in order to preserve work in Britain or to attract jobs from other parts of the EU and elsewhere.
- *Improving public and social services.* The essential purpose of trade unions is the representation of members at work. But workers also have other roles: parents, consumers, tenants, pensioners, the sick, the unemployed. Awareness of this wider context has led to union pressure for changes in society as a whole.
- *A voice in government.* British unions have had a direct relationship with the Labour Party since 1900 – initially it was organized to reflect their views. Many unions contributed funds to the Labour Party and, as the largest source of income, strongly influenced its policies and organization. Conservative legislation in the 1980s allowed members to opt out of their union's political fund, reducing this flow by around 20 per cent.

  The Labour Party itself concluded that identifying too closely with the trade union movement was counter-productive at the end of the 20th century. The proportion of British voters identifying themselves as 'working class' fell dramatically due to government initiatives such as council house sales to tenants and a general improvement in prosperity. The new middle class ('Thatcher's children') were portrayed as being scared of overtly socialist policies that might reduce their economic well-being, and are seen to have lost interest in the underprivileged. The Blair Labour government appears to be scarcely any more receptive to trade union influence.

- *Industrial democracy.* The Conservative government opted out of those sections of the Social Charter that required works councils to be formed in all large companies. The Labour government signed up when they achieved office and EU Directives are pushing them in the direction of recognizable continental forms of employee consultation.

  The pattern in other countries varies because of prevailing cultural, historical and legislative factors. These issues are reflected in the nature of employee relations as an activity undertaken by managers, employees and unions.

Activity 22:5   What should trade unions do to be 'new realists' in employee relations?

Summary

'Employee relations' is a relatively new term that broadens the study of industrial relations to include wider aspects of the employment relationship, including non-unionized workplaces, personal contracts and socio-emotional, rather than contractual, arrangements. This is an area with diverse ideological underpinnings and political ramifications. Governments have taken an active part in determining its conduct. In Europe, harmonization is leading to the establishment of works councils across the EU, giving a new role for collective representation.

Further reading

Industrial Relations by Mike Salaman (4th edition published by FT/Pitman in 2001), Employee Relations in Context by David Farnham (2nd edition, CIPD 2000) and Employment Relations by Ed Rose (FT Prentice Hall, 2000) all provide good overviews of the field. International and Comparative Industrial Relations edited by Greg Bamber and Russell Lansbury (published by Sage Publications, 1998) compares different countries.

Review questions

1   What are the key differences between unitarist and pluralist views of employee relations?

2   What is meant by the employment relationship? To what extent is it reasonable to say that employee relations should encompass all employment relationships?

3   Discuss the view that employee relations is an outmoded concept that has no place in organizations managed according to the principles of HRM.

4   Are works councils a handicap or a benefit to business efficiency?

5   What is enterprise bargaining?

6   Is it wise for governments to suppress independent trade unions?

Problems for discussion and analysis

Middletown Council

Middletown council covers a large urban area bordered by open country. Most of its 300 staff are located in the main office complex, Delta House, located in the old town centre. A new shopping mall has opened immediately between the council offices and the old market, transforming a derelict area into a fashionable district. The staff are delighted since they now work in a pleasant and prestigious locality with a massive choice of shops and eating places nearby.

The council have been re-elected after promising a considerable improvement in their services. However, all available funds have been devoted to maintaining things as they are. After much debate they have decided that their costs could be cut dramatically by renting out Delta House to a commercial firm and transferring the staff to much cheaper accommodation at the edge of town. The savings could be used to pay for the new services promised in the election.

The staff are unionized and have a reputation for resisting changes, no matter how small.

Question: How would you advise the council to proceed?

Euro Vehicles

Euro Vehicles manufactures vans and other light commercial vehicles. Due to severe competition and a declining market, the workforce has been reduced from 11 300 to 2800 in the last three years and the remaining employees are fearful of further redundancy. There are three unions in the two remaining plants, representing clerical, engineering and supervisory staff. Partly as a result of the recent cuts they are all suspicious of management intentions. Management is authoritarian, based on a rigid departmental structure and values technical competence and seniority over anything else. Most of the managers have been promoted from the engineering and production side of the company and are in their 40s and 50s.

The company's production is largely devoted to basic van models built to a 15-year-old design and sold to large utility companies at a very keen price. Marketing is almost non-existent and the research and development department was closed as a cost-cutting measure three years ago. The company is currently owned by a large conglomerate that left the management alone until recently but with strict, detailed financial controls. Consequently, the company has been consistently profitable but with a shrinking level of production and increasingly outdated manufacturing equipment. The conglomerate has decided that this 'hands-off' approach is no longer satisfactory. They are prepared to make a major investment but only if they can be convinced that this will be effectively managed.

Question: You have been brought in as a consultant to look at the current organization and to recommend changes that would improve the situation. How would you go about this? What are the implications for employee relations?

23

Conflict, bargaining, involvement and well-being

Objectives

The purpose of this chapter is to:

- Discuss the role of conflict in the workplace.
- Provide an overview of mediation and tribunal systems.
- Evaluate the relationship between employee involvement and workplace productivity.
- Discuss the role of HR practitioners in matters such as work–life balance, health and safety and stress reduction.

Employee relations as an activity

In many developed countries the industrial relations of the 1950s to the 1970s depended on the existence of company rules and regulations that served the purpose of clarifying what was expected of both employees and employers. Since then, the move towards flexibility and empowerment of staff has resulted in 'fuzzier' boundaries between required behaviour and that which is regarded as inappropriate. Employees – particularly managers – have been given greater discretion on decision making in free market economies. This has been encouraged by 'neo-liberal' governments throughout the world. Within the European Union, however, there has been a countervailing emphasis on formal rules because of the predominance of social market economies at the heart of the EU. Typically, most large organizations continue to have formal rules on:

1 *Timekeeping*
   - Normally expected times of attendance, often with monitoring ('clocking-in').
   - Sanctions for lateness.

2 *Absence*
   - An approval mechanism for absence.
   - Authorization for taking annual leave.
   - A reporting procedure when people are absent from the workplace.
   - The need for medical self-certification or a doctor's certificate.

3 *Health and safety*
   - Requirements for appearance or cleanliness – e.g. protective clothing, wearing jewellery.
   - Special hazards such as chemicals and dangerous machinery.
   - Prohibition of smoking, alcohol or drugs.

4 *Gross misconduct*
   - Offences regarded as being serious enough to lead to dismissal without notice.
   - Theft, fraud, deliberate falsification of records.
   - Fighting, assault on another person.
   - Deliberate damage to company property.
   - Serious incapability through alcohol or being under the influence of illegal drugs.
   - Serious negligence that causes unacceptable loss, damage or injury.
   - Serious acts of insubordination.
   - Unauthorized entry to computer records.

5 *Use of company facilities*
   - Use of telephone for private calls.
   - Admission to company premises outside working hours.
   - Use of company equipment – e.g. computers, photocopiers – for personal reasons.
   - Abuse of e-mails and the internet.

6 *Discrimination*
   - Overt discrimination but also sexual harassment and racial abuse.

The enforcement of such rules is a sensitive issue, requiring some form of formal or informal disciplinary system.

Discipline is not only negative, in the sense of being punitive or preventative, it also makes a positive contribution to organizational performance. An effective organization cannot survive if its members behave in an anarchic way. Order within an organization depends on an appropriate mixture of each of these forms of discipline. Within the context of HRM, however, the emphasis has moved away from managerial discipline towards self and, especially, team discipline. Nevertheless, most organizations continue to have institutionalized disciplinary procedures, largely determined by management.

Dismissal is the ultimate expression of such procedures and also one of the most unpleasant aspects of human resource management. It may arise because of disciplinary issues such as persistent absenteeism, failure of an employee to perform adequately despite support and training, or as a strategic requirement arising from a change in direction by the organization. Most managers regard the 'exiting' process with distaste – often it is more stressful for the sacking manager than for the victims.

HRM in reality

Big brother is watching

Some 80 per cent of large US businesses check their employees' e-mail, internet, or telephone calls or even videotape staff at work – up from 74 per cent last year. This is the conclusion of the American Management Association's (AMA) annual survey on workplace monitoring and surveillance. It compares with just 35 per cent in 1997.

According to the AMA survey of 1627 organizations, which focused on large and mid-sized firms:

- 63 per cent of major companies monitor employees' internet connections, compared with 54 per cent last year
- 47 per cent store and review employee e-mail, up from 38 per cent in 2000
- 40 per cent block connections to 'unauthorized or inappropriate' websites – again up from 29 per cent last year
- 27 per cent of major companies in the survey said that they had fired employees for misuse of office e-mail or internet connections
- 65 per cent said that there had been disciplinary measures for those offences
- 36 per cent stored and reviewed computer files
- 15 per cent video recorded employees at work
- 12 per cent recorded and reviewed telephone messages (43 per cent surveyed telephone numbers called and time spent on the phone).

'Privacy in today's workplace is largely illusory. In this era of open space cubicles, shared desk space, networked computers and teleworkers, it is hard to realistically hold onto a belief in private space,' said Ellen Bayer, AMA's human resources practice leader. 'Work is carried out on equipment belonging to employers who have a legal right to the work product of the employees using it.'

'The lines between one's personal and professional life can blur with expectations of a 24/7 work week, but employees ought to engage in some discretion about personal activities carried out during the official hours of work,' Bayer said. 'The obligations for respect are mutual. It is up to clear-thinking managers and realistic employees to leverage the good that monitoring can accomplish and work to assure those adequate safeguards are in place to avoid abuses.'

'It's not just a matter of corporate curiosity, but very real worries about productivity and liability that push these policies,' said Eric Rolfe Greenberg, director of management studies for AMA:

> Personal e-mail can clog a company's telecommunications system, and sexually explicit or other inappropriate material downloaded from the internet can lead to claims of a hostile work environment. It's important to note, however, that by far the greater share of this monitoring is performed on a spot-check basis rather than an ongoing, 24-hour basis. And, importantly, 90 per cent of the companies engaging in any of these practices inform their employees that they're doing so.

Source: *HRM Guide USA* (http://www.hrmguide.net/usa/), 18 April 2001.

Conflict

Only a portion of employee relations issues have a disciplinary element. Many cases arise from some form of conflict between management and employees, or between specific individuals. Conflict has both positive and negative aspects as we can see in Table 23.1. Where does conflict come from? A number of basic psychological causes are apparent, regardless of the overt justification for a dispute (McKenna, 1994, p.418; Torrington and Hall, 1995, p.641):

- *Frustration and aggression.* Disagreement often reflects frustration – feelings of being ignored, of being pressurized or of blocked promotion. Any point of difference, no matter how irrelevant, may spark a reaction to frustration. This may appear in the form of verbal aggression, seemingly out of proportion to the importance of the supposed dispute. Clearly, the dispute masks problems that are attributable to poor communication, lack of empowerment and mistrust.

- *Different objectives.* The rhetoric of HRM states that organizations should aim for shared goals between management and staff. However, in practice, managers and employees have different priorities. Managers may focus on efficiency and cost-effectiveness, whereas employees want higher pay and longer holidays. Unless there are mechanisms, such as team briefings or quality circles, by which mutual understanding of these goals can be improved, differences are likely to be brought to a head at some stage.

- *Different values.* These could be political – a difference in belief about the purpose of business for example – or a disagreement about the manager's right to manage. Many managers believe that they have the authority to issue instructions without being challenged by their staff. On the other hand, some employees consider that managers have this right only if they are prepared to explain their decisions, account for the consequences of their actions, and are prepared to accept questions and criticisms.

Table 23.1	Consequences of conflict	
Positive		*Negative*
'Clearing the air'. Allowing people to air their grievances can sometimes lead to an improved atmosphere after the disagreement has finished. This serves to bring 'hidden agendas' out into the open.		**Wasting time and energy.** A simple decision can be quick to implement, but negotiation can take an inordinate amount of time. Often participants forget the original purpose of negotiation and get caught up with fighting a war.
Understanding each other's position. When both sides of an agenda are brought out into the open, people must think through their own case in order to express it clearly; and grasp the other point of view in order to challenge it.		**Stress.** Conflicts can become quite personal, abusive and threatening. The postures taken by the two sides can lead to further stress. Mental exhaustion may come from prolonged debate.
Modification of goal. One side may realize how unpopular or impractical the consequences of their argument may be.		**Worsening the situation.** Conflict may highlight problems, dislikes and grievances better left unstated. Tension may escalate debate into action: strikes, lock-outs, work-to-rule, threatened or implied redundancies. Consequences may be unpleasantness with worse morale and industrial relations after negotiations than before.

Source: Based on Torrington and Hall (1995, p.642).

- *Jealousy*. Individual employees can be sensitive to other members of staff being paid more than them, or getting extra perks. The conflict arises from jealousy or loss of status.

- *Culture*. The tradition of 'us and them' (employees versus management) continues to exist in many organizations, particularly those using an authoritarian style of people management. New staff and management are quickly encouraged to accept the 'normality' of this perspective. In other cases, a change in the management approach disturbs the prevailing employee relations culture.

Conflict is an inevitable feature of negotiating and bargaining. Trained negotiators are taught to deal with conflict, expecting both negative and positive aspects to appear during the process. This will be easier to understand when we consider specific models of negotiation later in this chapter.

Issues of conflict and discipline may not be resolved at local level. Many countries have mechanisms by which disputes may be taken to an outside body, usually in the form of industrial tribunals or arbitration bodies.

Activity 23:1	Review the positive and negative aspects of conflict in the workplace. Are human resource strategies designed to minimize conflict necessarily beneficial?

Tribunals and arbitration systems

To what extent can differences between employers and workers be resolved through arbitration or legal tribunals? It is the view in many countries that an impartial, legally based process has a significant role to play in a number of circumstances. Industrial tribunals take many forms: in Germany the labour courts make legally binding judgements; in the UK tribunal decisions do not set a precedent in law and cannot establish criminal behaviour. Even in the latter case, however, they have a long-term effect since they establish a set of values and influence the behaviour of others. If there is a judgement on a case of significant racial discrimination, for example, the resulting publicity may lead to a moderation of racialist behaviour as people fear the possibility of similar action against themselves. In Australia, under the former Labor government's 13-year accord with the trade unions, the emphasis was on conciliation and cooperation. The Industrial Relations Commission (AIRC) could make binding rulings, as highlighted in the 'HRM in reality' example.

HRM in reality	**Individual contracts at Weipa**

The dispute originated between the mining group CRA and its workers at the Weipa bauxite mine in Queensland. CRA attempted to replace wage rates based on union-negotiated pay awards with individual staff contracts. Over 70 employees had refused to accept the new arrangements and were now complaining about discrimination. They claimed that workers on the new contracts were receiving as much as A$20 000 a year more for the same work. CRA's aluminium subsidiary Comalco admitted that 'differences averaging A$7000 have emerged'.

The dispute escalated into a national disagreement over collective bargaining rights as 3000 miners in CRA coal mines started a strike, joined by 17 000 others around the country. Port workers began industrial action and public support came from the Metal Trade Federation and the Australian Education Union. The Australian Council of Trade Unions (ACTU) initiated meetings to organize direct action against CRA.

The issue took on a political edge with ACTU officials arguing that this would be the prevailing industrial relations climate if the opposition came into power. In response, the opposition pointed out that CRA's action had taken place under the Labor government and that they 'would not sanction discrimination against workers doing the same work'.

The dispute ended in November 1995 when a full bench of the Australian Industrial Relations Commission, the country's highest arbitration body, imposed a settlement. They awarded an immediate 8 per cent pay rise to the 70 Weipa workers, backdated to March 1994. They required the ending of industrial action and lifting of all work bans as part of the settlement.

Source: *Financial Times*, 16 and 22 November 1995.

Discussion questions: (a) To what extent does an effective industrial tribunal system rely on an accord or consensus between the different stakeholders? (b) Should all industrial disputes be settled by arbitration?

When the new Liberal–National Party coalition took over, industrial unrest increased markedly. In the first three months alone, four times as many working days were lost through strikes. Some 20 000 trade unionists joined Aboriginal groups outside the Australian parliament to protest at drastic budget cuts and planned reductions in trade union rights. The Accord was dismantled and the emphasis changed to banning closed shops, restricting secondary picketing and increased flexibility in the workplace. As we have noted earlier, the role of the AIRC was much curtailed.

In the UK, ACAS plays a similar role to the Australian Industrial Relations Commission in relation to collective disputes. It provides the following services:

- *Binding arbitration.* ACAS can appoint an arbitrator provided that the two parties agree to accept the arbitrator's decision.
- *Voluntary conciliation.* ACAS provides a calm environment and help on defining the important issues. ACAS conciliation staff act as facilitators and do not make judgements or attempt to impose solutions.
- *Mediation.* Intermediate between arbitration and conciliation. ACAS mediators make advisory recommendations that are aimed at preventing disputes from degenerating into industrial action. These recommendations are not binding on the parties involved.

HRM in reality

ACAS Report 2002

ACAS will have a vital role to play in spreading good practice and resolving disputes over the next few years, according to ACAS chair Rita Donaghy. She explained:

This has been a year when employment relations have come back into the spotlight. There are some major legislative changes just round the corner – the Employment Act, Article 13 discrimination rights and the EC Directive on informing and consulting employees, to name a few. The challenge will be to help organizations take the changes on board smoothly and make the most of opportunities for improving their employment relations.

▶

◄

But with all the talk of more industrial unrest and economic uncertainty, how can people afford to think about best practice? This is just when it is vital and ACAS is ideally placed to deliver the agenda. We offer a wide range of services from advice on employment rights and how best to put legislation into practice through to help with workplace problems and disputes. We work with hundreds of organizations every day, using our first-hand knowledge of what can go wrong to help people get it right. We firmly believe that good employment relations have a direct effect on productivity and competitiveness – the bottom line.

Demand for our dispute resolution services may also increase although it is too early to identify any real upward trend here. No doubt the new legislation will have an impact on individual rights cases. On the collective dispute side we are seeing an increase in media profile rather than demand for conciliation. As always ACAS is ready to play its role if progress can be made through our services.

Some of the most significant details in the 2002 *Annual Report* include:

- There were 100 878 applications to tribunals (compared to 105 909 in 2000/01) covering 165 093 different complaints. Of these, 75 per cent were settled or withdrawn and went no further than the ACAS stage (compared with 71 per cent last year). Unfair dismissal remains the largest category of complaint.

- A total of 1270 collective conciliation cases were completed, compared with 1226 in 2000/01.

- ACAS helplines answered 755 449 calls around the country and Equality Direct a further 2686 on equality issues. Some 99 per cent of callers in recent research said they would use the service again and 80 per cent said the information provided helped them to decide on a course of action.

- ACAS delivered 1084 events – such as seminars for small businesses – compared with 649 in 2000/01. More than 11 000 delegates attended ACAS events with 95 per cent reporting that they were satisfied.

- A total of 385 requests for assistance over recognition were received and 64 per cent of completed cases resulted in full or partial recognition of the trade union.

- ACAS is now a partner in several major EC-funded projects such as those building an industrial relations framework in Slovakia, Latvia and Slovenia.

Source: *HRMGuide.co.uk* (http://www.hrmguide.co.uk), 12 August 2002.

ACAS also plays a major role in promoting agreed settlements in disputes taken to industrial tribunals. Of these, only about a third go to a full hearing by the tribunal – most are settled with ACAS assistance or withdrawn – and less than half of these are judged in favour of the complainant.

Tribunals are composed of a qualified lawyer as chair and two lay members – one employer and one trade unionist. The tribunals are informal by legal standards but continue to be intimidating for applicants.

The negotiating process

Negotiation is an ancient art. It is important in fields as diverse as diplomacy, buying and selling, arranging relationships (marriages, business partnerships) as well as employee relations. Negotiation is a form of decision making where two or more parties approach a problem or situation wanting to achieve their own objectives – which may or may not turn

Table 23.2	Communication in collective bargaining

Statement	Translation
We explored all options	Everybody talked a lot
A great deal of additional work will be necessary	Nobody understood it
The results were inconclusive	Nothing happened
While no agreement was reached, definite progress was made	Nobody budged an inch
It is hoped that this report will stimulate interest in the problem	Let somebody else do it next time

Source: Adapted from *Toctanic* (undated, circa 1989), unofficial staff publication, British Telecom International.

out to be the same. In the employee relations arena, negotiation usually takes place within the collective bargaining environment.

Participants enter the process with widely different views: some – typically on the employee side – will view it as being fundamental to industrial democracy, fairness and good business conduct; others see it as a barrier to efficiency – a view more prevalent on the management side. The latter view sees negotiation as compromise and second-best to winning: possibly worse than giving in! As can be seen from Table 23.2, the process also has its own jargon.

Negotiation is not simply a matter of 'splitting the difference' so that neither side achieves what it wants. It can produce an outcome that meets both sets of goals. In negotiating, both sides must have some goals in common and some that conflict. For example, employers and employees will all want the business to survive and expand. However, employers might resist high pay rises to keep costs down, whereas the staff side will want increases to boost employee morale. Usually, bargaining takes place because neither side has the power or the authority to force a decision on the other and at the same time preserve a harmonious working atmosphere.

Therefore, both sides will open negotiations knowing that they will have to move from the opening position and that there will have to be sacrifices on one item to achieve advantages on another. Even in those ideal circumstances, such as the German model, where deliberate confrontation is not acceptable, there will be an element of conflict between the two sides.

There is also an implicit assumption that the two parties have the same amount of power in the bargaining situation. This is almost certainly not the case and the degree of power will change during the process of negotiation; the location of greatest power may well switch backwards and forwards between the two sides as they achieve positions of advantage. Whatever the actual degree of power, advantages will come from both sides preserving the appearance or illusion of power. There is value, therefore, in playing a game of bluff.

Many texts imply that the methods of bargaining can only be learned through experience and may well suggest that negotiation, like most interpersonal skills, is instinctive rather than learned. Perhaps, the basic requirement is a combination of a competitive, assertive style with a devious and resilient personality. In fact, study of the bargaining process indicates regular patterns and processes that people tend to go through. Studies of industrial negotiations have indicated that many disputes worsen because of:

● lack of clarity of aims or goals by one or both sides

● poor understanding of the detailed situation

● the apparent dispute is not the real problem.

These points are well illustrated in the 'HRM in reality' case of Timex in which poor communication, cultural differences and a complete incompatibility of goals led to the closure of a factory.

HRM in reality

Timex

In 1992 Timex was a multinational company with world headquarters in Connecticut, USA. It was controlled by Fred Olsen, a Norwegian entrepreneur and owner of the Olsen shipping line. An electronics components factory in Dundee on the north-east coast of Scotland formed part of the group. Faced with falling orders and short-time working, negotiations began at the end of that year between local management and unions.

On Christmas Eve 1992, management informed its 343 largely female hourly paid workers that their numbers would have to be halved, at least until the latter part of 1993. Notwithstanding the holiday period, negotiations began immediately between officials of the Amalgamated Engineering and Electrical Union (AEEW) and managers from the plant. The management side was led by Timex UK president Peter Hall, described in one report as 'the Englishman from Surrey with the executive haircut and the tartan tie'. He had worked for the company for two years, having been headhunted for the Dundee post after his own electronics business had gone into receivership in the south-east of England.

The unions suggested that lay-offs should be organized on a rotating basis with the company supplementing state benefits. Timex managers did not support the concept of all staff working alternate weeks. They felt that the company should decide who should be laid off. A ballot of members indicated 92 per cent support for a strike that began on 29 January.

In mid-February, two corporate bosses travelled to the plant with a compromise formula. Among new 'fringe benefits' proposed were reductions in contributions to employee pension plans and an in-house savings scheme. The AEEU claimed there was a hidden agenda of more significant measures under consideration, including a pay freeze, cuts in holidays and overtime payments, and an increase in working hours from 37 to 40 each week.

On 14 February, union members voted to return to work 'under protest', accepting the revised plan for negotiating lay-offs but resisting any erosion of pay and conditions. On 15 February they found the factory gates locked. Two days later they received redundancy notices delivered by taxi. The first of an alternative workforce were bussed in the following day. The following months saw numerous violent clashes and arrests in the vicinity of the factory. The company unsuccessfully sought legal redress to limit the activities of pickets, who were supported by a number of high-profile politicians and unionists.

As positions polarized, cultural differences between the protagonists became increasingly evident. Timex was an elusive multinational foe with a reputation as a 'slash and burn' employer ready to redeploy in the interests of profit. Olsen was said to keep up to date with the smallest details of his extensive business empire while remaining unimpressed by consensus or prevailing business fashion. Timex had been based in Dundee for 46 years, entering the globally competitive electronics subcontracting field after watch production ceased in 1983. Dundee was a city in which the demise of traditional industries based on jute and jam-making had contributed to rising unemployment.

The majority of the Timex employees had worked for the company for a long time – ranging from ten to 40 years. There was a strong sense of community solidarity extending back over many generations and a tradition of labour activism among women. Non-unionized replacement workers were considered to be 'without dignity or conscience'. Workers were also critical of the AEEW president, Bill Jordan. 'Not for the first time, the focused fervour of a self-sufficient group of workers contrasts sharply with the inevitably distanced pragmatism of their union's top brass.' Within this emotional arena, Timex UK president Peter Hall's tone was described as 'studied, strategic blandness: as far as he is concerned, there is no industrial dispute; he is simply running a business'.

Any hope that Peter Hall was the main obstacle to a negotiated settlement received a major setback in June 1993 when he suddenly resigned. By the next meeting between the two sides Timex management had grown weary of trying to deal with a workforce it did not understand. Senior managers from the United States and union officials could find no common ground. The possible exception was the problem at the heart of the original dispute: a loss of £10 million between 1987 and 1992, coupled with a £2 million shortfall in the first six months of 1993. Timex threatened to close the Dundee factory by Christmas unless there was agreement to wage cuts and retraining to introduce conditions similar to those in Japanese companies operating in Britain.

The proposed deal was unanimously rejected and Timex announced 'an orderly withdrawal' from Dundee. Mohammed Saleh, corporate director of human resources, was reported as telling a press conference: 'I defy anybody to say we are not reasonable … It became clear that union members definitely did not want to work under conditions where they would have less wages, or less benefits, than what they had before the strike.' Gavin Laird, general secretary of the AEEW blamed the situation on the company's exploitation of 'brutal anti-union legislation', while the Scottish Trades Union Congress said responsibility lay with Timex 'management madness'.

The end could not have been more acrimonious. On Sunday evening, 29 August 1993, the Dundee factory was abruptly closed leaving John Monks, then general secretary-elect of the Trades Union Congress to comment: 'It is typical of Timex that they, in this very sorry and squalid affair, should have pulled out and in a sense done a moonlight flit.' In October 1993, a narrow majority voted to accept a pay-off from Timex as recommended by the AEEW union. This provided one week's pay for every year worked, in return for a promise not to use union funds to pursue claims for unfair dismissal and an end to the boycott of Timex products. Jimmy Airlie, the AEEW union leader 'fled Dundee amid accusations of blackmail and betrayal'. He commented that while he understood the bitterness of workers 'the factory has closed, that was the reality'.

In *Scotland on Sunday* (20 June 1993) Kamal Ahmed reflected:

> At its simplest the most bitter dispute to hit Britain since the 1980s was over 150 jobs and £30 a week. But at deeper, harsher levels, it became a battle for hearts and minds, a fight to the death between a management's right to manage and a worker's right to earn a decent wage … and to strike.

Sources: *The Guardian,* 15–19 June 1993; *Scotland on Sunday,* 20 June 1993; *The Scotsman,* 15 October 1993.

▶

◄

Discussion questions

1 What is the main problem underlying this case?

2 List the main parties/individuals involved and evaluate their: (a) objectives; (b) degree of flexibility; (c) effectiveness as negotiators.

3 What options were open to the negotiators?

4 Who made the final decision?

5 Was there a better way of dealing with the situation?

Models of bargaining

There are several models of the bargaining process, the clearest of which identifies four main stages (Lyons, 1988, p.110):

1 *Initial positioning.* Both parties set out their positions and requirements in an emphatic, firm way aimed at giving the impression that there is no possibility of budging from those positions. The situation can appear hopeless at this stage.

2 *Testing.* The next stage is a less formal probing of the other side's demands, testing out which are really unmovable and which might bend in the right circumstances.

3 *Concession.* Some tentative proposals and concessions are exchanged on which detailed negotiations can take place.

4 *Settlement.* Finally, agreement is reached and the package of new terms is settled and actioned.

Obviously, the model does not apply in every case: the Timex negotiations went awry from the beginning and came to an end somewhere in the middle of the sequence. Lyons argues that successful negotiation requires specific skills, examined in the following sub-sections. These skills were visibly missing at Timex, particularly on the management side:

Analysis

This may be defined as the ability to analyse a situation not only in terms of one's own position and goals but also those of the other side. There should be a long-term perspective – rarely is it clear that one should begin to consider the consequences of the whole process at this basic stage. The analysis must include a decision on which elements can be agreed on an 'I win/you win' basis, as opposed to those which are 'I win/you lose'. It is not worthwhile winning one of the latter if the advantage is trivial in comparison with the longer-term bad feelings that may arise as a consequence.

This phase is frequently glossed over but in fact is possibly the most important. It is the stage at which one should work out what the highest and lowest gains you and your opponent are likely to accept. Additionally, there must be a clear understanding of what the other side really want as opposed to what you think they might want. Clearly, in the Timex case we see little understanding of the opposing perspective and no evidence from the management side of a willingness to accept an 'I win/you win' position.

Effective argument

This has to be carefully balanced between being forceful and being reasonable. The whole point of negotiation is to convince the other side of the merits of your argument as against their own. It is a change process. It is important to avoid cheap point-scoring and abuse in order to preserve mutual respect and avoid distraction from irrelevant side issues. Again, the Timex managers were unable to convince the employees of the merits of their argument and were seemingly incapable of understanding the employees' point of view.

Signals of cooperation

The skill of sensing and giving signals of cooperation and possible compromise. Again, virtually absent in the Timex case. Kanter (1989, p.156) found that the participants in successful 'business partnerships' were 'very adept at "reading" signals that indicated whether partner representatives can be trusted'. On the 'tit-for-tat' principle, maximum opportunity comes from rewarding cooperation or compromise with a compromise of your own. On the other hand, one does not reward the opposition for sticking to an unmovable position: every offer one makes has to be conditional on cooperation in return. It may be necessary to keep communication going in order for this process to happen. In the case of a complete deadlock, it may even be necessary to have 'talks about talks'. All offers and threats must have credibility, remembering that it is not real power that matters but the appearance of it.

Attention to detail

Lastly, the final conclusion of negotiations requires the ability to attend to detail, making sure that all aspects are taken care of and there is no way for the other side to avoid its agreed obligations.

Employee involvement

Employee involvement is a wide-ranging topic that hinges on the notion that managers may have a prerogative to manage but this prerogative should not be exercised without considering the opinions of their employees. The concept of employee involvement has a moral, practical and legal basis. The moral dimension is difficult to resolve since it involves an ethical debate on the 'right' of managers to manage and the 'right' of employees to have a say in the way the organization is managed. Fundamentally, it is a matter of personal opinion. The practical and legal aspects are more easily explained and justified.

There are sound practical reasons for taking account of employee views before making significant decisions. They include an acknowledgement of the greater and more detailed knowledge that experienced employees may have of specific processes when compared with a manager who may be relatively new or who has never been involved at a working level with those processes. Changes may seem perfectly reasonable and desirable to the manager, operating at a distance from the activity to be changed. But skilled workers may be aware of implications that are invisible to the manager. In fact, as we observed in Part 1, the concept of knowledge management is based on the value of individual expertise and experience that need to be harnessed and used for the benefit of the organization – rather than being ignored by overconfident and unwise managers.

The authority of managers may be constrained by an organization's own rules in the form of company handbooks, job definitions, reporting paths and consultation procedures so that the involvement of employees in decision making cannot be avoided. We noted in previous chapters that legislation can also impose requirements for consultation, for example in the form of works councils required under European legislation. In practice, most countries have employment legislation in place that sets the rights of employees within a legal context. Their rights are usually prescribed both individually and collectively so that (theoretically, at least) it is impossible for an organization and its managers to have total discretion over consultation and, to a lesser extent, involvement.

> **Key concept 23:1**
>
> **Employee involvement**   An umbrella term that is inconsistently and imprecisely used to embrace a diverse range of management processes involving participation, communication, decision making, industrial democracy and employee motivation.

According to Holden (2001):

> There is an enormous range of employee involvement schemes, varying from those which are informational mechanisms to full-blown democratic systems where employees have as much say in the decision making as does management. This makes an all-encompassing definition problematic. In addition, different labels have been attached to these processes, such as employee or worker participation, industrial democracy, organizational communications, co-determination, employee influence, etc., each of which have their own definitions.

Marchington (2001) considers that employee involvement became prominent in the 1980s as an attempt by employers to find participative ways in which to manage staff. The trend in recent decades towards individual rather than collective employee relations may have encouraged interest in employee involvement. The UK 1998 Workplace Employee Relations Survey (Cully *et al.*, 1999) showed that even in firms that recognized trade unions, managers consulted individual employees (57 per cent) in preference to union representatives (36 per cent). In fact, 41 per cent of the companies surveyed did not have any union involvement but a mere 8 per cent stated that they never involved individual employees.

The nature of the relationship between employer and employed is described as the 'psychological contract' (see Key concept 23.2). Townley (1994) sees an inevitable gap between what is promised and what is realized: 'the naturally occurring space between expectation and deliverance of work'. The psychological contract implies some kind of exchange within the employment relationship but this is obscured by the power of the economic relationship between employer and employed.

> **Key concept 23:2**
>
> **The psychological contract**   An informal understanding between the employer and the employee. Unlike the formal employment contract, this has no physical existence. It is a set of expectations held by both employers and employees in terms of what they wish to give and receive from their working relationship (Rousseau and Parks, 1993).

Perhaps anticipating employer branding and its implications, Monks (1996) suggests that management of the psychological contract could be a suitable job for the human resource manager. In order for this to be possible, Townley (1994) points to three areas where knowledge is required:

- *Knowledge of the workforce as a population* – where human resource information systems, employee surveys and staff feedback are as important as traditional personnel records.
- *Knowledge of the activity or work to be performed* – detailed information obtainable through job analyses, quality circles and, more recently, the techniques elaborated for knowledge management.

● *Knowledge of individual workers* – through performance assessments and feedback interviews.

She sees the employment relationship becoming a 'calculable arena' – a transformation of 'soft' HR based on indeterminate and sometimes unspecified understanding into a harder form based on detailed information. In her view human resource practices are technologies through which 'activities and individuals become knowable and governable'. From this perspective, HRM becomes a powerful methodology that can turn the apparently imprecise and subjective topic that was once 'personnel' into a technology of people. Since Townley put forward her ideas, a raft of new hybrid HR/information technology techniques have been developed to make this technology of people more likely.

Activity 23:2	How might employee involvement increase the power of managers over employees?

Employee involvement in practice

Unlike Townley, Marchington (2001) sees employee involvement as a feature of soft rather than hard HRM. In firms with a hard orientation, Marchington considers that the 'numbers-driven', cost-cutting mentality reduces involvement to a one-way communication channel aimed at transmitting management decisions and propaganda to staff. This contrasts with organizations that are true believers in employees as their 'greatest asset' where there is a strategic commitment to sharing information and opinions and achieving a workplace culture that meets business needs.

Peccei and Rosenthal (2001) examined attempts to engender desirable customer-oriented behaviours among employees in the context of a major change initiative in a retail company. The change programme followed (by now) orthodox management theory which assumed that management behaviour, job design and values-based training would produce a feeling of empowerment among employees, and that this sense of empowerment would lead to prosocial customer-oriented behaviour. A large-scale employee survey showed that staff who took a positive view of management behaviour and who had also participated in values-based training were more likely to feel empowered. In turn, Peccei and Rosenthal found a positive relationship between psychological empowerment and customer-oriented behaviour.

Key concept 23:3	**Empowerment and empowering** Murrell and Meredith (2000, p.1) define empowering as: '… mutual influence; it is the creation of power; it is shared responsibility; it is vital and energetic, and it is inclusive, democratic and long-lasting.' They argue that 'empowerment' implies a finished process, a state of constancy. Whereas: 'Empowering … suggests action – enabling the growth of individuals and organizations as they add value to the products or services the organization delivers to its customers, and the promotion of continuous discovery and learning.'

Marchington (2001) identifies the following characteristics in employee involvement schemes:

1 Employee involvement is a process primarily instigated by management.

2 Employees are assumed to want greater involvement, regardless of its form.

3 A unity of purpose is thought to be achievable between employees and their managers.

4 There is an expectation that employee involvement will lead to greater commitment and productivity.

Marchington (2001) also states that:

> For many observers, notions of employee involvement (EI) and participation are central to any consideration of human resource management. Terms such as 'empowerment', 'team working', 'autonomy' and 'communications' are peppered throughout the management literature which publicizes and celebrates the latest initiatives in HRM. Similarly, the concepts of involvement form part of many academic discussions of HRM. Either as explicit elements of its policy and practice, or implicitly as a potential contributor to the achievement of higher levels of employee commitment.

He notes that belief in the link between direct employee involvement and high levels of commitment and performance is based on some questionable assumptions:

1 That line managers will be committed to employee involvement and will ensure that it happens in the workplace.

2 That employee involvement positively influences staff attitudes, causing them to change their working behaviour which, in turn, leads to greater effectiveness and productivity.

3 That trade union officials and other employee representatives will allow themselves to be marginalized or led into acceptance of the management agenda.

Schuster (1998) asks why managers have been so slow in adopting employee-centred management. He postulates five main reasons:

1 Complacency and inertia. He argues that, until recently, many executives had never questioned or considered changing the fairly comfortable status quo.

2 The short-term focus of 'management systems in general, and reward systems in particular'. Executive performance bonuses and incentive plans are tied to one year – and certainly not aimed at building a committed workforce over the long term.

3 Inability to measure the impact of HR practices. Schuster contends that: 'Until recently, little attention has been paid to executive performance regarding effective utilization of human resources, in part because standards for comparison did not exist. Our lack of *control* [original emphasis] over the efficient utilization of the most expensive single cost of operation in many organizations is indeed remarkable.'

4 Reluctance to give up their special status, executive privileges and managerial power.

5 Perhaps the most significant explanation of all – that many managers would like to introduce high-involvement practices 'but are unsure how to begin or exactly how to proceed'.

Pun, Chin and Gill (2001) investigated the characteristics of successful employee involvement initiatives in Hong Kong. They found the most critical factors to be: management commitment, rewards and motivation with a clear corporate mission, continuous improvement and both extrinsic rewards and intrinsic rewards being the main sub-factors. Contrary to the view that line managers are obstacles to employee involvement, Fenton-O'Creevy (2001) found that middle managers' attitudes were no more negative than those of senior managers. But there was a complex relationship between perceptions of their own degree of empowerment and attitudes towards employee involvement. Managers with experience of employee involvement were more likely to be supportive, but not if they had recently lost a job. Intriguingly, however, managers who had been through de-layering were more likely to support the involvement of employees.

According to Fisher (1999, p.3):

> Empowerment has clearly become the latest in a long litany of vogue practices that have ebbed and flowed over corporations like the changing of the tide. Today it is estimated that virtually every corporation in North America and western Europe is using various forms of empowerment somewhere in their organization. Many even utilize an advanced form of empowerment called *self-directed work teams* (SDWTs) – now more commonly called *high-performance work systems*.

In fact, SDWTs are in a direct line of descent from the 'socio-technical systems' of the 1950s. Fisher argues that companies that take the concept seriously consider empowerment to be more than a passing fad. He also sees the team leader as a key role in the empowerment process. In the past the equivalent would have been supervisors, 'foremen' or managers. Now their titles may include terms such as 'facilitator' or 'adviser' and 'lead', 'coach', or 'train' rather than 'plan', 'organize', 'direct' or 'control'. Under the traditional form of management, supervisors would control subordinates by telling them what to do. In other words, the supervisor was the boss. Fisher contends that all traditional managers are supervisors but, for empowerment to take effect, they must become team leaders. Fisher (1999, p.11) justifies this by saying that: 'Competitive advantage comes from fully utilizing the *discretionary* effort of the workforce, not from buying the latest gadget or using the latest management fad. Voluntary effort comes from employee commitment, and commitment comes from empowerment.'

Ramaswamy and Schiphorst (2000) found that employee empowerment was increasingly viewed as a serious strategic option by Indian companies whose profitability was being squeezed in a competitive market. On the face of it, power-sharing which resulted in workers taking responsibility for shop-floor decisions on quality, safety, productivity and material seemed attractive to both managers and employees. But trade unions might choose to obstruct or subvert the process. Gill and Krieger (1999) surveyed workplaces in ten European Union countries and found a considerable gap between the rhetoric and reality of direct participation. Different forms of direct participation were widespread in the ten countries but the scope was relatively limited. The survey also showed that works councils and union representatives were more likely to be 'agents of change' rather than barriers for achieving employee involvement.

For Murrell and Meredith (2000) managers in an empowering organization:

- Believe that leadership belongs to all employees – and not just a few.
- Know that the company is most likely to succeed when employees have the tools, training and authority to do their best work.
- Understand that information is power – and share it with all employees.
- Value employees enough to build a culture that values and supports individuals.
- Create opportunities for finding solutions and for designing what-can-be not searching for problems and what-should-have-been.
- Understand that fostering empowerment is a continuous effort – not an end-point to be checked off a list of objectives.

Lee and Koh (2001) argue that although empowerment has been actively practised, the exact meaning of the terms 'empowerment' and 'psychological empowerment' have not been thought through. They contend that empowerment is quite distinct from related concepts such as authority delegation, motivation, self-efficacy, job enrichment, employee ownership, autonomy, self-determination, self-management, self-control, self-influence, self-leadership, high-involvement and participative management. They conclude that empowerment is not just a fad, but a unique concept reflecting a new managerial approach. Conversely, Harley (1999), using data from the 1995 Australian Workplace Industrial Relations Survey could find no meaningful relationship between empowerment and employee autonomy.

| Activity 23:3 | Evaluate the proposition that empowerment is a unique and meaningful concept. |

Ichniowski *et al.* (2000) review a number of theories as to why high skill, high involvement workplaces are believed to be more effective than traditional 'top-down' management regimes. They divide these theories into two basic groups:

1 Those that focus on the effort and motivation of workers and work groups and suggest that people work harder.

2 Those that focus on changes in the structure of organizations that produce improvements in efficiency.

In the first group, the emphasis may be on 'working harder' and 'working smarter'. People may work harder if they find elements of a job to be interesting or enjoyable, and this may come from rewards or feedback. They are also less likely to resent aspects of the job if they have contributed to its design.

As regards working smarter, innovative work practices can lead to improved efficiency. Workers can suggest improved work practices because they have a more intimate knowledge of the job than managers or external consultants. Moreover, open discussion allows employees to modify their own work processes to fit more effectively with others as they become aware of the 'bigger picture'. Ichniowski *et al.* point to the need to change work culture from 'rate-busting' – discouraging high levels of performance – to one that values greater efficiency. This process can be encouraged by specifically rewarding high performance through collective bonuses. Helper, Levine and Bendoly (2002) surveyed the benefits of employee involvement practices for blue-collar workers in the auto-supply industry and found wages to be 3–5 per cent higher than would otherwise be the case. They attribute the cause to improved efficiency.

Theories in the second group may emphasize innovative work practices that can also lead to improvements in organizational structure that are independent of motivational effects. Ichniowski *et al.* (2000) give the following as examples:

● Cross-training and flexible job assignment may reduce the costs of absenteeism.

● Delegating decision making to self-directed teams can reduce the number of supervisors or middle managers and improve communication.

● Training in problem solving, statistical process control and computer skills may enhance the benefits of information technology.

● Involving workers and unions in decision making can reduce grievances and other sources of conflict.

It is clear that such changes associated with employee involvement are complex and make it 'difficult to isolate any single causal mechanism that produces their effects on economic performance'. Nevertheless, Ichniowski *et al.* conclude that the companies which adopt such practices 'should enjoy higher productivity and quality …, leading to lower costs and higher product demand, all else equal'. But this comes at a cost because employee involvement programmes can be expensive due to extra meetings and related activities.

Silvestro (2002) reports empirical findings from one of the UK's largest supermarket companies that seem to challenge the notion that employee satisfaction and loyalty are key drivers of productivity, efficiency and profit. The study shows an inverse correlation between employee satisfaction and the measures of productivity, efficiency and profitability. In fact, the most profitable stores were those in which employees were least satisfied and length of service tended to be lowest. One possible explanation is that managers at ground level were being pressurized to maximize store efficiency, leading to 'dysfunctional managerial behaviour at store level'.

What is the relationship between employee involvement and productivity?

CUPE attacks work overload

Around 100 delegates, representing more than 2200 PEI members of the Canadian Union of Public Employees (CUPE) voted overwhelmingly against 'unsafe and unhealthy' workload levels at the annual convention of CUPE PEI.

'It is time to demand more staff, take our breaks and refuse to work unpaid overtime. It is also time to be compensated for the damage workload and stress are wreaking on our bodies and our lives,' says CUPE national president Judy Darcy. 'The Canadian Union of Public Employees is declaring war on work overload.'

'We work through our breaks. We work through our lunches. We are working longer hours and additional unpaid hours,' says Donalda MacDonald, president of CUPE PEI. 'Enough is enough. Our members are telling us that workload is going to be a major issue in negotiations and in our workplaces.'

The vote was taken on an executive resolution stating that CUPE members in all sectors are dealing with increasing on-the-job stresses caused by chronic government underfunding, privatization, staffing shortages and workplace amalgamations. The resolution described work overload as a 'modern-day epidemic' that leads to unhealthy levels of stress and to on-the-job injuries. It called for CUPE PEI to focus on workload in this year's campaigns and negotiations.

Some 52 per cent of public sector workers identified heavy workload as a significant problem in a cross-Canada poll conducted by Ekos. This was particularly emphasized by people in the education (74 per cent) and social services sectors (72 per cent). The poll also showed that public sector workers work more overtime than those in the private sector.

'From coast to coast, our members are telling me that the pressure of excessive workload is costing them their health. We know of one member who experienced such incredible stress from work overload that he took his own life,' adds Judy Darcy, CUPE's national president. 'It is unacceptable that workers should have to choose between their jobs and their health. It is unacceptable that Premier Binns can brag about a budget surplus, yet he can't find the funds to address the workload crisis. In PEI, our members are fed up and we aren't going to take it any more.'

Source: *HRM Guide Canada* (http://www.hrmguide.net/canada/), 11 May 2001.

Work–life balance

The 'Work–Life Balance 2000' baseline study was conducted jointly by the Institute for Employment Research, University of Warwick and IFF Research. It was commissioned by the UK Department of Education and Employment (DfEE) to give baseline information for the department's work–life balance campaign (*HRMGuide.co.uk*, 20 November 2000). It is representative of national provision of work–life balance arrangements in places of work that have five or more employees. The study consists of two surveys: (a) a survey of employers responsible for 2500 workplaces in Great Britain; and (b) a further survey of around 7500 employees.

The study concludes that there is a widespread demand from employees for the right to balance work and home life. It also reveals that businesses prefer to offer stress counselling for the personal consequences of long working hours (49 per cent) rather than provide assistance for childcare (9 per cent).

One in nine of full-time employees (including men with children) work more than 60 hours every week. Two-thirds of male employees believe that part-time working would damage their career prospects. At the same there is a clear demand for greater flexibility – especially from fathers. In general, men seem to have a greater enthusiasm for working from home than do women. Virtually all the respondents to both surveys – employees and employers alike – agreed with the concept of work–life balance. But one in eight of employees still worked Saturdays and Sundays and around 20 per cent of employees worked for 24-hour/seven-day-week businesses.

Other conclusions of the study were:

- 80 per cent of workplaces had employees who worked more than their standard hours with 39 per cent doing so without extra pay.

- Just 20 per cent of employers were fully aware of increased maternity leave rights and 24 per cent fully aware of new paternal leave rights.

- 25 per cent of entitled female employees took less than 18 weeks' maternity leave.

- 55 per cent of employers consider it acceptable to allow staff to move from full-time to part-time work in some cases.

- 24 per cent of employees now work flexitime with 12 per cent working only during school terms.

- 56 per cent of women preferred flexible working – for example, part-time or home-based – after a pregnancy to having a longer maternity leave period.

HRM in reality

Work–life balance examples

Lloyds TSB and UNIFI

Lloyds TSB employees indicated in a survey that work–life balance was more important to many than improved pay and conditions. Focus groups were then used to find out more about staff views and consultants were asked to formulate policy. A system was then established allowing individual members of staff to: initiate requests for change; make business case applications using a guidance pack; and conduct dialogues with their line managers. The process is monitored and a staff newsletter used to keep people up to date on ideas.

Requests are approved if they do not have a negative impact on the business. According to Sally Evans, head of equal opportunities at Lloyds TSB: 'There is a very clear business imperative for us, as what differentiates us from our competitors is the quality of our people. To maintain that edge we need to recruit and retain the right calibre of personnel.'

This means that the bank will consider suggestions for part-time work, job share, compressed hours, teleworking or a combination of these. And Ed Sweeney, joint general secretary, UNIFI says: 'This is a good start to the long process of getting a sensible policy on work–life balance for staff and bank.'

Arla Foods and GMB

Arla Foods (GMB, T&G) is a multinational dairy company with six dairies in the UK. It supplies 20 per cent of milk to UK supermarkets. But the demand is seasonal and production is governed by the requirements of the supermarkets. This makes it difficult to give staff a choice over their hours and patterns of work.

Before the working time regulations were introduced many Arla employees regularly worked 50–60 hours a week – occasionally working as much as 80 hours per week. The GMB and T&G trade unions and Arla UK came up with a plan to reduce working time and offer employees more choice about how long they work. The new agreement uses an annualized hours scheme with the number of working hours per year specified (instead of the traditional number of hours per week). Workers have some degree of choice – a 40, 42, 44, 46 or 48 hours average working week throughout the year. And they can apply to increase or reduce their hours if circumstances or preferences change, providing that there is enough work to support their request.

At first the scheme did not work too well but Gerry Veart (GMB) and Paul Simpson (Arla) took responsibility for the scheme and worked together – along with the T&G – to redesign it. They say that, despite considerable constraints imposed by customer demand, by working in partnership with its trade unions, Arla has managed to reduce working time while maintaining the ability to meet tight production targets.

Source: *HRMGuide.co.uk* (http://www.hrmguide.co.uk), 5 February 2002.

Activity 23:5	What is 'work–life balance' and how can it be achieved?

Health and safety

According to Naidoo and Wills (2000, p.270):

> The relationship between work and health may appear substantial but it is viewed in different ways by different groups of people. One of the defining characteristics of the workplace setting is that it brings together a variety of groups who have different agendas with regard to work and health. The key parties are workers or employees and their trade unions or staff associations, employers and managers, occupational health staff, health and safety officers, environmental health officers and specialist health promoters.

Sickness absence in the UK due to workplace injury and illness amounts to 19 million days a year, or 40 times the amount lost because of industrial action. According to the TUC, sickness absence as a whole costs the British economy somewhere between £4 billion and £9 billion. Moreover, 27 000 people leave the employment market each year because of a workplace injury or illness.

An Australian Bureau of Statistics (ABS, 2000) report shows that 477 800 people experienced a work-related injury or illness in the year ending September 2000. This amounts to about 5 per cent of the 9 687 300 Australians aged 15 and over who worked at some time during that period. Broken down into major categories: 60 per 1000 males; 36 per 1000 females; 70 per 1000 males aged 35–44 years; and 41 per 1000 females aged 35–44 years.

The report indicates that, of people who had experienced a work-related injury or illness in the 12 months ending September 2000: 6 per cent were not working at September 2000; and 89 per cent were employees in the job where they experienced a work-related injury or illness. More than twice as many males (323 900) experienced a work-related injury or illness as female workers (154 000). Some 40 per cent of the 477 800 people who experienced a work-related injury or illness received workers' compensation for their most recent work-related injury or illness.

Around 259 900 did not apply for workers' compensation. Very nearly a half (49 per cent) of these said the main reason for not applying was that they considered the injury or illness to be minor. More than half (54 per cent) of those who did not apply for workers' compensation received no financial assistance for that injury or illness. Of the 46 per cent receiving financial assistance, the most common sources were Medicare and employer-provided sick leave.

Health and safety are workplace issues with considerable organizational and legal implications for HR and other managers. Naidoo and Wills (2000) identify the benefits to organizations from the promotion of health in the workplace as (a) 'hard' benefits, such as improvements in productivity as a result of reduced sickness, absence and staff turnover; and (b) 'soft' benefits, including enhanced corporate image.

Organizations may introduce specialist occupational health staff tasked with the following (Naidoo and Wills, 2000):

- surveillance of the work environment, such as monitoring the effects of new technology
- introducing initiatives and providing advice on the control of hazards
- surveillance of employee health including assessing fitness to work and analysing sickness/absence reports
- organizing first aid and emergency responses
- involvement with adaptation of work and working environment to the worker.

Changes away from large, labour-intensive manufacturing organizations towards more fragmented, technology-based industries have dramatically altered the nature of occupational health over the last few decades – in developed countries, at least. Boyd (2001) argues that health and safety (as a topic) occupies a somewhat rhetorical role in HRM literature. Boyd looked at HRM and the management of health and safety in the airline industry and found that airlines have adopted a short-term cost-cutting approach to both in response to increasingly competitive trading conditions. The focus has been on reducing operating costs, achieving immediate productivity gains and prioritizing profit over employee health and safety.

| **HRM in reality** | **Measuring employee wellness** |

There is growing concern over burned-out, stressed-out workforces, but widespread adoption of corporate wellness programs in Canada has been discouraged by an inability to make a solid business case and justify the costs, according to Buffett Taylor & Associates. They argue that most Canadian companies do not view wellness as a strategic business imperative because they cannot link it to the bottom line.

Buffett Taylor & Associates have launched a new and comprehensive cost/benefit tool which, they claim, 'enables organizations to rigorously evaluate the impact of their wellness investment on their employees' well-being, on their organization's well-being – and, ultimately, on the bottom line'. The company says that the software tracks, analyses and generates reports quantitatively and qualitatively. It also reveals return on investment as well as organizational trends in areas such as absenteeism, productivity, disability/benefit costs, company morale, employee attitudes and program participation.

Other features of the Buffett Taylor Employee Wellness Cost Benefit Software include the flexibility to accommodate different user requirements – e.g. multiple sites, multiple users, a variety of program initiatives with different measurement requirements, or other customized needs. The company cites, as an example, the ability to measure the effectiveness of an organization's cardiovascular wellness program by tracking health progress, absenteeism, medication usage, knowledge level and participant satisfaction – and provide reports in an aggregate manner. Additionally, it will calculate the return on investment of the program, showing the financial impact of outcomes such as reduced absenteeism, increased productivity, reduced medical claims and so on.

The software also allows for web-enabled data collection, for example through online questionnaires. Given the sensitivity of employee information, security features are included allowing users to access only at designated security levels. This means that reports and other information can be restricted to certain users.

'Workplace wellness has lagged in Canada because of an inability to validate and quantify the return on investment,' says Ed Buffett, founder and chairman of Buffett Taylor & Associates. 'And, while there is a growing base of evidence supporting the value of workplace wellness programs, organizations haven't had any feasible means to truly demonstrate the effectiveness of their own proprietary corporate wellness initiatives. With employee burn-out on the rise, the time is right to give wellness a proper seat at the boardroom table. But without the tools to properly evaluate how your wellness dollar is performing, this area will continue to be seen as another soft benefit.'

A recent survey (Buffett Taylor National Wellness Survey Report 2000) conducted for the company found that only 17 per cent of mid-to-large sized Canadian organizations said they offer a comprehensive employee wellness program. When asked to name the main health risks identified by their organizations, respondents ranked stress highest (cited by 83 per cent), then 'smoking' (57 per cent), 'unable to balance work and family' (55 per cent) and 'feeling of loss of control over work schedule and environment' (53 per cent).

'We are now living in a global economy where technology and intense competition are driving our employees faster than ever – and often on a 7/24 basis. Yet, while the heavy lifting of business comes from innovation and intellectual capital, we are at risk of burning out our most important asset,' says Buffett. 'We must do all we can to put wellness on the table as a business issue before it's too late to catch up.'

Source: *HRM Guide Canada* (http://www.hrmguide.net/canada), 1 May 2001.

Activity 23:6   Should human resource practitioners be involved with health and safety at work?

HRM in reality

Growing stress levels worry employers

A survey of 565 HR specialists (a 10 per cent response rate from questionnaires sent out to a random selection of 5600 by the Industrial Society) appears to show evidence of growing concern about worker stress among UK employers. The survey found that 74 per cent of respondents consider the incidence of workplace stress to be a faster growing health problem than back pain, smoking and drug or alcohol abuse.

Most employers treat worker health as a serious matter with 77 per cent having workplace health policies. But employers still seem tardy in dealing with the issue of stress. Just one-third actively monitor stress in the workplace and only 29 per cent have a stress policy. Almost two-thirds (63 per cent) of employers take no action to provide stress awareness coaching for their staff. A mere 8 per cent provide managers with training on health promotion issues.

According to Pat McGuinness of the Industrial Society:

> Employers are aware of stress and its consequences, but are still struggling to find ways of identifying and dealing with it. Having open and honest lines of communication where employees feel that they can freely acknowledge that they are under stress without fear of retribution can go some way to alleviating the problem.

Around 45 per cent of employers acknowledged that compliance with legislation was the main reason for promoting well-being but 39 per cent also claim that employee health promotion is a significant part of holistic people management.

Businesses surveyed tend to deal with health promotion by means of written advice and health screening (both 61 per cent). Some 53 per cent provide access to a trained counsellor; 46 per cent offer catering facilities with healthy eating alternatives; and 31 per cent now have employee assistance programmes (EAPs). More exotically, 5 per cent offer aromatherapy and 5 per cent reflexology.

Source: *HRMGuide.co.uk* (http://www.hrmguide.co.uk), 29 November 2000.

Stress

Stress is a commonly used word. It has been taken from physics where mechanical stress has been a long-standing concept. In its physical context it describes a strain leading to distortion of an object. For example, a steel girder may bend as the result of temporary forces such as strong winds acting against a bridge. Eventually, however, if the strain is long-lasting or excessive, the girder breaks. Psychological stress draws on the physical analogy but the strain on human beings is seen as coming from life's pressures, boredom, overwork, threat and ambiguity. In essence, pressure overcomes the ability to cope. The social readjustment rating scale shown in Table 23.3 gives an indication of the life events that individuals find most stressful.

Stress is a subjective experience: it is not necessarily easy to identify stress in another person. Neither is it clear that the experience is the same for different people. Indeed, it is apparent that similar situations will produce entirely different reactions in different individuals. Table 23.4 shows the wide range of symptoms that have been linked with stress. Burnout is a related concept (see Key concept 23.4).

Key concept 23:4

Burnout   This refers to a condition in which individuals are completely negative about themselves and their lives. This includes feeling worthless, physical and mental fatigue. They feel disregarded, pessimistic about the future and lacking in control of their lives. This state has been described particularly in professionals such as nurses.

Stressors include a long list of factors. Too much or too little work may both be stressful. De-layering, downsizing, rightsizing: the changes in organization and job structure are rife in modern industry and are perceived as stressful by those who are made to change.

Table 23.3	Social readjustment rating scale (excerpt items)		

Rank	Life event	Mean value
1	Death of partner	100
2	Divorce	73
3	Marital separation	65
4	Jail term	63
5	Death of close family member	63
6	Personal injury/illness	53
7	Marriage	50
8	Fired at work	47
9	Marital reconciliation	45
10	Retirement	45
11	Illness of family member	44
12	Pregnancy	40
13	Sex difficulties	39
14	Gain new family member	39
15	Business readjustment	39
16	Change in financial state	38
17	Death of close friend	37
21	Foreclosure of mortgage	30
27	Begin/end school	26
32	Change in residence	20
41	Holiday	13

Source: Adapted from Holmes and Rahe (1967).

Where job numbers are slashed, the remaining workforce may be pressurized and also be concerned about the future of their own jobs. The 2:3:2 formula – half the people doing three times the work for twice the money – brings its own pressures.

The UK Health and Safety Executive (HSE) has published research showing that teaching, nursing, and management and professional occupations report the highest levels of work-related stress (*HRMGuide.co.uk*, 20 December 2000). In order, occupational groups reporting high stress most commonly were teaching, nursing, management, professionals, other education and welfare (including social workers), road transport and security (including police and prison officers). In each of these groups at least one in five reported high stress (two in five among teachers). Full-time workers were more likely to report high stress than part-time employees.

High levels of stress were reported most frequently by people in managerial and technical occupations, those educated to degree level and those earning more than £20 000. Non-white employees reported comparatively higher levels of stress than white workers but it is pointed out that the numbers involved were small. Little difference was reported in stress levels between male and female workers.

Table 23.4	Symptoms of stress

Physical	Mental	Illnesses
Appetite loss	Irritability	Hypertension
Craving under pressure	Lack of interest in life	Coronary thrombosis
Indigestion	Unable to cope	Hay fever
Fatigue	Feeling a failure	Migraine
Insomnia	Self-dislike	Asthma
Sweating	Decisions hard	Colitis
Headaches	Hiding feelings	Dyspepsia
Cramps	Loss of humour	Skin disorders
Nausea	Dread of future	Diabetes
Fainting	Feeling ugly	Tuberculosis
Frequent crying/wanting to	Unable to finish one task before going on to next	Menstrual difficulties
Impotence	Fear of open or enclosed spaces	Hyperthyroidism
High blood pressure		Depression

Source: Adapted from Arnold, Robertson and Cooper (1991).

Alker and McHugh (2000) looked at the rationale used for introducing employee assistance or advisory programmes (EAPs) in UK organizations. They found that support was more likely to be given for organizational change than for more humanistic reasons. They offer the explanation that this is consistent with managers' work roles.

HRM in reality

Married to the job?

The partners of a third of people who work longer than 48 hours in a typical week reported that the long hours culture had a negative effect on their relationships. More than half of the partners interviewed by Taylor Nelson Sofres for the CIPD said that their sex life suffered as a result of the 'long hours' worker's tiredness. Some 43 per cent agreed that they were fed up with having to take responsibility for most of the domestic burden.

These were some of the findings reported by the CIPD in *Married to the Job?*, a report which looks at the impact of long working hours on relationships with family, friends and fellow workers. The report was based on two pieces of research conducted by Taylor Nelson Sofres for the CIPD. First, 486 people were interviewed by telephone in August 2000, including 291 people working over 48 hours and 139 partners of 'long hours' workers. The other telephone survey involved interviews with 589 people in paid work – part of a nationally representative survey of UK workers conducted between 15–17 December 2000.

The main findings included:

- Of partners with school-age or younger children, 29 per cent said that the time the 'long hours' worker spends at work has either a quite or a very negative effect on his/her relationship with their children. More than a third report that the children have complained that they don't see enough of the parent who works more than 48 hours a week (36 per cent).

- Some 27 per cent of partners say that the 'long hours' worker does not always arrive home before their children have gone to bed or have the time to help the kids with their homework.

- Most of the 'long hours' workers admitted feeling that they had struck the wrong work–life balance and 56 per cent conceded that they were spending too much time at work.

- Two-fifths of 'long hours' workers say that their work pattern has caused arguments with their partner in the last year, and a similar proportion admit to feeling guilty about not doing their fair share of domestic work. Almost one-third concede that their sex life is suffering because of work-related tiredness and 14 per cent report a reduction in sex drive or even a loss of libido in the previous 12 months.

- Long hours can also have a negative effect on job performance and cause accidents. A third of the 'long hours' sample said they had made mistakes, including fatigue-related mismanagement of people and projects to property damage and personal injury.

According to the report's author, Melissa Compton-Edwards:

While working long hours doesn't necessarily lead to marriage breakdown, it can put a strain on relationships with partners, children and friends. Long-suffering spouses and cohabiting partners tend to tolerate the situation and try to curb their criticism of their absentee other half. The Faustian pact seems to be that while they would rather their 'long hours' partner worked shorter hours, this is considered a price worth paying if it guarantees a decent standard of living.

What should not be overlooked is that excessive hours can have a negative effect on job performance and cause costly or reputation-damaging mistakes. Fatigue-related accidents are potentially life-threatening. Employers need to ensure that they do everything in their power to improve productivity through efficiency improvements rather than by overloading their staff.

Source: *HRMGuide.co.uk* (http://www.hrmguide.co.uk), 5 March 2001.

| HRM in reality | Stress levels rise as workers struggle to balance the demands of work and home |

A report from the Industrial Society, *Occupational Stress*, published earlier this year showed that almost 70 per cent of people surveyed cited difficulty in balancing work and home demands as a significant contributing factor to occupational stress. Nearly 50 per cent reported unrealistic deadlines and the consequent time pressure as a factor. More than 40 per cent identified poor communications as a factor in raising stress levels.

Other findings included:

- 86 per cent of respondents considered that stress was a problem in their organization, with 36 per cent rating it as being significantly so

◀

- 79 per cent identified increased absence as the main symptom of stress in an employee
- 53 per cent regard stress as something an organization can address proactively
- 95 per cent view supportive managers as the workplace factor most likely to help employees cope with stress.

Pat McGuinness, an occupational health expert, said:

> Employees need to feel they can talk about stress without fear of recrimination. In this way companies get a more accurate picture of negative processes, practices and bad job design which compromise employee performance. Successfully identifying and removing causes of negative stress brings real benefits.

The following were identified as positive measures for reducing stress:

- good employee communication (68 per cent)
- realistic deadlines (53 per cent)
- empowering staff (32 per cent)
- a 'no blame culture' (45 per cent)
- flexible working arrangements (44 per cent)
- promoting a family.

Interestingly, organizational and technological change seemed to feature as a major background with almost two-thirds reporting that their organization had undergone change programmes in the past year with 55 per cent stating that their organizations had introduced new technology.

Pat McGuiness commented:

> The pace of change in organizations is not being matched by the development of employee well-being safety nets such as effective stress policies and good job design. Having a comprehensive stress policy, which is part of the organizational fabric and develops with the organization, can help reduce the likelihood of individuals experiencing occupational stress, improve productivity levels and so benefit the bottom line.

Source: *HRMGuide.co.uk* (http://www.hrmguide.co.uk), 2 December 2001.

Summary

This chapter focused on employee relations as an activity extending through negotiation and bargaining, discipline and employee involvement. These activities involve a number of kills crucial to human resource managers. HR specialists are also involved in issues that are regulated by extensive legislation and touch on home life and health as well as more familiar workplace topics such as discipline and conflict. Competitive pressure has placed extra burdens on employees, especially those with career aspirations. These burdens can cause health problems, particularly those that are stress-related. HR practitioners have at least a moral responsibility to deal with such matters and encourage the setting up of supportive mechanisms such as employee assistance programmes.

Further reading

Harvard Business Review on Work and Life Balance (published by Harvard Business School, 2000) is a collection of articles on a range of issues. Beyond Work–Family Balance: Advancing Gender Equity and Workplace Performance by Rhona Rapoport, Lotte Bailyn, Joyce K. Fletcher and Bettye H. Pruitt (published by Jossey-Bass, 2001) argues that the concept of 'balance' is outmoded and why a new approach – work–personal life integration – offers greater promise. Tolley's Health and Safety at Work Handbook edited by Malcolm Dewis (Tolley Publishing, 2002) discusses health and safety in the UK legal context. The Mind and Heart of the Negotiator by Leigh L. Thomson (published by Prentice Hall, 2000) looks at the skills of negotiation and bargaining.

Review questions

1 What are the key skills of negotiation?
2 Should all disputes be resolved by arbitration?
3 Discuss the view that conflict is healthy.
4 Is work–life balance an impossible goal?
5 What is stress?
6 What can HR practitioners do to support stressed employees?

Problems for discussion and analysis

1 Read the following article. To what extent are managers and professionals better or worse able to deal with work–life balance?

Managers find it hard to care

It seems that managers find juggling successful careers with caring responsibilities more difficult than other professionals such as doctors. A new ESRC-funded cross-national study compares bankers and doctors in Britain, France and Norway and highlights a need for further policies to help both male and female employees attain a satisfactory work–life balance.

Professor Rosemary Crompton, a researcher from City University, London, considers that equal opportunities and 'affirmative action' policies help women to achieve equality in the workplace. She says that: 'Our study shows that we might now usefully shift the focus away from "women" as such and instead address the broader issue of how caring responsibilities might be combined with employment.'

Work–life balance is harder for managers to achieve than professional workers even in Norway, which is renowned for 'family friendly' policies. The study indicates that many women bankers – if they had children at all – restricted themselves to just one. But women doctors had more children (with 65 per cent having two or more children compared to 37 per cent of women bankers). And male doctors in the survey also had more children than male bankers.

◀

'All bankers, male and female, emphasized the difficulty of achieving individual success alongside substantial caring responsibilities – even in "family friendly" Norway,' Dr Crompton says. Only a few men with major caring responsibilities were interviewed but all reported that their careers had taken second place to their family life. 'Clearly the general argument relating to the possibility of flexibly combining professional employment with family life applies to men, as well as women,' suggests Professor Crompton. 'And perhaps the major contrast in debates relating to gender and careers should not be between masculine and feminine career paths, but rather between 'carer' and 'non-carer' careerists and how to combine a career with caring.'

She argues that the difference between the experience of doctors and managers in the study is due to the nature of professional qualifications. 'Whereas professional qualifications bestow a "licence to practice" which can be used flexibly over employment and family lives, managerial careers are subject to organizational constraints that hinder such flexibility.'

Doctors have 'substantial occupational power' and can work out their own ways of combining employment with family life. But this is more difficult to achieve in market-driven jobs such as banking.

'As managers of both sexes face similar difficulties and since society's caring needs are unlikely to be met simply by the re-domestication of women, then policy-makers need to address the issue of how caring can be combined with employment,' she advises.

A possible policy initiative would be to allow employees of both sexes the right to work part-time if they have caring responsibilities, instead of allowing the decision to an employer's discretion. The lesson from Norway is that 'family friendly' policies must force private companies into action. 'What we see even in Norway is that family friendly benefits are very well taken up in the state sector, but not in the highly competitive atmosphere of private companies. What we need is policies which regulate the behaviour of private companies,' she concludes.

Source: *HRMGuide.co.uk* (http://www.hrmguide.co.uk), 30 August 2001.

2 Read the following article and answer these questions:

● Do stress measurement questionnaires really measure stress in a reliable and valid way?

● Do they actually provide the information that organizations need to tackle workplace stress?

Evaluating stress measurement questionnaires

In a paper presented at the British Psychological Society Occupational Psychology Conference today, researchers are revealing the findings from the first-ever large-scale review of stress measures. The strengths and weaknesses of different approaches to measuring stress are highlighted in their report, which also discusses implications for organizations trying to measure and tackle stress at work.

The report was commissioned by the Health and Safety Executive (HSE) with a remit to review measures of workplace 'stressors' – measures of those aspects or characteristics of jobs, such as workload or lack of control, which, when present at excessive levels, are believed to lead to poor psychological or physical health.

A team of independent organizational psychologists led by Dr Jo Rick from the Institute for Employment Studies (IES) and Dr Rob Briner from Birkbeck College, University of London conducted the research. They used a set of rigorous standards to evaluate over 25 different stress measures that are widely used in the UK. The researchers came up with a number of surprising findings:

1 The amount and quality of evidence they could find about different measures was quite limited. In fact there was only sufficient evidence to allow a detailed analysis of five measures. The lack of evidence suggests that many stress measures have not been adequately developed. In many cases it seems that we do not know if these instruments are accurately measuring stress at all!

2 Even where particular stress measures are supported by evidence, results are inconsistent and mixed in a number of ways. This suggests that these stress measures are not very reliable tools for assessing workplace stress.

3 Most surprisingly, there was an almost complete absence of evidence about the predictive power of these stress measures. This is a worrying finding because the main reason for measuring stress is to assess aspects of work that are likely to lead to health problems so that these harmful aspects can be changed. But it seems that virtually all the available evidence comes from one-off 'snap-shot' studies and these cannot show if the stressful aspects of work tapped by these measures actually lead to ill-health.

Dr Jo Rick (principal research fellow, Institute for Employment Studies) said: 'I was very surprised by the lack of evidence linking the workplace stress measured by these scales to possible ill-health outcomes. This has serious implications for organizations using these measures to help them tackle stress at work.'

Dr Rob Briner (senior lecturer in organizational psychology, Birkbeck College) added: 'This report shows the need for a fundamental rethink of the way in which stress is measured at work and how more valid and reliable tools for assessing stress can be developed.'

What are the implications of the research? Organizations are required to assess stress but this research indicates that the tools by which they can make an assessment have severe limitations. In fact, organizations that are using commonly available stress measures may not be accurately measuring aspects of the work environment that might lead to ill-health. So they could be focusing on relatively harmless issues and missing real stress problems in the workplace.

The researchers argue that 'it is not clear, therefore, that using these measures either on their own or as part of a broader stress assessment process fulfils the requirements of health and safety legislation to identify and control those aspects of work that are likely to lead to ill-health or harm.'

They conclude that we need more information about the reliability and validity of existing stress measures but it may be that the existing approach to stress measurement is questionable and new methods and techniques should be considered.

Source: *HRMGuide.co.uk* (http://www.hrmguide.co.uk), 3 January 2002.

24 | Conclusion

Objectives

The purpose of this chapter is to:

- Evaluate whether or not HRM has been meaningfully implemented and, if so, to what extent.

- Investigate the form it may take.

- Determine the principal driving forces for the implementation of HRM.

- Summarize evidence for its effectiveness.

- Consider trends and future developments for the human resource function.

The status and significance of HRM

We began this volume with an analysis of the concept of HRM. We found that interpretations of human resource management range from formal models to comparatively loose portrayals of the territory with which HRM should be concerned. There is general agreement on its underlying philosophy, linking people management to business objectives in a strategic, integrated and coherent way. Beyond that, however, commentators and practitioners interpret HRM in different ways, depending on personal agendas and vested interests. As a result HRM ranges from soft, humanistic attempts to win over staff and achieve heart-felt commitment, to hard-nosed extraction of maximum effort at minimum cost.

Regardless of the rationale or the nature of its practice, HRM has become a common label for various forms and functions of people management. In English-speaking countries, the term has replaced 'personnel management' in many contexts. For example, academic courses, journals and textbooks formerly labelled as 'personnel management' are now described as 'human resource management'. However, and particularly at practitioner level, relabelling does not mean necessarily that either the approach or the content has changed (Sisson, 1995, p.87). The diverse interpretations of HRM are apparent when we compare practices in different countries and organizations. We noted earlier that 'personnel' and 'human resources' can co-exist and many organizations throughout the developed world follow North American practice, using the terms interchangeably.

Following a South African study by Wood and Els (2000) we can identify four distinct patterns of practice:

1 A simple change in nomenclature of relevant personnel sections where, in a number of cases, staff were not seen as managers but instead they were viewed as a distinct, relatively junior category of employee.

2 A broadened personnel function encompassing clearly delineated areas such as training and development.

3 HRM practitioners play an important strategic role as facilitators in the adoption of progressive industrial relations policies, rather than developing a vision for managing human resources across the organization.

4 True strategic HRM.

In the South African instance, Wood and Els (2000) found that, whatever the pattern of practice, all the HR practitioners they studied deviated from the 'conventional wisdom' definition of HRM. They attribute this partly to the persistence of effective and militant trade unions, requiring the use of hybrid HR–industrial relations practices. But they also point to the fact that HRM is a complex package of concepts and practices which are adopted and adjusted flexibly to fit the prevailing economic situation and managerial traditions. Studies in the UK show that its introduction has been a slow process (Guest and Hoque, 1993). Often it has been introduced as a cosmetic exercise, changing the nameplate on the 'Personnel' office door to 'Human Resources'. A decade ago, Blyton and Turnbull (1992, p.1) wrote that:

… in the UK, there is widespread agreement that, in one way or another, the adoption of HRM has so far been limited: limited to a small number of (largely foreign-owned) 'exemplar' companies; limited in the sense of organizations adopting HRM in a very partial and piecemeal way; and limited in many cases to a mere relabelling of existing activity and positions.

To what extent has the situation changed? Since the nature of human resource management still remains a matter of debate, it is scarcely surprising that practitioners interpret it in a variety of ways. Some organizations have taken pragmatic, local initiatives based on specific problems and solutions developed by their own managers, whereas others, particularly in foreign-owned workplaces, have been heavily influenced by managerial practices from elsewhere.

Why is HRM considered to be a complex and diverse concept?

HRM and globalization

Faulkner, Pitkethly and Child (2002) investigated HR practices adopted by companies from the USA, Japan, Germany and France in UK acquisitions compared to British companies acquired by other UK firms. They found some convergence in HR practices. For example, businesses from all the countries surveyed used performance-related pay and increased the level of training in their new subsidiaries. But HRM practices varied considerably between each nationality and these were strongly influential in changing practices within acquisitions. Walsh (2001) drew on the 1995 Australian Workplace Industrial Relations Survey to investigate the characteristics of HRM in multinational companies operating in Australia. The study suggests that investments in the human resource function and the use of HR practices were generally more prevalent in foreign-owned than Australian organizations. Walsh observes that this was particularly the case for workplaces belonging to US and British-owned firms. Geary and Roche (2001), reviewing evidence in an Irish context, point to the predominance of 'country-of-origin effects' over 'host country effects', particularly in countries with weak industrial relations systems. They found employment relations practices in foreign-owned (especially US-owned) workplaces to be very different from those in Irish-owned establishments.

To an extent, the penetration of HRM reflects a complex interaction between globalization (primarily driven by transnational companies), the distinctiveness of local culture and awareness of management literature through education or contact with external agencies. Selmer and de Leon (2001), for example, found that the style of human resource practices in the Philippines is distinctively Pinoy (Filipino). Pinoy HRM has its basis in a system of indigenous core values that emphasize social acceptance. Globalization has had a limited impact since subtle and intricate (but also powerful) local cultural imperatives have strongly influenced HR practices in foreign-owned companies. In an African context, Harvey (2002) states that Western managers can view human resource management on the continent as a dreamlike experience because of the sheer complexity and diversity found there. The 'rules, regulations and laws' of many African nations, and the degree to which many African organizations and employees ignore or bend the rules can seem surreal.

Taylor and Walley (2002) argue that central and eastern European countries have been a kind of test-bed for HRM since 1989 as communism has been replaced with market economies. Gurkov (2002) reports on a survey of over 700 Russian chief executive officers (CEOs) conducted in 1998, with a similar number surveyed in 2000, on HR practices in Russian industrial companies. There was a significant move towards modern HR practices but most were being implemented on a trial and error basis, without any reference to international practices. Taylor and Walley (2002), in a review of 21 Croatian companies, suggest that subsidiaries of multinational companies are leading the way towards HRM, with industry sector and size of company being other significant factors. They found evidence of a 'hijacking' of HRM by reactionary managers trying to maintain the status quo in some Croatian companies. But younger Croatian managers had a positive attitude towards progressive HR practices and generally identified with HRM except for some lingering suspicions about 'mindset control' which they saw underpinning HRM and also associated with the previous regime.

Hetrick (2002) explored the ways in which HRM emerged as a set of concepts, policies and practices within multinational subsidiaries in Poland between 1996 and 1999. HRM was clearly viewed as an imported 'Anglo-American concept' bearing no resemblance to people management as practised in Polish organizations. Hetrick comments that multinational firms are increasingly viewing HRM as one of the main control mechanisms by which employees can be integrated across national boundaries. Expatriate managers are important in this process as:

- *Role models*, displaying appropriate company behaviours, values and ways of doing things.
- *Fixers*, adapting corporate values and mission statements to local circumstances.
- *Key actors*, enacting the HRM practices.
- *Networkers* or *boundary spanners*, making connections between local managers and other parts of the business.
- *Agents of the owners*, overseeing the new subsidiary company.
- *Coaches* or *mentors*, transferring knowledge to local managers.

HRM is not necessarily strong in all Western countries. Wächter and Muller-Camen (2002), noting the importance of German businesses to the European economy, suggest that a well-functioning HR system would be expected. But a number of comparative studies have found HRM in German companies to be less strategically integrated and proactive than that of similar businesses in other countries. They attribute these findings, at least partly, to the co-determination structure of German employee relations where the *Betriebsrat* (works council) has an important strategic role. Hence HRM has to be integrated with a pre-existing local system which, according to Wächter and Muller-Camen, might even be a strategic resource.

Papalexandris and Chalikias (2002) compared the practice of HRM in Greek organizations, using Cranet survey results from 1992 to 1999, with a focus on specific core functions such as performance management, employee communications and training and development. It was clear that Greece was following a general European trend towards a more strategic role for human resource management. But the rate of change differed with more improvement in training and development and performance management compared to employee communications. Also Greek companies were generally slower in following the trend than organizations from many other EU countries.

| Activity 24:2 | Why is HRM not practised in exactly the same way in all countries? |

HRM and 'best practice'

It is relevant to ask if HRM is a prescriptive, ideal model of people management or simply a description of 'best practices' in competitive organizations. As we saw in Part 1 of this book, Jeffrey Pfeffer has inspired a considerable interest in the concept of 'best practice' in HRM. Marchington and Grugulis (2000) question whether the practices typically assumed to be 'good' are actually beneficial to workers. They argue that the literature is underpinned by unitarist thinking and also that the notion of 'best practice' is problematic despite its superficial attractiveness. In particular, they point to weaknesses in relation to the meaning of specific practices, their consistency with each other, and the supposed universal applicability of this version of HRM. Truss (2001) found that the informal organization played a significant role in the process and implementation of HR policies and that successful organizations do not always implement 'best practice' HRM even if intended. Conversely, Hughes (2002) argues that empirical support for universal HRM is growing.

Boxall and Purcell (2000) argue that there is a complex relationship between HRM and the achievement of organizational outcomes and that HR strategies are strongly influenced by national, sectoral and organizational factors. But this conclusion does not necessarily invalidate the concept of 'best practice' because basic principles of people management underpin practice and are essential to the competitiveness of business organizations.

However, there is increasing evidence supporting the notion that HR practices are more effective when combined. For example, Laursen (2002) studied 726 Danish firms with more than 50 employees and found that HR practices influence innovation performance more when applied together than as individual practices. Additionally, application of complementary HR practices is most effective for firms in knowledge-intensive industries.

Using data from the 1998 Workplace Employee Relations Survey, Lucas (2002) searched for 'fragments of HRM' within the hospitality industry as compared with all industries and services in Great Britain. Lucas found that HRM in the hospitality industry shared little of the 'soft' aspects of HRM found elsewhere. On the contrary, power and cost-control were emphasized in an industry that exemplified 'hard' HRM in action. Paradoxically, employees in the hospitality industry were generally more content than their counterparts in the broad stream of industries, despite indicators of dissatisfaction.

Guest (2001) argues that attempts to relate HRM to specific outcomes such as business performance suffer from a number of significant practical difficulties. However, he acknowledges that progress has been made, particularly in the area of measuring HRM, but there remains a need for more clearly specified theory, particularly about the nature of HRM itself. Part of the confusion comes from the indistinct boundaries between HRM and a plethora of other fashionable management programmes. Often HRM is used as a label for a collection of different people management techniques, described by Legge (1995, p.34) as 'symbiotic buzz-words'. A specific people management initiative may be regarded as HRM – or, alternatively, bundled up with total quality management, customer care, business process re-engineering and so on.

Recent years have seen an increasing momentum in the implementation of radical management developments. Managers may use a number of simultaneous initiatives without any real awareness or understanding that they are part of 'HRM'. Indeed, a small study of major organizations (Armstrong, 1994) produced evidence of 'strategic HRM' being applied but none of them used the term!

According to Storey (1989, p.1):

> One cannot help but be impressed by the widespread awareness among practitioners of such experimentation; meetings with managers at all levels even in conventional mainstream organizations soon reveal the fact that current 'flavours' have permeated the managerial consciousness and imagination in a way that was never the case with, for example, OD, job enrichment, QWL and other much-vaunted 'movements' of previous decades which some critics cite as equivalents.

Many of these concepts are presented as 'quick fixes' that are found to be attractive by senior managers with little time before objectives have to be achieved, or contracts run out.

Activity 24:3   What are the advantages and disadvantages of using 'best practices'?

Driving forces of HRM

Whether as a label or a variable combination of specific initiatives, we can justifiably ask if the uptake of HRM has been driven by practitioners – people involved in practical people management – and then attracted wider attention; or if it is a creation of academics and consultants with some (and only some) practitioners following on? What is apparent is that the practitioners involved in the introduction of HRM are often line or general managers rather than personnel managers. Clearly, there are many 'stakeholders' in HRM.

Managerialists

Management power increased significantly in the 1980s, especially in English-speaking countries with 'New Right' governments. Keenoy (1990, p.371) calls HRM 'a deliberate and brilliant ambiguity', suspecting a hidden political agenda arising from right-wing government policies. This perspective sees HRM as a reflection of Thatcherite and Reaganite policies which were translated into a wave of managerialism, first in industry and then the public sector.

Certainly, it is evident that politicians take a particular interest in people management when its development affects their view of society. Managerialism's new legitimacy is most clearly seen in the public sector, where government has imposed 'market conditions' and new management structures. Ironically, business concepts such as HRM have been adopted most widely in organizations that are not true 'businesses' at all. These issues are particularly evident when such organizations are privatized. Van der Zwaan, von Eije and de Witte (2002) looked at the organizational and HR changes accompanying the transformation from public to private in a sample of 28 Dutch organizations. They found growth in the culture of efficiency and accountability, together with an increased relationship between financial participation and performance, suggesting a link between the adoption of HRM and privatization.

Senior managers

The strategic nature of HRM, conventionally owned and driven from the top, has been of great interest to senior managers. It is compatible with the power needs of top managers who want the reins in their own hands. In effect, HRM is part of the fashionable 'ideas industry' which fuels modern management.

In our discussion on the management of change we saw that HRM has been associated with programmes such as TQM, culture change, downsizing and business process re-engineering. Ideas for increasing the effectiveness of business management come and go in a constant stream. Management education and the writings of management gurus alike provide ideas and legitimize their adoption. The concepts they spawn flow in tidal waves across the face of industry. Managerial behaviour follows current fads, conforming to each change in fashion as if they were skirt lengths or hairstyles.

Caldwell (2001) observes that the HR professional has often been viewed as a change agent and that there is evidence for the increased significance of that role. Hailey (2001) describes how HRM interventions and the structure of the HR function itself have been used as change levers to support a shift in business strategy from cost-cutting and acquisition to innovation. Khatri and Budhwar (2002) found that the role and status of the HR function depend on a combination of top management 'enlightenment' and the level of HR competencies. They noted that the businesses they studied pursued four types of HR strategies: informal and not communicated; informal and communicated; formal but not communicated; and formal and communicated. There is also evidence that HR strategies can potentially lower staff turnover by increasing organizational commitment (Buck and Watson, 2002).

Patrickson and Hartmann (2001) argue that in Australia, as an instance, the workforce is currently more qualified, casualized and diverse than at any previous point in history. HR practitioners have responded to the situation with an increased emphasis on aligning HR strategy with corporate strategy, giving performance management a higher priority, exploring alternative forms of flexible work arrangements, making greater use of legal expertise, and increasingly adopting human resource information systems.

Senior executives do not have a consistent view of HRM – any more than they have a shared understanding of management. Many do not perceive any distinction between general management and managing people. Even less do they wish to be involved with fine academic distinctions between different models of HRM: 'As chief executive I have to have the organization I want, and if it doesn't marry up with any particular model that the world of HRM has thrown up, well, too bad' (quoted in Armstrong, 1994).

The actual 'doing' of HRM is passed to middle managers who are responsible for its implementation and can be held (conveniently) accountable for any failures. People policies and practices must be integrated and coherent for HRM to be effective but this division of labour leads to a significant weakness: it offers scope for a dislocation between strategic intentions and the conduct of people management at ground level. Teo (2002) examined the effectiveness of the strategic HRM in an Australian public sector entity, before and after corporatization, and found that the rating of strategic HRM role effectiveness remained low despite overall improvement in the integration of HRM and strategic management. Results showed that the corporate strategic HRM function was more effective in an administrative role than as a value-adding, strategic business partner to line managers. On the other hand, Björkman and Xiucheng (2002) found positive relationships between business performance and the use of 'high performance' HRM systems and integrated HR and business strategies in a number of Chinese–Western joint ventures and subsidiaries.

Nankervis, Compton and Savery (2002) observe that while recent Australian research studies report a gradual but apparently growing convergence between the theory and practice of strategic HRM in large organizations there is little empirical evidence on HR strategies and practices in small and medium enterprises (SMEs), or on the opinions of their chief executive officers (CEOs). They sampled CEOs in Australian SMEs and found some limited evidence that SMEs may eventually adopt recognizable strategic HRM.

What is clear is that the central tenet of 'soft' HRM – the belief that HRM regards employees as valuable assets and not just costs – is rarely translated into action. The practices associated with HRM are often introduced for reasons of expediency rather than any serious belief in its principles. Indeed, it is arguable that the practice of HRM is rife with hypocrisy and rhetoric. Many organizations in free market countries feel that competitive forces make it impossible to commit themselves to their employees. People management in these firms is firmly focused on cost-cutting. A conflict arises from the inherent contradiction between typical HRM themes such as encouraging long-term employee commitment and short-term cost-effectiveness. According to Gratton (*Financial Times: Mastering Management*, 1995), employees are left:

> to make sense of the paradoxes and mixed messages with which they are faced, who try to understand the underlying message of customer delight when no attempt is made to provide them with the skills necessary to deliver it, who are rewarded and promoted for delivering short-term financial targets and who see the people who try hardest to understand customers' needs penalized for the time they take to do so.

This leads to the question of whether HRM is no more than a matter of fine words. Employees quickly learn to mistrust official rhetoric and instead practise the art of 'sense-making': looking for cues that indicate the route for success or, at least, survival. Informal messages are transmitted through the choice of people who are rewarded and those whose skills are developed. For example, large-scale redundancies – determined at short notice by senior managers – have followed soothing statements about the importance of human resources to an organization's future.

Activity 24:4	Does HRM represent a totally managerialist philosophy?

Academics

Market forces have given academics an added interest in HRM (Townley, 1994, p.22; Legge, 1995, p.48). With the reduction in the perceived importance of industrial relations due to government action in a number of countries, academics have had to look elsewhere for research funding and new courses to teach. HRM offers an opportunity for people with expertise in work psychology and industrial sociology to continue with the subjects that interest them – but under a more marketable label.

Townley, for example, regards academics as 'participant constructors' rather than neutral observers. In her view HRM has been 'constructed' as a discipline in order to attract (often private) finance to investigate a new phenomenon – HRM itself – which appears to meet the requirements of flexibility and the free market. HRM has become an academic cottage industry, churning out degree courses, collected papers, journals, texts and professorial chairs. Paradoxically, some of the most successful products of this industry have been attempts to 'deconstruct' the contradictions and rhetoric of HRM itself (Legge, 1995, p.49)!

Muller (1999) reviewed the German HRM debate and showed it to be dominated by business administration academics specializing in the topic. In the past, these academics – together with practitioners – had generally embraced the techniques and ideology of HRM somewhat uncritically. Muller attributes this to a comparatively low emphasis on empirical research, neglect of industrial relations aspects, and the strong impact of US-developed theories and concepts. More recently, the US approach to HRM has been viewed more critically, along with a more positive assessment of the German HRM model.

The personnel profession

Personnel practitioners have long held ambiguous views on the subject of HRM. Opinion in the profession has swung between various extremes:

- *Ignore it.* It will go away. It is just another fad that will be replaced by another soon enough.

- *Embrace it.* It will give us prestige. We can repackage personnel management as a marketing exercise. Lots more money.

- *Believe in it.* Always a minority position. People are *really* the most valuable resources? So how come I'm not paid as much as the finance manager?

- *Live with it.* OK, so it's an American import, a fad, and something economists will never understand. But it gives me a bit more clout right now.

Hoque and Noon (2001) examined data from the 1998 UK Workplace Employee Relations Survey to establish differences between the characteristics and job-related activities of specialists who used the title 'human resources' and those using the title 'personnel'. They found that practitioners using the HR title were better qualified than their counterparts who used the personnel title and were more involved with strategic planning. Human resource development was more likely to be included in strategic plans in such cases. Additionally, a number of specific practices commonly associated with HRM – for example personality tests, attitude surveys and off-the-job training – were more likely to have been adopted in workplaces with HR specialists than in those with personnel specialists.

Armstrong (2000) contends that many so-called 'HRM' practices were in widespread use before HRM came on the scene in the 1980s. He argues that there has been no great revolution as a result of HRM theory. Instead there has been a process of evolution. The rate of change may have increased but, according to Armstrong, this is not attributable to the arrival of HRM as a philosophy. Rather, rapid changes in the business, political, economic and social environment have forced organizations to respond. Armstrong also points to increasing professionalism among personnel practitioners encouraged by bodies such as the UK's Chartered Institute of Personnel and Development and the dissemination of ideas about HRM by academics publishing in an increasing range of publications.

Rynes, Colbert and Brown (2002) tested such claims on responses obtained from 959 US human resource professionals, specifically focused on their agreement with various HR research findings. They found large discrepancies between research findings and practitioners' beliefs in a number of areas. This was particularly so in the case of employee selection where practitioners seemed to have considerably less faith in the use of intelligence and personality tests than HR research would recommend. Practitioners at higher levels, with SPHR certification and those who read the academic literature, were more likely to agree with research findings. Shepherd and Mathews (2000) examined academic research on employee commitment, a central part of HR models, in relation to the views of practitioners. They surveyed 300 HRM managers and found wide recognition of commitment in terms of its desirability and benefits. But academics and practitioners conceptualized and measured commitment in entirely different ways. Practitioners adopted a subjective and ad hoc approach, generally ignoring the formal measuring tools and structured, 'objective' approaches developed by academics.

Moreover, change initiatives – particularly business process re-engineering – frequently led to a questioning of the need for any personnel or human resource specialists. Storey (1995, p.384) finds this to be a common theme at consultant-organized conferences. Of course, this is consistent with HRM models that place the responsibility for people management in the hands of line managers. Together with marketing and research, it is difficult to measure the effect that HR specialists have on the well-being of a company. Paperwork-obsessed personnel administrators, ignorant of wider business issues do not help. They make ripe targets for short-termists working to 'zero-based budgeting' and City analysts with no industrial experience.

Activity 24:5	Why do practitioners and academic researchers have different views on HRM?

HRM in reality	**Confidence in big bosses declines**

A recent Watson Wyatt survey shows that declining employee confidence in corporate leadership is threatening Canadian competitiveness.

Canadian employees are increasingly committed to the organizations they work for but their trust and confidence in senior management have fallen, according to the 2002 Watson Wyatt WorkCanada® survey – including over 2300 Canadian employees at all job levels and in all major industries. Employee engagement is also weak and the growing distrust of corporate leadership and a poor opinion of management effectiveness are damaging the financial performance of their companies. Just 51 per cent of Canadian workers have trust and confidence in senior management and even fewer (45 per cent) consider that their organizations are being managed effectively.

Yet employee commitment has increased by 12 per cent since 2000 to reach 61 per cent today. How can we explain this increase? The report suggests that the jump is likely to be due to a general belief that the risks of job-changing during an economic downturn are greater than any potential benefits. A mere 31 per cent of Canadian employees feel that they are involved in the activities of their employers. The result is that engagement and productivity levels may suffer.

'It is quickly evident that few companies have escaped untouched by the fallout from the recent turmoil in the business environment,' says Jan Grude, national practice director, Human Capital Group. 'Corporate Canada needs to work on repairing that damage before future financial performance and competitiveness are further hindered. Employees who are committed, but not engaged, do not actively contribute to the organization's success. To ensure that employees stay engaged, organizations need to effectively evaluate and recognize employee performance.'

But addressing these issues can lead to improved financial performance and return on investment in human capital. The study shows that total returns to shareholders are nine times higher for firms with high trust and confidence levels in senior managers and 12 times higher for businesses with high management effectiveness. The results also indicate that firms with engaged employees are worth five times more than companies with workers who are disengaged.

Other significant findings from the survey include:

- Only 31 per cent of employees are actively involved in management decisions.
- Only 39 per cent of employees consider that their companies effectively evaluate and reward employees for performance.
- Only 50 per cent of workers are satisfied with their compensation and benefits.
- Only 50 per cent of employees give their companies a high rating for training and development.

Compared to a similar survey of US companies conducted earlier this year, Canadian businesses are faring only slightly better than their US counterparts. But employee commitment in Canadian firms is significantly higher (65 per cent) than in the USA (57 per cent).

'By assessing just how far trust levels have fallen at their specific organizations, companies can gain insight into the depth of the problem among their workers and establish a baseline against which to measure the success of their efforts to restore trust,' says Dawn Bell, organizational effectiveness leader, Watson Wyatt Canada. 'To increase employee engagement, the workforce must be motivated to bring their capabilities to work each day; feel the organization is attracting the best talent and surrounding them with highly qualified people; and believe that there is a convincing plan to grow and manage the business, including keeping costs under control.'

Source: *HRM Guide Canada* (http://www.hrmguide.net/canada/), 22 October 2002.

The impact of HRM

Is there any evidence that the implementation of HRM has a significant effect on national or organizational economic performance? After all, this is the justification implicit in HRM models for valuing the human resource above all others. When the first edition of this book was written (in the mid-1990s) the conclusion was that we simply did not know. The following were given as possible explanations:

- *Insufficient research.* Not because of lack of effort but due to the absence of clear, agreed frameworks within which to conduct comparative research. The root cause of this was perceived as HRM's own ambiguity. How were we to look for evidence of HRM and its effects if we had no agreement on what HRM was?

- *Intangibility.* If people are an 'intangible resource' we have an insurmountable problem – by definition intangibles are unmeasurable!

Since then, progress has been made in conceptualizing the problem and measuring results (see the 'HRM in reality' article on HRM and shareholder value). For example, Huang (2000) looked at 315 firms in Taiwan and related their human resource practices to their organizational performance. Huang's study shows a significant relationship between performance and the effectiveness of their HR functions, including planning, staffing, appraisal, compensation, and training and development. Michie and Sheehan-Quinn (2001) surveyed over 200 manufacturing firms in the UK to investigate the relationship between corporate performance and the use of flexible work practices, human resource systems and industrial relations. They found that 'low-road' practices – including short-term contracts, lack of employer commitment to job security, low levels of training and unsophisticated human resource practices – were negatively correlated with corporate performance. In contrast, they established a positive correlation between good corporate performance and 'high-road' work practices – 'high-commitment' organizations or 'transformed' workplaces. They also found that HR practices are more likely to make a contribution to competitive success when introduced as a comprehensive package, or 'bundle' of practices.

Kelliher and Riley (2002), highlighting evidence to support the view that the impact of HRM is greatest when it involves a set of coherent policies and practices, also consider that HR initiatives should be implemented as part of an integrated package. They instance functional flexibility, which leads to an intensification of work, but in the cases they studied this was less of an issue when supported by higher levels of remuneration.

Michie and Sheehan (1999) used evidence from the UK 1990 Workplace Industrial Relations Survey to show that 'low-road' HRM practices also appeared to be negatively correlated with investment in R&D and new technology. By contrast, 'high-road' work practices were positively correlated with investment in R&D and new technology. Cooke, F.L. (2001) reviewed a number of British studies on the use of 'high-road' and 'low-road' HRM strategies and concludes that high-road HRM may lead to better organizational performance. But firms do not necessarily opt for this because of the historical, social and institutional context of employment relationships in Britain.

Rondeau and Wager (2001) focused on the ability of certain 'progressive' or 'high performance' human resource management practices to enhance organizational effectiveness, noting growing evidence that the impact of various HRM practices on performance is contingent on a number of contextual factors, including workplace climate. They conducted a postal survey of 283 Canadian nursing homes which included questions about human resource practices, programmes and policies impacting on workplace climate. The survey also included a variety of performance indicators. Their results indicated that nursing homes with more 'progressive' HRM practices and which also reported a workplace climate valuing employee participation, empowerment and accountability tended to be viewed as better performers. The best performers overall were those nursing homes that had implemented more HRM practices and also reported workplace climates reflecting a strong commitment to their human resources.

Capital investment is another important moderator of HRM's effectiveness. Richard and Johnson (2001) found that strategic HRM significantly reduces employee turnover and increases overall market performance assessment. But the effect of SHRM on firm productivity and return on equity depends on the level of capital investment.

HRM delivers shareholder value

Call it human resource management, personnel or high-performance management, the evidence for the financial benefit from good people management continues to grow. Companies using the best people management practices deliver nearly twice as much value to shareholders as their average competitors, according to a study by consultants Watson Wyatt.

This study is the fourth iteration of Watson Wyatt's respected Human Capital Index (HCI) research. It covers HR practices in more than 600 companies from 16 countries across Europe, combined with independent financial data. The study demonstrates a clear link between specific HR practices and financial performance. Watson Wyatt's North American and Asia-Pacific HCI studies showed similar results.

The new study found that: good people management was linked to a 90 per cent increase in shareholder value; companies with weak people management practices produced negative returns on equity over the past two years; and the best companies are pulling ahead from the rest. Companies with the best people management practices gain tremendous value while the difference between average and poor performers in HR is negligible in terms of creating shareholder value.

'The perception that HR is a non-strategic business overhead still persists,' says Steven Dicker, a partner at Watson Wyatt and co-author of the HCI report. 'But this is wrong. Our HCI research has again demonstrated the strong link between effective human capital management and shareholder value.'

Commenting on the finding that companies with the best people management deliver nearly twice as much value to their shareholders as their average competitors, Steven Dicker said:

> Great people management is linked with a 90 per cent increase in shareholder value. It is an amazing figure at first sight. As well as highlighting the gulf between the best and the rest, we believe it reflects the growing emphasis on people management within businesses as other sources of competitive advantage prove increasingly difficult to sustain.
>
> With the return to real-world economics after the bursting of the 'tech' bubble and unwinding of the 1990s creative accounting, most businesses are fundamentally 'people businesses'. Increasingly, it is the quality of a company's people management that determines its real success or failure.

'However, it is not surprising that many business leaders are sceptical about the value of human resources departments when there is so much poor practice around,' said Doug Ross, also a partner at Watson Wyatt and co-author of the report. 'Human resources has a key role in facilitating good people management throughout the business, and our study shows this can have great value. But in too many cases human resources activity becomes an end in itself, failing to align with the business needs, failing to control costs, failing to manage risks effectively or failing to focus on its contribution to growing revenues.'

Doug Ross highlights three practices that stand out in the Watson Wyatt study as undermining financial performance: using contract workers to provide 'a disposable workforce'; developmental training; and excessive paternalism.

▶

The disposable workforce

'The approach to using temporary workers to provide a cushion of "disposable workers" in case of an economic slowdown or cancellation of non-core projects seems reasonable in principle,' says Doug Ross. 'However, our experience suggests that the temporary workers cause tensions and jealousies with permanent employees in good times because of the different terms and lack of commitment to the company, and now the "disposals" are being implemented the permanent employees feel just as exposed as if permanent employees were being cut.' According to the HCI study, companies that have avoided the 'disposable worker' approach delivered up to 5.6 per cent more shareholder value than average performing companies.

Developmental training

'Development training appears to increase the value of the individual but not necessarily the value of the company,' says Doug Ross. 'This is either because the training is not well timed or good enough, or the costs of employment rise as the employee either demands more pay or moves to another employer to realize their newly enhanced value.' According to the HCI study, companies that limit their use of developmental training deliver up to 5.2 per cent more shareholder value than average companies.

Excessive paternalism

'Providing a secure working environment, coupled with effective performance management can create a high value workplace,' says Doug Ross. 'However, some people management practices are excessively paternalistic, such as maintaining training regardless of economic circumstances and avoiding at almost all costs the termination of employees; these undermine shareholder value.' According to the HCI study, companies that were overly paternalistic lost up to 5.2 per cent of shareholder value compared with average companies.

Watson Wyatt's global HCI is in its fourth year and has become the leading measure of the financial effectiveness of human capital management. The new study, the second time it has been carried out in Europe, confirms the findings of the previous European HCI, undertaken when stock markets were at their heights in 2000. This year's study demonstrates that the key HR practices associated with higher value continue to show up in bear as well as bull markets. The same applies to people management practices that are linked with a reduction in shareholder value.

'The Human Capital Index brings up evidence supporting our belief that enhanced people management leads to better financial performance, rather than the other way around,' said Steven Dicker. 'In other words, HCI can be a leading indicator of financial performance.'

Watson Wyatt examined return on equity over the past two years for the companies that participated in both the 2000 and 2002 European HCI studies. High scoring companies (top quartile) in the 2000 Human Capital Index study produced returns of over 20 per cent. Conversely, companies that scored low on HCI in 2000 showed a negative return on equity during the same period.

'For many companies, business is now tougher than ever. With no let up in sight, the need to focus on maximizing real, sustainable value from their human capital has never been greater,' said Steven Dicker. 'The good news is that Watson Wyatt's Human Capital Index now provides a clearer, more global route map to maximizing the value of human capital than ever before.'

Source: *HRMGuide.co.uk* (http://www.hrmguide.co.uk), 24 September 2002.

Further explanations given in the mid-1990s for not being able to assess the impact of HRM were:

- *Confusion with other management initiatives.* We have observed already that it is difficult to untangle the effects of true 'HRM' from other strategic initiatives. HRM is accompanied almost invariably by other packaged programmes such as total quality management (TQM). A US study by Buch and Rivers (2001) looked at the effects of a TQM initiative on a department in a mid-sized utility company. Immediately after the intervention there appeared to be a culture change that was characterized by empowerment, employee development and teamwork. But eventually there was a shift back to the culture that prevailed before the intervention, accompanied by a significant decline in employee job satisfaction.

- *Situational effects.* HRM is not – and, arguably, cannot be – implemented uniformly. It is found mainly in specific areas. In private industry it has been adopted by large, sophisticated and often non-unionized organizations. These businesses have particular characteristics that are appropriate for HRM. The classic examples of success come from greenfield sites that provide a 'clean slate' with no previous practices or cultural history to prevent management action. HRM may not be appropriate in firms that have strong unions or depend on a low-skilled workforce (Hollinshead and Leat, 1995, p.319). Tansley, Newell and Williams (2001) argue that the term 'greenfield' helps to conceptualize a break with prevailing employee relations practices but it can be a philosophical break with the past rather than a physical change of location. They suggest that the implementation of a human resource information system (HRIS) offers an opportunity to break with the past.

Flexibility and the introduction of managerialism into non-profits and the public sector also test the applicability of HRM. For example, human resource practitioners face dilemmas in preparing HR strategies in situations where the workforce is largely seasonal or made up of volunteers as is the case in the Scottish heritage industry (Graham and Lennon, 2002). In fact, employer–employee relationships are blurred in project-based or virtual organizations where self-employed, contract and salaried employees work together. Rubery *et al.* (2002) contend that complex organizational forms – they instance cross-organization networking, partnerships, alliances, the use of external providers for core as well as peripheral activities, multi-employer sites and blurring of the public/private sector divide – have major implications for the employment relationship.

Greenwood (2002) reviewed the ethical position of HRM and concluded that even when judged by minimum standards, HRM is seriously lacking, not least because of a general disregard of stakeholder theory. Foote (2001) investigated the ethical behaviour of HR managers working in a sample of UK and Irish charities. The study highlights the ethical inconsistency between the application of strong, explicit organizational values to external clients and the limited influence of those values on HR strategies and practices within organizations. HR professionals no longer thought that the HRM function should be the conscience of the organization, but felt that they had a significant role in the provision of advice on ethical action to senior management.

What do people 'at the coal face' feel about the prevalence and effectiveness of human resource management? Gibb (2001) describes a survey of the views of 2632 employees on HRM in the 73 organizations for which they worked. In this study employees were found to be positive about some elements of HRM, including training and development, rewards and levels of personal motivation. They also gave high ratings for the performance of HR staff across a range of services. But the survey found negative employee views on the management of staffing levels, aspects of recruitment and retention, communication and overall levels of morale in their organizations.

Activity 24:6 Review the evidence for the effectiveness of human resource management. What would make HRM more effective?

What next?

Can we expect a never-ending succession of fashionable ideas? There are enough up-and-coming authors and consultants to drive the process. Some of them derive from the ideas industry itself: a generation of middle managers evicted by downsizing and de-layering. At the same time there are a few hopeful signs of disillusion with simplistic approaches – a call for pragmatism that recognizes the complexities involved in managing people. But 'pragmatic management' implies experience, expertise and common sense. It sounds boring. It is not likely to satisfy the ambitious.

At present there are indications that 'knowledge management' and 'human capital management' are overlapping with many features of human resource management.

The SHRM surveyed 170 senior HR professionals in the USA to find their views on the top ten trends for human resource management (Patel, 2002). The following themes were identified as most significant from a choice of 85:

1 Use of technology to communicate with employees.
2 Rising healthcare costs.
3 Increased vulnerability of intellectual property.
4 Managing talent.
5 Greater demand for high-skilled workers than for low-skilled workers.
6 Labour shortage.
7 Change from manufacturing to information/service economy.
8 Increase in employment-related government regulations.
9 Focus on domestic safety and security.
10 Ability to use technology to more closely monitor employees.

These views represent an American perspective, but practitioners in other countries would probably identify with a number of these trends.

Another SHRM study (SHRM, 2002) took the views of eight major management consultancy firms. Overall, technology and talent management were identified as the two major drivers of change in HR: 'Specifically, continuous innovations in technology will fundamentally change the way HR work is accomplished. Further, talent management will become a critical priority for the nation's business – and the strategic purpose of HR's future role within organizations.' The main impacts of technology were seen to be:

● employee self-service through web-based portals
● increasingly sophisticated call-centres
● aggressive new entrants into the outsourcing market.

These studies are consistent with heavily publicized developments in information technology (IT) applications for HRM. But how much use is made of IT in reality? As an example, West and Berman (2001) surveyed HR managers in US city administrations with populations over 50 000 on their use of IT and how it affected HRM work. Managers agreed that IT was important but few cities used IT extensively in their human resource management. The widest use was in payroll and benefits administration and online recruiting. IT applications were not much used for training, job analysis and evaluation, position classification, personnel testing and background checks.

Raich (2002) argues that the HR function is clearly shifting from being a 'service provider' to a 'business partner' but the requirements and needs of this new role can also be met by line managers or external providers. Hence the change of roles is both an immense opportunity and a threat for human resource managers. Raich (2002) considers that the HR function of the future will be significantly different from that in the past and that organizations need to recognize this in order to make the most of knowledge workers and knowledge professionals. According to Boxall and Purcell (2000) strategic literature is increasingly emphasizing intellectual capital, learning processes and organizational adaptability. They argue that HRM specialists could play a central role because questions of how to attract, motivate and develop workers with scarce but critical abilities, and developing effective processes of work organization are fundamental to knowledge-based competition.

In the past, new management concepts have generally come from North America but the worldwide economy is changing, with ever-stronger regional groupings challenging individual nation states in importance. East Asia and the European Union appear destined to be major influences at the beginning of the 21st century and neither is entirely dominated by US-style free market ideas. Whereas American concepts reign in business schools, people are being managed increasingly through methods forged within different cultural ideologies. The collectivist traditions of the East and the 'social partner' philosophy of the EU may foster philosophies of people management that value employees more than the 'hard HRM' of the free market. Only time will tell.

Further reading

For advanced students, *Human Resource Management: A Critical Text*, 2nd edition, edited by John Storey (published by Thomson Learning in 2001) provides an excellent survey of the field. The contributors are acknowledged experts and each chapter reviews a specific topic critically. *The Future of the HR Profession*, published by the Society for Human Resource Management (2002), encapsulates the thoughts and opinions of four major management consultancy firms. Dave Patel's *SHRM Workplace Forecast: A Strategic Outlook 2002–2003*, also published by the Society for Human Resource Management in 2002, takes a measured view of the processes affecting the practice of HRM.

Review questions

1 What evidence is there for the effectiveness of HRM?

2 To what degree is the adoption of HRM driven by globalization?

3 Discuss the view that the concepts of 'fit' and 'best practice' are modern versions of 'hard' and 'soft' HRM.

4 What impact does 'bundling' have on the success of human resource initiatives?

5 How will information technology affect the human resource profession in the next decade?

6 Does the welfare tradition of personnel management have any role in modern HRM?

7 To what extent is information technology likely to transform the practice of HRM?

Problem for discussion and analysis

Creating an HR function

Jenny is the new human resource manager at a medium-sized catering supplies company. Prior to her arrival all HR activities were dealt with by the General Manager (hiring, training and personnel administration) and the Finance Manager (pay and benefits, annual leave monitoring, sickness, etc.). Jenny has to create her own HR function and absorb the responsibilities previously handled by these managers. She has a capital budget for IT and a staff budget for three employees who would need to be transferred from other parts of the company.

Discussion question: How would you advise Jenny to proceed and what should be her priorities for the new HR function?

Glossary

Action learning Reg Revans argued that classroom-based management education is not adequate. He devised a systematic, experiential or action learning programme based on job exchanges which place managers in unfamiliar situations and ask them to take on challenging tasks.

Action research Organizational development – particularly in its 1960s and 70s form – relied on a methodology described as action research. This was an undramatic but effective long-term change process based on incremental improvements and a continuous flow of emergent strategies. Action research has become unfashionable with the advent of 'packaged' techniques such as business process re-engineering.

Added-worker hypothesis A hypothesis that predicts an increase in employment participation rates during periods of high unemployment. The premise is that partners go to work to compensate for the lost income of main wage earners who are made redundant.

Adult learning It has been argued that adult learning is qualitatively different from learning in childhood. The 'andragogy' approach emphasizes the importance of self-directed learning for adults, integrating new material and ideas with current and previous experience.

Advisory, Conciliation and Arbitration Service (ACAS) Founded in 1974, this is a UK public body whose core function is 'preventing and resolving problems in the workplace'. It is run by a council of 12 members from business, unions and the independent sector and has approximately 800 staff in England, Scotland and Wales. There are 11 main regional centres plus a head office in London. ACAS defines its services as follows: (a) *conciliating* – the act of reconciling or bringing together the parties in a dispute with the aim of moving forward to a settlement acceptable to all sides; (b) *arbitrating* – an independent arbitrator or arbiter (in Scotland) deciding the outcome of a dispute (the decision may well be binding in law); and (c) *mediating* – acting as an intermediary in talking to both sides. The aim is for the parties to resolve the problem between themselves but the mediator will make suggestions along the way.

Affective identification A real intellectual and emotional identification with the organization.

Affirmative action Or positive discrimination. A long-standing approach in the USA, designed to advantage the disadvantaged, including women, African-Americans and Hispanics. Laws only applied to the public sector and its suppliers.

Ageism Discrimination on the grounds of age is prevalent but often unrecognized. Some countries such as Canada, France, New Zealand and the USA have legislated against ageism. In other countries employers are allowed to specify age ranges for job applications. The European Union has issued a Directive compelling all member states to introduce anti-ageism legislation.

Alienation A state of estrangement, or a feeling of being an outsider from society. Dull, boring and repetitive work induces a feeling of alienation. Assembly line workers are involved with a small part of the final product, have little control over the rhythm of their work and may have no idea of the significance of their contribution. Their work can appear to be alien with no relationship or meaning to their lives other than to produce income. As a consequence they may feel little enthusiasm and, often, active hostility towards what seems like forced labour.

Alternative dispute resolution (ADR) The term has been in use for decades but the various forms of ADR have become increasingly used in recent years. The US Federal Administrative Dispute Resolution Act 1995 states that 'alternative means of dispute resolution' means any procedure that is used to resolve issues in controversy, including, but not limited to, conciliation, facilitation, mediation, fact-finding, minitrials, arbitration, and use of ombuds, or any combination thereof.

American Arbitration Association The American Arbitration Association makes itself available to resolve a wide range of disputes (including labour/employment issues) through mediation, arbitration, elections and other out-of-court settlement procedures. A not-for-profit organization, it claims to be the largest provider of ADR (alternative dispute resolution) procedures in the USA. It also provides panels, education and training services.

Americans with Disabilities Act (ADA) The Americans with Disabilities Act prohibits discrimination against people with disabilities in employment, transportation, public accommodation, communications, and activities of state and local government. The Act was signed into law in 1990 but its various elements came into force on different dates including: state and local government activities, 26 January 1992; employers with 25 or more workers, 26 July 1992; employers with 15 or more workers, 26 July 1994. The Act requires that employers, employment agencies, labour organizations and joint labour–management committees must have non-discriminatory application procedures, qualification standards, and selection criteria and in all other terms and conditions of employment, and make reasonable accommodation to the known limitations of a qualified applicant or employee unless to do so would cause an undue hardship. There are exceptions regarding the employment of a person with a contagious disease, a person who illegally uses drugs or alcohol, employment of someone by a religious entity and private membership clubs.

Application forms (blanks)   Usually sent out to job-seekers who respond to some kind of job advertising. The form or blank is a template for the presentation of personal information that should be relevant to the job applied for. This ensures that all candidates provide the desired range of information in the same order of presentation to facilitate comparison and preparation of a shortlist for further selection procedures.

Application letters   Traditionally used for job applications they have tended to become little more than cover letters in English-speaking countries, generally being discounted in the selection process. However, in a number of continental European countries, especially France and Switzerland, they are requested to be handwritten and may be subject to graphological analysis as one (sometimes the main) selection procedure.

Appraisals   Appraisals rate individuals on quasi-objective criteria or standards deemed to be relevant to performance. Traditional appraisals rated individuals on a list of qualities – primarily work-related attitudes and personality traits. See also 'Performance assessment'.

Arbitration   Arbitration is a long-standing alternative to court-based litigation. For example, the first institute for arbitration in Denmark was set up in Copenhagen in 1894. The process has a number of variant forms but, in essence, nominated third parties (arbitrators) can make decisions that are binding on the parties to a dispute. Arbitration procedures can range between the informal and more rule-based systems, similar to court procedures. Generally, arbitration is seen as providing such benefits as confidentiality, flexibility, speed and relative cheapness.

Assessment   See 'Appraisals', 'Assessment centre', 'Performance assessment'.

Assessment centre   A concept and not necessarily a place. Normally used for selection or employee development. Participants are given a variety of exercises, tests, role-plays, interviews, etc. over a period of days. Several rates contribute to the assessment.

Attitudes   Attitudes are dispositions held by people, towards or against people, things and ideas. They have individual components based on factors such as personality and understanding, and social elements derived from shared experiences and cultural history. Attitudes are complex systems of belief, evaluation, emotion and behaviour.

Australian Council of Trade Unions (ACTU)   Formed in 1927, ACTU is the peak council and national centre representing the unionized Australian workforce. The ACTU holds a Congress every three years that sets out a clear set of policies and objectives for unions. The core activity of unions remains the improvement and representation of workers through workplace and industry activity and collective bargaining. The ACTU also has policies on a range of other issues that affect workers, their families and their communities.

Australian Industrial Relations Commission (AIRC)   The functions of the AIRC are broadly summarized as follows: (a) to facilitate agreement-making between employers and employees or organizations of employees about wages and conditions of employment; (b) to ensure that a safety net of fair minimum wages and conditions of employment is established and maintained; (c) to prevent and settle industrial disputes, so far as possible by conciliation, and, where appropriate within the limits specified by the Workplace Relations Act 1996, by arbitration; (d) to facilitate equal remuneration for work of equal value; (e) to conciliate claims for relief in relation to termination of employment, and if necessary to arbitrate whether a termination is harsh, unjust or unreasonable; and (f) to deal with matters concerning organizations, particularly registration, amalgamation, cancellation, representation rights, alteration of eligibility rules and change of name.

Australian Workplace Agreement (AWA)   An AWA is an individual written agreement between an employer and employee about the employee's terms and conditions of employment, such as pay, hours of work, annual leave and sick leave. AWAs are made under the federal Workplace Relations Act 1996. An AWA must be developed through a voluntary process. This means that an employee cannot be forced to sign an AWA against his or her will. It is against the law for employers or employees to use duress, or to give false information when making an

AWA. Once an AWA is approved it takes the place of any federal or state award that would otherwise apply. An AWA can change working conditions; for example, it could change hours of work, rosters, leave entitlements or pay.

Balanced scorecard A conceptual framework used to translate an organization's vision into a set of performance indicators, including measures of: financial performance; customer satisfaction; internal business processes; and learning and growth. Both current performance and efforts to learn and improve can be monitored using these measures.

Bargaining See 'Collective bargaining'.

Benchmarking Direct comparisons of different measures between an organization and 'best practice' competitors in the same business sector. This indicates the gap in performance, costs, morale, etc., between that organization and industry best practice.

Behavioural compliance Simply presenting an appearance of the attitudes and behaviours expected by senior managers. Not a true commitment.

Behavioural consistency Maintaining a set of desired behaviours consistently in the workplace. Desired behaviours may be agreed ways of behaving towards customers, team behaviour, etc.

Best practice Strategies, activities or techniques that are viewed as being highly effective. Note that what is best practice in one context may not work in another.

Biodata Roberts (1997, p.10) describes biodata as a 'set of questions framed around "coincidences" in the lives of good performers.' People who are good at a particular job are likely to be more similar to each other than to individuals selected at random from the general population. Such similarities extend beyond work-related factors into hobbies, sports and social activities.

Business culture See 'Corporate culture'.

Business environment Everything outside a business organization that interacts with that organization. Traditionally, human resource managers have been closely involved with employment legislation, industrial tribunals and trade unions at a functional level. HRM's strategic emphasis requires a focus on other environmental variables. Government economic, social security, education and training policies affect the availability, cost and quality of employees. International competition, strategic alliances and supranational organizations such as the European Union are exercising increasing influence on people management.

Business goals The strategic objectives of a business.

Business process re-engineering A 'fundamental rethinking and radical redesign of business processes to achieve dramatic improvements in critical contemporary measures of performance, such as cost, quality, service and speed' (Hammer and Champy, 1993).

Centralization An organizational process in which an activity or function (including control) is concentrated in one place.

Change Businesses must change to survive. However, change is a difficult management task. Effective change requires sure-footed, considerate people managers who can take employees through the process with minimum anxiety and maximum enthusiasm. It requires the recognition that an organization's people should not be the pawns of strategy but active participants in change.

Change strategy An organizational or HR strategy aimed at implementing planned change.

Charisma Weber regarded charisma as one of three sources of authority (the other two being 'rational' and 'traditional'), portraying it as a magical and hypnotic force based on direct personal contact. In modern life charisma is often fake – a product of carefully orchestrated mass communications.

Childcare In the HR context, a facility that looks after a child during a parent's working hours (including travelling time). May be provided by an employer as a benefit.

Cloning Cloning, or 'elective homogeneity' is the tendency for selectors to pick people like themselves, thereby reducing the breadth of skills and personalities in an organization. Simply matching the set of characteristics possessed by previous successful post-holders, it is a safe, conservative way of filling jobs. As a low-risk, but backward-looking approach, it is unlikely to meet the future needs of the organization.

Co-determination Cooperation between employees and management in policymaking.

Coherence HR strategies and actions must be consistent with each other. For example, if a business has a strategy of increasing sales of high profit margin products, rewards in the sales department should be focused on these products rather than less profitable items.

Collaborative entrepreneurship Cooperation between two or more individuals in order to found or acquire a business. The degree and nature of collaboration may vary from one company to another in terms of financial input, time devoted, skills and knowledge.

Collective bargaining Collective bargaining takes place between employers and trade unions when: employees are members of trade unions that undertake to negotiate on their behalf in matters such as pay, working conditions, other benefits and work allocation; and employers recognize trade unions and their officials as legitimate bargaining agents.

Collectivism The opposite of individualism – a preference for being part of a group. In employment relations, a process of combining into unions or staff associations for the purpose of negotiation with management.

Collectivization As individuals, most employees have a limited amount of power in comparison to their employers. But employees can pool the power they have. Through collectivization, workers are able to band together to protect their mutual interests. From the late 19th century onwards, trade unions have fought to improve pay and conditions for their members.

Commission for Racial Equality (CRE) The CRE is a publicly funded, non-governmental body set up under the UK Race Relations Act 1976 to tackle racial discrimination and promote racial equality. It works in both the public and private sectors to encourage fair treatment and to promote equal opportunities for everyone, regardless of their race, colour, nationality, or national or ethnic origin.

Commitment Commitment is defined as the degree of identification and involvement that individuals have with their organization's mission, values and goals. This translates into: their desire to stay with the organization; belief in its objectives and values; and the strength of employee effort in the pursuit of business objectives.

Communication Good communication is essential to the smooth running of the people management system. It must be a two-way process. This can involve a cascaded flow of information from the top and also feedback from lower levels through surveys, performance measures and open meetings.

Competence Organizations must have the capability to meet changing needs. In current parlance this is often expressed in terms of competencies – skills, knowledge and abilities. These are qualities possessed by the people who work for those organizations. Competencies can be brought into businesses through the recruitment of skilled individuals. They can also be developed within existing people by investing in training, education and experiential programmes.

Competitive advantage A concept popularized by Michael Porter. A condition that enables an organization to operate in a more efficient or otherwise higher-quality manner than the organizations it competes with.

Comprehensiveness All people management activities should be part of a single, comprehensive system. This implies that the attitudes, behaviour and culture of every individual in an organization – especially those with people management responsibilities – should be integrated within a deliberate framework.

Conflict Disagreement that may result in withdrawal of cooperation or, in an employee relations context, may result in some form of industrial action.

Conformity Opposite of creativity. A tendency to obey rules and stick to procedures or conventional ways of doing things.

Confucian dynamism Acceptance of the legitimacy of hierarchy and valuing of perseverance and thrift, without undue emphasis on tradition and social obligations that could impede business initiative.

Congruence One of the 'four Cs' of the Harvard model. An organization should be regarded as a system whose elements and activities have to fit together.

Contingency theory A theory that takes account of the circumstances in one situation at one point in time. Allows for multiple ways of doing things to fit different circumstances.

Contingent employees Temporary, intermittent or seasonal workers. The US Bureau of Labor Statistics' definition of contingent worker includes all salary and wage workers who do not expect their employment to last.

Continuous improvement Operational philosophy based on the view that performance improvement is the ongoing responsibility of everyone in an organization in order to achieve higher levels of performance, profitability and customer satisfaction.

Control HRM is aimed at directing and coordinating employees to meet an organization's objectives and cannot be anarchic nor totally democratic in its approach. Human resource literature mostly advocates a participative approach with a high degree of empowerment and delegation. An autocratic approach is unlikely to encourage good communication and employee commitment.

Cooperatives A cooperative is an autonomous association of persons united voluntarily to meet their common economic, social, and cultural needs and aspirations through a jointly owned and democratically controlled enterprise.

Coordination Tasks divided among a group of individuals must be synchronized and integrated in some way so as to achieve the overall objectives of the group. Jobs must fit into a coherent flow of work. Coordination involves the distribution of decision making. This can be formal, with rigid rules and regulations, or informal, giving freedom for local decisions. Coordination may be routine, because of structure and control mechanisms, including a performance management system, or direct, by management action.

Core and peripheral staff Core staff are those

employees regarded as essential to the organization; peripheral staff are there to meet operational needs but are not regarded as indispensable. Core staff have greater security and may also have better terms and conditions of employment.

Corporate culture Defined by Bower (1966) as 'the way we do things around here'. Trice and Beyer (1984) elaborated this as: 'the system of ... publicly and collectively accepted meanings operating for a given group at a given time'. Hofstede (1994) describes corporate culture as 'the psychological assets of an organization, which can be used to predict what will happen to its financial assets in five years time'. (See also 'Culture'.)

Cost-effectiveness Expressed in terms of profitability, cost-effectiveness has been used extensively as the justification for large-scale job cuts. But as a reflection of the value of its human assets, an organization has a duty to use its people wisely. In itself, there is nothing wrong with an attention to cost, provided that it does not become the one and only management criterion.

Counselling interview In the context of performance and employee development, an interview in which strengths and weaknesses and development actions are discussed. Typically, it follows a performance assessment.

Creativity Creativity can lead to new products and services, novel applications and cost-savings. A creative environment develops from a trusting, open culture with good communication and a blame-free atmosphere. Conversely, creativity is inhibited by lack of trust or commitment and fear of the consequences of change.

Credibility Managers and the organizations they represent must have credibility in the eyes of their employees if they are to expect the best performance. A degree of healthy cynicism is unavoidable, but in today's downsized workplaces this frequently extends into mistrust of and contempt for senior management. This feeling reflects the way many staff feel they are themselves regarded by management. Regaining trust depends on personal credibility, which, in turn, can only come from honesty and sincerity.

Critical incidents technique A set of procedures for systematically identifying behaviours that contribute to success or failure of individuals or organizations in specific situations.

Culture An all-pervasive system of beliefs and behaviours transmitted socially. Specifically it consists of the set of values – abstract ideals – and norms or rules held by a society, together with its material expressions. (See also 'Corporate culture'.)

Data Hard, factual information often in numerical form. It can tell you when, and how often something happened, how much it cost and so on, but it does not say why it happened. (See also 'Knowledge'.)

De-layering Removing one or more levels in a management hierarchy, thereby creating a flatter organization.

Demographic trends Long-term changes in a country's population density, age profile, etc.

Direct discrimination Treating an individual or group less favourably on grounds such as disability, race, religion, age, gender or sexual orientation. Direct discrimination is fairly obvious because of its explicit nature. The use of different criteria for promoting or paying male or female employees is an example of direct discrimination.

Disability The Americans with Disabilities Act 1990 defines disability as follows: 'Anyone with a physical or mental impairment substantially limiting one or more major life activities; has a record of such impairment; or is regarded as having such an impairment, is considered a person with a disability.' In terms of employment, the law defines a 'qualified individual with a disability' as a person with a disability who can perform the essential functions of the job with or without reasonable accommodation.

Disability Discrimination Act – Australia The Australian federal Disability Discrimination Act 1992 provides protection in Australia against discrimination based on disability. It encourages everyone to be involved in implementing the Act and to share in the overall benefits to the community and the economy that flow from participation by the widest range of people. According to the Australian Human Rights and Equal Opportunities Commission, disability discrimination happens when people with a disability are treated less fairly than people without a disability. Disability discrimination also occurs when people are treated less fairly because they are relatives, friends, carers, co-workers or associates of a person with a disability.

Disability Discrimination Act – UK The Disability Discrimination Act 1995 gives disabled people rights in the areas of: employment; access to goods, facilities and services; and buying or renting land or property. The employment rights and first rights of access came into force on 2 December 1996; further rights of access came into force on 1 October 1999; and the final rights of access will come into force in October 2004.

Discouraged worker hypothesis More people would work if jobs were easy to find – but they do not search when work is scarce. Workers calculate the probability of finding a job in relation to the wage they are likely to get and conclude that the effort is not worthwhile.

Discrimination   See 'Direct discrimination', 'Indirect discrimination'.

Diversity   'Diversity is the variation of social and cultural identities among people existing together in a defined employment or marketing systems' (Cox, O'Neill and Quinn, 2001).

Divisional structure   Organizational structure based on semi-autonomous units operating outside the centre.

Division of labour   The subdivision of work so that specific tasks or jobs are allocated to individuals deemed most suitable on the basis of skill, experience or cultural tradition.

Downsizing   Term used to describe sacking, dismissing or otherwise making redundant a substantial proportion of an organization's workforce.

Economically active   Includes the employed (those in paid work) and the unemployed (those who are looking for paid work but are unable to find it).

Economic turbulence   Cyclical and non-cyclical changes in the economy that cause periods of high or low demand for goods, services and employees.

Education   Formal learning outside (and often before entering) the workplace.

Employee analysis   Modern computer packages offer extensive possibilities for modelling the total profile of an organization's human resources. Employees can be classified in a variety of ways, such as function, department or grade.

Employee demand   Need for staff.

Employee involvement   An umbrella term that is inconsistently and imprecisely used to embrace a diverse range of management processes involving participation, communication, decision making, industrial democracy and employee motivation.

Employee relations   Employee relations is an alternative label for 'industrial relations'. It is not confined to unionized collective bargaining but encompasses all employment relationships. It goes beyond the negotiation of pay and benefits to include the conduct of the power relationship between employee and employer.

Employee resourcing   Resourcing is the process by which people are identified and allocated to perform necessary work. Resourcing has two strategic imperatives: first, minimizing employee costs and maximizing employee value to the organization; secondly, obtaining the correct behavioural mix of attitude and commitment in the workforce

Employee self-service   Employees can view company information, change selected personal details, make benefit enquiries (pension plans, sick pay entitlement, etc.), book leave and apply for training programmes through a company's HR portal or intranet. (See also 'Manager self-service'.)

Employee supply   Available staff in the employment market.

Employee turnover   Measurable incidence of people joining and leaving the organization.

Employer branding   The practice of developing, differentiating and leveraging an organization's brand message to its current and future workforce in a manner meaningful to them. Using the methodology of corporate brand-building strategy to attract and keep quality employees. Employer branding is aimed at motivating and securing employees' alignment with the vision and the values of the company.

Employment market   The employment market comprises all those people who are available for work. Neo-classical economics views this potential workforce as forming a labour market. The market is affected by national or regional supply and demand for appropriately skilled employees. It is constrained by demographic factors such as the number of young people leaving schools and universities and by cultural variables such as expectations for mothers to stay at home looking after children.

Employment relationship   A formal and informal relationship between the employing organization and an employee. The informal element is sometimes referred to as the psychological contract – an undocumented understanding about the nature of employment within the organization. Regarded by neo-classical economists as an exchange of labour for pay, The employment relationship is also a power relationship in which the employer has the formal authority to direct effort towards specific goals, whereas the employee can – informally – frustrate the achievements of those objectives.

Empowerment   Being in control of one's own destiny. Enabling someone to take decisions, think, behave and control work in their own way.

Entrepreneurship   A classic definition of entrepreneurship is provided by Timmons (1994, p.7): 'Entrepreneurship is the process of creating or seizing an opportunity and pursuing it regardless of the resources currently controlled.'

Equal access   A situation where disadvantaged groups are not barred from entry into organizations but may be confined to lower levels of work.

Equal chance   A situation where everyone has the same right, for example, to apply for a vacancy or be considered for promotion.

Equal Opportunities Commission   The UK Equal Opportunities Commission (EOC) was established under the Sex Discrimination Act 1975. It is an independent public body charged with the following tasks: (a) to work towards the elimination of discrimination on the grounds of sex or marriage; (b) to promote equality of opportunity for women and men; (c) to keep under review the Sex Discrimination Act and the Equal Pay Act; and (d) to provide legal advice and assistance to individuals who have been discriminated against.

Equal opportunity policy   A written statement of commitment to fair, non-discriminatory human resource management.

Equal Pay Act 1970   Applies to England, Scotland and Wales. Gives an individual a right to the same contractual pay and benefits as a person of the opposite sex in the same employment, where the man and the woman are doing: like work; or work rated as equivalent under an analytical job evaluation study; or work that is proved to be of equal value. The employer will not be required to provide the same pay and benefits if it can prove that the difference in pay or benefits is genuinely due to a reason other than one related to sex.

Equal share   Access is free to any position within an organization and all groups are represented at all levels. May require a quota system or affirmative action (q.v.) to achieve this situation.

Ethnic discrimination   See 'Race discrimination'.

Explicit knowledge   The obvious knowledge found in manuals, documentation, files and other accessible sources. (See also 'Tacit knowledge'.)

Federation   A loosely connected arrangement of businesses with a single holding company or separate firms in alliance.

Flexibility   The concept covers a combination of practices that enable organizations to react quickly and cheaply to environmental changes. In essence, flexibility is demanded from the workforce in terms of pay, contractual rights, hours and conditions, and working practices. This extends to the employment market, requiring job-seekers to show a willingness to move location, change occupation and accept radically different terms of employment. (See 'Numerical flexibility', 'Functional flexibility', 'Flexible firm', 'Flexible pay', 'Flexible specialization'.

Flexible firm   Atkinson's model combining flexibility with Japanese concepts of 'core' and 'peripheral' workforces.

Flexible specialization   Allocation of time and labour according to consumer demand. Staff receive extra training and resources to widen their specialist skills.

Fordism   Named after the mass production, assembly line methods used by Henry Ford for automobile manufacturing.

Functional flexibility   Abolishing demarcation rules and skill barriers so that workers can take on a variety of jobs.

Functional structure   Form of organization divided into relatively simple parts with defined areas of activity such as production, marketing or personnel.

Gender   All human societies divide themselves into two social categories called 'female' and 'male' (this does not exclude other categories). Each category is defined on the basis of varying cultural assumptions about the attributes, beliefs and behaviours expected from males and females. The gender of any individual depends on a complex combination of genetic, body, social, psychological and social elements, none of which is free from possible ambiguity or anomaly. Traditionally, sexual differences have been used to justify male-dominated societies in which women have been given inferior and secondary roles in their working lives.

Gender discrimination   Many countries, including all members of the EU, have sex discrimination and equal pay legislation. However, informal psychological and organizational barriers continue to bar the progress of women. The processes of occupational segregation and sex-typing of jobs continue so that women tend to be concentrated at the base of most organizational hierarchies in jobs that are less prestigious and lower paid than those favoured by men.

Gender legislation   In December 1975, South Australia became the first state in Australia to have sex discrimination laws.

Glass ceiling   The term 'glass ceiling' describes the process that bars women from promotion by means of an invisible barrier. This involves a number of factors, including attitudes of people in power and the inflexible processes and requirements geared to the cloning process which ensures that 'men of a certain type' will generally succeed. In the USA the term is also used to describe the barrier that prevents progress for other disadvantaged groups – for example ethnic minorities.

Glass Ceiling Commission (USA)   Created under the Civil Rights Act 1991 and chaired by the Secretary of State for Labor. According to the mission statement: the Glass Ceiling Commission was formed in order to: (1) build public awareness of the specific behaviours, practices and attitudes that either cause or prevent advancement by minorities and women to leadership and management positions; (2) develop concrete policy recommendations for improving and expanding employment opportunities for minorities and women; and (3) provide leadership in developing and communicating the Commission's equal employment opportunity agenda. The Glass Ceiling Commission produced a number of reports between 1991 and 1995.

Globalization   A systematic trend towards integration of production and marketing with brand-named goods and virtually identical 'badge-engineered' products such as cars being made available throughout the world. This process has been fostered by 'transnational' or 'multinational' companies operating in more than one country.

Graphology   Handwriting analysis to identify features of personality. Popular in continental Europe as a selection technique.

Hard HRM   Storey (1989) distinguished between hard and soft forms of HRM, typified by the Michigan and Harvard models, respectively. 'Hard' HRM focuses on the resource side of human resources. It emphasizes costs in the form of 'headcounts' and places control firmly in the hands of management. Their role is to manage numbers effectively, keeping the workforce closely matched with requirements in terms of both bodies and behaviour. (See also 'Soft HRM'.)

Harvard model   The Harvard Business School generated one of the most influential models of HRM. The Harvard view provides a strategic map of HRM territory, which guides all managers in their relations with employees. Beer *et al.* (1984) who devised this approach recognized an element of mutuality in all businesses – that employees are significant stakeholders in an organization.

Headhunting   Recruitment method aimed at identifying star performers.

Heroes   Personifications of the organization's values according to a number of management theorists: achievers who provide role models for success within the company.

Hierarchy   Pattern of responsibility and authority, usually represented by a tree and branch organization chart.

High-performance work system   'A comprehensive customer-driven system that aligns all of the activities in an organization with the common focus of customer satisfaction through continuous improvement in the quality of goods and services.' (US Department of Labor).

Human capital   Economic growth creates employment, but economic growth partly depends on skilled human resources – a country's human capital. The concept encompasses investment in the skills of the labour force, including education and vocational training to develop specific skills.

Human relations   A humanistic approach to management popularized by Elton Mayo and based on the Hawthorne experiments.

Human resource development (HRD)   A strategic approach to investing in human capital. It draws on other human resource processes, including resourcing and performance assessment to identify actual and potential talent. HRD provides a framework for self-development, training programmes and career progression to meet an organization's future skill requirements.

Human Resources Development Canada (HRDC)   HRDC, under the authority of the Department of Human Resources Development Act 1996, fulfils its mandate by administering the Employment Insurance Act, the Canada Pension Plan, the Old Age Security Act, the Canada Labour Code and the Acts and Regulations Governing Human Resources Development Canada with the objective of enhancing employment, encouraging equality and promoting social security.

Human resource flow   Movement of people through an organization commencing with recruitment.

Human resource information systems (HRIS)   'The HRIS system is the primary transaction processor, editor, record-keeper, and functional application system which lies at the heart of all computerized HR work. It maintains employee, organizational and HR plan data sufficient to support most, if not all, of the HR functions depending on the modules installed' (Walker, 2001).

Human resource management   A philosophy of people management based on the belief that human resources are uniquely important to sustained business success. An organization gains competitive advantage by using its people effectively, drawing on their expertise and ingenuity to meet clearly defined objectives. HRM is aimed at recruiting capable, flexible and committed people, managing and rewarding their performance and developing key competencies. (See 'Hard HRM', 'Soft HRM'.)

Human resource planning (HRP)   A process that anticipates and maps out the consequences of business strategy on an organization's human resource requirements. This is reflected in planning of skill and competence needs as well as total headcounts.

Human resource service centres   One of the most widely used solutions to re-engineered HR in large organizations. Such centres centralize a number of HR processes and may deal with geographically widespread users. Enquiries can be taken by voice, e-mail or internet forms.

Human resource strategy   Overall plan for staffing, developing and rewarding employees and outsourced human resources tied to business objectives.

Human Rights and Equal Opportunities Commission (HREOC, Australia)   The HREOC is a national independent statutory government body, established in 1986 by an Act of the federal parliament, the Human Rights and Equal Opportunity Commission Act. The federal Attorney General is the minister responsible in parliament for the Commission. The Commission is administered by the president, who is the chief executive officer. She is assisted by the Human Rights, Race, Sex, Disability and Aboriginal and Torres Strait Islander Social Justice Commissioners. Matters that can be investigated by the HREOC include discrimination on the grounds of race, colour or ethnic origin, racial vilification, sex, sexual harassment, marital status, pregnancy or disability.

Image The apparent totality of knowledge and abilities as outwardly presented by an individual or group. Can be false. (See also 'Impression management'.)

Implicit knowledge See 'Tacit knowledge'.

Implicit theory An internal or mental model of how and why a set of events or behaviours takes place. A belief system developed by individuals to explain part of their world or organization based on their own interpretations and experiences.

Impression management A deliberate process in which a personal image is learned or acquired through training. (See also 'Image'.)

Indirect discrimination A less obvious form of discrimination than direct discrimination. This may take the form of applying certain conditions or requirements that are more easily satisfied by one group than another. One example would be to specify a fixed minimum height requirement for entry into a police force. This is a requirement that would be more easily met by male than female applicants. Another example would be a requirement for an unnecessarily high standard of spoken or written English that would favour people with a particular educational background. (See also 'Direct discrimination'.)

Individualism Opposite of collectivism. Preference to work individually rather than as part of a group.

Induction Initial orientation and training of a new recruit.

Industrial democracy Egalitarian notion of worker involvement in decision making.

Informal organization An organization is both a formal and informal entity. The formal aspect of an organization is its official structure and public image visible in organization charts and annual reports. The informal organization is a more elusive concept, describing the complex network of psychological and social relationships between its people. The informal organization is an unrecognized world of cliques and politics, friendships and enmities, gossip and affairs.

In-group Favoured and usually long-standing members of a society, department or organization.

Insecurity thesis Heery and Salmon (2000) identify a connection between globalization and the 'insecurity thesis' – a belief that: 'Employment in the developed economies has become more insecure or unstable in the sense that both continued employment and the level of remuneration have become less predictable and contingent on factors that lie beyond the employee's control.'

Institutionalized racism An indirect and largely invisible process that can be compared with cloning and the glass ceiling. It is a term encompassing the, often unintentional, barriers and selection/promotion procedures that serve to disadvantage members of ethnic minority groups.

Japanization A term that first came into vogue in the mid-1980s. It is used as a label for the attempts of Western firms to make practical use of 'Japanese' ideas and practices and as a description of the presence and impact of Japanese subsidiaries overseas.

Job analysis The process of job analysis is that of gathering and analysing job-related information. This includes details about tasks to be performed as part of a job and the personal qualities required to do so. Job analysis can provide information for a variety of purposes including: determining training needs; development criteria; and appropriate pay and productivity improvements. For resourcing purposes, job analysis can generate job and personnel specifications.

Job description List of essential tasks involved in a particular job.

Job market See 'Employment market', 'Labour market'.

Knowledge 'Knowledge is a fluid mix of framed expertise, values, contextual information and expert insight that provides a framework for evaluating and incorporating new experiences and information. It originates from and is applied in the minds of knowers. In organizations it often becomes embedded not only in documents or repositories but also in organizational routines, processes, practices and norms' (Davenport and Prusack, 2000).

Knowledge management 'Knowledge management caters to the critical issues of organizational adaption, survival and competence in face of increasingly discontinuous environmental change.... Essentially, it embodies organizational processes that seek synergistic combination of data and information processing capacity, of information technologies and the creative and innovative capacity of human beings' (Malhotra, 1998).

Labour market The setting in which people who can provide labour meet those who need labour. Labour markets can be internal, within an organization, or external, outside the organization. Labour market is a somewhat old-fashioned term which implies physical labour as opposed to the time, knowledge and intellectual effort required in many modern jobs. 'Job market' or 'employment market' is more meaningful in today's context. (See 'Employment market'.)

Learning organization An organization that 'lives and breathes' learning and knowledge acquisition.

Management by objectives A technique to establish individual performance objectives that are tangible, measurable and verifiable. Individual objectives are derived or cascaded from organizational goals. Top managers agree their own specific objectives compatible with the organization's goals but restricted to their own areas of responsibility. Subordinates do the same at each lower level, forming an interlocked and coherent hierarchy of performance targets.

Managing diversity The management of diversity goes beyond equal opportunity and embodies the belief that people should be valued for their differences and variety. Diversity is perceived to enrich an organization's human capital. Whereas equal opportunity focuses on various disadvantaged groups, the management of diversity is about individuals.

Manager self-service Managers can have access to 'front-end' applications on their desktops in the form of HR portals. Typically, they are able to view a range of personal details and aggregate information. They are also allowed to change and input certain details and model the consequences on their budgets of salary increases or bonus payments. (See also 'Employee self-service'.)

Manpower planning Now obsolete. 'A strategy for the acquisition, utilization, improvement and retention of an enterprise's human resources' (anonymous government publication cited in Pratt and Bennett, 1989, p.101). (See 'Human resource planning'.)

Matching model See 'Michigan model'.

Matrix structures Organizational structures focused on project teams, bringing skilled individuals together from different parts of the organization. Individuals are responsible to their line manager and to the project manager for different aspects of their jobs.

Mentoring Individual–individual support in an organization providing guidance on career development, learning and performance.

Meritocracy Meritocratic procedures aim to make judgements on the basis of evidence of competence such as examination results or the achievement of targets.

Meta analysis Statistical technique in which results from a large number of (comparatively) small studies are combined.

Michigan model of HRM The Michigan model is strongly influenced by strategic management literature. HRM is seen as a strategic process, making the most effective use of an organization's human resources. Hence there must be coherent human resource policies that 'fit' closely with overall business strategies.

Minimum wage Lowest allowable level of pay within a state or country.

Mission statement A mission statement should convey the essence of what an organization is about: why it exists, what kind of business it intends to be and who its intended customers are. The mission is translated into objectives or goals within the strategic management process.

Numerical flexibility Matching employee numbers to fluctuating production levels or service requirements.

Occupational segregation Disproportionate representation of particular groups in specific sectors, job types or levels of responsibility. Horizontal segregation places men and women, for example, in different jobs, such as chambermaids (women) and porters (men). Vertical segregation places one group in better-paid positions than another group, so that men are better represented at managerial levels while women are concentrated in lower, administrative jobs.

Option scheme Right to buy shares in an employing organization, often at a favourable price.

Organizational design The 'design' of an organization patterns its formal structure and culture. It allocates purpose and power to departments and individuals. It lays down guidelines for authoritarian or participative management by its rigidity or flexibility, its hierarchical or non-hierarchical structure.

Organizational development (OD) Methodology of change characterized by an ongoing series of relatively small improvements.

Organizational goals The logical starting point for human resource management lies in an organization's goals – the reasons for its existence. Most modern businesses express these goals in the form of a mission statement. The allocation and control of human resources serves to assist or constrain the achievement of these objectives.

Organizations The means by which human and other

resources are deployed so that work gets done. They are social entities with purposes expressed in the form of common goals and boundaries between themselves and the rest of the world.

Particularism A form of discrimination favouring particular groups and individuals over others. It derives from a reliance on personal relationships such as ethnic origin, religion or tribal community. It contrasts with universalism in which personal relationships are ignored and emphasis is on other criteria such as qualifications, expertise and ability to do the job.

Pay flexibility Offering different rates of pay for the same work, depending on geographical location and skills availability.

Performance assessment One of the many people management techniques that 'classify and order individuals hierarchically' (Townley, 1994, p.33). Modern assessment is often focused on competencies. (See also 'Appraisals'.)

Performance management 'A strategic and integrated approach to increasing the effectiveness of organizations by improving the performance of the people who work in them and by developing the capabilities of teams and individual contributors.' (Armstrong and Baron, 1998).

Performance-related pay (PRP) Pay based on merit as assessed by a performance management process.

Personality Generally expressed in terms of types or traits, the latter form the basis of most personality tests used for resourcing and the documentation employed for many performance appraisal systems. An alternative approach is to regard personality as an artefact of a particular set of circumstances. In other words, apparent personality depends on the meaning individuals give to a particular situation.

Personnel specification 'The demands of the job translated into human terms' (Arnold, Robertson and Cooper, 1991, p.95). Personnel specifications list 'essential' criteria that must be satisfied, and other criteria which rule out certain people from being able to do the job.

Person perception The perception of other people. Cues such as facial expression, posture, gesture, body movement, tone of voice, etc., are used to evaluate their current mood and overall personalities (McKenna, 1994, p.144). Each one of us has an 'implicit personality theory' based on our experience, assumptions about people, beliefs and prejudices. The evidence of our senses is used to collect data about the perceived person and attribute characteristics to them according to our implicit theory.

Pluralism The acceptance of several alternative approaches, interests or goals within the same organization or society. A view which recognizes that every organization is composed of different interests which are not balanced. Pluralists accept that conflict is natural and are concerned with the means by which it can be managed.

Positive action Measures to prevent discrimination by insisting, for example, on non-discriminatory recruitment procedures, training programmes and pay rates. This does not include any preferential treatment for disadvantaged groups.

Positive discrimination See 'Affirmative action'.

Power distance The perceived status differences between people with high and low degrees of power.

Productivity The amount of output (what is produced) per unit of input used. Labour is one input among many. Total productivity is dependent upon a variety of diverse and hard to measure inputs. One simple measure of productivity is the gross domestic product (GDP) per person-hour worked. But it is also a simplistic measure of productivity because it neglects a number of factors such as capital investment.

Psychological contract An informal understanding between the employer and employee. Unlike the formal employment contract, this has no physical existence. It is a set of expectations held by both employers and employees in terms of what they wish to give and receive from their working relationship (Rousseau and Parks, 1993).

Psychometric model The dominant approach to selection in British and US textbooks. In its traditional form, it grounds the 'best-person' model in psychological theory and testing. It embodies the use of refined techniques to achieve the best 'match' between job characteristics identified by formal job analysis and individual characteristics measured by psychological tests, structured interviews and other assessment methods.

Race discrimination Unfavourable treatment on the grounds of race or ethnic origin.

Recruitment Attracting candidates prior to selection.

Reorganization A move from one form of organization to another. For example, a business may change from a divisional to a network structure.

Resourcing See 'Employee resourcing'.

Restructuring Breaking up and recombining organizational structures in order to reduce costs, eliminate duplication and achieve greater efficiency.

Retrenchment Downsizing or reducing the number of staff on the payroll.

Reward management Management of pay, benefits and other forms of compensation.

Scientific management F.W. Taylor devised 'scientific management' as a systematic but controversial programme based on rudimentary time and motion studies, selection of 'first-class men' for the job and premium pay for a 'fair day's work'.

Sexual discrimination   See 'Gender discrimination'.

Sexual harassment   Definitions vary considerably but most are agreed that it is sexual attention that is unwanted, repeated, and affects a person's work performance or expectations from her job. However, it is possible for one incident to be sufficiently severe to be regarded as harassment. It differs from sexual banter or flirting since it is one-way; it does not have the involvement and acceptance of both parties. In the USA, the Equal Employment Opportunity Commission has extended the definition of sexual harassment to include a range of actions that lead to a 'hostile work environment'. This definition includes unwelcome touching, joking, teasing, innuendoes, slurs and the display of sexually explicit materials.

Social dumping   The concept of social dumping describes the practice of switching production from countries with relatively high employee costs to those with cheap labour. It is an accusation made against large multinational corporations. Social dumping has led to long-term structural changes including the closure of older heavy manufacturing industries such as steel and shipbuilding in established industrial countries.

Social market   A term coined by Alfred Müller-Armack, Secretary of State at the Economics Ministry in Bonn, Federal Republic of Germany between 1958 and 1963. He defined the social market as an economic system that combined market freedom with social equilibrium. In this kind of economic system the government plays a regulating role and creates the framework for market processes, going beyond securing competition to ensure social equity.

Social protection   According to the World Bank, social protection measures improve or protect human capital, ranging from labour market interventions, unemployment or old-age insurance, to income support, for individuals, households and communities.

Soft HRM   Storey (1989) distinguished between hard and soft forms of HRM, typified by the Michigan and Harvard models, respectively. 'Soft' HRM stresses the 'human' aspects of HRM. Its concerns are with communication and motivation. People are led rather than managed. They are involved in determining and realizing strategic objectives.

Soft planning   Human resource planning based on factors other than numbers of employees.

Specialization   The division of work between individuals or departments, allocating responsibilities for specific activities or functions to people who can achieve a high standard of work in a relatively narrow range of activities. They may require specific training or expertise. For example, HR managers are concerned with organization of the HR function and resourcing of all other functions.

Stakeholders   Recognizably separate groups or institutions with a special interest in an organization. These include shareholders, employees, managers, customers, suppliers, lenders and government. Each group has its own priorities and demands and fits into the power structure controlling the organization.

Strategic HRM   Directing people, processes and HR systems to achieve strategic objectives so that individual goals are tied to the business needs of the whole organization.

Strategy   A strategy is the means by which an organization seeks to meet its objectives. It is a deliberate choice, a decision to take a course of action rather than reacting to circumstances. It focuses on significant, long-term goals rather than day-to-day operating matters.

Substance   The body of competencies, knowledge and experience required to fulfil a particular function.

Synergy   Making the new whole worth more than its old parts, sometimes described as '2+2=5'. Synergies involve economies from integrating activities, horizontally or vertically; but also unrealized potential for new ideas, products or processes by melding expertise from the different sources into centres of excellence.

Tacit or implicit knowledge   This is found in the heads of an organization's employees. It is difficult to access and use – for obvious reasons. Typically, an organization does not even know what this knowledge is. Worse, the knee-jerk reaction of top managers who fire employees at the first sign of any downturn means that the knowledge is often lost.

Targeting   Quotas for the employment of particular groups have been enforced in the USA. In Europe quota systems commonly apply to the disabled and, in a few countries, other groups such as ex-servicemen, but enforcement is not usually strict. (See also 'Affirmative action'.)

Taylorism   An approach to management based on the theories of F.W. Taylor. (See 'Scientific management'.)

Tokenism   The employment or promotion of isolated individuals to represent their gender or colour. For example, a 12-member board of directors with one token woman and one token ethnic minority person.

Total quality management (TQM)   A methodology focused on continuous improvement, quality assurance and zero faults. TQM programmes are geared to organizational processes such as production. HR involvement includes the selection of flexible people who are amenable to increasingly demanding levels of quality.

Turnover   See 'Employee turnover'.

Uncertainty avoidance   How people deal with conflict, particularly aggression and the expression of feelings. High uncertainty avoidance favours precise rules, teachers who are always right and superiors who should be obeyed without question. Low uncertainty avoidance favours flexibility, discussion and delegation of decision making.

Unitarism   A managerialist stance which assumes that everyone in an organization is a member of a team with a common purpose. The unitarist view is implicit in American models of HRM. It embodies a central concern of HRM, that an organization's people, whether managers or lower-level employees, should share the same objectives and work together harmoniously. From this perspective, conflicting objectives are seen as negative and dysfunctional.

Values   Values are at the heart of corporate culture. They are made up of the key beliefs and concepts shared by an organization's employees. Successful companies are clear about these values and their managers publicly reinforce them. Often values are unwritten and operate at a subconscious level.

Virtual organizations   Advancing technology allows firms to extend the network concept to form enterprises with no permanent structures. They bring people together for specific projects. Teams dissolve on completion, to reappear in new combinations for other tasks.

Work ethic   The belief that work is virtuous in itself. Hard work is to be admired and leisure is equated with laziness. In some societies the work ethic became a fundamental religious principle, the Puritans and Calvinists holding it to be such a virtue that Max Weber termed it the protestant work ethic. The concept is sometimes extended to include the virtue of frugality as against waste. It justifies regarding the poor as sinful, since success and ambition are virtuous and wealth is a sign of God's favour.

World view   A set of values and beliefs held by members of a particular culture. This is meaningful to its members but alien to others.

References

Abrahart, A. and Verme, P. (2001) 'Labor market policies: theoretical background', in I.D. Ortitz (ed.) *Social Protection in Asia and the Pacific*, Asian Development Bank.

Abrashoff, D.M. (2002) *It's Your Ship: Management Techniques from the Best Damn Ship in the Navy*, Warner Books.

ABS (2000) *Work-Related Injuries, Australia, September 2000*, (Cat. No. 6324.0), Australian Bureau of Statistics.

ACAS (1990) *Appraisal Related Pay*, ACAS Advisory Booklet No. 14, Advisory, Conciliation and Arbitration Service.

Ackoff, R.L. (1999) *Re-Creating the Corporation: A Design of Organizations for the 21st Century*, Oxford University Press.

Adams, K. (1991) 'Externalisation vs specialisation: what is happening to personnel?', *Human Resource Management Journal* 1(4):40–54.

Addison, J., Siebert, S., Wagner, J. and Wei, X. (2000) 'Worker participation and firm performance: evidence from Germany and Britain', *British Journal of Industrial Relations* 38(1):7–48.

Addison, J.T., Schnabel, C. and Wagner, J. (2001) 'Works councils in Germany: their effects on establishment performance', *Oxford Economic Papers* 53(4):659–94.

Adjibolosoo, S.B.S.K. (1999) *Rethinking Development Theory and Policy: A Human Factor Critique*, Praeger Publications.

Adler, N.J. (1997) Preface to Lane, H.W., Distefano, J.J. and Maznevski, M.L., *International Management Behavior*, Blackwell.

Ahlrichs, N. (2000) *Competing for Talent: Key Recruitment and Retention Strategies for Becoming an Employer of Choice*, Davies-Black Publishing.

Ajuwon, J. (2002) 'Gatekeepers or innovators,' Forum, *Conspectus*, January 2002, Prime Marketing Publications Ltd.

Akinnusi, D. (1991) 'Personnel management in Africa', in C. Brewster and S. Tyson (eds) *International Comparisons in Human Resource Management*, Pitman.

Alcock, P., Beatty, C., Fothergill, S., MacMillan, R. and Yeandle, S. (2002) *Work to Welfare: How Men Become Detached from the Labour Market*, Cambridge University Press.

Aldrich, H.E. (1999) *Organizations Evolving*, Sage.

Aldrich, H.E. (2000) 'Learning together: national differences in entrepreneurship research', in D.L. Sexton and H. Landstrom (eds) *The Blackwell Handbook of Entrepreneurship* (Blackwell Handbooks in Management), Blackwell.

Alker, L. and McHugh, D. (2000) 'Human resource maintenance? Organizational rationales for the introduction of employee assistance programmes', *Journal of Managerial Psychology* 15(4):303–23.

Allan, C., Brosnan, P. and Walsh, P. (1999) 'Human resource strategies, workplace reform and industrial restructuring in Australia and New Zealand', *International Journal of Human Resource Management* 10(5):828–41.

Allen, N.J. and Meyer, M.P. (1990) 'The measurement of antecedents of affective, continuance and normative commitment to the organisation', *Journal of Occupational Psychology* 63: 1–8.

Altman, M. (2002) 'Economic theory and the challenge of innovative work practices', *Economic and Industrial Democracy* 23(2):271–88.

American Management Association (2000) *Auditing Your Human Resources Department*, AMACOM.

Anderson, N. and Herriot, P. (1997) *Assessment and Selection in Organizations: Methods and Practice for Recruitment and Appraisal, Volume 2, International Handbook of Selection and Assessment*, John Wiley & Son.

Andrisani, P. and Nestel, G. (1976) 'Internal-external control as contributor to and outcome of work experience', *Journal of Applied Psychology* 61:156–65.

Ansoff, H.I. (1968) *Corporate Strategy*, Penguin.

Argyle, M. (1991) *Cooperation: The Basis of Sociability*, Routledge.

Argyris, C. (1957) *Personality and Organization*, Harper and Row.

Armstrong, M. (1987) 'Human resource management: a case of the emperor's new clothes?', *Personnel Management* (August):31–4.

Armstrong, M. (1992) *Human Resource Management: Strategy and Action*, Kogan Page.

Armstrong, M. (1994) *The Reality of Strategic HRM*, paper presented at the Strategic Direction of Human Resource Management Conference, Nottingham Trent University, 14 December.

Armstrong, M. (2000) 'The name has changed but has the game remained the same?' *Employee Relations* 22(6):576–93.

Armstrong, M. and Baron, A. (1998) *Performance Management: The New Realities*, Chartered Institute of Personnel and Development (CIPD).

Armstrong, P. (1989) 'Limits and possibilities for HRM in an age of management accountancy', in J. Storey (ed.) *New Perspectives in Human Resource Management*, Routledge.

Arnold, J., Robertson, I.T. and Cooper, C.L. (1991) *Work Psychology*, Pitman.

Ashton, D. and Felstead, A. (1995) 'Training and development' in J. Storey (ed.) *Human Resource Management: A Critical Text*, Routledge.

Atkinson, J. (1984) 'Manpower strategies for flexible organizations', *Personnel Management*, August:28–31.

Auer, P. (ed.) (2001) *Changing Labour Markets in Europe: The Role of Institutions and Policies*, International Labour Office.

Augoustinos, M., Tuffin, K. and Rapley, M. (1999) 'Genocide or a failure to gel? Racism, history and nationalism in Australian talk', *Discourse and Society* 10(3):351–78.

Bacon, N. and Blyton, P. (1999) 'Co-operation and conflict in industrial relations: what are the implications for employees and trade unions?' *International Journal of Human Resource Management* 10(4):638–54.

Bakke, E.W. (1950) *Bonds of Organization*, Harper and Row.

Barak, M.E.M. and Levin, A. (2002) 'Outside of the corporate mainstream and excluded from the work community: a study of diversity, job satisfaction and well-being', *Community, Work and Family* 5(2):133–57.

Barclay, J.M. (2001) 'Improving selection interviews with structure: organisations' use of "behavioural" interviews', *Personnel Review* 30(1):81–101.

Barnard, C., Deakin, S., and Kilpatrick, C. (2002) 'Equality, non-discrimination and the labour market in the UK', *International Journal of Comparative Labour Law and Industrial Relations* 18(2):129–47.

Barr, M.D. (2000) 'Trade unions in an elitist society: the Singapore story', *Australian Journal of Politics & History* 46(4):480–96.

Barsoux, J.-L. and Lawrence, P. (1990) *Management in France*, Cassell.

Bartram, D. (1991) 'Addressing the abuse of psychological tests', *Personnel Management* (April):34–9.

Bassanini, A. and Ernst, E. (2002) 'Labour market regulation, industrial relations and technological regimes: a tale of comparative advantage', *Industrial and Corporate Change* 11(3):391–426.

Bates, R. (2002) 'Liking and similarity as predictors of multi-source ratings', *Personnel Review* 31(5):540–552.

Beardwell, I. (2001) 'An introduction to human resource management: strategy, style or outcome', in I. Beardwell and L. Holden (eds) *Human Resource Management: A Contemporary Perspective*, 3rd edition, Financial Times/Prentice-Hall.

Beardwell, I. and Holden, L. (eds) (1994) *Human Resource Management: A Contemporary Perspective*, Pitman.

Beaumont, P.B. (1992) 'The US human resource management literature: a review', in G. Salaman (ed.) *Human Resource Strategies*, Sage.

Becker, G.S. (1965) 'A theory of the allocation of time', *Economic Journal* 75(299):493–517.

Beehr, T.A., Glaser, K.M., Canali, K.G. and Wallwey, D.A. (2001) 'Back to basics: re-examination of demand-control theory of occupational stress', *Work and Stress* 15(2):115–30.

Beer, M., Spector, B.A., Lawrence, P.R., Mills, Q. and Walton, R.E. (1984). *Managing Human Assets*, The Free Press.

Bekker, M.H.J., Nijssen, A. and Hens, G. (2001) 'Stress prevention training: sex differences in types of stressors, coping, and training effects', *Stress and Health* 17(4):207–18.

Bennington, L. (2001) 'Age discrimination: converging evidence from four Australian studies', *Employee Responsibilities and Rights Journal* 13(3):125–34.

Bennington, L. and Wein, R. (2002) 'Aiding and abetting employer discrimination: the job applicant's role', *Employee Responsibilities and Rights Journal* 14(1):3–16.

Bennis, W. (1990) 'Managing the dream: leadership in the 21st century', *Training: The Magazine of Human Resource Development*, 27(5):44–6.

Ben-Tovim, G., Gabriel, J., Law, I. and Stredder, K. (1992) 'A political analysis of local struggles for racial equality', in P. Braham, A. Rattansi and R. Skellington (eds) *Racism and Antiracism*, Sage.

Bercusson, B. (2002) 'The European social model comes to Britain', *Industrial Law Journal* 31(3):209–244.

Berger, L.A. and Berger, D.R. (1999) *The Compensation Handbook*, 4th edition, McGraw-Hill.

Bermeo, N. (ed.) (2001) *Unemployment in the New Europe*, Cambridge University Press.

Bertozzi, F. and Bonoli, G. (2002) 'Europeanisation and the convergence of national social and employment policies: what can the open method of co-ordination achieve?' First draft of paper prepared for the workshop 'Europeanisation of national political institutions', ECPR joint-session, Turin 22–27 March 2002.

Bertsch, B. and Williams, R. (1994) 'How multinational CEOs make change programmes stick', *Long Range Planning* 27(5):12–24.

Best Practice LLC (2001) *Strategies for Outsourcing HR Tasks*, Best Practice LLC Reports.

Bevan, S. and Thompson, M. (1992) *Merit Pay, Performance Appraisals and Attitudes to Women's Work*, IMS Publications.

Beynon, H. (1973) *Working for Ford*, Pelican Paperback, Penguin.

Biagi, M. (2000) 'The impact of European employment strategy on the role of labour law and industrial relations', *International Journal of Comparative Labour Law and Industrial Relations* 16(2):155–73.

Biech, E. (2001) *The Consultant's Quick Start Guide: An Action Plan for Your First Year in Business*, John Wiley & Sons.

Björkman, I. and Xiucheng, F. (2002) 'Human resource management and the performance of Western firms in China', *International Journal of Human Resource Management* 13(6):853–64.

Black, B. (2001) 'National culture and industrial relations and pay structures', *Labour* 15(2):257–77.

Black, S. and Gregersen, H.B. (2002) *Leading Strategic Change*, Financial Times, Prentice-Hall.

Blackaby, D., Leslie, D., Murphy, P. and O'Leary, N. (1999) 'Unemployment among Britain's ethnic minorities', *The Manchester School* 67(1):1–20.

Blackman M.C. (2002a) 'The employment interview via the telephone: are we sacrificing accurate personality judgments for cost efficiency?' *Journal of Research in Personality* 36(3):208–23.

Blackman M.C. (2002b) 'Personality judgment and the utility of the unstructured employment interview', *Basic and Applied Social Psychology* 24(3):241–50.

Blair, A., Karsten, L. and Leopold, J. (2001) 'Britain and the working time regulations', *Politics* 21(1):40–6.

Blake, R. and Mouton, J. (1964) *The Managerial Grid*, Gulf Publishing.

Blanksby, M. and Iles, P. (1990) 'Recent developments in assessment centre theory, practice and operation', *Personnel Review* 19(6):33–42.

Blanpain, R. (2002) *European Labour Law*, 8th and revised edition, Kluwer Academic Publishers.

Blanton, H., George, G. and Crocker, J. (2001) 'Contexts of system justification and system evaluation: exploring the social comparison strategies of the (not yet) contented female worker', *Group Processes and Intergroup Relations* 4(2):126–37.

Blau, P.M. and Schoenherr, R.A. (1971) *The Structure of Organizations*, Basic Books.

Blinkhorn, S. and Johnson, C. (1990) 'The insignificance of personality testing', *Nature* 348:671–2.

Blumenthal, D. (2001) *Internal Branding: Does It Improve Employees' Quality Of Life?*, paper presented at the ISQOLS Conference, Washington DC, 29 November.

Blyton, P. and Turnbull, P. (1992) *Reassessing Human Resource Management*, Sage.

Blyton, P. and Turnbull, P. (1994) *The Dynamics of Employee Relations*, Macmillan.

Bolkestein, F. (2000) *The Future of the Social Market Economy*, speech by Commissioner Frits Bolkestein, Brussels, 5 December 2000.

Booth, A.L. and McCulloch, A. (1999) 'Redundancy pay, unions and employment', *The Manchester School* 67(3):346–66.

Bourantas, D. and Papalexandris, N. (1990) 'Sex differences in leadership: leadership styles and subordinate satisfaction', *Journal of Managerial Psychology* 5:7–10.

Bower, M. (1966) *The Will to Manage*, McGraw-Hill.

Boxall, P. (1996) 'The strategic HRM debate and the resource-based view of the firm', *Human Resource Management Journal* 6(3):59–75.

Boxall, P. and Purcell, J. (2000) 'Strategic human resource management: where have we come from and where should we be going?' *International Journal of Management Reviews* 2(2):183–203.

Boyatzis, R.E. (1982) *The Competent Manager*, John Wiley & Sons.

Boyd, C. (2001) 'HRM in the airline industry: strategies and outcomes', *Personnel Review* 30(4):438–53.

Brading, E. and Wright, V. (1990) 'Performance-related pay', *Personnel Management Factsheet*, June.

Bradley, J.R. and Cartwright, S. (2002) 'Social support, job stress, health, and job satisfaction among nurses in the United Kingdom', *International Journal of Stress Management* 9(3):163–82.

Braham, P., Rattansi, A. and Skellington, R. (eds) (1992) *Racism and Antiracism*, Sage.

Braverman, H. (1974) *Labor and Monopoly Capital: The Degradation of Work in the Twentieth Century*, Monthly Review Press.

Breakwell, G.M. (1990) *Interviewing*, BPS/Routledge.

Brennan, A., Chugh, J.S. and Kline, T. (2002) 'Traditional versus open office design: a longitudinal field study', *Environment and Behavior* 34(3):279–99.

Brewster, C. (1994) 'European HRM: reflection of, or challenge to, the American concept?', in P.S. Kirkbride (ed.) *Human Resource Management in Europe: Perspectives for the 1990s*, Routledge.

Brewster, C. and Tyson, S. (eds) (1991) *International Comparisons in Human Resource Management*, Pitman.

Briggs, C. (2001) 'Australian exceptionalism: the role of trade unions in the emergence of enterprise bargaining', *The Journal of Industrial Relations* 43(1):27–43.

Briggs, P. (1991) 'Organizational commitment: the key to Japanese success', in C. Brewster and S. Tyson (eds) *International Comparisons in Human Resource Management*, Pitman.

Brody, D. (2001) 'Why no shop committees in America: a narrative history', *Industrial Relations* 40(3):356–76.

Broman, C.L., Hamilton, V.L. and Hoffman, W.S. (2001) *Stress and Distress Among the Unemployed: Hard Times and Vulnerable People* (Plenum Studies in Work and Industry), Plenum Publications.

Brown, S. and Seidner, C. (1998) *Evaluating Corporate Training: Models and Issues*, Kluwer Academic Publishers.

Brown, W. (1994) *Bargaining for Full Employment*, Employment Policy Institute.

Brown, W., Deakin, S., Hudson, M. and Pratten, C. (2001) 'The limits of statutory trade union recognition', *Industrial Relations Journal* 32(3):180–94.

Brunsson, N. (1989) *The Organization of Hypocrisy: Talk, Decisions and Action in Organizations*, Wiley.

Bryman, A. (1992) *Charisma and Leadership in Organizations*, Sage.

Buch, K. and Rivers, E. (2001) 'TQM: the role of leadership and culture', *Leadership and Organization Development Journal* 22(8):365–71.

Buchanan, D. and Boddy, D. (1992) *The Expertise of the Change Agent*, Prentice-Hall.

Buck, J.M. and Watson, J.L. (2002) 'Retaining staff employees: the relationship between human resources management strategies and organizational commitment', *Innovative Higher Education* 26(3):175–93.

Bunge, M. and Ardila, R. (1987) *Philosophy of Psychology*, Springer-Verlag.

Buono, A.F. (1991) 'Managing strategic alliances: organizational and human resource considerations', *Business and the Contemporary World* 3(4):92–101.

Burke, G. and Peppard, J. (eds) (1995) *Examining Business Process Re-engineering: Current Perspectives and Research Directions*, Kogan Page.

Burke, R.J. (2001) 'Organizational values, work experiences and satisfactions among managerial and professional women', *The Journal of Management Development* 20(4):346–54.

Burke, R.J. (2002). 'Organizational values, job experiences and satisfactions among managerial and professional women and men: advantage men?' *Women in Management Review* 17(5):228–36.

Burns, T. and Stalker, G.M. (1961) *The Management of Innovation*, Tavistock Publications.

Burstein, P. (1998) *Discrimination, Jobs and Politics: The Struggle for Equal Employment Opportunity in the United States Since the New Deal*, University of Chicago Press.

Butler, R. (1991) *Designing Organizations: A Decision-Making Perspective*, Routledge.

Byham, W. (1984) 'Assessing employees without resorting to a "centre"', *Personnel Management* (October):55.

Cahn, S.M. (ed.) (2002) *The Affirmative Action Debate*, 2nd edition, Routledge.

Cakar, F. and Bititci, U.S. (2001) *Human Resource Management as a Strategic Input to Manufacturing*, paper presented at the International Working Conference on Strategic Manufacturing, 26–29 August 2001, Aalborg, Denmark.

Caldwell, R. (2001) 'Champions, adapters, consultants and synergists: the new change agents in HRM', *Human Resource Management Journal* 11(3):39–52.

Callaghan, G. and Thompson, P. (2002) 'We recruit attitude': the selection and shaping of routine call centre labour', *Journal of Management Studies* 39(2):233–54.

Campbell, J.P., Dunnette, M., Lawler, E. and Weick, K. (1970) *Managerial Behavior, Performance and Effectiveness*, McGraw-Hill.

Cannadine, D. (1992) 'The present and the past in the English Industrial Revolution', in L.R. Berlanstein (ed.) *The Industrial Revolution and Work in Nineteenth-Century Europe*, Routledge.

Carmichael, F. and Woods, R. (2000) 'Ethnic penalties in unemployment and occupational attainment: evidence for Britain', *International Review of Applied Economics* 14(1):71–98.

Cascio, W.F. (1998) *Applied Psychology in Human Resource Management*, Prentice-Hall.

Catlin, K. and Matthews, J. (2001) *Leading at the Speed of Growth: Journey from Entrepreneur to CEO*, John Wiley & Sons.

Chaffee, E. (1985) 'Three models of strategy', *Academy of Management Review* 10(1):89–98.

Chan, A.W. and Snape, E. (2000) 'Union weakness in Hong Kong: workplace industrial relations and the federation of trade unions', *Economic and Industrial Democracy* 21(2):117–46.

Chandler, A. (1962) *Strategy and Structure*, MIT Press.

Cheal, D. (2002) *Aging and Demographic Change in a Canadian Context* (Trends Project), University of Toronto Press.

Checkland, P.B. (1981) *Systems Thinking, Systems Practice,* John Wiley and Sons.

Chiu, W.C.K., Chan, A.W., Snape, E. and Redman, T. (2001) 'Age stereotypes and discriminatory attitudes towards older workers: an East–West comparison', *Human Relations* 54(5):629–61.

Chung, T.Z. (1991) 'Culture: a key to management communication between the Asian-Pacific area and Europe', *European Management Journal* 9(4):419–24.

CIPD (2000) *Recruitment Survey Report 14*, June, Chartered Institute of Personnel and Development.

Clarke, A.C. (1973) *Profiles of the Future: An Inquiry into the Limits of the Possible*, HarperCollins.

Claydon, T. (2001) 'Human resource management and the labour market', in I. Beardwell and L. Holden (eds) *Human Resource Management: A Contemporary Approach*, Pearson.

Clemente, M.N. and Greenspan, D.S. (1999) *Empowering Human Resources in the Merger and Acquisition Process: Guidance for HR Professionals in the Key Areas of M&A Planning and Integration*, Clemente, Greenspan and Co.

Clements, P. and Jones, J. (2002) *The Diversity Training Handbook,* Kogan Page.

Conference Board (2002) Performance 2001: Productivity, Employment, and Income in the World's Economies, *Report No. 1313–02-RR*, The Conference Board.

Conlon, G. and Chevalier, A. (2002) *Rates of Return to Qualifications: A Summary of Recent Evidence*, Council for Industry and Higher Education.

Cooke, F.L. (2001) 'Human resource strategy to improve organizational performance: a route for firms in Britain?' *International Journal of Management Reviews* 3(4):321–39.

Cooke, W.N. (2001) 'The effects of labour costs and workplace constraints on foreign direct investment among highly industrialized countries', *International Journal of Human Resource Management* 12(5):697–716.

Corbridg, M. and Pilbeam, S. (1998) *Employment Resourcing*, Financial Times Pitman Publishing.

Corrall, S. (1999) 'Knowledge management: are we in the knowledge management business?' *Ariadne* (http://www.ariadne.ac.uk/issue18/knowledge-mgt/).

Cox, J. and Tapsell, J. (1991) *The Writing on the Wall: Graphology and its Validity in Personality Assessments'*, paper presented at the British Psychological Society Conference, Cardiff.

Cox, T. Jr, O'Neill, P.H. and Quinn, R.E. (2001) *Creating the Multicultural Organization: A Strategy for Capturing the Power of Diversity*, John Wiley & Sons.

Cressey, P. (1993) 'Employee participation', in M. Gold (ed.) *The Social Dimension: Employment Policy in the European Community*, Macmillan.

Crittan, P. (1993) *Investing in People: Towards Corporate Capability*, Butterworth-Heinemann.

Crofts, A. (1991) 'Learning to lead', *Management Today* (June):68.

Cropanzano, R. (ed.) (2000) *Justice in the Workplace: From Theory to Practice,* Applied Psychology Series, Lawrence Erlbaum Associates Inc.

Crouch, C. (2000) 'The snakes and ladders of 21st-century trade unionism', *Oxford Review of Economic Policy* 16(1):70–83.

Croucher, R. and Druker, J. (2001) 'Decision-taking on human resource issues', *Employee Relations* 23(1):55–74.

Cully, M., Woodland, S., O'Reilly, A. and Dix, G. (1999) *Britain at Work*, Routledge.

Cunha, R.C. and Cooper, C.L. (2002) 'Does privatization affect corporate culture and employee wellbeing?' *Journal of Managerial Psychology* 17(1):21–49.

Curran, J. and Stanworth, J. (1988) 'The small firm: a neglected area of management', in A.G. Cowling, M.J.K. Stanworth, R.D. Bennett, J. Curran and P. Lyons (eds) *Behavioural Science for Managers*, 2nd edition, Edward Arnold.

Daft, R.L. (2000) *Organization Theory and Design*, 7th edition, South-Western College Publishing.

Dar, A. and Tzannatos, Z. (1999) 'Active labor market programs: a review of the evidence based on evaluations', *Social Protection Discussion Paper 9901*, World Bank.

Davenport, T.H. and Prusak, L. (2000) *Working Knowledge*, Harvard Business School Press.

Davidson, M.J. and Earnshaw, J. (1991) 'Policies, pracrices and attitudes towards sexual harassment in UK organizations', *Women in Management Review and Abstracts* 6(6):15–21.

Davison, H.K. and Burke, M.J. (2000) 'Sex discrimination in simulated employment contexts: a meta-analytic investigation', *Journal of Vocational Behavior* 56(2):225–48.

Deal, T. and Kennedy, A. (1982) *Corporate Cultures: The Rites and Rituals of Corporate Life*, Addison-Wesley.

Dean, P. (1998) 'Editorial: action learning and performance improvement', *Performance Improvement Quarterly* 11(1):3.

Deery, S., Iverson, R. and Erwin, P. (1999) 'Industrial relations climate, attendance behaviour and the role of trade unions', *British Journal of Industrial Relations* 37(4):533–58.

Deery, S., Walsh, J. and Knox, A. (2001) 'The non-union workplace in Australia: bleak house or human resource innovator?' *International Journal of Human Resource Management* 12(4):669–83.

Delery, J.E. and Doty, D.H. (1996) 'Modes of theorizing in strategic human resource management: Tests of universalistic, contingency, and configurational performance predictions', *Academy of Management Journal* 39(4):802–35.

Dibble, S. (1999) *Keeping Your Valuable Employees: Retention Strategies for Your Organization's Most Important Resource*, John Wiley & Sons.

Dicken, P. (1998) *Global Shift: Transforming the World Economy*, 3rd edition, The Guilford Press.

Dineen, B.R., Ash, S.R. and Noe, R.A. (2002) 'A web of applicant attraction: person–organization fit in the context of web-based recruitment', *Journal of Applied Psychology* 87(4):723–34.

Dipboye, R.L., Gaugler, B.B., Hayes, T.L. and Parker, D. (2001) 'The validity of unstructured panel interviews: more than meets the eye?' *Journal of Business and Psychology* 16(1):35–49.

Dominelli, L. (1992) 'An uncaring profession: an examination of racism in social work', in P. Braham, A. Rattansi and R. Skellington (eds) *Racism and Antiracism*, Sage.

Donaldson, T. and Preston, L.E. (1995) 'The stakeholder theory of the corporation', *Academy of Management Review* 20:65–91.

Donnelly, E. (2001) 'Borrowing from Europe? Employers' views on associability and collective bargaining reform in the new South Africa', *International Journal of Human Resource Management* 12(4):551–67.

Dowling, P., Welch, D.E. and Schuler, R.S. (1998) *International Human Resource Management: Managing People in a Multinational Context*, South-Western Publishing.

Drenth, P. (1978) 'Personnel selection', in P.B. Warr (ed.) *Psychology at Work*, 2nd edition, Penguin.

Drucker, P. (1998) 'The coming of the new organization' in *The Harvard Business Review on Knowledge Management* (Harvard Business Review Series), Harvard University Press.

Due, J., Madsen, J.S. and Jense, C.S. (1991) 'The social dimension: convergence or diversification of industrial relations in the single European market?' *Industrial Relations Journal* 22(2):85–102.

Dulewicz, V. (1991) 'Improving assessment centres', *Personnel Management* (June):50–5.

Duncan, C. (2001) 'The impact of two decades of reform of British public sector industrial relations', *Public Money and Management* 21(1):27–34.

Economic Research Forum (2000) *MENA Trends 2000*, Economic Research Forum.

Edenborough, R. (2002) *Effective Interviewing*, Kogan Page.

Eder, R. and Harris, M. (1999) 'Employment interview research: historical update and introduction,' in R. Eder and M. Harris (eds) *The Employment Interview Handbook*, Sage Publications.

Eiser, J.R. (1994) *Attitudes, Chaos and the Connectivist Mind*, Blackwell.

Elangovan, A.R. (2001) 'Causal ordering of stress, satisfaction and commitment, and intention to quit: a structural equations analysis', *Leadership and Organization Development Journal* 22(4):159–65.

Elkjaer, B. (2001) 'The learning organization: an undelivered promise', *Management Learning* 32(4):437–52.

Ellinger, A.D., Ellinger, A.E., Yang, B. and Howton, S.W. (2002) 'The relationship between the learning organization concept and firms' finanacial performance: An empirical assessment', *Human Resource Development Quarterly* 13(1):5–21.

Elvira, M.M. and Zatzick, C.D. (2002) 'Who's displaced first? The role of race in layoff decisions', *Industrial Relations* 41(2):329–61.

English, G. (1991) 'Tuning up for performance management', *Training and Development Journal* (April):56–60.

Entrekin, L. and Chung, Y.W. (2001) 'Attitudes towards different sources of executive appraisal: a comparison of Hong Kong Chinese and American managers in Hong Kong', *International Journal of Human Resource Management* 12(6):965–87.

Esping-Andersen, G. and Regini, M. (eds) (2000) *Why Deregulate Labour Markets?*, Oxford University Press.

Evans, A. (2001) *Staff Recruitment and Retention*, Chandos Publishing.

Evans, P., Pucik, V. and Barsoux, J-L. (2002) *The Global Challenge: Frameworks for International Human Resource Management*, Irwin/McGraw-Hill.

Ewing, K. (1999) 'Freedom of association and the Employment Relations Act 1999', *Industrial Law Journal* 28(4):283–98.

Faulkner, D., Pitkethly, R. and Child, J. (2002) 'International mergers and acquisitions in the UK 1985–94: a comparison of national HRM practices', *International Journal of Human Resource Management* 13(1):106–22.

Fayol, H. (1949) *General and Industrial Management*, Pitman.

Feather, N.T. (2002) 'Values and value dilemmas in relation to judgments concerning outcomes of an industrial conflict', *Personality and Social Psychology Bulletin* 28(4):446–59.

Fenton-O'Creevy, M. (2001) 'Employee involvement and the middle manager: saboteur or scapegoat?' *Human Resource Management Journal* 11(1):24–40.

Ferris, G.R., Hochwarter, W.A., Buckley, M.R., Harrell-Cook, G. and Frink, D.D. (1999) 'Human resources management: some new directions', *Journal of Management* 25(3):385–415.

Fisher, K. (1999) *Leading Self-Directed Work Teams*, McGraw-Hill.

Fishlow, A. and Parker, K. (eds) (1999) *Growing Apart: The Causes and Consequences of Global Wage Inequality*, Council on Foreign Relations.

Fitz-Enz, J. (1994) *How To Measure Human Resource Management*, 2nd edition (McGraw-Hill Training Series), McGraw-Hill.

Fitz-Enz, J. and Davison, B. (2001) *How to Measure Human Resource Management*, 3rd edition, McGraw-Hill.

Flamholtz, E.G. and Randle, Y. (2000) *Growing Pains: Transitioning from an Entrepreneurship to a Professionally Managed Firm*, Jossey-Bass.

Flanders, A. (1970) *Management and Unions*, Faber & Faber.

Flecker, J. and Schulten, T. (1999) 'The end of institutional stability: what future for the 'German model'? *Economic and Industrial Democracy* 20(1):81–115.

Fletcher, C. (2001) 'Performance appraisal and management: the developing research agenda', *Journal of Occupational and Organizational Psychology* 74(4):473–87.

Fletcher, C. and Williams, R. (1992) 'The route to performance management', *Personnel Management* (October):42–7.

Foley, P. and Green, H. (eds) (1989) *Small Business Success*, Paul Chapman Publishing.

Foote, D. (2001) 'The question of ethical hypocrisy in human resource management in the U.K. and Irish charity sectors', *Journal of Business Ethics* 34(1):25–38.

Forbes, R. (1996) 'Performance management', *HR Monthly*, November 1996, Australian Human Resource Institute.

Ford, T.E. (2000) 'Effects of sexist humor on tolerance of sexist events', *Personality and Social Psychology Bulletin* 26(9):1094–107.

Forrant, R. (2000) 'Between a rock and a hard place: US industrial unions, shop-floor participation and the lean, mean global economy', *Cambridge Journal of Economics* 24(6):751–69.

Fossum, J. and Fitch, M. (1985) 'The effects of individual and contextual attributes on the sizes of recommended salary increases', *Personnel Psychology* 38 (autumn):587–602.

Foucault, M. (1977) *Discipline and Punish*, Allen Lane.

Fowler, A. (1987) 'When chief executives discover HRM', *Personnel Management* (January):3.

Fowler, A. (1991) 'How to identify training needs', *Personnel Management Plus* (November):22.

Fowler, A. (1993) 'How to manage cultural change', *Personnel Management Plus* (November):25–6.

Frazer, R.A. and Wiersma, J.J. (2001) 'Prejudice versus discrimination in the employment interview: we may hire equally, but our memories harbour prejudice', *Human Relations* 54(2):173–91.

Fredman, S. (2001) 'Equality: a new generation?' *Industrial Law Journal* 30(2):145–68.

French, W.L. and Bell, C.H. (1990) *Organization Development: Behavioral Science Interventions for Organization Improvement*, 4th edition, Prentice-Hall.

Fritz, R. (1996) *Corporate Tides: The Inescapable Laws of Organizational Structure*, Berrett-Koehler.

Fullan, M. (2001) *Leading in a Culture of Change*, Jossey-Bass.

Furnham, A. (1990) *The Protestant Work Ethic: The Psychology of Work-related Beliefs and Behaviours*, Routledge.

Furnham, A. (1992) *Personality at Work*, Routledge.

Gahan, P.G. (2002) 'What do unions maximise? Evidence from survey data', *Cambridge Journal of Economics* 26(3):279–97.

Galbraith, J.K. (1967) *The New Industrial State*, H. Hamilton.

Gardiner, G.A. (1923) *Life of George Cadbury*, Cassell.

Gardner, T.M., Wright, P.M. and Gerhart, B.A. (2000) 'The HR-firm relationship: can it be in the mind of the beholder?' *CAHRS Working Paper 00–02*, Cornell University.

Garrahan, P. and Stewart, P. (1992) *The Nissan Enigma: Flexibility at Work in the Local Economy*, Mansell.

Garvin, D. (1993) 'Building a learning organization', *Harvard Business Review* (July–August):78–91.

Gatewood, R. and Field, H. (2000) *Human Resource Selection*, 5th edition, Thomson Learning.

Gaugler, E. (1988) 'HR management: an international comparison', *Personnel* (August):24–30.

Geary, J.F. and Roche, W.K. (2001) 'Multinationals and human resource practices in Ireland: a rejection of the 'new conformance thesis'', *International Journal of Human Resource Management* 12(1):109–27.

Gibb, S. (2000) 'Evaluating HRM effectiveness: the stereotype connection', *Employee Relations* 22(1):58–75.

Gibb, S. (2001) 'The state of human resource management: evidence from employees' views of HRM systems and staff', *Library Review* 23(4):318–36.

Gibb, S. (2002) *Learning and Development: Processes, Practices and Perspectives at Work*, Palgrave/Macmillan.

Giddens, A. (1989) *Sociology*, Polity Press.

Giles, E. and Williams, R. (1991) 'Can the personnel department survive quality management?', *Personnel Management* (April): 23–33.

Gill, C. and Krieger, H. (1999) 'Direct and representative participation in Europe: recent survey evidence', *International Journal of Human Resource Management* 10(4):572–91.

Gill, S. and Davidson, M.J. (2001) 'Problems and pressures facing lone mothers in management and professional occupations – a pilot study', *Women in Management Review* 16(8):383–99.

Glover, J. (1988) *I: The Philosophy and Psychology of Personal Identity*, Penguin.

Gold, M. (1993) 'Overview of the social dimension', in M. Gold (ed.) *The Social Dimension: Employment Policy in the European Community*, Macmillan.

Gollan, P.J. (1999) 'Tunnel vision: non-union employee representation at Eurotunnel', *Employee Relations* 23(4):376–400.

Gollan, P.J. (2002) 'So what's the news? Management strategies towards non-union employee representation at News International', *Industrial Relations Journal* 33(4):316–31.

Goltz, J. (1998) *The Street Smart Entrepreneur: 133 Tough Lessons I Learned the Hard Way*, LPC.

Gomez, R., Gunderson, M. and Luchak, A. (2002) 'Mandatory retirement: a constraint in transitions to retirement?' *Employee Relations* 24(4):403–22.

Goss, D. (1994) *Principles of Human Resource Management*, Routledge.

Gotsi, M. and Wilson, A. (2001) 'Corporate reputation management: "living the brand"', *Management Decision* 39(2):99–104.

Graham, H.T. and Bennett, R. (1992) *Human Resources Management*, 7th edition, M&E Handbook Series, Pitman.

Graham, M and Lennon, J.J. (2002) 'The dilemma of operating a strategic approach to human resource management in the Scottish visitor attraction sector', *International Journal of Contemporary Hospitality Management* 14(5):213–20.

Grant, R.M. (1997) 'The knowledge-based view of the firm: Implications for management practice', *Long Range Planning*, 30(3):450–4.

Greenwood, M.R. (2002) 'Ethics and HRM: a review and conceptual analysis', *Journal of Business Ethics* 36(3):261–78.

Gregory, M., Salverda, W. and Bazen, S. (eds) *Labour Market Inequalities: Problems and Policies of Low-Wage Employment in an International Perspective*, Oxford University Press (2000).

Griffin, R.W. and Bateman, T.S. (1986) 'Job satisfaction and organizational commitment' in C.L. Cooper and I.T. Robertson (eds) *International Review of Industrial and Organizational Psychology*, 1986, John Wiley.

Grint, K. (1995) *Management: A Sociological Introduction*, Polity Press.

Grubb, D., Lippoldt, D. and Tergeist, P. (2001) *Innovations in Labour Market Policies: The Australian Way*, OECD.

Guest, D. (1987) 'Human resource management and industrial relations', *Journal of Management Studies* 24(5):503–21.

Guest, D. (1989) 'Personnel and HRM: can you tell the difference?', *Personnel Management* (January):48–51.

Guest, D. (1992) 'Right enough to be dangerously wrong: an analysis of the In Search of Excellence phenomenon', in G. Salaman (ed.) *Human Resource Strategies*, Sage.

Guest, D. (1993) 'Current perspectives on human resource management in the United Kingdom', in J. Storey (ed.) *Human Resource Management: A Critical Text*, Routledge.

Guest, D. and Hoque, K. (1993) 'The mystery of the missing human resource manager', *Personnel Management* (June):40–1.

Guest, D.E. (2001) 'Human resource management: when research confronts theory', *International Journal of Human Resource Management* 12(7):1092–106.

Guest, D.E. and Conway, N. (2002) 'Communicating the psychological contract: an employer perspective', *Human Resource Management Journal* 12(2):22–38.

Gunnigle, P., Flood, P., Morley, M. and Turner, T. (1994) *Continuity and Change in Irish Employee Relations*, Oak Tree Press.

Gunnigle, P., MacCurtain, S. and Morley, M. (2001) 'Dismantling pluralism: industrial relations in Irish greenfield sites', *Personnel Review* 30(3):263–79.

Gunz, H. (1989) 'The dual meaning of managerial careers: organizational and individual levels of analysis', *Journal of Management Studies* 26(3): 225–50.

Gurkov, I. (2002) 'Innovations and legacies in Russian human resource management practices: surveys of 700 chief executive officers', *Post-Communist Economies* 14(1):137–44.

Hackett, P. (1998) *The Selection Interview*, CIPD.

Hailey, V.H. (2001) 'Breaking the mould? Innovation as a strategy for corporate renewal', *International Journal of Human Resource Management* 12(7):1126–40.

Haire, M. (1959) 'Psychological problems relevant to business and industry', *Psychological Bulletin* 56:169–94.

Haire, M., Ghiselli, E.E. and Porter, L.W. (1966) *Managerial Thinking: An International Study*, John Wiley.

Hamblin, A.C. (1974) *Evaluation and Control of Training*, McGraw-Hill.

Hammer, M. (1990) 'Reengineering work: don't automate, obliterate', *Harvard Business Review* (November–December): 119–31.

Hammer, M. (2001) *The Agenda: What Every Business Must Do to Dominate the Decade*, Crown Publications.

Hammer, M. and Champy, J. (1993) *Re-engineering the Corporation: A Manifesto for Business Revolution*, Harper Business.

Hammond, K.H. (2001) 'Michael Porter's Big Ideas', *Fast Company* 44:150.

Hammond, V. (1993) 'Women and development', *Training and Development* (December):10–11.

Hancke, B. (2000) 'European works councils and industrial restructuring in the european motor industry', *European Journal of Industrial Relations* 6(1):35–59.

Handy, C. (1989) *The Age of Unreason*, Business Books.

Handy, C. (1993) *Understanding Organizations*, 4th edition, Oxford University Press.

Handy, C. (2002) *The Future of Work*, Blackwell.

Hansen, L. (2002) 'Rethinking the industrial relations tradition from a gender perspective: an invitation to integration', *Employee Relations* 24(2):190–210.

Hanson, P. (2001) *The M&A Transition Guide: A 10-Step Roadmap for Workforce Integration*, John Wiley & Sons.

Harbridge, R. and Walsh, P. (2002) 'Globalisation and labour market deregulation in Australia and New Zealand: different approaches, similar outcomes', *Employee Relations* 24(4):423–36.

Harfield, T. (1998) 'Strategic management and Michael Porter: a postmodern reading', http://www.mngt.waikato.ac.nz/depts/sml/journal/special/harfield.htm

Harley, B. (1999) 'The myth of empowerment: work organisation, hierarchy and employee autonomy in contemporary Australian workplaces', *Work, Employment and Society* 13(1):41–66.

Harper, B. (2000) 'Beauty, stature and the labour market: a British cohort study', *Oxford Bulletin of Economics and Statistics* 62(1):771–800.

Harper, B. and Haq, M. (2001) 'Ambition, discrimination, and occupational attainment: a study of a British cohort', *Oxford Economic Papers* 53(4):695–720.

Harris, L. (2000) 'Rewarding employee performance: line managers' values, beliefs and perspectives', *International Journal of Human Resource Management* 12(7):1182–92.

Hart, R.A. and Kawasaki, S. (1999) *Work and Pay in Japan*, Cambridge University Press.

Harvey, M. (2002) 'Human resource management in Africa: Alice's adventures in wonderland', *International Journal of Human Resource Management* 13(7):1119–45.

Haslam, N. and Baron, J. (1994) 'Intelligence, personality, and prudence' Sternberg, R.J. and Ruzgis, P. (eds) in *Personality and Intelligence*, Cambridge University Press.

Hassel, A. (1999) 'The erosion of the German system of industrial relations', *British Journal of Industrial Relations* 37(3):483–505.

Haynes, P. and Allen, M. (2001) 'Partnership as union strategy: a preliminary evaluation', *Employee Relations* 23(2):164–93.

Heasman, K. (1993) 'The case against ageism', *NATFHE Journal* (autumn):28.

Heeks, R. (1996) 'Global software outsourcing to India by multinational corporations', in P. Palvia, S.C. Palvia and E.M. Roche (eds) *Global Information Technology and Systems Management: Key Issues and Trends*, Ivy League Publishing.

Heery, E. and Salmon, J. (2000) 'The insecurity thesis' in E. Heery and J. Salmon (eds) *The Insecure Workforce*, Routledge.

Hegewisch, A. and Brewster, C. (1993) *European Developments in Human Resource Management*, Kogan Page.

Hellgren, J. and Sverke, M. (2001) 'Unionized employees' perceptions of role stress and fairness during organizational downsizing: consequences for job satisfaction, union satisfaction and well-being', *Economic and Industrial Democracy* 22(4):543–67.

Helman, C.G. (1990) *Culture, Health and Illness*, 2nd edition, Butterworth-Heinemann.

Helper, S., Levine, D.I. and Bendoly, E. (2002) 'Employee involvement and pay at US and Canadian auto suppliers', *Journal of Economics and Management Strategy* 11(2):329–77.

Hempel, P.S. (2001) 'Differences between Chinese and Western managerial views of performance', *Personnel Review* 30(2):203–26.

Hendry, C. (1994) 'The Single European Market and the HRM response', in P.S. Kirkbride (ed.) *Human Resource Management: Perspectives for the 1990s*, Routledge.

Hendry, C. (1995) *Human Resource Management: A Strategic Approach to Employment*, Butterworth-Heinemann.

Heneman, R.L., Tansky, J.W., Camp, S.M. (2000) 'Human resource management practices in small and medium-sized enterprises: Unanswered questions and future research perspectives', *Entrepreneurship Theory and Practice* 25(1):11–26.

Herriot, P. and Fletcher, C. (1990) 'Candidate-friendly selection for the 1990s', *Personnel Management* (February):32–5.

Hertz, N. (2002) *The Silent Takeover: Global Capitalism and the Death of Democracy,* Free Press.

Hetrick, S. (2002) 'Transferring HR ideas and practices: globalization and convergence in Poland', *Human Resource Development International* 5(3):333–51.

Hinton, P.R. (1993) *The Psychology of Interpersonal Perception*, Routledge.

Hitzeman, S.E. (1997) *The Strategic Positioning of Today's Benefit Department*, IAHRM.

Hodgkinson, G.P. and Sparrow, P.R. (2002) *Re-framing Strategic Competence: A Psychological Perspective on the Strategic Management Process*, paper presented at the Strategy World Congress, Said Business School, University of Oxford, 18–19 March 2002.

Hofstede, G. (1980) *Culture's Consequences: International Differences in Work-Related Values*, Sage.

Hofstede, G. (1991) *Cultures and Organizations*, McGraw-Hill.

Hofstede, G. (1994) *Cultures and Organizations*, HarperCollins (amended paperback edition of the 1991 McGraw-Hill publication).

Hofstede, G. and Bond, M.H. (1988) 'The Confucius connection: from cultural roots to economic growth', *Organizational Dynamics*, 16(4):4–21.

Holden, L. (2001) 'Employee involvement and empowerment', in I. Beardwell and L. Holden (eds) *Human Resource Management: A Contemporary Approach*, 3rd edition, Financial Times/ Prentice-Hall.

Hollinsead, G. and Leat, M. (1995) *Human Resource Management: An International and Comparative Perspective*, Pitman.

Holloway, W. (1991) *Work Psychology and Organizational Behaviour: Managing the Individual at Work*, Sage Publications.

Holman, D., Chissick, C. and Totterdell, P. (2002) 'The effects of performance monitoring on emotional labor and well-being in call centers', *Motivation and Emotion* 26(1):57–81.

Holmes, T.H. and Rahe, R.H. (1967) 'The social readjustment rating scale', *Journal of Psychosomatic Research* 11:213–8.

Hoque K. and Noon M. (2001) 'Counting angels: a comparison of personnel and HR specialists', *Human Resource Management Journal* 11(3):5–22.

Hornaday, R.W. (1990) 'Dropping the E-word from small business research', *Journal of Small Business Research* (October):22–33.

Horwitz, F.M. and Smith, D.A. (1998) 'Flexible work practices and human resource management: a comparison of South African and foreign-owned companies, *International Journal of Human Resource Management*, 9:4.

Horwitz, F.M., Browning, V., Jain, H. and Steenkamp, A.J. (2002) 'Human resource practices and discrimination in South Africa: overcoming the apartheid legacy', *International Journal of Human Resource Management* 13(7):1105–18.

Howell, C. (2000) 'From New Labour to no labour? The industrial relations project of the Blair government', *New Political Science* 22(2):201–29.

Howitt, D. and Owusu-Bempah, J. (1990) 'Racism in a British journal', *Psychologist* (September):396–9.

Hoxie, R.F. (1923) *Trade Unionism in the United States*, 2nd edition, Appleton-Century Crofts; reproduced in W.E.J. McCarthy (ed.) (1972) *Trade Unions*, Penguin.

Huang, T-C. (2000) 'Are the human resource practices of effective firms distinctly different from those of poorly performing ones? Evidence from Taiwanese enterprises', *International Journal of Human Resource Management* 11(2):436–51.

Huczynski, A. and Buchanan, D. (2000) *Organizational Behaviour: An Introductory Text*, 4th edition, FT Prentice-Hall.

Hughes, J.M.C. (2002) 'HRM and universalism: is there one best way?' *International Journal of Contemporary Hospitality Management* 14(5):221–8.

Hui, C.H. (1990) 'Work attitudes, leadership styles, and managerial behaviours in different cultures', in R.W. Brislin (ed.) *Applied Cross-Cultural Psychology*, Sage.

Hursthouse, P. and Kolb, D. (2001) 'Cultivating culture in greenfields: The Heinz Wattie's case', *Personnel Review* 30(3):317–30.

Husband, C. (1991) *Race, Conflictual Politics and Anti-racist Social Work: Lessons From the Past for Action in the 90s*, Northern Curriculum Development Project Setting the Context for Change, Central Council for Education and Training in Social Work, Leeds.

Hutri, M. and Lindeman, M. (2002) 'The role of stress and negative emotions in an occupational crisis', *Journal of Career Development* 29(1):19–36.

Huysman, M. (2000) 'An organizational learning approach to the learning organization', *European Journal of Work and Organizational Psychology* 9(2):133–45.

Huzzard, T. (2001) 'Discourse for normalizing what? – The learning organization and the workplace trade union response', *Economic and Industrial Democracy* 22(3):407–31.

Hyman, R. (1988) 'Flexible specialization: miracle or myth?' in R. Hyman and W. Streek (eds) *New Technology and Industrial Relations*, Blackwell.

Ichniowski, C., Kochan, T.A., Levine, D.I., Olson, C. and Strauss, G. (2000) 'What works at work: overview and assessment', in C. Icniowski, T.A. Kochan, D.I. Levine, C. Olson and G. Strauss (eds) *The American Workplace: Skills, Compensation, and Employee Involvement*, Cambridge University Press.

Iles, P. (2001) 'Employee resourcing' in J. Storey (ed.) *Human Resource Management: A Critical Text*, 2nd edition, Thomson Learning.

Iles, P. and Mabey, C. (1992) 'Personnel strategies', in G. Salaman (ed.) *Human Resource Strategies*, Sage.

Iles, P. and Salaman, G. (1995) 'Recruitment, selection and assessment' in J. Storey (ed.) *Human Resource Management: A Critical Text*, Routledge.

IMF (1999) *World Economic Outlook*, October, International Monetary Fund.

Industrial Society (2000) *Experience Necessary: The Business Case for Wisdom*, Industrial Society.

Industrial Society (2001) *Valuing Diversity: Managing Best Practice 78*, Industrial Society.

Institute of Work Psychology (2001) *What is a High-performance Work System*, University of Sheffield.

International Labour Organization (2000) *Decent Work and Poverty Reduction in the Global Economy*, paper submitted by the International Labour Office to the Second Session of the Preparatory Committee for the Special Session of the General Assembly on the Implementation of the Outcome of the World Summit for Social Development and Further Initiatives, April 2000.

IRS (1997) 'The state of selection: an IRS survey', *Employee Development Bulletin*, 85, Industrial Relations Services.

Isaac, J.E. (2001) 'Performance related pay: the importance of fairness', *The Journal of Industrial Relations* 43(2):111–23.

Jackson, G. (1998) 'Globalization, wages, jobs and myths', *The New Australian*, 60:6–12.

Jacobi, O. and Muller-Jentsch (1990) 'West Germany: continuity and structural change', in G. Baglioni and C. Crouch (eds) *European Industrial Relations: The Challenge of Flexibility*, Sage.

Jacoby, S.M. (2001) 'Unnatural extinction: the rise and fall of the independent local union', *Industrial Relations* 40(3):377–404.

Jacques, R. (1997) 'Review of *Early Management Thought*, D.A. Wren (ed.), Dartmouth', *Electronic Journal of Radical Organisation Theory*, III(2):http://www.mngt.waikato.ac.nz/depts/sml/journal/vol3_2/jacques.htm.

Jenkins, A. (2001) *Companies' Use of Psychometric Testing and the Changing Demand for Skills: A Review of the Literature*, Centre for the Economics of Education, London School of Economics and Political Science.

Johnson, S. (2002) 'Card check or mandatory representation vote? How the type of union recognition procedure affects union certification success.' *Economic Journal* (April):344–61.

Johnson, G. and Scholes, K. (1984) *Exploring Corporate Strategy*, Prentice-Hall.

Kahn, H. (1979) *World Economic Development: 1979 and Beyond*, Westview.

Kakabadse, A. and Kakabadse, N. (2002) *Smart Sourcing: International Best Practice,* St. Martin's Press.

Kamel, R. and Hoffman, A. (eds) (1999) *The Maquiladora Reader: Cross-Border Organizing Since NAFTA,* American Friends Service Committee.

Kanai, A. and Wakabayashi, M. (2001) 'Workaholism among Japanese blue-collar employees', *International Journal of Stress Management* 8(2):129–45.

Kandola, R., Wood, R., Dholakia, B. and Keane, C. (2001) *The Graduate Recruitment Manual*, Gower Publishing Limited.

Kane, B., Crawford, J. and Grant, D. (1999) 'Barriers to effective HRM', *International Journal of Manpower*, 20(8):494–515.

Kanter, R.M. (1989) *When Giants Learn to Dance*, Simon and Schuster.

Keenoy, T. (1990) 'HRM: a case of the wolf in sheep's clothing', *Personnel Review* 19(2):3–9.

Keenoy, T. (1999) 'HRM as hologram: a polemic', *Journal of Management Studies* 36(1):1–23.

Keenoy, T. and Anthony, P.D. (1992) 'HRM: metaphor, meaning and morality', in P. Blyton and P. Turnbull (eds) *Reassessing Human Resource Management*, Sage.

Kelliher, C. and Riley, M. (2002) 'Making functional flexibility stick: an assessment of the outcomes for stakeholders', *International Journal of Contemporary Hospitality Management* 14(5):237–42.

Kellough, J.E. and Nigro, L.G. (2002) 'Pay for performance in Georgia state government: employee perspectives on GeorgiaGain after 5 years', *Review of Public Personnel Administration* 22(2):146–66.

Kessler, I. (1995) 'Reward systems', in J. Storey (ed.) *Human Resource Management: A Critical Text*, Routledge.

Kessler, I. (2001) 'Reward system choices', in J. Storey (ed.) *Human Resource Management: A Critical Text*, 2nd edition, Thomson Learning.

Kettley, P. (1996) *Personal Feedback: Cases in Point*, IES Report 326, Institute of Employment Studies.

Kettley, P. and Hirsh, W. (2000) *Learning from Cross-functional Teamwork*, IES Report 356, October, Institute of Employment Studies.

Khatri, N. and Budhwar, P.S. (2002) 'A study of strategic HR issues in an Asian context', *Personnel Review* 31(2):166–88.

Kinman, G. (2001) 'Pressure points: A review of research on stressors and strains in UK academics', *Educational Psychology* 21(4):473–92.

Kirkpatrick, D. (1994) *Evaluating Training Programs: The Four Levels*, Berrett-Koehler Publishers, Inc.

Kirton, G. and Greene, A. (2000) *Dynamics of Managing Diversity,* Butterworth-Heinemann.

Klikauer, T. (2002) 'Stability in Germany's industrial relations: a critique on Hassel's erosion thesis', *British Journal of Industrial Relations* 40(2):295–308.

Kline, B. (1993) *The Handbook of Psychological Testing*, Routledge.

Knapp, D.E. and Hart, C.W. (1999) *The Brand Mindset: Five Essential Strategies for Building Brand Advantage Throughout Your Company,* McGraw-Hill.

Kobayashi, N. (1992) 'Japan's global and regional roles', *Business and the Contemporary World* 4(4):18–24.

Kochan, T. and Dyer, L. (2001) 'HRM: an American view', in J. Storey (ed.) *Human Resource Management: A Critical Text*, Thomson Learning.

Koehoorn, M. and Lowe, G.S., Rondeau, K.V., Schellenberg, G. Wagar, T.H. (2002) 'Creating high-quality health care workplaces', *CPRN Discussion Paper No/W14*, Canadian Policy Research Networks.

Kram, K.E. (1983) 'Phases of the mentor relationship', *Academy of Management Journal* 26(4):608–25.

Kramer, L.A. and Lambert, S. (2001) 'Sex-linked bias in chances of being promoted to supervisor', *Sociological Perspectives* 44(1):111–27.

Kramer, S.N. (1963) *The Sumerians*, The University of Chicago Press.

Kraus, V. and Yonay, Y.P. (2000) 'The effect of occupational sex composition on the gender gap in workplace authority', *Social Science Research* 29(4):583–605.

Kuhn, P.J. (2002) *Losing Work, Moving On: International Perspectives On Worker Displacement,* W.E. Upjohn Institute.

Kuhn, T.S. (1962) *The Structure of Scientific Revolutions*, University of Chicago Press.

Kuruvilla, S. and Erickson, C.L. (2002) 'Change and transformation in Asian industrial relations', *Industrial Relations* 41(2):171–227.

Labovitz, G. and Rosansky, V. (1997) *The Power of Alignment: How Great Companies Stay Centered and Accomplish Extraordinary Things*, John Wiley & Sons.

Lancaster, L.C. and Stillman, D. (2002) *When Generations Collide*, Harper Business.

Lane, H.W., Distefano, J.J. and Maznevski, M.L. (1997) *International Management Behavior*, Blackwell.

Langtry, R. and Langtry, B. (1991) 'Why managers keep an eye on their image', *The Independent Business News*, 3 November.

Lapidus, J. and Figart, D.M. (1998) 'Remedying 'unfair acts': U.S. pay equity by race and gender', *Feminist Economics* 4(3):7–28.

Lappalainen, P. (2001) '*The Challenges Posed by the EU Anti-Discrimination Directives*', paper presented at the Sixth International Metropolis Conference, Workshop on Anti-discrimination legislation, 27 November 2001, Rotterdam, the Netherlands.

Lasserre, P. and Schutte, H. (1999) *Strategies for Asia Pacific: Beyond the Crisis*, Macmillan Business.

Laursen, K. (2002) 'The importance of sectoral differences in the application of complementary HRM practices for innovation performance', *International Journal of the Economics of Business* 9(1):139–56.

Lautenschlager, G.J. (1994) 'Accuracy and faking of background data', in G.A. Stokes, M.D. Mumford and W.A. Owens (eds) *Biodata Handbook*, Consulting Psychologists Press.

Lawler, Edward E., III (1991) *High-Involvement Management: Participative Strategies for Improving Organizational Performance*, Jossey-Bass.

Lawrence, A. (2000) 'Codetermination in post-apartheid South Africa?' *Politikon: South African Journal of Political Studies* 27(1):117–32.

Lawrence, P. (1993) 'Human resource management in Germany', in S. Tyson, P. Lawrence, P. Poirson, L. Manzolini and C.F. Vincente (eds) *Human Resource Management in Europe: Strategic Issues and Cases*, Kogan Page.

Lee, M. and Koh, J. (2001) 'Is empowerment really a new concept?' *International Journal of Human Resource Management* 12(4):684–95.

Leeds, C., Kirkbride, P.S. and Duncan, J. (1994) 'The cultural context of Europe: a tentative mapping', in P.S. Kirkbride (ed.) *Human Resource Management in Europe: Perspectives for the 1990s*, Routledge.

Legge, K. (1989) 'Human resource management: a critical analysis', in J. Storey (ed.) *New Perspectives in Human Resource Management*, Routledge.

Legge, K. (1995) *Human Resource Management: Rhetorics and Realities*, Macmillan Business.

Legge, K. (2001) 'Silver bullet or spent round? Assessing the meaning of the high commitment management/performance relationship', in J. Storey (ed.) *Human Resource Management: A Critical Text*, Thomson Learning.

Leibfried, S. and Pearson, P. (2000) 'Social policy: left to courts and markets?' in H. Wallace and W. Wallace (eds) *Policy-Making in the European Union*, Oxford University Press.

Lengnick-Hall, C.A. and Lengnick-Hall, M.L. (1988) 'Strategic HRM: a review of the literature and a proposed typology', *Academy of Management Review* 13(3):454–70.

LePla, F.J. and Parker, L.M. (1999) *Integrated Branding: Becoming Brand-Driven Through Companywide Action*, Quorum Books.

Lesonsky, R. (2001) *Start Your Own Business: The Only Start-Up Book You'll Ever Need*, 2nd edition, Entrepreneur Media Inc.

Lewis, C. (1985) *Employee Selection*, Hutchinson.

Lewis, P. (1991) 'Eight steps to the successful appointment of a training consultant', *Journal of European Industrial Training* 15(6):25–9.

Lewis, R.D. (2000) *When Cultures Collide*, Nicholas Brealey.

Lindbeck, A. and Snower, D. (1988) *The Insider-Outsider Theory of Unemployment and Employment*, MIT Press.

Lingard, H. and Sublet, A. (2002) 'The impact of job and organizational demands on marital or relationship satisfaction and conflict among Australian civil engineers', *Construction Management and Economics* 20(6):507–21.

London, M. and Stumpf, S.A. (1984) *Managing Careers*, Addison-Wesley.

Loretto, W., Duncan, C. and White, P.J. (2000) 'Industrial relations codes of practice: the 1999 Age Discrimination Code in context', *Employee Relations* 22(2):146–63.

Lu, L., Kao, S-F., Cooper, C.L. and Spector, P.E. (2000) 'Managerial stress, locus of control, and job strain in Taiwan and UK: a comparative study', *International Journal of Stress Management* 7(3):209–26.

Lucas, R. (2002) 'Fragments of HRM in hospitality? Evidence from the 1998 Workplace Employee Relations Survey', *International Journal of Contemporary Hospitality Management* 14(5):207–12.

Lyons, P. (1988) 'Social interaction', in A.G. Cowling, M.J.K. Stanworth, R.D. Bennett, J. Curran and P. Lyons (eds) *Behavioural Sciences for Managers*, 2nd edition, Edward Arnold.

Mabey, C., Salaman, G. and Storey, J. (eds) (1998) *Strategic Human Resource Management: A Reader*, The Open University/Sage.

Machiavelli, N. (1515/2003) *The Prince*, translated by George Bull, Penguin.

Mackay, J. (1992) 'Tying the knot: the human side of acquisitions', *Human Resources* (autumn):10–14.

Magnusson, L. and Ottosson, J. (eds) (2002) *Europe: One Labour Market (Work and Society)*, Peter Lang Publishing.

Malhotra, Y. (1998) 'Tools@work: deciphering the knowledge management hype', *Journal for Quality and Participation*, special issue on Learning and Information Management, 21(4):58–60.

Marchington, M. (2001) 'Employee involvement at work', in J. Storey (ed.) *Human Resource Management: A Critical Text*, 2nd edition, Thomson Learning.

Marchington, M. and Grugulis, I. (2000) '"Best practice" human resource management: perfect opportunity or dangerous illusion?' *International Journal of Human Resource Management* 11(6):1104–24.

Marcoux, A.M. (2000) 'Business ethics gone wrong', *CATO Policy Report*, CATO Institute, 24 July 2000.

Maresh, N. (1999) *ASTD Handbook of Training Design and Delivery*, 2nd edition, American Society for Training and Development.

Margerison, C. (1991) *Making Management Development Work*, McGraw-Hill.

Margerison, C. (2002) 'Careering ahead via work-based learning', *Training Journal*, October:24.

Marginson, P., Edwards, P., Martin, R., Purcell, J. and Sisson, K. (1988) *Beyond the Workplace: Managing Industrial Relations in the Multi-establishment Enterprise*, Blackwell.

Marginson, P., Edwards, P.K., Armstrong, P. and Purcell, J. (1993a) Executive Summary of Findings. *Second Company Level Industrial Relations Survey*, Industrial Relations Research Unit (mimeo).

Marginson, P., Edwards, P.K., Armstrong, P., Purcell, J. and Hubbard, N. (1993b) Report of the Initial Findings from the Second Company Level Industrial Relations Survey, *Warwick Papers in Industrial Relations*, no.45, University of Warwick.

Marquardt, M.J. and Revans, R. (1999) *Action Learning in Action: Transforming Problems and People for World-Class Organizational Learning*, Davies-Black Publishing.

Marsden, D., French, S. and Kobi, K. (2000) *Why Does Performance Pay Demotivate? Financial Incentives Versus Performance Appraisal*, Centre for Economic Performance, London School of Economics and Political Science.

Marti, M., Bobier, D. and Baron, R.S. (2000) 'Right before our eyes: the failure to recognize non-prototypical forms of prejudice', *Group Processes and Intergroup Relations* 3(4):403–18.

Martin, J.P. and Stancanelli, E. (2002) 'Tackling some myths about temporary jobs', *OECD Observer*, 26 June 2002.

Mason, P.L. (2000) 'Understanding recent empirical evidence on race and labor market outcomes in the USA', *Review of Social Economy* 58(3):319–38.

Matlay, H. (2002) 'Industrial relations in the SME sector of the British economy: an empirical perspective', *Journal of Small Business and Enterprise Development* 9(3):307–18.

Maurer, R. (1996) *Beyond the Wall of Resistance: Unconventional Strategies That Build Support for Change*, Bard Press.

Mayo, G.E. (1933) *The Human Problems of an Industrial Civilization*, Macmillan.

McCormick, E.J. and Ilgen, D. (1987) *Industrial and Organizational Psychology*, 8th edition, Unwin Hyman.

McGregor, D. (1960) *The Human Side of Enterprise*, McGraw-Hill.

McIlwee, T. and Roberts, I. (1991) *Human Resource Management*, Elm Publications.

McIntosh, T. (ed.) (2001) *Federalism, Democracy and Labour Market Policy in Canada* (Social Union Series), McGill-Queen's University Press.

McKenna, E. (1994) *Business Psychology and Organizational Behaviour*, Lawrence Erlbaum Associates.

Meek, V.L. (1988) 'Organizational culture: origins and weaknesses', *Organization Studies* 9(4):453–73.

Metcalf, D., Hansen, K. and Charlwood, A. (2001) 'Unions and the sword of justice: unions and pay systems, pay inequality, pay discrimination and low pay', *National Institute Economic Review* 176(1):61–75.

Metochi, M. (2002) 'The influence of leadership and member attitudes in understanding the nature of union participation', *British Journal of Industrial Relations* 40(1):87–111.

Michelson, G. and Mouly, S. (2000) 'Gender in organizational rumour and gossip: a conceptual study', *Management Decision* 38(5):339–46.

Michie, J. and Sheehan, M. (1999) 'HRM practices, R&D expenditure and innovative investment: evidence from the UK's 1990 Workplace Industrial Relations Survey (WIRS)', *Industrial and Corporate Change* 8(2):211–34.

Michie, J. and Sheehan-Quinn, M. (2001) 'Labour market flexibility, human resource management and corporate performance', *British Journal of Management* 12(4):287–306.

Milcovich, G.T., Newman, J.M. and Milcovich, C. (2001) *Compensation*, 7th edition, McGraw-Hill.

Miles, R. and Snow, C. (1978) *Organizational Strategy, Structure and Process*, McGraw-Hill.

Miles, R.E. and Snow, C.C. (1984) 'Designing strategic human resource systems', *Organizational Dynamics* (Summer):36–52.

Miller, A.F., Jnr and Hanson, M. (1991) 'The smile on the face of the leadership tiger', *Personnel Management* (October):54–7.

Miller, P. (1989) 'Managing corporate identity in the diversified business', *Personnel Management* (March):36–9.

Mills, A.J. and Murgatroyd, S.J. (1991) *Organizational Rules: A Framework for Understanding Organizational Action,* Open University.

Millward, N., Forth, J. and Bryson, A. (2000) *All Change at Work*, Routledge.

Mintzberg, H. (1983) *Structure in Fives: Designing Effective Organizations*, Prentice-Hall.

Mintzberg, H. (1994) *The Rise and Fall of Strategic Planning*, Prentice-Hall.

Mintzberg, H. and Waters, J.A. (1985) 'Of strategies deliberate and emergent', *Strategic Management Journal* 6:257–72.

Mintzberg, H., Ahlstrand, B. and Lampel, J. (1998) *Strategy Safari: A Guided Tour Through the Wilds of Strategic Management*, Free Press.

Misra, R. and Panigrahi, B. (1996) 'Effects of age on attitudes towards working women', *International Journal of Manpower* 17(2):3–17.

Molander, C. and Winterton, J. (1994) *Managing Human Resources*, Routledge.

Monks, K. (1996) *Roles in Personnel Management From Welfarism to Modernism: Fast Track or Back Track?* DCU Research Paper No.17, Dublin City University Business School.

Morgan, G. (1986) *Images of Organization*, Sage.

Morris, G.S. (2001) 'The Employment Relations Act 1999 and collective labour standards', *International Journal of Comparative Labour Law and Industrial Relations* 17(1):63–78.

Morris, L. (1987) 'The household in the labour market', in C.C. Harris (ed.) *Redundancy and Recession*, Blackwell.

Moscoso, S. (2000) 'Selection interview: a review of validity evidence, adverse impact and applicant reactions', *International Journal of Selection and Assessment* 8(4):237–47.

Mosel, J.N. and Goheen, H.W. (1958) 'The validity of the employment recommendation questionnaire in personnel selection', *Personnel Psychology* 2:487–90.

Moss, G. (1992) 'Different European perspectives on selection techniques: the case of graphology in business', in S. Vickerstaff (ed.) *Human Resource Management in Europe: Text and Cases*, Chapman & Hall.

Mowday, R., Steers, R. and Porter, L. (1979) 'The measurement of organizational commitment', *Journal of Vocational Behaviour* 14:224–47.

Moynahan, B. (1993) 'Creating harassment-free work zones', *Training and Development* (May):67–70.

Muller, M. (1999) 'Enthusiastic embrace or critical reception? The German HRM debate', *Journal of Management Studies* 36(4):465–82.

Mullins, L.J. (1996) *Management and Organisational Behaviour*, 4th edition, Pitman.

Murliss, H. (1987) 'Performance-related pay in the public sector', *Public Money* (March):29–33.

Murphy, K.R. (1994) 'Meta-analysis and validity generalization', in N. Anderson and P. Herriot (eds) *Assessment and Selection in Organizations: Methods and Practice for Recruitment and Appraisal*, First Update and Supplement 1994, Wiley.

Murphy, K.R. and Cleveland, J.N. (1995) *Understanding Performance Appraisal: Social, Organizational and Goal-based Perspectives*, Sage.

Murrell, K.L. and Meredith, M. (2000) *Empowering Employees*, McGraw-Hill.

Nadler, D.A., Gerstein, M.C., Shaw, R.B. and Associates (1992) *Organizational Architecture: Designs for Changing Organizations*, Jossey-Bass.

Nadler, L. and Nadler, Z. (1989) *Developing Human Resources*, Jossey-Bass.

Nadler, D. and Tushman, M.L. (1997) *Competing by Design: The Power of Organizational Architecture,* 2nd edition, Oxford University Press.

Naidoo, J. and Wills, J. (2000) *Health Promotion: Foundations for Practice*, 2nd edition, Balliere Tindall/RCN.

Nankervis, A., Compton, R. and Savery, L. (2002) 'Strategic HRM in small and medium enterprises: A CEO's perspective?' *Asia Pacific Journal of Human Resources* 40(2):260–73.

Needle, D. (1994) *Business in Context: An Introduction to Business and its Environment*, 2nd edition, Chapman and Hall.

Nelkin, D. and Tancredi, L. (1989) *Dangerous Diagnostics*, Basic Books.

Nelson L. and Holland P. (2002) 'Industrial relations 2001: A new spirit of compromise?' *Asia Pacific Journal of Human Resources* 40(2):246–59.

Noblet, A., Rodwell, J. and McWilliams, J. (2001) 'The job strain model is enough for managers: no augmentation needed', *Journal of Managerial Psychology* 16(8):635–49.

Noonan, C. (1985) *Practical Export Management: Developing International Business*, George Allen & Unwin.

Nowack, K.M. (1991) 'A true training needs analysis', *Training & Development Journal* (April):69–73.

Nowicki, M.D. and Rosse J.G. (2002) 'Managers' views of how to hire: building bridges between science and practice', *Journal of Business and Psychology* 17(2):157–70.

O'Dell, C.S. and Essaides, N. (1998) *If Only We Knew What We Know: The Transfer of Internal Knowledge and Best Practice*, Free Press.

O'Doherty, D. (1997) 'Human resource planning: control to seduction', in I. Beardwell and L. Holden (eds) *Human Resource Management: A Contemporary Perspective*, 2nd edition, Pitman Publishing.

O'Malley, M. (2000) *Creating Commitment: How to Attract and Retain Talented Employees by Building Relationships That Last*, John Wiley.

Olie, R. (1990) 'Culture and integration problems in international mergers and acquisitions', *European Management Journal* 8(2):206–15.

Osborne, R.L. and Cowen, S.S. (2002) 'High-performance companies: the distinguishing profile', *Management Decision* 40(3):227–31.

Ouchi, W. (1981) *Theory Z: How American Business Can Meet the Japanese Challenge*, Addison-Wesley.

Oxenbridge, S. and Brown, W. (2002) 'The two faces of partnership?: an assessment of partnership and co-operative employer/trade union relationships', *Employee Relations* 24(3):262–76.

Paauwe, J. and Williams, R. (2001) 'Management development revisited', *The Journal of Management Development* 20(2):180–91.

Paik, Y., Vance, C.M. and Stage, H.D. (2000) 'A test of assumed cluster homogeneity for performance appraisal management in four Southeast Asian countries', *International Journal of Human Resource Management* 11(4):736–50.

Palmer, C., Moon, G., Gill, T., Monaghan, K. and Stacey, M. (2002) *Discrimination Law Handbook*, Legal Action Group.

Papalexandris, N. (1991) 'A comparative study of human resource management in selected Greek and foreign-owned subsidiaries in Greece', in C. Brewster and S. Tyson (eds) *International Comparisons in Human Resource Management*, Pitman.

Papalexandris, N. and Chalikias, J. (2002) 'Changes in training, performance management and communication issues among Greek firms in the 1990s: intercountry and intracountry comparisons', *Journal of European Industrial Training* 26(7):342–52.

Parekh, B. (2000) *Commission on the Future of Multi-Ethnic Britain*, Runnymede Trust.

Pascale, R.T. and Athos, A.G. (1981) *The Art of Japanese Management*, Simon and Schuster.

Patel, D. (2002) *SHRM Workplace Forecast: A Strategic Outlook 2002–2003*, Society for Human Resource Management.

Patrickson, M. and Hartmann, L. (2001) 'Human resource management in Australia: prospects for the twenty-first century', *International Journal of Manpower* 22(3):198–206.

Pearson, R., Jagger, N., Connor, H. and Perryman, S. with de Grip, A., Marey, P. and Corvers, F. (2001) 'Assessing the supply and demand for scientists and technologists in Europe', *IES Report 377*, February 2001.

Peccei, R. and Rosenthal, P. (2001) 'Delivering customer-oriented behaviour through empowerment: an empirical test of HRM assumptions', *Journal of Management Studies* 38(6):831–857.

Pedler, M., Boydell, T.H. and Burgoyne, J.G. (1989) 'Towards a learning company', *Management Education and Development* 2(3):19–41.

Peetz, D. and Todd, P. (2001) 'Otherwise you're on your own': unions and bargaining in Malaysian banking', *International Journal of Manpower* 22(4):333–48.

Perkins, D. and Snapes, A. (1992) 'Developing the best managers: an assessment centre for general managers in the NHS', in S. Vickerstaff (ed.) *Human Resource Management in Europe: Text and Cases*, Chapman and Hall.

Perkins, S.J. and Banham J. (2000) *Globalization – The People Dimension: Human Resource Strategies for Global Expansion*, Kogan Page.

Peters, T.J. (1987) *Thriving on Chaos*, Alfred A. Knopf.

Peters, T.J. and Waterman, R.H. (1982) *In Search of Excellence*, Harper and Row.

Pettijohn, L.S., Parker, R.S., Pettijohn, C.E. and Kent O.L. (2001) 'Performance appraisals: usage, criteria and observation', *The Journal of Management Development* 20(9):754–71.

Pfeffer, J. (1998) *The Human Equation: Building Profits by Putting People First*, Harvard Business School Press.

Pheng, L.S. and Yuquan, S. (2002) 'An exploratory study of Hofstede's cross-cultural dimensions in construction projects', *Management Decision* 40(1):7–16.

Phillimore, J. (2000) 'The limits of supply-side social democracy: Australian labor, 1983–96', *Politics & Society* 28(4):557–87.

Philp, T. (1990) *Appraising Performance for Results*, McGraw-Hill.

Pieper, R. (ed.) (1990) *Human Resource Management: An International Comparison*, De Gruyter.

Pink, D. (2001) 'Who has the next big idea?' *Fast Company*, September, 50:108.

Pizzey, E., Shackleton, J.R. and Unwin, P. (2000) *Women or Men: Who are the Victims?*, CIVITAS: The Institute for the Study of Civil Society.

Poirson, P. (1993) 'The characteristics and dynamics of human resource management in France', in S. Tyson *et al.* (eds) (1993) *Human Resource Management in Europe*, Kogan Page.

Pollard, T.M. (2001) 'Changes in mental well-being, blood pressure and total cholesterol levels during workplace reorganization: the impact of uncertainty', *Work and Stress* 15(1):14–28.

Poole, M. (1990) 'Editorial: human resource management in an international perspective', *The International Journal of Human Resource Management* 1(1):1–16.

Porter, M. (1990) *The Competitive Advantage of Nations*, Free Press.

Porter, M.E. (1980) *Competitive Strategy: Techniques for Analyzing Industries and Competitors*, Free Press.

PPRU (1999) *Report for The Office of The Data Protection Registrar (UK)*, Personnel Policy Research Unit.

Pratt, K.J. and Bennett, S.G. (1989) *Elements of Personnel Management*, Chapman and Hall.

Price, A.J. (1997) *Human Resource Management in a Business Context*, Thomson Learning.

Price, A.J. (2000) *Principles of Human Resource Management: An Action-Learning Approach*, Blackwell.

Pringle, H. and Gordon, W. (2001) *Brand Manners: How to Create the Self Confident Organization to Live the Brand,* John Wiley.

Pun, K.F., Chin, K.S. and Gill, R. (2001) 'Determinants of employee involvement practices in manufacturing enterprises', *Total Quality Management* 12(1):95–109.

Purcell, J. (1989) 'The impact of corporate strategy on human resource management', in J. Storey (ed.) *New Perspectives on Human Resource Management*, Routledge.

Purcell, J. (1995) 'Corporate strategy and its link with human resource strategy', in J. Storey (ed.) *Human Resource Management: A Critical Text*, Routledge.

Purcell, J. (2001) 'The meaning of strategy in human resource management', in J. Storey (ed.) *Human Resource Management: A Critical Text*, 2nd edition, Thomson Learning.

Purcell, J. and Sisson, K. (1983) 'Strategies and practice in the management of industrial relations', in G.S. Bain (ed.) *Industrial Relations in Britain*, Blackwell.

Purcell, K. (2002) *Employers in the New Graduate Labour Market: Recruiting From a Wider Spectrum of Graduates*, Employment Studies Research Unit, University of the West of England.

Quince, T. (2001) *Entrepreneurial Collaboration: Terms of Endearment or Rules of Engagement*, Working Papers, ESRC Centre for Business Research, University of Cambridge.

Raelin, J.A. (1991) *The Clash of Cultures: Managers Managing Professionals*, 2nd edition, Harvard Business School.

Raia, A.P. (1974) *Managing by Objectives*, Scott, Foresman.

Raich, M. (2002) 'HRM in the knowledge-based economy: is there an afterlife?' *Journal of European Industrial Training* 26(6):269–73.

Rainbird, H. and Maguire, M. (1993) 'When corporate need supercedes employee development', Personnel Management (February):34–7.

Ramaswamy, E.A. and Schiphorst, F.B. (2000) 'Human resource management, trade unions and empowerment: two cases from India', *International Journal of Human Resource Management* 11(4):664–80.

Randlesome, C. (1994) *The Business Culture in Germany*, Butterworth-Heinemann.

Ransom, D. (1994) 'Maquila sunrise', *New Internationalist* 251:7.

Reed, S.F. and Lajoux, A.R. (1998) *The Art of M&A: A Merger, Acquisition, Buyout Guide*, 3rd edition, McGraw-Hill.

Reilly, P.A. (2001) *Flexibility at Work: Balancing the Interests of Employer and Employee*, Ashgate Publishing Company.

Revans, R.W. (1972) 'Action learning – a management development programme', *Personnel Review* (autumn).

Reynolds, P.D. (1994) *Reducing Barriers to New Firm Gestation: Prevalence and Success of Nascent Entrepreneurs*, paper presented at the Academy of Management, Dallas, Texas.

Reynolds, P.D. and White, S.B. (1997) *The Entrepreneurial Process: Economic Growth, Men, Women, and Minorities*, Greenwood Publishing Group.

Rhinesmith, S. (1996) *A Manager's Guide to Globalization*, McGraw-Hill.

Rice, A.K., Hull, J.M. and Trist, E.L. (1950) 'The representation of labour turnover as a social process', *Journal of Human Relations* 3.

Richard, O.C. and Johnson, N.B. (2001) 'Strategic human resource management effectiveness and firm performance', *International Journal of Human Resource Management* 12(2):299–310.

Rigby, M. and Aledo, M.L.M. (2001) 'The worst record in Europe? A comparative analysis of industrial conflict in Spain', *European Journal of Industrial Relations* 7(3):287–305.

Roberts, G. (1997) *Recruitment and Selection: A Competency Approach*, Chartered Institute of Personnel and Development.

Robertson, I.T. and Makin, P.J. (1986) 'Management selection in Britain: a survey and critique', *Journal of Occupational Psychology* 59(1):45–57.

Roche, B. (2000) 'The end of new industrial relations?' *European Journal of Industrial Relations* 6(3):261–82.

Roche, W.K. (2001) 'The individualization of Irish industrial relations?', *British Journal of Industrial Relations* 39(2):183–206.

Rodger, A. (1952) *The Seven Point Plan*, National Institute of Industrial Psychology.

Rondeau, K.V. and Wager, T.H. (2001) 'Impact of human resource management practices on nursing home performance', *Health Services Management Research* 14(3):192–202.

Ronen, S. and Shenkar, O. (1985) 'Clustering countries on attitudinal dimensions: a review and synthesis', *Academy of Management Review* 10(7):445–54.

Rosania, R.J. (2000) *The Credible Trainer*, American Society for Training and Development.

Rose, M. (1975) *Industrial Behaviour: Theoretical Developments Since Taylor*, Penguin.

Rosenbloom, J.S. (2001) *The Handbook of Employee Benefits*, 5th edition, McGraw-Hill.

Ross, R. and Schneider, R. (1992) *From Equality to Diversity: A Business Case for Equal Opportunities*, Pitman.

Rothwell, S. (1992) 'The development of the international manager', *Personnel Management* (January):33–5.

Rothwell, W.J. (1999) *The Action Learning Guidebook: A Real-Time Strategy for Problem Solving*, Jossey-Bass.

Rothwell, W.J., Prescott, R.K. and Taylor, M.W. (1998) *The Strategic Human Resource Leader: How to Prepare Your Organization for the Six Key Trends Shaping the Future*, Davies-Black Publications.

Rousseau, D.M. (1995) *Psychological Contracts in Organizations: Understanding Written and Unwritten Agreements*, Sage.

Rousseau, D.M. and Parks, J.M. (1993) 'The contracts of individuals and organizations', in L.L. Cummings and B.M. Staw (eds) *Research in Organizational Behavior, Volume 15*, JAI Press.

Rowden, R.W. (2001) 'Exploring methods to evaluate the return from training', *American Business Review* 19(1):6–12.

Rubery, J., Earnshaw, J., Marchington, M., Cooke, F.L. and Vincent, S. (2002) 'Changing organizational forms and the employment relationship', *Journal of Management Studies* 39(5):645–72.

Russell, C., Mattson, J., Devlin, S. and Atwater, D. (1990) 'Predictive validity of biodata items generated from retrospective life experience essays', *Journal of Applied Psychology* 75:569–80.

Rynes, S.L., Colbert, A.E. and Brown, K.G. (2002) '"HR Professionals" beliefs about effective human resource practices: correspondence between research and practice', *Human Resource Management* 41(2):149–74.

Sadler, P. and Milner, K. (1993) *The Talent-Intensive Organization: Optimising Your Company's Human Resource Strategies*, Economist Intelligence Unit.

Salaman, G. and Butler, J. (1994) 'Why managers won't learn', in C. Mabey and P. Iles (eds) *Managing Learning*, Routledge/Open University.

Salancik, G.R. (1977) 'Commitment and control of organizational behavior and beliefs', in B.M. Staw and G.R. Salancik (eds) *New Directions in Organizational Behavior*, St Clair Press.

Salgado, J.F. and Moscoso, S. (2002) 'Comprehensive meta-analysis of the construct validity of the employment interview', *European Journal of Work and Organizational Psychology* 11(3):299–324.

Sambrook, S. (2001) 'HRD as an emergent and negotiated evolution: an ethnographic case study in the British National Health Service', *Human Resource Development Quarterly* 12(2):169–93.

Sampson, A. (1995) *Company Man: The Rise and Fall of Corporate Life*, Random House.

Sanz-Valle, R., Sabater-Sanchez, R. and Aragon-Sanchez, A. (1998) 'Human resource management and business strategy links: an empirical study', *International Journal of Human Resource Management* 10(4): 655–71.

Sapsford, D. and Tzannatos, Z. (1993) *The Economics of the Labour Market*, Macmillan.

Sargeant, M. (2001) 'Lifelong learning and age discrimination in employment', *Education and the Law* 13(2):141–54.

Savery, L.K. and Luks, J.A. (2001) 'The relationship between empowerment, job satisfaction and reported stress levels: some Australian evidence', *Leadership and Organization Development Journal* 22(3):97–104.

Sayal, A. (1990) 'Black women and mental health', *Psychologist* (January):24–7.

Scase, R. and Goffee, R. (1990) 'Women in management: towards a research agenda', *International Journal of Human Resource Management* 1(1):107–25.

Schein, E.H. (1988) *Organizational Psychology*, 3rd edition, Prentice-Hall.

Scholte, J.A. (2000) *Globalization: A Critical Introduction*, Macmillan.

Schuler, R.S. (1990) *Personnel and Human Resource Management*, 4th edition, West Publishing.

Schuler, R.S. (1992) 'Strategic human resource management: linking the people with the strategic needs of the business,' *Organizational Dynamics* Summer:18–23.

Schuler, R.S., Jackson, S.E. and Storey, J. (2001) 'HRM and its link with strategic management', in J. Storey (ed.) *Human Resource Management: A Critical Text*, 2nd edition, Thomson Learning.

Schuster, F.E. (1998) *Employee-Centered Management: A Strategy for High Commitment and Involvement*, Quorum Books.

Schwab, K., Porter, M.E. and Sachs, J.D. (2002) *The Global Competitiveness Report 2001–2: World Economic Forum,* Oxford University Press.

Scullion, H. and Starkey, K. (2000) 'In search of the changing role of the corporate human resource function in the international firm', *International Journal of Human Resource Management* 11(6):1061–81.

Selmer, J. and de Leon, C. (2001) 'Pinoy-style HRM: human resource management in the Philippines', *Asia Pacific Business Review* 8(1):127–44.

Seltzer, A. and Merrett, D.T. (2000) 'Personnel policies at the Union Bank of Australia: Evidence from the 1888–1900 entry cohorts,' *Journal of Labor Economics* 18(4):573–613.

Sen, A. (2002) 'How to judge globalism', *The American Prospect* 13(1):1–14.

Shackleton, V. and Newell, S. (1991) 'Management selection: a comparative survey of methods used in top British and French companies', *Journal of Occupational Psychology* 64:23–36.

Shepherd, J.L. and Mathews, B.P. (2000) 'Employee commitment: academic vs practitioner perspectives', *Employee Relations* 22(6):555–75.

Shiner, M. and Modood, T. (2002) 'Help or hindrance? Higher education and the route to ethnic equality', *British Journal of Sociology of Education* 23(2):209–32.

SHRM (2002) *The Future of the HR Profession*, Society for Human Resource Management.

Shugrue, E., Berland, J., Gonzales, R. and Duke, K. (1997) 'How IBM reengineered its benefits center into a national HR service center', *Compensation Benefits and Review* March–April:41.

Silvestro, R. (2002) 'Dispelling the modern myth: employee satisfaction and loyalty drive service profitability', *International Journal of Operations and Production Management* 22(1):30–49.

Simon, H.A. (1955) *Recent Advances in Organization Theory*, Research Frontiers in Politics and Government, Brookings Institution, Washington, DC.

Simon, H.A. (1960) *The New Science of Management Decision*, Harper and Row.

Sisson, K. (1990) 'Introducing the *Human Resource Management Journal*', *Human Resource Management Journal* 1(1):1–11.

Sisson, K. (1995) 'Human resource management and the personnel function', in J. Storey (ed.) *Human Resource Management: A Critical Text*, Routledge.

Sisson, K. (2001) 'Human resource management and the personnel function – a case of partial impact?' in J. Storey (ed.) *Human Resource Management: A Critical Text*, 2nd edition, Thomson Learning.

Sisson, K. and Marginson, P. (2002) 'Co-ordinated bargaining: a process for our times?' *British Journal of Industrial Relations* 40(2):197–220.

Sivanandan, A. (1991) *Black Struggles Against Racism*, Northern Curriculum Development Project Setting the Context for Change: Anti-Racist Social Work Education, Central Council For Education and Training in Social Work, Leeds.

Sloman, M. (1993) 'Training to play a lead role', *Personnel Management* (July):40–4.

Sloman, M. (1994) 'Coming in from the cold: a new role for trainers', *Personnel Management* (January):24–7.

Sloman, M. (2001) *The E-learning Revolution*, CIPD.

Small, M.H. and Yasin, M. (2000) 'Human factors in the adoption and performance of advanced manufacturing technology in unionized firms', *Industrial Management and Data Systems* 100(8):389–402.

Smircich, L. (1983) 'Concepts of culture and organizational analysis', *Administrative Science Quarterly* 28:339–85.

Smith, A. (1776/1995) *An Inquiry into the Nature and Causes of the Wealth of Nations*, Hackett Publishing Company, Inc.

Smith, C., Child, J. and Rowlinson, M. (1990) *Reshaping Work: The Cadbury Experience*, Cambridge University Press.

Smith, M. (1948) *An Introduction to Industrial Psychology*, 4th edition, Cassell.

Smith, M. (1991) 'Selection in organizations', in M. Smith (ed.) *Analysing Organizational Behaviour*, Macmillan.

Smith, M. and Robertson, I.T. (1993) *The Theory and Practice of Systematic Personnel Selection*, 2nd edition, Macmillan.

Smith, M., Gregg, M. and Andrews, R. (1989) *Selection and Assessment: A New Appraisal*, Pitman.

Smither, R.D. (1994) *The Psychology of Work and Human Performance*, 2nd edition, HarperCollins.

Snell, A.F., Sydell, E.J. and Lueke, S.B. (1999) 'Towards a theory of applicant faking: Integrating studies of deception', *Human Resources Management Review* 9:219–42.

Snow, C.C., Miles, R.E. and Coleman, H.J. (1992) 'Managing 21st century organizations', *Organizational Dynamics* 20(3):5–20.

Snyder, M. (1974) 'The self-monitoring of expressive behaviour', *Journal of Personality and Social Psychology* 30:526–37.

Solomon, C. (1994) 'HR facilitates the learning organization concept', *Personnel Journal* 73(11):56–66.

Sonnenfeld, J.A., Peiperl, M.A. and Kotter, J.P. (1988) 'Strategic determinants of managerial labor markets: a career systems view', *Human Resource Management* 27(4):369–88.

Sparrow, P. (1994) 'Organizational competencies: creating a strategic behavioural framework for selection and assessment', in N. Anderson and P. Herriot (eds) *Assessment and Selection in Organizations: Methods and Practice for Recruitment and Appraisal*, First Update and Supplement 1994, Wiley.

Sparrow, P. and Hiltrop, J.-M. (1994) *European Human Resource Management in Transition*, Prentice-Hall.

Stacey, R.D. (1993) *Strategic Management and Organizational Dynamics*, Pitman.

Steedman, H. and Wagner, K. (1987) 'A second look at productivity, machinery and skills in Britain and Germany', *National Institute Economic Review* (November):57–71.

Steiner, G.A. (1969) *Top Management Planning*, Macmillan.

Stelcner, M. (2000) 'Earnings differentials among ethnic groups in Canada: a review of the research', *Review of Social Economy* 58(3):295–317.

Sternberg, R.J. (1994) 'Thinking styles: theory and assessment at the interface between intelligence and personality', in R.J. Sternberg and P. Ruzgis (eds) *Personality and Intelligence*, Cambridge University Press.

Stevens, J. and Walsh, T. (1991) 'Training and competitiveness', in J. Stevens and R. Mackay (eds) *Training and Competitiveness*, NEDO/ Kogan Page.

Stewart, L.D. and Perlow, R. (2001) 'Applicant race, job status, and racial attitude as predictors of employment discrimination', *Journal of Business and Psychology* 16(2):259–75.

Stewart, R. (1993) *The Reality of Management*, 2nd edition, Heinemann.

Stewart, T.A. (2001) *The Wealth of Knowledge: Intellectual Capital and the Twenty-first Century Organization*, Doubleday.

Stiglitz, J.E. (2002) *Globalization and Its Discontents*, W.W. Norton.

Stolze, W.J. (1999) *Start Up: An Entrepreneur's Guide to Launching and Managing a New Business*, Career Press.

Storey, J. (ed.) (1989) *New Perspectives on Human Resource Management*, Routledge.

Storey, J. (1992) *Developments in the Management of Human Resources*, Blackwell.

Storey, J. (1994a) 'How new-style management is taking hold', *Personnel Management* (January):32–5.

Storey, J. (ed.) (1994b) *New Wave Manufacturing Strategies: Organizational and Human Resource Management Dimensions*, Paul Chapman Publishing.

Storey, J. (ed.) (2001) *Human Resource Management: A Critical Text*, 2nd edition, Thomson Learning.

Storey, J., Ackers, P.B., Bacon, N.A., Buchanan, D.A., Coates, D.S., Preston, D. and Walley, P. (1993) *Human Resource Management Practices in Leicestershire: A Trends Monitor*, Leicestershire Training and Enterprise Council.

Storey, J. and Quintas, P. (2001) 'Knowledge management and HRM', in Storey, J. (ed.) *Human Resource Management: A Critical Text*, 2nd edition, Thomson Learning.

Straw, J.M. (1989) *Equal Opportunities: The Way Ahead*, Institute for Personnel Management.

Strebler, M.T., Robinson, D. and Bevan, S. (2001) *Performance Review: Balancing Objectives and Content*, IES Report 370, Institute of Employment Studies.

Stuart, M. and Lucio, M.M. (2002) 'Social partnership and the mutual gains organization: remaking involvement and trust at the British Workplace', *Economic and Industrial Democracy* 23(2):177–200.

Swain, J.W. (2002) 'Machiavelli and modern management', *Management Decision* 40(3):281–7.

Sweet, P. (2002) 'Backs to the wall', *Conspectus Report on Human Resource Management Systems*, January, PMP (UK) Ltd.

Tackey, N.D., Tamkin, P. and Sheppard, E. (2001) *The Problem of Minority Performance in Organizations* IES Report 375, Institute of Employment Studies.

Takeshi, I. (2001) 'From industrial relations to investor relations? Persistence and change in Japanese corporate governance, employment practices and industrial relations', *Social Science Japan Journal* 4(2):225–41.

Tamkin, P., Barber, L. and Dench, S. (1997) 'From admin to strategy: the changing face of the HR function', *Institute of Employment Studies, Report 332*, June 1997.

Tamkin, P., Yarnall, J. and Kerrin, M. (2002) *Kirkpatrick and Beyond: A Review of Models of Training Evaluation*, IES Report 392, Institute for Employment Studies.

Tansley, C., Newell, S. and Williams, H. (2001) 'Effecting HRM-style practices through an integrated human resource information system: An e-greenfield site?' *Personnel Review* 30(3):351–71.

Taylor, D. and Walley, E.E. (2002) 'Hijacking the Holy Grail? Emerging HR practices in Croatia', *European Business Review* 14(4):294–303.

Taylor, F. (1903) *Shop Management*, paper read before the American Society of Mechanical Engineers, Saratoga, June 1903.

Taylor, F. (1911) *The Principles of Scientific Management*, Harper Bros.

Taylor, F. (1947) *Scientific Management*, Harper and Row.

Teagarden, M.B., Butler, M.C. and Von Glinow, M.A. (1992) 'Mexico's maquiladora industry: where strategic human resource management makes a difference', *Organizational Dynamics* 21(3):34–47.

Tebbel, C. (2000) 'HR just makes the grade', *HRMonthly*, February, Australian Human Resources Institute.

Teo, S.T.T. (2002) 'Effectiveness of a corporate HR department in an Australian public-sector entity during commercialization and corporatization', *International Journal of Human Resource Management* 13(1):89–105.

Thompson, A.A. and Strickland, A.J. (1998) *Crafting and Implementing Strategy*, 10th edition, McGraw-Hill.

Thompson, J.L. (1993) *Strategic Management: Awareness and Change*, 2nd edition, Chapman & Hall.

Thompson, N. (2001) *Anti-discriminatory Practice*, 3rd edition, Palgrave Macmillan.

Thomson, R. (1968) *A Pelican History of Psychology*, Penguin.

Thomson, R. and Mabey, C. (1994) *Developing Human Resources*, Butterworth-Heinemann.

Thornqvist, C. (1999) 'The decentralization of industrial relations: the Swedish case in comparative perspective', *European Journal of Industrial Relations* 5(1):71–87.

Thurley, K. and Wirdenius, H. (1990) *Towards European Management*, Pitman.

Tichy, N.M., Fombrun, C.J. and Devanna, M.A. (1982) 'Strategic human resource management', *Sloan Management Review* 23(2):47–61.

Tight, M. (2000) 'Critical perspectives on management learning: a view from adult/continuing/lifelong education', *Management Learning* 31(1):103–19.

Tilly, C. (1999) *Durable Inequality,* University of California Press.

Timmons, J.A. (1994) *New Venture Creation: Entrepreneurship for the 21st Century*, 4th edition, Irwin Press.

Tinaikar, R., Hartman, A. and Nath, R. (1995) 'Rethinking business process re-engineering: a social constructivist perspective', in G. Burke and J. Peppard (eds) *Examining Business Process Re-engineering: Current Perspectives and Research Directions*, Kogan Page.

Tiwana, A. (1999) *The Knowledge Management Toolkit: Practical Techniques for Building a Knowledge Management System*, Prentice-Hall.

Todd, P. and Peetz, D. (2001) 'Malaysian industrial relations at century's turn: vision 2020 or a spectre of the past?' *International Journal of Human Resource Management* 12(8):1365–82.

Torrington, D. (1994) *International Human Resource Management: Think Globally, Act Locally*, Prentice-Hall.

Torrington, D. and Hall, L. (1991) *Personnel Management: A New Approach*, 2nd edition, Prentice-Hall.

Torrington, D. and Hall, L. (1995) *Personnel Management: HRM in Action*, 3rd edition, Prentice-Hall.

Townley, B. (1989) 'Selection and appraisal: reconstituting "social relations"?' in J. Storey (ed.) *New Perspectives on Human Resource Management*, Routledge.

Townley, B. (1994) *Reframing Human Resource Management*, Sage.

Townsend, R. (1970) *Up the Organization*, Michael Joseph.

Traxler, F. (2002) 'Wage regulation between industrial democracy and market pressures: towards a European model?' *European Sociological Review* 18(1):1–16.

Triandis, H.C. (1990) 'Theoretical concepts that are applicable to the analysis of ethnocentrism', in R.W. Brislin (ed.) *Applied Cross-Cultural Psychology*, Sage.

Triandis, H.C. (1995) 'A theoretical framework for the study of diversity', in M.M. Chemers, S. Oskamp and M.A. Costanzo (eds) *Diversity in Organizations: New Perspectives for a Changing Workplace*, Sage.

Trice, H.M. and Beyer, J.M. (1984) 'Studying organizational cultures through rites and rituals', *Academy of Management Review* 9:653–69.

Trompenaars, F. and Hampden-Turner, C. (1997) *Riding the Waves of Culture: Understanding Diversity in Global Business*, 2nd edition, McGraw-Hill.

Truss, C. (1999) 'Soft and hard HRM', in L. Gratton (ed.) *Strategic Human Resource Management: Corporate Rhetoric and Human Reality*, Oxford University Press.

Truss, C. (2001) 'Complexities and controversies in linking HRM with organizational outcomes', *Journal of Management Studies* 38(8):1121–49.

TUC (2002) *Racism at Work*, Trades Union Congress.

Turnasella, T. (1999) 'The salary trap', *Compensation and Benefits Review* 31(6):2–3.

Turok, I. (1999) *The Jobs Gap in Britain's Cities: Employment Loss and Labour Market Consequences,* Policy Press.

Tylor, E.B. (1871) *Primitive Culture*, Henry Holt.

Tyson, S. (1989) 'The management of the personnel function', *Journal of Management Studies* 24(September):523–32.

Tyson, S. (1995) *Human Resource Strategy*, Pitman.

Tyson, S., Lawrence, P., Poirson, P., Manzolini, L. and Vincente, C.F. (1993) *Human Resource Management in Europe: Strategic Issues and Cases*, Kogan Page.

Tziner, A., Joanis, C. and Murphy, K.R. (2000) 'A comparison of three methods of performance appraisal with regard to goal properties, goal perception, and ratee satisfaction', *Group and Organization Management* 25(2):175–90.

Ulrich, D. (1997) *Human Resource Champions: The Next Agenda for Adding Value and Delivering Results*, Harvard Business School Press.

UNIDO (1993) *United Nations Industrial Development Organization, Annual Report 1993*, United Nations Publications.

United Nations (1995) *The Copenhagen Declaration and Programme of Action*, United Nations.

US Department of Labor (1998) *Government as a High-Performance Employer*, SCANS Report for America 2000, US Department of Labor.

Vagg, P.R., Spielberger, C.D. and Wasala, C.F. (2002) 'Effects of organizational level and gender on stress in the workplace', *International Journal of Stress Management* 9(4):243–61.

van de Vliet, A. (1993) 'Assess for success', *Management Today* (July):60–5.

van der Zwaan, A.H., von Eije, J.H. and de Witte, M.C. (2002) 'HRM consequences of going public', *International Journal of Manpower* 23(2):126–36.

Van Ours, J. and Ridder, G. (1992) 'Vacancies and the recruitment of new employees', *Journal of Labor Economics* 10(2):138–55.

Van Ruysseveldt, J., Huiskamp, R. and van Hoof, J. (1995) *Comparative Industrial and Employment Relations*, Sage.

Vandenberghe, C. (1999) 'Organizational culture, person-culture fit, and turnover: a replication in the health care industry', *Journal of Organizational Behavior* 20:175–84.

Vickerstaff, S. (1992) *Human Resource Management in Europe: Text and Cases*, Chapman and Hall.

Vranken, M. (1999) 'The role of specialist labour courts in an environment of substantive labour law deregulation: a New Zealand case study', *International Journal of Comparative Labour Law and Industrial Relations* 15(3):303–28.

Wächter, H. and Muller-Camen, M. (2002) 'Co-determination and strategic integration in German firms', *Human Resource Management Journal* 12(3):76–87.

Waldman, D.A. and Atwater, L.E. (2001) 'Attitudinal and behavioral outcomes of an upward feedback process', *Group and Organization Management* 26(2):189–205.

Walker, A.J. (2001) 'Best practices in HR technology', in A.J. Walker (ed.) *Web-Based Human Resources*, McGraw-Hill.

Walker, S.F. and Marr, J.W. (2001) *Stakeholder Power: A Winning Plan for Building Stakeholder Commitment and Driving Corporate Growth*, Perseus Publishing.

Walsh, J. (2001) 'Human resource management in foreign-owned workplaces: evidence from Australia', *International Journal of Human Resource Management* 12(3):425–44.

Walton, J. (1999) *Strategic Human Resource Development*, Financial Times/Prentice-Hall.

Warr, P. (1987) *Psychology at Work*, 2nd edition, Penguin.

Watkins, L.M. and Johnston, L. (2000) 'Screening job applicants: the impact of physical attractiveness and application quality', *International Journal of Selection and Assessment* 8(2):76–84.

Watson, T.J. (1994) *In Search of Management: Culture, Chaos and Control in Management Work*, Routledge.

Weber, M. (1947) *Max Weber: The Theory of Social and Economic Organization*, translated by A.M. Henderson and Talcott Parsons, The Free Press.

Webster, E.C. (1964) *Decision Making in the Employment Interview*, Industrial Relations Centre, McGill University, Montreal.

Webster, W. (1990) *Not a Man to Match Her: The Marketing of a Prime Minister*, Women's Press.

Weinberger, C.J. (1998) 'Race and gender wage gaps in the market for recent college graduates', *Industrial Relations* 37(1):67–84.

Weisbrot, M. (2002) 'The mirage of progress', *The American Prospect* 13(1): 1–14.

Weisner, W.H. and Cronshaw, S.F. (1988) 'A meta-analytic investigation of the impact of interview format and degree of structure on the validity of the employment interview', *Journal of Occupational Psychology* 61:275–90.

Weiss, D.S. (1999) *High Performance HR: Leveraging Human Resources for Competitive Advantage*, John Wiley and Son Ltd.

Weiss, M. (2002) 'Modernizing the German works council system: a recent amendment', *International Journal of Comparative Labour Law and Industrial Relations* 18(3):251–64.

West, J.P. and Berman E.M. (2001) 'From traditional to virtual HR: is the transition occurring in local government?' *Review of Public Personnel Administration* 21(1):38–64.

Whipp, R. (1992) 'Human resource management, competition and strategy: some productive tensions', in P. Blyton and P. Turnbull (eds) *Reassessing Human Resource Management*, Sage.

Whitehill, A.M. (1991) *Japanese Management: Tradition and Transition*, Routledge.

Whittaker, H. (1999) *Entrepreneurs as Co-operative Capitalists: High-tech CEOs in the UK*, ESRC Centre for Business Research, Working Paper Series No.125, University of Cambridge.

Wilkinson, F. (2000) *Human Resource Management And Business Objectives And Strategies In Small And Medium Sized Business*, Working Papers, ESRC Centre for Business Research, University of Cambridge.

Willmott, H. (1993) 'Strength is ignorance; slavery is freedom: managing culture in modern organizations', *Journal of Management Studies*, 30(4):515–52.

Willmott, H. (1995) 'Will the turkeys vote for Christmas? The re-engineering of human resources', in G. Burke and J. Peppard (eds) *Examining Business Process Re-engineering: Current Perspectives and Research Directions*, Kogan Page.

Wilson, F.M. (1995) *Organizational Behaviour and Gender*, McGraw-Hill.

Wilson, T. (2002) *Global Diversity at Work: Winning the War for Talent*, 2nd edition, John Wiley & Son.

Windsor, D. (1998) *The Definition of Stakeholder Status*, paper presented at the International Association for Business and Society (IABS) annual conference in Kona-Kailua, Hawaii (June 1998).

Wirth, W. (2001) *Breaking Through the Glass Ceiling*, International Labour Office.

Wolf, M.G. (1999) 'Compensation: an overview', in L.A. Berger and D.R. Berger (eds) *The Compensation Handbook*, 4th edition, McGraw-Hill.

Wood, D. (1983) 'Uses and abuses of personnel consultants', *Personnel Management* (October):407.

Wood, G. and Els, C. (2000) 'The making and remaking of HRM: the practice of managing people in the Eastern Cape Province, South Africa', *International Journal of Human Resource Management* 11(1):112–25.

Wood, R. and Baron, H. (1992) 'Psychological testing free from prejudice', *Personnel Management* (December):34–7.

Wood, R. and Payne, T. (1998) *Competency-Based Recruitment and Selection*, John Wiley & Son.

Wooden, M. and Bora, B. (1999) 'Workplace characteristics and their effects on wages: Australian evidence', *Australian Economic Papers* 38(3):276–89.

Woodward, J. (1980) *Industrial Organization: Theory and Practice*, 2nd edition, Oxford University Press.

World Bank (1999) *World Development Report*, World Bank.

Wright, M. and Storey, J. (1994) 'Recruitment', in I. Beardwell and L. Holden (eds) *Human Resource Management*, Pitman.

Wright, P.C. and Bean, S.A. (1993) 'Sexual harassment: an issue of employee effectiveness', *Journal of Managerial Psychology* 8(2):30–6.

Wright, P.M. and McMahan, G.C. (1992) 'Theoretical perspectives for strategic human resource management'. *Journal of Management* 18:295–320.

Wright, P.M. and Snell, S.A. (1998) 'Toward a unifying framework for exploring fit and flexibility in strategic human resource management', *Academy of Management Review* 23(4):756–72.

Yousef, D.A. (2002) 'Job satisfaction as a mediator of the relationship between job stressors and affective, continuance, and normative commitment: a path analytical approach', *International Journal of Stress Management* 9(2):99–112.

Index